LEAGUE
Publications Ltd

RUGBY LEAGUE
2009-2010
A new generation

League Publications Ltd

First published in Great Britain in 2009 by
League Publications Ltd
Wellington House
Briggate
Brighouse
West Yorkshire HD6 1DN

A CIP catalogue record for this book is available from the British Library
ISBN 978-1-901347-21-0

Designed and Typeset by League Publications Limited
Printed by TJ International, Padstow, Cornwall

Contributing Editor	Tim Butcher		
Statistics, production and design	Daniel Spencer		
Design assistant	Lorraine Marsden		
Contributors	Gareth Walker	**Pictures**	Rugby League Photos
	Malcolm Andrews		Varley Picture Agency
	Raymond Fletcher		Peter Morley
	Mike Sterriker		Action Photographics, Australia
	Phil Caplan		Max Flego
	Ian Bridge		Gordon Clayton
	Neil Barraclough		Ian Lovell
	Tony Hannan		Mike McKenzie
	Martyn Sadler		
	James Gosling		
	Simon Fitzjohn		
	Ross Heppenstall		
	Phil Hodgson		
	David Parkinson		
	David Lawrenson		
	David Rees		
	Mike Latham		
	Steve Mascord		
	Mike Rylance		
	Richard de la Riviere		
	Ben Collins		
	Keith McGhie		
	Joanna Lester		
	Trevor Hunt		

CONTENTS

ACKNOWLEDGEMENTS

Gillette Rugby League 2009-2010 is the 14th in League Publications Ltd's annual series of Rugby League Yearbooks, the seventh year of its production with the backing of world-leading brand Gillette.

In compiling this historical record of the Rugby League year, we rely on the hard work and dedication of all the contributors to *Rugby Leaguer & Rugby League Express* and *Rugby League World* magazine. Without their efforts this yearbook would not be possible.

We are able to include some wonderful action photography provided by, in particular Varley Picture Agency, RLphotos.com, Action Photographics in Sydney and Peter Morley of RL Images.

Thanks are due to the Rugby Football League for their help during the year, and in particular Gavin Wild and Tom Hoyle for their assistance in helping track down the dates of birth of players.

The magnificent statistical review was put together meticulously, as always, by Daniel Spencer, who also designed the book.

Special mentions for Gareth Walker and Malcolm Andrews who wrote the Championship and NRL/State of Origin sections. Thanks also to Opta Sportdata, who compiled the Opta Analysis in our jam-packed statistical section.

TIM BUTCHER
Contributing Editor
Rugby League 2009-2010

FOREWORD

Welcome to *Gillette Rugby League 2009-10*. This is the seventh year Gillette has sponsored this book, and we once again congratulate League Publications for producing a valuable and detailed account of a memorable Rugby League year, and a vital source of reference for years to come.

Having first become involved with Rugby League in 2003 with the sponsorship of the Great Britain team, Gillette has increased its commitment year on year via the Gillette Tri-Nations, various one-off internationals and its continued backing of Great Britain and England. We are also entering our sixth year as sponsors of the Gillette Rugby League Heritage Centre in Huddersfield.

In 2009, Gillette sponsored England's two internationals against France in Paris and Wales in Bridgend, and we were particularly delighted to build on the Tri-Nations success as France entered the fray to contest the inaugural Four Nations, which produced some sensational games and action, as a new-look England narrowly lost out to Australia, with Darren Lockyer crowning a marvellous career by lifting the trophy.

Gillette has played a key role in the development of Rugby League over the last six years, and we look forward to it continuing.

NATHAN HOMER
Managing Director
Gillette UK

INTRODUCTION

How we remember the Rugby League year of 2009 will depend on a number of factors, including which club you support or in which part of the world you live.

For England supporters the season ended in a familiar way, with the national side - now known as England and not Great Britain - falling short against Australia in the final game of a series. There was however a glimmer of hope in the eventual 46-16 defeat in the Gillette Four Nations Final. Firstly, England had reached the final in the first place, a 20-12 win over New Zealand in their final group game a vast improvement on the disappointing World Cup campaign of the year before when they had twice lost to the Kiwis on their way out of the competition. Secondly, the side which competed in the final featured a threequarter line and two halfbacks new to full Test rugby in 2009 and, combined with a forward pack that could claim to be the best in the world, England produced a style of football against the Australians rarely seen over recent years.

The Four Nations Final was Tony Smith's last act as England coach. Despite telling journalists at the post-match press conference that he would be sitting down with the Rugby Football League to discuss the future, it transpired he had already informed them he would be standing down at the end of the tournament, at the end of his three-year contract.

Smith's situation had changed since he originally took up the role in 2007. Three games into the Super League XIV season he answered the call at Warrington Wolves, who despite some high-profile recruitment in recent seasons, were bottom of the table at the end of February. The former coach of Huddersfield and Leeds, who he steered to Super League titles in 2004 and 2007, didn't have an immediate impact on the Wolves' performance, and they failed to make the play-offs. But the 25-16 win over Huddersfield at Wembley at the end of August marked the first silverware for the club since 1991. Progress indeed, and a number of signings for 2010 are going to make for a very interesting season for Warrington.

The main prize went once again to Leeds Rhinos, their third successive title and a second in a row under genial coach Brian McClennan. Kevin Sinfield held aloft the Super League trophy for a record fourth time and in doing so became the most successful captain in Championship history, leaving behind such legendary leaders as Harold Wagstaff, Gus Risman and Ellery Hanley, among others, who lifted the old trophy three times. Sinfield also became the first to lead a side to three successive Grand Final titles. Half way through the season, McClennan was already hailing Sinfield as the greatest leader in Leeds' illustrious history and by the end of the year he was proven right. 2009 was also the year when Sinfield established his credentials as an international footballer with shining performances in England's win over New Zealand and in the second-half comeback against Australia at Wigan the week before.

St Helens proved themselves to still possess a great side, in a year when they were widely expected to fail to live up to their magnificent standards. The decline and fall never happened, despite the absence for almost the whole season of prop Jason Cayless and an injury-hit season all round. New coach Mick Potter fielded no less than ten players aged 20 or under - including the English game's most exciting prospect, Kyle Eastmond - during the course of the season and still managed to be within seven minutes of winning the title, Lee

Smith's try in the 73rd minute of the Grand Final at Old Trafford finally deciding the outcome.

If Leeds and Saints were the undisputed top two, there were credible challengers, who ultimately fell short, though the experience should stand them in good stead in years to come.

Of the chasing pack, Huddersfield got the closest, with a new coach in Nathan Brown and a new captain in experienced Australian Brett Hodgson. Hodgson won the Man of Steel for his assuredness at fullback in a Giants side that found consistency towards the end of the season before losing momentum after their Challenge Cup final defeat by Warrington. Eorl Crabtree also started to fulfil his potential and he too stood up on the international stage.

Hull KR also progressed tremendously, a fourth placed finish reward for their best season, their third in Super League. Rovers had much to owe to ever-present Michael Dobson, the former Catalans and Wigan halfback skilfully moving them around the park on the back of the wiles of Clint Newton and Ben Galea, for the likes of Shaun Briscoe and Peter Fox to prosper and secure England caps at the end of the season. Dobson was the runaway winner of the Albert Goldthorpe Medal as the season's outstanding player.

Hull KR, as well as the Giants, exited the play-offs with two straight losses, as the new top-eight play-off system introduced in 2009, with the Super League expanded to 14 teams, came under some criticism. The first week Qualifying Play-offs lacked intensity, with the losers knowing they would have a home tie the next week. If there was a tactic in that it backfired as they both lost, Huddersfield beaten by Catalans and Hull KR falling to Wigan.

Both the Dragons and the Warriors timed their runs, almost but not quite, to perfection. Wigan's campaign ended at St Helens in the penultimate weekend, but it was mighty close, Sean Long saving Saints in his last home game at Knowsley Road with a match-winning tackle three minutes from time. After the game, Brian Noble announced he was leaving Wigan, not a big surprise with rumours throughout the season of discord between him and club owner Ian Lenagan. It was a near miraculous ending for the faithful Wigan supporters, who had seen their side lose their first three games of the season, overseas signing Tim Smith fail to hit form, and international back-rower Gareth Hock banned from the game for two years, after testing positive for cocaine. But then there was Sam Tomkins, who made his Super League debut in 2009 and went on to be named Albert Goldthorpe Rookie of the Year.

Kevin Walters had an even worse start with Catalans Dragons, who under Mick Potter had finished third in 2008, losing six of their first seven games and not climbing into the top eight until round 24. Even then they only made the play-offs with an amazing 24-12 win at St Helens on the last Friday of the regular season. They proved it wasn't a fluke, winning at Wakefield and Huddersfield with commanding displays in the following two weeks before losing with honour at Leeds. Perpignan (and Barcelona) remained one of the best places to watch Super League and the introduction of Toulouse into the Championship in 2009, and a potential move for a Super League franchise in Paris, has bolstered hopes that French Rugby League is on the rise once again.

Wakefield Wildcats finished fifth in the table, their best ever campaign, but were eliminated in the first week of the play-offs by the Dragons. It was significant they were without their inspiration for much of the season, 2008 Albert Goldthorpe Medal winner Danny Brough, out injured that night. John Kear was selected as Rugby League World magazine's coach of the year after the Wildcats' most consistent season to date. The club's battling spirit was a tribute to the late Adam Watene and to young forward Leon Walker, who tragically died in a reserve match early in the season.

Castleford Tigers fans can also reflect on a season in which their team improved from wooden spoonists to a seventh placed finish, despite a week one play-off exit at Wigan. Tigers centre Michael Shenton had proved himself an international calibre centre by the end of the year and youngster Richard Owen also marked himself down as a potential performer on the world stage. Cas fans also had the privilege of seeing the first Challenge Cup tie to be decided by a golden point (since 1941) when Brent Sherwin broke Halifax hearts at the

Introduction

Jungle in May.

Bradford didn't make the play-offs for the first time since they were introduced in 1998. In the end they were denied only by Catalans' stunning last-round win at St Helens after they had won six of their last seven matches, having been totally written off in the middle of July. A turnaround in personnel, including the departure of captain Paul Deacon to Wigan, is going to make Odsal a compelling place to be in 2010

Of the other teams not making the play-offs, Hull FC were the biggest disappointment, slumping to a 12th placed finish despite having won their opening five rounds and riding high in second place. They had another horror run with injuries - fullback Todd Byrne having his season and Hull career ended in round 2 - and the failure of their marquee signing, Michael Crocker, to get a visa was a major blow. Prop Epalahame Lauaki was allowed to enter the UK, but only in time for the last three games of the season.

Harlequins coach Brian McDermott stated in pre-season his aim was to win the competition, which seemed outrageous at the time, but by the middle of June Quins were in fourth spot after a brilliant 40-10 win at Hull KR, having beaten Leeds, almost nilling them, at Headingley at the end of April. But they had peaked too early and collapsed big style, losing eleven of their last 12 games.

The bottom two sides in Super League were predicted to be Salford and new franchise Celtic Crusaders and they didn't disappoint. The City Reds did muster seven wins, the high point the 30-20 win at Leeds on Easter Monday, and they also beat St Helens at home. The uncertainty about halfback Richie Myler's future certainly didn't help, and his confirmed move to Warrington eventually ended the saga.

Celtic by the end of the season had taken up the mantle of crisis club, with plenty of knives stuck into them for being awarded a Super League franchise. Rumours of financial collapse were capped by the expulsion of six of their players by the UK Border Agency for visa transgressions in previous years. 2009 ended with their new coach, Brian Noble, desperately trying to cobble together a team for the new season. Noble will have taken some heart from the emergence of a number of Super League players in the making in the Wales team that won the European Cup.

The next Super League franchises were due to be up for grabs for the 2012 season and one of the criteria for clubs to make applications was fulfilled by Barrow Raiders, the champions, and Halifax, for reaching the Championship Grand Final and Widnes Vikings, who won the Northern Rail Cup.

Gateshead and Doncaster were the teams relegated into Championship One, a complicated story even by lower league standards, with Dewsbury - who won every game in their league campaign - and Keighley Cougars moving up.

We hope you enjoy leafing through this record of another Rugby League year to savour. The Gillette Yearbook contains the full story of the domestic year, full details of the international season and the Australian NRL season, and match facts for every Super League, Challenge Cup games involving professional teams, National League One and Two and Northern Rail Cup game. Every player who has played Super League is also listed along with those players to have made their debuts this year. We have also selected five individuals who we judge to have made the biggest impact on Rugby League in 2009.

League Publications publishes the weekly newspaper Rugby Leaguer & Rugby League Express, as well as the monthly glossy magazine Rugby League World and the website 'totalrugbyleague.com'.

Many thanks once again to Gillette for their support for both this yearbook, and for the sport of Rugby League.

TIM BUTCHER
Contributing Editor
Rugby League 2009-2010

1
THE 2009 SEASON

DECEMBER 2008
Bigger and better

New Zealand's triumph in the World Cup was welcomed, at least outside Australia, but in England that quickly gave way to the nagging question: why had England performed so badly, winning only one of their three pool games before their elimination by the Kiwis in the semi-final? The Rugby Football League promised an in-house inquiry. Nathan Cayless, the Kiwis' World Cup-winning captain, told Rugby League World magazine that criticism of the England team after their failed World Cup bid was unwarranted. The Parramatta prop pointed out that the difference in refereeing interpretations hurt the English, and called for the officiating of the sport to be the same in the two hemispheres. Cayless said that England had every chance of winning the expanded Four Nations, involving Australia, England, New Zealand and France, to be staged in England and France in the autumn of 2009. 'It's always different playing a series in England, so I think England can bounce back.'

England's coach Tony Smith, speaking on the BBC's 'Super League Show', claimed his side didn't deserve much of the criticism they had attracted, criticising the negativity of the British press and also pointing out the difference in refereeing interpretations between Super League and the NRL.

But the northern and southern hemispheres looked set to grow further apart, with the NRL deciding that matches in their competition would be controlled by two referees. Chief executive Nigel Wood confirmed to League Express that the RFL had no plans to introduce the innovation in the domestic competitions.

As well as rule interpretations, the quality of the Super League competition came under scrutiny, particularly the lack of opportunity for home-grown players to develop because of the number of overseas imports. Rugby League World's list of the 50 best teenagers in the world seemed to bear this out. Northern Hemisphere representation in the list had dropped from 21 to 11. Australia's Israel Folau topped the ratings with Castleford's Joe Westerman third on the list, having climbed from 14th place in 2008. St Helens' Kyle Eastmond, in eighth place, was the only other English player to feature in the top ten.

One direct casualty of the World Cup was Ricky Stuart, who quit as Australia coach in the wake of his behaviour towards World Cup officials following his side's shock 34-20 defeat in the final. Stuart was widely condemned for his outbursts at match referee Ashley Klein and British referees' boss Stuart Cummings in a hotel lobby the morning after the game.

The year ended better for England captain Jamie Peacock with the news that his pregnant wife, his four-year-old son and mother-in-law would be safely back in the UK after anti-government protesters forced the closure of Bangkok's two airports, stranding thousands of holidaymakers for several days.

The 2009 season was set to be another season of innovation, both in Super League and in the National Leagues, which from this season would be called the Championship and Championship One.

In Super League, there were to be 14 teams in the competition for the first time since 1999; and an eight-team play-off giving more than half the teams in Super League a chance of reaching the Grand Final. One significant addition was that the highest qualifying team from week one would be able to choose its opponents from the two teams that had battled through to the semi-final stage from week two.

Meanwhile the Northern Rail Cup was to be played to a new formula, and on finals weekend in Blackpool in July the clubs that didn't reach the final were to take part in a Nines competition at the Fylde rugby union ground. The Championship was to include Toulouse Olympique.

The sport received a huge boost in December when Sport England announced it would award a grant of £29,408,341 to develop the grass roots over a four-year period from 1st April 2009 to 31st March 2013, a significant increase on prior awards to the RFL, which had received just over £18 million in the previous four-year period. The RFL, which that month signed up to gay pressure group Stonewall's 'Diversity Champions Programme', would use the funding to increase the overall participation in Rugby League and to assist the community game. None of it was to be used to support the England national team or other elite elements of the sport.

> **SUPER LEAGUE -**
> **TOP-EIGHT PLAY-OFF SYSTEM**
>
> **WEEK 1**
> *Qualifying play-off 1:* 1st v 4th
> *Qualifying play-off 2:* 2nd v 3rd
> *Elimination play-off 1:* 5th v 8th
> *Elimination play-off 2:* 6th v 7th
>
> **WEEK 2**
> *Preliminary semi-final 1:* Highest placed QPO Loser
> v lowest placed EPO Winner
> *Preliminary semi-final 2:*
> Remaining QPO Loser v remaining EPO Winner
>
> **WEEK 3**
> *Qualifying semi-final 1:*
> QPO 1 Winner v PSF Winner *
> *Qualifying semi-final 2:*
> QPO 2 Winner v PSF Winner *
> * subject to choice of highest placed winner in week one
>
> **WEEK 4**
> *Grand Final:*
> QSF 1 Winner v QSF 2 Winner

The British and the world economy was in recession, but officials predicted that Rugby League was better equipped to survive than many other professional sports. The RFL had a TV deal in the bag until the end of 2011, boosting each Super League club's income to around £1.2 million per annum from the £900,000 that they were all receiving in 2008.

Huddersfield Giants were still confident that Todd Carney, their new signing from Canberra Raiders, would be with them for SLXIV, despite his protracted wait for a visa. There was speculation that Carney, who had a history of transgressions off the pitch, could be turned down. The Giants meanwhile signed 17-year-old scrum-half Gregg McNally from Whitehaven but immediately loaned him back to the Cumbrian side to allow him more first-team experience and the chance to finish studying for his A-Levels.

Whitehaven were one of several clubs in the Co-operative Championship and Championship One competitions to have suffered following a ruling by the UK Border Agency that effectively prevented clubs from employing overseas players on an amateur basis while they were working in alternative employment or as students.

Super League's new club, Celtic Crusaders went into a three-week training camp in Brisbane with nine new signings, although Cook Islander Ben Vaeau asked to be released from his contract, citing family reasons. Additionally the Crusaders signed three players from Super League clubs - Matty Smith and Steve Tyrer, who both joined on season-long loan deals from St Helens, and Peter Lupton, 26, from Castleford Tigers. The Crusaders announced plans for a new 15,000-capacity stadium by the start of the 2012 season.

Over the Christmas period, the Centurions moved into the Leigh Sports Village as Salford beat them in a friendly by 26-6; Wigan's Karl Pryce and Mark Riddell played their first games for the club in a convincing 44-4 pre-season win at Warrington against a near Academy line-up; and Wakefield beat Leeds at Headingley by 22-16. The new Wildcats shirt was to include Adam Watene's signature sewn into the front, in tribute to their teammate who had tragically collapsed and died during a weight-training session in October.

In the annual League Express readers' poll, St Helens' James Graham was voted Super League Player of the Year, capping an outstanding individual year that saw him win a place in the World XIII, as well as taking the Man of Steel award; the
Rugby League Writers' award and the Rugby League World magazine Player of the Year award. The latest accolade came two weeks after the death of another Saints and Great Britain great, Hall of Famer Vince Karalius, who succumbed to cancer on the Isle of Man at the age of 76.

JANUARY
Red taped

England captain Jamie Peacock fired a broadside at the Rugby Football League as the new season approached, with his club Leeds again due to start a week in advance of round one to accommodate the World Club Challenge. Peacock, angered by another short pre-season, a situation endured by all international players in the UK, slammed League bosses, suggesting a longer off-season would increase England's chances of regaining superiority in the international game. Peacock said: 'I've not had a pre-season longer than 15 days for ten years now, and it needs to be improved and changed. It's always been down to the financial problems. But now there's an extra £300,000 for the clubs (from the renewed TV contract), and there is still no talk of reducing the games. Basically it's a load of crap – that's what it feels like as a player.' Keith Senior had already pulled the plug on his international career. The 32-year-old Rhinos veteran, in the final year of his current contract, admitted he wanted to apply himself exclusively to club football in the final stages of his career.

Brent Webb, carrying an injury from 2008, didn't travel to the Rhinos' pre-season training camp in Florida, which ended with a 12-10 win over Salford before 5,750 spectators at Hodges Stadium in Jacksonville. The City Reds used 26 players and led 10-0 after the first two quarters, but a late Ashley Gibson try sealed Leeds' win. Peacock, who signed a new three-year contract before the trip, had returned home on match eve to be with his pregnant wife Faye. Brian McClennan signed a one-year extension to his current two-year deal with the Rhinos.

Salford's week in Jacksonville had repercussions, with Malcolm Alker stripped of the Reds' captaincy after club rules were broken during the trip, including the breaking of late-night curfews. New signing Rob Parker was named new team captain. City Reds Chairman John Wilkinson also conceded that the Reds would not start the 2010 season in their new stadium, but insisted that 2009 would be the club's last full year at The Willows.

Meanwhile, the British High Commission in Canberra was doing its utmost to disrupt the preparations of some Super League clubs. Michael Crocker vowed to appeal against the decision to deny him a visa to play with Hull FC because of a conviction for affray. But despite a setback, Bradford Bulls were still confident that Greg Bird would to play in Super League in 2009. Leeds chief executive Gary Hetherington was highly critical of the Bulls over their signing of Bird, who parted company with his club Cronulla on the condition he did not play in Australia in 2009. He called for players delisted by the NRL for disciplinary reasons to also be banned in the northern hemisphere. Rhinos signing Greg Eastwood had still not received clearance to fly to the UK. Eastwood, a New Zealander whose father was born in Huddersfield, had applied for a British passport.

Meanwhile the Bulls' boom forward Sam Burgess got the go-ahead to resume full training after a major shoulder operation in July the previous year.

Scotland World Cup captain Danny Brough was eligible to play for England in the 2009 Four Nations tournament, according to Rugby League World magazine and the Rugby League International Federation, despite an RFL spokesman erroneously telling the Press Association he would have to wait two years. The Wakefield scrum-half, the winner of the inaugural Albert Goldthorpe Medal in 2008 but sidelined after off-season shoulder surgery, was being offered at 33/1 to win the Medal again in 2009 by bookmaker William Hill. Nine players shared favouritism for the Medal, each priced at 20/1. The favourites included Leeds' Rob Burrow, Jamie Peacock and Danny Buderus and St Helens' James Graham, Leon Pryce and Sean Long, while Sam Burgess, Joe Westerman (Castleford) and Thomas Bosc (Catalans) made up the nine.

Harlequins coach Brian McDermott insisted his side's aim was to win October's Grand Final at Old Trafford. 'There is going to be no messing around this year - I am here to win the competition,' he said. 'I have been wishy-washy with my goals in the past, but it has been a long off-season, and that gives you a lot of time to think.' Harlequins defeated Halifax 28-4 in a friendly at the Twickenham Stoop, with re-signing Luke Dorn scoring three tries.

Quins Chairman Keith Hogg stepped down with David Hughes taking the role. Hughes won an apology from the London Evening Standard newspaper for an article suggesting two of his companies had gone into liquidation, implying Harlequins could be heading for trouble. The Standard had confused Hughes with another businessman with the same name.

Celtic Crusaders signed Papua New Guinea World Cup forward Jason Chan from the Windsor Wolves, a feeder club to the Penrith Panthers. The Crusaders had been the hardest hit of all 14 Super League clubs in visa delays for overseas players.

Wakefield's acting coach Paul Broadbent - John Kear was recovering from a hip replacement - denied any knowledge of stand-off Jamie Rooney joining Huddersfield Giants, and Rooney backed him up in League Express.

Tony Puletua enjoyed a tryscoring St Helens debut against Wakefield in Paul Wellens' testimonial at Knowsley Road, a match that his side won 26-22; Bradford's new signing Steve Menzies made his debut for the Bulls in a muddy 20-8 win against Dewsbury Rams at the Tetley's Stadium; Wigan stole a last-gasp victory at Huddersfield with two tries in the last three minutes; and Michael Shenton scored a hat-trick in the Tigers' 32-12 win over Wakefield in a game played in the memory of former Castleford and Wakefield prop Adam Watene.

Severe weather conditions across the south-west of France forced a pre-season fixture between Toulouse Olympique and the Catalans Dragons to be called off. Winds gusting up to 100 miles an hour put paid to any hope of playing the match in safety.

And Super League referee Ashley Klein, who refereed the World Cup Final, returned to live in Australia. The RFL appointed Frenchman Thierry Alibert as a full-time match official on a one-year contract.

CARNEGIE CHALLENGE CUP - ROUND 1

Saturday 24th January 2009

The Army 72 Northumbria University 0; Bradford-Dudley Hill 19 Widnes St Maries 24; Egremont Rangers 0 Wath Brow Hornets 42; Featherstone Lions 18 Hull University 12; Hull Isberg 12 Saddleworth Rangers 36; Kells 26 Eastmoor Dragons 14; Leigh East 68 Orchard Park & Greenwood 0; Loughborough University 40 St Mary's University 12; Milford Marlins 14 Pilkington Recs 24; Queens 13 Halton Simms Cross 0; Waterhead 14 Castleford Lock Lane 16; West Bowling 32 East Hull 6; West Hull 56 East Leeds 0; Wigan St Judes 34 Myton Warriors 20; Wigan St Patricks 24 Skirlaugh 18

Sunday 25th January 2009

Leeds Met Carnegie 36 Warrington Wizards 6; RAF 16 Edinburgh Eagles 18; Royal Navy 38 Valley Cougars 28

Saturday 31st January 2009

Castleford Panthers 12 Leigh Miners Rangers 26; Crosfields 10 Sharlston Rovers 36; Hull Dockers 34 Ovenden 4; Siddal 36 Thatto Heath Crusaders 12

FEBRUARY
Hull fire

Celtic Crusaders made their Super League debut on the first Friday of February with a 28-6 defeat against Leeds Rhinos at Headingley. It was a credible result in the most testing of circumstances. Eight Celtic players - Tony Duggan, Josh Hannay, Mark Dalle-Cort, Damien Quinn, Jace Van Dijk, Darren Mapp, who had all played for the club in 2008, along with new forwards Ryan O'Hara and Jason Chan - had been stranded in Australia awaiting clearance to enter the UK, victims of the British government's new stringent immigration system, and only arrived in south Wales the Sunday before the season opener.

With Britain snowbound and frozen for the rest of the week, John Dixon's squad managed just one full training session and two new signings, utility star Marshall Chalk and hooker Lincoln Withers had to pull out of the game, Chalk with 'flu, and Withers with injury. Headingley groundsman Jason Booth was nominated as League Express gamestar for getting the game on, Booth and his staff removing 500 tons of snow before the kick-off.

Having gone 16 points down inside the opening quarter there was a fear that the Crusaders would be slaughtered by a Leeds team missing Danny Buderus, Brent Webb and Rob Burrow but Dixon's men showed sufficient resolve to make a real game of it, keeping the defending champions scoreless for all but the final play of the second half.

Jamie Peacock's deft offload set up the opening score of 2009, Danny McGuire's long pass freeing Keith Senior, who broke through and fed Jamie Jones-Buchanan on the inside, and he sent in Lee Smith. In the second half, Jace Van Dijk set up a landmark, Chris Beasley timing his return pass to his skipper to perfection and the scrum-half sliding in an early kick behind the Rhinos cover for Luke Dyer to score Celtic's first Super League try.

The inhospitable weather meant that for the final quarter the pitch was frozen – accounting for Luke Burgess's mild concussion when he fell attempting a big hit. Adam Peek and Peacock attempted to sort out their differences at a scrum and were given the final ten minutes off for their trouble.

Not only Leeds' game had been

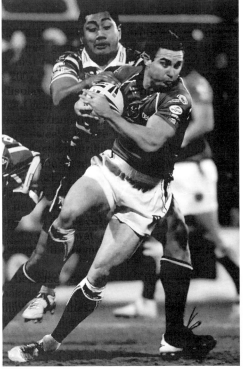

Tony Duggan collared by Ali Lauitiiti as Celtic Crusaders make their Super League bow

brought forward, to accommodate their World Club Challenge with Manly on the weekend of round three, but the RFL had allowed Harlequins to bring their round two game forward against Bradford Bulls, in order for them to give the Australian Premiers a warm-up match. As it turned out, the scheduled game at the Twickenham Stoop was postponed because of the icy weather, which led to Bradford chairman Peter Hood calling for a later start to the Super League season.

A third game to be brought forward went ahead on the Sunday and Wakefield coach John Kear revealed how a rousing speech by captain Jason Demetriou in honour of the late Wildcats prop Adam Watene played a major part in his injury-hit side's surprise 12-6 round 17 victory over Wigan at the JJB Stadium. Wakefield were missing Jamie Rooney, Danny Brough, Danny Sculthorpe, Tevita Leo-Latu, Ryan Atkins, Matt Peterson, Richard Moore and Aaron Murphy and were expected to be on the end of a hammering. Kear's men also came into the game having faced the potential disruption caused by a reported attempt by Huddersfield to lure Brad Drew to the Galpharm. Drew picked up three Albert Goldthorpe points with a superb display. Although Wakefield only led 10-0 at the break - thanks to two Dave Halley tries, the Bradford winger on a month's loan to cover the injury crisis, and a Tony Martin goal - they dominated. Joel Tomkins got Wigan's only try six minutes into the second half.

Catalans' new coach Kevin Walters declared himself pleased with his side's first match under his control, after the Dragons defeated a President's XIII drawn from the French Championship by 36 points to 18 on a wet Saturday evening at Gilbert Brutus.

Meanwhile, Championship clubs were frantically trying to rearrange matches after the entire first weekend of Northern Rail Cup was wiped out by the weather.

Round 1

Super League XIV officially kicked-off as Leeds made it two straight wins with an 18-4 Friday-night home success over Wakefield. Leeds were without Kevin Sinfield and Keith Senior, as well as still-absent Rob Burrow but their star capture for 2009, former Kangaroo skipper Danny Buderus, made a highly encouraging debut after six months on the sidelines with a torn bicep, coming from the bench after 24 minutes.

Wakefield went into the game with a host of first-team regulars missing due to injury, after a week in which prop forward Richard Moore was diagnosed with Crohn's disease, after suffering a mysterious weight loss, while halfback Jamie Rooney was involved in a frightening drama after his heart stopped beating for 30 seconds while he was under anaesthetic during a routine knee operation. To compound John Kear's problems, Sam Obst withdrew after pulling a hamstring in the warm-up and centre Tony Martin had to play scrum-half.

The day after, Leeds revealed that their second overseas signing, Brisbane's Greg Eastwood had been refused a visa because of previous driving convictions. The Rhinos said they would wait 'as long as it takes' for the New Zealand World Cup star to appeal against the decision of the UK Border Agency.

Eastwood was the latest player to have had his visa application rejected, following in the footsteps of Todd Carney, who had been hoping to join Huddersfield, Michael Crocker, Hull FC, and Greg Bird, who had signed a contract with Bradford but was facing a trial in April on charges of maliciously wounding his girlfriend. St Helens coach Mick Potter confirmed that Francis Meli was still waiting for a new visa. Meli went back to New Zealand after representing Samoa in the World Cup and had been stranded after failing to submit his application in time.

CARNEGIE CHALLENGE CUP - ROUND 2

Saturday 14th February 2009

Featherstone Lions 12 The Army 30; Kells 31 Leigh Miners Rangers 22; Saddleworth Rangers 20 Castleford Lock Lane 16; Sharlston Rovers 24 Leigh East 10; Siddal 34 West Bowling 10; Wath Brow Hornets 40 Hull Dockers 22; Widnes St Maries 8 Queens 15; Wigan St Judes 24 Pilkington Recs 28; Wigan St Patricks 20 West Hull 16

Sunday 15th February 2009

Leeds Met Carnegie 20 Edinburgh Eagles 8; Loughborough University 20 Royal Navy 18

That meant a full debut for St Helens' teenage winger Tom Armstrong in the highly anticipated match-up with Warrington Wolves. With new coach James Lowes having had a full off-season with the Wolves, and two big signings in Mickey Higham and Garreth Carvell brought in, a first ever Super League victory at Knowsley Road looked highly possible as Warrington led 14-0 after 46 minutes, through tries by Higham and Paul Rauhihi. But in 31 second-half minutes Saints showed they remained as ruthless as ever under Potter, running in six unanswered tries to win 26-14. Lee Gilmour sparked the seemingly inevitable Saints fightback with a 49th-minute try as he skinned opposite centre Paul Johnson for pace from a scrum, and was quickly followed over by Ade Gardner and Matt Gidley (twice). James Graham ensured Saints were still unbeaten in 25 games against Warrington, who had won just one of their 34 Super League meetings, before 19-year-old Armstrong scored late on after a great Tony Puletua break.

New Huddersfield boss Nathan Brown got his season off with a bang with a 30-8 victory against the Catalans in France on the Saturday. The success was achieved without former Kiwi Test hooker David Faiumu, who had flown back home following the death of his grandfather, allowing winter recruits Scott Moore and Shaun Lunt to shine in his absence. The game provided a painful Super League debut for former Australian Test star Jason Ryles, who staggered off in a daze early on after a huge hit by Darrell Griffin and Moore.

Hull KR captain Mick Vella suffered a medial ligament strain to his knee at Bradford in a thrilling 13-13 draw, while Bulls back-rowers David Solomona and Jamie Langley both dislocated shoulders. It was a dramatic finish. After 78 minutes, home scrum-half Paul Deacon appeared to have nicked it for Bradford by kicking a field goal that just about climbed over the crossbar. The Bulls were then awarded a penalty in their own half with the seconds ticking away and had to play out the set for the one-point win. They spilled the ball however. Rovers worked the ball back towards the Rooley Lane end where, with the hooter already sounding, Deacon's opposite number Michael Dobson scraped over a one-pointer that earned his side a valuable opening-day draw.

Harlequins got of to a good start with a 12-8 victory at Castleford. Luke Dorn, who had played at the Tigers in 2008, grabbed both Quins tries, registered in a matter of seconds in a stunning period straddling the break. Castleford fielded nine new players for the first time in a competitive game, and were missing Brett Sherwin with an ankle problem.

Hull halfback Richard Horne looked set for a big season after his 2008 season had been wiped out by injury and illness, as he played a key role in an impressive 18-10 home defeat of Wigan Warriors. Horne opened Hull's scoring with his 99th try for the club and followed it with a sky-high kick that led to a crucial second-half touchdown, as well as producing a raking 40/20 touchfinder. Wigan led twice and put in plenty of effort but they were down to only 11 fit players by the finish. The match was well balanced until Peter Cusack's converted try gave Hull an eight-point lead with just over ten minutes left.

In the Saturday night clash of the two promoted teams, Salford blitzed Celtic Crusaders early on and eventually ran out 28-16 winners. Just like in their opener at Leeds eight days earlier, Celtic were guilty of a slow start. Salford took full advantage to lead by 20 points after the same number of minutes. But Celtic took a lot of heart from the way they performed in the last 60 minutes. The Welsh team played some great stuff in attack, with fullback Tony Duggan grabbing his 99th and 100th tries for the club. And they looked set to pull off a stunning comeback win before a Malcolm Alker-inspired Salford found a second wind late on. Rob Parker captained Salford for the first time since being named as Alker's permanent successor. It was Parker's first Super League appearance for the Reds and for Willie Talau, Mark Henry, Jeremy Smith, Ray Cashmere and Luke Swain plus Richard Myler and Craig Stapleton.

* That weekend it was reported the RFL was set to clinch a landmark deal to play England Rugby League games at the 2012 Olympic Stadium in east London.

Round 2

Celtic Crusaders welcomed Super League to south Wales on the Saturday night with a colourful display to greet 5,272 excited fans in Bridgend. But Danny Tickle punctured the party atmosphere with a hat-trick of tries as Hull withstood an early onslaught by the Crusaders to seal an impressive 28-20 win. It was a genuine hat-trick as the former Halifax and Wigan back-rower tore over for two scores leading up to the break, before racing over for his third minutes after the restart.

Hull coach Richard Agar was pleased to come away from Bridgend with the points after Celtic, slow starters in their previous two games, had come out firing in their first home fixture and raced into a 10-nil lead with tries from Damien Quinn and debutant Marshall Chalk. A knee injury to fullback Todd Byrne in the build-up to the first try compounded Hull's woeful start but they responded in fine style as Shaun Berrigan went from dummy-half close to the line and Tickle's conversion brought the visitors to within four points. Tickle levelled the game with a powerful score on 35 minutes off Richard Horne's deft pass. The resulting conversion meant Hull were in the lead for the first time and just before the half-time hooter they extended the lead from a great set move. Straight from a scrum, a grubber kick by Richard Horne bounced up for Tickle, out at stand-off, to dance through and score his second try. More indiscipline in the Crusaders defence cost them early in the second half as Tickle took full advantage of a penalty to complete his hat-trick. Berrigan slipped the ball inside to Tickle and he barged through the Crusaders defence to extend his side's lead.

England winger Mark Calderwood was sent to the sin bin for lying on, three minutes later, and the momentum swung back in the Crusaders' favour. The Welsh side battled back and a Mark Dalle Court run eventually led to the former Canberra player Chalk scoring his second try through the right channel from a Van Dijk pass. But on his return to the field of battle, Calderwood sealed the game for Hull with his side's fifth and final try of the night. The Crusaders scored through fullback Tony Duggan with seconds left on the clock to salvage a measure of pride, but it was ultimately a disappointing defeat in their first home game.

Castleford piled the pressure on Wigan coach Brian Noble by holding off a second-half fightback to condemn the Warriors to their worst start in 24 years, with a 28-22 victory at the JJB Stadium. Not since the 1985-86 season had Wigan lost their opening three games - and each of those defeats had come against teams that didn't make the previous year's play-offs.

Tigers coach Terry Matterson hailed the return to action of Australian scrum-half Brent Sherwin as the big difference. And the fact that the two sides scored five tries apiece showed the significance of Kirk Dixon's two penalties during the opening quarter and how much Wigan missed regular kicker Pat Richards. Already without the suspended Richard Mathers - who received a two-match ban for tripping in the opener against Wakefield - Wigan lost Richards, Cameron Phelps and Phil Bailey to injury, resulting in try-scoring debuts for the fit-again Karl Pryce, after missing the whole of 2008, and 19-year-old Shaun Ainscough on the wings.

Brett Ferres's second try opened up a 14-point cushion in the 51st minute, and although Wigan went close, that proved to be just enough. Tigers captain Ryan Hudson escaped disciplinary action after he was placed on report for allegedly barging into referee Steve Ganson.

Ireland World Cup captain Scott Grix was facing more than a month on the sidelines after suffering an ankle injury during Wakefield's 29-10 home victory over Salford on the Sunday. Wakefield were already missing seven senior players but racked up a deserved 19-0 lead at half-time and rarely looked likely to succumb to a Salford fight-back after the break. Damien Blanch and Ryan Atkins both touched down twice. Brad Drew's field goal just before half-time put Wakefield four scores clear and well beyond Salford's reach.

Warrington coach James Lowes was left looking for clues after his side's latest second-half capitulation, this time to Catalans Dragons in the Saturday TV game. Leading 18-6 with only seconds of the first half remaining, the Wolves conceded two tries either side of half-time and fell away badly in the second half, as the Catalans recorded their first win of the season by 40-20, this despite the Frenchmen being reduced to 12 men after the 57th-minute sin-binning of substitute prop David Ferriol. Second-rower Ben Westwood was put on report by World Club Challenge referee Jason Robinson in the ninth minute, after a high-shot that left Catalans prop Dane Carlaw concussed, and ended his involvement in the game. He was banned for five matches.

St Helens finally shook off a resilient Huddersfield Giants at the Galpharm Stadium. The Giants had high hopes of snatching at least a point before Tony Puletua crowned a powerful performance by crashing over for the match-breaking try on 75 minutes. Gary Wheeler gave the victory margin a flattering look at 23-6 with a last-minute try.

Injured Mick Vella missed Rovers' 19-10 defeat by Leeds at Craven Park, in a closely-fought Friday night TV game. Video referee Ian Smith's controversial decision to rule out a Jake Webster score 14 minutes from the end, when the official judged that the Kiwi had knocked on before touching the ball down, proved to be the Robins' last shout. Any hopes Rovers had of victory evaporated in the 71st minute, when Ryan Bailey broke away down the left flank and sent Kallum Watkins over for the winning try. Bailey was knocked out in a collision with Briscoe as he offloaded the ball, and he received eight minutes' treatment before being carried off to a tremendous reception from both sets of supporters. Kevin Sinfield's conversion extended Leeds' lead to eight points, with the captain's field goal two minutes from the final hooter proving academic.

Danny Buderus, Brent Webb, Rob Burrow and Ali Lauitiiti did not play and were set for a race against time in a bid to prove their fitness for the following Sunday's Carnegie World Club Challenge against Manly Sea Eagles. The NRL Premiers that weekend notched a 34-26 warm-up win against Harlequins, which the Quins led 20-0 at half-time after Manly fielded an inexperienced line-up for the first half.

Off the field, it was confirmed that Executive Chairman Richard Lewis had been appointed the new Chair of Sport England from 1st April, but would still keep his role as chairman of the RFL.

Round 3

Warrington coach James Lowes was the red hot favourite to be the first top flight coach to leave his position in 2009, according to bookmaker William Hill, after the Wolves crashed to a heavy 48-22 defeat at Wakefield on the Friday night. After the game, Wolves owner Simon Moran entered the post-match press conference to ask what Lowes had said and was surprised to hear that he had praised a defence that had conceded eight tries.

Trinity produced a remarkable performance considering they were still without eight first-team squad players, inspired by the mid-field scheming of makeshift halfback Tony Martin and hooker Brad Drew, who paired up after the returning Sam Obst went off injured early on. Prop James Stosic was another early casualty, leaving coach John Kear with only 15 fit men for most of the game. Drew or Martin were involved in seven of Wakefield's eight tries, including setting up Matt Blaymire's hat-trick. The fullback opened the scoring by touching down Martin's short kick, then crashed over from the halfback's pass before grabbing a third late on off Drew's kick. Martin also sent up the high kick that led to the first of Dave Halley's two tries and sparked off the brilliant move that ended with a spectacular score for Luke George, while Drew produced the passes for Dale Ferguson's two touchdowns.

Warrington did have their moments and put in plenty of effort but their performance was epitomised by Chris Riley. The young fullback tried desperately to turn the tide and broke through to set up a wonderful try for Chris Bridge, only to spoil his efforts with a couple of mistakes that led to Trinity tries. Warrington were 24-0 down in 25 minutes. Wakefield finished the game in style when Martin sent Ryan Atkins on a superb cross field run to link with Sean Gleeson before George finished it all off in great style just after going on as a substitute for his first appearance in 12 months.

The pressure was relieved on Brian Noble as Wigan got off the mark in London with a 24-18 victory at Harlequins. Harlequins were leading 18-14 with five minutes left on the clock following Chris Melling's 70th minute try. The otherwise outstanding Chad Randall threw a long cut-out ball to his left, which was snapped up by winger Amos Roberts and the former Sydney Rooster raced over from 40 metres out. The try completely reversed the momentum of a pulsating game. Danny Orr's kick-off went straight out on the full and victory was secured when youngster Shaun Ainscough capped a strong performance by winning the race to Sean O'Loughlin's kick to prevent a fourth straight loss for Noble's side.

Noble had rung the changes, with Karl Pryce dropped after just one game and Sam Tomkins outstanding on his Super League debut. Richie Mathers was not recalled after suspension.

Huddersfield Giants' 16-12 win on the Friday night saw them pick up their second win in their opening three fixtures and put an end to a 40-year losing run against Bradford Bulls at Odsal. As in Perpignan a fortnight previously, having successfully weathered an early onslaught from their hosts, the impressive Giants frustrated then forced their opponents into submission.

Bradford opened up a 6-0 lead, courtesy of three Paul Deacon penalties. But the Bulls were caught accidentally offside when the third restart was fumbled by Terry Newton straight into the hands of a surprised Steve Menzies and, following back-to-back sets, Leroy Cudjoe's sleight of hand put Martin Aspinwall over in the corner. Then as the timekeepers reached for the hooter, Brett Hodgson's final grubber was scooped up and touched down by Jamahl Lolesi. Three minutes into the second half Ben Jeffries sent Glenn Morrison skipping his way to the line, with Deacon's conversion restoring the Bulls' lead. But, having already lost Wayne Godwin to a head knock, Bradford were reduced to 15 fit men when Deacon also left the field dazed and with blood gushing from a wound. The Giants started to dominate from then on, and it was no surprise when Hodgson put Kevin Brown through a gap and Stephen Wild, up in support, raced over.

Hull FC made it three wins from three with Richard Horne scoring his 100th try for the club in a convincing 28-12 home win over Catalans, missing Jamal Fakir, who had been suspended for one game after being cited for a high tackle in the win at Warrington. Hull's first-half performance was particularly impressive, with tries by Shaun Berrigan and Craig Hall, in his first start of the year for Hull, deputising at fullback for the injured Todd Byrne - both converted by Danny Tickle, plus a 14th minute penalty.

Hull, who that week announced the signing of New Zealand and Tongan Test forward Epalahame Lauaki from NZ Warriors, had never before managed three wins on the bounce to open a Super League season.

Nick Fozzard made a triumphant return to St Helens on the Friday night as his new team, Hull KR, ripped up the formbook to record a sensational 20-19 win. More late heroics from Michael Dobson gave Hull KR their first win at St Helens for 24 years. Sean Long's one-pointer ten minutes from time looked to have extended Saints' club record of 19 regular-season games unbeaten since losing away to Castleford in Round 10 in 2008. But Dobson, who had kicked a last-gasp field goal to secure a 13-13 draw at Bradford in Round 1, held his nerve to convert a 77th-minute penalty and edge the Robins in front for the first time. Four times Saints led, with converted tries by Tony Puletua, Gary Wheeler and Paul Wellens coming before Long's field goal. But led by Dobson's relentless probing of the Saints line, Rovers fought back, Ben Galea crossing before the break, while Peter Fox and Jake Webster followed in the second half.

Castleford followed up their victory at Wigan by demolishing new boys Salford 52-16 at the Jungle. From the very first minute, when Kirk Dixon - the kicker of eight goals on the night - was bundled into touch at the corner, to two minutes from time, when substitute Dean Widders scampered over to ensure a 50-plus point rout, the nine-try Tigers showed absolute authority. The Reds trailed 28-0 at one point, just a week after falling 19-0 behind at Wakefield before eventually losing 29-10.

That weekend the French Federation appointed Bobbie Goulding, whose experience as a professional coach extended to two spells with Rochdale, as head coach of the France national side.

SUPER LEAGUE TABLE - *Saturday 28th February*

	P	W	D	L	F	A	D	PTS
Leeds Rhinos	3	3	0	0	65	20	45	6
Wakefield T Wildcats	4	3	0	1	93	56	37	6
Hull FC	3	3	0	0	74	42	32	6
Castleford Tigers	3	2	0	1	88	50	38	4
St Helens	3	2	0	1	68	40	28	4
Huddersfield Giants	3	2	0	1	52	43	9	4
Hull Kingston Rovers	3	1	1	1	43	51	-8	3
Harlequins	2	1	0	1	30	32	-2	2
Wigan Warriors	4	1	0	3	62	76	-14	2
Catalans Dragons	3	1	0	2	60	78	-18	2
Salford City Reds	3	1	0	2	54	97	-43	2
Bradford Bulls	2	0	1	1	25	29	-4	1
Celtic Crusaders	3	0	0	3	42	84	-42	0
Warrington Wolves	3	0	0	3	56	114	-58	0

World Club Challenge

There was no fairytale successive win for Leeds in the World Club Challenge, NRL Premiers Manly Sea Eagles proving a much different proposition than Melbourne Storm at Elland Road twelve months before and winning 28-20. A three-try, five-minute blitz at the start of the second half did for the Rhinos but in truth they were second best for most of the game.

Leeds were given a pre-match boost when Rob Burrow was passed fit to start at scrum-half while Ali Lauitiiti also returned to the 17-man squad with a spot on the bench. But Anthony Watmough and Brett Stewart both crossed twice and it was only in the final quarter, with the match already won, that Leeds were able to claw back some respectability with tries from Keith Senior, Ryan Hall and Danny McGuire.

Jamie Peacock and Josh Perry were sin-binned in the first half after an all-in fight broke out, while Ryan Bailey exchanged punches with Matt Ballin in the closing stages.

Burrow left the field after just 17 minutes after a monster tackle from Watmough. Sea Eagles fullback Brett Stewart scored first, dummying from the play the ball after both sides had been temporarily reduced to 12 men thanks to an all-in melee sparked by Peacock's flurry of punches on his opposite number Perry. Five minutes later, Matt Orford slipped Watmough clear to swerve around Lee Smith and suddenly Leeds were staring down the barrel of a potential massacre.

Any chance of a comeback would have been even more remote had Watmough's pass stuck to the supporting Brett Stewart as Leeds were left exposed again, but the Rhinos dragged themselves back into contention just before the break. Kevin Sinfield's kick was charged down as the seconds ticked away but Jamie Jones-Buchanan reacted first, feeding McGuire on his inside shoulder and supporting the stand-off as he hared towards the line. When Stewart held up McGuire over the line, it was Jones-Buchanan who was on hand to ground the loose ball, with the try eventually being confirmed by video referee Steve Ganson.

That score may have buoyed the crowd and lifted Leeds' hopes, but it did nothing to

Jamie Jones-Buchanan tries to escape the attentions of Jamie Lyon

affect a ruthless Manly outfit. Instead, they left the Rhinos for dead with a devastating five-minute burst after the interval. Brett Stewart bagged his brace in the 43rd minute after pouncing on Carl Ablett's mistake, before Watmough completed his double three minutes later following Stewart's break. Steve Matai wrapped things up with a juggling effort in the 48th minute and Leeds' only challenge was to avoid humiliation, with Senior crossing after collecting Ali Lauitiiti's wonder pass before Ryan Hall was the beneficiary of more mesmerising skills from the Kiwi forward. McGuire closed the scoring by finishing Senior's break in the final minute but Matt Orford's penalty goal a few minutes earlier meant there was never any chance of a shock Rhinos win.

CARNEGIE WORLD CLUB CHALLENGE

Sunday 1st March 2009

LEEDS RHINOS 20 MANLY SEA EAGLES 28

RHINOS: 3 Lee Smith; 2 Scott Donald; 18 Carl Ablett; 4 Keith Senior; 5 Ryan Hall; 6 Danny McGuire; 7 Rob Burrow; 8 Kylie Leuluai; 14 Matt Diskin; 10 Jamie Peacock; 11 Jamie Jones-Buchanan; 17 Ian Kirke; 13 Kevin Sinfield (C). Subs (all used): 12 Ali Lauitiiti; 16 Ryan Bailey; 19 Luke Burgess; 23 Kallum Watkins.
Tries: Jones-Buchanan (37), Senior (64), Hall (72), McGuire (79); **Goals:** Sinfield 2/4.
Sin bin: Peacock (20) - fighting.
SEA EAGLES: 1 Brett Stewart; 2 Michael Robertson; 3 Jamie Lyon; 4 Steve Matai; 5 David Williams; 6 Chris Bailey; 7 Matt Orford (C); 8 Jason King; 9 Matt Ballin; 10 Josh Perry; 11 Anthony Watmough; 12 Glenn Hall; 13 Glenn Stewart. Subs (all used): 14 Heath L'Estrange; 15 Adam Cuthbertson; 16 George Rose; 17 Shane Rodney.
Tries: B Stewart (22, 43), Watmough (28, 46), Matai (48); **Goals:** Orford 4/6.
Sin bin: Perry (20) - fighting.
Rugby Leaguer & League Express Men of the Match:
Rhinos: Danny McGuire; *Sea Eagles:* Anthony Watmough.
Penalty count: 12-11; **Half-time:** 4-12;
Referee: Jason Robinson;
Attendance: 32,569 *(at Elland Road, Leeds).*

MARCH
Bird flies in

Round 4

The bookies were right about the tenuousness of James Lowes position. The appointment of England coach Tony Smith as Warrington's head of coaching and rugby was announced on the first Tuesday of March. Lowes had effectively been demoted to a number-two role, with Smith signing a three-year deal to lead the Wolves, although the former Bradford hooker did retain the title of first team coach. Eventually, the bookmakers paid out on bets. Smith was to stay on as coach of England on a part-time basis, although he stood down from his job as Technical Director at the Rugby Football League.

Smith's arrival at the Wolves didn't reap immediate results as one of his former clubs Leeds shrugged off their World Club Championship disappointment with a 20-14 win at the Halliwell Jones Stadium. It was a bruised and battered Rhinos side lacking six first team regulars. Two quick-fire tries from the Rhinos in the opening six minutes ensured Warrington's new dawn got off to the worst possible start. The home sided rallied to tie the scores on the hour mark, but having soaked up the pressure Leeds made a rare break into the home half on 70 minutes. Jamie Jones-Buchanan slipped the ball to Rob Burrow, keeping the ball alive on the final tackle and Ali Lauitiiti lobbed it on to Lee Smith. The fullback's downfield kick was fielded by Chris Riley who set about clearing his line only to be scythed down by a stunning Jones-Buchanan tackle that jolted the ball free. Danny McGuire swooped on it and galloped between the sticks for the score, with Sinfield tagging on the conversion to seal victory.

The other huge story of the week was Catalans Dragons' signing of Greg Bird, who in February had signed for Bradford Bulls before being refused a visa to work in the UK. Bird made his bow in the 20th minute of his side's 24-22 home defeat against Castleford on the Saturday night. The former Cronulla star was released by his Australian club and banned by the NRL as a result of an impending court case for the alleged assault of his girlfriend. Bird had signed a nine-month contract with the Dragons, and replaced long-term injury casualty Sébastien Raguin, who had been deregistered from the club's 25-man squad. There was uncertainty over whether border officials would allow him into the UK for away games but the club was confident they would because he had a French work visa.

Following the defeat, the Catalans lay in tenth place after losing for the third time. Thomas Bosc's inability to add the goal to Cyril Stacul's second try less than a minute before the final whistle meant the Tigers, guided expertly by Brent Sherwin, went home with the two points, and finished the weekend in third place in the Super League table.

Hull were in second spot behind Leeds after their 24-20 win at Huddersfield, their fourth win in a row - the club's best start to a season since 1991. The two sides each scored four tries, with the goalkicking of Danny Tickle eventually proving to be the difference on the scoreboard, but Hull were much the better side as the Giants underperformed in front of the TV cameras.

Richard Horne, voted the Player of the Month for February by Rugby League World magazine, took his outstanding form into March. Horne had shot into the lead in the year's Albert Goldthorpe Medal table with eleven points after four rounds. Halfback partner and former Giants captain Chris Thorman was also a standout behind a dominant pack that didn't seem weakened by the non-arrival of Michael Crocker. Hull coach Richard Agar gave new signing Sam Moa what he described as a 'cameo' debut appearance during the second half. The powerful Tongan World Cup star played just 12 minutes and looked far from match fit, but made several blockbusting runs.

Wigan coach Brian Noble reckoned his side was beginning to take shape after claiming their first home win of the season - a comprehensive 44-10 victory against Bradford on the Saturday, with Sam Tomkins handed his first Super League start after coming off the bench in the win at Harlequins the previous week. The Warriors romped to a seven-try win, with Gareth Hock and Harrison Hansen scoring two tries apiece. The Bulls seldom threatened on a miserable evening for Steve McNamara's men, who lost hooker Wayne Godwin in the second half through a broken leg and were still looking for their first win of the season after three games.

Hull KR coach Justin Morgan paid tribute to John Kear's injury-ravaged Wakefield after watching his Rovers side emerge 31-18 winners at Craven Park on the Sunday. Kear had been voted the Coach of the Month by Rugby League World, but the Wildcats started without ten first-team regulars, and then lost Brad Drew inside the first 40 seconds after a perfectly timed hit by Scott Murrell. Trinity were already without a recognised halfback and Drew's departure forced an early introduction for 19-year-old call centre worker Luke Blake.

Inspired by Shaun Briscoe and Michael Dobson, who kicked five goals from five attempts, Rovers led 30-6 midway through the second half before a late Trinity resurgence forced Dobson into knocking over a field goal to make certain of the points.

Salford were starting to look well off the pace and were booed off at half-time on the Friday night as Harlequins led 30-6 at the Willows. Quins' halfback combination of Danny Orr and former Red Luke Dorn cut Salford to shreds with their pace, slick passing and deadly kicking. Salford looked a different side in the second half but fell to a 48-18 defeat.

St Helens skipper Keiron Cunningham hit out at the slow play-the-balls in Super League in 2009 after his side's 4-0 win over Celtic Crusaders in the mud of Bridgend on the Saturday night. The only score came from winger Tom Armstrong on 55 minutes. However, Cunningham praised the Super League new boys, who mounted a valiant display against the Challenge Cup holders in front of a club record crowd of 6,351. Lincoln Withers made his Crusaders debut after a ten-month absence due to an anterior cruciate ligament injury.

* The third round of the Carnegie Challenge Cup threw up just one shock, with West Cumbrian amateurs Wath Brow Hornets edging out Championship One side London Skolars 14-12. Two tries from loose forward Scott Teare saw the National Conference League Division One outfit home at a water-logged Recreation Ground. Doncaster went through to the fourth round after the RFL ruled the result of their abandoned tie with Leeds amateurs Queens should stand. The tie was called off after 63 minutes because of violence in the stands between supporters. Doncaster, who had been trailing 2-0 at half-time, had edged 16-12 ahead by the time of the abandonment. South Yorkshire Police arrested three people for public order offences.

Round 5

Hull marched to a fifth victory on the trot, while winless Bradford stayed rooted in Super League's bottom three after the Airlie Birds' 36-24 win at Odsal. For the second week in a row, the final scoreboard scarcely reflected just how dominant Richard Agar's Hull side were. The Bulls were 12-0 down after the first six minutes as the black and whites scored six tries in all and defended resolutely throughout. A Bradford side lacking in confidence battled but never looked like taking anything from a match in which Chris Thorman had an outstanding game at scrum-half for the visitors, ably backed up by second-rower Willie Manu and double-try-scoring pair Kirk Yeaman and Craig Hall. Bulls coach Steve McNamara, who gave a debut to young centre Jason Crookes, maintained it was not the time to panic. William Hill made him the new favourite to leave his post.

Tigers coach Terry Matterson accused Huddersfield of making constant grapple tackles during the 26-24 Saturday night defeat to the Giants at the Jungle - a claim that was strenuously denied by counterpart Nathan Brown. Matterson said the Giants were 'round our heads all day' after Huddersfield ended up on the wrong end of a 14-5 penalty count.

Captain Brett Hodgson came up with two pieces of decisive action when most needed to swing the game Huddersfield's way – in defence and attack. With the score locked at 20-20, Tigers winger Richard Owen went hard for the corner in the 62nd minute. It looked like a certain try until Hodgson crashed him into touch with a flying tackle inches short of the goal line. Within two minutes the fullback was at the other end of the field and plunging over from a play-the-ball under the posts. He then tagged on the goal that was to prove all-important. The fullback had also linked up to send in David Hodgson for the first of his three tries to put Huddersfield back in front at 14-12 just before half-time.

Clint Newton celebrated his contract extension by scoring a hat-trick of tries as Hull KR put Super League new boys Celtic Crusaders to the sword at Craven Park, by 48-18. Newton took over the captain's arm-band following the late withdrawal of skipper Shaun Briscoe with a dead-leg. The Australian, who signed a new deal until the end of 2013, claimed in Rugby League World magazine that the NRL's treatment of some of their players was one reason for him not wanting to return to Australia, specifically referring to the de-registering of Greg Bird without the player being found guilty of an alleged offence.

It was the first time Rovers had won three consecutive Super League games and left the visitors still searching for their first win of the season, although a Darren Mapp try and Josh Hannay goal had the scores level on 35 minutes. The victory took Rovers into fifth place in the table with seven points from their opening five matches.

If Tony Smith had any illusions over the size of the task facing him at Warrington, they were blown away after a Danny Orr-inspired Harlequins ran in ten tries to destroy the Wolves by 60-8 at the Stoop. It was the Wolves' worst-ever start to a league season, and with five defeats in their opening five games they remained rooted to the foot of the Super League table. Aussie centre Matt King later apologised for aiming a one-finger insult at Warrington fans after the humiliation. For the rampant Harlequins it was a third win in four matches.

Salford coach Shaun McRae remained confident the City Reds could kick-start their season after a 38-12 Friday-night defeat at St Helens, their fourth straight defeat after winning their opener against the Celtic Crusaders. Hooker Malcolm Alker admitted he had 'learned lessons' after he was restored to the captaincy. Alker had been sacked in pre-season after incidents during the training camp in Florida but had been brought back as team captain, with Rob Parker taking up the position of club captain. Saints, with Jon Wilkin on top form, managed to score four tries in an error-strewn first half, adding another three after the break before Salford even troubled the scorers.

John Kear hailed Wakefield's youngsters after another battling victory took the Wildcats into the top four - this time a 30-10 win over Catalans without nine first team regulars. The Wildcats took a slender 12-10 advantage into the changing rooms at half-time and then stonewall defence kept the Dragons pointless during a second half when the visitors' chances were restricted to a couple of close calls near to the corner flag. Greg Bird made a surprise debut on British soil, having been expected to miss the game due to being recalled to his homeland to deal with pre-trial legal matters. Catalans coach Kevin Walters promised to instigate a stern examination of his side's discipline after a fourth defeat in five games on the back of a 15-6 caning in the penalty count.

The big game of the weekend was unbeaten Leeds' clash with resurgent Wigan at Headingley, a searing point-a-minute opening quarter the foundation of the Rhinos' 34-10 win. The Rhinos were without a recognised first team hooker Danny Buderus, recovering from knee surgery, and Matt Diskin still ruled out with a neck injury, forcing Jamie Jones-Buchanan, Rob Burrow and Kevin Sinfield to share the role. Ryan Hall scored twice for Leeds whilst Carl Ablett produced a man of the match performance with some powerful runs

Leeds' early control of the game was absolute, right from the moment Rob Burrow kicked a 40/20 at the end of the first set. It was hard to recall a more one-sided opening 25 minutes and 16 seconds of Super League. At that stage of the game, Leeds - Brent Webb making his first start of the season - made their first handling error, Kevin Sinfield knocking the ball on, and then Lee Smith's interference at the tackle saw Ian Smith award the first penalty of the night. Wigan got the ball into the Rhinos' half of the field for the first time. At 18-0 down, that gave the shell-shocked Warriors some hope even though, to the utter dismay of their fans, possession was lost, not for the first time, by Gareth Hock. Lee Smith produced a 40/20 from dummy-half reminiscent of the one he kicked in last year's Grand Final, and before too long Ali Lauitiiti's trademark looping pass to the left was putting Hall into the left corner.

After the game, coach Brian McClennan hailed Sinfield the greatest on-field leader in Leeds' illustrious history.

The previous Thursday Toulouse Olympique made a disastrous start to their debut season in English Rugby League - a 70-0 hammering in a televised match at Widnes - in the week it was confirmed they would be exempt from relegation from the Co-operative Championship.

* The number of penalties awarded in Super League in 2009 had plummeted, according to figures obtained by League Express. Statistics from Opta showed a total of 123 fewer penalties had been awarded during the first four rounds - a drop of more than 28 per cent.

Round 6

The Rhinos lost their unbeaten record in Super League XIV with a 26-18 defeat to St Helens at Knowsley Road. An incendiary atmosphere threatened to blow up after a Ryan Bailey tackle knocked out Maurie Fa'asavalu in the 47th minute, just after Saints had received a penalty following a dust up between Lee Gilmour and Lee Smith at a play-the-ball. After he was brought round, a bloodied Fa'asavalu walked off the Knowsley Road pitch. Bailey was not penalised, but Saints coach Mick Potter remained unimpressed by the incident when contacted by League Express. 'It was a shoulder to the head, and he smashed his nose,' the former Catalans coach said. Rhinos coach Brian McClennan defended Bailey. 'The tackle was absolutely fine,' McClennan insisted. The RFL Match Review Panel agreed with him when it met the following Monday, adjudging that Fa'asavalu had dropped into Bailey's shoulder, but after the incident Bailey was a target, with James Graham hunting him down at every opportunity.

It was a sensational game without all that. St Helens led 18-6 at half-time after an action-packed first half that boasted four tries, all of them converted, five goal-line drop-outs, all eight substitutes deployed, an injury to Rob Burrow, loads of forceful running, stinging defence, the occasional handling error, plus a keep-the-ball-alive-at-all-costs mentality from both teams. Ryan Hall's second-half try got Leeds back in it, but Gary Wheeler's 63rd minute effort regained the home initiative. When, on 69 minutes, Chris Flannery skipped away past Rob Burrow just inside his own half, Matt Gidley was on hand to score his second try. The Rhinos continued to scrap on, and forced another two GLDOs before Keith Senior completed his brace in the dying seconds of what was Saints' night.

Tony Smith's back-to-basics approach finally saw Warrington return to winning ways. The Wolves stopped the rot with a 24-12 home win over Hull KR on the Sunday, halting a ten-match losing streak which stretched back to early August 2008. Two tries from Paul Johnson, a solid defensive display, a belting first-half effort from Michael Monaghan and some good work off the bench by Lee Briers, a battling effort from Ben Harrison and some sparkling stuff from fullback Chris Riley all highlighted a much improved display. The much maligned Matt King even managed to raise a cheer when he scored. More bad news for the Robins was the shoulder injury to Chev Walker who was facing another lengthy spell on the sidelines.

Castleford shattered Hull's 100 per cent record on the Friday night with a dramatic 19-18 victory to secure the Tigers' first win at either the Boulevard or the KC Stadium in nine years. Brent Sherwin was the headline match-winner with a 77th minute field goal on his 31st birthday, but it was former Hull player Kirk Dixon's three-out-of-three conversions from near touch against his old club that put them in that position after Hull's Danny Tickle managed only one from four, despite going into the game as this season's lead goal scorer. Graeme Horne scored three tries for Hull, who missed a chance to go top after Leeds' defeat on the same night.

Dave Halley returned to Odsal from his loan spell at Wakefield and came off the bench in France on the Saturday night to score the winning try with just seconds left, as the Bulls secured a dramatic 30-24 victory against Catalans Dragons. The Bulls' first win of the season saw them leapfrog the Dragons in the Super League table.

Dragons coach Kevin Walters had awarded the captaincy of his team to newly arrived Greg Bird, and Jean-Philippe Baile's converted try on 66 minutes had given the Dragons a 24-18 lead, but Terry Newton replied and though Paul Sykes missed the easy conversion he kicked a penalty goal minutes later to set up a thrilling climax. Bradford went for a long-range field goal through Sykes, which drifted narrowly wide. On the subsequent set Thomas Bosc's clearance kick went out on the full, giving the visitors one last chance to claim victory. The ball went back to Sykes for another drop goal but instead he shifted the ball to Ben Jeffries who skipped through to the right and put Halley over with a handful of seconds left on the clock. Sykes added his second goal to complete the action of another dramatic match.

Brian McDermott defended his players after a 'bad day at the office' saw Harlequins' promising start to Super League XIV derailed by a 46-6 thumping at Huddersfield. The Londoners had won three of their first four games, including wins at Castleford and Salford, as well as a 60-8 humbling of Warrington just eight days beforehand. The Giants, despite three straight wins away this season, had not won at the Galpharm Stadium since July 6th 2008 and had already lost to St Helens and Hull on home soil this term. Scott Moore, on a year's loan from St Helens after a similar arrangement in 2008 with Castleford, continued his brilliant form at hooker. Quins, who began round six as top scorers in the division despite playing one less match than most, began promisingly, with Chris Melling almost scoring in the opening two minutes. But they trudged off at the break 28-0 down, as the Giants wrapped up the game with a clinical first-half performance that resulted in five tries, four of them converted by Brett Hodgson.

Wigan coach Brian Noble warned fans not to expect too much too soon from youngsters Sam Tomkins and Shaun Ainscough, after they starred in a 38-12 victory at Salford on the Friday. The youngsters scored two tries apiece at The Willows after Noble had dropped experienced players Richard Mathers, Amos Roberts and Tim Smith. Salford coach Shaun McRae hailed young scrum-half Richie Myler after seeing further evidence of his developing talent. The 18-year-old returned from a hand injury and scored both Salford's tries.

March

Earlier that week, Reds forward Ian Sibbit spoke of his 'massive relief' after escaping a potential two-year ban for high levels of the asthma drug Salbutamol in his system, despite the World Anti Doping Agency appealing against the RFL's initial decision that Sibbit had no case to answer. The appeal tribunal reprimanded Sibbit for the use of the drug contained in his asthma inhaler.

* Round six of Super League XIV will live in the memory for the saddest of reasons. Wakefield were due to play the last fixture of the weekend in a televised clash at Celtic Crusaders on the Sunday evening, but 35 minutes before kick-off the fixture was called off after Leon Walker died playing for the Wildcats' reserve-grade side against the Crusaders at Maesteg. Walker, 20, a Churwell Chiefs junior and England Academy international who had signed from Salford over the winter and had played for Wakefield in the Boxing Day friendly at Leeds, collapsed after making a tackle. He was flown to hospital in Swansea by air ambulance but was later pronounced dead. The news shocked and saddened everyone involved in the sport.

Round 7

Wakefield Wildcats went down to a 42-18 defeat on the Friday against St Helens at Belle Vue on what must have been one of the most emotional nights in the history of the game. The crowd applauded when Leon Walker's parents and family walked out onto the pitch prior to kick-off, and watched a heartrending interview on the big screen and a minute's silence as both teams lined up facing each other along with Leon's teammates and Wakefield Trinity legends.

Wakefield captain Jason Demetriou suggested the team had let down Leon with their worst display of the season but Leon's father, Steve Walker, insisted the Wakefield players could hold their heads high. A post-mortem was unable to reach a conclusion about the cause of Leon's death, while confirming he hadn't suffered a broken neck.

Wildcats coach John Kear had said the result would not matter and Wakefield, despite being level on the hour mark weren't at the races after that. Leon Pryce came up with an outstanding performance, the day after a judge had warned him he faced a jail sentence for common assault, highlighted by a quality hat-trick of tries. Down on the team sheet at scrum-half to replace injured Sean Long, Pryce's style differed little from his usual stand-off role and he set a great example to the youngsters in the Saints team. Pryce reserved the best till last when he completed his hat-trick in great style, dummying and breaking through on a diagonal 40-metre sprint to the corner.

On the same night, Catalans boss Kevin Walters sent out a stark warning to his side that they had to improve quickly if they wanted to avoid their season collapsing completely. Walters had presided over six defeats out of seven in 2009, with their latest heavy loss coming at Headingley when they went down 42-14 against Leeds.

The Giants went into third place after a Friday 22-8 win at Wigan. Huddersfield - their side containing five ex-Warriors - won the contest on the back of a kicking game better suited to conditions that produced an arm-wrestle of a contest. As well as that, the Wigan faithful left the JJB Stadium cursing their side's inability to convert possession, a ten-minute numerical advantage and a favourable penalty count into anything more than two tries. The final margin of victory flattered the Giants - the score was blown out by two late Giants tries. Brett Hodgson was magnificent at fullback, and kicked five goals from as many attempts.

Salford winger Paul White was ruled out for the season after sustaining a knee injury in Salford's 48-12 defeat at Hull KR, this after his early try had put the Reds into a shock lead, and they led until the 34th minute. Michael Dobson and Peter Fox crossed for hat-tricks as Hull KR produced a stunning second-half performance.

Gareth Haggerty and Jon Wells made comebacks for Harlequins in the 22-12 bruising Saturday win over Hull FC, as torrential rain and strong winds battered the Stoop. The game was all square going into the final 20 minutes, but after Danny Orr had kicked a penalty and in-form Chad Randall produced a superb 40/20 kick, David Howell crashed over after some Quins pressure on the line. With time ticking away, Orr stepped up to land a long-range penalty and secure the win.

After an hour of the Sunday clash at Warrington, Celtic Crusaders looked capable of gaining their first Super League victory, but the Wolves showed real resolve to come from behind and secure a 27-22 win at the Halliwell Jones. The late sin-binning of Ryan O'Hara and a return to form for Lee Briers, who returned to the starting line-up for the injured Michael Monaghan, meant John Dixon's men lost out in a gripping contest. The Crusaders played some expansive stuff as they recovered from an early Warrington try to lead 18-12 at half-time. Luke Dyer's second-half try staved off the Wolves a little longer but the hosts made it 22-22 on the hour mark through a converted Lee Mitchell try, which set up an enthralling finale.

With the pressure mounting, O'Hara was shown a yellow card with seven minutes left for kneeling on the face of Chris Riley after stopping a 60-metre break by the Warrington fullback. Briers then kicked a 77th-minute field goal before Chris Hicks' late try secured a back-to-back win for Warrington, after the Wolves had lost their first five games of the season.

Castleford were up to fourth after a stunning 28-26 home win over Bradford. The Tigers were trailing by 16 points, after substitute Dave Halley, with his first touch of the game, had just crossed to seemingly guarantee victory for the visitors with 12 minutes to go.

The fightback began immediately upon the restart as Bradford let the kick bounce into touch, gifting Cas the scrum. From the possession, a superb back-of-hand pass from Dean Widders sent Kirk Dixon in for his second try of the game. Moments later, gamestar Michael Shenton also completed a brace, after Ryan McGoldrick took a lovely Brent Sherwin chip before providing the killer pass. Despite being scored out wide, both of those tries were converted by Dixon who, in a frantic finale, also found time to be bundled into touch in a superb double tackle by Michael Platt and Paul Deacon. And when Rangi Chase then brought he house down with a try on the end of a wonderful solo weaving run, Dixon kept his nerve to kick the winning conversion.

SUPER LEAGUE TABLE - *Sunday 29th March*

	P	W	D	L	F	A	D	PTS
Leeds Rhinos	7	6	0	1	179	84	95	12
St Helens	7	6	0	1	178	88	90	12
Huddersfield Giants	7	5	0	2	166	105	61	10
Castleford Tigers	7	5	0	2	183	142	41	10
Hull FC	7	5	0	2	164	127	37	10
Hull Kingston Rovers	7	4	1	2	182	123	59	9
Harlequins	6	4	0	2	166	116	50	8
Wakefield T Wildcats	7	4	0	3	159	139	20	8
Wigan Warriors	8	3	0	5	162	154	8	6
Warrington Wolves	7	2	0	5	129	228	-99	4
Bradford Bulls	6	1	1	4	115	161	-46	3
Catalans Dragons	7	1	0	6	130	204	-74	2
Salford City Reds	7	1	0	6	108	269	-161	2
Celtic Crusaders	6	0	0	6	82	163	-81	0

APRIL
Fight in the Bulls

Challenge Cup Round 4

One of the Cup favourites were eliminated on the first Sunday of April as St Helens beat Leeds at Headingley by 22-18. Sean Long was missing but Jon Wilkin took man of the match honours, with two momentum changing 40/10s, along with some great distribution. James Roby was also magnificent on his introduction, Lee Gilmour impenetrable, Tony Puletua a huge presence up the middle, Paul Wellens back to his best with some outstanding heroism near his own whitewash and Matt Gidley was chief tormentor out wide. Gidley's 55th minute, classic centre's try opened up a 14-point gap that was a true reflection of the difference between the teams, one that was big enough to ultimately secure victory. Bad news for Saints was that Jason Cayless sustained a shoulder injury that ended his season and ultimately his St Helens career.

In the other all-Super League clashes, Huddersfield performed their second demolition job on Harlequins within a fortnight, this time at the Stoop. Luke Robinson and Kevin Brown pulled the strings on the back of a mighty forward effort led by Eorl Crabtree, and the star performer was once again Brett Hodgson in a 42-16 romp; Hull KR breezed past injury-hit Celtic Crusaders at Craven Park, Michael Dobson kicking six out of six goals in a 32-6 win; and Richie Myler's try three minutes from time gave Salford a surprise 22-18 win at Hull FC, with props Ray Cashmere and Craig Stapleton outstanding as the previous year's runners-up crashed out of the Cup.

In the first of two games televised by the BBC on the Sunday afternoon, there was an amazing clash between Catalans and Bradford in Perpignan. TV viewers looked on in amazement as the Bulls led 26-0 early in the second half, and then crashed to a 40-38 defeat - just one week after throwing away a 16-point advantage at Castleford in the last ten minutes. This after the Catalans, desperate to impress an impatient home crowd who had had little to cheer so far this season, suffered an early blow when Adam Mogg, taking over at stand-off for the first time, pulled a hamstring and went off. The home crowd's first-half misery was compounded soon after the interval when Steve Menzies was put into a gap by Michael Platt, taking a short pass from Deacon to put the visitors 26 points ahead without the Dragons offering even token resistance. But when Olivier Elima made no mistake from Greg Bird's fine offload to open the Dragons' account after 48 minutes, the home side found their self-belief to stage an amazing comeback win.

Gateshead went into the fifth round for the first time in history with a 32-18 win at Doncaster. Former Australian Schoolboys scrum-half Luke Branighan's virtuoso first-half performance capped by a brace of tries put the game beyond Doncaster.

There was almost a massive shock at rejuvenated Barrow, the Raiders falling to a stirring 32-20 defeat by Wigan on the Sunday. Dave Clark's side trailed 24-20 on 61 minutes, when Liam Harrison had a try ruled out for a forward pass, in a game watched by 6,278 people – Barrow's biggest crowd in a quarter of a century.

The big breaking story in League Express was that Warrington centre Martin Gleeson was to sign for Wigan. The Great Britain and England Test centre had been 'rested' by Wolves coach Tony Smith from Warrington's fourth round 56-10 Challenge Cup victory against York City Knights on the Saturday, meaning he would be eligible to play for Wigan in the succeeding rounds of the competition. That week, Gleeson signed a three-and-a-half-year deal with the Warriors for a transfer fee reported to be in the region of £110,000, with Richie Mathers joining the Wolves.

Round 8

Super League set a new attendance record over the Easter period, with an aggregate attendance of 84,474 attending the seven fixtures on the Thursday and Good Friday. Both Wigan and Hull FC posted crowds in excess of 20,000 for their local derbies against St Helens and Hull KR.

Martin Gleeson was pitched straight into battle on the Thursday night against one of his former clubs in a tight game at the JJB Stadium that St Helens edged 19-12. And although he had little to show for some neat touches on a promising debut, there were signs of better times ahead for the cherry and whites as Gleeson's arrival seemed to galvanise the Warriors in a gripping derby. Shaun Ainscough's second try in the 52nd minute gave Wigan a 12-6 lead. But Saints hit back with two tries in four minutes around the hour mark through Matt Gidley and Leon Pryce and stood firm before Kyle Eastmond sealed the win with a late field goal.

The next day the 207th Hull derby produced a game full of fierce pride and passion fought out before a KC Stadium packed with 22,337 fanatical fans. Hull's battling comeback after being 18-4 down early in the second half raised the atmosphere to fever pitch before Rovers came home 18-14. Rovers owed much to Michael Dobson for his midfield guidance and kicking game. With both sides scoring three tries, his conversion of all three for Rovers made all the difference and took them above Hull in the Super League table.

Hull FC's new signing till the end of the season, Stuart Reardon, was expected to make his debut the following week. Reardon was due to be sentenced on 23rd April after admitting common assault against his estranged wife and her partner in 2008, a district judge telling Reardon and Leon Pryce, who was also involved in the incident, that they could be imprisoned.

In an unconnected incident, Rovers' utility Ben Cockayne had been suspended by the club until 1st June, after being found guilty by a court of assault and given a 12-month suspended prison sentence and a community service order. Castleford had terminated the contract of reserve grade player Steve Hayward, who was found guilty of assault in the same incident.

The third big derby of the weekend at Odsal drew fewer than 15,000 fans, but those who stayed away missed a dramatic game as the Bulls stunned their neighbours with a 10-6 win. The game was tied at 6-all, with converted first-half tries from Jamie Jones-Buchanan for Leeds and Michael Worrincy for Bradford. On the hour, Rob Burrow had a spectacular try controversially disallowed by video referee Thierry Alibert. Burrow set off on a blind-side run just outside his own 20-metre line before working a one-two with Brent Webb on his way the line. But Webb had joined the move from an offside position and, instead of being at least four points down, Bradford were the recipients of a kickable penalty which Paul Sykes put wide.

On 66 minutes, the balance of play tilted once more when centre Carl Ablett was sin-binned for a professional foul, as he cynically bundled a grounded Rikki Sheriffe into touch at the end of a searing 60-metre break. Two minutes later, after electing to run the penalty, Ben Jeffries sent over a kick to the Leeds left-side corner where Steve Menzies and Ryan Hall challenged for possession. The ball came loose and Sheriffe beat Keith

Senior and Hall to the touchdown, again on the nod of the video ref. Sykes again missed the conversion.

Then, three minutes before time, Kevin Sinfield chipped over Bradford's stretched defensive line. It bounced nicely for Kallum Watkins on the wing who, although halted by Semi Tadulala, somehow got a one-handed pass inside to Sinfield who then sent the supporting Danny McGuire on a 20-metre run to the corner. The touch-judge had stood his ground and when the final decision was once again referred to Alibert, Jones-Buchanan, drifting between Watkins and Sinfield, was spotted to have knocked the ball on in flight.

The Rugby League Players' Association said it was ready to give its backing to Bulls winger Tame Tupou, who was told that week by a RFL Tribunal that the termination of his contract with six months' notice by the Bulls in February did not breach the RFL's operational rules.

There had already been a major shock earlier on Good Friday when Salford beat Warrington at the Willows by 18-16. Ben Westwood's last-gasp try looked to have secured the Wolves a point but the usually reliable Chris Hicks missed the kickable conversion. Richard Myler took full advantage of the opportunity to impress England coach Tony Smith as he bagged an impressive brace of tries.

Wakefield claimed 21 points in the last 17 minutes at the Jungle to stun the Tigers 35-6. The Wildcats kept Castleford, missing the suspended Ryan McGoldrick (two matches for an elbow in a Cup win at Keighley), at bay until the 57th minute despite playing in slippery conditions and had already scored twice by that point to establish a 14-point buffer. Ryan Atkins' try at the start of the second half put Castleford three scores behind as Danny Brough kept his side heading in the right direction.

Jerome Guisset admitted the Catalans side was still far from its best, despite claiming its second impressive victory in five days - a 28-24 win at Harlequins on the Thursday night. Guisset scored two crucial tries.

And Huddersfield's new acquisition, Liam Fulton, made a tryscoring debut in a 30-10 defeat of Celtic Crusaders on Friday night, as the Giants moved level in the table with Leeds Rhinos. Kevin Brown's 66th-minute try put the game out of the Crusaders' reach, with Brett Hodgson superb at the back once again.

Round 9

Shaun McRae's rejuvenated Reds created history on Easter Monday by becoming the first ever Salford side to take Super League points from Leeds with a stunning 30-20 success - only Salford's third win in 50 years at Headingley. Of the Salford side, only Robbie Paul was born the last time the Reds came away with the spoils in 1977. The win was ensured when Jordan Turner picked off Brent Webb's pass to race home from 60 metres four minutes from time.

Huddersfield's 30-8 win at Hull KR moved them to giddy heights as they rose above Leeds into second spot. They had to recover from 8-0 down after tries to Kris Welham and Liam Colbon, hitting back to lead 10-8 at the break through Michael Lawrence and David Hodgson tries. As the Robins tired, the Brett Hodgson-inspired Giants, who lost new signing Liam Fulton to a knee injury in the first half after a big tackle from Jake Webster, wrapped up victory with further scores from Shaun Lunt and Stephen Wild before Lawrence took a Michael Dobson kick on his own ten-metre line and raced clear. The hooter sounded as the centre had the pace to finish and Hodgson added his fifth goal.

Clint Greenshields and Jason Ryles scored two tries apiece as the Dragons moved level in the table with opponents Wigan after a 40-24 win in Perpignan. Dimitri Pelo, Greg Bird and Gregory Mounis were the other home try-scorers, with Thomas Bosc kicking six goals as the Catalans eventually ran riot against an exhausted looking Wigan side.

The Warriors, on the back of a ferocious derby with St Helens just four days previously and pulling the short straw for the Easter weekend trip to France, faded after a bright opening after which they led 14-4. The arrival of David Ferriol coincided with the Catalans' revival begun by captain Greg Bird stretching over the line. After shipping 36-unanswered points, Wigan scored late consolation tries through Sam Tomkins and Pat Richards.

Two tries each for Danny Orr and Luke Dorn sealed a convincing 40-18 victory for Harlequins at Celtic Crusaders as they bounced back from the home defeat to the Catalans on the previous Thursday evening. Early tries from Tony Clubb, David Howell and Orr shot Quins into an 18-0 lead before the home side responded with an Adam Peek try before half-time. Chris Melling went over on 46 minutes followed by Orr's second - on 50 minutes. Dorn got his first on the 68th minute, and then completed his brace in the final minute. Marshall Chalk and Mark Dalle Cort got second-half tries for the Welsh side, who saw the return of skipper Jace Van Dijk from injury, but they were well beaten and left seeking their first Super League win.

Leaders St Helens, with Sean Long back after a three-match absence, beat Hull FC 44-22 at Knowsley Road. Saints were in command from the eighth minute when Tony Puletua powered over from dummy-half and three minutes later they doubled their advantage when Lee Gilmour stretched over after good work in the build-up from Keiron Cunningham and Leon Pryce. The one-way traffic continued and Saints added to their tally when Jon Wilkin zipped in on the left after neat work in the build-up from Pryce. A full-length converted interception try from Graeme Horne was Hull's reply but Saints had the last word of the half with Pryce sending Paul Wellens through on the left. Long's conversion made it 22-6 at the break. Two minutes after the restart a Pryce try ended the game as a contest. Willie Manu got a try back before Kyle Eastmond scored with his first touch of the ball; then sent youngster Chris Dean in; Mark Calderwood and Ade Gardner swapped scores and Eastmond and Horne both got second tries.

Castleford bounced back in style from their derby drubbing by Wakefield on Good Friday with a merited five-try, 28-6 win at Warrington. It was a tight first half but the Tigers finally broke the deadlock on 33 minutes when Brett Ferres took Michael Wainwright's inside pass to go over in the corner. Kirk Dixon kicked the touchline conversion. Desperate Cas defence held up Matt King over the line as the Tigers, still missing the suspended Ryan McGoldrick, led 6-0 at the break. Cas extended their lead 11 minutes after the restart with Brent Sherwin's long pass finding Michael Wainwright and Dixon added the goal. Then Michael Monaghan's hesitancy from Sherwin's kick allowed Rangi Chase to touch down and make it 18-0. The Wolves, still missing Lee Briers but with Kevin Penny back, gave their fans something to cheer on the hour with Chris Bridge forcing his way over and Chris Hicks landing the goal. But further tries from Michael Shenton and Chase reasserted Cas's dominance.

The superb goal-kicking of Danny Brough - three out his four conversions were off the touchline - was all that separated the Wildcats and Bulls as Bradford came back from 24-10 down to almost snatch a dramatic victory. The final act saw a high bomb bounce in the Wakefield in-goal after the hooter had sounded with a posse of players trying to get their hand to the ball before it was thumped dead, and Wakefield had secured a 24-22 victory.

Steve Menzies scored a brace of tries in the right corner for the visitors in the first half but Damien Blanch, Brough and Ryan Atkins ensured the Wildcats took an 18-10 lead into the interval. Steve Snitch's short-ranger gave Wakefield a 14-point lead before the inspired Terry Newton led a Bulls revival, setting up converted tries for Michael Worrincy and Michael Platt.

Richard Moore played his first game since August 2008, after he was diagnosed with Crohn's disease earlier in the year, and the Bulls had former Wakefield favourite David Solomona back from a shoulder injury. But Jason Crookes was out for the rest of the campaign after an MRI scan revealed he damaged his cruciate ligament in the game.

* The debate about playing two games over the Easter weekend reared its head again. Jamie Peacock had called for the Rugby Football League to reduce the Easter fixture programme to just one match per club. The England captain, along with many other leading players and coaches, believed that one single round of games should be staggered over the five days to ease the burden on the players.

Round 10

Two-try David Solomona publicly backed under-fire coach Steve McNamara after sections of the Odsal crowd called for McNamara to be sacked during the Bulls' 58-22 televised home defeat to Warrington Wolves, a game between twelfth and thirteenth in the table. After 20 minutes the Wolves were 22-0 ahead, and the game was already as good as lost for the Bulls. Chris Hicks piled up 30 points from three tries and nine goals, Lee Briers had an outstanding game in midfield and captain Adrian Morley led by example up front. The most spectacular of Warrington's ten tries was a marvellous 90-metre effort by Chris Riley. Paul Johnson collected a high kick near his own line and did well to slip the ball out to Riley. The young fullback shot away and when opposite number Dave Halley blocked his path he kicked ahead and took the ball on the bounce without breaking his stride to finish well ahead of any pursuers.

Wigan coach Brian Noble hailed Shaun Ainscough and Sam Tomkins after leaving the youngsters out of the starting line-up for the 44-10 Sunday home win over the Celtic Crusaders. Although Tomkins featured from the bench, and scored two tries to take his tally to six in nine games, Ainscough was left out completely as the squad's 18th man. Noble explained that Ainscough wasn't injured, but he felt the time was right to give him a breather. The Crusaders never really threatened their first win. Marshall Chalk switched from loose forward to fullback amidst an injury crisis, while Damien Quinn became the first player to reach 100 competitive appearances for the Crusaders.

Wakefield Trinity racked up a third victory in eight days with a 21-14 Friday night win at Hull FC. Brad Drew controlled most of Trinity's play in both attack and defence. 'He played in a dinner jacket,' said Hull coach Richard Agar. Only when Oliver Wilkes went over inside the final ten minutes, five minutes after Danny Brough had given Wakefield a one-point lead with a field goal, could Wakefield finally relax after moving two scores clear with time ticking away. The KC Stadium's lowest Super League crowd of the season rang out with boos at full time, having watched Hull fall from a 12-8 half-time lead to a well-deserved defeat. The Airlie Birds had now lost their last six competitive fixtures.

That week a Wakefield-based property development company announced plans for a new community stadium, with a 12,000 capacity, just off of Junction 30 of the M62.

Darrell Goulding made his Salford debut in the Saturday night 38-6 away defeat to Catalans after moving to the Willows on a month's loan from Wigan, as the Dragons made it an impressive four wins on the bounce. It was a tough game, with Salford's defence magnificent at times, especially at the end of the first half when they withstood six sets on the trot. But then they gifted Dimitri Pelo a try when Goulding and Richie Myler each left a Greg Bird kick for each other and Pelo swooped for an easy touchdown and a telling 14-6 interval lead. The second half was nearly all Catalans, who lost ex-Australia Test prop Jason Ryles with a quadriceps injury.

Hull KR coach Justin Morgan hailed the return of skipper Mick Vella after the former Australian Test prop came off the bench in his side's historic win in the capital against Harlequins. Rovers had never won at the Stoop, but they recovered from 12-4 down to run out comfortable 32-12 victors. Vella returned after missing eight rounds of Super League with a knee ligament injury suffered in the opening game. He had two stints from the bench as Rovers bounced back from their Easter Monday loss to Huddersfield Giants. Paul Cooke and Michael Dobson were both outstanding.

Saturday night at the Galpharm had promised much with second placed Huddersfield meeting third-placed Leeds, but the contest never took off as the Rhinos eased home 34-6. A clinical first-half display saw Leeds stroll to a 22-0 lead at the break on the back of some admirable defence and two classy tries in the final four minutes before half-time. It had been a bad start for the pretenders as Brett Hodgson knocked on straight from the kick-off and, after just 75 seconds, his opposite number Brent Webb was waltzing in under the posts from a Matt Diskin pass, Kevin Sinfield adding the first in a perfect seven conversion rate.

There were concerns that Castleford Tigers' Joe Westerman suffered a serious injury during Sunday's 68-22 home defeat by St Helens. The match was halted on the half hour for 12 minutes, after St Helens players had waved wildly to attract referee Ian Smith's attention, while medics attended to Westerman, who appeared to have collapsed in back play and suffered fits. The 19-year old was eventually carried off on a stretcher, but Tigers coach Terry Matterson was able to inform his players at the interval that their teammate was conscious and reasonably lucid in hospital, where he was kept overnight for tests and observation. St Helens were 32-0 ahead when Westerman departed. Leon Pryce's try in the fourth minute after Castleford had kicked out on the full following Tony Puletua's opener made it clear it was to be a one-sided affair. Puletua ended the game with four tries.

Round 11

The last Friday of April provided two of the biggest shocks of Super League XIV. Bradford coach Steve McNamara began the weekend as the odds-on favourite to become the next Super League coach to be given the sack. But, after the Bulls' 34-30 victory over St Helens at the GPW Recruitment Stadium on Friday night his position looked secured.

Meanwhile, Brian McClennan admitted that Leeds' 21-4 home defeat to Harlequins was the Rhinos' lowest point of the season. Quins inflicted Leeds' fifth defeat in seven games, and were seconds away from becoming the first side to nil the Rhinos since Halifax in 1998. Only Rob Burrow's last-minute try prevented Brian McDermott's men achieving that goal. The Rhinos were booed off at half-time and full-time by disgruntled fans.

The finish, though not the outcome, may have been different if Scott Donald's length-of-the-field interception try - taken off the master-interceptor Luke Dorn - had not been recalled for Brent Webb apparently being offside inside him, a likely 10-6 becoming 12-0, but anything other than a Harlequins win would have been a travesty. Rob Purdham's 73rd minute field goal to make it 13-0 ensured that the visitors would deservedly claim the spoils.

At half-time at Knowsley Road, with St Helens leading 26-10, the bookies were offering 1/100 against a St Helens win, and 16/1 against Bradford. The Bulls had shot out to a 10-0 lead, and then video-referee Ian Smith turned down what should have been a try for Sam Burgess after 16 minutes that would have put them three scores ahead. It all looked so good for the Bulls until the point at which David Solomona was injured after 20 minutes when he was tackling Lee Gilmour. Saints scored their first try through Ade Gardner after 27 minutes, and eleven minutes later Francis Meli was touching down for their fifth, giving Saints a 26-10 half-time lead. It seemed certain to be a one-sided second half. It was, but amazingly in the Bulls' favour, with them scoring 24 points in the second half to St Helens' four. Two late Michael Worrincy tries decided the game in the Bulls' favour.

Bradford gave a debut off the bench to Julien Rinaldi, signed until the end of June. Rinaldi left Harlequins at the end of the 2008 season, after he was forced out of the club by the new Super League rules on home-grown players. The rules were subsequently modified in favour of players who were already playing in Super League, but it was too late for Rinaldi to find another club. He promised to sue the RFL for his loss of earnings and had engaged the services of former Bradford chairman Chris Caisley to fight his case. Solomona dislocated his shoulder and was later ruled out for the season.

April

With St Helens and Leeds both suffering defeat, there was a chance for the chasing pack to close the gap and Hull KR took advantage as a 44-10 home win over the Catalans took them into second spot. The Robins ran in eight tries against the French side who arrived in Hull having won their last four matches but were without the services of a number of key regulars including the injured Thomas Bosc, Adam Mogg and Jason Ryles and their current playmaking talisman, Greg Bird, who was back in Australia to make his court appearance. Michael Dobson was outstanding against one of his former clubs, tackling fearlessly, leading his team around the park impeccably and chipping in with another 16 points.

Wakefield could have moved into second but they sank to a 40-26 defeat to Wigan at Belle Vue. Wildcats coach John Kear urged England boss Tony Smith to consider Wigan flyer Shaun Ainscough for the mid-season international against France after his four-try haul. The 19-year-old winger raced in for a first-half hat-trick, before grabbing a final try 11 minutes before full-time. Earlier in the week, Thomas Leuluai signed a new contract until the end of 2012, after agreeing a three-year extension with the club. Kear's afternoon was made even worse by a season-ending knee injury to winger Damien Blanch in the closing stages. Blanch had earlier scored two tries.

Wolves coach Tony Smith refused to rule out the possibility of Michael Monaghan leaving the club at the end of the season, after more speculation over the player's possible return to Australia in the wake of a new tax crackdowns on sports clubs. The Wolves' 40-18 home win over the Giants was built on a terrific effort up front from Adrian Morley and Garreth Carvell, allowing several outside backs to shine. Chris Bridge had what Smith described as his best game for the club during his tenure, while fullback Chris Riley scored two well-taken tries. But the pick was right winger Chris Hicks, who helped himself to a first half hat-trick and 24 points in total, to follow up the three tries and 30 points he accumulated at the Grattan Stadium the previous Friday.

The Crusaders lost 34-22 at home to Castleford despite leading 10-0 after 25 minutes and then 22-18 with 13 minutes to go before the Brent Sherwin-inspired Tigers hit back and stole all the points in a late rally.

City Reds coach Shaun McRae confirmed that his club wanted to retain the services of on-loan winger Darrell Goulding, once the 21-year-old's initial one-month loan period from Wigan was up. Goulding, playing on the wing rather than his usual position at centre, made an impressive home debut in the Saturday night 18-14 defeat to Hull at the Willows, scoring two tries.

Reds forward Ian Sibbit missed the game after being suspended for one match by the RFL Disciplinary Committee for a reckless high tackle committed in the clash against the Dragons. Despite trailing 10-0 on six minutes, Richard Agar's Hull were dominant and had eased their way back to a 16-10 lead at half-time, using the kicking skills of their scrum-half Chris Thorman to perfection. Ultimately, John Wilshere's missed goal kicks proved crucial.

SUPER LEAGUE TABLE - *Sunday 26th April*

	P	W	D	L	F	A	D	PTS
St Helens	11	9	0	2	339	178	161	18
Hull Kingston Rovers	11	7	1	3	284	189	95	15
Leeds Rhinos	11	7	0	4	243	151	92	14
Huddersfield Giants	11	7	0	4	250	197	53	14
Wakefield T Wildcats	11	7	0	4	265	221	44	14
Castleford Tigers	11	7	0	4	273	273	0	14
Harlequins	10	6	0	4	263	198	65	12
Hull FC	11	6	0	5	232	224	8	12
Wigan Warriors	12	5	0	7	282	249	33	10
Catalans Dragons	11	4	0	7	246	302	-56	8
Warrington Wolves	11	4	0	7	249	314	-65	8
Bradford Bulls	10	3	1	6	203	279	-76	7
Salford City Reds	11	3	0	8	176	361	-185	6
Celtic Crusaders	10	0	0	10	142	311	-169	0

* On Wednesday 8th April the Rugby Football League held a press briefing to at last give its verdict on the disappointing World Cup performance by England. Invited journalists were told that the players had accepted their collective responsibility for the debacle. Neither coach Tony Smith nor tour manager Graeme Thompson were present to discuss their roles in England's series of embarrassing defeats. RFL Chairman Lewis explicitly denied reports that had suggested part of the problem was caused by conflict between the players of Leeds and St Helens.

MAY
Border crossing

Round 12 - Murrayfield Magic

Super League decamped to Edinburgh on the first weekend in May. The weekend in the Scottish capital was a qualified success as an aggregate attendance of 59,749 watched the full round of matches played over two days at the Scottish Rugby Union's Murrayfield Stadium. The standard of the games - all covered by Sky Sports - was variable, but the impression created in Scotland was almost all positive. Around 5,000 Scots attended the event over the two days.

The fans were rewarded with reasonable weather and clearly had a great time. A minority of players questioned the wisdom of taking a whole round of games to a venue outside the game's heartlands. Saints' James Graham and Keiron Cunningham were lukewarm about the weekend and the lack of enthusiasm for the venture rubbed off on St Helens as they were soundly beaten, 38-18, by Wigan in the last of the three games on the Saturday, their second defeat in a row. The RFL had abandoned playing extra derbies on the weekend but an open draw had pitted the two great rivals together. In the build-up, Wigan coach Brian Noble made his team watch their lamentable performance the previous year in Cardiff, when they lost by 57-16 to St Helens. Noble would have faced a barrage of criticism if Wigan had lost after he dropped new wing sensation Shaun Ainscough, despite the youngster scoring four tries the week before. And none did better than Pat Richards, who was switched from fullback to take Ainscough's wing spot. The experienced Australian scored two tries, created another and gave a perfect seven-out-of-seven goal kicking display. Cameron Phelps also did a top job at fullback.

For Saints, Leon Pryce's effort could not be faulted. The stand-off continued his top-class form, stepping through for a smart try and doing well to get the ball away in the move that led to Paul Wellens scoring. Having recently escaped a jail sentence for assault, Pryce was booed every time he received the ball, but it did not seem to affect him.

After the game, Noble insisted he had no desire to leave Wigan at the end of the season, when his current contract expired, and despite rumours linking him with a return to Bradford. The rumours caused the Bulls to put out a statement denying any intention to make a move for Noble.

In the first game of the weekend Harlequins ground out a 24-16 win over Salford City Reds. They were helped by a refereeing decision that allowed Luke Dorn to wriggle over for the match-winning try and left Reds coach Shaun McRae seething. However, Salford had missed probably their best chance two minutes earlier when Tony Clubb shoved Robbie Paul into touch just as the former Bradford star looked set to mark his 400th professional appearance in fairytale style. That did not stop McRae making his feelings known on Gareth Hewer's inability to spot what he thought was a blatant knock on by Danny Ward on the tackle before Dorn's try took the scores to 24-10 with nine minutes remaining. Despite being on the losing side, stand-off Stefan Ratchford was outstanding for the Reds.

The most spectacular performance of the weekend came in the second Saturday game as Bradford took revenge for their Easter Monday defeat at Belle Vue with a 32-16 win over Wakefield. A Paul Sykes hat-trick-inspired the Bulls to repel a sterling second-half effort from Wakefield and earn them a third win in five games as they played some truly exciting rugby. An impressive first-half showing had Bradford leading 20-6 at the break, but only a stonewall defensive display throughout most of the second period kept Trinity at bay before a late flurry left a slightly misleading final score. The Wildcats' persistence finally reaped two late tries and got them back to 20-16. It was an effort earlier in the half, ruled out by video referee Richard Silverwood, which coach John Kear felt was unjust and came at a crucial time. Dale Ferguson raced onto a Danny Brough grubber and most camera angles were inconclusive, though there was no benefit of doubt for the attacking team. The match was finally won for the Bulls by a majestically timed Ben Jeffries pass that sent Mike Worrincy on the way to scoring his fifth try in five games for the Bulls.

Huddersfield Giants coach Nathan Brown saw his side retain fourth place in Super League with their comfortable seven-try 40-16 win against Celtic Crusaders in the opening game on Sunday. The Crusaders were without six first-choice players through injury, including Tony Duggan and Darren Mapp, and the Giants were ruthless in exposing their opponents' flaws. Shaun Lunt crossed in either half, while Brett Hodgson amassed a personal haul of 16 points from a try and six goals as Huddersfield let rip. Only in the final quarter, when they were trailing 34-0, did Celtic come to life with late tries from Chris Beasley, Anthony Blackwood and David Tangata-Toa. After the game, Brown confirmed Wakefield halfback Danny Brough was a transfer target for the Giants, after rumours of a £100,000 bid.

Catalans captain Greg Bird injured his hamstring in a 36-16 reverse at the hands of Leeds. Bird was a virtual passenger when he was on the field after returning from Australia after being found guilty in a Sydney court of smashing a glass into his girlfriend's face and blaming the attack on his flatmate. Richard Lewis issued a statement after the court case, saying the RFL would take no action against the former Cronulla Test star, at least for the time being. Bird was due to return to Sydney for sentencing on 22nd June, although he would lodge an appeal against his conviction before that date. The Rhinos were 30-0 up at half-time, Ryan Hall's second touchdown, a classic winger's effort from a delightful Ali Lauitiiti offload, completing back-to-back efforts that ended their first-half spree and left them in seemingly total control, although the Dragons came back strongly from a hopeless position after the break.

Hull FC beat Castleford 24-16. The Airlie Birds weathered a difficult opening half hour to edge a see-saw encounter and gain some revenge for their single point defeat by Castleford at the KC Stadium in March. Level at the break, the Black and Whites heeded coach Richard Agar's half-time team talk with two late kick-and-chase orientated tries snatching the verdict. A controversial Danny Tickle penalty 12 minutes from time with the scores level at 16-16, for the tiniest of play-the-ball offences by winger Michael Wainwright proved crucial. Mark Calderwood's never-say-die persistence was instrumental in forcing an error and putting Hull in a position to finally seal the two points – Danny Washbrook subsequently chasing a Richard Horne kick under the posts, with Tickle putting the icing on the cake with his fourth goal from five attempts.

The final curtain came down on Murrayfield Magic in exciting style as Hull KR moved to within a point of league leaders St Helens courtesy of a 36-28 victory over Warrington. The Wolves went into the game shorn of key men Lee Briers, Adrian Morley, Louis Anderson and Paul Wood, but led 16-6 after an impressive opening quarter. Rovers wrestled control of the game either side of half-time, with Michael Dobson and Ben Galea providing some crucial contributions. Both players impressed, with Galea the best on the field after creating two tries, scoring the all-important fifth Robins effort with ten minutes remaining, and crossing for a second in the final minute. Dobson also touched down himself, while his faultless goal kicking proved invaluable in an often see-saw encounter.

RFL chief executive Nigel Wood said he was keen to build on the relationship with the Scottish Rugby Union and other tourist bodies in Edinburgh to develop the Magic concept in the city the following year. Wood confirmed, however, that the RFL would continue to look at the prospect of other cities hosting the Magic Weekend beyond 2010.

Challenge Cup Round 5

St Helens, chasing their fourth successive Challenge Cup, were overwhelming favourites to lift the famous trophy at Wembley in August, according to bookmakers William Hill, after they hammered 2007 finalists Catalans Dragons 42-8, and were handed a tie quarter-final tie against Gateshead Thunder, the only representatives of the Championship left in the Challenge Cup. Gary Wheeler's try bang on half-time killed off the disappointing Dragons in a televised Sunday game at Knowsley Road.

Gateshead celebrated new coach Steve McCormack's first game in charge with a 34-16 win over Oldham at the 25,500-capacity Northern Echo Darlington Arena, the Thunderdome being unavailable. Victory meant Gateshead had reached the quarter-finals for the first time. Later in the week BBC commentator Dave Woods apologised for an off-the-cuff remark after the televised draw that St Helens had drawn a bye into the semi-finals.

After being drawn at home to Salford, Wigan were second favourites at 4/1. Two fine late solo scores from Stuart Fielden - his first try for over two years - and Sam Tomkins sealed a 28-17 televised win at Wakefield. Wakefield rocketed into a 10-0 lead after seven minutes before being pegged back in a see-saw encounter, with Andy Coley repeatedly putting Trinity on the back foot.

Mark Henry scored four tries as Salford won at Batley 66-4, while Huddersfield were far from convincing against a Rochdale side forced to sign three loan players on the Friday afternoon just to raise a team. Hooker Shaun Lunt helped himself to a hat-trick of tries in the 38-12 win at the Galpharm. Tony Smith praised Michael Monaghan after the Australian produced a sensational display in the Wolves' 10-try, 56-8 romp at Featherstone Rovers.

There were almost two huge shocks. Hull KR beat Sheffield Eagles 34-24 at Craven Park after the Eagles came desperately close to producing a major upset. Rovers cruised through the first half without getting out of first gear and led 22-4 at the break, but with ten minutes to go a Kyle Wood try pegged it back to 28-24 before Ben Fisher dived in from dummy-half to take the Robins into the last eight.

It was even closer at the Jungle on the Saturday night, where Championship leaders Halifax led Castleford 34-30 in the closing stages, only for a Brent Sherwin try to take the game into extra time. Sherwin's conversion attempt hit the post, but he then kicked the winning field goal in the first minute of golden-point extra time - the first golden-point decider in the Challenge Cup since 1941, when Castleford won at Featherstone. Joe Westerman returned to the Castleford side for the first time since suffering fits on the field after taking a heavy hit in the round-ten game against St Helens.

Hull, who had exited the Challenge Cup in the previous round, finally gave up their visa battle to sign Michael Crocker. Instead he joined South Sydney Rabbitohs on a three-and-a-half-year deal. Hull were still awaiting a visa for Kiwi forward Epalahame Lauaki. They had also released former Warrington Wolves star Stuart Reardon after eleven days, when he failed a medical on an Achilles tendon injury. The 27-year-old had been released by the Wolves in the lead up to his sentencing for assaulting his estranged wife, and he was snapped up by Hull just two days later. Reardon underwent a second operation on the injury that had already seen him out of action for 12 months, and turned his sights to a full recovery and finding a new club for 2010. Hull FC imposed a ban on all access to players, coaches and staff by Radio Humberside and BBC TV Look North employees after what they saw as biased reporting.

Round 13

Celtic Crusaders finally got off the mark, with a shock 30-24 win at Odsal against in-form Bradford Bulls. Luke Dyer crossed twice and the Crusaders, who dominated from start to finish, were always in front after Chris Beasley's ninth-minute try. Bulls coach Steve McNamara admitted he could not explain Bradford's low-key performance. After leading 8-6 at the break, the men from Bridgend were 24-12 in front going into the final quarter, before a 67th-minute try by Steve Menzies, goaled by Paul Deacon, threatened to spark a Bulls fightback and spoil the visitors' party. And although that was soon followed by a 40-metre penalty goal by the impressive Josh Hannay, Celtic nerves continued to jangle when Paul Sykes darted over and Deacon again added the extras with a couple of minutes left on the clock. The Crusaders, however, were not to be denied. And when gamestar Dyer sealed matters in the dying seconds, on the end of a typically barnstorming run to the corner by second-rower Jason Chan, the Welsh side and its small band of followers were able to enjoy their first win in over 1,000 minutes of top-flight football.

Stuart Cummings, the RFL's controller of referees, suggested the Wigan club should invest in a louder hooter after referee Richard Silverwood allowed a crucial Hull Kingston Rovers try to stand after the 40-minute mark in the Friday night game between the two sides. Wigan led 6-0 through a Sean O'Loughlin try when the hooter sounded with Rovers attacking the Warriors' line with the tackled player wrapped up. Surprisingly, Silverwood didn't blow his whistle, the ball was played and Michael Dobson, the former Wigan player, touched down and levelled the scores by converting his own try. Boos rang around the stadium as the players left the pitch, with abuse raining down on the official. O'Loughlin added his second in the first two minutes of the second half, but Rovers hit back through Paul Cooke and Jake Webster to emerge 20-12 winners, which ended a Wigan run of four straight wins.

That weekend Wigan coach Brian Noble was strongly tipped to become the director of rugby at Sydney Roosters, struggling in 15th place in the NRL table under their club legend Brad Fittler, in his first full season in charge of the club.

Lee Briers, who had been rumoured to be on the way out of the club, inspired Warrington to a sensational 18-16 victory as they battled back from 16-6 down to shock Hull at the KC Stadium. The Wolves scored three tries during a ten-minute spell in the final quarter to snatch a dramatic victory.

Hull were believed to be chasing Manly scrum-half Matt Orford as they looked to follow up their signing of Australian Test second-row forward Craig Fitzgibbon for 2010.

Huddersfield had that week announced the signing of New Zealand World Cup winner David Fa'alogo on a three-year deal and on the Sunday they missed their inspirational captain Brett Hodgson as they crashed to a 24-4 home defeat by Salford. Clinical finishing was the secret behind Salford going in at half-time already leading 12-4, in contrast to Huddersfield's failure to convert both territory and possession into points. Richie Myler's 55th minute interception try, celebrated with a knowing fist in the air, visibly took stuffing out of Giants as halfback partner Stefan Ratchford once again shone.

Captain Rob Purdham committed his future to Harlequins by agreeing a two-year contract extension and landed four goals as they defeated Wakefield Trinity Wildcats 24-17 at the Twickenham Stoop on the Sunday. David Howell also celebrated a new two-year deal by scoring an important second-half try. It was a fourth successive League or Cup defeat for Wakefield - a run that had seen them fall to sixth place in Super League.

Greg Bird was watched by his cheering girlfriend Kate Milligan as the Dragons went down to a 32-28 defeat to St Helens at the Stade Gilbert Brutus in Perpignan on the Saturday. St Helens, who had announced the signing of New Zealand Test centre Iosia Soliola on a three-year deal, returned to the top of the table but only after a late Gary Wheeler score rescued the result.

That exciting finish could not top the final stages of the Castleford-Leeds clash on the Friday night. A match of high drama ended with the Tigers having a deserved point cruelly snatched away by a Kevin Sinfield penalty goal in the dying seconds, the Rhinos winning 24-22. Played out with a Wagnerian backing of thunder and lightning the match reached a dramatic climax when Castleford scrum-half Brent Sherwin lost the ball near his own line and colleague Michael Shenton had little option but to pick it up in an offside position. The full-time hooter sounded as Sinfield prepared to take the penalty kick and he had little difficulty popping it over from about ten metres right of the posts. Sinfield had the grace not to show any elation.

Round 14

Warrington Wolves got their play-off challenge into top gear with a 16-8 win over Wigan in a magnificent televised Friday-night game at the Halliwell Jones Stadium. A year before, it would probably have been a game the Wolves would have lost: trailing 6-0 inside the first five minutes, starved of any possession for the first nine minutes and then riddled with errors for much of the first half. Chris Bridge's touchline conversion of Chris Riley's try on 56 minutes edged the hosts ahead for the first time but they still needed at least one more score to be able to feel confident about their position. Michael Monaghan duly gave it to them, jinking his way through the Warriors' line before grounding the ball under pressure from Sam Tomkins to stretch Warrington's unbeaten home run against Wigan to a sixth year.

Wakefield coach John Kear denied that Wakefield's 54-6 home defeat by Huddersfield Giants on the Sunday had anything to do with his decision the previous week to suspend Danny Brough and Danny Sculthorpe for seven days without pay for defying an alcohol ban on the return coach trip from their defeat at Harlequins. Brough apologised for his indiscretion, but Sculthorpe was thought to be considering taking legal action in an effort to overturn the ban, and in particular his financial losses because of it. Kear watched his outclassed Wildcats team leak ten tries to a rampant Huddersfield, who had young on-loan Wigan forward Lee Mossop on debut off the bench.

Catalans Dragons lifted themselves up another notch in the table with a nervous 30-18 win at Celtic Crusaders in the first Super League game not to feature an English side. The French connection grabbed their first win following three straight defeats with an avalanche of points in the first half, featuring four tries and three conversions to end a dominant first half 22-6 ahead. The game hinged on a fantastic piece of defence by Clint Greenshields under his own sticks when Mark Bryant crashed over to seemingly give the Crusaders the lead in the 60th minute. The video showed that the Dragons fullback had managed to dislodge the ball as the Aussie forward crashed through. Instead of Celtic going on to win the game, the momentum turned once more and the Catalans dominated from then on, Steven Bell and Cyril Stacul scoring clinching tries.

All eyes were on Sean Long on the Friday night in the 22-12 home win over Harlequins after he revealed St Helens were only willing to offer him a one-year extension to his current deal, which expired at the end of the season, and he admitted he had already spoken to a number of other Super League coaches. While it was no vintage performance from Long, he gave the Saints hierarchy a glimpse of what they stood to lose. Tries from Chris Flannery and Paul Wellens gave Saints a 10-0 lead after an arm wrestle of a first half before a flash of brilliance from Long looked to have sealed it in the 53rd minute. Long dummied and darted his way through the Harlequins line before being stopped just short but, virtually on his back, the former Test star dumped the ball off perfectly for James Roby to collect and touch down. Quins made a spirited fightback with converted tries from Louie McCarthy-Scarsbrook and Luke Dorn putting them back within four points. But a trademark try by Keiron Cunningham secured victory and kept Saints a point clear of Hull KR at the Super League summit.

Justin Morgan was confident that Michael Dobson, runaway leader in the Albert Goldthorpe Medal standings, would remain at Hull Kingston Rovers despite speculation that he could be targeted by St Helens as a replacement for Long. Dobson was overshadowed in the Friday-night 16-6 home win over Castleford by Shaun Briscoe, who took another big stride towards taking over the England fullback spot with an outstanding role. A faultless performance in defence was topped off by a first class attacking display that brought him two of Rovers' three tries, and he had a big hand in the other. Chev Walker returned for his first game since round six, when he dislocated a shoulder in Rovers' 24-12 loss at Warrington.

Rovers needed that extra surge from the back because the Tigers matched them in almost every other department, despite going down to their first away defeat of the season.

Rising Salford stars Luke Adamson and Richie Myler heaped more agony on Bradford with an 18-10 win at the Willows and, despite dire predictions early-season, the Reds were now above the Bulls in the Super League table. All of their points came in a 12-minute purple patch midway through the second half and Bradford would have had the game won by then had they not spilled the ball over the try line on four occasions. Young second-rower Adamson had been one of Salford's best performers all season and he capped off an all-action performance by setting up Salford's second try with a glorious offload and scoring their third.

On the Tuesday night of the Bank Holiday weekend, Keith Senior stormed in for two tries - to celebrate his 300th blue and amber appearance - and had a third disallowed to maintain his phenomenal try every other game ratio. But it was Kevin Sinfield who Hull had no answer to, having moved to stand-off in the absence of Rob Burrow, in a 46-16 home win.

Another centre celebrating a milestone, Kirk Yeaman, had put the black and whites back in contention with his 100th touchdown for the club, superbly gathering a Richard Horne grubber in the 38th minute to make it 16-10.

Senior became only the eighth player in the club's history to reach the double target of scoring 150 or more tries in over 300 matches, joining Eric Harris, John Atkinson, Alan Smith, Les Dyl, Francis Cummins, Syd Hynes and John Holmes in reaching that milestone. The previous week 33-year-old Senior sealed a deal to keep him at the club until the end of 2010.

Challenge Cup Quarter Finals

St Helens were red-hot 1/2 clear favourites to win the Carnegie Challenge Cup after the Sunday semi-final draw pitted them against Huddersfield. Saints were the first club to be drawn out of the hat against the Giants, the only remaining Yorkshire team in the competition, who edged out Castleford Tigers by two points on the Sunday, while Wigan were drawn against Warrington Wolves.

On the Saturday, St Helens nosed one ahead of their old rivals Wigan by earning themselves a record ninth consecutive appearance in the semi-finals with a 66-6 win at Gateshead Thunder. Matt Gidley, Paul Wellens, Leon Pryce and Chris Flannery each notched a brace apiece. After a minute's silence for the absent Andrew Henderson's recently deceased father, Saints took the game by the scruff of the neck from the start. A colourful crowd of 4,325 was an indication of the potential for the code that was cast adrift on Tyneside, after one so far solitary, still-born season in the top flight in 1999. Ben McAlpine did get some tangible reward for his side's efforts when he intercepted a Tony Puletua pass before racing away over 50 metres to score, Nick Youngquest converting. But by then it was 36-0.

Wigan had beaten Salford 28-6 at the JJB Stadium on the Friday night, transforming a tenuous 10-6 interval lead with a further three second-half tries to leave Salford's hopes of ending a 40-year drought since they last appeared on the Wembley stage in tatters. Gareth Hock and skipper Sean O'Loughlin led the way with what Brian Noble later called 'world-class performances' while Pat Richards, restored to the wing spot with Shaun Ainscough back on half-time presentation duty to sponsors, provided the cutting edge. Richards scored three tries and added four goals. Salford, despite the benefit of a 4-0 penalty count in the first 24 minutes, threatened only once and scored the game's best try when Ray Cashmere superbly slipped out the ball in a massed tackle to create the opportunity for Luke Adamson to combine with Jordan Turner and dash over.

Stand-off Tim Smith was absent after returning to Australia on compassionate leave and Stuart Fielden missed the match after picking up a one-match ban for using a raised knee while in possession of the ball in Wigan's round-14 Super League loss to Warrington. Fielden escaped a charge of using foul and abusive language against match officials when he fronted the RFL Disciplinary Committee. The former Great Britain prop was accused of pointing and shouting comments questioning the integrity of referee Ben Thaler after Chris Riley's 56th-minute try for the Wolves. But Fielden successfully argued his comments were directed at Wolves' stand-off Lee Briers.

The other two ties - both televised, were thrillers. On the Sunday the Giants came back from the dead to edge Castleford Tigers 16-14. With ten minutes to play, hard-tackling Cas were 14-6 clear and an error-ridden Giants had already bombed enough chances to have taken them all the way to the final and beyond. But Stephen Wild finally managed to finish a fine move created by Kevin Brown and a deft Luke Robinson flick and Brett Hodgson's conversion, plus Danny Kirmond's late effort, sent Huddersfield into the semi-finals for the third time in barely five years.

On the Saturday, Lee Briers proved himself the ultimate match winner at Craven Park, as a pulsating quarter-final was decided in dramatic style by the first televised golden point. It had been a terrific comeback after Rovers had led 22-12 on the hour mark. But Warrington finished the stronger to continue their revival, and they could have won the tie in normal time after scoring two tries in five minutes to edge 24-22 ahead. But Michael Dobson levelled the scores with a 78th-minute penalty to set up the most dramatic of finishes. Briers had already sent three extra-time efforts wide of the posts when he finally landed the winning field goal with 85 minutes on the clock.

* In a postponed game from Round 6, Wakefield bounced back from their public flogging by the Giants with an impressive 50-6 victory against the out-gunned Celtic Crusaders. A minute's silence was perfectly observed before kick-off in memory of Leon Walker, whose tragic death in a reserve contest saw the original fixture in March cancelled.

Brad Drew and Jamie Rooney both grabbed a brace of tries apiece and returned prodigal Danny Brough shone throughout, finishing the game with an 18-point haul as the Wildcats ended a run of five successive defeats and moved up to sixth in the table. Michael Korkidas, re-signed for the club on loan from Huddersfield for the remainder of the season, seized on a clever inside pass from Danny Brough to make an immediate impact on the contest with a try with his first touch of the game. The loan deal saw Wakefield forward Danny Sculthorpe go in the opposite direction to spend the rest of the year with the Giants.

SUPER LEAGUE TABLE - *Saturday 30th May*

	P	W	D	L	F	A	D	PTS
St Helens	14	11	0	3	411	256	155	22
Hull Kingston Rovers	14	10	1	3	356	235	121	21
Leeds Rhinos	14	10	0	4	349	205	144	20
Huddersfield Giants	14	9	0	5	348	243	105	18
Harlequins	13	8	0	5	323	253	70	16
Wakefield T Wildcats	15	8	0	7	354	337	17	16
Hull FC	14	7	0	7	288	304	-16	14
Castleford Tigers	14	7	0	7	317	337	-20	14
Wigan Warriors	15	6	0	9	340	303	37	12
Warrington Wolves	14	6	0	8	311	374	-63	12
Catalans Dragons	14	5	0	9	320	388	-68	10
Salford City Reds	14	5	0	9	234	399	-165	10
Bradford Bulls	13	4	1	8	269	343	-74	9
Celtic Crusaders	14	1	0	13	212	455	-243	2

JUNE
The Long goodbye

Round 15

On the first day of June, Sean Long agreed to play for Hull FC for the following two years, after 13 glorious seasons at St Helens. Long expressed his disappointment to League Express that Saints failed to offer him the two-year deal he wanted, but Saints chairman Eamonn McManus explained salary cap constraints and his keenness to see the club retain some of its up and coming stars had prevented that. There was no sign of any resentment on the Friday night when, as chance would have it, Saints travelled to the KC Stadium with Long having a part in two of Paul Wellens' hat-trick of tries and a big say in another in a 30-6 victory. Just a few days after being dropped from England's squad, Wellens responded with an outstanding performance that was the highlight of Saints' record equalling 15th successive Super League away victory. One of Hull's better performances could not prevent a sixth successive home defeat.

The win moved St Helens three points clear at the top of the table as second-placed Hull KR and third-placed Leeds both lost. On a wet Friday, Hull KR went down at Huddersfield by 22-6, as the Giants ended Rovers' five-match winning run. The architects-in-chief of the victory were Scott Moore and Eorl Crabtree, who both celebrated international call-ups to the England squad to play France in Paris the following Saturday. On-loan for the season Moore indicated he could return to parent club St Helens at the end of the season after having already spent 2008 on loan at Castleford. Another on-loan player, Lee Mossop from Wigan, scored a crucial try seven minutes before half-time that gave the Giants an 18-6 lead going into the break.

Ben Cockayne returned to the Hull KR side after serving a club suspension. He hadn't played a Super League match since round seven on 29th March against Salford, after which he was found guilty of a street assault and banned by the club until 1st June. His absence hadn't tempered his robust approach to the game and he was suspended for one game the following Tuesday after being charged by the RFL Match Review Panel for a grapple tackle. The highlight of the match was a massive collision between the ball carrying Eorl Crabtree and Nick Fozzard, who was left groggy and dazed as he was bumped off in the tackle.

Huddersfield went into joint third with the Rhinos, who lost a stunning match in Perpignan. The Dragons claimed an unbelievable 32-30 win they deserved on the final play of a match they had seemingly lost just as astonishingly. Leeds held a narrow lead at the break, cut by a contentious penalty that proved to be the difference after both sides had scored five tries, just as the half-time hooter sounded. Having twice attempted to run the award but brought back by Steve Ganson, Thomas Bosc eventually elected to put over the two points.

As they had done at Murrayfield, in the second of their two convincing defeats to the Rhinos in 2009, Catalans dominated the majority of the second half, superbly served by an explosive pack led initially by Dane Carlaw and then Remi Casty and Cyrille Gossard, turning a two-point deficit into a seemingly winning lead of 28-12 with barely 11 minutes left. Leeds weren't done yet. Ryan Hall, another England call-up, conjured a fine solo try when grubbering for himself and winning the chase to give Leeds a glimmer, Kevin Sinfield landing a magnificent touchline conversion. The Rhinos skipper then produced a wondrous short ball to send Matt Diskin into a hole, he picked up Brent Webb and Ali Lauitiiti powered over to cut the gap to one score. That score came immediately afterwards, Danny Buderus shooting through in midfield and Webb supporting on a 50-metre dash to the posts, Sinfield's conversion seemingly completing one of the great escapes.

 But Lee Smith failed to gather the restart, and the Dragons showed their expertise from a set play by constructing a try from the scrum with barely 80 seconds left, to snatch the euphoric acclaim from 8,000 delirious 'sang et or' fans. Adam Mogg, Bosc and Greg Bird were at the core of the move, aided by a typically belligerent David Ferriol charge; Mogg's supreme pass giving Jason Croker the room to send Cyril Stacul over out wide to be the hero.

Catalans were without fullback Clint Greenshields for the first time since he joined them from St George in 2007, a run of 68 consecutive matches.

Wigan replaced Hull FC in the top-eight after a 34-18 home win over Salford, a week after knocking them out of the Challenge Cup at the same venue. With the Cup semi-final on the back-burner, Brian Noble's side set about improving their league position in their last home game for a month and after dominating the opening quarter and building a 22-0 lead the issue was never in doubt. Captain Sean O'Loughlin led from the front for Wigan, while Pat Richards again provided the cutting edge, taking his tally to 52 points in three games against the Reds that season with a 16-point haul. Reds' Rob Parker suffered a fractured skull after he clashed with Jordan Turner's elbow in one of the last tackles of the game.

Steve McNamara watched his Bulls side edge past Wakefield 36-22 at Odsal and declared: 'I believe the Bulls are just about to start for 2009.' Steve Menzies and Chris Nero both crossed twice for the hosts. In the end it was Paul Deacon's eight goals from eight attempts against one out of five from Danny Brough that separated the two sides.

That week the Bulls announced they were confident the scheme to create an Odsal Sports Village would give them a new home by 2012 at the latest, after Bradford Council agreed to proceed with a £75 million total redevelopment option for the land.

Terry Matterson blasted Castleford's all-action style in the wake of the Tigers' 34-18 home defeat by Warrington on the Saturday night after he saw his side throw away another commanding lead – they were 8-0 ahead after the first 20 minutes. Warrington were boosted by the return of Chris Hicks after a three-week absence due to a groin strain, while Matterson was still without injured duo Brent Sherwin and Ryan Hudson. Vinnie Anderson's quick-fire double at the start of the last quarter put an end to any thoughts of a Castleford comeback after Michael Shenton had struck from long range to cut the deficit to 20-14. Acting Cas captain Ryan McGoldrick was sin-binned for dissent after Anderson's first. Mickey Higham tore his bicep in the Wolves' win and faced 12 weeks on the sidelines

In the capital, Harlequins moved two points clear of Wakefield into fifth spot with a Saturday 26-6 win over Celtic Crusaders, although Luke Dorn suffered a broken fibula. David Howell had a hand in two tries in a less than memorable game.

Round 16

Celtic Crusaders stunned Wigan Warriors and grabbed their first home win of the season - a 22-16 victory at Brewery Field. Peter Lupton grabbed the winning try with only five minutes left on the clock after Wigan had clawed back from a 16-6 deficit to level the game and looked likely to go on and complete the win. But the crowd erupted as an Iafeta Palea'aesina knock-on almost underneath his own posts turned the game in the

Crusaders' favour. The Welsh side quickly shipped the ball wide and Lupton crashed through the despairing tackles of Amos Roberts and Martin Gleeson. Mark Lennon easily added the extra two points as the Crusaders hung on.

Glenn Morrison returned to the Bradford side for his first game since the end of March in the Bulls' 21-10 victory at Warrington Wolves on the Sunday. A 13th minute hamstring injury to Lee Briers was the final blow for a Warrington side already deprived of Ben Westwood and Adrian Morley through England International duty and Mickey Higham with a torn bicep.

The Bulls were also without their international Sam Burgess, but his absence was hardly noticed after huge displays from Morrison and Steve Menzies.

A Friday-night 40-10 victory at Hull KR was hailed as Harlequins' best ever performance, with Chad Randall outstanding on his 100th appearance for the club. Randall's track back and hauling down of Michael Dobson in the 77th minute showed Quins' commitment to the cause. Quins boss Brian McDermott heaped praise on young halfback Luke Gale after he produced a strong performance, getting his chance after Luke Dorn's injury. Winger Will Sharp scored two tries.

St Helens ended the weekend four points clear at the top of Super League and seemingly on course for their fifth successive league leaders' shield after they brushed aside a weakened Cas side 50-10 at Knowsley Road. Saints coped better without James Graham and James Roby than the Tigers without Michael Shenton and Joe Westerman, and the continued absences of Ryan Hudson and Brent Sherwin. The Tigers were now in tenth place in Super League, although level on points with seventh-placed Wigan, on points difference in the table along with Hull and Warrington, both of whom lost, but by smaller margins.

Hull fell to a 37-22 defeat at Wakefield. Two 50-50 video replay decisions went against Hull and resulted in 12 points for Trinity, who only made it six tries to four in the last second. But it had all gone horribly wrong for Hull in the first half, Wakefield holding a 23-0 interval lead. Man of the match was 2008 Albert Goldthorpe medallist Danny Brough, who shot up to third in the 2009 table, picking up another three points. The crafty scrum-half led his old team a merry dance with a superb demonstration of his all-round skills that included an 85-metre interception try. He also set up two tries and landed five goals plus a field goal.

Leeds were back in second spot after a close 20-12 win over Huddersfield at Headingley. The Giants were a pass away from achieving a win. If Brett Hodgson's last-gasp wide ball had found one of three men in white lurking it would have meant their first victory at Headingley in 50 years, Instead it was picked off by Kallum Watkins to secure a home victory.

* That Saturday England coach Tony Smith claimed the national team needed tougher opposition than the French side they demolished 66-12 in Paris. Salford's teenage scrum-half Richie Myler scored a hat-trick and finished with 30 points – an English record against France. France coach Bobbie Goulding hit back at a suggestion made by Smith that England should play an 'Other Nationalities' side rather than France as a mid-season Test match. 'I can think of at least five games in the last decade when Australia or New Zealand absolutely hammered Great Britain or England, yet they were still decent enough to carry on playing Tests against them,' argued Goulding.

Round 17

On Saturday 20th June 2009, three Super League matches took place simultaneously in London, Barcelona and south Wales.

Warrington coach Tony Smith and Catalans Dragons counterpart Kevin Walters both backed the prospect of staging an annual Super League match in Barcelona after the

Wolves ran out 24-12 winners at the Olympic Stadium in Super League's first game in Spain. The game drew a crowd of 18,150, with around 12,000 fans travelling to the Catalan capital from southwest France, and 4,000 locals coming to the game.

The Dragons' France internationals were in more destructive mood than they were for the previous week's 66-12 defeat by England and helped Catalans recover from an early Chris Bridge try to lead 10-6 at half-time after Jason Croker and Cyril Stacul touched down. Thomas Bosc's 46th-minute penalty made it 12-6 but that was the home side's only score in the second half as Warrington provided further evidence of their new-found defensive solidity. That provided the platform for Matt King, Chris Riley and Jon Clarke to cross and ensure the Wolves got back to winning ways with a sixth victory in seven games. There was no debut for Brian Carney though after his surprise return to League. The Dragons were without star halfback Greg Bird, back in Australia awaiting sentencing for assault, but Clint Greenshields, Jamal Fakir and Jason Ryles all returned.

Wigan coach Brian Noble's future at the JJB Stadium beyond the end of 2009 looked increasingly unsure, after reports that Wigan Chairman Ian Lenagan had unsuccessfully tried to lure Stephen Kearney to the club in 2010. Wigan had a week off because they had played their round 17 game at home to Wakefield at the beginning of the year.

Richie Myler turned down Salford City Reds' offer of a new contract. Warrington were heading the list of clubs interested in signing the 19-year-old. The scrum-half had probably his quietest game of the season in a 14-12 defeat at Hull. His only notable contribution was a perfectly-judged little kick that enabled Jeremy Smith to dive on the ball for his first try for the club.

Hull, aiming to end a run of four defeats, looked extra cautious after a promising start. Only two Danny Tickle penalty goals maintained their record of never having lost at home to Salford in Super League. Victory also ended a run of six successive home defeats.

Hull KR captain Mick Vella returned on the Saturday as Rovers defeated Celtic Crusaders 32-18 in Bridgend. Vella injured his knee in round one against Bradford Bulls at Odsal before picking up another knee injury three games into his comeback against Warrington at the Magic Weekend. It was the first match that Hull KR had won in the month of June since entering Super League in 2007.

Rangi Chase produced a match-winning display for Castleford against Huddersfield on the Friday night. Chase landed a vital late field goal to ensure the Tigers claimed their first victory in six games. His performance in the 13-6 triumph saw him claim three points in the Albert Goldthorpe Medal standings. Three weeks before Terry Matterson's side lost their cup quarter-final after Huddersfield produced a thrilling comeback – but there was rarely any danger of a repeat, despite Leroy Cudjoe's late try. Richard Owen's hauling into touch of Paul Whatuira approaching the hour mark, when Owen was Castleford's last line of defence and the Giants were bursting forward, was the gamebreaker.

England winger Lee Smith told Leeds that he was quitting the club at the end of the season to cross codes to play for London Wasps, and on the Saturday was a try-scorer in the Rhinos' 48-18 win at Harlequins. What looked a mouth-watering clash on paper was a one-sided contest on the pitch as the Rhinos ripped the home defence to shreds in the second half.

The hosts - missing captain Rob Purdham because of a blood clot discovered in his hand - were made to pay severely for not making more of early dominance, and with halfbacks Danny McGuire and Rob Burrow pulling the strings, Leeds avenged their shock 21-4 loss at Headingley in round 11. There was little suggestion of a riot in the opening quarter of an hour – the Londoners bossing the early exchanges, with both Tony Clubb and Louie McCarthy-Scarsbrook being held just short.

Leeds had signed Mike Coady, a former Bristol Sonics player, from his current club, financially-troubled Doncaster. Coady agreed a three-and-a-half year deal with the Rhinos, but was to spend the remainder of this season on loan at the Dons.

June

Glenn Morrison, just returned from three months out, picked up a rib cartilage injury in the 44-18 defeat to St Helens at Odsal on the Sunday, Julien Rinaldi was also in the wars, picking up a foot injury, effectively ending his loan spell.

Round 18

June ended in battling fashion for Wigan Warriors. On Monday 23rd, the Rugby Football League suspended the club's England forward Gareth Hock after he tested positive for benzoylecgonine, a metabolite of cocaine, after Wigan's home league win against Salford earlier in the month. Combined with the uncertainty over the future of coach Brian Noble, and the shock defeat at Celtic Crusaders in their last game, the club looked in real trouble.

But on the Sunday night, in a televised game, Wigan produced a stunning 36-28 win over Hull KR at Craven Park. Rovers made a sensational start with two tries from Peter Fox in the opening four minutes. Australian stand-off Tim Smith left the field on five minutes with a dislocated shoulder in an attempted tackle on the Rovers back-rower Clint Newton, desperately trying to prevent Fox scoring his second try. It was his last act of SLXIV. The Australian was helped from the field after little more than five minutes of the game, and was replaced by eventual match winner Sam Tomkins.

The game swung dramatically in the Warriors' favour during the third quarter with three tries in 11 minutes. Sam Tomkins sent Phil Bailey over; Tomkins then kicked a stunning 40/20 to keep his side on the front foot and Harrison Hansen used the position to storm over off Sean O'Loughlin's pass; and finally Tomkins raced over for the Warriors' sixth try after Rovers had gifted them more cheap possession in their own '20'. Rovers set up a tremendous finale when Daniel Fitzhenry crashed over through Tomkins' tackle and then Jake Webster stretched over. Wigan's lead was down to just two points. But Richards ran across field in his own '20' and sent Roberts sprinting down the best stand touchline and then finished the length of the field move under the Robins posts.

The RFL were ready to take action against Castleford, after bottles were thrown onto the field in the wake of the Tigers' 22-20 home defeat to Catalans Dragons on the Saturday night. Home supporters had been angered over several decisions throughout the game by referee Ian Smith, who was escorted off the field by a steward after the game, and had to leave the stadium by a back exit.

Richard Owen came up with another fine performance, but it was not enough to stop the Dragons snatching a victory that kept their play-off hopes flickering after trailing 10-0 inside seven minutes. The 19-year-old Tigers fullback's powerful finishing brought him two tries and he went very close to a hat-trick, but video referee Phil Bentham detected the slightest of wobbles as he tried to get the ball down when Clint Greenshields made a superb try-saving tackle. Castleford fans did not like that decision and were equally incensed when match referee Smith did not ask Bentham to look at two debatable Catalans touchdowns. The first was when Dimitri Pelo went over in the corner and the big screen suggested, at least to Cas fans, there may have been a double movement. The home fans voiced their disapproval and booed even louder when Clint Greenshields was awarded another try without the referee going to the screen. It was a 50-50 call with Greenshields probably just onside when he set off to brilliantly catch and touch down Thomas Bosc's kick. The home fans also protested loudly when Rangi Chase was penalised for a voluntary tackle shortly before Dane Carlaw scored the Catalans' vital late try.

In Sydney, a magistrate ordered Dragons captain Greg Bird to be jailed for 18 months, with a non-parole period of eight months, for the reckless wounding of his girlfriend Katie Milligan with a broken glass. After launching a Supreme Court appeal against the conviction and the penalty, Bird received bail, which would enable him to play out the Super League season with the Catalans, although Bird faced another Sydney court two weeks later over the alleged assault of a woman at a Cronulla nightclub.

Keiron Cunningham (knee), Jon Wilkin (neck) and James Graham (head) all picked up knocks in the 30-0 demolition of Celtic Crusaders. St Helens were 24-0 ahead and in total control by half-time after tries from Lee Gilmour, Paul Wellens, Tony Puletua and Matt Gidley. Celtic arrived at Knowsley Road minus the services of Tony Duggan, Darren Mapp, Josh Hannay, David Tangata Toa, Chris Beasley and on-loan Saints scrum-half Matty Smith. Two Welsh products - Lloyd White and Geraint Davies - made their Super League debuts.

Salford coach Shaun McRae denied the uncertainty about the future of halfback Richie Myler, out with a heel injury, played any part in the Reds' disappointing performance on the Friday night that led to a 34-10 home defeat by Huddersfield Giants. Trailing just 18-6 at the break, the City Reds still had hope of a turnaround but when Leroy Cudjoe went in for the first of two tries to restore his side's three-try advantage on 62 minutes, the Giants had put the result to bed.

John Kear hailed Wakefield hero Danny Brough after the scrum-half kicked a touchline conversion to snatch a dramatic 20-18 victory over Harlequins at Belle Vue, now known as Hearwell Stadium. Trinity trailed 18-14 going into the final minute but Brough combined with Sean Gleeson to send Scott Grix diving over in the corner. The timekeepers sounded the hooter after Grix's score, leaving all the pressure on Brough's shoulders. The Wildcats scrum-half kept his nerve and slotted the ball straight between the posts to send the Wakefield fans delirious.

Hull FC coach Richard Agar left halfback Chris Thorman out for the Sunday 24-12 defeat at Warrington. The Wolves' backline was in superb form as they stretched their recent run to seven wins in nine games. Matt King and Chris Riley scored a try apiece while fullback Richard Mathers continued his renaissance following his mid-season move from Wigan.

The Leeds-Bradford derby at Headingley was missing from the television schedules, and turned out to be one of the best derby games of the season. There was no big screen replay and Bradford coach Steve McNamara was left ruing the disallowing of winger Rikki Sheriffe's 76th minute effort in the corner, on a last-tackle power play, that would have made it 26-24 with a kick to come.

The winger was certain that he had got the ball down before being rolled into touch by the scrambling cavalry led by Rob Burrow, but the officials thought otherwise. By then, Rhinos skipper Kevin Sinfield had already tried and missed two field goals. From the re-start tap following Sheriffe's disappointment, Danny Buderus freed Lee Smith; Danny McGuire's grubber forced a drop out and, at the end of the set, Sinfield had a third one-point attempt superbly charged down by Jamie Langley. The ball fell to Smith and he calmly did the honours; Scott Donald's searing late try completing a 33-20 Leeds win.

SUPER LEAGUE TABLE - *Sunday 28th June*

	P	W	D	L	F	A	D	PTS
St Helens	18	15	0	3	565	290	275	30
Leeds Rhinos	18	13	0	5	480	283	197	26
Hull Kingston Rovers	18	11	1	6	432	351	81	23
Huddersfield Giants	18	11	0	7	422	292	130	22
Harlequins	17	10	0	7	421	337	84	20
Wakefield T Wildcats	18	10	0	8	433	413	20	20
Warrington Wolves	18	9	0	9	403	437	-34	18
Wigan Warriors	18	8	0	10	426	371	55	16
Hull FC	18	8	0	10	342	407	-65	16
Castleford Tigers	18	8	0	10	378	449	-71	16
Catalans Dragons	17	7	0	10	386	462	-76	14
Bradford Bulls	17	6	1	10	364	452	-88	13
Salford City Reds	17	5	0	12	274	481	-207	10
Celtic Crusaders	18	2	0	16	258	559	-301	4

* At the end of June, Hull KR's Michael Dobson still had a healthy lead in the Albert Goldthorpe Medal table, but the chasing pack was beginning to close the gap. Huddersfield's Brett Hodgson, in second place, was now just eight points behind on 21, while Albert Goldthorpe Medal holder Danny Brough was in top form and now had 18 points.

JULY
Warriors bouncing back

Round 19

Shaun McRae hailed Stefan Ratchford after the 20-year-old star produced an inspirational performance on the Friday night to help the Reds to a stunning 20-10 home victory over St Helens, the Reds' sixth win of the season. Ratchford scored twice in the first ten minutes, and created Salford's other two tries.

Salford produced a dominant performance from start to finish and only for a brief spell did St Helens look capable of overturning a 16-0 half-time deficit. Saints lined up with Kyle Eastmond at stand-off after Leon Pryce was forced to withdraw with a thigh injury. Salford were missing their own pivot, with Richard Myler still sidelined, but it hardly showed during a blistering first 40 minutes. Even when Salford were reduced to 12 men after Smith was sin-binned for striking Paul Wellens, the Reds proved the more clinical. Ratchford's grubber kick was swallowed up by Mark Henry to puncture Saints' momentum, meaning Francis Meli's late try meant nothing to the visitors.

It was a double blow for St Helens. Their lead at the top of the table over Leeds was reduced to two points and Sean Long broke his jaw during an attempted tackle on Henry. The prognosis was that Long would be in line for a comeback in the Challenge Cup final – should St Helens defeat Huddersfield in August's semi-final.

Huddersfield beat Wakefield 30-14 at the Galpharm Stadium to surge into third spot. The Giants were emerging as the biggest threat to Leeds and St Helens and outscored the Wildcats by five tries to three in an entertaining derby which erupted into life in the second half. Nathan Brown's side led 12-4 at the break, thanks to early tries from Scott Moore and David Faiumu, but the Wildcats hit back through Scott Grix. Huddersfield added further scores from Faiumu, David Hodgson and Liam Fulton. But Wakefield remained a threat, and crossed twice themselves in the second period through Tony Martin and Matt Petersen. Wakefield coach John Kear refused to comment on speculation linking the Wildcats with a move for Bradford hooker Terry Newton.

The midfield mastery of Michael Monaghan and Jon Clarke helped Warrington to a 22-6 win over Celtic Crusaders in Bridgend. The Wolves needed a touch of second-half magic from Monaghan, Matt King and Richie Mathers to open up the Welsh side's dogged defence and secure their eighth win in ten matches. With Jon Clarke slotting into midfield and taking on some of injured Lee Briers' organisational duties, Monaghan had a hand in all four of the visitors' tries. Briers, linked with a move from the Halliwell Jones Stadium, signed a new twelve-month deal at the Wolves.

That weekend Crusaders owner Leighton Samuel dispelled rumours about the financial instability of Super League's Welsh franchise, putting out a statement to assure fans of his long-term commitment to Rugby League in Wales. Crusaders players Peter Lupton and Damien Quinn denied reports that the club's players were owed a substantial amount of their wages.

Sam Tomkins celebrated his new five-year deal with Wigan by producing an outstanding performance as the Warriors beat Harlequins 40-12 on the Friday evening.

After a nightmare couple of weeks in June, consecutive wins boosted spirits at the JJB Stadium as the Warriors looked set to repeat their usual end-of-season surge, even though they were still in eighth place. The televised game was effectively decided when David Howell was shown a 28th-minute red card for recklessly hitting Sam Tomkins with his elbow after the whistle had blown. The home side, already eight points up, closed the game out in impressive fashion from there, prompted largely by Sam Tomkins, who was sin-binned late on for dissent.

Castleford Tigers produced a stunning 40-38 win over Bradford at Odsal on the Sunday. The matchwinning try came from Dean Widders' 80-metre interception. Widders plucked a loose Terry Newton pass out of the air on his own 20-metre line before tearing away upfield with Nick Scruton, Semi Tadulala and Newton himself in hot pursuit. It had been a topsy-turvy game. The Bulls had already clawed their way back to a 22-12 half-time lead, and looked likely to move three points clear of Celtic and Salford at the foot of the table. But then came four Tigers tries in eleven second-half minutes, to turn the game on its head. Stung, the Bulls again fought back to level the scores before, with eight minutes remaining, Widders' intervention.

Even then, there was time for a sting in the tail. In the last minute, with the Tigers again pressing the Bradford line, instead of retaining possession, winger Michael Wainwright opted to dab a kick through. It was collected ten metres out by Bradford's Dave Halley, who tore away up the touchline on a 90-metre run of his own. Halley didn't quite have the legs to go the distance but he did find the supporting Ben Jeffries who touched down. Crucially, though, the halfback was forced out towards the touchline. With the hooter almost ready to sound, Paul Deacon lined up the potential leveller. The ball drifted just wide of the upright.

Jean-Philippe Baile scored a hat-trick of tries against Hull KR on the Saturday in the Dragons' 23-12 victory in Perpignan, which kept their play-off hopes alive and moved them above Hull FC in the table. For Rovers it was a fifth defeat in six games, continuing their terrible record in the summer months. The Dragons included French international prop Sebastien Martins in the seventeen for the first time since he re-joined the club.

One of Leeds Rhinos' longest-serving players held centre stage in a 43-30 Saturday night victory over a spirited Hull FC at the KC Stadium. Keith Senior marked his 500th club and representative appearance by getting Leeds off to a flying start with a big hand in the Rhinos' first three tries. Hull might have made it even closer had Richard Horne not retired with a badly cut eye midway through the first half.

That week Hull FC announced the signing of Mark O'Meley - released from the final year of his contract with the Sydney Roosters - who promised to test out a few of the big name British forwards when he arrived in Super League in 2010. 'There will be no holding back when I get there,' he said. 'I already have my eye on a few Pommy blokes.'

Round 20

Wigan managed to hold on to a delicate two-point lead to beat Catalans 24-22 at the JJB Stadium, taking them to fifth in the table, ahead of Harlequins, Wakefield, Warrington and Castleford, also on 20 competition points. Their winning try was scored by Darrell Goulding, the out-of-favour centre who had been on loan at Salford. Only an injury crisis had brought him back and he squeezed into the right-hand corner with just six minutes remaining. Lee Mossop, another on-loan player recalled by Wigan, from Huddersfield, played off the bench.

The Dragons were forced into a late change, with Adam Mogg pulling out with a groin injury sustained in the warm up. Greg Bird, who had only flown in from Australia on the morning of the Friday-night match, was promoted from the bench. Dragons coach Kevin Walters was, according to press reports in Australia about to be sacked.

That weekend, banned second-row forward Gareth Hock spoke in the News of the

World of his shame and embarrassment in testing positive for cocaine. Hock, whose salary had been stopped by the Warriors, was keen to help convey an anti-drugs message to children.

Hull FC gave a full debut to their new signing, Australian prop forward Josh Cordoba, in their 40-18 defeat by Castleford Tigers at the Jungle on the Sunday. With props Peter Cusack (wrist), Ewan Dowes (calf muscle) and Jamie Thackray (hamstring) on the injury list, Cordoba arrived from Parramatta on a short-term deal until the end of the season. He was unable to prevent Hull from going down to their twelfth Super League defeat of 2009.

With two-try halfback Rangi Chase the architect, the Tigers bossed the game from the start and were full value for a rare home win of their own. Ryan Hudson returned after a 12-match absence with a broken arm and was outstanding, while young guns Michael Shenton and Richard Owen, Rugby League World's player of the month in June, also shone.

That day, former Leeds utility back Jordan Tansey landed in England. Tansey was signed by the Airlie Birds from NRL club Sydney Roosters for 2010, but the club had managed to negotiate his early release. Meanwhile Hull FC lifted their ban on BBC Radio Humberside and Look North, imposed in response to comments made on BBC Radio Humberside in April by the station's sports editor.

Leeds secured a classic 32-30 victory at Belle Vue in the televised game on Friday. Down 30-16 with 15 minutes left, the Rhinos broke Trinity hearts with just 37 seconds remaining when Scott Donald went in for the winning try, to give his side a 15th straight win at Belle Vue. Leeds had been reduced to 12 men when Brent Webb was sin-binned with eleven minutes remaining, but they refused to surrender and ultimately outscored John Kear's side by six tries to four. The winning try deserved to win any match. It still looked odds against Leeds winning with only a minute left when play restarted following Rob Burrow's converted try that made it 30-28. But Leeds battled back to halfway before opening up in a last desperate bid for victory. Danny McGuire chipped ahead and Carl Ablett collected before passing to Danny Buderus. McGuire rejoined the attack only to stumble and fall. But he managed to pop the ball out to Donald and the winger dived over in the corner. Lee Smith missed the goal. It didn't matter. The hooter sounded and Leeds had won.

Celtic Crusaders were desperate for a bit of good fortune to brighten up what had been a dismal week for Wales' Super League club with bad news and malicious rumours spreading through the national media like wildfire. They got it with a 25-12 win over Salford City Reds at Brewery Field on the Saturday night. The day had started with the announcement that David Watkins was to replace Jonathan Davies as club President, adding fuel to the fire to many fans that a move to Newport Gwent Dragons' Rodney Parade ground could be imminent. On-loan from St Helens Matty Smith's try just before the hour was the last try of the game and made it 24-12 to the Welsh side. A late Smith field goal, his second attempt in the final five minutes, completed the night and secured the points.

Harlequins were clinging to play-off hopes by their fingernails after a fourth straight defeat, to Huddersfield by 32-16 at the Stoop. The Giants made it three straight wins as Brett Hodgson was flawless, his two tries in the last two minutes halting a mini-Quins revival.

Hull KR kept their dream of a top-four finish alive with a comprehensive 32-12 victory against the struggling Bulls. With Wakefield and Harlequins both suffering round 20 defeats, the win kept Rovers just one point behind third-placed Huddersfield and put some daylight between themselves and the chasing pack. The teams had fought out a thrilling 13-13 draw on the opening day of the season at the Grattan Stadium, but Bradford had won only six of their 18 Super League games and arrived at Craven Park third from the bottom of the table. Wakefield loan signing Kyle Bibb started from the

Rovers bench as Shaun Briscoe produced another superb performance at the back, producing try-savers on Chris Nero, Matt Cook and Rikki Sheriffe.

Kyle Eastmond created three of Saints' tries and his own touchdown on 66 minutes proved decisive in turning a pulsating encounter at Warrington the way of St Helens. It put the visitors into a 30-26 lead, killing off a Warrington rally that had turned an 18-12 half-time deficit into a short-lived 24-18 advantage. Further scores from James Graham and Francis Meli completed a 40-26 win. Saints remained two points clear of Leeds at the top of the table, but prop forward Maurie Fa'asavalu was ruled out for three months after suffering a broken arm.

* That weekend Widnes Vikings became the first Championship club to earn the right to make a Super League licence application for 2012 after a 34-18 Northern Rail Cup final win over Barrow Raiders at Bloomfield Road

Round 21

Wakefield Wildcats' 22-20 TV win at St Helens on the Friday night brought the leaders back to the pack. The game will be remembered mainly for Paul Wellens' six failed goal attempts. The only easy kick that Wellens missed was the final one that came from a penalty when Leon Pryce lost the ball in a tackle by Steve Snitch, with the suspicion that Pryce might have let go of the ball in order to persuade referee Thierry Alibert to award the penalty.

Wakefield hadn't won at St Helens since 2003, and only Michael Korkidas and Snitch, who had both spent time at other clubs since then, survived from that encounter. The Wildcats had endure a nervous final ten minutes after Chris Dean's 69th minute try gave the home side hope and Wellens' last kick should have given Saints the draw. That week the Wildcats confirmed the signing of Terry Newton from Bradford Bulls on a two-year contract from 2010 but released young prop Jay Pitts to join Leeds Rhinos.

Wakefield needed the two points as Castleford, still without halfback Brent Sherwin, were on a roll, claiming their fourth victory in five games at a rain-sodden Salford on the Friday, by 18-12. Ryan McGoldrick controlled the Castleford effort and deputised well at fullback when Richard Owen had to go off with an eye injury. Salford coach Shaun McRae conceded that the City Reds' play-off hopes were all but dead. The match was McRae's 400th as a first-grade coach, in a career that had taken in St Helens, Gateshead Thunder, Hull FC and South Sydney, as well as the Reds.

Leeds moved level with St Helens at the top after they emerged 24-14 winners from a slugfest with Hull KR at Headingley on the same night. Rovers coach Justin Morgan stressed beforehand that the match would be a good indicator of how his charges were shaping up for the finals series and, having controlled the first half and gone 14-6 up at the start of the second, they showed they could be contenders.

In a deluge, Leeds were without captain Kevin Sinfield and blooded another with potential in 20-year-old former Dewsbury Celtic back-rower Dane Manning. The Rhinos were leading 18-14 with eight minutes to go when Dobson put up a bomb that Lee Smith snaffled before outpacing Ben Cockayne on the outside to slide in at the corner on a 70-metre run. For good measure Smith then kicked the conversion.

Huddersfield moved three points clear in third after an impressive 28-10 home win over Warrington on the Sunday. Luke Robinson, Brett Hodgson and Eorl Crabtree all had top games. Robinson was irrepressible, running at every opportunity and providing the passes that led to three tries. Behind him, Brett Hodgson came up with another wonderful fullback performance. He entered the Huddersfield attack in great style, twice timing his incursion perfectly to send in Leroy Cudjoe for tries.

Greg Bird and Thomas Bosc provided the class, and Dimitri Pelo twice proved an arch finisher as Catalans hammered Harlequins 38-16. Harlequins, severely depleted but lacking nothing in spirit, ultimately had no answer to the Dragons' superior quality in the searing 30-degree heat of Perpignan. Bosc's audacious effort in the 51st minute saw him chip the ball over the first line of defence with his left foot, then chip Harlequins fullback Will Sharp with his right to ground between the posts for one of the best tries of SLXIV or any other season.

Quins hooker Chad Randall's club record of 101 consecutive appearances came to an end after picking up a leg injury the week before against Huddersfield Giants.

Hull FC produced an amazing climax in the last 12 minutes of a game that for long periods they looked like losing, to score three tries and finally overcome an enthusiastic and gutsy challenge from the Crusaders by 22-6. Although Hull had won their first five matches in Super League XIV they'd managed to win only three of their subsequent 15 games. The home crowd was again less than impressed with their team's efforts and vented their frustration with a series of boos and slow-handclaps. Jordan Tansey made his debut for the club and Josh Cordoba made his first home start, whilst Craig Hall, fresh from a successful month's loan at Widnes, returned at centre for the injured Kirk Yeaman. New-boy Tansey was the pick of a below-par Hull side.

On the Sunday, a late two-try burst involving Wigan's Martin Gleeson left Bradford Bulls as rank outsiders for the play-offs after a 20-14 defeat at Odsal. Brian Noble's in-form Warriors had led 6-0 at half-time and when Pat Richards touched down six minutes into the second half, the Bulls' mathematical chances of making the last eight looked done remote.

But after a try from rookie James Donaldson hauled them back into the picture, Bradford fought a courageous rearguard action that eventually saw them hit the front with a Paul Deacon penalty on 68 minutes. Holding on, though, proved to be beyond them after a double-whammy from Gleeson - back in the side after a three-match absence with a hamstring injury - and Amos Roberts in the closing minutes.

Round 22

It was billed 'The Big One' and the match lived up to the hype as Wigan rampaged to a 28-10 win over Leeds at the last game at the JJB Stadium before it was renamed the DW Stadium. After bossing the first half territorially, if not on the scoreboard, Leeds led 10-6 at half-time. That margin would have been wider had George Carmont not nicked a try back for his side shortly before the break. Roared on by a 20,295 crowd - the biggest ever for a Wigan-Leeds fixture at the ground - after scoring three minutes into the second half, the Warriors contrived to keep Leeds entirely at bay while running in two further tries of their own. On a night filled with heroic goal-line defence, skill and entertaining open rugby, Warriors' stand-off Sam Tomkins once again stood out. The influence of Wigan's more aged Aussie contingent was also crucial, with the likes of Cameron Phelps, Pat Richards, George Carmont and Mark Riddell all having big games. Danny Buderus fractured his fibula in trying to kick a loose ball that Andy Coley bravely got down to collect and was out for the season.

Saints went two clear again at the top of the table after their whopping 44-24 win at Harlequins. Leading the way for Saints was hooker Keiron Cunningham, who, along with Kyle Eastmond and Leon Pryce, tore the home defence to shreds. A breathtaking opening period of attacking rugby saw St Helens leading 34-0 at half-time, their four-try burst at the end of the first half killing the game as a contest. It was Harlequins' sixth successive defeat and they dropped out of the play-off places.

Paul Cooke was the match winner once again in a Hull derby as the red and whites proved their dominance with a 24-18 win at Craven Park. Cooke was at his typical best. His decisive action brought him two tries and the creation of another. He also booted a great 40/20 in the closing minutes to further deflate Hull.

Cooke struck twice in the first five minutes to help Rovers to a 12-0 lead. First, he collected Michael Dobson's kick before passing superbly out of a tackle to put the scrum-half over. Two minutes later Cooke hoisted his own high kick, and when Jordan Tansey let the ball bounce it came off the post for the Rovers' stand-off to pounce for the touchdown. Little was seen of Cooke for a while, as Hull battled back to be only 14-12 behind, but then he struck them another deadly blow in the 58th minute as he powered in from a play-the-ball close to the Hull line, following a terrific '40/20' by Dobson. A Mark Calderwood try, converted by Danny Tickle, following an enterprising crossfield run by Gareth Raynor brought Hull back to 20-18. They appeared to have gone ahead a few minutes later when Raynor went in off Craig Hall's pass, but the referee said it was forward. Hull were still reeling from that decision when Rovers' Ben Fisher made a tremendous break and flung out a pass for Jake Webster to score the match-clinching try in the 67th minute.

Eorl Crabtree celebrated a new six-year contract with Huddersfield by helping the Giants to a convincing 36-12 home win over Catalans Dragons on the Sunday, a win that took them to within two points of second-placed Leeds. The Giants, inspired by a Leroy Cudjoe hat-trick, overcame a difficult start to sweep aside the challenge of the recently resurgent Catalans, whose head coach Kevin Walters was optimistic of making the play-offs. The Dragons remained four points short of a place in the end of season shoot-out, but with a game in hand on most of their rivals.

Lee Briers scored two and made four of Warrington's eleven tries as the Wolves bounced back with 50-unanswered points against Salford at the Halliwell Jones, after trailing 20-12 at half-time. Warrington's biggest Super League win of the season sent them back into the play-off places with five games remaining.

Castleford went two points clear into level fifth after a 20-12 win at Wakefield. Dean Widders proved the quickest off the mark as the Tigers leapfrogged their local rivals on the top eight ladder in a scrappy derby. The former South Sydney back-rower, filling in at left centre for the Tigers, scored tries within seconds of the start of both halves to help Terry Matterson's side to a fourth consecutive win. With loose forward Joe Westerman adding six goals from as many attempts and Rangi Chase effective all afternoon, that proved just enough in a tight tussle in which the two sides equally shared four tries, Danny Brough also getting a brace.

Bradford Bulls forward Steve Menzies was hit by a suspected case of swine flu - which hit the UK in the summer of 2009 - after being taken ill on the eve of the Bulls' crunch game with Celtic Crusaders in Bridgend. Menzies was isolated from the first-team squad and sent back to Bradford for further tests. Bradford won the game 34-12, keeping alive their slim chances of making the top eight. A stunning burst of attacking rugby midway through the first half set the Bulls on their way to victory. Three tries in six minutes on the back of barnstorming runs from Chris Nero, Glenn Morrison and Sam Burgess gave the Bulls an unassailable 18-0 lead, and dented the fragile confidence of the previously impressive Crusaders. Gamestar Andy Lynch's try on 50 minutes effectively snuffed out any hopes of a Celtic comeback

Meanwhile the Bulls' hopes of signing Australian Test star Craig Wing ended after the South Sydney utility star announced that he would be playing rugby union in Japan the following season.

SUPER LEAGUE TABLE - *Sunday 26th July*

	P	W	D	L	F	A	D	PTS
St Helens	22	17	0	5	679	382	297	34
Leeds Rhinos	22	16	0	6	589	385	204	32
Huddersfield Giants	22	15	0	7	548	344	204	30
Hull Kingston Rovers	22	13	1	8	514	428	86	27
Wigan Warriors	22	12	0	10	538	429	109	24
Castleford Tigers	22	12	0	10	496	529	-33	24
Wakefield T Wildcats	22	11	0	11	511	515	-4	22
Warrington Wolves	22	11	0	11	523	531	-8	22
Harlequins	21	10	0	11	489	491	-2	20
Catalans Dragons	21	9	0	12	481	550	-69	18
Hull FC	22	9	0	13	430	520	-90	18
Bradford Bulls	21	7	1	13	462	556	-94	15
Salford City Reds	21	6	0	15	338	596	-258	12
Celtic Crusaders	22	3	0	19	307	649	-342	6

AUGUST
New horizons

Round 23

Kyle Eastmond snatched a 10-6 win from under the noses of Wigan at Knowsley Road on the first Friday night of August, sliding in for the go-ahead try three minutes from the end to extend Saints' six-year unbeaten home run against the Warriors. Wigan had out-enthused the subdued Saints and looked set to take the spoils from a vintage slugfest. But Eastmond - denied three times by last-gasp tackles - took the ball on the '20', darted between two tacklers, bounced, spun and finally slid between the posts, with Paul Prescott clinging on for dear life.

Rainy weather ensured the game never really developed as an attacking spectacle but it was a great derby battle. Saints were buoyed by Paul Wellens' rapid recovery from a hand injury and edged into an early lead, Matt Gidley riding a large slice of luck to pluck Wellens' deflected grubber out of the air and plunge over at right centre. Wigan refused to panic and when Keiron Cunningham left the field on 20 minutes - with no James Roby to replace him - the pendulum looked set to swing their way. Having soaked up Saints' best, the Warriors spent the final minutes of the half raiding the Saints line. Twice they threatened to break down the left before Sam Tomkins pounced on a Francis Meli howler to score, Meli exposed as he spilled a grubber in-goal. Pat Richards' conversion snatched a 6-4 half-time lead against the run of play.

The tide began to turn Saints' way when Cameron Phelps mishandled a bomb on his own 15 metres. Eastmond was again thwarted inches short, and Lee Gilmour just failed to reel-in a slick offload from Leon Pryce with the line open. Saints continued to throw what they had at the Warriors as time ran down, but it was stodgy stuff until Eastmond's grubber trapped Thomas Leuluai in-goal and in the following set Eastmond's incisive break saw him slide in for the killer try. Darrell Goulding was ruled out of Wigan's Challenge Cup semi-final against Warrington the following weekend with a dislocated shoulder.

The win meant Saints stayed two points clear of Leeds at the top after the Rhinos snatched an even more dramatic win, Kevin Sinfield kicking a last-minute conversion to Scott Donald's equalising try for a 24-22 victory over Warrington at Headingley. Having missed all but one of his previous four shots, Sinfield was left with the defining moment from the touchline, on his wrong side, and delivered the knock out blow. Victory rewarded the efforts of Jamie Peacock, who included an astonishing drop-goal charge down when Lee Briers looked set to break Leeds hearts with a one-pointer for the third time at Headingley in eight seasons, and a magnificent offload that led to Lee Smith crossing to bring the hosts level with 15 minutes to go.

Defeat was harsh on the Wolves who strove manfully to cover the early loss of Brian Carney with a broken arm and later Simon Grix with a damaged shoulder. Wolves coach Tony Smith called for the scrapping of video referees, but claimed his views were not the result of the Wolves' narrow loss.

Huddersfield stayed three points clear of Hull KR in third after the Giants whitewashed Hull at the KC Stadium 24-0. The visitors led 12-0 at half-time and repeated that margin in the second half. Kevin Brown was involved in the first three of Huddersfield's four tries, creating two of them with perfectly timed passes that left Hull's defence in tatters. Michael Lawrence's try early in the second half took the game beyond Hull's reach.

A hat-trick from Shaun Briscoe and another outstanding performance from Michael Dobson were the individual highlights of Hull Kingston Rovers' first victory at Castleford for 17 years on the Sunday, in a midday kick-off at the request of the police. It was never as easy as the 46-28 scoreline suggested. Castleford raced into an early 12-0 lead and led 20-18 at half-time before Rovers stepped up a gear and outscored the Tigers five tries to one in the second half to end a run of four successive defeats at Castleford. Dobson's 44th minute try and goal put Rovers 24-22 ahead and began their second-half dominance.

Harlequins centre David Howell produced a man-of-the-match performance at Bradford Bulls on the Sunday after returning from a three-match suspension. The 25-year-old had been watching from the stands after being the first player to be red-carded in 2009 in the game against Wigan at the start of July. His two tries in the final 15 minutes of the game on Sunday ensured a 22-14 win for the London side, bringing to a halt their six-match losing run. The Bulls were now seven points adrift of the play-off spots.

Catalans Dragons' chance of making the top-eight looked stronger as a 34-0 win over Celtic Crusaders in Perpignan moved them within two points of eighth-placed Harlequins. The Dragons' new signing Sebastien Martins made a big impact from the bench with some barnstorming runs and deft handling.

A Friday-night scrum-half masterclass at the Willows from Danny Brough helped Wakefield Trinity Wildcats consolidate a place in the top eight with a 30-24 win, condemning Salford to a fourth defeat on the bounce. City Reds' substitute prop Philip Leuluai twice barged his way over for a last-gasp quickfire brace to make the winning margin six points, but Brough-inspired Wakefield controlled proceedings for most of the game. Bad news for Wakefield fans came the following Monday when League Express revealed that Ryan Atkins would be joining Warrington at the end of the season.

Challenge Cup Semi-finals

Warrington won 39-26 in a thrilling semi-final against Wigan to go through to Wembley for the first time since they were beaten by Wigan in 1990. Lee Briers was the official man of the match and Michael Monaghan was another key man with a virtuoso dummy-half display, in particular his constant targeting of Iafeta Palea'aesina in Wigan's defensive line. Monaghan was also quick to heap praise on Briers, who dedicated the victory to his late brother, Brian, who died eight years before. The day of the semi-final would have been his birthday.

Wigan welcomed captain Sean O'Loughlin and second-rower Phil Bailey back into their starting line-up, while Matt King and Chris Riley returned for Warrington. O'Loughlin fought hard but struggled to impose himself and after scoring the game's opening try on seven minutes, Bailey limped from the field a quarter of an hour later with an Achilles injury. Around the hour mark, Riley's head collided with the knee of Joel Tomkins and his neck twisted awkwardly in the fall. The game was held up for almost ten minutes before Riley was stretchered from the field, to applause from both sets of fans.

The thrills were provided by Wigan's three-try second-half fightback after Warrington had earlier overturned an 8-0 deficit themselves, before building up a 28-8 half-time lead that was increased to 32-8 by King's hat-trick try shortly after the break. The outcome was settled only by Briers' 71st-minute field goal, a trademark one-pointer which calmed Warrington's fears and ensured that Chris Hicks' late score was icing on the cake.

Huddersfield confounded the bookies the next day with a 24-14 victory over St Helens at Warrington to reach Wembley for the first time since 1962. Before kick-off St

Helens were 4/6 favourites to win the Cup for the fourth season in a row and the Giants the rank outsiders at 13/2, despite going into their semi-final on the back of a six-match winning streak.

Saints coach Mick Potter sprang a surprise by including hookers Keiron Cunningham and James Roby, both of whom had been doubtful with injury. Sean Long, however, who was surprisingly named in the initial 19 during the week, missed out, with Kyle Eastmond starting at scrum-half.

The Giants led 10-4 at the break with tries to on-form captain Brett Hodgson and Stephen Wild against one from Francis Meli. Hodgson's defence as well as his attacking incursions proved crucial, performing miracles to hold up both Leon Pryce and later Eastmond over his own line in the first half.

The Giants' matchwinning score came with five minutes left. Brett Hodgson, shaping to kick, dummied and broke through and, calmness personified, he kicked ahead for Wild to win the race for the ball to touch down. Ian Smith gave the nod, sending the Giants to Wembley for the first time for 47 years. There was still time for Meli's third try late on, but nothing was going to silence the celebrating Huddersfield fans.

Round 2: *In the game moved to the week before the season proper to accommodate Harlequins' friendly with Manly, but which was postponed because of a frozen pitch, Bradford turned the tables on the London side from the week before with a 42-18 win at the Stoop. Dave Halley was the star of the show early on, being the man on the spot to mop up a first-half hat-trick as the Bulls built an unassailable 36-6 half-time lead.*

Round 16: *Salford and Catalans played their catch-up game on the Friday night, the game originally postponed because of the Dragons' international player commitments in France's defeat by England. The Dragons heaped more misery on Salford as they snatched an 18-16 victory through Casey McGuire's last-gasp try to cap a late fightback after trailing 14-0. The visitors were in front for barely 30 seconds of the entire match.*

Round 24

Rugby League broke more new ground on Saturday 15th August when Super League was played at the Stade de la Méditerranée in Béziers. Catalans Dragons chairman Bernard Guasch was a happy man at the outcome of his side's 18-6 defeat of Hull. The Dragons' victory moved them into the top eight, while the attendance of just under 10,000 was the Perpignan club's second highest of the season after their match in Barcelona. The win also took some of the pressure off coach Kevin Walters, whose position had been seen as under threat. The defeat saw Hull FC's play-off hopes effectively ended.

The Airlie Birds were six points off eighth place with three games remaining. They took a 6-0 lead, but a second-half Olivier Elima hat-trick saw them beaten. Teenage winger Tom Briscoe came back from a four-month injury lay-off with an ankle-ligament injury suffered in the second half of the Hull derby on Good Friday. Later that week Hull confirmed Kirk Yeaman and Shaun Berrigan would miss the remainder of the year. Berrigan suffered a dislocated shoulder, while Yeaman tore two tendons off his hip bone.

Hull Kingston Rovers consolidated fourth place in the table, maintaining their five-point advantage over fifth-place Wigan, when they defeated St Helens 26-10 at Craven Park on the Sunday. The Robins produced a stunning second-half performance, including three tries in nine minutes, to complete their first double over the Saints for 27 years. A thrilling third quarter saw Rovers race into a 22-4 lead - a deficit that Mick Potter's patched-up and out-of-sorts side looked unlikely to close - and ultimately seal a comprehensive win. Daniel Fitzhenry, winger turned hooker, produced a stand-out display capped by two crucial tries

Leeds Rhinos posted the highest score of the season with a 14-try, 76-12 triumph over Castleford at Headingley, with 50 points coming after the break. It was a record against derby rivals Castleford and brought Leeds level on points with St Helens. Winger Ryan Hall extended his lead at the top of the Super League try-scoring charts with a five-try haul.

That week Greg Eastwood learned his appeal against the refusal earlier in the year by the UK Border Agency to grant him a visa to join Leeds Rhinos had been successful. Eastwood, playing this season for Canterbury Bulldogs, was now set to join the Rhinos in December under the terms of a three-year contract.

Wigan prop Iafeta Palea'aesina bounced back from a Challenge Cup semi-final nightmare as Wigan beat Warrington 36-16 to help avenge their Cup exit. Martin Gleeson's early second-half try took the game from his former club and when George Carmont scored his second try in ten minutes just before the hour mark, Wigan led 32-4. Tries to Vinnie Anderson and Chris Bridge were pure consolation. Former Irish Students international Tyrone McCarthy made an impressive debut off the bench for the Wolves.

Where Warrington went on Friday, so did their fellow Challenge Cup finalists Huddersfield on Sunday night, as a much-improved Bradford Bulls kept their mathematically slim hopes of a play-off place alive with a fiery 28-18 victory at the Galpharm Stadium. The damage was done in a first half that Bradford ended 24-6 in front, thanks to a four-try burst in 15 minutes. Steve McNamara's men seemed to be coasting it when Paul Deacon added a 50th-minute penalty goal. In an ill-tempered second half, however, the Giants came out fighting - literally at times - and with a little more composure might well have sprung an unlikely turnaround. As it was, a mixture of over-excitement from the Giants and some impressive Bradford defence saw the Bulls end their opponents' seven-match winning run.

Newport Titans Academy prop Lewis Mills made his debut for Celtic Crusaders against Wakefield Trinity Wildcats on the Sunday, as the injury-hit Crusaders were outclassed 46-12 at Belle Vue. There were four native-born Welsh players in their 17-man squad - the Crusaders' biggest Welsh representation since earning a Super League place. Marshall Chalk, Chris Beasley and Mark Lennon all pulled out of the Crusaders' side through injury the day before.

Danny Brough was awarded three Albert Goldthorpe points by match reporter Raymond Fletcher but blew his chances of winning the medal for a second year running when he was sent off for abusing a match official. The scrum-half was dismissed two minutes from the end after earlier being sent to the sin bin. He scored one try, had a big say in three others, kicked seven goals, including two from touch, and brought off the game's best tackle. Ironically, it was the tackle that led to Brough receiving the red card from referee James Child. He had raced across field to bring down Celtic prop Ryan O'Hara and roll him into touch. But the referee reckoned the tackle had been completed bcforc hc wcnt into touch. So he penalised Brough, who objected and was sent off.

Round 25

The last round of Super League before the Challenge Cup final was dominated by the news that six Celtic Crusaders players were to be deported by the UK Border Agency for visa violations. Australian stars Jace van Dijk, Damian Quinn, Tony Duggan, Mark Dalle Cort, Josh Hannay and Darren Mapp were ordered to leave the country by 7th September. The six were found to have been playing for the Crusaders on holiday and student visas during the club's early days in the Co-operative Championship and Championship One. Their current visas were valid, but the players were told that they couldn't re-enter the UK for ten years.

Following his side's crushing 68-0 defeat at the hands of Leeds Rhinos at Newport's Rodney Parade stadium on the Saturday, coach John Dixon was close to tears as he praised the contribution made to the club by the so-called 'Bridgend Six'. Another 13 clubs had recruited players who were in the United Kingdom on 'working holiday visas' and played them supposedly as amateurs, in contravention of visa regulations – which had been changed in 2005 - in the period between 2006 and 2008.

Predictably, the Rhinos were unstoppable. There were hat-tricks for Brent Webb and Jamie Peacock – his first for the club – and a typically lively display at seven from Rob Burrow, who exploited the space offered by the Crusaders to turn on the style.

Sam Burgess delivered a big hit to Catalans Dragons' play-off hopes at Odsal. Burgess, who was considering offers from NRL clubs, came on with the Dragons leading 6-0, and totally transformed the course of the game. He immediately scored and had a large hand in a couple of other tries, as the Bulls maintained their own slim top-eight hopes by extending their winning streak to three, the season's best, with a 42-18 success.

An ultimately comfortable eight try to three success over the Dragons also cast doubt over the French club's ability to reach the end of term finale. Three wins on the trot had previously hoisted Catalans back into the top eight, but their play-off prospects now revolved around the visit of Wakefield to Perpignan on September 5th and a trip to St Helens on the final weekend of the scheduled season.

Wakefield made mathematically certain of reaching the play-offs on the Friday night by winning at Challenge Cup finalists Warrington. Their coach John Kear believed his spell on the sidelines at the start of the year, when he was recovering from a hip operation, had contributed to the Wildcats' strong finish, in sharp contrast to 2007 and 2008, when weak finishes cost them a chance to compete in the Super League play-offs.

The Wildcats were superb in beating the Wolves 40-28, especially without two of their most influential players, Jason Demetriou and the suspended Danny Brough. Luke George and Sam Obst both scored twice for Trinity as the Wolves' fifth defeat in six Super League fixtures left their play-off hopes hanging by a thread. Dale Morton's first senior try on 69 minutes killed off any hopes Warrington had of travelling to Wembley on the back of two valuable Super League points.

Castleford's top-eight hopes were precarious too after they lost 29-22 at home to Wigan on the Sunday night - despite each team scoring five tries. The result left the Tigers in eighth place. Sam Tomkins confirmed his rating as one of the hottest young properties in Rugby League by steering Wigan to a hard-earned victory, grabbing a sparkling hat-trick, and a late field goal for good measure.

The Tigers, meanwhile, secured the services of their outstanding Australian halfback Rangi Chase for a further four years, while young Warriors utility star Mark Flanagan had signed a two-season deal to play in the NRL with Wests Tigers – joining fellow Englishman Gareth Ellis.

With just three games left of the season, Hull FC's Epalahame Lauaki finally made his debut for the club in the 26-6 home win over Harlequins on the Friday night. The Tongan forward initially signed with the black and whites in February, but only arrived at the club in July after red tape delayed his move. Despite having lived in New Zealand for 20 years, Lauaki's visa application was held up, as he had to prove he could speak English. Then the 25-year-old had to complete his recovery from a freak injury sustained at home, in which he damaged a tendon in his arm.

With the pressure off after failing to make the top eight, Hull played with the shackles off. They were classy, at least for an hour, especially Craig Hall, who scored a first-class hat-trick of tries.

It was a good night for Hull to conduct a ticket promotion that drew a crowd of 15,592, but the following Tuesday Jordan Tansey and Danny Tickle were both suspended for two matches by the RFL Disciplinary Committee after being found guilty of illegal tackles. Hull named both in their squad for the following Wednesday's Carnegie 9s. And the Disciplinary Committee decided that would count as their first game, much to round 27 opponents' Bradford's amazement, with the Super League round 26 fixture at Wigan Warriors on Friday September 4th counting as the second. Tickle's suspension was subsequently quashed on appeal anyway.

A big effort by Hull Kingston Rovers proved just enough to overcome a dogged Salford City Reds side at the Willows on the Friday night, and move them into third place in the table. For Rovers, the 14-10 victory was just about deserved but far from certain until a timely Shaun Briscoe try in the final minute.

A thrilling contest did not end without a note of controversy. Leading by only two points and with the seconds ticking away, Michael Dobson's in-goal kick appeared to hit a Hull KR player and go dead. Referee Jamie Leahy, however, spotted a Robbie Paul knock-on in the field of play and awarded Rovers the scrum. In the subsequent skirmishes, Briscoe took a Dobson pass before determinedly ducking in under the Salford defence and striking the killer blow, Dobson converting. There was still time for Stefan Ratchford to make the most of a Jeremy Smith kick with a try at the other end. But as John Wilshere's conversion attempt sailed wide, the hooter sounded and Justin Morgan's men had confirmed a top-four place for the first time ever.

St Helens scrum-half Sean Long made a successful return to action on the Friday night, helping his side to an unconvincing 12-10 win over an under-strength Huddersfield at Knowsley Road. The three-times Lance Todd Trophy winner sustained a jaw injury in the round-19 defeat at Salford in early July, which resulted in a six-week lay-off. Long had been unable to close one of his eyes, as a result of nerve damage caused by the repair to the jaw. Saints had lost three of the six games that Long missed, including the Challenge Cup semi-final defeat to Huddersfield. And they were now no longer top of Super League, having been overtaken by Leeds on points difference.

Saints struggled to see off a gallant effort from a virtual reserve grade Huddersfield outfit, rallying from 10-0 down. Just a week before their first Wembley appearance since 1962 the Giants team sheet lacked eleven of the semi-final winning side, with coach Nathan Brown opting to hand debuts to fullback Elliot Hodgson and winger Alex Brown in an all-English line-up. The big downside for them was a medial knee ligament injury to second-rower Danny Kirmond, which ruled him out of the following Saturday's showpiece. Francis Meli's 64th-minute try finally edged Saints ahead.

SUPER LEAGUE TABLE - *Sunday 23rd August*

	P	W	D	L	F	A	D	PTS
Leeds Rhinos	25	19	0	6	757	419	338	38
St Helens	25	19	0	6	711	424	287	38
Hull Kingston Rovers	25	16	1	8	600	476	124	33
Huddersfield Giants	25	16	0	9	600	384	216	32
Wigan Warriors	25	14	0	11	609	481	128	28
Wakefield T Wildcats	25	14	0	11	627	579	48	28
Catalans Dragons	25	12	0	13	569	614	-45	24
Castleford Tigers	25	12	0	13	562	680	-118	24
Warrington Wolves	25	11	0	14	589	631	-42	22
Harlequins	25	11	0	14	557	599	-42	22
Bradford Bulls	25	10	1	14	588	632	-44	21
Hull FC	25	10	0	15	462	568	-106	20
Salford City Reds	25	7	0	18	414	680	-266	14
Celtic Crusaders	25	3	0	22	319	797	-478	6

* On the Wednesday night before the Wembley final, Hull FC beat Leeds Rhinos in the final at Headingley to win the Carnegie Floodlit Nines, with Craig Hall voted man of the tournament.

CHALLENGE CUP FINAL
Howlin' Wolves!

Wolves chief executive Andy Gatcliffe predicted his club was entering a new era after the Wolves' 25-16 victory over Huddersfield Giants at Wembley took the Challenge Cup back to Warrington for the first time since 1974, their first silverware since the now defunct Regal Trophy in 1991. Marshalled superbly by scrum-half Lee Briers and Lance Todd Trophy-winner Michael Monaghan, after building an 18-10 lead at the break the Wolves were able to keep their noses in front, scrapping and rallying for every loose piece of possession. There were also big contributions from Adrian Morley, Vinnie Anderson (in the unfamiliar position of stand-off), his brother Louis, Garreth Carvell and Chris Hicks

Tony Smith's Wolves made a free-scoring start, running in three tries in the most frantic of opening quarters, as Nathan Brown's Giants were denied the right to settle. An initial indication that this might not be the Giants' day came at the end of the very first set. As Huddersfield skipper Brett Hodgson shaped to clear his lines on the last tackle, his kick was charged down by Louis Anderson.

The Kiwi second-rower couldn't quite get the ball away to Carvell in support and took the tackle five metres from his opponents' tryline. With only one minute and five seconds on the clock, Monaghan hit Richie Mathers with a pass from dummy-half and the fullback was just able to squeeze over by the side of the posts, despite the attentions of a clutch of Giants defenders, on the nod of video referee Phil Bentham.

Bentham was called on again on seven minutes when he disallowed what looked a try by Huddersfield hooker Shaun Lunt for a double movement. Two minutes later Lunt was in again. David Faiumu's great offload sent his captain, Hodgson, scampering away from just inside halfway and, with 30 metres to go, Lunt was there in support to take the final pass and score. Brett Hodgson's conversion levelled Chris Bridge's earlier goal and it was all square.

Three minutes later, at the other end of the field, Darrell Griffin coughed up possession under pressure from Morley. In the resulting set, Luke Robinson stepped too quickly out of the defensive line and Monaghan darted through the hole from dummy-half, Bridge again converting. When Hicks went in for a try on 14 minutes, and Bridge's third goal made it 18-6, people were beginning to question Huddersfield's wisdom in resting so many of their front-line players against St Helens the week before.

CARNEGIE CHALLENGE CUP FINAL

Saturday 29th August 2009

HUDDERSFIELD GIANTS 16 WARRINGTON WOLVES 25

GIANTS: 1 Brett Hodgson (C); 21 Leroy Cudjoe; 11 Jamahl Lolesi; 4 Paul Whatuira; 5 David Hodgson; 3 Kevin Brown; 7 Luke Robinson; 16 Keith Mason; 24 Shaun Lunt; 10 Darrell Griffin; 6 Liam Fulton; 13 Stephen Wild; 9 David Faiumu. Subs (all used): 8 Eorl Crabtree; 15 Paul Jackson; 20 Scott Moore; 2 Martin Aspinwall.
Tries: Lunt (9), B Hodgson (37), D Hodgson (76);
Goals: B Hodgson 2/3.
WOLVES: 30 Richard Mathers; 23 Chris Hicks; 25 Chris Bridge; 4 Matt King; 19 Chris Riley; 13 Vinnie Anderson; 6 Lee Briers; 8 Adrian Morley (C); 7 Michael Monaghan; 16 Garreth Carvell; 11 Louis Anderson; 24 Ben Harrison; 12 Ben Westwood. Subs (all used): 18 Michael Cooper; 2 Paul Johnson; 14 Mick Higham; 28 Tyrone McCarthy.
Tries: Mathers (2), Monaghan (12), Hicks (14), V Anderson (61); **Goals:** Bridge 4/5; **Field goal:** Briers (78).
Rugby Leaguer & League Express Men of the Match: *Giants:* Shaun Lunt; *Wolves:* Michael Monaghan.
Penalty count: 11-10; **Half-time:** 10-18;
Referee: Steve Ganson;
Attendance: 76,560 *(at Wembley Stadium).*

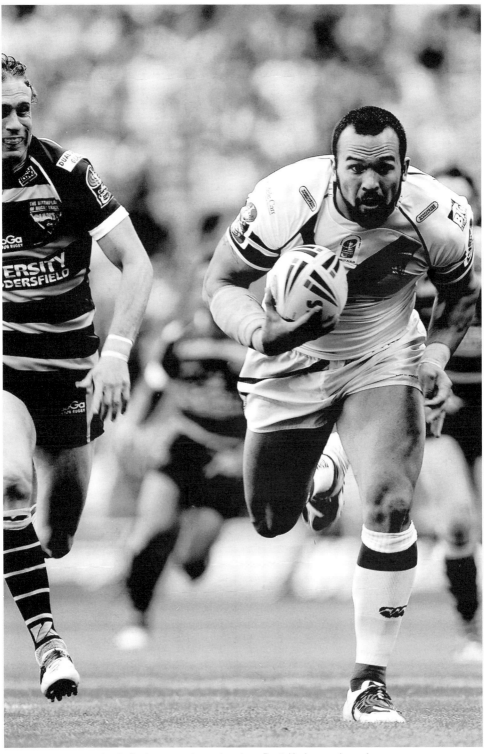

Louis Anderson makes a break as Brett Hodgson gives chase

Challenge Cup Final

Two Huddersfield penalties moved the Giants upfield where Robinson's pass to Kevin Brown was shipped on, one-handed, to 'scorer' David Hodgson. It was a lovely try denied only by the video ref spotting Lunt's supposed obstruction on Bridge in backplay.

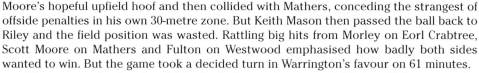

Huddersfield's task grew harder on the half-hour when stand-off Brown was led up the Wembley tunnel with a medial knee ligament injury. His opposite number Vinnie Anderson departed too for six stitches in a cut head, but he was destined to return.

Warrington could do little about Brett Hodgson's try three minutes before the break, as Huddersfield kept the ball alive through six sets of hands before Cudjoe flicked the ball back to Hodgson, whose subsequent touchline conversion attempt sailed wide.

Huddersfield had their best chance of the second half on 55 minutes when Chris Riley collected Scott Moore's hopeful upfield hoof and then collided with Mathers, conceding the strangest of offside penalties in his own 30-metre zone. But Keith Mason then passed the ball back to Riley and the field position was wasted. Rattling big hits from Morley on Eorl Crabtree, Scott Moore on Mathers and Fulton on Westwood emphasised how badly both sides wanted to win. But the game took a decided turn in Warrington's favour on 61 minutes.

The return of a bandaged Vinnie Anderson in place of Mickey Higham was the catalyst. After Warrington's first and only goal-line drop-out, Monaghan fed the Kiwi international after another dart from dummy-half and Anderson sailed between Robinson and Paul Whatuira to score. Bridge's conversion made it 24-10. Even when Bridge, inexplicably, put a 65th-minute penalty goal attempt wide, the day belonged to Warrington.

The Giants had a consolation, of sorts, when David Hodgson rode out Ben Westwood's valiant tackle to score with the approval of the video ref with three minutes left, namesake Brett converting. But when Briers then added a trademark last-minute field goal - his 60th in Warrington colours - that seemed a far more appropriate way to bring down the curtain.

The Wolves' success was a fairytale for youngster Tyrone McCarthy, who won a winners medal after making his first-team debut against Wigan just two weeks before.

David Hodgson scores a late Huddersfield consolation try

SEPTEMBER
Eight men standing

Round 26

Leeds and St Helens laid down a marker on the first Friday night of September with a thunderous and controversial clash at Headingley that the Rhinos won 18-10 to all but secure the League Leaders' Shield. James Graham was the victim of an alleged 'chicken wing' tackle on 11 minutes, for which Jamie Jones-Buchanan was put on report, and at the end of the game the Saints prop refused to shake hands with his opponents and was seen to have a verbal altercation with Rhinos coach Brian McClennan going back up the tunnel.

Keith Senior ended the game in the cooler after a dust up with Jon Wilkin. Senior seemed eager to carry on with the fight while teammates were trying to calm him down. At the end of the game Senior came back onto the field to shake hands with his opponents, but he seemed to grasp the hand of Wilkin and was unwilling to let go.

Saints had opened the brighter, and despite having Leon Pryce in the sin bin for a professional foul. After the 'chicken wing' tackle, Graham produced a peach of a pass to send Lee Gilmour arcing away from Brent Webb for the opening try, his career 100th. Kyle Eastmond converted from out wide and Saints held a lead as Pryce returned.

Leeds gained a foothold that they turned into a trench for the remainder of the first half. Tony Puletua somehow denied Burrow but the pressure told on 24 minutes, Carl Ablett twisting over and Sinfield levelling. Sinfield's bomb on the last tackle saw Donald impeded by Pryce, Gilmour downed Sinfield from the quickly-taken penalty but quick hands to the left saw Ryan Hall over in the corner, despite cries of the last pass being forward. Sinfield landed a superb touchline goal and in the last few seconds had a field-goal attempt charged down by the tireless Graham.

Defences were brutal at the start of the second half. Brent Webb went high on James Roby and the visitors were rewarded for not taking the two on offer. Eastmond, in the centre, toyed the cover across before sending Chris Flannery over on the inside with a perfectly-timed ball. Eastmond dragged the conversion attempt across the face of the posts.

Sean Long, trying to raise a mounting siege, kicked out on the full and, from the turnover on half way, Ron Burrow reacted quickest to a loose ball and shot clear. A super-quick play the ball saw Senior in stride and Hall majestically stepped Ade Gardner for another fine winger's try. Saints were caught offside and then not square as Diskin punished them, Kevin Sinfield putting his side into an eight-point winning lead with eight minutes to go.

After the game it emerged Sinfield had played for an hour with a suspected fractured cheekbone following a clash of heads, refusing to be withdrawn at half-time when diagnosed. Senior and Jones-Buchanan were each suspended for one game. JJB unsuccessfully appealed but the appeal committee stressed the foul tackle was not a 'chicken wing' but 'undue pressure on the shoulder joint'.

Saints and Leeds were jockeying for first and second positions, and there were plenty of sub-battles going on below them for play-off spots. The RFL's decision to increase the number of participants in Super League's play-offs from six to eight for SLXIV had resulted in four clubs fighting for the final eighth place on the last weekend of the regular season.

The top seven teams were now guaranteed to make the play-offs, leaving Catalans, Bradford, Warrington and Harlequins to battle out for eighth place. The Bulls were now strong favourites, with William Hill making them 8/13 to grab the last play-off spot by winning at Hull after they recorded their biggest win of the year - a 44-18 home victory over Salford, Chris Nero scoring a clinical hat-trick.

Catalans remained in eighth after a 34-20 defeat at home by Wakefield Trinity Wildcats, and faced the daunting task of having to get a result at St Helens the following Friday to make certain of a play-off spot. Sean Gleeson broke his cheekbone during Wakefield's win.

The Catalans had battled to a 20-18 lead on 50 minutes but a moment of Wakefield brilliance in the 55th minute from a 20-metre restart turned the game. Back from suspension Danny Brough hammered a quick punt up field for the chasing Luke George and the in-form winger ended up scoring with no Catalans players in sight. Then Michael Korkidas broke away to set up the position for Ryan Atkins to dance through the Dragons defence for a wonderful try. Brough added the goal and Luke George scored another fine try down the right after Tevita Leo-Latu's break and clever dummy-half work from captain Jason Demetriou. Wakefield were sure of at least sixth spot.

Super League's oldest player, Jason Croker, was thought to have played the final game of his 19-season Rugby League career after aggravating an Achilles injury. Croker, who debuted for Canberra Raiders in 1991, had already announced that 2009 would be his final season.

If the Dragons failed to win at Saints in Round 27, the Bulls would clinch eighth if they beat Hull. If the Catalans and Bradford both lost on the Friday, then the winners of the Warrington-Harlequins fixture on the Sunday would make the cut, although Quins could still miss out on points difference to the Dragons after a 48-0 thrashing by Castleford Tigers at the Stoop. Joe Westerman ran in a hat-trick of tries, ending the Tigers' three-match losing run to secure a top-eight finish at the expense of their hosts. Westerman also kicked five goals for a personal haul of 22 points to send a free-falling Quins spinning to a tenth defeat in the last 11 games. The Sunday afternoon win was a tenth win on the road for Castleford and secured their play-off spot.

Warrington started off brightly enough in their first post-Wembley game at Hull KR, leading 12-10 after 30 minutes, but there was no stopping the Robins securing their fifth successive win by 40-16. Clint Newton gave one of the top second-row performances of the season, highlighted by a superb hat-trick of tries.

Challenge Cup runners-up Huddersfield had a more comfortable return to Super League action, securing a 42-16 win at Celtic Crusaders, securing a top-four place.

And, Pat Richards kicked five goals from six attempts in Wigan's Friday 34-22 win over Hull FC at the DW Stadium. Two tries apiece from Amos Roberts and George Carmont ensured Wigan a home berth in the play-offs. Sam Tomkins was in great form again, scoring a splendid individual try that gave Hull an unlikely target of 16 points in the final nine minutes.

Round 27

Catalans Dragons clinched a play-off spot for the second consecutive year with a stunning first ever win, by 24-12, at Knowsley Road on the Friday night.

Catalans scored first with a sweeping move from their own quarter, initiated by Greg Bird, ending with Dimitri Pelo stepping inside Lee Gilmour's tackle to score wide out. Back-to-back penalties then gave Saints their first platform inside the Dragons '20', which ended with Tony Puletua crashing over by the posts from Sean Long's pass. Jonny Lomax converted. The Dragons hit back as Adam Mogg, Casey McGuire and Bird dominated the midfield, their forwards continually making ground. McGuire took Bird's crash-ball five metres out to score by the left upright and Thomas Bosc's conversion edged the Dragons into a 10-6 lead. A Bosc penalty after the restart extended the Dragons lead to six points. An electrifying break from Kyle Eastmond was halted only by a terrific cover tackle from Pelo before Olivier Elima punished a Saints error, crashing over at the left corner after Francis Meli's fumble had gifted the Dragons field position. Bosc converted from the touchline. The French extended their lead, with Clint Greenshields repeating Elima's effort in the left corner. Bosc again converted to make it 24-6 and put the game beyond Saints' reach, despite Keiron Cunningham's converted try eight minutes from time. Gregory Mounis and Cyril Stacul were to miss the rest of Dragons' season after picking up knee and ankle injuries respectively.

Catalans' shock win meant heartbreak for Bradford, who the same night had done all they could at the KC Stadium with a 21-18 win. Despite winning their last five matches Bradford failed to reach the play-offs for the first time since they were introduced in 1998. Bradford's match winner was Paul Deacon, who had played in six Grand Finals with the Bulls. Long before he snatched victory with a superb 40-metre 73rd minute field goal and sealed it with a last-minute penalty, the scrum-half had laid the foundations with a try-making pass and a brilliant touchdown of his own plus three other goals. It was a disappointing end to Glenn Morrison's Bradford career as, in addition to losing out on a play-off place, the Wakefield-bound Australian spent the last ten minutes in the sin bin for a high tackle. He was also a central figure in a brief brawl as tempers became frayed in a fiery finish.

Hull ended the Super League campaign in twelfth place and their performance reflected their disappointing season. They began in a way that promised much, stuttered midway through and then produced a spirited finish that still ended with nothing to show for their efforts. The club had already started a clear out, releasing Chris Thorman, Paul King, Jamie Thackray, Dominic Maloney, Tommy Lee, Graeme Horne, Motu Tony, Todd Byrne and Josh Cordoba, and football operations manager Jon Sharp was also released.

Leeds were presented the League Leaders Shield at the Willows after their 30-24 win over Salford City Reds. Even lacking two major playmakers in the injured Kevin Sinfield

Leeds Rhinos celebrate winning the League Leaders Shield

and Danny McGuire - a late withdrawal on compassionate grounds - and suspended pair Jamie Jones-Buchanan and Keith Senior, the Rhinos were expected to make light work of a Reds side who could finish no higher than 13th in the table. Salford, though, were determined to send departing Super League stalwart Robbie Paul, bound for Leigh, and home favourite John Wilshere out on a high, and they produced a gutsy performance that ended with their tenth defeat by eight points or less in SLXIV, as well as scoring one of the tries of the year in a highly entertaining encounter. They led 12-0 with 30 minutes gone and the game was all square at half-time. Carl Ablett's 70th-minute try seemed like icing when he scored it, but it proved to be crucial as Stuart Littler and Stefan Ratchford score tries in the last six minutes.

The last effort was magnificent, and featured both Paul and Wilshere, the latter launching the move with a belligerent upfield break almost from the restart from Littler's try. Paul was in support and it was his pass that sent Ratchford romping in for a score that brought the house down.

Hull KR needed to win at Wakefield in the televised Saturday night game to ensure they finished third in the table, but lost 24-10 and ended fourth, meaning a trip to Leeds Rhinos in the first round of the new play-off system. Sam Obst inspired the Wildcats to a sixth win in seven games. The Australian livewire scored one try and made others for Dale Ferguson and Aaron Murphy as John Kear's side finished the regular season on 32 points, their highest ever tally in Super League, securing a fifth-place finish.

Huddersfield went into third - a Super League best - to earn a trip to St Helens after a resounding 48-16 win over Wigan Warriors at the Galpharm Stadium, and that without Scott Moore and Keith Mason, both suspended by the club for reportedly missing training after a drinking session in London with Hollywood actor Mickey Rourke. Leroy Cudjoe collected three of the Giants' tries, but Brett Hodgson was the inspiration behind the success, seemingly omnipresent in attack and defence and slotting eight immaculate conversions from all over the pitch.

Wigan finished sixth to secure a home eliminator with Castleford and were thought to be considering appointing reserve team coach and former player Shaun Wane to the head coach's position, with Brian Noble rumoured to be heading to Celtic Crusaders at the end of the season.

Noble's move to south Wales moved a step closer when the Crusaders announced its current coach John Dixon was to return to Australia. The denuded Crusaders, with six home-grown players, finished their campaign on an optimistic note at Castleford, leading 22-18 until the 50th minute, and on level terms with 13 minutes to go. Craig Huby's try, two minutes from time, finally ended the Crusaders' hopes and a 35-22 Tigers win.

Warrington and Harlequins had gone into the weekend as play-off hopefuls but the events of Friday night at Knowsley Road made their Sunday game the deadest of rubbers, the Wolves winning 44-34. A carnival atmosphere picked up after the final whistle as the visitors were cheered from the field by the bumper crowd and the Challenge Cup was paraded around the pitch.

FINAL SUPER LEAGUE TABLE - *Sunday 13th September*

	P	W	D	L	F	A	D	PTS
Leeds Rhinos	27	21	0	6	805	453	352	42
St Helens	27	19	0	8	733	466	267	38
Huddersfield Giants	27	18	0	9	690	416	274	36
Hull Kingston Rovers	27	17	1	9	650	516	134	35
Wakefield T Wildcats	27	16	0	11	685	609	76	32
Wigan Warriors	27	15	0	12	659	551	108	30
Castleford Tigers	27	14	0	13	645	702	-57	28
Catalans Dragons	27	13	0	14	613	660	-47	26
Bradford Bulls	27	12	1	14	653	668	-15	25
Warrington Wolves	27	12	0	15	649	705	-56	24
Harlequins	27	11	0	16	591	691	-100	22
Hull FC	27	10	0	17	502	623	-121	20
Salford City Reds	27	7	0	20	456	754	-298	14
Celtic Crusaders	27	3	0	24	357	874	-517	6

* The Rugby Football League and the Australian Rugby League abandoned their plans to have England and Australia play for the Ashes trophy when they met at Wigan in the Gillette Four Nations tournament on 31st October. The plan had been almost universally condemned.

SUPER LEAGUE PLAY-OFFS
Dragons breathe fire

Week One

Qualifying Play-offs

LEEDS RHINOS 44 HULL KINGSTON ROVERS 8

A dominant second half - that harnessed 34 unanswered points - by the defending Champions showed the Rhinos were in no mood to relinquish the title. Even allowing for the disruptions the Robins were caused by the late withdrawal of Scott Murrell, who was earmarked for hooker, due to a wisdom tooth infection, the desperate early loss of Chev Walker, which meant a spell in the centres for Michael Vella, and the hurried but encouraging debut of second-rower Scott Taylor, there was a stark difference between a side in their first Super League play-off and one that had been there every season since their inception.

Walker was taken to hospital with a compound fracture of the tibia after his leg buckled as Keith Senior tackled him after just eleven minutes of the game. The Leeds player heard the snap and saw bone protruding from Walker's ankle before frantically beckoning medical attention. Hull KR were already without Shaun Briscoe and Ben Galea, although coach Justin Morgan admitted all would have all played in an eliminator. 'We have a second bite of the cherry and we weren't prepared to risk them,' said Morgan.

Six second-half tries saw the Rhinos quell the Robins, with Jamie Peacock's return the key to their dominance, along with two-try Ali Lauitiiti and the scheming of Danny McGuire and Matt Diskin.

ST HELENS 15 HUDDERSFIELD GIANTS 2

St Helens' win over Huddersfield also handed them a route straight through to week three of the play-offs. Three tries in the opening quarter were enough to put Saints 80 minutes from a third consecutive Grand Final appearance, in a low-key play-off encounter.

In an echo of their recent Wembley disappointment, the Giants gifted Saints an early try. Liam Fulton's desperate offload as he was caught in possession flew straight into the arms of Tony Puletua and the big Kiwi rumbled 40 metres to touch down by the posts, despite the attentions of Leroy Cudjoe and Brett Hodgson. Kyle Eastmond converted. A combination of solid home defence and a conservative game plan restricted the Giants' scoring opportunities. So much so that Brett Hodgson opted to kick a 30-metre penalty.

Leon Pryce ghosted through from close range to add a second try for Saints on 13 minutes, this after Eastmond had forced the ball from Brett Hodgson's grasp on a kick return. And on 20 minutes, after Ade Gardner was corralled on the right wing, a five-man passing move saw the ball whipped wide left where Eastmond's pace and direct running drew in the defence, allowing him to send Francis Meli diving in at the left corner. Sean Long effectively killed-off the slim Giants comeback chances when he slotted over a 73rd minute field goal to edge the Saints three scores clear.

Elimination Play-offs

WAKEFIELD TRINITY WILDCATS 16 CATALANS DRAGONS 25

Fifth-placed Wakefield were the first team to be eliminated on the Saturday night as, without Danny Brough, sidelined with a hip injury, they stuttered through the first half against a Catalans side visibly coming into form. The French side swept into a 22-2 lead after 47 minutes, but then had to withstand a terrific Wakefield fightback.

The victory was due mainly to a big team effort plus the craft of Casey McGuire, who controlled play from dummy-half. Clint Greenshields stood out at fullback, timing his linking up to perfection as he gave the final pass for a couple of tries. Adam Mogg also produced a touch of class when he cut through with a dummy to send in Olivier Elima for a try, while Thomas Bosc's kicking was another key factor.

Wildcats winger Luke George scored two tries, set up another and made a tremendous 40-metre clearance run from his own line. It all came in a 21-minute second-half spell to raise Trinity hopes of snatching a win. The 21-year-old's first try was a classic winger's score. When Wakefield moved the ball round the blind side of a scrum near halfway, Ryan Atkins slipped his winger a neat pass. George took it in full stride, raced down the touchline and sped past Greenshields' flying tackle attempt to finish off in great style.

Eight minutes later George was haring down the left again. This time he burst on to Scott Grix's kick before passing inside for Atkins to complete a spectacular 80-metre raid with a try.

WIGAN WARRIORS 18 CASTLEFORD TIGERS 12

Wigan emerged victorious on the Sunday night, earning a place against Hull Kingston Rovers in the following Saturday's preliminary semi-final. It was a nervous opening from both sides until 22 minutes when Pat Richards and Kirk Dixon contested Thomas Leuluai's kick to the left corner. The ball came loose and Harrison Hansen pounced to touch down on the say-so of video referee Phil Bentham, Richards converting. Eight minutes before the break scrum-half Leuluai's kick to the same corner this time taken cleanly by Richards. The winger fed George Carmont, who nipped around his provider to score in the corner before Richards sent over the extras from the touchline.

The Tigers, though out of sorts with ball in hand, continued to battle, but they were lucky to escape lightly when Joel Tomkins picked up a loose ball and sped away, the second-rower only just being hauled down by the outstanding Richard Owen, before Amos Roberts defused a Brent Sherwin bomb at the other end as the first-half seconds ticked away. A Richards penalty three minutes after the break extended the lead to 14 points and when Richards narrowly failed to reach Sean O'Loughlin's kick to the corner, Cas conceded their own first GLDO, allowing Sam Tomkins and then Cameron Phelps to send Roberts scampering over unopposed in the corner.

There was a great comeback by the Tigers, Craig Huby barging his way over and Joe Westerman ensured a lively last five minutes by taking a juggled Owen pass and coasting through for a try, before slotting a cool conversion.

Clint Greenshields all wrapped up by Brett Hodgson and Darrell Griffin

Week Two

Preliminary Semi-finals

HUDDERSFIELD GIANTS 6 CATALANS DRAGONS 16

The Catalans recorded their fourth away win in three weeks, making a mockery of odds as 50-1 pre-play-off outsiders to win the Grand Final. Third-placed Huddersfield Giants had begun as 12-1 dark horses, but a second play-off defeat meant it was a disappointing end to their best ever Super League season.

The clash between the 2008 and 2009 Dream Team fullbacks ended in a clear victory for the previous year's selection, Clint Greenshields, over current choice Brett Hodgson. A top-class performance brought Greenshields one try and a big hand in the match-clinching touchdown. Greenshields powered through Brett Hodgson on the line when scoring his try after the hint of a dummy took him over from ten metres off Adam Mogg's pass. Casey McGuire was a key figure in midfield. It was his quick pass that set up Dimitri Pelo for the try that regained Catalans the lead in the 62nd minute.

After grinding out a victory for most of the game, Catalans finished it off in style. Greenshields, inevitably, was involved in the build-up and a bewildering bout of passing that involved Greg Bird twice ended with Olivier Elima taking Bosc's inside pass. It was Elima's 18th touchdown this season. Huddersfield's only try had put them ahead in the 35th minute, a brilliant solo effort from Luke Robinson. Receiving the ball 20 metres out from the Dragons' posts, he burst through two defenders, and wrong-footed Greenshields, before just holding off a double-tackle attempt to scramble over.

73

Nick Fozzard and Ben Galea get to grips with Andy Coley

HULL KINGSTON ROVERS 16 WIGAN WARRIORS 30

A gallant second-half fightback by Hull Kingston Rovers was not enough to deny Wigan as the 2009 Super League play-offs finally exploded into life at Craven Park on the Saturday. Leading 18-0 at the break, the Warriors looked odds-on favourites to go through, as Rovers were made to pay for a nervous start by a team seemingly determined to send coach Brian Noble out on a high. George Carmont went in for the game's opening try on 16 minutes; Iafeta Palea'aesina crashed clean through off a tap penalty; and then Pat Richards burst through Shaun Briscoe and Michael Dobson in the corner, after his provider Sean O'Loughlin had burst into the attacking line superbly.

But when Kris Welham finally got his side on the scoreboard four minutes into the second half, the home side's self-belief rose to the extent that, going into the final quarter, after tries to Peter Fox and Chaz l'Anson there were only two points in it, and it was Rovers who had the wind in their sails. Then on 63 minutes, Wigan skipper O'Loughlin went into a tackle with Scott Murrell and Mick Vella. The ball came loose and Richard Silverwood, the referee, awarded a penalty, 30 metres away from the Hull KR line.

A minute later, after Wigan ran it, gamestar Martin Gleeson - having his best game of the season by far - was forcing his way over despite the valiant attentions of Rovers fullback Shaun Briscoe, allowing Richards' conversion to make it 24-16. Gleeson's second, a minute before time, was the icing on the cake for a Wigan side whose impressive late-season run was now just 80 minutes away from a near-perfect finish.

* On the Sunday lunchtime, live on terrestrial and satellite TV, Leeds Rhinos chief executive Gary Hetherington announced the club had selected Catalans Dragons as their opponents in the following Friday's Qualifying Semi-final. The first ever 'Clubcall' meant that St Helens would meet Wigan in the other tie.

Kevin Sinfield gets the ball away as Jason Ryles closes in

Week Three

Qualifying Semi-finals

LEEDS RHINOS 27 CATALANS DRAGONS 20

On the Friday night over one hundred family members, former teammates and Leeds directors lined up on the halfway line at Headingley to form a guard of honour, as the two teams took to the field and a crowd of 13,409 prepared to pay its own respects to former great John Holmes, who had died at the age of 57. After the emotional tributes, an industrious victory over the obdurate Dragons saw the Rhinos qualify for their fifth title decider in six seasons, with the chance to claim an unprecedented Grand Final treble, a run of success that was without parallel for Leeds.

It seemed fitting the home number six shirt, Danny McGuire, opened the scoring, his majestic step inside an already fooled cover from a deceiving dummy - a trademark Holmes calling card. Beforehand Kevin Sinfield said that he hoped his side would carry the spirit of the lost legend and this fiercely contested clash was effectively settled with a three-try barrage in five blistering minutes in the run up to half-time, in which Sinfield played the key part with a trio of different, unlocking passes. An overhead lob to Luke Burgess kept the ball alive for the first, a delicate flicked offload sent Jamie Jones-Buchanan rampaging clear for the second and a long ball put Scott Donald away out wide for the third. Sinfield's calming field goal proved to be the ultimately decisive factor.

Much was made over whether the Rhinos' decision to choose their opponents would provide their foes with added motivation and, in Adam Mogg and Greg Bird especially, they had the individual stand outs, the visitors earning praise for winning the second half 16-5 when their cause seemed shot at the break. Vincent Duport finished with a hat-trick and Sinfield's one-point cushion proved significant when Mogg ghosted in with six minutes left to make it 27-20.

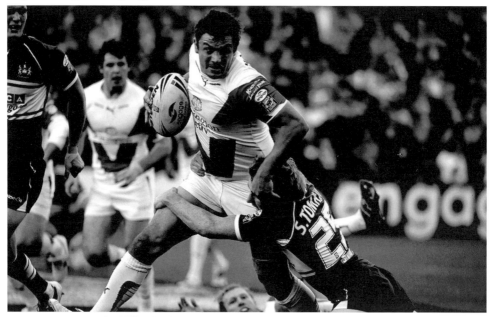

Jon Wilkin looks for support as he is tackled by Sam Tomkins

ST HELENS 14 WIGAN WARRIORS 10

Just hours before kick-off on the Saturday, Sean Long was signing copies of his controversial autobiography in a local bookshop. But he showed the signing session hadn't taken anything away from his game with some crucial interventions that took Saints through to their fourth consecutive Grand Final. He produced a magnificent flying cover tackle on Pat Richards to prevent the winger scoring in the left corner after nine minutes and scored a vital try after 36 minutes, enabling Saints to take the lead just before half-time. This after Saints got off to an explosive start, with Kyle Eastmond breaking through Sam and Joel Tomkins' attempted tackles on the left flank, before racing clear from half way to send Francis Meli in at the left corner. Then, on 49 minutes, a superb Long pass to Meli enabled the Samoan to touch down in the corner to give Saints an eight-point lead.

Wigan were magnificent in trying to get back on terms, and when Richards scored a brilliant try it looked as though the momentum might be with them for the final ten minutes. But it was Long who would pull off the vital play for Saints, when he tackled Joel Tomkins with less than three minutes to go and managed to plant Joel's foot onto the touchline. On another day it could have been a penalty to Wigan, but a Saints scrum was called, and after that Long kept Wigan deep in their own half.

It was the third successive season that Brian Noble had taken Wigan to within one game of the Grand Final. Everyone knew that this would be Noble's last game in charge, but it was still a dramatic moment when, after the game, he finally revealed that he would be leaving the club.

* Barrow coach Dave Clark confirmed that Barrow would apply for a Super League licence in 2011 after their Co-operative Championship Grand Final 26-18 victory over Halifax at Warrington.

And 20-year old superstar Sam Burgess announced that week he had signed a four-year deal with South Sydney Rabbitohs, who had paid a significant transfer fee to Bradford Bulls in order to release him from the last year of his current contract.

SUPER LEAGUE GRAND FINAL
Three-peat for Rhinos

Kevin Sinfield was confirmed as one of Leeds' greatest ever players as he lifted the Super League trophy as winning captain for the fourth time. Sinfield had already lifted the trophy in 2004, 2007 and 2008, and had now eclipsed the record set by Chris Joynt, who led St Helens to success in 1999, 2000 and 2002.

Life goes on, was Sean Long's initial reaction to Saints' third successive defeat at Old Trafford to a Rhinos side. Saints had won two of the previous three encounters in 2009 between, indubitably, the best sides that year, and they gave it their all, but when it mattered most, Leeds had the resolve to come up trumps. As Long failed to conjure a fairytale finish to his wonderful Saints career, Sinfield added the Harry Sunderland Trophy to his Lance Todd Trophy of 2005.

Sinfield shrugged off suggestions that he had not fully recovered from a cheekbone injury suffered against St

ENGAGE SUPER LEAGUE GRAND FINAL

Saturday 10th October 2009

LEEDS RHINOS 18 ST HELENS 10

RHINOS: 1 Brent Webb; 2 Scott Donald; 3 Lee Smith; 4 Keith Senior; 5 Ryan Hall; 6 Danny McGuire; 7 Rob Burrow; 8 Kylie Leuluai; 14 Matt Diskin; 10 Jamie Peacock; 11 Jamie Jones-Buchanan; 18 Carl Ablett; 13 Kevin Sinfield (C). Subs (all used): 16 Ryan Bailey for Leuluai (19); 19 Luke Burgess for Peacock (29); 17 Ian Kirke for Jones-Buchanan (29); 12 Ali Lauitiiti for Ablett (29); Jones-Buchanan for Lauitiiti (36); Peacock for Burgess (46); Leuluai for Bailey (53); Ablett for Kirke (57); Burgess for Diskin (62); Bailey for Leuluai (67); Diskin for Burgess (69); Kirke for Jones-Buchanan (76).
Tries: Diskin (30), Smith (37, 72); **Goals:** Sinfield 2/4;
Field goals: Sinfield (42), Burrow (78).
SAINTS: 1 Paul Wellens; 2 Ade Gardner; 3 Matt Gidley; 18 Kyle Eastmond; 5 Francis Meli; 6 Leon Pryce; 7 Sean Long; 10 James Graham; 9 Keiron Cunningham (C); 16 Tony Puletua; 12 Jon Wilkin; 11 Lee Gilmour; 13 Chris Flannery. Subs (all used): 14 James Roby for Cunningham (25); 15 Bryn Hargreaves for Puletua (24); 17 Paul Clough for Gilmour (31); 23 Maurie Fa'asavalu for Graham (31); Graham for Fa'asavalu (48); Puletua for Hargreaves (50); Gilmour for Wilkin (55); Cunningham for Clough (61); Wilkin for Roby (65); Roby for Flannery (73).
Try: Eastmond (13); **Goals:** Eastmond 3/3.
Rugby Leaguer & League Express Men of the Match:
Rhinos: Kevin Sinfield; *Saints:* James Graham.
Penalty count: 8-7; **Half-time:** 8-8; **Referee:** Steve Ganson;
Attendance: 63,259 *(at Old Trafford, Manchester).*

Helens in round 26. Tremendous in defence, he brought off a great try-saving and possibly match-saving tackle that smashed Kyle Eastmond into the corner flag, and his kicking game played a vital role again. A booming 50-metre '40/20' increased the pressure on St Helens, and Leeds scored their first try a few minutes later.

Having come back from 8-0 down, Leeds were level at half-time, and coach Brian McClennan sent them out with orders not to come back without a point from their first attack. Sinfield carried out those orders to perfection. His well-placed second-half kick-off forced Ade Gardner into an error ten metres from his own line and the ball bounced into touch. It gave Leeds possession, and after four tackles Sinfield stepped up to land a field goal from 12 metres to edge them in front. It seemed of little relevance with 39 minutes left to play, but by the time Lee Smith tore over for his second try on 73 minutes, the game was up for Saints, seven, not six points behind.

The mistake that gave Leeds position and possession for that fateful attack came from Francis Meli, who spilled the ball at first receiver coming away from his own line.

Leeds put him under pressure at every opportunity. He had responded magnificently with some bulldozing kick returns - added to lots of bullocking runs from first receiver. But by the last quarter of the game, Meli and Saints were visibly tiring. That became obvious in the 63rd minute when Matt Gidley got back to dummy half after another long raking kick had turned around Paul Wellens. Gidley, another industrious Saint, didn't have the energy to perform a service from dummy half and his pass to Gardner was wayward, deemed forward by referee Steve Ganson.

When Meli handed possession to Leeds, something had to crack. Sinfield's dab to the line caught Tony Puletua's foot, winning a repeat set, and Matt Diskin was held up magnificently by Wellens. But, after Jamie Peacock - extending his own record to six Grand Final wins, three with Bradford, now three with Leeds - had a second tilt at the line, the ball was shipped right. Under pressure, Danny McGuire hooked a kick around Leon Pryce for Smith to scoop up on a diagonal run and tear behind the posts.

It looked a dead-set try but the video referee was called into play and numerous replays suggested Smith was just in front of the kicker when he set off on his chase. The try was given, Smith was just behind the ball when it was kicked.

With seven points in it after Sinfield's conversion and six minutes to go, Saints needed the ball back but when Ryan Hall caught the short restart it was effectively game over, and Rob Burrow's 78th minute field goal confirmed that. There was one last hurrah from St Helens as Kyle Eastmond broke through but Leon Pryce had unwittingly obstructed the Leeds defence.

This was the tightest final since 1999 and though Leeds were deserved champions, St Helens played a huge part in the drama, dominating the first half hour of the game, leading 8-0 up to the point when Diskin forced his way over from dummy half for the Rhinos' opening try in the right corner, after Sinfield had just been stopped short.

And Saints had two very close calls, one in either corner, in the second half. Six minutes after Sinfield's field goal had given Leeds the lead for the first time, Gidley broke his shackles down the right centre and lobbed a one-handed pass out to Gardner, who showed terrific pace down the wing. It looked a try but Ryan Hall's desperate tackle took Gardner into the corner post as he touched down, although Brent Webb conceded a penalty, adjudged by the video referee to have fallen into the Saints winger with his knees. The next Saints attack broke down as a misguided pass from James Roby at dummy-half missed Long and was knocked on by Maurie Fa'asavalu.

Then, with the score at 11-10 after the sides had swapped easy penalties - Eastmond regaining the lead at 10-9 after a tackle by Burrow on Long was adjudged high, and Sinfield replying when Keiron Cunningham knocked the ball out of Kylie Leuluai's hands

under his own posts - Eastmond was bundled into the corner post by that magnificent Sinfield cover tackle after Meli had made the bust and sent him tearing down the wing into the corner.

Four minutes later Smith, with Sinfield's conversion, had decided the outcome of the game. The centre - playing his last game for Leeds before moving to rugby union with Wasps - and McGuire might have featured in Meli's dreams on the Saturday night. It was Meli's indecision three minutes before the break in dealing with a McGuire grubber to the in-goal that had allowed Leeds to draw level. The back-tracking winger could have scooped the ball dead, but instead tried to gather it in. The ball popped out of his grasp and Smith gleefully touched it down before it rolled dead.

Sinfield couldn't convert from the touchline -

Brent Webb and Sean Long contest a high ball

and he had already hit the post for the ball to bounce out after Diskin's try - but the two tries in seven minutes had cancelled out all the good work that St Helens had done in the first 30.

In an electric atmosphere, St Helens had got off to a great start on 12 minutes when a Jon Wilkin grubber took a deflection off Sinfield's leg; and Eastmond snatched the ball before Scott Donald could get to it and tore away behind the posts to give himself an easy conversion. A magnificent spiralling, almost uncatchable bomb from Long produced Saints' next points, an Eastmond penalty goal, Hall getting finger tips only to the ball, and Keith Senior being penalised for a shove on Chris Flannery.

A penalty against Eastmond for not letting Smith get a quick play-the-ball, as Brian McClennan brought three subs off the bench, gave Leeds great field position and Ali Lauitiiti made an immediate impact with an offload and then a great run before Diskin changed the course of the game, and history, with his try. Lauitiiti hobbled off shortly afterwards never to return and Leeds played the rest of the game with 16 men. But it was the Rhinos who had enough gas in the tank to wear down Saints into submission.

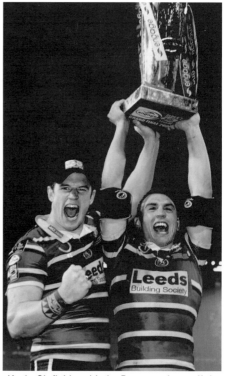

Kevin Sinfield and Luke Burgess show off the Super League Trophy

SUPER LEAGUE XIV AWARDS

MAN OF STEEL: Brett Hodgson (Huddersfield Giants)

(chosen by players poll)

YOUNG PLAYER OF THE YEAR: Sam Tomkins (Wigan Warriors)

COACH OF THE YEAR: Nathan Brown (Huddersfield Giants)

TOP TRY SCORER: Ryan Hall (Leeds Rhinos) *for scoring 28 regular season tries*

TOP METRE-MAKER: James Graham (St Helens) *for making 4,752 regular season metres*

TOP TACKLER: Malcolm Alker (Salford City Reds) *for making 981 regular season tackles*

SUPER LEAGUE DREAM TEAM *(previous appearances in italics)*
1 Brett Hodgson (Huddersfield Giants)
2 Peter Fox (Hull Kingston Rovers)
3 Matt Gidley (St Helens) *2008*
4 Keith Senior (Leeds Rhinos) *2002, 2003, 2004*
5 Ryan Hall (Leeds Rhinos)
6 Sam Tomkins (Wigan Warriors)
7 Michael Dobson (Hull Kingston Rovers)
8 Adrian Morley (Warrington Wolves) *1998, 1999*
9 Scott Moore (Huddersfield Giants)
10 Jamie Peacock (Leeds Rhinos) *2000, 2001, 2002, 2005, 2006, 2008*
11 Ben Galea (Hull Kingston Rovers)
12 Clint Newton (Hull Kingston Rovers)
13 Kevin Sinfield (Leeds Rhinos) *2005, 2006, 2008*

ALBERT GOLDTHORPE MEDAL: Michael Dobson (Hull Kingston Rovers)

ROOKIE OF THE YEAR: Sam Tomkins (Wigan Warriors)

MIKE GREGORY SPIRIT OF RUGBY LEAGUE AWARD: Steve Prescott

2
CHAMPIONSHIPS 2009

CHAMPIONSHIP SEASON
Fire in the Furness

BARROW RAIDERS' 2009 campaign will go down not only as one of the most remarkable in the club's own history, but of any club in the recent past. Promoted from the old National League Two, they first made their first final in over 20 years, signed a host of players in mid-season who helped them to finish top of the table, and ended up as Grand Final winners. And they made three coaching changes during the course of the year as well.

The abiding memory for most Barrow fans will be their 26-18 Grand Final win over Halifax, which was witnessed by the club's biggest travelling support in probably a generation. For coach Dave Clark - who rode the Raiders rollercoaster as hard as anyone - chairman Des Johnston, and the committed squad of players, it was rich reward for the hard work of recent years.

In that game, veteran fullback Gary Broadbent was magnificent, providing the perfect finale to an outstanding all-round season. Similarly prop Brett McDermott played his full part, alongside workaholic hooker Andy Ellis, whose campaign was topped off with the Championship Player of the Year award and a move to Super League club Harlequins.

The popular Clark was named Coach of the Year after a surreal season in which he was replaced by Steve Deakin in the wake of July's 34-18 Northern Rail Cup final defeat to Widnes, reinstated just weeks later, and finally moved to assistant to incoming boss Steve McCormack after the Grand Final.

McCormack inherited a richly talented squad that included Jamie Rooney, James Coyle and Zebastian Luisi, who were all key mid-season captures.

HALIFAX started the season like a steam train, faltered midway through the campaign, and eventually fell just short of Grand Final glory after recovering in the closing weeks.

By mid-May there looked as though there could be no other winners of the Championship, as Fax stood top of the competition, unbeaten and, in the Cup, having pushed Super League side Castleford all the way to golden point extra time in one of the season's best games.

But in the wake of that match coach Matt Calland produced one of the quotes of the year when he stated his side was the best in the Championship "by a country mile".

The following week they lost to Sheffield at home, and by the end of the season had gone down a further six times in the league and been knocked out of the Northern Rail Cup by Widnes.

They then lost at Barrow in the play-offs before recovering to beat Featherstone in a sudden-death shoot-out, but ultimately came up just short again when they faced the Raiders in the Grand Final.

Still, that appearance at Warrington helped the club to their main 2009 objective, to be in a position to apply for a Super League licence.

Calland's side were frequently the entertainers of their division, with the likes of Mark Gleeson, Ben Black, Shad Royston and Dave Larder all catching the eye at various points.

SHEFFIELD EAGLES marked their continuing emergence as a force by finishing the season in third place in the the the table.

Their campaign ended in ultimate disappointment when they crashed out of the play-offs with a 32-8 defeat at home to Featherstone, but that should not overshadow what was generally a season of success.

Mark Aston looked to the 2008 World Cup for inspiration in his close-season captures, and unearthed a real gem in Papua New Guinean centre Menzie Yere, who was nominated for the Championship Player of the Year award and made the All Stars team.

In addition, fellow Kumul Trevor Exton and Samoan centre Tangi Ropati also made an impact; with the only disappointment being a serious knee injury sustained by Fiji scrum-half Aaron Groom just five games into his Sheffield career. That could have derailed many teams' seasons, but the Eagles recovered well, with Huddersfield-bound halfback Kyle Wood rising to the fore.

Sheffield beat every team in the top six apart from Widnes, and also pushed Super League high-flyers Hull Kingston Rovers close in the Challenge Cup.

WIDNES VIKINGS may have fallen short of their competition favourites tag, but 2009 achieved their main objective – to be in a position to apply for a 2012 Super League licence.

That box was ticked when Paul Cullen's side lifted the Northern Rail Cup at Blackpool in July following a stirring 34-18 win over Barrow.

With the club completely focused on returning to the top flight in two years' time, that was always going to be the season highlight, and though they finished fourth in the Championship and then beat Whitehaven in the opening play-off game, they succumbed to in-form Featherstone the following week.

Cullen arrived at the club after the start of the season following the sudden and shock departure of Steve McCormack, and initially endured a difficult time as the Vikings lost to Leigh twice, among others.

But they avenged two defeats by Halifax with an outstanding 27-22 NRC semi-final win at the Shay, which was arguably their best performance of the season.

Cullen brought Kevin Penny and Steve Pickersgill on loan from his former club Warrington and both made an impact, while second row Richard Fletcher was named in the All Stars team after another consistent campaign.

The experienced Mark Smith and James Webster remained key figures, while out wide Paddy Flynn and Richard Varkulis had strong years.

WHITEHAVEN overcame several hurdles to exceed most people's expectations and finish fifth.

They were flying as high as second with two league games remaining, only for heavy defeats to Widnes and Leigh to see them slip down the table.

They were then dumped out of the play-offs by the Vikings – although not before an almighty effort in a gripping 26-21 defeat at the Stobart Stadium.

Coach Ged Stokes had a much lower budget to work with than most of his competitors, and at times the Haven squad was stretched to its limit. But they still produced several moments to savour, not least home wins over Sheffield, Barrow and Widnes, and a remarkable 50-42 win at Halifax in August.

Teenage scrum-half Gregg McNally made a stunning start to the season and looked set to break all kinds of points scoring records, but by the end of the season was struggling to get into the side.

That left a lot of playmaking responsibilities with the evergreen Leroy Joe, who notably played at both scrum-half and prop during the season.

In the front row, both Karl Edmondson and Kyle Amor were deservedly named in the All Stars team, with Amor earning a lucrative move to Super League champions Leeds Rhinos.

Flying winger Craig Calvert ran in 17 tries in 21 starts, Aussie Jamie Theoharous was a non-stop worker from loose forward, and there was also the emergence of yet more talented young Cumbrians.

FEATHERSTONE ROVERS' first season under Daryl Powell ended just one game short of the Grand Final after a stirring finish to the season.

Inspired by Iestyn Harris in the final games of his illustrious career, away play-off wins at Sheffield and Widnes raised genuine hopes that they could make the Grand Final. They then led in the Final Eliminator at Halifax, only for the home side to battle back and seal a thrilling 36-30 win at the Shay.

They also were also within 80 minutes of the Northern Rail Cup final, only to lose out 16-10 in a tense semi-final against Barrow.

Still, Powell had undoubtedly made a mark in his debut year at the Chris Moyles Stadium.

Scrum-half Andy Kain was named in the All Stars team, while prop Stuart Dickens was again a model of consistency up front.

Ian Hardman was among the competition's best outside backs, particularly when playing at fullback, and Tommy Saxton also posed constant problems for defences.

Kyle Briggs emerged as a credible successor to Harris at stand-off for 2010, while ex-Hull KR winger Jon Steel finished the season with an impressive 17 tries.

It was another year of trials and tribulations in the North East, as **GATESHEAD THUNDER** first staged a stunning recovery to avoid relegation, and ended the year in Championship One anyway after another financial crisis.

On the field, the newly-promoted Thunder looked doomed to relegation midway through the year, only for coach Steve McCormack and a handful of high-profile Australian signings to stage their own version of the Great Escape.

Of their last ten games they won seven and drew one, with Aussies Kris Kahler, Russ Aitken, Paul Franze and especially Nick Youngquest playing their full part. Existing squad members Michael Knowles – who was selected in the All Stars side – Andrew Henderson and Luke Branighan were also outstanding members of McCormack's team.

Survival was effectively secured with a 16-12 win away at Barrow in the penultimate game of the season, though it wasn't long before the club began to unravel off the field.

Chairman Steve Garside wound the club's holding company up following a shareholding dispute, and the club was once again forced to reform, this time under the new banner of Thunder Rugby Limited.

It was decided that they would compete in Championship One from next year, on minus six points, and the team was likely to comprise of locally-produced players again.

BATLEY BULLDOGS were another team to stage a late-season revival under a new coach, as the experienced Karl Harrison guided them away from the relegation trapdoor after a shaky start.

Harrison took over from the long-serving Gary Thornton with the Bulldogs at the foot of the Championship, but just four defeats in their final 12 games saw them eventually finish eighth.

Their safety was not confirmed, however, until the final day of the season, when Kevin Crouthers and Paul Mennell inspired them to come from behind and win 30-26 at Featherstone.

Mennell again had an influential year, although it was the arrival of the well-travelled Paul Handforth midway through the season that really kick-started the Bulldogs campaign. The experienced head helped get the best out of forwards such as Byron Smith and Craig Potter.

Ash Lindsay was little short of a revelation at times from loose forward, particularly late in the season, while Jermaine McGilvary earned a Young Player of the Year nomination after finishing with 21 tries while on loan from Huddersfield.

Ian Preece and Danny Maun also chipped in with some vital tries, and home wins over Halifax, Barrow and Widnes showed the Bulldogs could mix it with the best on their day.

LEIGH CENTURIONS eventually retained their place in the Championship, but not before they thought they had been relegated after finishing a disappointing ninth.

The Centurions were handed a late reprieve when Gateshead Thunder asked to compete in Championship One following their financial difficulties – ensuring that the returning Ian Millward and a host of high-profile signings started at the higher level the next year. Robbie Paul, Ricky Bibey and John Duffy had all signed for 2010.

Paul Rowley took over the coaching reins from Neil Kelly when he moved to be director of rugby, but all too often he was forced to work with a crippling injury list in an already stretched squad.

Following an opening day win at eventual high flyers Sheffield, the Centurions slowly lost their way, and in July were hammered 74-6 at Barrow.

They regrouped a little and threw themselves a survival lifeline with wins over Doncaster and Toulouse, but eventually not even a thumping win over Whitehaven was enough to save them finishing as one of the bottom two English sides.

Rowley had plenty of players who put their hands up consistently in trying circumstances, not least experienced scrum-half Ian Watson and former Castleford loose forward Aaron Smith.

Top try scorer was Jamie Durbin with 13, closely followed by the promising Ian Mort.

TOULOUSE OLYMPIQUE's debut campaign in the Championship was an overall success, with the French side chalking up nine league wins.

It didn't look very promising when they were hammered 70-0 in their opening Championship match at Widnes, live on television.

But after competitive displays against Sheffield and Whitehaven, they then won five matches on the trot under coach Gilles Dumas, including victories at Batley and Doncaster.

They also won at Featherstone and Gateshead, while at home they accounted for eventual champions Barrow 22-14 in May. Dumas had several consistent performers in his ranks, with centres Sebastien Planas and Damien Couturier among those to catch the eye. Australian fullback Rory Bromley was another to impress, while scrum-half Nathan Wynn earned plenty of man of the match awards.

In the forwards, big prop Brendan Worth was always a handful up front, while most defences will remember the work of feisty hooker Martin Mitchell.

French international Eric Anselme was a steadying influence in the back row and Constant Villegas had his moments at stand-off, and there was certainly plenty for Dumas and the club to build on ahead of their second season in England.

DONCASTER supporters were forced to endure another torrid campaign after the major highs of 2008, as more financial problems at the club led to a nine-point deduction and just one league win in 2009.

Just months after the club had been promoted on the crest of a wave, they again found themselves struggling to survive.

The result was the points deduction that was always going to result in them finishing bottom of the ultra-competitive Championship, and long-suffering coach Tony Miller had to put up with a threadbare squad. Miller worked minor miracles in getting a team on the field every week, and eventually had to use 52 players in total.

After more mid-season uncertainty about the club's future, popular former player Carl Hall eventually had his rescue package approved by the RFL.

There were high points, the main one being a televised one-point win at local rivals Sheffield Eagles in April, which ended up being their only victory of the league season. The Dons also won at Batley in the Northern Rail Cup, though it wasn't enough to see them progress to the knockout stages.

Among their best players was Australian Josh Weeden, who was almost carrying the team mid-season before his switch to Hunslet Hawks.He was joint top try scorer with Craig Cook, while the likes of Ryan Steen and Wayne Opie never wavered in their efforts.

CHAMPIONSHIP ONE SEASON
Battering Rams

DEWSBURY RAMS made history as only the second team ever to finish their league campaign with a 100 per cent record after a remarkable year under Warren Jowitt. Only Hull FC during the 1978-79 season had managed the feat before, and the Rams swept all before them in a season of remarkable consistency.

From the moment they clinically beat expected title rivals York 28-2 at the Tetley's Stadium, they were always a cut above the chasing pack, and came within two points of knocking Championship side Barrow out of the Northern Rail Cup.

Jowitt was rewarded with the Coach of the Year award in his first full season in charge, having got the most out of a squad that included few, if any star names.

Instead they relied on sheer hard work and organisation, and simply out-enthused most teams on a weekly basis. They had their key players of course, with Irish international scrum-half Liam Finn named as the Championship One Player of the Year for his efforts during the season.

He was joined in the competition's All Stars selection by five of his Rams teammates – Bryn Powell, Kane Epati, Patrick Walker, Andrew Bostock and Adam Hayes.

The likes of Rob Spicer, Mike Emmett and Alex Bretherton cannot have been far from selection either.

In short it was a superb all-round team effort by Dewsbury and Jowitt was relishing the challenge of making an impact in the Championship in 2010.

KEIGHLEY COUGARS continued their steady ascent under highly-rated coach Barry Eaton by finishing second and then earning promotion to the Championship.

The Cougars' 28-26 Grand Final win over Oldham ensured that three years of continuing development under Eaton was rewarded with elevation to the higher level. Star man on the day for Keighley was scrum-half Danny Jones, who scored two tries and created another to win the man of the match award.

His halfback partnership with Jon Presley proved potent all season, with Presley finishing as top try scorer with 25 in all competitions. They worked off the platform built by a solid pack, with props Andy Shickell and Scott Law – the latter of whom made the All Stars team alongside winger Gavin Duffy – setting the lead up front.

Hooker James Feather had another big year, capped off remarkably when he returned early from a serious facial injury to skipper the side in the final against Oldham.

Elsewhere, Will Cartledge, Daley Williams, George Rayner and Carl Hughes all played their part in the season, which included just four defeats in the league.

Two of those were heavy setbacks against champions Dewsbury, but those matches aside, Cougars supporters can look back on 2009 with genuine pride.

YORK CITY KNIGHTS supporters went through a range of emotions during the season, as the controversial mid-season departure of coach Paul March led to a disappointing conclusion to the campaign.

March was sacked after speaking out about a suspension handed to him and members of his squad following an alleged incident at a Leeds Rhinos function.

Within days he had been appointed at rivals Hunslet Hawks, and he was soon followed by a steady trickle of players to the South Leeds Stadium.

The controversy undoubtedly unsettled the Knights squad, and made it difficult for new coach James Ratcliffe to get the most out of his charges before the end of the year.

Despite defeat to a March-inspired Hawks in July, Ratcliffe guided the side to a third-place finish, but their hopes of promotion were dashed when they lost to both Keighley and Oldham in the play-offs.

Ratcliffe has since overseen a major overhaul of the squad, with the most eye-catching arrival being that of the vastly experienced Chris Thorman in a player-coach role.

Of the class of 2009, hooker Paul Hughes was as consistent as most, while Danny Ratcliffe finished as top try scorer from fullback.

Prop Mark Applegarth made the All Stars team after a strong second half to the year, with fellow front-rowers Adam Sullivan and late-season arrival Sean Hesketh also producing some big displays.

The 2010 season marked the start of a new era under James Ratcliffe and Thorman – and they set out with promotion as their primary goal.

OLDHAM were another club to experience repeated uncertainty over their future during 2009, and they also suffered a third consecutive Grand Final defeat when losing to Keighley.

By that stage of the year, just making the final had been seen as a significant achievement, after owner Bill Quinn ended his funding midway through the season and a host of players left for Barrow on transfer deadline day.

The departures of James Coyle, Danny Halliwell, Dave Allen and the already released Rob Roberts hurt Tony Benson's squad considerably, and the way they recovered in the play-offs was admirable.

They also hit back in the Grand Final against the Cougars before eventually losing 28-26, but the biggest battle still loomed large after it emerged that the club owed the Inland Revenue £48,000.

That could not be paid until former owner Chris Hamilton completed his move to take control of the club again from Quinn, which he did with just a day to spare. It was an all too familiar story for the Roughyeds faithful, whose hope to finally find some stability at the club were struck a blow when the club was told it had to leave Boundary Park.

They did have plenty of wins to cheer in 2009, however, culminating in a stirring play-offs campaign that included victories over Swinton, Hunslet and most impressively York.

Scrum-half Thomas Coyle was a constant menace for opposition defences even after the departure of brother James, while Chris Baines made the All Stars team after a rousing finish to the season.

Lucas Onyango and Marcus St Hilaire reached double figures in the try charts, as did non-stop second row Tommy Goulden.

BLACKPOOL PANTHERS marked their return as a genuine force by finishing the season in fifth place under coach Martin Crompton.

The former Wigan and Warrington scrum-half attracted several significant names to the club and moulded them into a side capable of competing with most teams in the division.

Had it not been for a stuttering start that included a series of narrow defeats, they could have finished even higher.

As it was, a mid-season run of just one defeat in eight games lifted the Panthers towards the top end of the table, before they finished in somewhat disappointing fashion by losing at home to Hunslet in the play-offs.

Crompton felt that his side didn't do themselves justice in that game, but with a host of experienced Championship players having joined the club, he was aiming higher than fifth in 2010.

Also back will be fullback and top try-scorer Jonny Leather, who was deservedly named as the Championship One Young Player of the Year.

The experienced Damian Munro was not far behind him in the try-scoring stakes, while Kris Ratcliffe, Ian Hodson and John Clough were consistent members of a hard-working pack.

Now settled at Fylde RU – with tentative plans to return to Blackpool at some stage in the future – and with a new, ambitious chairman on board in Bobby Hope, the Panthers were looking to make an even bigger impact in 2010.

HUNSLET HAWKS continued their rise, eventually falling just two games short of the Grand Final after Paul March took over as coach midway through the campaign.

March replaced Graeme Hallas in the South Leeds Stadium hot seat, and immediately brought a host of York City Knights players with him to give the Hawks a late-season lift.

York, Blackpool and Oldham were among their conquests in the closing weeks of the campaign, and they then knocked the Panthers out of the play-offs with an impressive 21-18 win on the west coast.

They came unstuck the following week against the Roughyeds, but March still had plenty of positives to build on for 2010.

The year started with the arrival of three Papua New Guinean internationals at the club and Charlie Wabo, Nicko Slain and Michael Mark all had an impact, with the latter finishing as joint top try-scorer with Michael Brown.

A genuine lack of firepower may have been among the reasons why the Hawks didn't finish higher, although Wayne McHugh – one of those to switch from the Knights to Hunslet late in the year – scored eight tries in six games after his arrival.

March made a big difference himself on the field, and having made several impressive captures for the new season – including brother David – he set his targets higher next time around.

With the PNG trio all back on board as well, Hunslet supporters had every reason to feel optimistic about 2010.

SWINTON LIONS will have felt they should have finished higher than seventh, though they pushed eventual Grand Finalists Oldham all the way in the play-offs before going down 31-26.

Paul Kidd's side won their first three league games, including impressive victories over Keighley and Blackpool, to set out an early stall.

But they twice suffered long losing runs – one of four matches and one of five – and were hardly helped by a five-match suspension handed out to captain Graham Holroyd after he was sent off against Rochdale for dissent. Kidd also had to deal with injuries throughout the campaign, stretching the Lions' already limited squad.

There were plenty of bright spots however, with Richie Hawkyard proving something of a revelation once he was moved from halfback to fullback. Young Carl Sneyd ended up as top pointscorer after his move from local rivals Rochdale, while the hard-working Dave Hull topped the try column with 12 in all competitions.

Kidd, who was the longest serving coach in the professional game, made the decision to move upstairs at the end of the campaign and become director of coaching.

He was succeeded by experienced back-rower Paul Smith in a player-coaching role, with fellow ex-Lions favourite Ian Watson as his assistant.

ROCHDALE HORNETS were always going to be up against it after receiving a nine-point penalty for entering administration but, after a traumatic close season, just finishing the campaign without any more major dramas was an achievement.

The first club in the professional game to become a co-operative and be owned by its supporters, Hornets RL as they were known in 2009 – for legal reasons – were effectively starting from scratch.

Coach Darren Shaw and his assistant Paul Anderson deserved great credit for pulling together a competitive squad at short notice, though both had been replaced by the end of the year in somewhat mysterious circumstances over an undisclosed breach of club discipline. Shaw was replaced by former St Helens and Widnes back-rower John Stankevitch, who set about building a new squad with great earnest during the winter.

In 2009, Shaw produced a side that managed to chalk up credible wins over York, Hunslet and Swinton, though they were never realistically in play-off contention.

Another significant achievement was a gutsy 38-12 Challenge Cup defeat at eventual finalists Huddersfield, when Shaw had to sign three loan players from Widnes just to make up a team.

Stand-off Martin Ainscough was again a shining light, scoring 18 tries in 25 appearances before switching to Blackpool at the end of the campaign.

The experienced Leroy Rivett, Ian Sinfield and Paul Raftrey also played their part, while the electric Casey Mayberry earned an All Stars selection at centre for his performances over the course of the year.

WORKINGTON TOWN finished the year with just 14 men fit to play at Rochdale and with only two wins in the entire 2009 campaign to their name.

That makes pretty miserable reading for the Derwent Park faithful, but at least the club had a more optimistic feel to it following the appointment of former players Gary Charlton and Martin Oglanby as joint coaches. The pair managed to oversee one win of their own, at London Skolars in August, and Town were generally competitive for much of the year.

But the new hope comes from a host of new signings and the promise of a more physical side in 2010. The season high came in the first game of the season when Town – then under the experienced Dave Rotheram – beat Rochdale 21-14 at home.

But the fifth-placed position they earned from that win was as good as it got for the Cumbrians, and low points came at home to the Skolars and then in conceding 76 points against champions Dewsbury.

Only Stephen Dawes reached double figures in the try-scoring charts before his year was ended by injury, with Australian prop Jarrad Stack the most impressive performer over the course of the entire season.

Hooker Jack Pedley and utility Jamie Marshall also had their moments, but Workington were hoping for much better in the new campaign.

LONDON SKOLARS finished bottom of the pile for the first time since 2005, which was a significant disappointment for the capital club.

They made a conscious effort to move more towards London-produced players under bright coach Callum Irving, but by the middle of the season he had moved to pastures new. He did oversee their only victory before then, as they shocked Workington Town 24-18 at Derwent Park.

But by the time Town avenged that win in London in August, Skolars had slipped back to the bottom, and they never recovered.

They still had a stirring performance at Oldham to cherish though, as caretaker coach Jermaine Coleman saw his charges push the high-flying Roughyeds close before losing 28-22.

And with Londoner James Massara in charge from 2010, they were hoping that the experience gained by a host of rookies in 2009 would benefit them considerably in the future.

Star man was undoubtedly centre Matt Thomas, who top scored with 11 tries and finished the year wearing a Welsh shirt in the European Cup. Several other players helped keep the team together on a week-to-week basis, including Skolars stalwarts Austen Aggrey, Gareth Honor and Paul Thorman.

But the club was hoping to celebrate more wins in 2009 to supplement its outstanding work in the North London community.

NORTHERN RAIL CUP FINAL
Vikings on track

A superb spell of dummy-half play from substitute John Duffy played a significant role as Widnes Vikings clinched their second Northern Rail Cup success in three years – and with it the golden ticket of a Super League licence application.

Widnes scored three tries in the ten minutes leading up to half-time, turning a two-point deficit into a 14-point interval lead. Alongside the display of Duffy, Widnes also had big performances from Anthony Thackeray, Mark Smith and Iain Morrison, while on-loan winger Kevin Penny scored twice inside four minutes during that spell leading up to the break.

Barrow coach Dave Clark could also hold his head high after a gutsy display from his side, who were missing the suspended Ned Catic. The likes of Martin Ostler, Gary Broadbent, Brett McDermott and Darren Holt never wavered in their efforts.

Holt landed a penalty to put his side two points in front, but Richard Fletcher snared the game's first try before Zebastien Luisi took Holt's pass and pushed off Richard Varkulis to score. Holt's conversion made it 8-6 just before the half-hour mark.

But the period leading up to half-time belonged firmly to Paul Cullen's side. Duffy scored Widnes' second try by cheekily throwing a huge dummy at the play-the-ball. Four minutes later a perfectly flighted kick from James Webster allowed Penny to touch down for his first try. Penny had his second moments later as on-loan from Hull Craig Hall flicked out a brilliant pass to allow him to stroll in again. Two Hall conversions from three attempts made it 8-22 at the interval.

James Nixon got a try back after the break but Widnes pushed their lead out to 16 points when Toa Kohe-Love fought his way over the line close to the posts, before Scott Kaighan and Richard Varkulis swapped late tries.

NORTHERN RAIL CUP FINAL

Sunday 12th July 2009

BARROW RAIDERS 18 WIDNES VIKINGS 34

RAIDERS: 1 Gary Broadbent; 19 Chris Larkin; 32 Andreas Bauer; 4 Liam Harrison; 5 James Nixon; 6 Liam Finch; 27 Darren Holt; 8 Brett McDermott; 9 Andy Ellis; 13 Andy Bracek; 12 Martin Ostler; 14 Paul Noone; 26 Zebastian Luisi. Subs (all used): 15 Chris Young; 16 Jamie Butler; 28 Nathan Mossop; 17 Scott Kaighan.
Tries: Luisi (26), Nixon (54), Kaighan (72); **Goals:** Holt 3/4.
Sin bin: McDermott (6) - fighting.
VIKINGS: 16 Gavin Dodd; 2 Dean Gaskell; 4 Toa Kohe-Love; 32 Craig Hall; 29 Kevin Penny; 6 Anthony Thackeray; 7 James Webster; 28 Steve Pickersgill; 9 Mark Smith; 10 Jim Gannon; 3 Richard Varkulis; 12 Richard Fletcher; 8 Iain Morrison. Subs (all used): 14 John Duffy; 11 Lee Doran; 15 Tim Hartley; 17 Ben Kavanagh.
Tries: Fletcher (12), Duffy (30), Penny (34, 38), Kohe-Love (56), Varkulis (80); **Goals:** Hall 5/6.
Sin bin: Gannon (6) - fighting.
Rugby Leaguer & League Express Men of the Match:
Raiders: Martin Ostler; *Vikings:* John Duffy.
Penalty count: 6-9; **Half-time:** 8-22; **Referee:** Gareth Hewer; **Attendance:** 8,720 *(at Bloomfield Road, Blackpool).*

CHAMPIONSHIP PLAY-OFFS
Raiders red-letter day

Featherstone Rovers sprung the shock of the opening weekend when they comprehensively accounted for Sheffield Eagles at the Don Valley Stadium.

The two teams were involved in an almighty first-minute dust-up that saw players from each side sent to the sin bin, and by half-time there had been four yellow cards and two reds as tempers boiled over. It was Rovers who regained their composure the better, and with Tommy Haughey grabbing two second-half tries from centre they eventually eased to a 32-8 win.

The previous night Widnes Vikings had moved through to the next stage by seeing off Whitehaven 26-21 in a televised thriller at the Stobart Stadium. Haven, despite their squad being stretched to its limits, led 18-8 at half-time, with second-minute try scorer Leroy Joe inspiring them from scrum-half.

The Vikings battled back after the break with Tim Hartley completing a double, but when Carl Rudd slotted a 71st minute field goal the Cumbrians were back in front. But Widnes then regained a smart short kick-off that led to James Webster's match-winning try, and Paul Cullen's side held on in the desperate closing stages.

Their reward was a home tie with in-form Featherstone, and with Iestyn Harris in majestic form, Rovers won on the road for the second week running, 32-24.

Playing at loose forward, Harris helped Rovers establish a 14-12 half-time lead with tries to Andy Kirk and Kyle Briggs, after Widnes had led 12-0. The Vikings battled back after the break and were within a score when Richard Varkulis crossed in the 73rd minute, only for Harris to fittingly cross for the winning score in the final seconds.

Meanwhile Barrow had booked their place in the Grand Final with a thoroughly professional 35-12 win over Halifax in front of the television cameras at Craven Park.

The Raiders rarely looked in danger of losing from the moment top try-scorer James Nixon crossed in the 14th minute, though Fax did threaten briefly when Shad Royston crossed after the break.

It proved to be false dawn for Fax however, as further Barrow tries from man of the match Ned Catic, Nixon again and Andy Bracek put Dave Clark's side on the road to Warrington.

It also left Halifax needing to win the final eliminator at home to Featherstone in order to tick the Super League licence box they so coveted. They managed to do that – but not before an almighty scare against Daryl Powell's Rovers.

With Harris again in fine form, Featherstone led on two occasions during a pulsating contest. But the tie was eventually settled when Australian Royston romped over with eight minutes remaining, breaking the hearts of a large travelling Featherstone support.

CHAMPIONSHIP GRAND FINAL

Barrow confirmed their re-emergence as a significant Rugby League force with a pulsating Championship Grand Final win against gallant Halifax, as Dave Clark's side battled back from an early ten-point deficit in a thrilling contest.

The game was still in the balance right until the 78th minute, when Raiders centre Andreas Bauer crossed for his second try. That sealed a memorable victory in front of a noisy Barrow travelling support.

After losing the Northern Rail Cup final to Widnes, it was rich reward for the work of coach Clark and the considerable investment of his chairman Des Johnston, who cut a passionate figure in the main stand as his side eventually emerged victorious.

That they did was down to outstanding performances from a host of players, headed by evergreen fullback Gary Broadbent, who was an absolute rock for the Raiders.

In attack, loose forward Zebastien Luisi was a constant menace and had a hand in three of Barrow's tries, while up front Brett McDermott and Rob Roberts were effective battering rams who also provided smart offloads.

At hooker, Championship Player of the Year Andy Ellis put in his usual unstinting effort around the play-the-balls, and halfbacks Jamie Rooney and James Coyle both provided crucial contributions.

Halifax played their full part in a terrific game, and could have been further in front than 10-0 after starting the contest in fine style.

They led again early in the second half, when the impressive Mick Govin scored out wide, but were not helped by four missed kicks at goal from Lee Patterson, who had previously been a revelation in the role this season.

Two Barrow tries just before half-time marked the game's main turning point after Calland's side dominated the first ten minutes. After Barrow's Liam Harrison had lost possession in the tackle on halfway, Fax attacked down the left, where Govin's clever no-look pass allowed James Haley to step inside the defence, juggle the ball and score. Just after the half-hour mark Halifax's second try initiated a flurry of points before the interval.

Mark Gleeson's scampering break laid the foundations for the try, which was finished by Shad Royston from a well-weighted Black kick by the posts. That made it 10-0 to Calland's team, but by half-time the Raiders were level.

Directly from the kick-off following Royston's try, Fax prop Said Tamghart knocked the ball on to gift Barrow possession. They took full advantage when Rooney's kick saw Harrison out-jump Black to score, with the Raiders stand-off adding the conversion from out wide.

Five minutes later it was veteran prop McDermott whose smart pass started it, before Luisi, Broadbent and Bauer all handled to send Andy Ballard racing over in the right-hand corner.

THE CO-OPERATIVE CHAMPIONSHIP GRAND FINAL

Sunday 4th October 2009

BARROW RAIDERS 26 HALIFAX 18

RAIDERS: 1 Gary Broadbent; 36 Andy Ballard; 32 Andreas Bauer; 4 Liam Harrison; 5 James Nixon; 24 Jamie Rooney; 31 James Coyle; 34 Rob Roberts; 9 Andy Ellis; 8 Brett McDermott; 33 Dave Allen; 22 Ned Catic; 26 Zebastian Luisi. Subs (all used): 15 Chris Young; 13 Andy Bracek; 35 Danny Halliwell; 14 Paul Noone.
Tries: Harrison (33), Ballard (37), Allen (61), Bauer (66, 78);
Goals: Rooney 3/5.
HALIFAX: 4 Shad Royston; 5 James Haley; 15 Mark Roberts; 2 Lee Patterson; 23 Rob Worrincy; 19 Mick Govin; 7 Ben Black; 21 Neil Cherryholme; 9 Sean Penkywicz; 22 David Wrench; 11 David Larder; 27 Steve Bannister; 12 Paul Smith. Subs (all used): 13 Bob Beswick; 14 Mark Gleeson; 16 Said Tamghart; 26 Dominic Maloney.
Tries: Haley (12), Royston (31), Black (45), Govin (70);
Goals: Patterson 1/5.
Rugby Leaguer & League Express Men of the Match:
Raiders: Gary Broadbent; *Halifax:* Mick Govin.
Penalty count: 8-5; **Half-time:** 10-10; **Referee:** Phil Bentham;
Attendance: 11,398 *(at Halliwell Jones Stadium, Warrington).*

Gary Broadbent driven back by strong Halifax defence

Handling errors littered the first few minutes of the second half, but it was one by Barrow's Bauer that proved the most costly. Moments after his knock-on, Black picked up a Gleeson pass on the bounce and threw a host of dummies before getting on the outside of Coyle to touch down out wide. Paterson pulled the difficult conversion wide, and more surprisingly then missed a penalty from just to the right of the posts after Broadbent had been caught not square at marker.

The Raiders took the lead for the first time in the 61st minute, handed the field position when Neil Cherryholme was penalised for a high tackle on Andy Ellis, and capitalising as Luisi's superb delayed pass allowed Allen to stride through for a converted try.

Five minutes later and the Cumbrians were over again. Allen was this time stopped just short by the Fax defence, but on the next tackle Bauer made no mistake from dummy half, the video referee ruling he had made the line.

Rooney had the chance to make the gap eight points, but pulled his conversion wide – and Fax made him pay when they forced a mistake from the kick-off. In the resulting set of six, Govin repeated Black's trick of dummying and arcing over in the left corner, and he even managed to improve the angle of Paterson's conversion.

But the Fax centre, usually so reliable, missed for the fourth time of the afternoon to leave the score at 20-18.

And that allowed one final Raiders flourish, as Allen offloaded in the tackle for Luisi, who sent Bauer in for his second and the match-clinching score.

CHAMPIONSHIP ONE PLAY-OFFS
Cougars on the rise

Hunslet Hawks produced a superb late effort to come from behind and beat much-fancied Blackpool on the west coast. The Panthers led 16-12 at half-time of an intriguing contest between two well-matched sides, before Wayne McHugh's second-half try saw the Hawks move level.

With the clash very much in the balance, a late Darren Robinson penalty and Josh Weeden drop goal finally saw off Martin Crompton's resilient side.

Elsewhere, Oldham – with a cloud of uncertainty hanging over their existence – produced the first of three backs-to-the-wall efforts to account for Swinton Lions 31-26. Back-rower Chris Baines would emerge as a key figure in their play-offs charge, and having only just taken over the kicking responsibilities at the club he landed five from six in a tense Lancashire derby.

Andy Saywell's second try in the 73rd minute kept the Lions right in the contest until the final hooter, only for Tony Benson's Roughyeds to hang on.

That win gave them a home clash with Hunslet, and it was Baines again who stepped forward with a magnificent performance. The former Warrington Academy second-rower broke the club record for points in a match as his four tries and nine goals saw him finish with 34 in a 54-30 win.

The Hawks showed plenty of invention with the ball, with winger Wayne Reittie finishing with a double, but their frail defence ensured their Grand Final dreams were ended at Boundary Park.

On the same afternoon Keighley were realising their Halliwell Stadium dreams by seeing off third-placed York City Knights 32-18 at Cougar Park. Barry Eaton's side were in control almost from the word go and led 20-12 at the break after a try double from Daley Williams.

And when man of the match Jon Presley crossed ten minutes after the restart, Keighley were always likely to have enough to see off the Knights.

York still had a second chance to make the Grand Final the following Sunday against Oldham, but were brushed aside 44-14 by Benson's charges.

The Roughyeds led 24-4 at the interval after early tries from Ben Heaton, Baines, Tommy Goulden and Paul Reilly had blitzed the Knights.

Another effort from Reilly soon after the restart ensured there was only going to be one winner, and Matt Ashe's late double ensured that Oldham booked their Cougars clash in style.

CHAMPIONSHIP ONE GRAND FINAL

Danny Jones inspired Keighley Cougars to victory in the Co-operative Championship One Grand Final – but nearly cost his side by getting sin-binned five minutes from time.

Oldham, who were trailing 28-16 at that point, crossed twice in the final four minutes through Luke Menzies and Wayne Kerr. But Chris Baines' missed conversion to Menzies' effort meant the Cougars survived the most frightening of late scares and could start planning for life in Rugby League's second tier.

THE CO-OPERATIVE CHAMPIONSHIP ONE GRAND FINAL

Sunday 4th October 2009

KEIGHLEY COUGARS 28 OLDHAM 26

COUGARS: 1 George Rayner; 2 Sam Gardner; 3 Dan Potter; 4 Oliver Purseglove; 5 Gavin Duffy; 6 Jon Presley; 7 Danny Jones; 17 Scott Law; 14 Jamaine Wray; 8 Andy Shickell; 11 Will Cartledge; 18 Greg Nicholson; 13 Carl Hughes. Subs (all used): 21 Ryan Smith; 28 Ryan Benjafield; 9 James Feather; 16 Brendan Rawlins.
Tries: Gardner (24), Jones (42, 50), Presley (63), Purseglove (67);
Goals: Jones 4/5.
OLDHAM: 4 Paul Reilly; 21 Lucas Onyango; 24 Marcus St Hilaire; 22 Phil Joseph; 1 Paul O'Connor; 18 Neil Roden; 7 Thomas Coyle; 15 Jason Boults; 30 Martin Roden; 16 Wayne Kerr; 23 Chris Baines; 12 Tommy Goulden; 28 Craig Lawton. Subs (all used): 10 Jamie I'Anson; 25 Luke Menzies; 27 Matt Ashe; 29 Ben Heaton.
Tries: Menzies (35, 76), N Roden (54), St Hilaire (70), Kerr (78);
Goals: Baines 3/4, Ashe 0/1.
Rugby Leaguer & League Express Men of the Match:
Cougars: Danny Jones; *Oldham:* Luke Menzies.
Penalty count: 9-2; **Half-time:** 4-6; **Referee:** Ronnie Laughton.
(at Halliwell Jones Stadium, Warrington).

The Cougars came into their biggest game of the season having only played once in the last five weeks and in an error-ridden opening quarter they largely looked second best as Oldham were twice denied by the video referee. First George Rayner held up Neil Roden under the posts, then replays showed Tommy Goulden had knocked on while he tried to ground the ball.

It meant Sam Gardner's effort proved the game's opening score. And with James Feather – who was returning from a fractured cheekbone – directing play after being a shock inclusion on Eaton's bench, Keighley looked to be taking control.

But Keighley fell behind when Luke Menzies marked his last game with Oldham by crashing over from Martin Roden's flat pass.

That blow could have killed off Keighley but they responded well, with Jones reclaiming his own short kick-off at the start of the second half and then touching down from Jon Presley's kick 60 seconds later. When Feather's pass spun out of Brendon Rawlins' grasp but fell into Jones' hands for his second try in eight minutes, the Cougars looked to be cruising.

Neil Roden and Presley exchanged scores midway through the second half but Keighley's lead remained at 10 points going into the final 15 minutes. When Jones' long pass from dummy half flew into Presley's grasp and his pass met Oliver Pursglove's angled run perfectly, Eaton's men could sense victory was within reach.

However, former Leeds and Huddersfield flyer Marcus St Hilaire crashed on to Thomas Coyle's pass and Jones' yellow-card, after he held down Coyle for a couple of seconds too long as Keighley scrambled back in desperation, paved the way for a thrilling end.

Menzies went over from Matt Ashe's pass before Wayne Kerr provided a fitting climax by bursting through from 40 metres out after Baines' great break out of his own half.

Time, however, was to run out on the Roughyeds.

Keighley Cougars, Championship One Grand Final Winners

THE CO-OPERATIVE CHAMPIONSHIP AWARDS

CHAMPIONSHIP PLAYER OF THE YEAR
Andy Ellis
(Barrow Raiders)

CHAMPIONSHIP ONE PLAYER OF THE YEAR
Liam Finn
(Dewsbury Rams)

CHAMPIONSHIP

PLAYER OF THE YEAR
Andy Ellis (Barrow Raiders)
Other nominees: Ben Black (Halifax)
Menzie Yere (Sheffield Eagles)

YOUNG PLAYER OF THE YEAR
Kyle Amor (Whitehaven)
Other nominees: Kyle Briggs (Featherstone Rovers)
Jermaine McGilvary (Batley Bulldogs)

COACH OF THE YEAR
Dave Clark (Barrow Raiders)
Other nominees: Mark Aston (Sheffield Eagles)
Karl Harrison (Batley Bulldogs)

RUGBY LEAGUE WORLD TEAM OF THE YEAR
1 Gary Broadbent (Barrow Raiders)
2 James Nixon (Barrow Raiders)
3 Menzie Yere (Sheffield Eagles)
4 Liam Harrison (Barrow Raiders)
5 Jermaine McGilvary (Batley Bulldogs)
6 Brendon Lindsay (Sheffield Eagles)
7 Ben Black (Halifax)
8 Kyle Amor (Whitehaven)
9 Andy Ellis (Barrow Raiders)
10 Said Tamghart (Halifax)
11 Michael Knowles (Gateshead Thunder)
12 David Larder (Halifax)
13 Zebastian Luisi (Barrow Raiders)

CLUB OF THE YEAR
Dewsbury Rams

BEST COMMUNITY PROGRAMME
Sheffield Eagles

REFEREE OF THE YEAR
Ronnie Laughton
Other nominees: James Child, Jamie Leahy

CHAMPIONSHIP ONE

PLAYER OF THE YEAR
Liam Finn (Dewsbury Rams)
Other nominees: Andrew Bostock (Dewsbury Rams)
Jon Presley (Keighley Cougars)

YOUNG PLAYER OF THE YEAR
Jonny Leather (Blackpool Panthers)
Other nominees: Danny Ratcliffe (York City Knights)
Jarrad Stack (Workington Town)

COACH OF THE YEAR
Warren Jowitt (Dewsbury Rams)
Other nominees: Martin Crompton (Blackpool Panthers)
Barry Eaton (Keighley Cougars)

RUGBY LEAGUE WORLD TEAM OF THE YEAR
1 Jonny Leather (Blackpool Panthers)
2 Bryn Powell (Dewsbury Rams)
3 Kane Epati (Dewsbury Rams)
4 Casey Mayberry (Rochdale Hornets)
5 Gavin Duffy (Keighley Cougars)
6 Jon Presley (Keighley Cougars)
7 Liam Finn (Dewsbury Rams)
8 Scott Law (Keighley Cougars)
9 James Feather (Keighley Cougars)
10 Jarrad Stack (Workington Town)
11 Andrew Bostock (Dewsbury Rams)
12 Chris Baines (Oldham)
13 Adam Hayes (Dewsbury Rams)

RUGBY LEAGUE CONFERENCE NATIONAL

PLAYER OF THE YEAR
Adam Millward (Nottingham Outlaws)

YOUNG PLAYER OF THE YEAR
Billy Sheen (Warrington Wizards)

COACH OF THE YEAR
Mark Butterill (Bramley Buffaloes)

2009 SUPER LEAGUE SEASON

Leeds

Building Society

Leeds

Building Society

engage

SUPER

Rugby

LEAGUE

ROUND 1

ABOVE: Kevin Brown in the thick of it as the Giants start with a win in Perpignan

BELOW: Michael Dobson steals a point for Hull KR in a thriller at Bradford

ROUND 3

ABOVE: Nick Fozzard looks to get away from Paul Clough and Jon Wilkin as Hull KR win on his return to Knowsley Road

BELOW: Jamie Jones-Buchanan wrapped up by Adrian Morley in Tony Smith's first game in charge at Warrington

Brett Ferres beats Tim Smith and Karl Pryce to score for the Tigers in their stunning win at Wigan

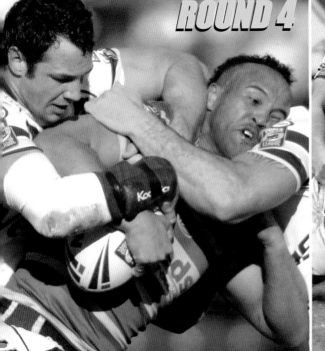

ROUND 4

ROUND 2

ABOVE: Things get heated at Knowsley Road as St Helens end Leeds' unbeaten run

LEFT: Rob Burrow looks to escape the clutches of Sean O'Loughlin as the Rhinos see off Wigan

ROUND 5

ROUND 7

ROUND

The most emotional night of Super League XIV as the teammates and family of Wakefield reserve player Leon Walker line up before the Wildcats-St Helens match

[AB]OVE: Stanley Gene skips past the [wo]unded Richard Horne as the Robins win [the] first Hull derby on Good Friday

[RIG]HT: Leon Pryce and Tony Puletua [com]bine to bring down Andy Coley in Saints' [win] at the JJB Stadium

[BEL]OW: Michael Worrincy crosses for a try [at O]dsal as the Bulls stun Leeds

ROUND 13

ROUND 9

ABOVE: Danny McGuire and John Wilshere compete in Salford's first win at Leeds since 1977

BELOW: Oliver Wilkes is stopped by the Hull FC defence but Wakefield win at the KC Stadium

Celtic Crusaders celebrate their first ever Super League victory - away at Bradford

ROUND 10

LEFT: Jamie Peacock and the Rhinos are grounded by Harlequins at Headingley

RIGHT: No way through for Jamie Langley but the Bulls come back to win at Knowsley Road

ROUND 12

Thomas Leuluai shoots over for a try as Wigan beat Saints at Murrayfield

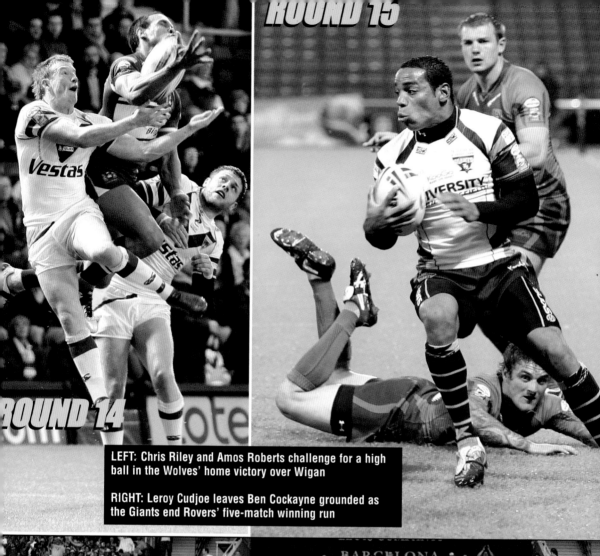

ROUND 14

ROUND 15

LEFT: Chris Riley and Amos Roberts challenge for a high ball in the Wolves' home victory over Wigan

RIGHT: Leroy Cudjoe leaves Ben Cockayne grounded as the Giants end Rovers' five-match winning run

Catalans and Warrington enter the Olympic Stadium in Barcelona as Super League hits Spain

ROUND 17

Jafeta Palea'aesina takes some stopping but Celtic get their first home win

BELOW: Danny McGuire collared as Leeds battle to home win over the Bulls

Rookie of the Year Sam Tomkins goes over as Wigan shock Hull KR at Craven Park

ROUND 19

ROUND 20

ABOVE: Rangi Chase beats Jamie Langley to score as Cas notch late Odsal win

RIGHT: Robbie Paul leads Salford to an eye-opening home win over Saints

BELOW: Leeds Rhinos celebrate Scott Donald's last gasp try against Wakefield

Joel Tomkins touches down as Wigan win 'The Big One' against Leeds

BELOW: Scott Grix sums up Wakefield's defensive steel in their shock win at Saints

ROUND 22

Paul Cooke wins a high ball

ROUND 21

ROUND 23

Kevin Sinfield coolly kicks a goal from the Headingley touchline to sink the Wolves

BELOW: Michael Platt, Rikki Sheriffe and David Hodgson compete for a high ball as Bulls win at Huddersfield

Kyle Eastmond got Saints home against Wigan with a stunning late try at Knowsley Road

ROUND 24

ROUND 25

ROUND 27

ROUND 26

LEFT: Danny Houghton is wrapped up as Hull beat Quins

BELOW: Danny McGuire and Paul Wellens chase a loose ball in fiery Leeds home win

ABOVE: Dimitri Pelo is brought down

RIGHT: Kevin Sinfield and Brian McClennan at Salford with the League Leaders shield

Luke Robinson gets to grips with Leon Pryce as Saints progress

BELOW: Ali Lauitiiti gets away fro Michael Vella in Leeds' big win

QUALIFYING PLAY-OFFS

ELIMINATION PLAY-OFFS

Richard Moore gets wrapped up by the Catalans defence

RIGHT: Harrison Hansen crosses for a try against Castleford

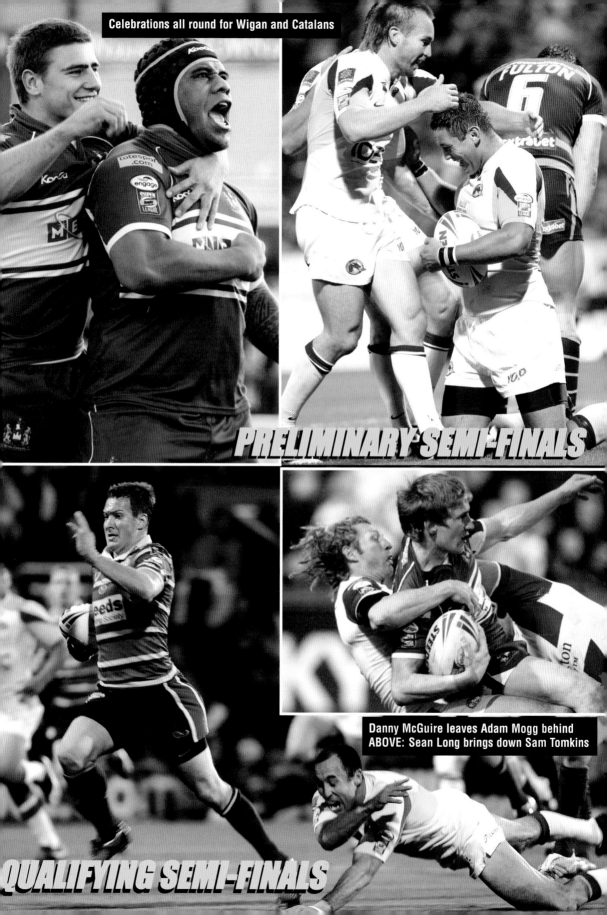

Celebrations all round for Wigan and Catalans

PRELIMINARY SEMI-FINALS

Danny McGuire leaves Adam Mogg behind
ABOVE: Sean Long brings down Sam Tomkins

QUALIFYING SEMI-FINALS

Kyle Eastmond is dramatically forced into the corner post by Kevin Sinfield

Jamie Jones-Buchanan tussles with James Graham

Lee Smith heads for the line

RIGHT: Kevin Sinfield lifts the Super League trophy aloft

3
PERSONALITIES OF 2009

Kevin Sinfield

When a 22-year-old Kevin Sinfield was appointed as Leeds Rhinos captain by then coach Daryl Powell for the start of the 2003 season, he could only have dreamed he would within seven years become the greatest leader in the club's illustrious history.

By the end of Super League XIV, Oldham-born Sinfield had achieved that status after he led Leeds to their third consecutive Championship title with an 18-10 win over St Helens at Old Trafford. By carrying off the Super League trophy for a fourth time (2004 was the first) he became the most successful captain in Championship history, leaving behind such legendary leaders as Harold Wagstaff, Gus Risman and Ellery Hanley, among others, who lifted the old trophy three times. Sinfield also became the first to lead a side to three successive Grand Final wins.

In being handed the Harry Sunderland Trophy for his performance in the 2009 finale, Sinfield joined the elite band who have also won the Lance Todd Trophy. He was on the losing side when awarded the latter trophy in the Challenge Cup final against Hull in 2005, but he was an inspirational winner against St Helens.

With St Helens racing into an 8-0 lead, it was from Sinfield's short drive to the line that Matt Diskin squeezed over at a play-the-ball to turn the tide. Sinfield was also tremendous in defence, and brought off a great try-saving and ultimately match-saving tackle that knocked Kyle Eastmond into the corner post.

And his kicking game was instrumental. Leeds were level at half-time, and coach Brian McClennan sent them out with orders not to come back without a point from their first attack. Sinfield carried out those orders to perfection. First, his well placed second-half kick-off

forced Ade Gardner into an error 10 metres from his own line. It gave Leeds possession, and after four tackles Sinfield stepped up to land a field goal from 12 metres to edge them in front for the first time.

Sinfield made his debut as a 16-year old against Sheffield at Headingley in 1997, but though not quite wrapped in cotton wool he didn't become a first-team regular until 1999 and even then was left out of the Challenge Cup final teams of 1999 and 2000. But since 2003, Sinfield has been central to the Rhinos' rise and rise. 2009 was also the year he finally established himself as a player able to dominate on the international stage with his man of the match performance in England's Gillette Four Nations win over New Zealand, and with Gareth Ellis, was one of two English nominations for the Rugby League World Golden Boot.

Sam Tomkins

In the League Express season preview at the beginning of 2009, Wigan's Sam Tomkins was picked out as a rookie to watch out for in Super League XIV.

The selection couldn't have been more prescient as at the end of the season the 20-year-old had picked up the Albert Goldthorpe Rookie of the Year award.

The pre-season tip wasn't that outrageous, although the leggy stand-off had played only one senior game in 2008 - a big Challenge Cup win against Whitehaven. But Tomkins, born in Milton Keynes before his family relocated to Chorley, did score five tries in an amazing debut, and it was a surprise he didn't get more first team chances that year.

In 2009, he enjoyed a magnificent year after making his Super League debut against Harlequins in February. The game at the Stoop saw Tomkins pick up two Albert Goldthorpe Medal points after his substitute appearance helped the Warriors overturn a 10-6 half-time deficit to record their first win of the season in their fourth game. At the end of June, Wigan had already tied Tomkins up on a five-year contract to the end of 2014.

Tomkins went from strength to strength during the course of the season, firmly cementing a regular starting place for himself, and helping the side to a fifth-placed finish in the table, and to the penultimate weekend of the play-offs when Wigan only just fell short at St Helens. He finished fourth in the overall Albert Goldthorpe Medal table, amassing 14 points more than any other Wigan player.

Thirteen months after Tomkins was picking up the man of the match award in Wigan's reserve team grand final victory over St Helens, he was playing for England in the Gillette Four Nations against Australia at Wigan, having made his debut in the 48-12 warm-up win against Wales, scoring a typical hat-trick of tries. So meteoric was his rise, he'd had to cancel an end-of-season holiday with big brother and teammate Joel to answer his country's call, expecting his season to end at the same time as Wigan's.

At international level it took him half a game to settle but in the next two games and a half he was part of the national team's most promising performances for many a year. A level-headed young man, Sam Tomkins had the world at his feet by the end of 2009.

Tony Smith

Tony Smith resigned as the England Head Coach the day after England lost the Gillette Four Nations final 46-16 to Australia. It was the end of a taxing year for the 42-year-old.

He revealed that he had told the Rugby Football League of his decision to stand down before the competition, wishing to concentrate on making his club Warrington a force in Super League and to devote more time to his family.

Smith had been appointed as Head Coach of Great Britain and England in March 2007 on a full-time basis. But on the 5th March 2009, he was unveiled as head of coaching and rugby at the Wolves on a two-and-half-year contract. Warrington, under coach James Lowes, who was moved to a number two position, had endured a poor start to Super League XIV, losing their first three games, including a home capitulation to Catalans.

Smith's impact wasn't immediate, losing his first two games, at home to one of his former clubs, Leeds and then at Harlequins in a 60-8 monstering. After that a home win over in-form Hull KR wasn't the immediate start of great things. But by the end of the year, Warrington had won their first Challenge Cup since 1974 with an impressive 25-16 win over Huddersfield Giants at Wembley, as well as Smith becoming the first coach of a Super League team to win in Spain after the Wolves' 24-12 victory over Catalans in Barcelona.

Smith, who became a naturalised Briton in 2008, first arrived in England as a player at Workington in 1996, and returned in mid-season in 2001 to coach struggling Huddersfield. He couldn't prevent them being relegated but brought the Giants straight back up the following year. At the end of 2003 he joined Leeds and in his first season took the Rhinos to the Super League title, repeating the feat in his last game in 2007.

Smith's first series as Head Coach of Great Britain and England, against New Zealand at the end of 2007 was won 3-0.

His England side of the 2008 World Cup in Australia didn't back that up as they sank to a big defeat against Australia and two disappointing losses to New Zealand. The national team's showing even prompted an inquiry by the Rugby Football League.

The 2009 Gillette Four Nations was a chance to make amends and England's progress to the final against Australia went some way towards achieving that aim.

Michael Dobson

Hull Kingston Rovers scrum-half Michael Dobson capped off a marvellous campaign buy winning the Albert Goldthorpe Medal as Super League's best player of 2009.

The 23-year-old harvested 40 points to top the Albert Goldthorpe table, with 2008 winner Danny Brough fully nine points behind him and Man of Steel winner Brett Hodgson in third. Dobson helped steer Hull Kingston Rovers to a fourth-placed finish in the Super League table and was awarded the solid gold medal and a prize of £2,000 at the Albert Goldthorpe Medal luncheon at Headingley Carnegie.

Dobson's kicking game was superb all season and his organisational skills were pivotal in guiding the Robins to their best ever finish. An ever present in Super League's 27 rounds, League Express match reporters awarded the Australian at least two points in 17 of those games. Right from round one he was deciding the outcome of matches, dropping a last-gasp field goal to earn Hull KR a point at Bradford.

Dobson admitted he still harboured hopes of making his name in the NRL, but he must be sorely tempted to stay in the northern hemisphere after his experiences at three Super League clubs.

He first came north in 2006 as a 19-year-old former Australian Schoolboy when Catalans Dragons' star signing for their first season, Stacey Jones, broke an arm during the second round match at Salford.

Dobson was a massive success, scoring 103 points under difficult circumstances. When his 12-match spell was up, unsurprisingly he was

chased by other clubs, ending up at Wigan, again a club under pressure. At the end of May, the Warriors were bottom of the Super League table, six points behind the nearest team, Castleford, and heading towards relegation. Dobson's impact was immense and Wigan survived. He scored another 142 points and guided the Warriors around the park like a veteran half.

At the end of that season he returned to Canberra, and English audiences thought they had seen the back of him. But things didn't work out as planned, and after a frustrating season and a half he was back in England, with Hull KR. He made a dream debut in round 15 of 2008 scoring two tries in a 22-8 home win over Harlequins; his season's highlight the four tries he scored against former club Wigan later in the year.

But in 2009, Dobson and his club Hull KR went up another notch. It was little surprise then that in mid-season Rovers extended his contract to the end of 2012.

Greg Inglis

Australia centre Greg Inglis was crowned the greatest Rugby League player in the world after the final whistle of the Gillette Four Nations final.

At just 22, Inglis became the youngest winner of the Golden Boot. He enjoyed a tremendous year in 2009, being part of the Melbourne Storm side that won its second Premiership in four years, the Queensland team that won its fourth-straight State of Origin series and the Australia team which won its first international competition since 2006.

He won the Wally Lewis Medal as the outstanding player in the Origin series, and was also named the Four Nations player of the tournament after three outstanding performances against New Zealand and England twice.

Australia's left-hand attack, Inglis included, had destroyed England in the 2008 World Cup, and in the autumn series in 2009, England did all they could to counter the threat. It proved impossible, as the rangy centre, compared by many to the great Mal Meninga, tore England to shreds in the first half of their game at Wigan and two weeks later scored a crucial try in the Gillette Four Nations final in Leeds.

Inglis was the third Melbourne player in a row to win the Golden Boot, after Cameron Smith in 2007 and Billy Slater in 2008. Both players were on the shortlist of six in 2009, along with England's Kevin Sinfield and Gareth Ellis and New Zealand's Fuifui Moimoi.

The Golden Boot, which is presented annually by Rugby League World magazine, was first awarded in 1985 to the Australian captain Wally Lewis, who in 2009 was one of seven members of a voting panel made up of former players and writers.

All the votes were cast immediately after the final hooter of the Elland Road final, in which Australia triumphed 46-16. Inglis received a standing ovation from his jubilant teammates upon receiving the award.

GOLDEN BOOT - ROLL OF HONOUR

1985 Wally Lewis (Australia)
1986 Brett Kenny (Australia)
1987 Garry Jack (Australia)
1988 Hugh McGahan (New Zealand) & Peter Sterling (Australia)
1989 Ellery Hanley (Great Britain)
1990 Mal Meninga (Australia)
1991-1998 *No award given*
1999 Andrew Johns (Australia)
2000 Brad Fittler (Australia)
2001 Andrew Johns (Australia)
2002 Stacey Jones (New Zealand)
2003 Darren Lockyer (Australia)
2004 Andrew Farrell (Great Britain)
2005 Anthony Minichiello (Australia)
2006 Darren Lockyer (Australia)
2007 Cameron Smith (Australia)
2008 Billy Slater (Australia)
2009 Greg Inglis (Australia)

4
INTERNATIONAL YEAR

GILLETTE FOUR NATIONS
Land of hope...

Australia, coached by Tim Sheens, won the first ever Four Nations tournament played in England and France in the autumn of 2009, as the Tri-Nations concept begun in 2004 was expanded to include France.

In the final at Elland Road in Leeds, Australia met an England side with a backline completely new to the full Test arena, none of whom had been part of the England squad which had competed in the 2008 World Cup. The final scoreline of 46-16 gave little indication of an England performance full of promise that saw the game finely balanced just before the hour mark.

England had won through to the final by beating New Zealand by 20-12, the Kiwis having been unlucky to only draw with Australia in their opener at the Stoop, and all three teams having beaten France.

France's three defeats were expected. But after former Great Britain scrum-half Bobbie Goulding's appointment as successor to coach John Monie, the French performed with great credit, competing in all three games before fading in the later stages.

The morning after England's defeat in the final, coach Tony Smith, who had taken over as club coach at Warrington earlier in the season and was at the end of his three-year contract, announced he was resigning.

England coach Tony Smith opted for young Salford scrum-half Richie Myler over Wigan's Sam Tomkins and St Helens' Kyle Eastmond for the Four Nations opener at Doncaster and it was Myler's two quickfire tries after France led 12-4 at the interval that began England's victory roll.

Myler had been outplayed by his opposite number James Wynne in the first half, but within three minutes of the break Myler slipped through from 15 metres out and survived a three-man tackle under the posts to get the ball down. Seven minutes later great support play saw Myler swoop in off Kevin Sinfield's pass to go over again.

Sinfield was another who stood out after an anonymous first half. His dummy and pass to send in Myler was a classic touch, and two minutes later he showed his own support play to go in off Jamie Peacock's offload.

Eastmond was sent on to replace England number one Shaun Briscoe in the 55th minute. He marked his international debut with a delightful kick that he slotted through for Tom Briscoe to touch down and complete the try scoring.

Scott Moore was taken off after a bad few minutes in the first half. The hooker's knock-on at a play-the-ball led to France's first try, and a few minutes later his pass went straight to Julien Touxagas, who made a deep run into the home half. From the position gained, opposite number Kane Bentley scooted in from a play-the-ball after stepping away from Moore's tackle.

England had gone 4-0 ahead after only 12 minutes when Lee Smith took advantage of a big overlap to touch down. France's response was to build immediate pressure, and when Clint Greenshields linked onto Sébastien Raguin's hit and offload, he spun round to put Vincent Duport in near the corner flag. Thomas Bosc's touchline kick went in off a post, and he added the goal to Bentley's try three minutes later. A 12-4 interval lead was as good as it got for the French.

Myler's two tries and one from Sinfield were all converted by the latter to sweep England into a 22-12 lead after 52 minutes. Any hopes France had of pulling the game back were dashed in the 64th minute, when Bosc's pass that might have created a try was intercepted by Ryan Hall, and the Leeds winger streaked 90 metres for a spectacular touchdown.

On the Saturday night of the first weekend the Australians snatched a dramatic draw at the Stoop, after Frank Pritchard had scored a try minutes from the end for a seemingly winning 20-14 scoreline. But the short kick-off was regathered, a penalty went the Aussies' way and hooker Cameron Smith, backing up a charge from Greg Inglis, managed to force his way over for a try which scrum-half Johnathan Thurston converted.

It was a thrill-a-minute contest. Rookie Kiwi prop Frank-Paul Nuuausala crossed after five minutes after a great short ball from Adam Blair. Australia's response came 26 minutes later when Smith scooped up a loose ball on his own '20', raced away and slipped a lovely pass

---

GILLETTE FOUR NATIONS - GAME ONE

Friday 23rd October 2009

ENGLAND 34 FRANCE 12

ENGLAND: 1 Shaun Briscoe (Hull Kingston Rovers); 2 Tom Briscoe (Hull FC); 3 Lee Smith (Leeds Rhinos); 4 Michael Shenton (Castleford Tigers); 5 Ryan Hall (Leeds Rhinos); 6 Danny McGuire (Leeds Rhinos); 7 Richard Myler (Salford City Reds); 8 Adrian Morley (Warrington Wolves); 9 Scott Moore (Huddersfield Giants); 10 Jamie Peacock (Leeds Rhinos) (C); 11 Gareth Ellis (Wests Tigers); 12 Sam Burgess (Bradford Bulls); 13 Kevin Sinfield (Leeds Rhinos). Subs (all used): 14 James Graham (St Helens); 15 James Roby (St Helens); 16 Ben Westwood (Warrington Wolves); 17 Kyle Eastmond (St Helens). **Tries:** Smith (12), Myler (43, 50), Sinfield (52), Hall (64), T Briscoe (76); **Goals:** Sinfield 5/6.
FRANCE: 1 Clint Greenshields (Catalans Dragons); 2 Vincent Duport (Catalans Dragons); 4 Sebastien Raguin (Catalans Dragons); 3 Jean-Phillipe Baile (Catalans Dragons); 5 Dimitri Pelo (Catalans Dragons); 6 Thomas Bosc (Catalans Dragons); 7 James Wynne (Lezignan); 8 David Ferriol (Catalans Dragons); 9 Kane Bentley (Catalans Dragons); 10 Remi Casty (Catalans Dragons); 11 Olivier Elima (Catalans Dragons) (C); 12 Julien Touxagas (Catalans Dragons); 13 Jamal Fakir (Catalans Dragons). Subs (all used): 14 Constant Villegas (Toulouse Olympique); 15 Teddy Sadaoui (Carcassonne); 16 Sebastien Martins (Catalans Dragons); 17 Romain Gagliazzo (Carcassonne). **Tries:** Duport (16), K Bentley (19); **Goals:** Bosc 2/2. **Dismissal:** Baile (79) - high tackle on Myler. **On report:** Ferriol (72) - alleged use of the elbow on Sinfield. **Rugby Leaguer & League Express Men of the Match:** *England:* Richard Myler; *France:* Kane Bentley. **Penalty count:** 13-9; **Half-time:** 4-12; **Referee:** Leon Williamson (New Zealand); **Attendance:** 11,529 *(at Keepmoat Stadium, Doncaster).*

GILLETTE FOUR NATIONS - GAME TWO

Saturday 24th October 2009

AUSTRALIA 20 NEW ZEALAND 20

AUSTRALIA: 1 Billy Slater (Melbourne Storm); 2 Brett Morris (St George-Illawarra Dragons); 3 Greg Inglis (Melbourne Storm); 4 Justin Hodges (Brisbane Broncos); 5 Jarryd Hayne (Parramatta Eels); 6 Darren Lockyer (Brisbane Broncos) (C); 7 Johnathan Thurston (North Queensland Cowboys); 8 Ben Hannant (Bulldogs); 9 Cameron Smith (Melbourne Storm); 10 Petero Civoniceva (Penrith Panthers); 11 Trent Waterhouse (Penrith Panthers); 12 Ryan Hoffman (Melbourne Storm); 13 Anthony Watmough (Manly Sea Eagles). Subs (all used): 14 Brett White (Melbourne Storm); 15 Sam Thaiday (Brisbane Broncos); 16 Paul Gallen (Cronulla Sharks); 17 Kurt Gidley (Newcastle Knights). **Tries:** B Morris (31), Thurston (42), Smith (78); **Goals:** Thurston 4/4.
NEW ZEALAND: 1 Lance Hohaia (New Zealand Warriors); 2 Sam Perrett (Sydney Roosters); 3 Steve Matai (Manly Sea Eagles); 4 Junior Sau (Newcastle Knights); 5 Bryson Goodwin (Bulldogs); 6 Benji Marshall (Wests Tigers) (C); 7 Nathan Fien (St George-Illawarra Dragons); 15 Frank-Paul Nuuausala (Sydney Roosters); 14 Thomas Leuluai (Wigan Warriors); 10 Fuifui Moimoi (Parramatta Eels); 11 Bronson Harrison (Canberra Raiders); 12 Frank Pritchard (Penrith Panthers); 13 Adam Blair (Melbourne Storm). Subs (all used): 8 Jeff Lima (Melbourne Storm); 9 Issac Luke (South Sydney Rabbitohs); 16 Iosia Soliola (Sydney Roosters); 17 Jared Waerea-Hargreaves (Manly Sea Eagles). **Tries:** Nuuausala (5), Sau (56), Hohaia (70), Pritchard (72); **Goals:** Goodwin 2/3, Luke 0/1. **Rugby Leaguer & League Express Men of the Match:** *Australia:* Cameron Smith; *New Zealand:* Junior Sau. **Penalty count:** 11-10; **Half-time:** 6-6; **Referee:** Steve Ganson (England); **Attendance:** 12,360 *(at Twickenham Stoop).*

to Melbourne clubmate Inglis, who perfectly positioned debutant Brett Morris to score in the left corner.

NZ fullback Lance Hohaia provided his own compelling sub-plot in the second half. Thurston pinched the ball off him to score a deadlock-breaker in the 42nd minute. Thurston converted and then edged his side 14-6 ahead with a penalty.

But Hohaia was a driving force in putting the Kiwis in position to win. New centre Junior Sau took three defenders with him when he scored on 56 minutes, substitute Issac Luke ruing his missed conversion attempt which hit the woodwork.

Then after the Aussies fluffed an attempt to take a spiralling kick and the Kiwis were awarded a scrum feed in striking distance, Hohaia stepped Billy Slater and dashed over to give his side the lead.

Second-rower Pritchard's impersonation of a missile as he shot across the line in the corner with eight minutes to go, after Nathan Fien and Benji Marshall combined at speed to get the ball wide to the left, brought the house down – prematurely as it turned out.

It was all over by half-time, with England facing a humiliation even greater than the one in the World Cup in Melbourne almost exactly a year before when Australia had beaten England 52-4. Shell-shocked England were booed by the crowd as they trooped off at half-time.

A reorganisation in which loose forward Kevin Sinfield had a greater say from dummy-half, and the introduction of Kyle Eastmond in the right centre, with Lee Smith shuffling out to the wing, was partly responsible for the turnaround. As was the barnstorming contribution of England's three other bench players, Sam Burgess, Eorl Crabtree and Ben Westwood. The net effect was three terrific tries to England and no more points to Australia.

A ten-point final margin certainly seemed unlikely when Aussie skipper Darren Lockyer opened the scoring with less than five minutes gone, equalling Ken Irvine's all-time try-scoring record of 33. He began the move too, sending out a long pass to Greg Inglis, who broke through a gap left by the bamboozled Smith and Danny McGuire, before finding his skipper in support, Johnathan Thurston converting.

Quick-fire Aussie handling enabled Billy Slater to round Smith, and he doubled his tally by taking an inside pass from Inglis before stepping Ryan Hall, after a terrific offload to Inglis in the build-up by Anthony Watmough. The Kangaroos were in for a fourth try five minutes later. Burgess, just on the field, could not take a forced McGuire pass and the ball came loose 25 metres from the Aussie line. Thurston scooped it up and in a flash fed Inglis, who roared away on an unstoppable race to the line. A scoreline of 22-0 against was bad enough but, eight minutes before the break, the mood of gloom further deepened when Brett Morris took another Inglis pass to score, after McGuire's attempted interception prolonged another spell of Aussie pressure.

The second half got off to a fiery start, Westwood being held up in-goal after some lovely interplay between McGuire and scrum-half Sam Tomkins. Then Burgess took Sinfield's inside pass and burst through three tacklers to touch down on the nod of the video ref, Sinfield converting. Jarryd Hayne had a try ruled out for a forward pass and the game surged towards an increasingly frantic final ten minutes.

GILLETTE FOUR NATIONS - GAME THREE

Saturday 31st October 2009

ENGLAND 16 AUSTRALIA 26

ENGLAND: 1 Shaun Briscoe (Hull Kingston Rovers); 2 Tom Briscoe (Hull FC); 3 Lee Smith (Leeds Rhinos); 4 Michael Shenton (Castleford Tigers); 5 Ryan Hall (Leeds Rhinos); 6 Danny McGuire (Leeds Rhinos); 7 Sam Tomkins (Wigan Warriors); 8 Adrian Morley (Warrington Wolves); 9 James Roby (St Helens); 10 James Graham (St Helens); 11 Jamie Peacock (Leeds Rhinos) (C); 12 Gareth Ellis (Wests Tigers); 13 Kevin Sinfield (Leeds Rhinos). Subs (all used): 14 Eorl Crabtree (Huddersfield Giants); 15 Sam Burgess (Bradford Bulls); 16 Ben Westwood (Warrington Wolves); 17 Kyle Eastmond (St Helens).
Tries: Burgess (42), Ellis (68), Smith (74); **Goals:** Sinfield 1/2, Smith 1/1.
AUSTRALIA: 1 Billy Slater (Melbourne Storm); 2 Brett Morris (St George-Illawarra Dragons); 3 Greg Inglis (Melbourne Storm); 4 Justin Hodges (Brisbane Broncos); 5 Jarryd Hayne (Parramatta Eels); 6 Darren Lockyer (Brisbane Broncos); 7 Johnathan Thurston (North Queensland Cowboys); 8 Ben Hannant (Bulldogs); 9 Cameron Smith (Melbourne Storm); 10 Petero Civoniceva (Penrith Panthers); 11 Anthony Watmough (Manly Sea Eagles); 12 Paul Gallen (Cronulla Sharks); 13 Nathan Hindmarsh (Parramatta Eels). Subs (all used): 14 Brett White (Melbourne Storm); 15 David Shillington (Canberra Raiders); 16 Luke Lewis (Penrith Panthers); 17 Robbie Farah (Wests Tigers).
Tries: Lockyer (5), Slater (16, 18), Inglis (22), B Morris (31);
Goals: Thurston 3/5.
Sin bin: Thurston (72) - persistent interference.
Rugby Leaguer & League Express Men of the Match:
England: Sam Burgess; *Australia:* Greg Inglis.
Penalty count: 13-6; **Half-time:** 0-26; **Referee:** Steve Ganson (England); **Attendance:** 23,122 *(at DW Stadium, Wigan).*

England clawed their way further back after a piece of individual Tomkins magic. The halfback's jinking inside step created the space and a surging run from Gareth Ellis did the rest, Lee Smith this time adding the extras on 68 minutes.

Shortly after Thurston was sin-binned for a professional foul by referee Steve Ganson, Michael Shenton was tackled short on England's left. After which, the ball was moved right where Eastmond's floated cut-out pass to the wing gave Smith just enough room to sneak in at the corner.

But those five first-half tries meant England always had just too much to do.

Later that Saturday, New Zealand were looking rocky at the Stade Ernest Wallon in Toulouse, after a desperately depleted French had narrowed the score to just 12-16 with a 41st minute James Wynne try. But after that the Kiwis ran in eight unanswered tries.

Captain Benji Marshall's fourth-minute try was worryingly easy – hooker Thomas Leuluai waltzed through a chasm in mid-field to set it up. Then Sam Perrett flew high to field Nathan Fien's raking effort and Bryson Goodwin's goal made it 10-0. In the 21st minute Sebastien Martins took Hohaia and Moimoi over the line with him for France's first try. But Issac Luke's break to put Lance Hohaia over after the ball fortuitously bounced into a couple of Kiwi hands from would-be errors, made the French pay for not converting pressure – but they still had some fight left in them as, just after half-time, Adam Blair dropped the kick from stand-off Bosc and Lézignan's Wynne scored.

GILLETTE FOUR NATIONS - GAME FOUR

Saturday 31st October 2009

FRANCE 12 NEW ZEALAND 62

FRANCE: 1 Constant Villegas (Toulouse Olympique); 2 Nicolas Piquemal (Lezignan); 3 Teddy Sadaoui (Carcassonne); 4 Vincent Duport (Catalans Dragons); 5 Frederic Vaccari (Lezignan); 6 Thomas Bosc (Catalans Dragons); 7 James Wynne (Lezignan); 8 Artie Shead (Limoux); 9 Kane Bentley (Catalans Dragons); 10 Mathieu Griffi (Toulouse Olympique); 11 Olivier Elima (Catalans Dragons); 12 Julien Touxagas (Catalans Dragons); 13 Jamal Fakir (Catalans Dragons). Subs (all used): 14 Christophe Moly (Carcassonne); 15 Andrew Bentley (Catalans Dragons); 16 Sebastien Martins (Catalans Dragons); 18 Romain Gagliazzo (Carcassonne).
Tries: Martins (22), Wynne (41); **Goals:** Bosc 2/2.
NEW ZEALAND: 1 Lance Hohaia (New Zealand Warriors); 2 Sam Perrett (Sydney Roosters); 3 Steve Matai (Manly Sea Eagles); 4 Junior Sau (Newcastle Knights); 5 Bryson Goodwin (Bulldogs); 6 Benji Marshall (Wests Tigers) (C); 7 Nathan Fien (St George-Illawarra Dragons); 8 Frank-Paul Nuuausala (Sydney Roosters); 9 Thomas Leuluai (Wigan Warriors); 10 Fuifui Moimoi (Parramatta Eels); 11 Adam Blair (Melbourne Storm); 12 Frank Pritchard (Penrith Panthers); 13 Iosia Soliola (Sydney Roosters). Subs (all used): 14 Issac Luke (South Sydney Rabbitohs); 15 Greg Eastwood (Bulldogs); 16 Ben Matulino (New Zealand Warriors); 17 Jared Waerea-Hargreaves (Manly Sea Eagles).
Tries: Marshall (4), Perrett (11, 50, 73), Hohaia (40, 59), Waerea-Hargreaves (53, 80), Nuuausala (57), Sau (62), Goodwin (76); **Goals:** Goodwin 9/11.
Rugby Leaguer & League Express Men of the Match:
France: James Wynne; *New Zealand:* Sam Perrett.
Penalty count: 5-3; **Half-time:** 6-16; **Referee:** Shayne Hayne (Australia); **Attendance:** 12,410 (*at Stade Ernest Wallon, Toulouse).*

But after punishing the French with their defence and pinning them in their own territory for several minutes, the Kiwis kicked off their rout. A quick spread put Perrett over; substitute Jared Waerea-Hargreaves benefited from Hohaia's pass and video referee Phil Bentham's decision, and prop Frank-Paul Nuuausala made it two touchdowns in as many Tests.

Warrior Hohaia's 60-metre individual effort was pretty to watch, while Marshall's kick and Perrett's flick put centre Junior Sau over.

Manly's Waerea-Hargreaves was denied by Bentham in the 71st minute, but Perrett fittingly brought up the half-century with seven to go, before Bryson Goodwin won the race for a loose ball in the in-goal and then substitute Waerea-Hargreaves completed the pasting on the buzzer.

Kiwis coach Stephen Kearney was counting the cost as Greg Eastwood, with a broken hand and Steve Matai (eye) joined first-game victim Bronson Harrison (calf) in being ruled out for the rest of the tournament.

Restricting tournament favourites Australia to just two unconverted tries in the first half at the Stade Charléty in Paris was a significant achievement from a French side which again suffered from last-minute reshuffles, injury problems revealing an all too obvious lack of strength in depth.

Though Clint Greenshields and Dimitri Pelo returned after a bout of swine flu, Sébastien Raguin from injury and David Ferriol from suspension, fellow Catalan Dragons

Jean-Philippe Baile, Rémi Casty, Cyrille Gossard and Jamal Fakir, who had broken his jaw against New Zealand, were all missing.

Tim Sheens left out seven of the side which had beaten England, but he still retained a core of experience which the French could not match, with Darren Lockyer, Johnathan Thurston, Petero Civoniceva, who became Australia's most capped forward, and Nathan Hindmarsh supported by an array of young stars from the NRL conveyor belt.

Lockyer captained Australia for the 28th time, breaking Clive Churchill's record, which had lasted 54 years. In his 49th appearance, he had already become Australia's most capped player, beating Mal Meninga's record of 46.

It was not a day to remember as the Aussies put on what must have been one

GILLETTE FOUR NATIONS - GAME FIVE

Saturday 7th November 2009

FRANCE 4 AUSTRALIA 42

FRANCE: 1 Clint Greenshields (Catalans Dragons); 2 Vincent Duport (Catalans Dragons); 3 Sebastien Raguin (Catalans Dragons); 4 Dimitri Pelo (Catalans Dragons); 5 Constant Villegas (Toulouse Olympique); 6 Thomas Bosc (Catalans Dragons); 7 James Wynne (Lezignan); 8 David Ferriol (Catalans Dragons); 9 Kane Bentley (Catalans Dragons); 10 Artie Shead (Limoux); 11 Olivier Elima (Catalans Dragons) (C); 15 Julien Touxagas (Catalans Dragons); 13 Andrew Bentley (Catalans Dragons). Subs (all used): 14 Christophe Moly (Carcassonne); 17 Teddy Sadaoui (Carcassonne); 12 Sebastien Martins (Catalans Dragons); 16 Mathieu Griffi (Toulouse Olympique).
Try: Elima (61); **Goals:** Bosc 0/1.
On report: Shead (42) - alleged dangerous tackle.
AUSTRALIA: 1 Kurt Gidley (Newcastle Knights); 2 Brett Morris (St George-Illawarra Dragons); 3 Josh Morris (Bulldogs); 4 Michael Jennings (Penrith Panthers); 5 Jarryd Hayne (Parramatta Eels); 6 Darren Lockyer (Brisbane Broncos) (C); 7 Johnathan Thurston (North Queensland Cowboys); 8 Ben Hannant (Bulldogs); 9 Robbie Farah (Wests Tigers); 10 Petero Civoniceva (Penrith Panthers); 11 Trent Waterhouse (Penrith Panthers); 12 Ryan Hoffman (Melbourne Storm); 13 Nathan Hindmarsh (Parramatta Eels). Subs (all used): 14 Sam Thaiday (Brisbane Broncos); 15 David Shillington (Canberra Raiders); 16 Luke Lewis (Penrith Panthers); 17 Cooper Cronk (Melbourne Storm).
Tries: Jennings (22, 26, 56), Lewis (42), B Morris (45, 49), J Morris (66, 71); **Goals:** Thurston 3/5, Gidley 2/3.
Rugby Leaguer & League Express Men of the Match:
France: Olivier Elima; *Australia:* Michael Jennings.
Penalty count: 5-9; **Half-time:** 0-8; **Referee:** Leon Williamson (New Zealand); **Attendance:** 8,656 *(at Charlety Stadium, Paris).*

of their worst first-half performances. As against England and New Zealand, France produced a gutsy first-half display, two unconverted debut tries for Tongan Michael Jennings all that separated the sides.

But when Artie Shead was placed on report for a dangerous throw, Luke Lewis drove through the French line for a try, goaled by Gidley, which began to alter the balance of the game.

Brett Morris's two tries in four minutes compounded it and Australia went further ahead when Greenshields lost the ball in Jarryd Hayne's crunching tackle and Jennings went 65 metres for his hat-trick try, converted by the returning Thurston to give Australia a 30-0 lead.

Well led by Olivier Elima, the French came back into the game for their only try, scored just after the hour. Fittingly it was scored by the French captain, who plucked Bosc's beautifully weighted kick out of the air to touch down for his 20th try of a remarkable season.

But Ryan Hoffman broke before Josh Morris took a pass back inside from brother Brett to claim his first try on his debut. Like his brother, he added another minutes later when Jennings foxed the defence and squeezed out the pass, both tries converted by Thurston.

Tony Smith had good reason to be well satisfied at the way his new-look England knocked out the World Champions at Huddersfield. The England coach showed a ruthless streak by dropping his right wing combination and axed the experienced Danny McGuire to bring in Kyle Eastmond at halfback. Then Smith sprang a late shock when he changed the announced team to switch Kevin Sinfield from loose forward to hooker.

The result was Peter Fox scored two tries on his recall to the wing and Eastmond grabbed England's other try, while Sinfield carried off the man of the match award. Sinfield had made an early impact in his new hooking role when moving smartly from a play-the-ball to send Burgess charging forward and putting Eastmond over for a 10th minute try between the posts. Sam Tomkins set up the next with a perfectly placed crossfield kick that caught the visitors' defence off guard and gave Fox an unimpeded dive to touch down.

Sinfield's quick pass from the base of the scrum paved the way, via Eastmond's smart hands, for Chris Bridge, another surprise selection at centre, to send in his winger. Sinfield also popped over the penalty that gave England a vital eight-point lead with only eight minutes left.

New Zealand's biggest threat came from substitute hooker Issac Luke. His strong midfield burst set up the best try of the match early in the second half. Lance Hohaia came up in support and handed on to Ben Matulino, who exchanged passes with Junior Sau before dummying his way through for a spectacular touchdown.

After two poor first halves against France and Australia, England grew in confidence after Eastmond's early try was converted by Sinfield and were not shaken when New Zealand responded with a try four minutes later, Hohaia's perfect cut out pass enabling debutant Kieran Foran, selected ahead of Krisnan Inu, to put in Bryson Goodwin near the corner flag.

Goodwin failed with the conversion attempt but put New Zealand level with a 29th minute goal when Eorl Crabtree was penalised for holding down. Still England retained their composure and Fox's two tries in the closing few minutes of the half set up the victory.

	P	W	D	L	F	A	D	Pts
Australia	3	2	1	0	88	40	48	5
England	3	2	0	1	70	50	20	4
New Zealand	3	1	1	1	94	52	42	3
France	3	0	0	3	28	138	-110	0

GILLETTE FOUR NATIONS

FOUR NATIONS FINAL

For around 60 minutes of a pulsating Gillette Four Nations final, England went toe to toe with odds-on favourites Australia and had realistic hopes of victory.

Just a try and a goal separated the two at 16-22 when Castleford centre Michael Shenton, who had defended magnificently, was stretchered from the field.

Seven minutes later, Billy Slater's miraculous in-goal flick and knock back of a Darren Lockyer kick that was heading for the stands allowed Cameron Smith to score the first of what would turn out to be four killer tries in the final 13 minutes.

Smith's try was followed, two minutes later, by the middle try in a Slater hat-trick. Smith tore out of dummy-half down the right that Shenton had previously policed superbly, Lockyer was in support and the fullback from Melbourne cantered home.

On 73 minutes, Lockyer's perfectly paced kick to the left corner allowed left

GILLETTE FOUR NATIONS - GAME SIX

Saturday 7th November 2009

ENGLAND 20 NEW ZEALAND 12

ENGLAND: 1 Shaun Briscoe (Hull Kingston Rovers); 2 Peter Fox (Hull Kingston Rovers); 3 Chris Bridge (Warrington Wolves); 4 Michael Shenton (Castleford Tigers); 5 Ryan Hall (Leeds Rhinos); 6 Sam Tomkins (Wigan Warriors); 7 Kyle Eastmond (St Helens); 8 Adrian Morley (Warrington Wolves); 9 Kevin Sinfield (Leeds Rhinos); 10 James Graham (St Helens); 11 Jamie Peacock (Leeds Rhinos) (C); 12 Gareth Ellis (Wests Tigers); 13 Sam Burgess (Bradford Bulls). Subs (all used): 14 Eorl Crabtree (Huddersfield Giants); 15 Jon Wilkin (St Helens); 16 Ben Westwood (Warrington Wolves); 17 James Roby (St Helens). **Tries:** Eastmond (10), Fox (34, 38); **Goals:** Sinfield 4/4.
NEW ZEALAND: 1 Lance Hohaia (New Zealand Warriors); 2 Sam Perrett (Sydney Roosters); 3 Kieran Foran (Manly Sea Eagles); 4 Junior Sau (Newcastle Knights); 5 Bryson Goodwin (Bulldogs); 6 Benji Marshall (Wests Tigers) (C); 7 Nathan Fien (St George-Illawarra Dragons); 8 Frank-Paul Nuuausala (Sydney Roosters); 9 Thomas Leuluai (Wigan Warriors); 10 Fuifui Moimoi (Parramatta Eels); 11 Iosia Soliola (Sydney Roosters); 12 Frank Pritchard (Penrith Panthers); 13 Adam Blair (Melbourne Storm). Subs (all used): 14 Issac Luke (South Sydney Rabbitohs); 15 Jeff Lima (Melbourne Storm); 16 Ben Matulino (New Zealand Warriors); 17 Jared Waerea-Hargreaves (Manly Sea Eagles). **Tries:** Goodwin (14), Matulino (43); **Goals:** Goodwin 2/3.
Rugby Leaguer & League Express Men of the Match:
England: Kevin Sinfield; *New Zealand:* Issac Luke.
Penalty count: 8-10; **Half-time:** 18-6; **Referee:** Thierry Alibert (France); **Attendance:** 19,390 *(at Galpharm Stadium, Huddersfield).*

GILLETTE FOUR NATIONS FINAL

Saturday 14th November 2009

ENGLAND 16 AUSTRALIA 46

ENGLAND: 1 Shaun Briscoe (Hull Kingston Rovers); 2 Peter Fox (Hull Kingston Rovers); 3 Chris Bridge (Warrington Wolves); 4 Michael Shenton (Castleford Tigers); 5 Ryan Hall (Leeds Rhinos); 6 Sam Tomkins (Wigan Warriors); 7 Kyle Eastmond (St Helens); 8 Adrian Morley (Warrington Wolves); 9 Kevin Sinfield (Leeds Rhinos); 10 James Graham (St Helens); 11 Jamie Peacock (Leeds Rhinos) (C); 12 Gareth Ellis (Wests Tigers); 13 Sam Burgess (Bradford Bulls). Subs (all used): 14 Eorl Crabtree (Huddersfield Giants); 15 Jon Wilkin (St Helens); 16 Ben Westwood (Warrington Wolves); 17 James Roby (St Helens). **Tries:** Burgess (10, 50), Fox (19); **Goals:** Sinfield 2/3.
AUSTRALIA: 1 Billy Slater (Melbourne Storm); 2 Brett Morris (St George-Illawarra Dragons); 3 Greg Inglis (Melbourne Storm); 4 Justin Hodges (Brisbane Broncos); 5 Jarryd Hayne (Parramatta Eels); 6 Darren Lockyer (Brisbane Broncos) (C); 7 Johnathan Thurston (North Queensland Cowboys); 8 Ben Hannant (Bulldogs); 9 Cameron Smith (Melbourne Storm); 10 Petero Civoniceva (Penrith Panthers); 11 Luke Lewis (Penrith Panthers); 12 Paul Gallen (Cronulla Sharks); 13 Nathan Hindmarsh (Parramatta Eels). Subs (all used): 14 Kurt Gidley (Newcastle Knights); 15 Brett White (Melbourne Storm); 16 Anthony Watmough (Manly Sea Eagles); 17 Sam Thaiday (Brisbane Broncos).
Tries: B Morris (14, 58), Inglis (25), Slater (54, 68, 77), Smith (67), Hayne (73); **Goals:** Thurston 7/9.
Rugby Leaguer & League Express Men of the Match:
England: Sam Burgess; *Australia:* Billy Slater.
Penalty count: 8-5; **Half-time:** 10-14;
Referee: Leon Williamson (New Zealand);
Attendance: 31,042 *(at Elland Road, Leeds).*

winger Jarryd Hayne to touch down, before the climax of a remarkable final quarter came with Slater's third. This time the fullback made the most of Kurt Gidley's burst up the right channel by collecting a nicely bouncing kick on the end of the substitute centre's run.

Official man of the match Johnathan Thurston completed a quartet of late conversions in a seven-goal haul to ensure an ultimately flattering 30-point difference

The preceding hour had been a fabulous contest. After Aussie winger Brett Morris had a try disallowed by video ref Phil Bentham the home side crossed first. From almost halfway, Sam Burgess stepped Petero Civoniceva and then dummied his way around a floundering Slater in a blink of an eye, Kevin Sinfield converting.

Eorl Crabtree swamped by the Australian defence during the Four Nations Final

Almost immediately, when Smith kicked out on the full from the restart, another scintillating break by Burgess nearly led to a second try, but the former Bradford man was brought down after ignoring Sam Tomkins in support. As England continued to press, James Graham's pushed pass was intercepted by Thurston, who raced away and fed Greg Inglis on halfway. And although Shenton chased back brilliantly to haul the centre down, on the last tackle, Thurston's pass was flicked on by Justin Hodges to Morris who, this time, finished the job.

On 19 minutes, though, England were in front again, Peter Fox leaping high above Hayne to collect Eastmond's perfect bomb to the corner. Sinfield couldn't add the touchline conversion and the miss allowed Thurston's second conversion of the game, to a wonderful try by Inglis, to push the Aussies ahead for the first time six minutes later. Again, Thurston's pass did the initial damage, his inside ball sending Hayne racing clear. And when the winger kicked ahead with 25 metres to go, Inglis beat Peter Fox in a foot race to the ball, on the nod of the video ref.

A Thurston penalty on the half-hour, after Gareth Ellis had blocked the scrum-half as he was chasing his own chip kick, gave Australia a 14-10 half-time lead.

England regained the lead on 50 minutes. A superb back-of-hand pass from Sam Tomkins fed an inside run from Ellis, before Burgess changed the angle of attack again and went in under the posts, Sinfield converting.

Once more, England were not allowed to settle on their advantage, as Slater showed terrific awareness from dummy-half in ducking under Tomkins' attempted tackle close to the line four minutes later.

Thurston couldn't add that goal but he had no difficulty after creating a second try for Morris with a sublime last-tackle cross-field dab - and then the floodgates opened.

* *Immediately after the final, the Rugby League World Golden Boot was presented to Melbourne's 22-year-old centre Greg Inglis, adjudged the world's best player in 2009.*

OTHER INTERNATIONALS
League unlimited

The year 2009 was the busiest ever year in international Rugby League history. "The potential for the international game is unlimited," Colin Love, the Australian Chairman of the Rugby League International Federation told Rugby League Express on a weekend when Papua New Guinea won the Pacific Cup in Port Moresby in a five-team competition, while Scotland and Wales won through to the final of the European Cup in a six-team competition that Wales eventually won. The Gillette Four Nations was also in full swing in England and France. In July, it had been announced the 2013 World Cup to be held in the United Kingdom would be the first in a four-year cycle.

GILLETTE FUSION INTERNATIONALS

GILLETTE FUSION INTERNATIONAL

Saturday 13th June 2009

FRANCE 12 ENGLAND 66

FRANCE: 1 Constant Villegas (Toulouse Olympique); 2 Frederic Vaccari (Catalans Dragons); 3 Jean-Phillipe Baile (Catalans Dragons); 4 Sebastien Planas (Toulouse Olympique); 5 Vincent Duport (Catalans Dragons); 6 Thomas Bosc (Catalans Dragons); 7 Mikael Murcia (Limoux); 8 Remi Casty (Catalans Dragons); 9 Kane Bentley (Catalans Dragons); 10 Jerome Guisset (Catalans Dragons) (C); 11 Gregory Mounis (Catalans Dragons); 12 Cyrille Gossard (Catalans Dragons); 13 Eric Anselme (Toulouse Olympique). Subs (all used): 14 Romain Gagliazzo (Carcassonne); 15 Sebastien Martins (Pia); 16 William Barthau (Catalans Dragons); 17 Mathieu Griffi (Toulouse Olympique).
Tries: Baile (43), Gossard (75); **Goals:** Bosc 2/2.
ENGLAND: 1 Shaun Briscoe (Hull Kingston Rovers); 2 Peter Fox (Hull Kingston Rovers); 3 Michael Shenton (Castleford Tigers); 4 Ryan Atkins (Wakefield Trinity Wildcats); 5 Ryan Hall (Leeds Rhinos); 6 Danny McGuire (Leeds Rhinos); 7 Richard Myler (Salford City Reds); 8 Adrian Morley (Warrington Wolves); 9 Scott Moore (Huddersfield Giants); 10 Jamie Peacock (Leeds Rhinos) (C); 11 Ben Westwood (Warrington Wolves); 12 Gareth Hock (Wigan Warriors); 13 Sam Burgess (Bradford Bulls). Subs (all used): 14 James Graham (St Helens); 15 James Roby (St Helens); 16 Eorl Crabtree (Huddersfield Giants); 17 Tony Clubb (Harlequins).
Tries: Atkins (8), McGuire (10), Myler (15, 17, 62), Fox (25, 70), Hall (27), Briscoe (35, 37), Roby (48), Burgess (65); **Goals:** Myler 9/12.
Rugby Leaguer & League Express Men of the Match:
France: Thomas Bosc; *England:* Richard Myler.
Penalty count: 2-4; **Half-time:** 0-44; **Referee:** Jarred Maxwell (Australia); **Attendance:** 7,200 *(at Stade Jean Bouin, Paris).*

England's 66-12 win over France at the Stade Jean Bouin in Paris in June was heralded as a bold new era after the disappointments of the 2008 World Cup. Richie Myler and his fellow youngsters grasped their opportunity as Tony Smith's side stampeded over their disappointing opponents in fine style. Myler finished with 30 points from a hat-trick of tries and nine goals – a record haul against the French.

Sam Burgess marked his return to the international fold as he consistently punched holes in the home side's defence. Alongside Myler at halfback was the impressive Danny McGuire, who seemed to relish a more responsible role as the senior playmaker.

Props Adrian Morley and Jamie Peacock were described as "warriors" by France's new coach Bobbie Goulding. Gareth Hock also made some typically stirring bursts and James Roby and James Graham contributed off the bench, while Scott Moore enjoyed an accomplished debut at hooker. Out wide was where most of the new faces could be found, and a second debutant, Ryan Hall, marked his first England appearance with a try while Shaun Briscoe, Peter Fox and Ryan Atkins also found themselves on the scoresheet.

This was also supposed to be a new start for France under Goulding, but the absence of seven key players was always going to make it difficult for the former Great Britain scrum-half. His side were completely out-gunned in the first half, and the interval scoreline of 44-0 left journalists reaching for the record books. They did regain some pride after the break, but there was much work to do before the autumn's Four Nations. The game was over as a contest by the time Myler crossed for his second try on 17 minutes, making it 24-0.

A headline-grabbing performance from young Wigan halfback Sam Tomkins helped England on their way to a 48-12 win against Iestyn Harris's new-look Wales team in Bridgend on the Saturday following the Super League Grand Final. The young Wigan stand-off scored a smart hat-trick of tries to push his claim for inclusion in Tony Smith's starting line-up for the Gillette Four Nations.

Tomkins made the headlines, but the real story to emerge from the contest on a cold Bridgend night was the home nation. Responding to the call-to-arms of new coaching team of Harris, Clive Griffiths and Kevin Ellis, Wales' youngsters took the game to England from the first whistle. Although they tired visibly late on, they were far more feisty, determined and committed than in recent years. With their Celtic Crusaders contingent to the fore, Harris's charges showed glimpses of class to upset Tony Smith's plans. Sean O'Loughlin's try on 62 minutes, which opened up a 16-point lead for England, finally ended Wales' brave resistance.

GILLETTE FUSION INTERNATIONAL

Saturday 17th October 2009

WALES 12 ENGLAND 48

WALES: 1 Elliot Kear (Celtic Crusaders); 2 Rhys Williams (Warrington Wolves); 3 Rhys Griffiths (Warrington Wolves); 4 Anthony Blackwood (Celtic Crusaders); 5 Ashley Bateman (Celtic Crusaders); 6 Lloyd White (Celtic Crusaders); 7 Ian Webster (Central Comets); 8 Jordan James (Celtic Crusaders) (C); 9 Neil Budworth (Celtic Crusaders); 10 Gil Dudson (Celtic Crusaders); 11 Craig Kopczak (Bradford Bulls); 12 Ben Flower (Celtic Crusaders); 13 Geraint Davies (Celtic Crusaders). Subs (all used): 14 Ian Watson (Leigh Centurions); 15 Lee Williams (Celtic Crusaders); 16 Ross Divorty (Featherstone Rovers); 17 Matt Barron (Gateshead Thunder).
Tries: Kopczak (1), Watson (49); **Goals:** White 2/3.
ENGLAND: 1 Paul Sykes (Bradford Bulls); 2 Tom Briscoe (Hull FC); 3 Michael Shenton (Castleford Tigers); 4 Sean O'Loughlin (Wigan Warriors); 5 Peter Fox (Hull Kingston Rovers); 6 Sam Tomkins (Wigan Warriors); 7 Richard Myler (Salford City Reds); 8 Adrian Morley (Warrington Wolves) (C); 9 Scott Moore (Huddersfield Giants); 10 Garreth Carvell (Warrington Wolves); 11 Gareth Ellis (Wests Tigers); 12 Ben Westwood (Warrington Wolves); 13 Sam Burgess (Bradford Bulls). Subs (all used): 14 Louie McCarthy-Scarsbrook (Harlequins); 15 Mick Higham (Warrington Wolves); 16 Danny Tickle (Hull FC); 17 Chris Bridge (Warrington Wolves).
Tries: Tomkins (7, 19, 77), McCarthy-Scarsbrook (27), Burgess (34), T Briscoe (57, 72), O'Loughlin (62), Morley (68); **Goals:** Sykes 6/9.
Rugby Leaguer & League Express Men of the Match:
Wales: Jordan James; *England:* Sam Burgess.
Penalty count: 4-8; **Half-time:** 6-20; **Referee:** Thierry Alibert (France); **Attendance:** 3,249 (at Brewery Field, Bridgend).

TRANS-TASMAN TEST

The media were talking up the Trans-Tasman Test in May as Australia's chance of retribution. Six months earlier the Kiwis had shocked the Aussies 34-20 in the final of the World Cup.

The Australian players weren't talking that way – just going about their business under new coach Tim Sheens. But at the end of the night at the same venue in Brisbane they had their revenge with a one-sided 38-10 victory. Except for the first half-hour the Test was never really a true contest. The all-star backline that had let Australia down so badly in the World Cup final turned in a vastly different display. And the Kiwis had no answer to their speed and class.

The only member of the back line not to score was inspirational Darren Lockyer. Billy Slater, whose moment of madness cost Australia so dearly in the World Cup final, made amends at the Lang Park arena. In doubt with an ankle injury until a few hours before the Test 'Billy the Kid' was at his magical best.

The defining moment of the encounter came as the clock ticked down towards half-time. Seven minutes before the interval, Slater made a long break but a pass was intercepted by Lance Hohaia. Within a blink of an eyelid, Benji Marshall split the Australian defence, and flung the ball back inside, but Slater was there to deny the New

Zealanders a try. It was a vital tackle. Play swung to the opposite end and Justin Hodges waltzed through a weak would-be tackle by David Fa'alogo to touch down between the uprights. Johnathan Thurston's conversion put the Australians ahead 16-6. Thurston figured prominently soon after play resumed in the second half. Lockyer threw a wonderful pass to send Glenn Stewart on his way to the line, but when collared by the Kiwis defence he released the ball, which bounced off Hohaia. Thurston pounced and dived over a couple of potential defenders to score.

Thurston converted his own try to stretch the lead to 16. The Australians were on a roll. Stewart was firing on all cylinders and took a pass off Lockyer to give Slater the slightest of breaks – and the fullback obliged. At 26-6, the Kiwis were dead ducks.

Manu Vatuvei scored a consolation try before an incredible display of athleticism gave Darius Boyd a try. The video replays showed how Boyd had rolled on his back, missed going into touch with either his body or legs and reached over his head to touch down. Hodges snared a second try as the clock ticked down.

The victory meant that the Australians once again had the international momentum in preparation for the Gillette Four Nations Tournament later in the year.

TRANS-TASMAN TEST

Friday 8th May 2009

AUSTRALIA 38 NEW ZEALAND 10

AUSTRALIA: 1 Billy Slater (Melbourne Storm); 2 Israel Folau (Brisbane Broncos); 3 Greg Inglis (Melbourne Storm); 4 Justin Hodges (Brisbane Broncos); 5 Darius Boyd (St George-Illawarra Dragons); 6 Darren Lockyer (Brisbane Broncos) (C); 7 Johnathan Thurston (North Queensland Cowboys); 8 Petero Civoniceva (Penrith Panthers); 9 Cameron Smith (Melbourne Storm); 10 Steve Price (New Zealand Warriors); 11 Anthony Laffranchi (Gold Coast Titans); 12 Paul Gallen (Cronulla Sharks); 13 Glenn Stewart (Manly Sea Eagles). Subs (all used): 14 Kurt Gidley (Newcastle Knights); 15 Brent Kite (Manly Sea Eagles); 16 Luke Bailey (Gold Coast Titans); 17 Anthony Watmough (Manly Sea Eagles).
Tries: Folau (6), Thurston (24, 43), Hodges (36, 72), Slater (56), Boyd (65); **Goals:** Thurston 5/7.
NEW ZEALAND: 1 Lance Hohaia (New Zealand Warriors); 2 Sam Perrett (Sydney Roosters); 17 Iosia Soliola (Sydney Roosters); 4 Jerome Ropati (New Zealand Warriors); 5 Manu Vatuvei (New Zealand Warriors); 6 Nathan Fien (New Zealand Warriors); 7 Benji Marshall (Wests Tigers) (C); 8 Roy Asotasi (South Sydney Rabbitohs); 9 Dene Halatau (Wests Tigers); 10 Adam Blair (Melbourne Storm); 11 David Fa'alogo (South Sydney Rabbitohs); 12 Bronson Harrison (Canberra Raiders); 3 Simon Mannering (New Zealand Warriors). Subs (all used): 14 Greg Eastwood (Bulldogs); 15 Jeff Lima (Melbourne Storm); 16 Jason Nightingale (St George-Illawarra Dragons); 18 Sika Manu (Melbourne Storm).
Tries: Perrett (18), Vatuvei (62); **Goals:** Marshall 1/2.
Rugby Leaguer & League Express Men of the Match:
Australia: Darren Lockyer; *New Zealand:* Adam Blair.
Half-time: 16-6; **Referee:** Richard Silverwood (England);
Attendance: 37,152 *(at Suncorp Stadium, Brisbane).*

EUROPEAN CUP

Wales produced a stunning second-half performance to beat Scotland by 28-16 and win the European Cup in front of a lively home crowd at Brewery Field in Bridgend. Trailing 16-14 at the break, Iestyn Harris's young Welsh side turned on the style in the second period, scoring three unanswered tries to claim their first international silverware since 1995.

Considering the inexperienced nature of the Wales side, it was a remarkable performance, built on a cluster of Celtic Crusaders players, namely Jordan James, Neil Budworth, Lloyd White and man-of-the-match Elliot Kear. The latter excelled in both attack and defence.

Scotland - who lost Iain Morrison on the morning of the game with a chest infection - had the better of the first half. Their forwards ran harder, their halfbacks looked sharper and hat-trick man Mick Nanyn gave them a 16-14 half-time lead, winger Ashley Bateman, Ben Flower and fullback prospect Elliot Kear getting Wales' tries.

Within five minutes of the restart, Wales had surged ahead once more – and this time they wouldn't be caught. On the back of some thrilling forward play, the impressive Lloyd White released centre Christiaan Roets 40 metres out. He pinned his ears back and won

EUROPEAN CUP FINAL

Sunday 8th November 2009

WALES 28 SCOTLAND 16

WALES: 1 Elliot Kear (Celtic Crusaders); 2 Rhys Williams (Warrington Wolves); 3 Lee Williams (Celtic Crusaders); 4 Christiaan Roets (Bridgend Blue Bulls); 5 Ashley Bateman (Celtic Crusaders); 6 Lloyd White (Celtic Crusaders); 7 Ian Watson (Leigh Centurions); 8 Jordan James (Celtic Crusaders) (C); 9 Neil Budworth (Celtic Crusaders); 10 Gil Dudson (Celtic Crusaders); 11 Chris Beasley (Celtic Crusaders); 12 Geraint Davies (Celtic Crusaders); 13 Ian Webster (Central Comets). Subs (all used): 14 Rhys Griffiths (Warrington Wolves); 15 Ross Divorty (Featherstone Rovers); 16 Ben Flower (Celtic Crusaders); 17 Matt Barron (Gateshead Thunder).
Tries: Bateman (16), Kear (26), Flower (32), Roets (46), White (59), R Williams (70);
Goals: White 2/5, L Williams 0/1.
SCOTLAND: 1 Jamie Benn (Castleford Panthers); 2 Jon Steel (Featherstone Rovers); 3 Kevin Henderson (Wakefield Trinity Wildcats); 4 Mick Nanyn (Leigh Centurions); 5 James Nixon (Barrow Raiders); 6 Brendon Lindsay (Sheffield Eagles); 7 Gareth Moore (York City Knights); 8 Mitchell Stringer (Sheffield Eagles); 9 Andrew Henderson (Gateshead Thunder) (C); 10 Neil Lowe (Hunslet Hawks); 11 Alox Szoctak (Sheffield Eagles); 12 Richard Fletcher (Widnes Vikings); 13 Lee Paterson (Widnes Vikings). Subs (all used): 12 John Duffy (Widnes Vikings); 15 John Cox (Edinburgh Eagles); 14 Paddy Coupar (Workington Town); 21 Rob Lunt (Workington Town).
Tries: Nanyn (8, 20, 39); **Goals:** Moore 2/3.
Rugby Leaguer & League Express Men of the Match:
Wales: Lloyd White; *Scotland:* Mick Nanyn.
Penalty count: 5-5; **Half-time:** 14-16; **Referee:** Shayne Hayne (Australia);
Attendance: 1,608 *(at Brewery Field, Bridgend).*

the race to the corner. White couldn't convert, but Wales were back in the driving seat.

Richard Fletcher thought he'd scored after touching down Moore's grubber, but video ref Ben Thaler ruled it out for offside. Within two minutes of the let-off, Wales extended their lead via a brilliant score from White. His attacking chip was collected on the bounce by centre Lee Williams. With Scotland fullback Jamie Benn charging across to cover, Williams slipped it back inside to the supporting White.

With little over ten minutes remaining, Wales got the knock-out blow. After a period of pressure, Kear's steepling crossfield kick was plucked out of the air by winger Rhys Williams.

* In the 3rd/4th place play-off Lebanon beat Ireland 40-16 in a game switched to Maesteg from Brewery Field because of heavy rain. Twin brothers Reece and Travis Robinson scored 24 of Lebanon's 40 points between them.

Italy beat Serbia 42-14 at the same venue to finish fifth. The win meant Italy stay in the European Cup for 2010 while Serbia were relegated and would compete in the European Shield, a competition they won in 2008.

EUROPEAN CUP RANKING GAMES

3RD/4TH PLAY-OFF

Sunday 8th November 2009

IRELAND 16 LEBANON 40

IRELAND: 1 Karl Fitzpatrick (Salford City Reds); 2 Tim Bergin (Laois Panthers); 3 Marcus St Hilaire (Oldham); 4 James Haley (Halifax); 5 Steve Gibbons (Carlow Crusaders); 6 James Coyle (Barrow Raiders); 7 Liam Finn (Dewsbury Rams); 8 Ryan Boyle (Castleford Tigers); 9 Bob Beswick (Halifax) (C); 10 Brett McDermott (Barrow Raiders); 11 Luke Ambler (Leeds Rhinos); 12 Dave Allen (Barrow Raiders); 13 Tyrone McCarthy (Warrington Wolves). Subs (all used): 14 Michael Haley (Sheffield Eagles); 15 Paddy Barcoe (Carlow Crusaders); 16 Sean Hesketh (York City Knights); 17 Wayne Kerr (Oldham).
Tries: J Haley (31, 36), Beswick (64); **Goals:** Finn 2/3.
LEBANON: 1 Adnan Saleh (Bankstown City); 2 Josh Mansour (South Sydney Rabbitohs); 3 Daniel Chiha (Windsor Wolves); 4 Reece Robinson (North Sydney Bears); 5 Travis Robinson (Chester Hill); 6 Liam Ayoub (Bulldogs); 7 George Ndaira (Newcastle Knights) (C); 8 Khaled Deeb (Newtown Jets); 9 Jamie Clark (Bulldogs); 10 John Koborsi (Wentworthville Magpies); 11 Ahmad Ellaz (Cronulla Sharks); 12 Steve Azzi (Sydney Roosters); 13 Chris Salem (Bankstown City). Subs (all used): 14 Allen Soultan (Wests Magpies); 15 Nick Kassis (Chester Hill); 16 Youssef El Helou (Jounieh); 17 Wael Harb (Wolves).
Tries: Saleh (2), Mansour (8), T Robinson (12, 26), Clark (22), R Robinson (40, 75), Chiha (49); **Goals:** R Robinson 4/5, Clark 0/2, T Robinson 0/1.
Rugby Leaguer & League Express Men of the Match:
Ireland: Liam Finn; *Lebanon:* Reece Robinson.
Penalty count: 2-0; **Half-time:** 10-30; **Referee:** Steve Ganson (England).

5TH/6TH PLAY-OFF

Sunday 8th November 2009

ITALY 42 SERBIA 14

ITALY: 1 Robert Quitadamo (Woy Woy); 2 Pierluigi Gentile (Piemonte); 3 Andrea Tagliavento (Milazzo); 4 Shane Pavan (unattached); 5 Filippo Veronese (La Rocha); 6 Benjamin Falcone (Balmain Tigers); 7 Raymond Nasso (Penrith Panthers); 8 Paul Stanica (Nafit); 9 John Grasso (Catania RU); 10 Ryan Tramonte (Windsor Wolves); 11 Dean Vicelich (Canterbury Bankstown); 12 Marco Ferrazzano (unattached) (C); 13 Ludovico Torreggiani (Nafit). Subs (all used): 14 Angelo Ricci (Queensbury); 15 Matthew Sands (Lyon); 16 Jason Dubas-Fisher (Leeds Akkies); 17 Edwardo Lerna (Redditch Ravens).
Tries: Falcone (28, 65, 76), Vicelich (30, 37, 69), Nasso (40); **Goals:** Veronese 7/7.
SERBIA: 1 Ivan Šušnjara (RK Beogradski Univerzitet); 2 Aleksandar Sic (Nis); 3 Marko Žebeljan (R13K Podbara); 4 Nenad Grbic (R13K Podbara); 5 Dimitris Dac (RK Dorćol); 6 Filip Brkic (RK Dorćol); 7 Austen Novakovic (Oldham); 8 Soni Radovanovic (Whitehaven); 9 Zoran Pešic (R13K Podbara); 10 Dejan Lukeni (RK Dorćol); 11 Milos Milanko (RK Dorćol); 12 Ivan Djordjevic (RLK Crvena Zvezda); 13 Dalibor Vukanovic (RK Dorćol) (C). Subs (all used): 14 Mario Milosavljevic (R13K Podbara); 15 Igor Kesegi (RK Dorćol); 16 Vuk Tvrdišic (RK Dorćol); 17 Milan Šušnjara (RK Dorćol).
Tries: Radovanovic (13), Vukanovic (16, 44); **Goals:** Brkic 1/3.
Rugby Leaguer & League Express Men of the Match:
Italy: Dean Vicelich; *Serbia:* Dalibor Vukanovic.
Penalty count: 7-7; **Half-time:** 24-10; **Referee:** Phil Bentham (England).

Attendance: 200 (at Old Parish, Maesteg).

EUROPEAN CUP GROUP A

Saturday 17th October 2009

ITALY 0 SCOTLAND 104

ITALY: 1 Edwardo Lerna (Redditch Ravens); 2 Pierluigi Gentile (Piamonte); 3 Jason Dubas-Fisher (Leeds Akkies); 4 Shane Pavan (unattached); 5 Manuelle Cipriani (Genoa); 6 Filippo Veronese (La Rocha); 7 John Grasso (Catania RU); 8 Paul Stanica (Nafit); 9 Greg Brincat (Randwick RU); 11 Matthew Sands (Lyon); 12 Marco Ferrazzano (unattached) (C); 13 Ludovico Torreggiani (Nafit). Subs (all used): 14 Angelo Ricci (Queensbury); 15 Rob Di Lera (unattached); 16 Filippo Maserati (Piamonte); 17 Andrew Zacchia (La Rocha).
SCOTLAND: 1 Jamie Benn (Castleford Panthers); 2 Jon Steel (Featherstone Rovers); 3 Kevin Henderson (Wakefield Trinity Wildcats); 4 Mick Nanyn (Leigh Centurions); 5 James Nixon (Barrow Raiders); 6 Brendon Lindsay (Sheffield Eagles); 7 Gareth Moore (York City Knights); 8 Mitchell Stringer (Sheffield Eagles); 9 Ben Fisher (Hull Kingston Rovers); 10 Neil Lowe (Hunslet Hawks); 11 Alex Szostak (Sheffield Eagles); 12 Richard Fletcher (Whitehaven); 13 Lee Paterson (Widnes Vikings). Subs (all used): 14 Paddy Coupar (Workington Town); 15 Andrew Henderson (Gateshead Thunder) (C); 16 Rob Lunt (Workington Town); 17 John Cox (Edinburgh Eagles).
Tries: Paterson (7), Steel (10, 54), K Henderson (13, 28), Fletcher (20, 57), Moore (23), Cox (31), Nixon (33, 41, 47, 78), Benn (36, 73), Nanyn (67, 76), Fisher (68); **Goals:** John Nixon 16/18.
Rugby Leaguer & League Express Men of the Match:
Italy: Ludovico Torreggiani; *Scotland:* Ben Fisher.
Penalty count: 0-4; **Half-time:** 0-54; **Referee:** Steve Ganson (England);
Attendance: 2,139 (at Stadio Del Plebiscito, Padova).

Saturday 24th October 2009

LEBANON 86 ITALY 0

LEBANON: 1 Adnan Saleh (Bankstown City); 2 Travis Robinson (Chester Hill); 3 Reece Robinson (North Sydney Bears); 4 Daniel Chiha (Windsor Wolves); 5 Josh Mansour (South Sydney Rabbitohs); 6 Liam Ayoub (Bulldogs); 7 George Ndaira (Newcastle Knights) (C); 8 Robin Hachache (LAU Immortals); 9 Jamie Clark (Bulldogs); 10 Khaled Deeb (Newtown Jets); 11 John Koborsi (Wentworthville Magpies); 12 Steve Azzi (Sydney Roosters); 13 Ahmad Ellaz (Cronulla Sharks). Subs (all used): 14 Wael Harb (Wolves); 15 Ghassan Dandach (Jounieh); 16 Youssef El Helou (Jounieh); 17 Jad Hachem (LAU Immortals).

Tries: T Robinson 2, Ellaz, Saleh 4, Mansour, R Robinson 3, Clark, Harb 2, El Helou; **Goals:** Ndaira 12/14, Clark 1/1.
ITALY: 1 Edwardo Lerna (Redditch Ravens); 2 Paul Stanica (Nafit); 3 Andrea Tagliavento (Milazzo); 4 Dean Vicelich (Canterbury Bankstown); 5 Filippo Veronese (La Rocha); 6 Pierluigi Gentile (Piamonte); 7 John Grasso (Catania RU); 8 Jason Dubas-Fisher (Leeds Akkies); 9 Angelo Ricci (Queensbury); 10 Greg Brincat (Randwick RU); 11 Matthew Sands (Lyon); 12 Marco Ferrazzano (unattached) (C); 13 Ludovico Torreggiani (Nafit). Subs (all used): 14 Rob Di Lera (unattached); 15 Tiziano Franchini (Nafit); 16 Shane Pavan (unattached); 17 Fabio Di Pietro (Nafit).
Rugby Leaguer & League Express Men of the Match:
Lebanon: Reece Robinson; *Italy:* Marco Ferrazzano.
Half-time: 40-0; **Referee:** Thierry Alibert (France). (at Tripoli Olympic Stadium).

Sunday 1st November 2009

SCOTLAND 22 LEBANON 10

SCOTLAND: 1 Jamie Benn (Castleford Panthers); 2 Jon Steel (Featherstone Rovers); 3 Kevin Henderson (Wakefield Trinity Wildcats); 4 Mick Nanyn (Leigh Centurions); 5 James Nixon (Barrow Raiders); 6 Brendon Lindsay (Sheffield Eagles); 7 Gareth Moore (York City Knights); 8 Mitchell Stringer (Sheffield Eagles); 9 Andrew Henderson (Gateshead Thunder) (C); 10 Neil Lowe (Hunslet Hawks); 12 Richard Fletcher (Widnes Vikings); 11 Alex Szostak (Sheffield Eagles); 13 Lee Paterson (Widnes Vikings). Subs (all used): 12 John Duffy (Widnes Vikings); 21 Iain Morrison (Widnes Vikings); 14 Paddy Coupar (Workington Town); 15 John Cox (Edinburgh Eagles).
Tries: Lindsay (29), Nixon (36), K Henderson (57); **Goals:** Nanyn 5/5.
Sin bin: Cox (24) - interference; Morrison (25) - interference, (66) - fighting.
LEBANON: 1 Adnan Saleh (Bankstown City); 2 Josh Mansour (South Sydney Rabbitohs); 3 Daniel Chiha (Windsor Wolves); 4 Reece Robinson (North Sydney Bears); 5 Travis Robinson (Chester Hill); 6 Liam Ayoub (Bulldogs); 7 George Ndaira (Newcastle Knights) (C); 8 Khaled Deeb (Newtown Jets); 9 Jamie Clark (Bulldogs); 10 John Koborsi (Wentworthville Magpies); 11 Ahmad Ellaz (Cronulla Sharks); 12 Steve Azzi (Sydney Roosters); 13 Chris Salem (Bankstown City). Subs (all used): 14 Allen Soultan (Wests Magpies); 15 Nick Kassis (Chester Hill); 16 Robin Hachache (LAU Immortals); 17 Wael Harb (Wolves).
Tries: Mansour (7), Kassis (73); **Goals:** Ndaira 1/2.
Sin bin: T Robinson (66) - fighting.
On report: Ayoub (76) - alleged use of the elbow.
Rugby Leaguer & League Express Men of the Match:
Scotland: Mick Nanyn; *Lebanon:* Chris Salem.
Penalty count: 13-5; **Half time:** 14-4;
Referee: Leon Williamson (New Zealand);
Attendance: 752 (at Old Anniesland, Glasgow).

GROUP A	P	W	D	L	F	A	D	Pts
Scotland	2	2	0	0	126	10	116	4
Lebanon	2	1	0	1	96	22	74	2
Italy	2	0	0	2	0	190	-190	0

EUROPEAN CUP GROUP B

Sunday 18th October 2009

IRELAND 82 SERBIA 0

IRELAND: 1 Karl Fitzpatrick (Salford City Reds); 2 John Coleman (Dublin City Exiles); 3 Tyrone McCarthy (Warrington Wolves); 4 Liam Harrison (Barrow Raiders); 5 Tim Bergin (Laois Panthers); 6 Steve Gibbons (Carlow Crusaders); 7 Liam Finn (Dewsbury Rams); 8 Ryan Boyle (Castleford Tigers); 9 Bob Beswick (Halifax) (C); 10 Luke Ambler (Leeds Rhinos); 11 Sean Hesketh (York City Knights); 12 Dave Allen (Barrow Raiders); 13 Jason Golden (Harlequins). Subs (all used): 14 Wayne Kerr (Oldham); 15 Paddy Barcoe (Carlow Crusaders); 16 Brendan Guilfoyle (Treaty City Titans); 17 James Coyle (Barrow Raiders).
Tries: Coleman (2), Bergin (10, 42), Ambler (13, 55), Finn (15), Fitzpatrick (18, 52, 66, 70), Allen (22), Hesketh (26), Harrison (38), Guilfoyle (74).
Goals: Finn 8/8, Coleman 1/1, Hesketh 4/5.
SERBIA: 1 Ivan Šušnjara (RK Beogradski Univerzitet); 2 Vladan Kikanovic (RK Dorćol); 3 Milos Milanko (RK Dorćol); 4 Nenad Grbic (R13K Podbara); 5 Nikša Unkovic (RK Dorćol); 6 Dalibor Vukanovic (RK Dorćol) (C); 7 Milan Šušnjara (RK Dorćol); 8 Dejan Lukeni (RK Dorćol); 9 Zoran Pešic (R13K Podbara); 10 Mario Milosavljevic (R13K Podbara); 11 Vuk Tvrdišic (RK Dorćol); 12 Stevan Stevanovic (RK Dorćol); 13 Soni Radovanovic (Whitehaven). Subs (all used): 14 Ivan Djordjevic (RLK Crvena Zvezda); 15 Marko Žebeljan (R13K Podbara); 16 Austen Novakovic (Oldham); 17 Alexsandar Sik (R13K Niš).
Rugby Leaguer & League Express Men of the Match:
Ireland: Tim Bergin; *Serbia:* Milos Milanko.
Penalty count: 4-4; **Half-time:** 46-0; **Referee:** Leon Williamson (New Zealand); **Attendance:** 250 *(at Tullamore RUFC).*

Sunday 25th October 2009

SERBIA 8 WALES 88

SERBIA: 1 Ivan Šušnjara (RK Beogradski Univerzitet); 2 Stevan Stevanovic (RK Dorćol); 3 Milan Radojevic (South Sunnybank); 4 Nenad Grbic (R13K Podbara); 5 Nikša Unkovic (RK Dorćol); 6 Filip Brkic (RK Dorćol); 7 Milan Šušnjara (RK Dorćol); 8 Soni Radovanovic (Whitehaven); 9 Zoran Pešic (R13K Podbara); 10 Mario Milosavljevic (R13K Podbara); 11 Vuk Tvrdišic (RK Dorćol); 12 Ivan Djordjevic (RLK Crvena Zvezda); 13 Austen Novakovic (Oldham). Subs (all used): 14 Igor Kesegi (RK Dorćol); 15 Dejan Lukeni (RK Dorćol); 16 Marko Žebeljan (R13K Podbara); 17 Vladan Kikanovic (RK Dorćol).

Tries: Novakovic (10); **Goals:** Brkic 2/2.
WALES: 1 Elliot Kear (Celtic Crusaders); 2 Rhys Williams (Warrington Wolves); 3 Matt Thomas (London Skolars); 4 Christiaan Roets (Bridgend Blue Bulls); 5 Ashley Bateman (Celtic Crusaders); 6 Ian Webster (Central Comets); 7 Ian Watson (Leigh Centurions); 8 Jordan James (Celtic Crusaders) (C); 9 Neil Budworth (Celtic Crusaders); 10 Gil Dudson (Celtic Crusaders); 11 Ben Flower (Celtic Crusaders); 12 Ross Divorty (Featherstone Rovers); 13 Geraint Davies (Celtic Crusaders). Subs (all used): 14 Lee Williams (Celtic Crusaders); 15 Chris Beasley (Celtic Crusaders); 16 Matt Barron (Gateshead Thunder); 17 Lewis Mills (Celtic Crusaders).
Tries: Kear (3), Roets (6, 54, 65), James (10, 19), Thomas (28), Divorty (31, 57), R Williams (34, 62), L Williams (59), Bateman (67), Webster (78); **Goals:** Webster 14/15.
Rugby Leaguer & League Express Men of the Match:
Serbia: Igor Kesegi; *Wales:* Christiaan Roets.
Penalty count: 5-4; **Half-time:** 8-40; **Referee:** Kevin Hale (Australia); **Attendance:** 437 *(at Fortress Stadium, Smederevo).*

Sunday 1st November 2009

WALES 42 IRELAND 12

WALES: 1 Elliot Kear (Celtic Crusaders); 2 Rhys Williams (Warrington Wolves); 3 Matt Thomas (London Skolars); 4 Christiaan Roets (Bridgend Blue Bulls); 5 Ashley Bateman (Celtic Crusaders); 6 Lloyd White (Celtic Crusaders); 7 Ian Watson (Leigh Centurions); 8 Jordan James (Celtic Crusaders) (C); 9 Neil Budworth (Celtic Crusaders); 10 Gil Dudson (Celtic Crusaders); 11 Chris Beasley (Celtic Crusaders); 12 Geraint Davies (Celtic Crusaders); 13 Ian Webster (Central Comets). Subs (all used): 14 Lee Williams (Celtic Crusaders); 15 Ross Divorty (Featherstone Rovers); 16 Matt Barron (Gateshead Thunder); 17 Lewis Mills (Celtic Crusaders).
Tries: Webster (31), L Williams (38), R Williams (48), Bateman (53), Davies (56), James (61), Kear (64), Dudson (72); **Goals:** White 5/8.
IRELAND: 1 Karl Fitzpatrick (Salford City Reds); 2 Tim Bergin (Laois Panthers); 3 Marcus St Hilaire (Oldham); 4 James Haley (Halifax); 5 Pat Richards (Wigan Warriors); 6 James Coyle (Barrow Raiders); 7 Liam Finn (Dewsbury Rams); 8 Ryan Boyle (Castleford Tigers); 9 Bob Beswick (Halifax) (C); 10 Luke Ambler (Leeds Rhinos); 11 Sean Hesketh (York City Knights); 12 Dave Allen (Barrow Raiders); 13 Tyrone McCarthy (Warrington Wolves). Subs (all used): 14 Wayne Kerr (Oldham); 15 Paddy Barcoe (Carlow Crusaders); 16 Michael Haley (Sheffield Eagles); 17 Steve Gibbons (Carlow Crusaders).
Tries: St Hilaire (8), Finn (19); **Goals:** Richards 2/2.
Rugby Leaguer & League Express Men of the Match:
Wales: Jordan James; *Ireland:* Pat Richards.
Penalty count: 7-7; **Half-time:** 12-12;
Referee: Thierry Alibert (France);
Attendance: 2,143 *(at Sardis Road, Pontypridd).*

			GROUP B				
	P	W	D	L	F	A	D	Pts
Wales	2	2	0	0	130	20	110	4
Ireland	2	1	0	1	94	42	52	2
Serbia	2	0	0	2	8	170	-162	0

PACIFIC CUP

Papua New Guinea qualified for the 2010 Four Nations tournament by defeating the Cook Islands 42-14 in the Pacific Cup Final in Port Moresby. The Kumuls enjoyed a comfortable 44-14 win over Tonga in the first round of the tournament, and were expected to face a tough challenge from a young Cooks side which had knocked out Samoa and Fiji over the previous fortnight.

The Kumuls' victory was expected to give a push to the PNG government's efforts to persuade the Australians to admit a team into the NRL competition within the next five years.

Hat-trick hero David Mead was dazzling in attack for the Kumuls against surprise package Cook Islands, coached by former St Helens prop David Fairleigh. Mead had changed his name from Moore since his debut in the 2008 World Cup. Sheffield Eagles centre Menzie Yere was in

Papua New Guinea's David Mead on the charge during the Kumuls' Pacific Cup Final win

robust form, and his try ten minutes into the second half gave the hosts an unassailable 26-10 lead and killed off any chance of a Cook Islands fightback.

"There are a lot of young players in our side and we've certainly got a great balance between them and our older guys," said Kumuls coach Adrian Lam. "I don't think it has really sunk in yet that we're in the Four Nations, but we're excited about it, and we'll get our heads around it soon enough."

In the play-off game between the two semi-finalists, Fiji beat Tonga 26-16.

Other Internationals

PACIFIC CUP FINAL

Sunday 1st November 2009

PAPUA NEW GUINEA 42 COOK ISLANDS 14

PAPUA NEW GUINEA: 1 David Mead (Gold Coast Titans); 2 Richard Kambo (Wentworthville Magpies); 3 Menzie Yere (Sheffield Eagles); 4 Anton Kui (Mendi Muruks); 5 John Wilshere (Salford City Reds) (C); 6 Dion Aiye (Island Gurias); 7 Keith Peters (Penrith Panthers); 8 Rodney Pora (Island Gurias); 9 Jay Aston (Northern Pride); 10 James Nightingale (Redcliffe Dolphins); 11 Jason Chan (Celtic Crusaders); 12 Siegfried Gande (Goroka Lahanis); 13 Glen Nami (Goroka Lahanis). Subs (all used): 14 Charlie Wabo (Hunslet Hawks); 15 Tu'u Maori (Sydney Roosters); 16 Tyson Martin (North Queensland Cowboys); 20 George Moni (Island Gurias).
Tries: Kambo (10, 67), Mead (15, 40, 58), Kui (35), Yere (49, 73); **Goals:** Wilshere 5/8.
COOK ISLANDS: 1 Monikura Tikinau (Wests Tigers); 2 Lulia Lulia (Newcastle Knights); 3 Keith Lulia (Newcastle Knights); 4 Anthony Gelling (Sydney Roosters); 5 Dominique Peyroux (Gold Coast Titans); 6 Sema Mataora (Otahuhu Leopards); 7 John Ford (Newcastle Knights); 8 Tere Glassie (Newtown Jets) (C); 9 Daniel Fepuleai (Shellharbour Dragons); 10 Ben Vaeau (Brisbane Easts Tigers); 11 Fred Makimare (Melbourne Storm); 12 Zane Tetevano (Newcastle Knights); 13 Tinirau Arona (Penrith Panthers). Subs (all used): 17 Joseph Matapuku (Bulldogs); 18 Ben Taia (Wentworthville Magpies); 19 Brad Takairangi (South Sydney Rabbitohs); 20 Leon Panapa (Wynnum Manly Dolphins).
Tries: Fepuleai (25), L Lulia (29), Peyroux (77); **Goals:** Taia 1/2, Takairangi 0/1.
Rugby Leaguer & League Express Men of the Match:
Papua New Guinea: David Mead; *Cook Islands:* Tere Glassie.
Penalty count: 5-9; **Half time:** 20-10; **Referee:** Chris James (Australia);
Attendance: 10,151 *(at Lloyd Robson Oval, Port Moresby).*

PACIFIC CUP SEMI-FINALS

Saturday 24th October 2009

COOK ISLANDS 24 FIJI 22

COOK ISLANDS: 1 Monikura Tikinau (Wests Tigers); 2 Lulia Lulia (Newcastle Knights); 3 Keith Lulia (Newcastle Knights); 4 Anthony Gelling (Sydney Roosters); 5 Dominique Peyroux (Gold Coast Titans); 6 John Ford (Newcastle Knights); 7 Daniel Fepuleai (Shellharbour Dragons); 8 Tere Glassie (Newtown Jets) (C); 9 Sam Brunton (Sydney Roosters); 10 Ben Vaeau (Brisbane Easts Tigers); 11 Fred Makimare (Melbourne Storm); 12 Zane Tetevano (Newcastle Knights); 13 Sema Mataora (Otahuhu Leopards). Subs (all used): 14 John Viiga (Cronulla Sharks); 16 Tinirau Arona (Penrith Panthers); 17 Joseph Matapuku (Bulldogs); 18 Ben Taia (Wentworthville Magpies).
Tries: Arona (5), Fepuleai (17, 55), Peyroux (50, 79); **Goals:** Fepuleai 2/3, Ford 0/1.
FIJI: 1 Kevin Naiqama (Newcastle Knights); 2 Akuila Uate (Newcastle Knights); 3 Mike Ratu (Leeds Rhinos); 4 Jone Macilai (Coral Coast Cowboys); 5 Joe Ravueta (Coral Coast Cowboys); 6 Wes Naiqama (Newcastle Knights) (C); 7 Ryan Millard (Newtown Jets); 8 Osea Sadrau (Police Sharks); 9 Hamilton Hughes (Moore Park Brumbies); 10 Iowane Divavesi (Lautoka Crushers); 11 Sitiveni Ralogaivau (Nadera Panthers); 12 Lepani Waqa (Wentworthville Magpies); 13 Jone Wesele (Police Sharks). Subs (all used): 14 Alipate Noilea (Coral Coast Cowboys); 15 Donas Gock (Cabramatta); 16 Sevanaia Koroi (Nadera Panthers); 17 Puna Rasaubale (Southern Districts Rebels).
Tries: Uate (21, 69), Waqa (24), Ratu (76); **Goals:** W Naiqama 3/4.
Rugby Leaguer & League Express Men of the Match:
Cook Islands: Daniel Fepuleai; *Fiji:* Akuila Uate.
Penalty count: 3-3; **Half time:** 10-10; **Referee:** Phil Haines (Australia);
Attendance: 3,269 *(at Lloyd Robson Oval, Port Moresby).*

Sunday 25th October 2009

PAPUA NEW GUINEA 44 TONGA 14

PAPUA NEW GUINEA: 1 David Mead (Gold Coast Titans); 2 Richard Kambo (Wentworthville Magpies); 3 Menzie Yere (Sheffield Eagles); 4 Anton Kui (Mendi Muruks); 5 John Wilshere (Salford City Reds) (C); 6 Dion Aiye (Island Gurias); 7 Keith Peters (Penrith Panthers); 8 Rodney Pora (Island Gurias); 9 Jay Aston (Northern Pride); 10 James Nightingale (Redcliffe Dolphins); 11 Jason Chan (Celtic Crusaders); 12 Siegfried Gande (Goroka Lahanis); 15 Jessie Joe Parker (Mendi Muruks). Subs (all used): 14 Charlie Wabo (Hunslet Hawks); 16 Tu'u Maori (Sydney Roosters); 17 Tyson Martin (North Queensland Cowboys); 18 Glen Nami (Goroka Lahanis).
Tries: Yere (6, 64), Chan (22), Kui (31), Mead (39, 50), Parker (43), Wabo (68);
Goals: Wilshere 6/8.
TONGA: 1 Toshio Laiseni (Papakura Sea Eagles); 2 Etuate Uaisele (Parramatta Eels); 3 Siuatonga Likiliki (New Zealand Warriors); 19 Sione Tongia (Auckland Vulcans); 5 Sam Huihahau (Canberra Raiders); 6 Feleti Mateo (Parramatta Eels) (C); 7 Eddie Paea (Cronulla Sharks); 8 Richard Fa'aoso (Newcastle Knights); 9 Kimi Uasi (Parramatta Eels); 10 Sione Tovo (Newcastle Knights); 11 Ukuma Ta'ai (New Zealand Warriors); 12 Niumataevatu Nasio (Wentworthville Magpies); 13 Atelea Vea (Cronulla Sharks). Subs (all used): 14 Joel Taufa'ao (Adelaide RU); 15 Siosaia Vave (Gold Coast Titans); 20 Soane Palau (Manly Sea Eagles); 17 Pakisonasi Afu (Bulldogs).
Tries: Tongia (12, 70), Vea (79); **Goals:** Paea 1/3.
Rugby Leaguer & League Express Men of the Match:
Papua New Guinea: Menzie Yere; *Tonga:* Sione Tongia.
Penalty count: 5-3; **Half-time:** 20-4; **Referee:** Chris James (Australia);
Attendance: 9,813 *(at Lloyd Robson Oval, Port Moresby).*

PACIFIC CUP QUALIFIER

Saturday 17th October 2009

COOK ISLANDS 22 SAMOA 20

COOK ISLANDS: 1 Monikura Tikinau (Wests Tigers); 2 Keith Lulia (Newcastle Knights); 3 Brad Takairangi (South Sydney Rabbitohs); 4 Anthony Gelling (Sydney Roosters); 5 Dominique Peyroux (Gold Coast Titans); 6 John Ford (Newcastle Knights); 7 Daniel Fepuleai (Shellharbour Dragons); 8 Tere Glassie (Newtown Jets) (C); 9 Sam Brunton (Sydney Roosters); 10 Ben Vaeau (Brisbane Easts Tigers); 11 Fred Makimare (Melbourne Storm); 12 Leon Panapa (Wynnum Manly Dolphins); 13 Sema Mataora (Otahuhu Leopards). Subs (all used): 14 John Viiga (Cronulla Sharks); 15 Vinnie Ngaro (North Sydney Bears); 16 Tinirau Arona (Penrith Panthers); 17 Fabien Sautar (Brisbane Easts Tigers).
Tries: Makimare 2, Ngaro, Fepuleai; **Goals:** Takairangi 3/4.
SAMOA: 1 Peter Mata'utia (Newcastle Knights); 2 Patrick Ah Van (New Zealand Warriors); 3 Sam Tagatese (Gold Coast Titans); 4 Tangi Ropati (Sheffield Eagles); 5 Misi Taulapapa (Cronulla Sharks); 6 Kyle Stanley (St George-Illawarra Dragons); 7 Albert Talipeau (Brisbane Easts Tigers); 8 Kylie Leuluai (Leeds Rhinos) (C); 9 Terence Seuseu (Cronulla Sharks); 10 Mark Taufua (Newcastle Knights); 11 Harrison Hansen (Wigan Warriors); 12 Phil Leuluai (Salford City Reds); 13 Joseph Paulo (Penrith Panthers). Subs (all used): 14 Masada Iosefa (Penrith Panthers); 15 Jack Afamasaga (Cronulla Sharks); 16 Paul Chan Tung (Saints); 17 Tanielu Pasene (Lions).
Tries: Taulapapa, Ah Van 2, Hansen; **Goals:** Mata'utia 2/4.
Half-time: 16-10; **Attendance:** 4,261 *(at Barlow Park, Cairns).*

GILLETTE FOUR NATIONS - WARM-UP GAME

Wednesday 14th October 2009

NEW ZEALAND 40 TONGA 24

NEW ZEALAND: 1 Lance Hohaia (New Zealand Warriors); 2 Bryson Goodwin (Bulldogs); 3 Steve Matai (Manly Sea Eagles); 4 Junior Sau (Newcastle Knights); 5 Sam Perrett (Sydney Roosters); 6 Benji Marshall (Wests Tigers) (C); 7 Nathan Fien (St George-Illawarra Dragons); 8 Jeff Lima (Melbourne Storm); 9 Issac Luke (South Sydney Rabbitohs); 10 Frank-Paul Nuuausala (Sydney Roosters); 11 Bronson Harrison (Canberra Raiders); 12 Frank Pritchard (Penrith Panthers); 13 Greg Eastwood (Bulldogs). Subs (all used): 14 Thomas Leuluai (Wigan Warriors); 15 Jared Waerea-Hargreaves (Manly Sea Eagles); 16 Iosia Soliola (Sydney Roosters); 17 Adam Blair (Melbourne Storm).
Tries: Marshall 2, Goodwin 2, Sau, Perrett, Fien, Matai; **Goals:** Luke 3/5, Marshall 1/3.
TONGA: 1 Toshio Laiseni (Papakura Sea Eagles); 2 Sam Huihahau (Canberra Raiders); 3 Pita Maile (Melbourne Storm); 4 Siuatonga Likiliki (New Zealand Warriors); 5 Etuate Uaisele (Parramatta Eels); 6 Feleti Mateo (Parramatta Eels) (C); 7 Eddie Paea (Cronulla Sharks); 8 Epalahame Lauaki (Hull FC); 9 Kimi Uasi (Parramatta Eels); 10 Richard Fa'aoso (Newcastle Knights); 11 Ukuma Ta'ai (New Zealand Warriors); 12 Viliami Mataka (Wests Tigers); 13 Atelea Vea (Cronulla Sharks). Subs (all used): 14 Joel Taufa'ao (Adelaide RU); 15 Sione Tovo (Newcastle Knights); 16 Siosaia Vave (Gold Coast Titans); 17 Pakisonasi Afu (Bulldogs).
Tries: Uaisele 2, Mateo, Huihahau, Mataka; **Goals:** Paea 2/5.
Rugby Leaguer & League Express Men of the Match: *New Zealand:* Frank Pritchard; *Tonga:* Feleti Mateo.
Penalty count: 7-7; **Half-time:** 24-8; **Referee:** Leon Williamson (New Zealand);
Attendance: 7,600 *(at Rotorua International Stadium).*

REPRESENTATIVE GAME

Saturday 26th September 2009

PAPUA NEW GUINEA 18 AUSTRALIAN PRIME MINISTER'S XIII 42

PAPUA NEW GUINEA: 1 Jessie Joe Parker (Mendi Muruks); 2 Kevin Frank (Port Moresby Vipers); 3 Anton Kui (Mendi Muruks); 4 Larsen Marabe (Island Gurias); 5 Elijah Riyong (Port Moresby Vipers); 6 Dion Aiye (Island Gurias); 7 Keith Peters (Penrith Panthers); 8 Rodney Pora (Island Gurias) (C); 9 Benjamin John (Port Moresby Rangers); 10 Nickson Kolo (Port Moresby Rangers); 11 George Moni (Island Gurias); 12 Siegfried Gande (Goroka Lahanis); 13 Rodney Griffin (Northern Pride) (C). Subs (all used): 14 Simon Young (Port Moresby Rangers); 15 Glen Nami (Goroka Lahanis); 16 Tommy Butterfield (Redcliffe Dolphins); 17 Tyson Martin (North Queensland Cowboys); 18 Kerry Tapako (Enga Mioks).
Tries: Gande, Butterfield, Parker; **Goals:** Nami 3/3.
PRIME MINISTER'S XIII: 1 Josh Dugan (Canberra Raiders); 2 Michael Robertson (Manly Sea Eagles); 3 Michael Jennings (Penrith Panthers); 4 Joel Monaghan (Canberra Raiders); 5 David Williams (Manly Sea Eagles); 6 Terry Campese (Canberra Raiders); 7 Johnathan Thurston (North Queensland Cowboys) (C); 8 David Shillington (Canberra Raiders); 9 Robbie Farah (Wests Tigers); 10 Matthew Scott (North Queensland Cowboys); 11 Trent Waterhouse (Penrith Panthers); 12 Luke O'Donnell (North Queensland Cowboys); 13 Glenn Stewart (Manly Sea Eagles). Subs (all used): 14 Chris Heighington (Wests Tigers); 15 Nate Myles (Sydney Roosters); 16 Tom Learoyd-Lahrs (Canberra Raiders); 17 George Rose (Manly Sea Eagles); 18 Ben Jones (Sydney Roosters).
Tries: Jennings 3, Shillington, Rose, Stewart, Scott; **Goals:** Thurston 7/7.
Half-time: 12-18; **Referee:** Brett Suttor (Australia);
Attendance: 9,800 *(at Lloyd Robson Oval, Port Moresby).*

RLEF EUROPEAN BOWL

4 July 2009
Latvia 6 Ukraine 40
in Riga
6 July 2009
Ukraine 86 Estonia 0
in Riga
8 August 2009
Estonia 4 Latvia 74
at Hippodroon, Tallinn

Winners: Ukraine

EURO MED CHALLENGE

4 July 2009
Catalonia 6 Morocco 29
at Torroella de Montgri
25 July 2009
Belgium 28 Catalonia 22
at Wavre
15 August 2009
Morocco 46 Belgium 12
at Beziers

RLEF EUROPEAN SHIELD

4 July 2009
Czech Republic 30 Germany 4
at Lokomotiva Olomouc
11 July 2009
Italy 38 Czech Republic 8
at Stadio Communale Anticha Mura
18 July 2009
Germany 30 Italy 42
at Heurth Stadion

Winners: Italy

AMATEUR HOME NATIONS CHAMPIONSHIP

13 June 2009
Wales Dragonhearts 42
England Lionhearts 4
at Brewery Field, Bridgend
Scotland Bravehearts 22
Irish Wolfhounds 30
at Preston Lodge, Edinburgh
11 July 2009
Wales Dragonhearts 32
Scotland Bravehearts 12
at Nelson RFC
England Lionhearts 28
Irish Wolfhounds 12
at Broughton Park
8 August 2009
Irish Wolfhounds 28
Wales Dragonhearts 26
at Dublin
England Lionhearts 24
Scotland Bravehearts 40
at Staines

Winners: Wales

MEDITERRANEAN SHIELD

at Marconi Stadium, Sydney

10 October 2009
Semi-finals
Greece 42 Portugal 16; Italy 34 Malta 10

17 October 2009
Final
Greece 34 Italy 14
3rd place play-off
Malta 62 Portugal 16

WOMENS INTERNATIONAL

25 July 2009
France 0 England 36
at Stade Ernest Argeles, Blagnac

RLEF EUROPEAN CUP UNDER 16s

at Aga Ciganlija, Belgrade
18-22 August 2009

Scotland 46 Euro Celts 12; Wales 0 England 44; Euro Celts 34 Serbia 8; France 54 Wales 18; Serbia 16 Scotland 26; England 22 France 14
Winners: England

ATLANTIC CUP

14 November 2009
USA 37 Jamaica 22
at University of N Florida, Jacksonville

SEASON DOWN UNDER
Going down a Storm

What a great game is Rugby League! No wonder the pioneering administrator Horrie Miller coined the phrase 'The Greatest Game Of All' in the 1920s. Ten decades later League showed just how it could overcome adversities.

There were a number of off-pitch incidents involving top NRL players that would have killed off a lesser sport. Even before the start of the season there were unwanted headlines. At the season launch for the reigning Premiers Manly, World Cup forward Anthony Watmough allegedly assaulted one of the Sea Eagles sponsors after the pair had words over a derogatory comment Watmough is said to have made about sponsor's 21-year-old daughter. And on the way home from the function, Manly fullback Brett Stewart, the face of the NRL's television adverting campaign, was involved in an incident which led to police charging him with sexual assault. The whole campaign had to be immediately scrapped. Greg Bird came back from Super League for his long-awaited court appearance and was found guilty of 'glassing' his girlfriend. The Sydney Roosters had to weather a succession of bad headlines, including assaults on women, Nate Myles defecating in the public area of a hotel and coach Brad Fittler caught out trying to enter the wrong hotel room while semi-naked.

But the fans shrugged off the bad publicity; embraced some of the most exciting rugby in years and flocked to the matches in record numbers, especially as the season headed for a dramatic conclusion. One preliminary final matched the Bulldogs, who had soared from the wooden spoon in 2009 to within one game of the season finale, and Parramatta, who when seemingly down and out had strung together an unbelievable number of victories to scrape into the play-offs. The Bulldogs-Eels match drew a Premiership record attendance for any single game other than a grand final.

Sadly, for Eels fans the fairytale came to an end when Parramatta reached the grand final from eighth spot after putting together 10 victories in 11 games. There the Melbourne Storm exorcised the memory of previous year's grand final thrashing by Manly to win their second Premiership in three seasons.

But they first had to hold off a remarkable late recovery by the Eels. The match seemed safely in the Storm's hands when they led 22-6 with 11 minutes left on the clock. However, the Storm players were suddenly faced with a Parramatta revival. Two tries in as many minutes gave the underdogs a real chance of an upset. The Eels were one converted try from forcing the match into 'golden point' extra time. It was only a field goal by Test star Greg Inglis from 20 metres out in the 77th minute that sealed victory.

The match lived up to all the hype. It was obvious from the start about what the players felt. Adam Blair and Dallas Johnson ferociously crashed Parramatta cult hero Fuifui Moimoi to the ground in the opening tackle. The Storm threw everything at Parramatta and it was only four minutes into the encounter that the Eels' defence cracked. Parramatta's former stand-off Brett Finch slipped a wonderful pass to a rampaging Ryan Hoffman who danced out of a desperation tackle by Hindmarsh to score wide on the left. Cameron Smith's conversion had the Storm ahead 6-0.

Midway through the half, a controversial penalty by referee Tony Archer gave the

Storm some more hope. And after a great break by scrum-half Cooper Cronk, Blair loomed up and raced away for his side's second try. The Storm must have been feeling confident with the 10-nil at the interval and their 86 per cent completion rate of six tackles. Nevertheless, the Eels weren't dead and buried just yet.

Early in the second spell the enigmatic Parramatta substitute Feleti Mateo produced a piece of brilliance, waltzing past several Melbourne players to set up the chance for Eric Grothe to score off an overhead pass from Jarryd Hayne. But the good work was all in vain. Minutes later Cronk put in what seemed an innocuous bomb. The Parramatta players were mesmerized and held off. But big Greg Inglis never took his eyes off the ball, leaped up to take it and was across to score without a hand being laid on him. The next to score was Billy Slater who ran onto a pass by Blair and, as it turned out, ensured a victory.

With 11 minutes remaining, the injured Reddy gave his side a faint chance of recovering by leaping high to take a Jeff Robson bomb and touch down. Then Moimoi charged 20 metres to the line to score a remarkable try and the Eels were back within six points and eight minutes remaining.

But, as history now shows, it was not enough. The Parramatta players helped end the season on a truly positive note with half-a-dozen of them and chief executive Paul Osborne flying to Rwanda to help build houses for the widows and orphans of the country's bloody civil war.

Here's how the NRL sides shaped up in 2009:

MELBOURNE STORM (Premiers)

The way the Storm players were performing towards the end of the season hardly encouraged their fans. They were struggling. But they had the draw in their favour. In the final two matches of the home-and-away games they came up against a couple of out-of-form sides – beating the Roosters 38-4 and the New Zealand Warriors 30-0.

Normally teams want tough matches as the play-offs approach, but these two big wins put the Melbourne players in the right frame of mind. They carried on the big scoring, eliminating their 2008 nemesis Manly 40-12 and the Brisbane Broncos 40-10 to storm into the grand final, where the roll continued.

No wonder there were six Melbourne players in the Australian squad for the Four Nations – Billy Slater, Greg Inglis, Cooper Cronk, Brett White, Cameron Smith and Ryan Hoffman – and two others Adam Blair (as vice-captain) and Jeff Lima in the Kiwis' line-up.

Coach Craig Bellamy and assistant coaches Stephen Kearney (the Kiwis mentor) and Wigan-bound Michael Maguire must take a lot of the credit for the success. They lost four internationals in the off-season but it didn't faze them.

They replaced them with some young lads and a few from other clubs who couldn't hold down a spot in the senior ranks. All of them came through with flying colours.

PARRAMATTA EELS (2nd)

It was not be a fairytale finish for Parramatta. But their fans would have been proud of the way the Eels fought back from being rank outsiders midway through the season to reach the grand final. Indeed after Round 18 they were just three points off the bottom of the NRL Ladder. 'No hope,' said the bookmakers. Even the fans were angry. They were looking at another wasted season.

But former St Helens coach Daniel Anderson had instilled some backbone in the Eels. He had dug deep to uncover their fighting spirit. And buoyed by some incredibly inspirational displays from fullback Jarryd Hayne, the Parramatta players lifted and turned it all around.

Hayne won seven successive man of the match awards in the voting for the Dally M Medal (and eventually accepted the coveted honour). And his teammates surged on his coat-tails. Big Fuifui Moimoi was almost unstoppable. He'd been a cult hero before. Now he was showing he was more than just a walking headline. He was averaging 130 metres per match in bruising runs, second only to Hayne at Parramatta.

Then there was the evergreen Nathan Hindmarsh, Not just a tackling machine, but a spirited attacking player, too. By the end of the season, he had an official career tally of 8,855 tackles and 3,542 runs, both NRL records. And there were still a few good years left in that battered body of his.

Captain Nathan Cayless continued to be forever young, Luke Burt was up there with the NRL top pointscorers, 20-year-old Daniel Mortimer established himself as a Test stand-off of the future and former Kiwi Test man Joe Galuvao found a new lease of life under the tutelage of Anderson.

BULLDOGS (3rd)

Only one club – Western Suburbs Magpies in 1934 – has gone from last to first in the space of a season. And late in the season it looked as if the Bulldogs could become the second.

Under new 'no frills' coach Kevin Moore they approached 2009 with a new enthusiasm. They could well have taken out the Minor Premiership but for being penalised two competition points for briefly having 14 players on the pitch in the second round of the season and then losing the final match of the season proper to Wests Tigers, when the Canterbury players were red-hot favourites.

After accounting for Newcastle in the first weekend of the finals, they then took on Parramatta in their preliminary final, one of the most eagerly anticipated play-off encounters since the NRL came into existence. So much so that it was a virtual sell-out, with 74,549 cramming into the former Olympic stadium at Homebush. That the Bulldogs were beaten was no disgrace.

Much of the Bulldogs success can be attributed to some clever off-season recruiting, luring the likes of Brett Kimmorley, Ben Hannant, Greg Eastwood, Josh Morris, Bryson Goodwin and Michael Ennis to Belmore. All except Kimmorley and Ennis headed off to the Northern Hemisphere for the end-of-season Gillette Four Nations Tournament, Ennis played State of Origin and Kimmorley was the linchpin in the Bulldogs' success.

Morris snared 21 tries in 20 appearances, while Goodwin, son of former Australian Test player 'Lord Ted' Goodwin, was across the whitewash 20 times in his 24 matches.

But as the Bulldogs bowed out against Parramatta, they also rang down the curtain on the wonderful career of Hazem El Masri. Not only was he the Premiership's record-breaking pointscorer – with his 2,418 points beating Andrew Johns' 2,176 – but six times he topped the NRL season's tally, with a best of 342 in 2004. El Masri may have been disappointed at the defeat but he was too gracious to show it. 'It was a great way to finish,' he said. 'I have been blessed.'

BRISBANE BRONCOS (4th)

New coach Ivan Henjak was on a hiding to nothing when he took over from the only other mentor the Brisbane Broncos had known in their 21 seasons in the big league. But he seemed unfazed and with some good early-season form seemed to have overcome the 'After-Bennett Syndrome'.

Then came seven losses in eight games, including a record 56-0 humiliation by Canberra, and the Broncos' hopes of making the finals were in complete disarray. But Henjak and his lads dug deep to post five straight victories and finish in fifth spot on the final NRL Ladder. Two more wins (40-32 over the Gold Coast and 24-10 over the Minor Premiers St George Illawarra) had them one win away from the grand final. But the

Broncos failed to clear the final hurdle, outclassed 40-10 by the eventual grand final winners Melbourne and conceding hat-tricks to both Billy Slater and Greg Inglis.

Nevertheless there was plenty to please Henjak. The two young wingers Jharal Yow Yeh and Antonio Winterstein nailed their colours to the mast, scoring nine tries (in 13 appearances) and 14 (in 27) respectively. Utility Alex Glenn made his senior debut and must have gone close to travelling to England and France with the Kiwis. Darren Lockyer, Justin Hodges and Sam Thaiday were in the green and gold in England. Karmichael Hunt could well have been there, too, but for his bizarre signing to play Australian Rules football in 2010, with a spell in French rugby union in the meantime.

The monster prop Dave Taylor terrorised opponents when lurking in the centres – but he has been lost to the Rabbitohs for 2010. How he was never named in the Four Nations squad is anyone's guess.

ST GEORGE-ILLAWARRA DRAGONS (5th)

Whatever happened to the Dragons? Early in the season it looked as if former Brisbane Broncos coach Wayne Bennett had brought his magic wand south with him as St George Illawarra looked to have a mortgage on the major title. With just seven losses the Dragons took out the Minor Premiership, conceding fewer tries (56) and fewer points (329) than any other club.

Forwards Michael Weyman, Justin Poore and Ben Creagh led from the front. Stand-off Jamie Soward was spoken of as Test match material. And wingers Brett Morris and Wendell Sailor were scoring heaps of tries.

The Dragons went into the finals series full of confidence after thrashing the team-of-the-moment Parramatta 37-nil in the last round of the season proper (with Morris snaring a hat-trick of touchdowns to top the NRL tryscoring table).

Then came two straight losses, leaving the Dragons' season in tatters. Within the space of a week Parramatta reversed the result 25-12 before the Broncos came out on top in Brisbane 24-10.

Bennett was not disappointed: 'If we were just a rag-tag team with a bunch of blokes who only performed in patches, then we wouldn't have won the Minor Premiership...you have to perform for 26 weeks.'

Morris finished the season with 25 tries in 24 games and was eventually rewarded with a trip to the Gillette Four Nations Tournament after Brisbane's Israel Folau was ruled out through injury. Soward was the NRL's second highest pointscorer with 234 – 14 fewer than scored by the retiring pointscoring whiz Hazem El Masri. Fullback Darius Boyd was a member of the Australian side that won the Trans-Tasman Test against the Kiwis.

GOLD COAST TITANS (6th)

The Titans got under the radar to reach the play-offs for the first time in their short three-season history. And they achieved more than anyone thought possible with a third-place finish in the table, with only St George Illawarra and the Bulldogs ahead of them by just two points.

But then the Titans undid all their good work, losing 40-32 to the Brisbane Broncos at home and then beaten 27-2 by the Eels at Parramatta. A quick farewell to the season!

Ironically, much of their success can be attributed to the wonderful form of hooker Nathan Friend, unwanted at the end of last season as the Gold Coast vainly chased first Cameron Smith and then Robbie Farah. Friend became only the fourth player in NRL history to notch 1,000 tackles – 1050 to be exact. With egg on their face the Titans have now tied him down to a new contract.

The poor finish to the season by the Gold Coast probably cost scrum-half Scott Prince and second-rower Anthony Laffranchi places in Australia's Four Nations squad.

But the latter did play in the mid-season Trans-Tasman Test against the Kiwis, as did Prince's co-captain Luke Bailey.

Young wingers Kevin Gordon and David Mead (the Kumuls' World Cup representative) were impressive, scoring 13 and eight tries respectively.

MANLY SEA EAGLES (7th)

So what happened to the side that thrashed Melbourne in the 2008 grand final and then beat Leeds Rhinos to win the World Club Challenge. Some critics had been hailing the Sea Eagles as the greatest club side in history.

Come again! They might have been soaring then. But they came down to earth with a thud at the side's season launch. Anthony Watmough allegedly assaulted a Manly sponsor. Then fullback Brett Stewart was charged with sexual assault of a 17-year-old girl in an incident that occurred on his way home.

From there the season disintegrated. The Sea Eagles lost six of their first eight matches and looked unlikely to make the play-offs – especially after Stewart, on his comeback from suspension over the pre-season incident, was lost for 19 weeks injured.

However Manly managed to find some late-season form to creep into the play-offs in fifth spot. In the first week of the finals they were humbled 40-12 by the Storm. And, when there were a couple of other upset results, the Sea Eagles found themselves out of the play-offs.

On the positive side, the Sea Eagles have a host of talented youngsters coming through the Toyota Cup (under-20s) ranks. And 19-year-old stand-off Kieran Foran has already graduated to the Kiwis Test squad after just nine senior appearances. Another talented rookie, Jared Waerea-Hargreaves, drafted into the Kiwi squad after only six games at senior level, has been lost to the Roosters.

NEWCASTLE KNIGHTS (8th)

The Knights made the play-offs for the first time in three seasons and beat several of the top sides. So one can only wonder what they could have done if they didn't have to face the mid-season upheaval of the projected departure of coach Brian Smith.

The side was travelling well when Smith dropped the bombshell – he had asked for a release from the final season of his contract to join the Sydney Roosters in 2010. That the Newcastle board agreed to let him go was no surprise – but critics wondered why, at first, they let him stay on in charge until the end of the year. After a few disastrous results the hierarchy saw the light and showed Smith the door, handing the coaching role to his popular assistant Rick Stone.

The Knights managed to scrape into the finals series, but once there they were hammered 26-12 by the Bulldogs, paying the price for playing Isaac De Gois and Zeb Taia even though they were injured. De Gois lasted just 33 seconds, forced off after the first tackle of the night, and Taia was of little use while he was on the pitch.

What they would have done during the year without captain Kurt Gidley is anyone's guess. He was a real motivator. Deservedly he took over from his former Newcastle teammate Danny Buderus as skipper of the NSW Origin side and was selected for both the Trans-Tasman Test and the Gillette Four Nations Tournament.

WESTS TIGERS (9th)

The Tigers beat five of the eight teams that made the play-offs during the season. But they lost five matches by two points or less, including four to finals participants, which cost them dearly. One point out of the top eight just wasn't good enough.

There is no doubt the fans would have loved to have had them in the final countdown, thanks to their razzle-dazzle style of rugby. Critics reckon their vital loss to Parramatta in the third-last round was one of the top half-dozen encounters in the past decade. A thrill a minute!

Injuries didn't help either, especially the ten weeks on the sideline for tough prop Keith Galloway. But for once the exciting Benji Marshall stayed on the pitch. He struggled early when coach Tim Sheens tried to convert him into a scrum-half. But late in the season back to stand-off, and with wonderful service from rookie No 7s Tim Moltzen and Robert Lui, Marshall inspired several victories. He matured into the captain of the Kiwis.

Blockbusting winger Taniela Tuiaki looked set to take the honours in the NRL tryscoring lists with 21 in 22 appearances before breaking a leg.

But perhaps the eye-opener was England Test forward Gareth Ellis, who took out the club's Player of the Year award in his first season in the NRL, averaging 28 tackles and 110 metres in runs per match.

Captain Robbie Farah made it into the Australian Four Nations squad, while Chris Heighington turned out for the Prime Minister's XIII against Papua New Guinea. And waiting in the wings are members of the under-20s side that was unlucky not to have won the Toyota Cup grand final.

SOUTH SYDNEY RABBITOHS (10th)

A team that offered so much finished the season on such a low that fisticuffs were exchanged by coach Jason Taylor and Huddersfield-bound David Fa'alogo at their end-of-year booze-up at an inner-Sydney hotel. Not a good look! This resulted in the sacking of Taylor and the immediate termination of Fa'alogo's contract, leaving him several thousands of dollars out of pocket.

Five straight losses mid-season proved Souths' undoing. So, too, did the hot-and-cold form of the enigmatic stand-off John Sutton, who at the start of the year was being touted as the man to orchestrate a NSW State of Origin revival but was found wanting when the going got tough.

Injuries to the experienced trio of Rhys Wesser, Craig Wing and Roy Asotasi didn't help the Rabbitohs' cause either. But veteran prop Luke Stuart showed some of the show ponies the true blue South Sydney spirit, playing all 24 matches and averaging 30 tackles and 115 metres in barnstorming runs.

Asotasi and Fa'alogo made the Kiwis Test side for the Trans-Tasman Test in May. And Wing and Michael Crocker played State of Origin.

The experienced John Lang will have the reins as coach in 2010 and will be buoyed by the arrival of England Test forward Sam Burgess from Bradford Bulls and the young forward 'discovery' of 2009, Dave Taylor from the Brisbane Broncos.

PENRITH PANTHERS (11th)

Near the end of 2008 the job of Penrith coach Matt Elliott was on the line – probably only the lack of money to pay out his contract saved the former Bradford Bulls mentor. This year the Panthers didn't fare much better, but it was through no fault of Elliott. Despite injuries to key players Petero Civoniceva and Luke Lewis (both who later earned selection in Australia's Four Nations squad), Penrith still managed to threaten for a place in the finals.

That they didn't make the eight means that they are the only NRL club who hasn't made it into the play-offs in the past five years.

Civoniceva broke a toe in Origin II and it took the rest of the season to heal properly. His loss was a body blow. He was an inspiration as captain, holding together a side that had so many talented, but young, players. Lewis also added experience. Even though he had not been in an Australian side since the 2003 Kangaroo tour, he was vital to Penrith's hopes, especially because of his utility value.

During the injury crisis, another former Test star who was to gain redemption and a Four-Nations berth, Trent Waterhouse, lifted personally to help guide the club's rookies. Sadly, it was not enough. They could have made the finals had they beaten Newcastle in the last round – but they collapsed in a heap and were beaten 35-nil.

However for a side that finished out of contention, the Panthers still had four players in the Australian Test squad for England and France – centre Michael Jennings was the fourth. Jennings sealed his spot with a hat-trick of tries for the Prime Minister's XIII against the Kumuls.

Another Panther, back-rower Frank Pritchard, was arguably New Zealand's best in the Test against Tonga in the lead-up to the Four Nations, despite not having played for more than a month.

NORTH QUEENSLAND COWBOYS (12th)

The return to Townsville of Neil Henry as coach of the Cowboys was tipped to be the catalyst for a revival of fortunes. But it wasn't to be.

The man who has carried their hopes in recent seasons, Test scrum-half Johnathan Thurston, tried hard – but there were not enough teammates with similar enthusiasm to keep the North Queensland hopes alive.

There were even rumblings of a major fallout between the two vital figures – Henry and Thurston. If true, it could account for some of the disappointing displays. You can't win games if the coach and the captain are at loggerheads.

The Cowboys lost a few crucial close games, but they never really threatened as Premiership contenders, even when winning five out of six encounters leading into the Origin series. A season-ending injury to playmaking hooker Aaron Payne in July didn't help. But his replacement Anthony Watts stepped up and negated much of the loss.

There was one positive aspect to the season. Despite their lowly finish, the Cowboys finished with a plus 85 points difference, the fifth best of all the NRL clubs.

Centre Willie Tonga won his way back onto the Origin arena after an absence of five years.

CANBERRA RAIDERS (13th)

One of these days the Raiders may learn how to perform consistently well away from home. They worry even the top sides at home but when they hit the road, they might as well not have made the journey.

Late-season wins over teams that made the play-offs – the Broncos, Dragons and Knights – showed Canberra's potential. Especially in the match against the Broncos! The Raiders inflicted a record 56-0 flogging on the Brisbane side. But incredibly the Brisbane players were able to regroup and beat Canberra 22-10 just five weeks later.

The real positive from the season was the emergence of a crop of exciting youngsters, who the previous season had won the Toyota Cup, especially the clever backs Josh Dugan, Daniel Vidot and Jarrod Croker (cousin of the Catalans' veteran Jason Croker).

Dugan showed how he was going to be a star when he won the Jack Gibson Medal as man of the match in the 2008 Toyota Cup grand final. And once in the senior ranks he did not disappoint, recording the most average metres in return kicks from open play (83 metres per match) as well as the most tackle-breaks per match (7). No wonder the Test selectors included him in the Prime Minister's XIII that took on the Papua New Guinea Kumuls in the end of season international in Port Moresby.

Canberra teammates Joel Monaghan, David Shillington and Tom Learoyd-Lahrs were also in that side, and prop Shillington's performance helped gain his selection in the Four Nations squad.

NEW ZEALAND WARRIORS (14th)

Many critics believe the Warriors' season ended before it began, with the drowning of exciting 20-year-old Sonny Fai. Not that he played a pivotal role in the Warriors' line-up. It was his popularity that was missed. The club even kept his locker intact, with his rugby gear inside and including him in the squad for the media guide. Perhaps the Warriors hierarchy overplayed its hand.

The Auckland club had a wretched season. Two key players, goalkicking stand-off Michael Witt and hooker/scrum half Nathan Fien were allowed to leave. The reasons were never quite explained, but later Fien was one of the first chosen to play for the Kiwis in the Gillette Four Nations Tournament.

Then there was the season-ending injury to Australian Test threequarter Brent Tate and many weeks lost through injury to his brother-in-law and inspirational captain Steve Price. Players like these are vital to any serious Premiership run.

In the absence of Price, loose forward Micheal Luck established his leadership credentials. And he topped the 1,000 tackles for the season, at a rate of 46 per appearance, almost twice as many as the next best Warrior, Sam Rapira (24.6).

Stacey Jones came out of retirement to a fanfare. He often played well but not enough times. However his tutelage of some of the younger players may bear fruit in years to come.

Perhaps the most impressive of these rookies was fullback/winger Kevin Locke, who ended the season in the Kiwi international squad.

CRONULLA SHARKS (15th)

It was only the Roosters' capitulation against the Cowboys in the former's final match of the season that saved Cronulla from the wooden spoon. There were scandals both on and off the pitch for the Sharks, including an alleged sexual harassment claim that led to the demise of chief executive Tony Zappia, a positive drugs test that resulted in a two-year ban for Reni Maitua and another embarrassment that saw Paul Gallen fined $10,000 and relieved of the Cronulla captaincy for a racial slur during a game. These only added to the injury problems that saw the Sharks savaged in what was supposed to be their comeback year.

But there were a few bright spots, not the least the consistently good form of prop Luke Douglas. Getting a break in the senior ranks when covering for injured teammates were a number of promising youngsters, including stand-off Blake Green, centre Matt Wright and utility back Blake Ferguson.

Before his season-ending injury Trent Barrett was recalled to the NSW Origin side after an absence of four years. Gallen also played Origin and in the Four Nations.

SYDNEY ROOSTERS (16th)

Sydney Roosters were handed their first wooden spoon since 1966. That was when they used to be known as Eastern Suburbs, played home games at the Sydney Sport Ground (the site of the current Sydney Football Stadium) and under British coach Bert Holcroft failed to win even one match. They did manage to win five in 2009 – the same number as Cronulla – but finished last on points-difference. The Roosters conceded an average of 28 points per match, while scoring only 16.

Plenty of dramas off the pitch didn't help. Neither did a rash of injuries, which saw no less than 32 different players appear in the senior side during the season. Coach Brad Fittler was eventually shown the door, replaced by Newcastle's Brian Smith. It was hardly a great start to his coaching career by Freddy.

If everyone had played with the heart of back-rower Craig Fitzgibbon it could very well have been a different finish for the Roosters. He won the Jack Gibson Medal as the club's Player of the Year for the fourth time and will be a welcome acquisition to the ranks of Hull after 285 senior appearances in 12 seasons of the Premiership.

NRL SCOREBOARD

FINAL NRL PREMIERSHIP TABLE

	P	W	L	D	B	F	A	Pts
St George-Illawarra Dragons	24	17	7	0	2	548	329	38
Bulldogs *	24	18	6	0	2	575	428	38
Gold Coast Titans	24	16	8	0	2	514	467	36
Melbourne Storm	24	14	9	1	2	505	348	33
Manly Sea Eagles	24	14	10	0	2	549	459	32
Brisbane Broncos	24	14	10	0	2	511	566	32
Newcastle Knights	24	13	11	0	2	508	491	30
Parramatta Eels	24	12	11	1	2	476	473	29
Wests Tigers	24	12	12	0	2	558	483	28
South Sydney Rabbitohs	24	11	12	1	2	566	549	27
Penrith Panthers	24	11	12	1	2	515	589	27
North Queensland Cowboys	24	11	13	0	2	558	474	26
Canberra Raiders	24	9	15	0	2	489	520	22
New Zealand Warriors	24	7	15	2	2	377	565	20
Cronulla Sharks	24	5	19	0	2	359	568	14
Sydney Roosters	24	5	19	0	2	382	681	14

* Two points deducted for 14 players on the pitch v Penrith

QUALIFYING FINALS

Friday 11th September 2009

MELBOURNE STORM 40 ....MANLY SEA EAGLES 12
Storm: Tries: Slater (3, 35, 44, 76), Neilsen (26), Smith (50),
Tolman (59); Goals: Smith 5/6, Turner 1/1
Sea Eagles: Tries: Matai (68), Foran (71); Goals: Orford 2/2
Half-time: 16-0; Referees: Shayne Hayne/Gavin Badger; Attendance: 21,155

Saturday 12th September 2009

GOLD COAST TITANS 32 ....BRISBANE BRONCOS 40
Titans: Tries: Campbell (6), Mead (24, 71), Gordon (48, 59), Meyers (53);
Goals: Prince 4/6
Broncos: Tries: McCulloch (12), Folau (15, 28, 62), Yow Yeh (32),
Lockyer (37), Taylor (75); Goals: Parker 6/8
Half-time: 10-28; Referees: Ben Cummins/Ashley Klein; Attendance: 27,227

BULLDOGS 26 ....NEWCASTLE KNIGHTS 12
Bulldogs: Tries: Morris (23), Patten (33, 38), Hannant (72);
Goals: El Masri 5/6
Knights: Tries: Sau (14), Dureau (51); Goals: Gidley 1/1, Dureau 1/1
Half-time: 18-6; Referees: Tony Archer/Jason Robinson; Attendance: 21,369

Sunday 13th September 2009

ST GEORGE-ILLAWARRA DRAGONS 12...........PARRAMATTA EELS 25
Dragons: Tries: Hunt (36), Morris (70); Goals: Soward 2/3
Eels: Tries: Burt (26), Mortimer (30), Grothe (61), Hayne (77);
Goals: Burt 4/4; Field goal: Burt (75)
Half-time: 8-12; Referees: Jared Maxwell/Matt Cecchin; Attendance: 18,174

SEMI-FINALS

Friday 18th September 2009

PARRAMATTA EELS 27 ....GOLD COAST TITANS 2
Eels: Tries: Mateo (20), Smith (34), Kingston (60), Wright (65);
Goals: Burt 5/5; Field goal: Hayne (40)
Titans: Goals: Prince 1/1
Half-time: 13-2; Referees: Shayne Hayne/Jared Maxwell; Attendance: 28,524

Saturday 19th September 2009

BRISBANE BRONCOS 24..........ST GEORGE-ILLAWARRA DRAGONS 10
Broncos: Tries: Hunt (14, 18), Yow Yeh (47), Setu (51); Goals: Parker 4/6
Dragons: Tries: Morris (22, 65); Goals: Soward 1/3
Half-time: 12-6; Referees: Tony Archer/Ben Cummins; Attendance: 50,225

PRELIMINARY FINALS

Friday 25th September 2009

BULLDOGS 12..........................PARRAMATTA EELS 22
Bulldogs: Tries: Goodwin (3), Morris (35); Goals: El Masri 2/3
Eels: Tries: Galuvao (25), Burt (50), Mannah (54), Mortimer (71);
Goals: Burt 3/4
Half-time: 12-6; Referees: Tony Archer/Ben Cummins; Attendance: 74,549

Saturday 26th September 2009

MELBOURNE STORM 40 ....BRISBANE BRONCOS 10
Storm: Tries: Chambers (3), Slater (19, 73), Johnson (24),
Inglis (38, 45, 69); Goals: Smith 6/7
Broncos: Tries: Glenn (58), Folau (80); Goals: Parker 1/2
Half-time: 22-0; Referees: Shayne Hayne/Jared Maxwell; Attendance: 27,687

GRAND FINAL

Sunday 4th October 2009

MELBOURNE STORM 23 PARRAMATTA EELS 16

STORM: 1 Billy Slater; 2 Steve Turner; 3 Will Chambers; 4 Greg Inglis; 5 Dane Nielsen; 6 Brett Finch; 7 Cooper Cronk; 8 Aiden Tolman; 9 Cameron Smith (C); 10 Brett White; 11 Adam Blair; 12 Ryan Hoffman; 13 Dallas Johnson. Subs (all used): 14 Ryan Hinchcliffe; 15 Jeff Lima; 16 Ryan Tandy; 17 Scott Anderson.
Tries: Hoffman (4), Blair (23), Inglis (48), Slater (55); **Goals:** Smith 3/4; **Field goal:** Inglis (77).
EELS: 1 Jarryd Hayne; 2 Luke Burt; 3 Kris Inu; 4 Joel Reddy; 5 Eric Grothe; 6 Daniel Mortimer; 7 Jeff Robson; 8 Nathan Cayless (C); 9 Matthew Keating; 10 Fuifui Moimoi; 11 Nathan Hindmarsh; 12 Ben Smith; 13 Todd Lowrie. Subs (all used): 14 Kevin Kingston; 15 Feleti Mateo; 16 Joe Galuvao; 17 Tim Mannah.
Tries: Grothe (44), Reddy (69), Moimoi (72); **Goals:** Burt 2/3.
Rugby Leaguer & League Express Men of the Match:
Storm: Cameron Smith; *Eels:* Fuifui Moimoi.
Clive Churchill Medal: Billy Slater (Melbourne Storm).
Half-time: 10-0; **Referees:** Tony Archer & Shayne Hayne;
Attendance: 82,538 *(at ANZ Stadium, Sydney).*

TOP POINTSCORERS

		T	G	FG	Pts
Hazem El Masri	Bulldogs	14	96	0	248
Jamie Soward	St George-Illawarra Dragons	12	90	6	234
Luke Burt	Parramatta Eels	15	77	3	217
Johnathan Thurston	North Queensland Cowboys	11	79	0	202
Scott Prince	Gold Coast Titans	7	81	0	182

TOP TRYSCORERS

Brett Morris	St George-Illawarra Dragons	25
Josh Morris	Bulldogs	22
Taniela Tuiaki	Wests Tigers	21
Bryson Goodwin	Bulldogs	20
Nathan Merritt	South Sydney Rabbitohs	19

OTHER GRAND FINALS

TOYOTA CUP (Under-20s)
Sunday 4th October 2009

MELBOURNE STORM 24 ....WESTS TIGERS 22
Storm: Tries: Duffie (20), Rogers (26), Widdop (36, 73), O'Neill (39);
Goals: Widdop 2/5
Tigers: Tries: Mullaney (12, 53), Curran (31), Lui (55); Goals: Mullaney 3/4
Half-time: 18-10; Referee: Gavin Reynolds. *(at ANZ Stadium, Sydney).*

NEW SOUTH WALES CUP
Sunday 4th October 2009

BANKSTOWN CITY BULLS 32 ....BALMAIN RYDE-EASTWOOD TIGERS 0
Bulls: Tries: Briggs (5), Barba (65, 70, 77), Williams (72); Goals: Crisp 6/7
Half-time: 6-0; Referee: Adam Gee. *(at ANZ Stadium, Sydney).*

QUEENSLAND CUP
Saturday 12th September 2009

NORTHERN PRIDE 18 ....SUNSHINE COAST SEA EAGLES 32
Pride: Tries: Jensen, Humble, Frizzo; Goals: Humble 3/3
Sea Eagles: Tries: Neumann 3, Hodkinson, Williams, Chapman, Walker;
Goals: Hodkinson 2/7
Half-time: 8-12; Referee: Clayton Sharpe.
Duncan Hall Medal (Man of the Match): Tony Williams (Sea Eagles).
Attendance: 3,200 *(at Stockland Park, Caloundra, Sunshine Coast).*

DALLY M AWARDS

Dally M Medal (Player of the Year): Jarryd Hayne (Parramatta Eels)
Provan Summons Medal (People's Choice):
Jamie Soward (St George-Illawarra Dragons)
Captain of the Year: Andrew Ryan (Bulldogs)
Coach of the Year: Kevin Moore (Bulldogs)
Rookie of the Year: Jamal Idris (Bulldogs)
Representative Player of the Year: Greg Inglis (Melbourne Storm)

Fullback: Jarryd Hayne (Parramatta Eels)
Winger: Taniela Tuiaki (Wests Tigers)
Centre: Josh Morris (Bulldogs)
Stand-off: Jamie Soward (St George-Illawarra Dragons)
Scrum half: Johnathan Thurston (North Queensland Cowboys)
Prop: Ben Hannant (Bulldogs)
Hooker: Michael Ennis (Bulldogs)
Second-rower: Anthony Watmough (Manly Sea Eagles)
Loose forward: David Stagg (Bulldogs)

Toyota Cup Player of the Year:
Beau Henry (St George-Illawarra Dragons)

Queensland rewrote the State of Origin record books in 2009 – becoming the first side to win four straight series in the three decades of the iconic clashes. Even the great Maroons teams of the Wally Lewis era and the NSW teams in the days of Laurie Daley could never make it four in a row. And though the Maroons were beaten in Origin III, the so-called 'dead rubber', they were already talking about extending the dynasty to an incredible five consecutive seasons.

ORIGIN I

The Queenslanders were red-hot favourites for the Origin opener at Melbourne's Etihad Stadium because of the inexperience at top level of so many of the Blues. As it turned out it was a controversial ruling by video referee Bill Harrigan that changed the whole momentum of the game.

Early in the clash Harrigan denied a try to winger Jarryd Hayne that had the Blues and their supporters fuming. It was only seven minutes into the action when dummy-half Robbie Farah sent the in-form Hayne on a long run down the left wing for what looked like being one of the great Origin tries of recent years. But after at least half-a-dozen replays Harrigan (assisted by Tim Mander) found Hayne had brushed the sideline.

After a penalty goal from in front by the Blues captain Kurt Gidley, the Hayne try could have extended the lead to eight. To rub salt into the wound, the Maroons went straight back on the attack. Hooker Cameron Smith put in a perfectly-weighted kick behind the NSW line. Storm teammate Billy Slater flew through and touched down millimetres inside the dead-ball line. This time the video referees awarded the try.

Darren Lockyer then switched the direction of the attack, threw a long pass and Greg Inglis took three would-be defenders with him across the stripe. Thurston booted the conversion from the sideline. He and Lockyer then combined to set up the third Queensland try in seven minutes. Quick hands across the backline from Lockyer saw the ball in the hands of Folau. As he was about to be flung into touch he short-kicked inside and Thurston grabbed a try for himself as Gidley and Luke Bailey looked on, as if shell-shocked. As the clock wound down to half-time, Hayne produced some more magic, flinging the ball back infield as he was hovering in the air over the sideline. And Ben Creagh backed up to score. The Blues went to the interval trailing by 18-6.

The second half started sensationally with Inglis making a 75-metre dash down the left flank, effortlessly standing up Gidley before posting his seventh try in eight Origin appearances.

Veteran utility Craig Wing came on for the Blues in the 55th minute and half a minute later he was over to score. Farah returned to the fray after a 12-minute rest on the bench and within 20 seconds he kicked from dummy half, re-gathered and sent Hayne in for a try.

Late in the game Gidley made a couple of uncharacteristic blunders – the second, a knock-on 20 metres out from the NSW line, which handed Queensland winger Darius Boyd a try with five seconds left on the clock for a final score of 28-18.

ORIGIN II

The anger of the NSW supporters over the Harrigan ruling in Origin I ensured what was virtually a full house at the Olympic stadium in Homebush for the vital second clash. The home fans who made up the majority of the 80,459 who packed the arena were hoping for revenge. But the incredible Queensland spirit came to the fore in the 24-14 victory that wrapped up the series.

Many of the Maroons had been laid low with a virus in the days leading up to Origin II. And they battled on after suffering an horrendous run of setbacks – Greg Inglis laid out with what was at first believed to be a broken jaw and other problems involving forwards Ben

Hannant (knee damage), Nate Myles (severe diarrhoea), Dallas Johnson (stomach cramps) and Ashley Harrison (torn rib cartilage).

The Maroons were given a penalty but rejected the chance of two points and ran the ball. They were rewarded when Inglis powered across the stripe with less than five minutes on the clock.

David 'The Wolfman' Williams was feeling the pinch as the Queenslanders defenders made him a target. Twice he was smashed in a tackle and lost the ball. On the second occasion his mistake cost New South Wales dearly. Israel Folau pounced and sped through to snare the Maroons' second try.

A few moments later Trent Barrett was placed on report for a high tackle on Inglis, who was helped off the pitch seeing stars. After the match Barrett pleaded guilty to making a reckless high tackle and was suspended for two matches.

The New South Welshmen looked determined to throw away the game. A long Farah pass went to ground 10 metres from the Blues' line and a delighted Lockyer swooped to score. The visitors were ahead 18-nil.

One NSW player who refused to capitulate was Jarryd Hayne. And he made a sensational intercept of a looping pass before running 92 metres to score. With two minutes of the half remaining, Hayne took centre-stage again. He jumped into dummy-half a metre or so out from the Queensland line, and spun away from potential defenders to touch down – and the Blues had reduced the deficit to eight.

It was nip and tuck in the second half. Sixty minutes into the encounter Hayne, looking for his hat-trick, was grassed a metre from the Maroons' line. It didn't matter. Some 40 seconds later, Williams was across the stripe to score. The wolf howls came from the NSW fans.

Then Joel Monaghan was held up over the line. The Queenslanders were certainly feeling the effects of the virus that swept through their camp. But they dug deep, clinging to their four-point lead until a Cameron Smith try off a Johnathan Thurston bomb with just two minutes to go ensured the Maroons of their place in history.

ORIGIN III

There was a full house at Lang Park despite the fact that Queensland had already won the 2009 Origin series. The 52,439 fans who turned up suspected the Blues would fight to regain some personal pride. And fight they did – with a passion. They had some scores to settle.

The first of a couple of melees erupted when NSW prop Brett White started throwing punches at Queensland stalwart Steve Price. Most were no more than air swings but one connected and as Price went down unconscious, players from both sides ran in to join in. Penrith's Trent Waterhouse tackled Price as he was going down. There was no hesitation by the referees. Waterhouse became the first NSW player to be sent off in the history of Origin encounters. Moments later the mayhem erupted again. This time Ben Creagh (NSW) and Sam Thaiday (Queensland) were sent to the sin bin for joining in.

It was excitement from start to finish. Twelve minutes into the encounter a wonderful short kick along the ground set up the first try for Queensland. It was a nightmare for David 'The Wolfman' Williams. He slipped over trying to punch the ball back to Hayne. But the ball went astray and Queensland loose forward Dallas Johnson charged through. Yet another controversial decision by the video referees – this time Paul Simpkins and Sean Hampstead – gave Johnson the benefit of the doubt even though it looked as if he may have fumbled when falling on the ball.

A few minutes later, a rare knock-on of a bomb by Greg Inglis gave the Blues good pitch position. They took full advantage and Creagh was across the stripe for a try.

Queensland missed another try – but not before one of the most spectacular personal displays in Origin history. Karmichael Hunt put in a kick that bounced up behind the tryline. Justin Hodges soared, took the ball as he was upside down and seemed to score one-handed in the corner. Sadly for the Queenslanders, the video showed the ball had also been forced on the touch-in-goal line.

From the restart the play surged to the other end of the pitch and New South Wales came away with an extremely-rare eight-point try – the first in Origin history. There was confusion behind the line, with Williams being given the benefit of the doubt for the try. But Johnathan Thurston was placed on report for kicking in the tackle. After the game he accepted an early guilty plea to enable him to escape a suspension. Once Kurt Gidley had converted, he was given a second kick in front of the posts. Success sent the visitors to the interval with a 14-6 lead.

The Queenslanders struck quickly after play restarted in the second half. After just 62 seconds Hodges was rewarded with a try, thanks to his brute strength in twisting out of a tackle. The Blues replied immediately. After Willie Tonga lost the ball, Josh Morris touched down for his first Origin try. Gidley's conversion extended the lead to 10 points.

Just when the Queenslanders looked out of it, there was some brilliance from Inglis to turn the momentum. He strode down the left flank, sent Williams sprawling with a solid fend and then kicked infield. Billy Slater flew through at top speed and forced the ball one handed for the four-pointer.

With 14 minutes remaining on the clock Anthony Watmough made a long run and Creagh followed it up by bursting past two or three Maroons to score his second try. Trysaving tackles by Brett Kimmorley and Gidley on Inglis and Darius Boyd respectively, in the dying minutes, stopped any miracle resurgence by the Maroons, who finally succumbed 28-16.

ORIGIN I

Wednesday 3rd June 2009

QUEENSLAND 28 NEW SOUTH WALES 18

QUEENSLAND: 1 Billy Slater (Melbourne Storm); 2 Darius Boyd (St George-Illawarra Dragons); 3 Greg Inglis (Melbourne Storm); 4 Justin Hodges (Brisbane Broncos); 5 Israel Folau (Brisbane Broncos); 6 Darren Lockyer (Brisbane Broncos) (C); 7 Johnathan Thurston (North Queensland Cowboys); 8 Steve Price (New Zealand Warriors); 9 Cameron Smith (Melbourne Storm); 10 Petero Civoniceva (Penrith Panthers); 11 Sam Thaiday (Brisbane Broncos); 12 Ashley Harrison (Gold Coast Titans); 13 Dallas Johnson (Melbourne Storm). Subs (all used): 14 Karmichael Hunt (Brisbane Broncos); 15 Ben Hannant (Bulldogs); 16 Nate Myles (Sydney Roosters); 17 Michael Crocker (South Sydney Rabbitohs).
Tries: Slater (10), Inglis (14, 42), Thurston (17), Boyd (80); **Goals:** Thurston 4/5.
NEW SOUTH WALES: 1 Kurt Gidley (Newcastle Knights) (C); 2 Jarryd Hayne (Parramatta Eels); 3 Michael Jennings (Penrith Panthers); 4 Jamie Lyon (Manly Sea Eagles); 5 James McManus (Newcastle Knights); 6 Terry Campese (Canberra Raiders); 7 Peter Wallace (Brisbane Broncos); 8 Brent Kite (Manly Sea Eagles); 9 Robbie Farah (Wests Tigers); 10 Luke Bailey (Gold Coast Titans); 11 Luke O'Donnell (North Queensland Cowboys); 12 Ben Creagh (St George-Illawarra Dragons); 13 Anthony Laffranchi (Gold Coast Titans). Subs (all used): 14 Craig Wing (South Sydney Rabbitohs); 15 Justin Poore (St George-Illawarra Dragons); 16 Michael Weyman (St George-Illawarra Dragons); 17 Luke Lewis (Penrith Panthers).
Tries: Creagh (32), Wing (55), Hayne (67); **Goals:** Gidley 3/4.
Rugby Leaguer & League Express Men of the Match:
Maroons: Billy Slater; *Blues:* Jarryd Hayne.
Half-time: 18-6; **Referees:** Tony Archer & Shayne Hayne;
Attendance: 50,967 *(at Etihad Stadium, Melbourne).*

ORIGIN II

Wednesday 24th June 2009

NEW SOUTH WALES 14 QUEENSLAND 24

NEW SOUTH WALES: 1 Kurt Gidley (Newcastle Knights) (C); 2 Jarryd Hayne (Parramatta Eels); 3 Joel Monaghan (Canberra Raiders); 4 Jamie Lyon (Manly Sea Eagles); 5 David Williams (Manly Sea Eagles); 6 Trent Barrett (Cronulla Sharks); 7 Peter Wallace (Brisbane Broncos); 8 Brent Kite (Manly Sea Eagles); 9 Robbie Farah (Wests Tigers); 10 Michael Weyman (St George-Illawarra Dragons); 11 Ben Creagh (St George-Illawarra Dragons); 12 Luke O'Donnell (North Queensland Cowboys); 13 Paul Gallen (Cronulla Sharks). Subs: 15 Justin Poore (St George-Illawarra Dragons); 16 Glenn Stewart (Manly Sea Eagles); 17 Anthony Watmough (Manly Sea Eagles); 19 Josh Morris (Bulldogs).
Tries: Hayne (27, 38), Williams (61); **Goals:** Gidley 1/3.
On report: Barrett (22) – alleged high tackle on Inglis.
QUEENSLAND: 1 Billy Slater (Melbourne Storm); 2 Darius Boyd (St George-Illawarra Dragons); 3 Greg Inglis (Melbourne Storm); 4 Willie Tonga (North Queensland Cowboys); 5 Israel Folau (Brisbane Broncos); 6 Darren Lockyer (Brisbane Broncos) (C); 7 Johnathan Thurston (North Queensland Cowboys); 8 Steve Price (New Zealand Warriors); 9 Cameron Smith (Melbourne Storm); 10 Petero Civoniceva (Penrith Panthers); 11 Ashley Harrison (Gold Coast Titans); 12 Sam Thaiday (Brisbane Broncos); 13 Dallas Johnson (Melbourne Storm). Subs (all used): 14 Karmichael Hunt (Brisbane Broncos); 15 Ben Hannant (Bulldogs); 16 Nate Myles (Sydney Roosters); 17 Michael Crocker (South Sydney Rabbitohs).
Tries: Inglis (5), Folau (16), Lockyer (23), Smith (78); **Goals:** Thurston 4/4.
Rugby Leaguer & League Express Men of the Match:
Blues: Jarryd Hayne; *Maroons:* Sam Thaiday.
Half-time: 10-18; **Referees:** Tony Archer & Shayne Hayne;
Attendance: 80,459 *(at ANZ Stadium, Sydney).*

ORIGIN III

Wednesday 15th July 2009

QUEENSLAND 16 NEW SOUTH WALES 28

QUEENSLAND: 1 Billy Slater (Melbourne Storm); 2 Darius Boyd (St George-Illawarra Dragons); 3 Greg Inglis (Melbourne Storm); 4 Justin Hodges (Brisbane Broncos); 5 Willie Tonga (North Queensland Cowboys); 6 Darren Lockyer (Brisbane Broncos) (C); 7 Johnathan Thurston (North Queensland Cowboys); 10 Steve Price (New Zealand Warriors); 9 Cameron Smith (Melbourne Storm); 16 David Shillington (Canberra Raiders); 11 Ashley Harrison (Gold Coast Titans); 17 Michael Crocker (South Sydney Rabbitohs); 13 Dallas Johnson (Melbourne Storm). Subs (all used): 8 Matthew Scott (North Queensland Cowboys); 12 Sam Thaiday (Brisbane Broncos); 14 Karmichael Hunt (Brisbane Broncos); 15 Neville Costigan (St George-Illawarra Dragons).
Tries: Johnson (12), Hodges (42), Slater (52); **Goals:** Thurston 2/3.
Sin bin: Thaiday (79) – fighting.
On report: Thurston (34) – alleged kicking.
NEW SOUTH WALES: 1 Kurt Gidley (Newcastle Knights) (C); 2 Jarryd Hayne (Parramatta Eels); 3 Josh Morris (Bulldogs); 4 Michael Jennings (Penrith Panthers); 5 David Williams (Manly Sea Eagles); 6 Trent Barrett (Cronulla Sharks); 7 Brett Kimmorley (Bulldogs); 8 Josh Perry (Manly Sea Eagles); 9 Michael Ennis (Bulldogs); 10 Justin Poore (St George-Illawarra Dragons); 11 Trent Waterhouse (Penrith Panthers); 12 Ben Creagh (St George-Illawarra Dragons); 13 Anthony Watmough (Manly Sea Eagles). Subs (all used): 14 Craig Wing (South Sydney Rabbitohs); 15 Tom Learoyd-Lahrs (Canberra Raiders); 16 Glenn Stewart (Manly Sea Eagles); 17 Brett White (Melbourne Storm).
Tries: Creagh (18, 66), Williams (33), Morris (45); **Goals:** Ennis 3/3, Gidley 3/3.
Dismissal: Waterhouse (79) – fighting.
Sin bin: Creagh (79) – fighting.
Rugby Leaguer & League Express Men of the Match:
Maroons: Greg Inglis; *Blues:* Anthony Watmough.
Half-time: 6-14; **Referees:** Tony Archer & Shayne Hayne;
Attendance: 52,439 *(at Suncorp Stadium, Brisbane).*

Wally Lewis Medal (Man of the Series): Greg Inglis (Queensland).

2009 REPRESENTATIVE SEASON

Gillette Four Nations ● Gillette Fusion Internationals ● European Cup ● Pacific Cup ● State Of Origin ● Trans-Tasman Test

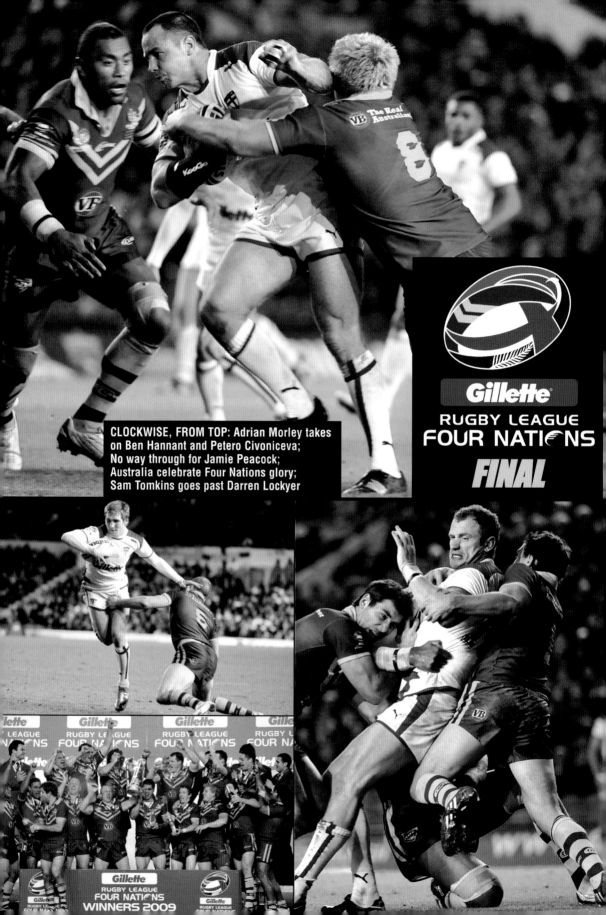

Gillette®

RUGBY LEAGUE FOUR NATIONS FINAL

CLOCKWISE, FROM TOP: Adrian Morley takes on Ben Hannant and Petero Civoniceva; No way through for Jamie Peacock; Australia celebrate Four Nations glory; Sam Tomkins goes past Darren Lockyer

Gillette
RUGBY LEAGUE
FOUR NATIONS
WINNERS 2009

RUGBY LEAGUE
OUR NATIONS

Kyle Eastmond scores England's opening try during their win over New Zealand

ABOVE: Eorl Crabtree feels the force of the New Zealand defence

RIGHT: Josh Morris beats the despairing dive of Clint Greenshields to score

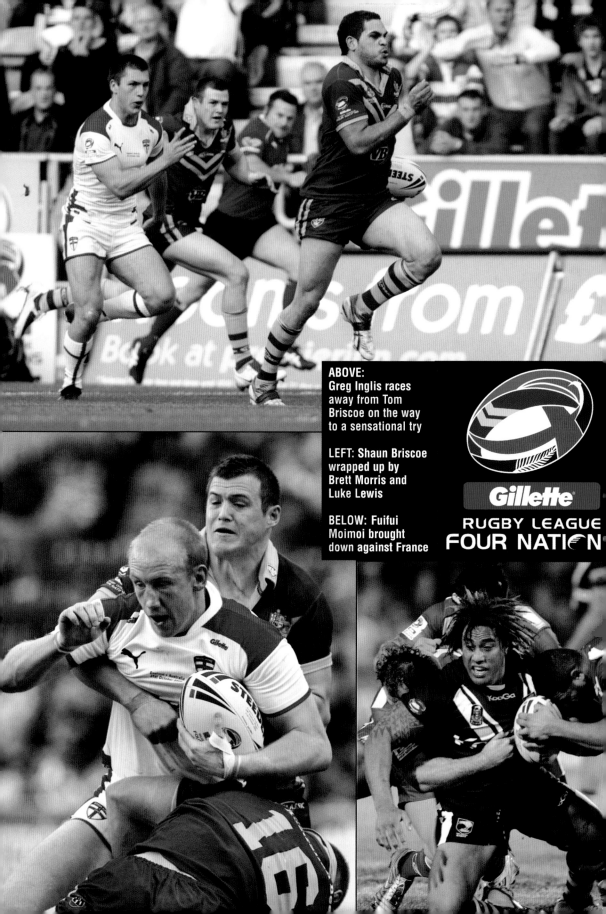

ABOVE: Greg Inglis races away from Tom Briscoe on the way to a sensational try

LEFT: Shaun Briscoe wrapped up by Brett Morris and Luke Lewis

BELOW: Fuifui Moimoi brought down against France

Gillette

RUGBY LEAGUE
FOUR NATION

RIGHT: Billy Slater collared by Frank Pritchard

BELOW: Frank-Paul Nuuausala celebrates scoring with Nathan Flen and Adam Blair

Ryan Hall heads for the tryline as Clint Greenshields gives chase

LEFT: Wales' Elliot Kear grounded by England's Sam Burgess

RIGHT: England's Ben Westwood in action against France

Captain Jordan James leads the celebrations as Wales win the European Cup

RIGHT: Ireland's Pat Richards has nowhere to go against Wales

ABOVE: Wales' Chris Beasley halted by the Scotland defence during the European Cup Final

RIGHT: Brett McDermott in action during Ireland's 3rd/4th place play-off defeat by Lebanon

BELOW RIGHT: Dean Vicelich scores against Serbia during the Italians' 5th/6th place play-off win

LEFT: Lebanon's John Korbosi dragged down against Scotland

RUGBY LEAGUE
PACIFIC CUP

ABOVE: David Mead bursts past Monikura Tikinau during the Pacific Cup Final

RIGHT: Papua New Guinea celebrate their Pacific Cup Final win over Cook Islands

ABOVE: Jessie Joe Parker mobbed after scoring against Tonga

A celebratory haka is underway as Cook Islands celebrate defeating Fiji

BELOW: Fiji on the attack

LEFT: Cook Islands stunned Samoa during the Pacific Cup Qualifier

STATE OF ORIGIN

RIGHT: Darren Lockyer lifts the Origin Shield

LEFT: New South Wales' Paul Gallen upended by Queensland duo Ashley Harrison and Dallas Johnson during Origin II

BELOW: Israel Folau dives past Manu Vatuvei for a try during Australia's win over New Zealand

TRANS-TASMAN TEST

Carnegie Challenge Cup

FINAL

CLOCKWISE, FROM TOP:
Chris Hicks shows his delight as he dives over to score; Brett Hodgson beats Mick Higham for a try; The champagne flows as Warrington celebrate their victory

Carnegie Challenge Cup
Winners 2009

Vinnie Anderson offloads to the supporting Michael Monaghan during Warrington's Semi-final success over Wigan

SEMI-FINALS

ABOVE: Stephen Wild mobbed by Leroy Cudjoe and Danny Kirmond as Huddersfield inflict St Helens' first Challenge Cup loss since 2005

BELOW: Wakefield's Jason Demetriou loses the ball under heavy pressure from Wigan's Andy Coley

Hull KR's Ben Galea wrongfoots Warrington's Richard Mathers for a try

QUARTER FINALS

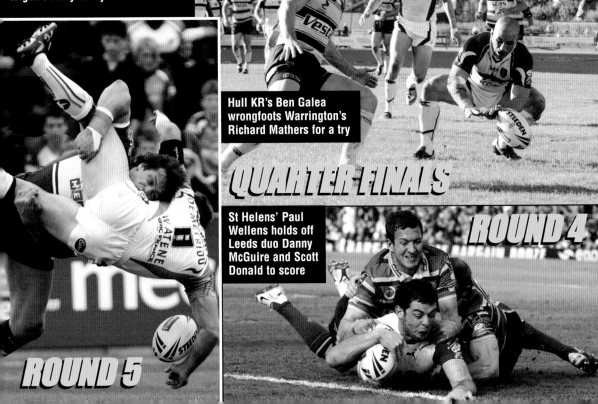

St Helens' Paul Wellens holds off Leeds duo Danny McGuire and Scott Donald to score

ROUND 4

ROUND 5

CLOCKWISE, FROM BELOW:
Melbourne Storm celebrate;
Adam Blair beats Daniel
Mortimer to score;
Cameron Smith shows off
the NRL trophy;
Fuifui Moimoi takes on the
Storm defence

NRL

GRAND FINAL

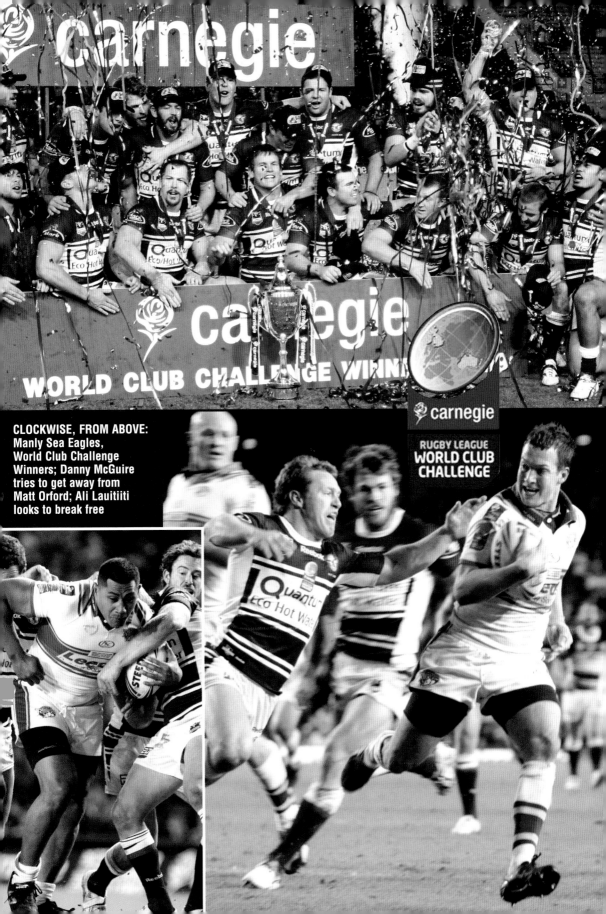

carnegie

WORLD CLUB CHALLENGE WINNERS

RUGBY LEAGUE
**WORLD CLUB
CHALLENGE**

CLOCKWISE, FROM ABOVE:
Manly Sea Eagles,
World Club Challenge
Winners; Danny McGuire
tries to get away from
Matt Orford; Ali Lauitiiti
looks to break free

The co-operative Championship Champions

The co-operative
CHAMPIONSHIP
GRAND FINAL

ABOVE: Barrow show their delight at becoming Champions

LEFT: Rob Worrincy all wrapped up

RIGHT: Zebastian Luisi gets the ball away

NORTHERN RAIL CUP

NORTHERN RAIL CUP

N northern

FINAL

Widnes, Northern Rail Cup Winners
BELOW LEFT: Richard Fletcher dives over
RIGHT: Kevin Penny jumps for joy

DORAN 11

Keighley's George Rayner finds a gap in the Oldham defence

BELOW LEFT: Cougars skipper James Feather and coach Barry Eaton celebrate

GRAND FINAL

The co-operative **CHAMPIONSHIP 1**

CHAMPIONS! Dewsbury captain Adam Hayes and coach Warren Jowitt show off the Championship 1 Trophy following the Rams' record-breaking unbeaten league season

Bramley's Paul Drake and Danny O'Connor lift the Conference National Trophy

Shaun Flynn takes on Huddersfield-Underbank's Joe Worthington

CONFERENCE NATIONAL GRAND FINAL

Gillette
RUGBY LEAGUE ACADEMY
GRAND FINAL

ABOVE: Wakefield Trinity Wildcats bask in the glory of being Academy Champions, after their Grand Final win over Wigan

RESERVE TEAM CHAMPIONSHIP - GRAND FINAL
Wigan Warriors celebrate victory over St Helens

NATIONAL CONFERENCE PREMIER DIVISION CHAMPIONS Siddal

RUGBY LEAGUE CONFERENCE CHAMPIONS West London Sharks

5
STATISTICAL REVIEW

SUPER LEAGUE PLAYERS
1996-2009

Super League Players 1996-2009

PLAYER	CLUB	YEAR	APP	TRIES	GOALS	FG	PTS
Carl Ablett	Leeds	2004, 2006-09	43(29)	13	0	0	52
	London	2005	3(2)	0	0	0	0
Darren Abram	Oldham	1996-97	25(2)	11	0	0	44
Darren Adams	Paris	1996	9(1)	1	0	0	4
Guy Adams	Huddersfield	1998	1(2)	0	0	0	0
Luke Adamson	Salford	2006-07, 2009	31(18)	6	0	0	24
Matt Adamson	Leeds	2002-04	54(8)	9	0	0	36
Phil Adamson	St Helens	1999	(1)	0	0	0	0
Ade Adebisi	London	2004	(1)	0	0	0	0
Jamie Ainscough	Wigan	2002-03	30(2)	18	0	0	72
Shaun Ainscough	Wigan	2009	11	13	0	0	52
Glen Air	London	1998-2001	57(13)	27	0	1	109
Makali Aizue	Hull KR	2007-09	18(32)	4	0	0	16
Darren Albert	St Helens	2002-05	105	77	0	0	308
Paul Alcock	Widnes	2003, 2005	1(7)	1	0	0	4
Neil Alexander	Salford	1998	(1)	0	0	0	0
Malcolm Alker	Salford	1997-2002, 2004-07, 2009	247(2)	40	0	1	161
Danny Allan	Leeds	2008-09	2(5)	0	0	0	0
Chris Allen	Castleford	1996	(1)	0	0	0	0
David Allen	Wigan	2003, 2005	6(15)	2	0	0	8
Gavin Allen	London	1996	10	0	0	0	0
John Allen	Workington	1996	20(1)	6	0	0	24
Ray Allen	London	1996	5(3)	3	0	0	12
Richard Allwood	Gateshead	1999	(4)	0	0	0	0
Sean Allwood	Gateshead	1999	3(17)	1	0	0	4
David Alstead	Warrington	2000-02	23(10)	3	0	0	12
Asa Amone	Halifax	1996-97	32(7)	10	0	0	40
Grant Anderson	Castleford	1996-97	15(6)	3	0	0	12
Louis Anderson	Warrington	2008-09	46	9	0	0	36
Paul Anderson	St Helens	2005-06	48(5)	7	1	0	30
	Bradford	1997-2004	74(104)	30	0	0	120
	Halifax	1996	5(1)	1	0	0	4
Paul Anderson	Sheffield	1999	3(7)	1	0	0	4
	St Helens	1996-98	2(28)	4	1	0	18
Vinnie Anderson	Warrington	2007-09	50(7)	20	0	0	80
	St Helens	2005-06	28(14)	17	0	0	68
Phil Anderton	St Helens	2004	1	0	0	0	0
Eric Anselme	Leeds	2008	2(2)	2	0	0	8
	Halifax	1997	(2)	0	0	0	0
Mark Applegarth	Wakefield	2004-07	20(5)	3	0	0	12
Graham Appo	Warrington	2002-05	60(13)	35	80	0	300
	Huddersfield	2001	7	4	0	0	16
Anthony Armour	London	2005	11(7)	1	0	0	4
Colin Armstrong	Workington	1996	11(2)	1	0	0	4
Tom Armstrong	St Helens	2009	5(1)	3	0	0	12
Richard Armswood	Workington	1996	5(1)	1	0	0	4
Danny Arnold	Salford	2001-02	26(13)	13	0	0	52
	Huddersfield	1998-2000	55(7)	26	0	0	104
	Castleford	2000	(4)	0	0	0	0
	St Helens	1996-97	40(1)	33	0	0	132
Joe Arundel	Castleford	2008	(1)	0	0	0	0
Craig Ashall	St Helens	2006	1	1	0	0	4
Chris Ashton	Wigan	2005-07	44(2)	25	2	0	104
Matty Ashurst	Wigan	2009	4(13)	0	0	0	0
Martin Aspinwall	Huddersfield	2006-09	64(5)	20	0	0	80
	Wigan	2001-05	85(13)	27	0	0	108
Mark Aston	Sheffield	1996-99	67(6)	6	243	6	516
Paul Atcheson	Widnes	2002-04	16(35)	4	0	0	16
	St Helens	1998-2000	58(4)	18	0	0	72
	Oldham	1996-97	40	21	0	0	84
David Atkins	Huddersfield	2001	26(1)	4	0	0	16
Ryan Atkins	Wakefield	2006-09	86(2)	45	0	0	180
Brad Attwood	Halifax	2003	(3)	0	0	0	0
Warren Ayres	Salford	1999	2(9)	1	2	0	8
Jerome Azema	Paris	1997	(1)	0	0	0	0
Marcus Bai	Bradford	2006	24	9	0	0	36
	Leeds	2004-05	57	42	0	0	168
David Baildon	Hull	1998-99	26(2)	4	0	0	16
Jean-Phillipe Baile	Catalans	2008-09	29(5)	12	0	0	48
Andy Bailey	Hull	2004-05	2(8)	1	0	0	4
Julian Bailey	Huddersfield	2003-04	47	13	0	0	52
Phil Bailey	Wigan	2007-09	71	13	0	0	52
Ryan Bailey	Leeds	2002-09	111(63)	8	0	0	32
Simon Baldwin	Salford	2004-06	20(29)	3	0	0	12
	Sheffield	1999	7(15)	2	0	0	8
	Halifax	1996-98	41(15)	16	0	1	65
Rob Ball	Wigan	1998-2000	3(4)	0	0	0	0
Paul Ballard	Celtic	2009	2	0	0	0	0
	Widnes	2005	3(1)	2	0	0	8
Darren Bamford	Salford	2005	2(1)	0	0	0	0
Michael Banks	Bradford	1998	(1)	0	0	0	0
Steve Bannister	Harlequins	2007	(6)	0	0	0	0
	St Helens	2006-07	(3)	0	0	0	0
Frederic Banquet	Paris	1996	16(2)	7	4	0	36
Lee Bardauskas	Castleford	1996-97	(2)	0	0	0	0
Craig Barker	Workington	1996	(2)	0	0	0	0
Dwayne Barker	Harlequins	2008	5(5)	1	0	0	4
	London	2004	3	1	0	0	4
	Hull	2003	(1)	0	0	0	0
Mark Barlow	Wakefield	2002	(1)	0	0	0	0
Danny Barnes	Halifax	1999	2	0	0	0	0
Richie Barnett	Salford	2007	7	4	0	0	16
	Warrington	2006-07	26(10)	15	0	0	60
	Hull	2004-05	21(5)	21	0	0	84
	Widnes	2005	4	2	0	0	8
Richie Barnett	Hull	2003-04	31(1)	17	0	0	68
	London	2001-02	31(4)	13	0	0	52
David Barnhill	Leeds	2000	20(8)	5	0	0	20
Trent Barrett	Wigan	2007-08	53(1)	22	0	4	92
Paul Barrow	Warrington	1996-97	1(10)	1	0	0	4
Scott Barrow	St Helens	1997-2000	9(13)	1	0	0	4
Steve Barrow	London	2000	2	0	0	0	0
	Hull	1998-99	4(17)	1	0	0	4
	Wigan	1996	(8)	3	0	0	12
Ben Barton	Huddersfield	1998	1(6)	1	0	0	4
Danny Barton	Salford	2001	1	0	0	0	0
Wayne Bartrim	Castleford	2002-03	41(2)	9	157	0	350
Greg Barwick	London	1996-97	30(4)	21	110	2	306
David Bastian	Halifax	1996	(2)	0	0	0	0
Ashley Bateman	Celtic	2009	1	0	0	0	0
David Bates	Castleford	2001-02	(4)	0	0	0	0
	Warrington	2001	1(2)	0	0	0	0
Nathan Batty	Wakefield	2001	1(1)	0	0	0	0
Andreas Bauer	Hull KR	2007	10(2)	5	0	0	20
Russell Bawden	London	1996-97, 2002-04	50(49)	15	0	0	60
Neil Baxter	Salford	2001	1	0	0	0	0
Neil Baynes	Salford	1999-2002, 2004	84(19)	10	0	0	40
	Wigan	1996-98	(10)	1	0	0	4
Chris Beasley	Celtic	2009	15(5)	2	0	0	8
Chris Beattie	Catalans	2006	22(5)	3	0	0	12
Robbie Beazley	London	1997-99	48(15)	13	0	0	52
Robbie Beckett	Halifax	2002	27	15	0	0	60
Dean Bell	Leeds	1996	1	1	0	0	4
Ian Bell	Hull	2003	(1)	0	0	0	0
Mark Bell	Wigan	1998	22	12	0	0	48
Paul Bell	Leeds	2000	1	0	0	0	0
Steven Bell	Catalans	2009	21	9	0	0	36
Troy Bellamy	Paris	1997	5(10)	0	0	0	0
Adrian Belle	Huddersfield	1998	10(2)	0	0	0	0
	Oldham	1996	19	8	0	0	32
Jamie Benn	Castleford	1998, 2000	3(8)	1	15	0	34
Andy Bennett	Warrington	1996	6(5)	1	0	0	4
Mike Bennett	St Helens	2000-08	74(70)	15	0	0	60
Andrew Bentley	Catalans	2007-08	9(7)	1	0	0	4
John Bentley	Huddersfield	1999	13(4)	3	0	0	12
	Halifax	1996, 1998	22(3)	24	0	0	96
Kane Bentley	Catalans	2007-09	3(14)	4	0	0	16
Phil Bergman	Paris	1997	20(1)	14	0	0	56
Shaun Berrigan	Hull	2008-09	41(4)	11	0	0	44
Joe Berry	Huddersfield	1998-99	25(14)	3	0	0	12
David Berthezene	Salford	2007	9(1)	0	0	0	0
	Catalans	2006-07	5(14)	0	0	0	0
Colin Best	Hull	2003-04	57	34	0	0	136
Roger Best	London	1997-98	1(5)	1	0	0	4
Bob Beswick	Wigan	2004-05	5(14)	2	0	0	8
Monty Betham	Wakefield	2006	26	2	0	0	8
Mike Bethwaite	Workington	1996	17(3)	1	0	0	4
Denis Betts	Wigan	1998-2001	82(24)	33	0	0	132
Cliff Beverley	Salford	2004-05	47(1)	14	0	0	56
Kyle Bibb	Wakefield	2008-09	1(22)	0	0	0	0
	Hull KR	2009	(2)	0	0	0	0
Adam Bibey	Widnes	2004	(1)	0	0	0	0
Ricky Bibey	Wakefield	2007-09	32(25)	1	0	0	4
	St Helens	2004	4(14)	0	0	0	0
	Wigan	2001-03	5(29)	0	0	0	0
Chris Birchall	Halifax	2002-03	24(22)	4	0	0	16
	Bradford	2000	(1)	0	0	0	0
Deon Bird	Castleford	2006	17(6)	5	0	0	20
	Widnes	2003-04	39(6)	9	0	0	36
	Wakefield	2002	10(1)	1	0	0	4
	Hull	2000-02	37(22)	20	0	0	80
	Gateshead	1999	19(3)	13	0	0	52
	Paris	1996-97	30	12	2	0	52
Greg Bird	Catalans	2009	20(2)	5	3	0	26
Nathan Blacklock	Hull	2005-06	44(5)	33	0	0	132
Richie Blackmore	Leeds	1997-2000	63	25	0	0	100
Anthony Blackwood	Celtic	2009	25	5	0	0	20
Luke Blake	Wakefield	2009	(2)	0	0	0	0
Matthew Blake	Wakefield	2003-04	1(5)	0	0	0	0
Steve Blakeley	Salford	1997-2002	103(5)	26	241	2	588
	Warrington	2000	4(3)	1	9	0	22
Richard Blakeway	Castleford	2002-04	1(14)	0	0	0	0
Damien Blanch	Wakefield	2008-09	24(2)	19	0	0	76
	Castleford	2006	3(2)	0	0	0	0
Matt Blaymire	Wakefield	2007-09	69(1)	21	0	0	84

PLAYER	CLUB	YEAR	APP	TRIES	GOALS	FG	PTS
Ian Blease	Salford	1997	(1)	0	0	0	0
Jamie Bloem	Huddersfield	2003	18(4)	3	11	0	34
	Halifax	1998-2002	82(25)	25	100	2	302
Vea Bloomfield	Paris	1996	4(14)	3	0	0	12
Matty Blythe	Warrington	2007-09	5(13)	2	0	0	8
Pascal Bomati	Paris	1996	17(1)	10	0	0	40
Simon Booth	Hull	1998-99	15(9)	2	0	0	8
	St Helens	1996-97	10(4)	1	0	0	4
Steve Booth	Huddersfield	1998-99	16(4)	2	3	0	14
Alan Boothroyd	Halifax	1997	2(3)	0	0	0	0
Thomas Bosc	Catalans	2006-09	82(3)	28	246	3	607
John Boslem	Paris	1996	(5)	0	0	0	0
Liam Bostock	St Helens	2004	1	0	0	0	0
Liam Botham	Wigan	2005	5	0	0	0	0
	Leeds	2003-05	2(11)	4	0	0	16
	London	2004	6(2)	3	6	0	24
Frano Botica	Castleford	1996	21	5	84	2	190
Matthew Bottom	Leigh	2005	(1)	0	0	0	0
Hadj Boudebza	Paris	1996	(2)	0	0	0	0
David Boughton	Huddersfield	1999	26(1)	4	0	0	16
David Bouveng	Halifax	1997-99	66(2)	19	0	0	76
Tony Bowes	Huddersfield	1998	3(2)	0	0	0	0
Radney Bowker	London	2004	3	1	0	0	4
	St Helens	2001	(1)	0	0	0	0
David Boyle	Bradford	1999-2000	36(13)	15	0	1	61
Ryan Boyle	Castleford	2006, 2008-09	(29)	2	0	0	8
Andy Bracek	Warrington	2005-08	7(49)	7	0	0	28
	St Helens	2004	(1)	0	0	0	0
David Bradbury	Hudds-Sheff	2000	21(2)	1	0	0	4
	Salford	1997-99	23(10)	6	0	0	24
	Oldham	1996-97	19(6)	9	0	0	36
John Braddish	St Helens	2001-02	1(1)	0	3	0	6
Graeme Bradley	Bradford	1996-98	62(1)	29	0	0	116
Nick Bradley-Qalilawa							
	Harlequins	2006	27	6	0	0	24
	London	2005	28	19	0	0	76
Darren Bradstreet	London	1999-2000	1(3)	0	0	0	0
Dominic Brambani							
	Castleford	2004	2(2)	0	0	0	0
Liam Bretherton	Wigan	1999	(5)	2	0	0	8
	Warrington	1997	(2)	0	0	0	0
Johnny Brewer	Halifax	1996	4(2)	2	0	0	8
Chris Bridge	Warrington	2005-09	74(8)	38	102	1	357
	Bradford	2003-04	2(14)	4	6	0	28
Lee Briers	Warrington	1997-2009	285(12)	98	742	57	1933
	St Helens	1997	3	0	11	0	22
Carl Briggs	Salford	1999	8(5)	3	0	1	13
	Halifax	1996	5(3)	1	0	0	4
Mike Briggs	Widnes	2002	1(2)	1	0	0	4
Shaun Briscoe	Hull KR	2008-09	44	13	0	0	52
	Hull	2004-07	83(9)	50	0	0	200
	Wigan	2002-03	23(5)	11	0	0	44
Tom Briscoe	Hull	2008-09	22(3)	13	0	0	52
Darren Britt	St Helens	2002-03	41	3	0	0	12
Gary Broadbent	Salford	1997-2002	117(2)	22	0	0	88
Paul Broadbent	Wakefield	2002	16(5)	0	0	0	0
	Hull	2000-01	40(9)	3	0	0	12
	Halifax	1999	26(1)	2	0	0	8
	Sheffield	1996-98	63(1)	6	0	0	24
Andrew Brocklehurst							
	Salford	2004-07	34(23)	5	0	0	20
	London	2004	12(6)	2	0	0	8
	Halifax	2001-03	37(8)	2	0	0	8
Justin Brooker	Wakefield	2001	25	9	0	0	36
	Bradford	2000	17(4)	11	0	0	44
Danny Brough	Wakefield	2008-09	44(1)	13	156	4	368
	Castleford	2006	10	1	31	2	68
	Hull	2005-06	25(12)	3	85	1	183
Judle Broughton	Hull	2008-09	9(3)	6	0	0	24
Alex Brown	Huddersfield	2009	1	0	0	0	0
Darren Brown	Salford	1999-2001	47(9)	11	6	0	56
Gavin Brown	Leeds	1996-97	5(2)	1	2	0	8
Kevin Brown	Huddersfield	2006-09	84	23	0	1	93
	Wigan	2003-06	46(18)	27	0	0	108
Lee Brown	Hull	1999	(1)	0	0	0	0
Michael Brown	Huddersfield	2008	(1)	0	0	0	0
Michael Brown	London	1996	(2)	0	0	0	0
Todd Brown	Paris	1996	8(1)	2	0	0	8
Adrian Brunker	Wakefield	1999	17	6	0	0	24
Lamont Bryan	Harlequins	2008-09	7(3)	0	0	0	0
Justin Bryant	Paris	1996	4(1)	0	0	0	0
	London	1996	7(8)	1	0	0	4
Mark Bryant	Celtic	2009	23(3)	0	0	0	0
Austin Buchanan	Wakefield	2005-06	6	2	0	0	8
	London	2003	3(1)	2	0	0	8
Danny Buderus	Leeds	2009	9(7)	2	0	0	8
Neil Budworth	Celtic	2009	8(19)	0	0	0	0
	Harlequins	2006	2(19)	0	0	0	0
	London	2002-05	59(11)	4	1	0	18
James Bunyan	Huddersfield	1998-99	8(7)	2	0	0	8
Andy Burgess	Salford	1997	3(12)	0	0	0	0
Luke Burgess	Leeds	2008-09	4(43)	6	0	0	24
	Harlequins	2007	(3)	0	0	0	0
Sam Burgess	Bradford	2006-09	46(34)	14	5	0	66
Mike Burnett	Hull	2008-09	9(17)	3	0	0	12
Darren Burns	Warrington	2002-04	66(6)	19	0	0	76
Gary Burns	Oldham	1996	6	1	0	0	4
Paul Burns	Workington	1996	5(2)	1	0	0	4
Rob Burrow	Leeds	2001-09	175(66)	107	107	4	646
Dean Busby	Warrington	1999-2002	34(34)	7	0	0	28
	Hull	1998	8(6)	0	0	0	0
	St Helens	1996-98	1(7)	0	0	0	0
Ikram Butt	London	1996	5(1)	0	0	0	0
Shane Byrne	Huddersfield	1998-99	1(5)	0	0	0	0
Todd Byrne	Hull	2008-09	20	4	0	0	16
Didier Cabestany	Paris	1996-97	20(6)	2	0	0	8
Joel Caine	Salford	2004	24	8	13	0	58
	London	2003	6	4	1	0	18
Mark Calderwood	Hull	2009	19	6	0	0	24
	Wigan	2006-08	64	23	0	0	92
	Leeds	2001-05	117(9)	88	0	0	352
Mike Callan	Warrington	2002	(4)	0	0	0	0
Matt Calland	Huddersfield	2003	2	0	0	0	0
	Hull	1999	1	0	0	0	0
	Bradford	1996-98	44(5)	24	0	0	96
Dean Callaway	London	1999-2000	26(24)	12	0	0	48
Laurent Cambres	Paris	1996	(1)	0	0	0	0
Chris Campbell	Warrington	2000	7(1)	2	0	0	8
Liam Campbell	Wakefield	2005	(1)	0	0	0	0
Logan Campbell	Hull	1998-99, 2001	70(13)	14	0	0	56
	Castleford	2000	14(2)	3	0	0	12
	Workington	1996	7(1)	1	0	0	4
Blake Cannova	Widnes	2002	(1)	0	0	0	0
Phil Cantillon	Widnes	2002-03	27(21)	18	0	0	72
	Leeds	1997	(1)	0	0	0	0
Daryl Cardiss	Warrington	2003-04	23(2)	3	4	0	20
	Halifax	1999-2003	91(8)	39	4	0	164
	Wigan	1996-98	12(6)	4	0	0	16
Dale Cardoza	Warrington	2002	5	1	0	0	4
	Halifax	2001	3	1	0	0	4
	Huddersfield	2000-01	20(9)	11	0	0	44
	Sheffield	1998-99	11(7)	3	0	0	12
Paul Carige	Salford	1999	24(1)	7	0	0	28
Dane Carlaw	Catalans	2008-09	37(10)	5	0	0	20
Keal Carlile	Huddersfield	2009	(1)	0	0	0	0
	Bradford	2008	(1)	0	0	0	0
Jim Carlton	Huddersfield	1999	3(11)	2	0	0	8
George Carmont	Wigan	2008-09	56	28	0	0	112
Brian Carney	Warrington	2009	4	2	0	0	8
	Wigan	2001-05	91(10)	42	1	0	170
	Hull	2000	13(3)	7	0	0	28
	Gateshead	1999	3(2)	2	0	0	8
Martin Carney	Warrington	1997	(1)	0	0	0	0
Paul Carr	Sheffield	1996-98	45(5)	15	0	0	60
Bernard Carroll	London	1996	2(1)	1	0	0	4
Mark Carroll	London	1998	15(3)	1	0	0	4
Tonie Carroll	Leeds	2001-02	42(2)	30	0	0	120
Darren Carter	Workington	1996	10(3)	0	1	0	2
Steve Carter	Widnes	2002	14(7)	4	0	0	16
John Cartwright	Salford	1997	9	0	0	0	0
Garreth Carvell	Warrington	2009	20(1)	4	0	0	16
	Hull	2001-08	69(83)	22	0	0	88
	Leeds	1997-2000	(4)	0	0	0	0
	Gateshead	1999	4(4)	1	0	0	4
Garen Casey	Salford	1999	13(5)	3	23	0	58
Ray Cashmere	Salford	2009	26(1)	0	0	0	0
Mick Cassidy	Widnes	2005	24	0	0	0	0
	Wigan	1996-2004	184(36)	30	0	0	120
Remi Casty	Catalans	2006-09	5(66)	4	0	0	16
Ned Catic	Castleford	2008	7(7)	3	0	0	12
	Wakefield	2006-07	17(29)	4	0	0	16
Chris Causey	Warrington	1997-99	(18)	1	0	0	4
Jason Cayless	St Helens	2006-09	62(9)	7	0	0	28
Arnaud Cervello	Paris	1996	4	4	0	0	16
Marshall Chalk	Celtic	2009	13	4	0	0	16
Gary Chambers	Warrington	1996-2000	65(28)	2	0	0	8
Pierre Chamorin	Paris	1996-97	27(3)	8	3	0	38
Alex Chan	Catalans	2006-08	59(19)	11	0	0	44
Jason Chan	Celtic	2009	17(6)	3	0	0	12
Joe Chandler	Leeds	2008	(1)	0	0	0	0
Chris Chapman	Leeds	1999	(1)	0	0	0	0
Damien Chapman	London	1998	6(2)	3	4	1	21
David Chapman	Castleford	1996-98	24(6)	8	0	0	32
Jaymes Chapman	Halifax	2002-03	5(8)	1	0	0	4
Richard Chapman							
	Sheffield	1996	1	2	0	0	8
Chris Charles	Salford	2004-06	59(16)	6	140	0	304
	Castleford	2001	1(4)	1	0	0	4
Olivier Charles	Catalans	2007	2	2	0	0	8
Rangi Chase	Castleford	2009	24(4)	10	0	1	41
Andy Cheetham	Huddersfield	1998-99	30	11	0	0	44
Kris Chesney	London	1998	1(2)	0	0	0	0
Chris Chester	Hull KR	2007-08	28(6)	4	0	0	16
	Hull	2002-06	67(25)	13	0	0	52
	Wigan	1999-2001	21(22)	5	0	0	20
	Halifax	1996-99	47(14)	16	15	1	95

Super League Players 1996-2009

PLAYER	CLUB	YEAR	APP	TRIES	GOALS	FG	PTS
Lee Chilton	Workington	1996	10(3)	6	0	0	24
Gary Christie	Bradford	1996-97	4(7)	1	0	0	4
Dean Clark	Leeds	1996	11(2)	3	0	0	12
Des Clark	St Helens	1999	4	0	0	0	0
	Halifax	1998-99	35(13)	6	0	0	24
Greg Clarke	Halifax	1997	1(1)	0	0	0	0
John Clarke	Oldham	1996-97	27(4)	5	0	0	20
Jon Clarke	Warrington	2001-09	210(8)	51	2	0	208
	London	2000-01	19(11)	2	0	0	8
	Wigan	1997-99	13(10)	3	0	0	12
Ryan Clayton	Castleford	2004, 2008-09	23(19)	3	0	0	12
	Salford	2006	3(8)	2	0	0	8
	Huddersfield	2005	4(6)	0	0	0	0
	Halifax	2000, 2002-03	28(12)	6	0	0	24
Gavin Clinch	Salford	2004	21(1)	1	0	1	5
	Halifax	1998-99, 2001-02	88(2)	26	45	5	199
	Hudds-Sheff	2000	18(2)	5	0	1	21
	Wigan	1999	10(2)	4	12	0	40
John Clough	Salford	2004-06	1(16)	0	0	0	0
Paul Clough	St Helens	2005-09	23(57)	12	0	0	48
Tony Clubb	Harlequins	2006-09	46(11)	14	0	0	56
Bradley Clyde	Leeds	2001	7(5)	1	0	0	4
Evan Cochrane	London	1996	5(1)	1	0	0	4
Ben Cockayne	Hull KR	2007-09	42(18)	15	0	0	60
Liam Colbon	Hull KR	2009	24	8	0	0	32
	Wigan	2004-05, 2007-08	37(14)	14	0	0	56
Anthony Colella	Huddersfield	2003	5(1)	2	0	0	8
Liam Coleman	Leigh	2005	1(4)	0	0	0	0
Andy Coley	Wigan	2008-09	55(4)	4	0	0	16
	Salford	2001-02, 2004-07	112(34)	34	0	0	136
Richard Colley	Bradford	2004	1	0	0	0	0
Steve Collins	Hull	2000	28	17	0	0	68
	Gateshead	1999	20(4)	13	0	0	52
Wayne Collins	Leeds	1997	21	3	0	0	12
Aurelien Cologni	Catalans	2006	4(1)	3	0	0	12
Gary Connolly	Widnes	2005	20	4	1	0	18
	Wigan	1996-2002, 2004	168(10)	70	5	0	290
	Leeds	2003-04	27	6	0	0	24
Matt Cook	Bradford	2005-09	11(52)	4	0	0	16
	Castleford	2008	2(1)	1	0	0	4
Mick Cook	Sheffield	1996	9(10)	2	0	0	8
Paul Cook	Huddersfield	1998-99	11(6)	2	13	0	34
	Bradford	1996-97	14(8)	7	38	1	105
Peter Cook	St Helens	2004	(1)	0	0	0	0
Paul Cooke	Hull KR	2007-09	51(5)	8	76	2	186
	Hull	1999-2007	177(27)	32	333	4	798
Ben Cooper	Leigh	2005	25(1)	5	0	0	20
	Huddersfield	2000-01, 2003-04	28(12)	3	0	0	12
Michael Cooper	Warrington	2006-09	1(31)	2	0	0	8
Ged Corcoran	Halifax	2003	1(11)	0	0	0	0
Wayne Corcoran	Halifax	2003	4(2)	0	0	0	0
Josh Cordoba	Hull	2009	8	1	0	0	4
Mark Corvo	Salford	2002	7(5)	0	0	0	0
Brandon Costin	Huddersfield	2001, 2003-04	69	42	93	3	357
	Bradford	2002	20(1)	8	0	0	32
Wes Cotton	London	1997-98	12	3	0	0	12
Phil Coussons	Salford	1997	7(2)	3	0	0	12
Alex Couttet	Paris	1997	1	0	0	0	0
Nick Couttet	Paris	1997	1	0	0	0	0
Jamie Coventry	Castleford	1996	1	0	0	0	0
Jimmy Cowan	Oldham	1996-97	2(8)	0	0	0	0
Will Cowell	Warrington	1998-2000	6(8)	1	0	0	4
Neil Cowie	Wigan	1996-2001	116(27)	10	0	1	41
Mark Cox	London	2003	(3)	0	0	0	0
James Coyle	Wigan	2005	2(3)	1	0	0	4
Thomas Coyle	Wigan	2008	2(1)	0	0	0	0
Eorl Crabtree	Huddersfield	2001, 2003-09	64(102)	18	0	0	72
Andy Craig	Halifax	1999	13(7)	1	3	0	10
	Wigan	1996	5(5)	2	0	0	8
Owen Craigie	Widnes	2005	15	7	0	2	30
Scott Cram	London	1999-2002	65(7)	4	0	0	16
Steve Craven	Hull	1998-2003	53(42)	4	0	0	16
Nicky Crellin	Workington	1996	(2)	0	0	0	0
Jason Critchley	Wakefield	2000	7(1)	4	0	0	16
	Castleford	1997-98	27(3)	11	0	0	44
Jason Croker	Catalans	2007-09	56(2)	11	0	1	45
Martin Crompton	Salford	1998-2000	30(6)	11	6	2	58
	Oldham	1996-97	36(1)	16	0	3	67
Paul Crook	Widnes	2005	2(2)	0	5	1	11
Paul Crook	Oldham	1996	4(9)	0	3	0	6
Jason Crookes	Bradford	2009	2(1)	0	0	0	0
Lee Crooks	Castleford	1996-97	27(2)	2	14	0	36
Alan Cross	St Helens	1997	(2)	0	0	0	0
Garret Crossman	Hull KR	2008	8(18)	0	0	0	0
Steve Crouch	Castleford	2004	4(1)	2	0	0	8

PLAYER	CLUB	YEAR	APP	TRIES	GOALS	FG	PTS
Kevin Crouthers	Warrington	2001-03	12(1)	4	0	0	16
	London	2000	6(4)	1	0	0	4
	Wakefield	1999	4(4)	1	0	0	4
	Bradford	1997-98	3(9)	2	0	0	8
Matt Crowther	Hull	2001-03	48	20	166	0	412
	Hudds-Sheff	2000	10(4)	5	22	0	64
	Sheffield	1996-99	43(4)	22	10	0	108
Heath Cruckshank	Halifax	2003	19(1)	0	0	0	0
	St Helens	2001	1(12)	0	0	0	0
Leroy Cudjoe	Huddersfield	2008-09	37(1)	19	27	0	130
Paul Cullen	Warrington	1996	19	3	0	0	12
Francis Cummins	Leeds	1996-2005	217(13)	120	26	2	534
Keiron Cunningham	St Helens	1996-2009	340(17)	133	0	0	532
Andy Currier	Warrington	1996-97	(2)	1	0	0	4
Peter Cusack	Hull	2008-09	26(6)	2	0	0	8
Joe Dakuitoga	Sheffield	1996	6(3)	0	0	0	0
Matty Dale	Hull	2006, 2008	(7)	1	0	0	4
	Wakefield	2008	1	0	0	0	0
Brett Dallas	Wigan	2000-06	156	89	0	0	356
Mark Dalle Cort	Celtic	2009	23	4	0	0	16
Paul Darbyshire	Warrington	1997	(6)	0	0	0	0
James Davey	Wakefield	2009	(1)	0	0	0	0
Maea David	Hull	1998	1	0	0	0	0
Paul Davidson	Halifax	2001-03	22(30)	10	0	0	40
	London	2000	6(10)	4	0	0	16
	St Helens	1998-99	27(16)	7	0	0	28
	Oldham	1996-97	17(18)	14	0	1	57
Gareth Davies	Warrington	1996-97	1(6)	0	0	0	0
Geraint Davies	Celtic	2009	(7)	0	0	0	0
Wes Davies	Wigan	1998-2001	22(22)	11	0	0	44
Brad Davis	Castleford	1997-2000, 2004, 2006	102(3)	31	43	10	220
	Wakefield	2001-03	51(12)	15	22	5	109
Matt Daylight	Hull	2000	17(1)	7	0	0	28
	Gateshead	1999	30	25	0	0	100
Michael De Vere	Huddersfield	2005-06	36	6	74	0	172
Paul Deacon	Bradford	1998-2009	258(43)	72	1029	23	2369
	Oldham	1997	(2)	0	0	0	0
Chris Dean	St Helens	2007-09	9(2)	6	0	0	24
Craig Dean	Halifax	1996-97	25(11)	12	1	1	51
Gareth Dean	London	2002	(4)	0	0	0	0
Yacine Dekkiche	Hudds-Sheff	2000	11(3)	3	0	0	12
Jason Demetriou	Wakefield	2004-09	149(2)	46	2	0	188
	Widnes	2002-03	47(1)	15	1	0	62
Martin Dermott	Warrington	1997	1	0	0	0	0
David Despin	Paris	1996	(1)	0	0	0	0
Fabien Devecchi	Paris	1996-97	17(10)	2	0	0	8
Paul Devlin	Widnes	2002-04	32	16	0	0	64
Stuart Dickens	Salford	2005	4(5)	0	4	0	8
Matt Diskin	Leeds	2001-09	187(23)	40	0	0	160
Andrew Dixon	St Helens	2009	6(3)	1	0	0	4
Kirk Dixon	Castleford	2008-09	47	23	89	0	270
	Hull	2004-06	13(4)	7	4	0	36
Paul Dixon	Sheffield	1996-97	5(9)	1	0	0	4
Gareth Dobson	Castleford	1998-2000	(10)	0	0	0	0
Michael Dobson	Hull KR	2008-09	42	19	125	3	329
	Wigan	2006	14	5	61	0	142
	Catalans	2006	10	4	31	1	79
Michael Docherty	Hull	2000-01	(6)	0	0	0	0
Sid Domic	Hull	2006-07	39(4)	15	0	0	60
	Wakefield	2004-05	48	30	0	0	120
	Warrington	2002-03	41(4)	17	0	0	68
Scott Donald	Leeds	2006-09	113	67	0	0	268
James Donaldson	Bradford	2009	(7)	2	0	0	8
Glen Donkin	Hull	2002-03	(10)	1	0	0	4
Stuart Donlan	Castleford	2008	20	8	0	0	32
	Huddersfield	2004-06	59(3)	15	0	0	60
	Halifax	2001-03	65(2)	22	0	0	88
Jason Donohue	Bradford	1996	(4)	0	0	0	0
Jeremy Donougher	Bradford	1996-99	40(21)	13	0	0	52
Justin Dooley	London	2000-01	37(18)	2	0	0	8
Dane Dorahy	Halifax	2003	20	7	45	0	118
	Wakefield	2000-01	16(2)	4	19	1	55
Luke Dorn	Harlequins	2006, 2009	45	26	0	0	104
	Castleford	2008	25(1)	19	0	0	76
	Salford	2007	19(8)	11	0	0	44
	London	2005	23	23	0	0	92
Ewan Dowes	Hull	2003-09	153(22)	9	0	0	36
	Leeds	2001-03	1(9)	0	0	0	0
Adam Doyle	Warrington	1998	9(3)	4	0	0	16
Rod Doyle	Sheffield	1997-99	52(10)	10	0	0	40
Brad Drew	Wakefield	2008-09	27(9)	7	14	1	57
	Huddersfield	2005-07	74(8)	17	13	1	95
Damien Driscoll	Salford	2001	23(1)	1	0	0	4
Gil Dudson	Celtic	2009	(1)	0	0	0	0
Jason Duffy	Leigh	2005	3(1)	0	0	0	0
John Duffy	Leigh	2005	21	6	0	0	24
	Salford	2000	3(11)	0	1	1	3
	Warrington	1997-99	12(12)	0	0	0	0
Tony Duggan	Celtic	2009	4	3	0	0	12

PLAYER	CLUB	YEAR	APP	TRIES	GOALS	FG	PTS
Andrew Duncan	London	1997	2(4)	2	0	0	8
	Warrington	1997	(1)	0	0	0	0
Andrew Dunemann							
	Salford	2006	25	1	0	2	6
	Leeds	2003-05	76(4)	11	0	2	46
	Halifax	1999-2002	68	19	0	1	77
Matt Dunford	London	1997-98	18(20)	3	0	1	13
Vincent Duport	Catalans	2007-09	27(14)	11	0	0	44
Jamie Durbin	Widnes	2005	1	0	0	0	0
	Warrington	2003	(1)	0	0	0	0
James Durkin	Paris	1997	(5)	0	0	0	0
Bernard Dwyer	Bradford	1996-2000	65(10)	14	0	0	56
Luke Dyer	Celtic	2009	21	6	0	0	24
	Hull KR	2007	26	13	0	0	52
	Castleford	2006	17(2)	5	0	0	20
Adam Dykes	Hull	2008	12	1	0	2	6
Jim Dymock	London	2001-04	94(1)	15	0	1	61
Leo Dynevor	London	1996	8(11)	5	7	0	34
Jason Eade	Paris	1997	9	4	0	0	16
Michael Eagar	Hull	2004-05	12	4	0	0	16
	Castleford	1999-2003	130(2)	60	0	0	240
	Warrington	1998	21	6	0	0	24
Kyle Eastmond	St Helens	2007-09	16(15)	15	50	1	161
Barry Eaton	Widnes	2002	25	2	49	4	110
	Castleford	2000	1(4)	0	3	0	6
Greg Ebrill	Salford	2002	15(6)	1	0	0	4
Cliff Eccles	Salford	1997-98	30(5)	1	0	0	4
Chris Eckersley	Warrington	1996	1	0	0	0	0
Steve Edmed	Sheffield	1997	15(1)	0	0	0	0
Mark Edmondson	Salford	2007	10(2)	0	0	0	0
	St Helens	1999-2005	27(75)	10	0	0	40
Diccon Edwards	Castleford	1996-97	10(5)	1	0	0	4
Grant Edwards	Castleford	2006	(2)	0	0	0	0
Peter Edwards	Salford	1997-98	35(2)	4	0	0	16
Shaun Edwards	London	1997-2000	32(8)	16	1	0	66
	Bradford	1998	8(2)	4	0	0	16
	Wigan	1996	17(3)	12	1	0	50
Danny Ekis	Halifax	2001	(1)	0	0	0	0
Abi Ekoku	Bradford	1997-98	21(4)	6	0	0	24
	Halifax	1996	15(1)	5	0	0	20
Shane Elford	Huddersfield	2007-08	26(1)	7	0	0	28
Olivier Elima	Catalans	2008-09	34(10)	25	0	0	100
	Wakefield	2003-07	40(47)	13	0	0	52
	Castleford	2002	(1)	1	0	0	4
Abderazak Elkhalouki							
	Paris	1997	(1)	0	0	0	0
Gareth Ellis	Leeds	2005-08	109	24	1	0	98
	Wakefield	1999-2004	86(17)	21	2	0	88
James Ellis	St Helens	2009	1(2)	0	1	0	2
Danny Ellison	Castleford	1998-99	7(16)	6	0	0	24
	Wigan	1996-97	15(1)	13	0	0	52
Andrew Emelio	Widnes	2005	22(2)	8	0	0	32
Jacob Emmitt	St Helens	2008-09	1(5)	0	0	0	0
Patrick Entat	Paris	1996	22	2	0	0	8
Jason Erba	Sheffield	1997	1(4)	0	0	0	0
Ryan Esders	Harlequins	2009	4(4)	2	0	0	8
	Hull KR	2009	(1)	0	0	0	0
James Evans	Castleford	2009	18(1)	8	0	0	32
	Bradford	2007-08	43(5)	20	0	0	80
	Wakefield	2006	6	3	0	0	12
	Huddersfield	2004-06	51	22	0	0	88
Paul Evans	Paris	1997	18	8	0	0	32
Wayne Evans	London	2002	11(6)	2	0	0	8
Richie Eyres	Warrington	1997	2(5)	0	0	0	0
	Sheffield	1997	2(3)	0	0	0	0
Henry Fa'afili	Warrington	2004-07	90(1)	70	0	0	280
Sala Fa'alogo	Widnes	2004-05	8(15)	2	0	0	8
Richard Fa'aoso	Castleford	2000	10(15)	5	0	0	20
Maurie Fa'asavalu							
	St Helens	2004-09	5(125)	27	0	0	108
Bolouagi Fagborun							
	Huddersfield	2004-06	4(2)	1	0	0	4
Esene Faimalo	Salford	1997-99	23(25)	2	0	0	8
	Leeds	1996	3(3)	0	0	0	0
Joe Faimalo	Salford	1998-2000	23(47)	7	0	0	28
	Oldham	1996-97	37(5)	7	0	0	28
Karl Fairbank	Bradford	1996	17(2)	4	0	0	16
David Fairleigh	St Helens	2001	26(1)	8	0	0	32
David Faiumu	Huddersfield	2008-09	8(18)	3	0	0	12
Jamal Fakir	Catalans	2006-09	38(25)	9	0	0	36
Jim Fallon	Leeds	1996	10	5	0	0	20
Danny Farrar	Warrington	1998-2000	76	13	0	0	52
Andy Farrell	Wigan	1996-2004	230	77	1026	16	2376
Anthony Farrell	Widnes	2002-03	24(22)	4	1	0	18
	Leeds	1997-2001	99(23)	18	0	0	72
	Sheffield	1996	14(5)	5	0	0	20
Craig Farrell	Hull	2000-01	1(3)	0	0	0	0
Abraham Fatnowna							
	London	1997-98	7(2)	2	0	0	8
	Workington	1996	5	2	0	0	8
Sione Faumuina	Castleford	2009	18	1	0	0	4
	Hull	2005	3	1	0	0	4

PLAYER	CLUB	YEAR	APP	TRIES	GOALS	FG	PTS
Vince Fawcett	Wakefield	1999	13(1)	2	0	0	8
	Warrington	1998	4(7)	1	0	0	4
	Oldham	1997	5	3	0	0	12
Danny Fearon	Huddersfield	2001	(1)	0	0	0	0
	Halifax	1999-2000	5(6)	0	0	0	0
Chris Feather	Castleford	2009	1(23)	0	0	0	0
	Bradford	2007-08	7(20)	1	0	0	4
	Leeds	2003-04,					
		2006	16(35)	6	0	0	24
	Wakefield	2001-02,					
		2004-05	29(32)	9	0	0	36
Dom Feaunati	Leigh	2005	4	1	0	0	4
	St Helens	2004	10(7)	7	0	0	28
Adel Fellous	Hull	2008	1(2)	0	0	0	0
	Catalans	2006-07	16(22)	4	0	0	16
Luke Felsch	Hull	2000-01	46(6)	7	0	0	28
	Gateshead	1999	28(1)	2	0	0	8
Leon Felton	Warrington	2002	4(2)	0	0	0	0
	St Helens	2001	1(1)	0	0	0	0
Dale Ferguson	Wakefield	2007-09	28(9)	8	0	0	32
Brett Ferres	Castleford	2009	23(2)	11	0	0	44
	Wakefield	2007-08	36(2)	6	5	0	34
	Bradford	2005-06	18(17)	11	2	0	48
David Ferriol	Catalans	2007-09	21(44)	5	0	0	20
Jason Ferris	Leigh	2005	4	1	0	0	4
Jamie Field	Wakefield	1999-2006	133(59)	19	0	0	76
	Huddersfield	1998	15(5)	0	0	0	0
	Leeds	1996-97	3(11)	0	0	0	0
Mark Field	Wakefield	2003-07	28(7)	3	0	0	12
Jamie Fielden	London	2003	(1)	0	0	0	0
	Huddersfield	1998-2000	4(8)	0	0	0	0
Stuart Fielden	Wigan	2006-09	76(22)	2	0	0	8
	Bradford	1998-2006	142(78)	41	0	0	164
Lafaele Filipo	Workington	1996	15(4)	3	0	0	12
Salesi Finau	Warrington	1996-97	16(15)	8	0	0	32
Liam Finn	Wakefield	2004	1(1)	0	1	0	2
	Halifax	2002-03	16(5)	2	30	1	69
Lee Finnerty	Halifax	2003	18(2)	5	2	0	24
Phil Finney	Warrington	1998	1	0	0	0	0
Simon Finnigan	Huddersfield	2009	19(1)	5	0	0	20
	Bradford	2008	14(13)	8	0	0	32
	Salford	2006-07	50	17	0	0	68
	Widnes	2003-05	51(19)	21	0	0	84
Matt Firth	Halifax	2000-01	12(2)	0	0	0	0
Andy Fisher	Wakefield	1999-2000	31(8)	4	0	0	16
Ben Fisher	Hull KR	2007-09	55(17)	10	0	0	40
Daniel Fitzhenry	Hull KR	2008-09	36(11)	14	0	0	56
Karl Fitzpatrick	Salford	2004-07,					
		2009	65(11)	24	2	0	100
Mark Flanagan	Wigan	2009	3(7)	1	0	0	4
Chris Flannery	St Helens	2007-09	52(3)	11	0	0	44
Darren Fleary	Leigh	2005	24	1	0	0	4
	Huddersfield	2003-04	43(8)	4	0	0	16
	Leeds	1997-2002	98(9)	3	0	0	12
Greg Fleming	London	1999-2001	64(1)	40	2	0	164
Adam Fletcher	Castleford	2006, 2008	16(7)	11	0	0	44
Bryan Fletcher	Wigan	2006-07	47(2)	14	0	0	56
Richard Fletcher	Castleford	2006	13(5)	3	4	0	20
	Hull	1999-2004	11(56)	5	0	0	20
Greg Florimo	Halifax	2000	26	6	4	0	32
	Wigan	1999	18(2)	7	1	0	30
Ben Flower	Celtic	2009	2(15)	0	0	0	0
Jason Flowers	Salford	2004	6(1)	0	0	0	0
	Halifax	2002	24(4)	4	0	0	16
	Castleford	1996-2001	119(19)	33	0	1	133
Stuart Flowers	Castleford	1996	(3)	0	0	0	0
Adrian Flynn	Castleford	1996-97	19(2)	10	0	0	40
Wayne Flynn	Sheffield	1997	3(5)	0	0	0	0
Adam Fogerty	Warrington	1998	4	0	0	0	0
	St Helens	1996	13	1	0	0	4
Carl Forber	Leigh	2005	4	1	0	0	4
	St Helens	2004	1(1)	0	6	0	12
Paul Forber	Salford	1997-98	19(12)	4	0	0	16
Byron Ford	Hull KR	2007	13	6	0	0	24
James Ford	Castleford	2009	3(5)	1	0	0	4
Mike Ford	Castleford	1997-98	25(12)	5	0	3	23
	Warrington	1996	3	0	0	0	0
Jim Forshaw	Salford	1999	(1)	0	0	0	0
Mike Forshaw	Warrington	2004	20(1)	5	0	0	20
	Bradford	1997-2003	162(7)	32	0	0	128
	Leeds	1996	11(3)	5	0	0	20
Mark Forster	Warrington	1996-2000	102(1)	40	0	0	160
David Foster	Halifax	2000-01	4(9)	0	0	0	0
Peter Fox	Hull KR	2008-09	49	31	0	0	124
	Wakefield	2007	23	11	0	0	44
Nick Fozzard	Hull KR	2009	18(1)	1	0	0	4
	St Helens	2004-08	92(17)	6	0	0	24
	Warrington	2002-03	43(11)	2	0	0	8
	Huddersfield	1998-2000	24(8)	2	0	0	8
	Leeds	1996-97	6(16)	3	0	0	12
David Fraisse	Workington	1996	8	0	0	0	0
Daniel Frame	Widnes	2002-05	100(6)	24	0	0	96

167

Super League Players 1996-2009

PLAYER	CLUB	YEAR	APP	TRIES	GOALS	FG	PTS
Paul Franze	Castleford	2006	2(1)	0	0	0	0
Laurent Frayssinous							
	Catalans	2006	14(2)	3	32	0	76
Andrew Frew	Halifax	2003	17	5	0	0	20
	Wakefield	2002	21	8	0	0	32
	Huddersfield	2001	26	15	0	0	60
Dale Fritz	Castleford	1999-2003	120(4)	9	0	0	36
Gareth Frodsham	St Helens	2008-09	1(9)	0	0	0	0
Liam Fulton	Huddersfield	2009	12(3)	4	0	0	16
David Furner	Leeds	2003-04	45	8	23	0	78
	Wigan	2001-02	51(2)	21	13	0	110
David Furness	Castleford	1996	(1)	0	0	0	0
Matt Gafa	Harlequins	2006-09	81	26	16	0	136
Luke Gale	Harlequins	2009	11(10)	6	2	0	28
Ben Galea	Hull KR	2008-09	49(1)	10	0	0	40
Tommy Gallagher	Hull KR	2007	1(7)	0	0	0	0
	Widnes	2004	(6)	0	0	0	0
	London	2003	1(9)	1	0	0	4
Mark Gamson	Sheffield	1996	3	0	0	0	0
Jim Gannon	Hull KR	2007	7(16)	1	0	0	4
	Huddersfield	2003-06	79(14)	11	0	0	44
	Halifax	1999-2002	83(4)	14	0	0	56
Steve Garces	Salford	2001	(1)	0	0	0	0
Jean-Marc Garcia	Sheffield	1996-97	35(3)	22	0	0	88
Ade Gardner	St Helens	2002-09	184(11)	114	0	0	456
Matt Gardner	Harlequins	2009	6(3)	2	0	0	8
	Huddersfield	2006-07	22(3)	7	0	0	28
	Castleford	2004	1	1	0	0	4
Steve Gartland	Oldham	1996	1(1)	0	1	0	2
Daniel Gartner	Bradford	2001-03	74(1)	26	0	0	104
Dean Gaskell	Warrington	2002-05	58(1)	10	0	0	40
George Gatis	Huddersfield	2008	5(5)	1	0	0	4
Richard Gay	Castleford	1996-2002	94(16)	39	0	0	156
Andrew Gee	Warrington	2000-01	33(1)	4	0	0	16
Stanley Gene	Hull KR	2007-09	37(17)	9	0	0	36
	Bradford	2006	5(16)	8	0	0	32
	Huddersfield	2001, 2003-05	70(6)	27	0	0	108
	Hull	2000-01	5(23)	6	0	0	24
Steve Georgallis	Warrington	2001	5(1)	2	0	0	8
Luke George	Wakefield	2007-09	11(3)	13	0	0	52
Shaun Geritas	Warrington	1997	(5)	1	0	0	4
Anthony Gibbons	Leeds	1996	9(4)	2	0	1	9
David Gibbons	Leeds	1996	3(4)	2	0	0	8
Scott Gibbs	St Helens	1996	9	3	0	0	12
Ashley Gibson	Leeds	2005-09	25(7)	13	9	0	70
Damian Gibson	Castleford	2003-04	40(3)	5	0	0	20
	Salford	2002	28	3	0	0	12
	Halifax	1998-2001	104(1)	39	0	0	156
	Leeds	1997	18	3	0	0	12
Matt Gidley	St Helens	2007-09	81	34	6	0	148
Ian Gildart	Oldham	1996-97	31(7)	0	0	0	0
Chris Giles	Widnes	2003-04	35	12	0	0	48
	St Helens	2002	(1)	0	0	0	0
Peter Gill	London	1996-99	75(6)	20	0	0	80
Carl Gillespie	Halifax	1996-99	47(36)	13	0	0	52
Michael Gillett	London	2001-02	23(21)	12	2	0	52
Simon Gillies	Warrington	1999	28	6	0	0	24
Lee Gilmour	St Helens	2004-09	149(3)	41	0	0	164
	Bradford	2001-03	44(31)	20	0	0	80
	Wigan	1997-2000	44(39)	22	0	0	88
Marc Glanville	Leeds	1998-99	43(3)	5	0	0	20
Eddie Glaze	Castleford	1996	1	0	0	0	0
Paul Gleadhill	Leeds	1996	4	0	0	0	0
Mark Gleeson	Warrington	2000-08	38(102)	12	0	0	48
Martin Gleeson	Wigan	2009	19	6	0	0	24
	Warrington	2005-09	110(1)	44	0	0	176
	St Helens	2002-04	56(1)	25	0	0	100
	Huddersfield	1999-2001	47(9)	18	0	0	72
Sean Gleeson	Wakefield	2007-09	49(5)	14	0	0	56
	Wigan	2005-06	3(3)	0	0	0	0
Jon Goddard	Hull KR	2007	20	2	0	0	8
	Castleford	2000-01	(2)	0	0	0	0
Richard Goddard	Castleford	1996-97	11(3)	2	10	0	28
Brad Godden	Leeds	1998-99	47	15	0	0	60
Wayne Godwin	Bradford	2008-09	10(23)	6	0	0	24
	Hull	2007	3(13)	1	0	0	4
	Wigan	2005-06	9(38)	6	0	0	24
	Castleford	2001-04	30(33)	18	56	0	184
Jason Golden	Harlequins	2009	16(8)	2	0	0	8
	Wakefield	2007-08	26(5)	1	0	0	4
Marvin Golden	Widnes	2003	4	1	0	0	4
	London	2001	17(2)	1	0	0	4
	Halifax	2000	20(2)	5	0	0	20
	Leeds	1996-99	43(11)	19	0	0	76
Brett Goldspink	Halifax	2000-02	64(5)	2	0	0	8
	Wigan	1999	6(16)	1	0	0	4
	St Helens	1998	19(4)	2	0	0	8
	Oldham	1997	13(2)	0	0	0	0
Lee Gomersall	Hull KR	2008	1	0	0	0	0
Luke Goodwin	London	1998	9(2)	3	1	1	15
	Oldham	1997	16(4)	10	17	2	76
Aaron Gorrell	Catalans	2007-08	23	6	14	0	52
Andy Gorski	Salford	2001-02	(2)	0	0	0	0

PLAYER	CLUB	YEAR	APP	TRIES	GOALS	FG	PTS
Cyrille Gossard	Catalans	2006-09	40(14)	4	0	0	16
Bobbie Goulding	Salford	2001-02	31(1)	2	56	4	124
	Wakefield	2000	12	3	25	3	65
	Huddersfield	1998-99	27(1)	3	65	4	146
	St Helens	1996-98	42(2)	9	210	4	460
Darrell Goulding	Wigan	2005-09	32(20)	19	0	0	76
	Salford	2009	9	5	0	0	20
Mick Govin	Leigh	2005	5(6)	4	0	0	16
David Gower	Salford	2006-07	(16)	0	0	0	0
James Graham	St Helens	2003-09	76(62)	35	0	0	140
Nathan Graham	Bradford	1996-98	17(28)	4	0	1	17
Nick Graham	Wigan	2003	13(1)	2	0	0	8
Jon Grayshon	Harlequins	2007-09	10(32)	4	0	0	16
	Huddersfield	2003-06	7(43)	5	0	0	20
Brett Green	Gateshead	1999	10(2)	0	0	0	0
Toby Green	Huddersfield	2001	3(1)	1	0	0	4
Craig Greenhill	Castleford	2004	21(4)	1	0	0	4
	Hull	2002-03	56	3	2	0	16
Clint Greenshields							
	Catalans	2007-09	83	41	0	0	164
Brandon Greenwood							
	Halifax	1996	1	0	0	0	0
Gareth Greenwood							
	Huddersfield	2003	(1)	0	0	0	0
	Halifax	2002	1	0	0	0	0
Lee Greenwood	Huddersfield	2005	7	3	0	0	12
	London	2004-05	30(2)	19	0	0	76
	Halifax	2000-03	38(2)	17	0	0	68
	Sheffield	1999	1(1)	0	0	0	0
Maxime Greseque							
	Wakefield	2007	2(1)	0	0	0	0
Mathieu Griffi	Catalans	2006-08	1(25)	0	0	0	0
Darrell Griffin	Huddersfield	2007-09	24(49)	8	0	0	32
	Wakefield	2003-06	55(37)	9	3	0	42
Josh Griffin	Huddersfield	2009	2	0	0	0	0
Jonathan Griffiths							
	Paris	1996	(4)	1	0	0	4
Andrew Grima	Workington	1996	2(9)	2	0	0	8
Tony Grimaldi	Hull	2000-01	56(1)	14	0	0	56
	Gateshead	1999	27(2)	10	0	0	40
Danny Grimley	Sheffield	1996	4(1)	1	0	0	4
Scott Grix	Wakefield	2008-09	39(3)	18	0	0	72
Simon Grix	Warrington	2006-09	36(11)	16	0	0	64
	Halifax	2003	2(4)	0	0	0	0
Brett Grogan	Gateshead	1999	14(7)	3	0	0	12
Brent Grose	Warrington	2003-07	134(1)	55	0	0	220
Renaud Guigue	Catalans	2006	14(4)	3	0	0	12
Jerome Guisset	Catalans	2006-09	86(17)	8	0	0	32
	Wigan	2005	20(2)	3	0	0	12
	Warrington	2000-04	59(65)	21	0	0	84
Awen Guttenbeil	Castleford	2008	19	0	0	0	0
Reece Guy	Oldham	1996	3(4)	0	0	0	0
Tom Haberecht	Castleford	2008	2(2)	1	0	0	4
Gareth Haggerty	Harlequins	2008-09	8(28)	6	0	0	24
	Salford	2004-07	1(93)	15	0	0	60
	Widnes	2002	1(2)	1	0	0	4
Andy Haigh	St Helens	1996-98	20(16)	11	0	0	44
Michael Haley	Leeds	2008	(1)	0	0	0	0
Carl Hall	Leeds	1996	7(2)	3	0	0	12
Craig Hall	Hull	2007-09	43(5)	30	8	0	136
Martin Hall	Halifax	1998	2(10)	0	0	0	0
	Hull	1999	7	0	0	0	0
	Castleford	1998	4	0	0	0	0
	Wigan	1996-97	31(5)	7	6	0	40
Ryan Hall	Leeds	2007-09	49(2)	43	0	0	172
Steve Hall	Widnes	2004	5	4	0	0	16
	London	2002-03	35(3)	10	0	0	40
	St Helens	1999-2001	36(22)	19	0	0	76
Graeme Hallas	Huddersfield	2001	1	0	0	0	0
	Hull	1998-99	30(10)	6	39	1	103
	Halifax	1996	11(4)	5	0	0	20
Dave Halley	Bradford	2007-09	40(12)	15	0	0	60
	Wakefield	2009	5	4	0	0	16
Danny Halliwell	Salford	2007	2(3)	0	0	0	0
	Leigh	2005	5	3	0	0	12
	Halifax	2000-03	17(8)	4	0	0	16
	Warrington	2002	9(1)	8	0	0	32
	Wakefield	2002	3	0	0	0	0
Colum Halpenny	Wakefield	2003-06	103(1)	36	0	0	144
	Halifax	2002	22	12	0	0	48
	Bradford	1996	(1)	0	0	0	0
Jon Hamer	Bradford	1996	(1)	0	0	0	0
Andrew Hamilton	London	1997, 2003	1(20)	3	0	0	12
John Hamilton	St Helens	1998	3	0	0	0	0
Karle Hammond	Halifax	2002	10(2)	2	14	0	36
	Salford	2001	2(3)	1	0	0	4
	London	1999-2000	47	23	2	3	99
	St Helens	1996-98	58(8)	28	0	0	116
Anthony Hancock	Paris	1997	8(6)	1	0	0	4
Michael Hancock	Salford	2001-02	12(24)	7	0	0	28
Gareth Handford	Castleford	2001	7(2)	0	0	0	0
	Bradford	2000	1(1)	0	0	0	0
Paul Handforth	Castleford	2006	2(15)	2	1	0	10
	Wakefield	2000-04	17(44)	10	13	0	66
Paddy Handley	Leeds	1996	1(1)	0	0	0	8

PLAYER	CLUB	YEAR	APP	TRIES	GOALS	FG	PTS
Dean Hanger	Warrington	1999	7(11)	3	0	0	12
	Huddersfield	1998	20(1)	5	0	0	20
Josh Hannay	Celtic	2009	17	2	24	0	56
Harrison Hansen	Wigan	2004-09	76(56)	25	0	0	100
Lee Hansen	Wigan	1997	10(5)	0	0	0	0
Shontayne Hape	Bradford	2003-08	123(2)	79	0	0	316
Lionel Harbin	Wakefield	2001	(1)	0	0	0	0
Ian Hardman	Hull KR	2007	18	4	0	0	16
	St Helens	2003-07	32(11)	9	5	0	46
Jeff Hardy	Hudds-Sheff	2000	20(5)	6	0	1	25
	Sheffield	1999	22(4)	7	0	0	28
Spencer Hargrave							
	Castleford	1996-99	(6)	0	0	0	0
Bryn Hargreaves	St Helens	2007-09	36(32)	5	0	0	20
	Wigan	2004-06	16(12)	1	0	0	4
Lee Harland	Castleford	1996-2004	148(35)	20	0	0	80
Neil Harmon	Halifax	2003	13(3)	0	0	0	0
	Salford	2001	6(5)	0	0	0	0
	Bradford	1998-2000	15(13)	2	0	0	8
	Huddersfield	1998	12	1	0	0	4
	Leeds	1996	10	1	0	0	4
Ben Harris	Bradford	2005-07	70(4)	24	0	0	96
Iestyn Harris	Bradford	2004-08	109(11)	35	87	2	316
	Leeds	1997-2001	111(7)	57	490	6	1214
	Warrington	1996	16	4	63	2	144
Ben Harrison	Warrington	2007-09	27(29)	4	0	0	16
Karl Harrison	Hull	1999	26	2	0	0	8
	Halifax	1996-98	60(2)	2	0	0	8
Andrew Hart	London	2004	12(1)	2	0	0	8
Tim Hartley	Harlequins	2006	2	1	0	0	4
	Salford	2004-05	6(7)	5	0	0	20
Carlos Hassan	Bradford	1996	6(4)	2	0	0	8
Phil Hassan	Wakefield	2002	9(1)	0	0	0	0
	Halifax	2000-01	25(4)	3	0	0	12
	Salford	1998	15	2	0	0	8
	Leeds	1996-97	38(4)	12	0	0	48
Tom Haughey	Castleford	2006	1(3)	1	0	0	4
	London	2003-04	10(8)	1	0	0	4
	Wakefield	2001-02	5(12)	0	0	0	0
Simon Haughton	Wigan	1996-2002	63(46)	32	0	0	128
Solomon Haumono							
	Harlequins	2006	10(9)	6	0	0	24
	London	2005	24(5)	8	0	0	32
Richie Hawkyard	Bradford	2007	1(2)	1	0	0	4
Andy Hay	Widnes	2003-04	50(2)	7	0	0	28
	Leeds	1997-2002	112(27)	43	0	0	172
	Sheffield	1996-97	17(3)	5	0	0	20
Adam Hayes	Hudds-Sheff	2000	2(1)	0	0	0	0
Joey Hayes	Salford	1999	9	2	0	0	8
	St Helens	1996-98	11(6)	7	0	0	28
James Haynes	Hull KR	2009	1	0	0	0	0
Mathew Head	Hull	2007	9(1)	1	0	1	5
Mitch Healey	Castleford	2001-03	68(1)	10	16	0	72
Daniel Heckenberg							
	Harlequins	2006-09	31(39)	4	0	0	16
Ricky Helliwell	Salford	1997-99	(2)	0	0	0	0
Tom Hemingway	Huddersfield	2005-09	7(7)	1	17	0	38
Bryan Henare	St Helens	2000-01	4(12)	1	0	0	4
Richard Henare	Warrington	1996-97	28(2)	24	0	0	96
Andrew Henderson							
	Castleford	2006, 2008	44(11)	4	0	0	16
Ian Henderson	Bradford	2005-07	33(37)	13	0	0	52
Kevin Henderson	Wakefield	2005-09	39(36)	7	0	0	28
	Leigh	2005	(1)	0	0	0	0
Mark Henry	Salford	2009	22	9	0	0	36
Brad Hepi	Castleford	1999, 2001	9(21)	3	0	0	12
	Salford	2000	3(5)	0	0	0	0
	Hull	1998	15(1)	3	0	0	12
Jon Hepworth	Castleford	2003-04	19(23)	7	8	0	44
	Leeds	2003	(1)	0	0	0	0
	London	2002	(2)	0	0	0	0
Ian Herron	Hull	2000	9	1	17	0	38
	Gateshead	1999	25	4	105	0	226
Jason Hetherington							
	London	2001-02	37	9	0	0	36
Gareth Hewitt	Salford	1999	2(1)	0	0	0	0
Andrew Hick	Hull	2000	9(9)	1	0	0	4
	Gateshead	1999	12(5)	2	0	0	8
Chris Hicks	Warrington	2008-09	48	32	119	0	366
Paul Hicks	Wakefield	1999	(1)	0	0	0	0
Darren Higgins	London	1998	5(6)	2	0	0	8
Iain Higgins	London	1997-98	1(7)	2	0	0	8
Liam Higgins	Castleford	2008-09	29(21)	1	0	0	4
	Hull	2003-06	1(34)	0	0	0	0
Mick Higham	Warrington	2009	9(8)	6	0	0	24
	Wigan	2006-08	61(28)	13	0	0	52
	St Helens	2001-05	43(56)	32	0	0	128
Chris Highton	Warrington	1997	1(1)	0	0	0	0
David Highton	London	2004-05	21(24)	2	0	0	8
	Salford	2002	4(5)	2	0	0	8
	Warrington	1998-2001	18(14)	2	0	0	8
Paul Highton	Salford	1998-2002, 2004-07	114(80)	14	0	0	56
	Halifax	1996-97	12(18)	2	0	0	8
Andy Hill	Huddersfield	1999	(4)	0	0	0	0
	Castleford	1999	4(4)	0	0	0	0
Chris Hill	Leigh	2005	(1)	0	0	0	0
Danny Hill	Wigan	2006-07	1(10)	0	0	0	0
	Hull KR	2007	2	0	0	0	0
	Hull	2004-06	4(6)	0	0	0	0
Howard Hill	Oldham	1996-97	22(12)	4	0	0	16
John Hill	St Helens	2003	(1)	0	0	0	0
	Halifax	2003	1(2)	0	0	0	0
	Warrington	2001-02	(4)	0	0	0	0
Scott Hill	Harlequins	2007-08	41(2)	13	0	0	52
Mark Hilton	Warrington	1996-2000, 2002	141(40)	7	0	0	28
Ian Hindmarsh	Catalans	2006	25	3	0	0	12
Brendan Hlad	Castleford	2008	(3)	0	0	0	0
Andy Hobson	Widnes	2004	5(13)	0	0	0	0
	Halifax	1998-2003	51(85)	8	0	0	32
Gareth Hock	Wigan	2003-09	98(37)	24	0	0	96
Tommy Hodgkinson							
	St Helens	2006	(1)	0	0	0	0
Andy Hodgson	Wakefield	1999	14(2)	2	1	0	10
	Bradford	1997-98	8(2)	4	0	0	16
Brett Hodgson	Huddersfield	2009	24	11	88	0	220
David Hodgson	Huddersfield	2008-09	36	22	0	0	88
	Salford	2005-07	81	30	47	0	214
	Wigan	2000-04	90(19)	43	0	0	172
	Halifax	1999	10(3)	5	0	0	20
Elliot Hodgson	Huddersfield	2009	1	0	0	0	0
Josh Hodgson	Hull	2009	(2)	0	0	0	0
Darren Hogg	London	1996	(1)	0	0	0	0
Michael Hogue	Paris	1997	5(7)	0	0	0	0
Chris Holden	Warrington	1996-97	2(1)	0	0	0	0
Stephen Holgate	Halifax	2000	1(10)	0	0	0	0
	Hull	1999	1	0	0	0	0
	Wigan	1997-98	11(26)	2	0	0	8
	Workington	1996	19	3	0	0	12
Martyn Holland	Wakefield	2000-03	52(3)	6	0	0	24
Tim Holmes	Widnes	2004-05	15(4)	0	0	0	0
Graham Holroyd	Huddersfield	2003	3(5)	0	0	0	0
	Salford	2000-02	40(11)	8	75	5	187
	Halifax	1999	24(2)	3	74	5	165
	Leeds	1996-98	40(26)	22	101	8	298
Dallas Hood	Wakefield	2003-04	18(9)	1	0	0	4
Jason Hooper	St Helens	2003-07	89(6)	35	30	0	200
Lee Hopkins	Harlequins	2006-07	44(3)	11	0	0	44
	London	2005	29	6	0	0	24
Sean Hoppe	St Helens	1999-2002	69(16)	32	0	0	128
Graeme Horne	Hull	2003-09	49(74)	24	0	0	96
Richard Horne	Hull	1999-2009	247(10)	92	12	6	398
John Hough	Warrington	1996-97	9	2	0	0	8
Danny Houghton	Hull	2007-09	17(35)	5	0	0	20
Sylvain Houles	Wakefield	2003, 2005	8(1)	1	0	0	4
	London	2001-02	17(10)	11	0	0	44
	Hudds-Sheff	2000	5(2)	1	0	0	4
Harvey Howard	Wigan	2001-02	25(27)	1	0	0	4
	Bradford	1998	4(2)	1	0	0	4
	Leeds	1996	8	0	0	0	0
Kim Howard	London	1997	4(5)	0	0	0	0
Stuart Howarth	Workington	1996	(2)	0	0	0	0
David Howell	Harlequins	2008-09	43	21	0	0	84
Phil Howlett	Bradford	1999	5(1)	2	0	0	8
Craig Huby	Castleford	2003-04, 2006, 2008-09	44(38)	12	34	0	116
Ryan Hudson	Castleford	2002-04, 2009	88(6)	24	0	0	96
	Huddersfield	1998-99, 2007-08	51(22)	10	0	0	40
	Wakefield	2000-01	42(9)	11	0	1	45
Adam Hughes	Widnes	2002-05	89(2)	45	51	0	282
	Halifax	2001	8(8)	8	0	0	32
	Wakefield	1999-2000	43(3)	21	34	0	152
	Leeds	1996-97	4(5)	4	0	0	16
Ian Hughes	Sheffield	1996	9(8)	4	0	0	16
Mark Hughes	Catalans	2006	23	9	0	0	36
Steffan Hughes	London	1999-2001	1(13)	1	0	0	4
David Hulme	Salford	1997-99	53(1)	5	0	0	20
	Leeds	1996	8(1)	2	0	0	8
Paul Hulme	Warrington	1996-97	23(1)	2	0	0	8
Gary Hulse	Widnes	2005	12(5)	2	0	0	8
	Warrington	2001-04	20(28)	8	0	1	33
Alan Hunte	Salford	2002	19(2)	9	0	0	36
	Warrington	1999-2001	83	49	0	0	196
	Hull	1998	21	7	0	0	28
	St Helens	1996-97	30(2)	28	0	0	112
Nick Hyde	Paris	1997	5(5)	1	0	0	4
Chaz I'Anson	Hull KR	2007-09	10(13)	3	0	0	12
Andy Ireland	Hull	1998-99	22(15)	0	0	0	0
	Bradford	1996	1	0	0	0	0
Kevin Iro	St Helens	1999-2001	76	39	0	0	156
	Leeds	1996	16	9	0	0	36
Andrew Isherwood							
	Wigan	1998-99	(5)	0	0	0	0
Olu Iwenofu	London	2000-01	2(1)	0	0	0	0

169

Super League Players 1996-2009

PLAYER	CLUB	YEAR	APP	TRIES	GOALS	FG	PTS
Chico Jackson	Hull	1999	(4)	0	0	0	0
Lee Jackson	Hull	2001-02	37(9)	12	1	0	50
	Leeds	1999-2000	28(24)	7	0	0	28
Michael Jackson	Sheffield	1998-99	17(17)	2	0	0	8
	Halifax	1996-97	27(6)	11	0	0	44
Paul Jackson	Huddersfield	1998, 2005-09	50(73)	4	0	0	16
	Castleford	2003-04	7(21)	0	0	0	0
	Wakefield	1999-2002	57(41)	2	0	0	8
Rob Jackson	Leigh	2005	20(3)	5	0	0	20
	London	2002-04	26(14)	9	0	0	36
Wayne Jackson	Halifax	1996-97	17(5)	2	0	0	8
Aled James	Celtic	2009	3(3)	0	0	0	0
	Widnes	2003	3	0	0	0	0
Andy James	Halifax	1996	(4)	0	0	0	0
Jordan James	Celtic	2009	17(4)	1	0	0	4
	Wigan	2006	2(4)	3	0	0	12
Matt James	Bradford	2006-09	1(23)	0	0	0	0
Pascal Jampy	Catalans	2006	4(7)	0	0	0	0
	Paris	1996-97	3(2)	0	0	0	0
Adam Janowski	Harlequins	2008	(1)	0	0	0	0
Ben Jeffries	Bradford	2008-09	43(3)	13	0	0	52
	Wakefield	2003-07	128(7)	62	14	4	280
Mick Jenkins	Hull	2000	24	2	0	0	8
	Gateshead	1999	16	3	0	0	12
Ed Jennings	London	1998-99	1(2)	0	0	0	0
Rod Jensen	Huddersfield	2007-08	26(3)	13	0	0	52
Anthony Jerram	Warrington	2007	(2)	0	0	0	0
Lee Jewitt	Salford	2007, 2009	4(25)	0	0	0	0
	Wigan	2005	(2)	0	0	0	0
Andrew Johns	Warrington	2005	3	1	12	1	29
Matthew Johns	Wigan	2001	24	3	0	1	13
Andy Johnson	Salford	2004-05	8(26)	7	0	0	28
	Castleford	2002-03	32(16)	11	0	0	44
	London	2000-01	24(21)	12	0	0	48
	Huddersfield	1999	5	1	0	0	4
	Wigan	1996-99	24(20)	19	0	0	76
Bruce Johnson	Widnes	2004-05	(4)	0	0	0	0
Jason Johnson	St Helens	1997-99	2	0	0	0	0
Mark Johnson	Salford	1999-2000	22(9)	16	0	0	64
	Hull	1998	10(1)	4	0	0	16
	Workington	1996	12	4	0	0	16
Nick Johnson	London	2003	(1)	0	0	0	0
Paul Johnson	Warrington	2007-09	37(9)	17	0	0	68
	Bradford	2004-06	46(8)	19	0	0	76
	Wigan	1996-2003	74(46)	54	0	0	216
Richard Johnson	Bradford	2008	(3)	0	0	0	0
Chris Jones	Leigh	2005	1(1)	0	0	0	0
Danny Jones	Halifax	2003	1	0	0	0	0
David Jones	Oldham	1997	14(1)	5	0	0	20
Mark Jones	Warrington	1996	8(11)	2	0	0	8
Phil Jones	Leigh	2005	16	8	31	0	94
	Wigan	1999-2001	14(7)	6	25	0	74
Stacey Jones	Catalans	2006-07	39	11	43	3	133
Stephen Jones	Huddersfield	2005	(1)	0	0	0	0
Stuart Jones	Castleford	2009	20(4)	1	0	0	4
	Huddersfield	2004-08	96(22)	17	0	0	68
	St Helens	2003	(18)	2	0	0	8
	Wigan	2002	5(3)	1	0	0	4
Ben Jones-Bishop	Leeds	2008-09	3(1)	0	0	0	0
Jamie Jones-Buchanan	Leeds	1999-2009	122(56)	38	0	0	152
Tim Jonkers	Wigan	2006	3(1)	0	0	0	0
	Salford	2004-06	5(11)	0	0	0	0
	St Helens	1999-2004	41(64)	12	0	0	48
Darren Jordan	Wakefield	2003	(1)	0	0	0	0
Phil Joseph	Huddersfield	2004	7(6)	0	0	0	0
Warren Jowitt	Hull	2003	(2)	0	0	0	0
	Salford	2001-02	17(4)	2	0	0	8
	Wakefield	2000	19(3)	8	0	0	32
	Bradford	1996-99	13(25)	5	0	0	20
Chris Joynt	St Helens	1996-2004	201(14)	68	0	0	272
Gregory Kacala	Paris	1996	7	1	0	0	4
Andy Kain	Castleford	2004, 2006	9(7)	3	10	0	32
Mal Kaufusi	London	2004	1(3)	0	0	0	0
Ben Kaye	Harlequins	2009	2(12)	0	0	0	0
	Leeds	2008	2(2)	1	0	0	4
Elliot Kear	Celtic	2009	3	0	0	0	0
Stephen Kearney	Hull	2005	22(2)	5	0	0	20
Damon Keating	Wakefield	2002	7(17)	1	0	0	4
Shaun Keating	London	1996	1(3)	0	0	0	0
Mark Keenan	Workington	1996	3(4)	1	0	0	4
Tony Kemp	Wakefield	1999-2000	15(5)	2	0	1	9
	Leeds	1996-98	23(2)	5	0	2	22
Damien Kennedy	London	2003	5(11)	1	0	0	4
Ian Kenny	St Helens	2004	(1)	0	0	0	0
Jason Kent	Leigh	2005	23	1	0	0	4
Shane Kenward	Wakefield	1999	28	6	0	0	24
	Salford	1998	1	0	0	0	0
Jason Keough	Paris	1997	2	1	0	0	4
Keiran Kerr	Widnes	2005	6	2	0	0	8
Martin Ketteridge	Halifax	1996	7(5)	0	0	0	0
Ronnie Kettlewell	Warrington	1996	(1)	0	0	0	0
Younes Khattabi	Catalans	2006-08	24(4)	10	0	0	40
David Kidwell	Warrington	2001-02	14(12)	9	0	0	36
Andrew King	London	2003	23(1)	15	0	0	60
Dave King	Huddersfield	1998-99	11(17)	2	0	0	8
James King	Leigh	2005	5(7)	0	0	0	0
Kevin King	Wakefield	2005	8(1)	2	0	0	8
	Castleford	2004	(1)	0	0	0	0
Matt King	Warrington	2008-09	47	20	0	0	80
Paul King	Hull	1999-2009	136(93)	20	0	1	81
Andy Kirk	Wakefield	2005	6(3)	1	0	0	4
	Salford	2004	20	5	0	0	20
	Leeds	2001-02	4(4)	0	0	0	0
Ian Kirke	Leeds	2006-09	25(42)	5	0	0	20
John Kirkpatrick	London	2004-05	18(1)	5	0	0	20
	St Helens	2001-03	10(11)	10	0	0	40
	Halifax	2003	4	1	0	0	4
Danny Kirmond	Huddersfield	2008-09	11(20)	6	0	0	24
Wayne Kitchin	Workington	1996	11(6)	3	17	1	47
Ian Knott	Leigh	2005	8(1)	2	0	0	8
	Wakefield	2002-03	34(5)	7	79	0	186
	Warrington	1996-2001	68(41)	24	18	0	132
Matt Knowles	Wigan	1996	(3)	0	0	0	0
Michael Knowles	Castleford	2006	(1)	0	0	0	0
Phil Knowles	Salford	1997	1	0	0	0	0
Simon Knox	Halifax	1999	(6)	0	0	0	0
	Salford	1998	1(1)	0	0	0	0
	Bradford	1996-98	9(19)	7	0	0	28
Toa Kohe-Love	Warrington	1996-2001, 2005-06	166(3)	90	0	0	360
	Bradford	2004	1(1)	0	0	0	0
	Hull	2002-03	42	19	0	0	76
Paul Koloi	Wigan	1997	1(2)	1	0	0	4
Craig Kopczak	Bradford	2006-09	4(44)	1	0	0	4
Michael Korkidas	Wakefield	2003-06, 2009	102(21)	13	0	0	52
	Huddersfield	2009	4(1)	1	0	0	4
	Castleford	2008	15(6)	1	0	0	4
	Salford	2007	26(1)	1	0	0	4
David Krause	London	1996-97	22(1)	7	0	0	28
Ben Kusto	Huddersfield	2001	21(4)	9	0	1	37
Adrian Lam	Wigan	2001-04	105(2)	40	1	9	171
Mark Lane	Paris	1996	(2)	0	0	0	0
Allan Langer	Warrington	2000-01	47	13	4	0	60
Kevin Langer	London	1996	12(4)	2	0	0	8
Junior Langi	Salford	2005-06	27(7)	7	0	0	28
Chris Langley	Huddersfield	2000-01	18(1)	3	0	0	12
Gareth Langley	St Helens	2006	1	1	3	0	10
Jamie Langley	Bradford	2002-09	117(47)	31	0	0	124
Andy Last	Hull	1999-2005	16(10)	4	0	0	16
Epalahame Lauaki	Hull	2009	(3)	0	0	0	0
Dale Laughton	Warrington	2002	15(1)	0	0	0	0
	Huddersfield	2000-01	36(2)	4	0	0	16
	Sheffield	1996-99	48(22)	5	0	0	20
Ali Lauitiiti	Leeds	2004-09	56(87)	47	0	0	188
Jason Laurence	Salford	1997	1	0	0	0	0
Graham Law	Wakefield	1999-2002	34(30)	6	40	0	104
Neil Law	Wakefield	1999-2002	83	39	0	0	156
	Sheffield	1998	1(1)	1	0	0	4
Dean Lawford	Widnes	2003-04	17(1)	5	2	4	28
	Halifax	2001	1(1)	0	0	0	0
	Leeds	1997-2000	15(8)	2	3	0	14
	Huddersfield	1999	6(1)	0	6	1	13
	Sheffield	1996	9(5)	2	1	1	11
Johnny Lawless	Halifax	2001-03	73(1)	10	0	0	40
	Hudds-Sheff	2000	19(6)	3	0	0	12
	Sheffield	1996-99	76(4)	11	0	0	44
Michael Lawrence	Huddersfield	2007-09	34(1)	13	0	0	52
Mark Leafa	Castleford	2008	5(9)	1	0	0	4
	Leigh	2005	28	2	0	0	8
Leroy Leapai	London	1996	2	0	0	0	0
Jim Leatham	Hull	1998-99	20(18)	4	0	0	16
	Leeds	1997	(1)	0	0	0	0
Andy Leathem	Warrington	1999	2(8)	0	0	0	0
	St Helens	1996-98	20(1)	1	0	0	4
Danny Lee	Gateshead	1999	16(2)	0	0	0	0
Jason Lee	Halifax	2001	10(1)	2	0	0	8
Mark Lee	Salford	1997-2000	25(11)	1	0	4	8
Robert Lee	Hull	1999	4(3)	0	0	0	0
Tommy Lee	Hull	2005-09	44(27)	6	0	0	24
Matthew Leigh	Salford	2000	(6)	0	0	0	0
Chris Leikvoll	Warrington	2004-07	72(18)	4	0	0	16
Jim Lenihan	Huddersfield	1999	19(1)	10	0	0	40
Mark Lennon	Celtic	2009	10(3)	1	8	0	20
	Hull KR	2007	11(4)	5	7	0	34
	Castleford	2001-03	30(21)	10	21	0	82
Tevita Leo-Latu	Wakefield	2006-09	9(44)	5	0	0	20
Gary Lester	Hull	1998-99	46	17	0	0	68
Stuart Lester	Wigan	1997	1(3)	0	0	0	0
Afi Leuila	Oldham	1996-97	17(3)	2	0	0	8
Kylie Leuluai	Leeds	2007-09	65(20)	10	0	0	40

PLAYER	CLUB	YEAR	APP	TRIES	GOALS	FG	PTS
Phil Leuluai	Salford	2007, 2009	4(28)	2	0	0	8
Thomas Leuluai	Wigan	2007-09	90	29	0	0	116
	Harlequins	2006	15(2)	6	0	0	24
	London	2005	20	13	0	0	52
Simon Lewis	Castleford	2001	4	3	0	0	12
Paul Leyland	St Helens	2006	1	0	0	0	0
Jon Liddell	Leeds	2001	1	0	0	0	0
Jason Lidden	Castleford	1997	15(1)	7	0	0	28
Danny Lima	Wakefield	2007	(3)	0	0	0	0
	Salford	2006	7(2)	0	0	0	0
	Warrington	2004-06	15(47)	9	0	0	36
Craig Littler	St Helens	2006	1	1	0	0	4
Stuart Littler	Salford	1998-2002, 2004-07, 2009	200(22)	60	0	0	240
Peter Livett	Workington	1996	3(1)	0	0	0	0
Scott Logan	Wigan	2006	10(11)	0	0	0	0
	Hull	2001-03	27(20)	5	0	0	20
Jamahl Lolesi	Huddersfield	2007-09	60(9)	23	0	0	92
Filimone Lolohea	Harlequins	2006	3(6)	0	0	0	0
	London	2005	8(15)	0	0	0	0
David Lomax	Huddersfield	2000-01	45(9)	4	0	0	16
	Paris	1997	19(2)	1	0	0	4
Jonny Lomax	St Helens	2009	5(2)	2	1	0	10
Dave Long	London	1999	(1)	0	0	0	0
Karl Long	London	2003	(1)	0	0	0	0
	Widnes	2002	4	1	0	0	4
Sean Long	St Helens	1997-2009	253(8)	126	826	20	2176
	Wigan	1996-97	1(5)	0	0	0	0
Davide Longo	Bradford	1996	1(3)	0	0	0	0
Gary Lord	Oldham	1996-97	28(12)	3	0	0	12
Paul Loughlin	Huddersfield	1998-99	34(2)	4	4	0	24
	Bradford	1996-97	36(4)	15	8	0	76
Rhys Lovegrove	Hull KR	2007-09	15(24)	7	0	0	28
Karl Lovell	Hudds-Sheff	2000	14	5	0	0	20
	Sheffield	1999	22(4)	8	0	0	32
James Lowes	Bradford	1996-2003	205	84	2	2	342
Laurent Lucchese	Paris	1996	13(5)	2	0	0	8
Zebastian Luisi	Harlequins	2006-07	23(2)	4	0	0	16
	London	2004-05	21(1)	7	0	0	28
Shaun Lunt	Huddersfield	2009	6(11)	11	0	0	44
Peter Lupton	Celtic	2009	16(4)	4	0	0	16
	Castleford	2006, 2008	40	11	0	0	44
	Hull	2003-06	19(26)	10	3	0	46
	London	2000-02	10(15)	2	2	0	12
Andy Lynch	Bradford	2005-09	107(29)	31	0	0	124
	Castleford	1999-2004	78(48)	15	0	0	60
Jamie Lyon	St Helens	2005-06	54(1)	39	172	0	500
Duncan MacGillivray	Wakefield	2004-08	75(18)	6	0	0	24
Brad Mackay	Bradford	2000	24(2)	8	0	0	32
Graham Mackay	Hull	2002	27	18	24	0	120
	Bradford	2001	16(3)	12	1	0	50
	Leeds	2000	12(8)	10	2	0	44
Keiron Maddocks	Leigh	2005	1(3)	0	0	0	0
Steve Maden	Leigh	2005	23	9	0	0	36
	Warrington	2002	3	0	0	0	0
Mateaki Mafi	Warrington	1996-97	7(8)	7	0	0	28
Brendan Magnus	London	2000	3	1	0	0	4
Mark Maguire	London	1996-97	11(4)	7	13	0	54
Adam Maher	Hull	2000-03	88(4)	24	0	0	96
	Gateshead	1999	21(5)	3	0	0	12
Lee Maher	Leeds	1996	4(1)	0	0	0	0
Shaun Mahony	Paris	1997	5	0	0	0	0
Hutch Maiava	Hull	2007	(19)	1	0	0	4
David Maiden	Hull	2000-01	32(10)	11	0	0	44
	Gateshead	1999	5(16)	8	0	0	32
Craig Makin	Salford	1999-2001	24(20)	2	0	0	8
Brady Malam	Wigan	2000	5(20)	1	0	0	4
Dominic Maloney	Hull	2009	(7)	0	0	0	0
Francis Maloney	Castleford	1998-99, 2003-04	71(7)	24	33	3	165
	Salford	2001-02	45(1)	26	5	0	114
	Wakefield	2000	11	1	1	0	6
	Oldham	1996-97	39(2)	12	91	2	232
George Mann	Warrington	1997	14(5)	1	0	0	4
	Leeds	1996	11(4)	2	0	0	8
Dane Manning	Leeds	2009	(1)	0	0	0	0
Misili Manu	Widnes	2005	1	0	0	0	0
Willie Manu	Hull	2007-09	58(11)	10	0	0	40
	Castleford	2006	19(4)	9	0	0	36
Darren Mapp	Celtic	2009	9(2)	1	0	0	4
David March	Wakefield	1999-2007	164(23)	34	126	0	388
Paul March	Wakefield	1999-2001, 2007	42(31)	17	23	0	114
	Huddersfield	2003-06	71(19)	17	36	1	141
Nick Mardon	London	1997-98	14	2	0	0	8
Oliver Marns	Halifax	1996-2002	54(19)	23	0	0	92
Paul Marquet	Warrington	2002	23(2)	0	0	0	0
Iain Marsh	Salford	1998-2001	1(4)	0	0	0	0
Lee Marsh	Salford	2001-02	3(4)	0	0	0	0

PLAYER	CLUB	YEAR	APP	TRIES	GOALS	FG	PTS
Richard Marshall	Leigh	2005	4(16)	0	0	0	0
	London	2002-03	33(11)	1	0	0	4
	Huddersfield	2000-01	35(14)	1	0	0	4
	Halifax	1996-99	38(34)	2	0	0	8
Jason Martin	Paris	1997	15(2)	3	0	0	12
Scott Martin	Salford	1997-99	32(18)	8	0	0	32
Tony Martin	Wakefield	2008-09	33	10	33	0	106
	London	1996-97, 2001-03	97(1)	36	170	1	485
Mick Martindale	Halifax	1996	(4)	0	0	0	0
Sebastien Martins	Catalans	2006, 2009	(5)	1	0	0	4
Tommy Martyn	St Helens	1996-2003	125(20)	87	63	12	486
Dean Marwood	Workington	1996	9(6)	0	22	0	44
Martin Masella	Warrington	2001	10(14)	5	0	0	20
	Wakefield	2000	14(8)	4	0	0	16
	Leeds	1997-1999	59(5)	1	0	0	4
Colin Maskill	Castleford	1996	8	1	1	0	6
Keith Mason	Huddersfield	2006-09	78(5)	3	0	0	12
	Castleford	2006	(2)	0	0	0	0
	St Helens	2003-05	33(23)	4	0	0	16
	Wakefield	2000-01	5(17)	0	0	0	0
Nathan Massey	Castleford	2008-09	1(4)	0	0	0	0
Vila Matautia	St Helens	1996-2001	31(68)	9	0	0	36
Feleti Mateo	London	2005	4(10)	1	0	0	4
Barrie-Jon Mather	Castleford	1998, 2000-02	50(12)	21	0	0	84
Richard Mathers	Warrington	2002, 2009	18(3)	3	0	0	12
	Wigan	2008-09	23(1)	2	0	0	8
	Leeds	2002-06	85(2)	26	0	0	104
Jamie Mathiou	Leeds	1997-2001	31(82)	3	0	0	12
Terry Matterson	London	1996-98	46	15	90	6	246
Luke May	Harlequins	2009	(1)	0	0	0	0
Casey Mayberry	Halifax	2000	1(1)	0	0	0	0
Chris Maye	Halifax	2003	3(4)	0	0	0	0
Joe Mbu	Harlequins	2006-09	33(20)	3	0	0	12
	London	2003-05	29(19)	4	0	0	16
Danny McAllister	Gateshead	1999	3(3)	1	0	0	4
	Sheffield	1996-97	33(7)	10	0	0	40
John McAtee	St Helens	1996	2(1)	0	0	0	0
Nathan McAvoy	Bradford	1998-2002, 2007	83(31)	46	0	0	184
	Wigan	2006	15(2)	5	0	0	20
	Salford	1997-98, 2004-05	57(4)	18	0	0	72
Tyrone McCarthy	Warrington	2009	1(3)	2	0	0	8
Louie McCarthy-Scarsbrook	Harlequins	2006-09	26(41)	16	0	0	64
Dave McConnell	London	2003	(4)	0	0	0	0
	St Helens	2001-02	3(2)	4	0	0	16
Robbie McCormack	Wigan	1998	24	2	0	0	8
Steve McCurrie	Leigh	2005	7(3)	1	0	0	4
	Widnes	2002-04	55(22)	10	0	0	40
	Warrington	1998-2001	69(26)	31	0	0	124
Barrie McDermott	Leeds	1996-2005	163(69)	28	0	0	112
Brian McDermott	Bradford	1996-2002	138(32)	33	0	0	132
Ryan McDonald	Widnes	2002-03	6(4)	0	0	0	0
Wayne McDonald	Huddersfield	2005-06	11(23)	1	0	0	4
	Wigan	2005	(4)	0	0	0	0
	Leeds	2002-05	34(47)	14	0	0	56
	St Helens	2001	7(11)	4	0	0	16
	Hull	2000	5(8)	4	0	0	16
	Wakefield	1999	9(17)	8	0	0	32
Craig McDowell	Huddersfield	2003	(1)	0	0	0	0
	Warrington	2002	(1)	0	0	0	0
	Bradford	2000	(1)	0	0	0	0
Wes McGibbon	Halifax	1999	1	0	0	0	0
Dean McGilvray	Salford	2009	12	4	0	0	16
	St Helens	2006-08	5(1)	1	0	0	4
Billy McGinty	Workington	1996	1	0	0	0	0
Ryan McGoldrick	Castleford	2006, 2008-09	78	15	10	0	80
Kevin McGuinness	Salford	2004-07	63(3)	11	0	0	44
Casey McGuire	Catalans	2007-09	65(4)	22	0	0	88
Danny McGuire	Leeds	2001-09	159(34)	147	0	2	590
Gary McGuirk	Workington	1996	(4)	0	0	0	0
Michael McIlorum	Wigan	2007-09	10(31)	3	0	0	12
Richard McKell	Castleford	1997-98	22(7)	2	0	0	8
Chris McKenna	Bradford	2006-07	40(7)	7	0	0	28
	Leeds	2003-05	65(4)	18	0	0	72
Phil McKenzie	Workington	1996	4	0	0	0	0
Chris McKinney	Oldham	1996-97	4(9)	2	0	0	8
Mark McLinden	Harlequins	2006-08	46(1)	20	0	1	81
	London	2005	22(3)	8	0	0	32
Shayne McMenemy	Hull	2003-07	80(8)	12	0	0	48
	Halifax	2001-03	63	11	0	0	44
Andy McNally	London	2004	5(3)	0	0	0	0
	Castleford	2001, 2003	2(5)	1	0	0	4

Super League Players 1996-2009

PLAYER	CLUB	YEAR	APP	TRIES	GOALS	FG	PTS
Steve McNamara	Huddersfield	2001, 2003	41(9)	3	134	1	281
	Wakefield	2000	15(2)	2	32	0	72
	Bradford	1996-99	90(3)	14	348	7	759
Paul McNicholas	Hull	2004-05	28(12)	4	0	0	16
Neil McPherson	Salford	1997	(1)	0	0	0	0
Duncan McRae	London	1996	11(2)	3	0	1	13
Paul McShane	Leeds	2009	1(2)	0	0	0	0
Derek McVey	St Helens	1996-97	28(4)	6	1	0	26
Dallas Mead	Warrington	1997	2	0	0	0	0
Robbie Mears	Leigh	2005	8(6)	0	0	0	0
	Leeds	2001	23	6	0	0	24
Paul Medley	Bradford	1996-98	6(35)	9	0	0	36
Francis Meli	St Helens	2006-09	96(1)	54	0	0	216
Chris Melling	Harlequins	2007-09	51(9)	21	3	0	90
	Wigan	2004-05	8(2)	1	3	0	10
Paul Mellor	Castleford	2003-04	36(3)	18	0	0	72
Craig Menkins	Paris	1997	4(5)	0	0	0	0
Luke Menzies	Hull KR	2008	(1)	0	0	0	0
Steve Menzies	Bradford	2009	25(1)	12	0	0	48
Gary Mercer	Castleford	2002	(1)	0	0	0	0
	Leeds	1996-97, 2001	40(2)	9	0	0	36
	Warrington	2001	18	2	0	0	8
	Halifax	1998-2001	73(2)	16	0	0	64
Tony Mestrov	London	1996-97, 2001	59(8)	4	0	0	16
	Wigan	1998-2000	39(39)	3	0	0	12
Keiran Meyer	London	1996	4	1	0	0	4
Brad Meyers	Bradford	2005-06	40(11)	13	0	0	52
Gary Middlehurst	Widnes	2004	(2)	0	0	0	0
Simon Middleton	Castleford	1996-97	19(3)	8	0	0	32
Shane Millard	Wigan	2007	19(6)	3	0	0	12
	Leeds	2006	6(21)	3	0	0	12
	Widnes	2003-05	69	23	0	0	92
	London	1998-2001	72(14)	11	1	0	46
David Mills	Hull KR	2008-09	20(11)	1	0	0	4
	Harlequins	2006-07	24(20)	2	0	0	8
	Widnes	2002-05	17(77)	8	0	0	32
Lewis Mills	Celtic	2009	(4)	0	0	0	0
Lee Milner	Halifax	1999	(1)	0	0	0	0
John Minto	London	1996	13	4	0	0	16
Lee Mitchell	Warrington	2007-09	8(17)	3	0	0	12
Sam Moa	Hull	2009	(14)	0	0	0	0
Martin Moana	Salford	2004	6(3)	1	0	0	4
	Halifax	1996-2001, 2003	126(22)	62	0	1	249
	Wakefield	2002	19(2)	10	0	0	40
	Huddersfield	2001	3(3)	2	0	0	8
Adam Mogg	Catalans	2007-09	70	19	0	1	77
Steve Molloy	Huddersfield	2000-01	26(20)	3	0	0	12
	Sheffield	1998-99	32(17)	3	0	0	12
Chris Molyneux	Huddersfield	2000-01	1(18)	0	0	0	0
	Sheffield	1999	1(2)	0	0	0	0
Michael Monaghan	Warrington	2008-09	50(1)	9	0	1	37
Adrian Moore	Huddersfield	1998-99	1(4)	0	0	0	0
Danny Moore	London	2000	7	0	0	0	0
	Wigan	1998-99	49(3)	18	0	0	72
Jason Moore	Workington	1996	(5)	0	0	0	0
Richard Moore	Wakefield	2007-09	36(32)	7	0	0	28
	Leigh	2005	2(5)	0	0	0	0
	Bradford	2002-04	1(26)	0	0	0	0
	London	2002, 2004	5(9)	2	0	0	8
Scott Moore	Huddersfield	2009	23(2)	9	0	0	36
	Castleford	2008	11(5)	1	0	0	4
	St Helens	2004-07	8(10)	2	0	0	8
Dennis Moran	Wigan	2005-06	39	17	1	1	71
	London	2001-04	107(2)	74	2	5	305
Willie Morganson	Sheffield	1997-98	18(12)	5	3	0	26
Paul Moriarty	Halifax	1996	3(2)	0	0	0	0
Adrian Morley	Warrington	2007-09	67(1)	2	0	0	8
	Bradford	2005	2(4)	0	0	0	0
	Leeds	1996-2000	95(14)	25	0	0	100
Chris Morley	Salford	1999	3(5)	0	0	0	0
	Warrington	1998	2(8)	0	0	0	0
	St Helens	1996-97	21(16)	4	0	0	16
Glenn Morrison	Bradford	2007-09	48(2)	19	0	0	76
Iain Morrison	Hull KR	2007	5(6)	1	0	0	4
	Huddersfield	2003-05	11(23)	1	0	0	4
	London	2001	(1)	0	0	0	0
Dale Morton	Wakefield	2009	2(1)	1	0	0	4
Gareth Morton	Hull KR	2007	7(4)	3	23	0	58
	Leeds	2001-02	1(1)	0	0	0	0
Lee Mossop	Wigan	2008-09	(12)	0	0	0	0
	Huddersfield	2009	1(4)	1	0	0	4
Aaron Moule	Salford	2006-07	45	17	0	0	68
	Widnes	2004-05	29	12	0	0	48
Wilfried Moulinec	Paris	1996	1	0	0	0	0
Gregory Mounis	Catalans	2006-09	70(29)	14	9	0	74
Mark Moxon	Huddersfield	1998-2001	20(5)	1	0	1	5
Brett Mullins	Leeds	2001	5(3)	1	0	0	4
Damian Munro	Salford	2002	8(2)	1	0	0	4
	Halifax	1996-97	9(6)	8	0	0	32
Matt Munro	Oldham	1996-97	26(5)	8	0	0	32

PLAYER	CLUB	YEAR	APP	TRIES	GOALS	FG	PTS
Craig Murdock	Salford	2000	(2)	0	0	0	0
	Hull	1998-99	21(6)	8	0	2	34
	Wigan	1996-98	18(17)	14	0	0	56
Aaron Murphy	Wakefield	2008-09	12(2)	5	0	0	20
Justin Murphy	Catalans	2006-08	59	49	0	0	196
	Widnes	2004	5	1	0	0	4
Doc Murray	Warrington	1997	(2)	0	0	0	0
	Wigan	1997	6(2)	0	0	0	0
Scott Murrell	Hull KR	2007-09	54(7)	11	17	0	78
	Leeds	2005	(1)	0	0	0	0
	London	2004	3(3)	2	0	0	8
David Mycoe	Sheffield	1996-97	12(13)	1	0	0	4
Richard Myler	Salford	2009	18	11	0	0	44
Rob Myler	Oldham	1996-97	19(2)	6	0	0	24
Stephen Myler	Salford	2006	4(8)	1	15	0	34
	Widnes	2003-05	35(14)	8	74	0	180
Vinny Myler	Salford	2004	(4)	0	0	0	0
	Bradford	2003	(1)	0	0	0	0
Matt Nable	London	1997	2(2)	1	0	0	4
Brad Nairn	Workington	1996	14	4	0	0	16
Frank Napoli	London	2000	14(6)	2	0	0	8
Carlo Napolitano	Salford	2000	(3)	1	0	0	4
Stephen Nash	Salford	2007, 2009	2(18)	1	0	0	4
	Widnes	2005	4(1)	0	0	0	0
Jim Naylor	Halifax	2000	7(6)	2	0	0	8
Scott Naylor	Salford	1997-98, 2004	30(1)	9	0	0	36
	Bradford	1999-2003	127(1)	51	0	0	204
Mike Neal	Salford	1998	(1)	0	0	0	0
	Oldham	1996-97	6(4)	3	0	0	12
Jonathan Neill	Huddersfield	1998-99	20(11)	0	0	0	0
	St Helens	1996	1	0	0	0	0
Chris Nero	Bradford	2008	41(5)	16	0	0	64
	Huddersfield	2004-07	97(8)	38	0	0	152
Jason Netherton	Hull KR	2007-09	22(33)	4	0	0	16
	London	2003-04	6	0	0	0	0
	Halifax	2002	2(3)	0	0	0	0
	Leeds	2001	(3)	0	0	0	0
Kirk Netherton	Castleford	2009	4(21)	3	0	0	12
	Hull KR	2007-08	9(15)	2	0	0	8
Paul Newlove	Castleford	2004	1	0	0	0	0
	St Helens	1996-2003	162	106	0	0	424
Richard Newlove	Wakefield	2003	17(5)	8	0	0	32
Clint Newton	Hull KR	2008-09	45(1)	16	0	0	64
Terry Newton	Bradford	2006-09	83(6)	26	0	0	104
	Wigan	2000-05	157(9)	62	0	0	248
	Leeds	1996-1999	55(14)	4	0	0	16
Gene Ngamu	Huddersfield	1999-2000	29(2)	9	67	0	170
Sonny Nickle	St Helens	1999-2002	86(18)	14	0	0	56
	Bradford	1996-98	25(16)	9	0	0	36
Jason Nicol	Salford	2000-02	52(7)	11	0	0	44
Tawera Nikau	Warrington	2000-01	51	7	0	0	28
Rob Nolan	Hull	1998-99	20(11)	6	0	0	24
Paul Noone	Harlequins	2006	5(2)	0	0	0	0
	Warrington	2000-06	60(59)	12	20	0	88
Chris Norman	Halifax	2003	13(3)	2	0	0	8
Paul Norman	Oldham	1996	1	0	0	0	0
Andy Northey	St Helens	1996-97	8(17)	2	0	0	8
Danny Nutley	Castleford	2006	28	3	0	0	12
	Warrington	1998-2001	94(1)	3	0	0	12
Tony Nuttall	Oldham	1996-97	1(7)	0	0	0	0
Clinton O'Brien	Wakefield	2003	(2)	0	0	0	0
Sam Obst	Wakefield	2005-09	79(25)	32	1	0	130
Jamie O'Callaghan	Harlequins	2008-09	7(1)	1	0	0	4
Eamon O'Carroll	Wigan	2006-09	2(44)	2	0	0	8
Matt O'Connor	Paris	1997	11(4)	1	26	2	58
Terry O'Connor	Widnes	2005	25	2	0	0	8
	Wigan	1996-2004	177(45)	9	0	0	36
Jarrod O'Doherty	Huddersfield	2003	26	3	0	0	12
David O'Donnell	Paris	1997	21	3	0	0	12
Martin Offiah	Salford	2000-01	41	20	0	2	82
	London	1996-99	29(3)	21	0	0	84
	Wigan	1996	8	7	0	0	28
Mark O'Halloran	London	2004-05	34(3)	10	0	0	40
Ryan O'Hara	Celtic	2009	27	3	0	0	12
Hefin O'Hare	Huddersfield	2001, 2003-05	72(10)	27	0	0	108
Hitro Okesene	Hull	1998	21(1)	0	0	0	0
Anderson Okiwe	Sheffield	1997	1	0	0	0	0
Tom Olbison	Bradford	2009	(1)	0	0	0	0
Jamie Olejnik	Paris	1997	11	8	0	0	32
Kevin O'Loughlin	Halifax	1997-98	2(4)	0	0	0	0
	St Helens	1997	(3)	0	0	0	0
Sean O'Loughlin	Wigan	2002-09	167(19)	35	2	2	146
Jules O'Neill	Widnes	2003-05	57(3)	14	158	7	379
	Wakefield	2005	10(2)	2	4	0	16
	Wigan	2002-03	29(1)	12	72	0	192
Julian O'Neill	Widnes	2002-05	57(39)	3	0	0	12
	Wakefield	2001	24(1)	2	0	0	8
	St Helens	1997-2000	95(8)	5	0	0	20
Mark O'Neill	Hull KR	2007	17	5	0	0	20
	Leeds	2006	1(8)	0	0	0	0
Steve O'Neill	Gateshead	1999	1(1)	0	0	0	0

PLAYER	CLUB	YEAR	APP	TRIES	GOALS	FG	PTS
Tom O'Reilly	Warrington	2001-02	8(6)	1	0	0	4
Chris Orr	Huddersfield	1998	19(3)	2	0	0	8
Danny Orr	Harlequins	2007-09	69(2)	9	44	0	124
	Wigan	2004-06	66(2)	18	11	0	94
	Castleford	1997-2003	150(18)	65	279	3	821
Nick Owen	Leigh	2005	8(1)	1	11	0	26
Richard Owen	Castleford	2008-09	44(3)	21	0	0	84
Iafeta Palea'aesina							
	Wigan	2006-09	55(57)	14	0	0	56
Jason Palmada	Workington	1996	12	2	0	0	8
Junior Paramore	Castleford	1996	5(5)	3	0	0	12
Paul Parker	Hull	1999-2002	23(18)	9	0	0	36
Rob Parker	Salford	2009	15	1	0	0	4
	Warrington	2006-08	10(56)	6	0	0	24
	Bradford	2000,					
		2002-05	19(76)	14	0	0	56
	London	2001	9	1	0	0	4
Wayne Parker	Halifax	1996-97	12(1)	0	0	0	0
Ian Parry	Warrington	2001	(1)	0	0	0	0
Jules Parry	Paris	1996	10(2)	0	0	0	0
Regis Pastre-Courtine	Paris	1996	4(3)	4	0	0	0
16							
Andrew Patmore	Oldham	1996	8(5)	3	0	0	12
Larne Patrick	Huddersfield	2009	2(5)	1	0	0	4
Henry Paul	Harlequins	2006-08	60(1)	8	94	2	222
	Bradford	1999-2001	81(5)	29	350	6	822
	Wigan	1996-98	60	37	23	0	194
Junior Paul	London	1996	3	1	0	0	4
Robbie Paul	Salford	2009	2(24)	2	0	0	8
	Huddersfield	2006-07	44(8)	7	0	0	28
	Bradford	1996-2005	198(31)	121	3	0	490
Jason Payne	Castleford	2006	1(1)	0	0	0	0
Danny Peacock	Bradford	1997-99	32(2)	15	0	0	60
Jamie Peacock	Leeds	2006-09	104(6)	16	0	0	64
	Bradford	1999-2005	163(25)	38	0	0	152
Martin Pearson	Wakefield	2001	21(1)	3	60	3	135
	Halifax	1997-98,					
		2000	55(6)	24	181	0	458
	Sheffield	1999	17(6)	9	36	2	110
Jacques Pech	Paris	1996	16	0	0	0	0
Mike Pechey	Warrington	1998	6(3)	2	0	0	8
Bill Peden	London	2003	21(3)	7	0	0	28
Adam Peek	Celtic	2009	5(12)	3	0	0	12
Dimitri Pelo	Catalans	2007-09	62	33	0	0	132
Sean Penkywicz	Huddersfield	2004-05	21(11)	7	0	0	28
	Halifax	2000-03	29(27)	8	0	0	32
Julian Penni	Salford	1998-99	4	0	0	0	0
Kevin Penny	Warrington	2006-09	39(1)	26	0	0	104
Lee Penny	Warrington	1996-2003	140(5)	54	0	0	216
Paul Penrice	Workington	1996	11(2)	2	0	0	8
Chris Percival	Widnes	2002-03	26	6	0	0	24
Apollo Perelini	St Helens	1996-2000	103(16)	27	0	0	108
Mark Perrett	Halifax	1996-97	15(4)	4	0	0	16
Shane Perry	Catalans	2009	8(8)	1	0	0	4
Adam Peters	Paris	1997	16(3)	0	0	0	0
Dominic Peters	London	1998-2003	58(11)	12	0	0	48
Mike Peters	Warrington	2000	2(12)	1	0	0	4
	Halifax	2000	1	0	0	0	0
Willie Peters	Widnes	2004	9	3	0	2	14
	Wigan	2000	29	15	5	6	76
	Gateshead	1999	27	11	1	6	52
Matt Petersen	Wakefield	2008-09	14	3	0	0	12
Adrian Petrie	Workington	1996	(1)	0	0	0	0
Cameron Phelps	Wigan	2008-09	37(1)	10	4	0	48
Rowland Phillips	Workington	1996	22	1	0	0	4
Nathan Picchi	Leeds	1996	(1)	0	0	0	0
Ian Pickavance	Hull	1999	4(2)	2	0	0	8
	Huddersfield	1999	3(14)	0	0	0	0
	St Helens	1996-98	12(44)	6	0	0	24
James Pickering	Castleford	1999	1(19)	0	0	0	0
Steve Pickersgill	Warrington	2005-09	1(36)	0	0	0	0
Nick Pinkney	Salford	2000-02	64	29	0	0	116
	Halifax	1999	26(2)	13	0	0	52
	Sheffield	1997-98	33	10	0	0	40
Mikhail Piskunov	Paris	1996	1(1)	1	0	0	4
Darryl Pitt	London	1996	2(16)	4	0	1	17
Jay Pitts	Leeds	2009	(1)	1	0	0	4
	Wakefield	2008-09	9(8)	2	0	0	8
Andy Platt	Salford	1997-98	20(3)	1	0	0	4
Michael Platt	Bradford	2007-09	58(3)	23	0	0	92
	Castleford	2006	26	7	0	0	28
	Salford	2001-02	3	1	0	0	4
Willie Poching	Leeds	2002-06	58(73)	44	0	0	176
	Wakefield	1999-2001	65(4)	20	0	0	80
Quentin Pongia	Wigan	2003-04	15(10)	0	0	0	0
Dan Potter	Widnes	2002-03	34(2)	6	0	0	24
	London	2001	1(3)	1	0	0	4
Craig Poucher	Hull	1999-2002	31(5)	5	0	0	20
Bryn Powell	Salford	2004	1(1)	0	0	0	0
Daio Powell	Sheffield	1999	13(1)	2	0	0	8
	Halifax	1997-98	30(3)	17	0	0	68
Daryl Powell	Leeds	1998-2000	49(30)	12	0	2	50
Karl Pratt	Bradford	2003-05	35(19)	18	0	0	72
	Leeds	1999-2002	62(12)	33	0	0	132

PLAYER	CLUB	YEAR	APP	TRIES	GOALS	FG	PTS
Paul Prescott	Wigan	2004-09	24(42)	1	0	0	4
Steve Prescott	Hull	1998-99,					
		2001-03	99	46	191	3	569
	Wakefield	2000	22(1)	3	13	0	38
	St Helens	1996-97	32	15	17	0	94
Lee Prest	Workington	1996	(1)	0	0	0	0
Gareth Price	Salford	2002	(2)	0	0	0	0
	London	2002	2(2)	3	0	0	12
	St Helens	1999	(11)	2	0	0	8
Gary Price	Wakefield	1999-2001	55(13)	11	0	0	44
Richard Price	Sheffield	1996	1(2)	0	0	0	0
Tony Priddle	Paris	1997	11(7)	3	0	0	12
Karl Pryce	Wigan	2009	4(2)	2	0	0	8
	Bradford	2003-06	28(19)	33	1	0	134
Leon Pryce	St Helens	2006-09	106(2)	56	0	0	224
	Bradford	1998-2005	159(29)	86	0	0	344
Waine Pryce	Wakefield	2007	10(2)	4	0	0	16
	Castleford	2000-06	97(12)	49	0	0	196
Tony Puletua	St Helens	2009	24(3)	14	0	0	56
Andrew Purcell	Castleford	2000	15(5)	3	0	0	12
	Hull	1999	27	4	0	0	16
Rob Purdham	Harlequins	2006-09	80(1)	14	117	1	291
	London	2002-05	53(15)	16	2	1	69
Luke Quigley	Catalans	2007	16(1)	1	0	0	4
Damien Quinn	Celtic	2009	20(1)	4	12	0	40
Scott Quinnell	Wigan	1996	6(3)	1	0	0	4
Florian Quintilla	Catalans	2008-09	1(4)	0	0	0	0
Lee Radford	Hull	1998,					
		2006-09	108(7)	13	1	0	54
	Bradford	1999-2005	79(65)	18	12	0	96
Kris Radlinski	Wigan	1996-2006	236(1)	134	1	0	538
Sebastien Raguin	Catalans	2007-09	45(7)	12	0	0	48
Adrian Rainey	Castleford	2002	4(7)	1	0	0	4
Andy Raleigh	Huddersfield	2006-09	60(32)	13	0	0	52
Jean-Luc Ramondou							
	Paris	1996	1(1)	1	0	0	4
Chad Randall	Harlequins	2006-09	98(2)	28	0	0	112
Craig Randall	Halifax	1999	8(11)	4	0	0	16
	Salford	1997-98	12(18)	4	0	0	16
Scott Ranson	Oldham	1996-97	19(2)	7	0	0	28
Aaron Raper	Castleford	1999-2001	48(4)	4	2	1	21
Stefan Ratchford	Salford	2007, 2009	27	9	10	0	56
Mike Ratu	Leeds	2007, 2009	1(5)	1	0	0	4
Paul Rauhihi	Warrington	2006-09	67(20)	10	0	0	40
Ben Rauter	Wakefield	2001	15(6)	4	0	0	16
Gareth Raynor	Hull	2001-09	186	102	0	0	408
	Leeds	2000	(3)	0	0	0	0
Tony Rea	London	1996	22	4	0	0	16
Stuart Reardon	Warrington	2006-08	48	12	0	0	48
	Bradford	2003-05	62(11)	32	0	0	128
	Salford	2002	7(1)	3	0	0	12
Mark Reber	Wigan	1999-2000	9(9)	5	0	0	20
Alan Reddicliffe	Warrington	2001	1	0	0	0	0
Tahi Reihana	Bradford	1997-98	17(21)	0	0	0	0
Paul Reilly	Wakefield	2008	5(2)	1	0	0	4
	Huddersfield	1999-2001,					
		2003-07	150(8)	35	1	0	142
Robert Relf	Widnes	2002-04	68(2)	5	0	0	20
Steve Renouf	Wigan	2000-01	55	40	0	0	160
Steele Retchless	London	1998-2004	177(6)	13	0	0	52
Scott Rhodes	Hull	2000	2	0	0	0	0
Phillipe Ricard	Paris	1996-97	2	0	0	0	0
Andy Rice	Huddersfield	2000-01	2(13)	1	0	0	4
Basil Richards	Huddersfield	1998-99	28(17)	1	0	0	4
Craig Richards	Oldham	1996	1	0	0	0	0
Pat Richards	Wigan	2006-09	107	64	325	3	909
Andy Richardson	Hudds-Sheff	2000	(2)	0	0	0	0
Sean Richardson	Widnes	2002	2(18)	1	0	0	4
	Wakefield	1999	5(1)	0	0	0	0
	Castleford	1996-97	3(8)	1	0	0	4
Mark Riddell	Wigan	2009	25(3)	3	0	0	12
Neil Rigby	St Helens	2006	(1)	0	0	0	0
Shane Rigon	Bradford	2001	14(11)	12	0	0	48
Craig Rika	Halifax	1996	2	0	0	0	0
Chris Riley	Warrington	2005-09	48(10)	26	0	0	104
Peter Riley	Workington	1996	7(5)	0	0	0	0
Julien Rinaldi	Bradford	2009	(7)	1	0	0	4
	Harlequins	2007-08	4(43)	9	0	0	36
	Catalans	2006	16(6)	3	1	0	14
	Wakefield	2002	(3)	0	0	0	0
Dean Ripley	Castleford	2004	3(4)	1	0	0	4
Leroy Rivett	Warrington	2002	9	1	0	0	4
	Hudds-Sheff		5(1)	1	0	0	4
	Leeds	1996-2000	39(15)	21	0	0	84
Jason Roach	Warrington	1998-99	29(7)	15	0	0	60
	Castleford	1997	7	4	0	0	16
Ben Roarty	Castleford	2006	11(6)	2	0	0	8
	Huddersfield	2003-05	52	5	0	0	20
Amos Roberts	Wigan	2009	29	12	5	0	58
Mark Roberts	Wigan	2003	(3)	0	0	0	0
Robert Roberts	Huddersfield	2001	(1)	0	0	0	0
	Halifax	2000	(3)	0	0	0	0
	Hull	1999	24(2)	4	13	4	46
Chad Robinson	Harlequins	2009	13(1)	2	0	0	8

173

Super League Players 1996-2009

PLAYER	CLUB	YEAR	APP	TRIES	GOALS	FG	PTS
Craig Robinson	Wakefield	2005	(1)	0	0	0	0
Jason Robinson	Wigan	1996-2000	126(1)	87	0	1	349
Jeremy Robinson	Paris	1997	10(3)	1	21	0	46
John Robinson	Widnes	2003-04	7	1	0	0	4
Luke Robinson	Huddersfield	2008-09	53	15	4	0	68
	Salford	2005-07	79	28	10	2	134
	Wigan	2002-04	17(25)	9	6	1	49
	Castleford	2004	9	4	3	0	22
Will Robinson	Hull	2000	22	4	0	0	16
	Gateshead	1999	28	9	0	0	36
James Roby	St Helens	2004-09	49(101)	38	0	0	152
Mike Roby	St Helens	2004	(1)	0	0	0	0
Carl Roden	Warrington	1997	1	0	0	0	0
Matt Rodwell	Warrington	2002	10	3	0	0	12
Darren Rogers	Castleford	1999-2004	162(1)	81	0	0	324
	Salford	1997-98	42	16	0	0	64
Jamie Rooney	Wakefield	2003-09	113(7)	60	314	21	889
	Castleford	2001	2(1)	0	6	0	12
Jonathan Roper	Castleford	2001	13	7	12	0	52
	Salford	2000	1(4)	1	3	0	10
	London	2000	4	0	0	0	0
	Warrington	1996-2000	75(8)	33	71	0	274
Scott Roskell	London	1996-97	30(2)	16	0	0	64
Steve Rosolen	London	1996-98	25(9)	10	0	0	40
Adam Ross	London	1996	(1)	0	0	0	0
Paul Round	Castleford	1996	(3)	0	0	0	0
Steve Rowlands	Widnes	2004-05	18(3)	2	15	0	38
	St Helens	2003	(1)	0	0	0	0
Paul Rowley	Leigh	2005	15(7)	3	0	0	12
	Huddersfield	2001	24	3	0	0	12
	Halifax	1996-2000	107(3)	27	1	3	113
Nigel Roy	London	2001-04	100	39	0	0	156
Nicky Royle	Widnes	2004	13	7	0	0	28
Chris Rudd	Warrington	1996-98	31(17)	10	16	0	72
Sean Rudder	Catalans	2006	22(1)	6	0	0	24
	Castleford	2004	9(3)	2	0	0	8
James Rushforth	Halifax	1997	(4)	0	0	0	0
Danny Russell	Huddersfield	1998-2000	50(13)	8	0	0	32
Ian Russell	Oldham	1997	1(3)	1	0	0	4
	Paris	1996	3	0	0	0	0
Richard Russell	Castleford	1996-98	37(4)	2	0	0	8
Robert Russell	Salford	1998-99	2(1)	0	1	0	2
Sean Rutgerson	Salford	2004-06	60(9)	4	0	0	16
Chris Ryan	London	1998-99	44(3)	17	10	0	88
Sean Ryan	Castleford	2004	11(5)	2	0	0	8
	Hull	2002-03	53	8	0	0	32
Justin Ryder	Wakefield	2004	19(3)	11	0	0	44
Jason Ryles	Catalans	2009	19(2)	2	0	0	8
Teddy Sadaoui	Catalans	2006	7	0	0	0	0
Matt Salter	London	1997-99	14(34)	0	0	0	0
Ben Sammut	Hull	2000	20	4	67	0	150
	Gateshead	1999	26(2)	6	17	0	58
Dean Sampson	Castleford	1996-2003	124(28)	24	0	0	96
Paul Sampson	London	2004	1(2)	1	0	0	4
	Wakefield	2000	17	8	0	0	32
Lee Sanderson	London	2004	1(5)	1	7	0	18
Jason Sands	Paris	1996-97	28	0	0	0	0
Mitchell Sargent	Castleford	2008-09	27(6)	4	0	0	16
Lokeni Savelio	Halifax	2000	2(11)	0	0	0	0
	Salford	1997-98	18(20)	0	0	0	0
Tom Saxton	Salford	2007	5	0	0	0	0
	Wakefield	2006	9(6)	2	0	0	8
	Hull	2005	19(8)	3	0	0	12
	Castleford	2002-04	37(12)	11	0	0	44
Jonathan Scales	Halifax	2000	1	0	0	0	0
	Bradford	1996-98	46(4)	24	0	0	96
Andrew Schick	Castleford	1996-98	45(13)	10	0	0	40
Garry Schofield	Huddersfield	1998	(2)	0	0	0	0
Gary Schubert	Workington	1996	(1)	0	0	0	0
Matt Schultz	Hull	1998-99	23(9)	2	0	0	8
	Leeds	1996	2(4)	0	0	0	0
John Schuster	Halifax	1996-97	31	9	127	3	293
Nick Scruton	Bradford	2009	22(5)	1	0	0	4
	Leeds	2002, 2004-08	11(53)	3	0	0	12
	Hull	2004	2(16)	3	0	0	12
Danny Sculthorpe							
	Huddersfield	2009	5(8)	0	0	0	0
	Wakefield	2007-09	14(28)	1	0	0	4
	Castleford	2006	18(1)	4	0	1	17
	Wigan	2002-05	13(49)	7	0	0	28
Paul Sculthorpe	St Helens	1998-2008	223(4)	94	356	7	1095
	Warrington	1996-97	40	6	0	0	24
Mick Seaby	London	1997	3(2)	1	0	0	4
Danny Seal	Halifax	1996-99	8(17)	3	0	0	12
Matt Seers	Wakefield	2003	11(1)	2	0	0	8
Anthony Seibold	London	1999-2000	33(19)	5	0	0	20
Keith Senior	Leeds	1999-2009	278(1)	145	0	0	580
	Sheffield	1996-99	90(2)	40	0	0	160
Fili Seru	Hull	1998-99	37(1)	13	0	0	52
Anthony Seuseu	Halifax	2003	1(11)	1	0	0	4
Jerry Seuseu	Wigan	2005-06	29(9)	1	0	0	4
Will Sharp	Harlequins	2008-09	38(1)	12	0	0	48

PLAYER	CLUB	YEAR	APP	TRIES	GOALS	FG	PTS
Darren Shaw	Salford	2002	5(9)	1	0	0	4
	London	1996, 2002	22(8)	3	0	0	12
	Castleford	2000-01	50(6)	1	0	0	4
	Sheffield	1998-99	51(1)	3	0	1	13
Mick Shaw	Halifax	1999	5	1	0	0	4
	Leeds	1996	12(2)	7	0	0	28
Phil Shead	Paris	1996	3(2)	0	0	0	0
Richard Sheil	St Helens	1997	(1)	0	0	0	0
Kelly Shelford	Warrington	1996-97	25(3)	4	0	2	18
Michael Shenton	Castleford	2004, 2006, 2008-09	75(2)	36	0	0	144
Ryan Sheridan	Castleford	2004	2	0	0	0	0
	Widnes	2003	14(3)	2	0	0	8
	Leeds	1997-2002	123(7)	46	0	1	185
	Sheffield	1996	9(3)	5	0	1	21
Rikki Sheriffe	Bradford	2009	27	6	0	0	24
	Harlequins	2006-08	35(1)	16	0	0	64
	Halifax	2003	6(1)	3	0	0	12
Ian Sherratt	Oldham	1996	5(3)	1	0	0	4
Brent Sherwin	Castleford	2008-09	37	1	0	3	7
Peter Shiels	St Helens	2001-02	44(3)	11	0	0	44
Gary Shillabeer	Huddersfield	1999	(2)	0	0	0	0
Mark Shipway	Salford	2004-05	30(12)	3	0	0	12
Ian Sibbit	Salford	2005-07, 2009	47(14)	10	0	0	40
	Warrington	1999-2001, 2003-04	63(18)	24	0	0	96
Mark Sibson	Huddersfield	1999	2	2	0	0	8
Adam Sidlow	Salford	2009	6(11)	1	0	0	4
Jon Simms	St Helens	2002	(1)	0	0	0	0
Craig Simon	Hull	2000	23(2)	8	0	0	32
	Gateshead	1999	25(4)	6	0	0	24
Darren Simpson	Huddersfield	1998-99	17(1)	5	0	0	20
Robbie Simpson	London	1999	6(7)	0	0	0	0
Kevin Sinfield	Leeds	1997-2009	271(25)	47	911	15	2025
Matt Sing	Hull	2007-08	41	14	0	0	56
Wayne Sing	Paris	1997	18(1)	2	0	0	8
Fata Sini	Salford	1997	22	7	0	0	28
John Skandalis	Huddersfield	2007-08	37(5)	4	0	0	16
Dylan Skee	Harlequins	2008-09	(3)	0	0	0	0
Ben Skerrett	Castleford	2003	(1)	0	0	0	0
Kelvin Skerrett	Halifax	1997-99	31(6)	2	0	0	8
	Wigan	1996	1(8)	0	0	0	0
Troy Slattery	Wakefield	2002-03	33(5)	4	0	0	16
	Huddersfield	1999	3	1	0	0	4
Mick Slicker	Huddersfield	2001, 2003-05	17(48)	2	0	0	8
	Sheffield	1999	(3)	1	0	0	4
	Halifax	1997	2(5)	0	0	0	0
Ian Smales	Castleford	1996-97	10(8)	5	0	0	20
Aaron Smith	Castleford	2006	(2)	0	0	0	0
	Bradford	2003-04	12(1)	3	0	0	12
Andy Smith	Harlequins	2007	6(3)	3	0	0	12
	Bradford	2004-06	9(9)	4	0	0	16
	Salford	2005	4	1	0	0	4
Byron Smith	Castleford	2004	(9)	0	0	0	0
	Halifax	2003	6(1)	0	0	0	0
Chris Smith	Hull	2001-02	12	3	0	0	12
	St Helens	1998-2000	62(9)	26	0	0	104
	Castleford	1996-97	36(1)	12	0	0	48
Craig Smith	Wigan	2002-04	77(3)	10	0	0	40
Damien Smith	St Helens	1998	21(1)	8	0	0	32
Danny Smith	Paris	1996	10(2)	1	15	0	34
	London	1996	2(1)	1	0	0	4
Darren Smith	St Helens	2003	25(1)	14	0	0	56
Gary Smith	Castleford	2001	(1)	0	0	0	0
Hudson Smith	Bradford	2000	8(22)	2	0	0	8
	Salford	1999	23(2)	5	0	0	20
James Smith	Salford	2000	23(3)	6	0	0	24
Jamie Smith	Hull	1998-99	24(6)	6	12	0	48
	Workington	1996	5(3)	0	1	0	2
Jason Smith	Hull	2001-04	61(3)	17	0	1	69
Jeremy Smith	Salford	2009	23(1)	2	0	0	8
Kris Smith	London	2001	(1)	0	0	0	0
	Halifax	2001	(1)	0	0	0	0
Lee Smith	Leeds	2005-09	86(5)	46	22	1	229
Leigh Smith	Workington	1996	9	4	0	0	16
Mark Smith	Widnes	2005	12(15)	4	0	0	16
	Wigan	1999-2004	35(77)	8	0	0	32
Matty Smith	Celtic	2009	15(1)	3	2	1	17
	St Helens	2006-08	14(2)	3	10	1	33
Michael Smith	Hull KR	2007	(3)	1	0	0	4
	Castleford	1998, 2001-04	86(33)	32	0	0	128
	Hull	1999	12(6)	3	0	0	12
Paul Smith	Huddersfield	2004-06	52(17)	13	0	0	52
Paul Smith	Warrington	2001	(1)	0	0	0	0
	Castleford	1997-2000	6(37)	3	0	0	12
Paul Smith	London	1997	7(1)	2	0	0	8
Peter Smith	Oldham	1996	2	0	0	0	0
Richard Smith	Wakefield	2001	8(1)	1	0	0	4
	Salford	1997	(1)	1	0	0	4
Tim Smith	Wigan	2008-09	13(8)	2	0	0	8

174

PLAYER	CLUB	YEAR	APP	TRIES	GOALS	FG	PTS
Tony Smith	Hull	2001-03	43(5)	26	0	0	104
	Wigan	1997-2000	66(5)	46	0	0	184
	Castleford	1996-97	18(2)	10	0	0	40
Tony Smith	Workington	1996	9	1	0	0	4
Tyrone Smith	Harlequins	2006-07	49(3)	13	0	0	52
	London	2005	20(4)	11	0	0	44
Rob Smyth	Leigh	2005	15(1)	4	0	0	16
	Warrington	2000-03	65	35	20	0	180
	London	1998-2000	32(2)	9	15	0	66
	Wigan	1996	11(5)	16	0	0	64
Steve Snitch	Wakefield	2002-05, 2009	33(55)	9	0	0	36
	Huddersfield	2006-08	24(35)	12	0	0	48
Bright Sodje	Wakefield	2000	15	4	0	0	16
	Sheffield	1996-99	54	34	0	0	136
David Solomona	Bradford	2007-09	44(9)	19	0	0	76
	Wakefield	2004-06	73(3)	26	0	0	104
Alfred Songoro	Wakefield	1999	8(5)	4	0	0	16
Romain Sort	Paris	1997	(1)	0	0	0	0
Paul Southern	Salford	1997-2002	79(33)	6	13	0	50
	St Helens	2002	1(1)	0	0	0	0
Roy Southernwood							
	Wakefield	1999	1	0	0	0	0
	Halifax	1996	2	0	0	0	0
Jason Southwell	Huddersfield	2004	(1)	0	0	0	0
Waisale Sovatabua							
	Wakefield	2001-03	44(3)	19	0	0	76
	Hudds-Sheff	2000	23(1)	8	0	0	32
	Sheffield	1996-99	56(17)	19	0	1	77
Yusef Sozi	London	2000-01	(5)	0	0	0	0
Andy Speak	Castleford	2001	4(4)	0	0	0	0
	Wakefield	2000	6(5)	2	0	0	8
	Leeds	1999	4	1	0	0	4
Tim Spears	Castleford	2003	(3)	0	0	0	0
Ady Spencer	London	1996-99	8(36)	5	0	0	20
Jack Spencer	Salford	2009	(1)	0	0	0	0
Rob Spicer	Wakefield	2002-05	28(18)	4	0	0	16
Stuart Spruce	Widnes	2002-03	45(4)	19	0	0	76
	Bradford	1996-2001	107(2)	57	0	0	228
Lee St Hilaire	Castleford	1997	4(2)	0	0	0	0
Marcus St Hilaire	Bradford	2006-07	34(1)	12	0	0	48
	Huddersfield	2003-05	72(2)	30	0	0	120
	Leeds	1996-2002	59(33)	31	0	0	124
Cyril Stacul	Catalans	2007-09	28	9	0	0	36
Dylan Stainton	Workington	1996	2(3)	0	0	0	0
Mark Stamper	Workington	1996	(1)	0	0	0	0
John Stankevitch	Widnes	2005	17(5)	0	0	0	0
	St Helens	2000-04	74(40)	25	0	0	100
Gareth Stanley	Bradford	2000	1	1	0	0	4
Craig Stapleton	Salford	2009	24	2	0	0	8
	Leigh	2005	27(1)	4	0	0	16
Graham Steadman							
	Castleford	1996-97	11(17)	5	0	0	20
Jon Steel	Hull KR	2007-08	18	6	0	0	24
Jamie Stenhouse	Warrington	2000-01	9(3)	3	0	0	12
Gareth Stephens	Sheffield	1997-99	23(6)	2	0	0	8
David Stephenson							
	Hull	1998	11(7)	3	0	0	12
	Oldham	1997	10(8)	2	0	0	8
Francis Stephenson							
	London	2002-05	42(34)	5	0	0	20
	Wigan	2001	2(9)	0	0	0	0
	Wakefield	1999-2000	50(1)	6	0	0	24
Paul Sterling	Leeds	1997-2000	79(12)	50	0	0	200
Paul Stevens	Oldham	1996	2(1)	0	0	0	0
	London	1996	(1)	0	0	0	0
Warren Stevens	Leigh	2005	4(14)	1	0	0	4
	Warrington	1996-99, 2002-05	17(66)	1	0	0	4
	Salford	2001	(8)	0	0	0	0
Anthony Stewart	Harlequins	2006	4	0	0	0	0
	Salford	2004-06	51(2)	15	0	0	60
	St Helens	1997-2003	93(23)	44	0	0	176
Troy Stone	Widnes	2002	18(6)	1	0	0	4
	Huddersfield	2001	12(1)	1	0	0	4
James Stosic	Wakefield	2009	8(10)	1	0	0	4
Lynton Stott	Wakefield	1999	21	4	6	1	29
	Sheffield	1996-98	40(4)	15	0	0	60
Mitchell Stringer	Salford	2005-06	12(4)	0	0	0	0
	London	2004-05	10(19)	0	0	0	0
Graham Strutton	London	1996	9(1)	2	0	0	8
Matt Sturm	Leigh	2005	8(19)	3	0	0	12
	Warrington	2002-04	1(18)	0	0	0	0
	Huddersfield	1998-99	46	8	0	0	32
Anthony Sullivan	St Helens	1996-2001	137(2)	105	0	0	420
Michael Sullivan	Warrington	2006-07	21(16)	8	1	0	34
Phil Sumner	Warrington	1996	(5)	0	0	0	0
Simon Svabic	Salford	1998-2000	13(5)	3	19	0	50
Luke Swain	Salford	2009	27	2	0	0	8
Richard Swain	Hull	2004-07	89	5	0	0	20
Anthony Swann	Warrington	2001	3	1	0	0	4
Logan Swann	Warrington	2005-06	49(1)	17	0	0	68
	Bradford	2004	25	6	0	0	24
Willie Swann	Warrington	1996-97	25(2)	6	0	0	24
Nathan Sykes	Castleford	1996-2004	158(52)	3	0	0	12
Paul Sykes	Bradford	1999-2002, 2008-09	56(4)	26	23	0	150
	Harlequins	2006-07	31(2)	15	47	1	155
	London	2001-05	95(1)	26	220	3	547
Wayne Sykes	London	1999	(2)	0	0	0	0
Semi Tadulala	Bradford	2008-09	49	30	0	0	120
	Wakefield	2004-07	85	36	0	0	144
Whetu Taewa	Sheffield	1997-98	33(7)	8	0	0	32
Alan Tait	Leeds	1996	3(3)	1	0	0	4
Willie Talau	Salford	2009	5	2	0	0	8
	St Helens	2003-08	130(1)	50	0	0	200
Ian Talbot	Wakefield	1999	9(5)	2	31	0	70
	Wigan	1997	3	1	0	0	4
Albert Talipeau	Wakefield	2004	2(3)	0	0	0	0
Gael Tallec	Halifax	2000	5(19)	3	0	0	12
	Castleford	1998-99	19(21)	3	0	0	12
	Wigan	1996-97	8(12)	3	0	0	12
Joe Tamani	Bradford	1996	11(3)	4	0	0	16
Ryan Tandy	Hull KR	2007	8(4)	2	0	0	8
Andrew Tangata-Toa							
	Huddersfield	1999	15	2	0	0	8
David Tangata-Toa							
	Celtic	2009	1(18)	4	0	0	16
	Hull KR	2007	(17)	3	0	0	12
Jordan Tansey	Hull	2009	6	1	0	0	4
	Leeds	2006-08	18(32)	19	3	0	82
Kris Tassell	Wakefield	2002	24	10	0	0	40
	Salford	2000-01	35(10)	12	0	0	48
Shem Tatupu	Wigan	1996	(3)	0	0	0	0
Tony Tatupu	Wakefield	2000-01	20	2	0	0	8
	Warrington	1997	21(1)	6	0	0	24
James Taylor	Leigh	2005	(4)	0	0	0	0
Joe Taylor	Paris	1997	9(5)	2	0	0	8
Lawrence Taylor	Sheffield	1996	(1)	0	0	0	0
Scott Taylor	Hull KR	2009	(1)	0	0	0	0
Frederic Teixido	Sheffield	1999	(4)	0	0	0	0
	Paris	1996-97	2(3)	1	0	0	4
Lionel Teixido	Catalans	2006-07	11(13)	3	0	0	12
Karl Temata	Harlequins	2006-09	72(10)	3	0	0	12
	London	2005	1(2)	1	0	0	4
Jason Temu	Hull	1998	13(2)	1	0	0	4
	Oldham	1996-97	25(3)	1	0	0	4
Paul Terry	London	1997	(1)	0	0	0	0
Anthony Thackeray							
	Castleford	2008	3(6)	0	0	0	0
	Hull	2007	2	0	0	0	0
Jamie Thackray	Hull	2005-06, 2008-09	37(45)	6	0	0	24
	Leeds	2006-07	5(27)	7	0	0	28
	Castleford	2003-04	7(11)	3	0	0	12
	Halifax	2000-02	10(38)	3	0	0	12
Adam Thaler	Castleford	2002	(1)	0	0	0	0
Giles Thomas	London	1997-99	1(2)	0	0	0	0
Steve Thomas	London	2004	4(2)	0	0	0	0
	Warrington	2001	2	0	0	0	0
Alex Thompson	Warrington	2009	(1)	1	0	0	4
Alex Thompson	Sheffield	1997	4(11)	0	0	0	0
Bobby Thompson	Salford	1999	28	5	2	0	24
Jordan Thompson							
	Castleford	2009	1(1)	1	0	0	4
Sam Thompson	Harlequins	2009	(2)	0	0	0	0
	St Helens	2008	(5)	0	0	0	0
Chris Thorman	Hull	2009	19(2)	1	0	0	4
	Huddersfield	2000-01, 2005-08	126(20)	51	320	3	847
	London	2003	26(1)	7	81	1	191
	Sheffield	1999	5(13)	2	8	1	25
Tony Thorniley	Warrington	1997	(5)	0	0	0	0
Andy Thornley	Salford	2009	(1)	1	0	0	4
Danny Tickle	Hull	2007-09	80	20	242	0	564
	Wigan	2002-06	94(36)	35	201	2	544
	Halifax	2000-02	25(17)	10	91	2	224
Kris Tickle	Warrington	2001	(1)	0	0	0	0
John Timu	London	1998-2000	57(3)	11	0	0	44
Kerrod Toby	London	1997	2(2)	0	0	0	0
Tulsen Tollett	London	1996-2001	105(5)	38	49	1	251
Joel Tomkins	Wigan	2005-09	40(36)	23	0	0	92
Sam Tomkins	Wigan	2009	18(5)	12	0	1	49
Glen Tomlinson	Wakefield	1999-2000	41(5)	8	0	0	32
	Hull	1998	5	1	0	0	4
	Bradford	1996-97	27(13)	12	0	0	48
Ian Tonks	Castleford	1996-2001	32(50)	11	13	0	70
Motu Tony	Hull	2005-09	76(20)	25	0	0	100
	Castleford	2004	8(1)	1	0	0	4
Mark Tookey	Harlequins	2006	12(14)	1	0	0	4
	London	2005	13(14)	5	0	0	20
	Castleford	2004	2(8)	1	0	0	4
Clinton Toopi	Leeds	2006-08	40(3)	9	0	0	36
David Tootill	Harlequins	2008	(4)	0	0	0	0
Paul Topping	Oldham	1996-97	23(10)	1	19	0	42
Patrick Torreilles	Paris	1996	9(1)	1	25	0	54
Albert Torrens	Huddersfield	2006	7	5	0	0	20
Mat Toshack	London	1998-2004	120(21)	24	0	0	96
Julien Touxagas	Catalans	2006-09	12(40)	3	0	0	12
Darren Treacy	Salford	2002	24(1)	6	1	0	26
Dean Treister	Hull	2003	16(1)	3	0	0	12
Steve Trindall	London	2003-05	40(20)	3	0	0	12
George Truelove	Wakefield	2002	2	1	0	0	4
	London	2000	5	1	0	0	4
Va'aiga Tuigamala	Wigan	1996	21	10	3	0	46

Super League Players 1996-2009

PLAYER	CLUB	YEAR	APP	TRIES	GOALS	FG	PTS
Fereti Tuilagi	St Helens	1999-2000	43(15)	21	0	0	84
	Halifax	1996-98	55(3)	27	0	0	108
Sateki Tuipulotu	Leeds	1996	6(3)	1	2	0	8
Tame Tupou	Bradford	2007-08	10(7)	8	0	0	32
Neil Turley	Leigh	2005	6(3)	2	20	1	49
Darren Turner	Huddersfield	2000-01, 2003-04	42(13)	13	0	0	52
	Sheffield	1996-99	41(29)	15	0	0	60
Ian Turner	Paris	1996	1(1)	1	0	0	4
Jordan Turner	Salford	2006-07, 2009	22(10)	4	1	0	18
Chris Tuson	Wigan	2008	(1)	0	0	0	0
Gregory Tutard	Paris	1996	1(1)	0	0	0	0
Brendon Tuuta	Warrington	1998	18(2)	4	0	0	16
	Castleford	1996-97	41(1)	3	0	0	12
Steve Tyrer	Celtic	2009	8	2	5	0	18
	St Helens	2006-08	17(3)	12	42	0	132
Mike Umaga	Halifax	1996-97	38(1)	16	5	0	74
Kava Utoikamanu	Paris	1996	6(3)	0	0	0	0
David Vaealiki	Wigan	2005-07	67(1)	17	0	0	68
Joe Vagana	Bradford	2001-08	176(44)	17	0	0	68
Nigel Vagana	Warrington	1997	20	17	0	0	68
Tevita Vaikona	Bradford	1998-2004	145(2)	89	0	0	356
Lesley Vainikolo	Bradford	2002-07	132(4)	136	1	0	546
Eric Van Brussell	Paris	1996	2	0	0	0	0
Jace Van Dijk	Celtic	2009	19	1	1	0	6
Richard Varkulis	Warrington	2004	4(1)	3	0	0	12
Marcus Vassilakopoulos	Sheffield	1997-99	15(11)	3	10	2	34
	Leeds	1996-97	1(3)	0	0	0	0
Phil Veivers	Huddersfield	1998	7(6)	1	0	0	4
	St Helens	1996	(1)	1	0	0	4
Michael Vella	Hull KR	2007-09	64(2)	11	0	0	44
Bruno Verges	Catalans	2006	25	6	0	0	24
Eric Vergniol	Paris	1996	14(1)	6	0	0	24
Gray Viane	Salford	2007	9	2	0	0	8
	Castleford	2006	20(7)	14	0	0	56
	Widnes	2005	20	13	0	0	52
	St Helens	2004	1	1	0	0	4
Adrian Vowles	Castleford	1997-2001, 2003	125(1)	29	1	1	119
	Wakefield	2002-03	24(3)	6	1	0	26
	Leeds	2002	14(3)	2	0	0	8
Michael Wainwright	Castleford	2008-09	45	12	0	0	48
	Wakefield	2004-05	21(10)	8	0	0	32
Mike Wainwright	Salford	2000-02, 2007	75(3)	9	0	0	36
	Warrington	1996-99, 2003-07	168(14)	23	0	0	92
Ben Walker	Leeds	2002	23(1)	8	100	0	232
Chev Walker	Hull KR	2008-09	24(7)	5	0	0	20
	Leeds	1999-2006	142(19)	77	0	0	308
Matt Walker	Huddersfield	2001	3(6)	0	0	0	0
Anthony Wall	Paris	1997	9	3	3	0	18
Mark Wallace	Workington	1996	14(1)	3	0	0	12
Joe Walsh	Huddersfield	2009	1(1)	1	0	0	4
	Harlequins	2007-08	1(4)	0	0	0	0
Kerrod Walters	Gateshead	1999	10(12)	2	1	0	10
Kevin Walters	Warrington	2001	1	0	0	0	0
Jason Walton	Salford	2009	(5)	0	0	0	0
Barry Ward	St Helens	2002-03	20(30)	4	0	0	16
Danny Ward	Harlequins	2008-09	45(3)	3	0	0	12
	Hull KR	2007	11(9)	0	0	0	0
	Castleford	2006	18(7)	2	0	0	8
	Leeds	1999-2005	70(48)	9	0	1	37
Phil Waring	Salford	1997-99	6(8)	2	0	0	8
Brett Warton	London	1999-2001	49(7)	14	133	0	322
Kyle Warren	Castleford	2002	13(14)	3	0	0	12
Danny Washbrook	Hull	2005-09	70(15)	9	0	0	36
Adam Watene	Wakefield	2006-08	45(8)	5	0	0	20
	Bradford	2006	(4)	0	0	0	0
Frank Watene	Wakefield	1999-2001	24(37)	6	0	0	24
Kallum Watkins	Leeds	2008-09	10(6)	6	0	0	24
Dave Watson	Sheffield	1998-99	41(4)	4	0	0	16
Ian Watson	Salford	1997, 2002	24(17)	8	3	5	43
	Workington	1996	4(1)	1	15	0	34
Kris Watson	Warrington	1996	11(2)	2	0	0	8
Brad Watts	Widnes	2005	6	3	0	0	12
Liam Watts	Hull KR	2008	(3)	0	0	0	0
Michael Watts	Warrington	2002	3	0	0	0	0
Brent Webb	Leeds	2007-09	75(1)	52	0	0	208
Jason Webber	Salford	2000	25(1)	10	0	0	40
Ian Webster	St Helens	2006	1	0	0	0	0
Jake Webster	Hull KR	2008-09	46(1)	18	7	0	86
James Webster	Hull	2008	1	0	0	0	0
	Hull KR	2007-08	36	0	0	2	10
Pat Weisner	Hull KR	2007	(2)	0	0	0	0
	Harlequins	2006	10(6)	3	0	0	12
Taylor Welch	Warrington	2008	1	0	0	0	0
Kris Welham	Hull KR	2007-09	40(2)	19	0	0	76
Paul Wellens	St Helens	1998-2009	284(23)	130	34	1	589
Jon Wells	Harlequins	2006-09	66	10	0	0	40
	London	2004-05	42(2)	19	0	0	76
	Wakefield	2003	22(1)	1	0	0	4
	Castleford	1996-2002	114(14)	49	0	0	196
Dwayne West	St Helens	2000-02	8(16)	6	0	0	24
	Wigan	1999	1(1)	0	0	0	0
Joe Westerman	Castleford	2008-09	43(7)	21	69	0	222
Craig Weston	Widnes	2002, 2004	23(9)	2	1	2	12
	Huddersfield	1998-99	46(1)	15	15	0	90
Ben Westwood	Warrington	2002-09	175(6)	64	5	0	266
	Wakefield	1999-2002	31(7)	8	1	0	34
Andrew Whalley	Workington	1996	(2)	0	0	0	0
Paul Whatuira	Huddersfield	2008-09	49	19	0	0	76
Scott Wheeldon	Hull KR	2009	17(5)	1	0	0	4
	Hull	2006-08	2(60)	4	0	0	16
Gary Wheeler	St Helens	2008-09	7(4)	6	3	0	30
Matt Whitaker	Castleford	2006	8(2)	0	0	0	0
	Widnes	2004-05	10(20)	9	0	0	36
	Huddersfield	2003-04	3(14)	0	0	0	0
David White	Wakefield	2000	1	0	0	0	0
Josh White	Salford	1998	18(3)	5	5	1	31
	London	1997	14(2)	8	0	1	33
Lloyd White	Celtic	2009	6	1	0	0	4
Paul White	Salford	2009	1	1	0	0	4
	Wakefield	2006-07	24(12)	12	0	0	48
	Huddersfield	2003-05	11(32)	17	16	0	100
Elliott Whitehead	Bradford	2009	3(4)	1	0	0	4
Richard Whiting	Hull	2004-09	77(30)	35	5	2	152
Danny Whittle	Warrington	1998	(2)	0	0	0	0
David Whittle	St Helens	2002	1(2)	0	0	0	0
	Warrington	2001	1(2)	0	0	0	0
Jon Whittle	Wakefield	2006	8(2)	3	0	0	12
	Widnes	2005	13	2	0	0	8
	Wigan	2003	1	0	0	0	0
Dean Widders	Castleford	2009	8(10)	6	0	0	24
Stephen Wild	Huddersfield	2006-09	97(2)	29	0	0	116
	Wigan	2001-05	67(20)	24	0	0	96
Oliver Wilkes	Wakefield	2008-09	41(13)	6	0	0	24
	Wigan	2006	1(5)	0	0	0	0
	Leigh	2005	13(1)	1	0	0	4
	Huddersfield	2000-01	1(6)	0	0	0	0
	Sheffield	1998	(1)	0	0	0	0
Jon Wilkin	St Helens	2003-09	130(25)	49	0	1	197
Alex Wilkinson	Hull	2003-04	11(4)	1	0	0	4
	Huddersfield	2003	8	4	0	0	16
	London	2002	5(1)	0	0	0	0
	Bradford	2000-01	3(3)	1	0	0	4
Bart Williams	London	1998	5(3)	1	0	0	4
Daley Williams	Salford	2006-07	9(2)	4	0	0	16
Danny Williams	Harlequins	2006	9(13)	4	0	0	16
	London	2005	1(16)	0	0	0	0
Danny Williams	Leeds	2006, 2008	13(2)	7	0	0	28
	Hull	2008	3	0	0	0	0
Dave Williams	Harlequins	2008-09	(2)	0	0	0	0
Desi Williams	Wigan	2004	2	0	0	0	0
Jonny Williams	London	2004	(4)	0	0	0	0
Luke Williamson	Harlequins	2009	21	3	0	0	12
John Wilshere	Salford	2006-07, 2009	72(2)	32	142	0	412
	Leigh	2005	26	8	6	0	44
	Warrington	2004	5	2	0	0	8
Craig Wilson	Hull	2000	2(16)	1	0	1	5
	Gateshead	1999	17(11)	5	0	1	21
George Wilson	Paris	1996	7(2)	3	0	0	12
John Wilson	Catalans	2006-08	69	23	0	0	92
Richard Wilson	Hull	1998-99	(13)	0	0	0	0
Scott Wilson	Warrington	1998-99	23(2)	6	0	0	24
Johan Windley	Hull	1999	2(2)	1	0	0	4
Paul Wingfield	Warrington	1997	5(3)	6	1	0	26
Frank Winterstein	Wakefield	2009	(5)	0	0	0	0
Lincoln Withers	Celtic	2009	21	6	0	0	24
Michael Withers	Wigan	2007	6(1)	1	0	0	4
	Bradford	1999-2006	156(6)	94	15	4	410
Jeff Wittenberg	Huddersfield	1998	18(1)	1	0	0	4
	Bradford	1997	8(9)	4	0	0	16
Martin Wood	Sheffield	1997-98	24(11)	4	18	2	54
Nathan Wood	Warrington	2002-05	90	38	0	3	155
	Wakefield	2002	11	2	0	0	8
Paul Wood	Warrington	2000-09	89(107)	31	0	0	124
Phil Wood	Widnes	2004	2(1)	0	0	0	0
Darren Woods	Widnes	2005	(1)	0	0	0	0
David Woods	Halifax	2002	18(2)	8	0	0	32
Simon Worrall	Leeds	2008-09	5(16)	1	0	0	4
Michael Worrincy	Bradford	2009	4(20)	10	0	0	40
	Harlequins	2006-08	20(12)	10	0	0	40
Rob Worrincy	Castleford	2004	1	0	0	0	0
Troy Wozniak	Widnes	2004	13(7)	1	0	0	4
Matthew Wray	Wakefield	2002-03	13(3)	2	0	0	8
David Wrench	Wakefield	2002-06	28(52)	6	0	0	24
	Leeds	1999-2001	7(17)	0	0	0	0
Craig Wright	Castleford	2000	1(9)	0	0	0	0
Nigel Wright	Huddersfield	1999	4(6)	1	0	0	4
	Wigan	1996-97	15(2)	2	0	1	9
Ricky Wright	Sheffield	1997-99	2(13)	0	0	0	0
Vincent Wulf	Paris	1996	13(4)	1	0	0	4
Andrew Wynyard	London	1999-2000	34(6)	4	0	0	16
Bagdad Yaha	Paris	1996	4(4)	2	4	0	16
Malakai Yasa	Sheffield	1996	1(3)	0	0	0	0
Kirk Yeaman	Hull	2001-09	165(17)	94	0	0	376
Grant Young	London	1998-99	22(2)	2	0	0	8
Ronel Zenon	Paris	1996	(4)	0	0	0	0
Nick Zisti	Bradford	1999	6(1)	0	0	0	0
Freddie Zitter	Catalans	2006	1	0	0	0	0

NEW FACES - Players making their Super League debuts in 2009

PLAYER	CLUB	DEBUT vs	ROUND	DATE
Shaun Ainscough	Wigan	Castleford (h)	2	20/2/09
Tom Armstrong	St Helens	Warrington (h)	1	13/2/09
Matty Ashurst	St Helens	Salford (h)	5	13/3/09
Ashley Bateman	Celtic	Castleford (a)	27	13/9/09
Chris Beasley	Celtic	Leeds (a)	3	6/2/09
(first team debut: Blackpool (a), NL2, 23/7/06)				
Steven Bell	Catalans	Huddersfield (h)	1	14/2/09
Greg Bird	Catalans	Castleford (h)	4	7/3/09
Anthony Blackwood	Celtic	Leeds (a)	3	6/2/09
(first team debut: Widnes (h), NRC, 9/2/07)				
Luke Blake	Wakefield	Leeds (a)	1	13/2/09
Alex Brown	Huddersfield	St Helens (a)	25	21/8/09
Mark Bryant	Celtic	Leeds (a)	3	6/2/09
Danny Buderus	Leeds	Wakefield (h)	1	13/2/09
Ray Cashmere	Salford	Celtic (h)	1	14/2/09
Marshall Chalk	Celtic	Hull (h)	2	21/2/09
Jason Chan	Celtic	Salford (a)	1	14/2/09
Rangi Chase	Castleford	Harlequins (h)	1	15/2/09
Josh Cordoba	Hull	Castleford (a)	20	12/7/09
Jason Crookes	Bradford	Hull (h)	5	15/3/09
Mark Dalle Cort	Celtic	Leeds (a)	3	6/2/09
(first team debut: Widnes (h), NRC, 9/2/07)				
James Davey	Wakefield	Hull KR (a)	4	8/3/09
Geraint Davies	Celtic	St Helens (a)	18	26/6/09
(first team debut: Hemel Hempstead (a), NRC, 12/2/06)				
Andrew Dixon	St Helens	Hull KR (h)	3	27/2/09
James Donaldson	Bradford	Castleford (h)	19	5/7/09
Gil Dudson	Celtic	Leeds (h)	25	22/8/09
Tony Duggan	Celtic	Leeds (a)	3	6/2/09
(first team debut: Hemel Hempstead (a), NRC, 12/2/06)				
James Ellis	St Helens	Salford (a)	19	3/7/09
Ryan Esders	Hull KR	Huddersfield (h)	9	13/4/09
(first team debut: Featherstone (h), NRC, 5/3/06)				
Mark Flanagan	Wigan	Celtic (a)	16	13/6/09
Ben Flower	Celtic	Leeds (a)	3	6/2/09
(first team debut: London Skolars (a), NRC, 10/2/08)				
James Ford	Castleford	Warrington (a)	9	13/4/09
(first team debut: Keighley (a), CCR4, 5/4/09)				
Liam Fulton	Huddersfield	Celtic (h)	8	10/4/09
Luke Gale	Harlequins	Wigan (h)	3	28/2/09
Josh Griffin	Huddersfield	St Helens (a)	25	21/8/09
(first team debut: Rochdale (h), CCR5, 10/5/09)				
Josh Hannay	Celtic	Leeds (a)	3	6/2/09
(first team debut: Keighley (a), NL2, 18/8/07)				
James Haynes	Hull KR	Harlequins (h)	16	12/6/09
Mark Henry	Salford	Celtic (h)	1	14/2/09
Brett Hodgson	Huddersfield	Catalans (a)	1	14/2/09
Elliot Hodgson	Huddersfield	St Helens (a)	25	21/8/09
Josh Hodgson	Hull	Warrington (h)	13	16/5/09
Elliot Kear	Celtic	Leeds (h)	25	22/8/09
Epalahame Lauaki	Hull	Harlequins (h)	25	21/8/09

PLAYER	CLUB	DEBUT vs	ROUND	DATE
Jonny Lomax	St Helens	Wakefield (a)	7	27/3/09
Shaun Lunt	Huddersfield	Catalans (a)	1	14/2/09
Dominic Maloney	Hull	St Helens (a)	9	13/4/09
Dane Manning	Leeds	Hull KR (h)	21	17/7/09
Darren Mapp	Celtic	Leeds (a)	3	6/2/09
(first team debut: Widnes (h), NRC, 9/2/07)				
Tyrone McCarthy	Warrington	Wigan (a)	24	14/8/09
Paul McShane	Leeds	Celtic (h)	3	6/2/09
Luke May	Harlequins	Catalans (a)	21	19/7/09
Steve Menzies	Bradford	Hull KR (h)	1	15/2/09
Lewis Mills	Celtic	Wakefield (a)	24	16/8/09
Sam Moa	Hull	Huddersfield (a)	4	6/3/09
Dale Morton	Wakefield	Salford (a)	23	31/7/09
Richard Myler	Salford	Celtic (h)	1	14/2/09
(first team debut: Rochdale (a), NRC, 3/2/08)				
Ryan O'Hara	Celtic	Leeds (a)	3	6/2/09
Tom Olbison	Bradford	Warrington (h)	10	17/4/09
Larne Patrick	Huddersfield	Castleford (a)	5	14/3/09
Adam Peek	Celtic	Leeds (a)	3	6/2/09
Shane Perry	Catalans	Huddersfield (h)	1	14/2/09
Tony Puletua	St Helens	Warrington (h)	1	13/2/09
Damien Quinn	Celtic	Leeds (a)	3	6/2/09
(first team debut: Hemel Hempstead (a), NRC, 12/2/06)				
Mark Riddell	Wigan	Wakefield (h)	17	8/2/09
Amos Roberts	Wigan	Wakefield (h)	17	8/2/09
Chad Robinson	Harlequins	Castleford (a)	1	15/2/09
Jason Ryles	Catalans	Huddersfield (h)	1	14/2/09
Adam Sidlow	Salford	Harlequins (h)	4	6/3/09
(first team debut: Bramley (h), NRC, 4/4/08)				
Jeremy Smith	Salford	Celtic (h)	1	14/2/09
Jack Spencer	Salford	Hull KR (h)	25	21/8/09
James Stosic	Wakefield	Wigan (a)	17	8/2/09
Luke Swain	Salford	Celtic (h)	1	14/2/09
Scott Taylor	Hull KR	Leeds (a)	QPO	18/9/09
Alex Thompson	Warrington	Harlequins (h)	27	13/9/09
Jordan Thompson	Castleford	St Helens (a)	16	12/6/09
Andy Thornley	Salford	St Helens (a)	5	13/3/09
Sam Tomkins	Wigan	Harlequins (a)	3	28/2/09
(first team debut: Whitehaven (h), CCR5, 12/5/08)				
Jace Van Dijk	Celtic	Leeds (a)	3	6/2/09
(first team debut: Hemel Hempstead (a), NRC, 12/2/06)				
Jason Walton	Salford	Harlequins (h)	4	6/3/09
(first team debut: Warrington Wizards (h), CCR3, 7/3/08)				
Lloyd White	Celtic	St Helens (a)	18	26/6/09
Elliott Whitehead	Bradford	Wakefield (h)	15	7/6/09
Dean Widders	Castleford	Harlequins (h)	1	15/2/09
Luke Williamson	Harlequins	Castleford (a)	1	15/2/09
Frank Winterstein	Wakefield	Leeds (a)	3	17/5/09
(first team debut: Wigan (h), CCR5, 9/5/09)				
Lincoln Withers	Celtic	St Helens (h)	4	7/3/09

Super League Players 1996-2009

OLD FACES - Players making their debuts for new clubs in 2009

PLAYER	CLUB	DEBUT vs	ROUND	DATE
Paul Ballard	Celtic	Castleford (h)	11	26/4/09
		(first team debut: Widnes (h), NRC, 9/2/07)		
Kyle Bibb	Hull KR	Bradford (h)	20	12/7/09
Jodie Broughton	Hull	Wakefield (h) (D2)	10	17/4/09
Neil Budworth	Celtic	Leeds (a)	3	6/2/09
		(first team debut: Widnes (h), NRC, 9/2/07)		
Mark Calderwood	Hull	Wigan (h)	1	13/2/09
Keal Carlile	Huddersfield	St Helens (a)	25	21/8/09
		(first team debut: Rochdale (h), CCR5, 10/5/09)		
Brian Carney	Warrington	St Helens (h)	20	11/7/09
Garreth Carvell	Warrington	St Helens (a)	1	13/2/09
Liam Colbon	Hull KR	Bradford (a)	1	15/2/09
Luke Dorn	Harlequins	Castleford (a) (D2)	1	15/2/09
Luke Dyer	Celtic	Leeds (a)	3	6/2/09
		(first team debut: Sheffield (a), NRC, 1/2/08)		
Ryan Esders	Harlequins	Huddersfield (h)	20	11/7/09
James Evans	Castleford	Harlequins (h)	1	15/2/09
Sione Faumuina	Castleford	Harlequins (h)	1	15/2/09
Chris Feather	Castleford	Harlequins (h)	1	15/2/09
Brett Ferres	Castleford	Harlequins (h)	1	15/2/09
Simon Finnigan	Huddersfield	Catalans (a)	1	14/2/09
Nick Fozzard	Hull KR	Bradford (a)	1	15/2/09
Matt Gardner	Harlequins	Catalans (h)	8	9/4/09
Martin Gleeson	Wigan	St Helens (h)	8	9/4/09
Jason Golden	Harlequins	Wigan (h)	3	28/2/09
Darrell Goulding	Salford	Catalans (a)	10	18/4/09
Dave Halley	Wakefield	Wigan (a)	17	8/2/09
Mick Higham	Warrington	St Helens (a)	1	13/2/09
Ryan Hudson	Castleford	Harlequins (h) (D2)	1	15/2/09
Aled James	Celtic	Huddersfield (a)	8	10/4/09
		(first team debut: Swinton (a), NL2, 11/6/06)		
Jordan James	Celtic	Leeds (a)	3	6/2/09
		(first team debut: Sheffield (a), NRC, 1/2/08)		
Stuart Jones	Castleford	Harlequins (h)	1	15/2/09
Ben Kaye	Harlequins	Castleford (a)	1	15/2/09
Michael Korkidas	Huddersfield	St Helens (h)	2	22/2/09
	Wakefield	Celtic (a) (D2)	6	30/5/09
Mark Lennon	Celtic	St Helens (h)	4	7/3/09
		(first team debut: Sheffield (h), NRC, 16/2/08)		
Peter Lupton	Celtic	Leeds (a)	3	6/2/09
Sebastien Martins	Catalans	Hull KR (h) (D2)	19	4/7/09
Richard Mathers	Warrington	Hull (a)	13	16/5/09
		(first team debut: Featherstone (a) (D2), CCR5, 10/5/09)		
Dean McGilvray	Salford	Hull KR (a)	7	29/3/09
Scott Moore	Huddersfield	Catalans (a)	1	14/2/09
Lee Mossop	Huddersfield	Wakefield (a)	14	24/5/09
Kirk Netherton	Castleford	Harlequins (h)	1	15/2/09
Rob Parker	Salford	Celtic (h)	1	14/2/09
Robbie Paul	Salford	Celtic (h)	1	14/2/09
		(first team debut: Bramley (h), NRC, 4/4/08)		
Jay Pitts	Leeds	Salford (a)	27	11/9/09
Karl Pryce	Wigan	Castleford (h)	2	20/2/09
Julien Rinaldi	Bradford	St Helens (a)	11	24/4/09
Nick Scruton	Bradford	Hull KR (h)	1	15/2/09
Danny Sculthorpe	Huddersfield	Leeds (a)	16	14/6/09
Rikki Sheriffe	Bradford	Hull KR (h)	1	15/2/09
Matty Smith	Celtic	Leeds (a)	3	6/2/09
Steve Snitch	Wakefield	Wigan (a) (D2)	17	8/2/09
Craig Stapleton	Salford	Celtic (h)	1	14/2/09
		(first team debut: Rochdale (a), NRC, 3/2/08)		
Willie Talau	Salford	Celtic (h)	1	14/2/09
David Tangata-Toa	Celtic	Salford (a)	1	14/2/09
		(first team debut: Sheffield (a), NRC, 1/2/08)		
Jordan Tansey	Hull	Celtic (h)	21	17/7/09
Sam Thompson	Harlequins	Celtic (h)	15	6/6/09
Chris Thorman	Hull	Wigan (h)	1	13/2/09
Steve Tyrer	Celtic	St Helens (a)	18	26/6/09
		(first team debut: Hull KR (a), CCR4, 3/4/09)		
Joe Walsh	Huddersfield	Hull (h)	4	6/3/09
Scott Wheeldon	Hull KR	Celtic (h)	5	15/3/09
Paul White	Salford	Hull KR (a)	7	29/3/09
		(first team debut: Rochdale (a), NRC, 3/2/08)		
Michael Worrincy	Bradford	Huddersfield (h)	3	27/2/09

SUPER LEAGUE XIV
Club by Club

17 January 2009 - Australian Test player Greg Bird signs one-year contract for 2009 with further two-year option.

8 February 2009 - opening (round 2) Super League match at Harlequins casualty of the big freeze.

13 February 2009 - Greg Bird refused visa by UK Border Agency because of pending court case.

15 February 2009 - 13-13 opening round draw with Hull KR at Odsal. Jamie Langley and David Solomona both suffer dislocated shoulders.

27 February 2009 - 16-12 defeat to Huddersfield at Odsal.

7 March 2009 - Wayne Godwin breaks right leg in 44-10 defeat at Wigan.

15 March 2009 - Andy Lynch plays first game of season after neck surgery, a 36-24 home defeat to Hull.

17 March 2009 - Dave Halley recalled from loan spell at Wakefield, Matt James returns to Halifax on loan.

21 March 2009 - last-second Dave Halley try secures first win of season, by 30-24 at Catalans Dragons.

29 March 2009 - vice-captain Glenn Morrison ruptures wrist ligaments in last-minute 28-26 defeat at Castleford.

5 April 2009 – Challenge Cup exit at Catalans as 26-0 lead ends in 40-38 loss.

8 April 2009 - Paul Deacon undergoes exploratory knee surgery.

11 April 2009 - shock 10-6 derby triumph over champions Leeds at Odsal.

13 April 2009 - Jason Crookes out for season with cruciate ligament damage during 24-22 Easter Monday defeat at Wakefield.

17 April 2009 - hooker Julien Rinaldi joins on temporary deal until June.

24 April 2009 - David Solomona ruled out for season after dislocating shoulder in stunning 34-30 win at St Helens.

KEY DATES - BRADFORD BULLS

2 May 2009 - Paul Sykes hat-trick in brilliant 32-16 win over Wakefield at Murrayfield.

17 May 2009 - Celtic Crusaders record first Super League win, by 30-24 at Odsal.

22 May 2009 - 18-10 defeat at Salford.

2 June 2009 - forward Glenn Hall signs from Manly on three-year contract from 2010.

7 June 2009 - Bulls complete double over Wakefield with 36-22 home victory.

11 June 2009 - Andy Lynch signs new three-year deal until 2012.

13 June 2009 - 21-10 victory at Warrington leaves Bulls one point off play-off places.

19 June 2009 - Dave Halley signs new two-year contract to end of 2011.

7 July 2009 - Paul Sykes signs new 12-month contract.

9 July 2009 - Terry Newton to leave at end of season after failing to agree new deal.

12 July 2009 - 32-12 defeat at Hull KR leaves Bulls seven points outside top eight.

17 July 2009 - Manly Sea Eagles hooker Heath L'Estrange signs for 2010 on two-year contract.

22 July 2009 - Glenn Morrison to leave at end of season.

12 August 2009 - Terry Newton undergoes surgery to repair cheekbone fractured in 42-18 win at Harlequins.

14 August 2009 - Steve Menzies agrees one-year contract extension.

17 August 2009 - Semi Tadulala fined £400 for pulling Eorl Crabtree's hair in 28-18 win at Huddersfield.

22 August 2009 - Elliott Whitehead given improved contract until the end of 2011.

23 August 2009 - 42-18 home win over Catalans is third on the trot.

6 September 2009 - Chris Nero hat-trick in 44-18 home win over Salford.

11 September 2009 - Ben Jeffries returns to Wakefield.

11 September 2009 - 21-18 win at Hull FC just not enough to make play-offs as Catalans gain shock win at St Helens.

17 September 2009 - Matt James signs for Harlequins.

29 September 2009 - Sam Burgess signs four-year contract with South Sydney from 2010

6 October 2009 - Cronulla Sharks utility back Brett Kearney signs two-year contract.

13 October 2009 - 18-year-old back row forward James Donaldson signs new three-year contract.

20 October 2009 - free agent Stuart Reardon returns to the club.

23 October 2009 - Danny Sculthorpe joins on two-year contract.

4 November 2009 - Heath L'Estrange and Brett Kearney granted visas.

12 November 2009 - Sam Burgess's twin brothers George and Tom Burgess sign new three-year contracts.

13 November 2009 - Glenn Hall granted entry visa.

16 November 2009 - Manly scrum-half Matt Orford signs three-year deal.

16 November 2009 - Gold Coast centre Chris Walker claims he signed contract with Bulls in August.

16 November 2009 - Paul Deacon joins Wigan.

BRADFORD BULLS

DATE	FIXTURE	RESULT	SCORERS	LGE	ATT
15/2/09	Hull KR (h)	D13-13	t:Tadulala,Nero g:Deacon(2) fg:Deacon	8th	12,141
27/2/09	Huddersfield (h)	L12-16	t:Morrison g:Deacon(4)	12th	10,186
7/3/09	Wigan (a)	L44-10	t:Sheriffe,Menzies g:Deacon	12th	12,588
15/3/09	Hull (h)	L24-36	t:Jeffries,Sheriffe,Tadulala,Menzies g:Deacon(4)	12th	11,327
21/3/09	Catalans (a)	W24-30	t:Menzies,Tadulala,Sheriffe,Newton,Halley g:Deacon(3),Sykes(2)	10th	7,620
29/3/09	Castleford (a)	L28-26	t:Platt,Tadulala,Lynch,Morrison,Halley g:Deacon(2),Sykes	11th	9,185
5/4/09	Catalans (a) (CCR4)	L40-38	t:Sykes,Sheriffe,Cook,Nero,Menzies,Tadulala,Halley g:Deacon(5)	N/A	6,450
10/4/09	Leeds (h)	W10-6	t:Worrincy,Sheriffe g:Sykes	10th	14,554
13/4/09	Wakefield (a)	L24-22	t:Menzies(2),Worrincy,Platt g:Sykes(3)	12th	6,516
17/4/09	Warrington (h)	L22-58	t:Solomona(2),Platt,Jeffries g:Sykes(3)	13th	8,643
24/4/09	St Helens (a)	W30-34	t:Tadulala(2),Kopczak,Burgess,Worrincy(2) g:Sykes(5)	12th	11,039
2/5/09	Wakefield (MM) ●	W32-16	t:Sykes(3),Newton,Menzies,Worrincy g:Deacon(4)	10th	N/A
17/5/09	Celtic Crusaders (h)	L24-30	t:Lynch,Worrincy,Menzies,Sykes g:Deacon(4)	11th	7,602
22/5/09	Salford (a)	L18-10	t:Sykes(2) g:Deacon	13th	4,383
7/6/09	Wakefield (h)	W36-22	t:Nero(2),Menzies(2),Rinaldi g:Deacon(8)	12th	8,387
14/6/09	Warrington (a)	W10-21	t:Nero,Morrison,Newton g:Deacon(4) fg:Deacon	11th	9,606
21/6/09	St Helens (h)	L18-44	t:Morrison,Sheriffe,Tadulala g:Deacon(3)	11th	10,599
26/6/09	Leeds (a)	L33-20	t:Tadulala,Deacon,Menzies g:Deacon(4)	12th	17,824
5/7/09	Castleford (h)	L38-40	t:Tadulala,Halley,Scruton,Worrincy,Burgess,Jeffries(2) g:Deacon(4),Sykes	12th	8,971
12/7/09	Hull KR (a)	L32-12	t:Halley,Worrincy g:Deacon,Sykes	12th	8,206
19/7/09	Wigan (h)	L14-20	t:Donaldson,Nero g:Deacon(3)	12th	9,487
25/7/09	Celtic Crusaders (a)	W12-34	t:Morrison,Whitehead,Halley,Lynch(2),Tadulala g:Deacon(5)	12th	3,081
2/8/09	Harlequins (h)	L14-22	t:Tadulala,Sykes,Nero g:Deacon	12th	7,813
8/8/09	Harlequins (a)	W18-42	t:Halley(3),Burgess,Menzies,Worrincy,Godwin g:Deacon(7)	12th	3,112
16/8/09	Huddersfield (a)	W18-28	t:Platt,Nero(2),Sykes g:Deacon(6)	11th	7,892
23/8/09	Catalans (h)	W42-18	t:Burgess,Sheriffe,Nero,Menzies,Godwin,Sykes,Deacon,Morrison g:Deacon(5)	11th	7,919
6/9/09	Salford (h)	W44-18	t:Nero(3),Tadulala(2),Langley(2),Lynch g:Deacon(6)	9th	8,167
11/9/09	Hull (a)	W18-21	t:Worrincy,Deacon,Donaldson g:Deacon(4) fg:Deacon	9th	13,412

● Played at Murrayfield, Edinburgh

		APP		TRIES		GOALS		FG		PTS	
	D.O.B.	ALL	SL	ALL	SL	ALL	SL	ALL	SL	ALL	SL
Sam Burgess	14/12/88	19(7)	18(7)	4	4	0	0	0	0	16	16
Matt Cook	14/11/86	6(10)	5(10)	1	0	0	0	0	0	4	0
Jason Crookes	21/4/90	2(1)	2(1)	0	0	0	0	0	0	0	0
Paul Deacon	13/2/79	24	23	3	3	91	86	3	3	197	187
James Donaldson	14/9/91	(7)	(7)	2	2	0	0	0	0	8	8
Wayne Godwin	13/3/82	6(7)	6(7)	2	2	0	0	0	0	8	8
Dave Halley	12/10/86	20(3)	20(2)	9	8	0	0	0	0	36	32
Matt James	26/3/87	(2)	(2)	0	0	0	0	0	0	0	0
Ben Jeffries	4/9/80	20(2)	19(2)	4	4	0	0	0	0	16	16
Craig Kopczak	20/12/86	3(23)	3(22)	1	1	0	0	0	0	4	4
Jamie Langley	21/12/83	25(1)	24(1)	2	2	0	0	0	0	8	8
Andy Lynch	20/10/79	25	24	5	5	0	0	0	0	20	20
Steve Menzies	4/12/73	26(1)	25(1)	13	12	0	0	0	0	52	48
Glenn Morrison	28/5/76	15	15	6	6	0	0	0	0	24	24
Chris Nero	14/2/81	24	23	13	12	0	0	0	0	52	48
Terry Newton	7/11/78	22(2)	21(2)	3	3	0	0	0	0	12	12
Tom Olbison	20/3/91	(1)	(1)	0	0	0	0	0	0	0	0
Michael Platt	23/3/84	17(3)	16(3)	4	4	0	0	0	0	16	16
Julien Rinaldi	27/4/79	(7)	(7)	1	1	0	0	0	0	4	4
Nick Scruton	24/12/84	22(6)	22(5)	1	1	0	0	0	0	4	4
Rikki Sheriffe	5/5/84	28	27	7	6	0	0	0	0	28	24
David Solomona	26/1/78	1(3)	1(3)	2	2	0	0	0	0	8	8
Paul Sykes	11/8/81	26	25	10	9	17	17	0	0	74	70
Semi Tadulala	3/3/78	26	25	14	13	0	0	0	0	56	52
Elliott Whitehead	4/9/89	3(4)	3(4)	1	1	0	0	0	0	4	4
Michael Worrincy	16/2/86	4(21)	4(20)	10	10	0	0	0	0	40	40

Steve Menzies

LEAGUE RECORD
P27-W12-D1-L14
(9th, SL)
F653, A668, Diff-15
25 points.

CHALLENGE CUP
Round Four

ATTENDANCES
Best - v Leeds (SL - 14,554)
Worst - v Celtic Crusaders
(SL - 7,602)
Total (SL only) - 125,796
Average (SL only) - 9,677
(Down by 610 on 2008)

KEY DATES - CASTLEFORD TIGERS

13 January 2009 - Ryan Hudson appointed captain for 2009.

15 February 2009 - 12-8 opening-round home defeat to Harlequins.

20 February 2009 - Ryan Hudson avoids punishment after coming into contact with referee Steve Ganson during 28-22 round 2 win at Wigan.

28 February 2009 - 52-16 round 3 thrashing of Salford at the Jungle.

7 March 2009 - 24-22 win over Dragons in Perpignan takes Tigers into third spot.

14 March 2009 - Terry Matterson accuses Huddersfield of grapple tackling after 26-24 home defeat to Giants

20 March 2009 - 77th minute Brent Sherwin field goal secures 19-18 win at unbeaten Hull FC.

29 March 2009 - Kirk Dixon kicks last minute conversion as Tigers come back from 26-10 down to secure 28-26 home win over Bradford.

5 April 2009 - 64-20 Challenge Cup victory over Keighley at Cougar Park.

13 April 2009 - captain Ryan Hudson breaks arm in 28-6 Easter Monday win at Warrington.

20 April 2009 - Joe Westerman suffers fits in 68-22 hammering by St Helens at the Jungle.

9 May 2009 - Brent Sherwin's 40-metre field goal 55 seconds into golden-point extra-time against Halifax seals Challenge Cup quarter-final place.

15 May 2009 - last-gasp Leeds penalty steals 24-22 win in Jungle derby.

22 May 2009 - 16-6 defeat at Hull KR - third league defeat in a row.

31 May 2009 - exit from Challenge Cup after 16-14 loss at Huddersfield.

6 June 2009 - 34-18 defeat by Warrington is fourth in five games.

11 June 2009 - Stuart Jones signs new two-year deal.

12 June 2009 - Jordan Thompson makes debut in 50-10 loss at St Helens.

15 June 2009 - Academy products Josh Nathaniel and Josh Parle sign three and two-year deals respectively.

15 June 2009 - Nathan Massey joins Gateshead on month's loan.

17 June 2009 - coach Terry Matterson signs new two-year contract to end of 2011.

2 July 2009 - Brett Ferres signs new three-year contract to end of 2012.

7 July 2009 - Kirk Dixon agrees new two-year deal.

12 July 2009 - Ryan Hudson returns from 12-match absence with a broken arm in 40-18 home win over Hull FC.

14 July 2009 - teenage back-row forward John Davies signs new three-year contract.

21 July 2009 - Brett Ferres suspended for one game for a dangerous tackle on Richie Myler in 18-12 win at Salford

26 July 2009 - 20-12 derby win at Wakefield.

4 August 2009 - Sione Faumuina sacked and returns to Australia. James Evans (two years) and Michael Wainwright (one) sign new deals.

11 August 2009 - Liam Higgins signs new one-year contract to end of 2010.

21 August 2009 - Rangi Chase signs new four-year contract.

23 August 2009 - Ryan Hudson suffers recurrence of broken arm in 29-26 home defeat to Wigan.

2 September 2009 - James Ford signs for Widnes.

4 September 2009 - Steve Snitch signs from Wakefield on three-year contract.

6 September 2009 - Joe Westerman scores hat-trick in 48-0 win at Harlequins as Tigers secure top-eight finish.

9 September 2009 - former Batley coach Gary Thornton appointed under-20s coach.

13 September 2009 - 35-22 win over Celtic at the Jungle secures seventh spot.

14 September 2009 - RFL fine of £40,000, half suspended, following crowd disturbance at home game against Catalans Dragons on June 27.

15 September 2009 - Huddersfield prop Paul Jackson returns on two-year deal.

20 September 2009 - elimination at Wigan after 18-12 defeat.

24 September 2009 - Chris Feather, Ryan Boyle and Ryan Clayton all released.

2 November 2009 - Ryan Clayton signs a new one-year contract after earlier being released.

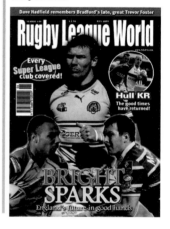

CASTLEFORD TIGERS

DATE	FIXTURE	RESULT	SCORERS	LGE	ATT
15/2/09	Harlequins (h)	L8-12	t:Evans,Owen	10th	7,049
20/2/09	Wigan (a)	W22-28	t:Westerman,Ferres(2),Dixon,Shenton g:Dixon(4)	7th	12,079
28/2/09	Salford (h)	W52-16	t:Shenton,Huby,Hudson,Owen(2),Westerman,Netherton,McGoldrick, Widders g:Dixon(8)	4th	7,052
7/3/09	Catalans (a)	W22-24	t:Dixon,Evans(2),Owen,Chase g:Dixon(2)	3rd	8,150
14/3/09	Huddersfield (h)	L24-26	t:Evans,Huby(2),Ferres(2) g:Dixon(2)	7th	6,572
20/3/09	Hull (a)	W18-19	t:Dixon,Westerman,McGoldrick g:Dixon(3) fg:Sherwin	6th	14,028
29/3/09	Bradford (h)	W28-26	t:Shenton(2),Dixon(2),Chase g:Dixon(4)	4th	9,185
5/4/09	Keighley (a) (CCR4)	W20-64	t:Shenton,Higgins,Dixon,Chase(3),Faumuina,Evans,Owen,Ford, Netherton g:Dixon(10)	N/A	3,255
10/4/09	Wakefield (h)	L6-35	t:Westerman g:Dixon	7th	10,155
13/4/09	Warrington (a)	W6-28	t:Ferres,Wainwright,Chase(2),Shenton g:Dixon(4)	5th	8,202
19/4/09	St Helens (h)	L22-68	t:Shenton,Sargent,Dixon,Faumuina g:Dixon(3)	6th	8,003
26/4/09	Celtic Crusaders (a)	W22-34	t:Boyle,Evans,Dixon,Wainwright,Shenton,Sherwin g:Dixon(5)	6th	2,017
3/5/09	Hull (MM) ●	L16-24	t:Ford,Dixon,Evans g:Dixon(2)	8th	N/A
9/5/09	Halifax (h) (CCR5)	W35-34 (aet)	t:McGoldrick(2),Evans,Shenton,Dixon,Chase,Sherwin g:Dixon(2),Sherwin fg:Sherwin	N/A	5,595
15/5/09	Leeds (h)	L22-24	t:Jones,Dixon,Chase,Shenton g:Dixon(3)	8th	8,082
22/5/09	Hull KR (a)	L16-6	t:Sargent g:Dixon	7th	8,104
31/5/09	Huddersfield (a) (CCQF)	L16-14	t:Shenton,Ferres g:Dixon(3)	N/A	6,359
6/6/09	Warrington (h)	L18-34	t:Dixon,Owen,Shenton,Evans g:Dixon	8th	5,628
12/6/09	St Helens (a)	L50-10	t:Ferres,Dixon g:Dixon	10th	9,680
19/6/09	Huddersfield (a)	W6-13	t:Dixon,McGoldrick g:Dixon(2) fg:Chase	9th	6,010
27/6/09	Catalans (h)	L20-22	t:Ferres,Owen(2) g:Dixon,Westerman(3)	11th	5,508
5/7/09	Bradford (a)	W38-40	t:Shenton(2),Chase(2),Thompson,Westerman,Widders g:Westerman(6)	9th	8,971
12/7/09	Hull (h)	W40-18	t:Chase(2),Huby,Wainwright(2),Hudson,Shenton g:Westerman(6)	9th	8,297
17/7/09	Salford (a)	W12-18	t:Ferres,Shenton,Netherton g:Westerman(3)	7th	3,487
26/7/09	Wakefield (a)	W12-20	t:Widders(2) g:Westerman(6)	6th	8,371
2/8/09	Hull KR (h)	L28-46	t:Ferres,Huby,Hudson,Netherton g:Westerman(5),Huby	7th	8,709
14/8/09	Leeds (a)	L76-12	t:Evans,Chase g:Westerman(2)	8th	16,931
23/8/09	Wigan (a)	L26-29	t:Dixon(2),Ferres,Widders,Shenton g:Westerman(2),Dixon	8th	6,579
6/9/09	Harlequins (a)	W0-48	t:Westerman(3),Dixon(2),Sargent,Widders,Higgins,Ferres g:Westerman(5),Dixon	7th	3,824
13/9/09	Celtic Crusaders (h)	W35-22	t:Dixon,Sargent,Wainwright,Owen,Shenton(2),Huby g:Westerman,Dixon(2) fg:Sherwin	7th	6,547
20/9/09	Wigan (a) (EPO)	L18-12	t:Huby,Westerman g:Westerman(2)	N/A	8,689

● Played at Murrayfield, Edinburgh

APP TRIES GOALS FG PTS

	D.O.B.	ALL	SL	ALL	SL	ALL	SL	ALL	SL	ALL	SL
Ryan Boyle	17/10/87	1(10)	(9)	1	1	0	0	0	0	4	4
Rangi Chase	11/4/86	27(4)	24(4)	14	10	0	0	1	1	57	41
Ryan Clayton	22/11/82	8(10)	8(8)	0	0	0	0	0	0	0	0
Kirk Dixon	19/7/84	29	26	19	17	66	51	0	0	208	170
James Evans	5/11/78	21(1)	18(1)	10	8	0	0	0	0	40	32
Sione Faumuina	27/3/81	19(2)	18	2	1	0	0	0	0	8	4
Chris Feather	7/12/81	2(25)	1(23)	0	0	0	0	0	0	0	0
Brett Ferres	17/4/86	25(2)	23(2)	12	11	0	0	0	0	48	44
James Ford	29/9/82	3(7)	3(5)	2	1	0	0	0	0	8	4
Liam Higgins	19/7/83	15(12)	14(10)	2	1	0	0	0	0	8	4
Craig Huby	21/5/86	21(6)	20(5)	7	7	1	1	0	0	30	30
Ryan Hudson	20/11/79	15	15	3	3	0	0	0	0	12	12
Stuart Jones	7/12/81	22(4)	20(4)	1	1	0	0	0	0	4	4
Nathan Massey	11/7/89	2(2)	1(2)	0	0	0	0	0	0	0	0
Ryan McGoldrick	12/1/81	28	25	5	3	0	0	0	0	20	12
Kirk Netherton	10/5/85	6(21)	4(21)	4	3	0	0	0	0	16	12
Richard Owen	25/4/90	24(1)	22(1)	9	8	0	0	0	0	36	32
Mitchell Sargent	2/7/77	27(3)	25(3)	4	4	0	0	0	0	16	16
Michael Shenton	22/7/86	30	27	19	16	0	0	0	0	76	64
Brent Sherwin	20/3/78	19	17	2	1	1	0	3	2	13	6
Jordan Thompson	4/9/91	1(1)	1(1)	1	1	0	0	0	0	4	4
Michael Wainwright	4/11/80	24	22	5	5	0	0	0	0	20	20
Joe Westerman	15/11/89	25(3)	22(3)	9	9	41	41	0	0	118	118
Dean Widders	25/10/79	9(10)	8(10)	6	6	0	0	0	0	24	24

Kirk Dixon

LEAGUE RECORD
P27-W14-D0-L13
(7th, SL/Elimination Play-Off)
F645, A702, Diff-57
28 points.

CHALLENGE CUP
Quarter Finalists

ATTENDANCES
Best - v Wakefield (SL - 10,155)
Worst - v Catalans (SL - 5,508)
Total (SL only) - 97,366
Average (SL only) - 7,490
(Down by 11 on 2008)

KEY DATES - CATALANS DRAGONS

24 January 2009 - warm-up match at Toulouse postponed because of storm winds.

31 January 2009 - French Federation agrees three-year deal with Orange TV to secure televising of Dragons games.

2 February 2009 - Sebastien Raguin suffers knee ligament damage in 36-18 win over French President's XIII.

14 February 2009 - 30-8 home defeat to Huddersfield. Jason Ryles damages shoulder.

21 February 2009 - 40-20 win at Warrington in round 2. Jamal Fakir is banned for one game for high tackle on Adrian Morley. Dane Carlaw is knocked out in high tackle and suffers knee ligament damage.

27 February 2009 - 28-12 defeat in round 3 at Hull FC.

4 March 2009 - Greg Bird, whose move to Bradford was denied by the UK Border Agency, signs until end of season.

20 March 2009 - Greg Bird takes over as captain from Casey McGuire and Bulls snatch late 30-24 win in Perpignan.

27 March 2009 - 42-14 defeat at Leeds Rhinos.

5 April 2009 - 40-38 home Challenge Cup win over Bradford Bulls, after trailing 26-0 just after half-time.

9 April 2009 - Jerome Guisset scores two tries in 28-24 win at Harlequins.

13 April 2009 - Easter Monday 40-24 win over Wigan at Gilbert Brutus.

18 April 2009 - Thomas Bosc sustains shoulder injury in 38-6 home win over Salford.

26 April 2009 - 44-10 hammering by Hull KR at Craven Park

27 April 2009 - Greg Bird lodges appeal after being found guilty in a Sydney court of smashing a glass into his girlfriend's face and blaming the attack on his flatmate.

3 May 2009 - Greg Bird suffers hamstring injury in 36-16 loss to Leeds at Murrayfield.

6 May 2009 - talks open with Greg Bird over new contract.

16 May 2009 - Thomas Bosc back in 32-28 home defeat to St Helens.

23 May 2009 - 30-18 victory at Celtic in the first all non-English Super League encounter.

Dimitri Pelo

6 June 2009 - Clint Greenshields misses first game since signing in 2007 as late Cyril Stacul try secures 32-30 home victory over champions Leeds.

20 June 2009 - 24-12 defeat by Warrington in Barcelona as the first-ever Super League game in Spain draws crowd of 18,150.

22 June 2009 - Greg Bird lodges appeal after being sentenced to 16 months in prison.

23 June 2009 - Jamal Fakir handed two-match ban for high tackle on Matt King in Barcelona.

26 June 2009 - 22-20 win at Castleford causes angry crowd scenes.

2 July 2009 - French Test prop Sebastian Martins joins from Pia until end of season.

9 July 2009 - teenage scrum-half William Barthau signs two-year contract after appearing as a substitute in France's 66-12 defeat by England in June.

26 July 2009 - 36-12 defeat at Huddersfield leaves Dragons four points off play-off spots.

31 July 2009 - Cyrille Gossard agrees new two-year contract.

1 August 2009 - 34-0 win over Celtic in Perpignan, captain Greg Bird handed one-match ban for a reckless tackle Ryan O'Hara.

7 August 2009 - last-gasp Casey McGuire try snatches 18-16 win at Salford in re-arranged round 16 game.

12 August 2009 - Jean-Philippe Baile agrees new two-year contract.

18 August 2009 - Rémi Casty signs new two-year contract.

11 September 2009 - 24-12 round 27 win at St Helens secures eighth spot.

19 September 2009 - Dimitri Pelo scores two tries in 25-16 Elimination Play-off win at Wakefield.

25 September 2009 - 16-6 Preliminary Semi-final win at Huddersfield takes Dragons 80 minutes away from Old Trafford.

27 September 2009 - Leeds Rhinos pick Dragons as opponents in Qualifying semi-final in first ever Club Call.

2 October 2009 - 27-20 defeat to Leeds at Headingley.

12 November 2009 - Melbourne loose forward Dallas Johnson signs three-year deal. Jason Ryles leaves.

13 November 2009 - New Zealand international Setaimata Sa signs on two-year contract.

CATALANS DRAGONS

DATE	FIXTURE	RESULT	SCORERS	LGE	ATT
14/2/09	Huddersfield (h)	L8-30	t:Pelo g:Bosc(2)	13th	7,533
21/2/09	Warrington (a)	W20-40	t:Mounis,Elima,Greenshields(2),Stacul,Baile,Pelo g:Bosc(6)	8th	7,947
27/2/09	Hull (a)	L28-12	t:Elima,Mogg g:Bosc(2)	10th	12,482
7/3/09	Castleford (h)	L22-24	t:Greenshields,Fakir,Stacul(2) g:Bosc(3)	10th	8,150
15/3/09	Wakefield (a)	L30-10	t:Baile,Pelo g:Bosc	10th	4,807
21/3/09	Bradford (h)	L24-30	t:Duport,Bird,Elima,Baile g:Bosc(4)	11th	7,620
27/3/09	Leeds (a)	L42-14	t:Bell,Bosc,Duport g:Bosc	12th	13,425
5/4/09	Bradford (h) (CCR4)	W40-38	t:Elima(2),Greenshields,Bosc(2),Baile,Gossard g:Bosc(6)	N/A	6,450
9/4/09	Harlequins (a)	W24-28	t:McGuire,Guisset(2),Greenshields,Elima g:Bosc(4)	11th	2,540
13/4/09	Wigan (h)	W40-24	t:Pelo,Bird,Mounis,Ryles(2),Greenshields(2) g:Bosc(6)	10th	9,490
18/4/09	Salford (h)	W38-6	t:Pelo(2),Casty,Baile(2),Guisset,Bentley,Bell g:Bosc,Bird(2)	10th	8,327
26/4/09	Hull KR (a)	L44-10	t:Greenshields,Pelo g:Mounis	10th	8,115
3/5/09	Leeds (MM) ●	L16-36	t:Bentley,Elima,McGuire g:Mounis(2)	12th	N/A
10/5/09	St Helens (a) (CCR5)	L42-8	t:Gossard g:Bosc(2)	N/A	7,176
16/5/09	St Helens (h)	L28-32	t:Bell(2),Bosc(2),Mogg g:Bosc(4)	12th	9,065
23/5/09	Celtic Crusaders (a)	W18-30	t:Bird,Elima,Mogg,Perry,Bell,Stacul g:Bosc(3)	11th	2,927
6/6/09	Leeds (h)	W32-30	t:Bell,Baile,Elima(2),Stacul g:Bosc(6)	11th	7,913
20/6/09	Warrington (h) ●●	L12-24	t:Croker,Stacul g:Bosc(2)	12th	18,150
27/6/09	Castleford (a)	W20-22	t:Pelo,Baile,Greenshields,Carlaw g:Bosc(3)	11th	5,508
4/7/09	Hull KR (h)	W23-12	t:Baile(3),Croker g:Bosc(3) fg:Bosc	10th	9,073
10/7/09	Wigan (a)	L24-22	t:Bell,Elima,Bird,Pelo g:Bosc(3)	10th	11,543
19/7/09	Harlequins (h)	W38-16	t:Elima,Pelo(2),Bosc,Baile,Bell,McGuire g:Bosc(5)	10th	8,324
26/7/09	Huddersfield (a)	L36-12	t:Greenshields,Pelo g:Bosc(2)	10th	5,823
1/8/09	Celtic Crusaders (h)	W34-0	t:Pelo,McGuire,Greenshields,Bird,Bentley,Croker,Bell g:Bosc(3)	10th	6,874
7/8/09	Salford (a)	W16-18	t:Elima,Carlaw,Mogg,McGuire g:Mounis	10th	2,475
15/8/09	Hull (h) ●●●	W18-6	t:Elima(3) g:Mounis(2),Bird	7th	9,083
23/8/09	Bradford (a)	L42-18	t:Raguin,Gossard,Martins g:Mounis(3)	7th	7,919
5/9/09	Wakefield (h)	L20-34	t:Raguin(2),McGuire(2) g:Bosc(2)	8th	8,755
11/9/09	St Helens (a)	W12-24	t:Pelo,McGuire,Elima,Greenshields g:Bosc(4)	8th	8,268
19/9/09	Wakefield (a) (EPO)	W16-25	t:Duport,Elima,Pelo(2) g:Bosc(4) fg:Bosc	N/A	4,008
25/9/09	Huddersfield (a) (PSF)	W6-16	t:Greenshields,Pelo,Elima g:Bosc(2)	N/A	4,263
2/10/09	Leeds (a) (QSF)	L27-20	t:Duport(3),Mogg g:Bosc(2)	N/A	13,409

● Played at Murrayfield, Edinburgh
●● Played at Olympic Stadium, Barcelona
●●● Played at Stade de la Mediterranee, Beziers

		APP		TRIES		GOALS		FG		PTS	
	D.O.B.	ALL	SL	ALL	SL	ALL	SL	ALL	SL	ALL	SL
Jean-Phillipe Baile	7/6/87	29(1)	27(1)	12	11	0	0	0	0	48	44
Steven Bell	28/5/76	23	21	9	9	0	0	0	0	36	36
Kane Bentley	16/4/87	3(9)	2(8)	3	3	0	0	0	0	12	12
Greg Bird	10/2/84	21(2)	20(2)	5	5	3	3	0	0	26	26
Thomas Bosc	5/8/83	28	26	6	4	86	78	2	2	198	174
Dane Carlaw	21/2/80	14(9)	14(7)	2	2	0	0	0	0	8	8
Remi Casty	5/2/85	2(27)	1(27)	1	1	0	0	0	0	4	4
Jason Croker	10/3/73	14(2)	13(2)	3	3	0	0	0	0	12	12
Vincent Duport	15/12/87	15(1)	13(1)	6	6	0	0	0	0	24	24
Olivier Elima	19/5/83	25(5)	23(5)	19	17	0	0	0	0	76	68
Jamal Fakir	30/8/82	10(6)	10(5)	1	1	0	0	0	0	4	4
David Ferriol	24/4/79	10(20)	10(18)	0	0	0	0	0	0	0	0
Cyrille Gossard	7/2/82	21(6)	20(5)	3	1	0	0	0	0	12	4
Clint Greenshields	11/1/82	29	27	13	12	0	0	0	0	52	48
Jerome Guisset	29/8/78	28(3)	26(3)	3	3	0	0	0	0	12	12
Sebastien Martins	18/11/84	(4)	(4)	1	1	0	0	0	0	4	4
Casey McGuire	24/1/80	29(1)	28	8	8	0	0	0	0	32	32
Adam Mogg	31/7/77	21	19	5	5	0	0	0	0	20	20
Gregory Mounis	18/1/85	15(11)	14(11)	2	2	9	9	0	0	26	26
Dimitri Pelo	17/4/85	29	27	17	17	0	0	0	0	68	68
Shane Perry	9/11/77	8(8)	8(8)	1	1	0	0	0	0	4	4
Florian Quintilla	20/10/88	1	1	0	0	0	0	0	0	0	0
Sebastien Raguin	14/2/79	7	7	3	3	0	0	0	0	12	12
Jason Ryles	17/1/79	20(2)	19(2)	2	2	0	0	0	0	8	8
Cyril Stacul	12/10/84	13	13	6	6	0	0	0	0	24	24
Julien Touxagas	12/2/84	1(11)	1(11)	0	0	0	0	0	0	0	0

Olivier Elima

LEAGUE RECORD
P27-W13-D0-L14
(8th, SL/Qualifying Semi-Final)
F613, A660, Diff-47
26 points.

CHALLENGE CUP
Round Five

ATTENDANCES
Best - v Warrington (SL - 18,150)
Worst - v Bradford (CC - 6,450)
Total (SL only) - 118,357
Average (SL only) - 9,104
(Up by 616 on 2008)

KEY DATES - CELTIC CRUSADERS

26 November 2008 - Crusaders confirm release of Paul Ballard, Philippe Gardent, Gareth Dean, Jamie I'Anson, Ian Webster and Neale Wyatt.

26 November 2008 - Matty Smith and Steve Tyrer join on season-long loans from St Helens

26 November 2008 - Peter Lupton joins from Castleford; Manly's Mark Bryant; Lincoln Withers and Marshall Chalk from Canberra; Wests Tigers Ryan O'Hara; Cronulla's Adam Peek; and Cook Islander Ben Vaeau from North Queensland all announced.

3 December 2008 - prop Ben Vaeau asks to be released from his contract for family reasons.

11 December 2008 - Crusaders announce plans for 15,000 capacity stadium at Island Farm, Bridgend.

12 January 2009 - Papua New Guinea international Jason Chan joins from Jim Beam Cup winners Windsor Wolves.

30 January 2009 - eight Australian players all granted visas and arrive five days before first Super League fixture.

3 February 2009 - chief executive David Thompson leaves the club.

6 February 2009 - 28-6 defeat in opening Super League game at Leeds.

14 February 2009 - 28-16 defeat at Salford after going 20-0 behind midway through first half.

16 February 2009 - winger Paul Ballard re-signs for 2009.

21 February 2009 - 28-20 defeat by Hull in first home game.

7 March 2009 - Mark Lennon fractures thumb in 4-0 home defeat by St Helens.

22 March 2009 - televised Sunday night round-six match at home to Wakefield postponed half an hour before kick-off following the death of Wildcats' Leon Walker in reserve match at Maesteg earlier that day.

29 March 2009 - 27-22 round seven defeat at Warrington.

1 April 2009 - Maesteg head coach Kevan Tee, 47, replaces departed Thibault Giroud as football manager.

3 April 2009 - 32-6 fourth-round Carnegie Challenge Cup defeat at Hull KR.

13 April 2009 - 40-18 Easter Monday defeat to Harlequins at Brewery Field.

26 April 2009 - Marshall Chalk out for at least two months with broken jaw after 34-22 home defeat to Castleford.

Jason Chan

1 May 2009 - on-loan St Helens centre Steve Tyrer joins Widnes on month's loan.

3 May 2009 - 40-16 defeat by Huddersfield at Murrayfield is eleventh on a row.

15 May 2009 - Tony Duggan out for season after being told he needs to undergo ankle surgery.

17 May 2009 - Luke Dyer scores two tries in first Super League win, by 30-24 at Bradford.

20 May 2009 - Mike Turner appointed Chief Executive.

23 May 2009 - 30-18 home defeat by Catalans in first all non-English Super League encounter.

30 May 2009 - 50-6 hammering by Wakefield leaves Celtic still searching for first home win.

6 June 2009 - 26-6 defeat at Harlequins on the back of a 10-4 penalty count.

13 June 2009 - Peter Lupton scores twice in 22-16 win over Wigan, marking the Crusaders' first home Super League victory. Darren Mapp sustains chest injury.

20 June 2009 - 32-18 home defeat by Hull KR.

2 July 2009 - Darren Mapp ruled out for rest of season after operation to repair torn pectoral muscle.

8 July 2009 - Damien Quinn and Tony Duggan to be released at end of season.

11 July 2009 - David Watkins replaces Jonathan Davies as club president.

17 July 2009 - Adam Peek suffers medial ligament damage in 22-6 defeat at Hull FC.

3 August 2009 - Peter Lupton to miss rest of season after deciding to undergo knee surgery.

18 August 2009 - Jace Van Dijk, Tony Duggan, Mark Dalle Cort, Josh Hannay, Darren Mapp and Damien Quinn ordered to leave UK after visa discrepancies in previous seasons.

21 August 2009 - Crusaders confirm two-year deal to ground-share with rugby union club Newport Gwent Dragons from 2010.

3 September 2009 - Crusaders confirm they will take a Super League match to Wrexham in 2010.

4 September 2009 - on-loan St Helens scrum-half Matty Smith signs for Salford in 2010.

8 September 2009 - Adam Peek signs new two-year contract.

12 September 2009 - coach John Dixon to be released after final Super League match of the season at Castleford.

13 September 2009 - 35-22 defeat at Castleford in last game of season.

7 October 2009 - 20-year-old fullback Elliot Kear signs full-time contract.

14 October 2009 - Brian Noble appointed head coach; Jon Sharp and Iestyn Harris as assistants.

2 November 2009 - Celtic name dropped from Crusaders Rugby League.

3 November 2009 - Lewis Mills signs full-time professional forms.

CELTIC CRUSADERS

DATE	FIXTURE	RESULT	SCORERS	LGE	ATT
6/2/09	Leeds (a)	L28-6	t:Dyer g:Hannay	N/A	14,827
14/2/09	Salford (a)	L28-16	t:Lupton,Duggan(2) g:Hannay(2)	14th	4,026
21/2/09	Hull (h)	L20-28	t:Quinn,Chalk(2),Duggan g:Hannay(2)	14th	5,272
7/3/09	St Helens (h)	L0-4		13th	6,351
15/3/09	Hull KR (a)	L48-18	t:Lupton,Mapp,Smith g:Hannay(3)	13th	8,046
29/3/09	Warrington (a)	L27-22	t:Blackwood,Withers,Hannay,Dyer g:Hannay(3)	14th	7,854
3/4/09	Hull KR (a) (CCR4)	L32-6	t:Tangata-Toa g:Hannay	N/A	7,104
10/4/09	Huddersfield (a)	L30-10	t:Peek,Blackwood g:Hannay	14th	6,407
13/4/09	Harlequins (h)	L18-40	t:Peek,Chalk,Dalle Cort g:Hannay(3)	14th	3,009
19/4/09	Wigan (a)	L44-10	t:Dyer,Dalle Cort g:Van Dijk	14th	12,371
26/4/09	Castleford (h)	L22-34	t:Quinn,Peek,Tangata-Toa,O'Hara g:Quinn(3)	14th	2,017
3/5/09	Huddersfield (MM) ●	L16-40	t:Beasley,Blackwood,Tangata-Toa g:Quinn(2)	14th	N/A
17/5/09	Bradford (a)	W24-30	t:Beasley,Tangata-Toa,Withers,Dyer(2) g:Hannay(5)	14th	7,602
23/5/09	Catalans (h)	L18-30	t:Hannay,Chan,J James g:Hannay(3)	14th	2,927
30/5/09	Wakefield (h)	L6-50	t:Tangata-Toa g:Hannay	14th	2,089
6/6/09	Harlequins (a)	L26-6	t:Quinn g:Lennon	14th	2,245
13/6/09	Wigan (h)	W22-16	t:Van Dijk,Lupton(2),Dalle Cort g:Lennon(3)	14th	5,253
20/6/09	Hull KR (h)	L18-32	t:Quinn,O'Hara,Chan g:Lennon(3)	14th	3,015
26/6/09	St Helens (a)	L30-0		14th	8,684
4/7/09	Warrington (h)	L6-22	t:Dyer g:Lennon	14th	3,231
11/7/09	Salford (h)	W25-12	t:Chalk,Blackwood,Withers,Smith g:Quinn(4) fg:Smith	14th	3,009
17/7/09	Hull (a)	L22-6	t:Chan g:Quinn	14th	10,397
25/7/09	Bradford (h)	L12-34	t:Withers,Smith g:Quinn(2)	14th	3,081
1/8/09	Catalans (a)	L34-0		14th	6,874
16/8/09	Wakefield (a)	L46-12	t:Dalle Cort,Tyrer g:Smith(2)	14th	7,893
22/8/09	Leeds (h) ●●	L0-68		14th	5,597
5/9/09	Huddersfield (h)	L16-42	t:Blackwood,Tyrer,Lennon g:Tyrer(2)	14th	1,988
13/9/09	Castleford (a)	L35-22	t:White,Withers(2),O'Hara g:Tyrer(3)	14th	6,547

● Played at Murrayfield, Edinburgh
●● Played at Rodney Parade, Newport

		APP		TRIES		GOALS		FG		PTS	
	D.O.B.	ALL	SL	ALL	SL	ALL	SL	ALL	SL	ALL	SL
Paul Ballard	4/9/84	2	2	0	0	0	0	0	0	0	0
Ashley Bateman	11/2/90	1	1	0	0	0	0	0	0	0	0
Chris Beasley	17/10/83	15(5)	15(5)	2	2	0	0	0	0	8	8
Anthony Blackwood	13/9/82	26	25	5	5	0	0	0	0	20	20
Mark Bryant	10/4/81	24(3)	23(3)	0	0	0	0	0	0	0	0
Neil Budworth	10/3/82	8(20)	8(19)	0	0	0	0	0	0	0	0
Marshall Chalk	13/3/81	14	13	4	4	0	0	0	0	16	16
Jason Chan	26/1/84	18(6)	17(6)	3	3	0	0	0	0	12	12
Mark Dalle Cort	19/5/82	24	23	4	4	0	0	0	0	16	16
Geraint Davies	7/3/86	(7)	(7)	0	0	0	0	0	0	0	0
Gil Dudson	16/6/90	(1)	(1)	0	0	0	0	0	0	0	0
Tony Duggan	29/8/78	5	4	3	3	0	0	0	0	12	12
Luke Dyer	15/8/81	22	21	6	6	0	0	0	0	24	24
Ben Flower	19/10/87	2(15)	2(15)	0	0	0	0	0	0	0	0
Josh Hannay	11/1/80	18	17	2	2	25	24	0	0	58	56
Aled James	17/2/82	3(3)	3(3)	0	0	0	0	0	0	0	0
Jordan James	24/5/80	17(5)	17(4)	1	1	0	0	0	0	4	4
Elliot Kear	29/11/88	3	3	0	0	0	0	0	0	0	0
Mark Lennon	17/8/80	10(3)	10(3)	1	1	8	8	0	0	20	20
Peter Lupton	7/3/82	17(4)	16(4)	4	4	0	0	0	0	16	16
Darren Mapp	8/10/80	9(2)	9(2)	1	1	0	0	0	0	4	4
Lewis Mills	30/3/89	(4)	(4)	0	0	0	0	0	0	0	0
Ryan O'Hara	18/8/80	28	27	3	3	0	0	0	0	12	12
Adam Peek	5/2/77	6(12)	5(12)	3	3	0	0	0	0	12	12
Damien Quinn	24/8/81	21(1)	20(1)	4	4	12	12	0	0	40	40
Matty Smith	23/7/87	15(1)	15(1)	3	3	2	2	1	1	17	17
David Tangata-Toa	15/7/81	1(19)	1(18)	5	4	0	0	0	0	20	16
Steve Tyrer	16/3/89	8(1)	8	2	2	5	5	0	0	18	18
Jace Van Dijk	25/2/81	19	19	1	1	1	1	0	0	6	6
Lloyd White	9/10/88	6	6	1	1	0	0	0	0	4	4
Lincoln Withers	7/5/81	22	21	6	6	0	0	0	0	24	24

Ryan O'Hara

LEAGUE RECORD
P27-W3-D0-L24
(14th, SL)
F357, A874, Diff-517
6 points.

CHALLENGE CUP
Round Four

ATTENDANCES
Best - v St Helens (SL - 6,351)
Worst - v Huddersfield
(SL - 1,988)
Total (SL only) - 46,839
Average (SL only) - 3,603
(Up by 1,674 on 2008, NL1)

KEY DATES - HARLEQUINS

Chad Randall

5 January 2009 - chairman Keith Hogg resigns because of family and business commitments. Long-serving director and investor David Hughes re-takes the role.

8 February 2009 - opening (round 2) Super League match at home to Bradford casualty of the big freeze.

15 February 2009 - two Luke Dorn tries secure opening-round 12-8 win at Castleford.

28 February 2009 - 24-18 home defeat to Wigan.

6 March 2009 - 48-18 hammering of Salford at the Willows.

14 March 2009 - 60-8 hammering of Warrington at the Stoop.

17 March 2009 - former Hull KR chief executive Paul Blanchard appointed general manager.

22 March 2009 - 46-6 humbling by Huddersfield.

28 March 2009 - back to winning ways with 22-12 home win over Hull FC.

9 April 2009 - 28-24 home defeat by Catalans.

13 April 2009 - 40-18 Easter Monday win at Celtic.

24 April 2009 - David Howell scores two tries in 21-4 win at Leeds.

7 May 2009 - Chris Melling signs new two-year contract until end 2011.

15 May 2009 - David Howell signs two-year contract extension until end of 2011 season.

17 May 2009 - 24-17 home win over Wakefield sees Quins move into fourth.

18 May 2009 - captain Rob Purdham agrees two-year contract extension until end of 2011.

20 May 2009 - Chad Randall signs contract until end of 2011.

22 May 2009 - 22-12 defeat to St Helens at GPW Recruitment Stadium.

6 June 2009 - Comfortable 26-6 home victory over Celtic.

9 June 2009 - Quins announce new partnership with London Skolars.

11 June 2009 - Will Sharp signs new contract to end of 2010.

11 June 2009 - Jon Grayshon joins Widnes on a month's loan.

12 June 2009 - Chad Randall plays 100th Quins game in 40-10 victory over second-placed Hull KR at Craven Park.

20 June 2009 - 48-18 defeat by Leeds at the Stoop.

3 July 2009 - David Howell becomes first player sent off in SLXIV for high tackle on Sam Tomkins in 40-12 defeat at Wigan.

7 July 2009 - ever-present David Howell handed three-match ban.

8 July 2009 - Hull KR second-rower Ryan Esders arrives on a month's loan.

13 July 2009 - Danny Ward signs new 12-month contract.

28 July 2009 - Tony Clubb suspended for two matches for a head slam tackle on St Helens halfback Kyle Eastmond during 44-24 home defeat.

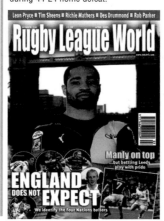

11 August 2009 - Ryan Esders loan spell extended to end of season.

3 September 2009 - Ryan Esders signs one-year deal.

4 September 2009 - Wakefield Wildcats forward Oliver Wilkes signs on two-year contract from 2010.

6 September 2009 - 48-0 home defeat to Castleford all but ends top-eight chances.

11 September 2009 - 20-year-old Londoner Luke May signs new contract for 2010.

13 September 2009 - 44-34 defeat at Warrington in round 17 means 11th placed finish.

17 September 2009 - Bradford Bulls prop Matt James signs two-year deal from 2010.

7 October 2009 - Championship player of the year Andy Ellis joins from Barrow on two-year contract.

16 October 2009 - Leeds Rhinos academy prop Ben Jones joins on one-year contract.

19 October 2009 - Leeds Rhinos junior Ben Jones-Bishop arrives on a year's loan.

21 October 2009 - Londoner Dave Williams signs new contract for 2010.

26 October 2009 - Lamont Bryan signs contract for 2010.

HARLEQUINS

DATE	FIXTURE	RESULT	SCORERS	LGE	ATT
15/2/09	Castleford (a)	W8-12	t:Dorn(2) g:Purdham(2)	6th	7,049
28/2/09	Wigan (h)	L18-24	t:Randall,Gafa,McCarthy-Scarsbrook,Melling g:Orr	8th	3,883
6/3/09	Salford (a)	W18-48	t:Gafa,Howell(2),Mbu,Melling(2),Randall,Dorn,Heckenberg g:Orr(6)	7th	3,367
14/3/09	Warrington (h)	W60-8	t:Dorn,Ward,Temata,Gafa,Orr,Randall,Howell,Gale(2),Melling g:Orr(10)	6th	3,206
22/3/09	Huddersfield (a)	L46-6	t:Ward g:Orr	8th	6,356
28/3/09	Hull (h)	W22-12	t:Clubb,Golden,Howell g:Orr(5)	7th	3,593
4/4/09	Huddersfield (h) (CCR4)	L16-42	t:Clubb,Temata,Howell g:Orr(2)	N/A	1,973
9/4/09	Catalans (h)	L24-28	t:Gardner,Golden,McCarthy-Scarsbrook,Melling g:Purdham(4)	8th	2,540
13/4/09	Celtic Crusaders (a)	W18-40	t:Clubb,Howell,Orr(2),Melling,Dorn(2) g:Purdham(5),Orr	7th	3,009
19/4/09	Hull KR (h)	L12-32	t:Gardner,Robinson g:Purdham(2)	7th	3,492
24/4/09	Leeds (a)	W4-21	t:Howell(2),Randall g:Purdham(4) fg:Purdham	7th	13,912
2/5/09	Salford (MM) ●	W24-16	t:Williamson,Clubb,Howell,Dorn g:Purdham(4)	5th	N/A
17/5/09	Wakefield (h)	W24-17	t:Dorn,Sharp,Howell,Williamson g:Purdham(4)	4th	3,612
22/5/09	St Helens (a)	L22-12	t:McCarthy-Scarsbrook,Dorn g:Purdham(2)	5th	9,359
6/6/09	Celtic Crusaders (h)	W26-6	t:McCarthy-Scarsbrook,Melling,Williamson,Randall g:Purdham(5)	5th	2,245
12/6/09	Hull KR (a)	W10-40	t:Randall,McCarthy-Scarsbrook,Sharp(2),Howell(2),Melling g:Purdham,Orr(3),Melling(2)	4th	7,874
20/6/09	Leeds (h)	L14-48	t:Melling,Howell,Randall g:Orr	5th	4,378
28/6/09	Wakefield (a)	L20-18	t:Orr,Gale,Randall g:Orr(3)	5th	5,079
3/7/09	Wigan (a)	L40-12	t:Gafa,Gale g:Orr(2)	5th	14,977
11/7/09	Huddersfield (h)	L16-32	t:Gale,Melling(2) g:Orr(2)	6th	3,916
19/7/09	Catalans (a)	L38-16	t:Esders,Gale,Haggerty g:Gale(2)	8th	8,324
25/7/09	St Helens (h)	L24-44	t:Haggerty,Robinson,Ward,Gafa g:Orr(4)	9th	4,258
2/8/09	Bradford (a)	W14-22	t:Gafa,Esders,Howell(2) g:Orr(3)	8th	7,813
8/8/09	Bradford (h)	L18-42	t:Purdham(2),Sharp g:Orr,Purdham(2)	9th	3,112
15/8/09	Salford (h)	L22-26	t:Dorn,Randall,Purdham,McCarthy-Scarsbrook g:Purdham(3)	9th	2,612
21/8/09	Hull (a)	L26-6	t:Sharp g:Purdham	10th	15,592
6/9/09	Castleford (h)	L0-48		11th	3,824
13/9/09	Warrington (a)	L44-34	t:Clubb,Dorn(3),O'Callaghan,Gafa g:Melling,Gafa(4)	11th	10,387

● Played at Murrayfield, Edinburgh

	D.O.B.	APP ALL	SL	TRIES ALL	SL	GOALS ALL	SL	FG ALL	SL	PTS ALL	SL
Lamont Bryan	12/4/88	2(3)	2(3)	0	0	0	0	0	0	0	0
Tony Clubb	12/6/87	16(7)	15(7)	5	4	0	0	0	0	20	16
Luke Dorn	2/7/82	22	21	13	13	0	0	0	0	52	52
Ryan Esders	20/10/86	4(4)	4(4)	2	2	0	0	0	0	8	8
Matt Gafa	31/8/78	25	24	7	7	4	4	0	0	36	36
Luke Gale	22/6/88	11(10)	11(10)	6	6	2	2	0	0	28	28
Matt Gardner	24/8/84	6(3)	6(3)	2	2	0	0	0	0	8	8
Jason Golden	6/11/85	16(9)	16(8)	2	2	0	0	0	0	8	8
Jon Grayshon	10/5/83	(2)	(2)	0	0	0	0	0	0	0	0
Gareth Haggerty	8/9/81	(13)	(13)	2	2	0	0	0	0	8	8
Daniel Heckenberg	27/10/79	4(19)	4(18)	1	1	0	0	0	0	4	4
David Howell	18/11/83	20	19	15	14	0	0	0	0	60	56
Ben Kaye	19/12/88	2(12)	2(12)	0	0	0	0	0	0	0	0
Luke May	23/8/89	(1)	(1)	0	0	0	0	0	0	0	0
Joe Mbu	6/11/83	4(2)	4(2)	1	1	0	0	0	0	4	4
Louie McCarthy-Scarsbrook	14/1/86	13(15)	13(14)	6	6	0	0	0	0	24	24
Chris Melling	21/9/84	27	26	11	11	3	3	0	0	50	50
Jamie O'Callaghan	21/9/90	4(1)	4(1)	1	1	0	0	0	0	4	4
Danny Orr	17/5/78	22(2)	21(2)	4	4	45	43	0	0	106	102
Rob Purdham	14/4/80	18	17	3	3	39	39	1	1	91	91
Chad Randall	30/12/80	25	24	9	9	0	0	0	0	36	36
Chad Robinson	20/10/80	14(1)	13(1)	2	2	0	0	0	0	8	8
Will Sharp	12/5/86	26	25	5	5	0	0	0	0	20	20
Dylan Skee	13/1/86	(2)	(2)	0	0	0	0	0	0	0	0
Karl Temata	12/7/78	22	21	2	1	0	0	0	0	8	4
Sam Thompson	9/10/86	(2)	(2)	0	0	0	0	0	0	0	0
Danny Ward	15/6/80	21(2)	20(2)	3	3	0	0	0	0	12	12
Jon Wells	23/9/78	19	18	0	0	0	0	0	0	0	0
Dave Williams	29/1/87	(1)	(1)	0	0	0	0	0	0	0	0
Luke Williamson	2/6/78	21(1)	21	3	3	0	0	0	0	12	12

Louie McCarthy-Scarsbrook

LEAGUE RECORD
P27-W11-D0-L16
(11th, SL)
F591, A691, Diff-100
22 points.

CHALLENGE CUP
Round Four

ATTENDANCES
Best - v Leeds (SL - 4,378)
Worst - v Huddersfield
(CC - 1,973)
Total (SL only) - 44,671
Average (SL only) - 3,436
(Down by 337 on 2008)

189

10 November 2008 - Paul Cook joins as assistant coach.

28 November 2008 - 17-year-old Whitehaven scrum-half Gregg McNally signs on three-year deal, and is loaned back to Whitehaven.

15 December 2008 - former Salford head coach Karl Harrison joins as Senior Scholarship coach.

8 January 2009 - new signing Todd Carney refused visa by UK Border Agency.

23 January 2009 - Jamahl Lolesi receives new visa after long wait.

2 February 2009 - Brett Hodgson appointed captain.

9 February 2009 - hooker David Faiumu flies home to New Zealand following family bereavement.

14 February 2009 - stunning 30-8 round one away win over Catalans.

22 February 2009 - 23-6 home defeat by St Helens.

27 February 2009 - Simon Finnigan damages knee ligaments in first win at Bradford for 40 years, by 16-12.

29 March 2009 - Liam Fulton arrives in the UK on contract to end of season.

31 March 2009 - Keith Mason escapes with fine after being found guilty of running in to fight in round-seven 22-8 win at Wigan. Giants go third in table.

4 April 2009 - 42-16 away Challenge Cup hammering of Harlequins at the Stoop.

10 April 2009 - Liam Fulton makes try-scoring debut in 30-10 home Good Friday win over Celtic Crusaders.

13 April 2009 - Liam Fulton suffers knee injury in 30-8 Easter Monday victory at Hull KR as Giants move into second spot.

18 April 2009 - 34-6 home defeat by Leeds.

26 April 2009 - 40-18 defeat at Warrington.

3 May 2009 - 40-16 win over Celtic at Murrayfield

10 May 2009 - Shaun Lunt scores hat-trick in 38-12 home Cup victory over Rochdale Hornets.

14 May 2009 - Halifax sign Tom Hemingway on month's loan.

14 May 2009 - World Cup winner David Fa'alogo agrees four-year deal from 2010 after securing release from final year of South Sydney contract.

17 May 2009 - Brett Hodgson out injured as Giants drop to fifth after 24-4 home defeat to Salford.

KEY DATES - HUDDERSFIELD GIANTS

David Hodgson

18 May 2009 - Wigan's Lee Mossop arrives on month's loan.

20 May 2009 - Danny Kirmond signs new four-year contract to end of 2013 season.

24 May 2009 - David Hodgson hat-trick in 54-6 thrashing of Wakefield.

27 May 2009 - Danny Sculthorpe signs on season-long loan, with Michael Korkidas returning to Wakefield.

31 May 2009 - Progress into Challenge Cup semi-final ensured in 16-14 victory over Castleford.

31 May 2009 - drawn against St Helens in the semi-final of the Challenge Cup.

5 June 2009 - Danny Kirmond sidelined after suffering depressed cheekbone in 22-6 home win over Hull KR.

12 June 2009 - Scott Moore and Eorl Crabtree named in England side against France.

14 June 2009 - Liam Fulton returns from injury in tight, late 20-12 loss at Leeds Rhinos.

17 June 2009 - Huddersfield and Wigan agree to extend loan deal of Lee Mossop on a week-to-week basis.

19 June 2009 - 13-6 home defeat to Castleford.

23 June 2009 - Darrell Griffin escapes ban for reckless tackle in Castleford defeat.

14 July 2009 - Lee Gilmour signs on two-year deal from St Helens from 2010.

16 July 2009 - Kevin Brown signs new three-year contract to end of 2012.

31 July 2009 - 24-0 win at Hull FC is sixth successive victory.

9 August 2009 - 24-14 win over St Helens in Cup semi-final at Warrington secures first Wembley appearance since 1962.

20 August 2009 - Darrell Griffin signs new three-year contract until end of 2012.

21 August 2009 - Danny Kirmond ruled out for season with cruciate ligament damage suffered during 12-10 defeat at St Helens.

29 August 2009 - 25-16 defeat to Warrington Wolves in Challenge Cup final.

5 September 2009 - Brad Drew to return for second spell on one-year deal.

5 September 2009 - Simon Finnigan suffers season-ending wrist ligament damage during Giants' 42-16 win at Celtic.

8 September 2009 - reserve winger Alex Brown handed one-year full-time contract.

9 September 2009 - Paul Jackson, Liam Fulton, Joe Walsh, Richard Lopag, Tom Hemingway and Chris Lawson to be released at the end of the season.

13 September 2009 - 48-16 last-day home thrashing of Wigan secures third spot. Scott Moore and Keith Mason dropped pending disciplinary investigation

15 September 2009 - Keith Mason and Scott Moore to sit out opening play-off match at St Helens because of internal suspension.

18 September 2009 - 19-year-old prop forward Jacob Fairbank signs on three-year contract from local junior rugby.

19 September 2009 - 15-2 Qualifying Play-off defeat at St Helens.

25 September 2009 - 16-6 elimination at home to Catalans.

5 October 2009 - Brett Hodgson named Man of Steel, Huddersfield club of the year and Nathan Brown coach of the year.

13 October 2009 - Sheffield Eagles halfback Kyle Wood joins on three-year contract.

HUDDERSFIELD GIANTS

DATE	FIXTURE	RESULT	SCORERS	LGE	ATT
14/2/09	Catalans (a)	W8-30	t:Finnigan(2),D Hodgson,Lunt,Raleigh g:B Hodgson(5)	2nd	7,533
22/2/09	St Helens (h)	L6-23	t:Whatuira g:B Hodgson	5th	11,338
27/2/09	Bradford (a)	W12-16	t:Aspinwall,Lolesi,Wild g:B Hodgson(2)	6th	10,186
6/3/09	Hull (h)	L20-24	t:B Hodgson,Walsh,K Brown,D Hodgson g:B Hodgson(2)	9th	10,459
14/3/09	Castleford (a)	W24-26	t:Lolesi,D Hodgson(3),B Hodgson g:B Hodgson(3)	8th	6,572
22/3/09	Harlequins (h)	W46-6	t:Wild,Mason,K Brown(2),B Hodgson,Robinson(2),Lunt g:B Hodgson(6),Cudjoe	4th	6,356
27/3/09	Wigan (a)	W8-22	t:Moore,Lawrence,K Brown g:B Hodgson(5)	3rd	11,670
4/4/09	Harlequins (a) (CCR4)	W16-42	t:Mason,Robinson(2),D Hodgson(2),Wild,Whatuira,B Hodgson g:B Hodgson(4),D Hodgson	N/A	1,973
10/4/09	Celtic Crusaders (h)	W30-10	t:D Hodgson(2),Fulton,K Brown,Lawrence g:B Hodgson(5)	3rd	6,407
13/4/09	Hull KR (a)	W8-30	t:Lawrence(2),D Hodgson,Lunt,Wild g:B Hodgson(5)	2nd	8,731
18/4/09	Leeds (h)	L6-34	t:Lawrence g:B Hodgson	3rd	11,593
26/4/09	Warrington (a)	L40-18	t:Finnigan,Whatuira,B Hodgson g:B Hodgson(3)	4th	8,005
3/5/09	Celtic Crusaders (MM) ●	W16-40	t:B Hodgson,Kirmond,Moore,Lunt(2),Korkidas,Finnigan g:B Hodgson(6)	4th	N/A
10/5/09	Rochdale (h) (CCR5)	W38-12	t:Robinson,Lunt(3),Patrick,Carlile,Lolesi g:Cudjoe(5)	N/A	2,859
17/5/09	Salford (h)	L4-24	t:Robinson	5th	6,903
24/5/09	Wakefield (a)	W6-54	t:Kirmond,D Hodgson(3),Cudjoe,K Brown,Moore(2),Whatuira,Lolesi g:Cudjoe(7)	4th	5,037
31/5/09	Castleford (h) (CCQF)	W16-14	t:K Brown,Wild,Kirmond g:B Hodgson(2)	N/A	6,359
5/6/09	Hull KR (h)	W22-6	t:Moore,Robinson,Mossop,Whatuira g:Cudjoe(3)	4th	6,346
14/6/09	Leeds (a)	L20-12	t:D Hodgson,K Brown g:B Hodgson(2)	5th	14,934
19/6/09	Castleford (h)	L6-13	t:Cudjoe g:B Hodgson	4th	6,010
26/6/09	Salford (a)	W10-34	t:Moore,B Hodgson,Lawrence,Cudjoe(2),Wild g:B Hodgson(5)	4th	3,721
5/7/09	Wakefield (h)	W30-14	t:Moore,Faiumu(2),D Hodgson,Fulton g:B Hodgson(5)	3rd	7,486
11/7/09	Harlequins (a)	W16-32	t:Cudjoe,D Hodgson,Lawrence,B Hodgson(2) g:B Hodgson(6)	3rd	3,916
19/7/09	Warrington (h)	W28-10	t:Jackson,Moore,Cudjoe(2),Lawrence g:B Hodgson(4)	3rd	7,107
26/7/09	Catalans (h)	W36-12	t:Cudjoe(3),B Hodgson,D Griffin,D Hodgson,Finnigan g:B Hodgson(4)	3rd	5,823
31/7/09	Hull (a)	W0-24	t:D Hodgson,Lunt,Lawrence,Cudjoe g:B Hodgson(4)	3rd	11,191
9/8/09	St Helens (CCSF) ●●	W24-14	t:B Hodgson,Wild(2),Cudjoe,K Brown g:B Hodgson(2)	N/A	10,638
16/8/09	Bradford (h)	L18-28	t:B Hodgson,Moore,Kirmond g:B Hodgson(3)	3rd	7,892
21/8/09	St Helens (a)	L12-10	t:Lunt,Cudjoe g:Cudjoe	4th	8,708
29/8/09	Warrington (CCF) ●●●	L16-25	t:Lunt,B Hodgson,D Hodgson g:B Hodgson(2)	N/A	76,560
5/9/09	Celtic Crusaders (a)	W16-42	t:D Hodgson,Fulton(2),Patrick,Whatuira,Lunt(2) g:Cudjoe(7)	4th	1,988
13/9/09	Wigan (h)	W48-16	t:B Hodgson,D Hodgson,Lunt(2),Cudjoe(3),Whatuira g:B Hodgson(8)	3rd	8,988
19/9/09	St Helens (a) (QPO)	L15-2	g:B Hodgson	N/A	6,157
25/9/09	Catalans (h) (PSF)	L6-16	t:Robinson g:B Hodgson	N/A	4,263

● Played at Murrayfield, Edinburgh
●● Played at Halliwell Jones Stadium, Warrington
●●● Played at Wembley Stadium

		APP		TRIES		GOALS		FG		PTS	
	D.O.B.	ALL	SL	ALL	SL	ALL	SL	ALL	SL	ALL	SL
Martin Aspinwall	21/10/81	17(6)	14(5)	1	1	0	0	0	0	4	4
Alex Brown	28/8/87	1	1	0	0	0	0	0	0	0	0
Kevin Brown	2/10/84	26	22	9	7	0	0	0	0	36	28
Keal Carlile	20/3/90	(2)	(1)	1	0	0	0	0	0	4	0
Eorl Crabtree	2/10/82	5(22)	5(17)	0	0	0	0	0	0	0	0
Leroy Cudjoe	7/4/88	25	22	16	15	24	19	0	0	112	98
David Faiumu	30/4/83	10(16)	7(15)	2	2	0	0	0	0	8	8
Simon Finnigan	8/12/81	21(1)	19(1)	5	5	0	0	0	0	20	20
Liam Fulton	8/8/84	14(3)	12(3)	4	4	0	0	0	0	16	16
Darrell Griffin	19/6/81	13(14)	11(11)	1	1	0	0	0	0	4	4
Josh Griffin	9/5/90	3	2	1	0	0	0	0	0	4	0
Tom Hemingway	6/12/86	2	1	0	0	0	0	0	0	0	0
Brett Hodgson	12/2/78	28	24	14	11	98	88	0	0	252	220
David Hodgson	8/8/81	32	28	21	18	1	0	0	0	86	72
Elliot Hodgson	2/11/90	1	1	0	0	0	0	0	0	0	0
Paul Jackson	29/9/78	15(12)	12(10)	1	1	0	0	0	0	4	4
Danny Kirmond	11/11/85	10(10)	9(8)	4	3	0	0	0	0	16	12
Michael Korkidas	12/1/81	5(1)	4(1)	1	1	0	0	0	0	4	4
Michael Lawrence	12/4/90	24	22	9	9	0	0	0	0	36	36
Jamahl Lolesi	20/3/81	18(6)	13(6)	4	3	0	0	0	0	16	12
Shaun Lunt	15/4/86	8(13)	6(11)	15	11	0	0	0	0	60	44
Keith Mason	20/1/82	28	24	2	1	0	0	0	0	8	4
Scott Moore	23/1/88	26(3)	23(2)	9	9	0	0	0	0	36	36
Lee Mossop	17/1/89	1(4)	1(4)	1	1	0	0	0	0	4	4
Larne Patrick	3/11/88	3(5)	2(5)	2	1	0	0	0	0	8	4
Andy Raleigh	17/3/81	11(7)	10(6)	1	1	0	0	0	0	4	4
Luke Robinson	25/7/84	33	28	8	5	0	0	0	0	32	20
Danny Sculthorpe	8/9/79	5(8)	5(8)	0	0	0	0	0	0	0	0
Joe Walsh	13/1/86	1(2)	1(1)	1	1	0	0	0	0	4	4
Paul Whatuira	31/7/81	27	23	7	6	0	0	0	0	28	24
Stephen Wild	26/4/81	29(1)	25(1)	8	4	0	0	0	0	32	16

Brett Hodgson

LEAGUE RECORD
P27-W18-D0-L9
(3rd, SL/Preliminary Semi-Final)
F690, A416, Diff+274
36 points.

CHALLENGE CUP
Runners-Up

ATTENDANCES
Best - v Leeds (SL - 11,593)
Worst - v Rochdale (CC - 2,859)
Total (SL, inc play-offs) - 106,971
Average (SL, inc play-offs) - 7,641
(Down by 205 on 2008)

9 January 2009 - Tonga World Cup prop Sam Moa joins from Cronulla Sharks on one-year contract.

12 January 2009 - Gareth Raynor undergoes second operation on big toe and could be out of action until April.

2 February 2009 - Michael Crocker refused visa by UK Border Agency due to a criminal conviction.

13 February 2009 - Richard Horne leads Hull to 18-10 home victory over Wigan in round 1.

21 February 2009 - Danny Tickle scores hat-trick in 28-20 round 2 win at Celtic. Todd Byrne suffers knee injury.

23 February 2009 - New Zealand and Tonga forward Epalahame Lauaki signs on a three-year deal subject to visa.

27 February 2009 - 28-12 home win over Catalans makes it three from three.

3 March 2009 - Todd Byrne out for season after being told he needs knee reconstruction.

13 March 2009 - Tom Briscoe signs new five-year contract to end of 2013.

15 March 2009 - 36-24 win at Bradford makes it record opening five wins from five.

20 March 2009 - 77th minute Brent Sherwin field goal secures 19-18 Castleford win at KC Stadium to end winning run.

5 April 2009 - controversial late try seals 22-18 home Challenge Cup exit to Salford.

10 April 2009 - Tom Briscoe suffers ankle injury in 18-14 home Good Friday defeat to Hull KR.

12 April 2009 - Stuart Reardon, awaiting sentencing for an assault conviction, joins until end of season after release by Wolves.

14 April 2009 - Hull cancel contract of out-for-the-season Todd Byrne.

16 April 2009 - Leeds centre Jodie Broughton joins on one-month loan.

22 April 2009 - Stuart Reardon released 11 days after signing as he fails medical.

25 April 2009 - 18-14 win at Salford ends six-match losing run.

1 May 2009 - Mike Burnett agrees two-year contract extension to end of 2011.

12 May 2009 - Graeme Horne ruled out for six weeks after surgery on injured thumb.

16 May 2009 - Craig Fitzgibbon signs from Sydney Roosters on a 12-month deal with an option of second year.

16 May 2009 - Peter Cusack undergoes wrist reconstruction and Danny Washbrook suffers knee ligament damage in 18-16 home defeat by Warrington.

KEY DATES - HULL F.C.

26 May 2009 - heavy 46-16 defeat to Leeds at Headingley.

1 June 2009 - Sean Long signs two-year deal from 2010.

4 June 2009 - Jordan Tansey signs for 2010 season from Roosters.

5 June 2009 - Sean Long stars in 30-6 home defeat to St Helens.

5 June 2009 - Craig Hall joins Widnes on month's loan.

11 June 2009 - Mark Calderwood to miss up to six weeks after suffering chest injury.

13 June 2009 - 37-22 defeat at Wakefield.

17 June 2009 - Peter Cusack signs new contract for 2010.

30 June 2009 - Epalahame Lauaki granted visa.

4 July 2009 - Sydney Roosters' Mark O'Meley joins on three-year-deal from 2010.

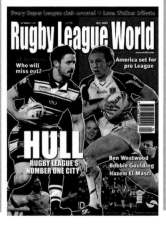

7 July 2009 - prop forward Josh Cordoba joins from Parramatta on short-term deal until end of season.

12 July 2009 - Josh Cordoba makes debut in 40-18 defeat at Castleford.

15 July 2009 - 2010 signing Jordan Tansey signed until the end of the year.

16 July 2009 - prop Dominic Maloney joins Halifax on loan to end of season.

17 July 2009 - second loan spell of Leeds winger Jodie Broughton until the end of the current season.

17 July 2009 - Jordan Tansey makes debut in 22-6 home win over Celtic.

21 August 2009 - Epalahame Lauaki makes debut; Craig Hall scores hat-trick in 26-6 home win over Harlequins.

24 August 2009 - 17-year-old Jack Briscoe, younger brother of Tom, given professional contract.

25 August 2009 - Jordan Tansey and Danny Tickle both suspended for two matches for illegal tackles in win over Harlequins; Carnegie Nines counts as one game.

26 August 2009 - Craig Hall player of tournament as Hull win Carnegie Floodlit Nines.

28 August 2009 - Richard Whiting signs new 12-month contract.

1 September 2009 - Tommy Lee and Mike Burnett suspended pending internal disciplinary investigation.

2 September 2009 - Danny Tickle has two-match ban reduced to one on appeal.

4 September 2009 - Dominic Maloney joins Halifax on permanent deal.

7 September 2009 - Jordan Turner joins from Salford on a three year deal.

11 September 2009 - 21-18 home defeat to Bradford ensures 12th-placed finish.

13 September 2009 - out-of-contract Chris Thorman, Paul King, Tommy Lee, Graeme Horne, Motu Tony, Todd Byrne, Josh Cordoba and Jamie Thackray released.

20 September 2009 - football operations manager Jon Sharp released.

3 October 2009 - Sam Moa agrees two-year contract.

27 October 2009 – 55-year-old former Manly assistant Dennis Moore joins as assistant coach for 2010.

28 October 2009 - Craig Fitzgibbon granted visa.

3 November 2009 - Mark O'Meley granted visa.

HULL FC

HULL F.C.

DATE	FIXTURE	RESULT	SCORERS	LGE	ATT
13/2/09	Wigan (h)	W18-10	t:R Horne,Radford,Cusack g:Tickle(3)	5th	14,523
21/2/09	Celtic Crusaders (a)	W20-28	t:Berrigan,Tickle(3),Calderwood g:Tickle(4)	3rd	5,272
27/2/09	Catalans (h)	W28-12	t:Berrigan,Hall,Briscoe,R Horne g:Tickle(6)	3rd	12,482
6/3/09	Huddersfield (a)	W20-24	t:Briscoe,R Horne,Thackray,Yeaman g:Tickle(4)	2nd	10,459
15/3/09	Bradford (a)	W24-36	t:R Horne,Yeaman(2),Hall(2),Thorman g:Tickle(6)	2nd	11,327
20/3/09	Castleford (h)	L18-19	t:R Horne,G Horne(3) g:Tickle	3rd	14,028
28/3/09	Harlequins (a)	L22-12	t:Yeaman,Hall g:Tickle(2)	5th	3,593
5/4/09	Salford (h) (CCR4)	L18-22	t:Yeaman(2),Briscoe g:Tickle(3)	N/A	8,945
10/4/09	Hull KR (h)	L14-18	t:Briscoe,Berrigan,Whiting g:Tickle	6th	22,337
13/4/09	St Helens (a)	L44-22	t:G Horne(2),Manu,Calderwood g:Tickle(3)	8th	13,684
17/4/09	Wakefield (h)	L14-21	t:Calderwood,Burnett g:Tickle(3)	8th	11,975
25/4/09	Salford (a)	W14-18	t:Calderwood,R Horne,Whiting g:Tickle(3)	8th	4,165
3/5/09	Castleford (MM) ●	W16-24	t:Burnett,Cusack,Whiting,Washbrook g:Tickle(4)	7th	N/A
16/5/09	Warrington (h)	L16-18	t:Whiting,Broughton g:Tickle(4)	7th	10,997
26/5/09	Leeds (a)	L46-16	t:Whiting,Yeaman,Radford g:Tickle(2)	6th	15,929
5/6/09	St Helens (h)	L6-30	t:Tickle g:Tickle	9th	12,009
13/6/09	Wakefield (a)	L37-22	t:Raynor,Broughton(2),Yeaman g:Tickle(3)	8th	4,721
19/6/09	Salford (h)	W14-12	t:Raynor,Tony g:Tickle(3)	8th	11,218
28/6/09	Warrington (a)	L24-12	t:Broughton,Yeaman g:Tickle(2)	9th	9,170
4/7/09	Leeds (h)	L30-43	t:Berrigan,Tickle,Raynor,Yeaman,Burnett g:Tickle(5)	11th	11,780
12/7/09	Castleford (a)	L40-18	t:Manu,Yeaman,Broughton g:Tickle,Whiting(2)	11th	8,297
17/7/09	Celtic Crusaders (h)	W22-6	t:Hall,Raynor,Calderwood,Cordoba g:Tickle(3)	11th	10,397
25/7/09	Hull KR (a)	L24-18	t:Tansey,Hall,Calderwood g:Tickle(3)	11th	9,450
31/7/09	Huddersfield (h)	L0-24		11th	11,191
15/8/09	Catalans (a) ●●	L18-6	t:Raynor g:Tickle	12th	9,083
21/8/09	Harlequins (h)	W26-6	t:Lee,Briscoe,Hall(3) g:Tickle(3)	12th	15,592
4/9/09	Wigan (a)	L34-22	t:Tickle,R Horne,Briscoe,Hall g:Tickle(2),Hall	12th	12,491
11/9/09	Bradford (h)	L18-21	t:Briscoe(2),Radford g:Tickle(3)	12th	13,412

● Played at Murrayfield, Edinburgh
●● Played at Stade de la Mediterranee, Beziers

	D.O.B.	APP		TRIES		GOALS		FG		PTS	
		ALL	SL	ALL	SL	ALL	SL	ALL	SL	ALL	SL
Shaun Berrigan	4/11/78	18(4)	17(4)	4	4	0	0	0	0	16	16
Tom Briscoe	19/3/90	13	12	8	7	0	0	0	0	32	28
Jodie Broughton	9/1/88	7	7	5	5	0	0	0	0	20	20
Mike Burnett	6/10/88	9(8)	9(8)	3	3	0	0	0	0	12	12
Todd Byrne	16/7/78	2	2	0	0	0	0	0	0	0	0
Mark Calderwood	25/10/81	20	19	6	6	0	0	0	0	24	24
Josh Cordoba	29/1/84	8	8	1	1	0	0	0	0	4	4
Peter Cusack	27/1/77	9(3)	8(3)	2	2	0	0	0	0	8	8
Ewan Dowes	4/3/81	23	22	0	0	0	0	0	0	0	0
Craig Hall	21/2/88	14(1)	13(1)	10	10	1	1	0	0	42	42
Josh Hodgson	31/10/89	(2)	(2)	0	0	0	0	0	0	0	0
Graeme Horne	22/3/85	20(4)	19(4)	5	5	0	0	0	0	20	20
Richard Horne	16/7/82	25	24	7	7	0	0	0	0	28	28
Danny Houghton	25/9/88	8(16)	8(16)	0	0	0	0	0	0	0	0
Paul King	28/6/79	5(14)	5(13)	0	0	0	0	0	0	0	0
Epalahame Lauaki	27/1/84	(3)	(3)	0	0	0	0	0	0	0	0
Tommy Lee	1/2/88	9(14)	9(13)	1	1	0	0	0	0	4	4
Dominic Maloney	12/3/87	(7)	(7)	0	0	0	0	0	0	0	0
Willie Manu	20/3/80	21(3)	20(3)	2	2	0	0	0	0	8	8
Sam Moa	14/6/86	(15)	(14)	0	0	0	0	0	0	0	0
Lee Radford	26/3/79	27	26	3	3	0	0	0	0	12	12
Gareth Raynor	24/2/78	14	14	5	5	0	0	0	0	20	20
Jordan Tansey	9/9/86	6	6	1	1	0	0	0	0	4	4
Jamie Thackray	30/9/79	10(8)	10(8)	1	1	0	0	0	0	4	4
Chris Thorman	26/9/80	20(2)	19(2)	1	1	0	0	0	0	4	4
Danny Tickle	10/3/83	28	27	6	6	79	76	0	0	182	176
Motu Tony	29/5/81	5	5	1	1	0	0	0	0	4	4
Danny Washbrook	18/9/85	8(3)	8(2)	1	1	0	0	0	0	4	4
Richard Whiting	20/12/84	13(5)	13(5)	5	5	2	2	0	0	24	24
Kirk Yeaman	15/9/83	22	21	11	9	0	0	0	0	44	36

Danny Tickle

LEAGUE RECORD
P27-W10-D0-L17
(12th, SL)
F502, A623, Diff-121
20 points.

CHALLENGE CUP
Round Four

ATTENDANCES
Best - v Hull KR (SL - 22,337)
Worst - v Salford (CC - 8,945)
Total (SL only) - 171,941
Average (SL only) - 13,226
(Down by 206 on 2008)

20 January 2009 - Chris Chester takes over as assistant coach as Lee Crooks, resigns 12 months into three-year contract.

15 February 2009 - last-second Michael Dobson field goal earns 13-13 opening-round draw at Bradford. Mick Vella suffers knee ligament damage.

17 February 2009 - Chev Walker banned for one game for leading with elbow in tackle by Glenn Morrison. Appeal is turned down.

20 February 2009 - 19-10 home defeat by Leeds in round 2. Paul Cooke suffers hand ligament damage.

27 February 2009 - late Michael Dobson penalty secures 20-19 win at St Helens.

12 March 2009 - Clint Newton signs new four-year contract to end of 2013 season.

22 March 2009 - Chev Walker ruled out for at least three months with dislocated shoulder sustained in 24-12 round-six defeat at Warrington.

29 March 2009 - 48-12 home win over Salford.

3 April 2009 - 32-6 fourth-round home Carnegie Challenge Cup win over Celtic Crusaders.

10 April 2009 - 18-14 Good Friday derby win at KC Stadium.

13 April 2009 - 30-8 Easter Monday defeat to Huddersfield at Craven Park.

15 April 2009 - coach Justin Morgan charged with misconduct by RFL over comments about referee Ben Thaler after 30-8 home Easter Monday defeat to Huddersfield.

19 April 2009 - 32-12 victory over Harlequins marks first ever win at the Stoop.

22 April 2009 - Justin Morgan fined £4,000 - half of it suspended - after being found guilty of misconduct.

26 April 2009 - 44-10 win over Catalans moves Rovers into second spot in table.

KEY DATES - HULL KINGSTON ROVERS

7 May 2009 - Peter Fox signs three-year contract extension until end of 2012.

10 May 2009 - last-minute Ben Fisher try clinches 34-24 victory over Sheffield Eagles to book place in Challenge Cup quarter-final.

15 May 2009 - 20-12 win at Wigan keeps Rovers in second.

22 May 2009 - 16-6 home victory against Castleford maintains title push.

30 May 2009 - 25-24 golden point loss to Warrington in quarter-final of Challenge Cup.

5 June 2009 - Michael Dobson commits future until 2012 by signing two-year contract extension.

5 June 2009 - Ben Cockayne returns from suspension in 22-6 loss at Huddersfield.

9 June 2009 - Ben Cockayne gets one-match ban after being found guilty of grapple tackle.

12 June 2009 - 40-10 home hammering by Harlequins.

20 June 2009 - captain Mick Vella returns in six-try 32-18 victory at Celtic Crusaders.

8 July 2009 - Ryan Esders joins Harlequins on month's loan.

25 July 2009 - Paul Cooke scores two tries in 24-18 home win over Hull FC.

5 August 2009 - Jason Netherton signs new two-year deal to end of 2011 season.

11 August 2009 - Ryan Esders loan spell at Harlequins RL extended to end of season.

16 August 2009 - Daniel Fitzhenry scores two tries in 26-10 home win over St Helens.

28 August 2009 - Rhys Lovegrove signs new contract for 2010.

1 September 2009 - Bradford second row Matt Cook joins on two-year contract from 2010.

3 September 2009 - Hull FC reserve team player of the year Josh Hodgson joins on two-year deal.

3 September 2009 - Ryan Esders leaves for Harlequins.

5 September 2009 - Scott Murrell breaks hand in 40-16 win over Warrington.

7 September 2009 - Justin Morgan signs extended contract to end of 2012 season.

8 September 2009 - released Makali Aizue signs for Halifax.

12 September 2009 - 24-10 defeat at Wakefield means fourth-placed finish.

16 September 2009 - Michael Dobson receives the Albert Goldthorpe Medal.

18 September 2009 - Chev Walker undergoes surgery on compound fracture of left leg sustained in 44-8 Super League play-off defeat at Leeds.

21 September 2009 - Nick Fozzard released from final year of contract to return to St Helens.

22 September 2009 - Michael Ratu joins from Leeds Rhinos on two-year deal.

26 September 2009 - eliminated from play-offs after 30-16 home defeat to Wigan.

10 October 2009 - Chaz l'Anson signs new contract for 2010.

6 October 2009 - Daniel Fitzhenry re-joins Wests Tigers.

31 October 2009 - reserve players Frankie Mariano and Richard Beaumont sign full-time 12-month contracts.

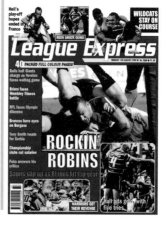

HULL KINGSTON ROVERS

DATE	FIXTURE	RESULT	SCORERS	LGE	ATT
15/2/09	Bradford (a)	D13-13	t:Fox(2) g:Dobson(2) fg:Dobson	8th	12,141
20/2/09	Leeds (h)	L10-19	t:Briscoe g:Dobson(3)	11th	8,623
27/2/09	St Helens (a)	W19-20	t:Galea,Fox,Webster g:Dobson(4)	7th	11,830
8/3/09	Wakefield (h)	W31-18	t:Briscoe,Newton,Murrell,Fisher,Colbon g:Dobson(5) fg:Dobson	6th	9,038
15/3/09	Celtic Crusaders (h)	W48-18	t:Welham,Fozzard,Newton(3),Walker,Galea,Dobson,Colbon g:Dobson(6)	5th	8,046
22/3/09	Warrington (a)	L24-12	t:Fox,Aizue g:Dobson(2)	7th	8,547
29/3/09	Salford (h)	W48-12	t:Murrell,Fox(3),Dobson(3),Welham(2) g:Dobson(6)	6th	8,104
3/4/09	Celtic Crusaders (h) (CCR4)	W32-6	t:Welham,Newton,Fitzhenry,Colbon,Webster g:Dobson(6)	N/A	7,104
10/4/09	Hull (a)	W14-18	t:Webster,Cooke,Fox g:Dobson(3)	4th	22,337
13/4/09	Huddersfield (h)	L8-30	t:Welham,Colbon	6th	8,731
19/4/09	Harlequins (a)	W12-32	t:Welham,Fox,Cooke,Colbon,Galea(2) g:Dobson(4)	5th	3,492
26/4/09	Catalans (h)	W44-10	t:Colbon,Murrell,Galea(2),Webster(2),Dobson,Fisher g:Dobson(6)	2nd	8,115
3/5/09	Warrington (MM) ●	W36-28	t:Briscoe,Dobson,Vella,Newton,Galea(2) g:Dobson(6)	2nd	N/A
10/5/09	Sheffield (h) (CCR5)	W34-24	t:Webster,Gene,Fisher(2),Newton,Briscoe g:Dobson(5)	N/A	4,955
15/5/09	Wigan (a)	W12-20	t:Dobson,Cooke,Webster g:Dobson(4)	2nd	13,415
22/5/09	Castleford (h)	W16-6	t:Fox,Briscoe(2) g:Dobson(2)	2nd	8,104
30/5/09	Warrington (h) (CCQF)	L24-25 (aet)	t:Welham,Newton,Galea,Webster g:Dobson(4)	N/A	7,671
5/6/09	Huddersfield (a)	L22-6	t:Welham g:Dobson	2nd	6,346
12/6/09	Harlequins (h)	L10-40	t:Gene,Wheeldon g:Dobson	3rd	7,874
20/6/09	Celtic Crusaders (a)	W18-32	t:Newton(2),Netherton,Welham,Dobson,Briscoe g:Dobson(4)	3rd	3,015
28/6/09	Wigan (h)	L28-36	t:Fox(2),Vella,Fitzhenry,Webster g:Dobson(4)	3rd	9,007
4/7/09	Catalans (a)	L23-12	t:Cockayne,Fitzhenry g:Dobson(2)	4th	9,073
12/7/09	Bradford (h)	W32-12	t:Murrell,Colbon(2),Welham(2),Fitzhenry g:Dobson(4)	4th	8,206
17/7/09	Leeds (a)	L24-14	t:Welham,Cockayne g:Dobson(3)	4th	16,192
25/7/09	Hull (h)	W24-18	t:Dobson,Cooke(2),Webster g:Dobson(4)	4th	9,450
2/8/09	Castleford (a)	W28-46	t:Fox(2),Briscoe(3),Dobson(2),Colbon g:Dobson(7)	4th	8,709
16/8/09	St Helens (h)	W26-10	t:Welham,Webster,Fitzhenry(2),Fox g:Dobson(3)	4th	8,976
21/8/09	Salford (a)	W10-14	t:Newton,Briscoe g:Dobson(3)	3rd	4,224
5/9/09	Warrington (h)	W40-16	t:Webster,Cooke,Newton(3),Welham,Fox g:Dobson(6)	3rd	8,579
12/9/09	Wakefield (a)	L24-10	t:Newton,Fox g:Dobson	4th	6,328
18/9/09	Leeds (a) (QPO)	L44-8	t:Fitzhenry g:Dobson(2)	N/A	11,220
26/9/09	Wigan (h) (PSF)	L16-30	t:Welham,Fox,I'Anson g:Dobson(2)	N/A	8,162

● Played at Murrayfield, Edinburgh

	D.O.B.	APP		TRIES		GOALS		FG		PTS	
		ALL	SL	ALL	SL	ALL	SL	ALL	SL	ALL	SL
Makali Aizue	30/12/77	3(14)	3(12)	1	1	0	0	0	0	4	4
Kyle Bibb	25/1/88	(2)	(2)	0	0	0	0	0	0	0	0
Shaun Briscoe	23/2/83	25	22	11	10	0	0	0	0	44	40
Ben Cockayne	20/7/83	11(4)	11(4)	2	2	0	0	0	0	8	8
Liam Colbon	30/9/84	26	24	9	8	0	0	0	0	36	32
Paul Cooke	17/4/81	26	23	6	6	0	0	0	0	24	24
Michael Dobson	29/5/86	32	29	11	11	115	100	2	2	276	246
Ryan Esders	20/10/86	(1)	(1)	0	0	0	0	0	0	0	0
Ben Fisher	4/2/81	18(10)	15(10)	4	2	0	0	0	0	16	8
Daniel Fitzhenry	8/12/79	16(13)	15(11)	7	6	0	0	0	0	28	24
Peter Fox	5/11/83	31	28	18	18	0	0	0	0	72	72
Nick Fozzard	22/7/77	20(4)	18(4)	1	1	0	0	0	0	4	4
Ben Galea	16/8/78	29(2)	27(1)	9	8	0	0	0	0	36	32
Stanley Gene	11/5/74	4(10)	2(9)	2	1	0	0	0	0	8	4
James Haynes	22/3/89	1	1	0	0	0	0	0	0	0	0
Chaz I'Anson	30/11/86	9(6)	8(6)	1	1	0	0	0	0	4	4
Rhys Lovegrove	11/3/87	3(14)	2(14)	0	0	0	0	0	0	0	0
Frankie Mariano	10/5/87	(1)	0	0	0	0	0	0	0	0	0
David Mills	1/6/81	1(5)	(4)	0	0	0	0	0	0	0	0
Scott Murrell	5/9/85	26(1)	24(1)	4	4	0	0	0	0	16	16
Jason Netherton	5/10/82	1(22)	1(21)	1	1	0	0	0	0	4	4
Clint Newton	18/6/81	31(1)	28(1)	15	12	0	0	0	0	60	48
Scott Taylor	27/2/91	(1)	(1)	0	0	0	0	0	0	0	0
Michael Vella	19/2/78	16(1)	16(1)	2	2	0	0	0	0	8	8
Chev Walker	9/10/82	12(8)	12(7)	1	1	0	0	0	0	4	4
Liam Watts	8/7/90	(1)	0	0	0	0	0	0	0	0	0
Jake Webster	29/10/83	25(1)	22(1)	12	9	0	0	0	0	48	36
Kris Welham	12/5/87	32	29	15	13	0	0	0	0	60	52
Scott Wheeldon	23/2/86	18(6)	17(5)	1	1	0	0	0	0	4	4

Michael Dobson

LEAGUE RECORD
P27-W17-D1-L9
(4th, SL/Preliminary Semi-Final)
F650, A516, Diff+134
35 points.

CHALLENGE CUP
Quarter Finalists

ATTENDANCES
Best - v Hull (SL - 9,450)
Worst - v Sheffield (CC - 4,955)
Total (SL, inc play-offs) - 119,015
Average (SL, inc play-offs) - 8,501
(Down by 53 on 2008)

16 December 2008 - 19 year old prop Luke Ambler signs from Salford on two-year contract after the clubs agree £12,000 fee.

22 December 2008 - Ryan Hall signs new three-year deal to end of 2011.

30 December 2008 - Barrie McDermott named new head of youth development.

17 January 2009 - Rhinos beat Salford 12-10 in Florida friendly in front of crowd of 6,000.

21 January 2009 - Jamie Jones-Buchanan agrees new four-year contract until end of 2012.

6 February 2009 - groundstaff move 500 tonnes of snow before 28-6 opening night (round 3) win over promoted Celtic.

13 February 2009 - 18-4 home win over Wakefield in Round 1. Rob Burrow, Brent Webb, Kevin Sinfield and Keith Senior absent through injury.

14 February 2009 - new signing Greg Eastwood denied work visa by UK Border Agency because of previous driving condition.

21 February 2009 - 19-10 win at Hull KR makes it three wins out of three, Ryan Bailey knocked out and carried off after making winning try.

24 February 2009 - Danny Buderus ruled out for at least six weeks after arthroscopy on his knee.

1 March 2009 - returning Rob Burrow knocked out after 17 minutes of 28-20 defeat by Manly Sea Eagles in Carnegie World Club Challenge at Elland Road.

13 March 2009 - Brent Webb plays first game of season in 34-10 home win over Wigan.

24 March 2009 - Matt Diskin found not guilty of making chicken wing tackle in previous Friday's 26-18 round six defeat at St Helens.

26 March 2009 - Lee Smith ruled out for four weeks after surgery on his knee following a reaction to an insect bite.

5 April 2009 - 22-18 Challenge Cup fourth round home defeat by St Helens.

8 April 2009 - Luke Burgess wins appeal against severity of one-match ban for reckless high tackle.

KEY DATES - LEEDS RHINOS

10 April 2009 - shock 10-6 derby defeat by Bradford at Odsal.

13 April 2009 - 30-20 home Easter Monday defeat to Salford drops Rhinos into third spot.

17 April 2009 - Scott Donald agrees 12-month contract extension to end of 2010.

18 April 2009 - 34-6 win at play-off challengers Huddersfield.

24 April 2009 - late Rob Burrow try avoids whitewash in shock home 21-4 home defeat by Harlequins.

15 May 2009 - last-second Kevin Sinfield penalty earns 24-22 win in rain-soaked Castleford.

26 May 2009 - comfortable 46-16 victory over Hull FC at Headingley.

6 June 2009 - Ian Kirke sustains broken leg in last-minute 32-30 defeat to Catalans in France.

14 June 2009 - Kallum Watkins brace in 20-12 victory over Huddersfield.

16 June 2009 - Michael Coady signs on three-and-a-half year deal from Doncaster.

19 June 2009 - Lee Smith to leave at end of season to play rugby union with Wasps.

20 June 2009 - Leeds overcome slow start to run in eight tries in 48-14 win at Harlequins.

4 July 2009 - Keith Senior scores 230th career try in his 500th senior appearance in 43–30 away win over Hull FC.

8 July 2009 - Carl Ablett signs contract extension to end of 2010 season.

9 July 2009 - prop Kyle Amor signs three-and-a-half-year deal but stays at Whitehaven on loan for rest of season.

14 July 2009 - Wakefield Wildcats' teenage forward Jay Pitts joins on three-and-half-year contract.

24 July 2009 - Danny Buderus out for season after breaking fibula in 28-10 defeat at Wigan.

3 August 2009 - Gold Coast centre Brett Delaney signs three-year contract from 2010.

13 August 2009 - Greg Eastwood wins appeal against visa refusal and will take up three year contract from 2010.

4 September 2009 - 18-10 round 26 home win over St Helens puts Leeds two points clear at the top with one game left of the regular season.

8 September 2009 - Jamie Jones-Buchanan gets one match ban for illegal tackle on James Graham; Keith Senior one match for punching.

11 September 2009 - Leeds presented League Leaders Shield following 30-24 victory at Salford.

18 September 2009 - 44-8 home win over Hull KR gives Leeds clubcall for the Qualifying Semi-final.

22 September 2009 - Michael Ratu leaves for Hull KR.

27 September 2009 - Leeds and Great Britain legend John Holmes loses battle with cancer at the age of 57.

27 September 2009 - Leeds choose Catalans Dragons as opponents in Qualifying semi-final.

1 October 2009 - Ashley Gibson leaves for Salford.

2 October 2009 - Ryan Hall and Danny McGuire each score twice in 27-20 triumph over Catalans.

10 October 2009 - 18-10 win over St Helens secures unprecedented hat-trick of Super League titles.

14 October 2009 - Danny Allan released from remaining two years of contract.

19 October 2009 - Ben Jones-Bishop signs one-year loan deal with Harlequins.

19 October 2009 - Simon Worrall signs new contract for 2010 season which he will spend in France with Championship club Toulouse. Dane Manning goes on season-long deal to Featherstone.

19 October 2009 - Kyle Amor and Michael Coady to be dual registered with Whitehaven and Featherstone respectively.

LEEDS RHINOS

DATE	FIXTURE	RESULT	SCORERS	LGE	ATT
6/2/09	Celtic Crusaders (h)	W28-6	t:Smith(2),Donald,Hall,Ablett g:Sinfield(4)	N/A	14,827
13/2/09	Wakefield (h)	W18-4	t:Lauitiiti,Jones-Buchanan,Kirke g:Smith(2),Gibson	1st	15,643
20/2/09	Hull KR (a)	W10-19	t:Ablett,Hall,Watkins g:Sinfield(3) fg:Sinfield	1st	8,623
1/3/09	Manly (WCC) ●	L20-28	t:Jones-Buchanan,Senior,Hall,McGuire g:Sinfield(2)	N/A	32,569
8/3/09	Warrington (a)	W14-20	t:Ablett,Sinfield,McGuire g:Sinfield(4)	1st	9,863
13/3/09	Wigan (h)	W34-10	t:Leuluai,Donald,Burrow,Hall(2),Peacock g:Sinfield(5)	1st	17,677
20/3/09	St Helens (a)	L26-18	t:Senior(2),Hall g:Sinfield(3)	1st	13,966
27/3/09	Catalans (h)	W42-14	t:Hall(2),Jones-Buchanan,McGuire,Webb,Gibson,Ablett,Diskin g:Sinfield(5)	1st	13,425
5/4/09	St Helens (h) (CCR4)	L18-22	t:Jones-Buchanan,Webb,Senior g:Sinfield(3)	N/A	17,689
10/4/09	Bradford (a)	L10-6	t:Jones-Buchanan g:Sinfield	2nd	14,554
13/4/09	Salford (h)	L20-30	t:Jones-Buchanan,Hall,Senior,Peacock g:Sinfield(2)	3rd	14,381
18/4/09	Huddersfield (a)	W6-34	t:Webb(2),Hall,McGuire,Diskin g:Sinfield(7)	2nd	11,593
24/4/09	Harlequins (h)	L4-21	t:Burrow	3rd	13,912
3/5/09	Catalans (MM) ●●	W16-36	t:Hall(2),Burrow,Peacock,Webb,Donald g:Sinfield(6)	3rd	N/A
15/5/09	Castleford (a)	W22-24	t:Burrow,McGuire(2),Hall g:Sinfield(4)	3rd	8,082
26/5/09	Hull (h)	W46-16	t:Smith(2),Senior(2),Webb,Ablett,Hall,Sinfield g:Sinfield(7)	3rd	15,929
6/6/09	Catalans (a)	L32-30	t:McGuire(2),Hall,Lauitiiti,Webb g:Sinfield(5)	3rd	7,913
14/6/09	Huddersfield (h)	W20-12	t:Watkins(2),Leuluai g:Sinfield(4)	2nd	14,934
20/6/09	Harlequins (a)	W14-48	t:Sinfield,McGuire,Jones-Buchanan,Donald,Webb,Buderus,Smith,Hall g:Sinfield(8)	2nd	4,378
26/6/09	Bradford (h)	W33-20	t:Hall(2),Jones-Buchanan,Burrow,Donald g:Sinfield(6) fg:Smith	2nd	17,824
4/7/09	Hull (a)	W30-43	t:Hall(2),Senior,Donald,Sinfield,Gibson,Smith g:Sinfield(7) fg:Burrow	2nd	11,780
10/7/09	Wakefield (a)	W30-32	t:Jones-Buchanan,Senior,Burrow(2),Lauitiiti,Donald g:Sinfield(3),Smith	2nd	6,425
17/7/09	Hull KR (h)	W24-14	t:Webb,Peacock,Buderus,Smith g:Smith(4)	2nd	16,192
24/7/09	Wigan (a)	L28-10	t:McGuire,Donald g:Sinfield	2nd	20,295
1/8/09	Warrington (h)	W24-22	t:Hall,Donald(2),McGuire,Smith g:Sinfield(2)	2nd	13,386
14/8/09	Castleford (h)	W76-12	t:Donald,Hall(5),Webb(2),Smith,Leuluai,Burrow,Peacock,Ratu,Lauitiiti g:Sinfield(10)	2nd	16,931
22/8/09	Celtic Crusaders (a) ●●●	W0-68	t:Senior(2),Hall,Donald,Webb(3),Peacock(3),Burrow,Jones-Buchanan,Diskin g:Sinfield(8)	1st	5,597
4/9/09	St Helens (h)	W18-10	t:Ablett,Hall(2) g:Sinfield(3)	1st	19,997
11/9/09	Salford (a)	W24-30	t:Watkins,Pitts,Burgess,Webb,Ablett g:Smith(5)	1st	6,101
18/9/09	Hull KR (h) (QPO)	W44-8	t:Smith(2),Webb,Lauitiiti(2),Peacock,Hall,Senior g:Sinfield(4),Smith(2)	N/A	11,220
2/10/09	Catalans (h) (QSF)	W27-20	t:McGuire(2),Hall(2),Donald g:Sinfield(3) fg:Sinfield	N/A	13,409
10/10/09	St Helens (GF) ●●●●	W18-10	t:Diskin,Smith(2) g:Sinfield(2) fg:Sinfield,Burrow	N/A	63,259

● Played at Elland Road, Leeds
●● Played at Murrayfield, Edinburgh
●●● Played at Rodney Parade, Newport
●●●● Played at Old Trafford, Manchester

		APP		TRIES		GOALS		FG		PTS	
	D.O.B.	ALL	SL	ALL	SL	ALL	SL	ALL	SL	ALL	SL
Carl Ablett	19/12/85	29(2)	27(2)	7	7	0	0	0	0	28	28
Danny Allan	9/4/89	1(4)	1(4)	0	0	0	0	0	0	0	0
Ryan Bailey	11/11/83	5(15)	5(14)	0	0	0	0	0	0	0	0
Danny Buderus	6/2/78	9(8)	9(7)	2	2	0	0	0	0	8	8
Luke Burgess	20/2/87	2(28)	2(26)	1	1	0	0	0	0	4	4
Rob Burrow	26/9/82	27	25	9	9	0	0	2	2	38	38
Matt Diskin	27/1/82	22(6)	20(6)	4	4	0	0	0	0	16	16
Scott Donald	14/2/80	29	27	13	13	0	0	0	0	52	52
Ashley Gibson	25/9/86	6(5)	5(5)	2	2	1	1	0	0	10	10
Ryan Hall	27/11/87	31	29	32	31	0	0	0	0	128	124
Ben Jones-Bishop	24/8/88	1(1)	1(1)	0	0	0	0	0	0	0	0
Jamie Jones-Buchanan	1/8/81	30	28	10	8	0	0	0	0	40	32
Ian Kirke	26/12/80	13(7)	12(6)	1	1	0	0	0	0	4	4
Ali Lauitiiti	13/7/79	7(22)	7(20)	6	6	0	0	0	0	24	24
Kylie Leuluai	29/3/78	29(2)	27(2)	3	3	0	0	0	0	12	12
Dane Manning	15/4/89	(1)	(1)	0	0	0	0	0	0	0	0
Danny McGuire	6/12/82	28(1)	26(1)	13	12	0	0	0	0	52	48
Paul McShane	19/11/89	1(2)	1(2)	0	0	0	0	0	0	0	0
Jamie Peacock	14/12/77	27(4)	25(4)	9	9	0	0	0	0	36	36
Jay Pitts	9/12/89	(1)	(1)	1	1	0	0	0	0	4	4
Mike Ratu	16/10/87	1(4)	1(4)	1	1	0	0	0	0	4	4
Keith Senior	24/4/76	28	26	12	10	0	0	0	0	48	40
Kevin Sinfield	12/9/80	29	27	4	4	122	117	3	3	263	253
Lee Smith	8/8/86	26	25	13	13	14	14	1	1	81	81
Kallum Watkins	12/3/91	9(5)	9(4)	4	4	0	0	0	0	16	16
Brent Webb	8/11/80	24(1)	23(1)	16	15	0	0	0	0	64	60
Simon Worrall	10/10/84	2(8)	2(8)	0	0	0	0	0	0	0	0

Ryan Hall

LEAGUE RECORD
P27-W21-D0-L6
(1st, SL/Grand Final Winners,
Champions)
F805, A453, Diff+352
42 points.

CHALLENGE CUP
Round Four

ATTENDANCES
Best - v St Helens (SL - 19,997)
Worst - v Hull KR (QPO - 11,220)
Total (SL, inc play-offs) - 229,687
Average (SL, inc play-offs) - 15,312
(Down by 1,444 on 2008)

23 July 2008 - North Queensland Cowboys prop Ray Cashmere signs on three-year deal from 2009.

31 July 2008 - Stefan Ratchford (three years) and Adam Sidlow (two) sign new contracts.

8 August 2008 - South Sydney halfback Jeremy Smith agrees two-year contract from 2009.

14 August 2008 - Gold Coast Titans back row forward Luke Swain joins on two-year deal from 2009.

1 September 2008 - Mark Henry joins from North Queensland Cowboys on two-year-deal.

1 September 2008 - Paul Highton, Matt Gardner, Chris Borgese, Andrew Brocklehurst, Daley Williams, Leon Walker, Luke Ambler and Andy Ballard all released.

1 October 2008 - Rob Parker signs from Warrington and Dean McGilvray from St Helens on one-year contracts.

7 October 2008 - St Helens centre Willie Talau signs two-year contract.

27 January 2009 - Malcolm Alker stripped of captaincy due to breach of discipline.

14 February 2009 - new captain Rob Parker leads City Reds to 28-16 home round 1 win over Celtic.

22 February 2009 - 29-10 defeat at Wakefield in round 2.

28 February 2009 - 52-16 hammering at Castleford in round 3.

5 March 2009 - three supporters banned from travelling to away fixtures for behaviour after the defeat at Castleford.

12 March 2009 - Malcolm Alker re-instated as captain six weeks after being stripped of the role.

29 March 2009 - Paul White to miss rest of season after aggravating knee injury in 48-12 defeat at Hull KR.

5 April 2009 - dramatic late Richie Myler try secures 22-18 Challenge Cup win at Hull FC.

10 April 2009 - Richie Myler scores two tries in 18-16 round eight home Good Friday win over Warrington.

13 April 2009 - Reds stun Leeds with 30-20 win - their first at Headingley since 1977.

14 April 2009 - Darrell Goulding joins on month's loan from Wigan.

21 April 2009 - Ian Sibbit gets one-match ban for high tackle in 38-6 defeat by Catalans Dragons.

KEY DATES - SALFORD CITY REDS

10 May 2009 - 66-4 Cup win over Batley Bulldogs at Mount Pleasant.

13 May 2009 - Darrell Goulding's initial one-month loan converted to rolling deal.

17 May 2009 - 24-4 win at Huddersfield.

22 May 2009 - 18-10 victory against Bradford at the Willows.

5 June 2009 - Willie Talau picks up season-ending scaphoid injury and Rob Parker suffers facial injury in 34-18 loss at Wigan.

10 June 2009 - Rob Parker injury, sustained in a collision with the elbow of Jordan Turner in Wigan defeat, confirmed as fractured skull.

13 June 2009 - Richie Myler scores 30 points for England against France with three tries and nine goals.

18 June 2009 - contract offer to Richie Myler to make him best-paid player in club's history.

19 June 2009 - Hull hold on in a tense finish to claim narrow 14-12 home win over Reds.

22 June 2009 - Richie Myler turns down contract offer, according to agent Martin Offiah.

26 June 2009 - John Wilshere makes 100th appearance for the club in 34-10 home defeat to Huddersfield.

4 July 2009 - Stefan Ratchford scores two early tries in 20-10 home win over St Helens.

10 July 2009 - Luke Adamson signs new contract to end of 2012 season.

11 July 2009 - 25-12 defeat at Celtic Crusaders.

14 July 2009 - John Wilkinson OBE awarded honorary degree by the University of Salford.

22 July 2009 - Salford one of five Super League clubs sent letter of warning re playing facilities.

24 July 2009 - Rob Parker, out for the season with fractured skull, signs new two-year contract at The Willows.

26 July 2009 - 62-20 hammering at Warrington after leading 20-12 at half-time.

4 August 2009 - Robbie Paul signs for Leigh for 2010.

7 August 2009 - Craig Stapleton sent off after final whistle as Catalans snatch last-gasp 18-16 win at the Willows.

11 August 2009 - Craig Stapleton gets one match for foul and abusive language.

15 August 2009 - Stuart Littler makes 300th appearance for club in late 26-22 win at Harlequins.

4 September 2009 - St Helens scrum-half Matty Smith, on loan at Celtic in 2009, joins on loan for 2010.

7 September 2009 - Richie Myler signs for Warrington; Jordan Turner for Hull FC.

10 September 2009 - Phil Leuluai signs new contract for 2010.

11 September 2009 - 30-24 last-day defeat at home to Leeds.

1 October 2009 - Leeds Rhinos centre Ashley Gibson signs a one-year deal.

27 October 2009 - captain Malcolm Alker becomes assistant coach.

27 October 2009 - Castleford Tigers prop Ryan Boyle joins on two-year deal.

1 November 2009 - John Wilshere leads PNG to Pacific Cup win.

SALFORD CITY REDS

DATE	FIXTURE	RESULT	SCORERS	LGE	ATT
14/2/09	Celtic Crusaders (h)	W28-16	t:Stapleton,Myler,Henry,Sibbit g:Wilshere(6)	3rd	4,026
22/2/09	Wakefield (a)	L29-10	t:Myler,Talau g:Wilshere	9th	6,578
28/2/09	Castleford (a)	L52-16	t:Talau,Fitzpatrick,Henry g:Wilshere(2)	11th	7,052
6/3/09	Harlequins (h)	L18-48	t:Parker,Wilshere,Paul g:Wilshere(3)	11th	3,367
13/3/09	St Helens (a)	L38-12	t:Fitzpatrick,Thornley g:Ratchford(2)	11th	9,723
20/3/09	Wigan (h)	L12-38	t:Myler(2) g:Turner,Ratchford	13th	7,016
29/3/09	Hull KR (a)	L48-12	t:White,Adamson g:Wilshere(2)	13th	8,104
5/4/09	Hull (a) (CCR4)	W18-22	t:Littler,Wilshere,Myler g:Wilshere(5)	N/A	8,945
10/4/09	Warrington (h)	W18-16	t:Myler(2),Adamson g:Wilshere(3)	13th	6,150
13/4/09	Leeds (a)	W20-30	t:Wilshere,Henry,Myler,Paul,Turner g:Wilshere(5)	11th	14,381
18/4/09	Catalans (a)	L38-6	t:Ratchford g:Wilshere	12th	8,327
25/4/09	Hull (h)	L14-18	t:Goulding(2),Myler g:Wilshere	13th	4,165
2/5/09	Harlequins (MM) ●	L24-16	t:Ratchford(2),Myler g:Wilshere(2)	13th	N/A
10/5/09	Batley (a) (CCR5)	W4-66	t:Wilshere,Myler,Henry(4),Ratchford,McGilvray,Alker,Paul,Adamson g:Wilshere(11)	N/A	1,298
17/5/09	Huddersfield (a)	W4-24	t:Wilshere,Goulding,Myler,Henry g:Wilshere(4)	13th	6,903
22/5/09	Bradford (h)	W18-10	t:Littler,Henry,Adamson g:Wilshere(3)	12th	4,383
29/5/09	Wigan (a) (CCQF)	L28-6	t:Adamson g:Wilshere	N/A	9,466
5/6/09	Wigan (h)	L34-18	t:Swain,Henry,Alker g:Wilshere(3)	13th	11,550
19/6/09	Hull (a)	L14-12	t:Smith,Goulding g:Wilshere(2)	13th	11,218
26/6/09	Huddersfield (h)	L10-34	t:Turner,Wilshere g:Wilshere	13th	3,721
3/7/09	St Helens (h)	W20-10	t:Ratchford(2),Goulding,Henry g:Wilshere(2)	13th	4,808
11/7/09	Celtic Crusaders (a)	L25-12	t:Adamson,Littler g:Wilshere(2)	13th	3,009
17/7/09	Castleford (h)	L12-18	t:McGilvray,Ratchford g:Wilshere(2)	13th	3,487
26/7/09	Warrington (a)	L62-20	t:Henry,Littler,Myler,Smith g:Wilshere(2)	13th	8,906
31/7/09	Wakefield (h)	L24-30	t:McGilvray(2),Leuluai(2) g:Wilshere(4)	13th	3,151
7/8/09	Catalans (h)	L16-18	t:Stapleton,Wilshere g:Ratchford(4)	13th	2,475
15/8/09	Harlequins (a)	W22-26	t:Wilshere(2),McGilvray,Nash,Swain g:Wilshere(3)	13th	2,612
21/8/09	Hull KR (h)	L10-14	t:Sidlow,Ratchford g:Wilshere	13th	4,224
6/9/09	Bradford (a)	L44-18	t:Wilshere(2),Henry g:Ratchford(3)	13th	8,167
11/9/09	Leeds (h)	L24-30	t:Adamson,Wilshere,Littler,Ratchford g:Wilshere(4)	13th	6,101

● Played at Murrayfield, Edinburgh

		APP		TRIES		GOALS		FG		PTS	
	D.O.B.	ALL	SL	ALL	SL	ALL	SL	ALL	SL	ALL	SL
Luke Adamson	17/11/87	28	25	7	5	0	0	0	0	28	20
Malcolm Alker	4/11/78	30	27	2	1	0	0	0	0	8	4
Ray Cashmere	12/1/80	29(1)	26(1)	0	0	0	0	0	0	0	0
Karl Fitzpatrick	13/9/80	12	11	2	2	0	0	0	0	8	8
Darrell Goulding	3/3/88	9	9	5	5	0	0	0	0	20	20
Mark Henry	19/4/81	24	22	13	9	0	0	0	0	52	36
Lee Jewitt	14/2/87	2(16)	1(14)	0	0	0	0	0	0	0	0
Phil Leuluai	16/7/77	1(29)	1(26)	2	2	0	0	0	0	8	8
Stuart Littler	19/2/79	26(4)	24(3)	5	4	0	0	0	0	20	16
Dean McGilvray	24/4/88	14	12	5	4	0	0	0	0	20	16
Richard Myler	21/5/90	21	18	13	11	0	0	0	0	52	44
Stephen Nash	14/1/86	(11)	(11)	1	1	0	0	0	0	4	4
Rob Parker	5/9/81	17(1)	15	1	1	0	0	0	0	4	4
Robbie Paul	3/2/76	2(27)	2(24)	3	2	0	0	0	0	12	8
Stefan Ratchford	19/7/88	25	23	9	8	10	10	0	0	56	52
Ian Sibbit	15/10/80	10(12)	9(10)	1	1	0	0	0	0	4	4
Adam Sidlow	25/10/87	6(11)	6(11)	1	1	0	0	0	0	4	4
Jeremy Smith	18/7/81	24(1)	23(1)	2	2	0	0	0	0	8	8
Jack Spencer	21/12/90	(1)	(1)	0	0	0	0	0	0	0	0
Craig Stapleton	13/8/78	26	24	2	2	0	0	0	0	8	8
Luke Swain	24/2/82	30	27	2	2	0	0	0	0	8	8
Willie Talau	25/1/76	7	5	2	2	0	0	0	0	8	8
Andy Thornley	1/3/89	(1)	(1)	1	1	0	0	0	0	4	4
Jordan Turner	9/1/89	18	15	2	2	1	1	0	0	10	10
Jason Walton	13/6/90	(5)	(5)	0	0	0	0	0	0	0	0
Paul White	7/12/82	1	1	1	1	0	0	0	0	4	4
John Wilshere	5/5/78	28	25	12	10	76	59	0	0	200	158

John Wilshere

LEAGUE RECORD
P27-W7-D0-L20
(13th, SL)
F456, A754, Diff-298
14 points.

CHALLENGE CUP
Quarter Finalists

ATTENDANCES
Best - v Wigan (SL - 7,016)
Worst - v Catalans (SL - 2,475)
Total (SL only) - 57,074
Average (SL only) - 4,390
(Up by 622 on 2008, NL1)

KEY DATES -
ST HELENS

5 April 2009 - 22-18 Challenge Cup fourth round win at Leeds.

10 April 2009 - 19-12 win at Wigan.

19 April 2009 - Tony Puletua and Jon Wilkin score hat-tricks in 68-22 win at Castleford as Saints go four points clear at top of table.

23 April 2009 – Leon Pryce gets 100 hours community service.

24 April 2009 - shock 34-30 defeat to Bradford at Knowsley Road.

2 May 2009 - 38-18 defeat by Wigan at Murrayfield

10 May 2009 - 42-8 Challenge Cup win over Catalans Dragons at Knowsley Road.

13 May 2009 - 22-year-old New Zealand international Sia Soliola signs on three-year contract from 2010.

16 May 2009 - Gary Wheeler try three minutes from time earns thrilling 32-28 win at Catalans.

20 May 2009 - 66-6 hammering of Gateshead earns place in Challenge Cup semi-final.

22 May 2009 - tight 22-12 home victory over Harlequins retains place at top of table.

27 May 2009 - Matty Ashurst signs three-year contract.

1 June 2009 - Sean Long to join Hull FC in 2010.

2 June 2009 - Gary Wheeler agrees three-year deal.

5 June 2009 - Paul Wellens hat-trick guides St Helens to 30-6 victory at Hull FC.

9 June 2009 - Andrew Dixon signs new three-year deal.

12 June 2009 - 50-10 hammering of Castleford keeps Saints at top of table.

23 June 2009 - Matt Gidley signs new one-year deal for 2010.

1 July 2009 - Keiron Cunningham undergoes minor knee operation.

3 July 2009 - Sean Long faces eight-week lay-off after breaking his jaw in shock 20-10 defeat at Salford.

11 July 2009 - Maurie Fa'asavalu suffers broken arm in 40-26 win at Warrington.

14 July 2009 - Lee Gilmour turns down one-year deal to join Huddersfield in 2010.

19 July 2009 - James Roby suffers broken hand in 22-20 home defeat by Wakefield; Jonny Lomax ankle damage.

9 August 2009 - 24-14 semi-final defeat by Huddersfield ends hopes of fourth successive Challenge Cup.

13 December 2008 - Saints legend Vince Karalius dies at the age of 76.

21 January 2009 - Keiron Cunningham to remain as captain.

13 February 2009 - Matt Gidley inspires come back from 14-0 to secure 26-14 home round one win over Warrington.

22 February 2009 - James Graham and Jason Cayless missing in 23-6 success at Huddersfield.

27 February 2009 - late Michael Dobson penalty secures 20-19 win for Hull KR at Knowsley Road.

10 March 2009 - Maurie Fa'asavalu handed one-match ban for chicken wing tackle in 4-0 win at Celtic Crusaders.

18 March 2009 - Francis Meli arrives after being stranded in Auckland by red tape over visa renewal.

20 March 2009 - Francis Meli plays first game of season in fiery 26-18 win over Leeds at Knowsley Road.

26 March 2009 - Leon Pryce pleads guilty to assault in Bradford court.

27 March 2009 - Leon Pryce scores hat-trick in 42-18 win at Belle Vue as Wakefield publically mourn death of reserve player Leon Walker.

16 August 2009 - 26-10 defeat at Hull KR.

4 September 2009 - Matty Smith, on loan at Celtic in 2009, joins Salford on loan for 2010.

4 September 2009 - 18-10 defeat at Leeds virtually ends chances of League Leaders title.

11 September 2009 - James Graham misses round 27, 24-12 home defeat by Catalans Dragons with shoulder injury.

15 September 2009 - captain Keiron Cunningham ends speculation by signing another 12-month contract.

19 September 2009 - 15-2 play-off win over Huddersfield Giants

21 September 2009 - Nick Fozzard released from final year of Hull KR contract to return to St Helens.

3 October 2009 - Sean Long stars as Saints reach record seventh Super League Grand Final after 14-10 win over Wigan at Knowsley Road.

10 October 2009 - 18-10 defeat to Leeds in Grand Final.

20 October 2009 - Scott Moore signs contract extension to the end of 2012.

ST HELENS

DATE	FIXTURE	RESULT	SCORERS	LGE	ATT
13/2/09	Warrington (h)	W26-14	t:Gilmour,Gardner,Gidley(2),Graham,Armstrong g:Long	4th	17,009
22/2/09	Huddersfield (a)	W6-23	t:Wellens,Gardner,Gilmour,Puletua,Wheeler g:Long fg:Long	2nd	11,338
27/2/09	Hull KR (h)	L19-20	t:Puletua,Wheeler,Wellens g:Long(3) fg:Long	5th	11,830
7/3/09	Celtic Crusaders (a)	W0-4	t:Armstrong	4th	6,351
13/3/09	Salford (h)	W38-12	t:Wilkin(2),Pryce,Flannery,Gardner,Graham,Cunningham g:Long(5)	3rd	9,723
20/3/09	Leeds (h)	W26-18	t:Gidley(2),Roby,Pryce,Wheeler g:Long(3)	2nd	13,966
27/3/09	Wakefield (a)	W18-42	t:Graham,Wheeler,Gidley,Pryce(3),Puletua,Gardner g:Wheeler(3),Gidley(2)	2nd	6,038
5/4/09	Leeds (a) (CCR4)	W18-22	t:Gardner,Roby,Wellens,Gidley g:Wellens(3)	N/A	17,689
9/4/09	Wigan (a)	W12-19	t:Cunningham,Gidley,Pryce g:Wellens,Eastmond(2) fg:Eastmond	1st	22,232
13/4/09	Hull (h)	W44-22	t:Puletua,Gilmour,Wilkin,Wellens,Pryce,Eastmond(2),Dean,Gardner g:Long(3),Eastmond	1st	13,684
19/4/09	Castleford (a)	W22-68	t:Puletua(4),Pryce(2),Gardner,Wilkin(3),Hargreaves,Fa'asavalu g:Long(10)	1st	8,003
24/4/09	Bradford (h)	L30-34	t:Gardner,Meli(2),Pryce,Wheeler,Long g:Long(3)	1st	11,039
2/5/09	Wigan (MM) ●	L18-38	t:Long,Pryce,Wellens g:Eastmond,Long(2)	1st	N/A
10/5/09	Catalans (h) (CCR5)	W42-8	t:Meli(2),Wheeler(2),Wellens(2),Clough,Pryce g:Long(4),Wheeler	N/A	7,176
16/5/09	Catalans (h)	W28-32	t:Gardner(2),Wellens,Meli,Pryce,Wheeler g:Long(4)	1st	9,065
22/5/09	Harlequins (h)	W22-12	t:Flannery,Wellens,Roby,Cunningham g:Long(3)	1st	9,359
30/5/09	Gateshead (a) (CCQF)	W6-66	t:Gidley(2),Roby,Wellens(2),Flannery(2),Fa'asavalu,Eastmond,Pryce(2),Ashurst g:Eastmond(8),Long	N/A	4,325
5/6/09	Hull (a)	W6-30	t:Lomax,Wellens(3),Gilmour,Fa'asavalu g:Long(3)	1st	12,009
12/6/09	Castleford (h)	W50-10	t:Pryce,Dean,Cunningham,Wilkin,Long,Lomax,Eastmond(2),Clough g:Long(3),Eastmond(4)	1st	9,680
21/6/09	Bradford (a)	W18-44	t:Meli(2),Roby,Wilkin,Flannery,Eastmond,Fa'asavalu,Puletua g:Eastmond(6)	1st	10,599
26/6/09	Celtic Crusaders (h)	W30-0	t:Gilmour,Wellens,Puletua,Gidley,Dean g:Long(5)	1st	8,684
3/7/09	Salford (a)	L20-10	t:Dixon,Meli g:Eastmond	1st	4,808
11/7/09	Warrington (a)	W26-40	t:Gilmour,Graham(2),Gardner,Wellens,Eastmond,Meli g:Eastmond(6)	1st	12,075
17/7/09	Wakefield (h)	L20-22	t:Gardner,Pryce,Dean(2),Meli	1st	8,651
25/7/09	Harlequins (a)	W24-44	t:Armstrong,Puletua(2),Graham,Eastmond,Pryce,Dean,Wilkin g:Eastmond(6)	1st	4,258
31/7/09	Wigan (h)	W10-6	t:Gidley,Eastmond g:Eastmond	1st	15,563
9/8/09	Huddersfield (CCSF) ●●	L24-14	t:Meli(3) g:Eastmond	N/A	10,638
16/8/09	Hull KR (a)	L26-10	t:Graham,Gardner g:Ellis	1st	8,976
21/8/09	Huddersfield (h)	W12-10	t:Gardner,Gidley,Meli	2nd	8,708
4/9/09	Leeds (a)	L18-10	t:Gilmour,Flannery g:Eastmond	2nd	19,997
11/9/09	Catalans (h)	L12-24	t:Puletua,Cunningham g:Lomax,Eastmond	2nd	8,268
19/9/09	Huddersfield (h) (QPO)	W15-2	t:Puletua,Pryce,Meli g:Eastmond fg:Long	N/A	6,157
3/10/09	Wigan (QSF)	W14-10	t:Meli(2),Long g:Eastmond	N/A	13,087
10/10/09	Leeds (GF) ●●●	L18-10	t:Eastmond g:Eastmond(3)	N/A	63,259

● Played at Murrayfield, Edinburgh
●● Played at Halliwell Jones Stadium, Warrington
●●● Played at Old Trafford, Manchester

		APP		TRIES		GOALS		FG		PTS	
	D.O.B.	ALL	SL	ALL	SL	ALL	SL	ALL	SL	ALL	SL
Tom Armstrong	12/9/89	5(1)	5(1)	3	3	0	0	0	0	12	12
Matty Ashurst	1/11/89	5(15)	4(13)	1	0	0	0	0	0	4	0
Jason Cayless	15/1/80	(6)	(5)	0	0	0	0	0	0	0	0
Paul Clough	27/9/87	13(21)	12(18)	2	1	0	0	0	0	8	4
Keiron Cunningham	28/10/76	29(2)	26(1)	5	5	0	0	0	0	20	20
Chris Dean	17/1/88	10	9	6	6	0	0	0	0	24	24
Andrew Dixon	28/2/90	6(4)	6(3)	1	1	0	0	0	0	4	4
Kyle Eastmond	17/7/89	11(6)	10(5)	10	9	44	35	1	1	129	107
James Ellis	4/10/89	1(2)	1(2)	0	0	1	1	0	0	2	2
Jacob Emmitt	4/10/88	1(4)	1(4)	0	0	0	0	0	0	0	0
Maurie Fa'asavalu	12/1/80	(27)	(24)	4	3	0	0	0	0	16	12
Chris Flannery	5/6/80	28	24	6	4	0	0	0	0	24	16
Gareth Frodsham	18/12/89	(3)	(3)	0	0	0	0	0	0	0	0
Ade Gardner	24/6/83	29	26	14	13	0	0	0	0	56	52
Matt Gidley	1/7/77	31	27	12	9	2	2	0	0	52	40
Lee Gilmour	12/3/78	32	29	7	7	0	0	0	0	28	28
James Graham	10/9/85	31	27	7	7	0	0	0	0	28	28
Bryn Hargreaves	14/11/85	19(12)	16(11)	1	1	0	0	0	0	4	4
Jonny Lomax	4/9/90	6(2)	5(2)	2	2	1	1	0	0	10	10
Sean Long	24/9/76	24	22	4	4	54	49	3	3	127	117
Francis Meli	20/8/80	26	23	17	12	0	0	0	0	68	48
Leon Pryce	9/10/81	32	28	19	16	0	0	0	0	76	64
Tony Puletua	25/6/79	28(3)	24(3)	14	14	0	0	0	0	56	56
James Roby	22/11/85	6(24)	5(21)	5	3	0	0	0	0	20	12
Paul Wellens	27/2/80	31	27	16	11	4	1	0	0	72	46
Gary Wheeler	30/9/89	8(4)	6(4)	8	6	4	3	0	0	40	30
Jon Wilkin	11/1/83	30	27	9	9	0	0	0	0	36	36

Sean Long

LEAGUE RECORD
P27-W19-D0-L8
(2nd, SL/Grand Final Runners-Up)
F733, A466, Diff+267
38 points.

CHALLENGE CUP
Semi Finalists

ATTENDANCES
Best - v Warrington (SL - 17,009)
Worst - v Huddersfield (QPO - 6,157)
Total (SL, inc play-offs) - 165,408
Average (SL, inc play-offs) - 11,027
(Up by 287 on 2008)

18 November 2008 - Ryan Atkins dismisses speculation he is to join Hull FC.

9 December 2008 - assistant Paul Broadbent takes charge of pre-season as head coach John Kear undergoes a hip replacement.

30 January 2009 - Bradford utility back Dave Halley joins on a month's loan.

8 February 2009 - 12-6 win at Wigan in first Super League (brought forward from round 17) match, despite missing eight regulars.

11 February 2009 - Wildcats reveal Richard Moore is suffering from Crohn's disease.

12 February 2009 - Jamie Rooney, out with a knee injury, facing two-month lay-off after undergoing a heart scare during operation.

13 February 2009 - 18-4 defeat at Leeds, Tony Martin plays scrum-half after Sam Obst injured in warm-up.

16 February 2009 - Frank Winterstein, Canterbury Bulldogs' Samoan back-rower, agrees contract for the rest of season.

22 February 2009 - 29-10 home win over Salford.

27 February 2009 - Sam Obst and James Stosic injured in 48-22 home romp over Warrington. Dave Halley loan extended for another month.

13 March 2009 - James Stosic ruled out for 12 weeks with damaged posterior cruciate ligament.

17 March 2009 - Dave Halley recalled from loan spell by Bradford.

22 March 2009 - televised Sunday night round-six match at Celtic Crusaders postponed half an hour before kick-off following the death of Leon Walker in reserve match earlier that day.

27 March 2009 - Wildcats thumped 42-18 by St Helens as club publically mourn death of reserve player Leon Walker.

3 April 2009 - 54-0 Challenge Cup demolition of Leigh Centurions at Belle Vue.

10 April 2009 - 35-6 Good Friday win at Castleford.

13 April 2009 - Richard Moore makes comeback in 24-22 Easter Monday win over Bradford at Belle Vue.

17 April 2009 - plans announced for new 12,000-capacity community stadium off junction 30 of M62; 21-14 win at Hull FC.

26 April 2009 - Damien Blanch out for season with ruptured cruciate knee ligament in 40-26 home defeat by Wigan.

KEY DATES - WAKEFIELD T WILDCATS

2 May 2009 - 32-16 defeat to Bradford at Murrayfield

9 May 2009 - 28-17 defeat by Wigan at Belle Vue sees Challenge Cup exit.

19 May 2009 - Danny Brough and Danny Sculthorpe suspended without pay for a week following breach of club discipline on journey home from 24-17 defeat at Harlequins.

24 May 2009 - suspended pair Brough and Sculthorpe missing for 54-6 home hammering by Huddersfield.

27 May 2009 - Danny Sculthorpe signs for Huddersfield on season-long loan, with Michael Korkidas returning to Wakefield.

27 May 2009 - Gary Thornton appointed Reserves Coach.

30 May 2009 - 50-6 thrashing of Celtic at Brewery Field.

7 June 2009 - 36-22 loss at Odsal, despite Sean Gleeson hat-trick.

13 June 2009 - Strong first-half performance ensures 37-22 victory over Hull FC at Belle Vue.

1 July 2009 - Jamie Rooney joins Barrow on loan until the end of the season.

14 July 2009 - Jay Pitts transferred to Leeds.

20 July 2009 - Terry Newton signs from Bradford on a two-year contract from 2010.

22 July 2009 - Wakefield one of five Super League clubs sent letter of warning re playing facilities.

24 July 2009 - Glenn Morrison signs from Bradford Bulls for 2010 season.

31 July 2009 - North Queensland prop Shane Tronc joins on two-year deal from 2010.

9 August 2009 - League Express reveals Ryan Atkins is to leave for Warrington.

18 August 2009 - Danny Brough suspended for one match for using foul and abusive language towards a touch-judge after being dismissed in the 77th minute of the Wildcats' 46-12 home win over Celtic.

28 August 2009 - Academy players Danny Cowling, James Davey, Dale Morton, Russ Spiers, Matt Wildie, Kyle Trout and Matt King all given two-year full-time contracts.

4 September 2009 - Steve Snitch to join Castleford in 2010.

4 September 2009 - Fiji World Cup centre Daryl Millard signs two-year deal from Canterbury Bulldogs.

4 September 2009 - Harlequins sign Oliver Wilkes for 2010.

5 September 2009 - Brad Drew to return to Huddersfield Giants in 2010.

5 September 2009 - Sean Gleeson breaks cheekbone in 34-20 win over Catalans Dragons in Perpignan.

7 September 2009 - Ryan Atkins announced as Warrington signing.

8 September 2009 - loan deal with Huddersfield Giants to retain the services of prop Michael Korkidas for 2010.

10 September 2009 - Matt Blaymire, the club's only ever-present in 2009, signs new two-year contract.

11 September 2009 - Ben Jeffries returns from Bradford on three-year deal from 2010.

12 September 2009 - last round 24-10 home win over Hull KR ensures fifth-placed finish.

16 September 2009 - Sam Obst signs new two-year contract.

19 September 2009 - 25-16 home elimination by Catalans Dragons.

21 September 2009 - Kevin Henderson signs new two-year contract.

25 September 2009 - Luke George signs new two-year contract.

3 October 2009 - Jamie Rooney makes permanent move to Barrow.

6 October 2009 - Damien Blanch signs new two-year contract until end of 2011.

7 October 2009 - Aaron Murphy signs new two-year contract to end of 2011.

8 October 2009 - Scott Grix departure to Huddersfield Giants confirmed.

WAKEFIELD T WILDCATS

DATE	FIXTURE	RESULT	SCORERS	LGE	ATT
8/2/09	Wigan (a)	W6-12	t:Halley(2) g:Martin(2)	N/A	14,377
13/2/09	Leeds (a)	L18-4	g:Martin(2)	7th	15,643
22/2/09	Salford (h)	W29-10	t:Blanch(2),Wilkes,Atkins(2) g:Martin(4) fg:Drew	4th	6,578
27/2/09	Warrington (h)	W48-22	t:Blaymire(3),Ferguson(2),Halley(2),George g:Martin(7),Drew	2nd	5,169
8/3/09	Hull KR (a)	L31-18	t:Henderson,Ferguson,Gleeson g:Martin(3)	5th	9,038
15/3/09	Catalans (h)	W30-10	t:Gleeson,Martin,Blanch,Atkins,Murphy g:Martin(4),Brough	4th	4,807
27/3/09	St Helens (h)	L18-42	t:Snitch,Murphy,Atkins g:Brough(3)	8th	6,038
3/4/09	Leigh (h) (CCR4)	W54-0	t:Brough,Blaymire(2),Murphy(2),Blanch,Obst(2),Sculthorpe,Leo-Latu g:Brough(7)	N/A	2,637
10/4/09	Castleford (a)	W6-35	t:Martin,Atkins(2),Blaymire,Gleeson g:Brough(4),Martin(3) fg:Brough	5th	10,155
13/4/09	Bradford (h)	W24-22	t:Blanch,Brough,Atkins,Snitch g:Brough(4)	4th	6,516
17/4/09	Hull (a)	W14-21	t:Demetriou,Grix,Pitts,Wilkes g:Brough(2) fg:Brough	4th	11,975
26/4/09	Wigan (a)	L26-40	t:Blanch(2),Brough(2) g:Brough(5)	5th	5,501
2/5/09	Bradford (MM) ●	L32-16	t:Demetriou,Snitch,Blaymire g:Brough,Martin	6th	N/A
9/5/09	Wigan (h) (CCR5)	L17-28	t:Demetriou,Leo-Latu,Martin g:Brough(2) fg:Brough	N/A	4,883
17/5/09	Harlequins (a)	L24-17	t:Brough,Moore,Martin g:Brough(2) fg:Brough	6th	3,612
24/5/09	Huddersfield (h)	L6-54	t:Blaymire g:Martin	8th	5,037
30/5/09	Celtic Crusaders (a)	W6-50	t:Atkins,Korkidas,Grix,Brough,Drew(2),Rooney(2),Snitch g:Brough(7)	6th	2,089
7/6/09	Bradford (h)	L36-22	t:Gleeson(3),Snitch,Grix g:Brough	6th	8,387
13/6/09	Hull (h)	W37-22	t:Ferguson,Brough,Martin(2),Petersen,Blaymire g:Brough(5),Martin fg:Brough	6th	4,721
28/6/09	Harlequins (h)	W20-18	t:Wilkes,Martin,Grix g:Brough(4)	6th	5,079
5/7/09	Huddersfield (a)	L30-14	t:Grix,Martin,Petersen g:Brough	6th	7,486
10/7/09	Leeds (a)	L30-32	t:Blaymire,Obst,Grix,Atkins g:Brough(7)	7th	6,425
17/7/09	St Helens (a)	W20-22	t:Atkins,Obst,Grix(2) g:Brough(3)	6th	8,651
26/7/09	Castleford (h)	L12-20	t:Brough(2) g:Brough(2)	7th	8,371
31/7/09	Salford (a)	W24-30	t:Wilkes,Gleeson,Korkidas,Grix,Ferguson g:Brough(5)	6th	3,151
16/8/09	Celtic Crusaders (h)	W46-12	t:George(2),Gleeson,Brough,Stosic,Leo-Latu(2),Demetriou g:Brough(7)	6th	7,893
21/8/09	Warrington (a)	W28-40	t:Ferguson,Obst(2),George(2),Gleeson,Morton g:Drew(6)	6th	8,681
5/9/09	Catalans (a)	W20-34	t:Atkins(2),Drew,George(2) g:Drew(4),Brough(3)	6th	8,755
12/9/09	Hull KR (h)	W24-10	t:Ferguson,Obst,Moore,Murphy g:Brough(3),Obst	5th	6,328
19/9/09	Catalans (h) (EPO)	L16-25	t:George(2),Atkins g:Drew(2)	N/A	4,008

● Played at Murrayfield, Edinburgh

		APP		TRIES		GOALS		FG		PTS	
	D.O.B.	ALL	SL	ALL	SL	ALL	SL	ALL	SL	ALL	SL
Ryan Atkins	7/10/85	25	23	13	13	0	0	0	0	52	52
Kyle Bibb	25/1/88	(17)	(15)	0	0	0	0	0	0	0	0
Ricky Bibey	22/9/81	13(5)	13(5)	0	0	0	0	0	0	0	0
Luke Blake	10/8/89	(2)	(2)	0	0	0	0	0	0	0	0
Damien Blanch	24/5/83	12	11	7	6	0	0	0	0	28	24
Matt Blaymire	10/6/82	30	28	10	8	0	0	0	0	40	32
Danny Brough	15/1/83	21(1)	19(1)	10	9	79	70	5	4	203	180
James Davey	21/8/89	(1)	(1)	0	0	0	0	0	0	0	0
Jason Demetriou	13/1/76	28	26	4	3	0	0	0	0	16	12
Brad Drew	25/8/75	16(6)	16(5)	3	3	13	13	1	1	39	39
Dale Ferguson	13/4/88	20(5)	19(5)	7	7	0	0	0	0	28	28
Luke George	30/10/87	6(1)	6(1)	9	9	0	0	0	0	36	36
Sean Gleeson	29/11/87	24	23	9	9	0	0	0	0	36	36
Scott Grix	1/5/84	24(1)	22(1)	9	9	0	0	0	0	36	36
Dave Halley	12/10/86	5	5	4	4	0	0	0	0	16	16
Kevin Henderson	1/10/81	10(12)	10(11)	1	1	0	0	0	0	4	4
Michael Korkidas	12/1/81	12(2)	12(2)	2	2	0	0	0	0	8	8
Tevita Leo-Latu	3/7/81	6(15)	5(14)	4	2	0	0	0	0	16	8
Tony Martin	7/10/78	19	18	8	7	28	28	0	0	88	84
Richard Moore	2/2/81	3(16)	2(16)	2	2	0	0	0	0	8	8
Dale Morton	31/10/90	2(1)	2(1)	1	1	0	0	0	0	4	4
Aaron Murphy	26/11/88	9	8	5	3	0	0	0	0	20	12
Sam Obst	26/11/80	19(3)	17(3)	7	5	1	1	0	0	30	22
Matt Petersen	27/3/80	9	8	2	2	0	0	0	0	8	8
Jay Pitts	9/12/89	10(5)	8(5)	1	1	0	0	0	0	4	4
Jamie Rooney	17/3/80	4(1)	4(1)	2	2	0	0	0	0	8	8
Danny Sculthorpe	8/9/79	1(8)	1(6)	1	0	0	0	0	0	4	0
Steve Snitch	22/2/83	25(2)	23(2)	5	5	0	0	0	0	20	20
James Stosic	22/9/81	8(10)	8(10)	1	1	0	0	0	0	4	4
Oliver Wilkes	2/5/80	29	27	4	4	0	0	0	0	16	16
Frank Winterstein	17/12/86	(6)	(5)	0	0	0	0	0	0	0	0

Matt Blaymire

LEAGUE RECORD
P27-W16-D0-L11
(5th, SL/Elimination Play-Off)
F685, A609, Diff+76
32 points.

CHALLENGE CUP
Round Five

ATTENDANCES
Best - v Castleford (SL - 8,371)
Worst - v Leigh (CC - 2,637)
Total (SL, inc play-offs) - 82,471
Average (SL, inc play-offs) - 5,891
(Down by 1,109 on 2008)

13 February 2009 - 26-14 defeat in round 1 at St Helens after leading 14-0 on 49 minutes.

21 February 2009 - 18-6 lead over Catalans ends in 40-20 home defeat. Ben Westwood on report for a high tackle on Dane Carlaw.

24 February 2009 - Ben Westwood suspended for five matches.

27 February 2009 - 48-22 defeat at Wakefield in round 3.

5 March 2009 - England head coach Tony Smith appointed head of coaching and rugby on a two-and-a-half-year contract.

8 March 2009 - Wolves just edged out 20-14 by Leeds in Tony Smith's first game in charge.

16 March 2009 - Matt King makes public apology for one-fingered gesture at Wolves fans after previous Saturday's 60-8 thrashing at Harlequins.

22 March 2009 - 24-12 home win over in-form Hull KR gets Wolves off the mark.

26 March 2009 - Stuart Reardon pleads guilty to assault in Bradford court and faces custodial sentence.

29 March 2009 - second successive win, 27-22 at home to Celtic Crusaders.

4 April 2009 - 56-10 home Challenge Cup win over York City Knights.

6 April 2009 - Martin Gleeson joins Wigan for a fee of around £100,000. Richard Mathers moves to Warrington.

9 April 2009 - Stuart Reardon released.

10 April 2009 - 18-16 round eight Good Friday defeat at Salford.

13 April 2009 - 28-6 home defeat to Castleford keeps Wolves next to bottom in table.

17 April 2009 - Chris Hicks gets hat-trick and kicks nine goals in stunning 58-22 win at Bradford.

KEY DATES - WARRINGTON WOLVES

23 April 2009 - Louis Anderson (two years), Chris Hicks and Paul Wood (both one year) sign contract extensions.

26 April 2009 - Chris Hicks scores hat-trick and kicks six goals in 40-18 home win over Huddersfield.

10 May 2009 - Richie Mathers scores two tries on debut in 56-8 win at Featherstone.

16 May 2009 - Simon Grix scores twice in 18-16 win at Hull FC.

19 May 2009 - Steve Pickersgill and Kevin Penny released on loan to Widnes for a month.

22 May 2009 - Michael Monaghan recovers from knock to lead his side to 16-8 victory over Wigan.

30 May 2009 - Lee Briers' field goal in sudden death extra time sends Warrington into Challenge Cup semi-final on back of 25-24 win at Hull KR.

2 June 2009 - former Irish International Brian Carney signs until end of season.

6 June 2009 - two tries each for Lee Briers and Vinnie Anderson ensure 34-18 victory at Castleford.

6 June 2009 - Mick Higham out for three months after tearing bicep against Castleford.

14 June 2009 - Lee Briers suffers hamstring injury early in 21-10 home defeat to Bradford.

20 June 2009 - 24-12 win over Catalans Dragons in Barcelona in first-ever Super League game in Spain.

24 June 2009 - Widnes Vikings extend loans of Kevin Penny and Steve Pickersgill.

2 July 2009 - Lee Briers, Vinnie Anderson and Mike Cooper agree new one-year contracts.

11 July 2009 - 40-26 home defeat by St Helens.

19 July 2009 - Warrington legend Ces Mountford dies at the age of 90.

21 July 2009 - Richie Mathers handed one-game ban for high tackle on Luke Robinson in 28-10 defeat at Huddersfield.

1 August 2009 - Brian Carney breaks arm in 24-22 defeat at Leeds

8 August 2009 - Matt King scores hat-trick in 39-26 defeat of Wigan at Widnes to end 19-year wait for trip to Wembley.

12 August 2009 - Kevin Penny and Steve Pickersgill brought back from loan spells at Widnes.

14 August 2009 - Lee Briers suffers facial injury in 36-16 defeat at Wigan.

18 August 2009 - X-rays clear Lee Briers to play at Wembley.

29 August 2009 - Michael Monaghan wins Lance Todd Trophy as 25-16 Wembley victory over Huddersfield secures first Challenge Cup win for 35 years.

7 September 2009 - transfer signings of Richie Myler and Ryan Atkins, both on four-year contracts, announced. David Solomona joins on free transfer on one-year deal.

13 September 2009 - 44-34 final-day home win over Harlequins means 10th place finish.

14 September 2009 - Steve Pickersgill leaves for Widnes Vikings.

24 September 2009 - coach James Lowes agrees new 12-month contract.

8 October 2009 - Adrian Morley extends contract to end of 2012. Ben Harrison and Chris Bridge sign two-year contract extensions.

15 October 2009 - Andrew Johns to return in January in a two-week coaching capacity.

4 November 2009 - stalwart club halfback Parry Gordon dies at the age of 64.

WARRINGTON WOLVES

DATE	FIXTURE	RESULT	SCORERS	LGE	ATT
13/2/09	St Helens (a)	L26-14	t:Higham,Rauhihi g:Hicks(3)	11th	17,009
21/2/09	Catalans (h)	L20-40	t:King,Carvell,Hicks g:Hicks(4)	13th	7,947
27/2/09	Wakefield (a)	L48-22	t:L Anderson(2),Hicks,Bridge g:Hicks(3)	14th	5,169
8/3/09	Leeds (h)	L14-20	t:Briers,Higham,Hicks g:Hicks	14th	9,863
14/3/09	Harlequins (a)	L60-8	t:V Anderson,Rauhihi	14th	3,206
22/3/09	Hull KR (h)	W24-12	t:Harrison,Monaghan,Johnson(2),King g:Hicks(2)	12th	8,547
29/3/09	Celtic Crusaders (h)	W27-22	t:Grix,Briers,King,Mitchell,Hicks g:Hicks(3) fg:Briers	10th	7,854
4/4/09	York (h) (CCR4)	W56-10	t:Grix,V Anderson(2),Harrison,Westwood,Cooper,Bridge,Briers, L Anderson,Johnson g:Hicks(8)	N/A	4,709
10/4/09	Salford (a)	L18-16	t:Johnson(2),Westwood g:Hicks(2)	12th	6,150
13/4/09	Castleford (h)	L6-28	t:Bridge g:Hicks	13th	8,202
17/4/09	Bradford (a)	W22-58	t:L Anderson,Hicks(3),King,Riley,Johnson,Higham(2),Briers g:Hicks(9)	11th	8,643
26/4/09	Huddersfield (h)	W40-18	t:King,Hicks(3),Monaghan,Riley(2) g:Hicks(6)	11th	8,005
3/5/09	Hull KR (MM) ●	L36-28	t:Hicks(2),Monaghan,V Anderson(2) g:Hicks(4)	11th	N/A
10/5/09	Featherstone (a) (CCR5)	W8-56	t:Grix,Mathers(2),Monaghan,Wood,Hicks(2),Harrison,Riley,Bridge g:Hicks(8)	N/A	3,127
16/5/09	Hull (a)	W16-18	t:Grix(2),Bridge,V Anderson g:Bridge	10th	10,997
22/5/09	Wigan (h)	W16-8	t:King,Riley,Monaghan g:Bridge(2)	10th	10,718
30/5/09	Hull KR (a) (CCQF)	W24-25 (aet)	t:V Anderson,Clarke,King,Bridge g:Bridge(4) fg:Briers	N/A	7,671
6/6/09	Castleford (a)	W18-34	t:Briers(2),L Anderson,King,V Anderson(2),Hicks g:Bridge(3)	10th	5,628
14/6/09	Bradford (h)	L10-21	t:Grix,Hicks g:Bridge	9th	9,606
20/6/09	Catalans (a) ●●	W12-24	t:Bridge,King,Riley,Clarke g:Hicks(4)	7th	18,150
28/6/09	Hull (h)	W24-12	t:Riley,Wood,King,Harrison g:Hicks(4)	7th	9,170
4/7/09	Celtic Crusaders (a)	W6-22	t:Clarke,Harrison,Mathers(2) g:Hicks(3)	7th	3,231
11/7/09	St Helens (h)	L26-40	t:Clarke,Bridge,Johnson,Carvell g:Bridge(5)	8th	12,075
19/7/09	Huddersfield (a)	L28-10	t:Westwood,Carney g:Bridge	9th	7,107
26/7/09	Salford (h)	W62-20	t:Briers(2),Carvell,Johnson,Grix,Westwood,Riley,Morley,Bridge, Carney,Hicks g:Bridge(9)	8th	8,906
1/8/09	Leeds (a)	L24-22	t:Mathers,V Anderson,L Anderson,Cooper g:Bridge(3)	9th	13,386
8/8/09	Wigan (CCSF) ●●●	W39-26	t:King(3),L Anderson,Briers,Cooper,Hicks g:Bridge(5) fg:Briers	N/A	12,975
14/8/09	Wigan (a)	L36-16	t:Bridge,V Anderson,Riley g:Bridge(2)	10th	13,452
21/8/09	Wakefield (a)	L28-40	t:Penny,Johnson,Riley,Monaghan,Carvell g:Bridge(4)	9th	8,681
29/8/09	Huddersfield (CCF) ●●●●	W16-25	t:Mathers,Monaghan,Hicks,V Anderson g:Bridge(4) fg:Briers	N/A	76,560
5/9/09	Hull KR (a)	L40-16	t:Higham,McCarthy,Hicks g:Briers(2)	10th	8,579
13/9/09	Harlequins (h)	W44-34	t:Penny(2),Westwood,Briers,Blythe,Thompson,Higham,McCarthy g:Bridge(6)	10th	10,387

● Played at Murrayfield, Edinburgh; ●● Played at Olympic Stadium, Barcelona; ●●● Played at Stobart Stadium, Widnes; ●●●● Played at Wembley Stadium

	D.O.B.	APP ALL	APP SL	TRIES ALL	TRIES SL	GOALS ALL	GOALS SL	FG ALL	FG SL	PTS ALL	PTS SL
Louis Anderson	27/6/85	28(1)	24	7	5	0	0	0	0	28	20
Vinnie Anderson	14/2/79	18(8)	15(7)	12	8	0	0	0	0	48	32
Matty Blythe	20/11/88	3(8)	3(7)	1	1	0	0	0	0	4	4
Chris Bridge	5/7/84	26(2)	21(2)	10	7	50	37	0	0	140	102
Lee Briers	14/6/78	23(1)	19(1)	10	8	2	2	4	1	48	37
Brian Carney	23/7/76	4	4	2	2	0	0	0	0	8	8
Garreth Carvell	21/4/80	25(1)	20(1)	4	4	0	0	0	0	16	16
Jon Clarke	4/4/79	17(6)	14(5)	4	3	0	0	0	0	16	12
Michael Cooper	15/9/88	1(18)	1(14)	3	1	0	0	0	0	12	4
Martin Gleeson	28/5/80	6	6	0	0	0	0	0	0	0	0
Simon Grix	28/9/85	19(1)	16(1)	7	5	0	0	0	0	28	20
Ben Harrison	24/2/88	25(5)	21(4)	5	3	0	0	0	0	20	12
Chris Hicks	19/3/77	24	20	20	16	65	49	0	0	210	162
Mick Higham	18/9/80	10(11)	9(8)	6	6	0	0	0	0	24	24
Paul Johnson	25/11/78	16(8)	14(6)	9	8	0	0	0	0	36	32
Matt King	22/8/80	26	21	13	9	0	0	0	0	52	36
Richard Mathers	24/10/83	18	14	6	3	0	0	0	0	24	12
Tyrone McCarthy	21/4/88	1(4)	1(3)	2	2	0	0	0	0	8	8
Lee Mitchell	8/9/88	3(12)	2(12)	1	1	0	0	0	0	4	4
Michael Monaghan	13/5/80	28(1)	24(1)	7	5	0	0	0	0	28	20
Adrian Morley	10/5/77	26	23	1	1	0	0	0	0	4	4
Kevin Penny	3/10/87	5	5	3	3	0	0	0	0	12	12
Steve Pickersgill	28/11/85	(4)	(4)	0	0	0	0	0	0	0	0
Paul Rauhihi	3/7/73	6(17)	6(14)	2	2	0	0	0	0	8	8
Chris Riley	22/2/88	27	23	10	9	0	0	0	0	40	36
Alex Thompson	11/2/90	(1)	(1)	1	1	0	0	0	0	4	4
Ben Westwood	25/7/81	26	21	5	4	0	0	0	0	20	16
Paul Wood	10/10/81	5(19)	4(17)	2	1	0	0	0	0	8	4

Adrian Morley

LEAGUE RECORD
P27-W12-D0-L15
(10th, SL)
F649, A705, Diff-56
24 points.

CHALLENGE CUP
Winners

ATTENDANCES
Best - v St Helens (SL - 12,075)
Worst - v York (CC - 4,709)
Total (SL only) - 119,961
Average (SL only) - 9,228
(Down by 268 on 2008)

205

21 January 2009 - former Sydney Roosters utility back Amos Roberts signs four-year contract after George Carmont's Samoan passport is approved.

8 February 2009 - 12-6 home defeat by Wakefield in first Super League (brought forward from round 17) match.

10 February 2009 - Richie Mathers cited for tripping and given two-match ban.

13 February 2009 - 18-10 defeat at Hull FC in round 1.

20 February 2009 - 28-22 loss at home to Castleford makes it three opening defeats on a row for first time since 1985.

24 February 2009 - Michael McIlorum cops one-match ban for dangerous throw on Mitchell Sargent.

28 February 2009 - youngsters Shaun Ainscough and Sam Tomkins star in 24-18 win comeback win at Harlequins.

6 March 2009 - 44-10 home romp over Bradford.

13 March 2009 - 34-10 defeat against Leeds Rhinos at Headingley,

18 March 2009 - Kris Radlinski placed in charge of scholarship scheme.

20 March 2009 - Sam Tomkins stars in 38-12 win at Salford; Eamon O'Carroll breaks bone in foot in reserves game.

27 March 2009 - 22-8 home defeat by Huddersfield leaves Wigan just outside top eight.

5 April 2009 - 32-20 Challenge Cup fourth round win at Barrow.

6 April 2009 - Martin Gleeson signs from Warrington Wolves for fee of around £100,000. Richard Mathers moves to Warrington.

10 April 2009 - 19-12 home defeat by St Helens.

13 April 2009 - Easter Monday 40-24 defeat at Catalans.

KEY DATES - WIGAN WARRIORS

22 April 2009 - Thomas Leuluai signs new three-year contract to end of 2012 season.

26 April 2009 - Shaun Ainscough scores four tries in 40-26 win at Wakefield.

2 May 2009 - 38-18 win over St Helens at Murrayfield

9 May 2009 - 28-17 Challenge Cup win over Wakefield at Belle Vue.

18 May 2009 - Lee Mossop goes to Huddersfield Giants on month's loan.

22 May 2009 - 16-8 defeat at Warrington.

29 May 2009 - Pat Richards scores hat-trick in 28-6 in Challenge Cup quarter-final win over Salford.

5 June 2009 - Pat Richards scores 18 points in 34-18 home victory over Salford.

13 June 2009 - 22-16 defeat at Celtic, the Crusaders' first home win in Super League.

16 June 2009 - Eamon O'Carroll undergoes surgery on ankle.

17 June 2009 - Lee Mossop loan deal at Huddersfield extended on week-by-week basis.

21 June 2009 - future of coach Brian Noble uncertain after Stephen Kearney turns down offer.

23 June 2009 - Wigan and England forward Gareth Hock tests positive for cocaine and provisionally suspended by RFL.

30 June 2009 - Sam Tomkins signs extended contract to end of 2014.

7 July 2009 - Gareth Hock's B Sample tests positive for Benzoylecgonine.

19 July 2009 - Wigan legend Ces Mountford dies at the age of 90.

23 July 2009 - Cameron Phelps and Andy Coley agree new one-year deals.

24 July 2009 - 28-10 home win over Leeds marks fifth successive win.

8 August 2009 - Phil Bailey ruptures Achilles in 39-26 Challenge Cup semi-final defeat by Warrington.

13 August 2009 - Shaun Ainscough out for season with scaphoid wrist damage.

14 August 2009 - 36-16 home win over Warrington.

26 August 2009 - RFL confirm Gareth Hock remains suspended from all competitions for a two-year period from June 23, 2009.

4 September 2009 - 34-22 home win over Hull FC secures play-off berth.

11 September 2009 - Mark Riddell returns to Australia on compassionate leave.

16 September 2009 - Sam Tomkins announced as Albert Goldthorpe Rookie of the Year.

18 September 2009 - Mark Flanagan to join Wests Tigers in 2010.

20 September 2009 - 18-12 Elimination play-off victory over Castleford at DW Stadium.

26 September 2009 - one game away from Grand Final after 30-16 win at Hull KR.

3 October 2009 - coach Brian Noble announces immediate departure after 14-10 play-off semi-final defeat at St Helens.

7 October 2009 - Melbourne Storm assistant Michael Maguire appointed new head coach; Shaun Wane assistant coach.

22 October 2009 - George Carmont signs new one-year contract, with an option for 2011 dependent on him playing a minimum, unspecified number of games.

16 November 2009 - Paul Deacon joins on one-year playing, three-year assistant coach contract.

WIGAN WARRIORS

DATE	FIXTURE	RESULT	SCORERS	LGE	ATT
8/2/09	Wakefield (h)	L6-12	t:J Tomkins g:Richards	N/A	14,377
13/2/09	Hull (a)	L18-10	t:Bailey,Richards g:Richards	12th	14,523
20/2/09	Castleford (h)	L22-28	t:Leuluai,Pryce,Goulding,J Tomkins,Ainscough g:Roberts	12th	12,079
28/2/09	Harlequins (a)	W18-24	t:Ainscough(2),Carmont,Bailey,Roberts g:Richards(2)	9th	3,883
7/3/09	Bradford (h)	W44-10	t:Richards,Hock(2),Carmont,Hansen(2),Palea'aesina g:Richards(8)	8th	12,588
13/3/09	Leeds (a)	L34-10	t:Ainscough,Hock g:Richards	9th	17,677
20/3/09	Salford (a)	W12-38	t:Ainscough(2),Leuluai(2),S Tomkins(2),Richards g:Richards(5)	9th	7,016
27/3/09	Huddersfield (h)	L8-22	t:Bailey,Roberts	9th	11,670
5/4/09	Barrow (a) (CCR4)	W20-32	t:Ainscough(4),Carmont,Pryce,S Tomkins g:Riddell,Roberts	N/A	6,275
9/4/09	St Helens (h)	L12-19	t:Ainscough(2) g:Roberts(2)	9th	22,232
13/4/09	Catalans (a)	L40-24	t:Roberts,Ainscough,Gleeson,S Tomkins,Richards g:Richards(2)	9th	9,490
19/4/09	Celtic Crusaders (h)	W44-10	t:Richards,O'Loughlin(2),Riddell,Roberts,S Tomkins(2),Carmont g:Richards(2),Roberts(2)	9th	12,371
26/4/09	Wakefield (a)	W26-40	t:Phelps(2),Ainscough(4),Gleeson g:Richards(6)	9th	5,501
2/5/09	St Helens (MM) ●	W18-38	t:O'Loughlin,Richards(2),Hock,J Tomkins,Leuluai g:Richards(7)	9th	N/A
9/5/09	Wakefield (a) (CCR5)	W17-28	t:Carmont,McIlorum,Phelps,Fielden,S Tomkins g:Richards(4)	N/A	4,883
15/5/09	Hull KR (h)	L12-20	t:O'Loughlin(2) g:Richards(2)	9th	13,415
22/5/09	Warrington (a)	L16-8	t:Phelps g:Richards(2)	9th	10,718
29/5/09	Salford (h) (CCQF)	W28-6	t:Hock(2),Richards(3) g:Richards(4)	N/A	9,466
5/6/09	Salford (h)	W34-18	t:Carmont,Smith,Richards(2),Riddell,Hansen g:Richards(5)	7th	11,550
13/6/09	Celtic Crusaders (a)	L22-16	t:Hansen,Phelps,Roberts g:Richards(2)	7th	5,253
28/6/09	Hull KR (a)	W28-36	t:Bailey(2),Carmont,Richards(2),Hansen,S Tomkins g:Richards(4)	8th	9,007
3/7/09	Harlequins (h)	W40-12	t:Richards,Riddell,Pryce,Carmont,Roberts,J Tomkins,Leuluai(2) g:Richards(4)	8th	14,977
10/7/09	Catalans (h)	W24-22	t:Carmont,Richards(2),Roberts,Goulding g:Richards(2)	5th	11,543
19/7/09	Bradford (a)	W14-20	t:J Tomkins,Richards,Gleeson,Roberts g:Richards(2)	5th	9,487
24/7/09	Leeds (h)	W28-10	t:Carmont,Hansen,J Tomkins,S Tomkins g:Richards(6)	5th	20,295
31/7/09	St Helens (a)	L10-6	t:S Tomkins g:Richards	5th	15,563
8/8/09	Warrington (CCSF) ●●	L39-26	t:Bailey,S Tomkins,Coley,Leuluai g:Richards(5)	N/A	12,975
14/8/09	Warrington (h)	W36-16	t:Richards,Roberts,Phelps,Leuluai,Gleeson,Carmont(2) g:Richards(4)	5th	13,452
23/8/09	Castleford (a)	W26-29	t:S Tomkins(3),Leuluai(2) g:Richards(4) fg:S Tomkins	5th	6,579
4/9/09	Hull (h)	W34-22	t:Roberts(2),Carmont(2),S Tomkins,Palea'aesina g:Richards(5)	5th	12,491
13/9/09	Huddersfield (a)	L48-16	t:Flanagan,J Tomkins g:Richards(2)	6th	8,988
20/9/09	Castleford (h) (EPO)	W18-12	t:Hansen,Carmont,Roberts g:Richards(3)	N/A	8,689
26/9/09	Hull KR (a) (PSF)	W16-30	t:Carmont,Palea'aesina,Richards,Gleeson(2) g:Richards(5)	N/A	8,162
3/10/09	St Helens (a) (QSF)	L14-10	t:Carmont,Richards g:Richards	N/A	13,087

● Played at Murrayfield, Edinburgh
●● Played at Stobart Stadium, Widnes

		APP		TRIES		GOALS		FG		PTS	
	D.O.B.	ALL	SL	ALL	SL	ALL	SL	ALL	SL	ALL	SL
Shaun Ainscough	27/11/89	12	11	17	13	0	0	0	0	68	52
Phil Bailey	25/5/80	22	18	6	5	0	0	0	0	24	20
George Carmont	30/6/78	30	26	17	15	0	0	0	0	68	60
Andy Coley	7/7/78	28(5)	25(4)	1	0	0	0	0	0	4	0
Stuart Fielden	14/9/79	14(18)	13(17)	1	0	0	0	0	0	4	0
Mark Flanagan	4/12/87	3(8)	3(7)	1	1	0	0	0	0	4	4
Martin Gleeson	28/5/80	22	19	6	6	0	0	0	0	24	24
Darrell Goulding	3/3/88	3(4)	3(3)	2	2	0	0	0	0	8	8
Harrison Hansen	26/10/85	19(10)	17(9)	7	7	0	0	0	0	28	28
Gareth Hock	5/9/83	17	15	6	4	0	0	0	0	24	16
Thomas Leuluai	22/6/85	34	30	10	9	0	0	0	0	40	36
Richard Mathers	24/10/83	1	1	0	0	0	0	0	0	0	0
Michael McIlorum	10/1/88	6(13)	5(12)	1	0	0	0	0	0	4	0
Lee Mossop	17/1/89	(10)	(9)	0	0	0	0	0	0	0	0
Eamon O'Carroll	13/6/87	2(4)	2(4)	0	0	0	0	0	0	0	0
Sean O'Loughlin	24/11/82	29	25	5	5	0	0	0	0	20	20
Iafeta Palea'aesina	10/2/82	4(30)	3(27)	3	3	0	0	0	0	12	12
Cameron Phelps	11/2/85	26	23	6	5	0	0	0	0	24	20
Paul Prescott	1/1/86	20(8)	17(7)	0	0	0	0	0	0	0	0
Karl Pryce	27/7/86	5(2)	4(2)	3	2	0	0	0	0	12	8
Pat Richards	27/2/82	31	28	23	20	102	89	0	0	296	258
Mark Riddell	9/12/80	28(3)	25(3)	3	3	1	0	0	0	14	12
Amos Roberts	2/11/80	33	29	12	12	6	5	0	0	60	58
Tim Smith	13/1/85	12(2)	11(1)	1	1	0	0	0	0	4	4
Joel Tomkins	21/3/87	20(13)	19(10)	7	7	0	0	0	0	28	28
Sam Tomkins	23/3/89	21(6)	18(5)	15	12	0	0	1	1	61	49

Sam Tomkins

LEAGUE RECORD
P27-W15-D0-L12
(6th, SL/Qualifying Semi-Final)
F659, A551, Diff+108
30 points.

CHALLENGE CUP
Semi Finalists

ATTENDANCES
Best - v St Helens (SL - 22,232)
Worst - v Castleford (EPO - 8,689)
Total (SL, inc play-offs) - 191,729
Average (SL, inc play-offs) - 13,695
(Down by 260 on 2008)

SUPER LEAGUE XIV
Round by Round

ROUND 3

Friday 6th February 2009

LEEDS RHINOS 28 CELTIC CRUSADERS 6

RHINOS: 3 Lee Smith; 2 Scott Donald; 23 Kallum Watkins; 4 Keith Senior; 5 Ryan Hall; 13 Kevin Sinfield (C); 6 Danny McGuire; 8 Kylie Leuluai; 14 Matt Diskin; 10 Jamie Peacock; 11 Jamie Jones-Buchanan; 12 Ali Lauitiiti; 18 Carl Ablett. Subs (all used): 19 Luke Burgess; 17 Ian Kirke; 26 Paul McShane (D); 22 Danny Allan.
Tries: Smith (10, 34), Donald (15), Hall (20), Ablett (79);
Goals: Sinfield 4/5.
Sin bin: Peacock (70) - fighting.
CRUSADERS: 1 Tony Duggan; 2 Luke Dyer; 3 Josh Hannay; 4 Mark Dalle Cort; 5 Anthony Blackwood; 14 Matty Smith (D); 7 Jace Van Dijk (C); 8 Ryan O'Hara (D); 23 Neil Budworth; 10 Mark Bryant (D); 11 Adam Peek (D); 12 Darren Mapp; 15 Peter Lupton (D). Subs (all used): 16 Ben Flower; 17 Jordan James; 6 Damien Quinn; 21 Chris Beasley.
Try: Dyer (55); **Goals:** Hannay 1/1.
Sin bin: Peek (70) - fighting.
Rugby Leaguer & League Express Men of the Match:
Rhinos: Kylie Leuluai; *Crusaders:* Darren Mapp.
Penalty count: 7-5; **Half-time:** 22-0;
Referee: Ben Thaler; **Attendance:** 14,827.

ROUND 17

Sunday 8th February 2009

WIGAN WARRIORS 6 WAKEFIELD TRINITY WILDCATS 12

WARRIORS: 1 Richard Mathers; 2 Amos Roberts (D); 21 Cameron Phelps; 4 George Carmont; 5 Pat Richards; 6 Tim Smith; 7 Thomas Leuluai; 8 Stuart Fielden; 9 Mark Riddell (D); 10 Iafeta Palea'aesina; 11 Gareth Hock; 12 Phil Bailey; 13 Sean O'Loughlin (C). Subs (all used): 14 Joel Tomkins; 15 Andy Coley; 16 Harrison Hansen; 23 Eamon O'Carroll.
Try: J Tomkins (46); **Goals:** Richards 1/1.
Sin bin: Mathers (66) - alleged trip on Halley.
On report: Mathers (66) - alleged trip on Halley.
WILDCATS: 1 Matt Blaymire; 2 Damien Blanch; 19 Sean Gleeson; 3 Tony Martin; 22 Dave Halley (D); 13 Scott Grix; 14 Sam Obst; 12 Oliver Wilkes; 9 Brad Drew; 15 James Stosic (D); 11 Steve Snitch (D2); 24 Dale Ferguson; 8 Jason Demetriou (C). Subs (all used): 16 Ricky Bibey; 17 Kevin Henderson; 28 Kyle Bibb; 29 Jay Pitts.
Tries: Halley (1, 13); **Goals:** Martin 2/4.
Rugby Leaguer & League Express Men of the Match:
Warriors: Thomas Leuluai; *Wildcats:* Brad Drew.
Penalty count: 7-11; **Half-time:** 0-10;
Referee: Ian Smith; **Attendance:** 14,377.

ROUND 1

Friday 13th February 2009

HULL FC 18 WIGAN WARRIORS 10

HULL: 3 Todd Byrne; 2 Mark Calderwood (D); 17 Graeme Horne; 4 Kirk Yeaman; 21 Tom Briscoe; 6 Richard Horne; 7 Chris Thorman (D); 8 Ewan Dowes; 9 Shaun Berrigan; 10 Peter Cusack; 22 Mike Burnett; 12 Danny Tickle; 11 Lee Radford (C). Subs (all used): 15 Danny Washbrook; 18 Jamie Thackray; 16 Willie Manu; 19 Paul King.
Tries: R Horne (18), Radford (55), Cusack (69);
Goals: Tickle 3/4.
WARRIORS: 2 Amos Roberts; 21 Cameron Phelps; 3 Darrell Goulding; 4 George Carmont; 5 Pat Richards; 6 Tim Smith; 7 Thomas Leuluai; 8 Stuart Fielden; 9 Mark Riddell; 23 Eamon O'Carroll; 11 Gareth Hock; 12 Phil Bailey; 13 Sean O'Loughlin (C). Subs (all used): 14 Joel Tomkins; 10 Iafeta Palea'aesina; 16 Harrison Hansen; 17 Michael McIlorum.
Tries: Bailey (10), Richards (41); **Goals:** Richards 1/2.
Rugby Leaguer & League Express Men of the Match:
Hull: Richard Horne; *Warriors:* Iafeta Palea'aesina.
Penalty count: 6-6; **Half-time:** 6-6;
Referee: Phil Bentham; **Attendance:** 14,523.

LEEDS RHINOS 18 WAKEFIELD TRINITY WILDCATS 4

RHINOS: 3 Lee Smith; 2 Scott Donald; 18 Carl Ablett; 23 Kallum Watkins; 5 Ryan Hall; 22 Danny Allan; 6 Danny McGuire; 8 Kylie Leuluai; 14 Matt Diskin; 10 Jamie Peacock (C); 12 Ali Lauitiiti; 17 Ian Kirke; 11 Jamie Jones-Buchanan. Subs (all used): 19 Luke Burgess; 9 Danny Buderus (D); 16 Ryan Bailey; 20 Ashley Gibson.
Tries: Lauitiiti (2), Jones-Buchanan (23), Kirke (73);
Goals: Smith 2/2, Gibson 1/1.
On report: Bailey (43) - alleged leading with the elbow.
WILDCATS: 1 Matt Blaymire; 2 Damien Blanch; 19 Sean Gleeson; 4 Ryan Atkins; 22 Dave Halley; 13 Scott Grix; 3 Tony Martin; 12 Oliver Wilkes; 9 Brad Drew; 15 James Stosic; 17 Kevin Henderson; 24 Dale Ferguson; 8 Jason Demetriou (C). Subs (all used): 16 Ricky Bibey; 29 Jay Pitts; 28 Kyle Bibb; 31 Luke Blake (D).
Goals: Martin 2/2.
Sin bin: Atkins (39) - late challenge.
Rugby Leaguer & League Express Men of the Match:
Rhinos: Lee Smith; *Wildcats:* Scott Grix.
Penalty count: 11-11; **Half time:** 12-2;
Referee: Steve Ganson; **Attendance:** 15,643.

ST HELENS 26 WARRINGTON WOLVES 14

SAINTS: 1 Paul Wellens; 2 Ade Gardner; 3 Matt Gidley; 11 Lee Gilmour; 29 Tom Armstrong (D); 6 Leon Pryce; 7 Sean Long; 10 James Graham; 9 Keiron Cunningham (C); 15 Bryn Hargreaves; 12 Jon Wilkin; 13 Chris Flannery; 16 Tony Puletua (D). Subs (all used): 8 Jason Cayless; 14 James Roby; 17 Paul Clough; 23 Maurie Fa'asavalu.
Tries: Gilmour (49), Gardner (54), Gidley (64, 69), Graham (74), Armstrong (80); **Goals:** Long 1/6.
WOLVES: 19 Chris Riley; 23 Chris Hicks; 2 Paul Johnson; 4 Matt King; 5 Kevin Penny; 6 Lee Briers; 7 Michael Monaghan; 8 Adrian Morley (C); 14 Mick Higham (D); 16 Garreth Carvell (D); 11 Louis Anderson; 12 Ben Westwood; 21 Matty Blythe. Subs (all used): 10 Paul Rauhihi; 15 Paul Wood; 24 Ben Harrison; 25 Chris Bridge.
Tries: Higham (35), Rauhihi (46); **Goals:** Hicks 3/3.
Rugby Leaguer & League Express Men of the Match:
Saints: Matt Gidley; *Wolves:* Mick Higham.
Penalty count: 10-6; **Half-time:** 0-8;
Referee: Ian Smith; **Attendance:** 17,009.

Saturday 14th February 2009

CATALANS DRAGONS 8 HUDDERSFIELD GIANTS 30

DRAGONS: 1 Clint Greenshields; 2 Cyril Stacul; 3 Steven Bell (D); 4 Adam Mogg; 5 Dimitri Pelo; 6 Thomas Bosc; 7 Shane Perry (D); 10 Jerome Guisset; 9 Casey McGuire (C); 23 Jason Ryles (D); 14 Dane Carlaw; 22 Jamal Fakir; 13 Gregory Mounis. Subs (all used): 8 David Ferriol; 12 Jason Croker; 16 Olivier Elima; 24 Remi Casty.
Try: Pelo (54); **Goals:** Bosc 2/2.
GIANTS: 1 Brett Hodgson (C) (D); 2 Martin Aspinwall; 19 Michael Lawrence; 4 Paul Whatuira; 5 David Hodgson; 3 Kevin Brown; 7 Luke Robinson; 16 Keith Mason; 20 Scott Moore (D); 10 Darrell Griffin; 13 Stephen Wild; 12 Andy Raleigh; 14 Simon Finnigan (D). Subs (all used): 8 Eorl Crabtree; 15 Paul Jackson; 18 Danny Kirmond; 24 Shaun Lunt (D).
Tries: Finnigan (19, 69), D Hodgson (33), Lunt (43), Raleigh (75); **Goals:** B Hodgson 5/6.
Rugby Leaguer & League Express Men of the Match:
Dragons: Jerome Guisset; *Giants:* Kevin Brown.
Penalty count: 9-11; **Half-time:** 2-12;
Referee: Gareth Hewer; **Attendance:** 7,533.

SALFORD CITY REDS 28 CELTIC CRUSADERS 16

CITY REDS: 1 Karl Fitzpatrick; 2 John Wilshere; 15 Stuart Littler; 4 Willie Talau (D); 3 Mark Henry (D); 6 Jeremy Smith (D); 7 Richard Myler; 8 Ray Cashmere (D); 9 Malcolm Alker; 10 Craig Stapleton; 20 Luke Adamson; 12 Rob Parker (C) (D); 13 Luke Swain (D). Subs (all used): 11 Ian Sibbit; 16 Phil Leuluai; 17 Robbie Paul; 22 Stephen Nash.
Tries: Stapleton (4), Myler (7), Henry (11), Sibbit (60);
Goals: Wilshere 6/7.
CRUSADERS: 1 Tony Duggan; 2 Luke Dyer; 3 Josh Hannay; 4 Mark Dalle Cort; 5 Anthony Blackwood; 6 Damien Quinn; 7 Jace Van Dijk (C); 8 Ryan O'Hara; 14 Matty Smith; 10 Mark Bryant; 11 Adam Peek; 12 Darren Mapp; 15 Peter Lupton. Subs (all used): 19 Jason Chan (D); 20 David Tangata-Toa; 21 Chris Beasley; 23 Neil Budworth.
Tries: Lupton (25), Duggan (49, 53); **Goals:** Hannay 2/3.
Rugby Leaguer & League Express Men of the Match:
City Reds: Malcolm Alker; *Crusaders:* Tony Duggan.
Penalty count: 9-7; **Half-time:** 20-4;
Referee: Thierry Alibert; **Attendance:** 4,026.

Sunday 15th February 2009

BRADFORD BULLS 13 HULL KINGSTON ROVERS 13

BULLS: 1 Michael Platt; 2 Rikki Sheriffe (D); 3 Paul Sykes; 4 Chris Nero; 5 Semi Tadulala; 6 Ben Jeffries; 7 Paul Deacon (C); 8 Sam Burgess; 9 Terry Newton; 17 Nick Scruton (D); 11 Steve Menzies (D); 12 Glenn Morrison; 13 Jamie Langley. Subs (all used): 15 Matt Cook; 14 Wayne Godwin; 26 David Solomona; 19 Craig Kopczak.
Tries: Tadulala (27), Nero (40); **Goals:** Deacon 2/3;
Field goal: Deacon (78).
ROVERS: 1 Shaun Briscoe; 2 Peter Fox; 3 Chev Walker; 19 Kris Welham; 5 Liam Colbon (D); 6 Paul Cooke; 7 Michael Dobson; 8 Nick Fozzard (D); 9 Ben Fisher; 20 Michael Vella (C); 11 Clint Newton; 12 Ben Galea; 13 Scott Murrell. Subs (all used): 14 Stanley Gene; 28 Ben Cockayne; 10 David Mills; 17 Makali Aizue.
Tries: Fox (2, 31); **Goals:** Dobson 2/3;
Field goal: Dobson (80).
Rugby Leaguer & League Express Men of the Match:
Bulls: Glenn Morrison; *Rovers:* Michael Dobson.
Penalty count: 10-4; **Half-time:** 10-12;
Referee: Ben Thaler; **Attendance:** 12,141.

CASTLEFORD TIGERS 8 HARLEQUINS 12

TIGERS: 23 Ryan McGoldrick; 2 Kirk Dixon; 4 James Evans (D); 3 Michael Shenton; 1 Richard Owen; 21 Sione Faumuina (D); 6 Rangi Chase (D); 8 Mitchell Sargent; 9 Ryan Hudson (C) (D2); 15 Liam Higgins; 11 Brett Ferres (D); 14 Stuart Jones (D); 13 Joe Westerman. Subs (all used): 10 Craig Huby; 16 Chris Feather (D); 19 Kirk Netherton (D); 25 Dean Widders (D).
Tries: Evans (21), Owen (75); **Goals:** Dixon 0/2.
HARLEQUINS: 2 Jon Wells; 1 Chris Melling; 3 Matt Gafa; 4 David Howell; 5 Will Sharp; 6 Luke Dorn (D2); 7 Danny Orr; 8 Karl Temata; 9 Chad Randall; 17 Danny Ward; 11 Luke Williamson (D); 12 Chad Robinson (D); 13 Rob Purdham (C). Subs (all used): 10 Louie McCarthy-Scarsbrook; 16 Gareth Haggerty; 15 Ben Kaye (D); 14 Tony Clubb.
Tries: Dorn (40, 41); **Goals:** Purdham 2/2.
Rugby Leaguer & League Express Men of the Match:
Tigers: Ryan McGoldrick; *Harlequins:* Luke Dorn.
Penalty count: 11-6; **Half-time:** 4-6;
Referee: Jamie Leahy; **Attendance:** 7,049.

ROUND 2

Friday 20th February 2009

HULL KINGSTON ROVERS 10 LEEDS RHINOS 19

ROVERS: 1 Shaun Briscoe (C); 2 Peter Fox; 19 Kris Welham; 4 Jake Webster; 5 Liam Colbon; 6 Paul Cooke; 7 Michael Dobson; 8 Nick Fozzard; 15 Daniel Fitzhenry; 17 Makali Aizue; 11 Clint Newton; 12 Ben Galea; 13 Scott Murrell. Subs (all used): 24 Rhys Lovegrove; 16 Jason Netherton; 9 Ben Fisher; 28 Ben Cockayne.
Try: Briscoe (9); **Goals:** Dobson 3/3.
Sin bin: Fox (68) - professional foul.
RHINOS: 3 Lee Smith; 2 Scott Donald; 18 Carl Ablett; 4 Keith Senior; 5 Ryan Hall; 13 Kevin Sinfield (C); 6 Danny McGuire; 8 Kylie Leuluai; 14 Matt Diskin; 16 Ryan Bailey; 17 Ian Kirke; 10 Jamie Peacock; 11 Jamie Jones-Buchanan. Subs (all used): 26 Paul McShane; 19 Luke Burgess; 22 Danny Allan; 23 Kallum Watkins.
Tries: Ablett (4), Hall (47), Watkins (71);
Goals: Sinfield 3/4; **Field goal:** Sinfield (78).
Sin bin: McShane (65) - persistent offside.
Rugby Leaguer & League Express Men of the Match:
Rovers: Michael Dobson; *Rhinos:* Danny McGuire.
Penalty count: 12-5; **Half-time:** 10-4;
Referee: Phil Bentham; **Attendance:** 8,623.

WIGAN WARRIORS 22 CASTLEFORD TIGERS 28

WARRIORS: 2 Amos Roberts; 20 Karl Pryce (D); 3 Darrell Goulding; 4 George Carmont; 28 Shaun Ainscough (D); 6 Tim Smith; 7 Thomas Leuluai; 8 Stuart Fielden; 9 Mark Riddell; 23 Eamon O'Carroll; 11 Gareth Hock; 14 Joel Tomkins; 13 Sean O'Loughlin (C). Subs (all used): 10 Iafeta Palea'aesina; 15 Andy Coley; 16 Harrison Hansen; 17 Michael McIlorum.
Tries: Leuluai (26), Pryce (44), Goulding (58), J Tomkins (63), Ainscough (66); **Goals:** Roberts 1/4, Riddell 0/1.
On report:
McIlorum (29) - alleged dangerous tackle on Sargent.
TIGERS: 23 Ryan McGoldrick; 2 Kirk Dixon; 4 James Evans; 3 Michael Shenton; 1 Richard Owen; 21 Sione Faumuina; 7 Brent Sherwin; 15 Liam Higgins; 9 Ryan Hudson (C); 10 Craig Huby; 11 Brett Ferres; 14 Stuart Jones; 13 Joe Westerman. Subs (all used): 6 Rangi Chase; 8 Mitchell Sargent; 16 Chris Feather; 19 Kirk Netherton.
Tries: Westerman (35), Ferres (37, 51), Dixon (48), Shenton (80); **Goals:** Dixon 4/7.
On report: Hudson (10) - alleged contact with referee.
Rugby Leaguer & League Express Men of the Match:
Warriors: Shaun Ainscough; *Tigers:* Brent Sherwin.
Penalty count: 4-7; **Half-time:** 6-16;
Referee: Steve Ganson; **Attendance:** 12,079.

Saturday 21st February 2009

CELTIC CRUSADERS 20 HULL FC 28

CRUSADERS: 1 Tony Duggan; 2 Luke Dyer; 3 Josh Hannay; 4 Mark Dalle Cort; 5 Anthony Blackwood; 6 Damien Quinn; 7 Jace Van Dijk (C); 8 Ryan O'Hara; 23 Neil Budworth; 10 Mark Bryant; 11 Adam Peek; 13 Marshall Chalk (D); 21 Chris Beasley. Subs (all used): 14 Matty Smith; 15 Peter Lupton; 16 Ben Flower; 17 Jordan James.
Tries: Quinn (9), Chalk (15, 48), Duggan (79);
Goals: Hannay 2/4.
HULL: 3 Todd Byrne; 2 Mark Calderwood; 17 Graeme Horne; 4 Kirk Yeaman; 21 Tom Briscoe; 6 Richard Horne; 7 Chris Thorman; 8 Ewan Dowes; 9 Shaun Berrigan; 10 Peter Cusack; 22 Mike Burnett; 12 Danny Tickle; 11 Lee Radford (C). Subs (all used): 15 Danny Washbrook; 18 Jamie Thackray; 16 Willie Manu; 20 Danny Houghton.
Tries: Berrigan (10), Tickle (35, 39, 42), Calderwood (75); **Goals:** Tickle 4/5.
Sin bin: Calderwood (44) - holding down.
Rugby Leaguer & League Express Men of the Match:
Crusaders: Marshall Chalk; *Hull:* Danny Tickle.
Penalty count: 10-4; **Half-time:** 10-18;
Referee: Jamie Leahy; **Attendance:** 5,272.

WARRINGTON WOLVES 20 CATALANS DRAGONS 40

WOLVES: 19 Chris Riley; 23 Chris Hicks; 3 Martin Gleeson; 25 Chris Bridge; 4 Matt King; 6 Lee Briers; 7 Michael Monaghan; 8 Adrian Morley (C); 14 Mick Higham; 16 Garreth Carvell; 11 Louis Anderson; 12 Ben Westwood; 13 Vinnie Anderson. Subs (all used): 24 Ben Harrison; 15 Paul Wood; 21 Matty Blythe; 10 Paul Rauhihi.
Tries: King (13), Carvell (20), Hicks (26);
Goals: Hicks 4/5.
On report: Westwood (9) - alleged high tackle on Carlaw.
DRAGONS: 1 Clint Greenshields; 2 Cyril Stacul; 3 Steven Bell; 4 Adam Mogg; 5 Dimitri Pelo; 6 Thomas Bosc (C); 7 Shane Perry; 14 Dane Carlaw; 15 Jean-Phillipe Baile; 10 Jerome Guisset; 22 Jamal Fakir; 12 Jason Croker; 13 Gregory Mounis. Subs (all used): 16 Olivier Elima; 8 David Ferriol; 24 Remi Casty; 17 Cyrille Gossard.
Tries: Mounis (10), Elima (40), Greenshields (44, 61), Stacul (66), Baile (69), Pelo (72); **Goals:** Bosc 6/8.
Sin bin: Ferriol (57) - interference.
Rugby Leaguer & League Express Men of the Match:
Wolves: Adrian Morley; *Dragons:* Thomas Bosc.
Penalty count: 15-11; **Half-time:** 18-12;
Referee: Jason Robinson; **Attendance:** 7,947.

Warrington's Lee Briers collared by Wakefield's Kyle Bibb

Sunday 22nd February 2009

HUDDERSFIELD GIANTS 6 ST HELENS 23

GIANTS: 1 Brett Hodgson (C); 2 Martin Aspinwall; 19 Michael Lawrence; 4 Paul Whatuira; 5 David Hodgson; 3 Kevin Brown; 7 Luke Robinson; 16 Keith Mason; 20 Scott Moore; 10 Darrell Griffin; 13 Stephen Wild; 12 Andy Raleigh; 14 Simon Finnigan. Subs (all used): 15 Paul Jackson; 17 Michael Korkidas (D); 24 Shaun Lunt; 11 Jamahl Lolesi.
Try: Whatuira (45); **Goals:** B Hodgson 1/2.
SAINTS: 1 Paul Wellens; 2 Ade Gardner; 3 Matt Gidley; 11 Lee Gilmour; 29 Tom Armstrong; 6 Leon Pryce; 7 Sean Long; 16 Tony Puletua; 9 Keiron Cunningham (C); 15 Bryn Hargreaves; 12 Jon Wilkin; 13 Chris Flannery; 17 Paul Clough. Subs (all used): 14 James Roby; 20 Gareth Frodsham; 23 Maurie Fa'asavalu; 21 Gary Wheeler.
Tries: Wellens (14), Gardner (19), Gilmour (32), Puletua (75), Wheeler (79); **Goals:** Long 1/5;
Field goal: Long (77).
Rugby Leaguer & League Express Men of the Match:
Giants: Scott Moore; *Saints:* Tony Puletua.
Penalty count: 6-5; **Half-time:** 2-12;
Referee: Thierry Alibert; **Attendance:** 11,338.

WAKEFIELD TRINITY WILDCATS 29 SALFORD CITY REDS 10

WILDCATS: 1 Matt Blaymire; 2 Damien Blanch; 19 Sean Gleeson; 4 Ryan Atkins; 22 Dave Halley; 3 Tony Martin; 13 Scott Grix; 12 Oliver Wilkes; 9 Brad Drew; 15 James Stosic; 24 Dale Ferguson; 17 Kevin Henderson; 8 Jason Demetriou (C). Subs (all used): 28 Kyle Bibb; 16 Ricky Bibey; 29 Jay Pitts; 11 Steve Snitch.
Tries: Blanch (3, 79), Wilkes (19), Atkins (23, 75);
Goals: Martin 4/6; **Field goal:** Drew (39).
CITY REDS: 1 Karl Fitzpatrick; 2 John Wilshere; 15 Stuart Littler; 4 Willie Talau; 3 Mark Henry; 6 Jeremy Smith; 7 Richard Myler; 8 Ray Cashmere; 9 Malcolm Alker; 10 Craig Stapleton; 12 Rob Parker (C); 20 Luke Adamson; 13 Luke Swain. Subs (all used): 11 Ian Sibbit; 17 Robbie Paul; 16 Phil Leuluai; 22 Stephen Nash.
Tries: Myler (41), Talau (78); **Goals:** Wilshere 1/2.
Rugby Leaguer & League Express Men of the Match:
Wildcats: Brad Drew; *City Reds:* Phil Leuluai.
Penalty count: 7-7; **Half-time:** 19-0;
Referee: Ian Smith; **Attendance:** 6,578.

ROUND 3

Friday 27th February 2009

BRADFORD BULLS 12 HUDDERSFIELD GIANTS 16

BULLS: 1 Michael Platt; 2 Rikki Sheriffe; 3 Paul Sykes; 4 Chris Nero; 5 Semi Tadulala; 6 Ben Jeffries; 7 Paul Deacon (C); 8 Sam Burgess; 9 Terry Newton; 17 Nick Scruton; 11 Steve Menzies; 15 Matt Cook; 12 Glenn Morrison. Subs (all used): 14 Wayne Godwin; 16 Michael Worrincy (D); 19 Craig Kopczak; 22 Matt James.
Try: Morrison (43); **Goals:** Deacon 4/4.
GIANTS: 1 Brett Hodgson (C); 2 Martin Aspinwall; 21 Leroy Cudjoe; 4 Paul Whatuira; 5 David Hodgson; 3 Kevin Brown; 7 Luke Robinson; 16 Keith Mason; 20 Scott Moore; 17 Michael Korkidas; 13 Stephen Wild; 12 Andy Raleigh; 14 Simon Finnigan. Subs (all used): 15 Paul Jackson; 9 David Faiumu; 11 Jamahl Lolesi; 18 Danny Kirmond.
Tries: Aspinwall (22), Lolesi (39), Wild (54);
Goals: B Hodgson 2/3.
On report: Cudjoe (46) – alleged dangerous tackle.
Rugby Leaguer & League Express Men of the Match:
Bulls: Glenn Morrison; *Giants:* Brett Hodgson.
Penalty count: 10-5; **Half-time:** 6-10;
Referee: Steve Ganson; **Attendance:** 10,186.

HULL FC 28 CATALANS DRAGONS 12

HULL: 24 Craig Hall; 2 Mark Calderwood; 17 Graeme Horne; 4 Kirk Yeaman; 21 Tom Briscoe; 6 Richard Horne; 7 Chris Thorman; 8 Ewan Dowes; 9 Shaun Berrigan; 10 Peter Cusack; 22 Mike Burnett; 12 Danny Tickle; 11 Lee Radford. Subs (all used): 23 Tommy Lee; 18 Jamie Thackray; 16 Willie Manu; 20 Danny Houghton.
Tries: Berrigan (24), Hall (37), Briscoe (61), R Horne (73); **Goals:** Tickle 6/6.
DRAGONS: 1 Clint Greenshields; 2 Cyril Stacul; 15 Jean-Phillipe Baile; 4 Adam Mogg; 5 Dimitri Pelo; 6 Thomas Bosc; 7 Shane Perry; 8 David Ferriol; 9 Casey McGuire (C); 10 Jerome Guisset; 16 Olivier Elima; 12 Jason Croker; 13 Gregory Mounis. Subs (all used): 17 Cyrille Gossard; 24 Remi Casty; 19 Julien Touxagas; 18 Vincent Duport.
Tries: Elima (45), Mogg (79); **Goals:** Bosc 2/2.
Rugby Leaguer & League Express Men of the Match:
Hull: Danny Tickle; *Dragons:* Adam Mogg.
Penalty count: 10-6; **Half-time:** 14-0;
Referee: Ben Thaler; **Attendance:** 12,482.

ST HELENS 19 HULL KINGSTON ROVERS 20

SAINTS: 1 Paul Wellens; 2 Ade Gardner; 3 Matt Gidley; 11 Lee Gilmour; 29 Tom Armstrong; 14 James Roby; 7 Sean Long; 10 James Graham; 9 Keiron Cunningham (C); 15 Bryn Hargreaves; 16 Tony Puletua; 12 Jon Wilkin; 17 Paul Clough. Subs (all used): 20 Gareth Frodsham; 21 Gary Wheeler; 23 Maurie Fa'asavalu; 24 Andrew Dixon (D).
Tries: Puletua (15), Wheeler (32), Wellens (47);
Goals: Long 3/3; **Field goal:** Long (70).
ROVERS: 1 Shaun Briscoe (C); 2 Peter Fox; 4 Jake

Webster; 19 Kris Welham; 28 Ben Cockayne; 21 Chaz I'Anson; 7 Michael Dobson; 8 Nick Fozzard; 15 Daniel Fitzhenry; 17 Makali Aizue; 3 Chev Walker; 12 Ben Galea; 13 Scott Murrell. Subs (all used): 9 Ben Fisher; 11 Clint Newton; 16 Jason Netherton; 24 Rhys Lovegrove.
Tries: Galea (21), Fox (44), Webster (65);
Goals: Dobson 4/4.
Rugby Leaguer & League Express Men of the Match:
Saints: Tony Puletua; *Rovers:* Michael Dobson.
Penalty count: 3-8; **Half-time:** 12-6;
Referee: Ian Smith; **Attendance:** 11,830.

WAKEFIELD TRINITY WILDCATS 48 WARRINGTON WOLVES 22

WILDCATS: 1 Matt Blaymire; 2 Damien Blanch; 19 Sean Gleeson; 4 Ryan Atkins; 22 Dave Halley; 3 Tony Martin; 14 Sam Obst; 12 Oliver Wilkes; 9 Brad Drew; 15 James Stosic; 24 Dale Ferguson; 11 Steve Snitch; 8 Jason Demetriou (C). Subs (all used): 28 Kyle Bibb; 16 Ricky Bibey; 29 Jay Pitts; 26 Luke George.
Tries: Blaymire (8, 11, 67), Ferguson (22, 49), Halley (25, 37), George (74); **Goals:** Martin 7/7, Drew 1/1.
WOLVES: 19 Chris Riley; 23 Chris Hicks; 3 Martin Gleeson; 25 Chris Bridge; 4 Matt King; 6 Lee Briers; 7 Michael Monaghan; 8 Adrian Morley (C); 14 Mick Higham; 10 Paul Rauhihi; 11 Louis Anderson; 24 Ben Harrison; 13 Vinnie Anderson. Subs (all used): 22 Lee Mitchell; 15 Paul Wood; 21 Matty Blythe; 17 Steve Pickersgill.
Tries: L Anderson (29, 33), Hicks (56), Bridge (70);
Goals: Hicks 3/4.
Rugby Leaguer & League Express Men of the Match:
Wildcats: Tony Martin; *Wolves:* Mick Higham.
Penalty count: 8-8; **Half-time:** 30-10;
Referee: Phil Bentham; **Attendance:** 5,169.

Saturday 28th February 2009

CASTLEFORD TIGERS 52 SALFORD CITY REDS 16

TIGERS: 23 Ryan McGoldrick; 5 Michael Wainwright; 2 Kirk Dixon; 3 Michael Shenton; 1 Richard Owen; 21 Sione Faumuina; 7 Brent Sherwin; 8 Mitchell Sargent; 9 Ryan Hudson (C); 10 Craig Huby; 11 Brett Ferres; 14 Stuart Jones; 13 Joe Westerman. Subs (all used): 6 Rangi Chase; 16 Chris Feather; 19 Kirk Netherton; 25 Dean Widders.
Tries: Shenton (3), Huby (9), Hudson (12), Owen (21, 57), Westerman (26), Netherton (43), McGoldrick (65), Widders (78); **Goals:** Dixon 8/9.
Sin bin: Huby (60) - fighting.
CITY REDS: 1 Karl Fitzpatrick; 2 John Wilshere; 15 Stuart Littler; 4 Willie Talau; 3 Mark Henry; 6 Jeremy Smith; 7 Richard Myler; 8 Ray Cashmere; 9 Malcolm Alker; 10 Craig Stapleton; 12 Rob Parker (C); 20 Luke Adamson; 13 Luke Swain. Subs (all used): 17 Robbie Paul; 11 Ian Sibbit; 16 Phil Leuluai; 22 Stephen Nash.

Tries: Talau (33), Fitzpatrick (70), Henry (75);
Goals: Wilshere 2/3.
Sin bin: Cashmere (60) - fighting.
Rugby Leaguer & League Express Men of the Match: *Tigers:* Brent Sherwin; *City Reds:* Jeremy Smith.
Penalty count: 8-8; **Half-time:** 28-6;
Referee: Gareth Hewer; **Attendance:** 7,052.

HARLEQUINS 18 WIGAN WARRIORS 24

HARLEQUINS: 2 Jon Wells; 1 Chris Melling; 3 Matt Gafa; 4 David Howell; 5 Will Sharp; 6 Luke Dorn; 7 Danny Orr; 8 Karl Temata; 9 Chad Randall; 17 Danny Ward; 12 Chad Robinson; 14 Tony Clubb; 13 Rob Purdham (C). Subs (all used): 10 Louie McCarthy-Scarsbrook; 19 Jason Golden (D); 23 Daniel Heckenberg; 21 Luke Gale (D).
Tries: Randall (18), Gafa (19), McCarthy-Scarsbrook (66), Melling (70); **Goals:** Orr 1/3, Gale 0/1.
WARRIORS: 5 Pat Richards; 2 Amos Roberts; 12 Phil Bailey; 4 George Carmont; 28 Shaun Ainscough; 6 Tim Smith; 7 Thomas Leuluai; 8 Stuart Fielden; 9 Mark Riddell; 15 Andy Coley; 11 Gareth Hock; 14 Joel Tomkins; 13 Sean O'Loughlin (C). Subs (all used): 10 Iafeta Palea'aesina; 16 Harrison Hansen; 23 Eamon O'Carroll; 25 Sam Tomkins.
Tries: Ainscough (12, 78), Carmont (41), Bailey (43), Roberts (74); **Goals:** Richards 2/5.
Rugby Leaguer & League Express Men of the Match: *Harlequins:* Chad Randall; *Warriors:* Gareth Hock.
Penalty count: 6-3; **Half-time:** 10-6;
Referee: Thierry Alibert; **Attendance:** 3,883.

ROUND 4

Friday 6th March 2009

HUDDERSFIELD GIANTS 20 HULL FC 24

GIANTS: 1 Brett Hodgson (C); 2 Martin Aspinwall; 21 Leroy Cudjoe; 4 Paul Whatuira; 5 David Hodgson; 3 Kevin Brown; 7 Luke Robinson; 16 Keith Mason; 20 Scott Moore; 17 Michael Korkidas; 12 Andy Raleigh; 13 Stephen Wild; 9 David Faiumu. Subs (all used): 15 Paul Jackson; 11 Jamahl Lolesi; 23 Joe Walsh (D); 18 Danny Kirmond.
Tries: B Hodgson (2), Walsh (29), K Brown (45), D Hodgson (80); **Goals:** B Hodgson 2/4.
HULL: 24 Craig Hall; 2 Mark Calderwood; 17 Graeme Horne; 4 Kirk Yeaman; 21 Tom Briscoe; 6 Richard Horne; 7 Chris Thorman; 10 Peter Cusack; 9 Shaun Berrigan; 8 Ewan Dowes; 16 Willie Manu; 12 Danny Tickle; 11 Lee Radford (C). Subs (all used): 20 Danny Houghton; 23 Tommy Lee; 27 Sam Moa (D); 18 Jamie Thackray.
Tries: Briscoe (9), R Horne (15), Thackray (32), Yeaman (53); **Goals:** Tickle 4/5.
Rugby Leaguer & League Express Men of the Match: *Giants:* Scott Moore; *Hull:* Richard Horne.
Penalty count: 5-7; **Half-time:** 10-18;
Referee: Ian Smith; **Attendance:** 10,459.

SALFORD CITY REDS 18 HARLEQUINS 48

CITY REDS: 1 Karl Fitzpatrick; 2 John Wilshere; 15 Stuart Littler; 14 Jordan Turner; 19 Stefan Ratchford; 6 Jeremy Smith; 17 Robbie Paul; 8 Ray Cashmere; 9 Malcolm Alker; 10 Craig Stapleton; 20 Luke Adamson; 12 Rob Parker (C); 13 Luke Swain. Subs (all used): 16 Phil Leuluai; 25 Jason Walton; 23 Adam Sidlow; 22 Stephen Nash.
Tries: Parker (39), Wilshere (55), Paul (61);
Goals: Wilshere 3/3.
HARLEQUINS: 2 Jon Wells; 1 Chris Melling; 3 Matt Gafa; 4 David Howell; 5 Will Sharp; 6 Luke Dorn; 7 Danny Orr (C); 10 Louie McCarthy-Scarsbrook; 9 Chad Randall; 17 Danny Ward; 12 Chad Robinson; 14 Tony Clubb; 18 Joe Mbu. Subs (all used): 23 Daniel Heckenberg; 20 Jon Grayshon; 19 Jason Golden; 21 Luke Gale.
Tries: Gafa (1), Howell (10, 12), Mbu (19), Melling (29, 34), Randall (68), Dorn (76), Heckenberg (80); **Goals:** Orr 6/9.
Rugby Leaguer & League Express Men of the Match: *City Reds:* Malcolm Alker; *Harlequins:* Danny Orr.
Penalty count: 6-9; **Half-time:** 6-30;
Referee: Jamie Leahy; **Attendance:** 3,387.

Saturday 7th March 2009

CATALANS DRAGONS 22 CASTLEFORD TIGERS 24

DRAGONS: 1 Clint Greenshields; 2 Cyril Stacul; 3 Steven Bell; 4 Adam Mogg; 5 Dimitri Pelo; 6 Thomas Bosc; 7 Shane Perry; 8 David Ferriol; 9 Casey McGuire (C); 10 Jerome Guisset; 12 Jason Croker; 22 Jamal Fakir; 13 Gregory Mounis. Subs (all used): 26 Greg Bird (D); 24 Remi Casty; 15 Jean-Phillipe Baile; 16 Olivier Elima.
Tries: Greenshields (22), Fakir (38), Stacul (59, 79);
Goals: Bosc 3/4.
TIGERS: 23 Ryan McGoldrick; 2 Kirk Dixon; 4 James Evans; 3 Michael Shenton; 1 Richard Owen; 21 Sione Faumuina; 7 Brent Sherwin; 8 Mitchell Sargent; 9 Ryan Hudson (C); 10 Craig Huby; 14 Stuart Jones; 11 Brett Ferres; 13 Joe Westerman. Subs (all used): 25 Dean Widders; 19 Kirk Netherton; 6 Rangi Chase; 16 Chris Feather.
Tries: Dixon (15), Evans (22, 43), Owen (35), Chase (70); **Goals:** Dixon 2/5.
Rugby Leaguer & League Express Men of the Match: *Dragons:* Jamal Fakir; *Tigers:* Brent Sherwin.
Penalty count: 5-5; **Half-time:** 12-14;
Referee: Richard Silverwood; **Attendance:** 8,150.

CELTIC CRUSADERS 0 ST HELENS 4

CRUSADERS: 13 Marshall Chalk; 18 Mark Lennon; 3 Josh Hannay; 4 Mark Dalle Cort; 5 Anthony Blackwood; 6 Damien Quinn; 14 Matty Smith; 8 Ryan O'Hara; 9 Lincoln Withers (D); 10 Mark Bryant; 21 Chris Beasley; 12 Darren Mapp (C); 15 Peter Lupton. Subs (all used): 11 Adam Peek; 16 Ben Flower; 19 Jason Chan; 23 Neil Budworth.
SAINTS: 1 Paul Wellens; 2 Ade Gardner; 3 Matt Gidley; 11 Lee Gilmour; 29 Tom Armstrong; 6 Leon Pryce; 7 Sean Long; 10 James Graham; 9 Keiron Cunningham (C); 15 Bryn Hargreaves; 12 Jon Wilkin; 24 Andrew Dixon; 16 Tony Puletua. Subs (all used): 8 Jason Cayless; 14 James Roby; 17 Paul Clough; 23 Maurie Fa'asavalu.
Try: Armstrong (55); **Goals:** Long 0/1.
Rugby Leaguer & League Express Men of the Match: *Crusaders:* Matty Smith; *Saints:* Tom Armstrong.
Penalty count: 3-11; **Half-time:** 0-0;
Referee: Phil Bentham; **Attendance:** 6,351.

WIGAN WARRIORS 44 BRADFORD BULLS 10

WARRIORS: 5 Pat Richards; 2 Amos Roberts; 12 Phil Bailey; 4 George Carmont; 28 Shaun Ainscough; 25 Sam Tomkins; 7 Thomas Leuluai; 8 Stuart Fielden; 9 Mark Riddell; 10 Iafeta Palea'aesina; 11 Gareth Hock; 14 Joel Tomkins; 13 Sean O'Loughlin (C). Subs (all used): 15 Andy Coley; 16 Harrison Hansen; 17 Michael McIlorum; 23 Eamon O'Carroll.
Tries: Richards (10), Hock (18, 53), Carmont (39), Hansen (58, 65), Palea'aesina (69); **Goals:** Richards 8/8.
BULLS: 1 Michael Platt; 2 Rikki Sheriffe; 3 Paul Sykes; 4 Chris Nero; 5 Semi Tadulala; 6 Ben Jeffries; 7 Paul Deacon (C); 8 Sam Burgess; 9 Terry Newton; 17 Nick Scruton; 11 Steve Menzies; 15 Matt Cook; 12 Glenn Morrison. Subs (all used): 14 Wayne Godwin; 16 Michael Worrincy; 19 Craig Kopczak; 22 Matt James.
Tries: Sheriffe (50), Menzies (76); **Goals:** Deacon 1/2.
Rugby Leaguer & League Express Men of the Match: *Warriors:* Gareth Hock; *Bulls:* Ben Jeffries.
Penalty count: 7-3; **Half-time:** 18-0;
Referee: Ben Thaler; **Attendance:** 12,588.

Sunday 8th March 2009

HULL KINGSTON ROVERS 31 WAKEFIELD TRINITY WILDCATS 18

ROVERS: 1 Shaun Briscoe (C); 2 Peter Fox; 19 Kris Welham; 4 Jake Webster; 5 Liam Colbon; 21 Chaz I'Anson; 7 Michael Dobson; 8 Nick Fozzard; 15 Daniel Fitzhenry; 11 Clint Newton; 3 Chev Walker; 12 Ben Galea; 13 Scott Murrell. Subs (all used): 9 Ben Fisher; 17 Makali Aizue; 16 Jason Netherton; 24 Rhys Lovegrove.
Tries: Briscoe (19), Newton (30), Murrell (35), Fisher (53), Colbon (58); **Goals:** Dobson 5/5;
Field goal: Dobson (77).
WILDCATS: 1 Matt Blaymire; 2 Damien Blanch; 19 Sean Gleeson; 17 Kevin Henderson; 22 Dave Halley; 3 Tony Martin; 8 Jason Demetriou (C); 12 Oliver Wilkes; 9 Brad Drew; 16 Ricky Bibey; 11 Steve Snitch; 29 Jay Pitts; 24 Dale Ferguson. Subs (all used): 32 James Davey (D); 31 Luke Blake; 28 Kyle Bibb; 10 Danny Sculthorpe.
Tries: Henderson (39), Ferguson (67), Gleeson (71);
Goals: Martin 3/3.
Rugby Leaguer & League Express Men of the Match: *Rovers:* Shaun Briscoe; *Wildcats:* Dale Ferguson.
Penalty count: 6-4; **Half-time:** 18-6;
Referee: Thierry Alibert; **Attendance:** 9,038.

WARRINGTON WOLVES 14 LEEDS RHINOS 20

WOLVES: 19 Chris Riley; 23 Chris Hicks; 3 Martin Gleeson; 2 Paul Johnson; 4 Matt King; 6 Lee Briers; 7 Michael Monaghan; 8 Adrian Morley (C); 9 Jon Clarke; 10 Paul Rauhihi; 11 Louis Anderson; 24 Ben Harrison; 13 Vinnie Anderson. Subs (all used): 15 Paul Wood; 22 Lee Mitchell; 14 Mick Higham; 17 Steve Pickersgill.
Tries: Briers (14), Higham (39), Hicks (57);
Goals: Hicks 1/3.
On report: Brawl (65).
RHINOS: 3 Lee Smith; 2 Scott Donald; 23 Kallum Watkins; 20 Ashley Gibson; 5 Ryan Hall; 6 Danny McGuire; 7 Rob Burrow; 16 Ryan Bailey; 26 Paul McShane; 19 Luke Burgess; 11 Jamie Jones-Buchanan; 18 Carl Ablett; 13 Kevin Sinfield (C). Subs (all used): 22 Danny Allan; 8 Kylie Leuluai; 12 Ali Lauitiiti; 10 Jamie Peacock.
Tries: Ablett (2), Sinfield (6), McGuire (71);
Goals: Sinfield 4/4.
On report: Brawl (65).
Rugby Leaguer & League Express Men of the Match: *Wolves:* Chris Hicks; *Rhinos:* Kevin Sinfield.
Penalty count: 6-5; **Half-time:** 10-14;
Referee: Steve Ganson; **Attendance:** 9,863.

ROUND 5

Friday 13th March 2009

LEEDS RHINOS 34 WIGAN WARRIORS 10

RHINOS: 3 Lee Smith; 2 Scott Donald; 20 Ashley Gibson; 23 Kallum Watkins; 5 Ryan Hall; 6 Danny McGuire; 7 Rob Burrow; 8 Kylie Leuluai; 11 Jamie Jones-Buchanan; 16 Ryan Bailey; 18 Carl Ablett; 17 Ian Kirke; 13 Kevin Sinfield (C). Subs (all used): 10 Jamie Peacock; 12 Ali Lauitiiti; 19 Luke Burgess; 1 Brent Webb.
Tries: Leuluai (3), Donald (11), Burrow (17), Hall (29, 51), Peacock (66); **Goals:** Sinfield 5/6.
WARRIORS: 5 Pat Richards; 2 Amos Roberts; 12 Phil Bailey; 4 George Carmont; 28 Shaun Ainscough; 25 Sam Tomkins; 7 Thomas Leuluai; 8 Stuart Fielden; 9 Mark Riddell; 10 Iafeta Palea'aesina; 11 Gareth Hock; 14 Joel Tomkins; 13 Sean O'Loughlin (C). Subs (all used): 15 Andy Coley; 16 Harrison Hansen; 17 Michael McIlorum; 23 Eamon O'Carroll.
Tries: Ainscough (36), Hock (78); **Goals:** Richards 1/2.
Rugby Leaguer & League Express Men of the Match: *Rhinos:* Carl Ablett; *Warriors:* Shaun Ainscough.
Penalty count: 6-6; **Half-time:** 22-6;
Referee: Ian Smith; **Attendance:** 17,677.

ST HELENS 38 SALFORD CITY REDS 12

SAINTS: 1 Paul Wellens; 2 Ade Gardner; 3 Matt Gidley; 13 Chris Flannery; 21 Gary Wheeler; 6 Leon Pryce; 7 Sean Long; 10 James Graham; 9 Keiron Cunningham (C); 15 Bryn Hargreaves; 12 Jon Wilkin; 24 Andrew Dixon; 17 Paul Clough. Subs (all used): 8 Jason Cayless; 14 James Roby; 28 Matty Ashurst (D); 31 Jacob Emmitt.
Tries: Wilkin (11, 37), Pryce (19), Flannery (40), Gardner (50), Graham (59), Cunningham (62);
Goals: Long 5/7.
CITY REDS: 1 Karl Fitzpatrick; 3 Mark Henry; 15 Stuart Littler; 14 Jordan Turner; 19 Stefan Ratchford; 6 Jeremy Smith; 17 Robbie Paul; 8 Ray Cashmere; 9 Malcolm Alker (C); 10 Craig Stapleton; 20 Luke Adamson; 12 Rob Parker; 13 Luke Swain. Subs (all used): 16 Phil Leuluai; 21 Andy Thornley (D); 22 Stephen Nash; 23 Adam Sidlow.
Tries: Fitzpatrick (70), Thornley (78);
Goals: Ratchford 2/2.
Rugby Leaguer & League Express Men of the Match: *Saints:* Jon Wilkin; *City Reds:* Malcolm Alker.
Penalty count: 9-6; **Half-time:** 20-0;
Referee: Richard Silverwood; **Attendance:** 9,723.

Saturday 14th March 2009

HARLEQUINS 60 WARRINGTON WOLVES 8

HARLEQUINS: 2 Jon Wells; 1 Chris Melling; 3 Matt Gafa; 4 David Howell; 5 Will Sharp; 6 Luke Dorn; 7 Danny Orr (C); 8 Karl Temata; 9 Chad Randall; 17 Danny Ward; 12 Chad Robinson; 14 Tony Clubb; 18 Joe Mbu. Subs (all used): 23 Daniel Heckenberg; 19 Jason Golden; 21 Luke Gale; 10 Louie McCarthy-Scarsbrook.
Tries: Dorn (2), Ward (18), Temata (24), Gafa (35), Orr (39), Randall (45), Howell (62), Gale (66, 78), Melling (73); **Goals:** Orr 10/10.
WOLVES: 23 Chris Hicks; 2 Paul Johnson; 3 Martin Gleeson; 20 Simon Grix; 4 Matt King; 6 Lee Briers; 7 Michael Monaghan; 8 Adrian Morley (C); 9 Jon Clarke; 10 Paul Rauhihi; 11 Louis Anderson; 13 Vinnie Anderson; 22 Lee Mitchell. Subs (all used): 15 Paul Wood; 14 Mick Higham; 17 Steve Pickersgill; 24 Ben Harrison.
Tries: V Anderson (9), Rauhihi (21); **Goals:** Hicks 0/2.
Rugby Leaguer & League Express Men of the Match: *Harlequins:* Danny Orr; *Wolves:* Paul Rauhihi.
Penalty count: 5-4; **Half-time:** 30-8;
Referee: Thierry Alibert; **Attendance:** 3,206.

CASTLEFORD TIGERS 24 HUDDERSFIELD GIANTS 26

TIGERS: 23 Ryan McGoldrick; 2 Kirk Dixon; 4 James Evans; 3 Michael Shenton; 1 Richard Owen; 21 Sione Faumuina; 7 Brent Sherwin; 8 Mitchell Sargent; 9 Ryan Hudson (C); 10 Craig Huby; 14 Stuart Jones; 11 Brett Ferres; 13 Joe Westerman. Subs (all used): 25 Dean Widders; 19 Kirk Netherton; 6 Rangi Chase; 16 Chris Feather.
Tries: Evans (8), Huby (11, 57), Ferres (59, 68);
Goals: Dixon 2/5.
On report: Huby (80) - alleged high tackle.
GIANTS: 1 Brett Hodgson (C); 21 Leroy Cudjoe; 19 Michael Lawrence; 4 Paul Whatuira; 5 David Hodgson; 3 Kevin Brown; 7 Luke Robinson; 16 Keith Mason; 20 Scott Moore; 15 Paul Jackson; 13 Stephen Wild; 11 Jamahl Lolesi; 23 Joe Walsh. Subs (all used): 18 Danny Kirmond; 30 Larne Patrick (D); 24 Shaun Lunt; 10 Darrell Griffin.
Tries: Lolesi (1), D Hodgson (15, 35, 50), B Hodgson (64); **Goals:** B Hodgson 3/5.
Sin bin: Cudjoe (68) - holding down.
Rugby Leaguer & League Express Men of the Match: *Tigers:* Brett Ferres; *Giants:* Brett Hodgson.
Penalty count: 14-5; **Half-time:** 12-14;
Referee: Steve Ganson; **Attendance:** 6,572.

Sunday 15th March 2009

BRADFORD BULLS 24 HULL FC 36

BULLS: 3 Paul Sykes; 2 Rikki Sheriffe; 23 Jason Crookes (D); 4 Chris Nero; 5 Semi Tadulala; 6 Ben Jeffries; 7 Paul Deacon (C); 10 Andy Lynch; 9 Terry Newton; 17 Nick Scruton; 11 Steve Menzies; 12 Glenn Morrison; 8 Sam Burgess. Subs (all used): 15 Matt Cook; 1 Michael Platt; 19 Craig Kopczak; 13 Jamie Langley.
Tries: Jeffries (21), Sheriffe (40), Tadulala (63), Menzies (72); **Goals:** Deacon 4/4.
HULL: 24 Craig Hall; 2 Mark Calderwood; 17 Graeme Horne; 4 Kirk Yeaman; 21 Tom Briscoe; 6 Richard Horne; 7 Chris Thorman; 8 Ewan Dowes; 9 Shaun Berrigan; 10 Peter Cusack; 16 Willie Manu; 12 Danny Tickle; 11 Lee Radford (C). Subs (all used): 20 Danny Houghton; 23 Tommy Lee; 27 Sam Moa; 18 Jamie Thackray.
Tries: R Horne (2), Yeaman (6, 27), Hall (36, 67), Thorman (47); **Goals:** Tickle 6/7.
Rugby Leaguer & League Express Men of the Match: *Bulls:* Ben Jeffries; *Hull:* Chris Thorman.
Penalty count: 5-6; **Half-time:** 12-22;
Referee: Phil Bentham; **Attendance:** 11,327.

HULL KINGSTON ROVERS 48 CELTIC CRUSADERS 18

ROVERS: 28 Ben Cockayne; 2 Peter Fox; 3 Chev Walker; 19 Kris Welham; 5 Liam Colbon; 21 Chaz I'Anson; 7 Michael Dobson; 8 Nick Fozzard; 15 Daniel Fitzhenry; 18 Scott Wheeldon (D); 11 Clint Newton (C); 12 Ben Galea;

13 Scott Murrell. Subs (all used): 4 Jake Webster; 9 Ben Fisher; 16 Jason Netherton; 24 Rhys Lovegrove.
Tries: Welham (21), Fozzard (28), Newton (39, 58, 68), Walker (44), Galea (51), Dobson (72), Colbon (79);
Goals: Dobson 6/8, Murrell 0/1.
CRUSADERS: 13 Marshall Chalk; 2 Luke Dyer; 3 Josh Hannay; 4 Mark Dalle Cort; 5 Anthony Blackwood; 6 Damien Quinn; 14 Matty Smith; 8 Ryan O'Hara; 9 Lincoln Withers; 10 Mark Bryant; 21 Chris Beasley; 12 Darren Mapp (C); 15 Peter Lupton. Subs (all used): 11 Adam Peek; 16 Ben Flower; 19 Jason Chan; 23 Neil Budworth.
Tries: Lupton (13), Mapp (35), Smith (76);
Goals: Hannay 3/3.
Rugby Leaguer & League Express Men of the Match:
Rovers: Clint Newton; *Crusaders:* Matty Smith.
Penalty count: 7-1; **Half-time:** 16-12;
Referee: Ben Thaler; **Attendance:** 8,046.

**WAKEFIELD TRINITY WILDCATS 30
CATALANS DRAGONS 10**

WILDCATS: 1 Matt Blaymire; 2 Damien Blanch; 19 Sean Gleeson; 4 Ryan Atkins; 27 Aaron Murphy; 3 Tony Martin; 7 Danny Brough; 12 Oliver Wilkes; 20 Tevita Leo-Latu; 16 Ricky Bibey; 11 Steve Snitch; 24 Dale Ferguson; 8 Jason Demetriou (C). Subs (all used): 28 Kyle Bibb; 17 Kevin Henderson; 29 Jay Pitts; 10 Danny Sculthorpe.
Tries: Gleeson (8), Martin (15), Blanch (48), Atkins (57), Murphy (80); **Goals:** Martin 4/7, Brough 1/1.
DRAGONS: 1 Clint Greenshields; 2 Cyril Stacul; 15 Jean-Phillipe Baile; 3 Steven Bell; 5 Dimitri Pelo; 6 Thomas Bosc; 7 Shane Perry; 8 David Ferriol; 9 Casey McGuire (C); 16 Olivier Elima; 17 Cyrille Gossard; 13 Gregory Mounis; 22 Jamal Fakir. Subs (all used): 19 Julien Touxagas; 10 Jerome Guisset; 26 Greg Bird; 24 Remi Casty.
Tries: Baile (21), Pelo (35); **Goals:** Bosc 1/2.
Rugby Leaguer & League Express Men of the Match:
Wildcats: Jason Demetriou; *Dragons:* Jamal Fakir.
Penalty count: 15-6; **Half-time:** 12-10;
Referee: James Child; **Attendance:** 4,807.

ROUND 6

Friday 20th March 2009

HULL FC 18 CASTLEFORD TIGERS 19

HULL: 24 Craig Hall; 2 Mark Calderwood; 17 Graeme Horne; 4 Kirk Yeaman; 21 Tom Briscoe; 6 Richard Horne; 7 Chris Thorman; 8 Ewan Dowes; 20 Danny Houghton; 10 Peter Cusack; 16 Willie Manu; 12 Danny Tickle; 11 Lee Radford (C). Subs (all used): 9 Shaun Berrigan; 23 Tommy Lee; 27 Sam Moa; 18 Jamie Thackray.
Tries: R Horne (1), G Horne (18, 49, 58);
Goals: Tickle 1/4.
TIGERS: 23 Ryan McGoldrick; 2 Kirk Dixon; 4 James Evans; 3 Michael Shenton; 1 Richard Owen; 6 Rangi Chase; 7 Brent Sherwin; 8 Mitchell Sargent; 9 Ryan Hudson (C); 16 Chris Feather; 14 Stuart Jones; 11 Brett Ferres; 21 Sione Faumuina. Subs (all used): 13 Joe Westerman; 19 Kirk Netherton; 10 Craig Huby; 15 Liam Higgins.
Tries: Dixon (7), Westerman (45), McGoldrick (64);
Goals: Dixon 3/3; **Field goal:** Sherwin (77).
Rugby Leaguer & League Express Men of the Match:
Hull: Graeme Horne; *Tigers:* Ryan McGoldrick.
Penalty count: 6-5; **Half-time:** 10-6;
Referee: Thierry Alibert; **Attendance:** 14,028.

SALFORD CITY REDS 12 WIGAN WARRIORS 38

CITY REDS: 1 Karl Fitzpatrick; 3 Mark Henry; 15 Stuart Littler; 14 Jordan Turner; 19 Stefan Ratchford; 6 Jeremy Smith; 7 Richard Myler; 18 Lee Jewitt; 9 Malcolm Alker (C); 10 Craig Stapleton; 20 Luke Adamson; 12 Rob Parker; 13 Luke Swain. Subs (all used): 16 Phil Leuluai; 8 Ray Cashmere; 23 Adam Sidlow; 17 Robbie Paul.
Tries: Myler (23, 68); **Goals:** Turner 1/1, Ratchford 1/1.
WARRIORS: 5 Pat Richards; 20 Karl Pryce; 12 Phil Bailey; 4 George Carmont; 28 Shaun Ainscough; 25 Sam Tomkins; 7 Thomas Leuluai; 19 Paul Prescott; 9 Mark Riddell; 15 Andy Coley; 16 Harrison Hansen; 11 Gareth Hock; 13 Sean O'Loughlin (C). Subs (all used): 6 Tim Smith; 8 Stuart Fielden; 10 Iafeta Palea'aesina; 14 Joel Tomkins.
Tries: Ainscough (10, 53), Leuluai (17, 74), S Tomkins (34, 48), Richards (38); **Goals:** Richards 5/7.
Rugby Leaguer & League Express Men of the Match:
City Reds: Richard Myler; *Warriors:* Sam Tomkins.
Penalty count: 5-3; **Half-time:** 6-22;
Referee: Gareth Hewer; **Attendance:** 7,016.

ST HELENS 26 LEEDS RHINOS 18

SAINTS: 1 Paul Wellens; 2 Ade Gardner; 3 Matt Gidley; 11 Lee Gilmour; 21 Gary Wheeler; 6 Leon Pryce; 7 Sean Long; 10 James Graham; 9 Keiron Cunningham (C); 15 Bryn Hargreaves; 12 Jon Wilkin; 13 Chris Flannery; 17 Paul Clough. Subs (all used): 8 Jason Cayless; 14 James Roby; 23 Maurie Fa'asavalu; 28 Matty Ashurst.
Tries: Gidley (14, 69), Roby (34), Pryce (38), Wheeler (63); **Goals:** Long 3/3, Wheeler 0/1, Gidley 0/1.
RHINOS: 1 Brent Webb; 2 Scott Donald; 3 Lee Smith; 4 Keith Senior; 5 Ryan Hall; 6 Danny McGuire; 7 Rob Burrow; 8 Kylie Leuluai; 14 Matt Diskin; 10 Jamie Peacock; 18 Carl Ablett; 11 Jamie Jones-Buchanan; 13 Kevin Sinfield (C). Subs (all used): 16 Ryan Bailey; 19 Luke Burgess; 20 Ashley Gibson; 22 Danny Allan.
Tries: Senior (24, 79), Hall (53); **Goals:** Sinfield 3/3.
Rugby Leaguer & League Express Men of the Match:
Saints: Chris Flannery; *Rhinos:* Keith Senior.
Penalty count: 9-6; **Half-time:** 18-6;
Referee: Phil Bentham; **Attendance:** 13,966.

Saturday 21st March 2009

CATALANS DRAGONS 24 BRADFORD BULLS 30

DRAGONS: 1 Clint Greenshields; 18 Vincent Duport; 3 Steven Bell; 15 Jean-Phillipe Baile; 5 Dimitri Pelo; 6 Thomas Bosc; 7 Shane Perry; 23 Jason Ryles; 9 Casey McGuire; 22 Jamal Fakir; 17 Cyrille Gossard; 13 Gregory Mounis; 26 Greg Bird (C). Subs (all used): 8 David Ferriol; 10 Jerome Guisset; 16 Olivier Elima; 24 Remi Casty.
Tries: Duport (17), Bird (33), Elima (36), Baile (66);
Goals: Bosc 4/6.
BULLS: 1 Michael Platt; 2 Rikki Sheriffe; 3 Paul Sykes; 4 Chris Nero; 5 Semi Tadulala; 6 Ben Jeffries; 7 Paul Deacon (C); 8 Sam Burgess; 9 Terry Newton; 10 Andy Lynch; 11 Steve Menzies; 12 Glenn Morrison; 13 Jamie Langley. Subs (all used): 16 Michael Worrincy; 17 Nick Scruton; 19 Craig Kopczak; 20 Dave Halley.
Tries: Menzies (6), Tadulala (13), Sheriffe (28), Newton (73), Halley (79); **Goals:** Deacon 3/5, Sykes 2/3.
Rugby Leaguer & League Express Men of the Match:
Dragons: Thomas Bosc; *Bulls:* Paul Sykes.
Penalty count: 8-9; **Half-time:** 18-18;
Referee: Ian Smith; **Attendance:** 7,620.

Sunday 22nd March 2009

HUDDERSFIELD GIANTS 46 HARLEQUINS 6

GIANTS: 1 Brett Hodgson (C); 21 Leroy Cudjoe; 19 Michael Lawrence; 4 Paul Whatuira; 5 David Hodgson; 3 Kevin Brown; 7 Luke Robinson; 16 Keith Mason; 20 Scott Moore; 15 Paul Jackson; 11 Jamahl Lolesi; 13 Stephen Wild; 14 Simon Finnigan. Subs (all used): 24 Shaun Lunt; 10 Darrell Griffin; 8 Eorl Crabtree; 18 Danny Kirmond.
Tries: Wild (6), Mason (18), K Brown (29, 67), B Hodgson (35), Robinson (40, 60), Lunt (75);
Goals: B Hodgson 6/7, Cudjoe 1/1.
HARLEQUINS: 1 Chris Melling; 14 Tony Clubb; 3 Matt Gafa; 4 David Howell; 5 Will Sharp; 6 Luke Dorn; 7 Danny Orr; 8 Karl Temata; 9 Chad Randall; 17 Danny Ward; 18 Joe Mbu; 12 Chad Robinson; 13 Rob Purdham (C). Subs (all used): 23 Daniel Heckenberg; 10 Louie McCarthy-Scarsbrook; 21 Luke Gale; 19 Jason Golden.
Try: Ward (70); **Goals:** Orr 1/1.
Rugby Leaguer & League Express Men of the Match:
Giants: Scott Moore; *Harlequins:* Chad Randall.
Penalty count: 6-2; **Half-time:** 28-0;
Referee: Ben Thaler; **Attendance:** 6,356.

**WARRINGTON WOLVES 24
HULL KINGSTON ROVERS 12**

WOLVES: 19 Chris Riley; 23 Chris Hicks; 20 Simon Grix; 2 Paul Johnson; 4 Matt King; 3 Martin Gleeson; 7 Michael Monaghan; 8 Adrian Morley (C); 14 Mick Higham; 10 Paul Rauhihi; 11 Louis Anderson; 13 Vinnie Anderson; 24 Ben Harrison. Subs (all used): 6 Lee Briers; 9 Jon Clarke; 18 Michael Cooper; 15 Paul Wood.
Tries: Harrison (6), Monaghan (28), Johnson (39, 57), King (69); **Goals:** Hicks 2/5.
ROVERS: 28 Ben Cockayne; 2 Peter Fox; 3 Chev Walker; 19 Kris Welham; 5 Liam Colbon; 21 Chaz l'Anson; 7 Michael Dobson; 8 Nick Fozzard; 15 Daniel Fitzhenry; 18 Scott Wheeldon; 11 Clint Newton (C); 12 Ben Galea; 13 Scott Murrell. Subs (all used): 14 Stanley Gene; 17 Makali Aizue; 9 Ben Fisher; 24 Rhys Lovegrove.
Tries: Fox (65), Aizue (75); **Goals:** Dobson 2/2.
Rugby Leaguer & League Express Men of the Match:
Wolves: Paul Johnson; *Rovers:* Michael Dobson.
Penalty count: 7-10; **Half-time:** 16-0;
Referee: Richard Silverwood; **Attendance:** 8,547.

ROUND 7

Friday 27th March 2009

LEEDS RHINOS 42 CATALANS DRAGONS 14

RHINOS: 1 Brent Webb; 2 Scott Donald; 20 Ashley Gibson; 4 Keith Senior; 5 Ryan Hall; 6 Danny McGuire; 7 Rob Burrow; 8 Kylie Leuluai; 14 Matt Diskin; 10 Jamie Peacock; 11 Jamie Jones-Buchanan; 18 Carl Ablett; 13 Kevin Sinfield (C). Subs (all used): 19 Luke Burgess; 17 Ian Kirke; 12 Ali Lauitiiti; 23 Kallum Watkins.
Tries: Hall (10, 37), Jones-Buchanan (15), McGuire (32), Webb (39), Gibson (53), Ablett (60), Diskin (76);
Goals: Sinfield 5/8.
DRAGONS: 1 Clint Greenshields; 18 Vincent Duport; 3 Steven Bell; 15 Jean-Phillipe Baile; 5 Dimitri Pelo; 6 Thomas Bosc; 7 Shane Perry; 23 Jason Ryles; 9 Casey McGuire; 16 Olivier Elima; 12 Jason Croker; 26 Greg Bird (C); 13 Gregory Mounis. Subs (all used): 10 Jerome Guisset; 17 Cyrille Gossard; 14 Dane Carlaw; 24 Remi Casty.
Tries: Bell (5), Bosc (56), Duport (66); **Goals:** Bosc 1/3.
Rugby Leaguer & League Express Men of the Match:
Rhinos: Kevin Sinfield; *Dragons:* Greg Bird.
Penalty count: 10-9; **Half-time:** 26-4;
Referee: Ben Thaler; **Attendance:** 13,425.

WAKEFIELD TRINITY WILDCATS 18 ST HELENS 42

WILDCATS: 1 Matt Blaymire; 2 Damien Blanch; 19 Sean Gleeson; 4 Ryan Atkins; 27 Aaron Murphy; 13 Scott Grix; 7 Danny Brough; 12 Oliver Wilkes; 20 Tevita Leo-Latu; 29 Jay Pitts; 24 Dale Ferguson; 11 Steve Snitch; 8 Jason Demetriou (C). Subs (all used): 28 Kyle Bibb; 17 Kevin Henderson; 14 Sam Obst; 10 Danny Sculthorpe.
Tries: Snitch (1), Murphy (30), Atkins (70);
Goals: Brough 3/3.
SAINTS: 30 Jonny Lomax (D); 2 Ade Gardner; 3 Matt Gidley; 11 Lee Gilmour; 5 Francis Meli; 21 Gary Wheeler; 6 Leon Pryce; 15 Bryn Hargreaves; 9 Keiron Cunningham (C); 10 James Graham; 12 Jon Wilkin; 13 Chris Flannery; 17 Paul Clough. Subs (all used): 16 Tony Puletua; 8 Jason Cayless; 23 Maurie Fa'asavalu; 28 Matty Ashurst.
Tries: Graham (20), Wheeler (24), Gidley (33), Pryce (37, 50, 76), Puletua (63), Gardner (66);
Goals: Wheeler 3/4, Gidley 2/4.
Rugby Leaguer & League Express Men of the Match:
Wildcats: Danny Brough; *Saints:* Leon Pryce.
Penalty count: 8-6; **Half-time:** 12-22;
Referee: Thierry Alibert; **Attendance:** 6,038.

WIGAN WARRIORS 8 HUDDERSFIELD GIANTS 22

WARRIORS: 5 Pat Richards; 2 Amos Roberts; 12 Phil Bailey; 4 George Carmont; 28 Shaun Ainscough; 25 Sam Tomkins; 7 Thomas Leuluai; 15 Andy Coley; 9 Mark Riddell; 19 Paul Prescott; 11 Gareth Hock; 16 Harrison Hansen; 13 Sean O'Loughlin (C). Subs (all used): 8 Stuart Fielden; 10 Iafeta Palea'aesina; 14 Joel Tomkins; 17 Michael McIlorum.
Tries: Bailey (17), Roberts (67); **Goals:** Richards 0/2.
Sin bin: Hansen (61) - fighting.
GIANTS: 1 Brett Hodgson (C); 2 Martin Aspinwall; 19 Michael Lawrence; 4 Paul Whatuira; 5 David Hodgson; 3 Kevin Brown; 7 Luke Robinson; 16 Keith Mason; 20 Scott Moore; 10 Darrell Griffin; 11 Jamahl Lolesi; 13 Stephen Wild; 14 Simon Finnigan. Subs (all used): 9 David Faiumu; 8 Eorl Crabtree; 12 Andy Raleigh; 18 Danny Kirmond.
Tries: Moore (29), Lawrence (75), K Brown (77);
Goals: B Hodgson 5/5.
Sin bin: Robinson (49) - delaying restart;
Griffin (61) - fighting.
Rugby Leaguer & League Express Men of the Match:
Warriors: Pat Richards; *Giants:* Brett Hodgson.
Penalty count: 11-6; **Half-time:** 4-10;
Referee: Phil Bentham; **Attendance:** 11,670.

Saturday 28th March 2009

HARLEQUINS 22 HULL FC 12

HARLEQUINS: 2 Jon Wells; 1 Chris Melling; 14 Tony Clubb; 4 David Howell; 27 Jamie O'Callaghan; 6 Luke Dorn; 7 Danny Orr; 10 Louie McCarthy-Scarsbrook; 9 Chad Randall; 17 Danny Ward; 8 Karl Temata; 13 Rob Purdham (C); 18 Joe Mbu. Subs (all used): 16 Gareth Haggerty; 21 Luke Gale; 23 Daniel Heckenberg; 19 Jason Golden.
Tries: Clubb (28), Golden (43), Howell (64);
Goals: Orr 5/5.
HULL: 24 Craig Hall; 2 Mark Calderwood; 17 Graeme Horne; 4 Kirk Yeaman; 21 Tom Briscoe; 6 Richard Horne; 7 Chris Thorman; 8 Ewan Dowes; 9 Shaun Berrigan; 10 Peter Cusack; 16 Willie Manu; 12 Danny Tickle; 11 Lee Radford (C). Subs (all used): 20 Danny Houghton; 23 Tommy Lee; 27 Sam Moa; 19 Paul King.
Tries: Yeaman (32), Hall (48); **Goals:** Tickle 2/3.
Rugby Leaguer & League Express Men of the Match:
Harlequins: Chad Randall; *Hull:* Craig Hall.
Penalty count: 5-4; **Half-time:** 6-6;
Referee: Richard Silverwood; **Attendance:** 3,593.

Sunday 29th March 2009

HULL KINGSTON ROVERS 48 SALFORD CITY REDS 12

ROVERS: 28 Ben Cockayne; 2 Peter Fox; 19 Kris Welham; 4 Jake Webster; 5 Liam Colbon; 21 Chaz l'Anson; 7 Michael Dobson; 8 Nick Fozzard; 15 Daniel Fitzhenry; 24 Rhys Lovegrove; 11 Clint Newton (C); 12 Ben Galea; 13 Scott Murrell. Subs (all used): 9 Ben Fisher; 17 Makali Aizue; 14 Stanley Gene; 16 Jason Netherton.
Tries: Murrell (10), Fox (20, 34, 48), Dobson (42, 65, 72), Welham (55, 79); **Goals:** Dobson 6/9.
CITY REDS: 2 John Wilshere; 24 Dean McGilvray (D); 15 Stuart Littler; 14 Jordan Turner; 5 Paul White; 6 Jeremy Smith; 7 Richard Myler; 8 Ray Cashmere; 9 Malcolm Alker (C); 10 Craig Stapleton; 20 Luke Adamson; 12 Rob Parker; 13 Luke Swain. Subs (all used): 16 Phil Leuluai; 17 Robbie Paul; 23 Adam Sidlow; 18 Lee Jewitt.
Tries: White (2), Adamson (16); **Goals:** Wilshere 2/2.
Rugby Leaguer & League Express Men of the Match:
Rovers: Peter Fox; *City Reds:* Malcolm Alker.
Penalty count: 7-2; **Half-time:** 12-12;
Referee: Steve Ganson; **Attendance:** 8,104.

WARRINGTON WOLVES 27 CELTIC CRUSADERS 22

WOLVES: 19 Chris Riley; 23 Chris Hicks; 2 Paul Johnson; 20 Simon Grix; 4 Matt King; 3 Martin Gleeson; 6 Lee Briers; 8 Adrian Morley (C); 14 Mick Higham; 10 Paul Rauhihi; 11 Louis Anderson; 13 Vinnie Anderson; 24 Ben Harrison. Subs (all used): 15 Paul Wood; 18 Michael Cooper; 25 Chris Bridge; 22 Lee Mitchell.
Tries: Grix (4), Briers (29), King (48), Mitchell (60), Hicks (79); **Goals:** Hicks 3/5; **Field goal:** Briers (77).
CRUSADERS: 1 Tony Duggan; 2 Luke Dyer; 3 Josh Hannay; 4 Mark Dalle Cort; 5 Anthony Blackwood; 6 Damien Quinn; 14 Matty Smith; 8 Ryan O'Hara; 9 Lincoln Withers; 10 Mark Bryant; 19 Jason Chan; 12 Darren Mapp (C); 13 Marshall Chalk. Subs (all used): 23 Neil Budworth; 11 Adam Peek; 15 Peter Lupton; 17 Jordan James.
Tries: Blackwood (19), Withers (22), Hannay (38), Dyer (54); **Goals:** Hannay 3/3, Smith 0/1.
Sin bin: O'Hara (73) - use of the knees.
Rugby Leaguer & League Express Men of the Match:
Wolves: Lee Briers; *Crusaders:* Tony Duggan.
Penalty count: 6-4; **Half-time:** 12-18;
Referee: Ian Smith; **Attendance:** 7,854.

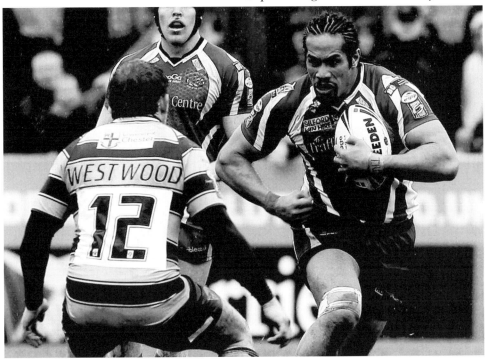

Salford's Phil Leuluai takes on Warrington's Ben Westwood

CASTLEFORD TIGERS 28 BRADFORD BULLS 26

TIGERS: 23 Ryan McGoldrick; 1 Richard Owen; 3 Michael Shenton; 2 Kirk Dixon; 5 Michael Wainwright; 6 Rangi Chase; 7 Brent Sherwin; 8 Mitchell Sargent; 9 Ryan Hudson (C); 10 Craig Huby; 11 Brett Ferres; 13 Joe Westerman; 21 Sione Faumuina. Subs (all used): 16 Chris Feather; 18 Nathan Massey; 19 Kirk Netherton; 25 Dean Widders.
Tries: Shenton (19, 73), Dixon (37, 71), Chase (79); **Goals:** Dixon 4/6.
On report:
Shenton (35) - alleged dangerous tackle on Deacon.
BULLS: 1 Michael Platt; 2 Rikki Sheriffe; 3 Paul Sykes; 4 Chris Nero; 5 Semi Tadulala; 6 Ben Jeffries; 7 Paul Deacon (C); 8 Sam Burgess; 9 Terry Newton; 10 Andy Lynch; 11 Steve Menzies; 12 Glenn Morrison; 13 Jamie Langley. Subs (all used): 20 Dave Halley; 16 Michael Worrincy; 19 Craig Kopczak; 17 Nick Scruton.
Tries: Platt (15), Tadulala (23), Lynch (28), Morrison (42), Halley (68); **Goals:** Deacon 2/4, Sykes 1/2.
Rugby Leaguer & League Express Men of the Match:
Tigers: Michael Shenton; *Bulls:* Michael Platt.
Penalty count: 8-6; **Half-time:** 10-16;
Referee: Gareth Hewer; **Attendance:** 9,185.

ROUND 8

Thursday 9th April 2009

HARLEQUINS 24 CATALANS DRAGONS 28

HARLEQUINS: 1 Chris Melling; 26 Matt Gardner (D); 14 Tony Clubb; 4 David Howell; 5 Will Sharp; 6 Luke Dorn; 21 Luke Gale; 8 Karl Temata; 9 Chad Randall; 23 Daniel Heckenberg; 19 Jason Golden; 11 Luke Williamson; 13 Rob Purdham (C). Subs (all used): 10 Louie McCarthy-Scarsbrook; 16 Gareth Haggerty; 18 Joe Mbu; 15 Ben Kaye.
Tries: Gardner (14), Golden (62), McCarthy-Scarsbrook (75), Melling (80); **Goals:** Purdham 4/4.
DRAGONS: 1 Clint Greenshields; 18 Vincent Duport; 3 Steven Bell; 15 Jean-Phillipe Baile; 5 Dimitri Pelo; 26 Greg Bird (C); 6 Thomas Bosc; 23 Jason Ryles; 9 Casey McGuire; 10 Jerome Guisset; 16 Olivier Elima; 12 Jason Croker; 17 Cyrille Gossard. Subs (all used): 14 Dane Carlaw; 8 David Ferriol; 20 Kane Bentley; 13 Gregory Mounis.
Tries: McGuire (10), Guisset (21, 71), Greenshields (31), Elima (51); **Goals:** Bosc 4/5.
Rugby Leaguer & League Express Men of the Match:
Harlequins: Chad Randall; *Dragons:* Thomas Bosc.
Penalty count: 7-6; **Half-time:** 6-16;
Referee: Thierry Alibert; **Attendance:** 2,540.

WIGAN WARRIORS 12 ST HELENS 19

WARRIORS: 21 Cameron Phelps; 2 Amos Roberts; 22 Martin Gleeson (D); 4 George Carmont; 28 Shaun Ainscough; 25 Sam Tomkins; 7 Thomas Leuluai; 8 Stuart Fielden; 9 Mark Riddell; 15 Andy Coley; 11 Gareth Hock; 12 Phil Bailey; 13 Sean O'Loughlin (C). Subs (all used): 10 Iafeta Palea'aesina; 16 Harrison Hansen; 17 Michael McIlorum; 19 Paul Prescott.
Tries: Ainscough (8, 52); **Goals:** Roberts 2/3.
SAINTS: 1 Paul Wellens; 2 Ade Gardner; 3 Matt Gidley; 11 Lee Gilmour; 5 Francis Meli; 12 Jon Wilkin; 6 Leon Pryce; 10 James Graham; 9 Keiron Cunningham (C); 15 Bryn Hargreaves; 16 Tony Puletua; 28 Matty Ashurst; 17 Paul Clough. Subs (all used): 23 Maurie Fa'asavalu; 14 James Roby; 20 Gareth Frodsham; 18 Kyle Eastmond.
Tries: Cunningham (12), Gidley (59), Pryce (62); **Goals:** Wellens 1/1, Eastmond 2/2.
Field goal: Eastmond (79).
Rugby Leaguer & League Express Men of the Match:
Warriors: Thomas Leuluai; *Saints:* Kyle Eastmond.
Penalty count: 5-4; **Half-time:** 6-6;
Referee: Ben Thaler; **Attendance:** 22,232.

Friday 10th April 2009

HULL FC 14 HULL KINGSTON ROVERS 18

HULL: 24 Craig Hall; 2 Mark Calderwood; 17 Graeme Horne; 4 Kirk Yeaman; 21 Tom Briscoe; 6 Richard Horne; 7 Chris Thorman; 8 Ewan Dowes; 9 Shaun Berrigan, 18 Jamie Thackray; 16 Willie Manu; 12 Danny Tickle; 11 Lee Radford (C). Subs (all used): 10 Peter Cusack; 23 Tommy Lee; 14 Richard Whiting; 19 Paul King.
Tries: Briscoe (19), Berrigan (53), Whiting (65);
Goals: Tickle 1/3.
ROVERS: 1 Shaun Briscoe (C); 2 Peter Fox; 19 Kris Welham; 4 Jake Webster; 5 Liam Colbon; 6 Paul Cooke; 7 Michael Dobson; 8 Nick Fozzard; 13 Scott Murrell; 18 Scott Wheeldon; 16 Jason Netherton; 11 Clint Newton; 12 Ben Galea. Subs (all used): 15 Daniel Fitzhenry; 17 Makali Aizue; 14 Stanley Gene; 24 Rhys Lovegrove.
Tries: Webster (1), Cooke (26), Fox (44);
Goals: Dobson 3/3.
Rugby Leaguer & League Express Men of the Match:
Hull: Shaun Berrigan; *Rovers:* Michael Dobson.
Penalty count: 4-1; **Half-time:** 4-12;
Referee: Steve Ganson; **Attendance:** 22,337.

SALFORD CITY REDS 18 WARRINGTON WOLVES 16

CITY REDS: 2 John Wilshere; 19 Stefan Ratchford; 15 Stuart Littler; 14 Jordan Turner; 24 Dean McGilvray; 6 Jeremy Smith; 7 Richard Myler; 8 Ray Cashmere; 9 Malcolm Alker (C); 10 Craig Stapleton; 20 Luke Adamson; 12 Rob Parker; 13 Luke Swain. Subs (all used): 16 Phil

Leuluai; 18 Lee Jewitt; 11 Ian Sibbit; 17 Robbie Paul.
Tries: Myler (21, 28), Adamson (76); **Goals:** Wilshere 3/3.
WOLVES: 23 Chris Hicks; 2 Paul Johnson; 13 Vinnie Anderson; 20 Simon Grix; 4 Matt King; 25 Chris Bridge; 7 Michael Monaghan; 8 Adrian Morley (C); 14 Mick Higham; 16 Garreth Carvell; 11 Louis Anderson; 12 Ben Westwood; 24 Ben Harrison. Subs (all used): 15 Paul Wood; 10 Paul Rauhihi; 22 Lee Mitchell; 9 Jon Clarke.
Tries: Johnson (6, 50), Westwood (79); **Goals:** Hicks 2/3.
Rugby Leaguer & League Express Men of the Match:
City Reds: Richard Myler; *Wolves:* Ben Westwood.
Penalty count: 7-5; **Half-time:** 12-6;
Referee: Jamie Leahy; **Attendance:** 6,150.

CASTLEFORD TIGERS 6 WAKEFIELD TRINITY WILDCATS 35

TIGERS: 1 Richard Owen; 5 Michael Wainwright; 3 Michael Shenton; 4 James Evans; 2 Kirk Dixon; 6 Rangi Chase; 7 Brent Sherwin; 8 Mitchell Sargent; 9 Ryan Hudson (C); 18 Nathan Massey; 10 Craig Huby; 21 Sione Faumuina; 13 Joe Westerman. Subs (all used): 15 Liam Higgins; 16 Chris Feather; 19 Kirk Netherton; 25 Dean Widders.
Try: Westerman (57); **Goals:** Dixon 1/2.
WILDCATS: 1 Matt Blaymire; 2 Damien Blanch; 19 Sean Gleeson; 4 Ryan Atkins; 27 Aaron Murphy; 3 Tony Martin; 7 Danny Brough; 12 Oliver Wilkes; 14 Sam Obst; 11 Steve Snitch; 29 Jay Pitts; 24 Dale Ferguson; 8 Jason Demetriou (C). Subs (all used): 28 Kyle Bibb; 17 Kevin Henderson; 9 Brad Drew; 10 Danny Sculthorpe.
Tries: Martin (29), Atkins (51, 78), Blaymire (60), Gleeson (71); **Goals:** Brough 4/5, Martin 3/3.
Field goal: Brough (76).
Rugby Leaguer & League Express Men of the Match:
Tigers: Rangi Chase; *Wildcats:* Danny Brough.
Penalty count: 6-12; **Half-time:** 0-8;
Referee: Phil Bentham; **Attendance:** 10,155.

HUDDERSFIELD GIANTS 30 CELTIC CRUSADERS 10

GIANTS: 1 Brett Hodgson (C); 2 Martin Aspinwall; 19 Michael Lawrence; 4 Paul Whatuira; 5 David Hodgson; 3 Kevin Brown; 7 Luke Robinson; 8 Eorl Crabtree; 20 Scott Moore; 15 Paul Jackson; 12 Andy Raleigh; 18 Danny Kirmond; 14 Simon Finnigan. Subs (all used): 9 Liam Fulton (D); 9 David Faiumu; 10 Darrell Griffin; 11 Jamahl Lolesi.
Tries: D Hodgson (8, 25), Fulton (48), K Brown (66), Lawrence (80); **Goals:** B Hodgson 5/5.
CRUSADERS: 5 Anthony Blackwood; 2 Luke Dyer; 3 Josh Hannay; 4 Mark Dalle Cort; 24 Aled James; 6 Damien Quinn (C); 9 Lincoln Withers; 8 Ryan O'Hara; 23 Neil Budworth; 17 Jordan James; 21 Chris Beasley; 15 Peter Lupton; 13 Marshall Chalk. Subs (all used): 16 Ben Flower; 11 Adam Peek; 20 David Tangata-Toa; 19 Jason Chan.

213

Hull's Willie Manu and Ewan Dowes close down St Helens' James Graham

Tries: Peek (44), Blackwood (60); **Goals:** Hannay 1/2.
Rugby Leaguer & League Express Men of the Match:
Giants: Brett Hodgson; *Crusaders:* Luke Dyer.
Penalty count: 4-5; **Half-time:** 12-0;
Referee: Richard Silverwood; **Attendance:** 6,407.

BRADFORD BULLS 10 LEEDS RHINOS 6

BULLS: 20 Dave Halley; 2 Rikki Sheriffe; 3 Paul Sykes; 4 Chris Nero; 5 Semi Tadulala; 11 Steve Menzies; 6 Ben Jeffries; 10 Andy Lynch (C); 7 Terry Newton; 19 Craig Kopczak; 13 Jamie Langley; 15 Matt Cook; 8 Sam Burgess. Subs: 17 Nick Scruton; 1 Michael Platt (not used); 23 Jason Crookes; 16 Michael Worrincy.
Tries: Worrincy (34), Sheriffe (68); **Goals:** Sykes 1/4.
RHINOS: 1 Brent Webb; 23 Kallum Watkins; 18 Carl Ablett; 4 Keith Senior; 5 Ryan Hall; 6 Danny McGuire; 7 Rob Burrow; 8 Kylie Leuluai; 14 Matt Diskin; 10 Jamie Peacock; 11 Jamie Jones-Buchanan; 17 Ian Kirke; 13 Kevin Sinfield (C). Subs (all used): 19 Luke Burgess; 9 Danny Buderus; 12 Ali Lauititi; 16 Ryan Bailey.
Try: Jones-Buchanan (21); **Goals:** Sinfield 1/1.
Sin bin: Ablett (66) - professional foul.
Rugby Leaguer & League Express Men of the Match:
Bulls: Dave Halley; *Rhinos:* Rob Burrow.
Penalty count: 12-6; **Half-time:** 6-6;
Referee: Ian Smith; **Attendance:** 14,554.

ROUND 9

Monday 13th April 2009

HULL KINGSTON ROVERS 8
HUDDERSFIELD GIANTS 30

ROVERS: 1 Shaun Briscoe (C); 2 Peter Fox; 19 Kris Welham; 4 Jake Webster; 5 Liam Colbon; 6 Paul Cooke; 7 Michael Dobson; 8 Nick Fozzard; 9 Ben Fisher; 18 Scott Wheeldon; 11 Clint Newton; 12 Ben Galea; 13 Scott Murrell. Subs (all used): 16 Jason Netherton; 24 Rhys Lovegrove; 15 Daniel Fitzhenry; 23 Ryan Esders.
Tries: Welham (2), Colbon (19); **Goals:** Dobson 0/2.
GIANTS: 1 Brett Hodgson (C); 21 Leroy Cudjoe; 19 Michael Lawrence; 11 Jamahl Lolesi; 5 David Hodgson; 6 Liam Fulton; 7 Luke Robinson; 16 Keith Mason; 24 Shaun Lunt; 15 Paul Jackson; 30 Larne Patrick; 13 Stephen Wild; 14 Simon Finnigan. Subs (all used): 8 Eorl Crabtree; 9 David Faiumu; 10 Darrell Griffin; 12 Andy Raleigh.
Tries: Lawrence (22, 80), D Hodgson (29), Lunt (52), Wild (63); **Goals:** B Hodgson 5/6.
Rugby Leaguer & League Express Men of the Match:
Rovers: Kris Welham; *Giants:* Brett Hodgson.
Penalty count: 5-5; **Half-time:** 8-10;
Referee: Ben Thaler; **Attendance:** 8,731.

CELTIC CRUSADERS 18 HARLEQUINS 40

CRUSADERS: 5 Anthony Blackwood; 2 Luke Dyer; 3 Josh Hannay; 4 Mark Dalle Cort; 24 Aled James; 6 Damien Quinn; 7 Jace Van Dijk (C); 8 Ryan O'Hara; 23 Neil Budworth; 10 Mark Bryant; 19 Jason Chan; 12 Darren Mapp; 13 Marshall Chalk. Subs (all used): 11 Adam Peek; 15 Peter Lupton; 20 David Tangata-Toa; 21 Chris Beasley.
Tries: Peek (27), Chalk (64), Dalle Cort (76);
Goals: Hannay 3/3.
HARLEQUINS: 1 Chris Melling; 26 Matt Gardner; 14 Tony Clubb; 4 David Howell; 5 Will Sharp; 6 Luke Dorn; 7 Danny Orr; 8 Karl Temata; 9 Chad Randall; 17 Danny Ward; 12 Chad Robinson; 11 Luke Williamson; 13 Rob Purdham (C). Subs (all used): 10 Louie McCarthy-Scarsbrook; 21 Luke Gale; 23 Daniel Heckenberg; 19 Jason Golden.
Tries: Clubb (14), Howell (18), Orr (27, 50), Melling (46), Dorn (68, 80); **Goals:** Purdham 5/5, Orr 1/2.
Rugby Leaguer & League Express Men of the Match:
Crusaders: Marshall Chalk; *Harlequins:* Danny Orr.
Penalty count: 5-4; **Half-time:** 6-18;
Referee: Ian Smith; **Attendance:** 3,009.

LEEDS RHINOS 20 SALFORD CITY REDS 30

RHINOS: 1 Brent Webb; 24 Ben Jones-Bishop; 18 Carl Ablett; 4 Keith Senior; 5 Ryan Hall; 6 Danny McGuire; 7 Rob Burrow; 19 Luke Burgess; 14 Matt Diskin; 16 Ryan Bailey; 11 Jamie Jones-Buchanan; 17 Ian Kirke; 13 Kevin Sinfield (C). Subs (all used): 10 Jamie Peacock; 8 Kylie Leuluai; 9 Danny Buderus; 12 Ali Lauititi.
Tries: Jones-Buchanan (30), Hall (53), Senior (66), Peacock (73); **Goals:** Sinfield 2/4.
CITY REDS: 2 John Wilshere; 3 Mark Henry; 15 Stuart Littler; 14 Jordan Turner; 19 Stefan Ratchford; 6 Jeremy Smith; 7 Richard Myler; 8 Ray Cashmere; 9 Malcolm Alker (C); 10 Craig Stapleton; 20 Luke Adamson; 12 Rob Parker; 13 Luke Swain. Subs (all used): 18 Lee Jewitt; 16 Phil Leuluai; 17 Robbie Paul; 11 Ian Sibbit.
Tries: Wilshere (6), Henry (14), Myler (39), Paul (49), Turner (76); **Goals:** Wilshere 5/6.
Rugby Leaguer & League Express Men of the Match:
Rhinos: Jamie Peacock; *City Reds:* Richard Myler.
Penalty count: 8-8; **Half-time:** 6-16;
Referee: James Child; **Attendance:** 14,381.

ST HELENS 44 HULL FC 22

SAINTS: 1 Paul Wellens; 2 Ade Gardner; 3 Matt Gidley; 19 Chris Dean; 5 Francis Meli; 6 Leon Pryce; 7 Sean Long; 10 James Graham; 9 Keiron Cunningham (C); 16 Tony Puletua; 11 Lee Gilmour; 12 Jon Wilkin; 17 Paul Clough. Subs (all used): 14 James Roby; 15 Bryn

Hargreaves; 18 Kyle Eastmond; 23 Maurie Fa'asavalu.
Tries: Puletua (8), Gilmour (11), Wilkin (19), Wellens (39), Pryce (41), Eastmond (55, 70), Dean (57), Gardner (67); **Goals:** Long 3/7, Eastmond 1/2.
HULL: 14 Richard Whiting; 2 Mark Calderwood; 15 Danny Washbrook; 4 Kirk Yeaman; 17 Graeme Horne; 6 Richard Horne; 7 Chris Thorman; 8 Ewan Dowes; 20 Danny Houghton; 18 Jamie Thackray; 16 Willie Manu; 12 Danny Tickle; 11 Lee Radford (C). Subs (all used): 9 Shaun Berrigan; 19 Paul King; 23 Tommy Lee; 25 Dominic Maloney (D).
Tries: G Horne (32, 74), Manu (50), Calderwood (64); **Goals:** Tickle 3/4.
Rugby Leaguer & League Express Men of the Match:
Saints: Leon Pryce; *Hull:* Graeme Horne.
Penalty count: 4-4; **Half-time:** 22-6;
Referee: Thierry Alibert; **Attendance:** 13,684.

WARRINGTON WOLVES 6 CASTLEFORD TIGERS 28

WOLVES: 23 Chris Hicks; 2 Paul Johnson; 20 Simon Grix; 4 Matt King; 5 Kevin Penny; 25 Chris Bridge; 7 Michael Monaghan; 8 Adrian Morley (C); 14 Mick Higham; 16 Garreth Carvell; 11 Louis Anderson; 12 Ben Westwood; 24 Ben Harrison. Subs (all used): 9 Jon Clarke; 10 Paul Rauhihi; 15 Paul Wood; 21 Matty Blythe.
Try: Bridge (60); **Goals:** Hicks 1/1.
TIGERS: 1 Richard Owen; 2 Kirk Dixon; 4 James Evans; 3 Michael Shenton; 5 Michael Wainwright; 6 Rangi Chase; 7 Brent Sherwin; 8 Mitchell Sargent; 9 Ryan Hudson (C); 15 Liam Higgins; 11 Brett Ferres; 21 Sione Faumuina; 13 Joe Westerman. Subs (all used): 10 Craig Huby; 16 Chris Feather; 19 James Ford.
Tries: Ferres (32), Wainwright (51), Chase (57, 76), Shenton (72); **Goals:** Dixon 4/5.
Rugby Leaguer & League Express Men of the Match:
Wolves: Ben Harrison; *Tigers:* Mitchell Sargent.
Penalty count: 2-1; **Half-time:** 0-6;
Referee: Steve Ganson; **Attendance:** 8,202.

WAKEFIELD TRINITY WILDCATS 24
BRADFORD BULLS 22

WILDCATS: 1 Matt Blaymire; 2 Damien Blanch; 19 Sean Gleeson; 4 Ryan Atkins; 27 Aaron Murphy; 3 Tony Martin; 7 Danny Brough; 12 Oliver Wilkes; 9 Brad Drew; 11 Steve Snitch; 29 Jay Pitts; 24 Dale Ferguson; 8 Jason Demetriou (C). Subs (all used): 28 Kyle Bibb; 17 Kevin Henderson; 20 Tevita Leo-Latu; 25 Richard Moore.
Tries: Blanch (9), Brough (27), Atkins (37), Snitch (52); **Goals:** Brough 4/4.
BULLS: 20 Dave Halley; 2 Rikki Sheriffe; 3 Paul Sykes; 23 Jason Crookes; 5 Semi Tadulala; 11 Steve Menzies; 6 Ben Jeffries; 10 Andy Lynch (C); 9 Terry Newton; 19 Craig Kopczak; 13 Jamie Langley; 15 Matt Cook; 8 Sam Burgess. Subs (all used): 1 Michael Platt; 16 Michael

Worrincy; 26 David Solomona; 17 Nick Scruton.
Tries: Menzies (6, 21), Worrincy (56), Platt (76);
Goals: Sykes 3/4.
Rugby Leaguer & League Express Men of the Match:
Wildcats: Danny Brough; *Bulls:* Terry Newton.
Penalty count: 8-6; **Half-time:** 18-10;
Referee: Richard Silverwood; **Attendance:** 6,516.

CATALANS DRAGONS 40 WIGAN WARRIORS 24

DRAGONS: 1 Clint Greenshields; 18 Vincent Duport; 3 Steven Bell; 15 Jean-Phillipe Baile; 5 Dimitri Pelo; 26 Greg Bird (C); 6 Thomas Bosc; 23 Jason Ryles; 9 Casey McGuire; 10 Jerome Guisset; 16 Olivier Elima; 12 Jason Croker; 14 Dane Carlaw. Subs (all used): 24 Remi Casty; 8 David Ferriol; 20 Kane Bentley; 13 Gregory Mounis.
Tries: Pelo (2), Bird (23), Mounis (30), Ryles (37, 72), Greenshields (54, 68); **Goals:** Bosc 6/7.
WARRIORS: 5 Pat Richards; 2 Amos Roberts; 22 Martin Gleeson; 20 Karl Pryce; 28 Shaun Ainscough; 25 Sam Tomkins; 7 Thomas Leuluai; 8 Stuart Fielden; 9 Mark Riddell; 15 Andy Coley; 16 Harrison Hansen; 12 Phil Bailey; 13 Sean O'Loughlin (C). Subs (all used): 10 Iafeta Palea'aesina; 14 Joel Tomkins; 17 Michael Mcllorum; 19 Paul Prescott.
Tries: Roberts (6), Ainscough (10), Gleeson (20), S Tomkins (75), Richards (79); **Goals:** Richards 2/5.
Rugby Leaguer & League Express Men of the Match:
Dragons: David Ferriol; *Warriors:* Thomas Leuluai.
Penalty count: 5-3; **Half-time:** 22-14;
Referee: Phil Bentham; **Attendance:** 9,490.

ROUND 10

Friday 17th April 2009

BRADFORD BULLS 22 WARRINGTON WOLVES 58

BULLS: 20 Dave Halley; 2 Rikki Sheriffe; 3 Paul Sykes; 1 Michael Platt; 5 Semi Tadulala; 11 Steve Menzies; 6 Ben Jeffries; 10 Andy Lynch (C); 9 Terry Newton; 19 Craig Kopczak; 13 Jamie Langley; 15 Matt Cook; 8 Sam Burgess. Subs (all used): 17 Nick Scruton; 29 Tom Olbison (D); 26 David Solomona; 16 Michael Worrincy.
Tries: Solomona (25, 44), Platt (39), Jeffries (72);
Goals: Sykes 3/4.
WOLVES: 19 Chris Riley; 23 Chris Hicks; 25 Chris Bridge; 4 Matt King; 2 Paul Johnson; 6 Lee Briers; 7 Michael Monaghan; 8 Adrian Morley (C); 9 Jon Clarke; 16 Garreth Carvell; 11 Louis Anderson; 12 Ben Westwood; 24 Ben Harrison. Subs (all used): 14 Mick Higham; 15 Paul Wood; 13 Vinnie Anderson; 18 Michael Cooper.
Tries: L Anderson (5), Hicks (11, 15, 61), King (19), Riley (32), Johnson (35), Higham (41, 65), Briers (52);
Goals: Hicks 9/10.
Rugby Leaguer & League Express Men of the Match:
Bulls: David Solomona; *Wolves:* Lee Briers.
Penalty count: 4-4; **Half-time:** 10-34;
Referee: Thierry Alibert; **Attendance:** 8,643.

HULL FC 14 WAKEFIELD TRINITY WILDCATS 21

HULL: 24 Craig Hall; 2 Mark Calderwood; 17 Graeme Horne; 4 Kirk Yeaman; 29 Jodie Broughton (D2); 15 Danny Washbrook; 7 Chris Thorman; 8 Ewan Dowes; 23 Tommy Lee; 18 Jamie Thackray; 16 Willie Manu; 12 Danny Tickle; 11 Lee Radford (C). Subs (all used): 9 Shaun Berrigan; 22 Mike Burnett; 14 Richard Whiting; 25 Dominic Maloney.
Tries: Calderwood (10), Burnett (34); **Goals:** Tickle 3/3.
WILDCATS: 1 Matt Blaymire; 2 Damien Blanch; 19 Sean Gleeson; 27 Aaron Murphy; 13 Scott Grix; 3 Tony Martin; 7 Danny Brough; 12 Oliver Wilkes; 9 Brad Drew; 11 Steve Snitch; 29 Jay Pitts; 24 Dale Ferguson; 8 Jason Demetriou (C). Subs (all used): 28 Kyle Bibb; 17 Kevin Henderson; 20 Tevita Leo-Latu; 25 Richard Moore.
Tries: Demetriou (23), Grix (28), Pitts (59), Wilkes (72);
Goals: Brough 2/4; **Field goal:** Brough (67).
Rugby Leaguer & League Express Men of the Match:
Hull: Danny Washbrook; *Wildcats:* Brad Drew.
Penalty count: 6-3; **Half-time:** 12-8;
Referee: Gareth Hewer; **Attendance:** 11,975.

Saturday 18th April 2009

CATALANS DRAGONS 38 SALFORD CITY REDS 6

DRAGONS: 1 Clint Greenshields; 18 Vincent Duport; 3 Steven Bell; 15 Jean-Phillipe Baile; 5 Dimitri Pelo; 26 Greg Bird (C); 6 Thomas Bosc; 23 Jason Ryles; 9 Casey McGuire; 10 Jerome Guisset; 13 Gregory Mounis; 16 Olivier Elima; 14 Dale Carlaw. Subs (all used): 8 David Ferriol; 17 Cyrille Gossard; 20 Kane Bentley; 24 Remi Casty.
Tries: Pelo (17, 35), Casty (28), Baile (56, 59), Guisset (68), Bentley (73), Bell (77); **Goals:** Bosc 1/4, Bird 2/4.
CITY REDS: 2 John Wilshere; 29 Darrell Goulding (D); 15 Stuart Littler; 14 Jordan Turner; 19 Stefan Ratchford; 6 Jeremy Smith; 7 Richard Myler; 8 Ray Cashmere; 9 Malcolm Alker (C); 10 Craig Stapleton; 20 Luke Adamson; 12 Rob Parker; 13 Luke Swain. Subs (all used): 11 Ian Sibbit; 16 Phil Leuluai; 17 Robbie Paul; 18 Lee Jewitt.
Try: Ratchford (12); **Goals:** Wilshere 1/1.
On report:
Cashmere (59) - alleged late challenge on Bosc.
Rugby Leaguer & League Express Men of the Match:
Dragons: Greg Bird; *City Reds:* Luke Swain.
Penalty count: 9-4; **Half-time:** 14-6;
Referee: Ben Thaler; **Attendance:** 8,327.

HUDDERSFIELD GIANTS 6 LEEDS RHINOS 34

GIANTS: 1 Brett Hodgson (C); 21 Leroy Cudjoe; 4 Paul Whatuira; 19 Michael Lawrence; 5 David Hodgson; 3 Kevin Brown; 7 Luke Robinson; 16 Keith Mason; 20 Scott Moore; 15 Paul Jackson; 13 Stephen Wild; 18 Danny Kirmond; 14 Simon Finnigan. Subs (all used): 8 Eorl Crabtree; 10 Darrell Griffin; 11 Jamahl Lolesi; 9 David Faiumu.
Try: Lawrence (45); **Goals:** B Hodgson 1/1.
RHINOS: 1 Brent Webb; 2 Scott Donald; 20 Ashley Gibson; 4 Keith Senior; 5 Ryan Hall; 6 Danny McGuire; 7 Rob Burrow; 17 Ian Kirke; 14 Matt Diskin; 10 Jamie Peacock; 11 Jamie Jones-Buchanan; 18 Carl Ablett; 13 Kevin Sinfield (C). Subs (all used): 9 Danny Buderus; 16 Ryan Bailey; 19 Luke Burgess; 12 Ali Lauitiiti.
Tries: Webb (2, 41), Hall (37), McGuire (40), Diskin (70); **Goals:** Sinfield 7/7.
Rugby Leaguer & League Express Men of the Match:
Giants: Eorl Crabtree; *Rhinos:* Kevin Sinfield.
Penalty count: 8-7; **Half-time:** 0-22;
Referee: Richard Silverwood; **Attendance:** 11,593.

Sunday 19th April 2009

HARLEQUINS 12 HULL KINGSTON ROVERS 32

HARLEQUINS: 1 Chris Melling; 26 Matt Gardner; 3 Matt Gafa; 4 David Howell; 5 Will Sharp; 6 Luke Dorn; 7 Danny Orr; 8 Karl Temata; 9 Chad Randall; 17 Danny Ward; 12 Chad Robinson; 11 Luke Williamson; 13 Rob Purdham (C). Subs (all used): 10 Louie McCarthy-Scarsbrook; 19 Jason Golden; 23 Daniel Heckenberg; 21 Luke Gale.
Tries: Gardner (11), Robinson (20); **Goals:** Purdham 2/2.
ROVERS: 15 Daniel Fitzhenry; 2 Peter Fox; 4 Jake Webster; 19 Kris Welham; 5 Liam Colbon; 6 Paul Cooke; 7 Michael Dobson; 11 Clint Newton; 9 Ben Fisher; 18 Scott Wheeldon; 14 Stanley Gene; 12 Ben Galea; 13 Scott Murrell. Subs (all used): 16 Jason Netherton; 21 Chaz I'Anson; 17 Makali Aizue; 20 Michael Vella (C).
Tries: Welham (16), Fox (27), Cooke (46), Colbon (49), Galea (63, 70); **Goals:** Dobson 4/6.
Rugby Leaguer & League Express Men of the Match:
Harlequins: Danny Orr; *Rovers:* Paul Cooke.
Penalty count: 4-3; **Half-time:** 12-8;
Referee: Phil Bentham; **Attendance:** 3,492.

WIGAN WARRIORS 44 CELTIC CRUSADERS 10

WARRIORS: 21 Cameron Phelps; 2 Amos Roberts; 22 Martin Gleeson; 4 George Carmont; 5 Pat Richards; 6 Tim Smith; 7 Thomas Leuluai; 8 Stuart Fielden; 9 Mark Riddell; 15 Andy Coley; 11 Gareth Hock; 12 Phil Bailey; 13 Sean O'Loughlin (C). Subs (all used): 10 Iafeta Palea'aesina; 14 Joel Tomkins; 19 Paul Prescott; 25 Sam Tomkins.
Tries: Richards (5, 69), O'Loughlin (12, 58), Riddell (18), Roberts (35), S Tomkins (44, 77), Carmont (51); **Goals:** Richards 2/5, Roberts 2/4.
CRUSADERS: 13 Marshall Chalk; 2 Luke Dyer; 3 Josh Hannay; 4 Mark Dalle Cort; 5 Anthony Blackwood; 6 Damien Quinn; 7 Jace Van Dijk (C); 8 Ryan O'Hara; 9 Lincoln Withers; 20 David Tangata-Toa; 11 Adam Peek; 12 Darren Mapp; 15 Peter Lupton. Subs (all used): 23 Neil Budworth; 10 Mark Bryant; 19 Jason Chan; 24 Aled James.
Tries: Dyer (3), Dalle Cort (72);
Goals: Hannay 0/1, Van Dijk 1/1.
Sin bin: Quinn (68) - dissent;
Chalk (78) - delaying restart.
Rugby Leaguer & League Express Men of the Match:
Warriors: Cameron Phelps; *Crusaders:* Marshall Chalk.
Penalty count: 9-4; **Half-time:** 20-4;
Referee: Steve Ganson; **Attendance:** 12,371.

CASTLEFORD TIGERS 22 ST HELENS 68

TIGERS: 23 Ryan McGoldrick; 1 Richard Owen; 2 Kirk Dixon; 3 Michael Shenton; 5 Michael Wainwright; 6 Rangi Chase; 7 Brent Sherwin (C); 8 Mitchell Sargent; 19 Kirk Netherton; 15 Liam Higgins; 10 Craig Huby; 21 Sione Faumuina; 13 Joe Westerman. Subs (all used): 12 Ryan Clayton; 17 Ryan Boyle; 18 Nathan Massey; 20 James Ford.
Tries: Shenton (37), Sargent (45), Dixon (55), Faumuina (66); **Goals:** Dixon 3/4.
On report: Alleged biting incident (57) on Pryce.
SAINTS: 1 Paul Wellens; 2 Ade Gardner; 3 Matt Gidley; 19 Chris Dean; 5 Francis Meli; 6 Leon Pryce; 7 Sean Long; 10 James Graham; 9 Keiron Cunningham (C); 16 Tony Puletua; 11 Lee Gilmour; 12 Jon Wilkin; 17 Paul Clough. Subs (all used): 23 Maurie Fa'asavalu; 14 James Roby; 15 Bryn Hargreaves; 28 Matty Ashurst.
Tries: Puletua (2, 12, 15, 59), Pryce (4, 74), Gardner (18), Wilkin (23, 31, 69), Hargreaves (48), Fa'asavalu (72); **Goals:** Long 10/12.
Rugby Leaguer & League Express Men of the Match:
Tigers: Ryan McGoldrick; *Saints:* James Graham.
Penalty count: 9-7; **Half-time:** 6-38;
Referee: Ian Smith; **Attendance:** 8,003.

ROUND 11

Friday 24th April 2009

LEEDS RHINOS 4 HARLEQUINS 21

RHINOS: 1 Brent Webb; 2 Scott Donald; 23 Kallum Watkins; 4 Keith Senior; 5 Ryan Hall; 6 Danny McGuire; 7 Rob Burrow; 8 Kylie Leuluai; 14 Matt Diskin; 10 Jamie Peacock; 11 Jamie Jones-Buchanan; 17 Ian Kirke; 13 Kevin Sinfield (C). Subs (all used): 16 Ryan Bailey; 9 Danny Buderus; 18 Carl Ablett; 12 Ali Lauitiiti.
Try: Burrow (79); **Goals:** Sinfield 0/1.
HARLEQUINS: 1 Chris Melling; 26 Matt Gardner; 3 Matt Gafa; 4 David Howell; 5 Will Sharp; 13 Rob Purdham (C); 6 Luke Dorn; 8 Karl Temata; 9 Chad Randall; 17 Danny Ward; 11 Luke Williamson; 12 Chad Robinson; 19 Jason Golden. Subs (all used): 10 Louie McCarthy-Scarsbrook; 16 Gareth Haggerty; 15 Ben Kaye; 14 Tony Clubb.
Tries: Howell (8, 75), Randall (13); **Goals:** Purdham 4/5;
Field goal: Purdham (73).
Rugby Leaguer & League Express Men of the Match:
Rhinos: Danny Buderus; *Harlequins:* Chad Randall.
Penalty count: 7-6; **Half-time:** 0-10;
Referee: Steve Ganson; **Attendance:** 13,912.

ST HELENS 30 BRADFORD BULLS 34

SAINTS: 1 Paul Wellens; 2 Ade Gardner; 19 Chris Dean; 11 Lee Gilmour; 5 Francis Meli; 6 Leon Pryce; 7 Sean Long; 10 James Graham; 9 Keiron Cunningham (C); 15 Bryn Hargreaves; 12 Jon Wilkin; 13 Chris Flannery; 17 Paul Clough. Subs (all used): 14 James Roby; 21 Gary Wheeler; 23 Maurie Fa'asavalu; 28 Matty Ashurst.
Tries: Gardner (28), Meli (31, 39), Pryce (34), Wheeler (37), Long (53); **Goals:** Long 3/6.
BULLS: 20 Dave Halley; 2 Rikki Sheriffe; 11 Steve Menzies; 1 Michael Platt; 5 Semi Tadulala; 3 Paul Sykes; 6 Ben Jeffries; 10 Andy Lynch (C); 9 Terry Newton; 17 Nick Scruton; 26 David Solomona; 8 Sam Burgess; 13 Jamie Langley. Subs (all used): 15 Matt Cook; 16 Michael Worrincy; 19 Craig Kopczak; 24 Julien Rinaldi (D).
Tries: Tadulala (2, 11), Kopczak (50), Burgess (63), Worrincy (65, 69); **Goals:** Sykes 5/6.
Rugby Leaguer & League Express Men of the Match:
Saints: Gary Wheeler; *Bulls:* Semi Tadulala.
Penalty count: 7-6; **Half-time:** 26-10;
Referee: Richard Silverwood; **Attendance:** 11,039.

Saturday 25th April 2009

SALFORD CITY REDS 14 HULL FC 18

CITY REDS: 2 John Wilshere; 19 Stefan Ratchford; 15 Stuart Littler; 14 Jordan Turner; 29 Darrell Goulding; 6 Jeremy Smith; 7 Richard Myler; 8 Ray Cashmere; 9 Malcolm Alker (C); 10 Craig Stapleton; 20 Luke Adamson; 12 Rob Parker; 13 Luke Swain. Subs (all used): 16 Phil Leuluai; 18 Lee Jewitt; 23 Adam Sidlow; 17 Robbie Paul.
Tries: Goulding (4, 50), Myler (6); **Goals:** Wilshere 1/4.
HULL: 6 Richard Horne; 2 Mark Calderwood; 14 Richard Whiting; 4 Kirk Yeaman; 17 Graeme Horne; 15 Danny Washbrook; 7 Chris Thorman; 8 Ewan Dowes; 23 Tommy Lee; 18 Jamie Thackray; 16 Willie Manu; 12 Danny Tickle; 11 Lee Radford (C). Subs (all used): 20 Danny Houghton; 22 Mike Burnett; 25 Dominic Maloney; 10 Peter Cusack.
Tries: Calderwood (11), R Horne (27), Whiting (30);
Goals: Tickle 3/4.
Rugby Leaguer & League Express Men of the Match:
City Reds: Darrell Goulding; *Hull:* Chris Thorman.
Penalty count: 7-9; **Half-time:** 10-16;
Referee: Jamie Leahy; **Attendance:** 4,165.

Sunday 26th April 2009

CELTIC CRUSADERS 22 CASTLEFORD TIGERS 34

CRUSADERS: 13 Marshall Chalk; 2 Luke Dyer; 3 Josh Hannay; 4 Mark Dalle Cort; 27 Paul Ballard; 6 Damien Quinn; 7 Jace Van Dijk (C); 8 Ryan O'Hara; 9 Lincoln Withers; 19 Jason Chan; 11 Adam Peek; 15 Peter Lupton; 21 Chris Beasley. Subs (all used): 10 Mark Bryant; 23 Neil Budworth; 24 Aled James; 20 David Tangata-Toa.
Tries: Quinn (12), Peek (14), Tangata-Toa (39), O'Hara (49); **Goals:** Quinn 3/4.
TIGERS: 1 Richard Owen; 2 Kirk Dixon; 4 James Evans; 3 Michael Shenton; 5 Michael Wainwright; 6 Rangi Chase; 7 Brent Sherwin (C); 8 Mitchell Sargent; 19 Kirk Netherton; 15 Liam Higgins; 14 Stuart Jones; 21 Sione Faumuina; 23 Ryan McGoldrick. Subs (all used): 11 Brett Ferres; 16 Chris Feather; 17 Ryan Boyle; 20 James Ford.
Tries: Boyle (26), Evans (38), Dixon (55), Wainwright (70), Shenton (78), Sherwin (79); **Goals:** Dixon 5/6.
Rugby Leaguer & League Express Men of the Match:
Crusaders: Ryan O'Hara; *Tigers:* Brent Sherwin.
Penalty count: 9-12; **Half-time:** 16-12;
Referee: Thierry Alibert; **Attendance:** 2,017.

HULL KINGSTON ROVERS 44 CATALANS DRAGONS 10

ROVERS: 1 Shaun Briscoe; 2 Peter Fox; 4 Jake Webster; 19 Kris Welham; 5 Liam Colbon; 6 Paul Cooke; 7 Michael Dobson; 18 Scott Wheeldon; 9 Ben Fisher; 20 Michael Vella (C); 11 Clint Newton; 12 Ben Galea; 13 Scott Murrell. Subs (all used): 15 Daniel Fitzhenry; 10 David Mills; 16 Jason Netherton; 17 Makali Aizue.
Tries: Colbon (5), Murrell (15), Galea (18, 70), Webster (49, 73), Dobson (54), Fisher (79); **Goals:** Dobson 6/8.
DRAGONS: 1 Clint Greenshields; 18 Vincent Duport; 3 Steven Bell; 15 Jean-Phillipe Baile; 5 Dimitri Pelo; 13 Gregory Mounis; 7 Shane Perry; 8 David Ferriol; 9 Casey McGuire (C); 10 Jerome Guisset; 16 Olivier Elima; 14 Dane Carlaw; 21 Florian Quintilla. Subs (all used): 24 Remi Casty; 20 Kane Bentley; 19 Julien Touxagas; 22 Jamal Fakir.
Tries: Greenshields (22), Pelo (62); **Goals:** Mounis 1/2.
Rugby Leaguer & League Express Men of the Match:
Rovers: Michael Dobson; *Dragons:* Gregory Mounis.
Penalty count: 9-6; **Half-time:** 18-6;
Referee: Ian Smith; **Attendance:** 8,115.

WARRINGTON WOLVES 40 HUDDERSFIELD GIANTS 18

WOLVES: 19 Chris Riley; 23 Chris Hicks; 25 Chris Bridge;

4 Matt King; 2 Paul Johnson; 6 Lee Briers; 7 Michael Monaghan; 8 Adrian Morley (C); 9 Jon Clarke; 16 Garreth Carvell; 13 Vinnie Anderson; 12 Ben Westwood; 24 Ben Harrison. Subs (all used): 10 Paul Rauhihi; 15 Paul Wood; 14 Mick Higham; 20 Simon Grix.
Tries: King (2), Hicks (5, 24, 30), Monaghan (56), Riley (63, 78); **Goals:** Hicks 6/9.
GIANTS: 1 Brett Hodgson (C); 2 Martin Aspinwall; 19 Michael Lawrence; 4 Paul Whatuira; 5 David Hodgson; 3 Kevin Brown; 7 Luke Robinson; 15 Paul Jackson; 20 Scott Moore; 16 Keith Mason; 13 Stephen Wild; 18 Danny Kirmond; 14 Simon Finnigan. Subs (all used): 8 Eorl Crabtree; 9 David Faiumu; 10 Darrell Griffin; 11 Jamahl Lolesi.
Tries: Finnigan (15), Whatuira (46), B Hodgson (76); **Goals:** B Hodgson 3/3.
Rugby Leaguer & League Express Men of the Match: *Wolves:* Chris Hicks; *Giants:* David Faiumu.
Penalty count: 10-4; **Half-time:** 20-6;
Referee: Phil Bentham; **Attendance:** 8,005.

WAKEFIELD TRINITY WILDCATS 26
WIGAN WARRIORS 40

WILDCATS: 1 Matt Blaymire; 2 Damien Blanch; 19 Sean Gleeson; 4 Ryan Atkins; 13 Scott Grix; 3 Tony Martin; 7 Danny Brough; 12 Oliver Wilkes; 9 Brad Drew; 11 Steve Snitch; 29 Jay Pitts; 24 Dale Ferguson; 8 Jason Demetriou (C). Subs (all used): 14 Sam Obst; 17 Kevin Henderson; 25 Richard Moore; 10 Danny Sculthorpe.
Tries: Blanch (4, 45), Brough (26, 36); **Goals:** Brough 5/5.
WARRIORS: 5 Pat Richards; 2 Amos Roberts; 22 Martin Gleeson; 21 Cameron Phelps; 28 Shaun Ainscough; 6 Tim Smith; 7 Thomas Leuluai; 8 Stuart Fielden; 9 Mark Riddell; 15 Andy Coley; 11 Gareth Hock; 12 Phil Bailey; 13 Sean O'Loughlin (C). Subs (all used): 10 Iafeta Palea'aesina; 14 Joel Tomkins; 19 Paul Prescott; 25 Sam Tomkins.
Tries: Phelps (9, 56), Ainscough (12, 18, 30, 69), Gleeson (75); **Goals:** Richards 6/7.
Rugby Leaguer & League Express Men of the Match: *Wildcats:* Danny Brough; *Warriors:* Shaun Ainscough.
Penalty count: 10-4; **Half-time:** 20-22;
Referee: Ben Thaler; **Attendance:** 5,501.

ROUND 12 - MURRAYFIELD MAGIC

Saturday 2nd May 2009

HARLEQUINS 24 SALFORD CITY REDS 16

HARLEQUINS: 1 Chris Melling; 26 Matt Gardner; 3 Matt Gafa; 4 David Howell; 5 Will Sharp; 6 Luke Dorn; 7 Danny Orr; 8 Karl Temata; 9 Chad Randall; 17 Danny Ward; 11 Luke Williamson; 12 Chad Robinson; 13 Rob Purdham (C). Subs (all used): 10 Louie McCarthy-Scarsbrook; 19 Jason Golden; 14 Tony Clubb; 15 Ben Kaye.
Tries: Williamson (4), Clubb (33), Howell (62), Dorn (71); **Goals:** Purdham 4/4.
CITY REDS: 2 John Wilshere; 3 Mark Henry; 15 Stuart Littler; 14 Jordan Turner; 29 Darrell Goulding; 19 Stefan Ratchford; 7 Richard Myler; 8 Ray Cashmere; 9 Malcolm Alker (C); 10 Craig Stapleton; 12 Rob Parker; 20 Luke Adamson; 13 Luke Swain. Subs (all used): 11 Ian Sibbit; 16 Phil Leuluai; 17 Robbie Paul; 18 Lee Jewitt.
Tries: Ratchford (7, 76), Myler (15); **Goals:** Wilshere 2/3.
Rugby Leaguer & League Express Men of the Match: *Harlequins:* Luke Dorn; *City Reds:* Stefan Ratchford.
Penalty count: 5-4; **Half-time:** 12-10;
Referee: Gareth Hewer.

BRADFORD BULLS 32
WAKEFIELD TRINITY WILDCATS 16

BULLS: 20 Dave Halley; 2 Rikki Sheriffe; 3 Paul Sykes; 4 Chris Nero; 5 Semi Tadulala; 6 Ben Jeffries; 7 Paul Deacon (C); 17 Nick Scruton; 9 Terry Newton; 10 Andy Lynch; 11 Steve Menzies; 8 Sam Burgess; 13 Jamie Langley. Subs (all used): 24 Julien Rinaldi; 15 Matt Cook; 16 Michael Worrincy; 19 Craig Kopczak.
Tries: Sykes (7, 33, 79), Newton (12), Menzies (35), Worrincy (75); **Goals:** Deacon 4/6.
WILDCATS: 1 Matt Blaymire; 5 Matt Petersen; 3 Tony Martin; 4 Ryan Atkins; 13 Scott Grix; 14 Sam Obst; 7 Danny Brough; 12 Oliver Wilkes; 9 Brad Drew; 25 Richard Moore; 11 Steve Snitch; 17 Kevin Henderson; 8 Jason Demetriou (C). Subs (all used): 10 Danny Sculthorpe; 20 Tevita Leo-Latu; 24 Dale Ferguson; 28 Kyle Bibb.
Tries: Demetriou (30), Snitch (66), Blaymire (69); **Goals:** Brough 1/2, Martin 1/1.
Rugby Leaguer & League Express Men of the Match: *Bulls:* Steve Menzies; *Wildcats:* Jason Demetriou.
Penalty count: 9-10; **Half-time:** 20-6; **Referee:** Ian Smith.

ST HELENS 18 WIGAN WARRIORS 38

SAINTS: 1 Paul Wellens; 2 Ade Gardner; 3 Matt Gidley; 11 Lee Gilmour; 5 Francis Meli; 6 Leon Pryce; 7 Sean Long; 16 Tony Puletua; 9 Keiron Cunningham (C); 10 James Graham; 28 Matty Ashurst; 13 Chris Flannery; 17 Paul Clough. Subs (all used): 15 Bryn Hargreaves; 14 James Roby; 23 Maurie Fa'asavalu; 18 Kyle Eastmond.
Tries: Long (36), Pryce (57), Wellens (73); **Goals:** Eastmond 1/1, Long 2/2.
WARRIORS: 21 Cameron Phelps; 2 Amos Roberts; 22 Martin Gleeson; 4 George Carmont; 5 Pat Richards; 6 Tim Smith; 7 Thomas Leuluai; 8 Stuart Fielden; 17 Michael McIlorum; 15 Andy Coley; 11 Gareth Hock; 12 Phil Bailey; 13 Sean O'Loughlin (C). Subs (all used): 10 Iafeta Palea'aesina; 14 Joel Tomkins; 19 Paul Prescott; 25 Sam Tomkins.
Tries: O'Loughlin (7), Richards (18, 76), Hock (31), J Tomkins (39), Leuluai (46); **Goals:** Richards 7/7.
Rugby Leaguer & League Express Men of the Match: *Saints:* Leon Pryce; *Warriors:* Pat Richards.
Penalty count: 6-4; **Half-time:** 6-24;
Referee: Steve Ganson.

Attendance: 29,627 *(at Murrayfield, Edinburgh).*

Sunday 3rd May 2009

CELTIC CRUSADERS 16 HUDDERSFIELD GIANTS 40

CRUSADERS: 5 Anthony Blackwood; 2 Luke Dyer; 3 Josh Hannay; 4 Mark Dalle Cort; 27 Paul Ballard; 6 Damien Quinn; 7 Jace Van Dijk (C); 8 Ryan O'Hara; 9 Lincoln Withers; 17 Jordan James; 19 Jason Chan; 21 Chris Beasley; 15 Peter Lupton. Subs (all used): 23 Neil Budworth; 20 David Tangata-Toa; 24 Aled James; 10 Mark Bryant.
Tries: Beasley (64), Blackwood (73), Tangata-Toa (77); **Goals:** Quinn 2/3.
GIANTS: 1 Brett Hodgson (C); 19 Michael Lawrence; 11 Jamahl Lolesi; 4 Paul Whatuira; 5 David Hodgson; 3 Kevin Brown; 7 Luke Robinson; 16 Keith Mason; 20 Scott Moore; 17 Michael Korkidas; 18 Danny Kirmond; 13 Stephen Wild; 9 David Faiumu. Subs (all used): 24 Shaun Lunt; 15 Paul Jackson; 8 Eorl Crabtree; 14 Simon Finnigan.
Tries: B Hodgson (4), Kirmond (14), Moore (29), Lunt (37, 61), Korkidas (56), Finnigan (69); **Goals:** B Hodgson 6/7.
Rugby Leaguer & League Express Men of the Match: *Crusaders:* David Tangata-Toa; *Giants:* Shaun Lunt.
Penalty count: 6-5; **Half-time:** 0-22; **Referee:** Ben Thaler.

CASTLEFORD TIGERS 16 HULL FC 24

TIGERS: 1 Richard Owen; 2 Kirk Dixon; 3 Michael Shenton; 4 James Evans; 5 Michael Wainwright; 6 Rangi Chase; 7 Brent Sherwin; 8 Mitchell Sargent; 14 Stuart Jones; 15 Liam Higgins; 11 Brett Ferres; 21 Sione Faumuina; 23 Ryan McGoldrick (C). Subs (all used): 16 Chris Feather; 17 Ryan Boyle; 19 Kirk Netherton; 20 James Ford.
Tries: Ford (7), Dixon (48), Evans (59); **Goals:** Dixon 2/3.
HULL: 6 Richard Horne; 2 Mark Calderwood; 14 Richard Whiting; 4 Kirk Yeaman; 17 Graeme Horne; 15 Danny Washbrook; 7 Chris Thorman; 8 Ewan Dowes; 23 Tommy Lee; 18 Jamie Thackray; 16 Willie Manu; 12 Danny Tickle; 11 Lee Radford (C). Subs (all used): 20 Danny Houghton; 22 Mike Burnett; 10 Peter Cusack; 25 Dominic Maloney.
Tries: Burnett (37), Cusack (54), Whiting (64), Washbrook (76); **Goals:** Tickle 4/5.
Rugby Leaguer & League Express Men of the Match: *Tigers:* Ryan McGoldrick; *Hull:* Danny Washbrook.
Penalty count: 2-7; **Half-time:** 6-6;
Referee: Phil Bentham.

CATALANS DRAGONS 16 LEEDS RHINOS 36

DRAGONS: 1 Clint Greenshields; 18 Vincent Duport; 3 Steven Bell; 15 Jean-Phillipe Baile; 5 Dimitri Pelo; 26 Greg Bird (C); 4 Adam Mogg; 24 Remi Casty; 9 Casey McGuire; 10 Jerome Guisset; 16 Olivier Elima; 14 Dane Carlaw; 13 Gregory Mounis. Subs (all used): 8 David Ferriol; 22 Jamal Fakir; 17 Cyrille Gossard; 20 Kane Bentley.
Tries: Bentley (41), Elima (47), McGuire (79); **Goals:** Mounis 2/3.
RHINOS: 1 Brent Webb; 2 Scott Donald; 3 Lee Smith; 4 Keith Senior; 5 Ryan Hall; 13 Kevin Sinfield (C); 7 Rob Burrow; 8 Kylie Leuluai; 9 Danny Buderus; 10 Jamie Peacock; 17 Ian Kirke; 11 Jamie Jones-Buchanan; 18 Carl Ablett. Subs (all used): 19 Luke Burgess; 12 Ali Lauitiiti; 14 Matt Diskin; 6 Danny McGuire.
Tries: Hall (9, 33), Burrow (15), Peacock (27), Webb (31), Donald (67); **Goals:** Sinfield 6/6.
Rugby Leaguer & League Express Men of the Match: *Dragons:* Casey McGuire; *Rhinos:* Ryan Hall.
Penalty count: 6-4; **Half-time:** 0-30;
Referee: Thierry Alibert.

HULL KINGSTON ROVERS 36
WARRINGTON WOLVES 28

ROVERS: 1 Shaun Briscoe; 2 Peter Fox; 4 Jake Webster; 19 Kris Welham; 5 Liam Colbon; 6 Paul Cooke; 7 Michael Dobson; 20 Michael Vella (C); 9 Ben Fisher; 18 Scott Wheeldon; 11 Clint Newton; 12 Ben Galea; 13 Scott Murrell. Subs (all used): 17 Makali Aizue; 10 David Mills; 16 Jason Netherton; 15 Daniel Fitzhenry.
Tries: Briscoe (8), Dobson (22), Vella (45), Newton (52), Galea (70, 80); **Goals:** Dobson 6/6.
WOLVES: 19 Chris Riley; 23 Chris Hicks; 2 Paul Johnson; 20 Simon Grix; 4 Matt King; 25 Chris Bridge; 7 Michael Monaghan (C); 16 Garreth Carvell; 9 Jon Clarke; 10 Paul Rauhihi; 13 Vinnie Anderson; 12 Ben Westwood; 24 Ben Harrison. Subs (all used): 14 Mick Higham; 18 Michael Cooper; 21 Matty Blythe; 22 Lee Mitchell.
Tries: Hicks (5, 75), Monaghan (12), V Anderson (16, 75); **Goals:** Hicks 4/5.
Rugby Leaguer & League Express Men of the Match: *Rovers:* Ben Galea; *Wolves:* Chris Hicks.
Penalty count: 8-8; **Half-time:** 12-16;
Referee: Richard Silverwood.

Attendance: 30,122 *(at Murrayfield, Edinburgh).*

ROUND 13

Friday 15th May 2009

CASTLEFORD TIGERS 22 LEEDS RHINOS 24

TIGERS: 23 Ryan McGoldrick (C); 2 Kirk Dixon; 3 Michael Shenton; 4 James Evans; 5 Michael Wainwright; 21 Sione Faumuina; 7 Brent Sherwin; 8 Mitchell Sargent; 6 Rangi Chase; 15 Liam Higgins; 11 Brett Ferres; 14 Stuart Jones; 13 Joe Westerman. Subs (all used): 12 Ryan Clayton; 16 Chris Feather; 17 Ryan Boyle; 20 James Ford.
Tries: Jones (16), Dixon (32), Chase (44), Shenton (67); **Goals:** Dixon 3/4.
RHINOS: 1 Brent Webb; 2 Scott Donald; 3 Lee Smith; 4 Keith Senior; 5 Ryan Hall; 6 Danny McGuire; 7 Rob Burrow; 8 Kylie Leuluai; 9 Danny Buderus; 10 Jamie Peacock; 17 Ian Kirke; 11 Jamie Jones-Buchanan; 13 Kevin Sinfield (C). Subs (all used): 12 Ali Lauitiiti; 14 Matt Diskin; 18 Carl Ablett; 19 Luke Burgess.
Tries: Burrow (6), McGuire (9, 48), Hall (14); **Goals:** Sinfield 4/5.
Rugby Leaguer & League Express Men of the Match: *Tigers:* Rangi Chase; *Rhinos:* Danny McGuire.
Penalty count: 9-6; **Half-time:** 10-16;
Referee: Ian Smith; **Attendance:** 8,082.

WIGAN WARRIORS 12 HULL KINGSTON ROVERS 20

WARRIORS: 21 Cameron Phelps; 2 Amos Roberts; 22 Martin Gleeson; 4 George Carmont; 5 Pat Richards; 6 Tim Smith; 7 Thomas Leuluai; 8 Stuart Fielden; 17 Michael McIlorum; 15 Andy Coley; 11 Gareth Hock; 12 Phil Bailey; 13 Sean O'Loughlin (C). Subs (all used): 9 Mark Riddell; 10 Iafeta Palea'aesina; 14 Joel Tomkins; 19 Paul Prescott.
Tries: O'Loughlin (7, 42); **Goals:** Richards 2/2.
ROVERS: 1 Shaun Briscoe (C); 5 Liam Colbon; 4 Jake Webster; 19 Kris Welham; 2 Peter Fox; 6 Paul Cooke; 7 Michael Dobson; 18 Scott Wheeldon; 9 Ben Fisher; 11 Clint Newton; 14 Stanley Gene; 12 Ben Galea; 13 Scott Murrell. Subs (all used): 17 Makali Aizue; 16 Jason Netherton; 15 Daniel Fitzhenry; 8 Nick Fozzard.
Tries: Dobson (40), Cooke (52), Webster (57); **Goals:** Dobson 4/4.
Rugby Leaguer & League Express Men of the Match: *Warriors:* Sean O'Loughlin; *Rovers:* Scott Murrell.
Penalty count: 7-8; **Half-time:** 6-6;
Referee: Richard Silverwood; **Attendance:** 13,415.

Saturday 16th May 2009

HULL FC 16 WARRINGTON WOLVES 18

HULL: 6 Richard Horne (C); 2 Mark Calderwood; 14 Richard Whiting; 4 Kirk Yeaman; 29 Jodie Broughton; 15 Danny Washbrook; 7 Chris Thorman; 10 Peter Cusack; 23 Tommy Lee; 18 Jamie Thackray; 8 Ewan Dowes; 22 Mike Burnett; 12 Danny Tickle. Subs (all used): 20 Danny Houghton; 19 Paul King; 25 Dominic Maloney; 26 Josh Hodgson (D).
Tries: Whiting (12), Broughton (14); **Goals:** Tickle 4/5.
WOLVES: 30 Richard Mathers; 25 Chris Bridge; 20 Simon Grix; 13 Vinnie Anderson; 19 Chris Riley; 6 Lee Briers; 7 Michael Monaghan; 8 Adrian Morley (C); 9 Jon Clarke; 16 Garreth Carvell; 11 Louis Anderson; 12 Ben Westwood; 24 Ben Harrison. Subs (all used): 14 Mick Higham; 10 Paul Rauhihi; 15 Paul Wood; 21 Matty Blythe.
Tries: Grix (24, 65), Bridge (62), V Anderson (72); **Goals:** Bridge 1/4.
Sin bin: Carvell (5) - high tackle on Dowes.
Rugby Leaguer & League Express Men of the Match: *Hull:* Ewan Dowes; *Wolves:* Lee Briers.
Penalty count: 5-5; **Half-time:** 14-6;
Referee: Steve Ganson; **Attendance:** 10,997.

CATALANS DRAGONS 28 ST HELENS 32

DRAGONS: 1 Clint Greenshields; 18 Vincent Duport; 3 Steven Bell; 15 Jean-Phillipe Baile; 5 Dimitri Pelo; 4 Adam Mogg; 6 Thomas Bosc; 14 Dane Carlaw; 9 Casey McGuire; 10 Jerome Guisset; 22 Jamal Fakir; 19 Julien Touxagas; 26 Greg Bird (C). Subs (all used): 8 David Ferriol; 13 Gregory Mounis; 20 Kane Bentley; 24 Remi Casty.
Tries: Bell (3, 38), Bosc (21, 33), Mogg (72); **Goals:** Bosc 4/5.
SAINTS: 1 Paul Wellens; 2 Ade Gardner; 3 Matt Gidley; 21 Gary Wheeler; 5 Francis Meli; 6 Leon Pryce; 7 Sean Long; 10 James Graham; 9 Keiron Cunningham (C); 15 Bryn Hargreaves; 11 Lee Gilmour; 13 Chris Flannery; 16 Tony Puletua. Subs (all used): 14 James Roby; 17 Paul Clough; 23 Maurie Fa'asavalu; 28 Matty Ashurst.
Tries: Gardner (15, 41), Wellens (27), Meli (50), Pryce (54), Wheeler (77); **Goals:** Long 4/6.
Rugby Leaguer & League Express Men of the Match: *Dragons:* Thomas Bosc; *Saints:* James Graham.
Penalty count: 7-7; **Half-time:** 22-10;
Referee: Phil Bentham; **Attendance:** 9,065.

Sunday 17th May 2009

BRADFORD BULLS 24 CELTIC CRUSADERS 30

BULLS: 20 Dave Halley; 2 Rikki Sheriffe; 3 Paul Sykes; 1 Michael Platt; 5 Semi Tadulala; 6 Ben Jeffries; 7 Paul Deacon (C); 10 Andy Lynch; 9 Terry Newton; 17 Nick Scruton; 11 Steve Menzies; 8 Sam Burgess; 13 Jamie Langley. Subs (all used): 19 Craig Kopczak; 24 Julien Rinaldi; 15 Matt Cook; 16 Michael Worrincy.
Tries: Lynch (40), Worrincy (57), Menzies (69), Sykes (78); **Goals:** Deacon 4/4.
CRUSADERS: 6 Damien Quinn; 2 Luke Dyer; 3 Josh Hannay; 4 Mark Dalle Cort; 5 Anthony Blackwood; 14 Matty Smith; 7 Jace Van Dijk (C); 8 Ryan O'Hara; 9 Lincoln Withers; 10 Mark Bryant; 17 Jordan James; 19 Jason Chan; 21 Chris Beasley. Subs (all used): 23 Neil Budworth; 20 David Tangata-Toa; 16 Ben Flower; 18 Mark Lennon.
Tries: Beasley (9), Tangata-Toa (43), Withers (50),

Hull KR's Clint Newton offloads as Castleford's Michael Shenton looks on

Dyer (61, 69); **Goals:** Hannay 5/8.
Rugby Leaguer & League Express Men of the Match:
Bulls: Ben Jeffries; *Crusaders:* Luke Dyer.
Penalty count: 7-7; **Half-time:** 6-8;
Referee: James Child; **Attendance:** 7,602.

HARLEQUINS 24 WAKEFIELD TRINITY WILDCATS 17

HARLEQUINS: 1 Chris Melling; 2 Jon Wells; 3 Matt Gafa;
4 David Howell; 5 Will Sharp; 6 Luke Dorn; 7 Danny Orr;
8 Karl Temata; 9 Chad Randall; 17 Danny Ward; 19
Jason Golden; 11 Luke Williamson; 13 Rob Purdham
(C). Subs (all used): 10 Louie McCarthy-Scarsbrook; 14
Tony Clubb; 15 Ben Kaye; 23 Daniel Heckenberg.
Tries: Dorn (17), Sharp (34), Howell (49),
Williamson (57); **Goals:** Purdham 4/4.
WILDCATS: 1 Matt Blaymire; 13 Scott Grix; 8 Jason
Demetriou (C); 4 Ryan Atkins; 26 Luke George; 3 Tony
Martin; 7 Danny Brough; 12 Oliver Wilkes; 14 Sam Obst;
10 Danny Sculthorpe; 11 Steve Snitch; 29 Jay Pitts; 17
Kevin Henderson. Subs (all used): 6 Jamie Rooney; 25
Richard Moore; 16 Ricky Bibey; 18 Frank Winterstein.
Tries: Brough (5), Moore (19), Martin (67);
Goals: Brough 2/3; **Field goal:** Brough (40).
Rugby Leaguer & League Express Men of the Match:
Harlequins: Luke Williamson; *Wildcats:* Danny Sculthorpe.
Penalty count: 5-8; **Half-time:** 12-11;
Referee: Ben Thaler; **Attendance:** 3,612.

HUDDERSFIELD GIANTS 4 SALFORD CITY REDS 24

GIANTS: 21 Leroy Cudjoe; 2 Martin Aspinwall; 11 Jamahl
Lolesi; 4 Paul Whatuira; 5 David Hodgson; 3 Kevin Brown;
7 Luke Robinson; 16 Keith Mason; 20 Scott Moore; 17
Michael Korkidas; 13 Stephen Wild (C); 30 Larne Patrick;
24 Shaun Lunt. Subs (all used): 8 Eorl Crabtree; 15 Paul
Jackson; 18 Danny Kirmond; 9 David Faiumu.
Try: Robinson (17); **Goals:** Cudjoe 0/1.
CITY REDS: 2 John Wilshere; 3 Mark Henry; 14 Jordan
Turner; 4 Willie Talau; 29 Darrell Goulding; 19 Stefan
Ratchford; 7 Richard Myler; 8 Ray Cashmere; 9 Malcolm
Alker (C); 12 Rob Parker; 11 Ian Sibbit; 20 Luke
Adamson; 13 Luke Swain. Subs (all used): 18 Lee
Jewitt; 16 Phil Leuluai; 17 Robbie Paul; 15 Stuart Littler.
Tries: Wilshere (5), Goulding (25), Myler (55),
Henry (72); **Goals:** Wilshere 4/5.
Rugby Leaguer & League Express Men of the Match:
Giants: Luke Robinson; *City Reds:* Stefan Ratchford.
Penalty count: 5-8; **Half-time:** 4-12;
Referee: Thierry Alibert; **Attendance:** 6,903.

ROUND 14

Friday 22nd May 2009

HULL KINGSTON ROVERS 16 CASTLEFORD TIGERS 6

ROVERS: 1 Shaun Briscoe (C); 2 Peter Fox; 19 Kris

Welham; 4 Jake Webster; 5 Liam Colbon; 6 Paul Cooke;
7 Michael Dobson; 8 Nick Fozzard; 15 Daniel Fitzhenry;
11 Clint Newton; 3 Chev Walker; 12 Ben Galea; 13 Scott
Murrell. Subs (all used): 9 Ben Fisher; 14 Stanley Gene;
17 Makali Aizue; 18 Scott Wheeldon.
Tries: Fox (6), Briscoe (44, 70); **Goals:** Dobson 2/3.
TIGERS: 20 James Ford; 2 Kirk Dixon; 3 Michael
Shenton; 4 James Evans; 5 Michael Wainwright; 21
Sione Faumuina; 7 Brent Sherwin (C); 8 Mitchell
Sargent; 6 Rangi Chase; 15 Liam Higgins; 11 Brett
Ferres; 14 Stuart Jones; 13 Joe Westerman. Subs (all
used): 10 Craig Huby; 12 Ryan Clayton; 16 Chris
Feather; 17 Ryan Boyle.
Try: Sargent (49); **Goals:** Dixon 1/1.
Rugby Leaguer & League Express Men of the Match:
Rovers: Shaun Briscoe; *Tigers:* Rangi Chase.
Penalty count: 13-7; **Half-time:** 4-0;
Referee: Gareth Hewer; **Attendance:** 8,104.

SALFORD CITY REDS 18 BRADFORD BULLS 10

CITY REDS: 2 John Wilshere; 3 Mark Henry; 4 Willie
Talau; 14 Jordan Turner; 29 Darrell Goulding; 19 Stefan
Ratchford; 7 Richard Myler; 8 Ray Cashmere; 9 Malcolm
Alker (C); 12 Rob Parker; 20 Luke Adamson; 11 Ian
Sibbit; 13 Luke Swain. Subs (all used): 16 Phil Leuluai;
18 Lee Jewitt; 15 Stuart Littler; 17 Robbie Paul.
Tries: Littler (54), Henry (62), Adamson (66);
Goals: Wilshere 3/3.
BULLS: 1 Michael Platt; 2 Rikki Sheriffe; 3 Paul Sykes; 4
Chris Nero; 20 Dave Halley; 6 Ben Jeffries; 7 Paul
Deacon (C); 10 Andy Lynch; 9 Terry Newton; 17 Nick
Scruton; 11 Steve Menzies; 8 Sam Burgess; 13 Jamie
Langley. Subs (all used): 15 Matt Cook; 24 Julien
Rinaldi; 16 Michael Worrincy; 19 Craig Kopczak.
Tries: Sykes (27, 70); **Goals:** Deacon 1/2.
Rugby Leaguer & League Express Men of the Match:
City Reds: Luke Adamson; *Bulls:* Paul Sykes.
Penalty count: 9-5; **Half-time:** 0-4;
Referee: Phil Bentham; **Attendance:** 4,383.

ST HELENS 22 HARLEQUINS 12

SAINTS: 1 Paul Wellens; 18 Kyle Eastmond; 3 Matt
Gidley; 11 Lee Gilmour; 21 Gary Wheeler; 6 Leon Pryce;
7 Sean Long; 10 James Graham; 9 Keiron Cunningham
(C); 31 Jacob Emmitt; 13 Chris Flannery; 12 Jon Wilkin;
16 Tony Puletua. Subs (all used): 14 James Roby; 17
Paul Clough; 23 Maurie Fa'asavalu; 28 Matty Ashurst.
Tries: Flannery (12), Wellens (39), Roby (53),
Cunningham (78); **Goals:** Long 3/4.
HARLEQUINS: 2 Jon Wells; 27 Jamie O'Callaghan; 3
Matt Gafa; 4 David Howell; 5 Will Sharp; 6 Luke Dorn; 7
Danny Orr; 8 Karl Temata; 9 Chad Randall; 23 Daniel
Heckenberg; 19 Jason Golden; 11 Luke Williamson; 13

Rob Purdham (C). Subs (all used): 10 Louie McCarthy-
Scarsbrook; 14 Tony Clubb; 15 Ben Kaye; 20 Jon
Grayshon.
Tries: McCarthy-Scarsbrook (58), Dorn (67);
Goals: Purdham 2/2.
Rugby Leaguer & League Express Men of the Match:
Saints: Sean Long; *Harlequins:* Jason Golden.
Penalty count: 6-4; **Half-time:** 10-0;
Referee: Steve Ganson; **Attendance:** 9,359.

WARRINGTON WOLVES 16 WIGAN WARRIORS 8

WOLVES: 30 Richard Mathers; 19 Chris Riley; 25 Chris
Bridge; 20 Simon Grix; 4 Matt King; 6 Lee Briers; 7
Michael Monaghan; 8 Adrian Morley (C); 9 Jon Clarke; 16
Garreth Carvell; 11 Louis Anderson; 12 Ben Westwood;
13 Vinnie Anderson. Subs (all used): 14 Mick Higham; 15
Paul Wood; 10 Paul Rauhihi; 24 Ben Harrison.
Tries: King (36), Riley (56), Monaghan (65);
Goals: Bridge 2/3.
WARRIORS: 5 Pat Richards; 2 Amos Roberts; 22 Martin
Gleeson; 21 Cameron Phelps; 28 Shaun Ainscough; 25
Sam Tomkins; 7 Thomas Leuluai; 8 Stuart Fielden; 17
Michael McIlorum; 15 Andy Coley; 11 Gareth Hock; 14
Joel Tomkins; 13 Sean O'Loughlin (C). Subs (all used):
10 Iafeta Palea'aesina; 9 Mark Riddell; 19 Paul Prescott;
16 Harrison Hansen.
Try: Phelps (4). **Goals:** Richards 2/2.
Rugby Leaguer & League Express Men of the Match:
Wolves: Adrian Morley; *Warriors:* Thomas Leuluai.
Penalty count: 11-5; **Half-time:** 4-6;
Referee: Ben Thaler; **Attendance:** 10,718.

Saturday 23rd May 2009

CELTIC CRUSADERS 18 CATALANS DRAGONS 30

CRUSADERS: 6 Damien Quinn; 2 Luke Dyer; 4 Mark
Dalle Cort; 3 Josh Hannay; 5 Anthony Blackwood; 14
Matty Smith; 7 Jace Van Dijk (C); 8 Ryan O'Hara; 9
Lincoln Withers; 17 Jordan James; 21 Chris Beasley; 10
Mark Bryant; 19 Jason Chan. Subs (all used): 23 Neil
Budworth; 20 David Tangata-Toa; 12 Darren Mapp; 16
Ben Flower.
Tries: Hannay (7), Chan (42), J James (57);
Goals: Hannay 3/3.
DRAGONS: 1 Clint Greenshields; 2 Cyril Stacul; 15 Jean-
Phillipe Baile; 4 Adam Mogg; 3 Steven Bell; 26 Greg Bird
(C); 6 Thomas Bosc; 16 Olivier Elima; 20 Kane Bentley;
10 Jerome Guisset; 17 Cyrille Gossard; 14 Dane Carlaw;
13 Gregory Mounis. Subs (all used): 7 Shane Perry; 8
David Ferriol; 24 Remi Casty; 19 Julien Touxagas.
Tries: Bird (9), Elima (20), Mogg (21), Perry (40),
Bell (68), Stacul (80); **Goals:** Bosc 3/6.
Rugby Leaguer & League Express Men of the Match:
Crusaders: Damien Quinn; *Dragons:* Cyrille Gossard.
Penalty count: 14-8; **Half-time:** 6-22;
Referee: Richard Silverwood; **Attendance:** 2,927.

Harlequins' Luke Williamson dives over despite the attentions of Celtic Crusaders' Mark Dalle Cort

Sunday 24th May 2009

WAKEFIELD TRINITY WILDCATS 6
HUDDERSFIELD GIANTS 54

WILDCATS: 1 Matt Blaymire; 19 Sean Gleeson; 8 Jason Demetriou (C); 4 Ryan Atkins; 26 Luke George; 3 Tony Martin; 6 Jamie Rooney; 16 Ricky Bibey; 14 Sam Obst; 25 Richard Moore; 29 Jay Pitts; 11 Steve Snitch; 17 Kevin Henderson. Subs (all used): 28 Kyle Bibb; 15 James Stosic; 13 Scott Grix; 20 Tevita Leo-Latu.
Try: Blaymire (24); **Goals:** Martin 1/1.
GIANTS: 21 Leroy Cudjoe; 2 Martin Aspinwall; 11 Jamahl Lolesi; 4 Paul Whatuira; 5 David Hodgson; 3 Kevin Brown; 7 Luke Robinson; 16 Keith Mason; 20 Scott Moore; 10 Darrell Griffin; 13 Stephen Wild (C); 18 Danny Kirmond; 9 David Faiumu; 12 Andy Raleigh; 32 Lee Mossop (D).
Tries: Kirmond (2), D Hodgson (32, 57, 73), Cudjoe (35), K Brown (44), Moore (47, 76), Whatuira (52), Lolesi (65); **Goals:** Cudjoe 7/10.
Rugby Leaguer & League Express Men of the Match: *Wildcats:* Sam Obst; *Giants:* Luke Robinson.
Penalty count: 10-4; **Half-time:** 6-14;
Referee: Phil Bentham; **Attendance:** 5,037.

Tuesday 26th May 2009

LEEDS RHINOS 46 HULL FC 16

RHINOS: 1 Brent Webb; 2 Scott Donald; 3 Lee Smith; 4 Keith Senior; 5 Ryan Hall; 13 Kevin Sinfield (C); 6 Danny McGuire; 8 Kylie Leuluai; 9 Danny Buderus; 10 Jamie Peacock; 11 Jamie Jones-Buchanan; 17 Ian Kirke; 18 Carl Ablett. Subs (all used): 14 Matt Diskin; 12 Ali Lauitiiti; 16 Ryan Bailey; 19 Luke Burgess.
Tries: Smith (6, 43), Senior (23, 67), Webb (35), Ablett (40), Hall (59), Sinfield (79); **Goals:** Sinfield 7/8.
HULL: 1 Motu Tony; 2 Mark Calderwood; 14 Richard Whiting; 4 Kirk Yeaman; 5 Gareth Raynor; 6 Richard Horne; 7 Chris Thorman; 8 Ewan Dowes; 9 Shaun Berrigan; 18 Jamie Thackray; 22 Mike Burnett; 12 Danny Tickle; 11 Lee Radford (C). Subs (all used): 19 Paul King; 20 Danny Houghton; 23 Tommy Lee; 27 Sam Moa.
Tries: Whiting (11), Yeaman (38), Radford (65);
Goals: Tickle 2/3.
Rugby Leaguer & League Express Men of the Match: *Rhinos:* Kevin Sinfield; *Hull:* Motu Tony.
Penalty count: 7-11; **Half-time:** 22-10;
Referee: Thierry Alibert; **Attendance:** 15,929.

ROUND 6

Saturday 30th May 2009

CELTIC CRUSADERS 6
WAKEFIELD TRINITY WILDCATS 50

CRUSADERS: 3 Josh Hannay; 2 Luke Dyer; 4 Mark Dalle Cort; 5 Anthony Blackwood; 18 Mark Lennon; 6 Damien Quinn; 7 Jace Van Dijk (C); 8 Ryan O'Hara; 9 Lincoln Withers; 17 Jordan James; 10 Mark Bryant; 21 Chris Beasley; 19 Jason Chan. Subs (all used): 12 Darren Mapp; 11 Adam Peek; 20 David Tangata-Toa; 23 Neil Budworth.
Try: Tangata-Toa (79); **Goals:** Hannay 1/1.
WILDCATS: 1 Matt Blaymire; 13 Scott Grix; 3 Tony Martin; 4 Ryan Atkins; 5 Matt Petersen; 6 Jamie Rooney; 7 Danny Brough; 12 Oliver Wilkes; 14 Sam Obst; 16 Ricky Bibey; 24 Dale Ferguson; 11 Steve Snitch; 8 Jason Demetriou (C). Subs (all used): 20 Tevita Leo-Latu; 9 Brad Drew; 23 Michael Korkidas (D2); 15 James Stosic.
Tries: Atkins (10), Korkidas (25), Grix (28), Brough (32), Drew (40, 71), Rooney (47, 50), Snitch (66);
Goals: Brough 7/9.
Rugby Leaguer & League Express Men of the Match: *Crusaders:* David Tangata-Toa; *Wildcats:* Danny Brough.
Penalty count: 5-11; **Half-time:** 0-30;
Referee: Ben Thaler; **Attendance:** 2,089.

ROUND 15

Friday 5th June 2009

HUDDERSFIELD GIANTS 22
HULL KINGSTON ROVERS 6

GIANTS: 21 Leroy Cudjoe; 2 Martin Aspinwall; 19 Michael Lawrence; 4 Paul Whatuira; 5 David Hodgson; 3 Kevin Brown; 7 Luke Robinson; 16 Keith Mason; 20 Scott Moore; 15 Paul Jackson; 12 Andy Raleigh; 18 Danny Kirmond; 13 Stephen Wild (C). Subs (all used): 24 Shaun Lunt; 32 Lee Mossop; 8 Eorl Crabtree; 9 David Faiumu.
Tries: Moore (12), Robinson (14), Mossop (33), Whatuira (70); **Goals:** Cudjoe 3/4.
ROVERS: 1 Shaun Briscoe (C); 2 Peter Fox; 19 Kris Welham; 28 Ben Cockayne; 5 Liam Colbon; 12 Ben Galea; 7 Michael Dobson; 8 Nick Fozzard; 15 Daniel Fitzhenry; 17 Makali Aizue; 11 Clint Newton; 3 Chev Walker; 13 Scott Murrell. Subs (all used): 16 Jason Netherton; 14 Stanley Gene; 10 David Mills; 9 Ben Fisher.
Try: Welham (22); **Goals:** Dobson 1/1.
Rugby Leaguer & League Express Men of the Match: *Giants:* Scott Moore; *Rovers:* Shaun Briscoe.
Penalty count: 7-6; **Half-time:** 18-6;
Referee: Richard Silverwood; **Attendance:** 6,346.

HULL FC 6 ST HELENS 30

HULL: 1 Motu Tony; 2 Mark Calderwood; 14 Richard Whiting; 4 Kirk Yeaman; 5 Gareth Raynor; 6 Richard Horne; 7 Chris Thorman; 8 Ewan Dowes; 9 Shaun Berrigan; 18 Jamie Thackray; 22 Mike Burnett; 12 Danny Tickle; 11 Lee Radford (C). Subs (all used): 25 Dominic Maloney; 23 Tommy Lee; 20 Danny Houghton; 19 Paul King.
Try: Tickle (4); **Goals:** Tickle 1/1.
SAINTS: 1 Paul Wellens; 30 Jonny Lomax; 3 Matt Gidley; 11 Lee Gilmour; 5 Francis Meli; 6 Leon Pryce; 7 Sean Long; 15 Bryn Hargreaves; 9 Keiron Cunningham (C); 10 James Graham; 12 Jon Wilkin; 13 Chris Flannery; 16 Tony Puletua. Subs (all used): 17 Paul Clough; 14 James Roby; 23 Maurie Fa'asavalu; 28 Matty Ashurst.
Tries: Lomax (12), Wellens (17, 39, 52), Gilmour (66), Fa'asavalu (75); **Goals:** Long 3/6.
Rugby Leaguer & League Express Men of the Match: *Hull:* Danny Tickle; *Saints:* Paul Wellens.
Penalty count: 7-3; **Half-time:** 6-14;
Referee: Phil Bentham; **Attendance:** 12,009.

WIGAN WARRIORS 34 SALFORD CITY REDS 18

WARRIORS: 21 Cameron Phelps; 2 Amos Roberts; 22 Martin Gleeson; 4 George Carmont; 5 Pat Richards; 6 Tim Smith; 7 Thomas Leuluai; 15 Andy Coley; 9 Mark Riddell; 19 Paul Prescott; 11 Gareth Hock; 14 Joel Tomkins; 13 Sean O'Loughlin (C). Subs (all used): 10 Iafeta Palea'aesina; 8 Stuart Fielden; 16 Harrison Hansen; 17 Michael McIlorum.
Tries: Carmont (4), Smith (6), Richards (12, 37), Riddell (16), Hansen (68); **Goals:** Richards 5/6.
CITY REDS: 2 John Wilshere; 29 Darrell Goulding; 15 Stuart Littler; 14 Jordan Turner; 3 Mark Henry; 19 Stefan Ratchford; 7 Richard Myler; 8 Ray Cashmere; 9 Malcolm Alker (C); 10 Craig Stapleton; 20 Luke Adamson; 12 Rob Parker; 13 Luke Swain. Subs (all used): 11 Ian Sibbit; 18 Lee Jewitt; 16 Phil Leuluai; 6 Jeremy Smith.
Tries: Swain (21), Henry (49), Alker (79);
Goals: Wilshere 3/3.
Rugby Leaguer & League Express Men of the Match: *Warriors:* Sean O'Loughlin; *City Reds:* Luke Adamson.
Penalty count: 9-11; **Half-time:** 28-6;
Referee: Ian Smith; **Attendance:** 11,550.

Saturday 6th June 2009

HARLEQUINS 26 CELTIC CRUSADERS 6

HARLEQUINS: 2 Jon Wells; 1 Chris Melling; 3 Matt Gafa; 4 David Howell; 5 Will Sharp; 6 Luke Dorn; 7 Danny Orr; 8 Karl Temata; 9 Chad Randall; 10 Louie McCarthy-

Scarsbrook; 19 Jason Golden; 11 Luke Williamson; 13 Rob Purdham (C). Subs (all used): 23 Daniel Heckenberg; 31 Sam Thompson (D); 14 Tony Clubb; 15 Ben Kaye.
Tries: McCarthy-Scarsbrook (14), Melling (47), Williamson (52), Randall (64); **Goals:** Purdham 5/6.
CRUSADERS: 6 Damien Quinn; 2 Luke Dyer; 24 Aled James; 4 Mark Dalle Cort; 18 Mark Lennon; 12 Darren Mapp; 7 Jace Van Dijk (C); 8 Ryan O'Hara; 9 Lincoln Withers; 10 Mark Bryant; 17 Jordan James; 15 Peter Lupton; 21 Chris Beasley. Subs (all used): 11 Adam Peek; 16 Ben Flower; 23 Neil Budworth; 20 David Tangata-Toa.
Try: Quinn (6); **Goals:** Lennon 1/1.
Rugby Leaguer & League Express Men of the Match: *Harlequins:* David Howell; *Crusaders:* Mark Dalle Cort.
Penalty count: 10-4; **Half-time:** 8-6;
Referee: Jamie Leahy; **Attendance:** 2,245.

CASTLEFORD TIGERS 18 WARRINGTON WOLVES 34

TIGERS: 23 Ryan McGoldrick (C); 1 Richard Owen; 3 Michael Shenton; 4 James Evans; 2 Kirk Dixon; 21 Sione Faumuina; 6 Rangi Chase; 8 Mitchell Sargent; 19 Kirk Netherton; 10 Craig Huby; 11 Brett Ferres; 14 Stuart Jones; 12 Ryan Clayton. Subs (all used): 16 Chris Feather; 13 Joe Westerman; 25 Dean Widders; 15 Liam Higgins.
Tries: Dixon (5), Owen (20), Shenton (59), Evans (71);
Goals: Dixon 1/4.
Sin bin: McGoldrick (63) - dissent.
WOLVES: 30 Richard Mathers; 19 Chris Riley; 20 Simon Grix; 4 Matt King; 23 Chris Hicks; 25 Chris Bridge; 6 Lee Briers; 8 Adrian Morley (C); 9 Jon Clarke; 16 Garreth Carvell; 11 Louis Anderson; 12 Ben Westwood; 24 Ben Harrison. Subs (all used): 14 Mick Higham; 15 Paul Wood; 10 Paul Rauhihi; 13 Vinnie Anderson.
Tries: Briers (25, 43), L Anderson (34), King (49), V Anderson (63, 67), Hicks (77); **Goals:** Bridge 3/7.
Rugby Leaguer & League Express Men of the Match: *Tigers:* Brett Ferres; *Wolves:* Vinnie Anderson.
Penalty count: 5-7; **Half-time:** 8-12;
Referee: Ben Thaler; **Attendance:** 5,628.

CATALANS DRAGONS 32 LEEDS RHINOS 30

DRAGONS: 6 Thomas Bosc; 2 Cyril Stacul; 12 Jason Croker; 15 Jean-Phillipe Baile; 3 Steven Bell; 26 Greg Bird (C); 4 Adam Mogg; 14 Dane Carlaw; 9 Casey McGuire; 10 Jerome Guisset; 16 Olivier Elima; 17 Cyrille Gossard; 13 Gregory Mounis. Subs (all used): 8 David Ferriol; 24 Remi Casty; 19 Julien Touxagas; 7 Shane Perry.
Tries: Bell (19), Baile (45), Elima (57, 65), Stacul (79);
Goals: Bosc 6/7.
RHINOS: 1 Brent Webb; 2 Scott Donald; 3 Lee Smith; 4 Keith Senior; 5 Ryan Hall; 13 Kevin Sinfield (C); 6 Danny McGuire; 8 Kylie Leuluai; 14 Matt Diskin; 10 Jamie Peacock; 17 Ian Kirke; 12 Ali Lauitiiti; 18 Carl Ablett. Subs (all used): 16 Ryan Bailey; 19 Luke Burgess; 9 Danny Buderus; 20 Ashley Gibson.
Tries: McGuire (25, 32), Hall (69), Lauitiiti (75), Webb (77); **Goals:** Sinfield 5/5.
On report: Leuluai (49) - alleged high tackle on Bird.
Rugby Leaguer & League Express Men of the Match: *Dragons:* Adam Mogg; *Rhinos:* Danny McGuire.
Penalty count: 12-6; **Half-time:** 10-12;
Referee: Steve Ganson; **Attendance:** 7,913.

Sunday 7th June 2009

BRADFORD BULLS 36
WAKEFIELD TRINITY WILDCATS 22

BULLS: 20 Dave Halley; 2 Rikki Sheriffe; 3 Paul Sykes; 4 Chris Nero; 5 Semi Tadulala; 6 Ben Jeffries; 7 Paul Deacon (C); 10 Andy Lynch; 9 Terry Newton; 17 Nick Scruton; 11 Steve Menzies; 8 Sam Burgess; 13 Jamie Langley. Subs (all used): 19 Craig Kopczak; 24 Julien Rinaldi; 28 Elliott Whitehead (D); 16 Michael Worrincy.
Tries: Nero (3, 56), Menzies (22, 37), Rinaldi (50);
Goals: Deacon 8/8.
Sin bin: Burgess (63) - fighting.
WILDCATS: 1 Matt Blaymire; 5 Matt Petersen; 3 Tony Martin; 19 Sean Gleeson; 13 Scott Grix; 6 Jamie Rooney; 7 Danny Brough; 16 Ricky Bibey; 14 Sam Obst; 12 Oliver Wilkes; 24 Dale Ferguson; 11 Steve Snitch; 8 Jason Demetriou (C). Subs (all used): 9 Brad Drew; 15 James Stosic; 20 Tevita Leo-Latu; 23 Michael Korkidas.
Tries: Gleeson (18, 25, 32), Snitch (47), Grix (67);
Goals: Brough 1/5.
Sin bin: Demetriou (63) - fighting.
Rugby Leaguer & League Express Men of the Match: *Bulls:* Dave Halley; *Wildcats:* Sean Gleeson.
Penalty count: 13-14; **Half-time:** 20-14;
Referee: Thierry Alibert; **Attendance:** 8,387.

ROUND 16

Friday 12th June 2009

HULL KINGSTON ROVERS 10 HARLEQUINS 40

ROVERS: 15 Daniel Fitzhenry; 21 Chaz l'Anson; 4 Jake Webster; 19 Kris Welham; 27 James Haynes (D); 6 Paul Cooke; 7 Michael Dobson; 8 Nick Fozzard; 13 Scott Murrell; 18 Scott Wheeldon; 11 Clint Newton (C); 3 Chev Walker; 12 Ben Galea. Subs (all used): 14 Stanley Gene; 9 Ben Fisher; 17 Makali Aizue; 16 Jason Netherton.
Tries: Gene (36), Wheeldon (48); **Goals:** Dobson 1/2.
HARLEQUINS: 2 Jon Wells; 1 Chris Melling; 3 Matt Gafa; 4 David Howell; 5 Will Sharp; 7 Danny Orr; 21 Luke Gale; 8 Karl Temata; 9 Chad Randall; 10 Louie McCarthy-Scarsbrook; 19 Jason Golden; 11 Luke Williamson; 13 Rob Purdham (C). Subs (all used): 15 Ben Kaye; 23 Daniel Heckenberg; 31 Sam Thompson; 26 Matt Gardner.
Tries: Randall (5), McCarthy-Scarsbrook (11), Sharp (29, 58), Howell (39, 79), Melling (77);
Goals: Purdham 1/1, Orr 3/5, Melling 2/2.
Rugby Leaguer & League Express Men of the Match: *Rovers:* Scott Wheeldon; *Harlequins:* Chad Randall.
Penalty count: 8-7; **Half-time:** 4-24;
Referee: Phil Bentham; **Attendance:** 7,874.

ST HELENS 50 CASTLEFORD TIGERS 10

SAINTS: 1 Paul Wellens; 30 Jonny Lomax; 3 Matt Gidley; 19 Chris Dean; 5 Francis Meli; 6 Leon Pryce; 7 Sean Long; 16 Tony Puletua; 9 Keiron Cunningham (C); 15 Bryn Hargreaves; 12 Jon Wilkin; 13 Chris Flannery; 11 Lee Gilmour. Subs (all used): 17 Paul Clough; 18 Kyle Eastmond; 23 Maurie Fa'asavalu; 28 Matty Ashurst.
Tries: Pryce (12), Dean (14), Cunningham (23), Wilkin (26), Long (52), Lomax (55), Eastmond (58, 76), Clough (73); **Goals:** Long 3/5, Eastmond 4/4.
TIGERS: 1 Richard Owen; 2 Kirk Dixon; 20 James Ford; 25 Dean Widders; 5 Michael Wainwright; 6 Rangi Chase; 23 Ryan McGoldrick (C); 15 Liam Higgins; 19 Kirk Netherton; 10 Craig Huby; 11 Brett Ferres; 14 Stuart Jones; 21 Sione Faumuina. Subs (all used): 8 Mitchell Sargent; 12 Ryan Clayton; 16 Chris Feather; 26 Jordan Thompson (D).
Tries: Ferres (4), Dixon (43); **Goals:** Dixon 1/2.
Rugby Leaguer & League Express Men of the Match: *Saints:* Jonny Lomax; *Tigers:* Sione Faumuina.
Penalty count: 10-6; **Half-time:** 20-6;
Referee: Ian Smith; **Attendance:** 9,680.

Saturday 13th June 2009

CELTIC CRUSADERS 22 WIGAN WARRIORS 16

CRUSADERS: 6 Damien Quinn; 2 Luke Dyer; 18 Mark Lennon; 4 Mark Dalle Cort; 5 Anthony Blackwood; 12 Darren Mapp; 7 Jace Van Dijk (C); 8 Ryan O'Hara; 9 Lincoln Withers; 10 Mark Bryant; 17 Jordan James; 19 Jason Chan; 21 Chris Beasley. Subs (all used): 15 Peter Lupton; 23 Neil Budworth; 11 Adam Peek; 20 David Tangata-Toa.
Tries: Van Dijk (15), Lupton (33, 75), Dalle Cort (54);
Goals: Lennon 3/4.
WARRIORS: 5 Pat Richards; 2 Amos Roberts; 22 Martin Gleeson; 21 Cameron Phelps; 28 Shaun Ainscough; 6 Tim Smith; 7 Thomas Leuluai (C); 15 Andy Coley; 9 Mark Riddell; 19 Paul Prescott; 12 Phil Bailey; 16 Harrison Hansen; 14 Joel Tomkins. Subs (all used): 10 Iafeta Palea'aesina; 17 Michael McIlorum; 8 Stuart Fielden; 26 Mark Flanagan (D).
Tries: Hansen (22), Phelps (61), Roberts (69);
Goals: Richards 2/3.
Rugby Leaguer & League Express Men of the Match: *Crusaders:* Peter Lupton; *Warriors:* Pat Richards.
Penalty count: 2-4; **Half-time:** 12-6;
Referee: Steve Ganson; **Attendance:** 5,253.

WAKEFIELD TRINITY WILDCATS 37 HULL FC 22

WILDCATS: 1 Matt Blaymire; 5 Matt Petersen; 3 Tony Martin; 19 Sean Gleeson; 13 Scott Grix; 6 Jamie Rooney; 7 Danny Brough; 23 Michael Korkidas; 9 Brad Drew (C); 16 Ricky Bibey; 12 Oliver Wilkes; 11 Steve Snitch; 24 Dale Ferguson. Subs (all used): 15 James Stosic; 25 Richard Moore; 18 Frank Winterstein; 20 Tevita Leo-Latu.
Tries: Ferguson (5), Brough (10), Martin (15, 48), Petersen (34), Blaymire (80);
Goals: Brough 5/6, Martin 1/1; **Field goal:** Brough (22).
HULL: 1 Motu Tony; 29 Jodie Broughton; 14 Richard Whiting; 4 Kirk Yeaman; 5 Gareth Raynor; 6 Richard Horne; 7 Chris Thorman; 8 Ewan Dowes; 9 Shaun Berrigan; 18 Jamie Thackray; 22 Mike Burnett; 12 Danny Tickle; 11 Lee Radford (C). Subs (all used): 25 Dominic Maloney; 23 Tommy Lee; 20 Danny Houghton; 19 Paul King.
Tries: Raynor (46), Broughton (60, 77), Yeaman (66);
Goals: Tickle 3/4.
Rugby Leaguer & League Express Men of the Match: *Wildcats:* Danny Brough; *Hull:* Motu Tony.
Penalty count: 7-8; **Half-time:** 23-0;
Referee: Ben Thaler; **Attendance:** 4,721.

Sunday 14th June 2009

LEEDS RHINOS 20 HUDDERSFIELD GIANTS 12

RHINOS: 1 Brent Webb; 2 Scott Donald; 3 Lee Smith; 4 Keith Senior; 23 Kallum Watkins; 13 Kevin Sinfield (C); 7 Rob Burrow; 8 Kylie Leuluai; 9 Danny Buderus; 16 Ryan Bailey; 11 Jamie Jones-Buchanan; 18 Carl Ablett; 14 Matt Diskin. Subs (all used): 21 Simon Worrall; 12 Ali Lauitiiti; 19 Luke Burgess; 20 Ashley Gibson.
Tries: Watkins (46, 78), Leuluai (68); **Goals:** Sinfield 4/4.
GIANTS: 1 Brett Hodgson (C); 2 Martin Aspinwall; 11 Jamahl Lolesi; 4 Paul Whatuira; 5 David Hodgson; 3 Kevin Brown; 7 Luke Robinson; 10 Darrell Griffin; 24 Shaun Lunt; 16 Keith Mason; 13 Stephen Wild; 12 Andy Raleigh; 32 Lee Mossop. Subs (all used): 15 Paul Jackson; 6 Liam Fulton; 33 Danny Sculthorpe (D); 9 David Faiumu.
Tries: D Hodgson (33), K Brown (42);
Goals: B Hodgson 2/2.
Rugby Leaguer & League Express Men of the Match: *Rhinos:* Brent Webb; *Giants:* Kevin Brown.
Penalty count: 7-7; **Half-time:** 0-6;
Referee: Thierry Alibert; **Attendance:** 14,934.

WARRINGTON WOLVES 10 BRADFORD BULLS 21

WOLVES: 30 Richard Mathers; 23 Chris Hicks; 20 Simon Grix; 4 Matt King; 19 Chris Riley; 25 Chris Bridge; 6 Lee Briers (C); 15 Paul Wood; 9 Jon Clarke; 16 Garreth Carvell; 11 Louis Anderson; 13 Vinnie Anderson; 24 Ben Harrison. Subs (all used): 10 Paul Rauhihi; 18 Michael Cooper; 7 Michael Monaghan; 2 Paul Johnson.
Tries: Grix (53), Hicks (75); **Goals:** Bridge 1/2.
BULLS: 20 Dave Halley; 2 Rikki Sheriffe; 11 Steve Menzies; 4 Chris Nero; 5 Semi Tadulala; 6 Ben Jeffries; 7 Paul Deacon (C); 10 Andy Lynch; 9 Terry Newton; 17 Nick Scruton; 16 Michael Worrincy; 12 Glenn Morrison; 13 Jamie Langley. Subs (all used): 1 Michael Platt; 24 Julien Rinaldi; 28 Elliott Whitehead; 19 Craig Kopczak.
Tries: Nero (14), Morrison (47), Newton (65);
Goals: Deacon 4/4; **Field goal:** Deacon (40).
Rugby Leaguer & League Express Men of the Match: *Wolves:* Richard Mathers; *Bulls:* Glenn Morrison.
Penalty count: 7-9; **Half-time:** 0-9;
Referee: Richard Silverwood; **Attendance:** 9,606.

ROUND 17

Friday 19th June 2009

HUDDERSFIELD GIANTS 6 CASTLEFORD TIGERS 13

GIANTS: 1 Brett Hodgson (C); 21 Leroy Cudjoe; 11 Jamahl Lolesi; 4 Paul Whatuira; 5 David Hodgson; 3 Kevin Brown; 7 Luke Robinson; 16 Keith Mason; 20 Scott Moore; 10 Darrell Griffin; 13 Stephen Wild; 8 Eorl Crabtree; 14 Simon Finnigan. Subs (all used): 9 David Faiumu; 6 Liam Fulton; 12 Andy Raleigh; 33 Danny Sculthorpe.
Try: Cudjoe (68); **Goals:** B Hodgson 1/1.
TIGERS: 1 Richard Owen; 5 Michael Wainwright; 3 Michael Shenton; 25 Dean Widders; 2 Kirk Dixon; 21 Sione Faumuina; 23 Ryan McGoldrick (C); 8 Mitchell Sargent; 6 Rangi Chase; 10 Craig Huby; 11 Brett Ferres; 14 Stuart Jones; 13 Joe Westerman. Subs (all used): 15 Liam Higgins; 17 Ryan Boyle; 12 Ryan Clayton; 19 Kirk Netherton.
Tries: Dixon (4), McGoldrick (18); **Goals:** Dixon 2/3;
Field goal: Chase (78).
Rugby Leaguer & League Express Men of the Match: *Giants:* Eorl Crabtree; *Tigers:* Rangi Chase.
Penalty count: 5-5; **Half-time:** 0-12;
Referee: Steve Ganson; **Attendance:** 6,010.

HULL FC 14 SALFORD CITY REDS 12

HULL: 1 Motu Tony; 29 Jodie Broughton; 17 Graeme Horne; 4 Kirk Yeaman; 5 Gareth Raynor; 6 Richard Horne; 7 Chris Thorman; 8 Ewan Dowes; 23 Tommy Lee; 11 Lee Radford (C); 22 Mike Burnett; 16 Willie Manu; 12 Danny Tickle. Subs (all used): 9 Shaun Berrigan; 18 Jamie Thackray; 20 Danny Houghton; 19 Paul King.
Tries: Raynor (10), Tony (32); **Goals:** Tickle 3/4.
CITY REDS: 2 John Wilshere; 29 Darrell Goulding; 19 Stefan Ratchford; 14 Jordan Turner; 3 Mark Henry; 6 Jeremy Smith; 7 Richard Myler; 8 Ray Cashmere; 9 Malcolm Alker (C); 10 Craig Stapleton; 11 Ian Sibbit; 15 Stuart Littler; 13 Luke Swain. Subs (all used): 17 Robbie Paul; 18 Lee Jewitt; 16 Phil Leuluai; 23 Adam Sidlow.
Tries: Smith (26), Goulding (57); **Goals:** Wilshere 2/2.
Rugby Leaguer & League Express Men of the Match: *Hull:* Gareth Raynor; *City Reds:* John Wilshere.
Penalty count: 13-7; **Half-time:** 12-6;
Referee: Phil Bentham; **Attendance:** 11,218.

Saturday 20th June 2009

CATALANS DRAGONS 12 WARRINGTON WOLVES 24

DRAGONS: 1 Clint Greenshields; 2 Cyril Stacul; 12 Jason Croker; 15 Jean-Phillipe Baile; 3 Steven Bell; 4 Adam Mogg; 6 Thomas Bosc; 14 Dane Carlaw; 9 Casey McGuire (C); 10 Jerome Guisset; 16 Olivier Elima; 17 Cyrille Gossard; 22 Jamal Fakir. Subs (all used): 7 Shane Perry; 8 David Ferriol; 19 Julien Touxagas; 23 Jason Ryles.
Tries: Croker (17), Stacul (20); **Goals:** Bosc 2/3.
On report:
Elima (53) - alleged late challenge on Monaghan.
WOLVES: 30 Richard Mathers; 23 Chris Hicks; 25 Chris Bridge; 4 Matt King; 19 Chris Riley; 20 Simon Grix; 7 Michael Monaghan; 8 Adrian Morley (C); 9 Jon Clarke; 16 Garreth Carvell; 11 Louis Anderson; 12 Ben Westwood; 24 Ben Harrison. Subs (all used): 2 Paul Johnson; 10 Paul Rauhihi; 13 Vinnie Anderson; 15 Paul Wood.
Tries: Bridge (7), King (18), Riley (60), Clarke (71);
Goals: Hicks 4/5.
Rugby Leaguer & League Express Men of the Match: *Dragons:* Steven Bell; *Wolves:* Simon Grix.
Penalty count: 6-9; **Half-time:** 10-6;
Referee: Thierry Alibert;
Attendance: 18,150 *(at Olympic Stadium, Barcelona).*

CELTIC CRUSADERS 18 HULL KINGSTON ROVERS 32

CRUSADERS: 6 Damien Quinn; 2 Luke Dyer; 3 Josh Hannay; 4 Mark Dalle Cort; 5 Anthony Blackwood; 18 Mark Lennon; 7 Jace Van Dijk (C); 8 Ryan O'Hara; 9 Lincoln Withers; 10 Mark Bryant; 17 Jordan James; 19 Jason Chan; 15 Peter Lupton. Subs (all used): 16 Ben Flower; 23 Neil Budworth; 11 Adam Peek; 20 David Tangata-Toa.
Tries: Quinn (45), O'Hara (50), Chan (72);
Goals: Lennon 3/5.
ROVERS: 1 Shaun Briscoe; 2 Peter Fox; 4 Jake Webster; 19 Kris Welham; 28 Ben Cockayne; 6 Paul Cooke; 7 Michael Dobson; 18 Scott Wheeldon; 9 Ben Fisher; 20 Michael Vella (C); 11 Clint Newton; 12 Ben Galea; 13 Scott Murrell. Subs (all used): 21 Chaz l'Anson; 16 Jason Netherton; 8 Nick Fozzard; 3 Chev Walker.
Tries: Newton (19, 64), Netherton (39), Welham (57), Dobson (70), Briscoe (79); **Goals:** Dobson 4/6.

Rugby Leaguer & League Express Men of the Match: *Crusaders:* Luke Dyer; *Rovers:* Shaun Briscoe.
Penalty count: 14-5; **Half-time:** 4-12;
Referee: James Child; **Attendance:** 3,015.

HARLEQUINS 14 LEEDS RHINOS 48

HARLEQUINS: 2 Jon Wells; 1 Chris Melling; 3 Matt Gafa; 4 David Howell; 5 Will Sharp; 7 Danny Orr (C); 21 Luke Gale; 8 Karl Temata; 9 Chad Randall; 10 Louie McCarthy-Scarsbrook; 11 Luke Williamson; 14 Tony Clubb; 19 Jason Golden. Subs (all used): 23 Daniel Heckenberg; 17 Danny Ward; 18 Joe Mbu; 26 Matt Gardner.
Tries: Melling (3), Howell (26), Randall (67);
Goals: Orr 1/3.
RHINOS: 1 Brent Webb; 2 Scott Donald; 3 Lee Smith; 4 Keith Senior; 5 Ryan Hall; 6 Danny McGuire; 7 Rob Burrow; 8 Kylie Leuluai; 9 Danny Buderus; 10 Jamie Peacock; 18 Carl Ablett; 11 Jamie Jones-Buchanan; 13 Kevin Sinfield (C). Subs (all used): 12 Ali Lauitiiti; 19 Luke Burgess; 21 Simon Worrall; 23 Kallum Watkins.
Tries: Sinfield (16), McGuire (20), Jones-Buchanan (37), Donald (42), Webb (47), Buderus (53), Smith (60), Hall (71); **Goals:** Sinfield 8/8, Burrow 0/1.
Rugby Leaguer & League Express Men of the Match: *Harlequins:* Danny Orr; *Rhinos:* Rob Burrow.
Penalty count: 8-6; **Half-time:** 8-20;
Referee: Ian Smith; **Attendance:** 4,378.

Sunday 21st June 2009

BRADFORD BULLS 18 ST HELENS 44

BULLS: 20 Dave Halley; 2 Rikki Sheriffe; 11 Steve Menzies; 4 Chris Nero; 5 Semi Tadulala; 6 Ben Jeffries; 7 Paul Deacon (C); 10 Andy Lynch; 9 Terry Newton; 17 Nick Scruton; 8 Sam Burgess; 12 Glenn Morrison; 13 Jamie Langley. Subs (all used): 16 Michael Worrincy; 24 Julien Rinaldi; 28 Elliott Whitehead; 19 Craig Kopczak.
Tries: Morrison (5), Sheriffe (11), Tadulala (62);
Goals: Deacon 3/4.
SAINTS: 1 Paul Wellens; 2 Ade Gardner; 3 Matt Gidley; 12 Jon Wilkin; 5 Francis Meli; 6 Leon Pryce; 18 Kyle Eastmond; 15 Bryn Hargreaves; 9 Keiron Cunningham (C); 10 James Graham; 19 Chris Dean; 13 Chris Flannery; 11 Lee Gilmour. Subs (all used): 17 Paul Clough; 14 James Roby; 23 Maurie Fa'asavalu; 16 Tony Puletua.
Tries: Meli (2, 78), Roby (25), Wilkin (31), Flannery (36), Eastmond (40), Fa'asavalu (71), Puletua (73); **Goals:** Eastmond 6/8.
Rugby Leaguer & League Express Men of the Match: *Bulls:* Chris Nero; *Saints:* James Roby.
Penalty count: 11-6; **Half-time:** 14-28;
Referee: Ben Thaler; **Attendance:** 10,599.

ROUND 18

Friday 26th June 2009

LEEDS RHINOS 33 BRADFORD BULLS 20

RHINOS: 1 Brent Webb; 2 Scott Donald; 3 Lee Smith; 4 Keith Senior; 5 Ryan Hall; 6 Danny McGuire; 7 Rob Burrow; 8 Kylie Leuluai; 9 Danny Buderus; 10 Jamie Peacock; 11 Jamie Jones-Buchanan; 18 Carl Ablett; 13 Kevin Sinfield (C). Subs (all used): 16 Ryan Bailey; 12 Ali Lauitiiti; 19 Luke Burgess; 20 Ashley Gibson.
Tries: Hall (5, 9), Jones-Buchanan (20), Burrow (65), Donald (79); **Goals:** Sinfield 6/7; **Field goal:** Smith (78).
BULLS: 20 Dave Halley; 2 Rikki Sheriffe; 3 Paul Sykes; 4 Chris Nero; 5 Semi Tadulala; 6 Ben Jeffries; 7 Paul Deacon (C); 10 Andy Lynch; 9 Terry Newton; 17 Nick Scruton; 11 Steve Menzies; 13 Jamie Langley; 8 Sam Burgess. Subs (all used): 19 Craig Kopczak; 16 Michael Worrincy; 15 Matt Cook; 28 Elliott Whitehead.
Tries: Tadulala (24), Deacon (50), Menzies (56);
Goals: Deacon 4/5.
Rugby Leaguer & League Express Men of the Match: *Rhinos:* Keith Senior; *Bulls:* Paul Deacon.
Penalty count: 6-9; **Half-time:** 18-8;
Referee: Phil Bentham; **Attendance:** 17,824.

SALFORD CITY REDS 10 HUDDERSFIELD GIANTS 34

CITY REDS: 2 John Wilshere; 3 Mark Henry; 15 Stuart Littler; 14 Jordan Turner; 29 Darrell Goulding; 19 Stefan Ratchford; 6 Jeremy Smith; 8 Ray Cashmere; 9 Malcolm Alker (C); 10 Craig Stapleton; 23 Adam Sidlow; 11 Ian Sibbit; 13 Luke Swain. Subs (all used): 16 Phil Leuluai; 18 Lee Jewitt; 25 Jason Walton; 17 Robbie Paul.
Tries: Turner (29), Wilshere (69); **Goals:** Wilshere 1/2.
GIANTS: 1 Brett Hodgson (C); 21 Leroy Cudjoe; 19 Michael Lawrence; 13 Stephen Wild; 5 David Hodgson; 3 Kevin Brown; 7 Luke Robinson; 16 Keith Mason; 20 Scott Moore; 10 Darrell Griffin; 6 Liam Fulton; 14 Simon Finnigan; 8 Eorl Crabtree. Subs (all used): 9 David Faiumu; 15 Paul Jackson; 33 Danny Sculthorpe; 32 Lee Mossop.
Tries: Moore (3), B Hodgson (6), Lawrence (21), Cudjoe (62, 75), Wild (79); **Goals:** B Hodgson 5/6.
Rugby Leaguer & League Express Men of the Match: *City Reds:* Luke Swain; *Giants:* Brett Hodgson.
Penalty count: 12-10; **Half-time:** 6-18;
Referee: Ben Thaler; **Attendance:** 3,721.

ST HELENS 30 CELTIC CRUSADERS 0

SAINTS: 1 Paul Wellens; 2 Ade Gardner; 3 Matt Gidley; 19 Chris Dean; 5 Francis Meli; 6 Leon Pryce; 7 Sean Long; 10 James Graham; 9 Keiron Cunningham (C); 15 Bryn Hargreaves; 13 Chris Flannery; 12 Jon Wilkin; 11 Lee Gilmour. Subs (all used): 14 James Roby; 16 Tony Puletua; 17 Paul Clough; 23 Maurie Fa'asavalu.
Tries: Gilmour (16), Wellens (19), Puletua (28), Gidley (40), Dean (79); **Goals:** Long 5/5.
CRUSADERS: 6 Damien Quinn; 18 Mark Lennon; 22 Steve Tyrer; 4 Mark Dalle Cort; 5 Anthony Blackwood; 28 Lloyd White (D); 7 Jace Van Dijk (C); 8 Ryan O'Hara; 9 Lincoln Withers; 10 Mark Bryant; 17 Jordan James; 19 Jason Chan; 15 Peter Lupton. Subs (all used): 11 Adam Peek; 16 Ben Flower; 23 Neil Budworth; 25 Geraint Davies.
Rugby Leaguer & League Express Men of the Match: *Saints:* Paul Wellens; *Crusaders:* Mark Bryant.
Penalty count: 8-5; **Half-time:** 24-0;
Referee: Gareth Hewer; **Attendance:** 8,684.

Saturday 27th June 2009

CASTLEFORD TIGERS 20 CATALANS DRAGONS 22

TIGERS: 1 Richard Owen; 2 Kirk Dixon; 3 Michael Shenton; 25 Dean Widders; 5 Michael Wainwright; 21 Sione Faumuina; 23 Ryan McGoldrick (C); 8 Mitchell Sargent; 6 Rangi Chase; 10 Craig Huby; 11 Brett Ferres; 14 Stuart Jones; 13 Joe Westerman. Subs (all used): 15 Liam Higgins; 12 Ryan Clayton; 19 Kirk Netherton; 17 Ryan Boyle.
Tries: Ferres (4), Owen (6, 76);
Goals: Dixon 1/2, Westerman 3/3.
DRAGONS: 1 Clint Greenshields; 5 Dimitri Pelo; 12 Jason Croker; 15 Jean-Phillipe Baile; 3 Steven Bell; 4 Adam Mogg; 6 Thomas Bosc; 8 David Ferriol; 9 Casey McGuire (C); 10 Jerome Guisset; 16 Olivier Elima; 17 Cyrille Gossard; 14 Dane Carlaw. Subs (all used): 7 Shane Perry; 13 Gregory Mounis; 23 Jason Ryles; 24 Remi Casty.
Tries: Pelo (21), Baile (27), Greenshields (53), Carlaw (66); **Goals:** Bosc 3/4.
Rugby Leaguer & League Express Men of the Match: *Tigers:* Richard Owen; *Dragons:* Thomas Bosc.
Penalty count: 8-6; **Half-time:** 10-10;
Referee: Ian Smith; **Attendance:** 5,508.

Sunday 28th June 2009

WARRINGTON WOLVES 24 HULL FC 12

WOLVES: 30 Richard Mathers; 23 Chris Hicks; 25 Chris Bridge; 4 Matt King; 19 Chris Riley; 20 Simon Grix; 7 Michael Monaghan; 8 Adrian Morley (C); 9 Jon Clarke; 16 Garreth Carvell; 11 Louis Anderson; 12 Ben Westwood; 24 Ben Harrison. Subs (all used): 15 Paul Wood; 18 Michael Cooper; 13 Vinnie Anderson; 2 Paul Johnson.
Tries: Riley (39), Wood (46), King (53), Harrison (56);
Goals: Hicks 4/4.
HULL: 1 Motu Tony; 29 Jodie Broughton; 17 Graeme Horne; 4 Kirk Yeaman; 5 Gareth Raynor; 6 Richard Horne; 9 Shaun Berrigan; 8 Ewan Dowes; 23 Tommy Lee; 11 Lee Radford (C); 22 Mike Burnett; 16 Willie Manu; 12 Danny Tickle. Subs (all used): 20 Danny Houghton; 14 Richard Whiting; 19 Paul King; 18 Jamie Thackray.
Tries: Broughton (26), Yeaman (62); **Goals:** Tickle 2/2.
Rugby Leaguer & League Express Men of the Match: *Wolves:* Matt King; *Hull:* Kirk Yeaman.
Penalty count: 2-2; **Half-time:** 6-6;
Referee: Steve Ganson; **Attendance:** 9,170.

WAKEFIELD TRINITY WILDCATS 20 HARLEQUINS 18

WILDCATS: 1 Matt Blaymire; 5 Matt Petersen; 4 Ryan Atkins; 19 Sean Gleeson; 13 Scott Grix; 3 Tony Martin; 7 Danny Brough; 16 Ricky Bibey; 9 Brad Drew; 23 Michael Korkidas; 12 Oliver Wilkes; 11 Steve Snitch; 8 Jason Demetriou (C). Subs (all used): 15 James Stosic; 25 Richard Moore; 18 Frank Winterstein; 20 Tevita Leo-Latu.
Tries: Wilkes (14), Martin (25), Grix (80);
Goals: Brough 4/6.
HARLEQUINS: 27 Jamie O'Callaghan; 1 Chris Melling; 3 Matt Gafa; 4 David Howell; 26 Matt Gardner; 21 Luke Gale; 7 Danny Orr (C); 17 Danny Ward; 9 Chad Randall; 10 Louie McCarthy-Scarsbrook; 8 Karl Temata; 11 Luke Williamson; 19 Jason Golden. Subs (all used): 16 Gareth Haggerty; 23 Daniel Heckenberg; 14 Tony Clubb; 29 Dylan Skee.
Tries: Orr (9), Gale (60), Randall (68); **Goals:** Orr 3/3.
Rugby Leaguer & League Express Men of the Match: *Wildcats:* Danny Brough; *Harlequins:* Chad Randall.
Penalty count: 12-7; **Half-time:** 10-6;
Referee: Richard Silverwood; **Attendance:** 5,079.

HULL KINGSTON ROVERS 28 WIGAN WARRIORS 36

ROVERS: 1 Shaun Briscoe; 2 Peter Fox; 19 Kris Welham; 4 Jake Webster; 28 Ben Cockayne; 6 Paul Cooke; 7 Michael Dobson; 20 Michael Vella (C); 9 Ben Fisher; 18 Scott Wheeldon; 11 Clint Newton; 12 Ben Galea; 13 Scott Murrell. Subs (all used): 8 Nick Fozzard; 16 Jason Netherton; 15 Daniel Fitzhenry; 3 Chev Walker.
Tries: Fox (3, 4), Vella (36), Fitzhenry (65), Webster (71); **Goals:** Dobson 4/5.
WARRIORS: 21 Cameron Phelps; 2 Amos Roberts; 12 Phil Bailey; 4 George Carmont; 5 Pat Richards; 6 Tim Smith; 7 Thomas Leuluai; 15 Andy Coley; 9 Mark Riddell; 19 Paul Prescott; 14 Joel Tomkins; 16 Harrison Hansen; 13 Sean O'Loughlin (C). Subs (all used): 8 Stuart Fielden; 10 Iafeta Palea'aesina; 17 Michael McIlorum; 25 Sam Tomkins.
Tries: Bailey (17, 43), Carmont (24), Richards (28, 78), Hansen (51), S Tomkins (54); **Goals:** Richards 4/7.
Rugby Leaguer & League Express Men of the Match: *Rovers:* Peter Fox; *Warriors:* Sam Tomkins.
Penalty count: 8-3; **Half-time:** 16-14;
Referee: Thierry Alibert; **Attendance:** 9,007.

ROUND 19

Friday 3rd July 2009

SALFORD CITY REDS 20 ST HELENS 10

CITY REDS: 2 John Wilshere; 3 Mark Henry; 15 Stuart Littler; 29 Darrell Goulding; 24 Dean McGilvray; 6 Jeremy Smith; 19 Stefan Ratchford; 8 Ray Cashmere; 9 Malcolm Alker (C); 10 Craig Stapleton; 20 Luke Adamson; 23 Adam Sidlow; 13 Luke Swain. Subs (all used): 16 Phil Leuluai; 18 Lee Jewitt; 25 Jason Walton; 17 Robbie Paul.
Tries: Ratchford (6, 10), Goulding (16), Henry (59);
Goals: Wilshere 2/4.
Sin bin: Smith (55) - punching Wellens.
SAINTS: 1 Paul Wellens (C); 2 Ade Gardner; 13 Chris Flannery; 19 Chris Dean; 5 Francis Meli; 18 Kyle Eastmond; 7 Sean Long; 10 James Graham; 14 James Roby; 15 Bryn Hargreaves; 28 Matty Ashurst; 16 Tony Puletua; 11 Lee Gilmour. Subs (all used): 23 Maurie Fa'asavalu; 27 James Ellis (D); 24 Andrew Dixon; 17 Paul Clough.
Tries: Dixon (44), Meli (79); **Goals:** Eastmond 1/2.
Rugby Leaguer & League Express Men of the Match: *City Reds:* John Wilshere; *Saints:* Andrew Dixon.
Penalty count: 2-7; **Half-time:** 16-0;
Referee: James Child; **Attendance:** 4,808.

WIGAN WARRIORS 40 HARLEQUINS 12

WARRIORS: 21 Cameron Phelps; 2 Amos Roberts; 20 Karl Pryce; 4 George Carmont; 5 Pat Richards; 25 Sam Tomkins; 7 Thomas Leuluai; 15 Andy Coley; 9 Mark Riddell; 19 Paul Prescott; 16 Harrison Hansen; 12 Phil Bailey; 13 Sean O'Loughlin (C). Subs (all used): 8 Stuart Fielden; 10 Iafeta Palea'aesina; 14 Joel Tomkins; 17 Michael McIlorum.
Tries: Richards (2), Riddell (8), Pryce (12), Carmont (29), Roberts (35), J Tomkins (46), Leuluai (56, 61); **Goals:** Richards 4/8.
Sin bin: S Tomkins (76) - dissent.
HARLEQUINS: 1 Chris Melling; 2 Jon Wells; 14 Tony Clubb; 4 David Howell; 5 Will Sharp; 7 Danny Orr (C); 21 Luke Gale; 10 Louie McCarthy-Scarsbrook; 9 Chad Randall; 17 Danny Ward; 11 Luke Williamson; 8 Karl Temata; 3 Matt Gafa. Subs (all used): 12 Chad Robinson; 16 Gareth Haggerty; 23 Daniel Heckenberg; 26 Matt Gardner.
Tries: Gafa (25), Gale (73); **Goals:** Orr 2/2.
Dismissal: Howell (28) - use of the elbow on S Tomkins.
Rugby Leaguer & League Express Men of the Match: *Warriors:* Sam Tomkins; *Harlequins:* Will Sharp.
Penalty count: 3-6; **Half-time:** 24-6;
Referee: Steve Ganson; **Attendance:** 14,977.

Saturday 4th July 2009

HULL FC 30 LEEDS RHINOS 43

HULL: 6 Richard Horne; 5 Gareth Raynor; 17 Graeme Horne; 4 Kirk Yeaman; 29 Jodie Broughton; 7 Chris Thorman; 9 Shaun Berrigan; 18 Jamie Thackray; 23 Tommy Lee; 19 Paul King; 12 Danny Tickle; 16 Willie Manu; 11 Lee Radford (C). Subs (all used): 20 Danny Houghton; 14 Richard Whiting; 22 Mike Burnett; 27 Sam Moa.
Tries: Berrigan (11), Tickle (35), Raynor (51), Yeaman (55), Burnett (70); **Goals:** Tickle 5/5.
RHINOS: 3 Lee Smith; 2 Scott Donald; 20 Ashley Gibson; 4 Keith Senior; 5 Ryan Hall; 13 Kevin Sinfield (C); 7 Rob Burrow; 8 Kylie Leuluai; 9 Danny Buderus; 10 Jamie Peacock; 11 Jamie Jones-Buchanan; 21 Simon Worrall; 18 Carl Ablett. Subs (all used): 14 Matt Diskin; 29 Mike Ratu; 12 Ali Lauitiiti; 19 Luke Burgess.
Tries: Hall (5, 8), Senior (14), Donald (19), Sinfield (32), Gibson (43), Smith (74); **Goals:** Sinfield 7/7;
Field goal: Burrow (64).
Rugby Leaguer & League Express Men of the Match: *Hull:* Shaun Berrigan; *Rhinos:* Kevin Sinfield.
Penalty count: 6-6; **Half-time:** 12-30;
Referee: Ian Smith; **Attendance:** 11,780.

CELTIC CRUSADERS 6 WARRINGTON WOLVES 22

CRUSADERS: 13 Marshall Chalk; 2 Luke Dyer; 22 Steve Tyrer; 4 Mark Dalle Cort; 5 Anthony Blackwood; 18 Mark Lennon; 7 Jace Van Dijk (C); 8 Ryan O'Hara; 9 Lincoln Withers; 10 Mark Bryant; 17 Jordan James; 21 Chris Beasley; 15 Peter Lupton. Subs (all used): 16 Ben Flower; 19 Jason Chan; 23 Neil Budworth; 25 Geraint Davies.
Try: Dyer (77); **Goals:** Lennon 1/1.
WOLVES: 30 Richard Mathers; 23 Chris Hicks; 25 Chris Bridge; 4 Matt King; 19 Chris Riley; 20 Simon Grix; 7 Michael Monaghan; 8 Adrian Morley (C); 9 Jon Clarke; 15 Paul Wood; 11 Louis Anderson; 12 Ben Westwood; 24 Ben Harrison. Subs (all used): 2 Paul Johnson; 13 Vinnie Anderson; 16 Garreth Carvell; 18 Michael Cooper.
Tries: Clarke (9), Harrison (52), Mathers (56, 65);
Goals: Hicks 3/4.
Rugby Leaguer & League Express Men of the Match: *Crusaders:* Jace Van Dijk; *Wolves:* Michael Monaghan.
Penalty count: 6-5; **Half-time:** 0-6;
Referee: Thierry Alibert; **Attendance:** 3,231.

CATALANS DRAGONS 23 HULL KINGSTON ROVERS 12

DRAGONS: 1 Clint Greenshields; 3 Steven Bell; 12 Jason Croker; 15 Jean-Phillipe Baile; 5 Dimitri Pelo; 4 Adam Mogg; 6 Thomas Bosc; 8 David Ferriol; 9 Casey McGuire (C); 10 Jerome Guisset; 16 Olivier Elima; 17 Cyrille Gossard; 23 Jason Ryles. Subs (all used): 7 Shane Perry; 13 Gregory Mounis; 24 Remi Casty; 27 Sebastien Martins (D2).

Catalans' Jason Croker charges towards Wigan's Cameron Phelps as Mark Riddell gives chase

Tries: Baile (9, 14, 79), Croker (39); **Goals:** Bosc 3/4; **Field goal:** Bosc (77).
ROVERS: 1 Shaun Briscoe; 2 Peter Fox; 19 Kris Welham; 3 Chev Walker; 28 Ben Cockayne; 6 Paul Cooke; 7 Michael Dobson; 18 Scott Wheeldon; 9 Ben Fisher; 24 Rhys Lovegrove; 11 Clint Newton; 20 Michael Vella (C); 12 Ben Galea. Subs (all used): 13 Scott Murrell; 15 Daniel Fitzhenry; 16 Jason Netherton; 21 Chaz I'Anson.
Tries: Cockayne (24), Fitzhenry (60); **Goals:** Dobson 2/3.
Rugby Leaguer & League Express Men of the Match:
Dragons: Clint Greenshields; *Rovers:* Clint Newton.
Penalty count: 10-8; **Half-time:** 18-6;
Referee: Richard Silverwood; **Attendance:** 9,073.

Sunday 5th July 2009

BRADFORD BULLS 38 CASTLEFORD TIGERS 40

BULLS: 20 Dave Halley; 2 Rikki Sheriffe; 3 Paul Sykes; 4 Chris Nero; 5 Semi Tadulala; 6 Ben Jeffries; 7 Paul Deacon (C); 10 Andy Lynch; 9 Terry Newton; 17 Nick Scruton; 8 Sam Burgess; 11 Steve Menzies; 13 Jamie Langley. Subs (all used): 16 Michael Worrincy; 14 Wayne Godwin; 30 James Donaldson (D); 19 Craig Kopczak.
Tries: Tadulala (11), Halley (22), Scruton (27), Worrincy (39), Burgess (60), Jeffries (66, 80);
Goals: Deacon 4/6, Sykes 1/1.
TIGERS: 1 Richard Owen; 26 Jordan Thompson; 25 Dean Widders; 3 Michael Shenton; 5 Michael Wainwright; 23 Ryan McGoldrick (C); 6 Rangi Chase; 8 Mitchell Sargent; 14 Stuart Jones; 15 Liam Higgins; 10 Craig Huby; 11 Brett Ferres; 13 Joe Westerman. Subs (all used): 17 Ryan Boyle; 16 Chris Feather; 12 Ryan Clayton; 19 Kirk Netherton.
Tries: Shenton (7, 46), Chase (19, 51), Thompson (44), Westerman (54), Widders (72); **Goals:** Westerman 6/7.
Rugby Leaguer & League Express Men of the Match:
Bulls: Dave Halley; *Tigers:* Rangi Chase.
Penalty count: 8-4; **Half-time:** 22-12;
Referee: Ben Thaler; **Attendance:** 8,971.

HUDDERSFIELD GIANTS 30
WAKEFIELD TRINITY WILDCATS 14

GIANTS: 1 Brett Hodgson (C); 21 Leroy Cudjoe; 11 Jamahl Lolesi; 19 Michael Lawrence; 5 David Hodgson; 6 Liam Fulton; 7 Luke Robinson; 16 Keith Mason; 20 Scott Moore; 10 Darrell Griffin; 13 Stephen Wild; 8 Eorl Crabtree; 9 David Faiumu. Subs (all used): 33 Danny Sculthorpe; 24 Shaun Lunt; 15 Paul Jackson; 32 Lee Mossop.
Tries: Moore (4), Faiumu (13, 59), D Hodgson (69), Fulton (79); **Goals:** B Hodgson 5/5.
WILDCATS: 1 Matt Blaymire; 13 Scott Grix; 19 Sean Gleeson; 4 Ryan Atkins; 5 Matt Petersen; 3 Tony Martin; 7 Danny Brough; 16 Ricky Bibey; 20 Tevita Leo-Latu; 23

Michael Korkidas; 11 Steve Snitch; 12 Oliver Wilkes; 8 Jason Demetriou (C). Subs (all used): 14 Sam Obst; 15 James Stosic; 24 Dale Ferguson; 25 Richard Moore.
Tries: Grix (30), Martin (50), Petersen (74);
Goals: Brough 1/3.
Rugby Leaguer & League Express Men of the Match:
Giants: David Faiumu; *Wildcats:* Michael Korkidas.
Penalty count: 10-7; **Half-time:** 12-4;
Referee: Phil Bentham; **Attendance:** 7,486.

ROUND 20

Friday 10th July 2009

WAKEFIELD TRINITY WILDCATS 30 LEEDS RHINOS 32

WILDCATS: 1 Matt Blaymire; 5 Matt Petersen; 4 Ryan Atkins; 19 Sean Gleeson; 13 Scott Grix; 8 Jason Demetriou (C); 7 Danny Brough; 23 Michael Korkidas; 14 Sam Obst; 16 Ricky Bibey; 12 Oliver Wilkes; 11 Steve Snitch; 20 Tevita Leo-Latu. Subs (all used): 15 James Stosic; 25 Richard Moore; 24 Dale Ferguson; 9 Brad Drew.
Tries: Blaymire (20), Obst (36), Grix (51), Atkins (55);
Goals: Brough 7/7.
Sin bin: Snitch (15) - delaying restart.
RHINOS: 1 Brent Webb; 2 Scott Donald; 3 Lee Smith; 4 Keith Senior; 5 Ryan Hall; 6 Danny McGuire; 7 Rob Burrow; 8 Kylie Leuluai; 9 Danny Buderus; 11 Jamie Jones-Buchanan; 12 Ali Lauitiiti; 18 Carl Ablett; 13 Kevin Sinfield (C). Subs (all used): 15 James Diskin; 21 Simon Worrall; 10 Jamie Peacock; 19 Luke Burgess.
Tries: Jones-Buchanan (8), Senior (30), Burrow (41, 78), Lauitiiti (65), Donald (80);
Goals: Sinfield 3/4, Smith 1/2.
Sin bin: Webb (68) - holding down.
On report: Lauitiiti (13) - alleged high tackle on Petersen.
Rugby Leaguer & League Express Men of the Match:
Wildcats: Danny Brough; *Rhinos:* Keith Senior.
Penalty count: 10-4; **Half-time:** 16-10;
Referee: Steve Ganson; **Attendance:** 6,425.

WIGAN WARRIORS 24 CATALANS DRAGONS 22

WARRIORS: 21 Cameron Phelps; 2 Amos Roberts; 3 Darrell Goulding; 4 George Carmont; 5 Pat Richards; 25 Sam Tomkins; 7 Thomas Leuluai (C); 15 Andy Coley; 9 Mark Riddell; 19 Paul Prescott; 16 Harrison Hansen; 12 Phil Bailey; 14 Joel Tomkins. Subs (all used): 8 Stuart Fielden; 10 Iafeta Palea'aesina; 20 Karl Pryce; 24 Lee Mossop.
Tries: Carmont (23), Richards (26, 64), Roberts (45), Goulding (74); **Goals:** Richards 2/5.
Sin bin: Leuluai (35) - dissent.
DRAGONS: 1 Clint Greenshields; 3 Steven Bell; 12 Jason

Croker; 15 Jean-Phillipe Baile; 5 Dimitri Pelo; 26 Greg Bird (C); 6 Thomas Bosc; 8 David Ferriol; 9 Casey McGuire; 10 Jerome Guisset; 16 Olivier Elima; 17 Cyrille Gossard; 23 Jason Ryles. Subs (all used): 7 Shane Perry; 13 Gregory Mounis; 22 Jamal Fakir; 24 Remi Casty.
Tries: Bell (35), Elima (39), Bird (50), Pelo (57);
Goals: Bosc 3/4.
Sin bin: Greenshields (26) - dissent.
Rugby Leaguer & League Express Men of the Match:
Warriors: Andy Coley; *Dragons:* Greg Bird.
Penalty count: 13-5; **Half-time:** 10-12;
Referee: Ben Thaler; **Attendance:** 11,543.

Saturday 11th July 2009

HARLEQUINS 16 HUDDERSFIELD GIANTS 32

HARLEQUINS: 1 Chris Melling; 2 Jon Wells; 3 Matt Gafa; 14 Tony Clubb; 5 Will Sharp; 21 Luke Gale; 7 Danny Orr (C); 17 Danny Ward; 9 Chad Randall; 10 Louie McCarthy-Scarsbrook; 11 Luke Williamson; 12 Chad Robinson; 8 Karl Temata. Subs (all used): 23 Daniel Heckenberg; 16 Gareth Haggerty; 32 Ryan Esders (D); 15 Ben Kaye.
Tries: Gale (13), Melling (70, 74); **Goals:** Orr 2/3.
GIANTS: 1 Brett Hodgson (C); 21 Leroy Cudjoe; 19 Michael Lawrence; 4 Paul Whatuira; 5 David Hodgson; 3 Kevin Brown; 7 Luke Robinson; 16 Keith Mason; 20 Scott Moore; 33 Danny Sculthorpe; 6 Liam Fulton; 13 Stephen Wild; 14 Simon Finnigan. Subs (all used): 9 David Faiumu; 2 Eorl Crabtree; 10 Darrell Griffin; 9 David Faiumu; 2 Martin Aspinwall.
Tries: Cudjoe (20), D Hodgson (38), Lawrence (47), B Hodgson (78, 80); **Goals:** B Hodgson 6/6.
Rugby Leaguer & League Express Men of the Match:
Harlequins: Luke Gale; *Giants:* Brett Hodgson.
Penalty count: 9-4; **Half-time:** 6-12;
Referee: Thierry Alibert; **Attendance:** 3,916.

CELTIC CRUSADERS 25 SALFORD CITY REDS 12

CRUSADERS: 6 Damien Quinn; 2 Luke Dyer; 13 Marshall Chalk; 4 Mark Dalle Cort; 5 Anthony Blackwood; 14 Matty Smith; 7 Jace Van Dijk (C); 8 Ryan O'Hara; 9 Lincoln Withers; 10 Mark Bryant; 17 Jordan James; 19 Jason Chan; 15 Peter Lupton. Subs (all used): 23 Neil Budworth; 11 Adam Peek; 21 Chris Beasley; 18 Mark Lennon.
Tries: Chalk (20), Blackwood (28), Withers (33), Smith (59); **Goals:** Quinn 4/4; **Field goal:** Smith (79).
CITY REDS: 2 John Wilshere; 24 Dean McGilvray; 15 Stuart Littler; 19 Stefan Ratchford; 3 Mark Henry; 6 Jeremy Smith; 7 Richard Myler; 8 Ray Cashmere; 9 Malcolm Alker (C); 10 Craig Stapleton; 20 Luke Adamson; 23 Adam Sidlow; 13 Luke Swain. Subs (all used): 17 Robbie Paul; 25 Jason Walton; 16 Phil Leuluai; 18 Lee Jewitt.

221

Castleford's Craig Huby brought down by Hull's Shaun Berrigan

Tries: Adamson (3), Littler (14); **Goals:** Wilshere 2/2.
Rugby Leaguer & League Express Men of the Match:
Crusaders: Matty Smith; *City Reds:* John Wilshere.
Penalty count: 6-6; **Half-time:** 18-12;
Referee: Phil Bentham; **Attendance:** 3,009.

WARRINGTON WOLVES 26 ST HELENS 40

WOLVES: 30 Richard Mathers; 32 Brian Carney (D); 20 Simon Grix; 4 Matt King; 19 Chris Riley; 25 Chris Bridge; 7 Michael Monaghan (C); 16 Garreth Carvell; 9 Jon Clarke; 15 Paul Wood; 11 Louis Anderson; 12 Ben Westwood; 24 Ben Harrison. Subs (all used): 13 Vinnie Anderson; 2 Paul Johnson; 22 Lee Mitchell; 18 Michael Cooper.
Tries: Clarke (9), Bridge (34), Johnson (43), Carvell (54); **Goals:** Bridge 5/5.
SAINTS: 1 Paul Wellens (C); 2 Ade Gardner; 21 Gary Wheeler; 11 Lee Gilmour; 5 Francis Meli; 6 Leon Pryce; 18 Kyle Eastmond; 10 James Graham; 14 James Roby; 17 Paul Clough; 13 Chris Flannery; 12 Jon Wilkin; 16 Tony Puletua. Subs (all used): 15 Bryn Hargreaves; 23 Maurie Fa'asavalu; 24 Andrew Dixon; 30 Jonny Lomax.
Tries: Gilmour (15), Graham (19, 75), Gardner (39), Wellens (57), Eastmond (70), Meli (79);
Goals: Eastmond 6/8.
On report:
Gilmour (33) - alleged late challenge on Mathers.
Rugby Leaguer & League Express Men of the Match:
Wolves: Garreth Carvell; *Saints:* Kyle Eastmond.
Penalty count: 6-6; **Half-time:** 12-18;
Referee: Richard Silverwood; **Attendance:** 12,075.

Sunday 12th July 2009

HULL KINGSTON ROVERS 32 BRADFORD BULLS 12

ROVERS: 1 Shaun Briscoe; 2 Peter Fox; 4 Jake Webster; 19 Kris Welham; 5 Liam Colbon; 6 Paul Cooke; 7 Michael Dobson; 20 Michael Vella (C); 9 Ben Fisher; 18 Scott Wheeldon; 11 Clint Newton; 12 Ben Galea; 13 Scott Murrell. Subs (all used): 3 Chev Walker; 15 Daniel Fitzhenry; 29 Kyle Bibb (D); 24 Rhys Lovegrove.
Tries: Murrell (18), Colbon (30, 64), Welham (36, 54), Fitzhenry (76); **Goals:** Dobson 4/7.
BULLS: 20 Dave Halley; 2 Rikki Sheriffe; 3 Paul Sykes; 4 Chris Nero; 5 Semi Tadulala; 6 Ben Jeffries; 7 Paul Deacon (C); 10 Andy Lynch; 9 Terry Newton; 17 Nick Scruton; 16 Michael Worrincy; 13 Jamie Langley; 8 Sam Burgess. Subs (all used): 15 Matt Cook; 11 Steve Menzies; 14 Wayne Godwin; 19 Craig Kopczak.
Tries: Halley (9), Worrincy (25);
Goals: Deacon 1/1, Sykes 1/1.
Rugby Leaguer & League Express Men of the Match:
Rovers: Shaun Briscoe; *Bulls:* Dave Halley.
Penalty count: 8-9; **Half-time:** 16-12;
Referee: Ian Smith; **Attendance:** 8,206.

CASTLEFORD TIGERS 40 HULL FC 18

TIGERS: 1 Richard Owen; 2 Kirk Dixon; 3 Michael Shenton; 25 Dean Widders; 5 Michael Wainwright; 6 Rangi Chase; 23 Ryan McGoldrick; 8 Mitchell Sargent; 9 Ryan Hudson (C); 10 Craig Huby; 11 Brett Ferres; 12 Ryan Clayton; 13 Joe Westerman. Subs (all used): 14 Stuart Jones; 16 Chris Feather; 19 Kirk Netherton; 15 Liam Higgins.
Tries: Chase (4, 46), Huby (17), Wainwright (21, 78), Hudson (24), Shenton (74); **Goals:** Westerman 6/7.
HULL: 6 Richard Horne; 29 Jodie Broughton; 17 Graeme Horne; 4 Kirk Yeaman; 5 Gareth Raynor; 7 Chris Thorman; 9 Shaun Berrigan; 19 Paul King; 23 Tommy Lee; 30 Josh Cordoba (D); 16 Willie Manu; 12 Danny Tickle; 11 Lee Radford (C). Subs (all used): 20 Danny Houghton; 14 Richard Whiting; 22 Mike Burnett; 27 Sam Moa.
Tries: Manu (31), Yeaman (58), Broughton (80);
Goals: Tickle 1/1, Whiting 2/2.
Rugby Leaguer & League Express Men of the Match:
Tigers: Rangi Chase; *Hull:* Richard Horne.
Penalty count: 8-7; **Half-time:** 24-6;
Referee: Jamie Leahy; **Attendance:** 8,297.

ROUND 21

Friday 17th July 2009

HULL FC 22 CELTIC CRUSADERS 6

HULL: 31 Jordan Tansey (D); 2 Mark Calderwood; 14 Richard Whiting; 24 Craig Hall; 5 Gareth Raynor; 6 Richard Horne; 9 Shaun Berrigan; 30 Josh Cordoba; 20 Danny Houghton; 19 Paul King; 12 Danny Tickle; 16 Willie Manu; 11 Lee Radford (C). Subs (all used): 23 Tommy Lee; 27 Sam Moa; 22 Mike Burnett; 17 Graeme Horne.
Tries: Hall (39), Raynor (68), Calderwood (73); Cordoba (79); **Goals:** Tickle 3/4.
CRUSADERS: 6 Damien Quinn; 2 Luke Dyer; 13 Marshall Chalk; 4 Mark Dalle Cort; 5 Anthony Blackwood; 14 Matty Smith; 7 Jace Van Dijk (C); 8 Ryan O'Hara; 9 Lincoln Withers; 10 Mark Bryant; 17 Jordan James; 19 Jason Chan; 15 Peter Lupton. Subs (all used): 23 Neil Budworth; 11 Adam Peek; 21 Chris Beasley; 20 David Tangata-Toa.
Try: Chan (49); **Goals:** Quinn 1/1.
Rugby Leaguer & League Express Men of the Match:
Hull: Richard Whiting; *Crusaders:* Matty Smith.
Penalty count: 6-6; **Half-time:** 4-0;
Referee: James Child; **Attendance:** 10,397.

LEEDS RHINOS 24 HULL KINGSTON ROVERS 14

RHINOS: 1 Brent Webb; 23 Kallum Watkins; 3 Lee Smith; 4 Keith Senior; 5 Ryan Hall; 6 Danny McGuire; 7 Rob Burrow; 8 Kylie Leuluai; 14 Matt Diskin; 10 Jamie

Peacock (C); 11 Jamie Jones-Buchanan; 12 Ali Lauitiiti; 18 Carl Ablett. Subs (all used): 19 Luke Burgess; 29 Mike Ratu; 9 Danny Buderus; 27 Dane Manning (D).
Tries: Webb (2), Peacock (55), Buderus (70), Smith (72); **Goals:** Smith 4/4.
ROVERS: 28 Ben Cockayne; 2 Peter Fox; 4 Jake Webster; 19 Kris Welham; 5 Liam Colbon; 6 Paul Cooke; 7 Michael Dobson; 8 Nick Fozzard; 9 Ben Fisher; 20 Michael Vella (C); 11 Clint Newton; 12 Ben Galea; 13 Scott Murrell. Subs (all used): 3 Chev Walker; 24 Rhys Lovegrove; 18 Scott Wheeldon; 15 Daniel Fitzhenry.
Tries: Welham (22), Cockayne (35); **Goals:** Dobson 3/3.
Rugby Leaguer & League Express Men of the Match:
Rhinos: Jamie Peacock; *Rovers:* Scott Murrell.
Penalty count: 6-4; **Half-time:** 6-12;
Referee: Ben Thaler; **Attendance:** 16,192.

SALFORD CITY REDS 12 CASTLEFORD TIGERS 18

CITY REDS: 2 John Wilshere; 3 Mark Henry; 14 Jordan Turner; 19 Stefan Ratchford; 24 Dean McGilvray; 6 Jeremy Smith; 7 Richard Myler; 8 Ray Cashmere; 9 Malcolm Alker (C); 10 Craig Stapleton; 20 Luke Adamson; 23 Adam Sidlow; 13 Luke Swain. Subs (all used): 16 Phil Leuluai; 18 Lee Jewitt; 15 Stuart Littler; 17 Robbie Paul.
Tries: McGilvray (54), Ratchford (75);
Goals: Wilshere 2/2.
TIGERS: 1 Richard Owen; 2 Kirk Dixon; 3 Michael Shenton; 25 Dean Widders; 5 Michael Wainwright; 6 Rangi Chase; 23 Ryan McGoldrick; 8 Mitchell Sargent; 9 Ryan Hudson (C); 10 Craig Huby; 11 Brett Ferres; 12 Ryan Clayton; 13 Joe Westerman. Subs (all used): 14 Stuart Jones; 15 Liam Higgins; 16 Chris Feather; 19 Kirk Netherton.
Tries: Ferres (32), Shenton (39), Netherton (59);
Goals: Westerman 3/3.
Rugby Leaguer & League Express Men of the Match:
City Reds: John Wilshere; *Tigers:* Ryan McGoldrick.
Penalty count: 10-5; **Half-time:** 0-12;
Referee: Gareth Hewer; **Attendance:** 3,487.

ST HELENS 20 WAKEFIELD TRINITY WILDCATS 22

SAINTS: 1 Paul Wellens; 2 Ade Gardner; 3 Matt Gidley; 19 Chris Dean; 5 Francis Meli; 6 Leon Pryce; 10 James Graham; 14 James Roby; 16 Tony Puletua; 18 Matty Ashurst; 24 Andrew Dixon; 11 Lee Gilmour. Subs (all used): 9 Keiron Cunningham (C); 15 Bryn Hargreaves; 17 Paul Clough; 30 Jonny Lomax.
Tries: Gardner (4), Pryce (24), Dean (27, 69), Meli (53);
Goals: Wellens 0/6.
WILDCATS: 1 Matt Blaymire; 5 Matt Petersen; 4 Ryan Atkins; 19 Sean Gleeson; 13 Scott Grix; 14 Sam Obst; 7 Danny Brough; 16 Ricky Bibey; 20 Tevita Leo-Latu; 23 Michael Korkidas; 11 Steve Snitch; 12 Oliver Wilkes; 8 Jason Demetriou (C). Subs (all used): 15 James Stosic;

25 Richard Moore; 24 Dale Ferguson; 17 Kevin Henderson.
Tries: Atkins (10), Obst (33), Grix (49, 56);
Goals: Brough 3/4.
Rugby Leaguer & League Express Men of the Match:
Saints: Paul Wellens; *Wildcats:* Jason Demetriou.
Penalty count: 9-2; **Half-time:** 12-12;
Referee: Thierry Alibert; **Attendance:** 8,651.

Sunday 19th July 2009

BRADFORD BULLS 14 WIGAN WARRIORS 20

BULLS: 1 Michael Platt; 2 Rikki Sheriffe; 11 Steve Menzies; 4 Chris Nero; 20 Dave Halley; 3 Paul Sykes; 7 Paul Deacon (C); 10 Andy Lynch; 9 Terry Newton; 17 Nick Scruton; 28 Elliott Whitehead; 16 Michael Worrincy; 13 Jamie Langley. Subs (all used): 8 Sam Burgess; 14 Wayne Godwin; 30 James Donaldson; 15 Matt Cook.
Tries: Donaldson (53), Nero (68); **Goals:** Deacon 3/3.
WARRIORS: 21 Cameron Phelps; 2 Amos Roberts; 22 Martin Gleeson; 4 George Carmont; 5 Pat Richards; 25 Sam Tomkins; 7 Thomas Leuluai (C); 15 Andy Coley; 9 Mark Riddell; 19 Paul Prescott; 16 Harrison Hansen; 12 Phil Bailey; 14 Joel Tomkins. Subs (all used): 8 Stuart Fielden; 10 Iafeta Palea'aesina; 3 Darrell Goulding; 24 Lee Mossop.
Tries: J Tomkins (22), Richards (46), Gleeson (74), Roberts (78); **Goals:** Richards 2/4.
Rugby Leaguer & League Express Men of the Match:
Bulls: Sam Burgess; *Warriors:* Joel Tomkins.
Penalty count: 9-7; **Half-time:** 0-6;
Referee: Richard Silverwood; **Attendance:** 9,487.

HUDDERSFIELD GIANTS 28 WARRINGTON WOLVES 10

GIANTS: 1 Brett Hodgson (C); 21 Leroy Cudjoe; 19 Michael Lawrence; 4 Paul Whatuira; 5 David Hodgson; 3 Kevin Brown; 7 Luke Robinson; 16 Keith Mason; 24 Shaun Lunt; 10 Darrell Griffin; 6 Liam Fulton; 13 Stephen Wild; 9 David Faiumu. Subs (all used): 2 Martin Aspinwall; 8 Eorl Crabtree; 15 Paul Jackson; 20 Scott Moore.
Tries: Jackson (18), Moore (28), Cudjoe (33, 50), Lawrence (61); **Goals:** B Hodgson 4/5.
WOLVES: 30 Richard Mathers; 32 Brian Carney; 2 Paul Johnson; 4 Matt King; 19 Chris Riley; 25 Chris Bridge; 6 Lee Briers (C); 15 Paul Wood; 7 Michael Monaghan; 16 Garreth Carvell; 11 Louis Anderson; 24 Ben Harrison; 12 Ben Westwood. Subs (all used): 9 Jon Clarke; 22 Lee Mitchell; 18 Michael Cooper; 21 Matty Blythe.
Tries: Westwood (44), Carney (79); **Goals:** Bridge 1/2.
Rugby Leaguer & League Express Men of the Match:
Giants: Luke Robinson; *Wolves:* Lee Briers.
Penalty count: 8-11; **Half-time:** 18-0;
Referee: Ian Smith; **Attendance:** 7,107.

CATALANS DRAGONS 38 HARLEQUINS 16

DRAGONS: 1 Clint Greenshields; 2 Cyril Stacul; 3 Steven Bell; 15 Jean-Phillipe Baile; 5 Dimitri Pelo; 26 Greg Bird (C); 6 Thomas Bosc; 8 David Ferriol; 9 Casey McGuire; 23 Jason Ryles; 16 Olivier Elima; 17 Cyrille Gossard; 14 Dane Carlaw. Subs (all used): 7 Shane Perry; 13 Gregory Mounis; 22 Jamal Fakir; 24 Remi Casty.
Tries: Elima (14), Pelo (37, 43), Bosc (51), Baile (64), Bell (70), McGuire (80); **Goals:** Bosc 5/7.
HARLEQUINS: 1 Chris Melling; 27 Jamie O'Callaghan; 14 Tony Clubb; 2 Jon Wells; 5 Will Sharp; 3 Matt Gafa; 21 Luke Gale; 8 Karl Temata; 15 Ben Kaye; 17 Danny Ward (C); 12 Chad Robinson; 32 Ryan Esders; 19 Jason Golden. Subs (all used): 10 Louie McCarthy-Scarsbrook; 16 Gareth Haggerty; 24 Luke May (D); 29 Dylan Skee.
Tries: Esders (48), Gale (57), Haggerty (76);
Goals: Melling 0/1, Gale 2/2.
Rugby Leaguer & League Express Men of the Match:
Dragons: Thomas Bosc; *Harlequins:* Luke Gale.
Penalty count: 7-6; **Half-time:** 8-0;
Referee: Steve Ganson; **Attendance:** 8,324.

ROUND 22

Friday 24th July 2009

WIGAN WARRIORS 28 LEEDS RHINOS 10

WARRIORS: 21 Cameron Phelps; 2 Amos Roberts; 22 Martin Gleeson (C); 4 George Carmont; 5 Pat Richards; 25 Sam Tomkins; 7 Thomas Leuluai; 15 Andy Coley; 9 Mark Riddell; 19 Paul Prescott; 14 Joel Tomkins; 16 Harrison Hansen; 26 Mark Flanagan. Subs (all used): 3 Darrell Goulding; 8 Stuart Fielden; 10 Iafeta Palea'aesina; 24 Lee Mossop.
Tries: Carmont (36), Hansen (43), J Tomkins (57), S Tomkins (71); **Goals:** Richards 6/7.
RHINOS: 3 Lee Smith; 2 Scott Donald; 29 Mike Ratu; 4 Keith Senior; 5 Ryan Hall; 6 Danny McGuire; 7 Rob Burrow; 8 Kylie Leuluai; 9 Danny Buderus; 10 Jamie Peacock; 11 Jamie Jones-Buchanan; 18 Carl Ablett; 13 Kevin Sinfield (C). Subs: 14 Matt Diskin; 12 Ali Lauitiiti; 19 Luke Burgess; 21 Simon Worrall (not used).
Tries: McGuire (21), Donald (25); **Goals:** Sinfield 1/2.
Rugby Leaguer & League Express Men of the Match:
Warriors: Sam Tomkins; *Rhinos:* Rob Burrow.
Penalty count: 13-7; **Half-time:** 6-10;
Referee: Phil Bentham; **Attendance:** 20,295.

Saturday 25th July 2009

HARLEQUINS 24 ST HELENS 44

HARLEQUINS: 5 Will Sharp; 2 Jon Wells; 3 Matt Gafa; 14 Tony Clubb; 1 Chris Melling; 6 Luke Dorn; 21 Luke Gale; 8 Karl Temata; 15 Ben Kaye; 17 Danny Ward; 11 Luke Williamson; 12 Chad Robinson; 19 Jason Golden. Subs (all used): 32 Ryan Esders; 10 Louie McCarthy-Scarsbrook; 16 Gareth Haggerty; 7 Danny Orr (C).
Tries: Haggerty (43), Robinson (50), Ward (70), Gafa (75); **Goals:** Orr 4/4.
SAINTS: 3 Matt Gidley; 29 Tom Armstrong; 19 Chris Dean; 11 Lee Gilmour; 5 Francis Meli; 6 Leon Pryce; 18 Kyle Eastmond; 10 James Graham; 9 Keiron Cunningham (C); 16 Tony Puletua; 12 Jon Wilkin; 13 Chris Flannery; 24 Andrew Dixon. Subs (all used): 28 Matty Ashurst; 17 Paul Clough; 15 Bryn Hargreaves; 27 James Ellis.
Tries: Armstrong (4), Puletua (16, 34), Graham (20), Eastmond (28), Pryce (37), Dean (46), Wilkin (56);
Goals: Eastmond 6/8.
Rugby Leaguer & League Express Men of the Match:
Harlequins: Danny Orr; *Saints:* Keiron Cunningham.
Penalty count: 7-12; **Half-time:** 0-34;
Referee: James Child; **Attendance:** 4,258.

CELTIC CRUSADERS 12 BRADFORD BULLS 34

CRUSADERS: 6 Damien Quinn; 22 Steve Tyrer; 3 Josh Hannay; 4 Mark Dalle Cort; 5 Anthony Blackwood; 14 Matty Smith; 7 Jace Van Dijk (C); 8 Ryan O'Hara; 9 Lincoln Withers; 10 Mark Bryant; 17 Jordan James; 21 Chris Beasley; 15 Peter Lupton. Subs (all used): 23 Neil Budworth; 16 Ben Flower; 20 David Tangata-Toa; 18 Mark Lennon.
Tries: Withers (58), Smith (72); **Goals:** Quinn 2/2.
BULLS: 20 Dave Halley; 2 Rikki Sheriffe; 1 Michael Platt; 4 Chris Nero; 5 Semi Tadulala; 3 Paul Sykes; 7 Paul Deacon (C); 10 Andy Lynch; 14 Wayne Godwin; 17 Nick Scruton; 28 Elliott Whitehead; 12 Glenn Morrison; 13 Jamie Langley. Subs (all used): 8 Sam Burgess; 30 James Donaldson; 9 Terry Newton; 16 Michael Worrincy.
Tries: Morrison (19), Whitehead (22), Halley (25), Lynch (50, 66), Tadulala (78); **Goals:** Deacon 5/7.
Rugby Leaguer & League Express Men of the Match:
Crusaders: Matty Smith; *Bulls:* Andy Lynch.
Penalty count: 9-4; **Half-time:** 0-18;
Referee: Thierry Alibert; **Attendance:** 3,081.

HULL KINGSTON ROVERS 24 HULL FC 18

ROVERS: 1 Shaun Briscoe; 2 Peter Fox; 19 Kris Welham; 4 Jake Webster; 5 Liam Colbon; 6 Paul Cooke; 7 Michael Dobson; 8 Nick Fozzard; 9 Ben Fisher; 20 Michael Vella (C); 11 Clint Newton; 12 Ben Galea; 13 Scott Murrell. Subs (all used): 3 Chev Walker; 15 Daniel Fitzhenry; 18 Scott Wheeldon; 24 Rhys Lovegrove.
Tries: Dobson (3), Cooke (5, 58), Webster (67);
Goals: Dobson 4/5.
HULL: 31 Jordan Tansey; 2 Mark Calderwood; 14 Richard Whiting; 24 Craig Hall; 5 Gareth Raynor; 6 Richard Horne; 9 Shaun Berrigan; 30 Josh Cordoba; 20 Danny Houghton; 19 Paul King; 16 Willie Manu; 12 Danny Tickle; 11 Lee Radford (C). Subs (all used): 17 Graeme Horne; 23 Tommy Lee; 22 Mike Burnett; 27 Sam Moa.
Tries: Tansey (38), Hall (52), Calderwood (64);
Goals: Tickle 3/3.
Rugby Leaguer & League Express Men of the Match:
Rovers: Paul Cooke; *Hull:* Jordan Tansey.
Penalty count: 5-5; **Half-time:** 12-6;
Referee: Richard Silverwood; **Attendance:** 9,450.

Sunday 26th July 2009

HUDDERSFIELD GIANTS 36 CATALANS DRAGONS 12

GIANTS: 1 Brett Hodgson (C); 21 Leroy Cudjoe; 19 Michael Lawrence; 13 Stephen Wild; 5 David Hodgson; 3 Kevin Brown; 7 Luke Robinson; 10 Darrell Griffin; 24 Shaun Lunt; 15 Paul Jackson; 14 Simon Finnigan; 18 Danny Kirmond; 6 Liam Fulton. Subs (all used): 33 Danny Sculthorpe; 20 Scott Moore; 2 Martin Aspinwall; 8 Eorl Crabtree.
Tries: Cudjoe (7, 29, 75), B Hodgson (12), D Griffin (20), D Hodgson (48), Finnigan (57); **Goals:** B Hodgson 4/7.
DRAGONS: 1 Clint Greenshields; 5 Dimitri Pelo; 15 Jean-Phillipe Baile; 17 Cyrille Gossard; 3 Steven Bell; 26 Greg Bird (C); 6 Thomas Bosc; 8 David Ferriol; 9 Casey McGuire; 10 Jerome Guisset; 16 Olivier Elima; 23 Jason Ryles; 13 Gregory Mounis. Subs (all used): 22 Jamal Fakir; 24 Remi Casty; 14 Dane Carlaw; 7 Shane Perry.
Tries: Greenshields (2), Pelo (31); **Goals:** Bosc 2/2.
Sin bin: Greenshields (10) - holding down.
On report:
Bird (37) - alleged late challenge on D Hodgson.
Rugby Leaguer & League Express Men of the Match:
Giants: Leroy Cudjoe; *Dragons:* Clint Greenshields.
Penalty count: 12-6; **Half-time:** 20-12;
Referee: Phil Bentham; **Attendance:** 5,823.

WARRINGTON WOLVES 62 SALFORD CITY REDS 20

WOLVES: 19 Chris Riley; 23 Chris Hicks; 25 Chris Bridge; 4 Matt King; 32 Brian Carney; 20 Simon Grix; 6 Lee Briers; 8 Adrian Morley (C); 7 Michael Monaghan; 16 Garreth Carvell; 11 Louis Anderson; 24 Ben Harrison; 12 Ben Westwood. Subs (all used): 15 Paul Wood; 18 Michael Cooper; 2 Paul Johnson; 22 Lee Mitchell.
Tries: Briers (6, 54), Carvell (9), Johnson (45), Grix (51), Westwood (59), Riley (62), Morley (65), Bridge (68), Carney (73), Hicks (79); **Goals:** Bridge 9/11.
CITY REDS: 2 John Wilshere; 24 Dean McGilvray; 15 Stuart Littler; 19 Stefan Ratchford; 3 Mark Henry; 6 Jeremy Smith; 7 Richard Myler; 8 Ray Cashmere; 9 Malcolm Alker (C); 10 Craig Stapleton; 20 Luke Adamson; 23 Adam Sidlow; 13 Luke Swain. Subs (all used): 17 Robbie Paul; 11 Ian Sibbit; 16 Phil Leuluai; 22 Stephen Nash.
Tries: Henry (13), Littler (27), Myler (36), Smith (39);
Goals: Wilshere 2/4.
Sin bin: Leuluai (78) - holding down.
Rugby Leaguer & League Express Men of the Match:
Wolves: Ben Westwood; *City Reds:* Stefan Ratchford.
Penalty count: 12-4; **Half-time:** 12-20;
Referee: Ben Thaler; **Attendance:** 8,906.

WAKEFIELD TRINITY WILDCATS 12
CASTLEFORD TIGERS 20

WILDCATS: 1 Matt Blaymire; 13 Scott Grix; 19 Sean Gleeson; 4 Ryan Atkins; 27 Aaron Murphy; 8 Jason Demetriou (C); 7 Danny Brough; 16 Ricky Bibey; 14 Sam Obst; 23 Michael Korkidas; 11 Steve Snitch; 12 Oliver Wilkes; 17 Kevin Henderson. Subs (all used): 15 James Stosic; 25 Richard Moore; 24 Dale Ferguson; 9 Brad Drew.
Tries: Brough (17, 53); **Goals:** Brough 2/2.
TIGERS: 1 Richard Owen; 5 Michael Wainwright; 3 Michael Shenton; 25 Dean Widders; 2 Kirk Dixon; 23 Ryan McGoldrick; 6 Rangi Chase; 8 Mitchell Sargent; 9 Ryan Hudson (C); 15 Liam Higgins; 10 Craig Huby; 12 Ryan Clayton; 13 Joe Westerman. Subs (all used): 4 James Evans; 14 Stuart Jones; 16 Chris Feather; 19 Kirk Netherton.
Tries: Widders (2, 42); **Goals:** Westerman 6/6.
Rugby Leaguer & League Express Men of the Match:
Wildcats: Danny Brough; *Tigers:* Rangi Chase.
Penalty count: 9-10; **Half-time:** 6-8;
Referee: Ian Smith; **Attendance:** 8,371.

ROUND 23

Friday 31st July 2009

HULL FC 0 HUDDERSFIELD GIANTS 24

HULL: 31 Jordan Tansey; 2 Mark Calderwood; 17 Graeme Horne; 24 Craig Hall; 5 Gareth Raynor; 6 Richard Horne; 9 Shaun Berrigan; 30 Josh Cordoba; 20 Danny Houghton; 19 Paul King; 12 Danny Tickle; 16 Willie Manu; 11 Lee Radford (C). Subs (all used): 26 Josh Hodgson; 27 Sam Moa; 22 Mike Burnett; 7 Chris Thorman.
GIANTS: 1 Brett Hodgson (C); 21 Leroy Cudjoe; 11 Jamahl Lolesi; 19 Michael Lawrence; 5 David Hodgson; 3 Kevin Brown; 7 Luke Robinson; 16 Keith Mason; 20 Scott Moore; 15 Paul Jackson; 6 Liam Fulton; 14 Simon Finnigan; 9 David Faiumu. Subs (all used): 24 Shaun Lunt; 18 Danny Kirmond; 33 Danny Sculthorpe; 2 Martin Aspinwall.
Tries: D Hodgson (28), Lunt (37), Lawrence (45), Cudjoe (79); **Goals:** B Hodgson 4/4.
Rugby Leaguer & League Express Men of the Match:
Hull: Shaun Berrigan; *Giants:* Kevin Brown.
Penalty count: 8-3; **Half-time:** 0-12;
Referee: Steve Ganson; **Attendance:** 11,191.

SALFORD CITY REDS 24
WAKEFIELD TRINITY WILDCATS 30

CITY REDS: 2 John Wilshere; 3 Mark Henry; 15 Stuart Littler; 19 Stefan Ratchford; 24 Dean McGilvray; 6 Jeremy Smith; 7 Richard Myler; 8 Ray Cashmere; 9 Malcolm Alker (C); 10 Craig Stapleton; 20 Luke Adamson; 23 Adam Sidlow; 13 Luke Swain. Subs (all used): 16 Phil Leuluai; 11 Ian Sibbit; 22 Stephen Nash; 17 Robbie Paul.
Tries: McGilvray (32, 54), Leuluai (77, 80);
Goals: Wilshere 4/5.
WILDCATS: 1 Matt Blaymire; 19 Sean Gleeson; 8 Jason Demetriou (C); 4 Ryan Atkins; 13 Scott Grix; 14 Sam Obst; 7 Danny Brough; 16 Ricky Bibey; 9 Brad Drew; 23 Michael Korkidas; 11 Steve Snitch; 12 Oliver Wilkes; 24 Dale Ferguson. Subs (all used): 33 Dale Morton (D); 17 Kevin Henderson; 20 Tevita Leo-Latu; 25 Richard Moore.
Tries: Wilkes (8), Gleeson (11), Korkidas (39), Grix (44), Ferguson (48); **Goals:** Brough 5/7.
Rugby Leaguer & League Express Men of the Match:
City Reds: Dean McGilvray; *Wildcats:* Danny Brough.
Penalty count: 8-13; **Half-time:** 8-18;
Referee: James Child; **Attendance:** 3,151.

ST HELENS 10 WIGAN WARRIORS 6

SAINTS: 1 Paul Wellens; 2 Ade Gardner; 3 Matt Gidley; 11 Lee Gilmour; 5 Francis Meli; 6 Leon Pryce; 18 Kyle Eastmond; 10 James Graham; 9 Keiron Cunningham (C); 16 Tony Puletua; 12 Jon Wilkin; 13 Chris Flannery; 21 Andrew Dixon. Subs (all used): 17 Paul Clough; 28 Matty Ashurst; 29 Tom Armstrong; 31 Jacob Emmitt.
Tries: Gidley (10), Eastmond (77); **Goals:** Eastmond 1/2.
WARRIORS: 21 Cameron Phelps; 2 Amos Roberts; 22 Martin Gleeson (C); 4 George Carmont; 5 Pat Richards; 25 Sam Tomkins; 7 Thomas Leuluai; 15 Andy Coley; 9 Mark Riddell; 19 Paul Prescott; 16 Harrison Hansen; 14 Joel Tomkins; 26 Mark Flanagan. Subs (all used): 8 Stuart Fielden; 10 Iafeta Palea'aesina; 3 Darrell Goulding; 24 Lee Mossop.
Try: S Tomkins (40); **Goals:** Richards 1/1.
Rugby Leaguer & League Express Men of the Match:
Saints: James Graham; *Warriors:* Sam Tomkins.
Penalty count: 6-4; **Half-time:** 4-6;
Referee: Ben Thaler; **Attendance:** 15,563.

Saturday 1st August 2009

LEEDS RHINOS 24 WARRINGTON WOLVES 22

RHINOS: 1 Brent Webb; 2 Scott Donald; 3 Lee Smith; 4 Keith Senior; 5 Ryan Hall; 6 Danny McGuire; 7 Rob Burrow; 8 Kylie Leuluai; 14 Matt Diskin; 10 Jamie Peacock; 11 Jamie Jones-Buchanan; 18 Carl Ablett; 13 Kevin Sinfield (C). Subs (all used): 19 Luke Burgess; 12 Ali Lauitiiti; 21 Simon Worrall; 29 Mike Ratu.

Tries: Hall (8), Donald (21, 78), McGuire (57), Smith (64); **Goals:** Sinfield 2/5.
WOLVES: 30 Richard Mathers; 23 Chris Hicks; 25 Chris Bridge; 2 Paul Johnson; 32 Brian Carney; 6 Lee Briers; 20 Simon Grix; 8 Adrian Morley (C); 7 Michael Monaghan; 16 Garreth Carvell; 11 Louis Anderson; 24 Ben Harrison; 12 Ben Westwood. Subs (all used): 13 Vinnie Anderson; 18 Michael Cooper; 9 Jon Clarke; 22 Lee Mitchell.
Tries: Mathers (3), V Anderson (16), L Anderson (50), Cooper (75); **Goals:** Bridge 3/4.
Rugby Leaguer & League Express Men of the Match: *Rhinos:* Matt Diskin; *Wolves:* Michael Monaghan.
Penalty count: 6-7; **Half-time:** 8-12;
Referee: Ian Smith; **Attendance:** 13,386.

CATALANS DRAGONS 34 CELTIC CRUSADERS 0

DRAGONS: 1 Clint Greenshields; 3 Steven Bell; 12 Jason Croker; 15 Jean-Phillipe Baile; 5 Dimitri Pelo; 6 Thomas Bosc; 26 Greg Bird (C); 10 Jerome Guisset; 9 Casey McGuire; 23 Jason Ryles; 17 Cyrille Gossard; 14 Dane Carlaw; 22 Jamal Fakir. Subs (all used): 13 Gregory Mounis; 20 Kane Bentley; 24 Remi Casty; 27 Sebastien Martins.
Tries: Pelo (9), McGuire (15), Greenshields (29), Bird (34), Bentley (39), Croker (49), Bell (75);
Goals: Bosc 3/7.
On report: Bird (77) - alleged late challenge.
CRUSADERS: 18 Mark Lennon; 2 Luke Dyer; 13 Marshall Chalk; 22 Steve Tyrer; 5 Anthony Blackwood; 28 Lloyd White; 14 Matty Smith; 8 Ryan O'Hara (C); 9 Lincoln Withers; 10 Mark Bryant; 17 Jordan James; 19 Jason Chan; 15 Peter Lupton. Subs (all used): 16 Ben Flower; 20 David Tangata-Toa; 23 Neil Budworth; 25 Geraint Davies.
Rugby Leaguer & League Express Men of the Match: *Dragons:* Sebastien Martins; *Crusaders:* Steve Tyrer.
Penalty count: 9-7; **Half-time:** 26-0;
Referee: Richard Silverwood; **Attendance:** 6,874

Sunday 2nd August 2009

CASTLEFORD TIGERS 28 HULL KINGSTON ROVERS 46

TIGERS: 1 Richard Owen; 2 Kirk Dixon; 3 Michael Shenton; 4 James Evans; 5 Michael Wainwright; 23 Ryan McGoldrick; 6 Rangi Chase; 10 Craig Huby; 9 Ryan Hudson (C); 15 Liam Higgins; 11 Brett Ferres; 14 Stuart Jones; 13 Joe Westerman. Subs (all used): 8 Mitchell Sargent; 16 Chris Feather; 19 Kirk Netherton; 25 Dean Widders.
Tries: Ferres (7), Huby (13), Hudson (37), Netherton (63); **Goals:** Westerman 5/5, Huby 1/1.
ROVERS: 1 Shaun Briscoe; 2 Peter Fox; 19 Kris Welham; 4 Jake Webster; 5 Liam Colbon; 6 Paul Cooke; 7 Michael Dobson; 18 Scott Wheeldon; 9 Ben Fisher; 20 Michael Vella (C); 11 Clint Newton; 12 Ben Galea; 13 Scott Murrell. Subs (all used): 15 Daniel Fitzhenry; 24 Rhys Lovegrove; 28 Ben Cockayne; 29 Kyle Bibb.
Tries: Fox (17, 52), Briscoe (30, 65, 78), Dobson (33, 44), Colbon (46); **Goals:** Dobson 7/8.
Rugby Leaguer & League Express Men of the Match: *Tigers:* Ryan Hudson; *Rovers:* Michael Dobson.
Penalty count: 8-6; **Half-time:** 20-18;
Referee: Thierry Alibert; **Attendance:** 8,709.

BRADFORD BULLS 14 HARLEQUINS 22

BULLS: 20 Dave Halley; 2 Rikki Sheriffe; 11 Steve Menzies; 4 Chris Nero; 5 Semi Tadulala; 3 Paul Sykes; 7 Paul Deacon (C); 10 Andy Lynch; 14 Wayne Godwin; 17 Nick Scruton; 28 Elliott Whitehead; 12 Glenn Morrison; 13 Jamie Langley. Subs (all used): 9 Terry Newton; 19 Craig Kopczak; 30 James Donaldson; 16 Michael Worrincy.
Tries: Tadulala (9), Sykes (55), Nero (61);
Goals: Deacon 1/3.
HARLEQUINS: 5 Will Sharp; 2 Jon Wells; 3 Matt Gafa; 4 David Howell; 1 Chris Melling; 6 Luke Dorn; 21 Luke Gale; 8 Karl Temata; 7 Danny Orr (C); 17 Danny Ward; 11 Luke Williamson; 12 Chad Robinson; 19 Jason Golden. Subs (all used): 32 Ryan Esders; 10 Louie McCarthy-Scarsbrook; 23 Daniel Heckenberg; 15 Ben Kaye.
Tries: Gafa (28), Esders (30), Howell (65, 75);
Goals: Orr 3/5.
Rugby Leaguer & League Express Men of the Match: *Bulls:* Dave Halley; *Harlequins:* David Howell.
Penalty count: 8-6; **Half-time:** 4-10;
Referee: Phil Bentham; **Attendance:** 7,813.

ROUND 16

Friday 7th August 2009

SALFORD CITY REDS 16 CATALANS DRAGONS 18

CITY REDS: 1 Karl Fitzpatrick; 2 John Wilshere; 3 Mark Henry; 15 Stuart Littler; 24 Dean McGilvray; 6 Jeremy Smith; 19 Stefan Ratchford; 8 Ray Cashmere; 9 Malcolm Alker (C); 10 Craig Stapleton; 11 Ian Sibbit; 20 Luke Adamson; 13 Luke Swain. Subs (all used): 16 Phil Leuluai; 23 Adam Sidlow; 22 Stephen Nash; 17 Robbie Paul.
Tries: Stapleton (10), Wilshere (23);
Goals: Ratchford 4/4.
DRAGONS: 6 Thomas Bosc; 2 Cyril Stacul; 15 Jean-Phillipe Baile; 12 Jason Croker; 5 Dimitri Pelo; 4 Adam Mogg; 9 Casey McGuire (C); 23 Jason Ryles; 20 Kane Bentley; 10 Jerome Guisset; 17 Cyrille Gossard; 14 Dane Carlaw; 22 Jamal Fakir. Subs (all used): 13 Gregory Mounis; 8 David Ferriol; 16 Olivier Elima; 24 Remi Casty.
Tries: Elima (56), Carlaw (65), Mogg (73), McGuire (79);
Goals: Mounis 1/4.
Rugby Leaguer & League Express Men of the Match: *City Reds:* Stefan Ratchford; *Dragons:* Casey McGuire.
Penalty count: 8-7; **Half-time:** 12-0;
Referee: Phil Bentham; **Attendance:** 2,475.

ROUND 2

Saturday 8th August 2009

HARLEQUINS 18 BRADFORD BULLS 42

HARLEQUINS: 1 Chris Melling; 2 Jon Wells; 3 Matt Gafa; 13 Rob Purdham (C); 5 Will Sharp; 6 Luke Dorn; 7 Danny Orr; 10 Louie McCarthy-Scarsbrook; 9 Chad Randall; 17 Danny Ward; 32 Ryan Esders; 19 Jason Golden; 11 Luke Williamson. Subs (all used): 23 Daniel Heckenberg; 16 Gareth Haggerty; 21 Luke Gale; 34 Lamont Bryan.
Tries: Purdham (16, 76), Sharp (80);
Goals: Orr 1/1, Purdham 2/2.
BULLS: 20 Dave Halley; 2 Rikki Sheriffe; 1 Michael Platt; 4 Chris Nero; 5 Semi Tadulala; 3 Paul Sykes; 7 Paul Deacon (C); 10 Andy Lynch; 9 Terry Newton; 17 Nick Scruton; 13 Jamie Langley; 12 Glenn Morrison; 11 Steve Menzies. Subs (all used): 8 Sam Burgess; 16 Michael Worrincy; 19 Craig Kopczak; 14 Wayne Godwin.
Tries: Halley (3, 6, 19), Burgess (22), Menzies (28), Worrincy (40), Godwin (59); **Goals:** Deacon 7/8.
Rugby Leaguer & League Express Men of the Match: *Harlequins:* Ryan Esders; *Bulls:* Paul Sykes.
Penalty count: 9-7; **Half-time:** 6-36;
Referee: Ian Smith; **Attendance:** 3,112.

ROUND 24

Friday 14th August 2009

LEEDS RHINOS 76 CASTLEFORD TIGERS 12

RHINOS: 1 Brent Webb; 2 Scott Donald; 3 Lee Smith; 4 Keith Senior; 5 Ryan Hall; 6 Danny McGuire; 7 Rob Burrow; 8 Kylie Leuluai; 14 Matt Diskin; 10 Jamie Peacock; 11 Jamie Jones-Buchanan; 18 Carl Ablett; 13 Kevin Sinfield (C). Subs (all used): 19 Luke Burgess; 12 Ali Lauitiiti; 21 Simon Worrall; 29 Mike Ratu.
Tries: Donald (11), Hall (23, 25, 37, 60, 73), Webb (31, 63), Smith (44), Leuluai (52), Burrow (65), Peacock (70), Ratu (76), Lauitiiti (79); **Goals:** Sinfield 10/14.
TIGERS: 23 Ryan McGoldrick; 20 James Ford; 3 Michael Shenton; 4 James Evans; 5 Michael Wainwright; 25 Dean Widders; 6 Rangi Chase; 8 Mitchell Sargent; 9 Ryan Hudson (C); 10 Craig Huby; 11 Brett Ferres; 12 Ryan Clayton; 13 Joe Westerman. Subs (all used): 15 Liam Higgins; 16 Chris Feather; 19 Kirk Netherton; 14 Stuart Jones.
Tries: Evans (14), Chase (48); **Goals:** Westerman 2/2.
Sin bin: McGoldrick (79) - professional foul.
Rugby Leaguer & League Express Men of the Match: *Rhinos:* Ryan Hall; *Tigers:* Rangi Chase.
Penalty count: 7-4; **Half-time:** 26-6;
Referee: Ben Thaler; **Attendance:** 16,931.

WIGAN WARRIORS 36 WARRINGTON WOLVES 16

WARRIORS: 21 Cameron Phelps; 2 Amos Roberts; 22 Martin Gleeson; 4 George Carmont; 5 Pat Richards; 25 Sam Tomkins; 7 Thomas Leuluai; 15 Andy Coley; 9 Mark Riddell; 19 Paul Prescott; 14 Joel Tomkins; 16 Harrison Hansen; 13 Sean O'Loughlin (C). Subs (all used): 8 Stuart Fielden; 10 Iafeta Palea'aesina; 24 Lee Mossop; 26 Mark Flanagan.
Tries: Richards (19), Roberts (26), Phelps (31), Leuluai (33), Gleeson (45), Carmont (47, 57);
Goals: Richards 4/7.
WOLVES: 30 Richard Mathers; 5 Kevin Penny; 2 Paul Johnson; 13 Vinnie Anderson; 19 Chris Riley; 25 Chris Bridge; 6 Lee Briers; 8 Adrian Morley (C); 7 Michael Monaghan; 18 Michael Cooper; 22 Lee Mitchell; 11 Louis Anderson; 12 Ben Westwood. Subs (all used): 17 Steve Pickersgill; 10 Paul Rauhihi; 21 Matty Blythe; 28 Tyrone McCarthy (D).
Tries: Bridge (12), V Anderson (63), Riley (74);
Goals: Bridge 2/3.
Rugby Leaguer & League Express Men of the Match: *Warriors:* Cameron Phelps; *Wolves:* Tyrone McCarthy.
Penalty count: 8-8; **Half-time:** 22-4;
Referee: Richard Silverwood; **Attendance:** 13,452.

Saturday 15th August 2009

HARLEQUINS 22 SALFORD CITY REDS 26

HARLEQUINS: 1 Chris Melling; 2 Jon Wells; 3 Matt Gafa; 14 Tony Clubb; 5 Will Sharp; 6 Luke Dorn; 21 Luke Gale; 17 Danny Ward; 9 Chad Randall; 10 Louie McCarthy-Scarsbrook; 11 Luke Williamson; 19 Jason Golden; 13 Rob Purdham (C). Subs (all used): 23 Daniel Heckenberg; 15 Ben Kaye; 16 Gareth Haggerty; 34 Lamont Bryan.
Tries: Dorn (22), Randall (26), Purdham (46), McCarthy-Scarsbrook (71); **Goals:** Purdham 3/4.
CITY REDS: 1 Karl Fitzpatrick; 24 Dean McGilvray; 15 Stuart Littler; 3 Mark Henry; 2 John Wilshere; 6 Jeremy Smith; 19 Stefan Ratchford; 8 Ray Cashmere; 9 Malcolm Alker (C); 16 Phil Leuluai; 11 Ian Sibbit; 20 Luke Adamson; 13 Luke Swain. Subs (all used): 17 Robbie Paul; 25 Jason Walton; 23 Adam Sidlow; 22 Stephen Nash.
Tries: Wilshere (13, 33), McGilvray (37), Nash (76), Swain (78); **Goals:** Wilshere 3/5.
Rugby Leaguer & League Express Men of the Match: *Harlequins:* Louie McCarthy-Scarsbrook; *City Reds:* Stefan Ratchford.
Penalty count: 7-6; **Half-time:** 10-14;
Referee: Thierry Alibert; **Attendance:** 2,612.

CATALANS DRAGONS 18 HULL FC 6

DRAGONS: 1 Clint Greenshields; 2 Cyril Stacul; 11 Sebastien Raguin; 15 Jean-Phillipe Baile; 5 Dimitri Pelo; 26 Greg Bird (C); 4 Adam Mogg; 23 Jason Ryles; 9 Casey McGuire; 10 Jerome Guisset; 16 Olivier Elima; 17 Cyrille Gossard; 22 Jamal Fakir. Subs (all used): 8 David Ferriol; 13 Gregory Mounis; 14 Dane Carlaw; 24 Remi Casty.
Tries: Elima (47, 54, 80); **Goals:** Mounis 2/2, Bird 1/1.
HULL: 14 Richard Whiting; 21 Tom Briscoe; 4 Kirk Yeaman; 17 Graeme Horne; 5 Gareth Raynor; 31 Jordan Tansey; 9 Shaun Berrigan; 30 Josh Cordoba; 20 Danny Houghton; 8 Ewan Dowes; 12 Danny Tickle; 16 Willie Manu; 11 Lee Radford (C). Subs (all used): 19 Paul King; 27 Sam Moa; 23 Tommy Lee; 24 Craig Hall.
Try: Raynor (7); **Goals:** Tickle 1/2.
Rugby Leaguer & League Express Men of the Match: *Dragons:* Remi Casty; *Hull:* Richard Whiting.
Penalty count: 11-12; **Half-time:** 0-6;
Referee: Ian Smith; **Attendance:** 9,083
(at Stade de la Mediterranee, Beziers).

Sunday 16th August 2009

HULL KINGSTON ROVERS 26 ST HELENS 10

ROVERS: 1 Shaun Briscoe; 2 Peter Fox; 4 Jake Webster; 19 Kris Welham; 5 Liam Colbon; 6 Paul Cooke; 7 Michael Dobson; 8 Nick Fozzard; 15 Daniel Fitzhenry; 20 Michael Vella (C); 11 Clint Newton; 12 Ben Galea; 28 Ben Cockayne. Subs (all used): 3 Chev Walker; 18 Scott Wheeldon; 16 Jason Netherton; 21 Chaz l'Anson.
Tries: Welham (39), Webster (44), Fitzhenry (47, 53), Fox (77); **Goals:** Dobson 3/5.
SAINTS: 1 Paul Wellens (C); 2 Ade Gardner; 3 Matt Gidley; 11 Lee Gilmour; 5 Francis Meli; 6 Leon Pryce; 27 James Ellis; 10 James Graham; 14 James Roby; 16 Tony Puletua; 12 Jon Wilkin; 13 Chris Flannery; 24 Andrew Dixon. Subs (all used): 15 Bryn Hargreaves; 17 Paul Clough; 28 Matty Ashurst; 21 Gary Wheeler.
Tries: Graham (21), Gardner (79); **Goals:** Ellis 1/2.
Rugby Leaguer & League Express Men of the Match: *Rovers:* Daniel Fitzhenry; *Saints:* James Roby.
Penalty count: 3-3; **Half-time:** 6-4;
Referee: Steve Ganson; **Attendance:** 8,976.

WAKEFIELD TRINITY WILDCATS 46 CELTIC CRUSADERS 12

WILDCATS: 1 Matt Blaymire; 26 Luke George; 4 Ryan Atkins; 19 Sean Gleeson; 13 Scott Grix; 14 Sam Obst; 7 Danny Brough; 23 Michael Korkidas; 9 Brad Drew; 16 Ricky Bibey; 12 Oliver Wilkes; 17 Kevin Henderson; 8 Jason Demetriou (C). Subs (all used): 15 James Stosic; 25 Richard Moore; 20 Tevita Leo-Latu; 28 Kyle Bibb.
Tries: George (11, 72), Gleeson (14), Brough (22), Stosic (31), Leo-Latu (42, 69), Demetriou (53);
Goals: Brough 7/8.
Dismissal: Brough (78) - dissent.
Sin bin: Brough (56) - fighting.
CRUSADERS: 5 Anthony Blackwood; 2 Luke Dyer; 3 Josh Hannay; 22 Steve Tyrer; 4 Mark Dalle Cort; 14 Matty Smith; 7 Jace Van Dijk (C); 8 Ryan O'Hara; 23 Neil Budworth; 10 Mark Bryant; 16 Ben Flower; 19 Jason Chan; 28 Lloyd White. Subs (all used): 17 Jordan James; 20 David Tangata-Toa; 25 Geraint Davies; 30 Lewis Mills (D).
Tries: Dalle Cort (64), Tyrer (75); **Goals:** Smith 2/2.
Sin bin: Tyrer (56) - fighting.
Rugby Leaguer & League Express Men of the Match: *Wildcats:* Danny Brough; *Crusaders:* Mark Dalle Cort.
Penalty count: 8-13; **Half-time:** 22-0;
Referee: James Child; **Attendance:** 7,893.

HUDDERSFIELD GIANTS 18 BRADFORD BULLS 28

GIANTS: 1 Brett Hodgson (C); 21 Leroy Cudjoe; 11 Jamahl Lolesi; 4 Paul Whatuira; 5 David Hodgson; 3 Kevin Brown; 7 Luke Robinson; 8 Eorl Crabtree; 20 Scott Moore; 16 Keith Mason; 6 Liam Fulton; 13 Stephen Wild; 18 Danny Kirmond. Subs (all used): 9 David Faiumu; 10 Darrell Griffin; 33 Danny Sculthorpe; 2 Martin Aspinwall.
Tries: B Hodgson (2), Moore (62), Kirmond (67);
Goals: B Hodgson 3/3.
Sin bin: Moore (47) - late challenge on Deacon.
BULLS: 20 Dave Halley; 2 Rikki Sheriffe; 1 Michael Platt; 4 Chris Nero; 5 Semi Tadulala; 3 Paul Sykes; 7 Paul Deacon (C); 17 Nick Scruton; 14 Wayne Godwin; 10 Andy Lynch; 12 Glenn Morrison; 13 Jamie Langley; 11 Steve Menzies. Subs (all used): 15 Matt Cook; 19 Craig Kopczak; 8 Sam Burgess; 30 James Donaldson.
Tries: Platt (14), Nero (16, 29), Sykes (21);
Goals: Deacon 6/6.
Sin bin: Sykes (65) - professional foul.
Rugby Leaguer & League Express Men of the Match: *Giants:* Danny Kirmond; *Bulls:* Jamie Langley.
Penalty count: 7-9; **Half-time:** 6-24;
Referee: Phil Bentham; **Attendance:** 7,892.

ROUND 25

Friday 21st August 2009

HULL FC 26 HARLEQUINS 6

HULL: 14 Richard Whiting; 2 Mark Calderwood; 21 Tom Briscoe; 24 Craig Hall; 5 Gareth Raynor; 15 Danny

Nowhere for Leeds' Danny McGuire to go against Celtic Crusaders

Washbrook; 31 Jordan Tansey; 30 Josh Cordoba; 23 Tommy Lee; 8 Ewan Dowes; 12 Danny Tickle; 16 Willie Manu; 11 Lee Radford (C). Subs (all used): 20 Danny Houghton; 17 Graeme Horne; 27 Sam Moa; 32 Epalahame Lauaki (D).
Tries: Lee (5), Briscoe (12), Hall (15, 30, 59); **Goals:** Tickle 3/5.
On report: Hall (9) - alleged dangerous tackle.
HARLEQUINS: 1 Chris Melling; 2 Jon Wells; 3 Matt Gafa; 13 Rob Purdham (C); 5 Will Sharp; 6 Luke Dorn; 21 Luke Gale; 10 Louie McCarthy-Scarsbrook; 9 Chad Randall; 23 Daniel Heckenberg; 19 Jason Golden; 34 Lamont Bryan; 11 Luke Williamson. Subs (all used): 7 Danny Orr; 15 Ben Kaye; 32 Ryan Esders; 17 Danny Ward.
Try: Sharp (63); **Goals:** Purdham 1/1.
Rugby Leaguer & League Express Men of the Match: *Hull:* Craig Hall; *Harlequins:* Louie McCarthy-Scarsbrook.
Penalty count: 6-8; **Half-time:** 22-0;
Referee: Phil Bentham; **Attendance:** 15,592.

SALFORD CITY REDS 10 HULL KINGSTON ROVERS 14

CITY REDS: 1 Karl Fitzpatrick; 2 John Wilshere; 3 Mark Henry; 15 Stuart Littler; 24 Dean McGilvray; 6 Jeremy Smith; 19 Stefan Ratchford; 8 Ray Cashmere; 9 Malcolm Alker (C); 10 Craig Stapleton, 11 Ian Sibbit; 20 Luke Adamson; 13 Luke Swain. Subs (all used): 16 Phil Leuluai; 17 Robbie Paul; 23 Adam Sidlow; 28 Jack Spencer (D).
Tries: Sidlow (48), Ratchford (80); **Goals:** Wilshere 1/2.
Sin bin: Stapleton (54) - late challenge on Dobson.
ROVERS: 1 Shaun Briscoe; 2 Peter Fox; 19 Kris Welham; 4 Jake Webster; 5 Liam Colbon; 6 Paul Cooke; 7 Michael Dobson; 8 Nick Fozzard; 9 Ben Fisher; 20 Michael Vella (C); 11 Clint Newton; 12 Ben Galea; 28 Ben Cockayne. Subs (all used): 16 Jason Netherton; 17 Makali Aizue; 21 Chaz I'Anson; 3 Chev Walker.
Tries: Newton (37), Briscoe (79); **Goals:** Dobson 3/3.
Sin bin: Cockayne (61) - late challenge on Paul.
Rugby Leaguer & League Express Men of the Match: *City Reds:* Stefan Ratchford; *Rovers:* Michael Vella.
Penalty count: 9-9; **Half-time:** 0-6;
Referee: Jamie Leahy; **Attendance:** 4,224.

ST HELENS 12 HUDDERSFIELD GIANTS 10

SAINTS: 1 Paul Wellens; 2 Ade Gardner; 3 Matt Gidley; 30 Jonny Lomax; 5 Francis Meli; 6 Leon Pryce; 7 Sean Long; 10 James Graham; 9 Keiron Cunningham (C); 16 Tony Puletua; 12 Jon Wilkin; 13 Chris Flannery; 11 Lee Gilmour. Subs (all used): 14 James Roby; 17 Paul Clough; 28 Matty Ashurst; 31 Jacob Emmitt.
Tries: Gardner (19), Gidley (48), Meli (64);
Goals: Lomax 0/3.
GIANTS: 34 Elliot Hodgson (D); 21 Leroy Cudjoe; 28

Josh Griffin; 19 Michael Lawrence; 36 Alex Brown (D); 26 Tom Hemingway; 10 Darrell Griffin; 20 Scott Moore; 24 Shaun Lunt; 15 Paul Jackson (C); 14 Simon Finnigan; 18 Danny Kirmond; 2 Martin Aspinwall. Subs (all used): 12 Andy Raleigh; 29 Keal Carlile; 30 Larne Patrick; 33 Danny Sculthorpe.
Tries: Lunt (1), Cudjoe (8); **Goals:** Cudjoe 1/2.
Rugby Leaguer & League Express Men of the Match: *Saints:* Francis Meli; *Giants:* Shaun Lunt.
Penalty count: 7-3; **Half-time:** 4-10;
Referee: Ian Smith; **Attendance:** 8,708.

WARRINGTON WOLVES 28
WAKEFIELD TRINITY WILDCATS 40

WOLVES: 30 Richard Mathers; 19 Chris Riley; 25 Chris Bridge; 2 Paul Johnson; 5 Kevin Penny; 6 Lee Briers; 9 Jon Clarke; 8 Adrian Morley (C); 7 Michael Monaghan; 16 Garreth Carvell; 11 Louis Anderson; 13 Vinnie Anderson; 12 Ben Westwood. Subs (all used): 18 Michael Cooper; 28 Tyrone McCarthy; 22 Lee Mitchell; 10 Paul Rauhihi.
Tries: Penny (5), Johnson (14), Riley (32), Monaghan (63), Carvell (79); **Goals:** Bridge 4/5.
WILDCATS: 1 Matt Blaymire; 33 Dale Morton; 19 Sean Gleeson; 4 Ryan Atkins; 26 Luke George; 13 Scott Grix; 14 Sam Obst; 23 Michael Korkidas; 9 Brad Drew (C); 15 James Stosic; 12 Oliver Wilkes; 17 Kevin Henderson; 24 Tevita Leo-Latu; 26 Richard Moore, 20 Kyle Bibb.
Tries: Ferguson (2), Obst (8, 61), George (18, 42), Gleeson (36), Morton (69); **Goals:** Drew 6/9.
Rugby Leaguer & League Express Men of the Match: *Wolves:* Adrian Morley; *Wildcats:* Brad Drew.
Penalty count: 4-6; **Half-time:** 16-20;
Referee: Ben Thaler; **Attendance:** 8,681.

Saturday 22nd August 2009

CELTIC CRUSADERS 0 LEEDS RHINOS 68

CRUSADERS: 31 Elliot Kear (D); 5 Anthony Blackwood; 13 Marshall Chalk; 19 Jason Chan; 22 Steve Tyrer; 28 Lloyd White; 14 Matty Smith; 8 Ryan O'Hara (C); 23 Neil Budworth; 17 Jordan James; 16 Ben Flower; 10 Mark Bryant; 21 Chris Beasley. Subs (all used): 20 David Tangata-Toa; 25 Geraint Davies; 29 Gil Dudson (D); 30 Lewis Mills.
RHINOS: 1 Brent Webb; 2 Scott Donald; 3 Lee Smith; 4 Keith Senior; 5 Ryan Hall; 6 Danny McGuire; 7 Rob Burrow; 8 Kylie Leuluai; 14 Matt Diskin; 10 Jamie Peacock; 12 Ali Lauitiiti; 11 Jamie Jones-Buchanan; 13 Kevin Sinfield (C). Subs (all used): 16 Ryan Bailey; 19 Luke Burgess; 21 Simon Worrall; 23 Kallum Watkins.
Tries: Senior (4, 24), Hall (9), Donald (14),

Webb (23, 38, 64), Peacock (29, 57, 80), Burrow (58), Jones-Buchanan (71), Diskin (74); **Goals:** Sinfield 8/13.
Rugby Leaguer & League Express Men of the Match: *Crusaders:* Elliot Kear; *Rhinos:* Rob Burrow.
Penalty count: 2-9; **Half-time:** 0-34;
Referee: Thierry Alibert; **Attendance:** 5,597
(at Rodney Parade, Newport).

Sunday 23rd August 2009

BRADFORD BULLS 42 CATALANS DRAGONS 18

BULLS: 20 Dave Halley; 2 Rikki Sheriffe; 1 Michael Platt; 4 Chris Nero; 5 Semi Tadulala; 3 Paul Sykes; 7 Paul Deacon (C); 10 Andy Lynch; 14 Wayne Godwin; 17 Nick Scruton; 13 Jamie Langley; 12 Glenn Morrison; 11 Steve Menzies. Subs (all used): 30 James Donaldson; 16 Michael Worrincy; 8 Sam Burgess; 19 Craig Kopczak.
Tries: Burgess (19), Sheriffe (30), Nero (34), Menzies (37), Godwin (51), Sykes (54), Deacon (58), Morrison (71); **Goals:** Deacon 5/8.
DRAGONS: 5 Dimitri Pelo; 18 Vincent Duport; 17 Cyrille Gossard; 11 Sebastien Raguin; 2 Cyril Stacul; 4 Adam Mogg; 26 Greg Bird (C); 23 Jason Ryles; 9 Casey McGuire; 10 Jerome Guisset; 13 Gregory Mounis; 16 Olivier Elima; 8 David Ferriol. Subs (all used): 19 Julien Touxagas; 20 Kane Bentley; 27 Sebastien Martins; 24 Remi Casty.
Tries: Raguin (11), Gossard (62), Martins (76);
Goals: Mounis 3/3.
Rugby Leaguer & League Express Men of the Match: *Bulls:* Sam Burgess; *Dragons:* Adam Mogg.
Penalty count: 10-4; **Half-time:** 20-6;
Referee: Richard Silverwood; **Attendance:** 7,919.

CASTLEFORD TIGERS 26 WIGAN WARRIORS 29

TIGERS: 23 Ryan McGoldrick; 2 Kirk Dixon; 3 Michael Shenton; 4 James Evans; 5 Michael Wainwright; 6 Rangi Chase; 7 Brent Sherwin; 8 Mitchell Sargent; 9 Ryan Hudson (C); 10 Craig Huby; 11 Brett Ferres; 14 Stuart Jones; 13 Joe Westerman. Subs (all used): 12 Ryan Clayton; 15 Liam Higgins; 17 Ryan Boyle; 25 Dean Widders.
Tries: Dixon (23, 58), Ferres (31), Widders (52), Shenton (78); **Goals:** Westerman 2/5, Dixon 1/1.
On report:
Sargent (20) - alleged late challenge on S Tomkins.
WARRIORS: 21 Cameron Phelps; 2 Amos Roberts; 22 Martin Gleeson; 4 George Carmont; 5 Pat Richards; 25 Sam Tomkins; 7 Thomas Leuluai; 15 Andy Coley; 9 Mark Riddell; 19 Paul Prescott; 14 Joel Tomkins; 16 Harrison Hansen; 13 Sean O'Loughlin (C). Subs (all used): 8 Stuart Fielden; 10 Iafeta Palea'aesina; 24 Lee Mossop; 26 Mark Flanagan.

Bradford's Steve Menzies makes a break as Salford's Luke Adamson moves in

Tries: S Tomkins (9, 38, 64), Leuluai (21, 45);
Goals: Richards 4/5; **Field goal:** S Tomkins (68).
Rugby Leaguer & League Express Men of the Match:
Tigers: Brett Ferres; *Warriors:* Sam Tomkins.
Penalty count: 6-5; **Half-time:** 8-16;
Referee: Steve Ganson; **Attendance:** 6,579.

ROUND 26

Friday 4th September 2009

LEEDS RHINOS 18 ST HELENS 10

RHINOS: 1 Brent Webb; 2 Scott Donald; 3 Lee Smith; 4
Keith Senior; 5 Ryan Hall; 6 Danny McGuire; 7 Rob
Burrow; 8 Kylie Leuluai; 14 Matt Diskin; 10 Jamie
Peacock; 11 Jamie Jones-Buchanan; 18 Carl Ablett; 13
Kevin Sinfield (C). Subs (all used): 19 Luke Burgess; 12
Ali Lauititi; 16 Ryan Bailey; 17 Ian Kirke.
Tries: Ablett (24), Hall (37, 60); **Goals:** Sinfield 3/4.
Sin bin: Senior (78) - punching Wilkin.
On report: Jones-Buchanan (13) - alleged dangerous
tackle on Graham.
SAINTS: 1 Paul Wellens; 2 Ade Gardner; 3 Matt Gidley;
18 Kyle Eastmond; 5 Francis Meli; 6 Leon Pryce; 7 Sean
Long; 10 James Graham; 9 Keiron Cunningham (C); 16
Tony Puletua; 11 Lee Gilmour; 13 Chris Flannery; 12 Jon
Wilkin. Subs (all used): 23 Maurie Fa'asavalu; 15 Bryn
Hargreaves; 14 James Roby; 17 Paul Clough.
Tries: Gilmour (12), Flannery (47); **Goals:** Eastmond 1/2.
Sin bin: Long (3) - professional foul.
Rugby Leaguer & League Express Men of the Match:
Rhinos: Ryan Hall; *Saints:* Tony Puletua.
Penalty count: 11-8; **Half-time:** 12-6;
Referee: Phil Bentham; **Attendance:** 19,997.

WIGAN WARRIORS 34 HULL FC 22

WARRIORS: 21 Cameron Phelps; 2 Amos Roberts; 22
Martin Gleeson; 4 George Carmont; 5 Pat Richards; 25
Sam Tomkins; 7 Thomas Leuluai; 15 Andy Coley; 9 Mark
Riddell; 19 Paul Prescott; 14 Joel Tomkins; 16 Harrison
Hansen; 13 Sean O'Loughlin (C). Subs (all used): 8
Stuart Fielden; 10 Iafeta Palea'aesina; 24 Lee Mossop;
26 Mark Flanagan.
Tries: Roberts (31, 45), Carmont (40, 41),
S Tomkins (71), Palea'aesina (79); **Goals:** Richards 5/6.
Sin bin: Coley (8) - professional foul.
HULL: 14 Richard Whiting; 5 Gareth Raynor; 24 Craig
Hall; 17 Graeme Horne; 21 Tom Briscoe; 15 Danny
Washbrook; 6 Richard Horne; 8 Ewan Dowes; 20 Danny
Houghton; 30 Josh Cordoba; 12 Danny Tickle; 16 Willie
Manu; 11 Lee Radford (C). Subs (all used): 7 Chris
Thorman; 19 Paul King; 27 Sam Moa; 32 Epalahame
Lauaki.
Tries: Tickle (34), R Horne (64), Briscoe (74), Hall (80);
Goals: Tickle 2/2, Hall 1/2.
Rugby Leaguer & League Express Men of the Match:
Warriors: Sam Tomkins; *Hull:* Epalahame Lauaki.
Penalty count: 4-4; **Half-time:** 10-6;
Referee: Ben Thaler; **Attendance:** 12,491.

Saturday 5th September 2009

HULL KINGSTON ROVERS 40 WARRINGTON WOLVES 16

ROVERS: 1 Shaun Briscoe; 2 Peter Fox; 19 Kris Welham;
4 Jake Webster; 5 Liam Colbon; 6 Paul Cooke; 7 Michael
Dobson; 18 Scott Wheeldon; 15 Daniel Fitzhenry; 20
Michael Vella (C); 11 Clint Newton; 3 Chev Walker; 13
Scott Murrell. Subs (all used): 12 Ben Galea; 28 Ben
Cockayne; 16 Jason Netherton; 8 Nick Fozzard.
Tries: Webster (8), Cooke (21), Newton (32, 69, 74),
Welham (40), Fox (55); **Goals:** Dobson 6/7.
WOLVES: 30 Richard Mathers; 23 Chris Hicks; 21 Matty
Blythe; 13 Vinnie Anderson; 19 Chris Riley; 6 Lee Briers; 7
Michael Monaghan; 8 Adrian Morley (C); 14 Mick Higham;
16 Garreth Carvell; 11 Louis Anderson; 24 Ben Harrison;
12 Ben Westwood. Subs (all used): 18 Michael Cooper;
10 Paul Rauhihi; 22 Lee Mitchell; 28 Tyrone McCarthy.
Tries: Higham (5), McCarthy (17), Hicks (65);
Goals: Briers 2/3.
Rugby Leaguer & League Express Men of the Match:
Rovers: Clint Newton; *Wolves:* Lee Briers.
Penalty count: 9-8; **Half-time:** 22-12;
Referee: Richard Silverwood; **Attendance:** 8,579.

CELTIC CRUSADERS 16 HUDDERSFIELD GIANTS 42

CRUSADERS: 31 Elliot Kear; 5 Anthony Blackwood; 19
Jason Chan; 22 Steve Tyrer; 18 Mark Lennon; 14 Matty
Smith; 9 Lincoln Withers; 8 Ryan O'Hara (C); 23 Neil
Budworth; 10 Mark Bryant; 17 Jordan James; 21 Chris
Beasley; 28 Lloyd White. Subs (all used): 16 Ben Flower;
20 David Tangata-Toa; 25 Geraint Davies; 30 Lewis Mills.
Tries: Blackwood (62), Tyrer (72), Lennon (79);
Goals: Tyrer 2/3.
GIANTS: 21 Leroy Cudjoe; 28 Josh Griffin; 19 Michael
Lawrence; 4 Paul Whatuira; 5 David Hodgson; 20 Scott
Moore; 7 Luke Robinson; 33 Danny Sculthorpe; 9 David
Faiumu; 16 Keith Mason; 6 Liam Fulton; 12 Andy Raleigh;
14 Simon Finnigan. Subs (all used): 13 Stephen Wild (C);
8 Eorl Crabtree; 24 Shaun Lunt; 30 Larne Patrick.
Tries: D Hodgson (4), Fulton (25, 67), Patrick (33),
Whatuira (45), Lunt (48, 52); **Goals:** Cudjoe 7/7.
Rugby Leaguer & League Express Men of the Match:
Crusaders: Steve Tyrer; *Giants:* Shaun Lunt.
Penalty count: 7-7; **Half-time:** 0-18;
Referee: Steve Ganson; **Attendance:** 1,988.

CATALANS DRAGONS 20 WAKEFIELD TRINITY WILDCATS 34

DRAGONS: 1 Clint Greenshields; 2 Cyril Stacul; 11
Sebastien Raguin; 15 Jean-Phillipe Baile; 5 Dimitri Pelo;
4 Adam Mogg; 6 Thomas Bosc; 23 Jason Ryles; 9 Casey
McGuire; 10 Jerome Guisset; 16 Olivier Elima; 17 Cyrille
Gossard; 26 Greg Bird (C). Subs (all used): 8 David
Ferriol; 12 Jason Croker; 13 Gregory Mounis; 24 Remi
Casty.
Tries: Raguin (21, 32), McGuire (45, 48);
Goals: Bosc 2/4.

WILDCATS: 1 Matt Blaymire; 19 Sean Gleeson; 8 Jason
Demetriou (C); 4 Ryan Atkins; 26 Luke George; 13 Scott
Grix; 14 Sam Obst; 15 James Stosic; 9 Brad Drew; 23
Michael Korkidas; 11 Steve Snitch; 12 Oliver Wilkes; 24
Dale Ferguson. Subs (all used): 7 Danny Brough; 17
Kevin Henderson; 20 Tevita Leo-Latu; 25 Richard Moore.
Tries: Atkins (17, 63), Drew (27), George (56, 74);
Goals: Drew 4/4, Brough 3/4.
Rugby Leaguer & League Express Men of the Match:
Dragons: Casey McGuire; *Wildcats:* Brad Drew.
Penalty count: 13-9; **Half-time:** 10-18;
Referee: Ian Smith; **Attendance:** 8,755.

Sunday 6th September 2009

BRADFORD BULLS 44 SALFORD CITY REDS 18

BULLS: 20 Dave Halley; 2 Rikki Sheriffe; 1 Michael Platt;
4 Chris Nero; 5 Semi Tadulala; 3 Paul Sykes; 7 Paul
Deacon (C); 10 Andy Lynch; 14 Wayne Godwin; 17 Nick
Scruton; 13 Jamie Langley; 12 Glenn Morrison; 11 Steve
Menzies. Subs (all used): 19 Craig Kopczak; 6 Ben
Jeffries; 8 Sam Burgess; 16 Michael Worrincy.
Tries: Nero (2, 48, 51), Tadulala (4, 56),
Langley (12, 29), Lynch (78); **Goals:** Deacon 6/8.
CITY REDS: 1 Karl Fitzpatrick; 2 John Wilshere; 3 Mark
Henry; 15 Stuart Littler; 24 Dean McGilvray; 6 Jeremy
Smith; 19 Stefan Ratchford; 8 Ray Cashmere; 9 Malcolm
Alker (C); 10 Craig Stapleton; 11 Ian Sibbit; 20 Luke
Adamson; 13 Luke Swain. Subs (all used): 16 Phil
Leuluai; 23 Adam Sidlow; 22 Stephen Nash; 17 Robbie
Paul.
Tries: Wilshere (16, 68), Henry (72);
Goals: Ratchford 3/3.
On report: Stapleton (8) - high tackle.
Rugby Leaguer & League Express Men of the Match:
Bulls: Chris Nero; *City Reds:* John Wilshere.
Penalty count: 12-7; **Half-time:** 24-6;
Referee: James Child; **Attendance:** 8,167.

HARLEQUINS 0 CASTLEFORD TIGERS 48

HARLEQUINS: 1 Chris Melling; 14 Tony Clubb; 3 Matt
Gafa; 13 Rob Purdham (C); 5 Will Sharp; 6 Luke Dorn; 7
Danny Orr; 17 Danny Ward; 9 Chad Randall; 10 Louie
McCarthy-Scarsbrook; 11 Luke Williamson; 32 Ryan
Esders; 19 Jason Golden. Subs (all used): 16 Gareth
Haggerty; 21 Luke Gale; 23 Daniel Heckenberg; 34
Lamont Bryan.
TIGERS: 23 Ryan McGoldrick; 2 Kirk Dixon; 3 Michael
Shenton; 4 James Evans; 5 Michael Wainwright; 6 Rangi
Chase; 7 Brent Sherwin (C); 8 Mitchell Sargent; 14 Stuart
Jones; 15 Liam Higgins; 10 Craig Huby; 12 Ryan Clayton;
13 Joe Westerman. Subs (all used): 11 Brett Ferres; 16
Chris Feather; 19 Kirk Netherton; 25 Dean Widders.
Tries: Westerman (16, 19, 51), Dixon (43, 68),
Sargent (47), Widders (56), Higgins (63), Ferres (80);
Goals: Westerman 5/7, Dixon 1/2.
Rugby Leaguer & League Express Men of the Match:
Harlequins: Will Sharp; *Tigers:* Rangi Chase.
Penalty count: 8-12; **Half-time:** 0-12;
Referee: Thierry Alibert; **Attendance:** 3,824.

Huddersfield's Liam Fulton looks to duck under the challenge of Wigan's Iafeta Palea'aesina

ROUND 27

Friday 11th September 2009

HULL FC 18 BRADFORD BULLS 21

HULL: 31 Jordan Tansey; 21 Tom Briscoe; 14 Richard Whiting; 24 Craig Hall; 5 Gareth Raynor; 6 Richard Horne; 15 Danny Washbrook; 30 Josh Cordoba; 20 Danny Houghton; 8 Ewan Dowes; 12 Danny Tickle; 16 Willie Manu; 11 Lee Radford (C). Subs (all used): 17 Graeme Horne; 19 Paul King; 27 Sam Moa; 32 Epalahame Lauaki.
Tries: Briscoe (7, 66), Radford (61); **Goals:** Tickle 3/3.
BULLS: 3 Paul Sykes; 2 Rikki Sheriffe; 1 Michael Platt; 4 Chris Nero; 5 Semi Tadulala; 12 Glenn Morrison; 7 Paul Deacon (C); 10 Andy Lynch; 14 Wayne Godwin; 17 Nick Scruton; 13 Jamie Langley; 16 Michael Worrincy; 11 Steve Menzies. Subs (all used): 6 Ben Jeffries; 8 Sam Burgess; 30 James Donaldson; 19 Craig Kopczak.
Tries: Worrincy (31), Deacon (38), Donaldson (58);
Goals: Deacon 4/5. **Field goal:** Deacon (73).
Rugby Leaguer & League Express Men of the Match:
Hull: Tom Briscoe; *Bulls:* Paul Deacon.
Penalty count: 9-8; **Half-time:** 6-12;
Referee: Richard Silverwood; **Attendance:** 13,412.

SALFORD CITY REDS 24 LEEDS RHINOS 30

CITY REDS: 1 Karl Fitzpatrick; 2 John Wilshere; 3 Mark Henry; 15 Stuart Littler; 24 Dean McGilvray; 6 Jeremy Smith; 19 Stefan Ratchford; 8 Ray Cashmere; 9 Malcolm Alker (C); 10 Craig Stapleton; 11 Ian Sibbit; 20 Luke Adamson; 13 Luke Swain. Subs (all used): 16 Phil Leuluai; 17 Robbie Paul; 23 Adam Sidlow; 22 Stephen Nash.
Tries: Adamson (16), Wilshere (25), Littler (74), Ratchford (76); **Goals:** Wilshere 4/5.
RHINOS: 1 Brent Webb; 2 Scott Donald; 3 Lee Smith; 23 Kallum Watkins; 5 Ryan Hall; 18 Carl Ablett; 7 Rob Burrow; 8 Kylie Leuluai; 14 Matt Diskin; 10 Jamie Peacock (C); 12 Ali Lauititi; 17 Ian Kirke; 21 Simon Worrall. Subs (all used): 24 Ben Jones-Bishop; 16 Ryan Bailey; 19 Luke Burgess; 30 Jay Pitts (D).
Tries: Watkins (30), Pitts (38), Burgess (49), Webb (55), Ablett (70); **Goals:** Smith 5/5.
Rugby Leaguer & League Express Men of the Match:
City Reds: Malcolm Alker; *Rhinos:* Rob Burrow.
Penalty count: 8-10; **Half-time:** 12-12;
Referee: Thierry Alibert; **Attendance:** 6,101.

ST HELENS 12 CATALANS DRAGONS 24

SAINTS: 30 Jonny Lomax; 2 Ade Gardner; 3 Matt Gidley; 11 Lee Gilmour; 5 Francis Meli; 6 Leon Pryce; 7 Sean Long; 15 Bryn Hargreaves; 9 Keiron Cunningham (C); 16 Tony Puletua; 12 Jon Wilkin; 13 Chris Flannery; 17 Paul Clough. Subs (all used): 14 James Roby; 18 Kyle Eastmond; 23 Maurie Fa'asavalu; 31 Jacob Emmitt.
Tries: Puletua (14), Cunningham (72);
Goals: Lomax 1/1, Eastmond 1/1.

DRAGONS: 1 Clint Greenshields; 18 Vincent Duport; 15 Jean-Phillipe Baile; 11 Sebastien Raguin; 5 Dimitri Pelo; 4 Adam Mogg; 6 Thomas Bosc; 10 Jerome Guisset; 9 Casey McGuire; 23 Jason Ryles; 16 Olivier Elima; 17 Cyrille Gossard; 26 Greg Bird (C). Subs (all used): 8 David Ferriol; 19 Julien Touxagas; 24 Remi Casty; 27 Sebastien Martins.
Tries: Pelo (4), McGuire (24), Elima (57), Greenshields (67); **Goals:** Bosc 4/5.
Rugby Leaguer & League Express Men of the Match:
Saints: James Roby; *Dragons:* Casey McGuire.
Penalty count: 8-6; **Half-time:** 6-10;
Referee: Ben Thaler; **Attendance:** 8,268.

Saturday 12th September 2009

WAKEFIELD TRINITY WILDCATS 24 HULL KINGSTON ROVERS 10

WILDCATS: 1 Matt Blaymire; 33 Dale Morton; 8 Jason Demetriou (C); 4 Ryan Atkins; 27 Aaron Murphy; 13 Scott Grix; 7 Danny Brough; 15 James Stosic; 14 Sam Obst; 23 Michael Korkidas; 12 Oliver Wilkes; 17 Kevin Henderson; 24 Dale Ferguson. Subs (all used): 28 Kyle Bibb; 25 Richard Moore; 18 Frank Winterstein; 20 Tevita Leo-Latu.
Tries: Ferguson (4), Obst (28), Moore (42), Murphy (64); **Goals:** Brough 3/3, Obst 1/2.
ROVERS: 1 Shaun Briscoe; 2 Peter Fox; 3 Chev Walker; 19 Kris Welham; 5 Liam Colbon; 6 Paul Cooke; 7 Michael Dobson; 18 Scott Wheeldon; 15 Daniel Fitzhenry; 20 Michael Volla (C); 11 Clint Newton; 14 Ben Galea; 21 Chaz I'Anson. Subs (all used): 14 Stanley Gene; 24 Rhys Lovegrove; 16 Jason Netherton; 9 Ben Fisher.
Tries: Newton (13), Fox (51); **Goals:** Dobson 1/2.
On report: Gene (39) - alleged high tackle;
Wheeldon (72) - alleged high tackle.
Rugby Leaguer & League Express Men of the Match:
Wildcats: Sam Obst; *Rovers:* Clint Newton.
Penalty count: 6-2; **Half-time:** 12-6;
Referee: Steve Ganson; **Attendance:** 6,328.

Sunday 13th September 2009

HUDDERSFIELD GIANTS 48 WIGAN WARRIORS 16

GIANTS: 1 Brett Hodgson (C); 21 Leroy Cudjoe; 19 Michael Lawrence; 4 Paul Whatuira; 5 David Hodgson; 6 Liam Fulton; 7 Luke Robinson; 33 Danny Sculthorpe; 9 David Faiumu; 15 Paul Jackson; 13 Stephen Wild; 12 Andy Raleigh; 2 Martin Aspinwall. Subs (all used): 8 Eorl Crabtree; 24 Shaun Lunt; 10 Darrell Griffin; 30 Larne Patrick.
Tries: B Hodgson (8), D Hodgson (27), Lunt (32, 50), Cudjoe (45, 61, 78), Whatuira (53);
Goals: B Hodgson 8/8.
WARRIORS: 21 Cameron Phelps; 2 Amos Roberts; 22 Martin Gleeson; 4 George Carmont; 5 Pat Richards; 13 Sean O'Loughlin (C); 7 Thomas Leuluai; 15 Andy Coley; 17 Michael McIlorum; 19 Paul Prescott; 16 Harrison Hansen; 14 Joel Tomkins; 26 Mark Flanagan. Subs (all used): 8 Stuart Fielden; 10 Iafeta Palea'aesina; 20 Karl

Pryce; 24 Lee Mossop.
Tries: Flanagan (12), Richards (37), J Tomkins (69);
Goals: Richards 2/3.
Rugby Leaguer & League Express Men of the Match:
Giants: Brett Hodgson; *Warriors:* Mark Flanagan.
Penalty count: 8-8; **Half-time:** 18-10;
Referee: Ian Smith; **Attendance:** 8,988.

WARRINGTON WOLVES 44 HARLEQUINS 34

WOLVES: 30 Richard Mathers; 5 Kevin Penny; 25 Chris Bridge; 21 Matty Blythe; 19 Chris Riley; 6 Lee Briers; 7 Michael Monaghan; 8 Adrian Morley (C); 14 Mick Higham; 16 Garreth Carvell; 12 Ben Westwood; 28 Tyrone McCarthy; 24 Ben Harrison. Subs (all used): 18 Alex Thompson (D).
Tries: Penny (23, 58), Westwood (28), Briers (39), Blythe (46), Thompson (53), Higham (68), McCarthy (78); **Goals:** Bridge 6/8.
HARLEQUINS: 1 Chris Melling; 14 Tony Clubb; 3 Matt Gafa; 34 Lamont Bryan; 5 Will Sharp; 6 Luke Dorn; 7 Danny Orr (C); 23 Daniel Heckenberg; 9 Chad Randall; 10 Louie McCarthy-Scarsbrook; 11 Luke Williamson; 32 Ryan Esders; 19 Jason Golden. Subs (all used): 21 Luke Gale; 16 Gareth Haggerty; 25 Dave Williams; 27 Jamie O'Callaghan.
Tries: Clubb (2), Dorn (8, 32, 70), O'Callaghan (62), Gafa (65); **Goals:** Melling 1/2, Gafa 4/4.
Sin bin: Williamson (38) - holding down.
Rugby Leaguer & League Express Men of the Match:
Wolves: Adrian Morley; *Harlequins:* Luke Dorn.
Penalty count: 8-7; **Half-time:** 16-16;
Referee: Phil Bentham; **Attendance:** 10,387.

CASTLEFORD TIGERS 35 CELTIC CRUSADERS 22

TIGERS: 23 Ryan McGoldrick; 2 Kirk Dixon; 3 Michael Shenton; 4 James Evans; 5 Michael Wainwright; 6 Rangi Chase; 7 Brent Sherwin (C); 8 Mitchell Sargent; 14 Stuart Jones; 15 Liam Higgins; 11 Brett Ferres; 12 Ryan Clayton; 13 Joe Westerman. Subs (all used): 1 Richard Owen; 10 Craig Huby; 16 Chris Feather; 19 Kirk Netherton.
Tries: Dixon (16), Sargent (20), Wainwright (29), Owen (45), Shenton (49, 62), Huby (78);
Goals: Westerman 1/5, Dixon 2/2;
Field goal: Sherwin (69).
CRUSADERS: 31 Elliot Kear; 32 Ashley Bateman (D); 5 Anthony Blackwood; 22 Steve Tyrer; 18 Mark Lennon; 9 Lincoln Withers; 14 Matty Smith; 8 Ryan O'Hara (C); 23 Neil Budworth; 10 Mark Bryant; 17 Jordan James; 19 Jason Chan; 28 Lloyd White. Subs (all used): 16 Ben Flower; 20 David Tangata-Toa; 30 Lewis Mills; 25 Geraint Davies.
Tries: White (7), Withers (21, 26), O'Hara (41);
Goals: Tyrer 3/4.
Rugby Leaguer & League Express Men of the Match:
Tigers: Brent Sherwin; *Crusaders:* Jason Chan.
Penalty count: 13-13; **Half-time:** 14-16;
Referee: James Child (replaced at half-time by Peter Brooke); **Attendance:** 6,547.

PLAY-OFFS

QUALIFYING PLAY-OFFS

Friday 18th September 2009

LEEDS RHINOS 44 HULL KINGSTON ROVERS 8

RHINOS: 1 Brent Webb; 2 Scott Donald; 3 Lee Smith; 4 Keith Senior; 5 Ryan Hall; 6 Danny McGuire; 7 Rob Burrow; 8 Kylie Leuluai; 14 Matt Diskin; 10 Jamie Peacock; 11 Jamie Jones-Buchanan; 18 Carl Ablett; 13 Kevin Sinfield (C). Subs (all used): 16 Ryan Bailey; 12 Ali Lauitiiti; 17 Ian Kirke; 21 Simon Worrall.
Tries: Smith (6, 74), Webb (31), Lauitiiti (48, 52), Peacock (63), Hall (66), Senior (79);
Goals: Sinfield 4/6, Smith 2/2.
ROVERS: 15 Daniel Fitzhenry; 2 Peter Fox; 3 Chev Walker; 19 Kris Welham; 5 Liam Colbon; 6 Paul Cooke; 7 Michael Dobson; 8 Nick Fozzard; 9 Ben Fisher; 18 Scott Wheeldon; 11 Clint Newton; 20 Michael Vella (C); 21 Chaz I'Anson. Subs (all used): 14 Stanley Gene; 24 Rhys Lovegrove; 16 Jason Netherton; 30 Scott Taylor (D).
Try: Fitzhenry (20); **Goals:** Dobson 2/2.
Rugby Leaguer & League Express Men of the Match: *Rhinos:* Jamie Peacock; *Rovers:* Kris Welham.
Penalty count: 2-6; **Half-time:** 10-8;
Referee: Steve Ganson; **Attendance:** 11,220.

Saturday 19th September 2009

ST HELENS 15 HUDDERSFIELD GIANTS 2

SAINTS: 1 Paul Wellens; 2 Ade Gardner; 3 Matt Gidley; 18 Kyle Eastmond; 5 Francis Meli; 6 Leon Pryce; 7 Sean Long; 10 James Graham; 9 Keiron Cunningham (C); 16 Tony Puletua; 12 Jon Wilkin; 13 Chris Flannery; 11 Lee Gilmour. Subs (all used): 14 James Roby; 15 Bryn Hargreaves; 17 Paul Clough; 23 Maurie Fa'asavalu.
Tries: Puletua (2), Pryce (13), Meli (20);
Goals: Eastmond 1/3; **Field goal:** Long (73).
GIANTS: 21 Leroy Cudjoe; 2 Martin Aspinwall; 19 Michael Lawrence; 14 Simon Finnigan; 5 David Hodgson; 1 Brett Hodgson (C); 7 Luke Robinson; 33 Danny Sculthorpe; 6 Liam Fulton; 15 Paul Jackson; 13 Stephen Wild; 12 Andy Raleigh; 4 Paul Whatuira. Subs (all used): 8 Eorl Crabtree; 10 Darrell Griffin; 24 Shaun Lunt; 30 Larne Patrick.
Goals: B Hodgson 1/1.
Rugby Leaguer & League Express Men of the Match: *Saints:* James Graham; *Giants:* Stephen Wild.
Penalty count: 6-10; **Half-time:** 14-2;
Referee: Richard Silverwood; **Attendance:** 6,157.

ELIMINATION PLAY-OFFS

Saturday 19th September 2009

WAKEFIELD TRINITY WILDCATS 16 CATALANS DRAGONS 25

WILDCATS: 1 Matt Blaymire; 27 Aaron Murphy; 8 Jason Demetriou (C); 4 Ryan Atkins; 26 Luke George; 13 Scott Grix; 14 Sam Obst; 23 Michael Korkidas; 9 Brad Drew; 15 James Stosic; 12 Oliver Wilkes; 11 Steve Snitch; 24 Dale Ferguson. Subs (all used): 18 Frank Winterstein; 25 Richard Moore; 20 Tevita Leo-Latu; 17 Kevin Henderson.
Tries: George (51, 72), Atkins (58); **Goals:** Drew 2/4.
DRAGONS: 1 Clint Greenshields; 18 Vincent Duport; 15 Jean-Phillipe Baile; 11 Sebastien Raguin; 5 Dimitri Pelo; 4 Adam Mogg; 6 Thomas Bosc; 23 Jason Ryles; 9 Casey McGuire; 10 Jerome Guisset; 16 Olivier Elima; 17 Cyrille Gossard; 26 Greg Bird (C). Subs (all used): 24 Remi Casty; 8 David Ferriol; 19 Julien Touxagas; 14 Dane Carlaw.
Tries: Duport (29), Elima (34), Pelo (37, 47);
Goals: Bosc 4/5; **Field goal:** Bosc (77).
Rugby Leaguer & League Express Men of the Match: *Wildcats:* Luke George; *Dragons:* Clint Greenshields.
Penalty count: 8-4; **Half-time:** 2-16;
Referee: Phil Bentham; **Attendance:** 4,008.

Sunday 20th September 2009

WIGAN WARRIORS 18 CASTLEFORD TIGERS 12

WARRIORS: 21 Cameron Phelps; 2 Amos Roberts; 22 Martin Gleeson; 4 George Carmont; 5 Pat Richards; 25 Sam Tomkins; 7 Thomas Leuluai; 15 Andy Coley; 17 Michael McIlorum; 19 Paul Prescott; 14 Joel Tomkins; 16 Harrison Hansen; 13 Sean O'Loughlin (C). Subs (all used): 8 Stuart Fielden; 9 Mark Riddell; 10 Iafeta Palea'aesina; 26 Mark Flanagan.
Tries: Hansen (22), Carmont (32), Roberts (52);
Goals: Richards 3/4.
TIGERS: 1 Richard Owen; 2 Kirk Dixon; 3 Michael Shenton; 4 James Evans; 5 Michael Wainwright; 23 Ryan McGoldrick; 7 Brent Sherwin (C); 8 Mitchell Sargent; 6 Rangi Chase; 10 Craig Huby; 11 Brett Ferres; 12 Ryan Clayton; 14 Stuart Jones. Subs (all used): 13 Joe Westerman; 15 Liam Higgins; 16 Chris Feather; 19 Kirk Netherton.
Tries: Huby (61), Westerman (75);
Goals: Westerman 2/2.
Rugby Leaguer & League Express Men of the Match: *Warriors:* Cameron Phelps; *Tigers:* Richard Owen.
Penalty count: 8-7; **Half-time:** 12-0;
Referee: Ian Smith; **Attendance:** 8,689.

Hull KR's Michael Dobson wrapped up by Wigan's Martin Gleeson

PRELIMINARY SEMI-FINALS

Friday 25th September 2009

HUDDERSFIELD GIANTS 6 CATALANS DRAGONS 16

GIANTS: 1 Brett Hodgson (C); 21 Leroy Cudjoe; 11 Jamahl Lolesi; 19 Michael Lawrence; 5 David Hodgson; 4 Paul Whatuira; 7 Luke Robinson; 16 Keith Mason; 20 Scott Moore; 33 Danny Sculthorpe; 14 Simon Finnigan; 6 Liam Fulton; 13 Stephen Wild. Subs (all used): 12 Andy Raleigh; 10 Darrell Griffin; 8 Eorl Crabtree; 9 David Faiumu.
Try: Robinson (35); **Goals:** B Hodgson 1/1.
DRAGONS: 1 Clint Greenshields; 18 Vincent Duport; 15 Jean-Phillipe Baile; 11 Sebastien Raguin; 5 Dimitri Pelo; 4 Adam Mogg; 6 Thomas Bosc; 23 Jason Ryles; 9 Casey McGuire; 10 Jerome Guisset; 16 Olivier Elima; 17 Cyrille Gossard; 26 Greg Bird (C). Subs (all used): 24 Remi Casty; 8 David Ferriol; 19 Julien Touxagas; 14 Dane Carlaw.
Tries: Greenshields (19), Pelo (62), Elima (70);
Goals: Bosc 2/3.
Rugby Leaguer & League Express Men of the Match: *Giants:* Luke Robinson; *Dragons:* Clint Greenshields.
Penalty count: 12-9; **Half-time:** 6-4;
Referee: Steve Ganson; **Attendance:** 4,263.

Saturday 26th September 2009

HULL KINGSTON ROVERS 16 WIGAN WARRIORS 30

ROVERS: 1 Shaun Briscoe; 2 Peter Fox; 4 Jake Webster; 19 Kris Welham; 5 Liam Colbon; 6 Paul Cooke; 7 Michael Dobson; 8 Nick Fozzard; 15 Daniel Fitzhenry; 20 Michael Vella (C); 11 Clint Newton; 12 Ben Galea; 13 Scott Murrell. Subs (all used): 18 Scott Wheeldon; 24 Rhys Lovegrove; 16 Jason Netherton; 21 Chaz I'Anson.
Tries: Welham (44), Fox (56), I'Anson (61);
Goals: Dobson 2/4.
WARRIORS: 21 Cameron Phelps; 2 Amos Roberts; 22 Martin Gleeson; 4 George Carmont; 5 Pat Richards; 25 Sam Tomkins; 7 Thomas Leuluai; 15 Andy Coley; 9 Mark Riddell; 19 Paul Prescott; 14 Joel Tomkins; 16 Harrison Hansen; 13 Sean O'Loughlin (C). Subs (all used): 8 Stuart Fielden; 10 Iafeta Palea'aesina; 17 Michael McIlorum; 26 Mark Flanagan.
Tries: Carmont (16), Palea'aesina (31), Richards (38), Gleeson (64, 79); **Goals:** Richards 5/7.
Rugby Leaguer & League Express Men of the Match: *Rovers:* Shaun Briscoe; *Warriors:* Martin Gleeson.
Penalty count: 8-9; **Half-time:** 0-18;
Referee: Richard Silverwood; **Attendance:** 8,162.

QUALIFYING SEMI-FINALS

Friday 2nd October 2009

LEEDS RHINOS 27 CATALANS DRAGONS 20

RHINOS: 1 Brent Webb; 2 Scott Donald; 3 Lee Smith; 4 Keith Senior; 5 Ryan Hall; 6 Danny McGuire; 7 Rob Burrow; 8 Kylie Leuluai; 14 Matt Diskin; 10 Jamie Peacock; 11 Jamie Jones-Buchanan; 18 Carl Ablett; 13 Kevin Sinfield (C). Subs (all used): 16 Ryan Bailey; 19 Luke Burgess; 17 Ian Kirke; 21 Simon Worrall.
Tries: McGuire (13, 37), Hall (32, 34), Donald (43);
Goals: Sinfield 3/5; **Field goal:** Sinfield (62).
DRAGONS: 1 Clint Greenshields; 18 Vincent Duport; 11 Sebastien Raguin; 15 Jean-Phillipe Baile; 5 Dimitri Pelo; 4 Adam Mogg; 6 Thomas Bosc; 23 Jason Ryles; 9 Casey McGuire; 10 Jerome Guisset; 16 Olivier Elima; 17 Cyrille Gossard; 26 Greg Bird (C). Subs (all used): 8 David Ferriol; 19 Julien Touxagas; 24 Remi Casty; 14 Dane Carlaw.
Tries: Duport (15, 46, 54), Mogg (74); **Goals:** Bosc 2/4.
Rugby Leaguer & League Express Men of the Match: *Rhinos:* Jamie Peacock; *Dragons:* Adam Mogg.
Penalty count: 15-10; **Half-time:** 22-4;
Referee: Richard Silverwood; **Attendance:** 13,409.

Saturday 3rd October 2009

ST HELENS 14 WIGAN WARRIORS 10

SAINTS: 1 Paul Wellens; 2 Ade Gardner; 3 Matt Gidley; 18 Kyle Eastmond; 5 Francis Meli; 6 Leon Pryce; 7 Sean Long; 10 James Graham; 9 Keiron Cunningham (C); 16 Tony Puletua; 12 Jon Wilkin; 13 Chris Flannery; 11 Lee Gilmour. Subs (all used): 14 James Roby; 15 Bryn Hargreaves; 17 Paul Clough; 23 Maurie Fa'asavalu.
Tries: Meli (2, 48), Long (37); **Goals:** Eastmond 1/3.
WARRIORS: 21 Cameron Phelps; 2 Amos Roberts; 22 Martin Gleeson; 4 George Carmont; 5 Pat Richards; 25 Sam Tomkins; 7 Thomas Leuluai; 15 Andy Coley; 9 Mark Riddell; 19 Paul Prescott; 16 Harrison Hansen; 14 Joel Tomkins; 13 Sean O'Loughlin (C). Subs (all used): 8 Stuart Fielden; 10 Iafeta Palea'aesina; 24 Lee Mossop; 26 Mark Flanagan.
Tries: Carmont (23), Richards (69); **Goals:** Richards 1/2.
On report: Coley (59) - alleged high tackle on Gilmour.
Rugby Leaguer & League Express Men of the Match: *Saints:* Sean Long; *Warriors:* Thomas Leuluai.
Penalty count: 6-7; **Half-time:** 10-6;
Referee: Steve Ganson; **Attendance:** 13,087.

GRAND FINAL

Saturday 10th October 2009

LEEDS RHINOS 18 ST HELENS 10

RHINOS: 1 Brent Webb; 2 Scott Donald; 3 Lee Smith; 4 Keith Senior; 5 Ryan Hall; 6 Danny McGuire; 7 Rob Burrow; 8 Kylie Leuluai; 14 Matt Diskin; 10 Jamie Peacock; 11 Jamie Jones-Buchanan; 18 Carl Ablett; 13 Kevin Sinfield (C). Subs (all used): 16 Ryan Bailey for Leuluai (19); 19 Luke Burgess for Peacock (29); 17 Ian Kirke for Jones-Buchanan (29); 12 Ali Lauitiiti for Ablett (29); Jones-Buchanan for Lauitiiti (36); Peacock for Burgess (46); Leuluai for Bailey (53); Ablett for Kirke (57); Burgess for Diskin (62); Bailey for Leuluai (67); Diskin for Burgess (69); Kirke for Jones-Buchanan (76).
Tries: Diskin (30), Smith (37, 72); **Goals:** Sinfield 2/4;
Field goals: Sinfield (42), Burrow (78).
SAINTS: 1 Paul Wellens; 2 Ade Gardner; 3 Matt Gidley; 18 Kyle Eastmond; 5 Francis Meli; 6 Leon Pryce; 7 Sean Long; 10 James Graham; 9 Keiron Cunningham (C); 16 Tony Puletua; 12 Jon Wilkin; 11 Lee Gilmour; 13 Chris Flannery. Subs (all used): 14 James Roby for Cunningham (25); 15 Bryn Hargreaves for Puletua (24); 17 Paul Clough for Gilmour (31); 23 Maurie Fa'asavalu for Graham (31); Graham for Fa'asavalu (48); Puletua for Hargreaves (50); Gilmour for Wilkin (55); Cunningham for Clough (61); Wilkin for Roby (65); Roby for Flannery (73).
Try: Eastmond (13); **Goals:** Eastmond 3/3.
Rugby Leaguer & League Express Men of the Match: *Rhinos:* Kevin Sinfield; *Saints:* James Graham.
Penalty count: 8-7; **Half-time:** 8-8;
Referee: Steve Ganson; **Attendance:** 63,259
(at Old Trafford, Manchester).

Leeds' Carl Ablett, Matt Diskin and Kylie Leuluai halt St Helens' Tony Puletua during the Grand Final

SUPER LEAGUE XIV
Opta Analysis

SUPER LEAGUE XIV
TOP PERFORMERS

TACKLES
Malcolm Alker	Salford	981
Luke Adamson	Salford	923
Jamie Langley	Bradford	893
Luke Swain	Salford	881
Lee Radford	Hull	858
Jon Wilkin	St Helens	856
Scott Murrell	Hull KR	831
Danny Tickle	Hull	812
Stephen Wild	Huddersfield	774
Ben Galea	Hull KR	758

TACKLES MADE *(% success)*
Jamie Thackray	Hull	97.66
Lee Mossop	Wigan/	
	Huddersfield	97.30
Adam Peek	Celtic Crusaders	97.28
Ryan Boyle	Castleford	97.04
Paul Clough	St Helens	97.04
Jason Golden	Harlequins	96.79
Simon Finnigan	Huddersfield	96.74
Danny Kirmond	Huddersfield	96.67
Jason Ryles	Catalans	96.56
Danny Sculthorpe		
	Huddersfield/	
	Wakefield	96.52

OFFLOADS
Andy Lynch	Bradford	63
Ray Cashmere	Salford	55
Ali Lauitiiti	Leeds	53
Keith Senior	Leeds	53
Eorl Crabtree	Huddersfield	51
Leon Pryce	St Helens	49
Danny Tickle	Hull	49
Steve Menzies	Bradford	46
Mark Bryant	Celtic Crusaders	42
Iafeta Palea'aesina		
	Wigan	42

CLEAN BREAKS
Ryan Hall	Leeds	29
Clint Greenshields		
	Catalans	23
David Hodgson	Huddersfield	23
Keith Senior	Leeds	23
Chris Melling	Harlequins	22
Amos Roberts	Wigan	21
Luke Robinson	Huddersfield	21
Danny McGuire	Leeds	20
Dimitri Pelo	Catalans	18
Sam Tomkins	Wigan	18

TRY ASSISTS
Danny Orr	Harlequins	24
Thomas Bosc	Catalans	20
Michael Dobson	Hull KR	20
Ben Jeffries	Bradford	19
Kevin Brown	Huddersfield	16
Luke Dorn	Harlequins	16
Lee Briers	Warrington	15
Danny Brough	Wakefield	15
Richard Myler	Salford	15
Leon Pryce	St Helens	15

Malcolm Alker

MARKER TACKLES
Jamie Langley	Bradford	158
Jon Wilkin	St Helens	130
Jason Golden	Harlequins	127
Lee Radford	Hull	126
Malcolm Alker	Salford	125
James Roby	St Helens	117
Ben Fisher	Hull KR	115
Jamie Peacock	Leeds	115
Joe Westerman	Castleford	113
Scott Murrell	Hull KR	110

METRES
James Graham	St Helens	4752
Jamie Peacock	Leeds	3764
Clint Greenshields		
	Catalans	3404
Will Sharp	Harlequins	3385
Ryan Hall	Leeds	3366
Tony Puletua	St Helens	3310
Pat Richards	Wigan	3294
Andy Lynch	Bradford	3277
Chris Melling	Harlequins	3179
Paul Clough	St Helens	3155

CARRIES
James Graham	St Helens	658
Jamie Peacock	Leeds	522
Andy Lynch	Bradford	465
Will Sharp	Harlequins	460
Paul Wellens	St Helens	444
Rangi Chase	Castleford	442
Danny Tickle	Hull	434
Ryan O'Hara	Celtic Crusaders	427
Clint Greenshields		
	Catalans	425
Pat Richards	Wigan	424

AVERAGE GAIN PER CARRY *(Metres)*
Francis Meli	St Helens	9.20
Damien Blanch	Wakefield	9.18
Vincent Duport	Catalans	9.06
Ryan Hall	Leeds	9.06
Tom Briscoe	Hull	8.83
Peter Fox	Hull KR	8.82
Craig Hall	Hull	8.76
Tony Puletua	St Helens	8.75
Garreth Carvell	Warrington	8.64
Chris Melling	Harlequins	8.64

TACKLE BUSTS
Rangi Chase	Castleford	111
Willie Manu	Hull	98
Will Sharp	Harlequins	93
Iafeta Palea'aesina		
	Wigan	89
Paul Wellens	St Helens	86
Jason Demetriou		
	Wakefield	85
John Wilshere	Salford	85
Maurie Fa'asavalu		
	St Helens	82
Louie McCarthy-Scarsbrook		
	Harlequins	80
Brett Hodgson	Huddersfield	79

40/20s
Malcolm Alker	Salford	5
Thomas Bosc	Catalans	4
Michael Dobson		
	Hull KR	4
Casey McGuire	Catalans	3
Scott Murrell	Hull KR	3
Leon Pryce	St Helens	3
Kevin Sinfield	Leeds	3

opta sportsdata

*All statistics in Opta Analysis include
Super League regular season games only*

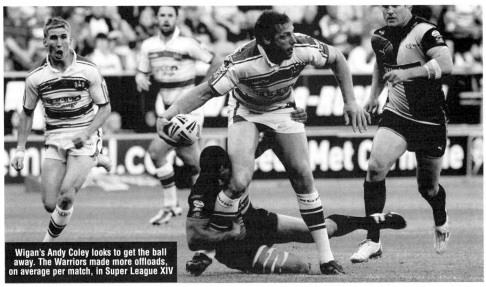

Wigan's Andy Coley looks to get the ball away. The Warriors made more offloads, on average per match, in Super League XIV

SUPER LEAGUE XIV AVERAGES PER MATCH

TACKLES		OFFLOADS		METRES		ERRORS	
Salford	326.9	Wigan	14.1	St Helens	1509.9	St Helens	21.9
St Helens	322.0	Hull	14.0	Hull	1350.3	Huddersfield	23.8
Huddersfield	320.9	Leeds	13.8	Leeds	1348.7	Catalans	26.1
Harlequins	319.2	Bradford	13.5	Warrington	1346.5	Leeds	26.2
Hull Kingston Rovers	315.1	Huddersfield	12.1	Hull Kingston Rovers	1325.6	Wigan	26.5
Hull	313.3	Warrington	12.0	Wigan	1319.6	Harlequins	27.0
Celtic Crusaders	311.0	Salford	11.9	Harlequins	1318.1	Salford	27.1
Wigan	298.3	Celtic Crusaders	11.5	Huddersfield	1312.0	Hull	27.6
Catalans	295.4	Harlequins	11.3	Bradford	1300.3	Celtic Crusaders	29.7
Bradford	294.7	St Helens	10.7	Castleford	1289.7	Wakefield	29.9
Warrington	290.9	Castleford	10.2	Wakefield	1269.4	Bradford	31.4
Leeds	290.5	Wakefield	8.8	Catalans	1255.9	Warrington	31.4
Wakefield	287.9	Catalans	8.7	Salford	1147.1	Castleford	32.2
Castleford	279.1	Hull Kingston Rovers	6.9	Celtic Crusaders	1119.3	Hull Kingston Rovers	35.4

MISSED TACKLES		CLEAN BREAKS		CARRIES		KICKS IN GENERAL PLAY	
St Helens	21.9	St Helens	7.2	St Helens	215.0	Hull Kingston Rovers	21.8
Huddersfield	23.8	Leeds	7.0	Harlequins	198.1	Hull	21.4
Catalans	26.1	Huddersfield	6.3	Leeds	198.0	Salford	21.1
Leeds	26.2	Wigan	6.1	Hull	197.8	Wakefield	20.7
Wigan	26.5	Warrington	5.9	Bradford	196.3	Celtic Crusaders	20.5
Harlequins	27.0	Bradford	5.5	Castleford	194.8	Harlequins	20.3
Salford	27.1	Castleford	5.4	Hull Kingston Rovers	190.5	Huddersfield	19.4
Hull	27.6	Wakefield	5.1	Warrington	187.7	Wigan	19.1
Celtic Crusaders	29.7	Hull Kingston Rovers	5.0	Wigan	187.3	Castleford	19.0
Wakefield	29.9	Catalans	4.9	Huddersfield	186.1	St Helens	18.6
Bradford	31.4	Harlequins	4.7	Wakefield	185.4	Catalans	18.1
Warrington	31.4	Hull	4.4	Celtic Crusaders	185.2	Leeds	18.0
Castleford	32.2	Salford	3.9	Salford	179.6	Warrington	17.5
Hull Kingston Rovers	35.4	Celtic Crusaders	3.8	Catalans	179.2	Bradford	17.0

SUPER LEAGUE XIV TRIES SCORED/CONCEDED

TOTAL TRIES SCORED		TOTAL TRIES CONCEDED		SCORED FROM KICKS		CONCEDED FROM KICKS	
Leeds	140	Celtic Crusaders	158	Harlequins	21	Wigan	25
St Helens	139	Salford	136	Wakefield	21	Salford	23
Huddersfield	122	Castleford	127	Hull Kingston Rovers	21	Catalans	22
Wigan	122	Harlequins	126	Salford	20	Leeds	19
Warrington	118	Warrington	124	Huddersfield	19	Hull Kingston Rovers	18
Castleford	115	Bradford	119	Hull	16	Warrington	18
Wakefield	115	Catalans	115	Wigan	16	Celtic Crusaders	17
Hull Kingston Rovers	114	Hull	110	Catalans	16	Harlequins	16
Catalans	112	Wakefield	107	Castleford	15	Hull	16
Bradford	111	Wigan	96	Leeds	15	Bradford	15
Harlequins	102	Hull Kingston Rovers	90	Bradford	14	Castleford	13
Hull	86	St Helens	80	Warrington	12	St Helens	12
Salford	79	Leeds	76	Celtic Crusaders	12	Wakefield	10
Celtic Crusaders	63	Huddersfield	74	St Helens	10	Huddersfield	4

231

Super League XIV - Opta Analysis

SUPER LEAGUE XIV TRIES SCORED/CONCEDED

TRIES SCORED FROM OWN HALF
Wigan	20
Leeds	19
Hull Kingston Rovers	14
Warrington	14
Hull	13
Bradford	13
Huddersfield	13
Wakefield	11
Salford	9
Celtic Crusaders	9
Harlequins	8
Castleford	7
St Helens	7
Catalans	3

TRIES CONCEDED FROM OVER 50M
Warrington	16
Harlequins	16
Bradford	15
Hull	13
Wakefield	13
Castleford	13
Catalans	13
Hull Kingston Rovers	11
Salford	11
Celtic Crusaders	10
St Helens	10
Wigan	8
Leeds	7
Huddersfield	4

TRIES SCORED FROM UNDER 10M
Warrington	67
St Helens	65
Leeds	63
Catalans	61
Wakefield	60
Castleford	55
Bradford	54
Wigan	54
Huddersfield	54
Hull Kingston Rovers	52
Harlequins	48
Hull	38
Salford	38
Celtic Crusaders	25

TRIES CONCEDED FROM UNDER 10M
Celtic Crusaders	80
Salford	66
Castleford	58
Catalans	57
Hull	56
Warrington	55
Harlequins	54
Bradford	53
St Helens	48
Hull Kingston Rovers	44
Leeds	42
Wakefield	42
Wigan	41
Huddersfield	38

TOTAL PENALTIES AWARDED
Wakefield	229
Bradford	213
Catalans	208
Castleford	195
Salford	194
Warrington	194
Hull Kingston Rovers	192
St Helens	192
Hull	187
Leeds	187
Harlequins	175
Wigan	172
Huddersfield	169
Celtic Crusaders	166

TOTAL PENALTIES CONCEDED
Catalans	235
Salford	223
Huddersfield	220
Leeds	209
Celtic Crusaders	204
Bradford	201
Castleford	198
Wakefield	194
Wigan	175
Warrington	173
Harlequins	171
St Helens	166
Hull Kingston Rovers	161
Hull	143

FOUL PLAY - AWARDED
Hull Kingston Rovers	50
Wakefield	45
Castleford	42
St Helens	40
Bradford	38
Warrington	38
Harlequins	36
Catalans	32
Huddersfield	32
Salford	29
Hull	28
Wigan	27
Celtic Crusaders	26
Leeds	25

FOUL PLAY - CONCEDED
Catalans	52
Salford	48
Warrington	40
Wakefield	39
Castleford	38
Huddersfield	38
Hull Kingston Rovers	38
Leeds	37
Celtic Crusaders	29
St Helens	29
Wigan	29
Harlequins	27
Bradford	23
Hull	21

OFFSIDE - AWARDED
Bradford	38
St Helens	35
Harlequins	34
Castleford	33
Hull Kingston Rovers	30
Hull	30
Salford	28
Huddersfield	24
Wigan	24
Warrington	23
Catalans	23
Wakefield	22
Leeds	22
Celtic Crusaders	20

OFFSIDE - CONCEDED
Huddersfield	46
Wakefield	37
Catalans	33
Leeds	31
Castleford	29
St Helens	29
Bradford	29
Harlequins	28
Wigan	25
Celtic Crusaders	25
Salford	22
Warrington	22
Hull Kingston Rovers	16
Hull	14

SUPER LEAGUE XIV PENALTIES

INTERFERENCE - AWARDED
Wakefield	97
Warrington	90
Salford	85
Leeds	82
Hull	81
Catalans	81
Castleford	80
Bradford	76
St Helens	73
Wigan	69
Hull Kingston Rovers	67
Celtic Crusaders	67
Harlequins	66
Huddersfield	65

INTERFERENCE - CONCEDED
Catalans	104
Celtic Crusaders	88
Salford	88
Bradford	87
Huddersfield	85
Castleford	85
Leeds	83
Wakefield	72
Wigan	72
Warrington	66
Hull Kingston Rovers	66
Harlequins	63
Hull	63
St Helens	57

OBSTRUCTION - AWARDED
Leeds	13
Wakefield	12
Bradford	12
Salford	9
Hull Kingston Rovers	8
Celtic Crusaders	8
Hull	7
Catalans	7
St Helens	7
Wigan	7
Warrington	6
Huddersfield	6
Harlequins	5
Castleford	3

OBSTRUCTION - CONCEDED
Bradford	17
Celtic Crusaders	13
Salford	13
Leeds	9
Huddersfield	8
Wakefield	7
Wigan	7
Warrington	6
Hull Kingston Rovers	6
Harlequins	6
Hull	6
St Helens	6
Catalans	5
Castleford	1

BALL STEALING - AWARDED
Catalans	30
Hull	22
Warrington	19
Celtic Crusaders	17
Wakefield	15
Bradford	15
Leeds	13
Wigan	13
Salford	12
Hull Kingston Rovers	11
St Helens	11
Harlequins	10
Castleford	9
Huddersfield	8

BALL STEALING - CONCEDED
Leeds	20
Bradford	18
Salford	18
Harlequins	17
Castleford	16
Wigan	15
Warrington	15
Celtic Crusaders	14
Hull	14
St Helens	14
Catalans	12
Wakefield	11
Hull Kingston Rovers	11
Huddersfield	10

OFFSIDE MARKERS - AWARDED
Catalans	14
Wakefield	13
Bradford	13
Huddersfield	12
Celtic Crusaders	11
Hull Kingston Rovers	11
Leeds	10
Wigan	8
Salford	8
Harlequins	8
Warrington	6
Hull	4
St Helens	4
Castleford	3

OFFSIDE MARKERS - CONCEDED
St Helens	17
Huddersfield	12
Catalans	11
Salford	10
Hull	10
Leeds	9
Bradford	9
Warrington	9
Wakefield	9
Hull Kingston Rovers	8
Wigan	6
Harlequins	5
Castleford	5
Celtic Crusaders	5

NOT PLAYING BALL CORRECTLY - AWARDED
Salford	11
Celtic Crusaders	6
Catalans	5
Wakefield	5
Bradford	4
Harlequins	4
Leeds	3
Wigan	3
Warrington	3
Huddersfield	2
Hull Kingston Rovers	2
Hull	2
Castleford	2
St Helens	1

NOT PLAYING BALL CORRECTLY - CONCEDED
Wigan	8
Salford	7
Leeds	6
Wakefield	5
St Helens	4
Catalans	4
Castleford	4
Huddersfield	3
Harlequins	3
Celtic Crusaders	3
Hull	2
Bradford	2
Warrington	2
Hull Kingston Rovers	0

DISSENT - AWARDED
Wakefield	6
Huddersfield	5
Harlequins	5
St Helens	5
Catalans	4
Castleford	4
Bradford	3
Wigan	3
Warrington	3
Salford	2
Celtic Crusaders	2
Leeds	2
Hull	2
Hull Kingston Rovers	1

DISSENT - CONCEDED
Leeds	9
Celtic Crusaders	7
Catalans	6
Wigan	6
Castleford	4
Wakefield	4
Harlequins	3
Huddersfield	3
Salford	2
Hull	2
Warrington	2
St Helens	1
Bradford	1
Hull Kingston Rovers	1

BRADFORD BULLS

Andy Lynch

MARKER TACKLES
Jamie Langley 158
Terry Newton 105
Nick Scruton 93
Andy Lynch 83
Michael Worrincy.............68

METRES
Andy Lynch 3277
Sam Burgess 2922
Rikki Sheriffe 2656
Dave Halley 2545
Semi Tadulala 2405

CARRIES
Andy Lynch 465
Sam Burgess 411
Jamie Langley 366
Rikki Sheriffe 364
Terry Newton 340

Dave Halley

TACKLES
Jamie Langley 893
Andy Lynch 740
Nick Scruton 634
Sam Burgess 600
Terry Newton 593

CLEAN BREAKS
Chris Nero 18
Semi Tadulala 16
Paul Sykes......................15
Steve Menzies 14
Dave Halley 11

TACKLE BUSTS
Rikki Sheriffe 77
Sam Burgess 63
Chris Nero 62
Andy Lynch 58
Semi Tadulala 56

OFFLOADS
Andy Lynch 63
Steve Menzies 46
Chris Nero 33
Sam Burgess 32
Terry Newton 23

TRY ASSISTS
Ben Jeffries 19
Paul Deacon 10
Chris Nero 6
Glenn Morrison 5
Paul Sykes........................5

TOTAL OPTA INDEX
Andy Lynch 18915
Dave Halley 15795
Jamie Langley 14858
Sam Burgess 14780
Steve Menzies 12795

CASTLEFORD TIGERS

Rangi Chase

MARKER TACKLES
Joe Westerman 113
Brett Ferres 76
Michael Shenton 74
Mitchell Sargent 71
Kirk Netherton 69

METRES
Ryan McGoldrick 2669
Richard Owen 2610
Mitchell Sargent 2553
Rangi Chase 2372
Craig Huby....................2301

CARRIES
Rangi Chase 442
Ryan McGoldrick 397
Richard Owen 347
Craig Huby....................346
Mitchell Sargent 339

Michael Shenton

TACKLES
Joe Westerman 699
Brett Ferres 638
Stuart Jones 581
Mitchell Sargent 561
Craig Huby.....................518

CLEAN BREAKS
Michael Shenton 18
Rangi Chase 17
Richard Owen 17
Ryan McGoldrick 11
Brett Ferres 10

TACKLE BUSTS
Rangi Chase 111
Richard Owen 69
Ryan McGoldrick 59
Michael Shenton 59
Joe Westerman 51

OFFLOADS
Rangi Chase 39
Craig Huby......................32
Sione Faumuina..............24
Ryan McGoldrick..............20
Joe Westerman 20

TRY ASSISTS
Brent Sherwin 14
Rangi Chase 10
Ryan McGoldrick 9
Michael Shenton 4
Dean Widders 4

TOTAL OPTA INDEX
Rangi Chase 18088
Michael Shenton 13938
Brett Ferres 13520
Ryan McGoldrick 13066
Joe Westerman 12572

233

CATALANS DRAGONS

TACKLES
Olivier Elima 696
Jerome Guisset 608
Gregory Mounis..............599
David Ferriol 546
Cyrille Gossard 529

OFFLOADS
Greg Bird.........................38
Olivier Elima 24
Jason Ryles.....................23
David Ferriol 19
Gregory Mounis...............14

CLEAN BREAKS
Clint Greenshields 23
Dimitri Pelo 18
Jean-Phillipe Baile 11
Olivier Elima 11
Steven Bell......................10

TRY ASSISTS
Thomas Bosc...................20
Adam Mogg.......................9
Jean-Phillipe Baile 8
Greg Bird...........................5
Casey McGuire 5

MARKER TACKLES
Olivier Elima 84
Jerome Guisset 63
Gregory Mounis...............62
Cyrille Gossard 55
Dane Carlaw 53

Clint Greenshields

METRES
Clint Greenshields 3404
David Ferriol 2771
Jerome Guisset 2536
Dimitri Pelo 2522
Jason Ryles.................2304

CARRIES
Clint Greenshields 425
David Ferriol 391
Jerome Guisset 345
Olivier Elima 305
Dimitri Pelo 304

TACKLE BUSTS
Clint Greenshields 78
Dimitri Pelo 73
Jean-Phillipe Baile 44
Greg Bird.........................38
Olivier Elima 35

TOTAL OPTA INDEX
Clint Greenshields 17808
Olivier Elima 14512
Dimitri Pelo 14338
Jerome Guisset 12905
David Ferriol 12303

Olivier Elima

CELTIC CRUSADERS

TACKLES
Ryan O'Hara 726
Mark Bryant...................673
Neil Budworth 580
Jason Chan 574
Peter Lupton 555

OFFLOADS
Mark Bryant.....................42
Ryan O'Hara 40
Mark Dalle Cort 37
Damien Quinn 34
Josh Hannay 14

CLEAN BREAKS
Mark Dalle Cort 11
Jason Chan 8
Damien Quinn 8
Luke Dyer 7
Anthony Blackwood............6

TRY ASSISTS
Jace Van Dijk..................11
Matty Smith.......................5
Mark Dalle Cort 2
Peter Lupton 2
David Tangata-Toa 2

MARKER TACKLES
Adam Peek 81
Neil Budworth 75
Ryan O'Hara 74
Jason Chan 71
Peter Lupton 68

Ryan O'Hara

METRES
Ryan O'Hara 2729
Mark Bryant.................2545
Mark Dalle Cort 2210
Anthony Blackwood.....1912
Luke Dyer 1838

CARRIES
Ryan O'Hara 427
Mark Bryant...................420
Mark Dalle Cort 321
Anthony Blackwood.......293
Luke Dyer 292

TACKLE BUSTS
Jason Chan 60
Damien Quinn 47
Luke Dyer 37
Neil Budworth 33
Anthony Blackwood..........26

TOTAL OPTA INDEX
Ryan O'Hara 13877
Mark Bryant...............13370
Jason Chan 11958
Mark Dalle Cort 10859
Neil Budworth 10248

Mark Bryant

HARLEQUINS

Louie
McCarthy-Scarsbrook

Will
Sharp

MARKER TACKLES
Jason Golden..................127
Luke Williamson 90
Chad Randall 79
Chad Robinson 75
Rob Purdham 73

METRES
Will Sharp 3385
Chris Melling 3179
Louie McCarthy-Scarsbrook 2828
Daniel Heckenberg........2088
Jon Wells.....................2042

CARRIES
Will Sharp 460
Chad Randall 401
Chris Melling 368
Louie McCarthy-Scarsbrook 367
Danny Orr 288

TACKLE BUSTS
Will Sharp 93
Louie McCarthy-Scarsbrook 80
Chris Melling 74
Tony Clubb......................56
David Howell 39

TOTAL OPTA INDEX
Louie
McCarthy-Scarsbrook..15938
Will Sharp 14800
Chad Randall 14577
Chris Melling 13584
Karl Temata 11075

TACKLES
Jason Golden...................754
Chad Randall 705
Louie McCarthy-Scarsbrook 652
Luke Williamson 615
Karl Temata 574

CLEAN BREAKS
Chris Melling 22
David Howell 15
Luke Dorn 14
Will Sharp 14
Louie McCarthy-Scarsbrook 8

OFFLOADS
Matt Gafa..........................36
Will Sharp 36
Louie McCarthy-Scarsbrook ..29
Danny Orr 26
Rob Purdham 19

TRY ASSISTS
Danny Orr 24
Luke Dorn 16
Chad Randall 8
Chris Melling 5
Luke Gale...........................4

HUDDERSFIELD GIANTS

Luke
Robinson

Brett
Hodgson

MARKER TACKLES
Stephen Wild 81
Danny Kirmond 64
Simon Finnigan 63
Liam Fulton 56
Paul Jackson 54

METRES
David Hodgson 3102
Keith Mason 2764
Brett Hodgson 2453
Leroy Cudjoe 2279
Eorl Crabtree 2012

CARRIES
Brett Hodgson 376
David Hodgson 371
Keith Mason 356
Leroy Cudjoe 283
Luke Robinson 282

TACKLES
Stephen Wild 774
Scott Moore....................635
Keith Mason 570
Simon Finnigan 564
Luke Robinson 487

CLEAN BREAKS
David Hodgson 23
Luke Robinson 21
Brett Hodgson 15
Kevin Brown 14
Leroy Cudjoe 13

TACKLE BUSTS
Brett Hodgson 79
Luke Robinson 70
David Hodgson 66
Eorl Crabtree 57
Leroy Cudjoe 40

OFFLOADS
Eorl Crabtree 51
David Faiumu....................28
Kevin Brown 25
Danny Sculthorpe 25
Brett Hodgson 20

TRY ASSISTS
Kevin Brown 16
Luke Robinson 13
Brett Hodgson 8
Leroy Cudjoe 6
Stephen Wild 6

TOTAL OPTA INDEX
Luke Robinson 16662
Brett Hodgson 16138
David Hodgson 15679
Kevin Brown 13133
Leroy Cudjoe 12863

HULL F C

HULL F.C.

Danny Tickle

TACKLES

Lee Radford	858
Danny Tickle	812
Ewan Dowes	739
Danny Houghton	612
Shaun Berrigan	492

OFFLOADS

Danny Tickle	49
Gareth Raynor	37
Willie Manu	35
Shaun Berrigan	29
Lee Radford	20

CLEAN BREAKS

Richard Horne	15
Craig Hall	11
Danny Tickle	9
Kirk Yeaman	9
Tom Briscoe	8

TRY ASSISTS

Richard Horne	10
Shaun Berrigan	5
Chris Thorman	4
Kirk Yeaman	4
Richard Whiting	3

METRES

Danny Tickle	2799
Lee Radford	2519
Ewan Dowes	2380
Willie Manu	2152
Shaun Berrigan	1956

TACKLE BUSTS

Willie Manu	98
Danny Tickle	63
Richard Horne	56
Gareth Raynor	50
Kirk Yeaman	40

MARKER TACKLES

Lee Radford	126
Ewan Dowes	82
Danny Houghton	78
Danny Tickle	78
Tommy Lee	62

CARRIES

Danny Tickle	434
Lee Radford	375
Richard Horne	352
Ewan Dowes	336
Shaun Berrigan	310

TOTAL OPTA INDEX

Danny Tickle	17274
Lee Radford	15695
Ewan Dowes	14157
Richard Horne	13629
Willie Manu	13347

Lee Radford

HULL KINGSTON ROVERS

Clint Newton

TACKLES

Scott Murrell	831
Ben Galea	758
Clint Newton	721
Ben Fisher	703
Paul Cooke	525

OFFLOADS

Clint Newton	28
Ben Galea	22
Chev Walker	19
Michael Dobson	15
Peter Fox	14

CLEAN BREAKS

Shaun Briscoe	17
Clint Newton	15
Kris Welham	15
Michael Dobson	11
Jake Webster	11

TRY ASSISTS

Michael Dobson	20
Paul Cooke	10
Ben Galea	5
Chaz I'Anson	3
Scott Murrell	3

METRES

Peter Fox	3133
Clint Newton	2648
Ben Galea	2580
Liam Colbon	2520
Shaun Briscoe	2270

TACKLE BUSTS

Clint Newton	68
Shaun Briscoe	64
Peter Fox	57
Ben Galea	56
Liam Colbon	48

MARKER TACKLES

Ben Fisher	115
Scott Murrell	110
Ben Galea	103
Jason Netherton	97
Scott Wheeldon	78

CARRIES

Ben Galea	401
Michael Dobson	361
Peter Fox	357
Clint Newton	349
Liam Colbon	320

TOTAL OPTA INDEX

Clint Newton	17464
Michael Dobson	17103
Ben Galea	16742
Peter Fox	13620
Shaun Briscoe	12945

Michael Dobson

LEEDS RHINOS

Jamie Peacock

MARKER TACKLES
Jamie Peacock.................115
Kevin Sinfield..................109
Carl Ablett 97
Jamie Jones-Buchanan 88
Matt Diskin 65

METRES
Jamie Peacock.............3764
Ryan Hall 3366
Brent Webb 2479
Keith Senior.................2307
Jamie Jones-Buchanan 2066

CARRIES
Jamie Peacock................522
Ryan Hall 375
Brent Webb 356
Danny McGuire 346
Kevin Sinfield.................336

Ryan Hall

TACKLES
Kevin Sinfield..................758
Jamie Peacock................745
Jamie Jones-Buchanan ..687
Carl Ablett 653
Matt Diskin 574

CLEAN BREAKS
Ryan Hall 29
Keith Senior......................23
Danny McGuire 20
Lee Smith 17
Scott Donald 16

TACKLE BUSTS
Ryan Hall 70
Lee Smith 65
Rob Burrow 64
Keith Senior......................60
Brent Webb 60

OFFLOADS
Ali Lauitiiti 53
Keith Senior......................53
Kevin Sinfield....................36
Danny McGuire 29
Luke Burgess....................25

TRY ASSISTS
Danny McGuire 13
Keith Senior......................13
Rob Burrow 12
Kevin Sinfield......................9
Brent Webb 7

TOTAL OPTA INDEX
Jamie Peacock............20051
Ryan Hall 17485
Danny McGuire 17393
Kevin Sinfield..............16229
Keith Senior................15935

SALFORD CITY REDS

Ray Cashmere

MARKER TACKLES
Malcolm Alker 125
Luke Adamson.................106
Luke Swain 81
Stuart Littler 65
Ray Cashmere 46

METRES
Ray Cashmere 2915
Phil Leuluai 2425
John Wilshere 2349
Luke Swain 1944
Craig Stapleton 1874

CARRIES
Ray Cashmere 403
John Wilshere 347
Phil Leuluai 330
Stuart Littler 326
Luke Swain 320

Luke Adamson

TACKLES
Malcolm Alker 981
Luke Adamson.................923
Luke Swain 881
Ray Cashmere 609
Stuart Littler 534

CLEAN BREAKS
John Wilshere 14
Richard Myler 12
Mark Henry 10
Luke Adamson....................8
Stefan Ratchford 8

TACKLE BUSTS
John Wilshere 85
Craig Stapleton 63
Stefan Ratchford 49
Luke Adamson....................40
Mark Henry 32

OFFLOADS
Ray Cashmere 55
Phil Leuluai 26
John Wilshere 25
Stuart Littler 20
Adam Sidlow 19

TRY ASSISTS
Richard Myler 15
Malcolm Alker 7
Stefan Ratchford 6
Jeremy Smith 6
Jordan Turner 5

TOTAL OPTA INDEX
Ray Cashmere 15490
Luke Adamson............15335
Malcolm Alker 15046
John Wilshere 14583
Luke Swain 13931

237

ST HELENS

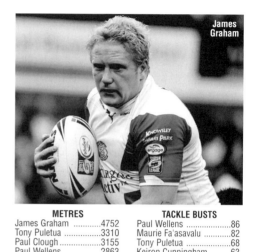

James Graham

TACKLES
Jon Wilkin	856
James Roby	720
Paul Clough	688
Chris Flannery	683
James Graham	619

OFFLOADS
Leon Pryce	49
Tony Puletua	29
Keiron Cunningham	24
James Graham	23
Paul Wellens	21

CLEAN BREAKS
Jon Wilkin	18
Leon Pryce	17
Lee Gilmour	14
Tony Puletua	14
Kyle Eastmond	13

TRY ASSISTS
Leon Pryce	15
Sean Long	12
Kyle Eastmond	7
Matt Gidley	7
Keiron Cunningham	6

METRES
James Graham	4752
Tony Puletua	3310
Paul Clough	3155
Paul Wellens	2863
James Roby	2545

TACKLE BUSTS
Paul Wellens	86
Maurie Fa'asavalu	82
Tony Puletua	68
Keiron Cunningham	63
Leon Pryce	63

MARKER TACKLES
Jon Wilkin	130
James Roby	117
Paul Clough	85
Chris Flannery	84
Matt Gidley	73

CARRIES
James Graham	658
Paul Wellens	444
Paul Clough	381
Tony Puletua	380
James Roby	367

TOTAL OPTA INDEX
James Graham	20962
Tony Puletua	17698
Leon Pryce	17325
Paul Wellens	16769
Jon Wilkin	15949

Tony Puletua

WAKEFIELD T WILDCATS

Jason Demetriou

TACKLES
Jason Demetriou	720
Dale Ferguson	706
Steve Snitch	544
Oliver Wilkes	515
Kevin Henderson	491

OFFLOADS
Ryan Atkins	32
Richard Moore	32
Matt Blaymire	15
Steve Snitch	14
Jason Demetriou	12

CLEAN BREAKS
Danny Brough	18
Ryan Atkins	12
Scott Grix	12
Sam Obst	9
Tony Martin	7

TRY ASSISTS
Danny Brough	15
Brad Drew	9
Tony Martin	8
Matt Blaymire	6
Jason Demetriou	5

METRES
Matt Blaymire	2682
Steve Snitch	2423
Oliver Wilkes	2421
Jason Demetriou	2025
Ryan Atkins	1997

TACKLE BUSTS
Jason Demetriou	85
Ryan Atkins	67
Steve Snitch	57
Scott Grix	48
Sam Obst	47

MARKER TACKLES
Dale Ferguson	99
Jason Demetriou	85
Sam Obst	82
Kevin Henderson	60
Oliver Wilkes	54

CARRIES
Matt Blaymire	413
Steve Snitch	359
Oliver Wilkes	329
Jason Demetriou	313
Brad Drew	280

TOTAL OPTA INDEX
Jason Demetriou	14360
Matt Blaymire	14176
Steve Snitch	12981
Dale Ferguson	12383
Oliver Wilkes	11845

Matt Blaymire

WARRINGTON WOLVES

Michael Monaghan

Adrian Morley

MARKER TACKLES
Vinnie Anderson 93
Ben Westwood.................92
Ben Harrison 89
Paul Wood 87
Mick Higham 81

METRES
Adrian Morley 3086
Garreth Carvell.............2653
Chris Riley 2487
Matt King......................2031
Vinnie Anderson 2020

CARRIES
Adrian Morley 382
Michael Monaghan 308
Garreth Carvell..............307
Chris Riley 295
Vinnie Anderson 277

TACKLES
Ben Westwood................602
Ben Harrison 599
Vinnie Anderson 596
Michael Monaghan 529
Mick Higham 521

CLEAN BREAKS
Chris Bridge.....................15
Lee Briers 15
Chris Riley 15
Vinnie Anderson 14
Chris Hicks 13

TACKLE BUSTS
Chris Riley 66
Chris Bridge......................65
Michael Monaghan 47
Ben Westwood..................47
Matt King...........................44

OFFLOADS
Vinnie Anderson 40
Paul Rauhihi 36
Michael Monaghan 25
Garreth Carvell.................23
Ben Westwood..................21

TRY ASSISTS
Lee Briers 15
Chris Bridge......................12
Michael Monaghan 7
Simon Grix 5
Martin Gleeson 4

TOTAL OPTA INDEX
Michael Monaghan 13809
Adrian Morley 13319
Vinnie Anderson 12976
Ben Westwood...........12489
Chris Riley 12115

WIGAN WARRIORS

Pat Richards

Thomas Leuluai

MARKER TACKLES
Harrison Hansen 108
Stuart Fielden 107
Sean O'Loughlin 102
Joel Tomkins 101
Andy Coley 82

METRES
Pat Richards 3294
Iafeta Palea'aesina........2519
Cameron Phelps 2371
Andy Coley 2359
Stuart Fielden 2345

CARRIES
Pat Richards 424
Thomas Leuluai 346
Andy Coley 328
Stuart Fielden 326
Cameron Phelps 325

TACKLES
Sean O'Loughlin 757
Stuart Fielden 679
Joel Tomkins 660
Harrison Hansen 623
Andy Coley 593

CLEAN BREAKS
Amos Roberts 21
Sam Tomkins...................18
Pat Richards 16
Shaun Ainscough 14
Thomas Leuluai 13

TACKLE BUSTS
Iafeta Palea'aesina...........89
Stuart Fielden 71
Thomas Leuluai 69
Pat Richards 62
Gareth Hock......................61

OFFLOADS
Iafeta Palea'aesina 42
Gareth Hock.....................39
George Carmont 37
Andy Coley 27
Amos Roberts 26

TRY ASSISTS
Thomas Leuluai 11
Sean O'Loughlin 10
Cameron Phelps 10
Tim Smith 7
Amos Roberts 6

TOTAL OPTA INDEX
Pat Richards 17205
Thomas Leuluai 16969
Sean O'Loughlin 14704
Iafeta Palea'aesina 14186
Stuart Fielden 14041

CHAMPIONSHIP 2009
Club by Club

BARROW RAIDERS

DATE	FIXTURE	RESULT	SCORERS	LGE	ATT
15/2/09	Rochdale (a) (NRC)	W12-54	t:Bell,Bracek,L Finch(2),Harrison,Backhouse(3),Ellis g:Noone(9)	2nd(P1)	501
22/2/09	Halifax (a) (NRC)	L40-10	t:Campbell,L Finch g:Noone	7th(P1)	1,687
1/3/09	Keighley (h) (NRC)	W34-7	t:Ellis(2),Campbell,L Finch,Brocklehurst,J Finch g:Noone(5)	5th(P1)	1,311
4/3/09	Widnes (h) (NRC)	W12-4	t:Harrison,Ellis g:Noone(2)	3rd(P1)	1,563
8/3/09	Blackpool (h) (CCR3)	W44-12	t:J Finch,Nixon(3),Dutton,McDermott,Ellis,Harrison(2) g:Noone(4)	N/A	1,187
14/3/09	Doncaster (h)	W34-14	t:Butler,Backhouse,McDermott,Nixon(2),Harrison,Campbell g:Noone(3)	4th	1,809
22/3/09	Gateshead (a)	W14-38	t:Ellis,Campbell,Bell,Nixon,Ostler,Noone,McDermott g:Noone(5)	2nd	502
28/3/09	Halifax (h)	L24-26	t:Campbell,Brocklehurst,Ostler,Young g:Noone(4)	3rd	1,918
5/4/09	Wigan (h) (CCR4)	L20-32	t:L Finch,Nixon,Campbell g:Noone(4)	N/A	6,275
10/4/09	Whitehaven (h)	W18-12	t:Butler,L Mossop,Brocklehurst,Noone(2)	2nd	3,202
13/4/09	Leigh (a)	W16-25	t:Nixon,L Finch,Ellis,Catic g:Holt(4) fg:Holt	1st	2,177
25/4/09	Batley (h)	W52-0	t:Larkin(3),Ellis,Broadbent,Catic,Luisi,Nixon(3) g:Holt(6)	3rd	1,757
1/5/09	Widnes (a)	W6-27	t:L Finch,Young,Harrison,Luisi g:Holt(5) fg:Holt	2nd	3,290
16/5/09	Toulouse (a)	L22-14	t:Nixon,Larkin g:Holt(3)	2nd	2,900
24/5/09	Featherstone (h)	W44-12	t:Nixon(4),Catic(3),Campbell g:Holt(6)	2nd	1,995
30/5/09	Sheffield (h)	W26-18	t:Nixon,Larkin(2),Young,Holt g:Holt(3)	1st	1,693
6/6/09	Dewsbury (h) (NRCQF)	W20-18	t:Broadbent,Catic,Bauer,Harrison g:Holt(2)	N/A	1,820
14/6/09	Halifax (a)	L30-24	t:Ellis(3),Luisi g:Holt(4)	2nd	2,872
18/6/09	Featherstone (h) (NRCSF)	W16-10	t:Ellis(2) g:Holt(4)	N/A	2,775
28/6/09	Batley (a)	L46-16	t:N Mossop,Bauer,Ellis g:Noone(2)	2nd	1,002
2/7/09	Toulouse (h)	W30-22	t:Nixon(2),Young,Ellis,Harrison g:Rooney(5)	2nd	2,456
12/7/09	Widnes (NRCF) ●	L18-34	t:Luisi,Nixon,Kaighan g:Holt(3)	N/A	8,720
16/7/09	Whitehaven (a)	L28-4	t:Nixon	2nd	2,708
25/7/09	Leigh (h)	W74-6	t:Larkin(2),Coyle(4),Nixon(3),Catic,Broadbent,Harrison,Ellis g:Rooney(7),Noone(4)	2nd	1,934
9/8/09	Doncaster (a)	W0-64	t:Luisi(2),Ellis,Ostler,Nixon,Catic(2),Bracek,Coyle(2),Harrison g:Ballard(10)	1st	481
13/8/09	Widnes (h)	W38-16	t:Noone,Bauer,Nixon,Broadbent,Ballard,Rooney g:Rooney(7)	1st	3,050
23/8/09	Featherstone (a)	W28-46	t:Harrison,Ballard,Coyle,Bauer,Rooney,Nixon(2) g:Rooney(9)	1st	2,099
31/8/09	Gateshead (h)	L12-16	t:Harrison,Ellis g:Rooney(2)	1st	2,981
3/9/09	Sheffield (a)	L29-22	t:Ostler,Nixon,Young g:Rooney(4) fg:Rooney(2)	1st	1,283
17/9/09	Halifax (h) (QSF)	W35-12	t:Nixon(2),Ballard,Catic,Bracek g:Rooney(7) fg:Rooney	N/A	2,823
4/10/09	Halifax (GF) ●●	W26-18	t:Harrison,Ballard,Allen,Bauer(2) g:Rooney(3)	N/A	11,398

● Played at Bloomfield Road, Blackpool
●● Played at Halliwell Jones Stadium, Warrington

		APP		TRIES		GOALS		FG		PTS	
	D.O.B.	ALL	Ch	ALL	Ch	ALL	Ch	ALL	Ch	ALL	Ch
Dave Allen	15/9/85	6(2)	6(2)	1	1	0	0	0	0	4	4
Mike Backhouse	14/6/82	8(1)	3	4	1	0	0	0	0	16	4
Andy Ballard	10/5/86	7	7	4	4	10	10	0	0	36	36
Andreas Bauer	26/9/82	14(1)	11(1)	6	5	0	0	0	0	24	20
Nick Beech	22/1/85	(2)	(2)	0	0	0	0	0	0	0	0
Ian Bell	28/1/83	5(2)	1(2)	2	1	0	0	0	0	8	4
Andy Bracek	21/3/84	20(5)	13(5)	3	2	0	0	0	0	12	8
Gary Broadbent	31/10/76	31	22	4	3	0	0	0	0	16	12
Andrew Brocklehurst	6/3/83	17(1)	11	3	2	1	1	0	0	14	10
Jamie Butler	29/8/80	13(10)	8(6)	2	2	0	0	0	0	8	8
Liam Campbell	5/6/86	10(2)	4(2)	7	4	0	0	0	0	28	16
Ned Catic	2/8/78	18(3)	16(2)	10	9	0	0	0	0	40	36
James Coyle	28/12/85	8	8	7	7	0	0	0	0	28	28
Lee Dutton	3/11/80	(5)	(2)	1	0	0	0	0	0	4	0
Andy Ellis	15/12/84	28(2)	20(1)	18	11	0	0	0	0	72	44
James Finch	9/7/83	5	2	2	0	0	0	0	0	8	0
Liam Finch	19/3/85	22	13	7	2	0	0	0	0	28	8
James Gordon	26/6/86	(1)	0	0	0	0	0	0	0	0	0
Danny Halliwell	23/3/81	(5)	(5)	0	0	0	0	0	0	0	0
Liam Harrison	3/12/82	31	22	13	8	0	0	0	0	52	32
Darren Holt	21/9/76	11(1)	8(1)	1	1	40	31	2	2	86	68
Scott Kaighan	11/11/88	(4)	(1)	1	0	0	0	0	0	4	0
Chris Larkin	20/6/86	16(1)	12(1)	8	8	0	0	0	0	32	32
Zebastian Luisi	22/12/84	23(1)	19(1)	6	5	0	0	0	0	24	20
Brett McDermott	10/9/78	24(4)	16(3)	3	2	0	0	0	0	12	8
Joe McKenna	21/8/87	(4)	(1)	0	0	0	0	0	0	0	0
Lee Mossop	17/1/89	1(3)	1(3)	1	1	0	0	0	0	4	4
Nathan Mossop	21/2/88	3(8)	2(3)	1	1	0	0	0	0	4	4
James Nixon	10/8/85	28	22	31	26	0	0	0	0	124	104
Paul Noone	22/4/81	23(8)	15(7)	2	2	45	20	0	0	98	48
Martin Ostler	21/6/80	14(13)	7(11)	4	4	0	0	0	0	16	16
Rob Roberts	21/6/78	6(1)	6(1)	0	0	0	0	0	0	0	0
Jamie Rooney	17/3/80	9	9	2	2	44	44	3	3	99	99
Sam Thompson	9/10/86	(2)	(2)	0	0	0	0	0	0	0	0
Chris Young	28/7/85	2(28)	2(19)	5	5	0	0	0	0	20	20

Gary Broadbent

LEAGUE RECORD
P20-W13-D0-L7-BP5
(1st, Championship/
Grand Final Winners, Champions)
F632, A361, Diff+271
44 points.

CHALLENGE CUP
Round Four

NORTHERN RAIL CUP
Runners-Up/3rd, Pool 1

ATTENDANCES
Best - v Wigan (CC - 6,275)
Worst - v Blackpool (CC - 1,187)
Total (excluding Challenge Cup) - 33,087
Average (excluding
Challenge Cup) - 2,206
(Up by 779 on 2008, NL2)

BATLEY BULLDOGS

DATE	FIXTURE	RESULT	SCORERS	LGE	ATT
15/2/09	Whitehaven (a) (NRC)	L52-30	t:Gallagher,Simpson,Cardiss,Flanagan,Maun g:Barlow(2),Flanagan(3)	6th(P2)	1,146
18/2/09	Doncaster (h) (NRC)	L18-22	t:Flanagan,Buttery(2) g:Flanagan(3)	7th(P2)	533
22/2/09	York (h) (NRC)	W40-28	t:Barlow(2),Cardiss(2),Simpson,Flanagan,Gallagher g:Flanagan(6)	7th(P2)	788
1/3/09	Dewsbury (a) (NRC)	L34-14	t:Preece,Stenchion,Armitage g:Flanagan	7th(P2)	1,512
8/3/09	Pilkington Recs (a) (CCR3) ●	W24-34	t:Lythe(2),Crouthers,Maun,Buttery,Cardoza,Preece g:Barlow(2),Flanagan	N/A	709
15/3/09	Featherstone (h)	L8-34	t:Feehan,McGilvary	10th	1,127
22/3/09	Leigh (a)	W28-34	t:Cardiss,McGilvary(2),Mennell(2),Preece g:Mennell(2),Flanagan(3)	8th	1,727
26/3/09	Gateshead (h)	D20-20	t:McGilvary,Flanagan,Simpson(2) g:Flanagan(2)	7th	650
5/4/09	Hunslet (h) (CCR4)	W28-24	t:Flanagan(3),McGilvary,Watson g:Flanagan(3),Mennell	N/A	633
9/4/09	Halifax (a)	L72-0		8th	2,184
13/4/09	Toulouse (h)	L22-60	t:McGilvary,Preece,Young,Lindsay g:Mennell(3)	9th	662
17/4/09	Widnes (a)	L40-18	t:Crouthers,Mennell,Watson g:Barlow(3)	11th	2,901
25/4/09	Barrow (a)	L52-0		11th	1,757
4/5/09	Leigh (h)	L16-18	t:McGilvary,Feehan(2) g:Barlow(2)	11th	1,055
10/5/09	Salford (h) (CCR5)	L4-66	t:Maun	N/A	1,298
24/5/09	Whitehaven (h)	W48-24	t:McGilvary(5),Potter,Crouthers,Simpson g:Mennell(7),McGilvary	10th	627
31/5/09	Widnes (h)	W40-34	t:McGilvary,Maun,Mennell,Lythe,Watson,Preece(2),Tootill g:Mennell(4)	9th	1,089
13/6/09	Toulouse (a)	L32-24	t:Mennell,Maun,Handforth,Simpson g:Mennell(3),Handforth	9th	2,176
21/6/09	Doncaster (a) ●●	W6-70	t:Gallagher,Potter,Campbell(4),Barlow,McGilvary,Handforth,Preece(2),Greenwood g:Mennell(11)	9th	565
28/6/09	Barrow (h)	W46-16	t:Smith,Lindsay(2),Mennell,Cardiss,Potter,Lythe,Maun g:Mennell(6),Barlow	8th	1,002
3/7/09	Sheffield (a)	L30-4	t:Preece	8th	1,286
19/7/09	Doncaster (h)	W56-12	t:Lindsay,Lythe,McGilvary(4),Simpson,Campbell,Handforth,Maun g:Handforth(3),Mennell(3)	8th	580
1/8/09	Gateshead (a)	D34-34	t:Tootill,Lythe,McGilvary,Crouthers(2),Preece g:Handforth(5)	8th	554
9/8/09	Sheffield (h)	L22-34	t:McGilvary(2),Maun,Preece g:Handforth(3)	8th	730
16/8/09	Whitehaven (a)	L20-12	t:Simpson,Mennell g:Mennell(2)	9th	1,550
20/8/09	Halifax (h)	W32-28	t:Smith,Toohey,Lindsay,Preece,Mennell,Maun g:Mennell(4)	8th	1,430
6/9/09	Featherstone (a)	W26-30	t:Crouthers,Lythe,Mennell(2),Buttery g:Mennell(5)	8th	2,076

● Played at GPW Recruitment Stadium, St Helens
●● Played at Chris Moyles Stadium, Featherstone

APP TRIES GOALS FG PTS

	D.O.B.	ALL	Ch	ALL	Ch	ALL	Ch	ALL	Ch	ALL	Ch
Nathan Armitage	15/10/88	7(2)	5(2)	1	0	0	0	0	0	4	0
Mark Barlow	16/2/84	19(2)	14(1)	3	1	10	6	0	0	32	16
Nathan Brown	7/4/89	3	0	0	0	0	0	0	0	0	0
Chris Buttery	23/12/85	12(4)	7(4)	4	1	0	0	0	0	16	4
John Campbell	17/7/87	18	17	5	5	0	0	0	0	20	20
Daryl Cardiss	13/7/77	15	10	5	2	0	0	0	0	20	8
Dale Cardoza	13/7/79	3(2)	2	1	0	0	0	0	0	4	0
Kevin Crouthers	3/1/76	18(2)	14	6	5	0	0	0	0	24	20
Ben Feehan	15/6/85	4	2	3	3	0	0	0	0	12	12
George Flanagan	8/10/86	3(6)	1(2)	7	1	22	5	0	0	72	14
John Gallagher	25/9/85	17(9)	11(8)	3	1	0	0	0	0	12	4
Gareth Greenwood	14/1/83	3(5)	3(5)	1	1	0	0	0	0	4	4
Paul Handforth	6/10/81	12	12	3	3	12	12	0	0	36	36
Anthony Henderson	9/12/82	9(1)	7	0	0	0	0	0	0	0	0
Ashley Lindsay	31/7/83	13(12)	12(7)	5	5	0	0	0	0	20	20
Kris Lythe	29/3/83	15	12	7	5	0	0	0	0	28	20
Danny Maun	5/1/81	26	20	10	7	0	0	0	0	40	28
Jermaine McGilvary	16/5/88	23(1)	16(1)	21	20	1	1	0	0	86	82
Paul Mennell	26/10/86	22	17	10	10	51	50	0	0	142	140
Craig Potter	17/12/80	21(4)	15(3)	3	3	0	0	0	0	12	12
Ian Preece	13/6/85	27	20	12	10	0	0	0	0	48	40
Damien Reid	14/3/84	1	0	0	0	0	0	0	0	0	0
Glen Reid	1/6/83	(1)	(1)	0	0	0	0	0	0	0	0
Danny Samuels	8/8/85	(1)	(1)	0	0	0	0	0	0	0	0
Jon Simpson	16/7/83	2(24)	2(18)	8	6	0	0	0	0	32	24
Byron Smith	5/3/84	21(1)	18(1)	2	2	0	0	0	0	8	8
Luke Stenchion	15/2/86	14(4)	8(4)	1	0	0	0	0	0	4	0
Mark Toohey	16/6/82	9(3)	4(3)	1	1	0	0	0	0	4	4
David Tootill	22/5/86	3(18)	2(15)	2	2	0	0	0	0	8	8
Jack Watson	29/9/86	9(6)	7(4)	3	2	0	0	0	0	12	8
Stuart Young	7/5/88	2	2	1	1	0	0	0	0	4	4

Jermaine McGilvary

LEAGUE RECORD
P20-W8-D2-L10-BP4
(8th, Championship)
F536, A620, Diff-84
32 points.

CHALLENGE CUP
Round Five

NORTHERN RAIL CUP
8th, Pool 2

ATTENDANCES
Best - v Halifax (Ch - 1,430)
Worst - v Doncaster (NRC - 533)
Total (excluding Challenge Cup) - 10,273
Average (excluding Challenge Cup) - 856
(Down by 114 on 2008)

DONCASTER

DATE	FIXTURE	RESULT	SCORERS	LGE	ATT
15/2/09	Featherstone (h) (NRC)	L6-32	t:Cook g:Briggs	8th(P2)	1,126
18/2/09	Batley (a) (NRC)	W18-22	t:Divorty,Colton,Cook,Steen g:Briggs(2),Speake	6th(P2)	533
22/2/09	London Skolars (a) (NRC)	W12-40	t:Bassinder,S Jones,Coady(4),Speake g:Speake(6)	6th(P2)	213
1/3/09	Swinton (h) (NRC)	W36-28	t:Green,Weeden(2),S Jones,Reittie,Ellery g:Briggs(6)	5th(P2)	645
7/3/09	Queens (a) (CCR3) ●	W12-16	t:Bovill,Weeden,Briggs g:Briggs(2)	N/A	595
14/3/09	Barrow (a)	L34-14	t:Bauer,May(2) g:S Jones	8th	1,809
29/3/09	Leigh (h)	L18-24	t:Carbutt,Cook,Bauer g:Briggs(3)	10th	827
5/4/09	Gateshead (h) (CCR4)	L18-32	t:Cook,Green,Carey g:Briggs,P Handforth(2)	N/A	458
9/4/09	Sheffield (a)	W22-23	t:Carey,P Handforth,Castle g:Briggs(5) fg:P Handforth	9th	1,209
13/4/09	Widnes (h)	L18-24	t:May,Weeden,P Handforth g:P Handforth(3)	8th	831
19/4/09	Halifax (a)	L44-12	t:P Handforth(2) g:P Handforth(2)	10th	2,002
26/4/09	Toulouse (h)	L18-48	t:Reittie,Holt,Castle,Opie g:Weeden	9th	1,089
1/5/09	Gateshead (a)	L45-42	t:Haley,Cook,Carey,Divorty(2),Steen(2) g:Weeden(6),Speake	10th	405
17/5/09	Featherstone (a)	L68-12	t:Divorty,Cook g:Weeden(2)	10th	1,577
21/5/09	Halifax (h)	L4-36	t:Bauer	11th	1,096
31/5/09	Whitehaven (a)	L50-12	t:Bassinder,Cook g:Weeden(2)	11th	1,362
21/6/09	Batley (h) ●●	L6-70	t:Ellery g:Weeden	11th	565
28/6/09	Sheffield (h) ●●	L8-78	t:Lawton,Coady	11th	275
4/7/09	Widnes (a)	L78-4	t:Weeden	11th	3,453
19/7/09	Batley (a)	L56-12	t:Weeden,McNamara(2)	11th	580
26/7/09	Whitehaven (h)	L10-19	t:Lawton,McDonald g:Weeden	11th	337
2/8/09	Leigh (a)	L31-28	t:McDonald,Griffiths,Colton,Leaf,Weeden g:Weeden(4)	11th	1,394
9/8/09	Barrow (h)	L0-64		11th	481
16/8/09	Featherstone (h)	L10-56	t:Vento,Stubbley g:McKinley	11th	641
22/8/09	Toulouse (a)	L52-6	t:Vento g:Speake	11th	1,200
6/9/09	Gateshead (h)	L0-56		11th	551

● Played at Keepmoat Stadium *(Match abandoned after 61 minutes, due to crowd trouble)*
●● Played at Chris Moyles Stadium, Featherstone

		APP		TRIES		GOALS		FG		PTS	
	D.O.B.	ALL	Ch	ALL	Ch	ALL	Ch	ALL	Ch	ALL	Ch
Jake Bassinder	15/7/90	6(18)	6(13)	2	1	0	0	0	0	8	4
David Bates	23/10/80	3(2)	3(2)	0	0	0	0	0	0	0	0
Andreas Bauer	26/9/82	13	10	3	3	0	0	0	0	12	12
Alex Benson	22/5/85	8(1)	8(1)	0	0	0	0	0	0	0	0
Liam Booth	4/3/89	(1)	(1)	0	0	0	0	0	0	0	0
Jamie Bovill	21/3/83	7(4)	4(3)	1	0	0	0	0	0	4	0
Kyle Briggs	7/12/87	7	2	1	0	20	8	0	0	44	16
Brooke Broughton	30/10/90	1(2)	1(2)	0	0	0	0	0	0	0	0
Matt Carbutt	3/10/85	9(1)	8(1)	1	1	0	0	0	0	4	4
Gareth Carey	17/10/87	7(1)	6(1)	3	2	0	0	0	0	12	8
Mark Castle	19/2/86	9(5)	8(1)	2	2	0	0	0	0	8	8
Mike Coady	15/4/87	9	5	5	1	0	0	0	0	20	4
Dean Colton	18/2/83	15(1)	12	2	1	0	0	0	0	8	4
Craig Cook	26/5/83	17	11	7	4	0	0	0	0	28	16
Ross Divorty	27/11/88	14	10	4	3	0	0	0	0	16	12
Kevin Eadie	13/12/88	(1)	0	0	0	0	0	0	0	0	0
Gary Ellery	29/6/85	6(8)	5(5)	2	1	0	0	0	0	8	4
Danny Flintoff	21/12/84	(1)	(1)	0	0	0	0	0	0	0	0
Nathan Freer	21/5/89	5(5)	(5)	0	0	0	0	0	0	0	0
Peter Green	2/12/81	14	8	2	0	0	0	0	0	8	0
Tommy Griffiths	8/12/86	5	5	1	1	0	0	0	0	4	4
Michael Haley	19/9/87	3(2)	2(2)	1	1	0	0	0	0	4	4
Steve Hall	13/1/86	7	7	0	0	0	0	0	0	0	0
Matthew Handforth	2/1/87	6	6	0	0	0	0	0	0	0	0
Paul Handforth	6/10/81	9	7	4	4	7	5	1	1	31	27
Craig Holt	20/12/90	8(5)	6(3)	1	1	0	0	0	0	4	4
Scott Howlett	23/2/92	(2)	(2)	0	0	0	0	0	0	0	0
Craig Jones	2/9/87	2(1)	2(1)	0	0	0	0	0	0	0	0
Scott Jones	4/4/90	4(3)	1(2)	2	0	1	1	0	0	10	2
Kyle Kesik	3/6/89	7	7	0	0	0	0	0	0	0	0
Craig Lawton	17/2/81	6	6	2	2	0	0	0	0	8	8
Shaun Leaf	10/7/84	13	8	1	1	0	0	0	0	4	4
Luke May	23/8/89	7	7	3	3	0	0	0	0	12	12
Scott McDonald	25/9/90	4	4	2	2	0	0	0	0	8	8
Mark McKinley	16/9/85	7(1)	7(1)	0	0	1	1	0	0	2	2
Chris McNamara	13/7/88	7	7	2	2	0	0	0	0	8	8
Wayne Opie	22/11/83	11(6)	10(6)	1	1	0	0	0	0	4	4
Alex Palmer	22/4/91	(1)	(1)	0	0	0	0	0	0	0	0
Lee Parnell	27/4/91	(1)	0	0	0	0	0	0	0	0	0
Wayne Reittie	21/1/88	13(1)	9(1)	2	1	0	0	0	0	8	4
Danny Richardson	25/6/88	(1)	(1)	0	0	0	0	0	0	0	0
Al Rounding	30/6/83	2(4)	1(2)	0	0	0	0	0	0	0	0
Carlos Sanchez	9/3/81	1(1)	1(1)	0	0	0	0	0	0	0	0
Tim Scire	17/3/91	1	1	0	0	0	0	0	0	0	0
Scott Smith	27/2/89	(2)	(2)	0	0	0	0	0	0	0	0
Andy Speake	28/9/86	11(5)	7(3)	1	0	9	2	0	0	22	4
Danny Stanley	15/8/86	1(6)	1(6)	0	0	0	0	0	0	0	0
Ryan Steen	26/6/82	26	20	3	2	0	0	0	0	12	8
Mark Stubbley	27/6/82	(5)	(5)	1	1	0	0	0	0	4	4
Lisiate Tafa	10/10/79	1	1	0	0	0	0	0	0	0	0
Danny Vento	29/9/85	3(2)	3(2)	2	2	0	0	0	0	8	8
Josh Weeden	10/11/83	23	17	7	4	17	17	0	0	62	50

Ryan Steen

LEAGUE RECORD
P20-W1-D0-L19-BP5
(11th, Championship)
F257, A955, Diff-698
-1 points. *(9 points deducted for entering administration)*

CHALLENGE CUP
Round Four

NORTHERN RAIL CUP
5th, Pool 2

ATTENDANCES
Best - v Featherstone (NRC - 1,126)
Worst - v Sheffield (Ch - 275)
Total (excluding Challenge Cup) - 8,464
Average (excluding Challenge Cup) - 705
(Down by 155 on 2008, NL2)

245

FEATHERSTONE ROVERS

DATE	FIXTURE	RESULT	SCORERS	LGE	ATT
15/2/09	Doncaster (a) (NRC)	W6-32	t:S Kain,A Kain,Harris,Steel,Smeaton,Field g:Harris(4)	3rd(P2)	1,126
18/2/09	Leigh (h) (NRC)	W10-6	t:Steel,Haughey g:Harris	2nd(P2)	1,487
22/2/09	Dewsbury (h) (NRC)	L26-28	t:McLocklan,A Kain,Pryce,Hardman g:McLocklan,Dickens(4)	4th(P2)	1,470
1/3/09	Workington (a) (NRC)	W6-38	t:Smeaton,Pryce(2),Harris,Hardman,Tonks,Blakeway g:Dickens(3),Harris(2)	3rd(P2)	477
8/3/09	The Army (h) (CCR3)	W94-2	t:Smeaton(2),A Kain(4),Saxton,Hirst(2),Tonks,Field,Pryce(2),Lee(2),Hesketh, Dale(2) g:A Kain,Dickens(6),Harris(4)	N/A	1,763
15/3/09	Batley (a)	W8-34	t:Hirst,Harris,Haughey(3),Hesketh g:Dickens(5)	2nd	1,127
22/3/09	Whitehaven (h)	L26-52	t:Hardman(2),Fallon,A Kain,Dale g:Harris(3)	7th	1,555
5/4/09	Wath Brow (h) (CCR4)	W54-16	t:McLocklan(2),A Kain(2),Saxton,Steel(3),Kirk,Haughey g:McLocklan(2),Harris,Dickens(4)	N/A	1,180
10/4/09	Gateshead (a)	W2-23	t:Field,Harris,Lee g:Dickens(5) fg:Harris	6th	651
13/4/09	Sheffield (h)	W20-12	t:Steel,A Kain,Kirk g:Dickens(4)	6th	1,612
19/4/09	Whitehaven (a)	W16-44	t:McLocklan(2),Field,Blakeway,Dale(2),A Kain,S Kain g:Dickens(4),Harris(2)	4th	1,411
23/4/09	Leigh (a)	W16-30	t:Dickens,Hardman,Haughey,S Kain,Tonks g:Dickens(5)	4th	2,307
30/4/09	Halifax (h)	L26-39	t:Harris,Steel,A Kain,Haughey,Hardman g:Harris,Dickens(2)	4th	2,673
10/5/09	Warrington (h) (CCR5)	L8-56	t:Saxton,Haughey	N/A	3,127
17/5/09	Doncaster (h)	W68-12	t:Steel,Bell(3),A Kain(2),Saxton(3),Hardman,Hesketh g:Harris,McLocklan(7)	4th	1,577
24/5/09	Barrow (a)	L44-12	t:McLocklan,Haughey g:Dickens(2)	4th	1,995
28/5/09	Leigh (h)	W30-24	t:Bell,Field,Saxton(2),Kirk,Hardman g:Briggs,Dickens(2)	4th	1,535
4/6/09	Oldham (a) (NRCQF) ●	W18-32	t:McLocklan,Haughey,Hirst,Steel,Dale,Kirk g:Dickens(4)	N/A	853
13/6/09	Widnes (a)	L46-22	t:Kirk,Haughey,Spears,Steel g:Dickens(3)	5th	3,278
18/6/09	Barrow (a) (NRCSF)	L16-10	t:Briggs,Haughey g:Hirst	N/A	2,775
27/6/09	Toulouse (a) ●●	W16-32	t:Hardman,Smeaton,Briggs(2),Spears g:Dickens(5),A Kain	4th	2,321
5/7/09	Gateshead (h)	W56-40	t:Haughey,Dickens,Briggs(2),Spears,Dale,Divorty,A Kain,Hardman,Steel g:Dickens(8)	4th	1,487
24/7/09	Halifax (a)	W20-22	t:Dale,A Kain,Tonks,Lee g:Briggs(2),Dickens	4th	2,456
1/8/09	Toulouse (h)	L18-34	t:Dale,Steel,Divorty g:Dickens(2),Briggs	6th	1,346
9/8/09	Widnes (h)	W34-29	t:Briggs,Steel,A Kain,Saxton(2),Dickens g:Dickens(5)	6th	2,125
16/8/09	Doncaster (a)	W10-56	t:Hardman(5),Briggs(2),Lee,Pryce,Haughey g:Dickens(8)	6th	641
23/8/09	Barrow (h)	L28-46	t:Steel,Harris,Hardman(2),Kirk,Pryce g:Briggs(2)	6th	2,099
27/8/09	Sheffield (a)	L28-12	t:Dale,Saxton g:Harris,Dickens	6th	1,028
6/9/09	Batley (h)	L26-30	t:Dale,Briggs,Steel,Barker,Divorty g:Briggs,Dickens(2)	6th	2,076
11/9/09	Sheffield (a) (EPO)	W8-32	t:Briggs,Spears,Saxton,Haughey(2),Lee g:Dickens,Harris(3)	N/A	802
18/9/09	Widnes (a) (ESF)	W24-32	t:Kirk,Briggs,Pryce,Lee,Harris g:Harris(6)	N/A	3,296
24/9/09	Halifax (a) (FE)	L36-30	t:Briggs,Hardman,Divorty,Spears g:Harris(7)	N/A	2,556

● Played at Leigh Sports Village
●● Played at Stade Ernest Argeles, Blagnac

	APP		TRIES		GOALS		FG		PTS	
	D.O.B.	ALL	Ch	ALL	Ch	ALL	Ch	ALL	Ch	ALL	Ch
Dwayne Barker	21/9/83	3(2)	3(2)	1	1	0	0	0	0	4	4
Ian Bell	28/1/83	1(1)	1(1)	4	4	0	0	0	0	16	16
Richard Blakeway	22/7/83	3(7)	(5)	2	1	0	0	0	0	8	4
Kyle Briggs	7/12/87	16(1)	14(1)	12	11	7	7	0	0	62	58
Matty Dale	10/10/86	30	22	11	8	0	0	0	0	44	32
Stuart Dickens	23/3/80	30	22	3	3	86	65	0	0	184	142
Ross Divorty	27/11/88	2(12)	2(11)	4	4	0	0	0	0	16	16
Aaron Dobek	10/9/87	(1)	(1)	0	0	0	0	0	0	0	0
Jon Fallon	11/5/87	4(13)	3(8)	1	1	0	0	0	0	4	4
Jamie Field	12/12/76	16	9	5	3	0	0	0	0	20	12
Matthew Handforth	2/1/87	1	0	0	0	0	0	0	0	0	0
Ian Hardman	8/12/84	32	23	18	16	0	0	0	0	72	64
Iestyn Harris	25/6/76	20(4)	14(4)	7	5	36	24	1	1	101	69
Tom Haughey	30/1/82	22(6)	18(3)	16	11	0	0	0	0	64	44
Sean Hesketh	17/8/86	3(4)	(3)	3	2	0	0	0	0	12	8
Joe Hirst	21/4/87	7(7)	5(3)	4	1	1	0	0	0	18	4
James Houston	28/12/82	12(11)	9(8)	0	0	0	0	0	0	0	0
Andy Kain	1/9/85	32	23	17	9	2	1	0	0	72	38
Stuart Kain	18/9/85	4(4)	1(3)	3	2	0	0	0	0	12	8
Andy Kirk	2/8/82	23(2)	19(2)	7	5	0	0	0	0	28	20
Jack Lee	1/11/88	9(17)	8(13)	7	5	0	0	0	0	28	20
Joe McLocklan	2/10/86	21(9)	14(7)	7	3	10	7	0	0	48	26
Waine Pryce	3/10/81	21(2)	14(1)	8	3	0	0	0	0	32	12
Tom Saxton	3/10/83	28(2)	20(1)	12	9	0	0	0	0	48	36
Sam Smeaton	26/10/88	12(4)	8(4)	5	1	0	0	0	0	20	4
Tim Spears	27/7/84	26(2)	20(1)	5	5	0	0	0	0	20	20
Jon Steel	14/3/80	23	17	17	11	0	0	0	0	68	44
Gareth Swift	3/8/90	1(1)	0	0	0	0	0	0	0	0	0
Tony Tonks	27/4/85	14(12)	10(9)	4	2	0	0	0	0	16	8

Ian Hardman

LEAGUE RECORD
P20-W12-D0-L8-BP1
(6th, Championship/Final Eliminator)
F619, A524, Diff+95
37 points.

CHALLENGE CUP
Round Five

NORTHERN RAIL CUP
Semi Finalists/4th, Pool 2

ATTENDANCES
Best - v Warrington (CC - 3,127)
Worst - v Wath Brow (CC - 1,180)
Total (excluding Challenge Cup) - 21,042
Average (excluding
Challenge Cup) - 1,754
(Up by 416 on 2008)

GATESHEAD THUNDER

DATE	FIXTURE	RESULT	SCORERS	LGE	ATT
10/2/09	Keighley (a) (NRC)	L40-20	t:McAlpine,Neighbour,Sanderson,Branighan g:Branighan(2)	N/A	337
15/2/09	Sheffield (h) (NRC)	W44-18	t:Arundel,Nash(3),Neighbour,Branighan,Sanderson,Peers g:Branighan(6)	4th(P1)	1,226
21/2/09	Widnes (a) (NRC)	L40-18	t:Thorman,Arundel(2),Sanderson g:Thorman	8th(P1)	3,001
1/3/09	Rochdale (h) (NRC)	W46-22	t:Sanderson(3),Henderson,Peers,Arundel,Parker,Neighbour,Nash g:Knowles(4),Branighan	6th(P1)	452
8/3/09	Whitehaven (h) (CCR3)	W42-38	t:Branighan(2),Henderson(2),Neighbour,Sanderson(2) g:Knowles(7)	N/A	501
15/3/09	Whitehaven (a)	L40-18	t:Thorman,McAlpine,Branighan g:Knowles(3)	9th	1,175
22/3/09	Barrow (h)	L14-38	t:McAlpine,Branighan,Sanderson g:Knowles	11th	502
26/3/09	Batley (a)	D20-20	t:Nash(2),Branighan g:Knowles(4)	9th	650
5/4/09	Doncaster (a) (CCR4)	W18-32	t:Knowles,Branighan(2),Sanderson,Henderson,Nash g:Knowles(2),McAlpine(2)	N/A	458
10/4/09	Featherstone (h)	L2-23	g:Knowles	10th	651
16/4/09	Sheffield (h)	W41-36	t:Peers,Branighan,McAlpine,Sanderson(2),Knowles,Parker g:Knowles(6) fg:Thorman	9th	715
26/4/09	Halifax (a)	L72-28	t:McAlpine(2),Peers,Cording(2),Sanderson g:Knowles,McAlpine	10th	2,022
1/5/09	Doncaster (h)	W45-42	t:Knowles(2),Henderson,McAlpine,Barron,Branighan,Peers,Sanderson g:Knowles(6) fg:Ryan Clarke	9th	405
9/5/09	Oldham (h) (CCR5) ●	W34-16	t:Knowles,Branighan(2),Barron,Sanderson,McAlpine g:Knowles(5)	N/A	929
17/5/09	Whitehaven (h)	L34-38	t:Cording,Franze(2),Youngquest(2),Kahler,McAlpine g:Knowles(2),McAlpine	9th	575
23/5/09	Widnes (a)	L46-30	t:Nash,Henderson,Youngquest,Branighan,Franze g:Knowles(5)	9th	5,236
30/5/09	St Helens (h) (CCQF)	L6-66	t:McAlpine g:Youngquest	N/A	4,325
7/6/09	Toulouse (h)	L16-52	t:Aitken(2),Franze g:Knowles(2)	10th	516
14/6/09	Leigh (a)	W12-40	t:Knowles,Youngquest(2),Nash,Franze,Cording,Sanderson g:Knowles(6)	10th	1,645
28/6/09	Halifax (h)	W34-28	t:Nash(3),Cording,Branighan,McAlpine g:Knowles(5)	10th	802
5/7/09	Featherstone (a)	L56-40	t:Sanderson(2),Branighan(2),Aitken,McAlpine,Youngquest g:Knowles(6)	10th	1,487
19/7/09	Widnes (h)	W34-18	t:Cording,Branighan,McAlpine,Thorman,Youngquest,England g:Knowles(5)	10th	717
23/7/09	Sheffield (a)	L46-30	t:Franze(2),Youngquest(3),Thorman g:Knowles(3)	10th	1,410
1/8/09	Batley (h)	D34-34	t:McAlpine(2),Youngquest(2),Branighan,Franze g:Knowles(5)	10th	554
8/8/09	Toulouse (a)	W20-48	t:Cording(2),McAlpine(2),Knowles,Aitken(2),Sanderson,Branighan g:Knowles(6)	10th	1,681
23/8/09	Leigh (h)	W30-24	t:Youngquest(3),Branighan,Sanderson g:Knowles(5)	10th	1,033
31/8/09	Barrow (a)	W12-16	t:Knowles,Nash g:Knowles(4)	9th	2,981
6/9/09	Doncaster (a)	W0-56	t:Franze(3),Kahler(2),Cording,Sanderson(2),McAlpine,Watts g:Knowles(8)	7th	551

● Played at Northern Echo Arena, Darlington

		APP		TRIES		GOALS		FG		PTS	
	D.O.B.	ALL	Ch	ALL	Ch	ALL	Ch	ALL	Ch	ALL	Ch
Russ Aitken	19/5/86	11	11	5	5	0	0	0	0	20	20
Dean Andrews	1/7/79	(2)	(2)	0	0	0	0	0	0	0	0
Joe Arundel	22/8/91	4	0	4	0	0	0	0	0	16	0
Matt Barron	17/11/86	1(15)	1(13)	2	1	0	0	0	0	8	4
Luke Branighan	29/6/81	26	18	21	13	9	0	0	0	102	52
Tabua Cakacaka	8/3/77	8(4)	5(3)	0	0	0	0	0	0	0	0
Rhys Clarke	12/3/91	6(7)	4(3)	0	0	0	0	0	0	0	0
Ryan Clarke	8/9/85	6(10)	4(8)	0	0	0	0	1	1	1	1
James Cording	30/12/89	24(1)	17(1)	9	9	0	0	0	0	36	36
Sam Crowther	21/10/86	1(5)	(4)	0	0	0	0	0	0	0	0
Mark Dack	28/8/91	(2)	(1)	0	0	0	0	0	0	0	0
Anthony England	19/10/86	1(8)	1(8)	1	1	0	0	0	0	4	4
Paul Franze	3/3/82	14	13	11	11	0	0	0	0	44	44
Andrew Henderson	17/6/79	26	19	6	2	0	0	0	0	24	8
Kris Kahler	12/2/83	14	13	3	3	0	0	0	0	12	12
Michael Knowles	2/5/87	27(1)	20	8	6	102	84	0	0	236	192
Nathan Massey	11/7/89	6(4)	6(4)	0	0	0	0	0	0	0	0
Crawford Matthews	23/11/91	2(1)	1	0	0	0	0	0	0	0	0
Ben McAlpine	21/6/84	27	20	18	15	4	2	0	0	80	64
Ryan McBride	7/5/84	9(16)	6(12)	0	0	0	0	0	0	0	0
Dylan Nash	28/12/86	26	19	13	8	0	0	0	0	52	32
Kevin Neighbour	10/7/83	10	4	4	0	0	0	0	0	16	0
Chris Parker	9/9/78	10(7)	6(3)	2	1	0	0	0	0	8	4
Jason Payne	20/1/88	10(1)	6	0	0	0	0	0	0	0	0
Robin Peers	18/1/82	19	11	5	3	0	0	0	0	20	12
Jamie Russo	16/4/81	7	4	0	0	0	0	0	0	0	0
Stewart Sanderson	10/4/85	25	17	22	12	0	0	0	0	88	48
Jonny Scott	13/3/87	(7)	(4)	0	0	0	0	0	0	0	0
Neil Thorman	4/6/84	20(8)	12(8)	4	3	1	0	1	1	19	13
David Vernon	17/6/84	(5)	(2)	0	0	0	0	0	0	0	0
Jonny Walker	20/2/91	2(5)	1(1)	0	0	0	0	0	0	0	0
Liam Watts	8/7/90	9(3)	9(3)	1	1	0	0	0	0	4	4
Nick Youngquest	28/7/83	13	12	15	15	0	0	0	0	62	60

Michael Knowles

LEAGUE RECORD
P20-W9-D2-L9-BP1
(7th, Championship)
F610, A657, Diff-47
32 points.

CHALLENGE CUP
Quarter Finalists

NORTHERN RAIL CUP
6th, Pool 1

ATTENDANCES
Best - v St Helens (CC - 4,325)
Worst - v Doncaster (Ch - 405)
Total (excluding Challenge Cup) - 8,148
Average (excluding Challenge Cup) - 679
(Up by 189 on 2008, NL2)

HALIFAX

DATE	FIXTURE	RESULT	SCORERS	LGE	ATT
15/2/09	Hunslet (a) (NRC)	W10-38	t:Tamghart,Black,Penkywicz(2),Greenwood,Moore,Cherryholme g:Black(3),Moore(2)	3rd(P1)	878
22/2/09	Barrow (h) (NRC)	W40-10	t:Goddard(2),Black,Gleeson,Patterson,James,Royston g:Haley(6)	3rd(P1)	1,687
1/3/09	Sheffield (a) (NRC)	W18-50	t:Penkywicz(2),Tamghart(2),Worrincy,Beswick,Royston,Haley(2),Patterson g:Haley(4),Govin	2nd(P1)	1,065
4/3/09	Blackpool (h) (NRC)	W50-28	t:Royston(2),Greenwood(2),Haley,Black,Tamghart,Barker(2) g:Govin(5),Black(2)	1st(P1)	1,291
8/3/09	Loughborough University (h) (CCR3)	W80-16	t:Barker(2),Wrench,Greenwood(2),Beswick,Gleeson(2),Tamghart(2),Worrincy, Penkywicz,Black,Patterson g:Govin(6),Black(5),Patterson	N/A	1,138
19/3/09	Widnes (h)	W24-14	t:Black,Cherryholme,Worrincy,Govin g:Black(2),Govin(2)	6th	3,274
28/3/09	Barrow (a)	W24-26	t:Larder,Greenwood,Penkywicz,James,Beswick g:Govin(3)	5th	1,918
3/4/09	Widnes (h) (CCR4)	W20-16	t:Black,Royston,Roberts g:Govin(4)	N/A	3,204
9/4/09	Batley (h)	W72-0	t:Royston,Penkywicz(2),James(2),Black,Andy Bowman(3),Worrincy,Greenwood, Gleeson g:Patterson(12)	4th	2,184
13/4/09	Whitehaven (a)	W18-34	t:Black,Royston,Gleeson,Barker g:Govin(4)	2nd	2,005
19/4/09	Doncaster (h)	W44-12	t:Worrincy(2),Larder,Black,Andy Bowman,Patterson(2),Haley g:Patterson(6)	1st	2,002
26/4/09	Gateshead (h)	W72-28	t:James(2),Royston(3),Black,Barker,Tamghart,Greenwood(2),Penkywicz,Wrench g:Patterson(12)	1st	2,022
30/4/09	Featherstone (a)	W26-39	t:Black(2),Royston(2),Tamghart,Penkywicz g:Patterson(7) fg:Penkywicz	1st	2,673
9/5/09	Castleford (a) (CCR5)	L35-34 (aet)	t:Royston,Barker,Beswick(3) g:Patterson(7)	N/A	5,595
17/5/09	Sheffield (h)	L26-40	t:Worrincy,Haley,Greenwood(3) g:Patterson(3)	1st	2,212
21/5/09	Doncaster (a)	W4-36	t:Barker,James,Tamghart,Penkywicz,Patterson,Gleeson,Royston g:Patterson(4)	1st	1,096
7/6/09	Leigh (h) (NRCQF)	W54-16	t:Worrincy(2),Larder,Black(2),Royston(2),Greenwood(2) g:Patterson(9)	N/A	2,186
14/6/09	Barrow (h)	W30-24	t:Haley,Watene,Gleeson,Patterson,Royston g:Patterson(5)	1st	2,872
21/6/09	Widnes (h) (NRCSF)	L22-27	t:Tamghart,Royston(2),Black g:Patterson(3)	N/A	3,972
28/6/09	Gateshead (a)	L34-28	t:Gleeson,Greenwood,Penkywicz(2),Worrincy g:Patterson(4)	1st	802
3/7/09	Leigh (h)	W48-16	t:Royston(2),Andy Bowman,Gleeson,Watene,Worrincy,Haley(2) g:Patterson(8)	1st	2,094
18/7/09	Toulouse (a)	W16-54	t:Penkywicz,Larder(2),Patterson,Black,Beswick,Worrincy,Tamghart,Greenwood g:Patterson(9)	1st	2,687
24/7/09	Featherstone (h)	L20-22	t:Gleeson,Maloney,Haley g:Patterson(4)	1st	2,456
31/7/09	Widnes (a)	L42-16	t:Haley,Patterson,Watene g:Patterson(2)	2nd	4,039
9/8/09	Whitehaven (h)	L42-50	t:Larder,Smith,Haley(2),Worrincy,Royston,Goddard,Penkywicz g:Patterson(5)	2nd	2,014
13/8/09	Sheffield (a)	L38-24	t:Patterson,Haley,Smith,Goddard g:Patterson(4)	3rd	1,457
20/8/09	Batley (a)	L32-28	t:Cherryholme,Larder(2),Gleeson,Tamghart g:Patterson(4)	4th	1,430
31/8/09	Leigh (a)	W18-27	t:Worrincy(3),Royston(2) g:Patterson(3) fg:Beswick	2nd	2,349
5/9/09	Toulouse (h)	W34-18	t:Worrincy,Larder,Penkywicz,Haley,Royston(2) g:Patterson(5)	2nd	2,128
17/9/09	Barrow (a) (QSF)	L35-12	t:Royston(2) g:Patterson(2)	N/A	2,823
24/9/09	Featherstone (h) (FE)	W36-30	t:Larder(2),Black,Beswick,Smith,Royston g:Patterson(6)	N/A	2,556
4/10/09	Barrow (GF) ●	L26-18	t:Haley,Royston,Black,Govin g:Patterson	N/A	11,398

● Played at Halliwell Jones Stadium, Warrington

		APP		TRIES		GOALS		FG		PTS	
	D.O.B.	ALL	Ch	ALL	Ch	ALL	Ch	ALL	Ch	ALL	Ch
Steve Bannister	10/10/87	6(3)	6(3)	0	0	0	0	0	0	0	0
Dwayne Barker	21/9/83	14(3)	9(1)	8	3	0	0	0	0	32	12
Bob Beswick	8/12/84	29(2)	21(2)	8	3	0	0	1	1	33	13
Ben Black	29/4/81	25(3)	17(2)	18	10	12	2	0	0	96	44
Andy Bowman	13/1/88	9(2)	8(2)	5	5	0	0	0	0	20	20
Anthony Bowman	18/3/92	1(2)	(2)	0	0	0	0	0	0	0	0
Graham Charlesworth	13/10/85	1	0	0	0	0	0	0	0	0	0
Neil Cherryholme	20/12/86	16(3)	12(2)	3	2	0	0	0	0	12	8
Mark Gleeson	16/6/82	10(17)	8(13)	11	8	0	0	0	0	44	32
Jon Goddard	21/6/82	16	11	4	2	0	0	0	0	16	8
Mick Govin	5/11/84	13(6)	8(5)	2	2	25	9	0	0	58	26
Miles Greenwood	30/7/87	22(2)	15	16	9	0	0	0	0	64	36
James Haley	2/7/85	29	22	15	12	10	0	0	0	80	48
Tom Hemingway	6/12/86	1(1)	1(1)	0	0	0	0	0	0	0	0
Matt James	26/3/87	8(2)	6(2)	7	6	0	0	0	0	28	24
David Larder	5/6/76	26	19	11	10	0	0	0	0	44	40
Dominic Maloney	12/3/87	7(3)	7(3)	1	1	0	0	0	0	4	4
Gareth Moore	3/6/89	(1)	0	1	0	2	0	0	0	8	0
Lee Patterson	20/7/82	32	23	10	7	126	106	0	0	292	240
Sean Penkywicz	18/5/82	24(8)	18(5)	16	11	0	0	1	1	65	45
Mark Roberts	9/11/82	18(7)	13(5)	1	0	0	0	0	0	4	0
Shad Royston	29/11/82	29	21	30	20	0	0	0	0	120	80
Paul Smith	17/5/77	26(1)	19	3	3	0	0	0	0	12	12
Said Tamghart	13/5/80	4(24)	2(18)	12	5	0	0	0	0	48	20
Frank Watene	15/2/77	1(25)	1(16)	3	3	0	0	0	0	12	12
Dana Wilson	22/5/83	11(7)	4(6)	0	0	0	0	0	0	0	0
Rob Worrincy	9/7/85	24	17	17	13	0	0	0	0	68	52
David Wrench	3/1/79	14(6)	11(4)	2	1	0	0	0	0	8	4

Lee Patterson

LEAGUE RECORD
P20-W13-D0-L7-BP4
(2nd, Championship/
Grand Final Runners-Up)
F714, A476, Diff+238
43 points.

CHALLENGE CUP
Round Five

NORTHERN RAIL CUP
Semi Finalists/1st, Pool 1

ATTENDANCES
Best - v Widnes (NRCSF - 3,972)
Worst - v Loughborough University
(CC - 1,138)
Total (excluding Challenge Cup - 34,950
Average (excluding
Challenge Cup) - 2,330
(Up by 331 on 2008)

LEIGH CENTURIONS

DATE	FIXTURE	RESULT	SCORERS	LGE	ATT
15/2/09	London Skolars (h) (NRC)	W74-6	t:Ridyard,Durbin(3),Mort,J Smith(2),Donlan,Reay,Maden(2),Watson,Stanton, Stewart g:Mort(9)	1st(P2)	1,375
18/2/09	Featherstone (a) (NRC)	L10-6	t:Durbin g:Ridyard	3rd(P2)	1,487
22/2/09	Swinton (a) (NRC)	W26-34	t:Stanton,Donlan,Watson,Maden,Ridyard,Hill g:Ridyard(5)	1st(P2)	857
1/3/09	Whitehaven (h) (NRC)	W24-22	t:Ridyard,Haggerty,Durbin,McConnell g:Ridyard(4)	2nd(P2)	1,789
8/3/09	Lokomotiv Moscow (h) (CCR3)	W82-6	t:Donlan,Rourke,Meekin,Higson,Reay(3),J Smith(2),Ridyard,Haggerty,Mort(2), Hobson,Wingfield g:Mort(11)	N/A	1,278
15/3/09	Sheffield (a)	W22-23	t:Higson(2),Donlan,Maden g:Mort(3) fg:Ridyard	5th	1,220
22/3/09	Batley (h)	L28-34	t:McConnell,Watson(2),Durbin,Donlan g:Mort(4)	5th	1,727
29/3/09	Doncaster (a)	W18-24	t:Mort(2),Haggerty,Hobson g:Mort(4)	4th	827
3/4/09	Wakefield (a) (CCR4)	L54-0		N/A	2,637
10/4/09	Widnes (a)	W8-10	t:Donlan,Mort g:Mort	3rd	4,354
13/4/09	Barrow (h)	L16-25	t:Rourke,Mort,Stanton g:Mort(2)	5th	2,177
18/4/09	Toulouse (a) ●	L46-10	t:Donlan,Durbin g:Mort	6th	3,507
23/4/09	Featherstone (h)	L16-30	t:Rudd,Mort,Durbin g:Mort(2)	6th	2,307
4/5/09	Batley (a)	W16-18	t:Durbin(2),Donlan g:Mort(3)	5th	1,055
14/5/09	Widnes (h)	W23-16	t:Hobson,Alstead(2),Donlan g:Mort(3) fg:Watson	6th	2,556
28/5/09	Featherstone (a)	L30-24	t:Maden,Nanyn(2),Morrison g:Mort(4)	6th	1,535
7/6/09	Halifax (a) (NRCQF)	L54-16	t:Leuluai,Ridyard,Mort g:Mort(2)	N/A	2,186
14/6/09	Gateshead (h)	L12-40	t:A Smith,Reay g:Stanton(2)	8th	1,645
28/6/09	Whitehaven (a)	L36-22	t:Alstead,Durbin,Maden,Watson g:Mort(3)	9th	1,310
3/7/09	Halifax (a)	L48-16	t:Mort,J Smith(2) g:Mort(2)	9th	2,094
19/7/09	Sheffield (h)	W32-24	t:McConnell,Nanyn(2),Durbin,Watson g:Mort(6)	9th	1,465
25/7/09	Barrow (a)	L74-6	t:Durbin g:Mort	9th	1,934
2/8/09	Doncaster (h)	W31-28	t:Leuluai(2),Watson,McConnell,Mort g:Mort(4),Nanyn fg:Hemingway	9th	1,394
15/8/09	Toulouse (h)	W26-6	t:Alstead,Stanton,Nanyn,Watson g:Mort(5)	8th	1,502
23/8/09	Gateshead (a)	L30-24	t:Taylor,Morrison,Stanton(2) g:Mort(4)	9th	1,033
31/8/09	Halifax (h)	L18-27	t:Nanyn,Ridyard,Donlan g:Nanyn(2),Ridyard	10th	2,349
6/9/09	Whitehaven (h)	W47-14	t:McConnell(2),Nanyn(2),Wingfield,Ridyard,Alstead(2) g:Nanyn(7) fg:Watson	9th	2,721

● Played at Stade Ernest Argeles, Blagnac

	APP		TRIES		GOALS		FG		PTS	
	D.O.B.	ALL	Ch	ALL	Ch	ALL	Ch	ALL	Ch	ALL	Ch
Andy Ainscough	24/4/90	(2)	(1)	0	0	0	0	0	0	0	0
David Alstead	18/2/82	11	10	6	6	0	0	0	0	24	24
Dave Armitstead	15/1/84	18(2)	15(2)	0	0	0	0	0	0	0	0
Mark Castle	19/2/86	1(3)	1(3)	0	0	0	0	0	0	0	0
John Cookson	12/12/84	(1)	0	0	0	0	0	0	0	0	0
Dean Dollin	27/10/89	(1)	(1)	0	0	0	0	0	0	0	0
Stuart Donlan	29/8/78	25	18	10	7	0	0	0	0	40	28
Jamie Durbin	7/9/84	6(15)	3(13)	13	8	0	0	0	0	52	32
Kurt Haggerty	8/1/89	8(2)	5(2)	3	1	0	0	0	0	12	4
Tom Hemingway	6/12/86	6	6	0	0	0	0	1	1	1	1
Adam Higson	19/5/87	11(4)	6(4)	3	2	0	0	0	0	12	8
Chris Hill	3/11/87	23(4)	17(3)	1	0	0	0	0	0	4	0
Andy Hobson	26/12/78	15(5)	10(3)	3	2	0	0	0	0	12	8
Macgraff Leuluai	9/2/90	8(5)	7(4)	3	2	0	0	0	0	12	8
Steve Maden	13/9/02	24	18	6	3	0	0	0	0	24	12
Lee Marsh	5/3/83	3	3	0	0	0	0	0	0	0	0
Dave McConnell	25/3/81	22(1)	18(1)	6	5	0	0	0	0	24	20
Danny Meekin	16/3/89	3(20)	2(15)	1	0	0	0	0	0	4	0
Mike Morrison	9/9/87	13(9)	11(8)	2	2	0	0	0	0	8	8
Ian Mort	21/6/88	22	17	11	7	74	52	0	0	192	132
Mick Nanyn	3/6/82	10(1)	9(1)	8	8	10	10	0	0	52	52
Sam Reay	23/5/84	8(4)	5(1)	5	1	0	0	0	0	20	4
Martyn Ridyard	25/7/86	13(1)	7(1)	7	2	11	1	1	1	51	11
Anthony Rourke	16/10/88	7(1)	4	2	1	0	0	0	0	8	4
Adam Rudd	29/7/86	3(1)	3(1)	1	1	0	0	0	0	4	4
Aaron Smith	10/9/82	13(1)	12(1)	1	1	0	0	0	0	4	4
Jamie Smith	8/6/87	6	1	6	2	0	0	0	0	24	8
Nicky Stanton	18/3/89	17	13	6	4	2	2	0	0	28	20
Anthony Stewart	5/3/79	9(10)	7(5)	1	0	0	0	0	0	4	0
James Taylor	11/9/84	18(7)	13(6)	1	1	0	0	0	0	4	4
Ian Watson	27/10/76	25	18	8	6	0	0	2	2	34	26
Lee Wingfield	9/6/81	3(8)	1(4)	2	1	0	0	0	0	8	4

Ian Mort

LEAGUE RECORD
P20-W9-D0-L11-BP5
(9th, Championship)
F426, A572, Diff-146
32 points.

CHALLENGE CUP
Round Four

NORTHERN RAIL CUP
Quarter Finalists/3rd, Pool 2

ATTENDANCES
Best - v Whitehaven (Ch - 2,721)
Worst - v Lokomotiv Moscow
(CC - 1,278)
Total (excluding Challenge Cup) - 23,007
Average (excluding
Challenge Cup) - 1,917
(Down by 521 on 2008)

SHEFFIELD EAGLES

DATE	FIXTURE	RESULT	SCORERS	LGE	ATT
11/2/09	Hunslet (h) (NRC)	W38-16	t:Brooks(2),Szostak,Roby,Lindsay,Boothroyd,Howieson g:Woodcock(5)	N/A	556
15/2/09	Gateshead (a) (NRC)	L44-18	t:Hepworth(2),Edwards g:Woodcock(3)	7th(P1)	1,226
22/2/09	Oldham (a) (NRC)	W22-34	t:Boothroyd,Woodcock,McDonald,Edwards,Brooks g:Woodcock(7)	4th(P1)	1,173
1/3/09	Halifax (h) (NRC)	L18-50	t:Woodcock,Gibson,Barlow g:Woodcock(3)	7th(P1)	1,065
8/3/09	Toulouse (h) (CCR3)	W22-6	t:Barlow,Lindsay,Gibson,Woodcock g:Woodcock(3)	N/A	1,554
15/3/09	Leigh (h)	L22-23	t:Gibson,Ropati(2),Stringer g:Woodcock(3)	6th	1,220
21/3/09	Toulouse (a)	W12-18	t:Stringer,Thackeray g:Woodcock(4),Lindsay	4th	1,923
28/3/09	Widnes (a)	L28-20	t:Ropati,Lindsay,Szostak,Wood g:Stringer(2)	6th	3,181
3/4/09	Dewsbury (h) (CCR4)	W28-18	t:Thackeray,McDonald,Woodcock,Brooks,Wood,Yere g:Woodcock(2)	N/A	597
9/4/09	Doncaster (h)	L22-23	t:Yere(3),Groom g:Woodcock(3)	7th	1,209
13/4/09	Featherstone (a)	L20-12	t:Thackeray,Hepworth g:Woodcock(2)	7th	1,612
16/4/09	Gateshead (a)	L41-36	t:Groom,Barlow,Ropati(2),McDonald,Fagborun,Hepworth g:Woodcock(4)	7th	715
26/4/09	Widnes (h)	L20-22	t:Fagborun,Ropati,Lindsay,Roby g:Woodcock(2)	8th	1,231
10/5/09	Hull KR (a) (CCR5)	L34-24	t:Yere,Barlow,Woodcock,Wood g:Woodcock(4)	N/A	4,955
17/5/09	Halifax (a)	W26-40	t:Woodcock(2),Gibson,Boothroyd,Barlow,Lindsay g:Woodcock(8)	8th	2,212
23/5/09	Toulouse (h)	W58-12	t:Szostak,Walsh(2),Ropati,Barlow(2),Gibson,Green,Boothroyd,Mills g:Woodcock(9)	8th	809
30/5/09	Barrow (a)	L26-18	t:Ropati,Lindsay,Szostak g:Ropati(3)	7th	1,693
13/6/09	Whitehaven (h)	W28-24	t:Brooks,Edwards,Szostak,Mills,Barlow g:Woodcock(4)	7th	811
28/6/09	Doncaster (a) ●	W8-78	t:Ropati(2),Yere(4),Mills,Cook,Wood,Lindsay,Gibson(3),Brooks g:Woodcock(11)	6th	275
3/7/09	Batley (h)	W30-4	t:Stringer(3),Ropati,Cook,Yere g:Woodcock(3)	5th	1,286
19/7/09	Leigh (a)	L32-24	t:Cook,Gibson,Mills,Woodcock g:Woodcock(4)	6th	1,465
23/7/09	Gateshead (h)	W46-30	t:Gibson(3),Yere,Thackeray(2),Hepworth,Lindsay,Wood g:Woodcock(5)	6th	1,410
2/8/09	Whitehaven (a)	L36-34	t:Mills,Barlow,Yere,Lindsay,Wood,Stringer g:Woodcock(3),Stringer(2)	5th	1,850
9/8/09	Batley (a)	W22-34	t:Mills(2),Lindsay(2),Wood,Hardbottle g:Woodcock(5)	5th	730
13/8/09	Halifax (h)	W38-24	t:Hepworth,Stringer,Exton,Thackeray,Ropati,Howieson,Mills g:Woodcock(5)	4th	1,457
27/8/09	Featherstone (h)	W28-12	t:Yere,Cook,Wood,Green,Lindsay g:Woodcock(4)	3rd	1,028
3/9/09	Barrow (h)	W29-22	t:Yere,Barlow,Stringer,Mills,Cook g:Woodcock(4) fg:Cook	3rd	1,283
11/9/09	Featherstone (h) (EPO)	L8-32	t:Mills g:Woodcock(2)	N/A	802

● Played at Chris Moyles Stadium, Featherstone

		APP		TRIES		GOALS		FG		PTS	
	D.O.B.	ALL	Ch	ALL	Ch	ALL	Ch	ALL	Ch	ALL	Ch
Sam Barlow	7/3/88	6(18)	4(15)	10	7	0	0	0	0	40	28
Andy Boothroyd	7/1/85	2(8)	1(5)	4	2	0	0	0	0	16	8
Matty Brooks	9/10/86	21(2)	15(2)	6	2	0	0	0	0	24	8
Gavin Brown	18/9/77	1(1)	1(1)	0	0	0	0	0	0	0	0
Tom Buckenham	15/8/84	(2)	(1)	0	0	0	0	0	0	0	0
Craig Cook	26/5/83	7(3)	7(3)	5	5	0	0	1	1	21	21
Ged Corcoran	28/3/83	9(1)	4(1)	0	0	0	0	0	0	0	0
Grant Edwards	22/3/87	13(4)	9(3)	3	1	0	0	0	0	12	4
Trevor Exton	8/11/81	4(6)	4(6)	1	1	0	0	0	0	4	4
Bolu Fagborun	28/3/86	7	4	2	2	0	0	0	0	8	8
Damian Gibson	14/5/75	20	16	12	10	0	0	0	0	48	40
Peter Green	2/12/81	11(2)	11(2)	2	2	0	0	0	0	8	8
Aaron Groom	23/6/87	3(2)	2(2)	2	2	0	0	0	0	8	8
Michael Haley	19/9/87	2(8)	2(8)	0	0	0	0	0	0	0	0
Luke Hardbottle	17/9/88	(1)	(1)	1	1	0	0	0	0	4	4
Ryan Hepworth	16/1/81	13(13)	11(9)	6	4	0	0	0	0	24	16
Joe Hirst	21/4/87	3(1)	3(1)	0	0	0	0	0	0	0	0
Jack Howieson	28/7/81	21	15	2	1	0	0	0	0	8	4
Brendon Lindsay	21/9/77	27	20	12	10	1	1	0	0	50	42
Dane McDonald	14/7/87	8(3)	2(3)	3	1	0	0	0	0	12	4
Danny Mills	10/8/82	14	14	10	10	0	0	0	0	40	40
James Morrow	8/3/83	(3)	(2)	0	0	0	0	0	0	0	0
Saqib Murtza	18/11/85	(3)	(1)	0	0	0	0	0	0	0	0
Mike Roby	2/4/86	4(4)	2(2)	2	1	0	0	0	0	8	4
Tangi Ropati	15/11/84	23(2)	18(2)	12	12	3	3	0	0	54	54
Mitchell Stringer	1/11/83	18(9)	14(7)	8	8	4	4	0	0	40	40
Alex Szostak	4/3/86	28	21	5	4	0	0	0	0	20	16
Ashley Thackeray	6/11/87	19	12	6	5	0	0	0	0	24	20
Tommy Trayler	27/4/83	5(1)	3	0	0	0	0	0	0	0	0
Nick Turnbull	22/11/82	(2)	0	0	0	0	0	0	0	0	0
Joe Walsh	13/1/86	1(3)	1(3)	2	2	0	0	0	0	8	8
Matt Whitaker	6/3/82	2(3)	1(1)	0	0	0	0	0	0	0	0
Kyle Wood	18/6/89	20(7)	17(3)	8	6	0	0	0	0	32	24
Jonny Woodcock	5/2/81	26	19	8	3	112	85	0	0	256	182
Menzie Yere	24/10/83	26	20	14	12	0	0	0	0	56	48

Menzie Yere

LEAGUE RECORD
P20-W11-D0-L9-BP9
(3rd, Championship/Elimination Play-Off)
F635, A447, Diff+188
42 points.

CHALLENGE CUP
Round Five

NORTHERN RAIL CUP
7th, Pool 1

ATTENDANCES
Best - v Toulouse (CC - 1,554)
Worst - v Hunslet (NRC - 556)
Total (excluding Challenge Cup) - 14,167
Average (excluding
Challenge Cup) - 1,090
(Up by 22 on 2008)

TOULOUSE OLYMPIQUE

DATE	FIXTURE	RESULT	SCORERS	LGE	ATT
8/3/09	Sheffield (a) (CCR3)	L22-6	t:Couturier g:N Wynn	N/A	1,554
12/3/09	Widnes (a)	L70-0		11th	5,071
21/3/09	Sheffield (h)	L12-18	t:Ormeno g:N Wynn(4)	9th	1,923
28/3/09	Whitehaven (a)	L40-26	t:N Wynn,Payen,Bromley,Villegas g:N Wynn(5)	11th	1,225
13/4/09	Batley (a)	W22-60	t:Houles,Ormeno(2),Almarcha,Maria(2),Payen,Couturier(2),N Wynn(2) g:N Wynn(7),Couturier	10th	662
18/4/09	Leigh (h) ●	W46-10	t:Bromley,Maria,Planas(2),Couturier,Bienes,Anselme,Griffi g:N Wynn(7)	8th	3,507
26/4/09	Doncaster (a)	W18-48	t:Mitchell(2),Almarcha,N Wynn,Bromley(2),T Wynn,Faure g:N Wynn(8)	7th	1,089
2/5/09	Whitehaven (h)	W38-12	t:Couturier,Villegas(2),Bromley,Anselme,Griffi g:N Wynn(7)	6th	2,121
16/5/09	Barrow (h)	W22-14	t:Planas,Gay,Villegas g:N Wynn(5)	7th	2,900
23/5/09	Sheffield (a)	L58-12	t:Bromley,Griffi g:N Wynn(2)	7th	809
7/6/09	Gateshead (a)	W16-52	t:Villegas(2),Bromley(2),Mitchell,Luguoro(2),Anselme,Planas g:N Wynn(8)	6th	516
13/6/09	Batley (h)	W32-24	t:Mitchell,Gay,Couturier,Bromley,T Wynn g:N Wynn(6)	4th	2,176
27/6/09	Featherstone (h) ●	L16-32	t:Couturier(2),Faure g:Couturier(2)	7th	2,321
2/7/09	Barrow (a)	L30-22	t:T Wynn,Bromley,Couturier(2) g:Couturier(3)	7th	2,456
18/7/09	Halifax (h)	L16-54	t:Payen,Couturier,Almarcha g:Couturier(2)	7th	2,687
25/7/09	Widnes (h) ●	L24-32	t:Mitchell,Bromley,Viala(2) g:Couturier(4)	7th	3,206
1/8/09	Featherstone (a)	W18-34	t:Couturier,Planas(2),Pramil,Gay(2) g:N Wynn(5)	7th	1,346
8/8/09	Gateshead (h)	L20-48	t:Griffi,Mendes Varela,Maria,Borlin g:N Wynn(2)	7th	1,681
15/8/09	Leigh (a)	L26-6	t:Couturier g:N Wynn	7th	1,502
22/8/09	Doncaster (h)	W52-6	t:Villegas(2),Bromley,Mendes Varela,Mitchell,Planas(2),Griffi,N Wynn,Tisseyre g:N Wynn(6)	7th	1,200
5/9/09	Halifax (a)	L34-18	t:Anselme,Tisseyre,Ormeno g:N Wynn(3)	10th	2,128

● Played at Stade Ernest Argeles, Blagnac

		APP		TRIES		GOALS		FG		PTS	
	D.O.B.	ALL	Ch	ALL	Ch	ALL	Ch	ALL	Ch	ALL	Ch
Matthieu Almarcha	29/11/83	7(9)	7(9)	3	3	0	0	0	0	12	12
Eric Anselme	20/5/79	12(6)	11(6)	4	4	0	0	0	0	16	16
Yohan Barthau	13/6/86	1(5)	1(5)	0	0	0	0	0	0	0	0
Clement Bienes	21/1/90	3	3	1	1	0	0	0	0	4	4
Jean-Christophe Borlin	21/12/76	3(9)	3(9)	1	1	0	0	0	0	4	4
Rory Bromley	1/5/84	18	18	12	12	0	0	0	0	48	48
Joris Canton	21/5/81	6	5	0	0	0	0	0	0	0	0
Damien Couturier	9/7/81	20(1)	19(1)	13	12	12	12	0	0	76	72
Nicholas Delgal	14/3/88	2(1)	1(1)	0	0	0	0	0	0	0	0
Nicholas Faure	30/5/84	(14)	(13)	2	2	0	0	0	0	8	8
Cedric Gay	12/3/82	5(4)	5(4)	4	4	0	0	0	0	16	16
Mathiou Griffi	2/3/83	18(1)	17(1)	5	5	0	0	0	0	20	20
Sylvain Houles	3/8/81	17	16	1	1	0	0	0	0	4	4
Kevin Luguoro	30/10/88	1	1	2	2	0	0	0	0	8	8
Anton Maria	21/3/87	10(10)	10(9)	4	4	0	0	0	0	16	16
Martin Mitchell	21/10/85	19	18	6	6	0	0	0	0	24	24
Bruno Ormeno	3/12/82	7(3)	7(3)	4	4	0	0	0	0	16	16
Sebastien Payen	12/7/86	17	16	3	3	0	0	0	0	12	12
Teli Pelo	22/7/84	3	3	0	0	0	0	0	0	0	0
Sebastien Planas	5/5/84	19	18	8	8	0	0	0	0	32	32
Olivier Pramil	4/6/79	(11)	(10)	1	1	0	0	0	0	4	4
Florian Quintilla	20/10/88	2(1)	2(1)	0	0	0	0	0	0	0	0
Yoan Tisseyre	8/5/89	(3)	(3)	2	2	0	0	0	0	8	8
Carlos Mendes Varela	28/12/84	4	4	2	2	0	0	0	0	8	8
Adrien Viala	22/2/82	2(6)	2(5)	2	2	0	0	0	0	8	8
Constant Villegas	21/10/86	20	19	8	8	0	0	0	0	32	32
Nathan Wynn	10/1/86	18	17	5	5	77	76	0	0	174	172
Tim Wynn	19/7/85	19	18	3	3	0	0	0	0	12	12
Brendan Worth	18/7/84	20	19	0	0	0	0	0	0	0	0

Damien Couturier

LEAGUE RECORD
P20-W9-D0-L11-BP3
(10th, Championship)
F556, A582, Diff-26
30 points.

CHALLENGE CUP
Round Three

NORTHERN RAIL CUP
Not entered

ATTENDANCES
Best - v Leigh (Ch - 3,507)
Worst - v Doncaster (Ch - 1,200)
Total (excluding Challenge Cup) - 23,722
Average (excluding
Challenge Cup) - 2,372

WHITEHAVEN

DATE	FIXTURE	RESULT	SCORERS	LGE	ATT
15/2/09	Batley (h) (NRC)	W52-30	t:Calvert,Mattinson,Patrick,Gorski(3),Eilbeck,McNally,M Jackson		1,146
			g:Rudd(6),McNally(2)	5th(P2)	
18/2/09	York (a) (NRC)	L36-6	t:C Smith g:McNally	5th(P2)	685
22/2/09	Workington (h) (NRC)	W26-12	t:Mattinson,Patrick,Calvert,McNally g:M Jackson(2),McNally(3)	5th(P2)	1,346
1/3/09	Leigh (a) (NRC)	L24-22	t:Eilbeck,McNally(2),Lavulavu g:M Jackson(3)	6th(P2)	1,789
8/3/09	Gateshead (a) (CCR3)	L42-38	t:Theohaurus,Adebisi(2),Benson(2),McNally(2),Eilbeck g:McNally(3)	N/A	501
15/3/09	Gateshead (h)	W40-18	t:Eilbeck(2),McNally(3),Amor,Adebisi g:McNally(6)	3rd	1,175
22/3/09	Featherstone (a)	W26-52	t:Joe,McNally(4),McAvoy,C Smith,R Jackson,Patrick g:McNally(8)	1st	1,555
28/3/09	Toulouse (h)	W40-26	t:Benson,Gorski,McNally,Mattinson,McAvoy,Patrick,Adebisi g:McNally(6)	1st	1,225
10/4/09	Barrow (a)	L18-12	t:Joe,McNally g:McNally(2)	1st	3,202
13/4/09	Halifax (h)	L18-24	t:McNally(3) g:McNally(3)	2nd	2,005
19/4/09	Featherstone (h)	L16-44	t:McAvoy,McNally,Adebisi g:McNally(2)	5th	1,411
2/5/09	Toulouse (a)	L38-12	t:Mattinson,Adebisi g:McNally(2)	7th	2,121
7/5/09	Widnes (h)	W26-22	t:McNally(2),D Miller,Calvert,Patrick g:McNally(3)	5th	2,102
17/5/09	Gateshead (a)	W34-38	t:Calvert(2),Rudd,R Jackson,McAvoy,McNally(2) g:McNally(5)	5th	575
24/5/09	Batley (a)	L48-24	t:Adebisi,Joe,Gorski,Rudd g:McNally(3),Rudd	5th	627
31/5/09	Doncaster (h)	W50-12	t:McNally,Amor(2),R Jackson,Ballard(3),C Smith,Adebisi g:McNally(7)	5th	1,362
13/6/09	Sheffield (a)	L28-24	t:McNally,Ballard,McAvoy,S Miller g:McNally(4)	6th	811
28/6/09	Leigh (h)	W36-22	t:Calvert(4),Adebisi(2),Joe	5th	1,310
16/7/09	Barrow (h)	W28-4	t:Ballard,Calvert,Gorski,R Jackson(2) g:McNally(4)	5th	2,708
26/7/09	Doncaster (a)	W10-19	t:Amor,Calvert,Rudd g:McNally(3) fg:Rudd	5th	337
2/8/09	Sheffield (h)	W36-34	t:Amor,Gorski,Calvert(2),Theohaurus(2) g:Rudd(6)	4th	1,850
9/8/09	Halifax (a)	W42-50	t:Calvert(4),Eilbeck(2),Theohaurus,Edmondson,Thornley		
			g:Rudd,M Jackson(3),Joe(3)	4th	2,014
16/8/09	Batley (h)	W20-12	t:Theohaurus,Amor,McAvoy g:Rudd(3),McNally	2nd	1,550
22/8/09	Widnes (a)	L58-10	t:R Jackson,McAvoy g:McNally	3rd	3,275
6/9/09	Leigh (a)	L47-14	t:Ballard(2),R Jackson g:Rudd	5th	2,721
10/9/09	Widnes (a) (EPO)	L26-21	t:Joe,R Jackson,Amor g:Rudd(4) fg:Rudd	N/A	2,375

		APP		TRIES		GOALS		FG		PTS	
	D.O.B.	ALL	Ch	ALL	Ch	ALL	Ch	ALL	Ch	ALL	Ch
Ade Adebisi	7/1/86	19	15	10	8	0	0	0	0	40	32
Kyle Amor	26/5/87	10(15)	9(12)	7	7	0	0	0	0	28	28
Marc Bainbridge	22/12/87	1	1	0	0	0	0	0	0	0	0
Paul Ballard	4/9/84	9	9	7	7	0	0	0	0	28	28
Daniel Barker	1/12/88	1(1)	1	0	0	0	0	0	0	0	0
Craig Benson	19/8/85	16	12	3	1	0	0	0	0	12	4
Craig Calvert	10/2/84	21	17	17	15	0	0	0	0	68	60
Ryan Campbell	23/9/81	1	0	0	0	0	0	0	0	0	0
Tyrone Dalton	7/1/89	1	0	0	0	0	0	0	0	0	0
Karl Edmondson	9/2/83	25(1)	21	1	1	0	0	0	0	4	4
Derry Eilbeck	1/6/84	14	10	7	4	0	0	0	0	28	16
Reece Fox	13/2/90	(1)	(1)	0	0	0	0	0	0	0	0
Andy Gorski	31/3/81	21(3)	17(3)	7	4	0	0	0	0	28	16
Howard Hill	16/1/75	5(7)	5(7)	0	0	0	0	0	0	0	0
Marc Jackson	21/8/79	4(13)	3(9)	1	0	8	3	0	0	20	6
Rob Jackson	4/9/81	20	16	8	8	0	0	0	0	32	32
Leroy Joe	31/12/74	25	21	4	4	4	4	0	0	24	24
Taani Lavulavu	22/3/76	5	1	1	0	0	0	0	0	4	0
John Lebbon	30/12/84	4	4	0	0	0	0	0	0	0	0
Scott Lofthouse	23/5/85	1	1	0	0	0	0	0	0	0	0
Karl Long	18/11/80	(4)	(4)	0	0	0	0	0	0	0	0
Tane Manihera	6/8/74	1	1	0	0	0	0	0	0	0	0
Graeme Mattinson	24/4/85	14(3)	11(3)	4	2	0	0	0	0	16	8
Scott McAvoy	9/4/86	18(3)	18(2)	7	7	0	0	0	0	28	28
Ryan McDonald	24/2/78	1(9)	(8)	0	0	0	0	0	0	0	0
Gregg McNally	2/1/91	19(5)	17(2)	25	19	74	65	0	0	248	206
Dexter Miller	3/6/82	1(11)	1(8)	1	1	0	0	0	0	4	4
Spencer Miller	27/2/80	25	21	1	1	0	0	0	0	4	4
John Patrick	29/11/82	9	6	5	3	0	0	0	0	20	12
Soni Radovanovic	31/3/88	2(1)	2(1)	0	0	0	0	0	0	0	0
Carl Rudd	10/10/82	21	17	3	3	22	16	2	2	58	46
Marc Shackley	14/1/89	1	0	0	0	0	0	0	0	0	0
Chris Smith	21/1/90	(13)	(12)	3	2	0	0	0	0	12	8
Daniel Smith	29/11/87	1	0	0	0	0	0	0	0	0	0
Jamie Theohaurus	23/1/88	18(5)	14(5)	5	4	0	0	0	0	20	16
Andy Thornley	1/3/89	1(4)	1(4)	1	1	0	0	0	0	4	4
Matthew Tunstall	7/9/77	3(5)	2(3)	0	0	0	0	0	0	0	0

Gregg McNally

LEAGUE RECORD
P20-W12-D0-L8-BP3
(5th, Championship/Elimination Play-Off)
F565, A567, Diff-2
39 points.

CHALLENGE CUP
Round Three

NORTHERN RAIL CUP
6th, Pool 2

ATTENDANCES
Best - v Barrow (Ch - 2,708)
Worst - v Batley (NRC - 1,146)
Total (excluding Challenge Cup) - 19,190
Average (excluding
Challenge Cup) - 1,599
(Down by 41 on 2008)

WIDNES VIKINGS

DATE	FIXTURE	RESULT	SCORERS	LGE	ATT
13/2/09	Oldham (h) (NRC)	L20-22	t:Dodd,Flynn,Duffy,Thackeray g:Dodd(2)	8th(P1)	2,783
21/2/09	Gateshead (h) (NRC)	W40-18	t:Gannon(3),Yates,Kohe-Love,Strong,Fletcher g:Yates(6)	5th(P1)	3,001
1/3/09	Blackpool (a) (NRC)	W16-46	t:Kohe-Love(2),Doran,Hartley,Fletcher,Flynn,Duffy,Yates g:Yates(7)	3rd(P1)	864
4/3/09	Barrow (a) (NRC)	L12-4	t:Gaskell	4th(P1)	1,563
7/3/09	Saddleworth (h) (CCR3)	W88-0	t:Gaskell,Dodd(2),Gannon,Ostick,Strong,Varkulis(2),Smith(3),Wildbore(2),Hartley,Thompson g:Hartley(14)	N/A	1,786
12/3/09	Toulouse (h)	W70-0	t:Duffy,Flynn(3),Yates,Fletcher(2),Wildbore(2),Webster,Grady,Doran g:Yates(11)	1st	5,071
19/3/09	Halifax (a)	L24-14	t:Flynn,Gaskell,Grady g:Dodd	3rd	3,274
28/3/09	Sheffield (h)	W28-20	t:Yates,Flynn(2),Doran,Smith(2) g:Dodd(2)	2nd	3,181
3/4/09	Halifax (a) (CCR4)	L20-16	t:Gannon,Thackeray g:Fletcher,Dodd(3)	N/A	3,204
10/4/09	Leigh (h)	L8-10	t:Wildbore g:Dodd(2)	5th	4,354
13/4/09	Doncaster (a)	W18-24	t:Yates,Dodd,Thompson,Thackeray,Doran g:Yates(2)	3rd	831
17/4/09	Batley (h)	W40-18	t:Varkulis,Gaskell,Yates,Thackeray,Kavanagh,Ostick,Dodd g:Yates(6)	2nd	2,901
26/4/09	Sheffield (a)	W20-22	t:Varkulis,Duffy,Webster,Fletcher g:Yates(3)	2nd	1,231
1/5/09	Barrow (h)	L6-27	t:Bannister g:Tyrer	3rd	3,290
7/5/09	Whitehaven (a)	L26-22	t:Bannister,Webster(3) g:Tyrer(3)	3rd	2,102
14/5/09	Leigh (a)	L23-16	t:Dodd,Webster,Ostick g:Tyrer,Bannister	3rd	2,556
23/5/09	Gateshead (h)	W46-30	t:Doran(2),Gannon,Thackeray,Dodd,Flynn,Penny,Bannister g:Hartley(5),Dodd(2)	3rd	5,236
31/5/09	Batley (a)	L40-34	t:Morrison(3),Flynn,Thackeray,Varkulis g:Hartley(5)	3rd	1,089
6/6/09	York (h) (NRCQF)	W44-18	t:Gaskell,Thackeray,Kavanagh,Varkulis,Kohe-Love(3),Fletcher g:Hall(6)	N/A	1,650
13/6/09	Featherstone (h)	W46-22	t:Penny,Grayshon,Morrison,Webster,Dodd,Smith,Kohe-Love,Gaskell g:Hall(7)	3rd	3,278
21/6/09	Halifax (a) (NRCSF)	W22-27	t:Thackeray(3),Dodd g:Hall(5) fg:Hall	N/A	3,972
4/7/09	Doncaster (h)	W78-4	t:Penny(3),Kohe-Love,Flynn(2),Hall,Grayshon,Varkulis(2),Dodd,Fletcher,Smith,Pickersgill g:Hall(8),Dodd(3)	3rd	3,453
12/7/09	Barrow (NRCF) •	W18-34	t:Fletcher,Duffy,Penny(2),Kohe-Love,Varkulis g:Hall(5)	N/A	8,720
19/7/09	Gateshead (a)	L34-18	t:Penny,Flynn,Thackeray g:Hartley(3)	3rd	717
25/7/09	Toulouse (a) ••	W24-32	t:Grayshon,Kavanagh,Penny(2),Gannon,Varkulis g:Dodd(4)	3rd	3,206
31/7/09	Halifax (h)	W42-16	t:Morrison,Flynn(3),Varkulis,Kohe-Love,Penny g:Hartley(7)	2nd	4,039
9/8/09	Featherstone (a)	L34-29	t:Kohe-Love,Flynn(2),Thackeray(2) g:Hartley(4) fg:Smith	3rd	2,125
13/8/09	Barrow (a)	L38-16	t:Dodd,Flynn,Hartley g:Hartley(2)	5th	3,050
22/8/09	Whitehaven (h)	W58-10	t:Thackeray,Varkulis(2),Gannon,Fletcher(2),Duffy,Flynn,Gaskell,Doran g:Hartley(9)	2nd	3,275
10/9/09	Whitehaven (h) (EPO)	W26-21	t:Grady,Hartley(2),Thackeray,Webster g:Hartley(3)	N/A	2,375
18/9/09	Featherstone (h) (ESF)	L24-32	t:Dodd,Doran,Grady,Varkulis g:Hartley(4)	N/A	3,296

● Played at Bloomfield Road, Blackpool
●● Played at Stade Ernest Argeles, Blagnac

		APP		TRIES		GOALS		FG		PTS	
	D.O.B.	ALL	Ch	ALL	Ch	ALL	Ch	ALL	Ch	ALL	Ch
Steve Bannister	10/10/87	3(1)	3(1)	3	3	1	1	0	0	14	14
Gavin Dodd	28/2/81	25(5)	18(3)	12	8	19	14	0	0	86	60
Lee Doran	23/3/81	23(6)	17(4)	8	7	0	0	0	0	32	28
John Duffy	2/7/80	16(7)	12(4)	6	3	0	0	0	0	24	12
Richard Fletcher	17/5/81	19	11	10	6	1	0	0	0	42	24
Paddy Flynn	11/12/87	25	20	20	18	0	0	0	0	80	72
Jim Gannon	16/6/77	30	21	8	3	0	0	0	0	32	12
Dean Gaskell	12/4/83	19(1)	13(1)	7	4	0	0	0	0	28	16
Shane Grady	13/12/89	6(7)	4(5)	4	4	0	0	0	0	16	16
Jon Grayshon	10/5/83	9	9	3	3	0	0	0	0	12	12
Craig Hall	21/2/88	5	2	1	1	31	15	1	0	67	34
Tim Hartley	2/1/86	11(7)	9(3)	5	3	56	42	0	0	132	96
David Houghton	2/11/89	(4)	(3)	0	0	0	0	0	0	0	0
Ben Kavanagh	4/3/88	2(29)	1(21)	3	2	0	0	0	0	12	8
Toa Kohe-Love	2/12/76	16	9	11	4	0	0	0	0	44	16
Danny Mills	10/8/82	(2)	(2)	0	0	0	0	0	0	0	0
Iain Morrison	6/5/83	9(2)	6(1)	5	5	0	0	0	0	20	20
Anthony Mullally	28/6/91	(1)		0	0	0	0	0	0	0	0
Michael Ostick	23/1/88	20(7)	14(6)	3	2	0	0	0	0	12	8
Lee Paterson	5/7/81	5(1)	5(1)	0	0	0	0	0	0	0	0
Kevin Penny	3/10/87	11	8	11	9	0	0	0	0	44	36
Steve Pickersgill	28/11/85	8(3)	5(3)	1	1	0	0	0	0	4	4
Josh Simm	8/11/89	9(7)	7(4)	0	0	0	0	0	0	0	0
Mark Smith	18/8/81	30	21	7	4	0	0	1	1	29	17
Matthew Strong	17/2/87	1(2)	0	2	0	0	0	0	0	8	0
Anthony Thackeray	19/2/86	23(8)	15(7)	15	9	0	0	0	0	60	36
Sam Thompson	9/10/86	(11)	(8)	2	1	0	0	0	0	8	4
Steve Tyrer	16/3/89	3	3	0	0	5	5	0	0	10	10
Richard Varkulis	21/5/82	26(4)	19(3)	14	10	0	0	0	0	56	40
James Webster	11/7/79	29(1)	21	8	8	0	0	0	0	32	32
Loz Wildbore	23/9/84	11(3)	7(3)	5	3	0	0	0	0	20	12
Scott Yates	8/9/88	9(3)	6(3)	6	4	35	22	0	0	94	60

Richard Varkulis

LEAGUE RECORD
P20-W11-D0-L9-BP6
(4th, Championship/
Elimination Semi-Final)
F649, A438, Diff+211
39 points.

CHALLENGE CUP
Round Four

NORTHERN RAIL CUP
Winners/4th, Pool 1

ATTENDANCES
Best - v Gateshead (Ch - 5,236)
Worst - v York (NRCQF - 1,650)
Total (excluding Challenge Cup) - 51,183
Average (excluding
Challenge Cup) - 3,412
(Down by 710 on 2008)

CHAMPIONSHIP 2009
Round by Round

ROUND 1

Thursday 12th March 2009

WIDNES VIKINGS 70 TOULOUSE OLYMPIQUE 0

VIKINGS: 21 Scott Yates; 22 Paddy Flynn; 23 Shane Grady; 4 Toa Kohe-Love; 2 Dean Gaskell; 14 John Duffy; 7 James Webster; 19 Michael Ostick; 9 Mark Smith; 10 Jim Gannon; 3 Richard Varkulis; 12 Richard Fletcher; 11 Lee Doran. Subs (all used): 1 Loz Wildbore; 6 Anthony Thackeray; 17 Ben Kavanagh; 24 Josh Simm.
Tries: Duffy (7), Flynn (11, 25, 30), Yates (14), Fletcher (17, 46), Wildbore (34, 80), Webster (54), Grady (58), Doran (71); **Goals:** Yates 11/12.
OLYMPIQUE: 6 Constant Villegas; 2 Sebastien Payen; 3 Sebastien Planas; 4 Damien Couturier; 5 Joris Canton; 19 Nicholas Delgal; 7 Nathan Wynn; 8 Brendan Worth; 9 Martin Mitchell; 10 Mathieu Griffi; 11 Tim Wynn; 13 Eric Anselme; 20 Sylvain Houles. Subs (all used): 14 Anton Maria; 16 Olivier Pramil; 21 Bruno Ormeno; 22 Nicholas Faure.
Rugby Leaguer & League Express Men of the Match: *Vikings:* John Duffy; *Olympique:* Brendan Worth.
Penalty count: 7-6; **Half-time:** 40-0;
Referee: Gareth Hewer; **Attendance:** 5,071.

Saturday 14th March 2009

BARROW RAIDERS 34 DONCASTER 14

RAIDERS: 1 Gary Broadbent; 2 Mike Backhouse; 18 James Finch; 4 Liam Harrison; 5 James Nixon; 6 Liam Finch; 7 Liam Campbell; 8 Brett McDermott; 9 Andy Ellis; 16 Jamie Butler; 14 Paul Noone; 12 Martin Ostler; 11 Andrew Brocklehurst. Subs (all used): 15 Chris Young; 10 Lee Dutton; 31 Nathan Mossop; 3 Ian Bell.
Tries: Butler (15), Backhouse (18), McDermott (22), Nixon (47, 52), Harrison (54), Campbell (70);
Goals: Noone 3/7.
Sin bin: McDermott (9) - fighting;
L Finch (34) - retaliation.
DONCASTER: 3 Andreas Bauer; 14 Scott Jones; 27 Al Rounding; 34 Luke May; 5 Wayne Reittie; 13 Josh Weeden; 7 Paul Handforth; 28 Jamie Bovill; 9 Craig Cook; 15 Mark Castle; 11 Peter Green; 17 Ross Divorty; 19 Ryan Steen. Subs (all used): 18 Craig Holt; 24 Jake Bassinder; 21 Gary Ellery; 16 Nathan Freer.
Tries: Bauer (10), May (75, 79); **Goals:** S Jones 1/3.
Dismissal: Cook (34) - headbutt on L Finch.
Sin bin: Bovill (9) - fighting; Divorty (20) - interference.
Rugby Leaguer & League Express Men of the Match: *Raiders:* Andrew Brocklehurst; *Doncaster:* Paul Handforth.
Penalty count: 10-9; **Half-time:** 16-4;
Referee: Jamie Leahy; **Attendance:** 1,809.

Sunday 15th March 2009

BATLEY BULLDOGS 8 FEATHERSTONE ROVERS 34

BULLDOGS: 1 Ian Preece; 2 Ben Feehan; 6 Mark Barlow; 4 Danny Maun; 18 Jermaine McGilvary; 12 Mark Toohey; 7 Paul Mennell; 8 Byron Smith; 19 George Flanagan; 10 Luke Stenchion; 11 Kevin Crouthers; 17 Craig Potter; 13 Ashley Lindsay. Subs (all used): 14 John Gallagher; 16 Jon Simpson; 35 Jack Watson; 23 Chris Buttery.
Tries: Feehan (38), McGilvary (40); **Goals:** Barlow 0/2.
ROVERS: 3 Ian Hardman; 2 Waine Pryce; 17 Joe Hirst; 1 Tom Saxton; 26 Sam Smeaton; 6 Iestyn Harris; 7 Andy Kain; 8 Tony Tonks; 16 Joe McLocklan; 10 Stuart Dickens; 11 Matty Dale; 18 Tim Spears; 12 Jamie Field. Subs (all used): 14 Tom Haughey; 9 Jack Lee; 19 Sean Hesketh; 15 James Houston.
Tries: Hirst (14), Harris (34), Haughey (45, 55, 78), Hesketh (59); **Goals:** Dickens 5/7.
Rugby Leaguer & League Express Men of the Match: *Bulldogs:* Danny Maun; *Rovers:* Tom Haughey.
Penalty count: 8-8; **Half-time:** 8-14;
Referee: Peter Brooke; **Attendance:** 1,127.

SHEFFIELD EAGLES 22 LEIGH CENTURIONS 23

EAGLES: 1 Jonny Woodcock; 28 Damian Gibson; 3 Menzie Yere; 23 Tangi Ropati; 5 Ashley Thackeray; 6 Brendon Lindsay; 19 Kyle Wood; 8 Jack Howieson; 20 Matty Brooks; 10 Mitchell Stringer; 11 Alex Szostak; 12 Ged Corcoran; 13 Dane McDonald. Subs (all used): 4 Mike Roby; 9 Grant Edwards; 15 Sam Barlow; 17 Tom Buckenham.
Tries: Gibson (2), Ropati (46, 75), Stringer (61);
Goals: Woodcock 3/5.
CENTURIONS: 1 Stuart Donlan; 3 Steve Maden; 15 Adam Higson; 18 Sam Reay; 14 Ian Mort; 23 Martyn Ridyard; 7 Ian Watson; 8 Andy Hobson; 9 Dave McConnell; 10 Mike Morrison; 37 Kurt Haggerty; 12 James Taylor; 40 Anthony Rourke. Subs (all used): 4 Anthony Stewart; 39 Jamie Durbin; 38 Danny Meekin; 16 Chris Hill.
Tries: Higson (6, 57), Donlan (37), Maden (51);
Goals: Mort 3/4; **Field goal:** Ridyard (78).
Rugby Leaguer & League Express Men of the Match: *Eagles:* Tangi Ropati; *Centurions:* Jamie Durbin.
Penalty count: 14-8; **Half-time:** 6-12;
Referee: Dave Merrick; **Attendance:** 1,220.

WHITEHAVEN 40 GATESHEAD THUNDER 18

WHITEHAVEN: 1 Craig Benson; 5 Ade Adebisi; 3 Rob Jackson; 4 Derry Eilbeck; 2 Craig Calvert; 6 Carl Rudd; 24 Gregg McNally; 21 Taani Lavulavu; 9 Graeme Mattinson; 10 Karl Edmondson; 12 Spencer Miller; 15 Andy Gorski; 7 Leroy Joe. Subs (all used): 25 Jamie Theohaurus; 13 Scott McAvoy; 34 Karl Long; 19 Kyle Amor.
Tries: Eilbeck (12, 46), McNally (27, 36, 41), Amor (52), Adebisi (64); **Goals:** McNally 6/7.
THUNDER: 1 Ben McAlpine; 18 Robin Peers; 3 Kevin Neighbour; 4 Dylan Nash; 5 Stewart Sanderson; 6 Neil Thorman; 7 Luke Branighan; 8 Jason Payne; 9 Andrew Henderson; 33 Jonny Walker; 32 James Cording; 29 Rhys Clarke; 12 Michael Knowles. Subs (all used): 14 Ryan Clarke; 23 Jonny Scott; 17 Chris Parker; 21 Ryan McBride.
Tries: Thorman (4), McAlpine (57), Branighan (61);
Goals: Knowles 3/3.
Sin bin: Nash (34) – holding down.
Rugby Leaguer & League Express Men of the Match: *Whitehaven:* Gregg McNally; *Thunder:* Stewart Sanderson.
Penalty count: 12-12; **Half-time:** 16-6;
Referee: Matthew Thomasson; **Attendance:** 1,175.

ROUND 2

Thursday 19th March 2009

HALIFAX 24 WIDNES VIKINGS 14

HALIFAX: 1 Miles Greenwood; 2 Lee Patterson; 6 Dwayne Barker; 4 Shad Royston; 23 Rob Worrincy; 13 Bob Beswick; 7 Ben Black; 21 Neil Cherryholme; 14 Mark Gleeson; 10 Dana Wilson; 11 David Larder; 15 Mark Roberts; 12 Paul Smith. Subs (all used): 9 Sean Penkywicz; 19 Mick Govin; 16 Said Tamghart; 17 Frank Watene.
Tries: Black (3), Cherryholme (16), Worrincy (36), Govin (76); **Goals:** Black 2/3, Govin 2/2.
VIKINGS: 21 Scott Yates; 2 Dean Gaskell; 23 Shane Grady; 4 Toa Kohe-Love; 22 Paddy Flynn; 14 John Duffy; 7 James Webster; 19 Michael Ostick; 9 Mark Smith; 10 Jim Gannon; 3 Richard Varkulis; 11 Lee Doran; 1 Loz Wildbore. Subs (all used): 6 Anthony Thackeray; 16 Gavin Dodd; 17 Ben Kavanagh; 24 Josh Simm.
Tries: Flynn (10), Gaskell (52), Grady (65);
Goals: Yates 0/1, Dodd 1/2.
Rugby Leaguer & League Express Men of the Match: *Halifax:* Shad Royston; *Vikings:* Ben Kavanagh.
Penalty count: 9-7; **Half-time:** 16-4;
Referee: Robert Hicks; **Attendance:** 3,274.

Saturday 21st March 2009

TOULOUSE OLYMPIQUE 12 SHEFFIELD EAGLES 18

OLYMPIQUE: 1 Rory Bromley; 31 Teli Pelo; 3 Sebastien Planas; 4 Damien Couturier; 21 Bruno Ormeno; 6 Constant Villegas; 7 Nathan Wynn; 8 Brendan Worth; 23 Cedric Gay; 10 Mathieu Griffi; 11 Tim Wynn; 14 Anton Maria; 20 Sylvain Houles. Subs (all used): 22 Nicholas Faure; 17 Yohan Barthau; 12 Matthieu Almarcha; 18 Adrien Viala.
Try: Ormeno (13); **Goals:** N Wynn 4/4.
EAGLES: 1 Jonny Woodcock; 28 Damian Gibson; 3 Menzie Yere; 23 Tangi Ropati; 5 Ashley Thackeray; 6 Brendon Lindsay; 19 Kyle Wood; 8 Jack Howieson; 20 Matty Brooks; 10 Mitchell Stringer; 11 Alex Szostak; 12 Ged Corcoran; 15 Sam Barlow. Subs (all used): 4 Mike Roby; 14 Andy Boothroyd; 22 Ryan Hepworth; 18 Saqib Murtza.
Tries: Stringer (4), Thackeray (80);
Goals: Woodcock 4/4, Lindsay 1/1.
Rugby Leaguer & League Express Men of the Match: *Olympique:* Nathan Wynn; *Eagles:* Ashley Thackeray.
Penalty count: 9-12; **Half-time:** 10-10;
Referee: Ronnie Laughton; **Attendance:** 1,923.

Sunday 22nd March 2009

FEATHERSTONE ROVERS 26 WHITEHAVEN 52

ROVERS: 3 Ian Hardman; 2 Waine Pryce; 17 Joe Hirst; 1 Tom Saxton; 26 Sam Smeaton; 6 Iestyn Harris; 7 Andy Kain; 8 Tony Tonks; 16 Joe McLocklan; 10 Stuart Dickens; 11 Matty Dale; 18 Tim Spears; 14 Tom Haughey. Subs (all used): 24 Jon Fallon; 9 Jack Lee; 19 Sean Hesketh; 13 Richard Blakeway.
Tries: Hardman (28, 37), Fallon (34), A Kain (75), Dale (77); **Goals:** Harris 3/5.
WHITEHAVEN: 1 Craig Benson; 5 Ade Adebisi; 3 Rob Jackson; 18 John Patrick; 4 Derry Eilbeck; 6 Carl Rudd; 24 Gregg McNally; 10 Karl Edmondson; 9 Graeme Mattinson; 7 Leroy Joe; 12 Spencer Miller; 13 Scott McAvoy; 25 Jamie Theohaurus. Subs (all used): 31 Dexter Miller; 34 Karl Long; 19 Kyle Amor; 32 Chris Smith.
Tries: Joe (3), McNally (8, 14, 49, 71), McAvoy (10), C Smith (20), R Jackson (54), Patrick (79);
Goals: McNally 8/11.
Rugby Leaguer & League Express Men of the Match: *Rovers:* Tom Saxton; *Whitehaven:* Gregg McNally.
Penalty count: 9-5; **Half-time:** 16-32;
Referee: Craig Halloran; **Attendance:** 1,555.

GATESHEAD THUNDER 14 BARROW RAIDERS 38

THUNDER: 3 Kevin Neighbour; 18 Robin Peers; 1 Ben McAlpine; 4 Dylan Nash; 5 Stewart Sanderson; 6 Neil Thorman; 7 Luke Branighan; 8 Jason Payne; 9 Andrew Henderson; 10 Tabua Cakacaka; 12 Michael Knowles; 22 Jamie Russo; 17 Chris Parker. Subs (all used): 14 Ryan Clarke; 21 Ryan McBride; 23 Jonny Scott; 29 Rhys Clarke.
Tries: McAlpine (23), Branighan (28), Sanderson (56);
Goals: Knowles 1/4.
RAIDERS: 1 Gary Broadbent; 2 Mike Backhouse; 18 James Finch; 4 Liam Harrison; 5 James Nixon; 6 Liam Finch; 7 Liam Campbell; 8 Brett McDermott; 9 Andy Ellis; 16 Jamie Butler; 14 Paul Noone; 12 Martin Ostler; 11 Andrew Brocklehurst. Subs (all used): 15 Chris Young; 10 Lee Dutton; 28 Nathan Mossop; 3 Ian Bell.
Tries: Ellis (9), Campbell (18), Bell (33), Nixon (44), Ostler (53), Noone (59), McDermott (77);
Goals: Noone 5/7.
Rugby Leaguer & League Express Men of the Match: *Thunder:* Michael Knowles; *Raiders:* Liam Campbell.
Penalty count: 9-6; **Half-time:** 10-18;
Referee: Peter Brooke; **Attendance:** 502.

LEIGH CENTURIONS 28 BATLEY BULLDOGS 34

CENTURIONS: 14 Ian Mort; 2 David Alstead; 1 Stuart Donlan; 15 Adam Higson; 3 Steve Maden; 23 Martyn Ridyard; 7 Ian Watson; 8 Andy Hobson; 9 Dave McConnell; 10 Mike Morrison; 37 Kurt Haggerty; 12 James Taylor; 27 Anthony Rourke. Subs (all used): 26 Jamie Durbin; 16 Chris Hill; 4 Anthony Stewart; 28 Danny Meekin.
Tries: McConnell (22), Watson (45, 67), Durbin (73), Donlan (77); **Goals:** Mort 4/5.
Sin bin: Maden (52) – retaliation; Higson (64) – fighting.
BULLDOGS: 1 Ian Preece; 5 John Campbell; 3 Dale Cardoza; 4 Danny Maun; 18 Jermaine McGilvary; 28 Daryl Cardiss; 7 Paul Mennell; 35 Jack Watson; 14 John Gallagher; 10 Luke Stenchion; 21 Nathan Armitage; 11 Kevin Crouthers; 8 Byron Smith. Subs (all used): 19 George Flanagan; 16 Jon Simpson; 20 David Tootill; 17 Craig Potter.
Tries: Cardiss (3), McGilvary (6, 27), Mennell (11, 34), Preece (54); **Goals:** Mennell 2/4, Flanagan 3/4.
Rugby Leaguer & League Express Men of the Match: *Centurions:* Dave McConnell; *Bulldogs:* Paul Mennell.
Sin bin: Flanagan (64) – fighting.
Penalty count: 12-11; **Half-time:** 6-24;
Referee: Jamie Leahy; **Attendance:** 1,727.

ROUND 3

Thursday 26th March 2009

BATLEY BULLDOGS 20 GATESHEAD THUNDER 20

BULLDOGS: 1 Ian Preece; 5 John Campbell; 3 Dale Cardoza; 4 Danny Maun; 18 Jermaine McGilvary; 6 Mark Barlow; 7 Paul Mennell; 35 Jack Watson; 14 John Gallagher; 10 Luke Stenchion; 21 Nathan Armitage; 17 Craig Potter; 12 Mark Toohey. Subs (all used): 19 George Flanagan; 20 David Tootill; 16 Jon Simpson; 13 Ashley Lindsay.
Tries: McGilvary (36), Flanagan (42), Simpson (48, 78);
Goals: Flanagan 2/4.
THUNDER: 3 Kevin Neighbour; 18 Robin Peers; 1 Ben McAlpine; 4 Dylan Nash; 5 Stewart Sanderson; 6 Neil Thorman; 7 Luke Branighan; 8 Jason Payne; 9 Andrew Henderson; 10 Tabua Cakacaka; 12 Michael Knowles; 29 Rhys Clarke; 22 Jamie Russo. Subs (all used): 14 Ryan Clarke; 17 Chris Parker; 21 Ryan McBride; 33 Jonny Walker.
Tries: Nash (19, 40), Branighan (27); **Goals:** Knowles 4/4.
Rugby Leaguer & League Express Men of the Match: *Bulldogs:* George Flanagan; *Thunder:* Michael Knowles.
Penalty count: 11-6; **Half-time:** 4-20;
Referee: Dave Merrick; **Attendance:** 650.

Saturday 28th March 2009

WHITEHAVEN 40 TOULOUSE OLYMPIQUE 26

WHITEHAVEN: 1 Craig Benson; 5 Ade Adebisi; 3 Rob Jackson; 18 John Patrick; 4 Derry Eilbeck; 6 Carl Rudd; 24 Gregg McNally; 15 Andy Gorski; 25 Jamie Theohaurus; 10 Karl Edmondson; 12 Spencer Miller; 13 Scott McAvoy; 7 Leroy Joe. Subs (all used): 19 Kyle Amor; 34 Karl Long; 16 Ryan McDonald; 9 Graeme Mattinson.
Tries: Benson (14), Gorski (30), McNally (52), Mattinson (64), McAvoy (69), Patrick (72), Adebisi (79);
Goals: McNally 6/7.
OLYMPIQUE: 1 Rory Bromley; 5 Joris Canton; 3 Sebastien Planas; 4 Damien Couturier; 2 Sebastien Payen; 6 Constant Villegas; 7 Nathan Wynn; 8 Brendan Worth; 23 Cedric Gay; 10 Mathieu Griffi; 11 Tim Wynn; 12 Matthieu Almarcha; 20 Sylvain Houles. Subs (all used): 14 Anton Maria; 13 Eric Anselme; 22 Nicholas Faure; 18 Adrien Viala.
Tries: N Wynn (4), Payen (6), Bromley (11), Villegas (39); **Goals:** N Wynn 5/5.
Rugby Leaguer & League Express Men of the Match: *Whitehaven:* Leroy Joe; *Olympique:* Nathan Wynn.
Penalty count: 10-7; **Half-time:** 12-24;
Referee: Robert Hicks; **Attendance:** 1,225.

WIDNES VIKINGS 28 SHEFFIELD EAGLES 20

VIKINGS: 21 Scott Yates; 22 Paddy Flynn; 3 Richard Varkulis; 23 Shane Grady; 2 Dean Gaskell; 6 Anthony Thackeray; 7 James Webster; 19 Michael Ostick; 9 Mark Smith; 10 Jim Gannon; 11 Lee Doran; 24 Josh Simm; 14 John Duffy. Subs (all used): 1 Loz Wildbore; 16 Gavin Dodd; 17 Ben Kavanagh; 20 Sam Thompson.
Tries: Yates (17), Flynn (40, 54), Doran (44), Smith (57, 64); **Goals:** Dodd 2/6.
EAGLES: 4 Mike Roby; 28 Damian Gibson; 3 Menzie Yere; 23 Tangi Ropati; 5 Ashley Thackeray; 6 Brendon Lindsay; 19 Kyle Wood; 8 Jack Howieson; 20 Matty Brooks; 10 Mitchell Stringer; 11 Alex Szostak; 12 Ged Corcoran; 27 Tommy Trayler. Subs (all used): 9 Grant Edwards; 14 Andy Boothroyd; 15 Sam Barlow; 22 Ryan Hepworth.
Tries: Ropati (15), Lindsay (18), Szostak (23), Wood (79); **Goals:** Stringer 2/2, Lindsay 0/2.
Rugby Leaguer & League Express Men of the Match: *Vikings:* John Duffy; *Eagles:* Brendon Lindsay.
Penalty count: 10-3; **Half-time:** 8-16;
Referee: James Child; **Attendance:** 3,181.

Leigh's Nicky Stanton finds his path blocked by Widnes duo Richard Varkulis and Lee Doran

BARROW RAIDERS 24 HALIFAX 26

RAIDERS: 1 Gary Broadbent; 2 Mike Backhouse; 3 Ian Bell; 4 Liam Harrison; 5 James Nixon; 6 Liam Finch; 7 Liam Campbell; 8 Brett McDermott; 9 Andy Ellis; 16 Jamie Butler; 14 Paul Noone; 12 Martin Ostler; 11 Andrew Brocklehurst. Subs: 15 Chris Young; 26 Zebastian Luisi; 21 Joe McKenna (not used); 28 Nathan Mossop (not used). **Tries:** Campbell (8), Brocklehurst (31), Ostler (40), Young (71); **Goals:** Noone 4/5.
HALIFAX: 4 Shad Royston; 1 Miles Greenwood; 6 Dwayne Barker; 2 Lee Patterson; 5 James Haley; 19 Mick Govin; 7 Ben Black; 21 Neil Cherryholme; 13 Bob Beswick; 8 Matt James; 11 David Larder; 15 Mark Roberts; 12 Paul Smith. Subs (all used): 9 Sean Penkywicz; 22 David Wrench; 16 Said Tamghart; 17 Frank Watene. **Tries:** Larder (14), Greenwood (20), Penkywicz (43), James (49), Beswick (60); **Goals:** Govin 3/5.
Rugby Leaguer & League Express Men of the Match: *Raiders:* Martin Ostler; *Halifax:* David Larder.
Penalty count: 9-10; **Half-time:** 16-8;
Referee: Matthew Thomasson; **Attendance:** 1,918.

Sunday 29th March 2009

DONCASTER 18 LEIGH CENTURIONS 24

DONCASTER: 3 Andreas Bauer; 26 Gareth Carey; 19 Ryan Steen; 34 Luke May; 5 Wayne Reittie; 6 Kyle Briggs; 7 Paul Handforth; 28 Jamie Bovill; 9 Craig Cook; 15 Mark Castle; 11 Peter Green; 17 Ross Divorty; 13 Josh Weeden. Subs (all used): 22 Andy Speake; 29 Matt Carbutt; 16 Nathan Freer; 27 Al Rounding. **Tries:** Carbutt (29, Cook (56), Bauer (67); **Goals:** Briggs 3/3.
CENTURIONS: 14 Ian Mort; 2 David Alstead; 1 Stuart Donlan; 15 Adam Higson; 3 Steve Maden; 17 Lee Marsh; 7 Ian Watson; 8 Andy Hobson; 9 Dave McConnell; 16 Chris Hill; 29 Lee Wingfield; 12 James Taylor; 27 Anthony Rourke. Subs (all used): 4 Anthony Stewart; 40 Kurt Haggerty; 28 Danny Meekin; 10 Mike Morrison. **Tries:** Mort (23, 25), Haggerty (39), Hobson (42); **Goals:** Mort 4/4.
Sin bin: Morrison (55) – high tackle.
Rugby Leaguer & League Express Men of the Match: *Doncaster:* Mark Castle; *Centurions:* Anthony Rourke.
Penalty count: 12-3; **Half-time:** 6-18;
Referee: Ronnie Laughton; **Attendance:** 827.

ROUND 4

Thursday 9th April 2009

SHEFFIELD EAGLES 22 DONCASTER 23

EAGLES: 1 Jonny Woodcock; 28 Damian Gibson; 3 Menzie Yere; 23 Tangi Ropati; 5 Ashley Thackeray; 6 Brendon Lindsay; 19 Kyle Wood; 8 Jack Howieson; 20 Matty Brooks; 10 Mitchell Stringer; 11 Alex Szostak; 12 Ged Corcoran; 13 Dane McDonald. Subs (all used): 21 Aaron Groom; 15 Sam Barlow; 24 Matt Whitaker; 22 Ryan Hepworth. **Tries:** Yere (18, 32, 51), Groom (43); **Goals:** Woodcock 3/4.
DONCASTER: 3 Andreas Bauer; 26 Gareth Carey; 19 Ryan Steen; 34 Luke May; 5 Wayne Reittie; 6 Kyle Briggs; 7 Paul Handforth; 15 Mark Castle; 9 Craig Cook; 29 Matt Carbutt; 11 Peter Green; 17 Ross Divorty; 13 Josh Weeden. Subs (all used): 27 Al Rounding; 24 Jake Bassinder; 16 Nathan Freer; 28 Jamie Bovill. **Tries:** Carey (1), P Handforth (3), Castle (46); **Goals:** Briggs 5/5; **Field goal:** P Handforth (76).
Rugby Leaguer & League Express Men of the Match: *Eagles:* Menzie Yere; *Doncaster:* Craig Cook.
Penalty count: 8-11; **Half-time:** 10-14;
Referee: Craig Halloran; **Attendance:** 1,209.

HALIFAX 72 BATLEY BULLDOGS 0

HALIFAX: 1 Miles Greenwood; 5 James Haley; 2 Lee Patterson; 4 Shad Royston; 23 Rob Worrincy; 9 Sean Penkywicz; 7 Ben Black; 21 Neil Cherryholme; 13 Bob Beswick; 22 David Wrench; 18 Andy Bowman; 15 Mark Roberts; 6 Dwayne Barker. Subs (all used): 8 Matt James; 10 Dana Wilson; 14 Mark Gleeson; 25 Anthony Bowman. **Tries:** Royston (17), Penkywicz (21, 53), James (33, 49), Black (42), Andy Bowman (45, 64, 70), Worrincy (53), Greenwood (55), Gleeson (75); **Goals:** Patterson 12/12.
BULLDOGS: 1 Ian Preece; 18 Jermaine McGilvary; 14 John Gallagher; 4 Danny Maun; 5 John Campbell; 31 Stuart Young; 7 Paul Mennell; 20 David Tootill; 6 Mark Barlow; 10 Luke Stenchion; 21 Nathan Armitage; 17 Craig Potter; 8 Byron Smith. Subs (all used): 13 Ashley Lindsay; 16 Jon Simpson; 25 Glen Reid; 33 Danny Samuels.
Sin bin: Reid (39) – interference.
Rugby Leaguer & League Express Men of the Match: *Halifax:* Andy Bowman; *Bulldogs:* Stuart Young.
Penalty count: 16-7; **Half-time:** 18-0;
Referee: James Child; **Attendance:** 2,184.

Friday 10th April 2009

BARROW RAIDERS 18 WHITEHAVEN 12

RAIDERS: 1 Gary Broadbent; 19 Chris Larkin; 26 Zebastian Luisi; 4 Liam Harrison; 5 James Nixon; 6 Liam Finch; 7 Liam Campbell; 8 Brett McDermott; 9 Andy Ellis; 16 Jamie Butler; 22 Ned Catic; 12 Martin Ostler; 11 Andrew Brocklehurst. Subs (all used): 15 Chris Young; 13 Andy Bracek; 34 Lee Mossop; 14 Paul Noone. **Tries:** Butler (9), L Mossop (34), Brocklehurst (37); **Goals:** Brocklehurst 1/1, Noone 2/2.
Sin bin: Brocklehurst (14) - fighting.
WHITEHAVEN: 1 Craig Benson; 5 Ade Adebisi; 4 Derry Eilbeck; 18 John Patrick; 2 Craig Calvert; 7 Leroy Joe; 24 Gregg McNally; 12 Spencer Miller; 9 Graeme Mattinson; 10 Karl Edmondson; 13 Scott McAvoy; 15 Andy Gorski; 25 Jamie Theoharurs. Subs (all used): 32 Chris Smith; 16 Ryan McDonald; 31 Dexter Miller; 19 Kyle Amor. **Tries:** Joe (22), McNally (64); **Goals:** McNally 2/3.
Sin bin: McDonald (14) - fighting.
Rugby Leaguer & League Express Men of the Match: *Raiders:* Gary Broadbent; *Whitehaven:* Leroy Joe.
Penalty count: 10-12; **Half-time:** 18-6;
Referee: Robert Hicks; **Attendance:** 3,202.

WIDNES VIKINGS 8 LEIGH CENTURIONS 10

VIKINGS: 1 Loz Wildbore; 2 Dean Gaskell; 3 Richard Varkulis; 16 Gavin Dodd; 22 Paddy Flynn; 6 Anthony Thackeray; 7 James Webster; 19 Michael Ostick; 9 Mark Smith; 10 Jim Gannon; 11 Lee Doran; 24 Josh Simm; 14 John Duffy. Subs: 17 Ben Kavanagh; 20 Sam Thompson; 21 Scott Yates; 23 Shane Grady (not used). **Try:** Wildbore (9); **Goals:** Dodd 2/2.
CENTURIONS: 14 Ian Mort; 5 Nicky Stanton; 1 Stuart Donlan; 18 Sam Reay; 3 Steve Maden; 17 Lee Marsh; 7 Ian Watson; 8 Andy Hobson; 9 Dave McConnell; 16 Chris Hill; 15 Adam Higson; 12 James Taylor; 36 Kurt Haggerty. Subs (all used): 10 Mike Morrison; 11 Dave Armitstead; 26 Jamie Durbin; 28 Danny Meekin. **Tries:** Donlan (63), Mort (79); **Goals:** Mort 1/2.
Rugby Leaguer & League Express Men of the Match: *Vikings:* Jim Gannon; *Centurions:* Dave Armitstead.
Penalty count: 15-9; **Half-time:** 6-0;
Referee: Ronnie Laughton; **Attendance:** 4,354.

GATESHEAD THUNDER 2 FEATHERSTONE ROVERS 23

THUNDER: 3 Kevin Neighbour; 18 Robin Peers; 1 Ben McAlpine; 4 Dylan Nash; 5 Stewart Sanderson; 6 Neil Thorman; 7 Luke Branighan; 8 Jason Payne; 9 Andrew Henderson; 17 Chris Parker; 12 Michael Knowles; 29 Rhys Clare; 22 Jamie Russo. Subs (all used): 14 Ryan Clarke; 32 James Cording; 23 Jonny Scott; 21 Ryan McBride.
Goals: Knowles 1/2.
ROVERS: 1 Tom Saxton; 26 Sam Smeaton; 4 Andy Kirk; 3 Ian Hardman; 5 Jon Steel; 6 Iestyn Harris; 7 Andy Kain; 8 Tony Tonks; 16 Joe McLocklan; 10 Stuart Dickens; 11 Matty Dale; 18 Tim Spears; 12 Jamie Field. Subs (all used): 14 Tom Haughey; 24 Jon Fallon; 9 Jack Lee; 13 Richard Blakeway. **Tries:** Field (14), Harris (45), Lee (77); **Goals:** Dickens 5/5; **Field goal:** Harris (72).
Rugby Leaguer & League Express Men of the Match: *Thunder:* Kevin Neighbour; *Rovers:* Tony Tonks.
Penalty count: 8-7; **Half-time:** 2-8;
Referee: Gareth Hewer; **Attendance:** 651.

ROUND 5

Monday 13th April 2009

LEIGH CENTURIONS 16 BARROW RAIDERS 25

CENTURIONS: 14 Ian Mort; 3 Steve Maden; 18 Sam Reay; 1 Stuart Donlan; 5 Nicky Stanton; 17 Lee Marsh; 7 Ian Watson; 10 Mike Morrison; 9 Dave McConnell; 16 Chris Hill; 27 Anthony Rourke; 12 James Taylor; 37 Kurt Haggerty. Subs (all used): 26 Jamie Durbin; 11 Dave Armitstead; 4 Anthony Stewart; 28 Danny Meekin.
Tries: Rourke (6), Mort (36), Stanton (39);
Goals: Mort 2/3.
RAIDERS: 1 Gary Broadbent; 19 Chris Larkin; 26 Zebastian Luisi; 4 Liam Harrison; 5 James Nixon; 6 Liam Finch; 27 Darren Holt; 16 Jamie Butler; 9 Andy Ellis; 13 Andy Bracek; 22 Ned Catic; 14 Paul Noone; 11 Andrew Brocklehurst. Subs (all used): 8 Brett McDermott; 15 Chris Young; 34 Lee Mossop; 12 Martin Ostler.
Tries: Nixon (50), L Finch (61), Ellis (73), Catic (75);
Goals: Holt 4/5; **Field goal:** Holt (79).
Rugby Leaguer & League Express Men of the Match:
Centurions: Dave McConnell; *Raiders:* Darren Holt.
Penalty count: 6-7; **Half-time:** 16-2;
Referee: Gareth Hewer; **Attendance:** 2,177.

BATLEY BULLDOGS 22 TOULOUSE OLYMPIQUE 60

BULLDOGS: 1 Ian Preece; 5 John Campbell; 28 Daryl Cardiss; 4 Danny Maun; 18 Jermaine McGilvary; 31 Stuart Young; 7 Paul Mennell; 8 Byron Smith; 29 Gareth Greenwood; 35 Jack Watson; 11 Kevin Crouthers; 21 Nathan Armitage; 14 John Gallagher. Subs (all used): 13 Ashley Lindsay; 17 Craig Potter; 16 Jon Simpson; 10 Luke Stenchion.
Tries: McGilvary (18), Preece (27), Young (62), Lindsay (64); **Goals:** Mennell 3/4.
OLYMPIQUE: 1 Rory Bromley; 2 Sebastien Payen; 3 Sebastian Planas; 4 Damien Couturier; 21 Bruno Ormeno; 6 Constant Villegas; 7 Nathan Wynn; 8 Brendan Worth; 9 Martin Mitchell; 10 Mathieu Griffi; 11 Tim Wynn; 14 Anton Maria; 20 Sylvain Houles. Subs (all used): 13 Eric Anselme; 16 Olivier Pramil; 12 Matthieu Almarcha; 22 Nicholas Faure.
Tries: Houles (10), Ormeno (21, 76), Almarcha (34), Maria (40, 41), Payen (50), Couturier (52, 78), N Wynn (56, 70); **Goals:** N Wynn 7/10, Couturier 1/1.
Sin bin: N Wynn (6) - dissent;
Mitchell (62) - late challenge.
Rugby Leaguer & League Express Men of the Match:
Bulldogs: Danny Maun; *Olympique:* Nathan Wynn.
Penalty count: 6-6; **Half-time:** 10-22;
Referee: Robert Hicks; **Attendance:** 662.

FEATHERSTONE ROVERS 20 SHEFFIELD EAGLES 12

ROVERS: 1 Tom Saxton; 26 Sam Smeaton; 3 Ian Hardman; 4 Andy Kirk; 5 Jon Steel; 6 Iestyn Harris; 7 Andy Kain; 8 Tony Tonks; 16 Joe McLocklan; 10 Stuart Dickens; 11 Matty Dale; 12 Jamie Field; 18 Tim Spears. Subs (all used): 9 Jack Lee; 24 Jon Fallon; 14 Tom Haughey; 13 Richard Blakeway.
Tries: Steel (28), A Kain (53), Kirk (65);
Goals: Dickens 4/4, Harris 0/1.
Sin bin: Hardman (79) - interference.
EAGLES: 1 Jonny Woodcock; 2 Bolu Fagborun; 3 Menzie Yere; 23 Tangi Ropati; 5 Ashley Thackeray; 6 Brendon Lindsay; 19 Kyle Wood; 8 Jack Howieson; 7 Gavin Brown; 10 Mitchell Stringer; 11 Alex Szostak; 27 Tommy Trayler; 9 Grant Edwards. Subs (all used): 21 Aaron Groom; 22 Ryan Hepworth; 13 Dane McDonald; 12 Ged Corcoran.
Tries: Thackeray (11), Hepworth (38);
Goals: Woodcock 2/3.
Sin bin: Hepworth (47) - high tackle;
Stringer (50) - interference.
Rugby Leaguer & League Express Men of the Match:
Rovers: Ian Hardman; *Eagles:* Gavin Brown.
Penalty count: 15-11; **Half-time:** 4-10;
Referee: Jamie Leahy; **Attendance:** 1,612.

WHITEHAVEN 18 HALIFAX 24

WHITEHAVEN: 1 Craig Benson; 5 Ade Adebisi; 4 Derry Filbeck; 18 John Patrick; 2 Craig Calvert; 6 Carl Rudd; 24 Gregg McNally; 19 Kyle Amor; 9 Graeme Mattinson; 10 Karl Edmondson; 12 Spencer Miller; 15 Andy Gorski; 7 Leroy Joe. Subs (all used): 8 Marc Jackson; 25 Jamie Theohaurus; 13 Scott McAvoy; 34 Karl Long.
Tries: McNally (49, 53, 65); **Goals:** McNally 3/3.
Sin bin: Calvert (73) - dissent.
HALIFAX: 1 Miles Greenwood; 5 James Haley; 2 Lee Patterson; 6 Dwayne Barker; 23 Rob Worrincy; 19 Mick Govin; 7 Ben Black; 10 Dana Wilson; 13 Bob Beswick; 8 Matt James; 11 David Larder; 15 Mark Roberts; 4 Shad Royston. Subs (all used): 9 Sean Penkywicz; 14 Mark Gleeson; 16 Said Tamghart; 17 Frank Watene.
Tries: Black (13), Royston (18), Gleeson (23), Barker (31); **Goals:** Govin 4/5.
Rugby Leaguer & League Express Men of the Match:
Whitehaven: Kyle Amor; *Halifax:* Mark Roberts.
Penalty count: 7-7; **Half-time:** 0-24;
Referee: Ronnie Laughton; **Attendance:** 2,005.

DONCASTER 18 WIDNES VIKINGS 24

DONCASTER: 26 Gareth Carey; 35 Wayne Opie; 34 Luke May; 3 Andreas Bauer; 5 Wayne Reittie; 13 Josh Weeden; 7 Paul Handforth; 29 Matt Carbutt; 9 Craig Cook; 15 Mark Castle; 11 Peter Green; 17 Ross Divorty; 19 Ryan Steen. Subs (all used): 22 Andy Speake; 24 Jake Bassinder; 28 Jamie Bovill; 16 Nathan Freer.
Tries: May (51), Weeden (58), P Handforth (65);
Goals: P Handforth 3/3.
VIKINGS: 21 Scott Yates; 22 Paddy Flynn; 3 Richard Varkulis; 16 Gavin Dodd; 2 Dean Gaskell; 6 Anthony Thackeray; 7 James Webster; 19 Michael Ostick; 9 Mark Smith; 10 Jim Gannon; 24 Josh Simm; 11 Lee Doran; 1 Loz Wildbore. Subs (all used): 5 Danny Mills; 17 Ben Kavanagh; 20 Sam Thompson; 23 Shane Grady.
Tries: Yates (13), Dodd (29), Thompson (35), Thackeray (39), Doran (43); **Goals:** Dodd 0/2, Yates 2/4.
Rugby Leaguer & League Express Men of the Match:
Doncaster: Paul Handforth; *Vikings:* Anthony Thackeray.
Penalty count: 9-7; **Half-time:** 0-24;
Referee: Matthew Thomasson; **Attendance:** 831.

ROUND 6

Thursday 16th April 2009

GATESHEAD THUNDER 41 SHEFFIELD EAGLES 36

THUNDER: 6 Neil Thorman; 18 Robin Peers; 1 Ben McAlpine; 22 Jamie Russo; 5 Stewart Sanderson; 14 Ryan Clarke; 7 Luke Branighan; 8 Jason Payne; 9 Andrew Henderson; 17 Chris Parker; 4 Dylan Nash; 32 James Cording; 12 Michael Knowles. Subs (all used): 29 Rhys Clarke; 20 David Vernon; 23 Jonny Scott; 21 Ryan McBride.
Tries: Peers (11), Branighan (16), McAlpine (21), Sanderson (29, 35), Knowles (62), Parker (74);
Goals: Knowles 6/8; **Field goal:** Thorman (33).
EAGLES: 1 Jonny Woodcock; 2 Bolu Fagborun; 3 Menzie Yere; 23 Tangi Ropati; 5 Ashley Thackeray; 6 Brendon Lindsay; 21 Aaron Groom; 8 Jack Howieson; 20 Matty Brooks; 10 Mitchell Stringer; 11 Alex Szostak; 27 Tommy Trayler; 9 Grant Edwards. Subs (all used): 7 Gavin Brown; 22 Ryan Hepworth; 15 Sam Barlow; 13 Dane McDonald.
Tries: Groom (6), Barlow (39), Ropati (41, 45), McDonald (54), Fagborun (58), Hepworth (79);
Goals: Woodcock 4/7.
Rugby Leaguer & League Express Men of the Match:
Thunder: Luke Branighan; *Eagles:* Tangi Ropati.
Penalty count: 4-5; **Half-time:** 31-12;
Referee: James Child; **Attendance:** 715.

Friday 17th April 2009

WIDNES VIKINGS 40 BATLEY BULLDOGS 18

VIKINGS: 21 Scott Yates; 22 Paddy Flynn; 3 Richard Varkulis; 16 Gavin Dodd; 2 Dean Gaskell; 6 Anthony Thackeray; 7 James Webster; 19 Michael Ostick; 9 Mark Smith; 10 Jim Gannon; 24 Josh Simm; 11 Lee Doran; 1 Loz Wildbore. Subs (all used): 5 Danny Mills; 17 Ben Kavanagh; 23 Shane Grady; 20 Sam Thompson.
Tries: Varkulis (3), Gaskell (7), Yates (14), Thackeray (21), Kavanagh (35), Ostick (60), Dodd (69);
Goals: Yates 6/7.
BULLDOGS: 1 Ian Preece; 18 Jermaine McGilvary; 28 Daryl Cardiss; 4 Danny Maun; 5 John Campbell; 6 Mark Barlow; 7 Paul Mennell; 10 Luke Stenchion; 29 Gareth Greenwood; 8 Byron Smith; 11 Kevin Crouthers; 21 Nathan Armitage; 14 John Gallagher. Subs (all used): 13 Ashley Lindsay; 20 David Tootill; 35 Jack Watson; 16 Jon Simpson.
Tries: Crouthers (26), Mennell (39), Watson (48);
Goals: Barlow 3/3.
Rugby Leaguer & League Express Men of the Match:
Vikings: Mark Smith; *Bulldogs:* Paul Mennell.
Penalty count: 9-14; **Half-time:** 28-12;
Referee: Jamie Leahy; **Attendance:** 2,901.

Saturday 18th April 2009

TOULOUSE OLYMPIQUE 46 LEIGH CENTURIONS 10

OLYMPIQUE: 1 Rory Bromley; 2 Sebastien Payen; 3 Sebastien Planas; 4 Damien Couturier; 31 Clement Bienes; 6 Constant Villegas; 7 Nathan Wynn; 8 Brendan Worth; 9 Martin Mitchell; 10 Mathieu Griffi; 11 Tim Wynn; 14 Anton Maria; 20 Sylvain Houles. Subs (all used): 12 Matthieu Almarcha; 13 Eric Anselme; 16 Olivier Pramil; 22 Nicholas Faure.
Tries: Bromley (7), Maria (17), Planas (20, 73), Couturier (39), Bienes (48), Anselme (50), Griffi (79);
Goals: N Wynn 7/8.
Sin bin: Griffi (11) - fighting.
CENTURIONS: 14 Ian Mort; 5 Nicky Stanton; 1 Stuart Donlan; 15 Adam Higson; 3 Steve Maden; 23 Martyn Ridyard; 7 Ian Watson; 8 Andy Hobson; 9 Dave McConnell; 16 Chris Hill; 37 Kurt Haggerty; 12 James Taylor; 11 Dave Armitstead. Subs (all used): 10 Mike Morrison; 18 Sam Reay; 26 Jamie Durbin; 28 Danny Meekin.
Tries: Donlan (42), Durbin (77); **Goals:** Mort 1/2.
Sin bin: Higson (11) - fighting.
Rugby Leaguer & League Express Men of the Match:
Olympique: Nathan Wynn; *Centurions:* Stuart Donlan.
Penalty count: 6-12; **Half-time:** 22-0;
Referee: Matthew Thomasson;
Attendance: 3,507 *(at Stade Ernest Argeles, Blagnac).*

Sunday 19th April 2009

HALIFAX 44 DONCASTER 12

HALIFAX: 1 Miles Greenwood; 5 James Haley; 2 Lee Patterson; 6 Dwayne Barker; 23 Rob Worrincy; 9 Sean Penkywicz; 7 Ben Black; 21 Neil Cherryholme; 13 Bob Beswick; 8 Matt James; 11 David Larder; 12 Paul Smith; 4 Shad Royston. Subs (all used): 14 Mark Gleeson; 17 Frank Watene; 18 Andy Bowman; 22 David Wrench.
Tries: Worrincy (11, 60), Larder (23), Black (32), Andy Bowman (42), Patterson (53, 78), Haley (64);
Goals: Patterson 6/8.
Dismissal: Greenwood (63) - kicking.
DONCASTER: 3 Andreas Bauer; 2 Dean Colton; 19 Ryan Steen; 34 Luke May; 5 Wayne Reittie; 13 Josh Weeden; 7 Paul Handforth; 28 Jamie Bovill; 9 Craig Cook; 29 Matt Carbutt; 18 Craig Holt; 17 Ross Divorty; 11 Peter Green. Subs (all used): 16 Nathan Freer; 24 Jake Bassinder; 26 Gareth Carey; 35 Wayne Opie.
Tries: P Handforth (5, 70); **Goals:** P Handforth 2/2.
Rugby Leaguer & League Express Men of the Match:
Halifax: Rob Worrincy; *Doncaster:* Paul Handforth.
Penalty count: 5-7; **Half-time:** 16-6;
Referee: Robert Hicks; **Attendance:** 2,002.

WHITEHAVEN 16 FEATHERSTONE ROVERS 44

WHITEHAVEN: 1 Craig Benson; 5 Ade Adebisi; 13 Scott McAvoy; 18 John Patrick; 2 Craig Calvert; 6 Carl Rudd; 24 Gregg McNally; 8 Marc Jackson; 9 Graeme Mattinson; 10 Karl Edmondson; 12 Spencer Miller; 15 Andy Gorski; 7 Leroy Joe. Subs (all used): 19 Kyle Amor; 25 Jamie Theohaurus; 16 Ryan McDonald; 31 Dexter Miller.
Tries: McAvoy (21), McNally (27), Adebisi (69);
Goals: McNally 2/3.
ROVERS: 3 Ian Hardman; 26 Sam Smeaton; 4 Andy Kirk; 14 Tom Haughey; 5 Jon Steel; 6 Iestyn Harris; 7 Andy Kain; 8 Tony Tonks; 16 Joe McLocklan; 10 Stuart Dickens; 11 Matty Dale; 18 Tim Spears; 12 Jamie Field. Subs (all used): 9 Jack Lee; 24 Jon Fallon; 13 Richard Blakeway; 20 Stuart Kain.
Tries: McLocklan (11, 31), Field (42), Blakeway (59), Dale (63, 79), A Kain (66), S Kain (73);
Goals: Dickens 4/6, Harris 2/2.
Rugby Leaguer & League Express Men of the Match:
Whitehaven: Scott McAvoy; *Rovers:* Iestyn Harris.
Penalty count: 8-7; **Half-time:** 12-12;
Referee: Ronnie Laughton; **Attendance:** 1,411.

ROUND 7

Thursday 23rd April 2009

LEIGH CENTURIONS 16 FEATHERSTONE ROVERS 30

CENTURIONS: 14 Ian Mort; 3 Steve Maden; 18 Sam Reay; 19 Adam Rudd; 5 Nicky Stanton; 1 Stuart Donlan; 7 Ian Watson; 8 Andy Hobson; 9 Dave McConnell; 10 Mike Morrison; 16 Chris Hill; 12 James Taylor; 11 Dave Armitstead. Subs (all used): 26 Jamie Durbin; 28 Danny Meekin; 37 Kurt Haggerty; 13 Aaron Smith.
Tries: Rudd (23), Mort (71), Durbin (74);
Goals: Mort 2/3.
ROVERS: 3 Ian Hardman; 26 Sam Smeaton; 4 Andy Kirk; 14 Tom Haughey; 1 Tom Saxton; 6 Iestyn Harris; 7 Andy Kain; 8 Tony Tonks; 16 Joe McLocklan; 10 Stuart Dickens; 11 Matty Dale; 18 Tim Spears; 12 Jamie Field. Subs (all used): 9 Jack Lee; 13 Richard Blakeway; 24 Jon Fallon; 20 Stuart Kain.
Tries: Dickens (13), Hardman (42), Haughey (48), S Kain (57), Tonks (78); **Goals:** Dickens 5/6.
Rugby Leaguer & League Express Men of the Match:
Centurions: Ian Mort; *Rovers:* Stuart Dickens.
Penalty count: 5-6; **Half-time:** 6-8;
Referee: Gareth Hewer; **Attendance:** 2,307.

Saturday 25th April 2009

BARROW RAIDERS 52 BATLEY BULLDOGS 0

RAIDERS: 1 Gary Broadbent; 19 Chris Larkin; 26 Zebastian Luisi; 4 Liam Harrison; 5 James Nixon; 6 Liam Finch; 27 Darren Holt; 8 Brett McDermott; 9 Andy Ellis; 13 Andy Bracek; 22 Ned Catic; 34 Lee Mossop; 11 Andrew Brocklehurst. Subs (all used): 15 Chris Young; 16 Jamie Butler; 12 Martin Ostler; 14 Paul Noone.
Tries: Larkin (9, 46, 61), Ellis (15), Broadbent (18), Catic (23), Luisi (31), Nixon (36, 53, 75); **Goals:** Holt 6/10.
BULLDOGS: 1 Ian Preece; 18 Jermaine McGilvary; 28 Daryl Cardiss; 4 Danny Maun; 5 John Campbell; 6 Mark Barlow; 7 Paul Mennell; 35 Jack Watson; 13 Ashley Lindsay; 10 Luke Stenchion; 11 Kevin Crouthers; 20 David Tootill; 14 John Gallagher. Subs (all used): 29 Gareth Greenwood; 16 Jon Simpson; 8 Byron Smith; 12 Mark Toohey.
Rugby Leaguer & League Express Men of the Match:
Raiders: Zebastian Luisi; *Bulldogs:* Mark Barlow.
Penalty count: 4-8; **Half-time:** 30-0;
Referee: Matthew Thomasson; **Attendance:** 1,757.

Sunday 26th April 2009

DONCASTER 18 TOULOUSE OLYMPIQUE 48

DONCASTER: 34 Luke May; 26 Gareth Carey; 19 Ryan Steen; 3 Andreas Bauer; 5 Wayne Reittie; 13 Josh Weeden; 7 Paul Handforth; 28 Jamie Bovill; 9 Craig Cook; 29 Matt Carbutt; 11 Peter Green; 17 Ross Divorty; 24 Jake Bassinder. Subs (all used): 30 Wayne Opie; 8 Michael Haley; 15 Mark Castle; 18 Craig Holt.
Tries: Reittie (8), Holt (42), Castle (55), Opie (72);
Goals: P Handforth 0/2, Weeden 1/2.
OLYMPIQUE: 1 Rory Bromley; 2 Sebastien Payen; 3 Sebastien Planas; 4 Damien Couturier; 31 Clement Bienes; 6 Constant Villegas; 7 Nathan Wynn; 8 Brendan Worth; 9 Martin Mitchell; 10 Mathieu Griffi; 11 Tim Wynn; 13 Eric Anselme; 20 Sylvain Houles. Subs (all used): 12 Matthieu Almarcha; 16 Olivier Pramil; 22 Nicholas Faure; 14 Anton Maria.
Tries: Mitchell (3, 40), Almarcha (37), N Wynn (60), Bromley (64, 76), T Wynn (67), Faure (80);
Goals: N Wynn 8/8.

Rugby Leaguer & League Express Men of the Match: *Doncaster:* Peter Green; *Olympique:* Rory Bromley.
Penalty count: 8-7; **Half-time:** 4-18;
Referee: James Child; **Attendance:** 1,089.

HALIFAX 72 GATESHEAD THUNDER 28

HALIFAX: 1 Miles Greenwood; 5 James Haley; 2 Lee Patterson; 6 Dwayne Barker; 23 Rob Worrincy; 9 Sean Penkywicz; 7 Ben Black; 21 Neil Cherryholme; 13 Bob Beswick; 8 Matt James; 15 Mark Roberts; 18 Andy Bowman; 4 Shad Royston. Subs (all used): 14 Mark Gleeson; 16 Said Tamghart; 19 Mick Govin; 22 David Wrench.
Tries: James (9, 69), Royston (12, 20, 45), Black (22), Barker (25), Tamghart (34), Greenwood (39, 47), Penkywicz (52), Wrench (64); **Goals:** Patterson 12/12.
THUNDER: 6 Neil Thorman; 18 Robin Peers; 1 Ben McAlpine; 4 Dylan Nash; 5 Stewart Sanderson; 14 Ryan Clarke; 7 Luke Branighan; 8 Jason Payne; 9 Andrew Henderson; 17 Chris Parker; 32 James Cording; 12 Michael Knowles; 29 Rhys Clarke. Subs (all used): 10 Tabua Cakacaka; 20 David Vernon; 28 Mark Dack; 34 Dean Andrews.
Tries: McAlpine (4, 28), Peers (33), Cording (60, 72), Sanderson (74); **Goals:** Knowles 1/5, McAlpine 1/1.
Rugby Leaguer & League Express Men of the Match: *Halifax:* Ben Black; *Thunder:* Dylan Nash.
Penalty count: 8-5; **Half-time:** 42-14;
Referee: Craig Halloran; **Attendance:** 2,022.

SHEFFIELD EAGLES 20 WIDNES VIKINGS 22

EAGLES: 1 Jonny Woodcock; 2 Bolu Fagborun; 3 Menzie Yere; 23 Tangi Ropati; 4 Mike Roby; 6 Brendon Lindsay; 21 Aaron Groom; 8 Jack Howieson; 14 Andy Boothroyd; 22 Ryan Hepworth; 11 Alex Szostak; 24 Matt Whitaker; 9 Grant Edwards. Subs (all used): 13 Dane McDonald; 19 Kyle Wood; 10 Mitchell Stringer; 15 Sam Barlow.
Tries: Fagborun (5), Ropati (58), Lindsay (63), Roby (78); **Goals:** Woodcock 2/5.
VIKINGS: 21 Scott Yates; 2 Dean Gaskell; 4 Toa Kohe-Love; 16 Gavin Dodd; 22 Paddy Flynn; 6 Anthony Thackeray; 7 James Webster; 19 Michael Ostick; 9 Mark Smith; 10 Jim Gannon; 24 Josh Simm; 12 Richard Fletcher; 14 John Duffy. Subs (all used): 1 Loz Wildbore; 3 Richard Varkulis; 17 Ben Kavanagh; 20 Sam Thompson.
Tries: Varkulis (15), Duffy (22), Webster (30), Fletcher (34); **Goals:** Yates 3/4.
Rugby Leaguer & League Express Men of the Match: *Eagles:* Brendon Lindsay; *Vikings:* Mark Smith.
Penalty count: 8-5; **Half-time:** 4-22;
Referee: Ronnie Laughton; **Attendance:** 1,231.

ROUND 8

Thursday 30th April 2009

FEATHERSTONE ROVERS 26 HALIFAX 39

ROVERS: 3 Ian Hardman; 1 Tom Saxton; 4 Andy Kirk; 14 Tom Haughey; 5 Jon Steel; 6 Iestyn Harris; 7 Andy Kain; 8 Tony Tonks; 16 Joe McLocklan; 10 Stuart Dickens; 11 Matty Dale; 18 Tim Spears; 12 Jamie Field. Subs (all used): 24 Jon Fallon; 9 Jack Lee; 20 Stuart Kain; 15 James Houston.
Tries: Harris (13), Steel (36), A Kain (54), Haughey (64), Hardman (79); **Goals:** Harris 1/2, Dickens 2/3.
HALIFAX: 1 Miles Greenwood; 2 Lee Patterson; 15 Mark Roberts; 6 Dwayne Barker; 5 James Haley; 9 Sean Penkywicz; 7 Ben Black; 22 David Wrench; 13 Bob Beswick; 8 Matt James; 11 David Larder; 12 Paul Smith; 4 Shad Royston. Subs (all used): 14 Mark Gleeson; 10 Dana Wilson; 16 Said Tamghart; 17 Frank Watene.
Tries: Black (3, 26), Royston (21, 74), Tamghart (42), Penkywicz (71); **Goals:** Patterson 7/7;
Field goal: Penkywicz (75).
Rugby Leaguer & League Express Men of the Match: *Rovers:* Tom Haughey; *Halifax:* Sean Penkywicz.
Penalty count: 12-9; **Half-time:** 10-20;
Referee: James Child; **Attendance:** 2,673.

Friday 1st May 2009

GATESHEAD THUNDER 45 DONCASTER 42

THUNDER: 5 Stewart Sanderson; 18 Robin Peers; 1 Ben McAlpine; 4 Dylan Nash; 26 Crawford Matthews; 6 Neil Thorman; 7 Luke Branighan; 17 Chris Parker; 9 Andrew Henderson; 10 Tabua Cakacaka; 12 Michael Knowles; 32 James Cording; 14 Ryan Clarke. Subs (all used): 15 Matt Barron; 29 Rhys Clarke; 21 Ryan McBride; 33 Sam Crowther.
Tries: Knowles (3, 9), Henderson (7), McAlpine (15), Barron (25), Branighan (46), Peers (63), Sanderson (73); **Goals:** Knowles 6/8; **Field goal:** Ryan Clarke (71).
DONCASTER: 34 Luke May; 26 Gareth Carey; 19 Ryan Steen; 3 Andreas Bauer; 5 Wayne Reittie; 13 Josh Weeden; 7 Paul Handforth; 15 Mark Castle; 9 Craig Cook; 29 Matt Carbutt; 18 Craig Holt; 17 Ross Divorty; 11 Peter Green. Subs (all used): 22 Andy Speake; 30 Wayne Opie; 8 Michael Haley; 24 Jake Bassinder.
Tries: Haley (32), Cook (51), Carey (53), Divorty (56, 69), Steen (59, 77); **Goals:** Weeden 6/6, Speake 1/1.
Sin bin: Castle (2) - interference.
Rugby Leaguer & League Express Men of the Match: *Thunder:* Michael Knowles; *Doncaster:* Josh Weeden.
Penalty count: 4-11; **Half-time:** 28-6;
Referee: Jamie Leahy; **Attendance:** 405.

WIDNES VIKINGS 6 BARROW RAIDERS 27

VIKINGS: 1 Loz Wildbore; 2 Dean Gaskell; 4 Toa Kohe-Love; 32 Steve Tyrer; 22 Paddy Flynn; 6 Anthony Thackeray; 7 James Webster; 19 Michael Ostick; 9 Mark Smith; 10 Jim Gannon; 11 Lee Doran; 3 Richard Varkulis; 14 John Duffy. Subs (all used): 26 Steve Bannister; 16 Gavin Dodd; 20 Sam Thompson; 17 Ben Kavanagh.
Try: Bannister (76); **Goals:** Tyrer 1/1.
RAIDERS: 1 Gary Broadbent; 19 Chris Larkin; 26 Zebastian Luisi; 4 Liam Harrison; 5 James Nixon; 27 Darren Holt; 6 Liam Finch; 8 Brett McDermott; 9 Andy Ellis; 16 Jamie Butler; 14 Paul Noone; 12 Martin Ostler; 11 Andrew Brocklehurst. Subs (all used): 15 Chris Young; 20 Nick Beech; 22 Ned Catic; 34 Lee Mossop.
Tries: L Finch (16), Young (34), Harrison (43), Luisi (46); **Goals:** Holt 5/5; **Field goal:** Holt (66).
Rugby Leaguer & League Express Men of the Match: *Vikings:* Jim Gannon; *Raiders:* Darren Holt.
Penalty count: 8-10; **Half-time:** 0-14;
Referee: Robert Hicks; **Attendance:** 3,290.

Saturday 2nd May 2009

TOULOUSE OLYMPIQUE 38 WHITEHAVEN 12

OLYMPIQUE: 1 Rory Bromley; 31 Teli Pelo; 3 Sebastien Planas; 4 Damien Couturier; 5 Joris Canton; 6 Constant Villegas; 7 Nathan Wynn; 11 Tim Wynn; 9 Martin Mitchell; 10 Mathieu Griffi; 13 Eric Anselme; 14 Anton Maria; 20 Sylvain Houles. Subs (all used): 12 Matthieu Almarcha; 16 Olivier Pramil; 23 Cedric Gay; 22 Nicholas Faure.
Tries: Couturier (4), Villegas (20, 55), Bromley (25), Anselme (50), Griffi (60); **Goals:** N Wynn 7/7.
Sin bin: Anselme (27) - late challenge.
WHITEHAVEN: 1 Craig Benson; 5 Ade Adebisi; 13 Scott McAvoy; 3 Rob Jackson; 2 Craig Calvert; 24 Gregg McNally; 34 Tane Manihera; 19 Kyle Amor; 9 Graeme Mattinson; 10 Karl Edmondson; 12 Spencer Miller; 15 Andy Gorski; 7 Leroy Joe. Subs (all used): 8 Marc Jackson; 25 Jamie Theohaurus; 16 Ryan McDonald; 11 Howard Hill.
Tries: Mattinson (36), Adebisi (79); **Goals:** McNally 2/2.
Rugby Leaguer & League Express Men of the Match: *Olympique:* Constant Villegas; *Whitehaven:* Graeme Mattinson.
Penalty count: 9-14; **Half-time:** 20-6;
Referee: Greg Dolan; **Attendance:** 2,121.

Monday 4th May 2009

BATLEY BULLDOGS 16 LEIGH CENTURIONS 18

BULLDOGS: 1 Ian Preece; 2 Ben Feehan; 6 Mark Barlow; 4 Danny Maun; 18 Jermaine McGilvary; 28 Daryl Cardiss; 7 Paul Mennell; 35 Jack Watson; 29 Gareth Greenwood; 10 Luke Stenchion; 11 Kevin Crouthers; 8 Byron Smith; 14 John Gallagher. Subs (all used): 23 Chris Buttery; 17 Craig Potter; 16 Jon Simpson; 13 Ashley Lindsay.
Tries: McGilvary (60), Feehan (68, 76); **Goals:** Barlow 2/3.
CENTURIONS: 14 Ian Mort; 1 Stuart Donlan; 2 David Alstead; 4 Anthony Stewart; 3 Steve Maden; 26 Jamie Durbin; 7 Ian Watson; 16 Chris Hill; 9 Dave McConnell; 10 Mike Morrison; 37 Macgraff Leuluai; 11 Dave Armitstead; 13 Aaron Smith. Subs (all used): 19 Adam Rudd; 12 James Taylor; 8 Andy Hobson; 28 Danny Meekin.
Tries: Durbin (4, 12), Donlan (17); **Goals:** Mort 3/3.
Sin bin: A Smith (48) - high tackle on McGilvary; Mort (76) - holding down.
Rugby Leaguer & League Express Men of the Match: *Bulldogs:* Ashley Lindsay; *Centurions:* Ian Watson.
Penalty count: 8-4; **Half-time:** 0-18;
Referee: Craig Halloran; **Attendance:** 1,055.

ROUND 9

Thursday 7th May 2009

WHITEHAVEN 26 WIDNES VIKINGS 22

WHITEHAVEN: 32 John Lebbon; 5 Ade Adebisi; 18 John Patrick; 13 Scott McAvoy; 2 Craig Calvert; 6 Carl Rudd; 24 Gregg McNally; 22 Matthew Tunstall; 7 Leroy Joe; 10 Karl Edmondson; 11 Howard Hill; 12 Spencer Miller; 25 Jamie Theohaurus. Subs (all used): 19 Kyle Amor; 31 Dexter Miller; 28 Chris Smith; 15 Andy Gorski.
Tries: McNally (20, 23), D Miller (43), Calvert (45), Patrick (74); **Goals:** McNally 3/5.
VIKINGS: 1 Loz Wildbore; 22 Paddy Flynn; 3 Richard Varkulis; 32 Steve Tyrer; 16 Gavin Dodd; 14 John Duffy; 7 James Webster; 19 Michael Ostick; 9 Mark Smith; 10 Jim Gannon; 24 Josh Simm; 26 Steve Bannister; 13 Lee Paterson. Subs (all used): 6 Anthony Thackeray; 11 Lee Doran; 17 Ben Kavanagh; 20 Sam Thompson.
Tries: Bannister (8), Webster (39, 53, 56);
Goals: Tyrer 3/5.
Rugby Leaguer & League Express Men of the Match: *Whitehaven:* John Lebbon; *Vikings:* James Webster.
Penalty count: 11-12; **Half-time:** 12-8;
Referee: Matthew Thomasson; **Attendance:** 2,102.

ROUND 10

Thursday 14th May 2009

LEIGH CENTURIONS 23 WIDNES VIKINGS 16

CENTURIONS: 14 Ian Mort; 3 Steve Maden; 2 David Alstead; 4 Anthony Stewart; 5 Nicky Stanton; 1 Stuart Donlan; 7 Ian Watson; 10 Mike Morrison; 9 Dave McConnell; 16 Chris Hill; 11 Dave Armitstead; 19 Adam Rudd; 13 Aaron Smith. Subs (all used): 26 Jamie Durbin; 12 James Taylor; 8 Andy Hobson; 29 Lee Wingfield.
Tries: Hobson (26), Alstead (34, 38), Donlan (52); **Goals:** Mort 3/6; **Field goal:** Watson (72).
VIKINGS: 1 Loz Wildbore; 22 Paddy Flynn; 3 Richard Varkulis; 32 Steve Tyrer; 16 Gavin Dodd; 14 John Duffy; 7 James Webster; 19 Michael Ostick; 9 Mark Smith; 10 Jim Gannon; 24 Josh Simm; 26 Steve Bannister; 13 Lee Paterson. Subs (all used): 6 Anthony Thackeray; 11 Lee Doran; 17 Ben Kavanagh; 20 Sam Thompson.
Tries: Dodd (13), Webster (18), Ostick (45);
Goals: Tyrer 1/2, Bannister 1/2.
Rugby Leaguer & League Express Men of the Match: *Centurions:* Ian Watson; *Vikings:* Michael Ostick.
Penalty count: 11-10; **Half-time:** 14-10;
Referee: Gareth Hewer; **Attendance:** 2,556.

Saturday 16th May 2009

TOULOUSE OLYMPIQUE 22 BARROW RAIDERS 14

OLYMPIQUE: 1 Rory Bromley; 2 Sebastien Payen; 3 Sebastien Planas; 4 Damien Couturier; 21 Bruno Ormeno; 6 Constant Villegas; 7 Nathan Wynn; 8 Brendan Worth; 9 Martin Mitchell; 10 Mathieu Griffi; 11 Tim Wynn; 13 Eric Anselme; 20 Sylvain Houles. Subs (all used): 14 Anton Maria; 22 Nicholas Faure; 23 Cedric Gay; 33 Jean-Christophe Borlin.
Tries: Planas (5), Gay (57), Villegas (78);
Goals: N Wynn 5/5.
RAIDERS: 1 Gary Broadbent; 19 Chris Larkin; 26 Zebastian Luisi; 4 Liam Harrison; 5 James Nixon; 6 Liam Finch; 27 Darren Holt; 8 Brett McDermott; 9 Andy Ellis; 16 Jamie Butler; 22 Ned Catic; 14 Paul Noone; 11 Andrew Brocklehurst. Subs (all used): 15 Chris Young; 13 Andy Bracek; 12 Martin Ostler; 7 Liam Campbell.
Tries: Nixon (19), Larkin (31); **Goals:** Holt 3/4.
Rugby Leaguer & League Express Men of the Match: *Olympique:* Martin Mitchell; *Raiders:* Chris Young.
Penalty count: 10-8; **Half-time:** 10-12;
Referee: Craig Halloran; **Attendance:** 2,900.

Sunday 17th May 2009

FEATHERSTONE ROVERS 68 DONCASTER 12

ROVERS: 3 Ian Hardman; 5 Jon Steel; 4 Andy Kirk; 1 Tom Saxton; 20 Stuart Kain; 6 Iestyn Harris; 7 Andy Kain; 24 Jon Fallon; 9 Jack Lee; 15 James Houston; 11 Matty Dale; 17 Joe Hirst; 12 Jamie Field. Subs (all used): 19 Sean Hesketh; 16 Joe McLocklan; 18 Tim Spears; 27 Ian Bell.
Tries: Steel (15, 35, 43), Bell (31, 53, 60), A Kain (37, 79), Saxton (42, 63, 69), Hardman (72), Hesketh (74); **Goals:** Harris 1/5, McLocklan 7/8.
DONCASTER: 3 Andreas Bauer; 26 Gareth Carey; 19 Ryan Steen; 30 Wayne Opie; 2 Dean Colton; 13 Josh Weeden; 22 Andy Speake; 8 Michael Haley; 9 Craig Cook; 15 Mark Castle; 18 Craig Holt; 17 Ross Divorty; 11 Peter Green. Subs (all used): 5 Wayne Reittie; 24 Jake Bassinder; 33 Danny Richardson; 10 Alex Benson.
Tries: Divorty (3), Cook (19); **Goals:** Weeden 2/2.
Rugby Leaguer & League Express Men of the Match: *Rovers:* Joe Hirst; *Doncaster:* Josh Weeden.
Penalty count: 7-8; **Half-time:** 18-12;
Referee: Robert Hicks; **Attendance:** 1,577.

GATESHEAD THUNDER 34 WHITEHAVEN 38

THUNDER: 19 Nick Youngquest; 18 Robin Peers; 4 Dylan Nash; 25 Paul Franze; 1 Ben McAlpine; 6 Neil Thorman; 7 Luke Branighan; 10 Tabua Cakacaka; 9 Andrew Henderson; 17 Chris Parker; 12 Michael Knowles; 32 James Cording; 24 Kris Kahler. Subs (all used): 14 Ryan Clarke; 15 Matt Barron; 33 Sam Crowther; 34 Dean Andrews.
Tries: Cording (8), Franze (11, 77), Youngquest (25, 46), Kahler (39), McAlpine (50);
Goals: Knowles 2/5, McAlpine 1/2.
Sin bin: Knowles (21) - dissent.
WHITEHAVEN: 32 John Lebbon; 5 Ade Adebisi; 3 Rob Jackson; 13 Scott McAvoy; 2 Craig Calvert; 6 Carl Rudd; 24 Gregg McNally; 22 Matthew Tunstall; 7 Leroy Joe; 10 Karl Edmondson; 12 Spencer Miller; 15 Andy Gorski; 25 Jamie Theohaurus. Subs (all used): 11 Howard Hill; 19 Kyle Amor; 31 Dexter Miller; 28 Chris Smith.
Tries: Calvert (2, 15), Rudd (28), R Jackson (40), McAvoy (41), McNally (63, 65); **Goals:** McNally 5/7.
Rugby Leaguer & League Express Men of the Match: *Thunder:* Nick Youngquest; *Whitehaven:* Gregg McNally.
Penalty count: 10-10; **Half-time:** 20-20;
Referee: Ronnie Laughton; **Attendance:** 575.

HALIFAX 26 SHEFFIELD EAGLES 40

HALIFAX: 1 Miles Greenwood; 2 Lee Patterson; 5 James Haley; 6 Dwayne Barker; 23 Rob Worrincy; 9 Sean Penkywicz; 7 Ben Black; 8 Matt James; 13 Bob Beswick; 11 David Larder; 12 Paul Smith; 15 Mark Roberts; 4 Shad Royston. Subs (all used): 10 Dana Wilson; 16 Said Tamghart; 21 Neil Cherryholme; 30 Tom Hemingway.
Tries: Worrincy (2), Haley (32), Greenwood (49, 67, 76);
Goals: Patterson 3/5.
EAGLES: 1 Jonny Woodcock; 32 Danny Mills; 28 Damian Gibson; 23 Tangi Ropati; 2 Bolu Fagborun; 6 Brendon Lindsay; 19 Kyle Wood; 8 Jack Howieson; 20 Matty Brooks; 22 Ryan Hepworth; 11 Alex Szostak; 15 Sam Barlow; 9 Grant Edwards. Subs (all used): 10 Mitchell Stringer; 25 James Morrow; 14 Andy Boothroyd; 33 Joe Walsh.
Tries: Woodcock (7, 56), Gibson (15), Boothroyd (51), Barlow (72), Lindsay (80); **Goals:** Woodcock 8/8.
Rugby Leaguer & League Express Men of the Match: *Halifax:* Miles Greenwood; *Eagles:* Kyle Wood.
Penalty count: 10-6; **Half-time:** 10-14;
Referee: Jamie Leahy; **Attendance:** 2,212.

Batley's five-try hero Jermaine McGilvary in action against Whitehaven

ROUND 11

Thursday 21st May 2009

DONCASTER 4 HALIFAX 36

DONCASTER: 3 Andreas Bauer; 2 Dean Colton; 20 Mike Coady; 30 Wayne Opie; 5 Wayne Reittie; 13 Josh Weeden; 22 Andy Speake; 15 Mark Castle; 9 Craig Cook; 10 Alex Benson; 18 Craig Holt; 17 Ross Divorty; 19 Ryan Steen. Subs (all used): 23 Scott Smith; 24 Jake Bassinder; 21 Gary Ellery; 32 Craig Jones.
Try: Bauer (17); **Goals:** Weeden 0/1.
HALIFAX: 1 Miles Greenwood; 2 Lee Patterson; 4 Shad Royston; 6 Dwayne Barker; 5 James Haley; 9 Sean Penkywicz; 30 Tom Hemingway; 22 David Wrench; 13 Bob Beswick; 10 Dana Wilson; 11 David Larder; 18 Andy Bowman; 12 Paul Smith. Subs (all used): 8 Matt James; 14 Mark Gleeson; 16 Said Tamghart; 17 Frank Watene.
Tries: Barker (8), James (35), Tamghart (38), Penkywicz (60), Patterson (68), Gleeson (71), Royston (79); **Goals:** Patterson 4/7.
Rugby Leaguer & League Express Men of the Match: *Doncaster:* Josh Weeden; *Halifax:* Matt James.
Penalty count: 6-5; **Half-time:** 4-16;
Referee: Robert Hicks; **Attendance:** 1,096.

Saturday 23rd May 2009

SHEFFIELD EAGLES 58 TOULOUSE OLYMPIQUE 12

EAGLES: 1 Jonny Woodcock; 32 Danny Mills; 3 Menzie Yere; 23 Tangi Ropati; 28 Damian Gibson; 6 Brendon Lindsay; 19 Kyle Wood; 8 Jack Howieson; 20 Matty Brooks; 22 Ryan Hepworth; 11 Alex Szostak; 15 Sam Barlow; 9 Grant Edwards. Subs (all used): 14 Andy Boothroyd; 29 Peter Green; 33 Joe Walsh; 10 Mitchell Stringer.
Tries: Szostak (24), Walsh (27, 35), Ropati (30), Barlow (37, 75), Gibson (43), Green (46), Boothroyd (63), Mills (80); **Goals:** Woodcock 9/10.
OLYMPIQUE: 1 Rory Bromley; 2 Sebastien Payen; 3 Sebastien Planas; 4 Damien Couturier; 21 Bruno Ormeno; 6 Constant Villegas; 7 Nathan Wynn; 8 Brendan Worth; 9 Martin Mitchell; 10 Mathieu Griffi; 11 Tim Wynn; 13 Eric Anselme; 20 Sylvain Houles. Subs (all used): 14 Anton Maria; 12 Matthieu Almarcha; 23 Cedric Gay; 33 Jean-Christophe Borlin.
Tries: Bromley (60), Griffi (73); **Goals:** N Wynn 2/2.
Rugby Leaguer & League Express Men of the Match: *Eagles:* Jonny Woodcock; *Olympique:* Martin Mitchell.
Penalty count: 13-5; **Half-time:** 28-0;
Referee: James Child; **Attendance:** 809.

WIDNES VIKINGS 46 GATESHEAD THUNDER 30

VIKINGS: 16 Gavin Dodd; 22 Paddy Flynn; 3 Richard Varkulis; 15 Tim Hartley; 29 Kevin Penny; 14 John Duffy; 7 James Webster; 17 Ben Kavanagh; 9 Mark Smith; 10 Jim Gannon; 11 Lee Doran; 26 Steve Bannister; 13 Lee Paterson. Subs (all used): 6 Anthony Thackeray; 8 Iain Morrison; 24 Josh Simm; 28 Steve Pickersgill.
Tries: Doran (30, 72), Gannon (36), Thackeray (47), Dodd (52), Flynn (56), Penny (70), Bannister (78); **Goals:** Hartley 5/5, Dodd 2/3.
THUNDER: 19 Nick Youngquest; 1 Ben McAlpine; 4 Dylan Nash; 25 Paul Franze; 5 Stewart Sanderson; 6 Neil Thorman; 7 Luke Branighan; 10 Tabua Cakacaka; 9 Andrew Henderson; 24 Kris Kahler; 15 Matt Barron; 32 James Cording; 12 Michael Knowles. Subs (all used): 14 Ryan Clarke; 21 Ryan McBride; 33 Sam Crowther; 34 Liam Watts.
Tries: Nash (2), Henderson (15), Youngquest (18), Branighan (24), Franze (42); **Goals:** Knowles 5/5.
Sin bin: Nash (63) - dangerous challenge on Hartley.
Rugby Leaguer & League Express Men of the Match: *Vikings:* Lee Doran; *Thunder:* Andrew Henderson.
Penalty count: 12-13; **Half-time:** 12-24;
Referee: Craig Halloran; **Attendance:** 5,236.

Sunday 24th May 2009

BARROW RAIDERS 44 FEATHERSTONE ROVERS 12

RAIDERS: 1 Gary Broadbent; 19 Chris Larkin; 26 Zebastian Luisi; 4 Liam Harrison; 5 James Nixon; 6 Liam Finch; 27 Darren Holt; 8 Brett McDermott; 9 Andy Ellis; 13 Andy Bracek; 22 Ned Catic; 14 Paul Noone; 11 Andrew Brocklehurst. Subs (all used): 15 Chris Young; 16 Jamie Butler; 12 Martin Ostler; 7 Liam Campbell.
Tries: Nixon (15, 44, 61, 70), Catic (48, 52, 58), Campbell (75); **Goals:** Holt 6/8.
ROVERS: 3 Ian Hardman; 5 Jon Steel; 4 Andy Kirk; 14 Tom Haughey; 1 Tom Saxton; 6 Iestyn Harris; 7 Andy Kain; 10 Stuart Dickens; 16 Joe McLocklan; 11 Matty Dale; 18 Tim Spears; 17 Joe Hirst; 12 Jamie Field. Subs (all used): 28 Kyle Briggs; 8 Tony Tonks; 15 James Houston; 26 Sam Smeaton.
Tries: McLocklan (12), Haughey (34); **Goals:** Dickens 2/3.
Rugby Leaguer & League Express Men of the Match: *Raiders:* James Nixon; *Rovers:* Andy Kain.
Penalty count: 3-5; **Half-time:** 4-12;
Referee: Matthew Thomasson; **Attendance:** 1,995.

BATLEY BULLDOGS 48 WHITEHAVEN 24

BULLDOGS: 1 Ian Preece; 5 John Campbell; 11 Kevin Crouthers; 4 Danny Maun; 18 Jermaine McGilvary; 30 Paul Handforth; 7 Paul Mennell; 35 Jack Watson; 9 Kris Lythe; 17 Craig Potter; 23 Chris Buttery; 8 Byron Smith; 14 John Gallagher. Subs (all used): 29 Gareth Greenwood; 13 Ashley Lindsay; 16 Jon Simpson; 20 David Tootill.
Tries: McGilvary (7, 23, 30, 44, 80), Potter (16), Crouthers (26), Simpson (71);
Goals: Mennell 7/7, McGilvary 1/1.
WHITEHAVEN: 32 John Lebbon; 5 Ade Adebisi; 13 Scott McAvoy; 3 Rob Jackson; 27 Paul Ballard; 6 Carl Rudd; 24 Gregg McNally; 19 Kyle Amor; 7 Leroy Joe; 10 Karl Edmondson; 12 Spencer Miller; 15 Andy Gorski; 14 Daniel Barker. Subs (all used): 28 Chris Smith; 11 Howard Hill; 26 Soni Radovanovic; 31 Dexter Miller.
Tries: Adebisi (35), Joe (42), Gorski (69), Rudd (77);
Goals: McNally 3/3, Rudd 1/1.
Rugby Leaguer & League Express Men of the Match: *Bulldogs:* Jermaine McGilvary; *Whitehaven:* Chris Smith.
Penalty count: 9-7; **Half-time:** 30-6;
Referee: Dave Merrick; **Attendance:** 627.

ROUND 12

Thursday 28th May 2009

FEATHERSTONE ROVERS 30 LEIGH CENTURIONS 24

ROVERS: 3 Ian Hardman; 5 Jon Steel; 4 Andy Kirk; 27 Ian Bell; 1 Tom Saxton; 28 Kyle Briggs; 7 Andy Kain; 24 Jon Fallon; 16 Joe McLocklan; 10 Stuart Dickens; 18 Tim Spears; 14 Tom Haughey; 12 Jamie Field. Subs (all used): 17 Joe Hirst; 15 James Houston; 26 Sam Smeaton; 9 Jack Lee.
Tries: Bell (12), Fiold (36), Saxton (47, 70), Kirk (49), Hardman (78); **Goals:** Briggs 1/1, Dickens 2/5.
CENTURIONS: 14 Ian Mort; 5 Nicky Stanton; 4 Anthony Stewart; 2 David Alstead; 3 Steve Maden; 1 Stuart Donlan; 7 Ian Watson; 16 Chris Hill; 9 Dave McConnell; 10 Mike Morrison; 11 Dave Armittstead; 19 Adam Rudd; 13 Aaron Smith. Subs (all used): 12 James Taylor; 8 Andy Hobson; 38 Mick Nanyn; 29 Lee Wingfield.
Tries: Maden (20), Nanyn (57, 66), Morrison (73);
Goals: Mort 4/5.
Rugby Leaguer & League Express Men of the Match: *Rovers:* Tom Saxton; *Centurions:* Ian Watson.
Penalty count: 6-9; **Half-time:** 12-6;
Referee: Matthew Thomasson; **Attendance:** 1,535.

Saturday 30th May 2009

BARROW RAIDERS 26 SHEFFIELD EAGLES 18

RAIDERS: 1 Gary Broadbent; 19 Chris Larkin; 26 Zebastian Luisi; 4 Liam Harrison; 5 James Nixon; 6 Liam Finch; 27 Darren Holt; 8 Brett McDermott; 28 Nathan Mossop; 13 Andy Bracek; 22 Ned Catic; 14 Paul Noone; 11 Andrew Brocklehurst. Subs: 15 Chris Young; 16 Jamie Butler; 12 Martin Ostler; 17 Scott Kaighan (not used).
Tries: Nixon (8), Larkin (28, 59), Young (65), Holt (77);
Goals: Holt 3/5.
EAGLES: 28 Damian Gibson; 32 Danny Mills; 3 Menzie Yere; 23 Tangi Ropati; 5 Ashley Thackeray; 6 Brendon Lindsay; 19 Kyle Wood; 8 Jack Howieson; 20

Sheffield's Alex Szostak crosses for a try against Whitehaven

Brooks; 22 Ryan Hepworth; 11 Alex Szostak; 15 Sam Barlow; 9 Grant Edwards. Subs (all used): 14 Andy Boothroyd; 10 Mitchell Stringer; 29 Peter Green; 33 Joe Walsh.
Tries: Ropati (2), Lindsay (5), Szostak (56); **Goals:** Ropati 3/4.
Rugby Leaguer & League Express Men of the Match: *Raiders:* Chris Young; *Eagles:* Tangi Ropati.
Penalty count: 9-6; **Half-time:** 10-12;
Referee: Dave Merrick; **Attendance:** 1,693.

Sunday 31st May 2009

BATLEY BULLDOGS 40 WIDNES VIKINGS 34

BULLDOGS: 1 Ian Preece; 18 Jermaine McGilvary; 11 Kevin Crouthers; 4 Danny Maun; 28 Daryl Cardiss; 30 Paul Handforth; 7 Paul Mennell; 35 Jack Watson; 9 Kris Lythe; 17 Craig Potter; 8 Byron Smith; 23 Chris Buttery; 14 John Gallagher. Subs (all used): 29 Gareth Greenwood; 13 Ashley Lindsay; 16 Jon Simpson; 20 David Tootill.
Tries: McGilvary (21), Maun (25), Mennell (34), Lythe (51), Watson (61), Preece (65, 78), Tootill (74); **Goals:** Mennell 4/8.
VIKINGS: 16 Gavin Dodd; 22 Paddy Flynn; 3 Richard Varkulis; 14 Tim Hartley; 29 Kevin Penny; 6 Anthony Thackeray; 7 James Webster; 10 Jim Gannon; 9 Mark Smith; 19 Michael Ostick; 12 Richard Fletcher; 8 Iain Morrison; 11 Lee Doran. Subs (all used): 14 John Duffy; 24 Josh Simm; 17 Ben Kavanagh; 28 Steve Pickersgill.
Tries: Morrison (5, 11, 30), Flynn (16), Thackeray (45), Varkulis (48); **Goals:** Hartley 5/6.
Rugby Leaguer & League Express Men of the Match: *Bulldogs:* Paul Handforth; *Vikings:* Anthony Thackeray.
Penalty count: 7-4; **Half time:** 16-22;
Referee: Ronnie Laughton; **Attendance:** 1,089.

WHITEHAVEN 50 DONCASTER 12

WHITEHAVEN: 32 John Lebbon; 5 Ade Adebisi; 13 Scott McAvoy; 3 Rob Jackson; 27 Paul Ballard; 6 Carl Rudd; 24 Gregg McNally; 26 Soni Radovanovic; 25 Jamie Theoharaus; 10 Karl Edmondson; 11 Howard Hill; 12 Spencer Miller; 7 Leroy Joe. Subs (all used): 19 Kyle Amor; 28 Chris Smith; 15 Andy Gorski; 22 Matthew Tunstall.
Tries: McNally (6), Amor (16, 45), R Jackson (26), Ballard (34, 67, 76), C Smith (50), Adebisi (78); **Goals:** McNally 7/9.
DONCASTER: 3 Andreas Bauer; 2 Dean Colton; 20 Mike Coady; 30 Wayne Opie; 5 Wayne Reittie; 13 Josh Weeden; 9 Craig Cook; 8 Michael Haley; 19 Ryan Steen; 10 Alex Benson; 15 Mark Castle; 17 Ross Divorty; 24 Jake Bassinder. Subs (all used): 23 Scott Smith; 21 Gary Ellery; 28 Jamie Bovill; 35 Alex Palmer.
Tries: Bassinder (8), Cook (61); **Goals:** Weeden 2/2.

Sin bin: Bovill (44) - high tackle on Rudd.
Rugby Leaguer & League Express Men of the Match: *Whitehaven:* Kyle Amor; *Doncaster:* Josh Weeden.
Penalty count: 8-5; **Half-time:** 20-6;
Referee: Greg Dolan; **Attendance:** 1,362.

Sunday 7th June 2009

GATESHEAD THUNDER 16 TOULOUSE OLYMPIQUE 52

THUNDER: 6 Neil Thorman; 18 Robin Peers; 1 Ben McAlpine; 25 Paul Franze; 5 Stewart Sanderson; 13 Russ Aitken; 7 Luke Branighan; 34 Liam Watts; 14 Ryan Clarke; 21 Ryan McBride; 12 Michael Knowles; 32 James Cording; 24 Kris Kahler. Subs (all used): 17 Chris Parker; 15 Matt Barron; 33 Sam Crowther; 10 Tabua Cakacaka.
Tries: Aitken (34, 57), Franze (64); **Goals:** Knowles 2/3.
Sin bin: McBride (39) - late challenge.
OLYMPIQUE: 1 Rory Bromley; 2 Sebastien Payen; 3 Sebastien Planas; 4 Damien Couturier; 31 Kevin Luguoro; 6 Constant Villegas; 7 Nathan Wynn; 8 Brendan Worth; 9 Martin Mitchell; 10 Mathieu Griffi; 14 Anton Maria; 12 Matthieu Almarcha; 13 Eric Anselme. Subs (all used): 16 Olivier Pramil; 33 Jean-Christophe Borlin; 17 Yohan Barthau; 18 Adrien Viala.
Tries: Villegas (11, 75), Bromley (17, 22), Mitchell (29), Luguoro (45, 79), Anselme (53), Planas (67); **Goals:** N Wynn 8/10.
Rugby Leaguer & League Express Men of the Match: *Thunder:* Russ Aitken; *Olympique:* Nathan Wynn.
Penalty count: 3-5; **Half-time:** 6-24;
Referee: Jarred Maxwell; **Attendance:** 516.

ROUND 13

Saturday 13th June 2009

SHEFFIELD EAGLES 28 WHITEHAVEN 24

EAGLES: 1 Jonny Woodcock; 32 Danny Mills; 3 Menzie Yere; 23 Tangi Ropati; 28 Damian Gibson; 6 Brendon Lindsay; 19 Kyle Wood; 22 Ryan Hepworth; 20 Matty Brooks; 10 Mitchell Stringer; 11 Alex Szostak; 33 Joe Walsh; 29 Peter Green. Subs (all used): 9 Grant Edwards; 15 Sam Barlow; 16 Trevor Exton; 30 Michael Haley.
Tries: Brooks (5), Edwards (18), Szostak (25), Mills (39), Barlow (46); **Goals:** Woodcock 4/5.
WHITEHAVEN: 27 Paul Ballard; 5 Ade Adebisi; 13 Scott McAvoy; 3 Rob Jackson; 2 Craig Calvert; 6 Carl Rudd; 24 Gregg McNally; 26 Soni Radovanovic; 25 Jamie Theoharaus; 10 Karl Edmondson; 11 Howard Hill; 12 Spencer Miller; 7 Leroy Joe. Subs (all used): 28 Chris Smith; 19 Kyle Amor; 15 Andy Gorski; 22 Matthew Tunstall.
Tries: McNally (29), Ballard (32), McAvoy (34),

S Miller (54); **Goals:** McNally 4/4.
Rugby Leaguer & League Express Men of the Match: *Eagles:* Mitchell Stringer; *Whitehaven:* Leroy Joe.
Penalty count: 16-5; **Half-time:** 22-18;
Referee: Craig Halloran; **Attendance:** 811.

WIDNES VIKINGS 46 FEATHERSTONE ROVERS 22

VIKINGS: 16 Gavin Dodd; 2 Dean Gaskell; 4 Toa Kohe-Love; 32 Craig Hall; 29 Kevin Penny; 6 Anthony Thackeray; 7 James Webster; 10 Jim Gannon; 9 Mark Smith; 28 Steve Pickersgill; 12 Richard Fletcher; 35 Jon Grayshon; 8 Iain Morrison. Subs (all used): 3 Richard Varkulis; 11 Lee Doran; 15 Tim Hartley; 17 Ben Kavanagh.
Tries: Penny (8), Grayshon (23), Morrison (25), Webster (31), Dodd (39), Smith (44), Kohe-Love (61), Gaskell (75); **Goals:** Hall 7/8.
ROVERS: 3 Ian Hardman; 1 Tom Saxton; 14 Tom Haughey; 4 Andy Kirk; 5 Jon Steel; 28 Kyle Briggs; 7 Andy Kain; 24 Jon Fallon; 16 Joe McLocklan; 10 Stuart Dickens; 11 Matty Dale; 18 Tim Spears; 17 Joe Hirst. Subs (all used): 2 Waine Pryce; 9 Jack Lee; 8 Tony Tonks; 29 Ross Divorty.
Tries: Kirk (50), Haughey (54), Spears (69), Steel (80); **Goals:** Dickens 3/4.
Sin bin: Kirk (18) - interference.
Rugby Leaguer & League Express Men of the Match: *Vikings:* James Webster; *Rovers:* Ian Hardman.
Penalty count: 15-5; **Half-time:** 28-0;
Referee: James Child; **Attendance:** 3,278.

TOULOUSE OLYMPIQUE 32 BATLEY BULLDOGS 24

OLYMPIQUE: 1 Rory Bromley; 2 Sebastien Payen; 32 Florian Quintilla; 4 Damien Couturier; 31 Clement Bienes; 7 Nathan Wynn; 9 Martin Mitchell; 8 Brendan Worth; 23 Cedric Gay; 24 Jean-Christophe Borlin; 11 Tim Wynn; 17 Yohan Barthau; 12 Matthieu Almarcha. Subs (all used): 16 Olivier Pramil; 18 Adrien Viala; 21 Bruno Ormeno; 22 Nicholas Faure.
Tries: Mitchell (22), Gay (32), Couturier (48), Bromley (50), T Wynn (57); **Goals:** N Wynn 6/6.
Sin bin: Barthau (67) - holding down.
BULLDOGS: 1 Ian Preece; 18 Jermaine McGilvary; 11 Kevin Crouthers; 4 Danny Maun; 5 John Campbell; 30 Paul Handforth; 7 Paul Mennell; 15 Anthony Henderson; 9 Kris Lythe; 17 Craig Potter; 8 Byron Smith; 23 Chris Buttery; 13 Ashley Lindsay. Subs (all used): 6 Mark Barlow; 14 John Gallagher; 16 Jon Simpson; 20 David Tootill.
Tries: Mennell (19), Maun (39), Handforth (65), Simpson (69); **Goals:** Mennell 3/3, Handforth 1/1.
Rugby Leaguer & League Express Men of the Match: *Olympique:* Martin Mitchell; *Bulldogs:* Paul Mennell.
Penalty count: 7-7; **Half-time:** 12-12;
Referee: Peter Brooke; **Attendance:** 2,176.

Sunday 14th June 2009

HALIFAX 30 BARROW RAIDERS 24

HALIFAX: 1 Miles Greenwood; 2 Lee Patterson; 3 Jon Goddard; 5 James Haley; 23 Rob Worrincy; 9 Sean Penkywicz; 7 Ben Black; 22 David Wrench; 13 Bob Beswick; 21 Neil Cherryholme; 11 David Larder; 12 Paul Smith; 4 Shad Royston. Subs (all used): 14 Mark Gleeson; 15 Mark Roberts; 16 Said Tamghart; 17 Frank Watene.
Tries: Haley (21), Watene (32), Gleeson (39), Patterson (53), Royston (80); **Goals:** Patterson 5/7.
RAIDERS: 1 Gary Broadbent; 19 Chris Larkin; 26 Zebastian Luisi; 4 Liam Harrison; 5 James Nixon; 6 Liam Finch; 27 Darren Holt; 8 Brett McDermott; 9 Andy Ellis; 13 Andy Bracek; 22 Ned Catic; 14 Paul Noone; 11 Andrew Brocklehurst. Subs (all used): 15 Chris Young; 12 Martin Ostler; 16 Jamie Butler; 32 Andreas Bauer.
Tries: Ellis (15, 68, 76), Luisi (59); **Goals:** Holt 4/4.
Rugby Leaguer & League Express Men of the Match:
Halifax: Bob Beswick; *Raiders:* Andy Ellis.
Penalty count: 8-7; **Half-time:** 18-6;
Referee: Gareth Hewer; **Attendance:** 2,872.

LEIGH CENTURIONS 12 GATESHEAD THUNDER 40

CENTURIONS: 1 Stuart Donlan; 5 Nicky Stanton; 18 Sam Reay; 37 Macgraff Leuluai; 3 Steve Maden; 23 Martyn Ridyard; 7 Ian Watson; 10 Mike Morrison; 9 Dave McConnell; 16 Chris Hill; 11 David Armitstead; 12 James Taylor; 13 Aaron Smith. Subs (all used): 26 Jamie Durbin; 28 Danny Meekin; 38 Mark Castle; 40 Andy Ainscough.
Tries: A Smith (9), Reay (22); **Goals:** Stanton 2/2.
Sin bin: Maden (49) - dissent.
THUNDER: 19 Nick Youngquest; 1 Ben McAlpine; 25 Paul Franze; 4 Dylan Nash; 5 Stewart Sanderson; 13 Russ Aitken; 7 Luke Branighan; 34 Liam Watts; 9 Andrew Henderson; 21 Ryan McBride; 32 James Cording; 12 Michael Knowles; 24 Kris Kahler. Subs (all used): 6 Neil Thorman; 33 Nathan Massey; 15 Matt Barron; 10 Tabua Cakacaka.
Tries: Knowles (3), Youngquest (19, 34), Nash (28), Franze (56), Cording (63), Sanderson (69);
Goals: Knowles 6/7.
Sin bin: Youngquest (80) – delaying restart.
Rugby Leaguer & League Express Men of the Match:
Centurions: Nicky Stanton; *Thunder:* Luke Branighan.
Penalty count: 8-8; **Half-time:** 12-22;
Referee: Ronnie Laughton; **Attendance:** 1,645.

ROUND 9

Sunday 21st June 2009

DONCASTER 6 BATLEY BULLDOGS 70

DONCASTER: 4 Shaun Leaf; 2 Dean Colton; 20 Mike Coady; 12 Craig Lawton; 30 Wayne Opie; 13 Josh Weeden; 22 Andy Speake; 10 Alex Benson; 9 Craig Cook; 29 Matt Carbutt; 8 Steve Hall; 18 Craig Holt; 19 Ryan Steen. Subs (all used): 15 Mark McKinley; 24 Jake Bassinder; 16 Craig Jones; 21 Gary Ellery.
Try: Ellery (76); **Goals:** Weeden 1/1.
BULLDOGS: 1 Ian Preece; 5 John Campbell; 6 Mark Barlow; 4 Danny Maun; 18 Jermaine McGilvary; 30 Paul Handforth; 7 Paul Mennell; 8 Byron Smith; 9 Kris Lythe; 15 Anthony Henderson; 23 Chris Buttery; 17 Craig Potter; 13 Ashley Lindsay. Subs (all used): 16 Jon Simpson; 20 David Tootill; 14 John Gallagher; 29 Gareth Greenwood.
Tries: Gallagher (16), Potter (20), Campbell (30, 48, 54, 59), Barlow (35), McGilvary (50), Handforth (65), Preece (70, 73), Greenwood (80); **Goals:** Mennell 11/12.
Rugby Leaguer & League Express Men of the Match:
Doncaster: Ryan Steen; *Bulldogs:* Paul Handforth.
Penalty count: 6-8; **Half-time:** 0-22;
Referee: Matthew Thomasson; **Attendance:** 565
(at Chris Moyles Stadium, Featherstone).

ROUND 14

Saturday 27th June 2009

TOULOUSE OLYMPIQUE 16 FEATHERSTONE ROVERS 32

OLYMPIQUE: 1 Rory Bromley; 2 Sebastien Payen; 3 Sebastien Planas; 4 Damien Couturier; 21 Bruno Ormeno; 6 Constant Villegas; 7 Nathan Wynn; 8 Brendan Worth; 9 Martin Mitchell; 10 Mathieu Griffi; 11 Tim Wynn; 12 Matthieu Almarcha; 13 Eric Anselme. Subs (all used): 14 Anton Maria; 22 Nicholas Faure; 24 Jean-Christophe Borlin; 32 Florian Quintilla.
Tries: Couturier (32, 65), Faure (48); **Goals:** Couturier 2/3.
ROVERS: 3 Ian Hardman; 26 Sam Smeaton; 4 Andy Kirk; 1 Tom Saxton; 2 Waine Pryce; 28 Kyle Briggs; 7 Andy Kain; 10 Stuart Dickens; 16 Joe McLocklan; 15 James Houston; 11 Matty Dale; 18 Tim Spears; 14 Tom Haughey. Subs (all used): 6 Iestyn Harris; 9 Jack Lee; 24 Jon Fallon; 29 Ross Divorty.
Tries: Hardman (8), Smeaton (20), Briggs (26, 55), Spears (44); **Goals:** Dickens 5/5, A Kain 1/1.
Rugby Leaguer & League Express Men of the Match:
Olympique: Damien Couturier; *Rovers:* Kyle Briggs.
Penalty count: 7-7; **Half-time:** 4-18;
Referee: Robert Hicks;
Attendance: 2,321 *(at Stade Ernest Argeles, Blagnac).*

Sunday 28th June 2009

BATLEY BULLDOGS 46 BARROW RAIDERS 16

BULLDOGS: 1 Ian Preece; 5 John Campbell; 6 Mark Barlow; 4 Danny Maun; 28 Daryl Cardiss; 30 Paul Handforth; 7 Paul Mennell; 15 Anthony Henderson; 9 Kris Lythe; 17 Craig Potter; 14 John Gallagher; 8 Byron Smith; 13 Ashley Lindsay. Subs (all used): 29 Gareth Greenwood; 16 Jon Simpson; 20 David Tootill; 35 Jack Watson.
Tries: Smith (5), Lindsay (11, 67), Mennell (14), Cardiss (45), Potter (71), Lythe (76), Maun (79);
Goals: Mennell 6/8, Barlow 1/1.
RAIDERS: 1 Gary Broadbent; 19 Chris Larkin; 32 Andreas Bauer; 4 Liam Harrison; 5 James Nixon; 6 Liam Finch; 27 Darren Holt; 8 Brett McDermott; 9 Andy Ellis; 13 Andy Bracek; 22 Ned Catic; 14 Paul Noone; 26 Zebastian Luisi. Subs (all used): 15 Chris Young; 16 Jamie Butler; 20 Nick Beech; 28 Nathan Mossop.
Tries: N Mossop (22), Bauer (58), Ellis (62);
Goals: Noone 2/3.
Dismissal: Catic (79) - dissent.
Sin bin: Catic (79) - high tackle.
Rugby Leaguer & League Express Men of the Match:
Bulldogs: Paul Handforth; *Raiders:* Zebastian Luisi.
Penalty count: 8-7; **Half-time:** 16-6;
Referee: Ronnie Laughton; **Attendance:** 1,002.

DONCASTER 8 SHEFFIELD EAGLES 78

DONCASTER: 4 Shaun Leaf; 2 Dean Colton; 20 Mike Coady; 1 Lisiate Tafa; 5 Chris McNamara; 13 Josh Weeden; 22 Andy Speake; 10 Alex Benson; 19 Ryan Steen; 33 Tim Scire; 18 Craig Holt; 12 Craig Lawton; 29 Matt Carbutt. Subs (all used): 14 Scott Jones; 34 Brooke Broughton; 24 Jake Bassinder; 17 Danny Flintoff.
Tries: Lawton (22), Coady (76);
Goals: Weeden 0/1, Speake 0/1.
EAGLES: 1 Jonny Woodcock; 28 Damian Gibson; 23 Tangi Ropati; 3 Menzie Yere; 32 Danny Mills; 6 Brendon Lindsay; 19 Kyle Wood; 22 Ryan Hepworth; 20 Matty Brooks; 10 Mitchell Stringer; 11 Alex Szostak; 29 Peter Green; 9 Grant Edwards. Subs (all used): 34 Craig Cook; 15 Sam Barlow; 16 Trevor Exton; 30 Michael Haley.
Tries: Ropati (17, 59), Yere (26, 30, 39, 50), Mills (34), Cook (45), Wood (48), Lindsay (56), Gibson (62, 66, 68), Brooks (79); **Goals:** Woodcock 11/14.
Rugby Leaguer & League Express Men of the Match:
Doncaster: Chris McNamara; *Eagles:* Menzie Yere.
Penalty count: 7-6; **Half-time:** 4-28;
Referee: Peter Brooke; **Attendance:** 275
(at Chris Moyles Stadium, Featherstone).

GATESHEAD THUNDER 34 HALIFAX 28

THUNDER: 19 Nick Youngquest; 1 Ben McAlpine; 4 Dylan Nash; 25 Paul Franze; 5 Stewart Sanderson; 13 Russ Aitken; 7 Luke Branighan; 33 Nathan Massey; 9 Andrew Henderson; 21 Ryan McBride; 12 Michael Knowles; 32 James Cording; 24 Kris Kahler. Subs (all used): 34 Liam Watts; 15 Matt Barron; 35 Anthony England; 6 Neil Thorman.
Tries: Nash (2, 8, 37), Cording (17), Branighan (22), McAlpine (33); **Goals:** Knowles 5/8.
HALIFAX: 1 Miles Greenwood; 2 Lee Patterson; 3 Jon Goddard; 5 James Haley; 23 Rob Worrincy; 13 Bob Beswick; 19 Mick Govin; 16 Said Tamghart; 9 Sean Penkywicz; 11 David Larder; 12 Paul Smith; 18 Andy Bowman; 4 Shad Royston. Subs (all used): 6 Dwayne Barker; 14 Mark Gleeson; 15 Mark Roberts; 17 Frank Watene.
Tries: Gleeson (43), Greenwood (47), Penkywicz (59, 71), Worrincy (76); **Goals:** Patterson 4/5.
Rugby Leaguer & League Express Men of the Match:
Thunder: Luke Branighan; *Halifax:* Sean Penkywicz.
Penalty count: 8-10; **Half-time:** 32-0;
Referee: Craig Halloran; **Attendance:** 802.

WHITEHAVEN 36 LEIGH CENTURIONS 22

WHITEHAVEN: 27 Paul Ballard; 5 Ade Adebisi; 13 Scott McAvoy; 3 Rob Jackson; 2 Craig Calvert; 7 Leroy Joe; 24 Gregg McNally; 19 Kyle Amor; 25 Jamie Theohaurus; 10 Karl Edmondson; 12 Spencer Miller; 15 Andy Gorski; 8 Marc Jackson. Subs (all used): 28 Chris Smith; 22 Matthew Tunstall; 16 Ryan McDonald; 11 Howard Hill.
Tries: Calvert (10, 16, 38, 79), Adebisi (31, 69);
Goals: McNally 5/6, Joe 1/1.
CENTURIONS: 14 Ian Mort; 5 Nicky Stanton; 38 Mick Nanyn; 2 David Alstead; 3 Steve Maden; 37 Tom Hemingway; 7 Ian Watson; 16 Chris Hill; 9 Dave McConnell; 8 Andy Hobson; 11 Dave Armitstead; 40 Macgraff Leuluai; 13 Aaron Smith. Subs (all used): 26 Jamie Durbin; 10 Mike Morrison; 36 Mark Castle; 28 Danny Meekin.
Tries: Alstead (6), Durbin (35), Maden (49), Watson (57); **Goals:** Mort 3/5.
Rugby Leaguer & League Express Men of the Match:
Whitehaven: Rob Jackson; *Centurions:* Jamie Durbin.
Penalty count: 10-8; **Half-time:** 22-12;
Referee: James Child; **Attendance:** 1,310.

ROUND 15

Thursday 2nd July 2009

BARROW RAIDERS 30 TOULOUSE OLYMPIQUE 22

RAIDERS: 1 Gary Broadbent; 19 Chris Larkin; 32 Andreas Bauer; 4 Liam Harrison; 5 James Nixon; 6 Liam Finch; 24 Jamie Rooney; 8 Brett McDermott; 9 Andy Ellis; 13 Andy Bracek; 22 Ned Catic; 14 Paul Noone; 26 Zebastian Luisi. Subs: 15 Chris Young; 16 Jamie Butler; 21 Joe McKenna (not used); 17 Scott Kaighan.
Tries: Nixon (19, 43), Young (37), Ellis (67), Harrison (70); **Goals:** Rooney 5/6.
OLYMPIQUE: 1 Rory Bromley; 2 Sebastien Payen; 32 Florian Quintilla; 4 Damien Couturier; 31 Teli Pelo; 6 Constant Villegas; 9 Martin Mitchell; 8 Brendan Worth; 18 Adrien Viala; 10 Mathieu Griffi; 11 Tim Wynn; 14 Anton Maria; 13 Eric Anselme. Subs (all used): 24 Jean-Christophe Borlin; 22 Nicholas Faure; 17 Yohan Barthau; 19 Nicholas Delgal.
Tries: T Wynn (11), Bromley (25), Couturier (75, 80);
Goals: Couturier 3/4.
Rugby Leaguer & League Express Men of the Match:
Raiders: Jamie Rooney; *Olympique:* Damien Couturier.
Penalty count: 8-7; **Half-time:** 12-12;
Referee: Gareth Hewer; **Attendance:** 2,456.

Friday 3rd July 2009

HALIFAX 48 LEIGH CENTURIONS 16

HALIFAX: 1 Miles Greenwood; 2 Lee Patterson; 3 Jon Goddard; 5 James Haley; 23 Rob Worrincy; 19 Mick Govin; 9 Sean Penkywicz; 10 Dana Wilson; 13 Bob Beswick; 11 David Larder; 18 Andy Bowman; 12 Paul Smith; 4 Shad Royston. Subs (all used): 14 Mark Gleeson; 15 Mark Roberts; 16 Said Tamghart; 17 Frank Watene.
Tries: Royston (6, 61), Andy Bowman (12), Gleeson (19), Watene (25), Worrincy (35), Haley (55, 70); **Goals:** Patterson 8/8.
CENTURIONS: 14 Ian Mort; 22 Jamie Smith; 38 Mick Nanyn; 4 Anthony Stewart; 3 Steve Maden; 37 Tom Hemingway; 7 Ian Watson; 36 Mark Castle; 26 Jamie Durbin; 8 Andy Hobson; 11 Dave Armitstead; 12 James Taylor; 13 Aaron Smith. Subs (all used): 23 Martyn Ridyard; 10 Mike Morrison; 16 Chris Hill; 30 Macgraff Leuluai.
Tries: Mort (29), J Smith (51, 67); **Goals:** Mort 2/3.
Sin bin: Morrison (22) - interference.
Rugby Leaguer & League Express Men of the Match:
Halifax: Bob Beswick; *Centurions:* Ian Watson.
Penalty count: 15-5; **Half-time:** 30-6;
Referee: Jamie Leahy; **Attendance:** 2,094.

SHEFFIELD EAGLES 30 BATLEY BULLDOGS 4

EAGLES: 1 Jonny Woodcock; 32 Danny Mills; 3 Menzie Yere; 23 Tangi Ropati; 28 Damian Gibson; 6 Brendon Lindsay; 19 Kyle Wood; 22 Ryan Hepworth; 20 Matty Brooks; 10 Mitchell Stringer; 11 Alex Szostak; 29 Peter Green; 9 Grant Edwards. Subs (all used): 34 Craig Cook; 15 Sam Barlow; 16 Trevor Exton; 30 Michael Haley.
Tries: Stringer (13, 64, 68), Ropati (19), Cook (36), Yere (39); **Goals:** Woodcock 3/6.
BULLDOGS: 1 Ian Preece; 28 Daryl Cardiss; 11 Kevin Crouthers; 4 Danny Maun; 5 John Campbell; 30 Paul Handforth; 6 Mark Barlow; 15 Anthony Henderson; 9 Kris Lythe; 17 Craig Potter; 14 John Gallagher; 8 Byron Smith; 13 Ashley Lindsay. Subs (all used): 18 Jermaine McGilvary; 35 Jack Watson; 16 Jon Simpson; 20 David Tootill.
Try: Preece (5); **Goals:** Barlow 0/1.
Sin bin: Crouthers (37) - interference.
Rugby Leaguer & League Express Men of the Match:
Eagles: Mitchell Stringer; *Bulldogs:* Paul Handforth.
Penalty count: 12-11; **Half-time:** 18-4;
Referee: Robert Hicks; **Attendance:** 1,286.

Saturday 4th July 2009

WIDNES VIKINGS 78 DONCASTER 4

VIKINGS: 16 Gavin Dodd; 22 Paddy Flynn; 4 Toa Kohe-Love; 32 Craig Hall; 29 Kevin Penny; 6 Anthony Thackeray; 14 John Duffy; 11 Lee Doran; 9 Mark Smith; 28 Steve Pickersgill; 12 Richard Fletcher; 35 Jon Grayshon; 13 Lee Paterson. Subs (all used): 3 Richard Varkulis; 15 Tim Hartley; 17 Ben Kavanagh; 19 Michael Ostick.
Tries: Penny (5, 45, 65), Kohe-Love (24), Flynn (27, 39), Hall (34), Grayshon (48), Varkulis (50, 64), Dodd (52), Fletcher (72), Smith (76), Pickersgill (78);
Goals: Hall 8/11, Dodd 3/3.
DONCASTER: 1 Tommy Griffiths; 5 Chris McNamara; 20 Mike Coady; 19 Ryan Steen; 2 Dean Colton; 15 Mark McKinley; 13 Josh Weeden; 29 Matt Carbutt; 22 Andy Speake; 10 Alex Benson; 8 Steve Hall; 33 Brooke Broughton; 24 Jake Bassinder. Subs (all used): 14 Scott Jones; 30 Wayne Opie; 16 Craig Jones; 21 Gary Ellery.
Try: Weeden (55); **Goals:** McKinley 0/1.
Rugby Leaguer & League Express Men of the Match:
Vikings: Craig Hall; *Doncaster:* Josh Weeden.
Penalty count: 5-5; **Half-time:** 28-0;
Referee: Greg Dolan; **Attendance:** 3,453.

Sunday 5th July 2009

FEATHERSTONE ROVERS 56 GATESHEAD THUNDER 40

ROVERS: 3 Ian Hardman; 5 Jon Steel; 26 Sam Smeaton; 4 Andy Kirk; 2 Waine Pryce; 28 Kyle Briggs; 7 Andy Kain; 15 James Houston; 16 Joe McLocklan; 10 Stuart Dickens; 18 Tim Spears; 11 Matty Dale; 14 Tom Haughey. Subs (all used): 29 Ross Divorty; 6 Iestyn Harris; 24 Jon Fallon; 9 Jack Lee.
Tries: Haughey (2), Dickens (14), Briggs (22, 76), Spears (30), Dale (47), Divorty (51), A Kain (56), Hardman (70), Steel (79); **Goals:** Dickens 8/9, A Kain 0/1.
THUNDER: 19 Nick Youngquest; 1 Ben McAlpine; 4 Dylan Nash; 25 Paul Franze; 5 Stewart Sanderson; 13 Russ Aitken; 7 Luke Branighan; 33 Nathan Massey; 9 Andrew Henderson; 21 Ryan McBride; 12 Michael Knowles; 32 James Cording; 24 Kris Kahler. Subs (all

used): 34 Liam Watts; 15 Matt Barron; 35 Anthony England; 6 Neil Thorman.
Tries: Sanderson (4, 39), Branighan (12, 43), Aitken (18), McAlpine (64), Youngquest (66);
Goals: Knowles 6/8.
Rugby Leaguer & League Express Men of the Match: *Rovers:* Kyle Briggs; *Thunder:* Michael Knowles.
Penalty count: 7-5; **Half-time:** 20-20;
Referee: Ronnie Laughton; **Attendance:** 1,487.

ROUND 16

Thursday 16th July 2009

WHITEHAVEN 28 BARROW RAIDERS 4

WHITEHAVEN: 32 Paul Ballard; 4 Derry Eilbeck; 3 Rob Jackson; 13 Scott McAvoy; 2 Craig Calvert; 6 Carl Rudd; 24 Gregg McNally; 19 Kyle Amor; 7 Leroy Joe; 10 Karl Edmondson; 15 Andy Gorski; 12 Spencer Miller; 25 Jamie Theohaurus. Subs (all used): 8 Marc Jackson; 11 Howard Hill; 16 Ryan McDonald; 9 Graeme Mattinson.
Tries: Ballard (22), Calvert (40), Gorski (57), R Jackson (65, 74); **Goals:** McNally 4/7.
Sin bin: M Jackson (24) - late challenge on Rooney.
RAIDERS: 1 Gary Broadbent; 19 Chris Larkin; 32 Andreas Bauer; 4 Liam Harrison; 5 James Nixon; 26 Zebastian Luisi; 24 Jamie Rooney; 8 Brett McDermott; 28 Nathan Mossop; 16 Jamie Butler; 13 Andy Bracek; 12 Martin Ostler; 14 Paul Noone. Subs (all used): 9 Andy Ellis; 15 Chris Young; 23 Sam Thompson; 21 Joe McKenna.
Try: Nixon (16); **Goals:** Rooney 0/1.
Rugby Leaguer & League Express Men of the Match: *Whitehaven:* Rob Jackson; *Raiders:* Zebastian Luisi.
Penalty count: 9-3; **Half-time:** 10-4;
Referee: Craig Halloran; **Attendance:** 2,708.

Saturday 18th July 2009

TOULOUSE OLYMPIQUE 16 HALIFAX 54

OLYMPIQUE: 1 Rory Bromley; 2 Sebastien Payen; 3 Sebastien Planas; 4 Damien Couturier; 21 Bruno Ormeno; 6 Constant Villegas; 9 Martin Mitchell; 8 Brendan Worth; 23 Cedric Gay; 10 Mathieu Griffi; 11 Tim Wynn; 13 Eric Anselme; 20 Sylvain Houles. Subs (all used): 12 Matthieu Almarcha; 14 Anton Maria; 22 Nicholas Faure; 24 Jean-Christophe Borlin.
Tries: Payen (36), Couturier (55), Almarcha (65);
Goals: Couturier 2/3.
HALIFAX: 1 Miles Greenwood; 2 Lee Patterson; 3 Jon Goddard; 5 James Haley; 23 Rob Worrincy; 9 Sean Penkywicz; 7 Ben Black; 26 Dominic Maloney; 14 Mark Gleeson; 21 Neil Cherryholme; 11 David Larder; 12 Paul Smith; 13 Bob Beswick. Subs (all used): 10 Dana Wilson; 15 Mark Roberts; 16 Said Tamghart; 17 Frank Watene.
Tries: Penkywicz (7), Larder (12, 29), Patterson (26), Black (34), Beswick (43), Worrincy (45), Tamghart (57), Greenwood (74); **Goals:** Patterson 9/9.
Rugby Leaguer & League Express Men of the Match: *Olympique:* Jean-Christophe Borlin; *Halifax:* Ben Black.
Penalty count: 7-7; **Half-time:** 6-30;
Referee: Peter Brooke; **Attendance:** 2,687.

Sunday 19th July 2009

BATLEY BULLDOGS 56 DONCASTER 12

BULLDOGS: 1 Ian Preece; 5 John Campbell; 6 Mark Barlow; 4 Danny Maun; 18 Jermaine McGilvary; 30 Paul Handforth; 7 Paul Mennell; 15 Anthony Henderson; 9 Kris Lythe; 17 Craig Potter; 23 Chris Buttery; 8 Byron Smith; 13 Ashley Lindsay. Subs (all used): 14 John Gallagher; 20 David Tootill; 16 Jon Simpson; 10 Luke Stenchion.
Tries: Lindsay (5), Lythe (15), McGilvary (20, 40, 52, 74), Simpson (37), Campbell (57), Handforth (68), Maun (70, 77); **Goals:** Handforth 3/3, Mennell 3/7, Barlow 0/1.
DONCASTER: 1 Tommy Griffiths; 5 Chris McNamara; 12 Craig Lawton; 19 Ryan Steen; 30 Wayne Opie; 6 Matthew Handforth; 13 Josh Weeden; 10 Alex Benson; 9 Kyle Kesik; 16 Craig Jones; 8 Steve Hall; 15 Mark McKinley; 25 Danny Stanley. Subs (all used): 35 Carlos Sanchez; 32 David Bates; 24 Jake Bassinder; 34 Brooke Broughton.
Tries: Weeden (29), McNamara (48, 80);
Goals: Weeden 0/2, McKinley 0/1.
Rugby Leaguer & League Express Men of the Match: *Bulldogs:* Danny Maun; *Doncaster:* Chris McNamara.
Penalty count: 8-5; **Half-time:** 26-4;
Referee: Dave Merrick; **Attendance:** 580.

GATESHEAD THUNDER 34 WIDNES VIKINGS 18

THUNDER: 19 Nick Youngquest; 1 Ben McAlpine; 4 Dylan Nash; 25 Paul Franze; 18 Robin Peers; 13 Russ Aitken; 7 Luke Branighan; 34 Liam Watts; 9 Andrew Henderson; 21 Ryan McBride; 12 Michael Knowles; 32 James Cording; 24 Kris Kahler. Subs (all used): 33 Nathan Massey; 15 Matt Barron; 35 Anthony England; 6 Neil Thorman.
Tries: Cording (15), Branighan (28), McAlpine (30), Thorman (60), Youngquest (64), England (75);
Goals: Knowles 5/6.
VIKINGS: 16 Gavin Dodd; 22 Paddy Flynn; 15 Tim Hartley; 3 Richard Varkulis; 29 Kevin Penny; 6 Anthony Thackeray; 7 James Webster; 28 Steve Pickersgill; 9 Mark Smith; 10 Jim Gannon; 35 Jon Grayshon; 12 Richard Fletcher; 11 Lee Doran. Subs (all used): 14 John Duffy; 13 Lee Paterson; 17 Ben Kavanagh; 19 Michael Ostick.
Tries: Penny (10), Flynn (40), Thackeray (71);
Goals: Hartley 3/3.
Rugby Leaguer & League Express Men of the Match: *Thunder:* Russ Aitken; *Vikings:* Kevin Penny.
Penalty count: 9-10; **Half-time:** 16-12;
Referee: Robert Hicks; **Attendance:** 717.

LEIGH CENTURIONS 32 SHEFFIELD EAGLES 24

CENTURIONS: 14 Ian Mort; 5 Nicky Stanton; 1 Stuart Donlan; 31 Mick Nanyn; 3 Steve Maden; 37 Tom Hemingway; 7 Ian Watson; 8 Andy Hobson; 9 Dave McConnell; 16 Chris Hill; 11 David Armitstead; 12 James Taylor; 13 Aaron Smith. Subs (all used): 26 Jamie Durbin; 30 Macgraff Leuluai; 10 Mike Morrison; 28 Danny Meekin.
Tries: McConnell (2), Nanyn (15, 66), Durbin (34), Watson (80); **Goals:** Mort 6/8.
EAGLES: 1 Jonny Woodcock; 32 Danny Mills; 3 Menzie Yere; 23 Tangi Ropati; 28 Damian Gibson; 6 Brendon Lindsay; 19 Kyle Wood; 22 Ryan Hepworth; 20 Matty Brooks; 10 Mitchell Stringer; 11 Alex Szostak; 29 Peter Green; 9 Grant Edwards. Subs (all used): 34 Craig Cook; 15 Sam Barlow; 16 Trevor Exton; 25 James Morrow.
Tries: Cook (55), Gibson (57), Mills (62), Woodcock (77); **Goals:** Woodcock 4/4.
Rugby Leaguer & League Express Men of the Match: *Centurions:* Chris Hill; *Eagles:* Craig Cook.
Penalty count: 7-13; **Half-time:** 18-0;
Referee: Mohammed Drizza; **Attendance:** 1,465.

ROUND 17

Thursday 23rd July 2009

SHEFFIELD EAGLES 46 GATESHEAD THUNDER 30

EAGLES: 1 Jonny Woodcock; 32 Danny Mills; 3 Menzie Yere; 28 Damian Gibson; 5 Ashley Thackeray; 6 Brendon Lindsay; 19 Kyle Wood; 30 Michael Haley; 34 Craig Cook; 10 Mitchell Stringer; 11 Alex Szostak; 29 Peter Green; 16 Trevor Exton. Subs (all used): 23 Tangi Ropati; 15 Sam Barlow; 20 Matty Brooks; 22 Ryan Hepworth.
Tries: Gibson (12, 19, 59), Yere (22), Thackeray (25, 56), Hepworth (39), Lindsay (49), Wood (62);
Goals: Woodcock 5/9.
THUNDER: 19 Nick Youngquest; 1 Ben McAlpine; 4 Dylan Nash; 25 Paul Franze; 18 Robin Peers; 13 Russ Aitken; 7 Luke Branighan; 34 Liam Watts; 9 Andrew Henderson; 21 Ryan McBride; 32 James Cording; 12 Michael Knowles; 24 Kris Kahler. Subs (all used): 33 Nathan Massey; 35 Anthony England; 15 Matt Barron; 6 Neil Thorman.
Tries: Franze (2, 43), Youngquest (29, 34, 70), Thorman (74); **Goals:** Knowles 3/6.
Sin bin: Franze (59) – interference.
Rugby Leaguer & League Express Men of the Match: *Eagles:* Trevor Exton; *Thunder:* Nick Youngquest.
Penalty count: 13-5; **Half-time:** 26-16;
Referee: Craig Halloran; **Attendance:** 1,410.

Friday 24th July 2009

HALIFAX 20 FEATHERSTONE ROVERS 22

HALIFAX: 1 Miles Greenwood; 2 Lee Patterson; 3 Jon Goddard; 5 James Haley; 23 Rob Worrincy; 9 Sean Penkywicz; 7 Ben Black; 21 Neil Cherryholme; 14 Mark Gleeson; 26 Dominic Maloney; 18 Andy Bowman; 12 Paul Smith; 13 Bob Beswick. Subs (all used): 10 Dana Wilson; 16 Said Tamghart; 17 Frank Watene; 27 Steve Bannister.
Tries: Gleeson (6), Maloney (14), Haley (20);
Goals: Patterson 4/4.
ROVERS: 3 Ian Hardman; 2 Waine Pryce; 1 Tom Saxton; 4 Andy Kirk; 5 Jon Steel; 28 Kyle Briggs; 7 Andy Kain; 8 Tony Tonks; 16 Joe McLocklan; 10 Stuart Dickens; 11 Matty Dale; 18 Tim Spears; 14 Tom Haughey. Subs (all used): 6 Iestyn Harris; 9 Jack Lee; 15 James Houston; 29 Ross Divorty.
Tries: Dale (51), A Kain (54), Tonks (61), Lee (79);
Goals: Briggs 2/3, Dickens 1/1.
On report: Dale and Harris (65) - alleged spear tackle.
Rugby Leaguer & League Express Men of the Match: *Halifax:* Said Tamghart; *Rovers:* Kyle Briggs.
Penalty count: 10-8; **Half-time:** 18-0;
Referee: Ronnie Laughton; **Attendance:** 2,456.

Saturday 25th July 2009

BARROW RAIDERS 74 LEIGH CENTURIONS 6

RAIDERS: 1 Gary Broadbent; 19 Chris Larkin; 32 Andreas Bauer; 4 Liam Harrison; 5 James Nixon; 24 Jamie Rooney; 31 James Coyle; 15 Chris Young; 9 Andy Ellis; 13 Andy Bracek; 22 Ned Catic; 14 Paul Noone; 26 Zebastian Luisi. Subs (all used): 33 Dave Allen; 23 Sam Thompson; 12 Martin Ostler; 27 Darren Holt.
Tries: Larkin (6, 14), Coyle (8, 27, 59, 73), Nixon (19, 53, 80), Catic (32), Broadbent (50), Harrison (69), Ellis (78); **Goals:** Rooney 7/7, Noone 4/6.
CENTURIONS: 14 Ian Mort; 5 Nicky Stanton; 1 Stuart Donlan; 31 Mick Nanyn; 3 Steve Maden; 37 Tom Hemingway; 7 Ian Watson; 8 Andy Hobson; 9 Dave McConnell; 16 Chris Hill; 11 Dave Armitstead; 12 James Taylor; 13 Aaron Smith. Subs (all used): 26 James Durbin; 30 Macgraff Leuluai; 10 Mike Morrison; 28 Danny Meekin.
Try: Durbin (64); **Goals:** Mort 1/1.
Rugby Leaguer & League Express Men of the Match: *Raiders:* Zebastian Luisi; *Centurions:* Macgraff Leuluai.
Penalty count: 5-3; **Half-time:** 36-0;
Referee: Robert Hicks; **Attendance:** 1,934.

TOULOUSE OLYMPIQUE 24 WIDNES VIKINGS 32

OLYMPIQUE: 1 Rory Bromley; 2 Sebastien Payen; 3 Sebastien Planas; 4 Damien Couturier; 21 Bruno Ormeno; 6 Constant Villegas; 9 Martin Mitchell; 8 Brendan Worth; 18 Adrien Viala; 10 Mathieu Griffi; 11 Tim Wynn; 14 Anton Maria; 20 Sylvain Houles. Subs (all used): 12 Matthieu Almarcha; 13 Eric Anselme; 16 Olivier Pramil; 24 Jean-Christophe Borlin.
Tries: Mitchell (9), Bromley (29), Viala (46, 49);
Goals: Couturier 4/4.
VIKINGS: 16 Gavin Dodd; 2 Dean Gaskell; 3 Richard Varkulis; 4 Toa Kohe-Love; 29 Kevin Penny; 6 Anthony Thackeray; 7 James Webster; 28 Steve Pickersgill; 9 Mark Smith; 10 Jim Gannon; 35 Jon Grayshon; 12 Richard Fletcher; 8 Iain Morrison. Subs (all used): 11 Lee Doran; 15 Tim Hartley; 17 Ben Kavanagh; 19 Michael Ostick.
Tries: Grayshon (14), Kavanagh (25), Penny (38, 74), Gannon (68), Varkulis (77); **Goals:** Dodd 4/6.
Rugby Leaguer & League Express Men of the Match: *Olympique:* Rory Bromley; *Vikings:* Jon Grayshon.
Penalty count: 7-7; **Half-time:** 12-16;
Referee: Matthew Thomasson;
Attendance: 3,206 *(at Stade Ernest Argeles, Blagnac).*

Sunday 26th July 2009

DONCASTER 10 WHITEHAVEN 19

DONCASTER: 1 Tommy Griffiths; 5 Scott McDonald; 4 Shaun Leaf; 19 Ryan Steen; 2 Dean Colton; 6 Matthew Handforth; 13 Josh Weeden; 35 Carlos Sanchez; 9 Kyle Kesik; 10 Alex Benson; 8 Steve Hall; 12 Craig Lawton; 15 Mark McKinley. Subs (all used): 25 Danny Stanley; 24 Jake Bassinder; 30 Wayne Opie; 34 Danny Vento.
Tries: Lawton (20), McDonald (79); **Goals:** Weeden 1/2.
Sin bin: Kesik (16) - late challenge on McNally.
WHITEHAVEN: 32 Paul Ballard; 4 Derry Eilbeck; 31 Dexter Miller; 3 Rob Jackson; 2 Craig Calvert; 6 Carl Rudd; 24 Gregg McNally; 19 Kyle Amor; 7 Leroy Joe; 10 Karl Edmondson; 12 Spencer Miller; 15 Andy Gorski; 25 Jamie Theohaurus. Subs (all used): 9 Graeme Mattinson; 11 Howard Hill; 8 Marc Jackson; 16 Ryan McDonald.
Tries: Amor (6), Calvert (11), Rudd (49);
Goals: McNally 3/3; **Field goal:** Rudd (65).
Dismissal: McDonald (40) - headbutt on Leaf.
Rugby Leaguer & League Express Men of the Match: *Doncaster:* Josh Weeden; *Whitehaven:* Gregg McNally.
Penalty count: 12-9; **Half-time:** 6-12;
Referee: Jamie Leahy; **Attendance:** 337.

ROUND 18

Friday 31st July 2009

WIDNES VIKINGS 42 HALIFAX 16

VIKINGS: 16 Gavin Dodd; 22 Paddy Flynn; 4 Toa Kohe-Love; 3 Richard Varkulis; 29 Kevin Penny; 15 Tim Hartley; 7 James Webster; 8 Iain Morrison; 14 John Duffy; 10 Jim Gannon; 12 Richard Fletcher; 35 Jon Grayshon; 11 Lee Doran. Subs (all used): 6 Anthony Thackeray; 17 Ben Kavanagh; 19 Michael Ostick; 28 Steve Pickersgill.
Tries: Morrison (8), Flynn (22, 36, 54), Varkulis (25), Kohe-Love (46), Penny (50); **Goals:** Hartley 7/9.
Sin bin: Pickersgill (42) - late challenge on Penkywicz.
HALIFAX: 1 Miles Greenwood; 2 Lee Patterson; 3 Jon Goddard; 4 Shad Royston; 5 James Haley; 9 Sean Penkywicz; 7 Ben Black; 21 Neil Cherryholme; 13 Bob Beswick; 26 Dominic Maloney; 18 Andy Bowman; 15 Mark Roberts; 12 Paul Smith. Subs (all used): 14 Mark Gleeson; 16 Said Tamghart; 17 Frank Watene; 27 Steve Bannister.
Tries: Haley (16), Patterson (68), Watene (80);
Goals: Patterson 2/3.
Sin bin: Tamghart (40) - dissent.
Rugby Leaguer & League Express Men of the Match: *Vikings:* Tim Hartley; *Halifax:* Lee Patterson.
Penalty count: 12-14; **Half-time:** 22-6;
Referee: Jamie Leahy; **Attendance:** 4,039.

Saturday 1st August 2009

FEATHERSTONE ROVERS 18 TOULOUSE OLYMPIQUE 34

ROVERS: 3 Ian Hardman; 5 Jon Steel; 14 Tom Haughey; 1 Tom Saxton; 2 Waine Pryce; 28 Kyle Briggs; 7 Andy Kain; 10 Stuart Dickens; 9 Jack Lee; 8 Tony Tonks; 18 Tim Spears; 11 Matty Dale; 6 Iestyn Harris. Subs (all used): 29 Ross Divorty; 30 Dwayne Barker; 15 James Houston; 4 Andy Kirk.
Tries: Dale (10), Steel (14), Divorty (41);
Goals: Dickens 2/2, Briggs 1/1.
OLYMPIQUE: 1 Rory Bromley; 5 Joris Canton; 3 Sebastien Planas; 4 Damien Couturier; 31 Carlos Mendes Varela; 6 Constant Villegas; 7 Nathan Wynn; 8 Brendan Worth; 9 Martin Mitchell; 10 Mathieu Griffi; 11 Tim Wynn; 12 Matthieu Almarcha; 20 Sylvain Houles. Subs (all used): 22 Nicholas Faure; 16 Olivier Pramil; 14 Anton Maria; 23 Cedric Gay.
Tries: Couturier (2), Planas (22, 79), Pramil (45), Gay (60, 62); **Goals:** N Wynn 5/8.
Sin bin: T Wynn (73) - interference.
Rugby Leaguer & League Express Men of the Match: *Rovers:* Tim Spears; *Olympique:* Nathan Wynn.
Penalty count: 11-11; **Half-time:** 12-14;
Referee: Mohammed Drizza; **Attendance:** 1,346.

GATESHEAD THUNDER 34 BATLEY BULLDOGS 34

THUNDER: 19 Nick Youngquest; 1 Ben McAlpine; 4 Dylan Nash; 25 Paul Franze; 5 Stewart Sanderson; 13 Russ Aitken; 7 Luke Branighan; 34 Liam Watts; 9 Andrew Henderson; 33 Nathan Massey; 12 Michael Knowles; 24 Kris Kahler; 32 James Cording. Subs (all used): 21 Ryan McBride; 15 Matt Barron; 35 Anthony England; 6 Neil Thorman.

Gateshead's Michael Knowles fends off Toulouse's Damien Couturier

Tries: McAlpine (2, 57), Youngquest (5, 43), Branighan (27), Franze (63); **Goals:** Knowles 5/8.
BULLDOGS: 1 Ian Preece; 18 Jermaine McGilvary; 11 Kevin Crouthers; 4 Danny Maun; 5 John Campbell; 6 Mark Barlow; 30 Paul Handforth; 8 Byron Smith; 9 Kris Lythe; 15 Anthony Henderson; 23 Chris Buttery; 17 Craig Potter; 13 Ashley Lindsay. Subs (all used): 14 John Gallagher; 16 Jon Simpson; 20 David Tootill; 21 Nathan Armitage.
Tries: Tootill (24), Lythe (31), McGilvary (37), Crouthers (50, 73), Preece (70); **Goals:** Handforth 5/6.
Rugby Leaguer & League Express Men of the Match:
Thunder: Nick Youngquest; *Bulldogs:* Paul Handforth.
Penalty count: 7-7; **Half-time:** 14-18;
Referee: Peter Brooke; **Attendance:** 554.

Sunday 2nd August 2009

LEIGH CENTURIONS 31 DONCASTER 28

CENTURIONS: 14 Ian Mort; 1 Stuart Donlan; 15 Adam Higson; 31 Mick Nanyn; 3 Steve Maden; 37 Tom Hemingway; 7 Ian Watson; 10 Mike Morrison; 9 Dave McConnell; 16 Chris Hill; 11 Dave Armitstead; 30 Macgraff Leuluai; 13 Aaron Smith. Subs (all used): 36 Mark Castle; 39 Dean Dollin; 12 James Taylor; 28 Danny Meekin
Tries: Leuluai (8, 65), Watson (12), McConnell (30), Mort (70); **Goals:** Mort 4/4, Nanyn 1/1;
Field goal: Hemingway (78).
DONCASTER: 1 Tommy Griffiths; 5 Scott McDonald; 19 Ryan Steen; 4 Shaun Leaf; 2 Dean Colton; 6 Matthew Handforth; 13 Josh Weeden; 16 Craig Jones; 9 Kyle Kesik; 21 Gary Ellery; 15 Mark McKinley; 12 Spencer Miller; 24 Jake Bassinder. Subs (all used): 30 Wayne Opie; 34 Danny Vento; 25 Danny Stanley; 31 Mark Stubbley.
Tries: McDonald (2), Griffiths (28), Colton (32), Leaf (50), Weeden (53); **Goals:** Weeden 4/5.
Rugby Leaguer & League Express Men of the Match:
Centurions: Chris Hill; *Doncaster:* Josh Weeden.
Penalty count: 5-5; **Half-time:** 18-16;
Referee: Greg Dolan; **Attendance:** 1,394.

WHITEHAVEN 36 SHEFFIELD EAGLES 34

WHITEHAVEN: 4 Derry Eilbeck; 33 Scott Lofthouse; 3 Rob Jackson; 13 Scott McAvoy; 2 Craig Calvert; 6 Carl Rudd; 7 Leroy Joe; 19 Kyle Amor; 9 Graeme Mattinson; 10 Karl Edmondson; 15 Andy Gorski; 12 Spencer Miller; 25 Jamie Theohaurus. Subs (all used): 8 Marc Jackson; 11 Howard Hill; 24 Gregg McNally; 26 Andy Thornley.
Tries: Amor (6), Gorski (13), Calvert (17, 58), Theohaurus (25, 44); **Goals:** Rudd 6/6.
EAGLES: 1 Jonny Woodcock; 32 Danny Mills; 3 Menzie Yere; 28 Damian Gibson; 5 Ashley Thackeray; 6 Brendon Lindsay; 19 Kyle Wood; 22 Ryan Hepworth; 34 Craig Cook; 10 Mitchell Stringer; 11 Alex Szostak; 29 Peter Green; 16 Trevor Exton. Subs (all used): 23 Tangi Ropati;

15 Sam Barlow; 31 Joe Hirst; 30 Michael Haley.
Tries: Mills (9), Barlow (34), Yere (39), Lindsay (41), Wood (62), Stringer (66);
Goals: Woodcock 3/4, Stringer 2/2.
Rugby Leaguer & League Express Men of the Match:
Whitehaven: Jamie Theohaurus; *Eagles:* Menzie Yere.
Penalty count: 7-7; **Half-time:** 24-16;
Referee: Robert Hicks; **Attendance:** 1,850.

ROUND 19

Saturday 8th August 2009

TOULOUSE OLYMPIQUE 20 GATESHEAD THUNDER 48

OLYMPIQUE: 1 Rory Bromley; 23 Cedric Gay; 3 Sebastien Planas; 4 Damien Couturier; 31 Carlos Mendes Varela; 6 Constant Villegas; 7 Nathan Wynn; 8 Brendan Worth; 9 Martin Mitchell; 24 Jean-Christophe Borlin; 11 Tim Wynn; 14 Anton Maria; 20 Sylvain Houles. Subs (all used): 10 Mathieu Griffi; 13 Eric Anselme; 16 Olivier Pramil; 32 Yoan Tisseyre.
Tries: Griffi (27), Mendes Varela (58), Maria (61), Borlin (75); **Goals:** N Wynn 2/4.
THUNDER: 19 Nick Youngquest; 1 Ben McAlpine; 4 Dylan Nash; 25 Paul Franze, 3 Stewart Sanderson; 7 Luke Branighan; 13 Russ Aitken; 34 Liam Watts; 9 Andrew Henderson; 33 Nathan Massey; 32 James Cording; 12 Michael Knowles; 24 Kris Kahler. Subs (all used): 21 Ryan McBride; 15 Matt Barron; 35 Anthony England; 6 Neil Thorman.
Tries: Cording (7, 46), McAlpine (11, 54), Knowles (20), Aitken (39, 52), Sanderson (67), Branighan (70);
Goals: Knowles 6/9.
Rugby Leaguer & League Express Men of the Match:
Olympique: Martin Mitchell; *Thunder:* Luke Branighan.
Penalty count: 7-7; **Half-time:** 6-18;
Referee: Ronnie Laughton; **Attendance:** 1,681.

Sunday 9th August 2009

BATLEY BULLDOGS 22 SHEFFIELD EAGLES 34

BULLDOGS: 1 Ian Preece; 5 John Campbell; 6 Mark Barlow; 4 Danny Maun; 18 Jermaine McGilvary; 23 Chris Buttery; 30 Paul Handforth; 8 Byron Smith; 9 Kris Lythe; 15 Anthony Henderson; 11 Kevin Crouthers; 17 Craig Potter; 13 Ashley Lindsay. Subs (all used): 12 Mark Toohey; 21 Nathan Armitage; 16 Jon Simpson; 20 David Tootill.
Tries: McGilvary (13, 78), Maun (38), Preece (74);
Goals: Handforth 3/6.
EAGLES: 1 Jonny Woodcock; 32 Danny Mills; 3 Menzie Yere; 23 Tangi Ropati; 5 Ashley Thackeray; 6 Brendon Lindsay; 19 Kyle Wood; 8 Jack Howieson; 34 Craig

Cook; 10 Mitchell Stringer; 11 Alex Szostak; 29 Peter Green; 31 Joe Hirst. Subs (all used): 35 Luke Hardbottle; 22 Ryan Hepworth; 16 Trevor Exton; 30 Michael Haley.
Tries: Mills (18, 43), Lindsay (35, 56), Wood (41), Hardbottle (46); **Goals:** Woodcock 5/6.
Sin bin: Hepworth (25) - tripping.
Rugby Leaguer & League Express Men of the Match:
Bulldogs: Jermaine McGilvary; *Eagles:* Brendon Lindsay.
Penalty count: 11-8; **Half-time:** 10-12;
Referee: Jamie Leahy; **Attendance:** 730.

DONCASTER 0 BARROW RAIDERS 64

DONCASTER: 1 Scott McDonald; 5 Chris McNamara; 19 Ryan Steen; 4 Shaun Leaf; 2 Dean Colton; 30 Wayne Opie; 13 Josh Weeden; 21 Gary Ellery; 9 Kyle Kesik; 10 Alex Benson; 34 Danny Vento; 12 Craig Lawton; 24 Jake Bassinder. Subs (all used): 25 Danny Stanley; 31 Mark Stubbley; 14 Craig Holt; 32 David Bates.
Goals: Weeden 0/1.
RAIDERS: 1 Gary Broadbent; 36 Andy Ballard; 32 Andreas Bauer; 4 Liam Harrison; 5 James Nixon; 33 Dave Allen; 31 James Coyle; 15 Chris Young; 9 Andy Ellis; 13 Andy Bracek; 22 Ned Catic; 14 Paul Noone; 26 Zebastian Luisi. Subs (all used): 19 Chris Larkin; 12 Martin Ostler; 34 Rob Roberts; 35 Danny Halliwell.
Tries: Luisi (24, 73), Ellis (33), Ostler (36), Nixon (41), Catic (44, 66), Bracek (49), Coyle (57, 79), Harrison (75); **Goals:** Ballard 10/11.
Rugby Leaguer & League Express Men of the Match:
Doncaster: Craig Lawton; *Raiders:* James Coyle.
Penalty count: 5-3; **Half-time:** 0-18;
Referee: Craig Halloran; **Attendance:** 481.

FEATHERSTONE ROVERS 34 WIDNES VIKINGS 29

ROVERS: 3 Ian Hardman; 5 Jon Steel; 4 Andy Kirk; 1 Tom Saxton; 2 Waine Pryce; 28 Kyle Briggs; 7 Andy Kain; 10 Stuart Dickens; 9 Jack Lee; 15 James Houston; 18 Tim Spears; 11 Matty Dale; 14 Tom Haughey. Subs (all used): 29 Ross Divorty; 30 Dwayne Barker; 16 Joe McLocklan; 8 Tony Tonks.
Tries: Briggs (8), Steel (38), A Kain (40), Saxton (42, 79), Dickens (74); **Goals:** Dickens 5/6.
VIKINGS: 16 Gavin Dodd; 22 Paddy Flynn; 3 Richard Varkulis; 4 Toa Kohe-Love; 29 Kevin Penny; 15 Tim Hartley; 7 James Webster; 28 Steve Pickersgill; 9 Mark Smith; 10 Jim Gannon; 11 Lee Doran; 35 Jon Grayshon; 14 John Duffy. Subs (all used): 2 Dean Gaskell; 6 Anthony Thackeray; 17 Ben Kavanagh; 19 Michael Ostick.
Tries: Kohe-Love (2), Flynn (28, 54), Thackeray (32, 48); **Goals:** Hartley 4/6; **Field goal:** Smith (72).
Rugby Leaguer & League Express Men of the Match:
Rovers: Stuart Dickens; *Vikings:* Anthony Thackeray.
Penalty count: 8-9; **Half-time:** 16-16;
Referee: Matthew Thomasson; **Attendance:** 2,125.

HALIFAX 42 WHITEHAVEN 50

HALIFAX: 4 Shad Royston; 2 Lee Patterson; 3 Jon Goddard; 5 James Haley; 23 Rob Worrincy; 13 Bob Beswick; 7 Ben Black; 26 Dominic Maloney; 14 Mark Gleeson; 22 David Wrench; 11 David Larder; 27 Steve Bannister; 12 Paul Smith. Subs (all used): 9 Sean Penkywicz; 16 Said Tamghart; 17 Frank Watene; 19 Mick Govin.
Tries: Larder (13), Smith (35), Haley (57, 68), Worrincy (64), Royston (71), Goddard (73), Penkywicz (78); **Goals:** Patterson 5/7, Govin 0/1.
Sin bin: Wrench (76) - late challenge.
WHITEHAVEN: 1 Craig Benson; 2 Craig Calvert; 13 Scott McAvoy; 3 Rob Jackson; 4 Derry Eilbeck; 6 Carl Rudd; 7 Leroy Joe; 11 Howard Hill; 9 Graeme Mattinson; 10 Karl Edmondson; 12 Spencer Miller; 15 Andy Gorski; 25 Jamie Theohaurus. Subs (all used): 8 Marc Jackson; 19 Kyle Amor; 26 Andy Thornley; 28 Chris Smith.
Tries: Calvert (4, 24, 48, 80), Eilbeck (16, 32), Theohaurus (38), Edmondson (40), Thornley (41); **Goals:** Rudd 1/2, M Jackson 3/5, Joe 3/4.
Rugby Leaguer & League Express Men of the Match: *Halifax:* David Larder; *Whitehaven:* Craig Calvert.
Penalty count: 10-8; **Half-time:** 10-34;
Referee: Peter Brooke; **Attendance:** 2,014.

ROUND 20

Thursday 13th August 2009

BARROW RAIDERS 38 WIDNES VIKINGS 16

RAIDERS: 1 Gary Broadbent; 36 Andy Ballard; 32 Andreas Bauer; 4 Liam Harrison; 5 James Nixon; 24 Jamie Rooney; 31 James Coyle; 34 Rob Roberts; 9 Andy Ellis; 13 Andy Bracek; 22 Ned Catic; 14 Paul Noone; 26 Zebastian Luisi. Subs (all used): 35 Danny Halliwell; 8 Brett McDermott; 12 Martin Ostler; 33 Dave Allen.
Tries: Noone (12), Bauer (48), Nixon (51), Broadbent (57), Ballard (69), Rooney (79); **Goals:** Rooney 7/7.
VIKINGS: 16 Gavin Dodd; 22 Paddy Flynn; 3 Richard Varkulis; 15 Tim Hartley; 2 Dean Gaskell; 6 Anthony Thackeray; 7 James Webster; 10 Jim Gannon; 9 Mark Smith; 19 Michael Ostick; 11 Lee Doran; 35 Jon Grayshon; 13 Lee Paterson. Subs (all used): 21 Scott Yates; 17 Ben Kavanagh; 23 Shane Grady; 31 David Houghton.
Tries: Dodd (18), Flynn (43), Hartley (66);
Goals: Hartley 2/3.
Rugby Leaguer & League Express Men of the Match: *Raiders:* Jamie Rooney; *Vikings:* Gavin Dodd.
Penalty count: 10-9; **Half-time:** 8-4;
Referee: Jamie Leahy; **Attendance:** 3,050.

SHEFFIELD EAGLES 38 HALIFAX 24

EAGLES: 1 Jonny Woodcock; 32 Danny Mills; 3 Menzie Yere; 23 Tangi Ropati; 5 Ashley Thackeray; 6 Brendon Lindsay; 20 Matty Brooks; 8 Jack Howieson; 34 Craig Cook; 22 Ryan Hepworth; 11 Alex Szostak; 29 Peter Green; 16 Trevor Exton. Subs (all used): 19 Kyle Wood; 30 Michael Haley; 15 Sam Barlow; 10 Mitchell Stringer.
Tries: Hepworth (9), Stringer (32), Exton (36), Thackeray (60), Ropati (66), Howieson (73), Mills (80);
Goals: Woodcock 5/8.
HALIFAX: 4 Shad Royston; 2 Lee Patterson; 3 Jon Goddard; 27 Steve Bannister; 5 James Haley; 19 Mick Govin; 9 Sean Penkywicz; 21 Neil Cherryholme; 14 Mark Gleeson; 22 David Wrench; 11 David Larder; 12 Paul Smith; 13 Bob Beswick. Subs (all used): 26 Dominic Maloney; 18 Andy Bowman; 17 Frank Watene; 7 Ben Black.
Tries: Patterson (14), Haley (17), Smith (25), Goddard (43); **Goals:** Patterson 4/4.
Rugby Leaguer & League Express Men of the Match: *Eagles:* Ryan Hepworth; *Halifax:* Sean Penkywicz.
Penalty count: 4-4; **Half-time:** 16-18;
Referee: Craig Halloran; **Attendance:** 1,457.

Saturday 15th August 2009

LEIGH CENTURIONS 26 TOULOUSE OLYMPIQUE 6

CENTURIONS: 1 Stuart Donlan; 5 Nicky Stanton; 31 Mick Nanyn; 2 David Alstead; 14 Ian Mort; 37 Tom Hemingway; 7 Ian Watson; 16 Chris Hill; 9 Dave McConnell; 10 Mike Morrison; 11 Dave Armitstead; 30 Macgraff Leuluai; 13 Aaron Smith. Subs (all used): 4 Anthony Stewart; 15 Adam Higson; 28 Danny Meekin; 12 James Taylor.
Tries: Alstead (3), Stanton (12), Nanyn (65), Watson (74); **Goals:** Mort 5/6.
OLYMPIQUE: 1 Rory Bromley; 2 Sebastien Payen; 3 Sebastien Planas; 4 Damien Couturier; 5 Joris Canton; 6 Constant Villegas; 7 Nathan Wynn; 8 Brendan Worth; 9 Martin Mitchell; 10 Mathieu Griffi; 11 Tim Wynn; 12 Matthieu Almarcha; 20 Sylvain Houles. Subs (all used): 24 Jean-Christophe Borlin; 17 Yohan Barthau; 14 Anton Maria; 13 Eric Anselme.
Try: Couturier (36); **Goals:** N Wynn 1/1.
Rugby Leaguer & League Express Men of the Match: *Centurions:* Stuart Donlan; *Olympique:* Brendan Worth.
Penalty count: 8-5; **Half-time:** 12-6;
Referee: Robert Hicks (replaced at half-time by Gordon Wallace); **Attendance:** 1,502.

Sunday 16th August 2009

DONCASTER 10 FEATHERSTONE ROVERS 56

DONCASTER: 1 Scott McDonald; 5 Chris McNamara; 30 Wayne Opie; 4 Shaun Leaf; 2 Dean Colton; 15 Mark McKinley; 6 Matthew Handforth; 21 Gary Ellery; 9 Kyle Kesik; 32 David Bates; 34 Danny Vento; 8 Steve Hall; 19 Ryan Steen. Subs (all used): 25 Danny Stanley; 31 Mark Stubbley; 24 Jake Bassinder; 16 Craig Jones.
Tries: Vento (4), Stubbley (71); **Goals:** McKinley 1/2.
ROVERS: 3 Ian Hardman; 5 Jon Steel; 1 Tom Saxton; 30 Dwayne Barker; 2 Waine Pryce; 28 Kyle Briggs; 7 Andy Kain; 15 James Houston; 9 Jack Lee; 10 Stuart Dickens; 11 Matty Dale; 18 Tim Spears; 14 Tom Haughey. Subs (all used): 33 Aaron Dobek; 4 Andy Kirk; 29 Ross Divorty; 8 Tony Tonks.
Tries: Hardman (1, 24, 26, 30, 47), Briggs (18, 36), Lee (42), Pryce (65), Haughey (75);
Goals: Dickens 8/9, Dobek 0/1.
Rugby Leaguer & League Express Men of the Match: *Doncaster:* Kyle Kesik; *Rovers:* Ian Hardman.
Penalty count: 8-7; **Half-time:** 4-34;
Referee: Ronnie Laughton; **Attendance:** 641.

Batley's Ashley Lindsay challenged by Halifax's Said Tamghart and David Larder

WHITEHAVEN 20 BATLEY BULLDOGS 12

WHITEHAVEN: 1 Craig Benson; 5 Ade Adebisi; 32 Paul Ballard; 13 Scott McAvoy; 2 Craig Calvert; 6 Carl Rudd; 7 Leroy Joe; 11 Howard Hill; 9 Graeme Mattinson; 10 Karl Edmondson; 12 Spencer Miller; 15 Andy Gorski; 25 Jamie Theohaurus. Subs (all used): 24 Gregg McNally; 8 Marc Jackson; 26 Andy Thornley; 19 Kyle Amor.
Tries: Theohaurus (2), Amor (18), McAvoy (27);
Goals: Rudd 3/3, McNally 1/2.
BULLDOGS: 1 Ian Preece; 18 Jermaine McGilvary; 6 Mark Barlow; 4 Danny Maun; 5 John Campbell; 30 Paul Handforth; 7 Paul Mennell; 8 Byron Smith; 9 Kris Lythe; 10 Luke Stenchion; 11 Kevin Crouthers; 17 Craig Potter; 13 Ashley Lindsay. Subs (all used): 16 Jon Simpson; 20 David Tootill; 14 John Gallagher; 12 Mark Toohey.
Tries: Simpson (71), Mennell (79); **Goals:** Mennell 2/2.
Rugby Leaguer & League Express Men of the Match: *Whitehaven:* Karl Edmondson; *Bulldogs:* Paul Mennell.
Penalty count: 11-13; **Half-time:** 18-0;
Referee: Mohammed Drizza; **Attendance:** 1,550.

ROUND 21

Thursday 20th August 2009

BATLEY BULLDOGS 32 HALIFAX 28

BULLDOGS: 1 Ian Preece; 28 Daryl Cardiss; 6 Mark Barlow; 4 Danny Maun; 5 John Campbell; 30 Paul Handforth; 7 Paul Mennell; 16 Jon Simpson; 9 Kris Lythe; 8 Byron Smith; 17 Craig Potter; 12 Mark Toohey; 13 Ashley Lindsay. Subs (all used): 14 John Gallagher; 23 Chris Buttery; 10 Luke Stenchion; 20 David Tootill.
Tries: Smith (3), Toohey (21), Lindsay (27), Preece (33), Mennell (38), Maun (76); **Goals:** Mennell 4/6.
HALIFAX: 4 Shad Royston; 2 Lee Patterson; 3 Jon Goddard; 15 Mark Roberts; 5 James Haley; 13 Bob Beswick; 7 Ben Black; 16 Said Tamghart; 14 Mark Gleeson; 26 Dominic Maloney; 11 David Larder; 18 Andy Bowman; 19 Mick Govin. Subs (all used): 9 Sean Penkywicz; 21 Neil Cherryholme; 22 David Wrench; 25 Anthony Bowman.
Tries: Cherryholme (31), Larder (43, 69), Gleeson (52), Tamghart (74); **Goals:** Patterson 4/5.
Rugby Leaguer & League Express Men of the Match: *Bulldogs:* Ashley Lindsay; *Halifax:* Ben Black.
Penalty count: 8-8; **Half time:** 28-6;
Referee: Matthew Thomasson; **Attendance:** 1,430.

Saturday 22nd August 2009

WIDNES VIKINGS 58 WHITEHAVEN 10

VIKINGS: 16 Gavin Dodd; 22 Paddy Flynn; 15 Tim Hartley; 3 Richard Varkulis; 2 Dean Gaskell; 6 Anthony Thackeray; 7 James Webster; 19 Michael Ostick; 9 Mark Smith; 10 Jim Gannon; 12 Richard Fletcher; 11 Lee Doran; 8 Iain Morrison. Subs (all used): 14 John Duffy; 17 Ben Kavanagh; 23 Shane Grady; 31 David Houghton.
Tries: Thackeray (8), Varkulis (12, 78), Gannon (15), Fletcher (27, 70), Duffy (40), Flynn (46), Gaskell (60), Doran (67); **Goals:** Hartley 9/11.
WHITEHAVEN: 1 Craig Benson; 5 Ade Adebisi; 32 Paul Ballard; 3 Rob Jackson; 2 Craig Calvert; 13 Scott McAvoy; 24 Greg McNally; 19 Kyle Amor; 8 Marc Jackson; 10 Karl Edmondson; 12 Spencer Miller; 15 Andy Gorski; 7 Leroy Joe. Subs (all used): 28 Chris Smith; 25 Jamie Theohaurus; 26 Andy Thornley; 16 Ryan McDonald.
Tries: R Jackson (2), McAvoy (38); **Goals:** McNally 1/2.
Sin bin: Theohaurus (29) - interference.
Rugby Leaguer & League Express Men of the Match: *Vikings:* Richard Fletcher; *Whitehaven:* Jamie Theohaurus.
Penalty count: 11-4; **Half-time:** 28-10;
Referee: Ronnie Laughton; **Attendance:** 3,275.

TOULOUSE OLYMPIQUE 52 DONCASTER 6

OLYMPIQUE: 1 Rory Bromley; 2 Sebastien Payen; 3 Sebastien Planas; 13 Eric Anselme; 31 Carlos Mendes Varela; 6 Constant Villegas; 7 Nathan Wynn; 8 Brendan Worth; 9 Martin Mitchell; 10 Mathieu Griffi; 11 Tim Wynn; 14 Anton Maria; 20 Sylvain Houles. Subs (all used): 24 Jean-Christophe Borlin; 12 Matthieu Almarcha; 4 Damien Couturier; 32 Yoan Tisseyre.
Tries: Villegas (3, 12), Bromley (9), Mendes Varela (18), Mitchell (28), Planas (33, 78), Griffi (39), N Wynn (51), Tisseyre (69); **Goals:** N Wynn 6/10.
Sin bin: Planas (67) - fighting.
DONCASTER: 4 Shaun Leaf; 5 Chris McNamara; 8 Steve Hall; 19 Ryan Steen; 30 Wayne Opie; 6 Matthew Handforth; 22 Andy Speake; 21 Gary Ellery; 9 Kyle Kesik; 32 David Bates; 34 Danny Vento; 24 Jake Bassinder; 15 Mark McKinley. Subs (all used): 1 Scott Howlett; 36 Liam Booth; 31 Mark Stubbley; 25 Danny Stanley.
Try: Vento (75); **Goals:** Speake 1/1.
Sin bin: Stanley (67) - fighting.
Rugby Leaguer & League Express Men of the Match: *Olympique:* Constant Villegas; *Doncaster:* Kyle Kesik.
Penalty count: 7-7; **Half-time:** 38-0;
Referee: Greg Dolan; **Attendance:** 1,200.

Sunday 23rd August 2009

FEATHERSTONE ROVERS 28 BARROW RAIDERS 46

ROVERS: 3 Ian Hardman; 5 Jon Steel; 4 Andy Kirk; 1 Tom Saxton; 2 Waine Pryce; 28 Kyle Briggs; 7 Andy Kain; 10 Stuart Dickens; 9 Jack Lee; 8 Tony Tonks; 11 Matty Dale; 18 Tim Spears; 14 Tom Haughey. Subs (all used): 16 Joe McLocklan; 15 James Houston; 29 Ross Divorty; 6 Iestyn Harris.
Tries: Steel (30), Harris (37), Hardman (44, 52), Kirk (60), Pryce (71); **Goals:** Dickens 0/1, Briggs 2/5.
RAIDERS: 1 Gary Broadbent; 36 Andy Ballard; 32 Andreas Bauer; 4 Liam Harrison; 5 James Nixon; 24 Jamie Rooney; 31 James Coyle; 34 Rob Roberts; 9 Andy Ellis; 13 Andy Bracek; 22 Ned Catic; 33 Dave Allen; 26 Zebastian Luisi. Subs (all used): 15 Chris Young; 35 Danny Halliwell; 12 Martin Ostler; 14 Paul Noone.
Tries: Harrison (6), Ballard (10), Coyle (12), Bauer (24), Rooney (34), Nixon (55, 65); **Goals:** Rooney 9/10.
Rugby Leaguer & League Express Men of the Match: *Rovers:* Iestyn Harris; *Raiders:* Jamie Rooney.
Penalty count: 11-7; **Half-time:** 8-30;
Referee: James Child; **Attendance:** 2,099.

GATESHEAD THUNDER 30 LEIGH CENTURIONS 24

THUNDER: 19 Nick Youngquest; 1 Ben McAlpine; 4 Dylan Nash; 25 Paul Franze; 5 Stewart Sanderson; 13 Russ Aitken; 7 Luke Branighan; 34 Liam Watts; 9 Andrew Henderson; 33 Nathan Massey; 12 Michael Knowles; 32 James Cording; 24 Kris Kahler. Subs (all used): 21 Ryan McBride; 15 Matt Barron; 35 Anthony England; 6 Neil Thorman.
Tries: Youngquest (18, 46, 52), Branighan (27), Sanderson (41); **Goals:** Knowles 5/6.
CENTURIONS: 1 Stuart Donlan; 5 Nicky Stanton; 31 Mick Nanyn; 2 David Alstead; 14 Ian Mort; 4 Anthony Stewart; 23 Martyn Ridyard; 16 Chris Hill; 9 Dave McConnell; 10 Mike Morrison; 30 Macgraff Leuluai; 11 Dave Armitstead; 13 Aaron Smith. Subs (all used): 26 Jamie Durbin; 15 Adam Higson; 12 James Taylor; 28 Danny Meekin.
Tries: Taylor (38), Morrison (48), Stanton (63, 73);
Goals: Mort 4/5.
Rugby Leaguer & League Express Men of the Match: *Thunder:* Nick Youngquest; *Centurions:* Stuart Donlan.
Penalty count: 12-13; **Half-time:** 14-8;
Referee: Craig Halloran; **Attendance:** 1,033.

Leigh's Danny Meekin meets Whitehaven's Graeme Mattinson head on

ROUND 9

Thursday 27th August 2009

SHEFFIELD EAGLES 28 FEATHERSTONE ROVERS 12

EAGLES: 1 Jonny Woodcock; 32 Danny Mills; 3 Menzie Yere; 23 Tangi Ropati; 28 Damian Gibson; 6 Brendon Lindsay; 20 Matty Brooks; 8 Jack Howieson; 34 Craig Cook; 22 Ryan Hepworth; 11 Alex Szostak; 29 Peter Green; 31 Joe Hirst. Subs (all used): 19 Kyle Wood; 30 Michael Haley; 15 Sam Barlow; 10 Mitchell Stringer.
Tries: Yere (1), Cook (16), Wood (26), Green (30), Lindsay (67); **Goals:** Woodcock 4/5.
ROVERS: 3 Ian Hardman; 5 Jon Steel; 4 Andy Kirk; 14 Tom Haughey; 2 Waine Pryce; 6 Iestyn Harris; 28 Kyle Briggs; 10 Stuart Dickens; 7 Andy Kain; 29 Ross Divorty; 11 Matty Dale; 18 Tim Spears; 30 Dwayne Barker. Subs (all used): 15 James Houston; 8 Tony Tonks; 16 Joe McLocklan; 1 Tom Saxton.
Tries: Dale (43), Saxton (63); **Goals:** Harris 1/1, Dickens 1/1.
Rugby Leaguer & League Express Men of the Match: *Eagles:* Sam Barlow; *Rovers:* Iestyn Harris.
Penalty count: 6-5; **Half-time:** 22-0;
Referee: Ronnie Laughton; **Attendance:** 1,028.

Monday 31st August 2009

LEIGH CENTURIONS 18 HALIFAX 27

CENTURIONS: 1 Stuart Donlan; 5 Nicky Stanton; 2 David Alstead; 31 Mick Nanyn; 3 Steve Maden; 4 Anthony Stewart; 23 Martyn Ridyard; 16 Chris Hill; 26 Jamie Durbin; 28 Danny Meekin; 12 James Taylor; 30 Macgraff Leuluai; 11 Dave Armitstead. Subs (all used): 15 Adam Higson; 9 Dave McConnell; 10 Mike Morrison; 29 Lee Wingfield.
Tries: Nanyn (8), Ridyard (29), Donlan (71);
Goals: Nanyn 2/4, Ridyard 1/1.
Sin bin: Nanyn (38) – holding down.
HALIFAX: 4 Shad Royston; 2 Lee Patterson; 3 Jon Goddard; 5 James Haley; 23 Rob Worrincy; 13 Bob Beswick; 9 Sean Penkywicz; 26 Dominic Maloney; 14 Mark Gleeson; 22 David Wrench; 11 David Larder; 15 Mark Roberts; 12 Paul Smith. Subs (all used): 10 Dana Wilson; 16 Said Tamghart; 19 Mick Govin; 27 Steve Bannister.
Tries: Worrincy (18, 31, 59), Royston (51, 77);
Goals: Patterson 3/5; **Field goal:** Beswick (79).
Rugby Leaguer & League Express Men of the Match: *Centurions:* Dave Armitstead; *Halifax:* Rob Worrincy.
Penalty count: 10-12; **Half-time:** 12-12;
Referee: Greg Dolan; **Attendance:** 2,349.

BARROW RAIDERS 12 GATESHEAD THUNDER 16

RAIDERS: 1 Gary Broadbent; 36 Andy Ballard; 32 Andreas Bauer; 4 Liam Harrison; 5 James Nixon; 24 Jamie Rooney; 31 James Coyle; 34 Rob Roberts; 9 Andy Ellis; 13 Andy Bracek; 22 Ned Catic; 33 Dave Allen; 26 Zebastian Luisi. Subs (all used): 15 Chris Young; 8 Brett McDermott; 12 Martin Ostler; 14 Paul Noone.
Tries: Harrison (12), Ellis (35); **Goals:** Rooney 2/3.
THUNDER: 19 Nick Youngquest; 1 Ben McAlpine; 4 Dylan Nash; 25 Paul Franze; 5 Stewart Sanderson; 13 Russ Aitken; 6 Neil Thorman; 34 Liam Watts; 9 Andrew Henderson; 35 Anthony England; 12 Michael Knowles; 32 James Cording; 24 Kris Kahler. Subs (all used): 21 Ryan McBride; 15 Matt Barron; 14 Ryan Clarke; 33 Nathan Massey.
Tries: Knowles (38), Nash (76); **Goals:** Knowles 4/4.
Rugby Leaguer & League Express Men of the Match: *Raiders:* Jamie Rooney; *Thunder:* Dylan Nash.
Penalty count: 12-12; **Half-time:** 12-8;
Referee: Ronnie Laughton; **Attendance:** 2,981.

ROUND 22

Thursday 3rd September 2009

SHEFFIELD EAGLES 29 BARROW RAIDERS 22

EAGLES: 1 Jonny Woodcock; 32 Danny Mills; 3 Menzie Yere; 23 Tangi Ropati; 28 Damian Gibson; 19 Kyle Wood; 20 Matty Brooks; 8 Jack Howieson; 34 Craig Cook; 30 Michael Haley; 11 Alex Szostak; 29 Peter Green; 31 Joe Hirst. Subs (all used): 22 Ryan Hepworth; 16 Trevor Exton; 15 Sam Barlow; 10 Mitchell Stringer.
Tries: Yere (4), Barlow (29), Stringer (39), Mills (48), Cook (79); **Goals:** Woodcock 4/5; **Field goal:** Cook (75).
RAIDERS: 1 Gary Broadbent; 36 Andy Ballard; 32 Andreas Bauer; 4 Liam Harrison; 5 James Nixon; 24 Jamie Rooney; 31 James Coyle; 34 Rob Roberts; 9 Andy Ellis; 8 Brett McDermott; 33 Dave Allen; 12 Martin Ostler; 26 Zebastian Luisi. Subs (all used): 15 Chris Young; 13 Andy Bracek; 22 Ned Catic; 14 Paul Noone.
Tries: Ostler (16), Nixon (20), Young (72);
Goals: Rooney 4/5; **Field goals:** Rooney (67, 69).
Rugby Leaguer & League Express Men of the Match: *Eagles:* Craig Cook; *Raiders:* Jamie Rooney.
Penalty count: 7-8; **Half-time:** 18-10;
Referee: Jamie Leahy; **Attendance:** 1,283.

Saturday 5th September 2009

HALIFAX 34 TOULOUSE OLYMPIQUE 10

HALIFAX: 4 Shad Royston; 2 Lee Patterson; 15 Mark Roberts; 5 James Haley; 23 Rob Worrincy; 13 Bob Beswick; 9 Sean Penkywicz; 26 Dominic Maloney; 14 Mark Gleeson; 22 David Wrench; 11 David Larder; 27 Steve Bannister; 12 Paul Smith. Subs (all used): 7 Ben Black; 16 Said Tamghart; 17 Frank Watene; 19 Mick Govin.
Tries: Worrincy (8), Larder (14), Penkywicz (44), Haley (53), Royston (69, 72); **Goals:** Patterson 5/6.
OLYMPIQUE: 4 Damien Couturier; 2 Sebastien Payen; 3 Sebastien Planas; 13 Eric Anselme; 31 Carlos Mendes Varela; 6 Constant Villegas; 7 Nathan Wynn; 8 Brendan Worth; 9 Martin Mitchell; 24 Jean-Christophe Borlin; 14 Anton Maria; 12 Matthieu Almarcha; 20 Sylvain Houles. Subs (all used): 18 Adrien Viala; 17 Yohan Barthau; 32 Yoan Tisseyre; 21 Bruno Ormeno.
Tries: Anselme (23), Tisseyre (48), Ormeno (64);
Goals: N Wynn 3/3.
Rugby Leaguer & League Express Men of the Match: *Halifax:* Shad Royston; *Olympique:* Brendan Worth.
Penalty count: 9-5; **Half-time:** 12-6;
Referee: Craig Halloran; **Attendance:** 2,128.

Sunday 6th September 2009

DONCASTER 0 GATESHEAD THUNDER 56

DONCASTER: 1 Tommy Griffiths; 2 Dean Colton; 30

Wayne Opie; 4 Shaun Leaf; 5 Chris McNamara; 6 Matthew Handforth; 22 Andy Speake; 32 David Bates; 9 Kyle Kesik; 21 Gary Ellery; 15 Mark McKinley; 8 Steve Hall; 19 Ryan Steen. Subs (all used): 25 Danny Stanley; 31 Mark Stubbley; 34 Scott Howlett; 24 Jake Bassinder.
Sin bin: Steen (36) – interference;
Stubbley (37) – interference.
THUNDER: 19 Nick Youngquest; 1 Ben McAlpine; 4 Dylan Nash; 25 Paul Franze; 5 Stewart Sanderson; 13 Russ Aitken; 6 Neil Thorman; 33 Nathan Massey; 9 Andrew Henderson; 34 Liam Watts; 32 James Cording; 12 Michael Knowles; 24 Kris Kahler. Subs (all used): 21 Ryan McBride; 35 Anthony England; 15 Matt Barron; 14 Ryan Clarke.
Tries: Franze (5, 27, 46), Kahler (11, 22), Cording (42), Sanderson (52, 66), McAlpine (57), Watts (59);
Goals: Knowles 8/10.
Rugby Leaguer & League Express Men of the Match: *Doncaster:* Chris McNamara; *Thunder:* Paul Franze.
Penalty count: 0-22; **Half-time:** 0-22;
Referee: Warren Turley; **Attendance:** 551.

FEATHERSTONE ROVERS 26 BATLEY BULLDOGS 30

ROVERS: 3 Ian Hardman; 1 Tom Saxton; 2 Waine Pryce; 28 Kyle Briggs; 7 Andy Kain; 10 Stuart Dickens; 29 James Houston; 11 Matty Dale; 14 Tom Haughey; 30 Dwayne Barker. Subs (all used): 3 Jack Lee; 8 Tony Tonks; 29 Ross Divorty; 26 Sam Smeaton.
Tries: Dale (4), Briggs (21), Steel (27), Barker (65), Divorty (80); **Goals:** Briggs 1/2, Dickens 2/3.
BULLDOGS: 1 Ian Preece; 28 Daryl Cardiss; 11 Kevin Crouthers; 4 Danny Maun; 5 John Campbell; 30 Paul Handforth; 7 Paul Mennell; 16 Jon Simpson; 9 Kris Lythe; 8 Byron Smith; 17 Craig Potter; 12 Mark Toohey; 13 Ashley Lindsay. Subs (all used): 14 John Gallagher; 23 Chris Buttery; 10 Luke Stenchion; 20 David Tootill.
Tries: Crouthers (34), Lythe (42), Mennell (45, 58), Buttery (55); **Goals:** Mennell 5/5.
Rugby Leaguer & League Express Men of the Match: *Rovers:* Ross Divorty; *Bulldogs:* Paul Mennell.
Penalty count: 5-10; **Half-time:** 14-6;
Referee: Matthew Thomasson; **Attendance:** 2,076.

LEIGH CENTURIONS 47 WHITEHAVEN 14

CENTURIONS: 1 Stuart Donlan; 2 David Alstead; 4 Anthony Stewart; 31 Mick Nanyn; 3 Steve Maden; 23 Martyn Ridyard; 7 Ian Watson; 16 Chris Hill; 9 Dave McConnell; 28 Danny Meekin; 12 James Taylor; 11 Dave Armitstead; 13 Aaron Smith. Subs (all used): 15 Adam Higson; 30 Macgraff Leuluai; 26 Jamie Durbin; 29 Lee Wingfield.
Tries: McConnell (10, 19), Nanyn (26, 66), Wingfield (36), Ridyard (45), Alstead (57, 77);
Goals: Nanyn 7/10; **Field goal:** Watson (59).
WHITEHAVEN: 1 Craig Benson; 32 Paul Ballard; 3 Rob Jackson; 13 Scott McAvoy; 2 Craig Calvert; 6 Carl Rudd; 24 Gregg McNally; 10 Karl Edmondson; 9 Graeme Mattinson; 7 Leroy Joe; 12 Spencer Miller; 15 Andy Gorski; 25 Jamie Theoharus. Subs (all used): 28 Chris Smith; 8 Marc Jackson; 19 Kyle Amor; 31 Dexter Miller.
Tries: Ballard (2, 62), R Jackson (71); **Goals:** Rudd 1/3.
Rugby Leaguer & League Express Men of the Match: *Centurions:* Martyn Ridyard; *Whitehaven:* Spencer Miller.
Penalty count: 5-5; **Half-time:** 22-4;
Referee: Ronnie Laughton; **Attendance:** 2,721.

Featherstone celebrate Iestyn Harris' late match-winning try against Widnes

PLAY-OFFS

ELIMINATION PLAY-OFFS

Thursday 10th September 2009

WIDNES VIKINGS 26 WHITEHAVEN 21

VIKINGS: 16 Gavin Dodd; 22 Paddy Flynn; 15 Tim Hartley; 23 Shane Grady; 3 Richard Varkulis; 6 Anthony Thackeray; 7 James Webster; 19 Michael Ostick; 9 Mark Smith; 10 Jim Gannon; 12 Richard Fletcher; 35 Jon Grayshon; 11 Lee Doran. Subs: 17 Ben Kavanagh; 21 Scott Yates; 31 David Houghton; 33 Danny Hulme (not used).
Tries: Grady (6), Hartley (38, 49), Thackeray (58), Webster (72); **Goals:** Hartley 3/5.
WHITEHAVEN: 1 Craig Benson; 2 Craig Calvert; 3 Rob Jackson; 13 Scott McAvoy; 4 Derry Eilbeck; 6 Carl Rudd; 7 Leroy Joe; 19 Kyle Amor; 9 Graeme Mattinson; 10 Karl Edmondson; 12 Spencer Miller; 15 Andy Gorski; 28 Andy Thornley. Subs (all used): 8 Marc Jackson; 28 Chris Smith; 31 Dexter Miller; 42 Reece Fox.
Tries: Joe (2), R Jackson (15), Amor (23);
Goals: Rudd 4/4; **Field goal:** Rudd (71).
Sin bin: S Miller (39) – persistent offside.
Rugby Leaguer & League Express Men of the Match:
Vikings: Anthony Thackeray;
Whitehaven: Graeme Mattinson.
Penalty count: 11-7; **Half-time:** 8-18;
Referee: Ronnie Laughton; **Attendance:** 2,375.

Friday 11th September 2009

SHEFFIELD EAGLES 8 FEATHERSTONE ROVERS 32

EAGLES: 1 Jonny Woodcock; 32 Danny Mills; 3 Menzie Yere; 28 Damian Gibson; 5 Ashley Thackeray; 6 Brendon Lindsay; 19 Kyle Wood; 8 Jack Howieson; 34 Craig Cook; 10 Mitchell Stringer; 11 Alex Szostak; 29 Peter Green; 16 Trevor Exton. Subs (all used): 20 Matty Brooks; 22 Ryan Hepworth; 30 Michael Haley; 15 Sam Barlow.
Try: Mills (50); **Goals:** Woodcock 2/2.
Dismissal: Hepworth (38) – punching.
Sin bin: Cook (1) - fighting; Barlow (38) - fighting.
On report: Brawl (1); Brawl (38).
ROVERS: 3 Ian Hardman; 1 Tom Saxton; 4 Andy Kirk; 14 Tom Haughey; 2 Waine Pryce; 28 Kyle Briggs; 7 Andy Kain; 15 James Houston; 9 Jack Lee; 10 Stuart Dickens; 11 Matty Dale; 18 Tim Spears; 6 Iestyn Harris. Subs: 8 Tony Tonks; 29 Ross Divorty; 16 Joe McLocklan; 5 Jon Steel (not used).
Tries: Briggs (10), Spears (18), Saxton (43), Haughey (63, 75), Lee (78); **Goals:** Dickens 1/3, Harris 3/5.
Dismissal: Hardman (38) – punching.
Sin bin: Harris (1) - fighting; A Kain (38) - fighting.
On report: Brawl (1); Brawl (38).
Rugby Leaguer & League Express Men of the Match:
Eagles: Craig Cook; *Rovers:* Andy Kain.
Penalty count: 13-14; **Half-time:** 2-14;
Referee: Jamie Leahy; **Attendance:** 802.

QUALIFYING SEMI-FINAL

Thursday 17th September 2009

BARROW RAIDERS 35 HALIFAX 12

RAIDERS: 1 Gary Broadbent; 36 Andy Ballard; 32 Andreas Bauer; 4 Liam Harrison; 5 James Nixon; 24 Jamie Rooney; 31 James Coyle; 34 Rob Roberts; 9 Andy Ellis; 8 Brett McDermott; 33 Dave Allen; 22 Ned Catic; 26 Zebastian Luisi. Subs (all used): 15 Chris Young; 13 Andy Bracek; 35 Danny Halliwell; 14 Paul Noone.
Tries: Nixon (14, 75), Ballard (33), Catic (64), Bracek (68); **Goals:** Rooney 7/7; **Field goal:** Rooney (28).
HALIFAX: 4 Shad Royston; 2 Lee Patterson; 3 Jon Goddard; 5 James Haley; 23 Rob Worrincy; 7 Ben Black; 9 Sean Penkywicz; 17 Frank Watene; 13 Bob Beswick; 22 David Wrench; 11 David Larder; 27 Steve Bannister; 12 Paul Smith. Subs (all used): 14 Mark Gleeson; 15 Mark Roberts; 16 Said Tamghart; 26 Dominic Maloney.
Tries: Royston (48, 79); **Goals:** Patterson 2/2.
Rugby Leaguer & League Express Men of the Match:
Raiders: Ned Catic; *Halifax:* Shad Royston.
Penalty count: 11-9; **Half-time:** 15-0;
Referee: Thierry Alibert; **Attendance:** 2,823.

ELIMINATION SEMI-FINAL

Friday 18th September 2009

WIDNES VIKINGS 24 FEATHERSTONE ROVERS 32

VIKINGS: 16 Gavin Dodd; 22 Paddy Flynn; 3 Richard Varkulis; 15 Tim Hartley; 2 Dean Gaskell; 6 Anthony Thackeray; 7 James Webster; 8 Iain Morrison; 9 Mark Smith; 10 Jim Gannon; 12 Richard Fletcher; 35 Jon Grayshon; 11 Lee Doran. Subs (all used): 14 John Duffy; 17 Ben Kavanagh; 19 Michael Ostick; 23 Shane Grady.
Tries: Dodd (12), Doran (14), Grady (64), Varkulis (73); **Goals:** Hartley 4/4.
ROVERS: 3 Ian Hardman; 5 Jon Steel; 4 Andy Kirk; 1 Tom Saxton; 2 Waine Pryce; 28 Kyle Briggs; 7 Andy Kain; 15 James Houston; 9 Jack Lee; 10 Stuart Dickens; 11 Matty Dale; 18 Tim Spears; 6 Iestyn Harris. Subs (all used): 8 Tony Tonks; 16 Joe McLocklan; 17 Joe Hirst; 26 Sam Smeaton.
Tries: Kirk (25), Briggs (37), Pryce (53), Lee (65), Harris (79); **Goals:** Harris 6/6.
Rugby Leaguer & League Express Men of the Match:
Vikings: James Webster; *Rovers:* Iestyn Harris.
Penalty count: 15-8; **Half-time:** 12-14;
Referee: Ben Thaler; **Attendance:** 3,296.

FINAL ELIMINATOR

Thursday 24th September 2009

HALIFAX 36 FEATHERSTONE ROVERS 30

HALIFAX: 4 Shad Royston; 2 Lee Patterson; 15 Mark Roberts; 5 James Haley; 23 Rob Worrincy; 19 Mick Govin; 7 Ben Black; 21 Neil Cherryholme; 9 Sean Penkywicz; 22 David Wrench; 11 David Larder; 27 Steve Bannister; 12 Paul Smith. Subs (all used): 13 Bob Beswick; 14 Mark Gleeson; 16 Said Tamghart; 17 Frank Watene.
Tries: Larder (6, 57), Black (38), Beswick (39), Smith (66), Royston (72); **Goals:** Patterson 6/6.
ROVERS: 3 Ian Hardman; 1 Tom Saxton; 4 Andy Kirk; 14 Tom Haughey; 2 Waine Pryce; 28 Kyle Briggs; 7 Andy Kain; 15 James Houston; 9 Jack Lee; 10 Stuart Dickens; 11 Matty Dale; 18 Tim Spears; 6 Iestyn Harris. Subs (all used): 8 Tony Tonks; 16 Joe McLocklan; 17 Joe Hirst; 29 Ross Divorty.
Tries: Briggs (13), Hardman (16), Divorty (52), Spears (77); **Goals:** Harris 7/7.
Rugby Leaguer & League Express Men of the Match:
Halifax: Ben Black; *Rovers:* Stuart Dickens.
Penalty count: 11-11; **Half-time:** 18-16;
Referee: Ian Smith; **Attendance:** 2,556.

GRAND FINAL

Sunday 4th October 2009

BARROW RAIDERS 26 HALIFAX 18

RAIDERS: 1 Gary Broadbent; 36 Andy Ballard; 32 Andreas Bauer; 4 Liam Harrison; 5 James Nixon; 24 Jamie Rooney; 31 James Coyle; 34 Rob Roberts; 9 Andy Ellis; 8 Brett McDermott; 33 Dave Allen; 22 Ned Catic; 26 Zebastian Luisi. Subs (all used): 15 Chris Young; 13 Andy Bracek; 35 Danny Halliwell; 14 Paul Noone.
Tries: Harrison (33), Ballard (37), Allen (61), Bauer (66, 78); **Goals:** Rooney 3/5.
HALIFAX: 4 Shad Royston; 5 James Haley; 15 Mark Roberts; 2 Lee Patterson; 23 Rob Worrincy; 19 Mick Govin; 7 Ben Black; 21 Neil Cherryholme; 9 Sean Penkywicz; 22 David Wrench; 11 David Larder; 27 Steve Bannister; 12 Paul Smith. Subs (all used): 13 Bob Beswick; 14 Mark Gleeson; 16 Said Tamghart; 26 Dominic Maloney.
Tries: Haley (12), Royston (31), Black (45), Govin (70);
Goals: Patterson 1/5.
Rugby Leaguer & League Express Men of the Match:
Raiders: Gary Broadbent; *Halifax:* Mick Govin.
Penalty count: 8-5; **Half-time:** 10-10;
Referee: Phil Bentham; **Attendance:** 11,398
(at Halliwell Jones Stadium, Warrington).

Barrow's Liam Harrison collars Halifax's Shad Royston during the Championship Grand Final

CHAMPIONSHIP ONE 2009
Club by Club

BLACKPOOL PANTHERS

DATE	FIXTURE	RESULT	SCORERS	LGE	ATT
15/2/09	Keighley (h) (NRC)	W16-14	t:McCully(2),Tucker g:Leather(2)	6th(P1)	400
22/2/09	Rochdale (a) (NRC)	L28-26	t:McCully(2),Leather,Keavney,Munro g:Leather(3)	6th(P1)	371
1/3/09	Widnes (h) (NRC)	L16-46	t:Munro,Alker,Forster g:Leather(2)	8th(P1)	864
4/3/09	Halifax (a) (NRC)	L50-28	t:Leather(2),Ratcliffe,Campbell,Tucker g:Leather(4)	8th(P1)	1,291
8/3/09	Barrow (a) (CCR3)	L44-12	t:Tucker,Leather g:Leather(2)	N/A	1,187
15/3/09	Oldham (a)	L36-18	t:Hatton,Woodcock,Langley(2) g:Langley	N/A	880
22/3/09	Hunslet (h)	W34-26	t:Hatton(2),Clough,Llewellyn(2),Alker g:Langley(5)	6th	265
29/3/09	York (a)	L22-20	t:Langley,McCully,Leather,Llewellyn g:Langley(2)	6th	900
10/4/09	Swinton (h)	L12-16	t:Leather,Ratcliffe g:Langley(2)	6th	411
13/4/09	London Skolars (a)	W10-48	t:Langley,Leather(2),Tucker,Forster,Keavney,Clough(2),Llewellyn g:Langley,Leather(5)	5th	215
26/4/09	Keighley (a)	L42-22	t:Keavney,Llewellyn,Clough,McCully g:Leather(3)	7th	534
4/5/09	Rochdale (h)	W24-12	t:Draper,Langley,Leather,Munro,Hatton g:Leather,Langley	7th	347
17/5/09	Dewsbury (a)	L42-16	t:Alcock,Munro,Tucker g:Leather(2)	7th	1,010
24/5/09	Keighley (h)	L26-30	t:Alcock(2),Forster,Winstanley,Leather g:Leather(3)	7th	500
28/6/09	Workington (h)	W46-18	t:Woodcock,Munro(3),Leather,Svabic,Thompson(2),McCully g:Leather(2),Forber(3)	7th	280
5/7/09	York (h)	W49-36	t:Munro(2),Thompson(2),Royle(2),Keavney,Leather,Hodson g:Leather(4),Duffy(2) fg:Leather	7th	443
19/7/09	Swinton (a)	W18-33	t:Forber,Woodcock,Munro(2),Leather,Royle g:Leather,Forber(3) fg:McCully	5th	440
25/7/09	London Skolars (h)	W46-22	t:Leather(2),Woodcock,Forber,Draper,Munro,Alcock,Keavney g:Leather(4),Forber(3)	5th	391
2/8/09	Hunslet (a)	L34-24	t:Royle,Bissell,Boland,Duffy g:Leather(3),Forber	6th	573
9/8/09	Rochdale (a)	W18-48	t:Keavney,Fairhurst(2),Woodcock,Alcock,Duffy,Thompson,Clough g:Forber(7),Leather	5th	527
16/8/09	Oldham (h)	D30-30	t:Royle(2),Woodcock,Alcock,Llewellyn g:Leather(4),Forber	5th	600
23/8/09	Workington (a)	W10-22	t:Munro,Clough(2),Draper g:Forber(3)	5th	405
6/9/09	Dewsbury (h)	L14-34	t:Woodcock,Llewellyn,Clough g:Forber	5th	975
13/9/09	Hunslet (h) (EPO)	L18-21	t:Hodson,Woodcock(2) g:Forber(3)	N/A	543

		APP		TRIES		GOALS		FG		PTS	
	D.O.B.	ALL	Ch1	ALL	Ch1	ALL	Ch1	ALL	Ch1	ALL	Ch1
Paul Alcock	12/11/82	17(3)	12(3)	6	6	0	0	0	0	24	24
Melvin Alker	6/3/80	5(1)	3	2	1	0	0	0	0	8	4
Simon Bissell	25/12/85	1(9)	1(9)	1	1	0	0	0	0	4	4
John Boland	7/1/86	5(8)	4(6)	1	1	0	0	0	0	4	4
Chris Campbell	2/12/80	6(1)	1(1)	1	0	0	0	0	0	4	0
John Clough	13/9/84	19(5)	14(5)	8	8	0	0	0	0	32	32
Rob Draper	30/11/87	12(6)	10(5)	3	3	0	0	0	0	12	12
Jay Duffy	16/4/87	5(6)	5(6)	2	2	2	2	0	0	12	12
Peter Fairhurst	8/4/83	14(3)	12(2)	2	2	0	0	0	0	8	8
Craig Farrimond	20/11/82	3(2)	1(2)	0	0	0	0	0	0	0	0
Carl Forber	17/3/85	10	10	2	2	25	25	0	0	58	58
Chris Forster	3/5/88	8	4	3	2	0	0	0	0	12	8
Dean Hatton	27/12/87	7(2)	7(2)	4	4	0	0	0	0	16	16
John Hill	7/10/81	2(2)	1(2)	0	0	0	0	0	0	0	0
Ian Hodson	23/10/81	19(1)	16(1)	2	2	0	0	0	0	8	8
Darryl Kay	6/11/87	5(6)	4(3)	0	0	0	0	0	0	0	0
Martin Keavney	5/12/87	7(17)	6(13)	6	5	0	0	0	0	24	20
Gareth Langley	24/10/84	9	9	5	5	12	12	0	0	44	44
Jonny Leather	29/7/89	22	17	15	11	46	33	1	1	153	111
Dave Llewellyn	3/12/82	11	11	7	7	0	0	0	0	28	28
Mark McCully	24/10/79	21	18	7	3	0	0	1	1	29	13
Liam McGovern	6/10/84	1(3)	0	0	0	0	0	0	0	0	0
Chris Mugan	28/12/88	3	0	0	0	0	0	0	0	0	0
Damian Munro	6/10/76	19(1)	16(1)	13	11	0	0	0	0	52	44
Kris Ratcliffe	28/5/81	22	17	2	1	0	0	0	0	8	4
Sam Reay	23/5/84	5	5	0	0	0	0	0	0	0	0
Nick Royle	25/9/83	7	7	6	6	0	0	0	0	24	24
Josh Simm	8/11/89	2(1)	2(1)	0	0	0	0	0	0	0	0
Simon Svabic	18/1/80	16(3)	12(2)	1	1	0	0	0	0	4	4
Dean Thompson	22/11/88	8	8	5	5	0	0	0	0	20	20
Keiron Tucker	16/10/87	3(6)	1(4)	5	2	0	0	0	0	20	8
Tom Wild	24/1/84	3(7)	2(5)	0	0	0	0	0	0	0	0
Scott Winstanley	23/2/83	1	1	1	1	0	0	0	0	4	4
Tom Woodcock	21/5/87	16(1)	12(1)	9	9	0	0	0	0	36	36

Jonny Leather

LEAGUE RECORD
P18-W9-D1-L8-BP4
(5th, Championship 1/
Elimination Play-Off)
F532, A456, Diff+76
33 points.

CHALLENGE CUP
Round Three

NORTHERN RAIL CUP
8th, Pool 1

ATTENDANCES
Best - v Dewsbury (Ch1 - 975)
Worst - v Hunslet (Ch1 - 265)
Total (excluding Challenge Cup) - 6,019
Average (excluding Challenge Cup) - 502
(Up by 63 on 2008)

DEWSBURY RAMS

DATE	FIXTURE	RESULT	SCORERS	LGE	ATT
15/2/09	Swinton (h) (NRC)	W50-0	t:Robinson,Powell,Spurr,Buchanan,Hirst,Epati(2) g:P Walker(11)	2nd(P2)	999
22/2/09	Featherstone (a) (NRC)	W26-28	t:Emmett,Epati(2),Buchanan,Lingard,Bostock g:P Walker(2)	4th(P2)	1,470
1/3/09	Batley (h) (NRC)	W34-14	t:Epati,Bretherton(2),Wildey,Finn(2) g:P Walker(5)	4th(P2)	1,512
8/3/09	Carcassonne (h) (CCR3)	W18-6	t:Lingard,Epati(2) g:P Walker(3)	N/A	998
15/3/09	London Skolars (a) (NRC)	W14-42	t:Crawley,North(2),Cook(2),Bostock,P Walker g:P Walker(7)	1st(P2)	314
22/3/09	York (h)	W28-2	t:Spicer,Finn,Lingard g:P Walker(8)	3rd	1,216
29/3/09	Rochdale (a)	W31-33	t:Bostock,Powell,Greenwood,Bretherton,Finn g:P Walker(6) fg:Finn	3rd	678
3/4/09	Sheffield (a) (CCR4)	L28-18	t:Bretherton,Powell g:P Walker(5)	N/A	597
10/4/09	London Skolars (h)	W70-0	t:Bostock(2),Epati(2),Spurr(3),Finn,Bretherton(2),Buchanan,Lingard g:Finn(11)	2nd	1,002
19/4/09	Oldham (a)	W12-36	t:Epati,Bostock,Wildey,Finn,Emmett,Smith g:P Walker(3),Finn(3)	1st	1,147
26/4/09	Hunslet (h)	W30-10	t:Powell(2),Finn,Spurr,Wildey g:P Walker(5)	1st	1,413
4/5/09	Swinton (a)	W22-35	t:P Walker,Lingard,Bostock(2),Spicer,Powell g:P Walker(5) fg:Finn	1st	661
17/5/09	Blackpool (h)	W42-16	t:Bostock(3),Powell,Finn,Bretherton,Epati g:P Walker(7)	1st	1,010
24/5/09	Workington (a)	W14-76	t:Wildey,Bostock(2),Lingard,Grice,P Walker,Buchanan(3),Bretherton(2),Powell,Spicer,Epati g:P Walker(10)	1st	319
31/5/09	York (a)	W18-24	t:Spurr,Finn,Buchanan,Bostock g:P Walker(4)	1st	1,326
6/6/09	Barrow (a) (NRCQF)	L20-18	t:Spurr,Buchanan(2) g:P Walker(3)	N/A	1,820
11/6/09	Keighley (h)	W46-6	t:Bostock(3),Epati(2),P Walker,Buchanan,Finn g:P Walker(6),Finn	1st	1,705
28/6/09	London Skolars (a)	W0-64	t:Spicer,Buchanan,Spurr,Wildbore(2),Powell(3),Hayes,Finn,Robinson g:P Walker(10)	1st	367
5/7/09	Swinton (h)	W36-8	t:Spurr(2),Bostock,Finn(2),Epati g:P Walker(6)	1st	940
19/7/09	Hunslet (a)	W6-24	t:Hirst,Finn,Epati g:P Walker(6)	1st	1,019
26/7/09	Oldham (h)	W38-8	t:Bostock(2),Lingard,Finn,Powell,Emmett g:P Walker(7)	1st	1,080
30/7/09	Keighley (a)	W14-54	t:Epati(2),Powell,Bretherton(2),Spurr,Robinson,Bostock,Smith g:P Walker(9)	1st	1,726
16/8/09	Workington (h)	W50-14	t:Spicer,Bostock,Bretherton(2),Smith,J Walker,Powell,Hayes,Epati g:P Walker(7)	1st	2,103
23/8/09	Rochdale (h)	W40-28	t:P Walker,Hayes,Robinson(2),Bretherton,Powell,Epati g:P Walker(6)	1st	912
6/9/09	Blackpool (a)	W14-34	t:Powell,Buchanan,Spurr(2),P Walker,Tonks g:P Walker(5)	1st	975

		APP		TRIES		GOALS		FG		PTS	
	D.O.B.	ALL	Ch1	ALL	Ch1	ALL	Ch1	ALL	Ch1	ALL	Ch1
Andrew Bostock	25/2/85	20(3)	16(1)	22	20	0	0	0	0	88	80
Craig Bower	1/5/80	1(1)	(1)	0	0	0	0	0	0	0	0
Alex Bretherton	5/12/82	14(9)	7(9)	14	11	0	0	0	0	56	44
Austin Buchanan	22/5/84	17(2)	11(2)	12	8	0	0	0	0	48	32
Tom Colleran	31/7/87	1(1)	1	0	0	0	0	0	0	0	0
Simon Cook	2/9/83	1(2)	0	2	0	0	0	0	0	8	0
Liam Crawley	18/4/87	1(16)	(10)	1	0	0	0	0	0	4	0
Jimmy Elston	8/12/79	(4)	(3)	0	0	0	0	0	0	0	0
Mike Emmett	13/5/87	24(1)	18	3	2	0	0	0	0	12	8
Kane Epati	13/8/81	24	18	20	13	0	0	0	0	80	52
Liam Finn	2/11/83	24	18	15	13	15	15	2	2	92	84
Gareth Greenwood	14/1/83	(4)	(2)	1	1	0	0	0	0	4	4
Chris Grice	26/5/87	2(6)	1(4)	1	1	0	0	0	0	4	4
Luke Haigh	24/7/87	1(1)	0	0	0	0	0	0	0	0	0
Chris Hall	12/12/82	1	1	0	0	0	0	0	0	0	0
Adam Hayes	30/11/81	22(1)	18	3	3	0	0	0	0	12	12
Keegan Hirst	13/12/88	23	17	2	1	0	0	0	0	8	4
Lee Lingard	21/10/83	21	15	7	5	0	0	0	0	28	20
James Lockwood	21/3/86	2(7)	2(7)	0	0	0	0	0	0	0	0
Allister McMaster	8/10/89	1	1	0	0	0	0	0	0	0	0
Gary North	5/12/86	1	0	2	0	0	0	0	0	8	0
Bryn Powell	5/9/79	25	18	16	14	0	0	0	0	64	56
Adam Robinson	8/4/87	16(2)	11(2)	5	4	0	0	0	0	20	16
Ryan Smith	25/10/88	2(13)	1(11)	3	3	0	0	0	0	12	12
Rob Spicer	22/9/84	22	18	5	5	0	0	0	0	20	20
Chris Spurr	7/7/80	22	16	13	11	0	0	0	0	52	44
Morgan Starkey	28/11/88	(1)	0	0	0	0	0	0	0	0	0
Andrew Tillotson	26/1/86	1	0	0	0	0	0	0	0	0	0
Josh Tonks	14/8/91	(2)	(1)	1	1	0	0	0	0	4	4
James Walker	15/4/77	(9)	(6)	1	1	0	0	0	0	4	4
Pat Walker	24/3/86	24	17	6	5	146	110	0	0	316	240
Tom Wandless	27/12/86	(1)	(1)	0	0	0	0	0	0	0	0
Loz Wildbore	23/9/84	1(2)	1(2)	2	2	0	0	0	0	8	8
Taron Wildey	11/9/87	10(7)	7(6)	4	3	0	0	0	0	16	12
Jake Wilson	23/3/89	(4)	(3)	0	0	0	0	0	0	0	0
Martin Woodhead	23/3/88	1	1	0	0	0	0	0	0	0	0

Andrew Bostock

LEAGUE RECORD
P18-W18-D0-L0-BP0
(Champions/1st, Championship 1)
F760, A223, Diff+537
54 points.

CHALLENGE CUP
Round Four

NORTHERN RAIL CUP
Quarter Finalists/1st, Pool 2

ATTENDANCES
Best - v Workington (Ch1 - 2,103)
Worst - v Rochdale (Ch1 - 912)
Total (excluding Challenge Cup) - 13,892
Average (excluding
Challenge Cup) - 1,263
(Up by 67 on 2008, NL1)

HUNSLET HAWKS

DATE	FIXTURE	RESULT	SCORERS	LGE	ATT
11/2/09	Sheffield (a) (NRC)	L38-16	t:Larvin,Mark,Brook g:McKinley,Chapman	N/A	556
15/2/09	Halifax (h) (NRC)	L10-38	t:Richardson,Brook g:Young	10th(P1)	878
22/2/09	Keighley (a) (NRC)	L44-6	t:Brook g:Sheldrake	10th(P1)	826
1/3/09	Oldham (h) (NRC)	L14-32	t:Faal,Larvin g:Robinson(2),Chapman	10th(P1)	582
14/3/09	Kells (a) (CCR3) ●	W12-22	t:Helme,Robinson,Watson,Williams g:Robinson(3)	N/A	251
22/3/09	Blackpool (a)	L34-26	t:Brown(2),Richardson,Robinson,Slain g:Robinson(3)	7th	265
29/3/09	London Skolars (h)	W71-0	t:Brown(2),Watson(2),Faal(4),Williams(3),Robinson g:Robinson(11) fg:Robinson	4th	527
5/4/09	Batley (a) (CCR4)	L28-24	t:Robinson,Slain,Firm,Watson g:Robinson(4)	N/A	633
10/4/09	Workington (a)	W16-24	t:Mark,Dooler,Firm,Wabo g:Robinson(4)	4th	543
13/4/09	Keighley (h)	W21-18	t:Chapman,Brown(2) g:Robinson fg:Chapman	2nd	697
26/4/09	Dewsbury (a)	L30-10	t:Brown,Watson g:Robinson	5th	1,413
4/5/09	Workington (h)	W28-12	t:Mark,Chapman,Robinson,Sheldrake,Childs g:Robinson(3),Sheldrake	3rd	515
17/5/09	Oldham (a)	L22-16	t:Chapman,Mark,Slain g:Sheldrake(2)	4th	1,136
24/5/09	Rochdale (h)	W56-30	t:Slain,Faal(3),Brook,Moxon,Williams,Robinson,Mark g:Sheldrake(4),Robinson(6)	5th	656
31/5/09	London Skolars (a)	W18-34	t:Mark,Howey,Faal,Moss,Wabo(2),Richardson g:Schofield(3)	4th	293
14/6/09	York (h)	L6-34	t:Mark g:Robinson	5th	716
28/6/09	Swinton (a)	L42-16	t:Young,Fawcett,Mark g:Chapman(2)	6th	537
5/7/09	Rochdale (a)	L41-22	t:Sheldrake,Dooler,Wabo,Brown g:Sheldrake(3)	6th	482
19/7/09	Dewsbury (h)	L6-24	t:Young g:Sheldrake	7th	1,019
26/7/09	York (a)	W8-20	t:Watson(2),March,Chapman g:Robinson(2)	6th	985
2/8/09	Blackpool (h)	W34-24	t:Young,Watson,McHugh,Dooler,Mark,Redfearn g:Robinson(5)	5th	573
16/8/09	Swinton (h)	W30-20	t:March,McHugh(2),Brown,Reittie g:Robinson(4),Weeden	6th	412
23/8/09	Keighley (a)	L20-16	t:Larvin,March,Mark g:McHugh(2)	6th	1,036
6/9/09	Oldham (h)	W36-18	t:Lowe,McHugh(3),Sheldrake,Wabo g:Young(2),McHugh(4)	6th	626
13/9/09	Blackpool (a) (EPO)	W18-21	t:Brown,Young,McHugh g:McHugh(2),Robinson(2) fg:Weeden	N/A	543
20/9/09	Oldham (a) (ESF)	L54-30	t:McHugh,Reittie(2),Brown,Mark,Weeden g:McHugh,Young,Robinson	N/A	801

● Played at Recreation Ground, Whitehaven

		APP		TRIES		GOALS		FG		PTS	
	D.O.B.	ALL	Ch1	ALL	Ch1	ALL	Ch1	ALL	Ch1	ALL	Ch1
Steve Brook	6/4/87	14(5)	9(4)	4	1	0	0	0	0	16	4
Michael Brown	9/9/86	23(1)	17(1)	11	11	0	0	0	0	44	44
Richard Chapman	5/9/75	17(8)	15(5)	4	4	4	2	1	1	25	21
Scott Childs	31/3/87	6	4	1	1	0	0	0	0	4	4
Danny Cook	14/10/81	2(3)	2(1)	0	0	0	0	0	0	0	0
Steve Dooler	31/12/77	19(4)	18(2)	3	3	0	0	0	0	12	12
Danny Ekis	17/1/82	(3)	(3)	0	0	0	0	0	0	0	0
Ayden Faal	12/12/86	16	10	9	8	0	0	0	0	36	32
Craig Fawcett	8/11/85	3	3	1	1	0	0	0	0	4	4
Gareth Firm	26/11/88	5(13)	1(12)	2	1	0	0	0	0	8	4
Ryan Glynn	3/9/87	(1)	(1)	0	0	0	0	0	0	0	0
Jason Hart	19/10/86	11(1)	8	0	0	0	0	0	0	0	0
Joe Helme	1/4/87	6(13)	3(11)	1	1	0	0	0	0	4	4
Joe Howey	27/4/89	5(4)	3(4)	1	1	0	0	0	0	4	4
Nathan Larvin	25/7/81	14	11	3	1	0	0	0	0	12	4
Neil Lowe	20/12/87	5(6)	5(6)	1	1	0	0	0	0	4	4
Paul March	25/7/79	8	8	3	3	0	0	0	0	12	12
Michael Mark	14/12/88	22	17	11	10	0	0	0	0	44	40
Wayne McHugh	1/2/80	5(1)	5(1)	8	8	9	9	0	0	50	50
Mark McKinley	16/9/85	1(1)	0	0	0	1	0	0	0	2	0
Craig Moss	4/8/84	5(1)	5(1)	1	1	0	0	0	0	4	4
Mark Moxon	22/8/80	11(1)	8	1	1	0	0	0	0	4	4
Chris Redfearn	4/12/80	13(8)	8(7)	1	1	0	0	0	0	4	4
Wayne Reittie	21/1/88	10	10	3	3	0	0	0	0	12	12
John Richardson	8/10/82	12(1)	7(1)	3	2	0	0	0	0	12	8
Darren Robinson	28/5/79	13(4)	9(4)	6	4	52	43	1	1	129	103
Jonathan Schofield	17/4/90	1	1	0	0	3	3	0	0	6	6
Tom Sheldrake	3/9/88	13(1)	10(1)	2	2	16	15	0	0	40	38
Nicko Slain	19/4/83	14(1)	9(1)	4	3	0	0	0	0	16	12
Charlie Wabo	19/9/83	13(8)	10(6)	5	5	0	0	0	0	20	20
Jonny Wainhouse	12/1/84	3	2	0	0	0	0	0	0	0	0
Ben Walkin	7/5/86	(8)	(4)	0	0	0	0	0	0	0	0
Scott Watson	16/3/88	23(3)	18(2)	8	6	0	0	0	0	32	24
Josh Weeden	10/11/83	5	5	2	2	1	1	1	1	11	11
Tony Williams	30/6/84	8(1)	7	5	4	0	0	0	0	20	16
Scott Woodcock	15/11/83	3	3	0	0	0	0	0	0	0	0
Stuart Young	7/5/88	9(3)	9(2)	4	4	4	3	0	0	24	22

Michael Mark

LEAGUE RECORD
P18-W10-D0-L8-BP3
(6th, Championship 1/
Elimination Semi-Final)
F472, A411, Diff+61
33 points.

CHALLENGE CUP
Round Four

NORTHERN RAIL CUP
10th, Pool 1

ATTENDANCES
Best - v Dewsbury (Ch1 - 1,019)
Worst - v Swinton (Ch1 - 412)
Total (excluding Challenge Cup) - 7,201
Average (excluding Challenge Cup) - 655
(Up by 97 on 2008)

KEIGHLEY COUGARS

DATE	FIXTURE	RESULT	SCORERS	LGE	ATT
10/2/09	Gateshead (h) (NRC)	W40-20	t:Rayner,Feather,Duffy,Presley(3),Purseglove g:Jones(6)	N/A	337
15/2/09	Blackpool (a) (NRC)	L16-14	t:Lowe,Bissell,Smith g:Jones	1st(P1)	400
22/2/09	Hunslet (h) (NRC)	W44-6	t:Cartledge,Presley(3),Mapals(2),Lowe,Purseglove,Rayner g:Jones(4)	1st(P1)	826
1/3/09	Barrow (a) (NRC)	L34-7	t:Presley g:Jones fg:Jones	4th(P1)	1,311
7/3/09	Pia (h) (CCR3)	W30-24	t:Presley(2),Cartledge,Potter,Duffy g:Jones(5)	N/A	447
22/3/09	Oldham (h)	W34-26	t:Presley(2),Bissell,Gardner,Williams,Hughes g:Jones(5)	4th	1,021
29/3/09	Swinton (a)	L36-28	t:Nicholson,Rayner,Law,Presley,Gardner g:Jones(4)	5th	540
5/4/09	Castleford (h) (CCR4)	L20-64	t:Presley,Mapals(3) g:Jones(2)	N/A	3,255
10/4/09	York (h)	W13-12	t:Lowe,Mapals g:Jones(2) fg:Presley	5th	770
13/4/09	Hunslet (a)	L21-18	t:Presley,Wray,Mapals g:Jones(3)	6th	697
26/4/09	Blackpool (h)	W42-22	t:Williams,Purseglove(2),Presley(2),Nicholson,Rayner,Potter g:Jones(5)	4th	534
4/5/09	York (a)	L24-22	t:Duffy,Mapals(2),Wray g:Jones(3)	6th	939
17/5/09	Swinton (h)	W32-16	t:Presley(2),Rayner,Shickell,Mapals g:Jones(6)	3rd	693
24/5/09	Blackpool (a)	W26-30	t:Law,Jones,Mapals,Duffy,Potter g:Jones(5)	3rd	500
31/5/09	Workington (h)	W58-6	t:Hughes(4),Feather,Mapals,Duffy(2),Potter(2),Jones g:Jones(7)	3rd	803
11/6/09	Dewsbury (a)	L46-6	t:Shickell g:Jones	4th	1,705
28/6/09	Rochdale (h)	W44-16	t:Hughes,Smith,Presley,Shickell,Jones,Williams,Rayner g:Jones(8)	3rd	901
5/7/09	London Skolars (h)	W60-28	t:Williams(2),Law(3),Potter(2),Presley(2),Hughes g:Jones(10)	2nd	838
19/7/09	Oldham (a)	W22-24	t:Williams(2),Feather,Rayner g:Jones(4)	2nd	848
30/7/09	Dewsbury (h)	L14-54	t:Presley(2) g:Jones(3)	4th	1,726
9/8/09	Workington (a)	W16-22	t:Rayner,Rawlins,Jones,Williams g:Jones(3)	3rd	417
16/8/09	Rochdale (h)	W18-44	t:Gardner,Potter,Purseglove,Benjafield,Rawlins,Nicholson,Rayner,Hughes g:Jones(6)	2nd	537
23/8/09	Hunslet (h)	W20-16	t:Gardner,Purseglove,Benjafield,Duffy g:Jones(2)	2nd	1,036
28/8/09	London Skolars (a)	W10-28	t:Williams,Rawlins(2),Potter,Gardner,Wray g:Jones(2)	2nd	1,156
20/9/09	York (h) (QSF)	W32-18	t:Duffy,Williams(2),Rayner,Presley,Jones g:Jones(4)	N/A	1,501
4/10/09	Oldham (GF) ●	W28-26	t:Gardner,Jones(2),Presley,Purseglove g:Jones(4)	N/A	N/A

● Played at Halliwell Jones Stadium, Warrington

		APP		TRIES		GOALS		FG		PTS	
	D.O.B.	ALL	Ch1	ALL	Ch1	ALL	Ch1	ALL	Ch1	ALL	Ch1
Ryan Benjafield	3/8/82	(11)	(11)	2	2	0	0	0	0	8	8
Simon Bissell	25/12/85	2(10)	2(4)	2	1	0	0	0	0	8	4
Craig Brown	2/12/80	2(8)	(7)	0	0	0	0	0	0	0	0
Will Cartledge	11/9/79	26	20	2	0	0	0	0	0	8	0
Gavin Duffy	9/4/87	24	18	8	6	0	0	0	0	32	24
Craig Fawcett	8/11/85	(1)	0	0	0	0	0	0	0	0	0
James Feather	15/4/84	23(1)	17(1)	3	2	0	0	0	0	12	8
Sam Gardner	28/8/77	13	8	6	6	0	0	0	0	24	24
Karl Gunney	18/1/87	2(9)	1(6)	0	0	0	0	0	0	0	0
James Haythornthwaite	19/10/90	(2)	(2)	0	0	0	0	0	0	0	0
Carl Hughes	30/11/82	12(4)	12(3)	8	8	0	0	0	0	32	32
Danny Jones	6/3/86	26	20	7	7	106	87	1	0	241	202
Scott Law	19/2/85	24(1)	19	5	5	0	0	0	0	20	20
Neil Lowe	20/12/78	5(4)	1(3)	3	1	0	0	0	0	12	4
Lee Mapals	17/7/85	13(2)	12	11	6	0	0	0	0	44	24
Greg Nicholson	24/9/85	14(9)	8(9)	3	3	0	0	0	0	12	12
Dan Potter	8/11/78	25	20	9	8	0	0	0	0	36	32
Jon Presley	8/7/84	26	20	25	15	0	0	1	1	101	61
Oliver Purseglove	18/1/86	26	20	8	6	0	0	0	0	32	24
Brendan Rawlins	28/1/86	(9)	(9)	4	4	0	0	0	0	16	16
George Rayner	19/9/80	26	20	10	8	0	0	0	0	40	32
Damien Reid	14/3/84	4	4	0	0	0	0	0	0	0	0
Ben Sagar	19/12/89	2(4)	2(4)	0	0	0	0	0	0	0	0
Andy Shickell	9/5/81	18	16	3	3	0	0	0	0	12	12
Ryan Smith	19/9/87	6(4)	2(2)	2	1	0	0	0	0	8	4
Daley Williams	15/5/86	16(1)	15(1)	11	11	0	0	0	0	44	44
Jamaine Wray	15/3/84	3(23)	3(17)	3	3	0	0	0	0	12	12

Danny Jones

LEAGUE RECORD
P18-W13-D0-L5-BP3
(2nd, Championship 1/
Grand Final Winners)
F539, A415, Diff+124
42 points.

CHALLENGE CUP
Round Four

NORTHERN RAIL CUP
5th, Pool 1

ATTENDANCES
Best - v Castleford (CC - 3,255)
Worst - v Gateshead (NRC - 337)
Total (excluding Challenge Cup) - 10,986
Average (excluding Challenge Cup) - 916
(Up by 48 on 2008)

LONDON SKOLARS

DATE	FIXTURE	RESULT	SCORERS	LGE	ATT
15/2/09	Leigh (a) (NRC)	L74-6	t:Aggrey g:Thorman	10th(P2)	1,375
22/2/09	Doncaster (h) (NRC)	L12-40	t:Aggrey(2),Bloom	10th(P2)	213
1/3/09	York (a) (NRC)	L58-12	t:Burke,M Thomas g:Thorman(2)	10th(P2)	1,003
8/3/09	Wath Brow (a) (CCR3) ●	L14-12	t:M Thomas,Fountain g:Thorman(2)	N/A	320
15/3/09	Dewsbury (h) (NRC)	L14-42	t:Iwenofu(3) g:Thorman	10th(P2)	314
22/3/09	Swinton (h)	L16-66	t:Obuchowski,Iwenofu,Thorman g:Thorman(2)	9th	637
29/3/09	Hunslet (a)	L71-0		9th	527
10/4/09	Dewsbury (a)	L70-0		9th	1,002
13/4/09	Blackpool (h)	L10-48	t:M Thomas,Paxton g:Thorman	9th	215
26/4/09	Rochdale (a)	L46-8	t:Paxton g:Thorman(2)	9th	480
2/5/09	Oldham (h)	L10-78	t:M Thomas(2) g:Thorman	9th	257
17/5/09	Workington (a)	W18-24	t:M Thomas,Paxton,Fountain(2) g:Thorman(4)	9th	353
24/5/09	York (h)	L6-80	t:M Thomas g:Thorman	9th	336
31/5/09	Hunslet (h)	L18-34	t:Bloom,M Thomas(2) g:Thorman(3)	9th	293
28/6/09	Dewsbury (h)	L0-64		9th	367
5/7/09	Keighley (a)	L60-28	t:Isles,Guiraud,Simms(2),Paxton g:Thorman(4)	10th	838
19/7/09	Rochdale (h)	L4-62	t:M Thomas	10th	485
25/7/09	Blackpool (a)	L46-22	t:Guiraud(2),Honor,Isles g:Thorman(3)	10th	391
2/8/09	Workington (h)	L18-24	t:Mbu,Thorman,Iwenofu g:Thorman(3)	10th	257
6/8/09	Oldham (a)	L28-22	t:Honor,Paxton,M Thomas g:Thorman(5)	10th	1,419
16/8/09	York (a)	L64-0		10th	629
23/8/09	Swinton (a)	L40-14	t:Kriouache,Simms,Paxton g:Thorman	10th	369
28/8/09	Keighley (h)	L10-28	t:Iwenofu(2) g:Thorman	10th	1,156

● Played at Recreation Ground, Whitehaven

		APP		TRIES		GOALS		FG		PTS	
	D.O.B.	ALL	Ch1	ALL	Ch1	ALL	Ch1	ALL	Ch1	ALL	Ch1
Orreiso Agbareh	17/9/88	(1)	0	0	0	0	0	0	0	0	0
Austen Aggrey	12/5/79	20(1)	15(1)	3	0	0	0	0	0	12	0
Keir Bell	14/6/85	(7)	(5)	0	0	0	0	0	0	0	0
Oliver Bloom	16/4/86	14(4)	10(4)	2	1	0	0	0	0	8	4
Danny Burke	26/7/86	8(9)	6(6)	1	0	0	0	0	0	4	0
Jaymes Chapman	17/12/83	3	1	0	0	0	0	0	0	0	0
Jermaine Coleman	17/6/82	2	2	0	0	0	0	0	0	0	0
Jy-Mel Coleman	13/10/88	5(2)	5(2)	0	0	0	0	0	0	0	0
Dave Ellison	2/4/82	10	5	0	0	0	0	0	0	0	0
Oliver Fountain	8/4/87	11(1)	7(1)	3	2	0	0	0	0	12	8
Jack Graves	4/1/89	1(2)	1(2)	0	0	0	0	0	0	0	0
Jeremy Guiraud	12/7/86	5	5	3	3	0	0	0	0	12	12
Kris Hodson	4/9/87	4(1)	4(1)	0	0	0	0	0	0	0	0
Gareth Honor	1/10/81	19(2)	16	2	2	0	0	0	0	8	8
Paul Hyder	28/2/85	1(6)	(3)	0	0	0	0	0	0	0	0
Chad Isles	7/2/87	15	10	2	2	0	0	0	0	8	8
Olu Iwenofu	28/9/81	15(2)	13(1)	7	4	0	0	0	0	28	16
Ben Joyce	13/2/80	16(1)	11(1)	0	0	0	0	0	0	0	0
Smokey Junor	15/4/90	2	2	0	0	0	0	0	0	0	0
Hosni Kriouache	15/1/88	1(2)	1(2)	1	1	0	0	0	0	4	4
Joe Mbu	6/11/83	3	3	1	1	0	0	0	0	4	4
Mark McLennan	18/12/85	2	2	0	0	0	0	0	0	0	0
Leigh Nissen	26/11/82	12(6)	8(5)	0	0	0	0	0	0	0	0
Jaroslaw Obuchowski	20/9/90	6(6)	5(6)	1	1	0	0	0	0	4	4
Jamie O'Callaghan	21/9/90	2	2	0	0	0	0	0	0	0	0
Glenn Osborn	17/8/83	1(2)	1(1)	0	0	0	0	0	0	0	0
John Paxton	20/4/85	15(1)	15(1)	6	6	0	0	0	0	24	24
Cedric Prizzon	10/6/84	4	4	0	0	0	0	0	0	0	0
Frank Reid	1/11/78	(7)	(4)	0	0	0	0	0	0	0	0
Florian Rolianet	21/2/86	(2)	(2)	0	0	0	0	0	0	0	0
Bernard Rule	17/5/76	3	3	0	0	0	0	0	0	0	0
Corey Simms	18/2/80	22	17	3	3	0	0	0	0	12	12
Graeme Spencer	3/9/85	3(14)	3(11)	0	0	0	0	0	0	0	0
Matt Thomas	8/1/80	21	16	11	9	0	0	0	0	44	36
Rob Thomas	9/10/90	2	2	0	0	0	0	0	0	0	0
Paul Thorman	28/9/82	23	18	2	2	37	31	0	0	82	70
Andre Vine	9/11/91	5(9)	5(9)	0	0	0	0	0	0	0	0
Bobby Wallis	7/1/83	5	3	0	0	0	0	0	0	0	0
Tony Williams	4/5/84	18(4)	13(4)	0	0	0	0	0	0	0	0

Matt Thomas

LEAGUE RECORD
P18-W1-D0-L17-BP2
(10th, Championship 1)
F210, A927, Diff-717
5 points.

CHALLENGE CUP
Round Three

NORTHERN RAIL CUP
10th, Pool 2

ATTENDANCES
Best - v Keighley (Ch1 - 1,156)
Worst - v Doncaster (NRC - 213)
Total (excluding Challenge Cup) - 4,530
Average (excluding Challenge Cup) - 412
(Down by 38 on 2008)

OLDHAM

DATE	FIXTURE	RESULT	SCORERS	LGE	ATT
13/2/09	Widnes (a) (NRC)	W20-22	t:Boults,Ballard g:Ballard(7)	5th(P1)	2,783
18/2/09	Rochdale (h) (NRC)	W54-4	t:Ballard(2),Kerr,St Hilaire,Halliwell(2),J Coyle(2),Goulden(2) g:Ballard(7)	1st(P1)	1,028
22/2/09	Sheffield (h) (NRC)	L22-34	t:O'Connor,I'Anson(2),Ballard g:Ballard(3)	2nd(P1)	1,173
1/3/09	Hunslet (a) (NRC)	W14-32	t:Onyango,Reilly(3),O'Connor,Halliwell g:Ballard(4)	1st(P1)	582
8/3/09	Sharlston (h) (CCR3)	W26-8	t:Onyango(2),J Coyle,N Roden,Roberts g:Halliwell(3)	N/A	800
15/3/09	Blackpool (h)	W36-18	t:Goulden,Reilly,Greenwood(2),Kerr(2),Ballard g:Ballard(4)	N/A	880
22/3/09	Keighley (a)	L34-26	t:Halliwell,T Coyle(2),J Coyle(2) g:Ballard(3)	1st	1,021
29/3/09	Workington (h)	W66-14	t:Ballard(3),T Coyle(3),Baines,Allen,J Coyle,O'Connor,Greenwood,St Hilaire g:Ballard(9)	1st	819
5/4/09	Lezignan (h) (CCR4)	W60-30	t:Onyango(3),St Hilaire(2),Ballard(2),T Coyle,Joseph,Mervill g:Ballard(10)	N/A	863
10/4/09	Rochdale (a)	W18-26	t:Baines,Greenwood,Gibbons,Ballard,J Coyle g:Ballard(3)	1st	1,249
19/4/09	Dewsbury (h)	L12-36	t:Highton,Greenwood g:Ballard(2)	4th	1,147
26/4/09	Swinton (h)	W52-36	t:Greenwood,Halliwell,O'Connor,Allen,Gibbons,I'Anson,Sykes,Goulden,T Coyle g:Ballard(8)	2nd	1,010
2/5/09	London Skolars (a)	W10-78	t:T Coyle(2),J Coyle(2),Ballard(2),Gibbons,Roberts,O'Connor,N Roden(2),Robinson,Onyango g:Ballard(13)	2nd	257
9/5/09	Gateshead (a) (CCR5) ●	L34-16	t:Goulden,Halliwell,Allen g:Ballard(2)	N/A	929
17/5/09	Hunslet (h)	W22-16	t:St Hilaire(2),Halliwell,Roberts g:Ballard(3)	2nd	1,136
24/5/09	Swinton (a)	W26-44	t:Allen(2),Ballard(3),St Hilaire(2),Joseph g:Ballard(6)	2nd	705
4/6/09	Featherstone (h) (NRCQF) ●●	L18-32	t:Ballard,Halliwell,Greenwood g:Ballard(3)	N/A	853
25/6/09	York (a)	L20-18	t:N Roden,Goulden,Baines g:Ballard(3)	4th	3,106
5/7/09	Workington (a)	W6-60	t:Allen,O'Connor(3),Goulden(2),J Coyle,St Hilaire,Sykes(2),Onyango g:Halliwell(2),J Coyle(5),Joseph	3rd	514
19/7/09	Keighley (h)	L22-24	t:Greenwood,Onyango,Baines,N Roden g:Ballard(3)	3rd	848
26/7/09	Dewsbury (a)	L38-8	t:Greenwood(2)	4th	1,080
2/8/09	Rochdale (h)	W48-28	t:Baines(2),Greenwood,Goulden,M Roden,Russo,Robinson,N Roden,O'Connor g:Ashe(4),O'Connor(2)	3rd	951
6/8/09	London Skolars (h)	W28-22	t:M Roden,Ashe,Russo,Littler,T Coyle,Greenwood g:Ashe,O'Connor	2nd	1,419
16/8/09	Blackpool (a)	D30-30	t:Onyango,Baines,Russo,T Coyle,Littler,Goulden g:Baines(3)	3rd	600
23/8/09	York (h)	L24-37	t:Onyango,T Coyle(2),Littler g:Baines(4)	4th	954
6/9/09	Hunslet (a)	L36-18	t:O'Connor,Onyango,Joseph g:Baines(3)	4th	626
13/9/09	Swinton (h) (EPO)	W31-26	t:Onyango,St Hilaire,T Coyle,O'Connor,Joseph g:Baines(5) fg:N Roden	N/A	745
20/9/09	Hunslet (h) (ESF)	W54-30	t:Baines(4),M Roden(2),O'Connor,Ashe,T Coyle g:Baines(9)	N/A	801
27/9/09	York (a) (FE)	W14-44	t:Heaton,Baines,Goulden,Reilly(2),Ashe(2),Onyango g:Baines(6)	N/A	1,164
4/10/09	Keighley (GF) ●●●	L28-26	t:Menzies(2),N Roden,St Hilaire,Kerr g:Baines(3)	N/A	N/A

● Played at Northern Echo Arena, Darlington
●● Played at Leigh Sports Village
●●● Played at Halliwell Jones Stadium, Warrington

		APP		TRIES		GOALS		FG		PTS	
	D.O.B.	ALL	Ch1	ALL	Ch1	ALL	Ch1	ALL	Ch1	ALL	Ch1
Dave Allen	15/9/85	17	10	6	5	0	0	0	0	24	20
Matt Ashe	4/9/85	2(5)	2(5)	4	4	5	5	0	0	26	26
Chris Baines	25/9/84	27(2)	21(1)	12	12	33	33	0	0	114	114
Andy Ballard	10/5/86	18	11	17	10	93	57	0	0	254	154
Andy Boothroyd	7/1/85	1(1)	1(1)	0	0	0	0	0	0	0	0
Jason Boults	7/9/83	17(3)	14(1)	1	0	0	0	0	0	4	0
James Coyle	28/12/85	20	12	10	7	5	5	0	0	50	38
Thomas Coyle	10/5/88	22(4)	17(4)	15	14	0	0	0	0	60	56
Steve Gibbons	27/9/88	4(3)	3(2)	3	3	0	0	0	0	12	12
Tommy Goulden	30/6/81	19(4)	14(3)	11	8	0	0	0	0	44	32
Lee Greenwood	28/9/80	21	16	12	11	0	0	0	0	48	44
Danny Halliwell	23/3/81	16(1)	10	8	3	5	2	0	0	42	16
Ben Heaton	12/3/90	1(2)	1(2)	1	1	0	0	0	0	4	4
Paul Highton	10/11/76	10(4)	7(1)	1	1	0	0	0	0	4	4
Jamie I'Anson	19/6/87	8(19)	4(16)	3	1	0	0	0	0	12	4
Phil Joseph	10/1/85	16(6)	11(5)	4	3	1	1	0	0	18	14
Wayne Kerr	18/3/84	10(14)	10(10)	4	3	0	0	0	0	16	12
Craig Lawton	17/2/81	4(1)	4(1)	0	0	0	0	0	0	0	0
Craig Littler	4/9/85	8	6	3	3	0	0	0	0	12	12
Luke Menzies	29/6/88	6(9)	4(8)	2	2	0	0	0	0	8	8
Richard Mervill	24/6/81	5(7)	1(6)	1	0	0	0	0	0	4	0
Paul O'Connor	3/6/84	28	21	12	10	3	3	0	0	54	46
Lucas Onyango	12/4/81	17(1)	13(1)	14	8	0	0	0	0	56	32
Paul Reilly	10/5/76	14(7)	12(3)	6	3	0	0	0	0	24	12
Rob Roberts	21/6/78	11(1)	6	3	2	0	0	0	0	12	8
Craig Robinson	30/7/85	8(8)	8(5)	2	2	0	0	0	0	8	8
Martin Roden	26/12/79	9(1)	9(1)	4	4	0	0	0	0	16	16
Neil Roden	9/4/80	16(7)	13(4)	7	6	0	0	1	1	29	25
Jamie Russo	16/4/81	5	5	3	3	0	0	0	0	12	12
Marcus St Hilaire	26/1/77	19(1)	12(1)	11	8	0	0	0	0	44	32
Luke Sutton	25/2/86	(1)	(1)	0	0	0	0	0	0	0	0
Gary Sykes	19/8/86	11(8)	8(6)	3	3	0	0	0	0	12	12

Thomas Coyle

LEAGUE RECORD
P18-W10-D1-L7-BP3
(4th, Championship 1/
Grand Final Runners-Up)
F618, A449, Diff+169
35 points.

CHALLENGE CUP
Round Five

NORTHERN RAIL CUP
Quarter Finalists/2nd, Pool 1

ATTENDANCES
Best - v London Skolars (Ch1 - 1,419)
Worst - v Swinton (EPO - 745)
Total (excluding Challenge Cup) - 13,764
Average (excluding Challenge Cup) - 983
(Down by 177 on 2008)

ROCHDALE HORNETS

DATE	FIXTURE	RESULT	SCORERS	LGE	ATT
15/2/09	Barrow (h) (NRC)	L12-54	t:Fogerty,Giles g:Corcoran(2)	9th(P1)	501
18/2/09	Oldham (a) (NRC)	L54-4	t:Walker	10th(P1)	1,028
22/2/09	Blackpool (h) (NRC)	W28-26	t:Donoghue,Mayberry,Ainscough,Walker,Gillam,Raftrey g:Corcoran(2)	9th(P1)	371
1/3/09	Gateshead (a) (NRC)	L46-22	t:Johnson,Cunniffe,Mayberry,Bretherton,Ainscough g:Giles	9th(P1)	452
8/3/09	Leeds Met Carnegie (a) (CCR3) ●	W24-38	t:Sinfield,Brocklehurst,Ainscough,Johnson,Gambles,Raftrey,Giles g:Giles(5)	N/A	221
22/3/09	Workington (a)	L21-14	t:Gillam(2),Giles g:Giles	10th	693
29/3/09	Dewsbury (h)	L31-33	t:Raftrey,Fogerty,Billings,McGovern,Sinfield,McLoughlin g:McGovern(3) fg:McGovern	10th	678
3/4/09	Swinton (a) (CCR4)	W22-28	t:Rivett,McLoughlin,Hough,Brocklehurst,Isherwood g:Hough(3),Corcoran	N/A	525
10/4/09	Oldham (h)	L18-26	t:Corcoran,Cunliffe,McGovern g:McGovern(3)	10th	1,249
13/4/09	York (a)	L44-14	t:Giles,Ainscough,Fogerty g:McGovern	10th	923
26/4/09	London Skolars (h)	W46-8	t:Gillam(2),Johnson,Ainscough,Mayberry,Donoghue,Brocklehurst(2) g:McGovern(7)	10th	480
4/5/09	Blackpool (a)	L24-12	t:Cunniffe(2),Fogerty	10th	347
10/5/09	Huddersfield (a) (CCR5)	L38-12	t:Fogerty,Ainscough g:Giles(2)	N/A	2,859
17/5/09	York (h)	W36-30	t:Rivett,Strong,Corcoran(2),Ainscough(2) g:Giles(6)	10th	717
24/5/09	Hunslet (a)	L56-30	t:Ainscough,Gallagher,Johnson,Fogerty,Mayberry g:Giles(2),McGovern(3)	10th	656
31/5/09	Swinton (a)	L23-22	t:Giles,Ainscough(2),Mayberry g:Giles(3)	10th	502
28/6/09	Keighley (a)	L44-16	t:Ainscough,Mayberry,Gillam g:Roper(2)	10th	901
5/7/09	Hunslet (h)	W41-22	t:Miller,Gallagher(2),Thomas(2),Rivett g:McGovern(8) fg:Ainscough	9th	482
19/7/09	London Skolars (a)	W4-62	t:Thomas,Ainscough,Miller,Sinfield(2),Isherwood(4),Johnson,Mayberry g:McGovern(9)	8th	485
26/7/09	Swinton (h)	W24-22	t:Mayberry(2),McGovern,Brocklehurst g:McGovern(4)	8th	576
2/8/09	Oldham (a)	L48-28	t:Gillam(3),McGovern(2) g:McGovern(4)	8th	951
9/8/09	Blackpool (h)	L18-48	t:Gallagher,McLoughlin,Ainscough,Raftrey g:Ainscough	8th	527
16/8/09	Keighley (h)	L18-44	t:Ainscough(2),Johnson g:Hatton,McGovern(2)	8th	537
23/8/09	Dewsbury (a)	L40-28	t:Ainscough,Thomas,Hatton,Rivett,Gillam g:Hatton(4)	8th	912
6/9/09	Workington (h)	W42-20	t:Gillam,Fogerty(2),Thomas,Miller(2),Ainscough,Isherwood g:Hatton(5)	8th	893

● Played at Headingley Carnegie, Leeds

	APP		TRIES		GOALS		FG		PTS	
	ALL	**Ch1**	**ALL**	**Ch1**	**ALL**	**Ch1**	**ALL**	**Ch1**	**ALL**	**Ch1**
	D.O.B.									
Martin Ainscough	23/10/85	25	18	18	14	1	1	1	1	75	59
Paul Anderson	2/4/77	(2)	(2)	0	0	0	0	0	0	0	0
David Best	1/5/79	14(4)	10(3)	0	0	0	0	0	0	0	0
Janan Billings	27/1/82	1(6)	(4)	1	1	0	0	0	0	4	4
Liam Bretherton	20/6/79	2(1)	0	1	0	0	0	0	0	4	0
Tommy Brindle	3/2/87	1(5)	1(5)	0	0	0	0	0	0	0	0
Mark Brocklehurst	27/9/86	13(2)	9(2)	5	3	0	0	0	0	20	12
Sam Butterworth	12/2/78	1(1)	0	0	0	0	0	0	0	0	0
Wayne Corcoran	10/7/85	16(5)	12(3)	3	3	5	0	0	0	22	12
Dave Cunliffe	15/1/80	3(2)	2(1)	1	1	0	0	0	0	4	4
Dale Cunniffe	25/3/87	12(1)	7(1)	3	2	0	0	0	0	12	8
Dayne Donoghue	22/9/88	19(2)	14(1)	2	1	0	0	0	0	8	4
Mick Fogerty	19/2/81	23(1)	16(1)	8	6	0	0	0	0	32	24
Tommy Gallagher	10/9/83	5(12)	5(9)	4	4	0	0	0	0	16	16
Martin Gambles	8/3/80	2(2)	0	1	0	0	0	0	0	4	0
Chris Giles	26/12/81	14	9	5	3	20	12	0	0	60	36
John Gillam	15/10/84	18	13	11	10	0	0	0	0	44	40
Liam Grundy	23/1/87	6(1)	2(1)	0	0	0	0	0	0	0	0
Dean Hatton	27/12/87	3	3	1	1	10	10	0	0	24	24
Mark Hobson	14/1/87	3(4)	3(4)	0	0	0	0	0	0	0	0
Chris Hough	30/8/81	5(1)	2	1	0	3	0	0	0	10	0
David Houghton	2/11/89	3(1)	2(1)	0	0	0	0	0	0	0	0
Andrew Isherwood	23/11/79	3(14)	3(9)	6	5	0	0	0	0	24	20
Craig Johnson	17/4/87	17(2)	10(2)	6	4	0	0	0	0	24	16
Darryl Kay	6/11/87	4(1)	4(1)	0	0	0	0	0	0	0	0
Casey Mayberry	19/12/81	16(1)	11(1)	9	7	0	0	0	0	36	28
Liam McGovern	6/10/84	9(2)	9(2)	5	5	44	44	1	1	109	109
Martin McLoughlin	2/8/80	2(13)	1(9)	3	2	0	0	0	0	12	8
Marlon Miller	28/10/78	4	4	4	4	0	0	0	0	16	16
Ryan Powell	3/2/88	3	3	0	0	0	0	0	0	0	0
Paul Raftrey	26/1/78	19(3)	13(3)	4	2	0	0	0	0	16	8
Leroy Rivett	17/12/76	14(1)	13	4	3	0	0	0	0	16	12
Brett Robinson	9/11/89	6(3)	5(3)	0	0	0	0	0	0	0	0
Steve Roper	10/11/86	1(2)	1(2)	0	0	2	2	0	0	4	4
Ian Sinfield	7/4/77	20(2)	15(2)	4	3	0	0	0	0	16	12
Andy Smith	6/7/84	1(1)	0	0	0	0	0	0	0	0	0
Matthew Strong	17/2/87	4	3	1	1	0	0	0	0	4	4
Adam Thomas	4/11/87	12	11	5	5	0	0	0	0	20	20
John Walker	26/3/88	1(2)	0	2	0	0	0	0	0	8	0

Ian Sinfield

LEAGUE RECORD
P18-W6-D0-L12-BP6
(8th, Championship 1)
F500, A557, Diff-57
15 points. *(9 points deducted for entering administration)*

CHALLENGE CUP
Round Five

NORTHERN RAIL CUP
9th, Pool 1

ATTENDANCES
Best - v Oldham (Ch1 - 1,249)
Worst - v Blackpool (NRC - 371)
Total (excluding Challenge Cup) - 7,011
Average (excluding Challenge Cup) - 637
(Up by 51 on 2008)

SWINTON LIONS

DATE	FIXTURE	RESULT	SCORERS	LGE	ATT
15/2/09	Dewsbury (a) (NRC)	L50-0		9th(P2)	999
22/2/09	Leigh (h) (NRC)	L26-34	t:Moana(2),McClurg,Hamilton,Wood g:Sneyd(3)	8th(P2)	857
1/3/09	Doncaster (a) (NRC)	L36-28	t:Rigby,Billy,Hayes,Newton,Hulse g:Sneyd(4)	8th(P2)	645
7/3/09	Siddal (a) (CCR3) ●	W6-10	t:Sneyd,Newton g:Sneyd	N/A	1,052
11/3/09	Workington (h) (NRC)	W31-24	t:Moana,Saywell,D Hull(2),Bamford,Ashall g:Crook(3) fg:Ashall	7th(P2)	242
22/3/09	London Skolars (a)	W16-66	t:Wood,Wainwright,Hulse,Bamford,D Hull(3),Newton,Holroyd,English,Grundy g:Sneyd(11)	2nd	637
29/3/09	Keighley (h)	W36-28	t:D Hull(3),Grundy(2),Sneyd g:Sneyd(6)	2nd	540
3/4/09	Rochdale (h) (CCR4)	L22-28	t:D Hull,Southern,Sneyd g:Sneyd(5)	N/A	525
10/4/09	Blackpool (a)	W12-16	t:Hulse,Rigby,Saywell g:Sneyd,Holroyd	3rd	411
13/4/09	Workington (h)	W42-28	t:Ashe,Saywell(2),Wainwright,Sneyd,Grundy,McClurg g:Sneyd(4),Holroyd	1st	404
26/4/09	Oldham (a)	L52-36	t:Hawkyard,D Hull,Wainwright,Ashall,Saywell,Hayes g:Holroyd(6)	3rd	1,010
4/5/09	Dewsbury (h)	L22-35	t:Ashall,Hawkyard,Holroyd,Heaton g:Sneyd(3)	5th	661
17/5/09	Keighley (a)	L32-16	t:Rigby,Johnson,English g:Sneyd(2)	6th	693
24/5/09	Oldham (h)	L26-44	t:Sneyd,Hulse(2),English,Bamford g:Sneyd(3)	6th	705
31/5/09	Rochdale (h)	W23-22	t:English,D Hull,Bamford,Rigby g:Sneyd(3) fg:Holroyd	6th	502
14/6/09	Workington (a)	W18-26	t:Sneyd,Ashall,Billy,English g:Sneyd(5)	6th	447
28/6/09	Hunslet (h)	W42-16	t:Rigby,Sneyd,Ashall,Hawkyard,Billy,Hayes,D Hull g:Sneyd(7)	5th	537
5/7/09	Dewsbury (a)	L36-8	t:C Hull,Moana	5th	940
19/7/09	Blackpool (h)	L18-33	t:C Hull,Hulse,Wood g:Sneyd(3)	6th	440
26/7/09	Rochdale (a)	L24-22	t:Tyrer,Holroyd,Saywell g:Sneyd(5)	7th	576
2/8/09	York (h)	L26-30	t:Grundy,Sneyd,Saywell,Southern,Holroyd g:Sneyd(3)	7th	452
16/8/09	Hunslet (a)	L30-20	t:Bamford,Grundy,Sneyd g:Sneyd(4)	7th	412
23/8/09	London Skolars (h)	W40-14	t:Billy,Bamford(2),Grundy,Moana,Johnson,Hawkyard g:Sneyd(6)	7th	369
5/9/09	York (a)	L46-28	t:Sneyd,Saywell(2),Ashall,Bamford g:Sneyd(4)	7th	844
13/9/09	Oldham (a) (EPO)	L31-26	t:Bamford,Hawkyard,Saywell(2) g:Sneyd(3),Holroyd(2)	N/A	745

● Played at The Shay, Halifax

APP   TRIES   GOALS   FG   PTS

	D.O.B.	ALL	Ch1	ALL	Ch1	ALL	Ch1	ALL	Ch1	ALL	Ch1
Craig Ashall	26/9/85	14(6)	8(6)	6	5	0	0	1	0	25	20
Matt Ashe	4/9/85	2(3)	2(2)	1	1	0	0	0	0	4	4
Darren Bamford	8/8/86	10(3)	7(3)	9	8	0	0	0	0	36	32
Adam Bibey	30/4/86	(1)	0	0	0	0	0	0	0	0	0
Marlon Billy	22/11/73	10(2)	7(1)	4	3	0	0	0	0	16	12
Paul Crook	28/8/86	2(1)	1(1)	0	0	3	0	0	0	6	0
Wayne English	8/3/80	12	10	5	5	0	0	0	0	20	20
Chris Frodsham	14/4/88	2(1)	1(1)	0	0	0	0	0	0	0	0
Dean Gorton	16/1/84	5	5	0	0	0	0	0	0	0	0
Tommy Grundy	17/4/85	17	12	7	7	0	0	0	0	28	28
Barry Hamilton	25/2/86	4	1	1	0	0	0	0	0	4	0
Richie Hawkyard	21/1/80	17(5)	11(5)	5	5	0	0	0	0	20	20
Gareth Hayes	15/6/85	4(8)	3(6)	3	2	0	0	0	0	12	8
Danny Heaton	19/4/81	17(5)	16(2)	1	1	0	0	0	0	4	4
Graham Holroyd	25/10/75	14(1)	13(1)	4	4	12	12	1	1	41	41
Chris Hull	4/12/86	7(1)	7(1)	2	2	0	0	0	0	8	8
Dave Hull	3/11/85	24	18	12	9	0	0	0	0	48	36
Gary Hulse	20/1/81	21	16	6	5	0	0	0	0	24	20
Bruce Johnson	26/1/84	6(13)	3(12)	2	2	0	0	0	0	8	8
Craig Littler	4/9/85	2	2	0	0	0	0	0	0	0	0
Richard Lopag	13/9/89	7	7	0	0	0	0	0	0	0	0
Alex McClurg	28/8/89	8(6)	6(2)	2	1	0	0	0	0	8	4
Martin Moana	13/8/73	8(14)	4(13)	5	2	0	0	0	0	20	8
Dave Newton	22/12/81	15(8)	12(5)	3	1	0	0	0	0	12	4
Neil Rigby	5/2/86	16(8)	13(6)	5	4	0	0	0	0	20	16
Andy Saywell	1/1/79	13	10	11	10	0	0	0	0	44	40
Carl Sneyd	11/4/87	23	18	10	8	86	73	0	0	212	178
Paul Southern	18/3/76	10(1)	5(1)	2	1	0	0	0	0	8	4
Chris Tyrer	10/10/85	7(5)	7(5)	1	1	0	0	0	0	4	4
Mike Wainwright	25/2/75	16(4)	14(1)	3	3	0	0	0	0	12	12
Phil Wood	25/10/83	12(3)	8(1)	3	2	0	0	0	0	12	8

Carl Sneyd

LEAGUE RECORD
P18-W8-D0-L10-BP3
(7th, Championship 1/
Elimination Play-Off)
F513, A516, Diff-3
27 points.

CHALLENGE CUP
Round Four

NORTHERN RAIL CUP
7th, Pool 2

ATTENDANCES
Best - v Leigh (NRC - 857)
Worst - v Workington (NRC - 242)
Total (excluding Challenge Cup) - 5,709
Average (excluding Challenge Cup) - 519
(Down by 18 on 2008)

WORKINGTON TOWN

DATE	FIXTURE	RESULT	SCORERS	LGE	ATT
15/2/09	York (h) (NRC)	L10-34	t:Stack,Dawes g:Forber	7th(P2)	513
22/2/09	Whitehaven (a) (NRC)	L26-12	t:Pedley,Frazer g:Forber(2)	9th(P2)	1,346
1/3/09	Featherstone (h) (NRC)	L6-38	t:Beattie g:Forber	9th(P2)	477
7/3/09	Lezignan (h) (CCR3)	L6-18	t:Stack g:Forber	N/A	314
11/3/09	Swinton (a) (NRC)	L31-24	t:Hodgson(2),Routledge,Brindle,Dawes g:Forber(2)	9th(P2)	242
22/3/09	Rochdale (h)	W21-14	t:Brindle(2),Dawes g:Forber(4) fg:Roper	5th	693
29/3/09	Oldham (a)	L66-14	t:Marshall,Hobson,Dawes g:Forber	8th	819
10/4/09	Hunslet (h)	L16-24	t:Dawes(3) g:Forber(2)	8th	543
13/4/09	Swinton (a)	L42-28	t:Dawes,Benjafield,Forber(2),Whitehead g:Forber(4)	8th	404
26/4/09	York (h)	L6-36	t:Marshall g:Forber	8th	530
4/5/09	Hunslet (a)	L28-12	t:Robinson,Pedley g:Roper(2)	8th	515
17/5/09	London Skolars (h)	L18-24	t:King,Wilson,Whitehead g:Forber(3)	8th	353
24/5/09	Dewsbury (h)	L14-76	t:S Burgess,Coupar,Marshall g:Roper	8th	319
31/5/09	Keighley (a)	L58-6	t:Dawes g:Bainbridge	8th	803
14/6/09	Swinton (h)	L18-26	t:King,Pedley,Beattie g:Bainbridge,S Burgess(2)	8th	447
28/6/09	Blackpool (a)	L46-18	t:King,Farrimond,S Burgess g:Bainbridge(3)	8th	280
5/7/09	Oldham (h)	L6-60	t:Mossop g:Lunt	8th	514
19/7/09	York (a)	L46-20	t:Pedley,King,Mossop,Scott g:Frodsham(2)	9th	653
2/8/09	London Skolars (a)	W18-24	t:Pedley,Beattie,Marshall,Ramsden g:Frodsham(4)	9th	257
9/8/09	Keighley (h)	L16-22	t:Robinson,Pedley,Marshall g:S Burgess(2)	9th	417
16/8/09	Dewsbury (a)	L50-14	t:Beattie,Rowley,Marshall g:Frodsham	9th	2,103
23/8/09	Blackpool (h)	L10-22	t:Stack,Marshall g:Frodsham	9th	405
6/9/09	Rochdale (a)	L42-20	t:Marshall,Dawes,Pedley,Robinson g:S Burgess(2)	9th	893

APP TRIES GOALS FG PTS

	D.O.B.	ALL	Ch1	ALL	Ch1	ALL	Ch1	ALL	Ch1	ALL	Ch1
Marc Bainbridge	22/12/87	3	3	0	0	5	5	0	0	10	10
Andrew Beattie	12/1/81	17(1)	12(1)	4	3	0	0	0	0	16	12
Ryan Benjafield	3/8/82	2(10)	(7)	1	1	0	0	0	0	4	4
Dean Bragg	14/1/82	2(1)	2(1)	0	0	0	0	0	0	0	0
Tommy Brindle	3/2/87	10	6	3	2	0	0	0	0	12	8
Dean Burgess	11/10/84	(1)	(1)	0	0	0	0	0	0	0	0
Scott Burgess	18/2/86	13(4)	11(3)	2	2	6	6	0	0	20	20
Brett Carter	9/7/88	5	5	0	0	0	0	0	0	0	0
Paddy Coupar	26/6/86	20(1)	16(1)	1	1	0	0	0	0	4	4
Kris Coward	1/10/81	8(2)	8(1)	0	0	0	0	0	0	0	0
Stephen Dawes	14/1/85	13	8	10	8	0	0	0	0	40	32
Peter Dobson	23/11/85	4(9)	3(8)	0	0	0	0	0	0	0	0
Jay Duffy	16/4/87	5	4	0	0	0	0	0	0	0	0
Craig Farrimond	20/11/82	8	8	1	1	0	0	0	0	4	4
Carl Forber	17/3/85	11	6	2	2	22	15	0	0	52	38
Neil Frazer	7/3/76	8	3	1	0	0	0	0	0	4	0
Chris Frodsham	14/4/88	6	6	0	0	8	8	0	0	16	16
Phillip Hewitt	10/12/78	(1)	(1)	0	0	0	0	0	0	0	0
Mark Hobson	14/1/87	12(1)	8	1	1	0	0	0	0	4	4
Craig Hodgson	14/1/86	4(3)	3(1)	2	0	0	0	0	0	8	0
Matthew Johnson	18/3/82	5	5	0	0	0	0	0	0	0	0
Harry Kaufman	20/12/91	(3)	(3)	0	0	0	0	0	0	0	0
Darren King	9/3/82	20	17	4	4	0	0	0	0	16	16
Rob Lunt	8/2/85	1	1	0	0	1	1	0	0	2	2
Jamie Marshall	17/7/78	20(1)	16	8	8	0	0	0	0	32	32
Ashley McDonald	21/1/89	(1)	(1)	0	0	0	0	0	0	0	0
Joe McKenna	21/8/87	(4)	(4)	0	0	0	0	0	0	0	0
Jason Mossop	12/9/85	15	12	2	2	0	0	0	0	8	8
Jack Pedley	9/11/89	1(14)	1(12)	7	6	0	0	0	0	28	24
Adam Ramsden	27/8/91	(2)	(2)	1	1	0	0	0	0	4	4
James Robinson	4/3/79	5(15)	5(11)	3	3	0	0	0	0	12	12
Steve Roper	10/11/86	13	8	0	0	3	3	1	1	7	7
Mark Routledge	24/1/88	6	4	1	0	0	0	0	0	4	0
Greg Rowley	9/4/82	3	3	1	1	0	0	0	0	4	4
Robert Scott	3/9/88	5	5	1	1	0	0	0	0	4	4
Marc Shackley	14/1/89	(3)	(3)	0	0	0	0	0	0	0	0
Brett Smith	17/10/77	1(3)	(1)	0	0	0	0	0	0	0	0
Jarrad Stack	13/2/88	21(2)	18	3	1	0	0	0	0	12	4
Mike Whitehead	25/8/78	20(3)	15(3)	2	2	0	0	0	0	8	8
Martyn Wilson	22/10/82	12(3)	12(3)	1	1	0	0	0	0	4	4

Jamie Marshall

LEAGUE RECORD
P18-W2-D0-L16-BP5
(9th, Championship 1)
F281, A700, Diff-419
11 points.

CHALLENGE CUP
Round Three

NORTHERN RAIL CUP
9th, Pool 2

ATTENDANCES
Best - v Rochdale (Ch1 - 693)
Worst - v Lezignan (CC - 314)
Total (excluding Challenge Cup) - 5,211
Average (excluding Challenge Cup) - 474
(Down by 243 on 2008)

YORK CITY KNIGHTS

DATE	FIXTURE	RESULT	SCORERS	LGE	ATT
15/2/09	Workington (a) (NRC)	W10-34	t:Haberecht(2),Oakes,M Mitchell,Clough,Ratcliffe g:A Mitchell(5)	4th(P2)	513
18/2/09	Whitehaven (h) (NRC)	W36-6	t:M Mitchell(2),Oakes,Ratcliffe,P March,Clough,McHugh g:Knight(3),Ratcliffe	1st(P2)	685
22/2/09	Batley (a) (NRC)	L40-28	t:Hughes(3),P March,Oakes g:A Mitchell(4)	2nd(P2)	788
1/3/09	London Skolars (h) (NRC)	W58-12	t:Ratcliffe(2),Clayton,Hughes,M Mitchell,Haberecht(2),Oakes,P March,D March,Grimshaw g:Knight(7)	1st(P2)	1,003
8/3/09	Wigan St Patricks (h) (CCR3)	W50-10	t:McHugh,Grimshaw,Oakes(2),Woodcock,Clough,Clayton,M Mitchell,Hodgson,Kelly g:A Mitchell(5)	N/A	936
22/3/09	Dewsbury (a)	L28-2	g:A Mitchell	8th	1,216
29/3/09	Blackpool (h)	W22-20	t:Haberecht,McHugh(2),Oakes,A Mitchell g:A Mitchell	7th	900
4/4/09	Warrington (a) (CCR4)	L56-10	t:Ratcliffe,Hughes g:Knight	N/A	4,709
10/4/09	Keighley (a)	L13-12	t:Clayton,Ratcliffe g:A Mitchell(2)	7th	770
13/4/09	Rochdale (h)	W44-14	t:Hughes,Applegarth,P March(2),Oakes,Grimshaw,M Mitchell,Hodgson g:McHugh(6)	7th	923
26/4/09	Workington (a)	W6-36	t:P March(3),Woodcock,Oakes,Hughes g:McHugh(6)	6th	530
4/5/09	Keighley (h)	W24-22	t:Clough,Hughes,Haberecht,Hodgson g:McHugh(4)	4th	939
17/5/09	Rochdale (a)	L36-30	t:Peacock,Hughes,P March,M Mitchell,Knight g:A Mitchell(5)	5th	717
24/5/09	London Skolars (a)	W6-80	t:Hughes(2),Haberecht(2),Knight(2),Ratcliffe(3),Hodgson(3),Applegarth,Sullivan g:A Mitchell(12)	4th	336
31/5/09	Dewsbury (h)	L18-24	t:Sullivan,Haberecht,Ratcliffe g:A Mitchell(3)	5th	1,326
6/6/09	Widnes (a) (NRCQF)	L44-18	t:Hughes(2),Ratcliffe g:A Mitchell(3)	N/A	1,650
14/6/09	Hunslet (a)	W6-34	t:P March(2),Hughes,Stancliffe,D March,A Mitchell g:A Mitchell(5)	3rd	716
25/6/09	Oldham (h)	W20-18	t:Oakes,Clayton,Haberecht,Hughes g:A Mitchell(2)	2nd	3,106
5/7/09	Blackpool (a)	L49-36	t:Knight(2),Lewis,Clough,Hodgson,Hesketh g:A Mitchell(6)	4th	443
19/7/09	Workington (h)	W46-20	t:Haberecht,Ratcliffe(2),Clough,Hesketh,Clayton,Moore,Waterman g:A Mitchell(7)	4th	653
26/7/09	Hunslet (h)	L8-20	t:Moore g:A Mitchell(2)	3rd	985
2/8/09	Swinton (a)	W26-30	t:Ratcliffe(2),Bell,Knight,Oakes,Waterman g:A Mitchell(3)	2nd	452
16/8/09	London Skolars (h)	W64-0	t:Lewis,Clayton(2),Moore(3),Haberecht,Hughes,Schofield(2),Wildbore(2) g:Schofield(8)	4th	629
23/8/09	Oldham (a)	W24-37	t:Ambler,Ross,Moore,Wildbore,Hesketh(2),Waterman g:Ratcliffe(2),Waterman(2) fg:Wildbore	3rd	954
5/9/09	Swinton (h)	W46-28	t:Ross(2),Wildbore(2),Ratcliffe(2),Oakes,Applegarth g:Waterman(7)	3rd	844
20/9/09	Keighley (a) (QSF)	L32-18	t:Hesketh,Ratcliffe,Wildbore g:Wildbore(2),A Mitchell	N/A	1,501
27/9/09	Oldham (h) (FE)	L14-44	t:Clough,Oakes(2) g:Wildbore	N/A	1,164

	APP		TRIES		GOALS		FG		PTS	
	D.O.B.	ALL	Ch1	ALL	Ch1	ALL	Ch1	ALL	Ch1	ALL	Ch1
Luke Ambler	18/12/89	(4)	(4)	1	1	0	0	0	0	4	4
Mark Applegarth	10/12/84	18(9)	15(5)	3	3	0	0	0	0	12	12
Carl Barrow	29/6/81	3(8)	2(6)	0	0	0	0	0	0	0	0
Ian Bell	28/1/83	2	2	1	1	0	0	0	0	4	4
Richard Blakeway	22/7/83	7(1)	7(1)	0	0	0	0	0	0	0	0
David Clayton	23/9/88	23	19	7	5	0	0	0	0	28	20
Chris Clough	20/1/87	7(16)	4(13)	7	4	0	0	0	0	28	16
Danny Ekis	17/1/82	3(5)	2(1)	0	0	0	0	0	0	0	0
Danny Grimshaw	25/2/86	9(1)	4(1)	3	1	0	0	0	0	12	4
Tom Haberecht	17/5/85	23	17	12	8	0	0	0	0	48	32
Sean Hesketh	17/8/86	6(6)	6(5)	5	5	0	0	0	0	20	20
Tom Hodgson	12/5/88	1(15)	1(10)	7	6	0	0	0	0	28	24
Paul Hughes	28/12/84	26	19	16	9	0	0	0	0	64	36
Adam Jones	31/5/90	2	1	0	0	0	0	0	0	0	0
Rob Kelly	1/3/86	19(1)	13(1)	1	0	0	0	0	0	4	0
Richard Knight	6/10/85	14(4)	8(3)	6	6	11	0	0	0	46	24
Steve Lewis	22/10/86	5(1)	5(1)	2	2	0	0	0	0	8	8
Tom Lineham	21/9/91	2	2	0	0	0	0	0	0	0	0
David March	25/5/79	20	14	2	1	0	0	0	0	8	4
Paul March	25/5/79	16	11	11	8	0	0	0	0	44	32
Wayne McHugh	1/2/80	11	7	4	2	16	16	0	0	48	40
Adam Mitchell	7/8/81	17(2)	13(2)	2	2	67	50	0	0	142	108
Mike Mitchell	7/4/85	16	11	7	2	0	0	0	0	28	8
Gareth Moore	3/6/89	6(2)	6(2)	6	6	0	0	0	0	24	24
John Oakes	12/2/88	26	19	14	8	0	0	0	0	56	32
Kris Peacock	11/2/87	4(4)	3(2)	1	1	0	0	0	0	4	4
Danny Ratcliffe	14/3/87	21	15	18	12	3	2	0	0	78	52
Jordan Ross	25/10/84	11(3)	11(3)	3	3	0	0	0	0	12	12
Jonathan Schofield	17/4/90	1	1	2	2	8	8	0	0	24	24
Tom Stancliffe	26/9/90	3	2	1	1	0	0	0	0	4	4
Jack Stearman	30/1/88	(2)	(1)	0	0	0	0	0	0	0	0
Adam Sullivan	14/11/82	20(6)	14(6)	2	2	0	0	0	0	8	8
Jonny Waldron	22/10/82	1	0	0	0	0	0	0	0	0	0
Lee Waterman	13/4/87	2(4)	2(4)	3	3	9	9	0	0	30	30
Loz Wildbore	23/9/84	3(2)	3(2)	6	6	3	3	1	1	31	31
Chris Williams	28/6/90	(1)	(1)	0	0	0	0	0	0	0	0
Scott Woodcock	15/11/83	2(11)	(8)	2	1	0	0	0	0	8	4

Adam Sullivan

LEAGUE RECORD
P18-W12-D0-L6-BP4
(3rd, Championship 1/Final Eliminator)
F589, A360, Diff+229
40 points.

CHALLENGE CUP
Round Four

NORTHERN RAIL CUP
Quarter Finalists/2nd, Pool 2

ATTENDANCES
Best - v Oldham (Ch1 - 3,106)
Worst - v London Skolars (Ch1 - 629)
Total (excluding Challenge Cup) - 13,157
Average (excluding
Challenge Cup) - 1,096
(Up by 156 on 2008)

CHAMPIONSHIP ONE 2009
Round by Round

ROUND 9

Sunday 15th March 2009

OLDHAM 36 BLACKPOOL PANTHERS 18

OLDHAM: 1 Paul O'Connor; 2 Andy Ballard; 3 Danny Halliwell; 4 Paul Reilly; 5 Lee Greenwood; 6 James Coyle; 7 Thomas Coyle; 8 Paul Highton; 9 Gary Sykes; 10 Jamie I'Anson; 11 Dave Allen; 23 Chris Baines; 13 Rob Roberts. Subs (all used): 12 Tommy Goulden; 14 Richard Mervill; 16 Wayne Kerr; 22 Phil Joseph.
Tries: Goulden (26), Reilly (50), Greenwood (59, 74), Kerr (62, 70), Ballard (79); **Goals:** Ballard 4/7.
Sin bin: Reilly (55) - fighting.
PANTHERS: 1 Jonny Leather; 28 Gareth Langley; 3 Tom Woodcock; 4 Mark McCully; 2 Damian Munro; 30 Dean Hatton; 6 Simon Svabic; 12 Kris Ratcliffe; 9 John Clough; 27 Craig Farrimond; 11 Paul Alcock; 15 Melvin Alker; 16 Ian Hodson. Subs (all used): 14 Martin Keavney; 10 John Hill; 13 Rob Draper; 22 Keiron Tucker.
Tries: Hatton (3), Woodcock (11), Langley (22, 34);
Goals: Leather 0/2, Hatton 0/1, Langley 1/1.
Sin bin: Clough (29) – late challenge;
Langley (55) – fighting; Farrimond (68) - interference.
Rugby Leaguer & League Express Men of the Match:
Oldham: Tommy Goulden; *Panthers:* Mark McCully.
Penalty count: 13-7; **Half-time:** 4-18;
Referee: Craig Halloran; **Attendance:** 880.

ROUND 1

Sunday 22nd March 2009

BLACKPOOL PANTHERS 34 HUNSLET HAWKS 26

PANTHERS: 1 Jonny Leather; 28 Gareth Langley; 17 Dave Llewellyn; 4 Mark McCully; 24 Chris Campbell; 30 Dean Hatton; 7 Chris Forster; 13 Rob Draper; 9 John Clough; 12 Kris Ratcliffe; 23 Darryl Kay; 15 Melvin Alker; 16 Ian Hodson. Subs (all used): 14 Martin Keavney; 11 Paul Alcock; 10 John Hill; 2 Damian Munro.
Tries: Hatton (6, 68), Clough (18), Llewellyn (26, 40), Alker (46); **Goals:** Langley 5/7.
HAWKS: 3 Tom Sheldrake; 5 John Richardson; 18 Ayden Faal; 4 Michael Brown; 25 Michael Mark; 6 Darren Robinson; 31 Tony Williams; 17 Steve Brook; 23 Jonny Wainhouse; 12 Jason Hart; 28 Steve Dooler; 26 Nicko Slain; 14 Chris Redfearn. Subs (all used): 9 Richard Chapman; 24 Charlie Wabo; 22 Scott Watson; 8 Joe Helme.
Tries: Brown (12, 31), Richardson (22), Robinson (37), Slain (50); **Goals:** Robinson 3/5.
Rugby Leaguer & League Express Men of the Match:
Panthers: Dave Llewellyn; *Hawks:* Michael Brown.
Penalty count: 10-12; **Half-time:** 20-20;
Referee: Warren Turley; **Attendance:** 265.

DEWSBURY RAMS 28 YORK CITY KNIGHTS 2

RAMS: 3 Lee Lingard; 15 Bryn Powell; 18 Chris Spurr; 22 Kane Epati; 16 Austin Buchanan; 13 Pat Walker; 19 Liam Finn; 23 Keegan Hirst; 9 Mike Emmett; 12 Taron Wildey; 20 Rob Spicer; 21 Andrew Bostock; 35 Adam Hayes. Subs (all used): 33 James Walker; 17 Alex Bretherton; 7 Gareth Greenwood; 28 Liam Crawley.
Tries: Spicer (53), Finn (59), Lingard (72);
Goals: P Walker 8/10.
CITY KNIGHTS: 1 Danny Ratcliffe; 34 Wayne McHugh; 3 John Oakes; 28 Mike Mitchell; 4 David Clayton; 6 Adam Mitchell; 7 Paul March; 15 Chris Clough; 9 Paul Hughes; 10 Adam Sullivan; 11 Rob Kelly; 12 Tom Haberecht; 21 David March. Subs (all used): 14 Tom Hodgson; 29 Mark Applegarth; 13 Richard Knight; 17 Scott Woodcock.
Goals: A Mitchell 1/2.
Sin bin: Sullivan (16) – late challenge;
P March (65) – dissent; Clough (70) – dissent.
On report: Hughes (66) – alleged punching;
Applegarth (78) – alleged dangerous tackle.
Rugby Leaguer & League Express Men of the Match:
Rams: Liam Finn; *City Knights:* Adam Mitchell.
Penalty count: 23-10; **Half-time:** 4-2;
Referee: Chris Leatherbarrow; **Attendance:** 1,216.

KEIGHLEY COUGARS 34 OLDHAM 26

COUGARS: 1 George Rayner; 2 Sam Gardner; 3 Dan Potter; 20 Daley Williams; 5 Gavin Duffy; 6 Jon Presley; 7 Danny Jones; 17 Scott Law; 9 James Feather; 10 Simon Bissell; 11 Will Cartledge; 4 Oliver Purseglove; 18 Greg Nicholson. Subs (all used): 14 Jamaine Wray; 12 Neil Lowe; 13 Carl Hughes; 29 Karl Gunney.
Tries: Presley (7, 80), Bissell (14), Gardner (31), Williams (42), Hughes (52); **Goals:** Jones 5/7.
OLDHAM: 1 Paul O'Connor; 2 Andy Ballard; 3 Danny Halliwell; 4 Paul Reilly; 5 Lee Greenwood; 6 James Coyle; 7 Thomas Coyle; 8 Paul Highton; 22 Phil Joseph; 10 Jamie I'Anson; 11 Dave Allen; 23 Chris Baines; 13 Rob Roberts. Subs (all used): 16 Wayne Kerr; 14 Richard Mervill; 24 Marcus St Hilaire; 18 Neil Roden.
Tries: Halliwell (2), T Coyle (39, 46), J Coyle (55, 60);
Goals: Ballard 3/5.
On report: T Coyle (76) - alleged high tackle.
Rugby Leaguer & League Express Men of the Match:
Cougars: Jon Presley; *Oldham:* Phil Joseph.
Penalty count: 6-13; **Half-time:** 14-8;
Referee: Matthew Thomasson; **Attendance:** 1,021.

LONDON SKOLARS 16 SWINTON LIONS 66

SKOLARS: 2 Corey Simms; 25 Jaroslaw Obuchowski; 17 Chad Isles; 11 Matt Thomas; 5 Austen Aggrey; 9 Gareth Honor; 7 Paul Thorman; 16 Tony Williams; 19 Leigh Nissen; 10 Glenn Osborn; 22 Danny Burke; 8 Dave Ellison; 21 Ben Joyce. Subs (all used): 14 Graeme Spencer; 1 Frank Reid; 27 Keir Bell; 26 Olu Iwenofu.
Tries: Obuchowski (9), Iwenofu (66), Thorman (70);
Goals: Thorman 2/3.
LIONS: 7 Richie Hawkyard; 22 Darren Bamford; 3 Dave Hull; 29 Carl Sneyd; 1 Wayne English; 6 Graham Holroyd; 15 Gary Hulse; 10 Bruce Johnson; 9 Phil Wood; 12 Danny Heaton; 11 Mike Wainwright; 17 Tommy Grundy; 14 Craig Ashall. Subs (all used): 16 Alex McClurg; 19 Neil Rigby; 28 Dave Newton; 27 Chris Tyrer.
Tries: Wood (5), Wainwright (17), Hulse (22), Bamford (25), D Hull (27, 53, 61), Newton (42), Holroyd (47), English (55), Grundy (64); **Goals:** Sneyd 11/11.
Rugby Leaguer & League Express Men of the Match:
Skolars: Tony Williams; *Lions:* Dave Hull.
Penalty count: 7-7; **Half-time:** 4-30;
Referee: Tim Roby; **Attendance:** 637.

WORKINGTON TOWN 21 ROCHDALE HORNETS 14

TOWN: 2 Neil Frazer; 20 Stephen Dawes; 21 Mark Routledge; 4 Jason Mossop; 5 Jamie Marshall; 6 Carl Forber; 7 Steve Roper; 16 Tommy Brindle; 31 Darren King; 24 Jarrad Stack; 22 Paddy Coupar; 12 Craig Hodgson; 13 Mark Hobson. Subs (all used): 9 Jack Pedley; 11 Mike Whitehead; 10 Dean Burgess; 8 Ryan Benjafield.
Tries: Brindle (6, 54), Dawes (14); **Goals:** Forber 4/4;
Field goal: Roper (77).
HORNETS: 19 Craig Johnson; 2 John Gillam; 3 Mick Fogerty; 4 Casey Mayberry; 1 Chris Giles; 6 Martin Ainscough; 24 Chris Hough; 8 David Best; 13 Wayne Corcoran; 10 Paul Raftrey; 33 Dale Cunniffe; 12 Ian Sinfield; 25 Dayne Donoghue. Subs (all used): 9 Janan Billings; 15 Martin McLoughlin; 17 Andrew Isherwood; 21 Tommy Gallagher.
Tries: Gillam (22, 42), Giles (64);
Goals: Giles 1/2, Hough 0/1.
Rugby Leaguer & League Express Men of the Match:
Town: Steve Roper; *Hornets:* Ian Sinfield.
Penalty count: 9-7; **Half-time:** 14-4;
Referee: Greg Dolan; **Attendance:** 693.

ROUND 2

Sunday 29th March 2009

OLDHAM 66 WORKINGTON TOWN 14

OLDHAM: 1 Paul O'Connor; 2 Andy Ballard; 3 Danny Halliwell; 24 Marcus St Hilaire; 5 Lee Greenwood; 6 James Coyle; 7 Thomas Coyle; 8 Paul Highton; 9 Gary Sykes; 10 Jamie I'Anson; 11 Dave Allen; 23 Chris Baines; 22 Phil Joseph. Subs (all used): 18 Neil Roden; 16 Wayne Kerr; 4 Paul Reilly; 17 Craig Robinson.
Tries: Ballard (8, 44, 73), T Coyle (23, 28, 39), Baines (26), Allen (32), J Coyle (45), O'Connor (56), Greenwood (64), St Hilaire (65); **Goals:** Ballard 9/12.
TOWN: 2 Neil Frazer; 20 Stephen Dawes; 21 Mark Routledge; 4 Jason Mossop; 5 Jamie Marshall; 6 Carl Forber; 7 Steve Roper; 16 Tommy Brindle; 31 Darren King; 24 Jarrad Stack; 22 Paddy Coupar; 12 Craig Hodgson; 13 Mark Hobson. Subs (all used): 9 Jack Pedley; 11 Mike Whitehead; 8 Ryan Benjafield; 17 Peter Dobson.
Tries: Marshall (2), Hobson (17), Dawes (50);
Goals: Forber 1/3.
Rugby Leaguer & League Express Men of the Match:
Oldham: Andy Ballard; *Town:* Steve Roper.
Penalty count: 8-8; **Half-time:** 34-8;
Referee: Peter Brooke; **Attendance:** 819.

ROCHDALE HORNETS 31 DEWSBURY RAMS 33

HORNETS: 16 Mark Brocklehurst; 2 John Gillam; 3 Mick Fogerty; 4 Casey Mayberry; 1 Chris Giles; 6 Martin Ainscough; 32 Liam McGovern; 11 Dave Cunliffe; 23 Liam Grundy; 10 Paul Raftrey; 33 Dale Cunniffe; 12 Ian Sinfield; 25 Dayne Donoghue. Subs (all used): 9 Janan Billings; 15 Martin McLoughlin; 17 Andrew Isherwood; 21 Tommy Gallagher.
Tries: Raftrey (10), Fogerty (27), Billings (48), McGovern (62), Sinfield (64), McLoughlin (67);
Goals: McGovern 3/6, Ainscough 0/1;
Field goal: McGovern (76).
RAMS: 1 Tom Colleran; 15 Bryn Powell; 17 Alex Bretherton; 22 Kane Epati; 16 Austin Buchanan; 13 Pat Walker; 19 Liam Finn; 12 Taron Wildey; 9 Mike Emmett; 23 Keegan Hirst; 20 Rob Spicer; 21 Andrew Bostock; 35 Adam Hayes. Subs (all used): 11 Adam Robinson; 33 James Walker; 27 Chris Grice; 7 Gareth Greenwood.
Tries: Bostock (16), Powell (19), Greenwood (32), Bretherton (45), Finn (54); **Goals:** P Walker 6/8;
Field goal: Finn (79).
Rugby Leaguer & League Express Men of the Match:
Hornets: Martin McLoughlin; *Rams:* Liam Finn.
Penalty count: 11-6; **Half-time:** 12-16;
Referee: Warren Turley; **Attendance:** 678.

SWINTON LIONS 36 KEIGHLEY COUGARS 28

LIONS: 7 Richie Hawkyard; 1 Wayne English; 3 Dave Hull; 29 Carl Sneyd; 22 Darren Bamford; 6 Graham Holroyd; 15 Gary Hulse; 8 Paul Southern; 9 Phil Wood; 10 Bruce Johnson; 11 Mike Wainwright; 17 Tommy Grundy; 14 Craig Ashall. Subs (all used): 16 Alex McClurg; 19 Neil Rigby; 28 Dave Newton; 12 Danny Heaton.
Tries: D Hull (3, 5, 70), Grundy (10, 13), Sneyd (30);
Goals: Sneyd 6/8.
COUGARS: 1 George Rayner; 2 Sam Gardner; 3 Dan Potter; 20 Daley Williams; 5 Gavin Duffy; 6 Jon Presley; 7 Danny Jones; 17 Scott Law; 9 James Feather; 10 Simon Bissell; 11 Will Cartledge; 4 Oliver Purseglove; 18 Greg Nicholson. Subs (all used): 14 Jamaine Wray; 12 Neil Lowe; 13 Carl Hughes; 29 Karl Gunney.
Tries: Nicholson (35), Rayner (39), Law (50), Presley (59), Gardner (64); **Goals:** Jones 4/5.
Sin bin: Gunney (25) - dissent.
Rugby Leaguer & League Express Men of the Match:
Lions: Graham Holroyd; *Cougars:* Jon Presley.
Penalty count: 10-9; **Half-time:** 26-10;
Referee: Chris Leatherbarrow; **Attendance:** 540.

YORK CITY KNIGHTS 22 BLACKPOOL PANTHERS 20

CITY KNIGHTS: 4 David Clayton; 3 John Oakes; 28 Mike Mitchell; 12 Tom Haberecht; 34 Wayne McHugh; 6 Adam Mitchell; 7 Paul March; 8 Danny Ekis; 9 Paul Hughes; 10 Adam Sullivan; 11 Rob Kelly; 13 Richard Knight; 21 David March. Subs (all used): 27 Danny Grimshaw; 29 Mark Applegarth; 30 Carl Barrow; 17 Scott Woodcock.
Tries: Haberecht (13), McHugh (32, 73), Oakes (40), A Mitchell (62); **Goals:** A Mitchell 1/4, Knight 0/1.
PANTHERS: 1 Jonny Leather; 28 Gareth Langley; 17 Dave Llewellyn; 4 Mark McCully; 2 Damian Munro; 30 Dean Hatton; 6 Simon Svabic; 12 Kris Ratcliffe; 9 John Clough; 13 Rob Draper; 23 Darryl Kay; 15 Melvin Alker; 16 Ian Hodson. Subs (all used): 14 Martin Keavney; 18 John Boland; 27 Craig Farrimond; 3 Tom Woodcock.
Tries: Langley (36), McCully (43), Leather (58), Llewellyn (80); **Goals:** Langley 2/4.
Rugby Leaguer & League Express Men of the Match:
City Knights: Adam Sullivan; *Panthers:* Mark McCully.
Penalty count: 9-7; **Half-time:** 12-4;
Referee: Craig Halloran; **Attendance:** 900.

HUNSLET HAWKS 71 LONDON SKOLARS 0

HAWKS: 3 Tom Sheldrake; 5 John Richardson; 4 Michael Brown; 18 Ayden Faal; 25 Michael Mark; 6 Darren Robinson; 31 Tony Williams; 17 Steve Brook; 27 Gareth Firm; 26 Nicko Slain; 28 Steve Dooler; 22 Scott Watson; 14 Chris Redfearn. Subs (all used): 9 Richard Chapman; 8 Joe Helme; 19 Ben Walkin; 24 Charlie Wabo.
Tries: Brown (9, 60), Watson (12, 30), Faal (16, 40, 76, 78), Williams (20, 42, 73), Robinson (55);
Goals: Robinson 11/12; **Field goal:** Robinson (37).
SKOLARS: 2 Corey Simms; 3 Oliver Fountain; 17 Chad Isles; 25 Jaroslaw Obuchowski; 5 Austen Aggrey; 29 Jermaine Coleman; 7 Paul Thorman; 16 Tony Williams; 9 Gareth Honor; 15 Bobby Wallis; 11 Matt Thomas; 28 Bernard Rule; 21 Ben Joyce. Subs (all used): 10 Glenn Osborn; 14 Graeme Spencer; 19 Leigh Nissen; 22 Danny Burke.
Rugby Leaguer & League Express Men of the Match:
Hawks: Darren Robinson; *Skolars:* Paul Thorman.
Penalty count: 5-9; **Half-time:** 35-0;
Referee: Greg Dolan; **Attendance:** 527.

ROUND 3

Friday 10th April 2009

BLACKPOOL PANTHERS 12 SWINTON LIONS 16

PANTHERS: 1 Jonny Leather; 2 Damian Munro; 3 Tom Woodcock; 17 Dave Llewellyn; 28 Gareth Langley; 6 Simon Svabic; 30 Dean Hatton; 13 Rob Draper; 9 John Clough; 10 John Hill; 16 Ian Hodson; 12 Kris Ratcliffe; 4 Mark McCully. Subs (all used): 14 Martin Keavney; 23 Darryl Kay; 20 Tom Wild; 11 Paul Alcock.
Tries: Leather (37), Ratcliffe (71); **Goals:** Langley 2/3.
LIONS: 7 Richie Hawkyard; 30 Andy Saywell; 3 Dave Hull; 29 Carl Sneyd; 1 Wayne English; 6 Graham Holroyd; 15 Gary Hulse; 12 Danny Heaton; 9 Phil Wood; 10 Bruce Johnson; 11 Mike Wainwright; 19 Neil Rigby; 13 Martin Moana. Subs (all used): 25 Matt Ashe; 14 Craig Ashall; 27 Chris Tyrer; 28 Dave Newton.
Tries: Hulse (11), Rigby (76), Saywell (80);
Goals: Sneyd 1/1, Holroyd 1/2.
Rugby Leaguer & League Express Men of the Match:
Panthers: Simon Svabic; *Lions:* Graham Holroyd.
Penalty count: 4-5; **Half-time:** 8-6;
Referee: Greg Dolan; **Attendance:** 411.

ROCHDALE HORNETS 18 OLDHAM 26

HORNETS: 16 Mark Brocklehurst; 26 Leroy Rivett; 3 Mick Fogerty; 4 Casey Mayberry; 1 Chris Giles; 6 Martin Ainscough; 32 Liam McGovern; 8 David Best; 13 Wayne Corcoran; 10 Paul Raftrey; 33 Dale Cunniffe; 12 Ian Sinfield; 25 Dayne Donoghue. Subs (all used): 11 Dave Cunliffe; 15 Martin McLoughlin; 19 Craig Johnson; 21 Tommy Gallagher.
Tries: Corcoran (7), Cunliffe (25), McGovern (41);
Goals: McGovern 3/3.
Sin bin: Best (67) - fighting.
On report: Brawl (79).
OLDHAM: 1 Paul O'Connor; 2 Andy Ballard; 3 Danny Halliwell; 24 Marcus St Hilaire; 5 Lee Greenwood; 6 James Coyle; 7 Thomas Coyle; 25 Luke Menzies; 9 Gary Sykes; 14 Richard Mervill; 11 Dave Allen; 23 Chris Baines; 22 Phil Joseph. Subs (all used): 16 Wayne Kerr; 17 Craig Robinson; 4 Paul Reilly; 29 Steve Gibbons.
Tries: Baines (23), Greenwood (38), Gibbons (48), Ballard (50), J Coyle (73); **Goals:** Ballard 3/5.
Sin bin: Allen (64) – dissent; Menzies (67) - fighting.
On report: Brawl (79).
Rugby Leaguer & League Express Men of the Match:
Hornets: Ian Sinfield; *Oldham:* Steve Gibbons.
Penalty count: 8-7; **Half-time:** 12-10;
Referee: Matthew Kidd; **Attendance:** 1,249.

Swinton's Mike Wainwright crashes over to score against Workington

WORKINGTON TOWN 16 HUNSLET HAWKS 24

TOWN: 1 Jay Duffy; 20 Stephen Dawes; 2 Neil Frazer; 4 Jason Mossop; 5 Jamie Marshall; 6 Carl Forber; 7 Steve Roper; 24 Jarrad Stack; 31 Darren King; 16 Tommy Brindle; 11 Mike Whitehead; 22 Paddy Coupar; 13 Mark Hobson. Subs (all used): 14 Brett Smith; 15 James Robinson; 19 Scott Burgess; 8 Ryan Benjafield. **Tries:** Dawes (4, 16, 57); **Goals:** Forber 2/3.
HAWKS: 3 Tom Sheldrake; 5 John Richardson; 4 Michael Brown; 18 Ayden Faal; 25 Michael Mark; 6 Darren Robinson; 31 Tony Williams; 17 Steve Brook; 24 Charlie Wabo; 26 Nicko Slain; 28 Steve Dooler; 22 Scott Watson; 9 Richard Chapman. Subs (all used): 27 Gareth Firm; 8 Joe Helme; 19 Ben Walkin; 14 Chris Redfearn.
Tries: Mark (20), Dooler (36), Firm (45), Wabo (52); **Goals:** Robinson 4/5.
Rugby Leaguer & League Express Men of the Match: *Town:* Stephen Dawes; *Hawks:* Charlie Wabo.
Penalty count: 6-3; **Half-time:** 12-10;
Referee: Peter Brooke; **Attendance:** 543.

DEWSBURY RAMS 70 LONDON SKOLARS 0

RAMS: 3 Lee Lingard; 15 Bryn Powell; 18 Chris Spurr; 22 Kane Epati; 16 Austin Buchanan; 6 Ryan Smith; 19 Liam Finn; 11 Adam Robinson; 9 Mike Emmett; 23 Keegan Hirst; 20 Rob Spicer; 21 Andrew Bostock; 35 Adam Hayes. Subs (all used): 17 Alex Bretherton; 12 Taron Wildey; 28 Liam Crawley; 8 Jimmy Elston.
Tries: Bostock (3, 70), Epati (5, 45), Spurr (18, 38, 75), Finn (30), Bretherton (36, 77), Buchanan (48), Lingard (66); **Goals:** Finn 11/12.
SKOLARS: 2 Corey Simms; 26 Olu Iwenofu; 17 Chad Isles; 13 Jaymes Chapman; 25 Jaroslaw Obuchowski; 9 Gareth Honor; 7 Paul Thorman; 8 Dave Ellison; 14 Graeme Spencer; 15 Bobby Wallis; 31 Mark McLennan; 5 Austen Aggrey; 11 Matt Thomas. Subs (all used): 23 Andre Vine; 16 Tony Williams; 19 Leigh Nissen; 32 John Paxton.
Rugby Leaguer & League Express Men of the Match: *Rams:* Liam Finn; *Skolars:* John Paxton.
Penalty count: 2-4; **Half-time:** 34-0;
Referee: Dave Merrick; **Attendance:** 1,002.

KEIGHLEY COUGARS 13 YORK CITY KNIGHTS 12

COUGARS: 1 George Rayner; 22 Lee Mapals; 3 Dan Potter; 20 Daley Williams; 5 Gavin Duffy; 6 Jon Presley; 7 Danny Jones; 17 Scott Law; 9 James Feather; 11 Will Cartledge; 29 Karl Gunney; 4 Oliver Purseglove; 18 Greg Nicholson. Subs (all used): 14 Jamaine Wray; 13 Carl Hughes; 12 Neil Lowe; 15 Craig Brown.
Tries: Lowe (22), Mapals (61); **Goals:** Jones 2/3;
Field goal: Presley (80).
CITY KNIGHTS: 1 Danny Ratcliffe; 34 Wayne McHugh; 28 Mike Mitchell; 4 David Clayton; 3 John Oakes; 6 Adam Mitchell; 7 Paul March; 8 Danny Ekis; 9 Paul Hughes; 10

Adam Sullivan; 11 Rob Kelly; 12 Tom Haberecht; 21 David March. Subs (all used): 14 Tom Hodgson; 29 Mark Applegarth; 15 Chris Clough; 19 Kris Peacock.
Tries: Clayton (26), Ratcliffe (45); **Goals:** A Mitchell 2/3.
Sin bin: Clough (22) - holding down;
P March (80) - late challenge.
On report: Ekis (17) - alleged use of the elbow;
D March (80) - alleged dangerous tackle.
Rugby Leaguer & League Express Men of the Match: *Cougars:* Daley Williams; *City Knights:* Paul March.
Penalty count: 15-7; **Half-time:** 8-8;
Referee: Matthew Thomasson; **Attendance:** 770.

ROUND 4

Monday 13th April 2009

LONDON SKOLARS 10 BLACKPOOL PANTHERS 48

SKOLARS: 2 Corey Simms; 3 Oliver Fountain; 32 John Paxton; 11 Matt Thomas; 25 Jaroslaw Obuchowski; 29 Jermaine Coleman; 7 Paul Thorman; 8 Dave Ellison; 9 Gareth Honor; 15 Bobby Wallis; 5 Austen Aggrey; 31 Mark McLennan; 23 Andre Vine. Subs (all used): 16 Tony Williams; 19 Leigh Nissen; 4 Oliver Bloom; 1 Frank Reid.
Tries: M Thomas (50), Paxton (62); **Goals:** Thorman 1/2.
PANTHERS: 22 Keiron Tucker; 2 Damian Munro; 17 Dave Llewellyn; 1 Jonny Leather; 28 Gareth Langley; 6 Simon Svabic; 7 Chris Forster; 20 Tom Wild; 9 John Clough; 8 Peter Fairhurst; 23 Darryl Kay; 12 Kris Ratcliffe; 16 Ian Hodson. Subs (all used): 14 Martin Keavney; 24 Chris Campbell; 18 John Boland; 30 Dean Hatton.
Tries: Langley (14), Leather (19, 66), Tucker (24), Forster (33), Keavney (54), Clough (74, 77), Llewellyn (80); **Goals:** Langley 1/4, Leather 5/5.
Rugby Leaguer & League Express Men of the Match: *Skolars:* Matt Thomas; *Panthers:* Jonny Leather.
Penalty count: 5-6; **Half-time:** 0-18;
Referee: Craig Halloran; **Attendance:** 215.

SWINTON LIONS 42 WORKINGTON TOWN 28

LIONS: 7 Richie Hawkyard; 1 Wayne English; 3 Dave Hull; 29 Carl Sneyd; 30 Andy Saywell; 6 Graham Holroyd; 25 Matt Ashe; 28 Dave Newton; 16 Alex McClurg; 12 Danny Heaton; 11 Mike Wainwright; 17 Tommy Grundy; 13 Martin Moana. Subs (all used): 14 Craig Ashall; 27 Chris Tyrer; 19 Neil Rigby; 18 Gareth Hayes.
Tries: Ashe (30), Saywell (35, 56), Wainwright (39), Sneyd (48), Grundy (68), McClurg (77);
Goals: Sneyd 4/5, Holroyd 3/3.
Sin bin: Holroyd (22) - dissent.
TOWN: 23 Martyn Wilson; 20 Stephen Dawes; 3 Andrew Beattie; 4 Jason Mossop; 5 Jamie Marshall; 6 Carl Forber; 7 Steve Roper; 16 Tommy Brindle; 26 Darren King; 24 Jarrad Stack; 11 Mike Whitehead; 22 Paddy Coupar; 13 Mark Hobson. Subs (all used): 9 Jack Pedley;

8 Ryan Benjafield; 17 Peter Dobson; 15 James Robinson.
Tries: Dawes (20), Benjafield (24), Forber (61, 63), Whitehead (74); **Goals:** Forber 4/5.
Rugby Leaguer & League Express Men of the Match: *Lions:* Graham Holroyd; *Town:* Carl Forber.
Penalty count: 10-9; **Half-time:** 16-12;
Referee: Chris Leatherbarrow; **Attendance:** 404.

YORK CITY KNIGHTS 44 ROCHDALE HORNETS 14

CITY KNIGHTS: 4 David Clayton; 20 Adam Jones; 3 John Oakes; 28 Mike Mitchell; 34 Wayne McHugh; 27 Danny Grimshaw; 7 Paul March; 29 Mark Applegarth; 9 Paul Hughes; 10 Adam Sullivan; 30 Carl Barrow; 16 Jordan Ross; 21 David March. Subs (all used): 14 Tom Hodgson; 15 Chris Clough; 8 Danny Ekis; 17 Scott Woodcock.
Tries: Hughes (2), Applegarth (11), P March (23, 55), Oakes (46), Grimshaw (49), M Mitchell (73), Hodgson (80); **Goals:** McHugh 6/8.
HORNETS: 16 Mark Brocklehurst; 26 Leroy Rivett; 3 Mick Fogerty; 4 Casey Mayberry; 1 Chris Giles; 6 Martin Ainscough; 32 Liam McGovern; 8 David Best; 13 Wayne Corcoran; 10 Paul Raftrey; 11 Dave Cunliffe; 12 Ian Sinfield; 25 Dayne Donoghue. Subs (all used): 15 Martin McLoughlin; 21 Tommy Gallagher; 23 Liam Grundy; 33 Dale Cunniffe.
Tries: Giles (17), Ainscough (32), Fogerty (64); **Goals:** McGovern 1/3.
Dismissal: Cunliffe (60) - dangerous tackle on D March.
Sin bin: Corcoran (79) - interference.
Rugby Leaguer & League Express Men of the Match: *City Knights:* Paul March; *Hornets:* Paul Raftrey.
Penalty count: 9-5; **Half-time:** 16-8;
Referee: Dave Merrick; **Attendance:** 923.

HUNSLET HAWKS 21 KEIGHLEY COUGARS 18

HAWKS: 3 Tom Sheldrake; 25 Michael Mark; 4 Michael Brown; 18 Ayden Faal; 5 John Richardson; 31 Tony Williams; 16 Mark Moxon; 17 Steve Brook; 9 Richard Chapman; 26 Nicko Slain; 28 Steve Dooler; 22 Scott Watson; 14 Chris Redfearn. Subs (all used): 27 Gareth Firm; 24 Charlie Wabo; 8 Joe Helme; 19 Ben Walkin.
Tries: Chapman (6), Brown (45, 60);
Goals: Sheldrake 4/5; **Field goal:** Chapman (64).
COUGARS: 1 George Rayner; 22 Lee Mapals; 3 Dan Potter; 20 Daley Williams; 5 Gavin Duffy; 6 Jon Presley; 7 Danny Jones; 11 Will Cartledge; 9 James Feather; 12 Neil Lowe; 18 Greg Nicholson; 4 Oliver Purseglove; 26 Ben Sagar. Subs: 14 Jamaine Wray; 10 Simon Bissell; 21 Ryan Smith; 2 Sam Gardner (not used).
Tries: Presley (23), Wray (38), Mapals (74);
Goals: Jones 3/3.
Sin bin: Smith (62) - interference.
Rugby Leaguer & League Express Men of the Match: *Hawks:* Michael Brown; *Cougars:* Jamaine Wray.
Penalty count: 10-10; **Half-time:** 10-12;
Referee: Warren Turley; **Attendance:** 697.

Sunday 19th April 2009

OLDHAM 12 DEWSBURY RAMS 36

OLDHAM: 1 Paul O'Connor; 2 Andy Ballard; 3 Danny Halliwell; 24 Marcus St Hilaire; 5 Lee Greenwood; 6 James Coyle; 7 Thomas Coyle; 8 Paul Highton; 29 Steve Gibbons; 25 Luke Menzies; 11 Dave Allen; 23 Chris Baines; 17 Craig Robinson. Subs (all used): 9 Gary Sykes; 12 Tommy Goulden; 14 Richard Mervill; 21 Lucas Onyango.
Tries: Highton (57), Greenwood (61); **Goals:** Ballard 2/2.
Sin bin: St Hilaire (76) - professional foul.
RAMS: 3 Lee Lingard; 15 Bryn Powell; 18 Chris Spurr; 22 Kane Epati; 16 Austin Buchanan; 13 Pat Walker; 19 Liam Finn; 11 Adam Robinson; 9 Mike Emmett; 23 Keegan Hirst; 20 Rob Spicer; 21 Andrew Bostock; 35 Adam Hayes. Subs: 6 Ryan Smith; 12 Taron Wildey; 17 Alex Bretherton (not used); 28 Liam Crawley.
Tries: Epati (8), Bostock (16), Wildey (27), Finn (39), Emmett (71), Smith (79); **Goals:** P Walker 3/4, Finn 3/4.
Rugby Leaguer & League Express Men of the Match:
Oldham: Dave Allen; *Rams:* Liam Finn.
Penalty count: 9-9; **Half-time:** 0-22;
Referee: Craig Halloran; **Attendance:** 1,147.

ROUND 5

Sunday 26th April 2009

DEWSBURY RAMS 30 HUNSLET HAWKS 10

RAMS: 3 Lee Lingard; 15 Bryn Powell; 18 Chris Spurr; 22 Kane Epati; 16 Austin Buchanan; 13 Pat Walker; 19 Liam Finn; 11 Adam Robinson; 9 Mike Emmett; 23 Keegan Hirst; 20 Rob Spicer; 21 Andrew Bostock; 35 Adam Hayes. Subs (all used): 8 Jimmy Elston; 17 Alex Bretherton; 12 Taron Wildey; 28 Liam Crawley.
Tries: Powell (3, 69), Finn (13), Spurr (38), Wildey (79);
Goals: P Walker 5/7.
Sin bin: Bostock (66) - high tackle.
HAWKS: 13 Craig Moss; 1 Nathan Larvin; 4 Michael Brown; 18 Ayden Faal; 25 Michael Mark; 6 Darren Robinson; 31 Tony Williams; 17 Steve Brook; 9 Richard Chapman; 26 Nicko Slain; 28 Steve Dooler; 22 Scott Watson; 24 Charlie Wabo. Subs (all used): 14 Chris Redfearn; 19 Ben Walkin; 8 Joe Helme; 27 Gareth Firm.
Tries: Brown (24), Watson (51); **Goals:** Robinson 1/2.
Sin bin: Redfearn (75) - high tackle.
Rugby Leaguer & League Express Men of the Match:
Rams: Bryn Powell; *Hawks:* Charlie Wabo.
Penalty count: 10-10; **Half-time:** 16-4;
Referee: Dave Merrick; **Attendance:** 1,413.

KEIGHLEY COUGARS 42 BLACKPOOL PANTHERS 22

COUGARS: 1 George Rayner; 22 Lee Mapals; 3 Dan Potter; 20 Daley Williams; 5 Gavin Duffy; 6 Jon Presley; 7 Danny Jones; 17 Scott Law; 9 James Feather; 8 Andy Shickell; 11 Will Cartledge; 4 Oliver Purseglove; 18 Greg Nicholson. Subs (all used): 14 Jamaine Wray; 26 Ben Sagar; 10 Simon Bissell; 15 Craig Brown.
Tries: Williams (8), Purseglove (14, 43), Presley (40, 53), Nicholson (48), Rayner (57), Potter (59);
Goals: Jones 5/8.
PANTHERS: 1 Jonny Leather; 2 Damian Munro; 17 Dave Llewellyn; 4 Mark McCully; 28 Gareth Langley; 6 Simon Svabic; 14 Martin Keavney; 13 Rob Draper; 9 John Clough; 20 Tom Wild; 23 Darryl Kay; 12 Kris Ratcliffe; 16 Ian Hodson. Subs (all used): 22 Keiron Tucker; 11 Paul Alcock; 30 Dean Hatton; 27 Craig Farrimond.
Tries: Keavney (8), Llewellyn (67), Clough (74), McCully (76); **Goals:** Leather 3/4.
Rugby Leaguer & League Express Men of the Match:
Cougars: Jon Presley; *Panthers:* Martin Keavney.
Penalty count: 9-9; **Half-time:** 16-6;
Referee: Warren Turley; **Attendance:** 534.

OLDHAM 52 SWINTON LIONS 36

OLDHAM: 1 Paul O'Connor; 2 Andy Ballard; 3 Danny Halliwell; 24 Marcus St Hilaire; 5 Lee Greenwood; 6 James Coyle; 7 Thomas Coyle; 8 Paul Highton; 9 Gary Sykes; 25 Luke Menzies; 11 Dave Allen; 12 Tommy Goulden; 13 Rob Roberts. Subs (all used): 10 Jamie I'Anson; 16 Wayne Kerr; 23 Chris Baines; 29 Steve Gibbons.
Tries: Greenwood (4), Halliwell (7), O'Connor (18), Allen (31), Gibbons (38), I'Anson (44), Sykes (58), Goulden (69), T Coyle (74); **Goals:** Ballard 8/10.
LIONS: 7 Richie Hawkyard; 1 Wayne English; 3 Dave Hull; 25 Matt Ashe; 30 Andy Saywell; 6 Graham Holroyd; 24 Paul Crook; 12 Danny Heaton; 16 Alex McClurg; 28 Dave Newton; 11 Mike Wainwright; 19 Neil Rigby; 13 Martin Moana. Subs (all used): 5 Marlon Billy; 14 Craig Ashall; 18 Gareth Hayes; 26 Chris Frodsham.
Tries: Hawkyard (13), D Hull (34), Wainwright (55), Ashall (61), Saywell (78), Hayes (80); **Goals:** Holroyd 6/6.
Rugby Leaguer & League Express Men of the Match:
Oldham: Thomas Coyle; *Lions:* Graham Holroyd.
Penalty count: 10-8; **Half-time:** 28-12;
Referee: Peter Brooke; **Attendance:** 1,010.

ROCHDALE HORNETS 46 LONDON SKOLARS 8

HORNETS: 1 Chris Giles; 2 John Gillam; 3 Mick Fogerty; 4 Casey Mayberry; 19 Craig Johnson; 6 Martin Ainscough; 32 Liam McGovern; 8 David Best; 23 Liam Grundy; 10 Paul Raftrey; 25 Dayne Donoghue; 12 Ian Sinfield; 13 Wayne Corcoran. Subs (all used): 9 Janan Billings; 15 Martin McLoughlin; 16 Mark Brocklehurst; 17 Andrew Isherwood.
Tries: Gillam (6, 19), Johnson (9), Ainscough (34), Mayberry (49), Donoghue (58), Brocklehurst (66, 78);
Goals: McGovern 7/8.
SKOLARS: 2 Corey Simms; 24 Smokey Junor; 17 Chad Isles; 32 John Paxton; 25 Jaroslaw Obuchowski; 9 Gareth Honor; 7 Paul Thorman; 8 Dave Ellison; 19 Leigh Nissen; 16 Tony Williams; 11 Matt Thomas; 5 Austen Aggrey; 23 Andre Vine. Subs (all used): 1 Frank Reid; 20 Paul Hyder; 4 Oliver Bloom; 22 Danny Burke.
Try: Paxton (15); **Goals:** Thorman 2/2.
Rugby Leaguer & League Express Men of the Match:
Hornets: Casey Mayberry; *Skolars:* Matt Thomas.
Penalty count: 9-10; **Half-time:** 24-8;
Referee: Greg Dolan; **Attendance:** 480.

WORKINGTON TOWN 6 YORK CITY KNIGHTS 36

TOWN: 1 Jay Duffy; 23 Martyn Wilson; 21 Mark Routledge; 4 Jason Mossop; 5 Jamie Marshall; 6 Carl Forber; 7 Steve Roper; 24 Jarrad Stack; 26 Darren King; 11 Mike Whitehead; 15 James Robinson; 22 Paddy Coupar; 13 Mark Hobson. Subs (all used): 19 Scott Burgess; 8 Ryan Benjafield; 12 Craig Hodgson; 17 Peter Dobson.
Try: Marshall (24); **Goals:** Forber 1/2.
Dismissal: Robinson (58) - kicking.
CITY KNIGHTS: 4 David Clayton; 3 John Oakes; 12 Tom Haberecht; 28 Mike Mitchell; 34 Wayne McHugh; 27 Danny Grimshaw; 7 Paul March; 29 Mark Applegarth; 9 Paul Hughes; 10 Adam Sullivan; 30 Carl Barrow; 16 Jordan Ross; 21 David March. Subs (all used): 14 Tom Hodgson; 15 Chris Clough; 11 Rob Kelly; 17 Scott Woodcock.
Tries: P March (18, 48, 67), Woodcock (52), Oakes (59), Hughes (62); **Goals:** McHugh 6/6.
Sin bin: Barrow (9) - late challenge on Roper.
Rugby Leaguer & League Express Men of the Match:
Town: Paddy Coupar; *City Knights:* Paul March.
Penalty count: 7-7; **Half-time:** 6-6;
Referee: Robert Hicks; **Attendance:** 530.

ROUND 6

Saturday 2nd May 2009

LONDON SKOLARS 10 OLDHAM 78

SKOLARS: 2 Corey Simms; 26 Olu Iwenofu; 32 John Paxton; 11 Matt Thomas; 24 Smokey Junor; 7 Paul Thorman; 5 Austen Aggrey; 8 Dave Ellison; 14 Graeme Spencer; 16 Tony Williams; 23 Andre Vine; 9 Gareth Honor; 21 Ben Joyce. Subs (all used): 20 Paul Hyder; 19 Leigh Nissen; 4 Oliver Bloom; 22 Danny Burke.
Tries: M Thomas (20, 47); **Goals:** Thorman 1/2.
Sin bin: Junor (15) – holding down.
OLDHAM: 1 Paul O'Connor; 2 Andy Ballard; 3 Danny Halliwell; 4 Paul Reilly; 21 Lucas Onyango; 6 James Coyle; 7 Thomas Coyle; 8 Paul Highton; 29 Steve Gibbons; 25 Luke Menzies; 12 Tommy Goulden; 23 Chris Baines; 13 Rob Roberts. Subs (all used): 10 Jamie I'Anson; 18 Neil Roden; 17 Craig Robinson; 16 Wayne Kerr.
Tries: T Coyle (4, 6), J Coyle (16, 29), Ballard (26, 40), Gibbons (31), Roberts (35), O'Connor (43), N Roden (51, 74), Robinson (70), Onyango (78);
Goals: Ballard 13/13.
Rugby Leaguer & League Express Men of the Match:
Skolars: Matt Thomas; *Oldham:* Andy Ballard.
Penalty count: 7-11; **Half-time:** 4-48;
Referee: Dave Merrick; **Attendance:** 257.

Monday 4th May 2009

BLACKPOOL PANTHERS 24 ROCHDALE HORNETS 12

PANTHERS: 1 Jonny Leather; 2 Damian Munro; 30 Dean Hatton; 4 Mark McCully; 28 Gareth Langley; 6 Simon Svabic; 7 Chris Forster; 8 Peter Fairhurst; 14 Martin Keavney; 13 Rob Draper; 11 Paul Alcock; 12 Kris Ratcliffe; 16 Ian Hodson. Subs (all used): 23 Darryl Kay; 20 Tom Wild; 22 Keiron Tucker; 9 John Clough.
Tries: Draper (5), Langley (18), Leather (25), Munro (47), Hatton (51); **Goals:** Leather 1/5, Langley 1/1.
HORNETS: 1 Chris Giles; 2 John Gillam; 3 Mick Fogerty; 16 Mark Brocklehurst; 19 Craig Johnson; 6 Martin Ainscough; 24 Chris Hough; 8 David Best; 13 Wayne Corcoran; 10 Paul Raftrey; 12 Ian Sinfield; 25 Dayne Donoghue; 33 Dale Cunniffe. Subs (all used): 15 Martin McLoughlin; 21 Tommy Gallagher; 9 Janan Billings; 17 Andrew Isherwood.
Tries: Cunniffe (4, 77), Fogerty (10); **Goals:** Corcoran 0/3.
Rugby Leaguer & League Express Men of the Match:
Panthers: Jonny Leather; *Hornets:* Dale Cunniffe.
Penalty count: 5-10; **Half-time:** 14-8;
Referee: Chris Leatherbarrow; **Attendance:** 347.

HUNSLET HAWKS 28 WORKINGTON TOWN 12

HAWKS: 3 Tom Sheldrake; 2 Scott Childs; 4 Michael Brown; 18 Ayden Faal; 25 Michael Mark; 6 Darren Robinson; 23 Jonny Wainhouse; 17 Steve Brook; 16 Mark Moxon; 8 Joe Helme; 28 Steve Dooler; 22 Scott Watson; 14 Chris Redfearn. Subs (all used): 9 Richard Chapman; 26 Nicko Slain; 24 Charlie Wabo; 21 Danny Cook.
Tries: Mark (25), Chapman (43), Robinson (58), Sheldrake (60), Childs (64);
Goals: Robinson 3/4, Sheldrake 1/1.
TOWN: 1 Jay Duffy; 23 Martyn Wilson; 21 Mark Routledge; 22 Paddy Coupar; 5 Jamie Marshall; 19 Scott Burgess; 7 Steve Roper; 24 Jarrad Stack; 26 Darren King; 11 Mike Whitehead; 15 James Robinson; 12 Craig Hodgson; 13 Mark Hobson. Subs (all used): 9 Jack Pedley; 8 Ryan Benjafield; 3 Andrew Beattie; 17 Peter Dobson.
Tries: Robinson (11), Pedley (70); **Goals:** Roper 2/2.
Rugby Leaguer & League Express Men of the Match:
Hawks: Richard Chapman; *Town:* Jack Pedley.
Penalty count: 8-7; **Half-time:** 6-6;
Referee: Matthew Kidd; **Attendance:** 515.

SWINTON LIONS 22 DEWSBURY RAMS 35

LIONS: 7 Richie Hawkyard; 2 Barry Hamilton; 3 Dave Hull; 29 Carl Sneyd; 30 Andy Saywell; 6 Graham Holroyd; 26 Chris Frodsham; 28 Dave Newton; 16 Alex McClurg; 12 Danny Heaton; 11 Mike Wainwright; 19 Neil Rigby; 14 Craig Ashall. Subs (all used): 25 Matt Ashe; 13 Martin Moana; 10 Bruce Johnson; 8 Paul Southern.
Tries: Ashall (5), Hawkyard (11), Holroyd (37), Heaton (53); **Goals:** Sneyd 3/4.
RAMS: 3 Lee Lingard; 15 Bryn Powell; 18 Chris Spurr; 22 Kane Epati; 30 Chris Hall; 13 Pat Walker; 19 Liam Finn; 11 Adam Robinson; 9 Mike Emmett; 23 Keegan Hirst; 20 Rob Spicer; 21 Andrew Bostock; 35 Adam Hayes. Subs (all used): 17 Alex Bretherton; 28 Liam Crawley; 8 Jimmy Elston; 26 Jake Wilson.
Tries: P Walker (17), Lingard (20), Bostock (27, 57), Spicer (68), Powell (73); **Goals:** P Walker 5/6;
Field goal: Finn (79).
Rugby Leaguer & League Express Men of the Match:
Lions: Graham Holroyd; *Rams:* Andrew Bostock.
Penalty count: 6-10; **Half-time:** 16-18;
Referee: Warren Turley; **Attendance:** 661.

YORK CITY KNIGHTS 24 KEIGHLEY COUGARS 22

CITY KNIGHTS: 4 David Clayton; 34 Wayne McHugh; 28 Mike Mitchell; 12 Tom Haberecht; 3 John Oakes; 27 Danny Grimshaw; 7 Paul March; 29 Mark Applegarth; 9 Paul Hughes; 10 Adam Sullivan; 11 Rob Kelly; 16 Jordan Ross; 21 David March. Subs (all used): 14 Tom Hodgson; 15 Chris Clough; 30 Carl Barrow; 17 Scott Woodcock.
Tries: Clough (24), Hughes (28), Haberecht (32), Hodgson (34); **Goals:** McHugh 4/5.
COUGARS: 1 George Rayner; 22 Lee Mapals; 3 Dan Potter; 20 Daley Williams; 5 Gavin Duffy; 6 Jon Presley; 7 Danny Jones; 8 Andy Shickell; 9 James Feather; 17 Scott Law; 11 Will Cartledge; 4 Oliver Purseglove; 18 Greg Nicholson. Subs (all used): 14 Jamaine Wray; 26 Ben Sagar; 10 Simon Bissell; 15 Craig Brown.
Tries: Duffy (15), Mapals (65, 74), Wray (78);
Goals: Jones 3/4.
Rugby Leaguer & League Express Men of the Match:
City Knights: David March; *Cougars:* Danny Jones.
Penalty count: 8-8; **Half-time:** 22-6;
Referee: Peter Brooke; **Attendance:** 939.

ROUND 7

Sunday 17th May 2009

WORKINGTON TOWN 18 LONDON SKOLARS 24

TOWN: 1 Jay Duffy; 23 Martyn Wilson; 3 Andrew Beattie; 20 Stephen Dawes; 5 Jamie Marshall; 6 Carl Forber; 7 Steve Roper; 16 Tommy Brindle; 26 Darren King; 24 Jarrad Stack; 15 James Robinson; 22 Paddy Coupar; 13 Mark Hobson. Subs (all used): 11 Mike Whitehead; 8 Ryan Benjafield; 33 Joe McKenna; 19 Scott Burgess.
Tries: King (27), Wilson (30), Whitehead (37);
Goals: Forber 3/3.
SKOLARS: 2 Corey Simms; 26 Olu Iwenofu; 32 John Paxton; 11 Matt Thomas; 3 Oliver Fountain; 9 Gareth Honor; 7 Paul Thorman; 16 Tony Williams; 19 Leigh Nissen; 28 Bernard Rule; 5 Austen Aggrey; 4 Oliver Bloom; 22 Danny Burke. Subs (all used): 27 Keir Bell; 23 Andre Vine; 14 Graeme Spencer; 25 Jaroslaw Obuchowski.
Tries: M Thomas (11), Paxton (22), Fountain (46, 68);
Goals: Thorman 4/4.
Rugby Leaguer & League Express Men of the Match:
Town: Paddy Coupar; *Skolars:* John Paxton.
Penalty count: 10-8; **Half-time:** 18-12;
Referee: Peter Brooke; **Attendance:** 353.

DEWSBURY RAMS 42 BLACKPOOL PANTHERS 16

RAMS: 3 Lee Lingard; 15 Bryn Powell; 22 Kane Epati; 18 Chris Spurr; 32 Martin Woodhead; 13 Pat Walker; 19 Liam Finn; 23 Keegan Hirst; 9 Mike Emmett; 12 Taron Wildey; 20 Rob Spicer; 21 Andrew Bostock; 35 Adam Hayes. Subs (all used): 28 Liam Crawley; 26 Jake Wilson; 17 Alex Bretherton; 16 Austin Buchanan.
Tries: Bostock (27, 38, 64), Powell (32), Finn (49), Bretherton (68), Epati (71); **Goals:** P Walker 7/7.
PANTHERS: 1 Jonny Leather; 2 Damian Munro; 3 Tom Woodcock; 4 Mark McCully; 28 Gareth Langley; 6 Simon Svabic; 30 Dean Hatton; 8 Peter Fairhurst; 14 Martin Keavney; 13 Rob Draper; 11 Paul Alcock; 12 Kris Ratcliffe; 16 Ian Hodson. Subs (all used): 9 John Clough; 23 Darryl Kay; 20 Tom Wild; 22 Keiron Tucker.
Tries: Alcock (22), Munro (60), Tucker (79);
Goals: Leather 2/3.
Rugby Leaguer & League Express Men of the Match:
Rams: Andrew Bostock; *Panthers:* Rob Draper.
Penalty count: 9-9; **Half-time:** 18-6;
Referee: Greg Dolan; **Attendance:** 1,010.

KEIGHLEY COUGARS 32 SWINTON LIONS 16

COUGARS: 1 George Rayner; 22 Lee Mapals; 3 Dan Potter; 27 Damien Reid; 5 Gavin Duffy; 6 Jon Presley; 7 Danny Jones; 17 Scott Law; 9 James Feather; 8 Andy Shickell; 11 Will Cartledge; 4 Oliver Purseglove; 18 Greg Nicholson. Subs (all used): 14 Jamaine Wray; 26 Ben Sagar; 10 Simon Bissell; 29 Karl Gunney.
Tries: Presley (5, 35), Rayner (66), Shickell (70), Mapals (80); **Goals:** Jones 6/6.

LIONS: 7 Richie Hawkyard; 1 Wayne English; 3 Dave Hull; 29 Carl Sneyd; 35 Richard Lopag; 6 Graham Holroyd; 15 Gary Hulse; 8 Paul Southern; 16 Alex McClurg; 28 Dave Newton; 11 Mike Wainwright; 19 Neil Rigby; 14 Craig Ashall. Subs: 22 Darren Bamford (not used); 13 Martin Moana; 18 Gareth Hayes; 10 Bruce Johnson.
Tries: Rigby (9), Johnson (42), English (57);
Goals: Sneyd 2/3.
Rugby Leaguer & League Express Men of the Match:
Cougars: Andy Shickell; *Lions:* Neil Rigby.
Penalty count: 9-14; **Half-time:** 12-4;
Referee: Dave Merrick; **Attendance:** 693.

OLDHAM 22 HUNSLET HAWKS 16

OLDHAM: 1 Paul O'Connor; 2 Andy Ballard; 3 Danny Halliwell; 24 Marcus St Hilaire; 5 Lee Greenwood; 6 James Coyle; 7 Thomas Coyle; 10 Jamie I'Anson; 29 Steve Gibbons; 15 Jason Boults; 11 Dave Allen; 23 Chris Baines; 13 Rob Roberts. Subs (all used): 4 Paul Reilly; 14 Richard Mervill; 16 Wayne Kerr; 22 Phil Joseph.
Tries: St Hilaire (16, 47), Halliwell (18), Roberts (31);
Goals: Ballard 3/5.
HAWKS: 3 Tom Sheldrake; 2 Scott Childs; 4 Michael Brown; 14 Chris Redfearn; 25 Michael Mark; 31 Tony Williams; 16 Mark Moxon; 17 Steve Brook; 9 Richard Chapman; 26 Nicko Slain; 28 Steve Dooler; 22 Scott Watson; 24 Charlie Wabo. Subs (all used): 7 Stuart Young; 8 Joe Helme; 11 Joe Howey; 27 Gareth Firm.
Tries: Chapman (14), Mark (28), Slain (39);
Goals: Sheldrake 2/3.
Rugby Leaguer & League Express Men of the Match:
Oldham: Paul O'Connor; *Hawks:* Gareth Firm.
Penalty count: 5-4; **Half-time:** 18-16;
Referee: Matthew Kidd; **Attendance:** 1,136.

ROCHDALE HORNETS 36 YORK CITY KNIGHTS 30

HORNETS: 1 Chris Giles; 26 Leroy Rivett; 3 Mick Fogerty; 20 Dale Cunniffe; 19 Craig Johnson; 6 Martin Ainscough; 34 Brett Robinson; 35 David Houghton; 13 Wayne Corcoran; 12 Ian Sinfield; 25 Dayne Donoghue; 14 Adam Thomas; 33 Matthew Strong. Subs (all used): 32 Liam McGovern; 17 Andrew Isherwood; 21 Tommy Gallagher; 22 Paul Anderson.
Tries: Rivett (22), Strong (28), Corcoran (30, 33), Ainscough (51, 61); **Goals:** Giles 6/7.
CITY KNIGHTS: 4 David Clayton; 1 Danny Ratcliffe; 28 Mike Mitchell; 12 Tom Haberecht; 3 John Oakes; 6 Adam Mitchell; 7 Paul March; 29 Mark Applegarth; 9 Paul Hughes; 10 Adam Sullivan; 11 Rob Kelly; 16 Jordan Ross; 19 Kris Peacock. Subs (all used): 14 Tom Hodgson; 15 Chris Clough; 13 Richard Knight; 17 Scott Woodcock.
Tries: Peacock (1), Hughes (5), P March (9), M Mitchell (41), Knight (72); **Goals:** A Mitchell 5/5.
Rugby Leaguer & League Express Men of the Match:
Hornets: Brett Robinson; *City Knights:* John Oakes.
Penalty count: 13-11; **Half-time:** 24-18;
Referee: Warren Turley; **Attendance:** 717.

ROUND 8

Sunday 24th May 2009

LONDON SKOLARS 6 YORK CITY KNIGHTS 80

SKOLARS: 2 Corey Simms; 26 Olu Iwenofu; 11 Matt Thomas; 32 John Paxton; 3 Oliver Fountain; 22 Danny Burke; 7 Paul Thorman; 28 Bernard Rule; 14 Graeme Spencer; 16 Tony Williams; 23 Andre Vine; 4 Oliver Bloom; 21 Ben Joyce. Subs (all used): 27 Keir Bell; 1 Frank Reid; 20 Paul Hyder; 25 Jaroslaw Obuchowski.
Try: M Thomas (78); **Goals:** Thorman 1/1.
CITY KNIGHTS: 1 Danny Ratcliffe; 34 Wayne McHugh; 12 Tom Haberecht; 4 David Clayton; 3 John Oakes; 6 Adam Mitchell; 7 Paul March; 16 Jordan Ross; 9 Paul Hughes; 10 Adam Sullivan; 11 Rob Kelly; 19 Kris Peacock; 13 Richard Knight. Subs (all used): 14 Tom Hodgson; 29 Mark Applegarth; 30 Carl Barrow; 17 Scott Woodcock.
Tries: Hughes (3, 72), Haberecht (8, 19), Knight (13, 54), Ratcliffe (14, 67, 70), Hodgson (30, 50, 62), Applegarth (35), Sullivan (79); **Goals:** A Mitchell 12/14.
Rugby Leaguer & League Express Men of the Match:
Skolars: Paul Thorman; *City Knights:* Danny Ratcliffe.
Penalty count: 8-7; **Half-time:** 0-40;
Referee: Chris Leatherbarrow; **Attendance:** 336.

BLACKPOOL PANTHERS 26 KEIGHLEY COUGARS 30

PANTHERS: 1 Jonny Leather; 2 Damian Munro; 17 Dave Llewellyn; 4 Mark McCully; 28 Gareth Langley; 30 Dean Hatton; 7 Chris Forster; 8 Peter Fairhurst; 9 John Clough; 12 Kris Ratcliffe; 11 Paul Alcock; 32 Scott Winstanley; 16 Ian Hodson. Subs (all used): 13 Rob Draper; 14 Martin Keavney; 18 John Boland; 37 Jay Duffy.
Tries: Alcock (3, 8), Forster (13), Winstanley (20), Leather (35); **Goals:** Leather 3/5.
COUGARS: 1 George Rayner; 22 Lee Mapals; 3 Dan Potter; 27 Damien Reid; 5 Gavin Duffy; 6 Jon Presley; 7 Danny Jones; 17 Scott Law; 9 James Feather; 8 Andy Shickell; 11 Will Cartledge; 4 Oliver Purseglove; 26 Ben Sagar. Subs (all used): 14 Jamaine Wray; 20 Daley Williams; 29 Karl Gunney; 15 Craig Brown.
Tries: Law (10), Jones (17), Mapals (49), Duffy (70), Potter (76); **Goals:** Jones 5/5.
Rugby Leaguer & League Express Men of the Match:
Panthers: Gareth Langley; *Cougars:* Danny Jones.
Penalty count: 3-3; **Half-time:** 26-12;
Referee: Matthew Kidd; **Attendance:** 500.

SWINTON LIONS 26 OLDHAM 44

LIONS: 7 Richie Hawkyard; 1 Wayne English; 3 Dave Hull; 29 Carl Sneyd; 35 Richard Lopag; 6 Graham Holroyd; 15 Gary Hulse; 28 Dave Newton; 16 Alex McClurg; 12 Danny Heaton; 19 Neil Rigby; 17 Tommy Grundy; 11 Mike Wainwright. Subs (all used): 22 Darren Bamford; 13 Martin Moana; 10 Bruce Johnson; 18 Gareth Hayes.
Tries: Sneyd (2), Hulse (9, 16), English (27), Bamford (77); **Goals:** Sneyd 3/6.
OLDHAM: 1 Paul O'Connor; 2 Andy Ballard; 4 Paul Reilly; 24 Marcus St Hilaire; 5 Lee Greenwood; 6 James Coyle; 7 Thomas Coyle; 15 Jason Boults; 22 Phil Joseph; 17 Craig Robinson; 11 Dave Allen; 23 Chris Baines; 13 Rob Roberts. Subs (all used): 10 Jamie I'Anson; 12 Tommy Goulden; 8 Paul Highton; 18 Neil Roden.
Tries: Allen (19, 38), Ballard (22, 67, 70), St Hilaire (32, 80), Joseph (50); **Goals:** Ballard 6/8.
Sin bin: O'Connor (75) - holding down.
On report:
T Coyle (23) - alleged spear tackle on Hawkyard.
Rugby Leaguer & League Express Men of the Match:
Lions: Graham Holroyd; *Oldham:* Dave Allen.
Penalty count: 10-7; **Half-time:** 20-22;
Referee: Ronnie Laughton; **Attendance:** 705.

WORKINGTON TOWN 14 DEWSBURY RAMS 76

TOWN: 23 Martyn Wilson; 32 Brett Carter; 3 Andrew Beattie; 20 Stephen Dawes; 5 Jamie Marshall; 19 Scott Burgess; 7 Steve Roper; 16 Tommy Brindle; 26 Darren King; 24 Jarrad Stack; 11 Mike Whitehead; 22 Paddy Coupar; 13 Mark Hobson. Subs (all used): 9 Jack Pedley; 15 James Robinson; 31 Joe McKenna; 17 Peter Dobson.
Try: S Burgess (34), Coupar (58), Marshall (75);
Goals: Roper 1/3.
RAMS: 3 Lee Lingard; 15 Bryn Powell; 18 Chris Spurr; 22 Kane Epati; 16 Austin Buchanan; 13 Pat Walker; 19 Liam Finn; 27 Chris Grice; 9 Mike Emmett; 12 Taron Wildey; 20 Rob Spicer; 21 Andrew Bostock; 35 Adam Hayes. Subs (all used): 6 Ryan Smith; 17 Alex Bretherton; 26 Jake Wilson; 4 Craig Bower.
Tries: Wildey (4), Bostock (11, 24), Lingard (20), Grice (26), P Walker (36), Buchanan (43, 64, 71), Bretherton (50, 61), Powell (52), Spicer (67), Epati (78);
Goals: P Walker 10/13, Finn 0/1.
Rugby Leaguer & League Express Men of the Match:
Town: Steve Roper; *Rams:* Alex Bretherton.
Penalty count: 4-11; **Half-time:** 6-36;
Referee: Warren Turley; **Attendance:** 319.

HUNSLET HAWKS 56 ROCHDALE HORNETS 30

HAWKS: 3 Tom Sheldrake; 25 Michael Mark; 18 Ayden Faal; 4 Michael Brown; 2 Scott Childs; 31 Tony Williams; 16 Mark Moxon; 26 Nicko Slain; 9 Richard Chapman; 17 Steve Brook; 11 Joe Howey; 22 Scott Watson; 14 Chris Redfearn. Subs (all used): 13 Craig Moss; 6 Darren Robinson; 28 Steve Dooler; 10 Neil Lowe.
Tries: Slain (3), Faal (7, 14, 17), Brook (12), Moxon (49), Williams (54), Robinson (58), Mark (77);
Goals: Sheldrake 4/5, Robinson 6/6.
HORNETS: 1 Chris Giles; 26 Leroy Rivett; 3 Mick Fogerty; 20 Dale Cunniffe; 19 Craig Johnson; 6 Martin Ainscough; 34 Brett Robinson; 35 David Houghton; 13 Wayne Corcoran; 12 Ian Sinfield; 14 Adam Thomas; 25 Dayne Donoghue; 33 Matthew Strong. Subs (all used): 4 Casey Mayberry; 21 Tommy Gallagher; 22 Paul Anderson; 32 Liam McGovern.
Tries: Ainscough (20), Gallagher (28), Johnson (45), Fogerty (67), Mayberry (69);
Goals: Giles 2/2, McGovern 3/3.
Dismissal: Anderson (42) - kicking.
Sin bin: Thomas (40) - high tackle.
Rugby Leaguer & League Express Men of the Match:
Hawks: Ayden Faal; *Hornets:* Wayne Corcoran.
Penalty count: 8-5; **Half-time:** 30-12;
Referee: Greg Dolan; **Attendance:** 656.

ROUND 9

Sunday 31st May 2009

KEIGHLEY COUGARS 58 WORKINGTON TOWN 6

COUGARS: 1 George Rayner; 22 Lee Mapals; 3 Dan Potter; 27 Damien Reid; 5 Gavin Duffy; 6 Jon Presley; 7 Danny Jones; 17 Scott Law; 9 James Feather; 8 Andy Shickell; 11 Will Cartledge; 4 Oliver Purseglove; 13 Carl Hughes. Subs (all used): 14 Jamaine Wray; 15 Craig Brown; 29 Karl Gunney; 28 Ryan Benjafield.
Tries: Hughes (9, 20, 65, 72), Feather (12), Purseglove (29), Duffy (37, 57), Potter (60, 80), Jones (63); **Goals:** Jones 7/11.
TOWN: 31 Brett Carter; 20 Stephen Dawes; 3 Andrew Beattie; 23 Martyn Wilson; 5 Jamie Marshall; 19 Scott Burgess; 32 Marc Bainbridge; 24 Jarrad Stack; 26 Darren King; 17 Peter Dobson; 15 James Robinson; 22 Paddy Coupar; 11 Mike Whitehead. Subs (all used): 9 Jack Pedley; 34 Joe McKenna; 18 Kris Coward; 33 Marc Shackley.
Try: Dawes (69); **Goals:** Bainbridge 1/1.
Rugby Leaguer & League Express Men of the Match:
Cougars: Danny Jones; *Town:* Marc Bainbridge.
Penalty count: 8-9; **Half-time:** 28-0;
Referee: Peter Brooke; **Attendance:** 803.

LONDON SKOLARS 18 HUNSLET HAWKS 34

SKOLARS: 33 Jamie O'Callaghan; 2 Corey Simms; 32 John Paxton; 11 Matt Thomas; 26 Olu Iwenofu; 22 Danny Burke; 7 Paul Thorman; 16 Tony Williams; 19 Leigh Nissen; 29 Rob Thomas; 4 Oliver Bloom; 5 Austen Aggrey; 21 Ben Joyce. Subs (all used): 23 Andre Vine; 34 Jack Graves; 27 Keir Bell; 25 Jaroslaw Obuchowski.
Tries: Bloom (6), M Thomas (54, 64);
Goals: Thorman 3/3.
HAWKS: 1 Nathan Larvin; 25 Michael Mark; 18 Ayden Faal; 13 Craig Moss; 5 John Richardson; 23 Jonathan Schofield; 16 Mark Moxon; 8 Joe Helme; 9 Richard Chapman; 10 Neil Lowe; 11 Joe Howey; 22 Scott Watson; 14 Chris Redfearn. Subs (all used): 3 Tom Sheldrake; 28 Steve Dooler; 17 Steve Brook; 24 Charlie Wabo.
Tries: Mark (15), Howey (20), Faal (23), Moss (32), Wabo (42, 50), Richardson (73); **Goals:** Schofield 3/7.
Rugby Leaguer & League Express Men of the Match:
Skolars: Matt Thomas; *Hawks:* Charlie Wabo.
Penalty count: 9-8; **Half-time:** 6-20;
Referee: Warren Turley; **Attendance:** 293.

SWINTON LIONS 23 ROCHDALE HORNETS 22

LIONS: 1 Wayne English; 35 Richard Lopag; 3 Dave Hull; 29 Carl Sneyd; 5 Marlon Billy; 6 Graham Holroyd; 15 Gary Hulse; 28 Dave Newton; 16 Alex McClurg; 27 Chris Tyrer; 19 Neil Rigby; 12 Danny Heaton; 13 Martin Moana. Subs (all used): 22 Darren Bamford; 9 Phil Wood; 14 Craig Ashall; 18 Gareth Hayes.
Tries: English (28), D Hull (49), Bamford (57), Rigby (71); **Goals:** Sneyd 3/4; **Field goal:** Holroyd (78).
Dismissal: Holroyd (79) - dissent.
Sin bin: Holroyd (79) - fighting.
HORNETS: 1 Chris Giles; 2 John Gillam; 3 Mick Fogerty; 4 Casey Mayberry; 26 Leroy Rivett; 6 Martin Ainscough; 34 Brett Robinson; 12 Ian Sinfield; 13 Wayne Corcoran; 10 Paul Raftrey; 14 Adam Thomas; 25 Dayne Donoghue; 33 Matthew Strong. Subs (all used): 7 Steve Roper; 27 Tommy Brindle; 28 Mark Hobson; 35 David Houghton.
Tries: Giles (4), Ainscough (37, 62), Mayberry (43);
Goals: Giles 3/4, Roper 0/1.
Rugby Leaguer & League Express Men of the Match:
Lions: Neil Rigby; *Hornets:* Matthew Strong.
Penalty count: 14-7; **Half-time:** 6-14;
Referee: Chris Leatherbarrow; **Attendance:** 502.

YORK CITY KNIGHTS 18 DEWSBURY RAMS 24

CITY KNIGHTS: 1 Danny Ratcliffe; 28 Mike Mitchell; 13 Richard Knight; 12 Tom Haberecht; 3 John Oakes; 6 Adam Mitchell; 7 Paul March; 16 Jordan Ross; 9 Paul Hughes; 10 Adam Sullivan; 11 Rob Kelly; 19 Kris Peacock; 21 David March. Subs (all used): 14 Tom Hodgson; 29 Mark Applegarth; 30 Carl Barrow; 17 Scott Woodcock.
Tries: Sullivan (10), Haberecht (61), Ratcliffe (67);
Goals: A Mitchell 3/4.
Sin bin: P March (40) - dissent.
RAMS: 3 Lee Lingard; 15 Bryn Powell; 18 Chris Spurr; 22 Kane Epati; 16 Austin Buchanan; 13 Pat Walker; 19 Liam Finn; 23 Keegan Hirst; 9 Mike Emmett; 11 Adam Robinson; 20 Rob Spicer; 21 Andrew Bostock; 35 Adam Hayes. Subs (all used): 17 Alex Bretherton; 6 Ryan Smith; 28 Liam Crawley; 27 Chris Grice.
Tries: Spurr (15), Finn (17), Buchanan (40), Bostock (47); **Goals:** P Walker 4/5.
Rugby Leaguer & League Express Men of the Match:
City Knights: Tom Haberecht; *Rams:* Liam Finn.
Penalty count: 10-7; **Half-time:** 8-16;
Referee: Craig Halloran; **Attendance:** 1,326.

ROUND 10

Thursday 11th June 2009

DEWSBURY RAMS 46 KEIGHLEY COUGARS 6

RAMS: 3 Lee Lingard; 15 Bryn Powell; 22 Kane Epati; 17 Alex Bretherton; 16 Austin Buchanan; 13 Pat Walker; 19 Liam Finn; 11 Adam Robinson; 9 Mike Emmett; 23 Keegan Hirst; 20 Rob Spicer; 21 Andrew Bostock; 35 Adam Hayes. Subs (all used): 28 Liam Crawley; 12 Taron Wildey; 6 Ryan Smith; 36 James Lockwood.
Tries: Bostock (14, 46, 52), Epati (16, 35), P Walker (42), Buchanan (67), Finn (75);
Goals: P Walker 6/8, Finn 1/1.
COUGARS: 1 George Rayner; 22 Lee Mapals; 3 Dan Potter; 27 Damien Reid; 5 Gavin Duffy; 6 Jon Presley; 7 Danny Jones; 17 Scott Law; 9 James Feather; 8 Andy Shickell; 11 Will Cartledge; 4 Oliver Purseglove; 13 Carl Hughes. Subs (all used): 14 Jamaine Wray; 29 Karl Gunney; 15 Craig Brown; 28 Ryan Benjafield.
Try: Shickell (9); **Goals:** Jones 1/1.
Rugby Leaguer & League Express Men of the Match:
Rams: Liam Finn; *Cougars:* Andy Shickell.
Penalty count: 8-9; **Half-time:** 18-6;
Referee: Robert Hicks; **Attendance:** 1,705.

Sunday 14th June 2009

WORKINGTON TOWN 18 SWINTON LIONS 26

TOWN: 23 Martyn Wilson; 31 Brett Carter; 3 Andrew Beattie; 4 Jason Mossop; 5 Jamie Marshall; 19 Scott Burgess; 32 Marc Bainbridge; 24 Jarrad Stack; 26 Darren King; 18 Kris Coward; 11 Mike Whitehead; 22 Paddy Coupar; 33 Craig Farrimond. Subs (all used): 9 Jack Pedley; 15 James Robinson; 31 Joe McKenna; 34 Marc Shackley.
Tries: King (1), Pedley (56), Beattie (72);
Goals: Bainbridge 1/1, S Burgess 2/2.
LIONS: 1 Wayne English; 35 Richard Lopag; 3 Dave Hull; 29 Carl Sneyd; 5 Marlon Billy; 11 Mike Wainwright; 15 Gary Hulse; 18 Gareth Hayes; 9 Phil Wood; 27 Chris Tyrer; 28 Dave Newton; 19 Neil Rigby; 14 Craig Ashall. Subs (all used): 7 Richie Hawkyard; 13 Martin Moana; 10 Bruce Johnson; 12 Danny Heaton.
Tries: Sneyd (21), Ashall (27), Billy (62), English (67);

York's Sean Hesketh feels the force of Oldham trio Jamie I'Anson, Chris Baines and Tommy Goulden

Goals: Sneyd 5/6.
Rugby Leaguer & League Express Men of the Match:
Town: Jamie Marshall; *Lions:* Gary Hulse.
Penalty count: 8-8; **Half-time:** 6-12;
Referee: Matthew Kidd; **Attendance:** 447.

HUNSLET HAWKS 6 YORK CITY KNIGHTS 34

HAWKS: 1 Nathan Larvin; 2 Wayne Reittie; 23 Craig Moss; 18 Ayden Faal; 25 Michael Mark; 6 Darren Robinson; 16 Mark Moxon; 26 Nicko Slain; 9 Richard Chapman; 17 Steve Brook; 28 Steve Dooler; 22 Scott Watson; 24 Charlie Wabo. Subs (all used): 14 Chris Redfearn; 10 Neil Lowe; 8 Joe Helme; 27 Gareth Firm.
Try: Mark (32); **Goals:** Robinson 1/1.
Dismissal: Lowe (15) - kick on D March.
CITY KNIGHTS: 1 Danny Ratcliffe; 28 Mike Mitchell; 3 John Oakes; 4 David Clayton; 22 Tom Stancliffe; 6 Adam Mitchell; 7 Paul March; 29 Mark Applegarth; 9 Paul Hughes; 10 Adam Sullivan; 11 Rob Kelly; 13 Richard Knight; 21 David March. Subs (all used): 14 Tom Hodgson; 15 Chris Clough; 16 Jordan Ross; 35 Sean Hesketh.
Tries: P March (10, 75), Hughes (10), Stancliffe (30), D March (52), A Mitchell (57); **Goals:** A Mitchell 5/6.
Rugby Leaguer & League Express Men of the Match:
Hawks: Mark Moxon; *City Knights:* Paul March.
Penalty count: 5-7; **Half-time:** 6-16;
Referee: Dave Merrick; **Attendance:** 716.

ROUND 11

Thursday 25th June 2009

YORK CITY KNIGHTS 20 OLDHAM 18

CITY KNIGHTS: 1 Danny Ratcliffe; 28 Mike Mitchell; 3 John Oakes; 12 Tom Haberecht; 4 David Clayton; 6 Adam Mitchell; 7 Paul March; 29 Mark Applegarth; 9 Paul Hughes; 10 Adam Sullivan; 11 Rob Kelly; 13 Richard Knight; 21 David March. Subs (all used): 14 Tom Hodgson; 15 Chris Clough; 16 Jordan Ross; 35 Sean Hesketh.
Tries: Oakes (16), Clayton (25), Haberecht (38), Hughes (61); **Goals:** A Mitchell 2/4.
OLDHAM: 1 Paul O'Connor; 2 Andy Ballard; 3 Danny Halliwell; 24 Marcus St Hilaire; 5 Lee Greenwood; 18 Neil Roden; 6 James Coyle; 8 Paul Highton; 9 Gary Sykes; 17 Craig Robinson; 4 Paul Reilly; 12 Tommy Goulden; 23 Chris Baines. Subs (all used): 15 Jason Boults; 10 Jamie I'Anson; 16 Wayne Kerr; 7 Thomas Coyle.

Tries: N Roden (8), Goulden (12), Baines (33);
Goals: Ballard 3/3.
Rugby Leaguer & League Express Men of the Match:
City Knights: Paul Hughes; *Oldham:* James Coyle.
Penalty count: 8-6; **Half-time:** 14-18;
Referee: Jamie Leahy; **Attendance:** 3,106.

Sunday 28th June 2009

BLACKPOOL PANTHERS 46 WORKINGTON TOWN 18

PANTHERS: 1 Jonny Leather; 2 Damian Munro; 33 Dean Thompson; 17 Dave Llewellyn; 3 Tom Woodcock; 6 Simon Svabic; 30 Carl Forber; 8 Peter Fairhurst; 9 John Clough; 12 Kris Ratcliffe; 11 Paul Alcock; 32 Josh Simm; 4 Mark McCully. Subs (all used): 14 Martin Keavney; 31 Simon Bissell; 37 Jay Duffy; 16 Ian Hodson.
Tries: Woodcock (4), Munro (8, 40, 56), Leather (13), Svabic (27), Thompson (61, 80), McCully (78);
Goals: Leather 2/4, Forber 3/5.
TOWN: 31 Brett Carter; 23 Martyn Wilson; 3 Andrew Beattie; 4 Jason Mossop; 5 Jamie Marshall; 19 Scott Burgess; 32 Marc Bainbridge; 24 Jarrad Stack; 26 Darren King; 18 Kris Coward; 11 Mike Whitehead; 22 Paddy Coupar; 33 Craig Farrimond. Subs (all used): 9 Jack Pedley; 15 James Robinson; 34 Marc Shackley; 17 Peter Dobson.
Tries: King (21), Farrimond (36), S Burgess (69);
Goals: Bainbridge 3/3.
Rugby Leaguer & League Express Men of the Match:
Panthers: Dean Thompson; *Town:* Scott Burgess.
Penalty count: 5-6; **Half-time:** 24-12;
Referee: Mohammed Drizza; **Attendance:** 280.

KEIGHLEY COUGARS 44 ROCHDALE HORNETS 16

COUGARS: 1 George Rayner; 22 Lee Mapals; 3 Dan Potter; 20 Daley Williams; 21 Ryan Smith; 6 Jon Presley; 7 Danny Jones; 17 Scott Law; 9 James Feather; 8 Andy Shickell; 11 Will Cartledge; 4 Oliver Purseglove; 13 Carl Hughes. Subs (all used): 14 Jamaine Wray; 15 Craig Brown; 18 Greg Nicholson; 28 Ryan Benjafield.
Tries: Hughes (2), Smith (21), Presley (23), Shickell (50), Jones (55), Williams (68), Rayner (72);
Goals: Jones 8/10.
HORNETS: 26 Leroy Rivett; 2 John Gillam; 3 Mick Fogerty; 4 Casey Mayberry; 19 Craig Johnson; 6 Martin Ainscough; 7 Steve Roper; 12 Ian Sinfield; 34 Brett Robinson; 10 Paul Raftrey; 14 Adam Thomas; 25 Dayne Donoghue; 20 Dale Cunniffe. Subs (all used): 17 Andrew Isherwood; 21 Tommy Gallagher; 27 Tommy Brindle; 28 Mark Hobson.
Tries: Ainscough (7), Mayberry (9), Gillam (43);

Goals: Roper 2/3, Ainscough 0/1.
Rugby Leaguer & League Express Men of the Match:
Cougars: Danny Jones; *Hornets:* Paul Raftrey.
Penalty count: 10-8; **Half-time:** 22-12;
Referee: Chris Leatherbarrow; **Attendance:** 901.

LONDON SKOLARS 0 DEWSBURY RAMS 64

SKOLARS: 2 Corey Simms; 32 Jeremy Guiraud; 30 John Paxton; 17 Chad Isles; 26 Olu Iwenofu; 29 Jy-Mel Coleman; 7 Paul Thorman; 21 Ben Joyce; 9 Gareth Honor; 27 Joe Mbu; 11 Matt Thomas; 5 Austen Aggrey; 19 Leigh Nissen. Subs (all used): 25 Jaroslaw Obuchowski; 14 Graeme Spencer; 4 Oliver Bloom; 16 Tony Williams.
RAMS: 3 Lee Lingard; 15 Bryn Powell; 18 Chris Spurr; 22 Kane Epati; 16 Austin Buchanan; 19 Liam Finn; 13 Pat Walker; 11 Adam Robinson; 9 Mike Emmett; 23 Keegan Hirst; 20 Rob Spicer; 12 Taron Wildey; 35 Adam Hayes. Subs (all used): 41 Loz Wildbore; 38 James Lockwood; 6 Ryan Smith; 27 Chris Grice.
Tries: Spicer (4), Buchanan (24), Spurr (29), Wildbore (38, 70), Powell (39, 49, 57), Hayes (47), Finn (52), Robinson (77); **Goals:** P Walker 10/11.
Rugby Leaguer & League Express Men of the Match:
Skolars: Jy-Mel Coleman; *Rams:* Bryn Powell.
Penalty count: 8-6; **Half-time:** 0-28;
Referee: Matthew Kidd; **Attendance:** 367.

SWINTON LIONS 42 HUNSLET HAWKS 16

LIONS: 29 Carl Sneyd; 36 Craig Littler; 3 Dave Hull; 4 Dean Gorton; 5 Marlon Billy; 11 Mike Wainwright; 15 Gary Hulse; 12 Danny Heaton; 9 Phil Wood; 27 Chris Tyrer; 17 Tommy Grundy; 19 Neil Rigby; 14 Craig Ashall. Subs (all used): 7 Richie Hawkyard; 13 Martin Moana; 18 Gareth Hayes; 10 Bruce Johnson.
Tries: Rigby (31), Sneyd (36), Ashall (56), Hawkyard (64), Billy (70), Hayes (74), D Hull (77);
Goals: Sneyd 7/7.
Sin bin: D Hull (46) – holding down.
HAWKS: 1 Nathan Larvin; 25 Michael Mark; 18 Ayden Faal; 23 Craig Moss; 2 Wayne Reittie; 31 James Fawcett; 16 Mark Moxon; 26 Nicko Slain; 14 Chris Redfearn; 22 Scott Watson; 28 Steve Dooler; 12 Jason Hart; 7 Stuart Young. Subs (all used): 4 Michael Brown; 24 Charlie Wabo; 8 Joe Helme; 9 Richard Chapman.
Tries: Young (14), Fawcett (30), Mark (80);
Goals: Young 0/1, Chapman 2/2.
Rugby Leaguer & League Express Men of the Match:
Lions: Richie Hawkyard; *Hawks:* Ayden Faal.
Penalty count: 7-8; **Half-time:** 12-10;
Referee: Greg Dolan; **Attendance:** 537.

Dewsbury's James Lockwood tries to find a way past Oldham's Phil Joseph

ROUND 12

Sunday 5th July 2009

BLACKPOOL PANTHERS 49 YORK CITY KNIGHTS 36

PANTHERS: 1 Jonny Leather; 2 Damian Munro; 3 Tom Woodcock; 33 Dean Thompson; 34 Nick Royle; 6 Simon Svabic; 30 Carl Forber; 8 Peter Fairhurst; 9 John Clough; 12 Kris Ratcliffe; 11 Paul Alcock; 32 Josh Simm; 4 Mark McCully. Subs (all used): 14 Martin Keavney; 37 Jay Duffy; 31 Simon Bissell; 16 Ian Hodson.
Tries: Munro (3, 31), Thompson (22, 76), Royle (25, 41), Keavney (45), Leather (54), Hodson (56);
Goals: Leather 4/6, Duffy 2/3; **Field goal:** Leather (73).
Sin bin: Keavney (30) – professional foul.
CITY KNIGHTS: 4 David Clayton; 22 Tom Stancliffe; 3 John Oakes; 12 Tom Haberecht; 28 Mike Mitchell; 6 Adam Mitchell; 27 Danny Grimshaw; 29 Mark Applegarth; 14 Tom Hodgson; 10 Adam Sullivan; 16 Jordan Ross; 35 Sean Hesketh; 13 Richard Knight. Subs (all used) 36 Chris Williams; 15 Chris Clough; 2 Steve Lewis; 30 Carl Barrow.
Tries: Knight (8, 61), Lewis (35), Clough (39), Hodgson (47), Hesketh (79); **Goals:** A Mitchell 6/7.
Rugby Leaguer & League Express Men of the Match:
Panthers: Nick Royle; *City Knights:* Adam Sullivan.
Penalty count: 4-13; **Half-time:** 20-16;
Referee: Chris Leatherbarrow; **Attendance:** 443.

DEWSBURY RAMS 36 SWINTON LIONS 8

RAMS: 3 Lee Lingard; 15 Bryn Powell; 18 Chris Spurr; 22 Kane Epati; 16 Austin Buchanan; 13 Pat Walker; 19 Liam Finn; 11 Adam Robinson; 9 Mike Emmett; 23 Keegan Hirst; 20 Rob Spicer; 12 Taron Wildey; 35 Adam Hayes. Subs (all used): 21 Andrew Bostock; 41 Loz Wildbore; 38 James Lockwood; 17 Alex Bretherton.
Tries: Spurr (7, 50), Bostock (19), Finn (37, 63), Epati (39); **Goals:** P Walker 6/6.
Sin bin: Lingard (77) – interference.
LIONS: 1 Wayne English; 35 Richard Lopag; 29 Carl Sneyd; 36 Craig Littler; 5 Marlon Billy; 34 Chris Hull; 15 Gary Hulse; 18 Gareth Hayes; 9 Phil Wood; 12 Danny Heaton; 17 Tommy Grundy; 19 Neil Rigby; 14 Craig Ashall. Subs (all used): 7 Richie Hawkyard; 13 Martin Moana; 28 Dave Newton; 10 Bruce Johnson.
Tries: C Hull (1), Moana (78); **Goals:** Sneyd 0/2.
Sin bin: Johnson (21) – professional foul;
Grundy (62) – high tackle.
Rugby Leaguer & League Express Men of the Match:
Rams: Liam Finn; *Lions:* Danny Heaton.
Penalty count: 12-7; **Half time:** 24-4;
Referee: Warren Turley; **Attendance:** 940.

KEIGHLEY COUGARS 60 LONDON SKOLARS 28

COUGARS: 1 George Rayner; 22 Lee Mapals; 3 Dan Potter; 20 Daley Williams; 21 Ryan Smith; 6 Jon Presley; 7 Danny Jones; 17 Scott Law; 9 James Feather; 8 Andy Shickell; 11 Will Cartledge; 4 Oliver Purseglove; 13 Carl Hughes. Subs (all used): 14 Jamaine Wray; 16 Brendan Rawlins; 18 Greg Nicholson; 28 Ryan Benjafield.
Tries: Williams (3, 44), Law (10, 57, 76), Potter (23, 34), Presley (62, 66), Hughes (74); **Goals:** Jones 10/10.
SKOLARS: 17 Chad Isles; 2 Corey Simms; 30 John Paxton; 11 Matt Thomas; 33 Jeremy Guiraud; 29 Jy-Mel Coleman; 7 Paul Thorman; 32 Joe Mbu; 9 Gareth Honor; 21 Ben Joyce; 5 Austen Aggrey; 4 Oliver Bloom; 23 Andre Vine. Subs (all used): 19 Leigh Nissen; 25 Jaroslaw Obuchowski; 27 Keir Bell; 34 Florian Rolianet.
Tries: Isles (15), Guiraud (18), Simms (39, 52), Paxton (70); **Goals:** Thorman 4/5.
Rugby Leaguer & League Express Men of the Match:
Cougars: Danny Jones; *Skolars:* Jy-Mel Coleman.
Penalty count: 8-5; **Half-time:** 24-18;
Referee: Dave Merrick; **Attendance:** 838.

ROCHDALE HORNETS 41 HUNSLET HAWKS 22

HORNETS: 26 Leroy Rivett; 2 John Gillam; 16 Mark Brocklehurst; 4 Casey Mayberry; 5 Marlon Miller; 6 Martin Ainscough; 32 Liam McGovern; 27 Tommy Brindle; 34 Brett Robinson; 12 Ian Sinfield; 14 Adam Thomas; 25 Dayne Donoghue; 21 Tommy Gallagher. Subs (all used): 8 David Best; 13 Wayne Corcoran; 10 Paul Raftrey; 28 Mark Hobson.
Tries: Miller (1), Gallagher (4, 34), Thomas (26, 64), Rivett (41); **Goals:** McGovern 8/8.
Field goal: Ainscough (76).
HAWKS: 3 Tom Sheldrake; 2 Wayne Reittie; 4 Michael Brown; 13 Craig Moss; 5 John Richardson; 23 Craig Fawcett; 16 Mark Moxon; 12 Jason Hart; 7 Stuart Young; 10 Neil Lowe; 24 Charlie Wabo; 22 Scott Watson; 28 Steve Dooler. Subs (all used): 31 Ryan Glynn; 14 Chris Redfearn; 8 Joe Helme; 9 Richard Chapman.
Tries: Sheldrake (8), Dooler (17), Wabo (47), Brown (52); **Goals:** Sheldrake 3/4.
Rugby Leaguer & League Express Men of the Match:
Hornets: Liam McGovern; *Hawks:* Richard Chapman.
Penalty count: 5-13; **Half-time:** 28-10;
Referee: Mohammed Drizza; **Attendance:** 482.

WORKINGTON TOWN 6 OLDHAM 60

TOWN: 31 Brett Carter; 32 Robert Scott; 3 Andrew Beattie; 4 Jason Mossop; 23 Martyn Wilson; 36 Rob Lunt; 35 Chris Frodsham; 24 Jarrad Stack; 26 Darren King; 18 Kris Coward; 11 Mike Whitehead; 22 Paddy Coupar; 33 Craig Farrimond. Subs (all used): 34 Ashley

McDonald; 15 James Robinson; 25 Harry Kaufman; 17 Peter Dobson.
Try: Mossop (39); **Goals:** Lunt 1/1.
Sin bin: Dobson (20) – fighting.
OLDHAM: 1 Paul O'Connor; 21 Lucas Onyango; 3 Danny Halliwell; 24 Marcus St Hilaire; 5 Lee Greenwood; 18 Neil Roden; 6 James Coyle; 15 Jason Boults; 9 Gary Sykes; 17 Craig Robinson; 11 Dave Allen; 12 Tommy Goulden; 23 Chris Baines. Subs (all used): 10 Jamie I'Anson; 16 Wayne Kerr; 22 Phil Joseph; 7 Thomas Coyle.
Tries: Allen (1), O'Connor (10, 26, 31), Goulden (37, 54), J Coyle (51), St Hilaire (56), Sykes (68, 75), Onyango (74); **Goals:** Halliwell 2/2, J Coyle 5/8, Joseph 1/1.
Dismissal: Halliwell (20) – fighting.
Sin bin: Joseph (28) – high tackle on Robinson.
Rugby Leaguer & League Express Men of the Match:
Town: Craig Farrimond; *Oldham:* Neil Roden.
Penalty count: 8-7; **Half-time:** 6-28;
Referee: Craig Halloran; **Attendance:** 514.

ROUND 13

Sunday 19th July 2009

LONDON SKOLARS 4 ROCHDALE HORNETS 62

SKOLARS: 2 Corey Simms; 26 Olu Iwenofu; 11 Matt Thomas; 30 John Paxton; 32 Jeremy Guiraud; 17 Chad Isles; 7 Paul Thorman; 29 Rob Thomas; 9 Gareth Honor; 21 Ben Joyce; 4 Oliver Bloom; 5 Austen Aggrey; 19 Leigh Nissen. Subs (all used): 14 Graeme Spencer; 34 Jack Graves; 32 Kris Hodson; 16 Tony Williams.
Try: M Thomas (55); **Goals:** Thorman 0/1.
Sin bin: Simms (57) – fighting; Aggrey (79) – fighting.
HORNETS: 19 Craig Johnson; 2 John Gillam; 16 Mark Brocklehurst; 4 Casey Mayberry; 5 Marlon Miller; 6 Martin Ainscough; 32 Liam McGovern; 12 Ian Sinfield; 13 Wayne Corcoran; 10 Paul Raftrey; 25 Dayne Donoghue; 28 Mark Hobson; 14 Adam Thomas. Subs (all used): 3 Mick Fogerty; 15 Martin McLoughlin; 17 Andrew Isherwood; 8 David Best.
Tries: Thomas (3), Ainscough (12), Miller (14), Sinfield (19, 73), Isherwood (33, 37, 48, 51), Johnson (46), Mayberry (58); **Goals:** McGovern 9/11.
Sin bin: Johnson (57) – fighting; Thomas (79) – fighting.
Rugby Leaguer & League Express Men of the Match:
Skolars: Matt Thomas; *Hornets:* Casey Mayberry.
Penalty count: 11-12; **Half-time:** 0-34;
Referee: Chris Leatherbarrow; **Attendance:** 485.

OLDHAM 22 KEIGHLEY COUGARS 24

OLDHAM: 4 Paul Reilly; 21 Lucas Onyango; 2 Andy

Ballard; 12 Tommy Goulden; 5 Lee Greenwood; 18 Neil Roden; 6 James Coyle; 15 Jason Boults; 9 Gary Sykes; 17 Craig Robinson; 11 Dave Allen; 23 Chris Baines; 22 Phil Joseph. Subs (all used): 7 Thomas Coyle; 10 Jamie I'Anson; 14 Richard Mervill; 16 Wayne Kerr.
Tries: Greenwood (31), Onyango (44), Baines (57), N Roden (77); **Goals:** Ballard 3/5.
Dismissal: T Coyle (28) - late challenge on Jones.
COUGARS: 1 George Rayner; 22 Lee Mapals; 3 Dan Potter; 20 Daley Williams; 5 Gavin Duffy; 6 Jon Presley; 7 Danny Jones; 8 Andy Shickell; 9 James Feather; 17 Scott Law; 11 Will Cartledge; 4 Oliver Purseglove; 13 Carl Hughes. Subs (all used): 14 Jamaine Wray; 16 Brendan Rawlins; 18 Greg Nicholson; 28 Ryan Benjafield.
Tries: Williams (10, 53), Feather (67), Rayner (69);
Goals: Jones 4/6.
Rugby Leaguer & League Express Men of the Match:
Oldham: James Coyle; *Cougars:* James Feather.
Penalty count: 15-11; **Half-time:** 8-6;
Referee: Jamie Leahy; **Attendance:** 848.

SWINTON LIONS 18 BLACKPOOL PANTHERS 33

LIONS: 29 Carl Sneyd; 35 Richard Lopag; 3 Dave Hull; 4 Dean Gorton; 30 Andy Saywell; 33 Chris Hull; 15 Gary Hulse; 8 Paul Southern; 9 Phil Wood; 12 Danny Heaton; 19 Neil Rigby; 17 Tommy Grundy; 11 Mike Wainwright. Subs (all used): 22 Darren Bamford; 13 Martin Moana; 27 Chris Tyrer; 10 Bruce Johnson.
Tries: C Hull (15), Hulse (27), Wood (77);
Goals: Sneyd 3/3.
Sin bin: Wood (50) - interference.
PANTHERS: 1 Jonny Leather; 2 Damian Munro; 3 Tom Woodcock; 33 Dean Thompson; 34 Nick Royle; 30 Carl Forber; 37 Jay Duffy; 8 Peter Fairhurst; 9 John Clough; 12 Kris Ratcliffe; 11 Paul Alcock; 16 Ian Hodson; 4 Mark McCully. Subs (all used): 14 Martin Keavney; 6 Simon Svabic; 31 Simon Bissell; 32 Josh Simm.
Tries: Forber (23), Woodcock (43), Munro (52, 79), Leather (55), Royle (68); **Goals:** Leather 1/2, Forber 3/4;
Field goal: McCully (74).
Rugby Leaguer & League Express Men of the Match:
Lions: Chris Hull; *Panthers:* Carl Forber.
Penalty count: 9-10; **Half-time:** 12-4;
Referee: Matthew Kidd; **Attendance:** 440.

YORK CITY KNIGHTS 46 WORKINGTON TOWN 20

CITY KNIGHTS: 34 Lee Waterman; 2 Steve Lewis; 12 Tom Haberecht; 4 David Clayton; 33 Tom Lineham; 6 Adam Mitchell; 1 Danny Ratcliffe; 29 Mark Applegarth; 9 Paul Hughes; 10 Adam Sullivan; 11 Rob Kelly; 13 Richard Knight; 21 David March. Subs (all used): 26 Gareth Moore; 15 Chris Clough; 36 Richard Blakeway; 35 Sean Hesketh.
Tries: Haberecht (5), Ratcliffe (10, 35), Clough (50), Hesketh (53), Clayton (56), Moore (67), Waterman (74);
Goals: A Mitchell 7/9.
TOWN: 23 Martyn Wilson; 36 Matthew Johnson; 3 Andrew Beattie; 4 Jason Mossop; 31 Robert Scott; 32 Chris Frodsham; 19 Scott Burgess; 24 Jarrad Stack; 26 Darren King; 18 Kris Coward; 11 Mike Whitehead; 22 Paddy Coupar; 33 Craig Farrimond. Subs (all used): 9 Jack Pedley; 15 James Robinson; 35 Adam Ramsden; 17 Peter Dobson.
Tries: Pedley (22), King (44), Mossop (70), Scott (78);
Goals: Frodsham 2/4.
Rugby Leaguer & League Express Men of the Match:
City Knights: Danny Ratcliffe; *Town:* Jack Pedley.
Penalty count: 8-8; **Half-time:** 18-6;
Referee: Greg Dolan; **Attendance:** 653.

HUNSLET HAWKS 6 DEWSBURY RAMS 24

HAWKS: 1 Nathan Larvin; 3 Tom Sheldrake; 4 Michael Brown; 21 Danny Cook; 5 John Richardson; 23 Craig Fawcett; 16 Paul March; 12 Jason Hart; 9 Richard Chapman; 22 Scott Watson; 24 Charlie Wabo; 28 Steve Dooler; 7 Stuart Young. Subs (all used): 17 Steve Brook; 11 Joe Howey; 14 Chris Redfearn; 6 Darren Robinson.
Try: Young (64); **Goals:** Sheldrake 1/1.
RAMS: 41 Loz Wildbore; 15 Bryn Powell; 18 Chris Spurr; 22 Kane Epati; 3 Lee Lingard; 13 Pat Walker; 19 Liam Finn; 11 Adam Robinson; 9 Mike Emmett; 23 Keegan Hirst; 20 Rob Spicer; 21 Andrew Bostock; 35 Adam Hayes. Subs (all used): 17 Alex Bretherton; 36 James Lockwood; 33 James Walker; 6 Ryan Smith.
Tries: Hirst (30), Finn (37), Epati (61);
Goals: P Walker 6/7.
Rugby Leaguer & League Express Men of the Match:
Hawks: Richard Chapman; *Rams:* Pat Walker.
Penalty count: 4-12; **Half-time:** 0-14;
Referee: Warren Turley; **Attendance:** 1,019.

ROUND 14

Saturday 25th July 2009

BLACKPOOL PANTHERS 46 LONDON SKOLARS 22

PANTHERS: 1 Jonny Leather; 2 Damian Munro; 3 Tom Woodcock; 33 Dean Thompson; 34 Nick Royle; 6 Simon Svabic; 30 Carl Forber; 18 John Boland; 9 John Clough; 8 Peter Fairhurst; 11 Paul Alcock; 12 Kris Ratcliffe; 4 Mark McCully. Subs (all used): 14 Martin Keavney; 31 Simon Bissell; 37 Jay Duffy; 13 Rob Draper.
Tries: Leather (6, 39), Woodcock (25), Forber (51), Draper (55), Munro (68), Alcock (74), Keavney (80);
Goals: Leather 4/4, Forber 3/4.
SKOLARS: 2 Corey Simms; 26 Olu Iwenofu; 30 John Paxton; 31 Kris Hodson; 33 Jeremy Guiraud; 17 Chad Isles; 7 Paul Thorman; 16 Tony Williams; 9 Gareth Honor; 21 Ben Joyce; 4 Oliver Bloom; 5 Austen Aggrey; 34 Jack Graves. Subs (all used): 14 Graeme Spencer; 23 Andre Vine; 22 Danny Burke; 3 Oliver Fountain.
Tries: Guiraud (11, 35), Honor (45), Isles (61);
Goals: Thorman 3/4.
Rugby Leaguer & League Express Men of the Match:
Panthers: Jonny Leather; *Skolars:* Jeremy Guiraud.
Penalty count: 12-6; **Half-time:** 16-10;
Referee: Warren Turley; **Attendance:** 391.

Sunday 26th July 2009

DEWSBURY RAMS 38 OLDHAM 8

RAMS: 3 Lee Lingard; 15 Bryn Powell; 17 Alex Bretherton; 22 Kane Epati; 18 Chris Spurr; 13 Pat Walker; 19 Liam Finn; 23 Keegan Hirst; 9 Mike Emmett; 11 Adam Robinson; 21 Andrew Bostock; 20 Rob Spicer; 35 Adam Hayes. Subs (all used): 6 Ryan Smith; 36 James Lockwood; 12 Taron Wildey; 27 Chris Grice.
Tries: Bostock (9, 28), Lingard (13), Finn (17), Powell (60), Emmett (78); **Goals:** P Walker 7/9.
OLDHAM: 1 Paul O'Connor; 21 Lucas Onyango; 12 Tommy Goulden; 23 Chris Baines; 5 Lee Greenwood; 18 Neil Roden; 7 Thomas Coyle; 15 Jason Boults; 9 Gary Sykes; 16 Wayne Kerr; 17 Craig Robinson; 31 Andy Boothroyd; 22 Phil Joseph. Subs (all used): 10 Jamie I'Anson; 26 Luke Sutton; 30 Martin Roden; 29 Ben Heaton.
Tries: Greenwood (39, 66); **Goals:** N Roden 0/2.
Rugby Leaguer & League Express Men of the Match:
Rams: Adam Robinson; *Oldham:* Lee Greenwood.
Penalty count: 17-8; **Half-time:** 22-4;
Referee: Mohammed Drizza; **Attendance:** 1,080.

ROCHDALE HORNETS 24 SWINTON LIONS 22

HORNETS: 26 Leroy Rivett; 19 Craig Johnson; 16 Mark Brocklehurst; 4 Casey Mayberry; 5 Marlon Miller; 6 Martin Ainscough; 32 Liam McGovern; 12 Ian Sinfield; 13 Wayne Corcoran; 10 Paul Raftrey; 3 Mick Fogerty; 28 Mark Hobson; 14 Adam Thomas. Subs (all used): 34 Brett Robinson; 8 David Best; 15 Martin McLoughlin; 17 Andrew Isherwood.
Tries: Mayberry (7, 70), McGovern (17), Brocklehurst (60); **Goals:** McGovern 4/6.
Sin bin: McLoughlin (29) – high tackle.
LIONS: 29 Carl Sneyd; 22 Darren Bamford; 3 Dave Hull; 4 Dean Gorton; 30 Andy Saywell; 6 Graham Holroyd; 15 Gary Hulse; 8 Paul Southern; 9 Phil Wood; 27 Chris Tyrer; 12 Danny Heaton; 17 Tommy Grundy; 11 Mike Wainwright. Subs (all used): 33 Chris Hull; 13 Martin Moana; 19 Neil Rigby; 28 Dave Newton.
Tries: Tyrer (2), Holroyd (32), Saywell (46);
Goals: Sneyd 5/5.
Rugby Leaguer & League Express Men of the Match:
Hornets: Casey Mayberry; *Lions:* Dean Gorton.
Penalty count: 13-14; **Half-time:** 14-16;
Referee: Peter Brooke; **Attendance:** 576.

YORK CITY KNIGHTS 8 HUNSLET HAWKS 20

CITY KNIGHTS: 1 Danny Ratcliffe; 2 Steve Lewis; 12 Tom Haberecht; 3 John Oakes; 4 David Clayton; 6 Adam Mitchell; 26 Gareth Moore; 29 Mark Applegarth; 9 Paul Hughes; 10 Adam Sullivan; 11 Rob Kelly; 36 Richard Blakeway; 21 David March. Subs (all used): 13 Richard Knight; 15 Chris Clough; 19 Kris Peacock; 35 Sean Hesketh.
Try: Moore (71); **Goals:** A Mitchell 2/2.
Dismissal: Kelly (18) – punching.
Sin bin: Moore (18) – fighting.
HAWKS: 1 Nathan Larvin; 2 Wayne Reittie; 21 Danny Cook; 4 Michael Brown; 3 Tom Sheldrake; 7 Stuart Young; 16 Paul March; 8 Joe Helme; 9 Richard Chapman; 12 Jason Hart; 22 Scott Watson; 28 Steve Dooler; 6 Darren Robinson. Subs (all used): 10 Neil Lowe; 14 Chris Redfearn; 27 Gareth Firm; 17 Steve Brook.
Tries: Watson (7, 9), March (36), Chapman (77);
Goals: Robinson 2/5.
Sin bin: Robinson (18) – fighting;
Lowe (39) – interference.
Rugby Leaguer & League Express Men of the Match:
City Knights: Paul Hughes; *Hawks:* Paul March.
Penalty count: 17-8; **Half-time:** 0-12;
Referee: Dave Merrick; **Attendance:** 985.

ROUND 15

Thursday 30th July 2009

KEIGHLEY COUGARS 14 DEWSBURY RAMS 54

COUGARS: 1 George Rayner; 22 Lee Mapals; 3 Dan Potter; 20 Daley Williams; 5 Gavin Duffy; 6 Jon Presley; 7 Danny Jones; 8 Andy Shickell; 9 James Feather; 17 Scott Law; 11 Will Cartledge; 4 Oliver Purseglove; 13 Carl Hughes. Subs (all used): 18 Greg Nicholson; 28 Ryan Benjafield; 14 Jamaine Wray; 16 Brendan Rawlins.
Tries: Presley (19, 76); **Goals:** Jones 3/3.
RAMS: 3 Lee Lingard; 15 Bryn Powell; 17 Alex Bretherton; 22 Kane Epati; 18 Chris Spurr; 13 Pat Walker; 19 Liam Finn; 23 Keegan Hirst; 9 Mike Emmett; 11 Adam Robinson; 20 Rob Spicer; 21 Andrew Bostock; 35 Adam Hayes. Subs (all used): 6 Ryan Smith; 12 Taron Wildey; 28 Liam Crawley; 36 James Lockwood.
Tries: Epati (23, 64), Powell (31), Bretherton (49, 66), Spurr (52), Robinson (55), Bostock (58), Smith (70);
Goals: P Walker 9/10.
Rugby Leaguer & League Express Men of the Match:
Cougars: Jon Presley; *Rams:* Liam Finn.
Penalty count: 6-9; **Half-time:** 8-14;
Referee: Ronnie Laughton; **Attendance:** 1,726.

Sunday 2nd August 2009

LONDON SKOLARS 18 WORKINGTON TOWN 24

SKOLARS: 32 Jeremy Guiraud; 26 Olu Iwenofu; 30 John Paxton; 33 Kris Hodson; 3 Oliver Fountain; 17 Chad Isles; 7 Paul Thorman; 16 Tony Williams; 9 Gareth Honor; 31 Joe Mbu; 4 Oliver Bloom; 5 Austen Aggrey; 19 Leigh Nissen. Subs (all used): 14 Graeme Spencer; 34 Florian Rolianet; 23 Andre Vine; 29 Jy-Mel Coleman.
Tries: Mbu (13), Thorman (55), Iwenofu (78);
Goals: Thorman 3/4.
TOWN: 23 Martyn Wilson; 31 Robert Scott; 3 Andrew Beattie; 4 Jason Mossop; 5 Jamie Marshall; 32 Chris Frodsham; 19 Scott Burgess; 17 Peter Dobson; 26 Darren King; 18 Kris Coward; 24 Jarrad Stack; 11 Mike Whitehead; 34 Craig Farrimond. Subs (all used): 9 Jack Pedley; 15 James Robinson; 33 Adam Ramsden; 22 Paddy Coupar.
Tries: Pedley (35), Beattie (40), Marshall (48), Ramsden (73); **Goals:** Frodsham 4/6.
Sin bin: Pedley (42) – delaying restart.
Rugby Leaguer & League Express Men of the Match:
Skolars: Oliver Bloom; *Town:* Jarrad Stack.
Penalty count: 11-9; **Half-time:** 8-12;
Referee: Matthew Kidd; **Attendance:** 257.

OLDHAM 48 ROCHDALE HORNETS 28

OLDHAM: 1 Paul O'Connor; 21 Lucas Onyango; 19 Craig Littler; 28 Jamie Russo; 5 Lee Greenwood; 27 Matt Ashe; 18 Neil Roden; 15 Jason Boults; 30 Martin Roden; 16 Wayne Kerr; 23 Chris Baines; 12 Tommy Goulden; 22 Phil Joseph. Subs (all used): 10 Jamie I'Anson; 14 Richard Mervill; 17 Craig Robinson; 31 Andy Boothroyd.
Tries: Baines (6, 37), Greenwood (12), Goulden (24), M Roden (30), Russo (44), Robinson (57), N Roden (62), O'Connor (69); **Goals:** Ashe 4/6, O'Connor 2/3.
Sin bin: Joseph (67) - fighting.
HORNETS: 16 Mark Brocklehurst; 26 Leroy Rivett; 14 Adam Thomas; 3 Mick Fogerty; 2 John Gillam; 6 Martin Ainscough; 32 Liam McGovern; 8 David Best; 13 Wayne Corcoran; 12 Ian Sinfield; 25 Dayne Donoghue; 28 Mark Hobson; 21 Tommy Gallagher. Subs (all used): 10 Paul Raftrey; 15 Martin McLoughlin; 34 Brett Robinson; 35 Darryl Kay.
Tries: Gillam (16, 52, 72), McGovern (49, 76);
Goals: McGovern 4/5.
Sin bin: Donoghue (23) - late challenge on N Roden; Best (67) - fighting.
Rugby Leaguer & League Express Men of the Match:
Oldham: Phil Joseph; *Hornets:* Martin Ainscough.
Penalty count: 9-13; **Half-time:** 26-6;
Referee: Dave Merrick; **Attendance:** 951.

SWINTON LIONS 26 YORK CITY KNIGHTS 30

LIONS: 7 Richie Hawkyard; 3 Dave Hull; 29 Carl Sneyd; 4 Dean Gorton; 30 Andy Saywell; 6 Graham Holroyd; 15 Gary Hulse; 8 Paul Southern; 33 Chris Hull; 27 Chris Tyrer; 12 Danny Heaton; 28 Dave Newton; 17 Tommy Grundy. Subs (all used): 14 Craig Ashall; 13 Martin Moana; 19 Neil Rigby; 10 Bruce Johnson.
Tries: Grundy (11), Sneyd (25), Saywell (34), Southern (76), Holroyd (79); **Goals:** Sneyd 3/5.
CITY KNIGHTS: 1 Danny Ratcliffe; 2 Steve Lewis; 3 John Oakes; 36 Ian Bell; 4 David Clayton; 34 Richard Blakeway; 6 Adam Mitchell; 29 Mark Applegarth; 9 Paul Hughes; 35 Sean Hesketh; 15 Chris Clough; 13 Richard Knight; 21 David March. Subs (all used): 26 Gareth Moore; 10 Adam Sullivan; 32 Lee Waterman; 30 Carl Barrow.
Tries: Ratcliffe (8, 15), Bell (21), Knight (47), Oakes (67), Waterman (73); **Goals:** A Mitchell 3/6, Knight 0/1.
Rugby Leaguer & League Express Men of the Match:
Lions: Graham Holroyd; *City Knights:* David March.
Penalty count: 9-6; **Half-time:** 14-16;
Referee: Matthew Thomasson; **Attendance:** 452.

HUNSLET HAWKS 34 BLACKPOOL PANTHERS 24

HAWKS: 1 Nathan Larvin; 2 Wayne Reittie; 4 Michael Brown; 21 Wayne McHugh; 25 Michael Mark; 7 Stuart Young; 16 Paul March; 12 Jason Hart; 9 Richard Chapman; 31 Scott Woodcock; 28 Steve Dooler; 22 Scott Watson; 6 Darren Robinson. Subs (all used): 27 Gareth Firm; 10 Neil Lowe; 13 Danny Ekis; 14 Chris Redfearn.
Tries: Young (20), Watson (28), McHugh (33), Dooler (60), Mark (63), Redfearn (68); **Goals:** Robinson 5/6.
PANTHERS: 1 Jonny Leather; 2 Damian Munro; 32 Sam Reay; 33 Dean Thompson; 34 Nick Royle; 37 Jay Duffy; 30 Carl Forber; 8 Peter Fairhurst; 9 John Clough; 13 Rob Draper; 11 Paul Alcock; 12 Kris Ratcliffe; 4 Mark McCully. Subs (all used): 14 Martin Keavney; 31 Simon Bissell; 20 Tom Wild; 18 John Boland.
Tries: Royle (9), Bissell (44), Boland (73), Duffy (77);
Goals: Leather 3/3, Forber 1/1.
Dismissal: Munro (23) - trip on Mark.
Rugby Leaguer & League Express Men of the Match:
Hawks: Wayne McHugh; *Panthers:* Jonny Leather.
Penalty count: 9-9; **Half-time:** 16-6;
Referee: Chris Leatherbarrow; **Attendance:** 573.

ROUND 10

Thursday 6th August 2009

OLDHAM 28 LONDON SKOLARS 22

OLDHAM: 1 Paul O'Connor; 21 Lucas Onyango; 19 Craig Littler; 28 Jamie Russo; 5 Lee Greenwood; 27 Matt Ashe; 18 Neil Roden; 15 Jason Boults; 30 Martin Roden; 16 Wayne Kerr; 23 Chris Baines; 12 Tommy Goulden; 22 Phil Joseph. Subs (all used): 7 Thomas Coyle; 10 Jamie

I'Anson; 17 Craig Robinson; 25 Luke Menzies.
Tries: M Roden (9), Ashe (51), Russo (65), Littler (72), T Coyle (75), Greenwood (79);
Goals: Ashe 1/2, O'Connor 1/4.
Sin bin: Russo (16) - fighting.
SKOLARS: 2 Corey Simms; 26 Olu Iwenofu; 30 John Paxton; 11 Matt Thomas; 3 Oliver Fountain; 17 Chad Isles; 7 Paul Thorman; 16 Tony Williams; 9 Gareth Honor; 32 Cedric Prizzon; 4 Oliver Bloom; 31 Kris Hodson; 19 Leigh Nissen. Subs (all used): 14 Graeme Spencer; 22 Danny Burke; 23 Andre Vine; 29 Jy-Mel Coleman.
Tries: Honor (4), Paxton (47), M Thomas (54);
Goals: Thorman 5/6.
Sin bin: Prizzon (16) - fighting.
Rugby Leaguer & League Express Men of the Match: *Oldham:* Chris Baines; *Skolars:* Gareth Honor.
Penalty count: 10-11; **Half-time:** 4-6;
Referee: Greg Dolan; **Attendance:** 1,419.

Sunday 9th August 2009

ROCHDALE HORNETS 18 BLACKPOOL PANTHERS 48

HORNETS: 6 Martin Ainscough; 2 John Gillam; 3 Mick Fogerty; 25 Dayne Donoghue; 16 Mark Brocklehurst; 4 Casey Mayberry; 13 Wayne Corcoran; 8 David Best; 21 Tommy Gallagher; 15 Martin McLoughlin; 17 Andrew Isherwood; 20 Darryl Kay; 26 Leroy Rivett. Subs (all used): 10 Paul Raftrey; 19 Craig Johnson; 28 Mark Hobson; 34 Brett Robinson.
Tries: Gallagher (27), McLoughlin (39), Ainscough (42), Raftrey (78); **Goals:** Ainscough 1/3, Corcoran 0/1.
Sin bin: Robinson (59) – fighting.
PANTHERS: 1 Jonny Leather; 3 Tom Woodcock; 17 Dave Llewellyn; 33 Dean Thompson; 34 Nick Royle; 32 Sam Reay; 30 Carl Forber; 13 Rob Draper; 14 Martin Keavney; 18 John Boland; 11 Paul Alcock; 16 Ian Hodson; 4 Mark McCully. Subs (all used): 37 Jay Duffy; 8 Peter Fairhurst; 9 John Clough; 31 Simon Bissell.
Tries: Keavney (10), Fairhurst (17, 45), Woodcock (21), Alcock (24), Duffy (54), Thompson (62), Clough (66);
Goals: Forber 7/8, Leather 1/1.
Sin bin: McCully (59) – fighting.
Rugby Leaguer & League Express Men of the Match: *Hornets:* Darryl Kay; *Panthers:* Carl Forber.
Penalty count: 11-11; **Half-time:** 10-24;
Referee: Greg Dolan; **Attendance:** 527.

ROUND 14

Sunday 9th August 2009

WORKINGTON TOWN 16 KEIGHLEY COUGARS 22

TOWN: 31 Greg Rowley; 32 Robert Scott; 35 Matthew Johnson; 4 Jason Mossop; 5 Jamie Marshall; 34 Craig Farrimond; 19 Scott Burgess; 17 Peter Dobson; 26 Darren King; 18 Kris Coward; 11 Mike Whitehead; 24 Jarrad Stack; 22 Paddy Coupar. Subs (all used): 9 Jack Pedley; 15 James Robinson; 23 Martyn Wilson; 25 Harry Kaufman.
Tries: Robinson (63), Pedley (66), Marshall (76);
Goals: S Burgess 2/3.
On report: Mossop (13) – alleged grapple tackle.
COUGARS: 1 George Rayner; 2 Sam Gardner; 3 Dan Potter; 20 Daley Williams; 5 Gavin Duffy; 6 Jon Presley; 7 Danny Jones; 17 Scott Law; 9 James Feather; 8 Andy Shickell; 11 Will Cartledge; 4 Oliver Purseglove; 13 Carl Hughes. Subs (all used): 14 Jamaine Wray; 18 Greg Nicholson; 28 Ryan Benjafield; 16 Brendan Rawlins.
Tries: Rayner (15), Rawlins (36), Jones (45), Williams (51); **Goals:** Jones 3/4.
Rugby Leaguer & League Express Men of the Match: *Town:* Mike Whitehead; *Cougars:* Danny Jones.
Penalty count: 9-7; **Half-time:** 0-12;
Referee: Dave Merrick; **Attendance:** 417.

ROUND 16

Sunday 16th August 2009

YORK CITY KNIGHTS 64 LONDON SKOLARS 0

CITY KNIGHTS: 1 Danny Ratcliffe; 2 Steve Lewis; 12 Tom Haberecht; 3 John Oakes; 4 David Clayton; 31 Jonathan Schofield; 26 Gareth Moore; 29 Mark Applegarth; 9 Paul Hughes; 35 Sean Hesketh; 15 Chris Clough; 30 Richard Blakeway; 21 David March. Subs (all used): 32 Loz Wildbore; 16 Jordan Ross; 10 Adam Sullivan; 36 Luke Ambler.
Tries: Lewis (4), Clayton (15, 57), Moore (20, 37, 68), Haberecht (26), Hughes (28), Schofield (49, 52), Wildbore (62, 77); **Goals:** Schofield 8/12.
SKOLARS: 2 Corey Simms; 26 Olu Iwenofu; 30 John Paxton; 11 Matt Thomas; 3 Oliver Fountain; 29 Jy-Mel Coleman; 7 Paul Thorman; 16 Tony Williams; 9 Gareth Honor; 32 Cedric Prizzon; 4 Oliver Bloom; 5 Austen Aggrey; 22 Danny Burke. Subs (all used): 23 Andre Vine; 21 Ben Joyce; 14 Graeme Spencer; 34 Hosni Kriouache.
Rugby Leaguer & League Express Men of the Match: *City Knights:* Gareth Moore; *Skolars:* Matt Thomas.
Penalty count: 6-8; **Half-time:** 32-0;
Referee: Peter Brooke; **Attendance:** 629.

BLACKPOOL PANTHERS 30 OLDHAM 30

PANTHERS: 1 Jonny Leather; 3 Tom Woodcock; 17 Dave Llewellyn; 33 Dean Thompson; 34 Nick Royle; 32 Sam Reay; 30 Carl Forber; 18 John Boland; 14 Martin Keavney; 13 Rob Draper; 11 Paul Alcock; 16 Ian Hodson; 4 Mark McCully. Subs (all used): 37 Jay Duffy; 31 Simon Bissell; 9 John Clough; 8 Peter Fairhurst.
Tries: Royle (6, 32), Woodcock (11), Alcock (20), Llewellyn (53); **Goals:** Leather 4/4, Forber 1/2.
Dismissal:
Bissell (61) – use of the elbow on Greenwood.
OLDHAM: 1 Paul O'Connor; 21 Lucas Onyango; 19 Craig Littler; 28 Jamie Russo; 5 Lee Greenwood; 18 Neil Roden; 7 Thomas Coyle; 15 Jason Boults; 30 Martin Roden; 16 Wayne Kerr; 12 Tommy Goulden; 23 Chris Baines; 4 Paul Reilly. Subs (all used): 10 Jamie I'Anson; 9 Gary Sykes; 25 Luke Menzies; 29 Craig Lawton.
Tries: Onyango (26), Baines (30), Russo (35), T Coyle (63), Littler (70), Goulden (73); **Goals:** Baines 3/6.
Sin bin: Greenwood (61) - retaliation.
Rugby Leaguer & League Express Men of the Match: *Panthers:* Ian Hodson; *Oldham:* Tommy Goulden.
Penalty count: 6-13; **Half-time:** 24-14;
Referee: Dave Merrick; **Attendance:** 600.

Hunslet's Wayne Reittie battles for the ball against Keighley

DEWSBURY RAMS 50 WORKINGTON TOWN 14

RAMS: 3 Lee Lingard; 15 Bryn Powell; 22 Kane Epati; 17 Alex Bretherton; 18 Chris Spurr; 13 Pat Walker; 19 Liam Finn; 36 James Lockwood; 9 Mike Emmett; 23 Keegan Hirst; 20 Rob Spicer; 21 Andrew Bostock; 35 Adam Hayes. Subs (all used): 6 Ryan Smith; 33 James Walker; 28 Liam Crawley; 16 Austin Buchanan.
Tries: Spicer (13), Bostock (18), Bretherton (29, 58), Smith (36), J Walker (39), Powell (52), Hayes (71), Epati (73); **Goals:** P Walker 7/9.
Sin bin: Epati (23) – professional foul.
TOWN: 31 Greg Rowley; 32 Robert Scott; 3 Andrew Beattie; 35 Matthew Johnson; 5 Jamie Marshall; 33 Chris Frodsham; 19 Scott Burgess; 24 Jarrad Stack; 26 Darren King; 18 Kris Coward; 11 Mike Whitehead; 22 Paddy Coupar; 34 Craig Farrimond. Subs (all used): 23 Martyn Wilson; 15 James Robinson; 36 Phillip Hewitt; 37 Dean Bragg.
Tries: Beattie (25), Rowley (68), Marshall (79);
Goals: Frodsham 1/3.
Rugby Leaguer & League Express Men of the Match: *Rams:* Adam Hayes; *Town:* Scott Burgess.
Penalty count: 8-7; **Half-time:** 28-6;
Referee: Tim Roby; **Attendance:** 2,103.

ROCHDALE HORNETS 18 KEIGHLEY COUGARS 44

HORNETS: 26 Leroy Rivett; 2 John Gillam; 3 Mick Fogerty; 14 Adam Thomas; 19 Craig Johnson; 6 Martin Ainscough; 24 Ryan Powell; 8 David Best; 32 Liam McGovern; 10 Paul Raftrey; 12 Ian Sinfield; 20 Darryl Kay; 11 Dean Hatton. Subs (all used): 17 Andrew Isherwood; 21 Tommy Gallagher; 25 Dayne Donoghue; 27 Tommy Brindle.
Tries: Ainscough (30, 47), Johnson (72);
Goals: Hatton 1/1, McGovern 2/2.
Sin bin: McGovern (20) – dissent.
COUGARS: 1 George Rayner; 2 Sam Gardner; 3 Dan Potter; 20 Daley Williams; 5 Gavin Duffy; 6 Jon Presley; 7 Danny Jones; 17 Scott Law; 9 James Feather; 8 Andy Shickell; 11 Will Cartledge; 4 Oliver Purseglove; 13 Carl Hughes. Subs (all used): 14 Jamaine Wray; 18 Greg Nicholson; 28 Ryan Benjafield; 16 Brendan Rawlins.
Tries: Gardner (12), Potter (15), Purseglove (20), Benjafield (23), Rawlins (27), Nicholson (37), Rayner (54), Hughes (64); **Goals:** Jones 6/8.
Rugby Leaguer & League Express Men of the Match: *Hornets:* Martin Ainscough; *Cougars:* Jamaine Wray.
Penalty count: 9-6; **Half-time:** 6-32;
Referee: Matthew Thomasson; **Attendance:** 537.

HUNSLET HAWKS 30 SWINTON LIONS 20

HAWKS: 1 Nathan Larvin; 25 Michael Mark; 21 Wayne McHugh; 4 Michael Brown; 2 Wayne Reittie; 23 Josh Weeden; 16 Paul March; 12 Jason Hart; 9 Richard Chapman; 31 Scott Woodcock; 28 Steve Dooler; 22 Scott Watson; 6 Darren Robinson. Subs (all used): 7 Stuart Young; 10 Neil Lowe; 13 Danny Ekis; 27 Gareth Firm.
Tries: March (17), McHugh (46, 70), Brown (73), Reittie (75); **Goals:** Robinson 4/4, Weeden 1/1.
Dismissal: Larvin (72) - dissent.
Sin bin: Robinson (77) - fighting.
LIONS: 22 Darren Bamford; 3 Dave Hull; 29 Carl Sneyd; 4 Dean Gorton; 5 Marlon Billy; 6 Graham Holroyd; 15 Gary Hulse; 12 Danny Heaton; 33 Chris Hull; 27 Chris Tyrer; 28 Dave Newton; 17 Tommy Grundy; 11 Mike Wainwright. Subs (all used): 7 Richie Hawkyard; 13 Martin Moana; 19 Neil Rigby; 10 Bruce Johnson.
Tries: Bamford (4), Grundy (19), Sneyd (43);
Goals: Sneyd 4/5.
Sin bin: Newton (8) - professional foul;
Gorton (77) - fighting.
Rugby Leaguer & League Express Men of the Match: *Hawks:* Wayne McHugh; *Lions:* Graham Holroyd.
Penalty count: 8-13; **Half-time:** 6-16;
Referee: Greg Dolan; **Attendance:** 412.

ROUND 17

Sunday 23rd August 2009

DEWSBURY RAMS 40 ROCHDALE HORNETS 28

RAMS: 17 Alex Bretherton; 15 Bryn Powell; 20 Rob Spicer; 22 Kane Epati; 18 Chris Spurr; 13 Pat Walker; 19 Liam Finn; 36 James Lockwood; 9 Mike Emmett; 23 Keegan Hirst; 38 Allister McMaster; 21 Andrew Bostock; 35 Adam Hayes. Subs (all used): 6 Ryan Smith; 11 Adam Robinson; 33 James Walker; 42 Tom Wandless.
Tries: P Walker (3), Hayes (11), Robinson (28, 42), Bretherton (32), Powell (74), Epati (80);
Goals: P Walker 6/9.
Sin bin: J Walker (52) – fighting.
HORNETS: 26 Leroy Rivett; 2 John Gillam; 3 Mick Fogerty; 14 Adam Thomas; 19 Craig Johnson; 6 Martin Ainscough; 24 Ryan Powell; 8 David Best; 11 Dean Hatton; 10 Paul Raftrey; 20 Darryl Kay; 17 Andrew Isherwood; 21 Tommy Gallagher. Subs (all used): 12 Ian Sinfield; 13 Wayne Corcoran; 16 Mark Brocklehurst; 27 Tommy Brindle.
Tries: Ainscough (9), Thomas (17), Hatton (21), Rivett (34), Gillam (79); **Goals:** Hatton 4/5.
Sin bin: Best (52) – fighting;
Brocklehurst (70) – late challenge.
Rugby Leaguer & League Express Men of the Match: *Rams:* Pat Walker; *Hornets:* Dean Hatton.
Penalty count: 11-5; **Half-time:** 22-24;
Referee: Warren Turley; **Attendance:** 912.

KEIGHLEY COUGARS 20 HUNSLET HAWKS 16

COUGARS: 1 George Rayner; 2 Sam Gardner; 3 Dan Potter; 20 Daley Williams; 5 Gavin Duffy; 6 Jon Presley; 7 Danny Jones; 17 Scott Law; 9 James Feather; 8 Andy Shickell; 11 Will Cartledge; 4 Oliver Purseglove; 13 Carl Hughes. Subs (all used): 14 Jamaine Wray; 16 Brendan Rawlins; 18 Greg Nicholson; 28 Ryan Benjafield.
Tries: Gardner (10), Purseglove (20), Benjafield (28), Duffy (62); **Goals:** Jones 2/4.
HAWKS: 1 Nathan Larvin; 2 Wayne Reittie; 4 Michael Brown; 21 Wayne McHugh; 25 Michael Mark; 23 Josh Weeden; 16 Paul March; 12 Jason Hart; 9 Richard Chapman; 31 Scott Woodcock; 24 Charlie Wabo; 28 Steve Dooler; 7 Stuart Young. Subs (all used): 10 Neil Lowe; 13 Danny Ekis; 22 Scott Watson; 27 Gareth Firm.
Tries: Larvin (5), March (34), Mark (79);
Goals: McHugh 2/3.
Rugby Leaguer & League Express Men of the Match: *Cougars:* Jamaine Wray; *Hawks:* Neil Lowe.
Penalty count: 10-6; **Half-time:** 14-10;
Referee: Dave Merrick; **Attendance:** 1,036.

OLDHAM 24 YORK CITY KNIGHTS 37

OLDHAM: 1 Paul O'Connor; 21 Lucas Onyango; 19 Craig Littler; 28 Jamie Russo; 5 Lee Greenwood; 18 Neil Roden; 7 Thomas Coyle; 15 Jason Boults; 30 Martin Roden; 16 Wayne Kerr; 23 Chris Baines; 12 Tommy Goulden; 29 Craig Lawton. Subs (all used): 9 Gary Sykes; 10 Jamie I'Anson; 22 Phil Joseph; 25 Luke Menzies.
Tries: Onyango (4), T Coyle (13, 76), Littler (79);
Goals: Baines 4/5.
CITY KNIGHTS: 1 Danny Ratcliffe; 3 John Oakes; 36 Ian Bell; 12 Tom Haberecht; 4 David Clayton; 6 Adam Mitchell; 26 Gareth Moore; 29 Mark Applegarth; 9 Paul Hughes; 35 Sean Hesketh; 16 Jordan Ross; 30 Richard Blakeway; 15 Chris Clough. Subs (all used): 32 Loz Wildbore; 34 Lee Waterman; 10 Adam Sullivan; 37 Luke Ambler.
Tries: Ambler (37), Ross (43), Moore (55), Wildbore (58), Hesketh (61, 80), Waterman (74);
Goals: Ratcliffe 2/3, Waterman 2/3, A Mitchell 0/2;
Field goal: Wildbore (69).
Rugby Leaguer & League Express Men of the Match: *Oldham:* Paul O'Connor; *City Knights:* Loz Wildbore.
Penalty count: 10-8; **Half-time:** 14-6;
Referee: Mohammed Drizza; **Attendance:** 954.

SWINTON LIONS 40 LONDON SKOLARS 14

LIONS: 22 Darren Bamford; 30 Andy Saywell; 29 Carl Sneyd; 3 Dave Hull; 5 Marlon Billy; 6 Graham Holroyd; 15 Gary Hulse; 12 Danny Heaton; 33 Chris Hull; 27 Chris Tyrer; 17 Tommy Grundy; 28 Dave Newton; 19 Neil Rigby. Subs (all used): 7 Richie Hawkyard; 13 Martin Moana; 11 Mike Wainwright; 10 Bruce Johnson.

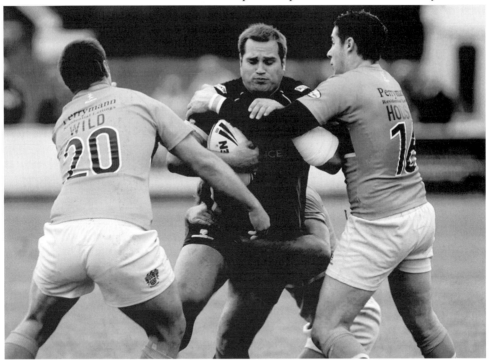

Dewsbury's James Walker takes on Blackpool's Tom Wild and Ian Hodson

Tries: Billy (9), Bamford (24, 39), Grundy (29), Moana (33), Johnson (47), Hawkyard (62); **Goals:** Sneyd 6/7.
SKOLARS: 2 Corey Simms; 26 Olu Iwenofu; 30 John Paxton; 11 Matt Thomas; 34 Hosni Kriouache; 29 Jy-Mel Coleman; 7 Paul Thorman; 16 Tony Williams; 9 Gareth Honor; 32 Cedric Prizzon; 4 Oliver Bloom; 22 Danny Burke; 21 Ben Joyce. Subs (all used): 5 Austen Aggrey; 23 Andre Vine; 14 Graeme Spencer; 25 Jaroslaw Obuchowski.
Tries: Kriouache (6), Simms (17), Paxton (78); **Goals:** Thorman 1/3.
Rugby Leaguer & League Express Men of the Match: *Lions:* Gary Hulse; *Skolars:* Jy-Mel Coleman.
Penalty count: 4-7; **Half-time:** 30-10;
Referee: Tim Roby; **Attendance:** 369.

WORKINGTON TOWN 10 BLACKPOOL PANTHERS 22

TOWN: 31 Greg Rowley; 35 Matthew Johnson; 3 Andrew Beattie; 4 Jason Mossop; 5 Jamie Marshall; 36 Chris Frodsham; 19 Scott Burgess; 33 Dean Bragg; 26 Darren King; 18 Kris Coward; 11 Mike Whitehead; 24 Jarrad Stack; 34 Craig Farrimond. Subs: 9 Jack Pedley; 15 James Robinson; 23 Martyn Wilson (not used).
Tries: Stack (10), Marshall (30); **Goals:** Frodsham 1/2.
PANTHERS: 2 Damian Munro; 3 Tom Woodcock; 33 Dean Thompson; 17 Dave Llewellyn; 34 Nick Royle, 37 Jay Duffy; 30 Carl Forber; 8 Peter Fairhurst; 14 Martin Keavney; 13 Rob Draper; 16 Ian Hodson; 12 Kris Ratcliffe; 4 Mark McCully. Subs (all used): 6 Simon Svabic; 31 Simon Bissell; 18 John Boland; 9 John Clough.
Tries: Munro (22), Clough (60, 66), Draper (69);
Goals: Forber 3/4.
Rugby Leaguer & League Express Men of the Match: *Town:* Jarrad Stack; *Panthers:* Carl Forber.
Penalty count: 4-7; **Half-time:** 10-6;
Referee: Matthew Thomasson; **Attendance:** 405.

ROUND 18

Friday 28th August 2009

LONDON SKOLARS 10 KEIGHLEY COUGARS 28

SKOLARS: 33 Jamie O'Callaghan; 2 Corey Simms; 30 John Paxton; 11 Matt Thomas; 26 Olu Iwenofu; 29 Jy-Mel Coleman; 7 Paul Thorman; 16 Tony Williams; 9 Gareth Honor; 32 Cedric Prizzon; 5 Austen Aggrey; 31 Kris Hodson; 21 Ben Joyce. Subs (all used): 14 Graeme Spencer; 23 Andre Vine; 22 Danny Burke; 34 Hosni Kriouache.
Tries: Iwenofu (8, 45); **Goals:** Thorman 1/2.
Sin bin: Hodson (33) - dissent.
COUGARS: 1 George Rayner; 2 Sam Gardner; 3 Dan

Potter; 20 Daley Williams; 5 Gavin Duffy; 6 Jon Presley; 7 Danny Jones; 17 Scott Law; 14 Jamaine Wray; 8 Andy Shickell; 11 Will Cartledge; 4 Oliver Purseglove; 13 Carl Hughes. Subs (all used): 33 James Haythornthwaite; 26 Ben Sagar; 18 Greg Nicholson; 16 Brendan Rawlins.
Tries: Williams (20), Rawlins (27, 40), Potter (32), Gardner (48), Wray (55); **Goals:** Jones 2/6.
Sin bin: Jones (65) – holding down.
Rugby Leaguer & League Express Men of the Match: *Skolars:* John Paxton; *Cougars:* Brendan Rawlins.
Penalty count: 8-3; **Half-time:** 6-18;
Referee: Matthew Thomasson; **Attendance:** 1,156.

Saturday 5th September 2009

YORK CITY KNIGHTS 46 SWINTON LIONS 28

CITY KNIGHTS: 1 Danny Ratcliffe; 34 Lee Waterman; 3 John Oakes; 12 Tom Haberecht; 4 David Clayton; 32 Loz Wildbore; 26 Gareth Moore; 29 Mark Applegarth; 9 Paul Hughes; 35 Sean Hesketh; 16 Jordan Ross; 30 Richard Blakeway; 21 David March. Subs (all used): 6 Adam Mitchell; 15 Chris Clough; 10 Adam Sullivan; 36 Luke Ambler.
Tries: Ross (3, 32), Wildbore (27, 79), Ratcliffe (34, 75), Oakes (57), Applegarth (67); **Goals:** Waterman 7/8.
LIONS: 22 Darren Bamford; 30 Andy Saywell; 3 Dave Hull; 29 Carl Sneyd; 36 Richard Lopag; 33 Chrio Hull; 15 Gary Hulse; 18 Gareth Hayes; 7 Richie Hawkyard; 12 Danny Heaton; 28 Dave Newton; 19 Neil Rigby; 14 Craig Ashall. Subs (all used): 24 Paul Crook; 13 Martin Moana; 27 Chris Tyrer; 10 Bruce Johnson.
Tries: Sneyd (29), Saywell (43, 61), Ashall (47), Bamford (70); **Goals:** Sneyd 4/5.
Sin bin: Johnson (12) – delaying restart.
Rugby Leaguer & League Express Men of the Match: *City Knights:* Gareth Moore; *Lions:* Gary Hulse.
Penalty count: 15-9; **Half-time:** 24-6;
Referee: Greg Dolan; **Attendance:** 844.

Sunday 6th September 2009

BLACKPOOL PANTHERS 14 DEWSBURY RAMS 34

PANTHERS: 37 Jay Duffy; 2 Damian Munro; 32 Sam Reay; 17 Dave Llewellyn; 3 Tom Woodcock; 6 Simon Svabic; 30 Carl Forber; 8 Peter Fairhurst; 9 John Clough; 31 Simon Bissell; 16 Ian Hodson; 12 Kris Ratcliffe; 4 Mark McCully. Subs (all used): 14 Martin Keavney; 13 Rob Draper; 18 John Boland; 20 Tom Wild.
Tries: Woodcock (9), Llewellyn (58), Clough (62);
Goals: Forber 1/3.
RAMS: 16 Austin Buchanan; 15 Bryn Powell; 22 Kane Epati; 17 Alex Bretherton; 18 Chris Spurr; 13 Pat Walker; 19 Liam Finn; 12 Taron Wildey; 9 Mike Emmett; 23 Keegan Hirst; 20 Rob Spicer; 21 Andrew Bostock; 35 Adam Hayes. Subs (all used): 6 Ryan Smith; 36 James

Lockwood; 33 James Walker; 34 Josh Tonks.
Tries: Powell (4), Buchanan (12), Spurr (17, 37), P Walker (25), Tonks (76); **Goals:** P Walker 5/6, Finn 0/1.
Rugby Leaguer & League Express Men of the Match: *Panthers:* Sam Reay; *Rams:* Liam Finn.
Penalty count: 6-7; **Half-time:** 4-28;
Referee: Peter Brooke; **Attendance:** 975.

ROCHDALE HORNETS 42 WORKINGTON TOWN 20

HORNETS: 26 Leroy Rivett; 2 John Gillam; 3 Mick Fogerty; 14 Adam Thomas; 5 Marlon Miller; 6 Martin Ainscough; 24 Ryan Powell; 8 David Best; 11 Dean Hatton; 10 Paul Raftrey; 17 Andrew Isherwood; 20 Darryl Kay; 21 Tommy Gallagher. Subs (all used): 7 Steve Roper; 12 Ian Sinfield; 13 Wayne Corcoran; 27 Tommy Brindle.
Tries: Gillam (8), Fogerty (14, 19), Thomas (27), Miller (38, 43), Ainscough (51), Isherwood (75);
Goals: Hatton 5/7, Ainscough 0/1.
TOWN: 3 Andrew Beattie; 5 Jamie Marshall; 31 Matthew Johnson; 20 Stephen Dawes; 23 Martyn Wilson; 32 Chris Frodsham; 19 Scott Burgess; 33 Dean Bragg; 9 Jack Pedley; 11 Mike Whitehead; 24 Jarrad Stack; 15 James Robinson; 22 Paddy Coupar. Subs (only three named): 25 Harry Kaufman; 2 Neil Frazer (not used); 17 Peter Dobson (not used).
Tries: Marshall (3), Dawes (50), Pedley (04), Robinson (69); **Goals:** Frodsham 0/2, S Burgess 2/2.
Rugby Leaguer & League Express Men of the Match: *Hornets:* Dean Hatton; *Town:* Scott Burgess.
Penalty count: 9-7; **Half-time:** 26-4;
Referee: Chris Leatherbarrow; **Attendance:** 893.

HUNSLET HAWKS 36 OLDHAM 18

HAWKS: 29 Scott Childs; 25 Michael Mark; 11 Joe Howey; 4 Michael Brown; 2 Wayne Reittie; 23 Josh Weeden; 16 Paul March; 10 Neil Lowe; 9 Richard Chapman; 22 Scott Watson; 24 Charlie Wabo; 28 Steve Dooler; 7 Stuart Young. Subs (all used): 27 Gareth Firm; 17 Steve Brook; 21 Wayne McHugh; 5 John Richardson.
Tries: Lowe (5), McHugh (35, 65, 77), Weeden (50), Wabo (54); **Goals:** Young 2/2, McHugh 4/4, Chapman 0/1.
OLDHAM: 4 Paul Reilly; 21 Lucas Onyango; 28 Jamie Russo; 24 Marcus St Hilaire; 1 Paul O'Connor; 18 Neil Roden; 7 Thomas Coyle; 15 Jason Boults; 30 Martin Roden; 16 Wayne Kerr; 17 Craig Robinson; 23 Chris Baines; 22 Phil Joseph. Subs (all used): 25 Luke Menzies; 27 Matt Ashe; 10 Jamie I'Anson; 9 Gary Sykes.
Tries: O'Connor (39), Onyango (47), Joseph (71);
Goals: Baines 3/3.
Rugby Leaguer & League Express Men of the Match: *Hawks:* Wayne McHugh; *Oldham:* Phil Joseph.
Penalty count: 10-13; **Half-time:** 12-6;
Referee: Dave Merrick; **Attendance:** 626.

Oldham's Craig Lawton caught high during his side's Final Eliminator win at York

PLAY-OFFS

ELIMINATION PLAY-OFFS

Sunday 13th September 2009

OLDHAM 31 SWINTON LIONS 26

OLDHAM: 4 Paul Reilly; 21 Lucas Onyango; 19 Craig Littler; 24 Marcus St Hilaire; 1 Paul O'Connor; 18 Neil Roden; 7 Thomas Coyle; 15 Jason Boults; 30 Martin Roden; 16 Wayne Kerr; 23 Chris Baines; 17 Craig Robinson; 12 Tommy Goulden. Subs (all used): 10 Jamie I'Anson; 22 Phil Joseph; 25 Luke Menzies; 27 Matt Ashe.
Tries: Onyango (7), St Hilaire (22), T Coyle (51), O'Connor (58), Joseph (76); **Goals:** Baines 5/6; **Field goal:** N Roden (65).
LIONS: 22 Darren Bamford; 30 Andy Saywell; 3 Dave Hull; 29 Carl Sneyd; 5 Marlon Billy; 33 Chris Hull; 15 Gary Hulse; 12 Danny Heaton; 7 Richie Hawkyard; 28 Dave Newton; 17 Tommy Grundy; 11 Mike Wainwright; 13 Neil Rigby. Subs (all used): 6 Graham Holroyd; 13 Martin Moana; 10 Bruce Johnson; 14 Craig Ashall.
Tries: Bamford (10), Hawkyard (13), Saywell (62, 73); **Goals:** Sneyd 3/3, Holroyd 2/2.
Rugby Leaguer & League Express Men of the Match: *Oldham:* Chris Baines; *Lions:* Gary Hulse.
Penalty count: 10-8; **Half-time:** 12-14;
Referee: Matthew Thomasson; **Attendance:** 745.

BLACKPOOL PANTHERS 18 HUNSLET HAWKS 21

PANTHERS: 1 Jonny Leather; 3 Tom Woodcock; 32 Sam Reay; 4 Mark McCully; 2 Damian Munro; 6 Simon Svabic; 30 Carl Forber; 8 Peter Fairhurst; 9 John Clough; 18 John Boland; 11 Paul Alcock; 12 Kris Ratcliffe; 16 Ian Hodson. Subs (all used): 14 Martin Keavney; 13 Rob Draper; 31 Simon Bissell; 37 Jay Duffy.
Tries: Hodson (9), Woodcock (15, 30); **Goals:** Forber 3/5.
HAWKS: 1 Nathan Larvin; 2 Wayne Reittie; 4 Michael Brown; 21 Wayne McHugh; 25 Michael Mark; 23 Josh Weeden; 16 Paul March; 10 Neil Lowe; 9 Richard Chapman; 22 Scott Watson; 24 Charlie Wabo; 28 Steve Dooler; 7 Stuart Young. Subs (all used): 27 Gareth Firm; 11 Joe Howey; 8 Joe Helme; 6 Darren Robinson.
Tries: Brown (23), Young (35), McHugh (53);
Goals: McHugh 2/3, Robinson 2/2;
Field goal: Weeden (76).
Rugby Leaguer & League Express Men of the Match: *Panthers:* Paul Alcock; *Hawks:* Josh Weeden.
Penalty count: 12-10; **Half-time:** 16-12;
Referee: Craig Halloran; **Attendance:** 543.

QUALIFYING SEMI-FINAL

Sunday 20th September 2009

KEIGHLEY COUGARS 32 YORK CITY KNIGHTS 18

COUGARS: 1 George Rayner; 2 Sam Gardner; 3 Dan Potter; 20 Daley Williams; 5 Gavin Duffy; 6 Jon Presley; 7 Danny Jones; 17 Scott Law; 14 Jamaine Wray; 8 Andy Shickell; 11 Will Cartledge; 4 Oliver Purseglove; 13 Carl Hughes. Subs (all used): 18 Greg Nicholson; 28 Ryan Benjafield; 33 James Haythornthwaite; 16 Brendan Rawlins.
Tries: Duffy (7), Williams (11, 32), Rayner (35), Presley (50), Jones (71); **Goals:** Jones 4/7.
On report: Williams (66) - alleged punch on Ratcliffe.
CITY KNIGHTS: 1 Danny Ratcliffe; 2 Steve Lewis; 3 John Oakes; 12 Tom Haberecht; 4 David Clayton; 32 Loz Wildbore; 26 Gareth Moore; 35 Sean Hesketh; 9 Paul Hughes; 29 Mark Applegarth; 11 Rob Kelly; 6 Adam Mitchell; 15 Chris Clough; 34 Lee Waterman; 10 Adam Sullivan.
Tries: Hesketh (16), Ratcliffe (26), Wildbore (79);
Goals: Wildbore 2/2, A Mitchell 1/1.
Rugby Leaguer & League Express Men of the Match: *Cougars:* Jon Presley; *City Knights:* Sean Hesketh.
Penalty count: 7-6; **Half-time:** 20-12;
Referee: Ronnie Laughton; **Attendance:** 1,501.

ELIMINATION SEMI-FINAL

Sunday 20th September 2009

OLDHAM 54 HUNSLET HAWKS 30

OLDHAM: 4 Paul Reilly; 21 Lucas Onyango; 19 Craig Littler; 24 Marcus St Hilaire; 1 Paul O'Connor; 18 Neil Roden; 7 Thomas Coyle; 15 Jason Boults; 30 Martin Roden; 16 Wayne Kerr; 23 Chris Baines; 12 Tommy Goulden; 28 Craig Lawton. Subs (all used): 9 Gary Sykes; 10 Jamie I'Anson; 25 Luke Menzies; 27 Matt Ashe.
Tries: Baines (13, 28, 37, 60), M Roden (18, 48), O'Connor (34), Ashe (45), T Coyle (53);
Goals: Baines 9/12.
Sin bin: Menzies (71) - punching.
HAWKS: 1 Nathan Larvin; 2 Wayne Reittie; 4 Michael Brown; 21 Wayne McHugh; 25 Michael Mark; 23 Josh Weeden; 16 Paul March; 10 Neil Lowe; 9 Richard Chapman; 22 Scott Watson; 24 Charlie Wabo; 28 Steve Dooler; 7 Stuart Young. Subs (all used): 6 Darren Robinson; 8 Joe Helme; 11 Joe Howey; 27 Gareth Firm.
Tries: McHugh (24), Reittie (39, 68), Brown (41), Mark (72), Weeden (77);
Goals: McHugh 1/2, Young 1/1, Robinson 1/3.
Sin bin: March (66) - dissent.
Rugby Leaguer & League Express Men of the Match: *Oldham:* Chris Baines; *Hawks:* Richard Chapman.
Penalty count: 15-10; **Half-time:** 28-10;
Referee: Jamie Leahy; **Attendance:** 801.

FINAL ELIMINATOR

Sunday 27th September 2009

YORK CITY KNIGHTS 14 OLDHAM 44

CITY KNIGHTS: 1 Danny Ratcliffe; 33 Tom Lineham; 3 John Oakes; 12 Tom Haberecht; 4 David Clayton; 32 Loz Wildbore; 26 Gareth Moore; 29 Mark Applegarth; 9 Paul Hughes; 35 Sean Hesketh; 16 Jordan Ross; 11 Rob Kelly; 30 Richard Blakeway. Subs (all used): 34 Lee Waterman; 15 Chris Clough; 10 Adam Sullivan; 36 Luke Ambler.
Tries: Clough (29), Oakes (48, 73); **Goals:** Wildbore 1/3.
OLDHAM: 4 Paul Reilly; 21 Lucas Onyango; 22 Phil Joseph; 29 Ben Heaton; 1 Paul O'Connor; 18 Neil Roden; 7 Thomas Coyle; 15 Jason Boults; 30 Martin Roden; 16 Wayne Kerr; 23 Chris Baines; 12 Tommy Goulden; 28 Craig Lawton. Subs (all used): 10 Jamie I'Anson; 25 Luke Menzies; 27 Matt Ashe; 9 Gary Sykes.
Tries: Heaton (5), Baines (9), Goulden (14), Reilly (18, 42), Ashe (67, 80), Onyango (75);
Goals: Baines 6/8, Onyango 0/1.
Rugby Leaguer & League Express Men of the Match: *City Knights:* Paul Hughes; *Oldham:* Thomas Coyle.
Penalty count: 8-7; **Half-time:** 4-24;
Referee: Phil Bentham; **Attendance:** 1,164.

GRAND FINAL

Sunday 4th October 2009

KEIGHLEY COUGARS 28 OLDHAM 26

COUGARS: 1 George Rayner; 2 Sam Gardner; 3 Dan Potter; 4 Oliver Purseglove; 5 Gavin Duffy; 6 Jon Presley; 7 Danny Jones; 17 Scott Law; 14 Jamaine Wray; 8 Andy Shickell; 11 Will Cartledge; 18 Greg Nicholson; 13 Carl Hughes. Subs (all used): 21 Ryan Smith; 28 Ryan Benjafield; 9 James Feather; 16 Brendan Rawlins.
Tries: Gardner (24), Jones (42, 50), Presley (63), Purseglove (67); **Goals:** Jones 4/5.
OLDHAM: 4 Paul Reilly; 21 Lucas Onyango; 24 Marcus St Hilaire; 22 Phil Joseph; 1 Paul O'Connor; 18 Neil Roden; 7 Thomas Coyle; 15 Jason Boults; 30 Martin Roden; 16 Wayne Kerr; 23 Chris Baines; 12 Tommy Goulden; 28 Craig Lawton. Subs (all used): 10 Jamie I'Anson; 25 Luke Menzies; 27 Matt Ashe; 29 Ben Heaton.
Tries: Menzies (35, 76), N Roden (54), St Hilaire (70), Kerr (78); **Goals:** Baines 3/4, Ashe 0/1.
Rugby Leaguer & League Express Men of the Match: *Cougars:* Danny Jones; *Oldham:* Luke Menzies.
Penalty count: 9-2; **Half-time:** 4-6; **Referee:** Ronnie Laughton. *(at Halliwell Jones Stadium, Warrington).*

Oldham's Chris Baines tackles Keighley's Jon Presley during the Championship One Grand Final

NORTHERN RAIL
CUP 2009
Round by Round

ROUND 1

Tuesday 10th February 2009

POOL 1

KEIGHLEY COUGARS 40 GATESHEAD THUNDER 20

COUGARS: 1 George Rayner; 2 Sam Gardner; 3 Dan Potter; 4 Oliver Purseglove; 5 Gavin Duffy; 6 Jon Presley; 7 Danny Jones; 8 Andy Shickell; 9 James Feather; 15 Craig Brown; 11 Will Cartledge; 12 Neil Lowe; 18 Greg Nicholson. Subs (all used): 14 Jamaine Wray; 21 Ryan Smith; 10 Simon Bissell; 17 Scott Law.
Tries: Rayner (18), Feather (29), Duffy (46), Presley (59, 77, 79), Purseglove (67); **Goals:** Jones 6/7.
THUNDER: 1 Ben McAlpine; 18 Robin Peers; 3 Kevin Neighbour; 32 James Cording; 5 Stewart Sanderson; 6 Neil Thorman; 7 Luke Branighan; 8 Jason Payne; 9 Andrew Henderson; 21 Ryan McBride; 29 Rhys Clarke; 4 Dylan Nash; 12 Michael Knowles. Subs (all used): 14 Ryan Clarke; 26 Crawford Matthews; 17 Chris Parker; 33 Jonny Walker.
Tries: McAlpine (5), Neighbour (24), Sanderson (39), Branighan (72); **Goals:** Branighan 2/4.
Rugby Leaguer & League Express Men of the Match: *Cougars:* Scott Law; *Thunder:* Andrew Henderson.
Penalty count: 7-5; **Half-time:** 12-14;
Referee: Gareth Hewer; **Attendance:** 337.

Wednesday 11th February 2009

POOL 1

SHEFFIELD EAGLES 38 HUNSLET HAWKS 16

EAGLES: 1 Jonny Woodcock; 2 Bolu Fagborun; 24 Matt Whitaker; 4 Mike Roby; 5 Ashley Thackeray; 6 Brendon Lindsay; 20 Matty Brooks; 8 Jack Howieson; 14 Andy Boothroyd; 10 Mitchell Stringer; 11 Alex Szostak; 12 Ged Corcoran; 13 Dane McDonald. Subs (all used): 18 Saqib Murtza; 19 Kyle Wood; 22 Ryan Hepworth; 31 Sam Barlow.
Tries: Brooks (19, 54), Szostak (23), Roby (30), Lindsay (61), Boothroyd (67), Howieson (70);
Goals: Woodcock 5/8.
HAWKS: 1 Nathan Larvin; 2 Scott Childs; 4 Michael Brown; 18 Ayden Faal; 25 Michael Mark; 16 Mark Moxon; 27 Gareth Firm; 17 Steve Brook; 9 Richard Chapman; 26 Nicko Slain; 11 Joe Howey; 12 Jason Hart; 13 Mark McKinley. Subs (all used): 22 Scott Watson; 19 Ben Walkin; 24 Charlie Wabo; 14 Chris Redfearn.
Tries: Larvin (34), Mark (43), Brook (78);
Goals: McKinley 1/2, Chapman 1/2.
Sin bin: Howey (49) – late challenge on Wood.
Rugby Leaguer & League Express Men of the Match: *Eagles:* Brendon Lindsay; *Hawks:* Richard Chapman.
Penalty count: 12-11; **Half-time:** 16-6;
Referee: Jamie Leahy; **Attendance:** 556.

ROUND 2

Friday 13th February 2009

POOL 1

WIDNES VIKINGS 20 OLDHAM 22

VIKINGS: 1 Loz Wildbore; 22 Paddy Flynn; 3 Richard Varkulis; 4 Toa Kohe-Love; 16 Gavin Dodd; 6 Anthony Thackeray; 7 James Webster; 19 Michael Ostick; 9 Mark Smith; 10 Jim Gannon; 11 Lee Doran; 12 Richard Fletcher; 14 John Duffy. Subs (all used): 8 Iain Morrison; 17 Ben Kavanagh; 23 Shane Grady; 24 Josh Simm.
Tries: Dodd (26), Flynn (61), Duffy (64), Thackeray (70);
Goals: Dodd 2/3, Fletcher 0/1.
Dismissal: Wildbore (32) - punching.
OLDHAM: 1 Paul O'Connor; 2 Andy Ballard; 3 Danny Halliwell; 24 Marcus St Hilaire; 5 Lee Greenwood; 6 James Coyle; 7 Thomas Coyle; 15 Jason Boults; 22 Phil Joseph; 10 Jamie I'Anson; 23 Chris Baines; 12 Tommy Goulden; 13 Rob Roberts. Subs (all used): 4 Paul Reilly; 8 Paul Highton; 16 Wayne Kerr; 20 Steve Gibbons.
Tries: Boults (4), Ballard (39); **Goals:** Ballard 7/7.
Sin bin: Boults (67) – high tackle on Ostick.
Rugby Leaguer & League Express Men of the Match: *Vikings:* Paddy Flynn; *Oldham:* Rob Roberts.
Penalty count: 9-11; **Half-time:** 4-14;
Referee: James Child; **Attendance:** 2,783.

Sunday 15th February 2009

POOL 1

BLACKPOOL PANTHERS 16 KEIGHLEY COUGARS 14

PANTHERS: 1 Jonny Leather; 2 Damian Munro; 3 Tom Woodcock; 4 Mark McCully; 24 Chris Campbell; 6 Simon Svabic; 14 Martin Keavney; 8 Peter Fairhurst; 9 John Clough; 12 Kris Ratcliffe; 11 Paul Alcock; 13 Rob Draper; 16 Ian Hodson. Subs (all used): 22 Kieron Tucker; 19 Liam McGovern; 23 Darryl Kay; 20 Tom Wild.
Tries: McCully (51, 57), Tucker (74); **Goals:** Leather 2/3.
COUGARS: 1 George Rayner; 2 Sam Gardner; 3 Dan Potter; 4 Oliver Purseglove; 5 Gavin Duffy; 6 Jon Presley; 7 Danny Jones; 8 Andy Shickell; 9 James Feather; 17 Scott Law; 11 Will Cartledge; 12 Neil Lowe; 18 Greg Nicholson. Subs (all used): 14 Jamaine Wray; 21 Ryan Smith; 10 Simon Bissell; 22 Lee Mapals.
Tries: Lowe (31), Bissell (45), Smith (63);
Goals: Jones 1/3.
Rugby Leaguer & League Express Men of the Match: *Panthers:* Simon Svabic; *Cougars:* Sam Gardner.
Penalty count: 8-7; **Half-time:** 0-6;
Referee: Dave Merrick; **Attendance:** 400.

GATESHEAD THUNDER 44 SHEFFIELD EAGLES 18

THUNDER: 1 Ben McAlpine; 18 Robin Peers; 3 Kevin Neighbour; 31 Joe Arundel; 5 Stewart Sanderson; 6 Neil Thorman; 7 Luke Branighan; 17 Chris Parker; 9 Andrew Henderson; 21 Ryan McBride; 4 Dylan Nash; 32 James Cording; 12 Michael Knowles. Subs (all used): 20 David Vernon; 29 Rhys Clarke; 33 Jonny Walker; 23 Jonny Scott.
Tries: Arundel (7), Nash (20, 31, 51), Neighbour (44), Branighan (61), Sanderson (63), Peers (76);
Goals: Branighan 6/9.
EAGLES: 1 Jonny Woodcock; 2 Bolu Fagborun; 3 Menzie Yere; 4 Mike Roby; 5 Ashley Thackeray; 6 Brendon Lindsay; 19 Kyle Wood; 8 Jack Howieson; 9 Grant Edwards; 22 Ryan Hepworth; 11 Alex Szostak; 27 Tommy Trayler; 13 Dane McDonald. Subs (all used): 18 Saqib Murtza; 10 Mitchell Stringer; 26 Nick Turnbull; 24 Matt Whitaker.
Tries: Hepworth (3, 56), Edwards (13);
Goals: Woodcock 3/3.
Rugby Leaguer & League Express Men of the Match: *Thunder:* Dylan Nash; *Eagles:* Grant Edwards.
Penalty count: 9-5; **Half-time:** 16-12;
Referee: Matthew Thomasson; **Attendance:** 1,226.

HUNSLET HAWKS 10 HALIFAX 38

HAWKS: 1 Nathan Larvin; 5 John Richardson; 4 Michael Brown; 18 Ayden Faal; 25 Michael Mark; 16 Mark Moxon; 27 Gareth Firm; 12 Jason Hart; 24 Charlie Wabo; 8 Joe Helme; 26 Nicko Slain; 22 Scott Watson; 14 Chris Redfearn. Subs (all used): 9 Richard Chapman; 19 Ben Walkin; 17 Steve Brook; 7 Stuart Young.
Tries: Richardson (18), Brook (79);
Goals: Brown 0/1, Young 1/1.
Sin bin: Faal (25) – holding down.
HALIFAX: 4 Shad Royston; 2 Lee Patterson; 3 Jon Goddard; 5 James Haley; 23 Rob Worrincy; 7 Ben Black; 9 Sean Penkywicz; 10 Dana Wilson; 13 Bob Beswick; 21 Neil Cherryholme; 11 David Larder; 15 Mark Roberts; 6 Dwayne Barker. Subs (all used): 1 Miles Greenwood; 16 Said Tamghart; 17 Frank Watene; 24 Gareth Moore.
Tries: Tamghart (25), Black (27), Penkywicz (32, 48), Greenwood (37), Moore (53), Cherryholme (62);
Goals: Black 3/5, Moore 2/2.
Rugby Leaguer & League Express Men of the Match: *Hawks:* Nathan Larvin; *Halifax:* Said Tamghart.
Penalty count: 4-8; **Half-time:** 4-20;
Referee: Greg Dolan; **Attendance:** 878.

ROCHDALE HORNETS 12 BARROW RAIDERS 54

HORNETS: 1 Chris Giles; 2 John Gillam; 3 Mick Fogerty; 4 Casey Mayberry; 19 Craig Johnson; 6 Martin Ainscough; 22 Martin Gambles; 8 David Best; 23 Liam Grundy; 10 Paul Raftrey; 13 Wayne Corcoran; 12 Ian Sinfield; 16 Mark Brocklehurst. Subs (all used): 14 Sam Butterworth; 15 Martin McLoughlin; 5 Andy Smith; 17 Andrew Isherwood.
Tries: Fogerty (7), Giles (13); **Goals:** Corcoran 2/2.
Sin bin: Mayberry (50) – fighting.
RAIDERS: 1 Gary Broadbent; 2 Mike Backhouse; 3 Ian Bell; 4 Liam Harrison; 5 James Nixon; 6 Liam Finch; 7 Liam Campbell; 8 Brett McDermott; 9 Andy Ellis; 16 Jamie Butler; 13 Andy Bracek; 14 Paul Noone; 11 Andrew Brocklehurst. Subs (all used): 15 Chris Young; 21 Joe McKenna; 12 Martin Ostler; 17 Scott Kaighan.
Tries: Bell (3), Bracek (24), L Finch (29, 72), Harrison (43), Backhouse (46, 65, 68), Ellis (80);
Goals: Noone 9/10.
Sin bin: Brocklehurst (50) - fighting.
Rugby Leaguer & League Express Men of the Match: *Hornets:* Martin Ainscough; *Raiders:* Liam Finch.
Penalty count: 7-12; **Half-time:** 12-16;
Referee: Tim Roby; **Attendance:** 501.

POOL 2

DEWSBURY RAMS 50 SWINTON LIONS 0

RAMS: 3 Lee Lingard; 15 Bryn Powell; 22 Kane Epati; 18 Chris Spurr; 16 Austin Buchanan; 13 Pat Walker; 19 Liam Finn; 11 Adam Robinson; 10 Luke Haigh; 23 Keegan Hirst; 17 Alex Bretherton; 12 Taron Wildey; 35 Adam Hayes. Subs (all used): 28 Liam Crawley; 24 Simon Cook; 27 Chris Grice; 9 Mike Emmett.
Tries: Robinson (2), Powell (18), Spurr (39), Buchanan (60), Hirst (62), Epati (72, 74); **Goals:** P Walker 11/11.
LIONS: 22 Darren Bamford; 30 Andy Saywell; 3 Dave Hull; 29 Carl Sneyd; 5 Marlon Billy; 7 Richie Hawkyard; 26 Chris Frodsham; 8 Paul Southern; 16 Alex McClurg; 10 Bruce Johnson; 17 Tommy Grundy; 11 Mike Wainwright; 14 Craig Ashall. Subs (all used): 9 Phil Wood; 13 Martin Moana; 28 Dave Newton; 12 Danny Heaton.
Sin bin: Ashall (30) – high tackle on Robinson.
Rugby Leaguer & League Express Men of the Match: *Rams:* Taron Wildey; *Lions:* Richie Hawkyard.
Penalty count: 11-10; **Half-time:** 24-0;
Referee: Peter Brooke; **Attendance:** 999.

DONCASTER 6 FEATHERSTONE ROVERS 32

DONCASTER: 14 Scott Jones; 20 Mike Coady; 19 Ryan Steen; 4 Shaun Leaf; 5 Wayne Reittie; 6 Kyle Briggs; 22 Andy Speake; 21 Gary Ellery; 9 Craig Cook; 16 Nathan Freer; 11 Peter Green; 17 Ross Divorty; 13 Josh Weeden. Subs (all used): 18 Craig Holt; 24 Jake Bassinder; 15 Mark Castle; 2 Dean Colton.
Try: Cook (59); **Goals:** Briggs 1/1.
ROVERS: 20 Stuart Kain; 2 Waine Pryce; 3 Ian Hardman; 34 Sam Smeaton; 5 Jon Steel; 6 Iestyn Harris; 7 Andy Kain; 15 James Houston; 16 Joe McLocklan; 19 Sean Hesketh; 12 Jamie Field; 14 Tom Haughey; 13 Richard Blakeway. Subs (all used): 1 Tom Saxton; 9 Jack Lee; 24 Jon Fallon; 17 Joe Hirst.
Tries: S Kain (9), A Kain (13), Harris (16), Steel (28), Smeaton (66), Field (76); **Goals:** Harris 4/6.
Rugby Leaguer & League Express Men of the Match: *Doncaster:* Craig Cook; *Rovers:* Andy Kain.
Penalty count: 9-7; **Half-time:** 0-22;
Referee: Mike Dawber; **Attendance:** 1,126.

LEIGH CENTURIONS 74 LONDON SKOLARS 6

CENTURIONS: 14 Ian Mort; 5 Nicky Stanton; 3 Steve Maden; 1 Stuart Donlan; 22 Jamie Smith; 23 Martyn Ridyard; 7 Ian Watson; 16 Chris Hill; 39 Jamie Durbin; 10 Mike Morrison; 15 Adam Higson; 12 James Taylor; 11 Dave Armitstead. Subs (all used): 18 Sam Reay; 4 Anthony Stewart; 8 Andy Hobson; 38 Danny Meekin.
Tries: Ridyard (5), Durbin (8, 30, 39), Mort (11), J Smith (24, 69), Donlan (37), Reay (42), Maden (46, 58), Watson (62), Stanton (72), Stewart (77); **Goals:** Mort 9/14.
SKOLARS: 2 Corey Simms; 26 Olu Iwenofu; 3 Oliver Fountain; 4 Oliver Bloom; 5 Austen Aggrey; 17 Chad Isles; 7 Paul Thorman; 8 Dave Ellison; 9 Gareth Honor; 20 Paul Hyder; 11 Matt Thomas; 16 Tony Williams; 21 Ben Joyce. Subs (all used): 19 Leigh Nissen; 1 Frank Reid; 22 Danny Burke; 27 Keir Bell.
Try: Aggrey (20); **Goals:** Thorman 1/1.
Rugby Leaguer & League Express Men of the Match: *Centurions:* Jamie Durbin; *Skolars:* Austen Aggrey.
Penalty count: 8-3; **Half-time:** 38-6;
Referee: Craig Halloran; **Attendance:** 1,375.

WHITEHAVEN 52 BATLEY BULLDOGS 30

WHITEHAVEN: 1 Craig Benson; 4 Derry Eilbeck; 3 Rob Jackson; 18 John Patrick; 2 Craig Calvert; 6 Carl Rudd; 25 Jamie Theohaurus; 16 Ryan McDonald; 9 Graeme Mattinson; 10 Karl Edmondson; 12 Spencer Miller; 15 Andy Gorski; 7 Leroy Joe. Subs (all used): 24 Gregg McNally; 8 Marc Jackson; 22 Matthew Tunstall; 14 Daniel Barker.
Tries: Calvert (11), Mattinson (17), Patrick (20), Gorski (22, 39, 66), Eilbeck (43), McNally (46), M Jackson (71); **Goals:** Rudd 6/7, McNally 2/2.
BULLDOGS: 1 Ian Preece; 18 Jermaine McGilvary; 28 Daryl Cardiss; 4 Danny Maun; 22 Nathan Brown; 12 Mark Toohey; 6 Mark Barlow; 17 Craig Potter; 14 John Gallagher; 10 Luke Stenchion; 20 David Tootill; 11 Kevin Crouthers; 23 Chris Buttery. Subs (all used): 13 Ashley Lindsay; 15 Anthony Henderson; 16 Jon Simpson; 19 George Flanagan.
Tries: Gallagher (7), Simpson (29), Cardiss (51), Flanagan (57), Maun (60);
Goals: Barlow 2/2, Flanagan 3/3.
Rugby Leaguer & League Express Men of the Match: *Whitehaven:* Andy Gorski; *Bulldogs:* George Flanagan.
Penalty count: 11-10; **Half-time:** 30-12;
Referee: Warren Turley; **Attendance:** 1,146.

WORKINGTON TOWN 10 YORK CITY KNIGHTS 34

TOWN: 1 Jay Duffy; 20 Stephen Dawes; 3 Andrew Beattie; 4 Jason Mossop; 2 Neil Frazer; 6 Carl Forber; 7 Steve Roper; 16 Tommy Brindle; 19 Scott Burgess; 24 Jarrad Stack; 11 Mike Whitehead; 22 Paddy Coupar; 13 Mark Hobson. Subs (all used): 15 James Robinson; 5 Jamie Marshall; 8 Ryan Benjafield; 17 Peter Dobson.
Tries: Stack (2), Dawes (67); **Goals:** Forber 1/2.
CITY KNIGHTS: 1 Danny Ratcliffe; 3 John Oakes; 32 Mike Mitchell; 12 Tom Haberecht; 5 Jonny Waldron; 6 Adam Mitchell; 33 Danny Grimshaw; 17 Scott Woodcock; 9 Paul Hughes; 10 Adam Sullivan; 11 Rob Kelly; 30 Carl Barrow; 34 Mark Applegarth. Subs (all used): 14 Tom Hodgson; 15 Chris Clough; 13 Richard Knight; 8 Danny Ekis.
Tries: Haberecht (6, 31), Oakes (13), M Mitchell (25), Clough (70), Ratcliffe (73); **Goals:** A Mitchell 5/6.
Rugby Leaguer & League Express Men of the Match: *Town:* Carl Forber; *City Knights:* Tom Haberecht.
Penalty count: 10-6; **Half-time:** 6-22;
Referee: James Child; **Attendance:** 513.

ROUND 1

Wednesday 18th February 2009

POOL 1

OLDHAM 54 ROCHDALE HORNETS 4

OLDHAM: 1 Paul O'Connor; 2 Andy Ballard; 3 Danny Halliwell; 24 Marcus St Hilaire; 5 Lee Greenwood; 18 Neil Roden; 6 James Coyle; 8 Paul Highton; 22 Phil Joseph; 10 Jamie I'Anson; 23 Chris Baines; 12 Tommy Goulden; 11 Dave Allen. Subs (all used): 16 Wayne Kerr; 15 Jason Boults; 4 Paul Reilly; 17 Craig Robinson.
Tries: Ballard (8, 40), Kerr (25), St Hilaire (38), Halliwell (44, 54), J Coyle (48, 76), Goulden (69, 73);
Goals: Ballard 7/10.
HORNETS: 1 Chris Giles; 19 Craig Johnson; 3 Mick Fogerty; 14 Sam Butterworth; 20 Liam Bretherton; 6 Martin Ainscough; 24 Chris Hough; 8 David Best; 9 Janan Billings; 10 Paul Raftrey; 18 John Walker; 33 Dale Cunniffe; 16 Mark Brocklehurst. Subs (all used): 22 Martin Gambles; 15 Martin McLoughlin; 17 Andrew Isherwood; 25 Dayne Donoghue.
Try: Walker (20); **Goals:** Butterworth 0/1.

Dismissal: McLoughlin (64) – headbutt.
Rugby Leaguer & League Express Men of the Match:
Oldham: Phil Joseph; *Hornets:* Paul Raftrey.
Penalty count: 12-6; **Half-time:** 22-4;
Referee: Craig Halloran; **Attendance:** 1,028.

POOL 2

BATLEY BULLDOGS 18 DONCASTER 22

BULLDOGS: 1 Ian Preece; 18 Jermaine McGilvary; 28 Daryl Cardiss; 4 Danny Maun; 2 Ben Feehan; 12 Mark Toohey; 23 Chris Buttery; 17 Craig Potter; 9 Kris Lythe; 10 Luke Stenchion; 21 Nathan Armitage; 15 Anthony Henderson; 13 Ashley Lindsay. Subs (all used): 11 Kevin Crouthers; 16 Jon Simpson; 14 John Gallagher; 19 George Flanagan.
Tries: Flanagan (20), Buttery (30, 50);
Goals: Flanagan 3/3.
DONCASTER: 14 Scott Jones; 20 Mike Coady; 19 Ryan Steen; 4 Shaun Leaf; 2 Dean Colton; 6 Kyle Briggs; 22 Andy Speake; 8 Michael Haley; 9 Craig Cook; 16 Nathan Freer; 11 Peter Green; 17 Ross Divorty; 13 Josh Weeden. Subs (all used): 18 Craig Holt; 15 Mark Castle; 24 Jake Bassinder; 28 Jamie Bovill.
Tries: Divorty (17), Colton (58), Cook (74), Steen (78);
Goals: Briggs 2/2, Speake 1/2.
Rugby Leaguer & League Express Men of the Match:
Bulldogs: Mark Toohey; *Doncaster:* Craig Cook.
Penalty count: 8-13; **Half-time:** 12-6;
Referee: Dave Merrick; **Attendance:** 533.

YORK CITY KNIGHTS 36 WHITEHAVEN 6

CITY KNIGHTS: 1 Danny Ratcliffe; 3 John Oakes; 12 Tom Haberecht; 32 Mike Mitchell; 29 Wayne McHugh; 33 Danny Grimshaw; 7 Paul March; 15 Chris Clough; 9 Paul Hughes; 10 Adam Sullivan; 11 Rob Kelly; 13 Richard Knight; 21 David March. Subs (all used): 14 Tom Hodgson; 8 Danny Ekis; 34 Mark Applegarth; 19 Kris Peacock.
Tries: M Mitchell (4, 79), Oakes (40), Ratcliffe (50), P March (57), Clough (68), McHugh (72);
Goals: Knight 3/6, Ratcliffe 1/2.
WHITEHAVEN: 20 Marc Bainbridge; 5 Ade Adebisi; 18 John Patrick; 4 Derry Eilbeck; 34 Daniel Smith; 24 Gregg McNally; 28 Tyrone Dalton; 21 Taani Lavulavu; 8 Marc Jackson; 22 Matthew Tunstall; 19 Kyle Amor; 23 Marc Shackley; 33 Ryan Campbell. Subs (all used): 32 Chris Smith; 31 Dexter Miller; 16 Ryan McDonald; 10 Karl Edmondson.
Try: C Smith (46); **Goals:** McNally 1/1.
Rugby Leaguer & League Express Men of the Match:
City Knights: Paul March; *Whitehaven:* Chris Smith.
Penalty count: 11-6; **Half-time:** 12-0;
Referee: Thierry Alibert; **Attendance:** 685.

FEATHERSTONE ROVERS 10 LEIGH CENTURIONS 6

ROVERS: 20 Stuart Kain; 2 Waine Pryce; 3 Ian Hardman; 1 Tom Saxton; 5 Jon Steel; 6 Iestyn Harris; 7 Andy Kain; 8 Tony Tonks; 9 Jack Lee; 10 Stuart Dickens; 11 Matty Dale; 18 Tim Spears; 12 Jamie Field. Subs (all used): 14 Tom Haughey; 13 Richard Blakeway; 24 Jon Fallon; 16 Joe McLocklan.
Tries: Steel (57), Haughey (63); **Goals:** Harris 1/2.
CENTURIONS: 1 Stuart Donlan; 5 Nicky Stanton; 15 Adam Higson; 3 Steve Maden; 22 Jamie Smith; 23 Martyn Ridyard; 7 Ian Watson; 8 Andy Hobson; 39 Jamie Durbin; 16 Chris Hill; 12 James Taylor; 37 Lee Wingfield; 11 Dave Armitstead. Subs (all used): 4 Anthony Stewart; 18 Sam Reay; 38 Danny Meekin; 20 John Cookson.
Try: Durbin (9); **Goals:** Ridyard 1/2.
Dismissal: Hobson (42) - use of forearm on Haughey.
Sin bin: Stewart (53) - holding down.
Rugby Leaguer & League Express Men of the Match:
Rovers: Ian Hardman; *Centurions:* Ian Watson.
Penalty count: 18-6; **Half-time:** 0-6;
Referee: James Child; **Attendance:** 1,487.

ROUND 3

Saturday 21st February 2009

POOL 1

WIDNES VIKINGS 40 GATESHEAD THUNDER 18

VIKINGS: 21 Scott Yates; 22 Paddy Flynn; 4 Toa Kohe-Love; 1 Loz Wildbore; 16 Gavin Dodd; 14 John Duffy; 7 James Webster; 19 Michael Ostick; 9 Mark Smith; 10 Jim Gannon; 11 Lee Doran; 3 Richard Varkulis; 12 Richard Fletcher. Subs (all used): 6 Anthony Thackeray; 17 Ben Kavanagh; 18 Matthew Strong; 23 Shane Grady.
Tries: Gannon (11, 24, 54), Yates (12), Kohe-Love (48), Strong (52), Fletcher (54); **Goals:** Yates 6/7.
THUNDER: 1 Ben McAlpine; 18 Robin Peers; 31 Joe Arundel; 3 Kevin Neighbour; 5 Stewart Sanderson; 6 Neil Thorman; 7 Luke Branighan; 8 Jason Payne; 9 Andrew Henderson; 21 Ryan McBride; 4 Dylan Nash; 32 James Cording; 12 Michael Knowles. Subs (all used): 17 Chris Parker; 20 David Vernon; 29 Rhys Clarke; 33 Jonny Walker.
Tries: Thorman (17), Arundel (52, 70), Sanderson (68);
Goals: Thorman 1/4.
Sin bin: Nash (10) - professional foul;
Payne (39) - holding down.
Rugby Leaguer & League Express Men of the Match:
Vikings: Jim Gannon; *Thunder:* Joe Arundel.
Penalty count: 15-5; **Half-time:** 18-6;
Referee: Craig Halloran; **Attendance:** 3,001.

Sunday 22nd February 2009

POOL 1

HALIFAX 40 BARROW RAIDERS 10

HALIFAX: 4 Shad Royston; 2 Lee Patterson; 3 Jon Goddard; 5 James Haley; 23 Rob Worrincy; 19 Mick Govin; 7 Ben Black; 8 Matt James; 9 Sean Penkywicz; 10 Dana Wilson; 15 Mark Roberts; 12 Paul Smith; 13 Bob Beswick. Subs (all used): 1 Miles Greenwood; 14 Mark Gleeson; 16 Said Tamghart; 17 Frank Watene.
Tries: Goddard (3, 55), Black (20), Gleeson (37), Patterson (50), James (66), Royston (71);
Goals: Haley 6/7.
RAIDERS: 1 Gary Broadbent; 2 Mike Backhouse; 14 Paul Noone; 4 Liam Harrison; 19 Chris Larkin; 6 Liam Finch; 7 Liam Campbell; 8 Brett McDermott; 9 Andy Ellis; 16 Jamie Butler; 13 Andy Bracek; 12 Martin Ostler; 11 Andrew Brocklehurst. Subs (all used): 34 James Gordon; 21 Joe McKenna; 15 Chris Young; 17 Scott Kaighan.
Tries: Campbell (62), L Finch (78); **Goals:** Noone 1/2.
Sin bin: L Finch (35) – holding down;
Larkin (40) – dissent.
Rugby Leaguer & League Express Men of the Match:
Halifax: Ben Black; *Raiders:* Andy Ellis.
Penalty count: 17-10; **Half-time:** 18-0;
Referee: James Child; **Attendance:** 1,687.

KEIGHLEY COUGARS 44 HUNSLET HAWKS 6

COUGARS: 1 George Rayner; 22 Lee Mapals; 3 Dan Potter; 21 Ryan Smith; 5 Gavin Duffy; 6 Jon Presley; 7 Danny Jones; 17 Scott Law; 9 James Feather; 12 Neil Lowe; 11 Will Cartledge; 4 Oliver Purseglove; 18 Greg Nicholson. Subs (all used): 14 Jamaine Wray; 19 Craig Fawcett; 10 Simon Bissell; 29 Karl Gunney.
Tries: Cartledge (20), Presley (26, 73, 79), Mapals (29, 46), Lowe (36), Purseglove (65), Rayner (76); **Goals:** Jones 4/8, Mapals 0/2.
HAWKS: 4 Michael Brown; 2 Scott Childs; 3 Tom Sheldrake; 18 Ayden Faal; 5 John Richardson; 23 Jonny Wainhouse; 27 Gareth Firm; 8 Joe Helme; 6 Darren Robinson; 17 Steve Brook; 22 Scott Watson; 11 Joe Howey; 14 Chris Redfearn. Subs (all used): 13 Mark McKinley; 19 Ben Walkin; 21 Danny Cook; 16 Mark Moxon.
Try: Brook (69); **Goals:** Sheldrake 1/1.
Rugby Leaguer & League Express Men of the Match:
Cougars: Scott Law; *Hawks:* Darren Robinson.
Penalty count: 12-6; **Half-time:** 20-0;
Referee: Gareth Hewer; **Attendance:** 826.

OLDHAM 22 SHEFFIELD EAGLES 34

OLDHAM: 1 Paul O'Connor; 2 Andy Ballard; 3 Danny Halliwell; 24 Marcus St Hilaire; 5 Lee Greenwood; 18 Neil Roden; 6 James Coyle; 8 Paul Highton; 22 Phil Joseph; 10 Jamie I'Anson; 23 Chris Baines; 11 Dave Allen; 13 Rob Roberts. Subs (all used): 4 Paul Reilly; 9 Gary Sykes; 15 Jason Boults; 16 Wayne Kerr.
Tries: O'Connor (55), I'Anson (58, 80), Ballard (61);
Goals: Ballard 3/5.
EAGLES: 1 Jonny Woodcock; 5 Ashley Thackeray; 23 Tangi Ropati; 3 Menzie Yere; 2 Bolu Fagborun; 6 Brendon Lindsay; 20 Matty Brooks; 10 Mitchell Stringer; 9 Grant Edwards; 12 Ged Corcoran; 11 Alex Szostak; 27 Tommy Trayler; 13 Dane McDonald. Subs (all used): 14 Andy Boothroyd; 19 Kyle Wood; 26 Nick Turnbull; 31 Sam Barlow.
Tries: Boothroyd (25), Woodcock (44), McDonald (53), Edwards (75), Brooks (78); **Goals:** Woodcock 7/7.
Rugby Leaguer & League Express Men of the Match:
Oldham: Paul O'Connor; *Eagles:* Jonny Woodcock.
Penalty count: 8-7; **Half-time:** 2-6;
Referee: Greg Dolan; **Attendance:** 1,173.

ROCHDALE HORNETS 28 BLACKPOOL PANTHERS 26

HORNETS: 19 Craig Johnson; 2 John Gillam; 3 Mick Fogerty; 4 Casey Mayberry; 5 Andy Smith; 6 Martin Ainscough; 24 Chris Hough; 15 Martin McLoughlin; 23 Liam Grundy; 10 Paul Raftrey; 25 Dayne Donoghue; 33 Dale Cunniffe; 13 Wayne Corcoran. Subs (all used): 9 Janan Billings; 17 Andrew Isherwood; 18 John Walker; 21 Tommy Gallagher.
Tries: Donoghue (11), Mayberry (15), Ainscough (31), Walker (43), Gillam (71), Raftrey (79);
Goals: Corcoran 2/5, Hough 0/1.
PANTHERS: 1 Jonny Leather; 2 Damian Munro; 3 Tom Woodcock; 4 Mark McCully; 24 Chris Campbell; 6 Simon Svabic; 7 Chris Forster; 12 Kris Ratcliffe; 9 John Clough; 20 Tom Wild; 13 Rob Draper; 11 Paul Alcock; 16 Ian Hodson. Subs (all used): 14 Martin Keavney; 22 Keiron Tucker; 15 Melvin Alker; 8 Peter Fairhurst.
Tries: McCully (20, 49), Leather (46), Keavney (55), Munro (67); **Goals:** Leather 3/5.
Rugby Leaguer & League Express Men of the Match:
Hornets: Paul Raftrey; *Panthers:* Jonny Leather.
Penalty count: 9-8; **Half-time:** 12-6;
Referee: Chris Leatherbarrow; **Attendance:** 371.

POOL 2

BATLEY BULLDOGS 40 YORK CITY KNIGHTS 28

BULLDOGS: 1 Ian Preece; 18 Jermaine McGilvary; 6 Mark Barlow; 4 Danny Maun; 28 Daryl Cardiss; 12 Mark Toohey; 7 Paul Mennell; 17 Craig Potter; 19 George Flanagan; 10 Luke Stenchion; 15 Anthony Henderson; 23 Chris Buttery; 14 John Gallagher. Subs (all used): 3 Dale Cardoza; 11 Kevin Crouthers; 16 Jon Simpson; 13 Ashley Lindsay.
Tries: Barlow (2, 15), Cardiss (4, 11), Simpson (18), Flanagan (35), Gallagher (79);
Goals: Flanagan 6/7, Barlow 0/1.
Dismissal: Flanagan (74) - punching.
CITY KNIGHTS: 1 Danny Ratcliffe; 3 John Oakes; 12 Tom Haberecht; 29 Wayne McHugh; 4 David Clayton; 6 Adam Mitchell; 7 Paul March; 34 Mark Applegarth; 9 Paul Hughes; 10 Adam Sullivan; 11 Rob Kelly; 13 Richard Knight; 21 David March. Subs: 30 Carl Barrow; 8 Danny Ekis; 17 Scott Woodcock; 19 Kris Peacock (not used).
Tries: Hughes (30, 62, 70), P March (38), Oakes (43);
Goals: A Mitchell 4/5.
Sin bin: Ratcliffe (21) - dissent;
P March (52) - holding down.
Rugby Leaguer & League Express Men of the Match:
Bulldogs: Mark Barlow; *City Knights:* Paul Hughes.
Penalty count: 9-10; **Half-time:** 34-12;
Referee: Mike Dawber; **Attendance:** 788.

FEATHERSTONE ROVERS 26 DEWSBURY RAMS 28

ROVERS: 20 Stuart Kain; 2 Waine Pryce; 3 Ian Hardman; 1 Tom Saxton; 34 Sam Smeaton; 7 Andy Kain; 16 Joe McLocklan; 15 James Houston; 23 Gareth Swift; 10 Stuart Dickens; 11 Matty Dale; 19 Sean Hesketh; 13 Richard Blakeway. Subs: 8 Tony Tonks; 18 Tim Spears; 25 Scott Wilson (not used); 17 Joe Hirst.
Tries: McLocklan (40), A Kain (54), Pryce (79), Hardman (80); **Goals:** McLocklan 1/1, Dickens 4/4.
Sin bin: Tonks (37) - fighting.
RAMS: 3 Lee Lingard; 15 Bryn Powell; 22 Kane Epati; 18 Chris Spurr; 16 Austin Buchanan; 13 Pat Walker; 19 Liam Finn; 11 Adam Robinson; 9 Mike Emmett; 23 Keegan Hirst; 17 Alex Bretherton; 12 Taron Wildey; 35 Adam Hayes. Subs (all used): 21 Andrew Bostock; 10 Luke Haigh; 28 Liam Crawley; 24 Simon Cook.
Tries: Emmett (12), Epati (21, 75), Buchanan (46), Lingard (63), Bostock (72); **Goals:** P Walker 2/6.
Sin bin: Bostock (37) - fighting;
Emmett (39) - holding down.
Rugby Leaguer & League Express Men of the Match:
Rovers: Andy Kain; *Rams:* Taron Wildey.
Penalty count: 12-6; **Half-time:** 8-10;
Referee: Dave Merrick; **Attendance:** 1,470.

LONDON SKOLARS 12 DONCASTER 40

SKOLARS: 2 Corey Simms; 3 Oliver Fountain; 13 Jaymes Chapman; 4 Oliver Bloom; 5 Austen Aggrey; 17 Chad Isles; 7 Paul Thorman; 8 Dave Ellison; 19 Leigh Nissen; 15 Bobby Wallis; 11 Matt Thomas; 16 Tony Williams; 21 Ben Joyce. Subs (all used): 9 Gareth Honor; 22 Danny Burke; 20 Paul Hyder; 18 Orreiso Agbareh.
Tries: Aggrey (15, 74), Bloom (45); **Goals:** Thorman 0/3.
DONCASTER: 14 Scott Jones; 20 Mike Coady; 19 Ryan Steen; 4 Shaun Leaf; 2 Dean Colton; 13 Josh Weeden; 22 Andy Speake; 28 Jamie Bovill; 9 Craig Cook; 16 Nathan Freer; 17 Ross Divorty; 18 Craig Holt; 11 Peter Green. Subs (all used): 25 Kevin Eadie; 24 Jake Bassinder; 27 Lee Parnell; 21 Gary Ellery.
Tries: Bassinder (19), S Jones (32), Coady (37, 55, 60, 67), Speake (47); **Goals:** Speake 6/7.
Sin bin: Weeden (78) - punching.
Rugby Leaguer & League Express Men of the Match:
Skolars: Austen Aggrey; *Doncaster:* Mike Coady.
Penalty count: 8-11; **Half-time:** 4-18;
Referee: Warren Turley; **Attendance:** 213.

SWINTON LIONS 26 LEIGH CENTURIONS 34

LIONS: 7 Richie Hawkyard; 30 Andy Saywell; 3 Dave Hull; 29 Carl Sneyd; 2 Barry Hamilton; 13 Martin Moana; 15 Gary Hulse; 8 Paul Southern; 9 Phil Wood; 28 Dave Newton; 17 Tommy Grundy; 19 Neil Rigby; 14 Craig Ashall. Subs (all used): 16 Alex McClurg; 11 Mike Wainwright; 12 Danny Heaton; 18 Gareth Hayes.
Tries: Moana (7, 57), McClurg (43), Hamilton (69), Wood (75); **Goals:** Sneyd 3/5.
CENTURIONS: 14 Ian Mort; 5 Nicky Stanton; 3 Steve Maden; 1 Stuart Donlan; 22 Jamie Smith; 23 Martyn Ridyard; 7 Ian Watson; 8 Andy Hobson; 39 Jamie Durbin; 16 Chris Hill; 15 Adam Higson; 12 James Taylor; 4 Anthony Stewart. Subs (all used): 18 Sam Reay; 36 Lee Wingfield; 38 Danny Meekin; 37 Anthony Rourke.
Tries: Stanton (3), Donlan (24), Watson (32), Maden (36), Ridyard (40), Hill (64); **Goals:** Ridyard 5/7.
Rugby Leaguer & League Express Men of the Match:
Lions: Richie Hawkyard; *Centurions:* Chris Hill.
Penalty count: 12-9; **Half-time:** 4-26;
Referee: Matthew Thomasson; **Attendance:** 857.

WHITEHAVEN 26 WORKINGTON TOWN 12

WHITEHAVEN: 1 Craig Benson; 5 Ade Adebisi; 3 Rob Jackson; 18 John Patrick; 2 Craig Calvert; 6 Carl Rudd; 25 Jamie Theohaurus; 21 Taani Lavulavu; 9 Graeme Mattinson; 10 Karl Edmondson; 12 Spencer Miller; 15 Andy Gorski; 7 Leroy Joe. Subs (all used): 24 Gregg McNally; 8 Marc Jackson; 22 Matthew Tunstall; 19 Kyle Amor.
Tries: Mattinson (15), Patrick (58), Calvert (69), McNally (72); **Goals:** M Jackson 2/2, McNally 3/3.
TOWN: 2 Neil Frazer; 20 Stephen Dawes; 3 Andrew Beattie; 4 Jason Mossop; 5 Jamie Marshall; 6 Carl Forber; 7 Steve Roper; 16 Tommy Brindle; 19 Scott Burgess; 24 Jarrad Stack; 11 Mike Whitehead; 22 Paddy Coupar; 13 Mark Hobson. Subs (all used): 14 Brett Smith; 15 James Robinson; 9 Jack Pedley; 8 Ryan Benjafield.
Tries: Pedley (25), Frazer (28); **Goals:** Forber 2/3.
Rugby Leaguer & League Express Men of the Match:
Whitehaven: Graeme Mattinson; *Town:* Jason Mossop.
Penalty count: 12-8; **Half time:** 6-12;
Referee: Peter Brooke; **Attendance:** 1,346.

ROUND 4

Sunday 1st March 2009

POOL 1

BARROW RAIDERS 34 KEIGHLEY COUGARS 7

RAIDERS: 1 Gary Broadbent; 2 Mike Backhouse; 3 Ian Bell; 4 Liam Harrison; 18 James Finch; 6 Liam Finch; 7 Liam Campbell; 8 Brett McDermott; 9 Andy Ellis; 13 Andy Bracek; 14 Paul Noone; 12 Martin Ostler; 11 Andrew Brocklehurst. Subs (all used): 15 Chris Young; 10 Lee Dutton; 31 Nathan Mossop; 16 Jamie Butler.
Tries: Ellis (15, 62), Campbell (42), L Finch (52), Brocklehurst (72), J Finch (75); **Goals:** Noone 5/6.
COUGARS: 1 George Rayner; 2 Sam Gardner; 3 Dan Potter; 21 Ryan Smith; 5 Gavin Duffy; 6 Jon Presley; 7 Danny Jones; 17 Scott Law; 9 James Feather; 12 Neil Lowe; 11 Will Cartledge; 4 Oliver Purseglove; 18 Greg Nicholson. Subs (all used): 14 Jamaine Wray; 10 Simon Bissell; 15 Craig Brown; 29 Karl Gunney.
Try: Presley (30); **Goals:** Jones 1/1;
Field goal: Jones (40).
Rugby Leaguer & League Express Men of the Match:
Raiders: Andy Ellis; *Cougars:* Jon Presley.
Penalty count: 7-8; **Half-time:** 6-7;
Referee: Richard Silverwood; **Attendance:** 1,311.

HUNSLET HAWKS 14 OLDHAM 32

HAWKS: 1 Nathan Larvin; 25 Michael Mark; 18 Ayden Faal; 4 Michael Brown; 5 John Richardson; 6 Darren Robinson; 16 Mark Moxon; 17 Steve Brook; 24 Charlie Wabo; 12 Jason Hart; 26 Nicko Slain; 22 Scott Watson; 14 Chris Redfearn. Subs (all used): 9 Richard Chapman; 21 Danny Cook; 28 Steve Dooler; 8 Joe Helme.
Tries: Faal (20), Larvin (26);
Goals: Robinson 2/2, Chapman 1/1.
OLDHAM: 1 Paul O'Connor; 2 Andy Ballard; 4 Paul Reilly; 24 Marcus St Hilaire; 21 Lucas Onyango; 6 James Coyle; 7 Thomas Coyle; 14 Richard Mervill; 22 Phil Joseph; 10 Jamie I'Anson; 11 Dave Allen; 12 Tommy Goulden; 13 Rob Roberts. Subs (all used): 25 Luke Menzies; 8 Paul Highton; 9 Gary Sykes; 3 Danny Halliwell.
Tries: Onyango (10), Reilly (38, 43, 48), O'Connor (62), Halliwell (66); **Goals:** Ballard 4/6.
On report: Roberts (40) - alleged punching.
Rugby Leaguer & League Express Men of the Match:
Hawks: Nathan Larvin; *Oldham:* Paul Reilly.
Penalty count: 9-6; **Half-time:** 14-10;
Referee: Chris Leatherbarrow; **Attendance:** 582.

BLACKPOOL PANTHERS 16 WIDNES VIKINGS 46

PANTHERS: 1 Jonny Leather; 5 Chris Mugan; 2 Damian Munro; 4 Mark McCully; 24 Chris Campbell; 7 Chris Forster; 19 Liam McGovern; 8 Peter Fairhurst; 9 John Clough; 12 Kris Ratcliffe; 11 Paul Alcock; 23 Darryl Kay; 15 Melvin Alker. Subs (all used): 14 Martin Keavney; 6 Simon Svabic; 18 John Boland; 13 Rob Draper.
Tries: Munro (23), Alker (38), Forster (77);
Goals: Leather 2/2, Forster 0/1.
VIKINGS: 21 Scott Yates; 22 Paddy Flynn; 4 Toa Kohe-Love; 18 Matthew Strong; 16 Gavin Dodd; 6 Anthony Thackeray; 7 James Webster; 19 Michael Ostick; 9 Mark Smith; 10 Jim Gannon; 17 Ben Kavanagh; 12 Richard Fletcher; 11 Lee Doran. Subs (all used): 14 John Duffy; 24 Josh Simm; 15 Tim Hartley; 32 David Houghton.
Tries: Kohe-Love (4, 46), Doran (10), Hartley (32), Fletcher (42), Flynn (50), Duffy (53), Yates (65);
Goals: Yates 7/8.
Rugby Leaguer & League Express Men of the Match:
Panthers: Damian Munro; *Vikings:* Toa Kohe-Love.
Penalty count: 6-9; **Half-time:** 12-18;
Referee: Warren Turley; **Attendance:** 864.

GATESHEAD THUNDER 46 ROCHDALE HORNETS 22

THUNDER: 6 Neil Thorman; 18 Robin Peers; 3 Kevin Neighbour; 31 Joe Arundel; 5 Stewart Sanderson; 22 Jamie Russo; 7 Luke Branighan; 10 Tabua Cakacaka; 9 Andrew Henderson; 33 Jonny Walker; 4 Dylan Nash; 32 James Cording; 17 Chris Parker. Subs (all used): 20 David Vernon; 8 Jason Payne; 12 Michael Knowles; 21 Ryan McBride.
Tries: Sanderson (7, 28, 51), Henderson (39), Peers (47), Arundel (65), Parker (70), Neighbour (73), Nash (80); **Goals:** Knowles 4/5, Branighan 1/4.
HORNETS: 19 Craig Johnson; 1 Chris Giles; 3 Mick Fogerty; 4 Casey Mayberry; 2 John Gillam; 6 Martin Ainscough; 20 Liam Bretherton; 8 David Best; 23 Liam Grundy; 10 Paul Raftrey; 33 Dale Cunniffe; 12 Ian Sinfield; 25 Dayne Donoghue. Subs (all used): 22 Martin Gambles; 18 John Walker; 13 Wayne Corcoran; 21 Tommy Gallagher.
Tries: Johnson (17), Cunniffe (34), Mayberry (42), Bretherton (55), Ainscough (77);
Goals: Giles 1/3, Corcoran 0/2.
Rugby Leaguer & League Express Men of the Match:
Thunder: Stewart Sanderson; *Hornets:* Mick Fogerty.
Penalty count: 5-5; **Half-time:** 14-8;
Referee: Peter Brooke; **Attendance:** 452.

SHEFFIELD EAGLES 18 HALIFAX 50

EAGLES: 1 Jonny Woodcock; 28 Damian Gibson; 3 Menzie Yere; 23 Tangi Ropati; 5 Ashley Thackeray; 6 Brendon Lindsay; 20 Matty Brooks; 8 Jack Howieson; 9 Grant Edwards; 12 Ged Corcoran; 11 Alex Szostak; 31 Sam Barlow; 13 Dane McDonald. Subs (all used): 19 Kyle Wood; 22 Ryan Hepworth; 25 James Morrow; 24 Matt Whitaker.
Tries: Woodcock (13), Gibson (44), Barlow (67);
Goals: Woodcock 3/3.
HALIFAX: 1 Miles Greenwood; 2 Lee Patterson; 4 Shad Royston; 5 James Haley; 23 Rob Worrincy; 19 Mick Govin; 7 Ben Black; 21 Neil Cherryholme; 9 Sean Penkywicz; 10 Dana Wilson; 15 Mark Roberts; 12 Paul Smith; 13 Bob Beswick. Subs (all used): 6 Dwayne Barker; 14 Mark Gleeson; 16 Said Tamghart; 17 Frank Watene.
Tries: Penkywicz (6, 30), Tamghart (25, 34), Worrincy (39), Beswick (47), Royston (51), Haley (55, 74), Patterson (79); **Goals:** Haley 4/8, Govin 1/2.
Rugby Leaguer & League Express Men of the Match:
Eagles: Alex Szostak; *Halifax:* Ben Black.
Penalty count: 6-10; **Half-time:** 6-28;
Referee: Mike Dawber; **Attendance:** 1,065.

POOL 2

DONCASTER 36 SWINTON LIONS 28

DONCASTER: 4 Shaun Leaf; 2 Dean Colton; 19 Ryan Steen; 3 Andreas Bauer; 5 Wayne Reittie; 6 Kyle Briggs; 22 Andy Speake; 28 Jamie Bovill; 9 Craig Cook; 16 Nathan Freer; 11 Peter Green; 27 Al Rounding; 13 Josh Weeden. Subs (all used): 14 Scott Jones; 15 Mark Castle; 24 Jake Bassinder; 21 Gary Ellery.
Tries: Green (32), Weeden (38, 62), S Jones (44), Reittie (48), Ellery (73); **Goals:** Briggs 6/6.
LIONS: 7 Richie Hawkyard; 2 Barry Hamilton; 3 Dave Hull; 29 Carl Sneyd; 5 Marlon Billy; 13 Martin Moana; 15 Gary Hulse; 8 Paul Southern; 9 Phil Wood; 28 Dave Newton; 17 Tommy Grundy; 19 Neil Rigby; 14 Craig Ashall. Subs (all used): 16 Alex McClurg; 11 Mike Wainwright; 12 Danny Heaton; 18 Gareth Hayes.
Tries: Rigby (6), Billy (12), Hayes (41), Newton (65), Hulse (80); **Goals:** Sneyd 4/5.
Rugby Leaguer & League Express Men of the Match:
Doncaster: Josh Weeden; *Lions:* Carl Sneyd.
Penalty count: 7-5; **Half-time:** 12-10;
Referee: Greg Dolan; **Attendance:** 645.

YORK CITY KNIGHTS 58 LONDON SKOLARS 12

CITY KNIGHTS: 1 Danny Ratcliffe; 4 David Clayton; 32 Mike Mitchell; 13 Richard Knight; 3 John Oakes; 33 Danny Grimshaw; 7 Paul March; 15 Chris Clough; 9 Paul Hughes; 10 Adam Sullivan; 19 Kris Peacock; 12 Tom Haberecht; 21 David March. Subs (all used): 14 Tom Hodgson; 29 Mark Applegarth; 30 Carl Barrow; 36 Jack Stearman.
Tries: Ratcliffe (4, 69), Clayton (9), Hughes (23), M Mitchell (34), Haberecht (36, 72), Oakes (47), P March (50), D March (58), Grimshaw (66);
Goals: Knight 7/11.
SKOLARS: 2 Corey Simms; 3 Oliver Fountain; 13 Jaymes Chapman; 4 Oliver Bloom; 5 Austen Aggrey; 17 Chad Isles; 7 Paul Thorman; 8 Dave Ellison; 19 Leigh Nissen; 16 Tony Williams; 11 Matt Thomas; 22 Danny Burke; 21 Ben Joyce. Subs (all used): 9 Gareth Honor; 20 Paul Hyder; 14 Graeme Spencer; 27 Keir Bell.
Tries: Burke (55), M Thomas (77); **Goals:** Thorman 2/2.
Sin bin: Burke (18) – interference.
Rugby Leaguer & League Express Men of the Match:
City Knights: David March; *Skolars:* Danny Burke.
Penalty count: 15-8; **Half-time:** 28-0;
Referee: Jamie Leahy; **Attendance:** 1,003.

DEWSBURY RAMS 34 BATLEY BULLDOGS 14

RAMS: 3 Lee Lingard; 15 Bryn Powell; 18 Chris Spurr; 22 Kane Epati; 16 Austin Buchanan; 13 Pat Walker; 19 Liam Finn; 11 Adam Robinson; 9 Mike Emmett; 23 Keegan Hirst; 17 Alex Bretherton; 21 Andrew Bostock; 35 Adam Hayes. Subs (all used): 12 Taron Wildey; 28 Liam Crawley; 27 Chris Grice; 7 Gareth Greenwood.
Tries: Epati (29), Bretherton (33, 53), Wildey (49), Finn (71, 76); **Goals:** P Walker 5/7.
BULLDOGS: 1 Ian Preece; 18 Jermaine McGilvary; 14 John Gallagher; 34 Damien Reid; 22 Nathan Brown; 6 Mark Barlow; 7 Paul Mennell; 10 Luke Stenchion; 19 George Flanagan; 8 Byron Smith; 17 Craig Potter; 21 Nathan Armitage; 12 Mark Toohey. Subs (all used): 20 David Tootill; 35 Jack Watson; 16 Jon Simpson; 3 Dale Cardoza.
Tries: Preece (9), Stenchion (22), Armitage (39);
Goals: Hanagan 1/3.
Rugby Leaguer & League Express Men of the Match:
Rams: Liam Finn; *Bulldogs:* Paul Mennell.
Penalty count: 8-9; **Half-time:** 8-14;
Referee: Matthew Thomasson; **Attendance:** 1,512.

LEIGH CENTURIONS 24 WHITEHAVEN 22

CENTURIONS: 1 Stuart Donlan; 5 Nicky Stanton; 18 Sam Reay; 15 Adam Higson; 3 Steve Maden; 23 Martyn Ridyard; 7 Ian Watson; 8 Andy Hobson; 9 Dave McConnell; 16 Chris Hill; 40 Kurt Haggerty; 12 James Taylor; 38 Anthony Rourke. Subs (all used): 39 Jamie Durbin; 36 Lee Wingfield; 4 Anthony Stewart; 37 Danny Meekin.
Tries: Ridyard (13), Haggerty (40), Durbin (48), McConnell (77); **Goals:** Ridyard 4/4.
WHITEHAVEN: 1 Craig Benson; 5 Ade Adebisi; 3 Rob Jackson; 4 Derry Eilbeck; 2 Craig Calvert; 6 Carl Rudd; 25 Jamie Theohaurus; 21 Taani Lavulavu; 9 Graeme Mattinson; 10 Karl Edmondson; 12 Spencer Miller; 15 Andy Gorski; 7 Leroy Joe. Subs (all used): 24 Gregg McNally; 8 Marc Jackson; 19 Kyle Amor; 31 Dexter Miller.
Tries: Eilbeck (22), McNally (33, 56), Lavulavu (53);
Goals: M Jackson 3/4.
Sin bin: Joe (36) – holding down;
M Jackson (39) – holding down.
On report:
Lavulavu (62) – alleged high tackle on Donlan.
Rugby Leaguer & League Express Men of the Match:
Centurions: Andy Hobson; *Whitehaven:* Spencer Miller.
Penalty count: 9-5; **Half-time:** 12-10;
Referee: Robert Hicks; **Attendance:** 1,789.

WORKINGTON TOWN 6 FEATHERSTONE ROVERS 38

TOWN: 2 Neil Frazer; 20 Stephen Dawes; 3 Andrew Beattie; 21 Mark Routledge; 5 Jamie Marshall; 6 Carl Forber; 7 Steve Roper; 8 Ryan Benjafield; 31 Darren King; 17 Peter Dobson; 11 Mike Whitehead; 12 Craig Hodgson; 14 Brett Smith. Subs (all used): 9 Jack Pedley; 18 Kris Coward; 13 Mark Hobson; 24 Jarrad Stack.
Try: Beattie (35); **Goals:** Forber 1/1.
On report:
Hobson (25) – alleged late challenge on Harris.
ROVERS: 3 Ian Hardman; 2 Waine Pryce; 17 Joe Hirst; 1 Tom Saxton; 34 Sam Smeaton; 6 Iestyn Harris; 7 Andy Kain; 8 Tony Tonks; 16 Joe McLocklan; 10 Stuart Dickens; 11 Matty Dale; 18 Tim Spears; 12 Jamie Field. Subs: 15 James Houston; 9 Jack Lee (not used); 20 Stuart Kain (not used); 13 Richard Blakeway.
Tries: Smeaton (7), Pryce (12, 57), Harris (42), Hardman (49), Tonks (67), Blakeway (74);
Goals: Dickens 3/3, Harris 2/4.
Rugby Leaguer & League Express Men of the Match:
Town: Neil Frazer; *Rovers:* Andy Kain.
Penalty count: 5-7; **Half-time:** 6-8;
Referee: Craig Halloran; **Attendance:** 477.

ROUND 1

Wednesday 4th March 2009

POOL 1

BARROW RAIDERS 12 WIDNES VIKINGS 4

RAIDERS: 1 Gary Broadbent; 2 Mike Backhouse; 3 Ian Bell; 4 Liam Harrison; 18 James Finch; 6 Liam Finch; 7 Liam Campbell; 8 Brett McDermott; 9 Andy Ellis; 13 Andy Bracek; 14 Paul Noone; 12 Martin Ostler; 11 Andrew Brocklehurst. Subs (all used): 15 Chris Young; 10 Lee Dutton; 31 Nathan Mossop; 16 Jamie Butler.
Tries: Harrison (18), Ellis (64); **Goals:** Noone 2/3.
VIKINGS: 21 Scott Yates; 22 Paddy Flynn; 4 Toa Kohe-Love; 15 Tim Hartley; 2 Dean Gaskell; 6 Anthony Thackeray; 14 John Duffy; 19 Michael Ostick; 9 Mark Smith; 10 Jim Gannon; 3 Richard Varkulis; 12 Richard Fletcher; 24 Josh Simm. Subs (all used): 7 James Webster; 17 Ben Kavanagh; 16 Gavin Dodd; 20 Sam Thompson.
Try: Gaskell (44); **Goals:** Yates 0/1.
Rugby Leaguer & League Express Men of the Match:
Raiders: Gary Broadbent; *Vikings:* Dean Gaskell.
Penalty count: 8-13; **Half-time:** 6-0;
Referee: Peter Brooke; **Attendance:** 1,563.

HALIFAX 50 BLACKPOOL PANTHERS 28

HALIFAX: 1 Miles Greenwood; 2 Lee Patterson; 6 Dwayne Barker; 5 James Haley; 20 Graham Charlesworth; 25 Anthony Bowman; 7 Ben Black; 21 Neil Cherryholme; 19 Mick Govin; 22 David Wrench; 18 Andy Bowman; 11 David Larder; 4 Shad Royston. Subs (all used): 9 Sean Penkywicz; 12 Paul Smith; 16 Said Tamghart; 17 Frank Watene.
Tries: Royston (11, 74), Greenwood (15, 50), Haley (24), Black (31), Tamghart (55), Barker (63, 79);
Goals: Govin 5/5, Haley 0/1, Black 2/3.
PANTHERS: 22 Keiron Tucker; 5 Chris Mugan; 3 Tom Woodcock; 1 Jonny Leather; 24 Chris Campbell; 6 Simon Svabic; 7 Chris Forster; 10 John Hill; 9 John Clough; 12 Kris Ratcliffe; 11 Paul Alcock; 15 Melvin Alker; 27 Craig Farrimond. Subs (all used): 14 Martin Keavney; 19 Liam McGovern; 18 John Boland; 23 Darryl Kay.
Tries: Leather (7, 43), Ratcliffe (19), Campbell (39), Tucker (46); **Goals:** Leather 4/5.
Sin bin: Mugan (73) – holding down.
Rugby Leaguer & League Express Men of the Match:
Halifax: Miles Greenwood; *Panthers:* Melvin Alker.
Penalty count: 13-4; **Half-time:** 22-18;
Referee: Matthew Thomasson; **Attendance:** 1,291.

Wednesday 11th March 2009

POOL 2

SWINTON LIONS 31 WORKINGTON TOWN 24

LIONS: 7 Richie Hawkyard; 30 Andy Saywell; 3 Dave Hull; 22 Darren Bamford; 1 Wayne English; 24 Paul Crook; 15 Gary Hulse; 18 Gareth Hayes; 16 Alex McClurg; 10 Bruce Johnson; 28 Dave Newton; 13 Martin Moana; 14 Craig Ashall. Subs (all used): 9 Phil Wood; 25 Matt Ashe; 5 Marlon Billy; 19 Neil Rigby.
Tries: Moana (11), Saywell (30), Hull (33, 62), Bamford (50), Ashall (79); **Goals:** Crook 3/6;
Field goal: Ashall (77).
TOWN: 2 Neil Frazer; 20 Stephen Dawes; 3 Andrew Beattie; 21 Mark Routledge; 5 Jamie Marshall; 6 Carl Forber; 7 Steve Roper; 24 Jarrad Stack; 31 Darren King; 16 Tommy Brindle; 11 Mike Whitehead; 22 Paddy Coupar; 13 Mark Hobson. Subs (all used): 19 Scott Burgess; 8 Ryan Benjafield; 15 James Robinson; 12 Craig Hodgson.
Tries: Hodgson (6, 19), Routledge (45), Brindle (48), Dawes (72); **Goals:** Forber 2/5.
Rugby Leaguer & League Express Men of the Match:
Lions: Richie Hawkyard; *Town:* Steve Roper.
Penalty count: 6-6; **Half-time:** 14-10;
Referee: Robert Hicks; **Attendance:** 242.

Sunday 15th March 2009

POOL 2

LONDON SKOLARS 14 DEWSBURY RAMS 42

SKOLARS: 2 Corey Simms; 26 Olu Iwenofu; 17 Chad Isles; 25 Jaroslaw Obuchowski; 5 Austen Aggrey; 9 Gareth Honor; 7 Paul Thorman; 8 Dave Ellison; 19 Leigh Nissen; 15 Bobby Wallis; 11 Matt Thomas; 16 Tony Williams; 21 Ben Joyce. Subs (all used): 14 Graeme Spencer; 10 Glenn Osborn; 22 Danny Burke; 1 Frank Reid. **Tries:** Iwenofu (17, 60, 70); **Goals:** Thorman 1/3.
RAMS: 4 Craig Bower; 15 Bryn Powell; 22 Kane Epati; 24 Simon Cook; 25 Gary North; 13 Pat Walker; 5 Andrew Tillotson; 23 Keegan Hirst; 9 Mike Emmett; 20 Rob Spicer; 17 Alex Bretherton; 21 Andrew Bostock; 28 Liam Crawley. Subs (all used): 34 Josh Tonks; 1 Tom Colleran; 2 Morgan Starkey; 33 James Walker. **Tries:** Crawley (2), North (21, 33), Cook (24, 38), Bostock (66), P Walker (74); **Goals:** P Walker 7/8.
Rugby Leaguer & League Express Men of the Match: *Skolars:* Olu Iwenofu; *Rams:* Pat Walker.
Penalty count: 15-11; **Half-time:** 6-28;
Referee: Warren Turley; **Attendance:** 314.

FINAL TABLES

POOL 1

	P	W	D	L	BP	F	A	Diff	Pts
Halifax	4	4	0	0	0	178	66	112	12
Oldham	4	3	0	1	1	130	72	58	10
Barrow	4	3	0	1	0	110	63	47	9
Widnes	4	2	0	2	2	110	68	42	8
Keighley	4	2	0	2	1	105	76	29	7
Gateshead	4	2	0	2	0	128	120	8	6
Sheffield	4	2	0	2	0	108	132	-24	6
Blackpool	4	1	0	3	1	86	138	-52	4
Rochdale	4	1	0	3	0	66	180	-114	3
Hunslet	4	0	0	4	0	46	152	-106	0

POOL 2

	P	W	D	L	BP	F	A	Diff	Pts
Dewsbury	4	4	0	0	0	154	54	100	12
York	4	3	0	1	1	156	68	88	10
Leigh	4	3	0	1	1	138	64	74	10
Featherstone	4	3	0	1	1	106	46	60	10
Doncaster	4	3	0	1	0	104	90	14	9
Whitehaven	4	2	0	2	1	106	102	4	7
Swinton	4	1	0	3	2	85	144	-59	5
Batley	4	1	0	3	1	102	136	-34	4
Workington	4	0	0	4	1	52	129	-77	1
London Skolars	4	0	0	4	0	44	214	-170	0

Top four teams from each Pool progressed to Quarter Finals.

QUARTER FINALS

Thursday 4th June 2009

OLDHAM 18 FEATHERSTONE ROVERS 32

OLDHAM: 4 Paul Reilly; 2 Andy Ballard; 3 Danny Halliwell; 24 Marcus St Hilaire; 5 Lee Greenwood; 18 Neil Roden; 6 James Coyle; 15 Jason Boults; 9 Gary Sykes; 14 Richard Mervill; 11 Dave Allen; 23 Chris Baines; 13 Rob Roberts. Subs (all used): 8 Paul Highton; 12 Tommy Goulden; 17 Craig Robinson; 22 Phil Joseph. **Tries:** Ballard (9), Halliwell (14), Greenwood (55); **Goals:** Ballard 3/3.
ROVERS: 3 Ian Hardman; 5 Jon Steel; 4 Andy Kirk; 14 Tom Haughey; 1 Tom Saxton; 28 Kyle Briggs; 7 Andy Kain; 24 Jon Fallon; 16 Joe McLocklan; 10 Stuart Dickens; 18 Tim Spears; 11 Matty Dale; 12 Jamie Field. Subs (all used): 2 Waine Pryce; 8 Tony Tonks; 9 Jack Lee; 17 Joe Hirst. **Tries:** McLocklan (5), Haughey (19), Hirst (42), Steel (47), Dale (51), Kirk (68); **Goals:** Dickens 4/5, Briggs 0/1.
Rugby Leaguer & League Express Men of the Match: *Oldham:* Paul Reilly; *Rovers:* Andy Kain.
Penalty count: 7-6; **Half-time:** 12-10; **Referee:** Gareth Hewer; **Attendance:** 853 *(at Leigh Sports Village).*

Saturday 6th June 2009

BARROW RAIDERS 20 DEWSBURY RAMS 18

RAIDERS: 1 Gary Broadbent; 19 Chris Larkin; 32 Andreas Bauer; 4 Liam Harrison; 5 James Nixon; 6 Liam Finch; 27 Darren Holt; 16 Jamie Butler; 9 Andy Ellis; 13 Andy Bracek; 22 Ned Catic; 12 Martin Ostler; 26 Zebastian Luisi. Subs (all used): 15 Chris Young; 14 Paul Noone; 8 Brett McDermott; 28 Nathan Mossop. **Tries:** Broadbent (6), Catic (22), Bauer (26), Harrison (78); **Goals:** Holt 2/4.
RAMS: 3 Lee Lingard; 15 Bryn Powell; 18 Chris Spurr; 22 Kane Epati; 16 Austin Buchanan; 13 Pat Walker; 19 Liam Finn; 11 Adam Robinson; 9 Mike Emmett; 23 Keegan Hirst; 17 Alex Bretherton; 20 Rob Spicer; 12 Taron Wildey. Subs (all used): 35 Adam Hayes; 21 Andrew Bostock; 28 Liam Crawley; 6 Ryan Smith. **Tries:** Spurr (31), Buchanan (70, 75); **Goals:** P Walker 3/4.
Rugby Leaguer & League Express Men of the Match: *Raiders:* Gary Broadbent; *Rams:* Lee Lingard.
Penalty count: 8-9; **Half-time:** 16-6;
Referee: Robert Hicks; **Attendance:** 1,820.

Rob Worrincy scores during Halifax's Quarter Final win over Leigh

WIDNES VIKINGS 44 YORK CITY KNIGHTS 18

VIKINGS: 16 Gavin Dodd; 2 Dean Gaskell; 4 Toa Kohe-Love; 32 Craig Hall; 29 Kevin Penny; 6 Anthony Thackeray; 7 James Webster; 28 Steve Pickersgill; 9 Mark Smith; 10 Jim Gannon; 8 Iain Morrison; 12 Richard Fletcher; 11 Lee Doran. Subs (all used): 3 Richard Varkulis; 15 Tim Hartley; 17 Ben Kavanagh; 19 Michael Ostick. **Tries:** Gaskell (5), Thackeray (8), Kavanagh (44), Varkulis (53), Kohe-Love (56, 57, 72), Fletcher (80); **Goals:** Hall 6/8.
CITY KNIGHTS: 1 Danny Ratcliffe; 22 Tom Stancliffe; 3 John Oakes; 12 Tom Haberecht; 4 David Clayton; 6 Adam Mitchell; 7 Paul March; 15 Chris Clough; 9 Paul Hughes; 10 Adam Sullivan; 13 Richard Knight; 11 Rob Kelly; 21 David March. Subs (all used): 35 Sean Hesketh; 29 Mark Applegarth; 19 Kris Peacock; 17 Scott Woodcock. **Tries:** Hughes (33, 38), Ratcliffe (49); **Goals:** A Mitchell 3/3.
Rugby Leaguer & League Express Men of the Match: *Vikings:* Toa Kohe-Love; *City Knights:* Paul March.
Penalty count: 10-11; **Half-time:** 10-12;
Referee: James Child; **Attendance:** 1,650.

Sunday 7th June 2009

HALIFAX 54 LEIGH CENTURIONS 16

HALIFAX: 1 Miles Greenwood; 2 Lee Patterson; 3 Jon Goddard; 5 James Haley; 23 Rob Worrincy; 9 Sean Penkywicz; 7 Ben Black; 8 Bob Beswick; 10 Dana Wilson; 11 David Larder; 12 Paul Smith; 4 Shad Royston. Subs (all used): 14 Mark Gleeson; 16 Said Tamghart; 17 Frank Watene. **Tries:** Worrincy (2, 62), Larder (13), Black (24, 65), Royston (29, 49), Greenwood (41, 73); **Goals:** Patterson 9/9.
CENTURIONS: 1 Stuart Donlan; 3 Steve Maden; 4 Anthony Stewart; 38 Mick Nanyn; 14 Ian Mort; 23 Martyn Ridyard; 7 Ian Watson; 16 Chris Hill; 9 Dave McConnell; 10 Mike Morrison; 11 Dave Armitstead; 40 Macgraff Leuluai; 13 Aaron Smith. Subs (all used): 8 Andy Hobson; 12 James Taylor; 29 Lee Wingfield; 37 Andy Ainscough. **Tries:** Leuluai (5), Ridyard (69), Mort (78); **Goals:** Mort 2/3.
Rugby Leaguer & League Express Men of the Match: *Halifax:* Ben Black; *Centurions:* Dave Armitstead.
Penalty count: 4-7; **Half-time:** 24-6;
Referee: Craig Halloran; **Attendance:** 2,186.

SEMI-FINALS

Thursday 18th June 2009

BARROW RAIDERS 16 FEATHERSTONE ROVERS 10

RAIDERS: 1 Gary Broadbent; 19 Chris Larkin; 32 Andreas Bauer; 4 Liam Harrison; 5 James Nixon; 6 Liam Finch; 27 Darren Holt; 8 Brett McDermott; 9 Andy Ellis; 13 Andy Bracek; 22 Ned Catic; 14 Paul Noone; 26 Zebastian Luisi. Subs (all used): 15 Chris Young; 16 Jamie Butler; 12 Martin Ostler; 11 Andrew Brocklehurst. **Tries:** Ellis (13, 78); **Goals:** Holt 4/4.
ROVERS: 3 Ian Hardman; 5 Jon Steel; 4 Andy Kirk; 1 Tom Saxton; 2 Wayne Pryce; 28 Kyle Briggs; 7 Andy Kain; 10 Stuart Dickens; 16 Joe McLocklan; 15 James Houston; 11 Matty Dale; 18 Tim Spears; 14 Tom Haughey. Subs (all used): 17 Joe Hirst; 29 Ross Divorty; 9 Jack Lee; 24 Jon Fallon. **Tries:** Briggs (31), Haughey (65); **Goals:** Hirst 1/1, Dickens 0/1.
Sin bin: Dickens (20) - late challenge on Holt.
Rugby Leaguer & League Express Men of the Match: *Raiders:* Gary Broadbent; *Rovers:* Ian Hardman.
Penalty count: 11-8; **Half-time:** 8-4;
Referee: Jamie Leahy; **Attendance:** 2,775.

Sunday 21st June 2009

HALIFAX 22 WIDNES VIKINGS 27

HALIFAX: 1 Miles Greenwood; 2 Lee Patterson; 3 Jon Goddard; 6 Dwayne Barker; 23 Rob Worrincy; 13 Bob Beswick; 7 Ben Black; 10 Dana Wilson; 14 Mark Gleeson; 16 Said Tamghart; 11 David Larder; 4 Shad Royston. Subs (all used): 9 Sean Penkywicz; 22 David Wrench; 17 Frank Watene; 19 Mick Govin. **Tries:** Tamghart (6), Royston (55, 63), Black (60); **Goals:** Patterson 3/4.
VIKINGS: 16 Gavin Dodd; 2 Dean Gaskell; 4 Toa Kohe-Love; 32 Craig Hall; 29 Kevin Penny; 6 Anthony Thackeray; 7 James Webster; 10 Jim Gannon; 9 Mark Smith; 28 Steve Pickersgill; 12 Richard Fletcher; 3 Richard Varkulis; 8 Iain Morrison. Subs (all used): 14 John Duffy; 11 Lee Doran; 17 Ben Kavanagh; 15 Tim Hartley. **Tries:** Thackeray (17, 50, 74), Dodd (30); **Goals:** Hall 5/6; **Field goal:** Hall (75).
Rugby Leaguer & League Express Men of the Match: *Halifax:* Said Tamghart; *Vikings:* Anthony Thackeray.
Penalty count: 3-11; **Half-time:** 6-14;
Referee: Ronnie Laughton; **Attendance:** 3,972.

FINAL

Sunday 12th July 2009

BARROW RAIDERS 18 WIDNES VIKINGS 34

RAIDERS: 1 Gary Broadbent; 19 Chris Larkin; 32 Andreas Bauer; 4 Liam Harrison; 5 James Nixon; 6 Liam Finch; 27 Darren Holt; 8 Brett McDermott; 9 Andy Ellis; 13 Andy Bracek; 12 Martin Ostler; 14 Paul Noone; 26 Zebastian Luisi. Subs (all used): 15 Chris Young; 16 Jamie Butler; 28 Nathan Mossop; 17 Scott Kaighan. **Tries:** Luisi (26), Nixon (54), Kaighan (72); **Goals:** Holt 3/4.
Sin bin: McDermott (6) - fighting.
VIKINGS: 16 Gavin Dodd; 2 Dean Gaskell; 4 Toa Kohe-Love; 32 Craig Hall; 29 Kevin Penny; 6 Anthony Thackeray; 7 James Webster; 28 Steve Pickersgill; 9 Mark Smith; 10 Jim Gannon; 3 Richard Varkulis; 12 Richard Fletcher; 8 Iain Morrison. Subs (all used): 14 John Duffy; 11 Lee Doran; 15 Tim Hartley; 17 Ben Kavanagh. **Tries:** Fletcher (12), Duffy (30), Penny (34, 38), Kohe-Love (56), Varkulis (80); **Goals:** Hall 5/6.
Sin bin: Gannon (6) - fighting.
Rugby Leaguer & League Express Men of the Match: *Raiders:* Martin Ostler; *Vikings:* John Duffy.
Penalty count: 6-9; **Half-time:** 8-22;
Referee: Gareth Hewer; **Attendance:** 8,720 *(at Bloomfield Road, Blackpool).*

Widnes' Toa Kohe-Love and John Duffy halt Barrow's Chris Young during the Northern Rail Cup Final

CHALLENGE CUP 2009
Round by Round

ROUND 3

Saturday 7th March 2009

SIDDAL 6 SWINTON LIONS 10

SIDDAL: 1 Brad Attwood; 2 Gareth Blackburn; 3 Chris Marsh; 4 Scott Caley; 5 Shaun Blackburn; 6 Shaun Garrod; 7 Lee Gudor; 8 Mark Boothroyd; 9 Craig Sanderson; 10 James Wrigley; 11 James Simeunovich; 12 Nick Smith; 13 Luke Simeunovich. Subs (all used): 14 John Birt; 15 George Ambler; 16 Luke Garnett; 17 Gary Lewis.
Try: Caley (34); **Goals:** S Blackburn 1/2.
LIONS: 7 Richie Hawkyard; 2 Barry Hamilton; 3 Dave Hull; 29 Carl Sneyd; 5 Marlon Billy; 13 Martin Moana; 15 Gary Hulse; 8 Paul Southern; 9 Phil Wood; 12 Danny Heaton; 19 Neil Rigby; 17 Tommy Grundy; 14 Craig Ashall. Subs (all used): 16 Alex McClurg; 11 Mike Wainwright; 28 Dave Newton; 10 Bruce Johnson.
Tries: Sneyd (10), Newton (67); **Goals:** Sneyd 1/2.
Rugby Leaguer & League Express Men of the Match: *Siddal:* Shaun Garrod; *Lions:* Richie Hawkyard.
Penalty count: 10-12; **Half-time:** 6-4; **Referee:** Clint Sharrad; **Attendance:** 1,052 *(at The Shay, Halifax).*

QUEENS 12 DONCASTER 16
(Match abandoned after 61 minutes, due to crowd trouble)

QUEENS: 1 Aaron Henry; 2 Omar Al'rawi; 3 Chris Munden; 4 Steve Morton; 5 John Winter; 6 John Milner; 7 Ryan Robinson; 8 Scott Houston; 9 Carl Luke; 10 James Brown; 11 Richard Hulme; 12 Craig Wright; 13 Robin Wilks. Subs: 14 Tom Primm; 15 Matt Stockdale; 16 Craig Boot; 17 Martin Slack (not used).
Tries: Munden (46), Milner (48); **Goals:** Milner 2/3.
Sin bin: Wright (40) - high tackle; Brown (55) - dissent.
DONCASTER: 4 Shaun Leaf; 20 Mike Coady; 3 Andreas Bauer; 19 Ryan Steen; 5 Wayne Reittie; 6 Kyle Briggs; 7 Paul Handforth; 28 Jamie Bovill; 9 Craig Cook; 16 Nathan Freer; 11 Peter Green; 18 Craig Holt; 13 Josh Weeden. Subs: 27 Al Rounding; 8 Michael Haley (not used); 15 Mark Castle; 22 Andy Speake.
Tries: Bovill (43), Weeden (54), Briggs (57);
Goals: Briggs 2/3.
Rugby Leaguer & League Express Men of the Match: *Queens:* Scott Houston; *Doncaster:* Kyle Briggs.
Penalty count: 6-11; **Half-time:** 2-0; **Referee:** Bob Everitt; **Attendance:** 595 *(at Keepmoat Stadium).*

WORKINGTON TOWN 6 LEZIGNAN 18

TOWN: 2 Neil Frazer; 20 Stephen Dawes; 3 Andrew Beattie; 4 Jason Mossop; 5 Jamie Marshall; 6 Carl Forber; 7 Steve Roper; 8 Ryan Benjafield; 31 Darren King; 16 Tommy Brindle; 11 Mike Whitehead; 22 Paddy Coupar; 13 Mark Hobson. Subs (all used): 12 Craig Hodgson; 14 Brett Smith; 15 James Robinson; 24 Jarrad Stack.
Try: Stack (78); **Goals:** Forber 1/1.
Sin bin: Robinson (21) - fighting.
LEZIGNAN: 1 Jarred Taylor; 2 Gregory Mazard; 3 Luke Hession; 4 Cedric Bringuier; 5 Aurelien Bourrel; 6 Aurelien Cologni; 7 James Wynne; 8 Chris Beattie; 9 Cedric Lacans; 10 Adel Fellous; 11 Phillippe Laurent; 12 Charly Clottes; 13 Alastair Brown. Subs (all used): 14 Nicolas Manessi; 15 Thibault Ancely; 16 Yoan Tisseyre; 17 Franck Rovira.
Tries: Brown (13), Taylor (26, 37);
Goals: Wynne 2/4, Cologni 1/1.
Dismissal: Laurent (21) – fighting.
Sin bin: Wynne (21) - fighting.
Rugby Leaguer & League Express Men of the Match: *Town:* Darren King; *Lezignan:* James Wynne.
Penalty count: 10-9; **Half-time:** 0-16;
Referee: Craig Halloran; **Attendance:** 314.

WIDNES VIKINGS 88 SADDLEWORTH RANGERS 0

VIKINGS: 1 Loz Wildbore; 2 Dean Gaskell; 15 Tim Hartley; 23 Shane Grady; 16 Gavin Dodd; 6 Anthony Thackeray; 7 James Webster; 19 Michael Ostick; 9 Mark Smith; 10 Jim Gannon; 24 Josh Simm; 3 Richard Varkulis; 11 Lee Doran. Subs (all used): 17 Ben Kavanagh; 18 Matthew Strong; 20 Sam Thompson; 25 Anthony Mullally.
Tries: Gaskell (4), Dodd (9, 25), Gannon (15), Ostick (18), Strong (31), Varkulis (36, 39), Smith (49, 50, 79), Wildbore (53, 72), Hartley (62), Thompson (77);
Goals: Hartley 14/15.
RANGERS: 1 Danny Attersall; 2 Fraser Coley; 3 James Whalley; 4 Tom Lever; 5 Shaun Robinson; 6 Michael Coates; 7 Lee Charlesworth; 8 Liam Hall; 9 Liam Coates; 10 Adam Walker; 11 Ben Walters; 12 Simon Parrish; 13 Emerson Jackman. Subs (all used): 14 Dale Lowe; 15 Gareth Davies; 16 Adam Jefferies; 17 Jack Brennan.
Rugby Leaguer & League Express Men of the Match: *Vikings:* Mark Smith; *Rangers:* Liam Coates.
Penalty count: 11-4; **Half-time:** 48-0;
Referee: Chris Leatherbarrow; **Attendance:** 1,786.

KEIGHLEY COUGARS 30 PIA 24

COUGARS: 1 George Rayner; 2 Sam Gardner; 3 Dan Potter; 21 Ryan Smith; 5 Gavin Duffy; 6 Jon Presley; 7 Danny Jones; 17 Scott Law; 9 James Feather; 15 Craig Brown; 11 Will Cartledge; 4 Oliver Purseglove; 18 Greg Nicholson. Subs (all used): 14 Jamaine Wray; 12 Neil Lowe; 10 Simon Bissell; 29 Karl Gunney.
Tries: Presley (7, 18), Cartledge (45), Potter (62), Duffy (72); **Goals:** Jones 5/8.
PIA: 1 Nick Youngquest; 2 Nicolas Piquemal; 3 Christophe Calegari; 4 Paul Franze; 5 Stephane Muniesa; 6 Dean Bosnich; 7 Sylvain Amigas; 8 Jerome Blazy; 9 Matthias Garrabe; 10 Kris Kahler; 11 Guillaume Knecht; 12 Mohammed Djalout; 13 Neale Wyatt. Subs (all used): 14 Samir Belkhiri; 15 Yannick Bois; 16 Maxime Greseque; 17 Thomas Ambert.
Tries: Amigas (14), Kahler (30, 52), Piquemal (42);
Goals: Youngquest 4/4.
Rugby Leaguer & League Express Men of the Match: *Cougars:* Jon Presley; *Pia:* Kris Kahler.
Penalty count: 11-7; **Half-time:** 18-12;
Referee: Gareth Hewer; **Attendance:** 447.

Sunday 8th March 2009

BARROW RAIDERS 44 BLACKPOOL PANTHERS 12

RAIDERS: 1 Gary Broadbent; 2 Mike Backhouse; 18 James Finch; 4 Liam Harrison; 5 James Nixon; 6 Liam Finch; 7 Liam Campbell; 8 Brett McDermott; 31 Nathan Mossop; 16 Jamie Butler; 14 Paul Noone; 12 Martin Ostler; 11 Andrew Brocklehurst. Subs (all used): 15 Chris Young; 10 Lee Dutton; 9 Andy Ellis; 21 Joe McKenna.
Tries: J Finch (17), Nixon (21, 29, 70), Dutton (25), McDermott (50), Ellis (59), Harrison (68, 79);
Goals: Noone 4/9.
PANTHERS: 22 Keiron Tucker; 5 Chris Mugan; 3 Tom Woodcock; 1 Jonny Leather; 24 Chris Campbell; 6 Simon Svabic; 7 Chris Forster; 18 John Boland; 9 John Clough; 12 Kris Ratcliffe; 11 Paul Alcock; 16 Ian Hodson; 27 Craig Farrimond. Subs (all used): 14 Martin Keavney; 19 Liam McGovern; 23 Darryl Kay; 20 Tom Wild.
Tries: Tucker (45), Leather (66); **Goals:** Leather 2/2.
Sin bin: Ratcliffe (74) - high tackle on Campbell.
Rugby Leaguer & League Express Men of the Match: *Raiders:* Liam Harrison; *Panthers:* Jonny Leather.
Penalty count: 9-8; **Half-time:** 22-0;
Referee: Matthew Thomasson; **Attendance:** 1,187.

LEEDS MET CARNEGIE 24 ROCHDALE HORNETS 38

CARNEGIE: 1 Ashley Huck; 2 Jon Paxton; 3 Rhys Griffiths; 4 Stuart Dunbar; 5 Rob Hill; 6 Iain Gordon; 7 Jymel Coleman; 8 Matt Carbutt; 9 Scott Ellan; 10 Danny Vento; 11 Lewis Wildridge; 12 Chris Clarke; 13 Kris Hodson. Subs (all used): 14 Liam Duffy; 15 Charles Paxton; 16 Dave Falcons; 17 Ben Parker.
Tries: Ellan (38), Paxton (43), Dunbar (46), Gordon (57);
Goals: Gordon 4/5.
HORNETS: 16 Mark Brocklehurst; 19 Craig Johnson; 3 Mick Fogerty; 4 Casey Mayberry; 1 Chris Giles; 6 Martin Ainscough; 22 Martin Gambles; 8 David Best; 13 Wayne Corcoran; 10 Paul Raftrey; 33 Dale Cunniffe; 12 Ian Sinfield; 25 Dayne Donoghue. Subs (all used): 20 Liam Bretherton; 15 Martin McLoughlin; 11 Dave Cunliffe; 21 Tommy Gallagher.
Tries: Sinfield (12), Brocklehurst (14), Ainscough (25), Johnson (30), Gambles (61), Raftrey (65), Giles (76);
Goals: Giles 5/7.
Rugby Leaguer & League Express Men of the Match: *Carnegie:* Iain Gordon; *Hornets:* Mark Brocklehurst.
Penalty count: 8-7; **Half-time:** 8-22; **Referee:** Greg Dolan; **Attendance:** 221 *(at Headingley Carnegie).*

WATH BROW HORNETS 14 LONDON SKOLARS 12

HORNETS: 1 Ryan Amor; 2 Michael Maxwell; 3 Fran King; 4 Gary Elliot; 5 Jamie Devine; 6 Craig Johnstone; 7 Ryan Robb; 8 David Pettit; 9 Dave Currie; 10 Mark Cox; 11 Mickey McAllister; 12 Kevin Thompson; 13 Scott Teare. Subs (all used): 14 David Byers; 15 James Toman; 16 James McClennan; 17 Phil Coyles.
Tries: Teare (65, 70); **Goals:** Robb 3/3.
SKOLARS: 2 Corey Simms; 3 Oliver Fountain; 17 Chad Isles; 4 Oliver Bloom; 5 Austen Aggrey; 9 Gareth Honor; 7 Paul Thorman; 8 Dave Ellison; 19 Leigh Nissen; 16 Tony Williams; 11 Matt Thomas; 22 Danny Burke; 21 Ben Joyce. Subs (all used): 1 Frank Reid; 14 Graeme Spencer; 26 Olu Iwenofu; 20 Paul Hyder.
Tries: M Thomas (25), Fountain (34); **Goals:** Thorman 2/3.
Rugby Leaguer & League Express Men of the Match: *Hornets:* Scott Teare; *Skolars:* Dave Ellison.
Penalty count: 11-9; **Half-time:** 2-12;
Referee: Andrew Smith; **Attendance:** 320 *(at Recreation Ground, Whitehaven).*

DEWSBURY RAMS 18 CARCASSONNE 6

RAMS: 3 Lee Lingard; 15 Bryn Powell; 18 Chris Spurr; 22 Kane Epati; 16 Austin Buchanan; 6 Ryan Smith; 19 Liam Finn; 27 Chris Grice; 9 Mike Emmett; 20 Rob Spicer; 17 Alex Bretherton; 21 Andrew Bostock; 13 Pat Walker. Subs (all used): 33 James Walker; 28 Liam Crawley; 26 Jake Wilson; 7 Gareth Greenwood.
Tries: Lingard (10), Epati (28, 34); **Goals:** P Walker 3/5.
CARCASSONNE: 1 Gregory Tiquet; 2 Thomas Barrau; 3 Sebastian Azema; 4 Saia Makisi; 5 Jeremy Guiraud; 6 Amar Sabri; 7 Francois Jovani; 8 Gareth Dean; 9 Matthieu Alberola; 10 Romain Gagliazzo; 11 Teddy Sadaoui; 12 David Delpoux; 13 Frederic Banquet. Subs (all used): 14 Tyrone Pau; 15 Arnaud Vital; 16 Florent Rouanet; 17 Nicolas De Martini.
Try: Jovani (56); **Goals:** Banquet 1/1.
Rugby Leaguer & League Express Men of the Match: *Rams:* Alex Bretherton; *Carcassonne:* Frederic Banquet.
Penalty count: 12-8; **Half-time:** 16-0;
Referee: Robert Hicks; **Attendance:** 998.

FEATHERSTONE ROVERS 94 THE ARMY 2

ROVERS: 3 Ian Hardman; 2 Waine Pryce; 17 Joe Hirst; 1 Tom Saxton; 34 Sam Smeaton; 6 Iestyn Harris; 7 Andy Kain; 8 Tony Tonks; 16 Joe McLocklan; 10 Stuart Dickens; 11 Matty Dale; 18 Tim Spears; 12 Jamie Field. Subs (all used): 14 Tom Haughey; 9 Jack Lee; 15 James Houston; 19 Sean Hesketh.
Tries: Smeaton (4, 40), A Kain (8, 27, 33, 49), Saxton (14), Hirst (17, 29), Tonks (21), Field (24), Pryce (36, 73), Lee (52, 79), Hesketh (62), Dale (64, 76);
Goals: A Kain 1/1, Dickens 6/8, Harris 4/9.
THE ARMY: 1 Tim Taman; 2 Sam Kataki; 3 Siona Tunisau; 4 Mosese Matau; 5 Andre Swinjen; 6 Paul Riley; 7 Rob Smart; 8 Inoke Veikune; 9 Tim Brewer; 10 Bruce Francis; 11 Dave Nunnerley; 12 Ben Taylor; 13 Darrell Winn. Subs (all used): 14 Andy Parkin; 15 Ryan Taylor; 16 Gary Debaughn; 17 Anthony Cowburn.
Goals: Smart 1/1.
Rugby Leaguer & League Express Men of the Match: *Rovers:* Andy Kain; *The Army:* Inoke Veikune.
Penalty count: 13-5; **Half-time:** 56-2;
Referee: Warren Turley; **Attendance:** 1,763.

GATESHEAD THUNDER 42 WHITEHAVEN 38

THUNDER: 1 Ben McAlpine; 18 Robin Peers; 3 Kevin Neighbour; 31 Joe Arundel; 5 Stewart Sanderson; 6 Neil Thorman; 7 Luke Branighan; 10 Tabua Cakacaka; 9 Andrew Henderson; 8 Jason Payne; 22 Jamie Russo; 32 James Cording; 12 Michael Knowles. Subs (all used): 17 Chris Parker; 23 Jonny Scott; 29 Rhys Clarke; 33 Jonny Walker.
Tries: Branighan (4, 58), Henderson (31, 47), Neighbour (44), Sanderson (75, 78); **Goals:** Knowles 7/8.
On report: Brawl (80).
WHITEHAVEN: 1 Craig Benson; 5 Ade Adebisi; 3 Rob Jackson; 4 Derry Eilbeck; 2 Craig Calvert; 6 Carl Rudd; 24 Gregg McNally; 21 Taani Lavulavu; 25 Jamie Theohaurus; 10 Karl Edmondson; 12 Spencer Miller; 15 Andy Gorski; 7 Leroy Joe. Subs (all used): 8 Marc Jackson; 19 Karl Amor; 31 Dexter Miller; 13 Scott McAvoy.
Tries: Theohaurus (13), Adebisi (17, 65), Benson (21, 70), McNally (24, 68), Eilbeck (56);
Goals: McNally 3/6, Rudd 0/2.
Dismissal: Lavulavu (80) - high tackle on Payne.
On report: Brawl (80).
Rugby Leaguer & League Express Men of the Match: *Thunder:* Michael Knowles; *Whitehaven:* Jamie Theohaurus.
Penalty count: 12-9; **Half-time:** 14-20;
Referee: Dave Merrick; **Attendance:** 501.

HALIFAX 80 LOUGHBOROUGH UNIVERSITY 16

HALIFAX: 1 Miles Greenwood; 2 Lee Patterson; 6 Dwayne Barker; 15 Mark Roberts; 23 Rob Worrincy; 19 Mick Govin; 9 Sean Penkywicz; 10 Dana Wilson; 13 Bob Beswick; 22 David Wrench; 11 David Larder; 12 Paul Smith; 4 Shad Royston. Subs (all used): 7 Ben Black; 14 Mark Gleeson; 16 Said Tamghart; 17 Frank Watene.
Tries: Barker (3, 56), Wrench (6), Greenwood (13, 61), Beswick (22), Gleeson (29, 37), Tamghart (45, 54), Worrincy (65), Penkywicz (68), Black (71), Patterson (79); **Goals:** Govin 6/6, Black 5/7, Patterson 1/1.
LOUGHBOROUGH: 1 Luke Dexter; 2 Johnny Farmer; 3 Jon Riley; 4 Mark Edwards; 5 Harry Mostyn; 6 Dan Kerr; 7 Andy Killerby; 8 Dan Ljazouli; 9 Jimmy Davis; 10 Ian Keevil; 11 Steve Hall; 12 Tom Howley; 13 Aiden Pritchard. Subs (all used): 14 Simon Greenwood; 15 Nick Van Buerren; 16 Hamish Locke; 17 Ed Branch.
Tries: Killerby (19, 32), Mostyn (42); **Goals:** Kerr 2/3.
Rugby Leaguer & League Express Men of the Match: *Halifax:* Mark Gleeson; *Loughborough:* Aiden Pritchard.
Penalty count: 1-4; **Half-time:** 36-10;
Referee: Tim Roby; **Attendance:** 1,138.

LEIGH CENTURIONS 82 LOKOMOTIV MOSCOW 6

CENTURIONS: 1 Stuart Donlan; 22 Jamie Smith; 18 Sam Reay; 3 Steve Maden; 14 Ian Mort; 23 Martyn Ridyard; 7 Ian Watson; 8 Andy Hobson; 9 Dave McConnell; 36 Danny Meekin; 15 Adam Higson; 37 Kurt Haggerty; 40 Anthony Rourke. Subs (all used): 39 Jamie Durbin; 38 Lee Wingfield; 4 Anthony Stewart; 16 Chris Hill.
Tries: Donlan (2), Rourke (5), Meekin (14), Higson (19), Reay (23, 34, 62), J Smith (29, 68), Ridyard (39), Haggerty (48), Mort (52, 65), Hobson (57), Wingfield (77); **Goals:** Mort 11/15.
LOKOMOTIV: 1 Valentin Baskakov; 2 Nikolay Zagoskin; 3 Sergey Dobrynin; 4 Andrey Koltykhov; 5 Alexander Klebanov; 6 Viktor Nechaev; 7 Mikhail Nisiforov; 8 Evgeny Bozhukov; 9 Roman Ovchinnikov; 10 Alexander Lysenkov; 11 Sergey Sidorov; 12 Georgy Vinogradov; 13 Oleg Smirnov. Subs (all used): 14 Denis Korolev; 15 Andrey Medvedev; 16 Sergey Matveev; 17 Denis Meshkov.
Try: Meshkov (42); **Goals:** Koltykhov 1/1.
Rugby Leaguer & League Express Men of the Match: *Centurions:* Danny Meekin; *Lokomotiv:* Roman Ovchinnikov.
Penalty count: 10-5; **Half-time:** 46-0;
Referee: James Child; **Attendance:** 1,278.

OLDHAM 26 SHARLSTON ROVERS 8

OLDHAM: 1 Paul O'Connor; 21 Lucas Onyango; 3 Danny Halliwell; 19 Craig Littler; 5 Lee Greenwood; 6 James Coyle; 7 Thomas Coyle; 25 Luke Menzies; 9 Gary Sykes; 14 Richard Mervill; 11 Dave Allen; 12 Tommy Goulden; 23 Chris Baines. Subs (all used): 10 Jamie I'Anson; 13 Rob Roberts; 16 Wayne Kerr; 18 Neil Roden.
Tries: Onyango (9, 79), J Coyle (30), N Roden (52), Roberts (55); **Goals:** Halliwell 3/5.
ROVERS: 1 Lee Maskill; 2 Dale Ferris; 3 Gareth Davies; 4 Dale Potter; 5 Brad Chatfield; 6 Thomas Wandless; 7 Lee Bettinson; 8 James Lockwood; 9 Carl Saville; 10 Bart Thompson; 11 Sean Emblem; 12 Jonathan Waddle; 13 Craig Miles. Subs (all used): 14 Andy Booth; 15 Tommy Crowther; 16 Chris Bingham; 17 Carl Spencer.
Try: Davies (33); **Goals:** Ferris 2/2.
Rugby Leaguer & League Express Men of the Match: *Oldham:* Dave Allen; *Rovers:* James Lockwood.
Penalty count: 11-16; **Half-time:** 12-8;
Referee: Brandon Robinson; **Attendance:** 800.

Challenge Cup 2009 - Round by Round

PILKINGTON RECS 24 BATLEY BULLDOGS 34

PILKINGTON: 1 Mark Ashton; 2 Mark Rigby; 3 Nigel Pratt; 4 Andy Lyons; 5 James Lacey; 6 Ryan Rogers; 7 Andy Burns; 8 Neil Morris; 9 Peter Cahalin; 10 Richard Rafferty; 11 John Rees; 12 Ricky Shaw; 13 Steve Rawsthorne. Subs (all used): 14 Danny Lynch; 15 Danny Mason; 16 Andy Parr; 17 Mike Loughlin.
Tries: Pratt (10), Ashton (30, 36, 49);
Goals: Rawsthorne 4/4.
BULLDOGS: 1 Ian Preece; 18 Jermaine McGilvary; 3 Dale Cardoza; 4 Danny Maun; 22 Nathan Brown; 6 Mark Barlow; 7 Paul Mennell; 10 Luke Stenchion; 9 Kris Lythe; 8 Byron Smith; 23 Chris Buttery; 11 Kevin Crouthers; 14 John Gallagher. Subs (all used): 13 Ashley Lindsay; 35 Jack Watson; 17 Craig Potter; 19 George Flanagan.
Tries: Lythe (4, 73), Crouthers (16), Maun (20), Buttery (25), Cardoza (39), Preece (45);
Goals: Barlow 2/6, Flanagan 1/1.
Rugby Leaguer & League Express Men of the Match: *Pilkington:* Steve Rawsthorne; *Bulldogs:* Chris Buttery.
Penalty count: 10-9; **Half-time:** 18-22;
Referee: Gareth Evans; **Attendance:** 709
(at GPW Recruitment Stadium, St Helens).

SHEFFIELD EAGLES 22 TOULOUSE OLYMPIQUE 6

EAGLES: 1 Jonny Woodcock; 28 Damian Gibson; 3 Menzie Yere; 23 Tangi Ropati; 5 Ashley Thackeray; 6 Brendon Lindsay; 19 Kyle Wood; 8 Jack Howieson; 20 Matty Brooks; 10 Mitchell Stringer; 11 Alex Szostak; 12 Ged Corcoran; 13 Dane McDonald. Subs (all used): 4 Mike Roby; 17 Tom Buckenham; 22 Ryan Hepworth; 15 Sam Barlow.
Tries: Barlow (44), Lindsay (50), Gibson (57), Woodcock (67); **Goals:** Woodcock 3/4.
Sin bin: Hepworth (47) - retaliation.
OLYMPIQUE: 6 Constant Villegas; 2 Sebastien Payen; 3 Sebastien Planas; 4 Damien Couturier; 5 Joris Canton; 19 Nicholas Delgal; 7 Nathan Wynn; 8 Brendan Worth; 9 Martin Mitchell; 10 Mathieu Griffi; 11 Tim Wynn; 12 Eric Anselme; 20 Sylvain Houles. Subs (all used): 14 Anton Maria; 16 Olivier Pramil; 18 Adrien Viala; 22 Nicholas Faure.
Try: Couturier (29); **Goals:** N Wynn 1/1.
Dismissal: Mitchell (47) - spear tackle on Hepworth.
Sin bin: Pramil (27) - interference.
Rugby Leaguer & League Express Men of the Match: *Eagles:* Kyle Wood; *Olympique:* Constant Villegas.
Penalty count: 11-4; **Half-time:** 0-6;
Referee: Jamie Leahy; **Attendance:** 1,554.

YORK CITY KNIGHTS 50 WIGAN ST PATRICKS 10

CITY KNIGHTS: 4 David Clayton; 34 Wayne McHugh; 3 John Oakes; 28 Mike Mitchell; 20 Adam Jones; 6 Adam Mitchell; 27 Danny Grimshaw; 17 Scott Woodcock; 9 Paul Hughes; 15 Chris Clough; 11 Rob Kelly; 13 Richard Knight; 21 David March. Subs (all used): 14 Tom Hodgson; 8 Danny Ekis; 29 Mark Applegarth; 36 Jack Stearman.
Tries: McHugh (1), Grimshaw (5), Oakes (8, 53), Woodcock (17), Clough (20), Clayton (42), M Mitchell (48), Hodgson (59), Kelly (78); **Goals:** A Mitchell 5/10.
On report: Hodgson (70) - alleged high tackle.
Sin bin: D March (42) - dissent.
ST PATRICKS: 1 Steven Simm; 2 Ian Schofield; 3 Damien Charnock; 4 Steven Bennett; 5 Sean O'Neill; 6 Ryan Baxter; 7 Anthony Atherton; 8 Lee Peacock; 9 Gary Phillips; 10 Dave Hales; 11 Tony Suffolk; 12 Richard Owen; 13 Mick Daniels. Subs (all used): 14 Reece Sedgwick; 15 Andy Rayburn; 16 Sean Selby; 17 Anthony Gallear.
Tries: Bennett (40), Charnock (64); **Goals:** Schofield 1/2.
Sin bin: Atherton (16) - holding down.
Rugby Leaguer & League Express Men of the Match: *City Knights:* Adam Mitchell; *St Patricks:* Gary Phillips.
Penalty count: 12-7; **Half-time:** 26-6;
Referee: Tony Mahar; **Attendance:** 936.

Saturday 14th March 2009

KELLS 12 HUNSLET HAWKS 22

KELLS: 1 Carl Sice; 2 Scott Nichol; 3 Steve McGrady; 4 Scott Lofthouse; 5 Ben Ferguson; 6 Greg Lofthouse; 7 Steve Kirkbride; 8 Dave Lowrey; 9 Kevin Agnew; 10 Paul Cullnean; 11 Scott Farmer; 12 Barry Boyd; 13 Tony Burns. Subs (all used): 14 Ross Gainford; 15 Carl Schofield; 16 Dave Dickinson; 17 Sean Flanagan.
Tries: Sice (47, 79); **Goals:** Burns 2/2.
HAWKS: 3 Tom Sheldrake; 25 Michael Mark; 18 Ayden Faal; 4 Michael Brown; 5 John Richardson; 6 Darren Robinson; 27 Gareth Firm; 8 Joe Helme; 24 Charlie Wabo; 17 Steve Brook; 26 Nicko Slain; 22 Scott Watson; 14 Chris Redfearn. Subs (all used): 9 Richard Chapman; 28 Steve Dooler; 31 Tony Williams; 12 Jason Hart.
Tries: Helme (8), Robinson (36), Watson (39), Williams (67); **Goals:** Robinson 3/4.
Rugby Leaguer & League Express Men of the Match: *Kells:* Steve Kirkbride; *Hawks:* Richard Chapman.
Penalty count: 9-10; **Half-time:** 0-18;
Referee: Matthew Kidd; **Attendance:** 251
(at Recreation Ground, Whitehaven).

ROUND 4

Friday 3rd April 2009

SWINTON LIONS 22 ROCHDALE HORNETS 28

LIONS: 7 Richie Hawkyard; 1 Wayne English; 3 Dave Hull; 29 Carl Sneyd; 22 Darren Bamford; 6 Graham Holroyd; 15 Gary Hulse; 8 Paul Southern; 9 Phil Wood; 10 Bruce Johnson; 11 Mike Wainwright; 17 Tommy Grundy; 14 Craig Ashall. Subs (all used): 16 Alex McClurg; 19 Neil Rigby; 28 Dave Newton; 20 Adam Bibey.
Tries: D Hull (5), Southern (21), Sneyd (53);
Goals: Sneyd 5/6.
Sin bin: Holroyd (32) - holding down.
HORNETS: 19 Craig Johnson; 2 John Gillam; 3 Mick Fogerty; 4 Casey Mayberry; 26 Leroy Rivett; 6 Martin Ainscough; 24 Chris Hough; 11 Dave Cunliffe; 23 Liam Grundy; 10 Paul Raftrey; 25 Dayne Donoghue; 12 Ian Sinfield; 16 Mark Brocklehurst. Subs (all used): 13 Wayne Corcoran; 15 Martin McLoughlin; 17 Andrew Isherwood; 8 David Best.
Tries: Rivett (24), McLoughlin (33), Hough (44), Brocklehurst (64), Isherwood (73);
Goals: Hough 3/4, Corcoran 1/1.
Sin bin: Best (38) - holding down.
Rugby Leaguer & League Express Men of the Match: *Lions:* Bruce Johnson; *Hornets:* Martin Ainscough.
Penalty count: 13-11; **Half-time:** 16-10;
Referee: Peter Brooke; **Attendance:** 525.

HALIFAX 20 WIDNES VIKINGS 16

HALIFAX: 4 Shad Royston; 1 Miles Greenwood; 2 Lee Patterson; 5 James Haley; 23 Rob Worrincy; 13 Bob Beswick; 7 Ben Black; 21 Neil Cherryholme; 19 Mick Govin; 22 David Wrench; 11 David Larder; 15 Mark Roberts; 12 Paul Smith. Subs (all used): 9 Sean Penkywicz; 10 Dana Wilson; 6 Dwayne Barker; 17 Frank Watene.
Tries: Black (10), Royston (48), Roberts (59);
Goals: Govin 4/4.
VIKINGS: 1 Loz Wildbore; 22 Paddy Flynn; 23 Shane Grady; 3 Richard Varkulis; 2 Dean Gaskell; 6 Anthony Thackeray; 7 James Webster; 19 Michael Ostick; 9 Mark Smith; 10 Jim Gannon; 12 Richard Fletcher; 11 Lee Doran; 14 John Duffy. Subs (all used): 20 Sam Thompson; 16 Gavin Dodd; 17 Ben Kavanagh; 24 Josh Simm.
Tries: Gannon (33), Thackeray (43);
Goals: Fletcher 1/1, Dodd 3/3.
Rugby Leaguer & League Express Men of the Match: *Halifax:* David Larder; *Vikings:* Loz Wildbore.
Penalty count: 9-10; **Half-time:** 6-8;
Referee: Richard Silverwood; **Attendance:** 3,204.

HULL KINGSTON ROVERS 32 CELTIC CRUSADERS 6

ROVERS: 1 Shaun Briscoe (C); 2 Peter Fox; 19 Kris Welham; 4 Jake Webster; 5 Liam Colbon; 6 Paul Cooke; 7 Michael Dobson; 8 Nick Fozzard; 9 Ben Fisher; 24 Rhys Lovegrove; 11 Clint Newton; 12 Ben Galea; 13 Scott Murrell. Subs (all used): 15 Daniel Fitzhenry; 17 Makali Aizue; 14 Stanley Gene; 10 David Mills.
Tries: Welham (8), Newton (29), Fitzhenry (46), Colbon (72), Webster (78); **Goals:** Dobson 6/6.
CRUSADERS: 1 Tony Duggan; 2 Luke Dyer; 3 Josh Hannay; 4 Mark Dalle Cort; 5 Anthony Blackwood; 6 Damien Quinn; 9 Lincoln Withers; 8 Ryan O'Hara; 15 Peter Lupton; 10 Mark Bryant; 11 Adam Peek (C); 19 Jason Chan; 13 Marshall Chalk. Subs (all used): 23 Neil Budworth; 22 Steve Tyrer (D); 20 David Tangata-Toa; 17 Jordan James.
Try: Tangata-Toa (61); **Goals:** Hannay 1/1.
Rugby Leaguer & League Express Men of the Match: *Rovers:* Jake Webster; *Crusaders:* Damien Quinn.
Penalty count: 9-8; **Half-time:** 12-0;
Referee: Thierry Alibert; **Attendance:** 7,104.

SHEFFIELD EAGLES 28 DEWSBURY RAMS 18

EAGLES: 1 Jonny Woodcock; 28 Damian Gibson; 3 Menzie Yere; 23 Tangi Ropati; 5 Ashley Thackeray; 6 Brendon Lindsay; 19 Kyle Wood; 8 Jack Howieson; 20 Matty Brooks; 10 Mitchell Stringer; 11 Alex Szostak; 12 Ged Corcoran; 13 Dane McDonald. Subs (all used): 14 Andy Boothroyd; 9 Grant Edwards; 27 Tommy Trayler; 22 Ryan Hepworth.
Tries: Thackeray (18), McDonald (33), Woodcock (58), Brooks (63), Wood (70), Yere (73); **Goals:** Woodcock 2/6.
RAMS: 3 Lee Lingard; 15 Bryn Powell; 18 Chris Spurr; 17 Alex Bretherton; 16 Austin Buchanan; 13 Pat Walker; 19 Liam Finn; 23 Keegan Hirst; 9 Mike Emmett; 11 Adam Robinson; 20 Rob Spicer; 21 Andrew Bostock; 35 Adam Hayes. Subs (all used): 33 James Walker; 28 Liam Crawley; 8 Jimmy Elston; 6 Ryan Smith.
Tries: Bretherton (24), Powell (49); **Goals:** P Walker 5/6.
Rugby Leaguer & League Express Men of the Match: *Eagles:* Kyle Wood; *Rams:* Alex Bretherton.
Penalty count: 6-6; **Half-time:** 8-12;
Referee: Robert Hicks; **Attendance:** 597.

WAKEFIELD TRINITY WILDCATS 54 LEIGH CENTURIONS 0

WILDCATS: 1 Matt Blaymire; 2 Damien Blanch; 19 Sean Gleeson; 4 Ryan Atkins; 27 Aaron Murphy; 13 Scott Grix; 7 Danny Brough; 12 Oliver Wilkes; 14 Sam Obst; 11 Steve Snitch; 29 Jay Pitts; 24 Dale Ferguson; 8 Jason Demetriou (C). Subs (all used): 28 Kyle Bibb; 17 Kevin Henderson; 20 Tevita Leo-Latu; 10 Danny Sculthorpe.
Tries: Brough (7), Blaymire (9, 44), Murphy (17, 34), Blanch (28), Obst (58, 60), Sculthorpe (71), Leo-Latu (74); **Goals:** Brough 7/10.
CENTURIONS: 14 Ian Mort; 2 David Alstead; 18 Sam Reay; 1 Stuart Donlan; 22 Jamie Smith; 40 Kurt Haggerty; 7 Ian Watson; 8 Andy Hobson; 9 Dave McConnell; 16 Chris Hill; 29 Lee Wingfield; 12 James Taylor; 27 Anthony Rourke. Subs (all used): 37 Macgraff Leuluai; 10 Mike Morrison; 28 Danny Meekin; 4 Anthony Stewart.
Rugby Leaguer & League Express Men of the Match: *Wildcats:* Sam Obst; *Centurions:* Stuart Donlan.
Penalty count: 6-5; **Half-time:** 26-0;
Referee: Gareth Hewer; **Attendance:** 2,637.

Saturday 4th April 2009

WARRINGTON WOLVES 56 YORK CITY KNIGHTS 10

WOLVES: 23 Chris Hicks; 2 Paul Johnson; 13 Vinnie Anderson; 20 Simon Grix; 4 Matt King; 25 Chris Bridge; 6 Lee Briers (C); 16 Garreth Carvell; 14 Mick Higham; 15 Paul Wood; 22 Lee Mitchell; 12 Ben Westwood; 24 Ben Harrison. Subs (all used): 10 Paul Rauhihi; 18 Michael Cooper; 11 Louis Anderson; 9 Jon Clarke.
Tries: Grix (2), V Anderson (10, 73), Harrison (17), Westwood (26), Cooper (39), Bridge (49), Briers (70), L Anderson (79), Johnson (80); **Goals:** Hicks 8/10.
On report: Alleged biting incident (63) on Clough; Brawl (65).
CITY KNIGHTS: 1 Danny Ratcliffe; 3 John Oakes; 28 Mike Mitchell; 12 Tom Haberecht; 34 Wayne McHugh; 27 Danny Grimshaw; 7 Paul March; 8 Danny Ekis; 9 Paul Hughes; 10 Adam Sullivan; 11 Rob Kelly; 13 Richard Knight; 21 David March. Subs (all used): 14 Tom Hodgson; 29 Mark Applegarth; 15 Chris Clough; 17 Scott Woodcock.
Tries: Ratcliffe (6), Hughes (23); **Goals:** Knight 1/2.
Dismissal: Ekis (65) – use of the elbow on L Anderson.
On report: Brawl (65).
Rugby Leaguer & League Express Men of the Match: *Wolves:* Garreth Carvell; *City Knights:* Adam Sullivan.
Penalty count: 9-11; **Half-time:** 28-10;
Referee: James Child; **Attendance:** 4,709.

HARLEQUINS 16 HUDDERSFIELD GIANTS 42

HARLEQUINS: 2 Jon Wells; 1 Chris Melling; 3 Matt Gafa; 4 David Howell; 5 Will Sharp; 6 Luke Dorn; 7 Danny Orr; 8 Karl Temata; 9 Chad Randall; 17 Danny Ward; 12 Chad Robinson; 14 Tony Clubb; 13 Rob Purdham (C). Subs (all used): 10 Louie McCarthy-Scarsbrook; 19 Jason Golden; 23 Daniel Heckenberg; 11 Luke Williamson.
Tries: Clubb (20), Temata (57), Howell (62);
Goals: Orr 2/3.
GIANTS: 1 Brett Hodgson (C); 2 Martin Aspinwall; 19 Michael Lawrence; 4 Paul Whatuira; 5 David Hodgson; 3 Kevin Brown; 7 Luke Robinson; 15 Paul Jackson; 20 Scott Moore; 16 Keith Mason; 11 Jamahl Lolesi; 13 Stephen Wild; 12 Andy Raleigh. Subs (all used): 8 Eorl Crabtree; 10 Darrell Griffin; 18 Danny Kirmond; 24 Shaun Lunt.
Tries: Mason (6), Robinson (24, 54), D Hodgson (28, 42), Wild (40), Whatuira (72), B Hodgson (77);
Goals: B Hodgson 4/7, D Hodgson 1/1.
Rugby Leaguer & League Express Men of the Match: *Harlequins:* Tony Clubb; *Giants:* Brett Hodgson.
Penalty count: 5-5; **Half-time:** 6-24;
Referee: Ben Thaler; **Attendance:** 1,973.

Sunday 5th April 2009

BATLEY BULLDOGS 28 HUNSLET HAWKS 24

BULLDOGS: 1 Ian Preece; 5 John Campbell; 28 Daryl Cardiss; 4 Danny Maun; 18 Jermaine McGilvary; 6 Mark Barlow; 7 Paul Mennell; 35 Jack Watson; 14 John Gallagher; 10 Luke Stenchion; 11 Kevin Crouthers; 17 Craig Potter; 12 Mark Toohey. Subs (all used): 19 George Flanagan; 20 David Tootill; 16 Jon Simpson; 13 Ashley Lindsay.
Tries: Flanagan (25, 38, 79), McGilvary (37), Watson (55); **Goals:** Flanagan 3/4, Mennell 1/1.
Sin bin: Mennell (18) - fighting.
HAWKS: 3 Tom Sheldrake; 5 John Richardson; 4 Michael Brown; 18 Ayden Faal; 25 Michael Mark; 28 Steve Dooler; 31 Tony Williams; 17 Steve Brook; 6 Darren Robinson; 26 Nicko Slain; 14 Chris Redfearn; 22 Scott Watson; 9 Richard Chapman. Subs (all used): 27 Gareth Firm; 8 Joe Helme; 24 Charlie Wabo; 19 Ben Walkin.
Tries: Robinson (5), Slain (11), Firm (45), Watson (68);
Goals: Robinson 4/4.
Sin bin: Chapman (18) – fighting, (80) - high tackle on Barlow.
Rugby Leaguer & League Express Men of the Match: *Bulldogs:* George Flanagan; *Hawks:* Gareth Firm.
Penalty count: 11-8; **Half-time:** 16-12;
Referee: Dave Merrick; **Attendance:** 633.

FEATHERSTONE ROVERS 54 WATH BROW HORNETS 16

ROVERS: 1 Tom Saxton; 2 Waine Pryce; 3 Ian Hardman; 4 Andy Kirk; 5 Jon Steel; 6 Iestyn Harris; 7 Andy Kain; 11 Matty Dale; 16 Joe McLocklan; 10 Stuart Dickens; 19 Sean Hesketh; 22 Matt Handforth; 12 Jamie Field. Subs (all used): 24 Jon Fallon; 8 Tony Tonks; 23 Gareth Swift; 14 Tom Haughey.
Tries: McLocklan (6, 67), A Kain (10, 21), Saxton (12), Steel (26, 28, 57), Kirk (41), Haughey (44);
Goals: McLocklan 2/2, Harris 1/3, Dickens 4/5.
Sin bin: Tonks (77) - fighting.
HORNETS: 1 Ryan Amor; 2 Glen Riley; 3 Fran King; 4 Gary Elliot; 5 Jamie Devine; 6 Craig Johnstone; 7 Andrew Hocking; 8 David Pettit; 9 Ryan Robb; 10 Dave Currie; 11 Mickey McAllister; 12 Kevin Thompson; 13 Scott Teare. Subs (all used): 14 David Byers; 15 James McClennan; 16 Phil Coyles; 17 Mark Cox.
Tries: Pettit (61), Thompson (64), King (72);
Goals: Robb 2/3.
Sin bin: Cox (77) - fighting.
Rugby Leaguer & League Express Men of the Match: *Rovers:* Jon Steel; *Hornets:* David Pettit.
Penalty count: 14-13; **Half-time:** 38-0;
Referee: Greg Dolan; **Attendance:** 1,180.

OLDHAM 60 LEZIGNAN 30

OLDHAM: 1 Paul O'Connor; 2 Andy Ballard; 19 Craig Littler; 24 Marcus St Hilaire; 21 Lucas Onyango; 6 James Coyle; 7 Thomas Coyle; 25 Luke Menzies; 9 Gary Sykes; 14 Richard Mervill; 11 Dave Allen; 23 Chris Baines; 22 Phil Joseph. Subs (all used): 10 Jamie I'Anson; 4 Paul Reilly; 17 Craig Robinson; 18 Neil Roden.
Tries: Onyango (8, 13, 45), St Hilaire (10, 16), Ballard (26, 74), T Coyle (29), Joseph (51), Mervill (68);
Goals: Ballard 10/11.
Sin bin: O'Connor (38) - holding down.
LEZIGNAN: 1 Jarred Taylor; 27 Aurelien Bourrel; 3 Luke Hession; 12 David Romero; 4 Cedric Bringuier; 13 Aurelien Cologni; 6 Nicolas Munoz; 8 Chris Beattie; 7 James Wynne; 10 Adel Fellous; 11 Phillippe Laurent; 30 Charly Clottes; 23 Alistair Brown. Subs (all used): 25 Cedric Lacans; 26 Thibault Ancely; 19 Yoan Tisseyre; 21 Franck Rovira.
Tries: Laurent (22), Beattie (32), Rovira (37, 40), Wynne (57); **Goals:** Munoz 5/5.
Sin bin: Taylor (10) - holding down.
Rugby Leaguer & League Express Men of the Match: *Oldham:* Thomas Coyle; *Lezignan:* James Wynne.
Penalty count: 9-8; **Half-time:** 34-24;
Referee: Ronnie Laughton; **Attendance:** 863.

CATALANS DRAGONS 40 BRADFORD BULLS 38

DRAGONS: 1 Clint Greenshields; 18 Vincent Duport; 3 Steven Bell; 15 Jean-Phillipe Baile; 5 Dimitri Pelo; 4 Adam Mogg; 6 Thomas Bosc; 23 Jason Ryles; 9 Casey McGuire; 10 Jerome Guisset; 12 Jason Croker; 16 Olivier Elima; 26 Greg Bird (C). Subs (all used): 17 Cyrille Gossard; 14 Dane Carlaw; 8 David Ferriol; 20 Kane Bentley.
Tries: Elima (48, 57), Greenshields (51), Bosc (53, 66), Baile (64), Gossard (72); **Goals:** Bosc 6/7.
BULLS: 1 Michael Platt; 2 Rikki Sheriffe; 3 Paul Sykes; 4 Chris Nero; 5 Semi Tadulala; 6 Ben Jeffries; 7 Paul Deacon (C); 8 Sam Burgess; 9 Terry Newton; 10 Andy Lynch; 11 Steve Menzies; 15 Matt Cook; 13 Jamie Langley. Subs (all used): 17 Nick Scruton; 16 Michael Worrincy; 19 Craig Kopczak; 20 Dave Halley.
Tries: Sykes (7), Sheriffe (9), Cook (20), Nero (22), Menzies (43), Tadulala (61), Halley (75, pen);
Goals: Deacon 5/7.
Rugby Leaguer & League Express Men of the Match: *Dragons:* Thomas Bosc; *Bulls:* Ben Jeffries.
Penalty count: 4-4; **Half-time:** 0-20;
Referee: Steve Ganson; **Attendance:** 6,450.

BARROW RAIDERS 20 WIGAN WARRIORS 32

RAIDERS: 1 Gary Broadbent; 3 Ian Bell; 26 Zebastian Luisi; 4 Liam Harrison; 5 James Nixon; 6 Liam Finch; 7 Liam Campbell; 8 Brett McDermott; 9 Andy Ellis; 16 Jamie Butler; 14 Paul Noone; 12 Martin Ostler; 11 Andrew Brocklehurst. Subs (all used): 15 Chris Young; 22 Ned Catic; 28 Nathan Mossop; 2 Mike Backhouse.
Tries: L Finch (10), Nixon (19), Campbell (49);
Goals: Noone 4/5.
WARRIORS: 2 Amos Roberts; 20 Karl Pryce; 12 Phil Bailey; 4 George Carmont; 28 Shaun Ainscough; 25 Sam Tomkins; 7 Thomas Leuluai; 19 Paul Prescott; 9 Mark Riddell; 10 Iafeta Palea'aesina; 14 Joel Tomkins; 16 Harrison Hansen; 13 Sean O'Loughlin (C). Subs (all used): 6 Tim Smith; 15 Andy Coley; 3 Darrell Goulding; 24 Lee Mossop.
Tries: Ainscough (6, 16, 28, 43), Carmont (38), Pryce (67), S Tomkins (73);
Goals: Riddell 1/4, Roberts 1/2, Pryce 0/1.
Rugby Leaguer & League Express Men of the Match: *Raiders:* Liam Finch; *Warriors:* Thomas Leuluai.
Penalty count: 11-9; **Half-time:** 14-20;
Referee: Jamie Leahy; **Attendance:** 6,275.

DONCASTER 18 GATESHEAD THUNDER 32

DONCASTER: 3 Andreas Bauer; 26 Gareth Carey; 19 Ryan Steen; 35 Wayne Opie; 5 Wayne Reittie; 6 Kyle Briggs; 7 Paul Handforth; 29 Matt Carbutt; 9 Craig Cook; 15 Mark Castle; 11 Peter Green; 17 Ross Divorty; 13 Josh Weeden. Subs (all used): 22 Andy Speake; 24 Jake Bassinder; 21 Gary Ellery; 27 Al Rounding.
Tries: Cook (3), Green (67), Carey (78);
Goals: Briggs 1/1, P Handforth 2/2.
THUNDER: 3 Kevin Neighbour; 18 Robin Peers; 1 Ben McAlpine; 4 Dylan Nash; 5 Stewart Sanderson; 6 Neil Thorman; 7 Luke Branighan; 8 Jason Payne; 9 Andrew Henderson; 17 Chris Parker; 29 Rhys Clarke; 12 Michael Knowles; 22 Jamie Russo. Subs (all used): 14 Ryan Clarke; 21 Ryan McBride; 23 Jonny Scott; 28 Mark Dack.
Tries: Knowles (10), Branighan (23, 30), Sanderson (36), Henderson (42), Nash (54);
Goals: Knowles 2/3, McAlpine 2/3.
Rugby Leaguer & League Express Men of the Match: *Doncaster:* Peter Green; *Thunder:* Luke Branighan.
Penalty count: 4-5; **Half-time:** 6-20;
Referee: Craig Halloran; **Attendance:** 458.

KEIGHLEY COUGARS 20 CASTLEFORD TIGERS 64

COUGARS: 1 George Rayner; 2 Sam Gardner; 21 Ryan Smith; 20 Daley Williams; 5 Gavin Duffy; 6 Jon Presley; 7 Danny Jones; 17 Scott Law; 9 James Feather; 11 Will Cartledge; 29 Karl Gunney; 4 Oliver Purseglove; 18 Greg Nicholson. Subs (all used): 14 Jamaine Wray; 22 Lee Mapals; 13 Carl Hughes; 10 Simon Bissell.
Tries: Presley (27), Mapals (53, 72, 80);
Goals: Jones 2/4.
Sin bin: Jones (62) - dissent.
TIGERS: 23 Ryan McGoldrick; 1 Richard Owen; 3 Michael Shenton; 4 James Evans; 2 Kirk Dixon; 6 Rangi Chase; 7 Brent Sherwin (C); 16 Chris Feather; 19 Kirk Netherton; 18 Nathan Massey; 10 Craig Huby; 25 Dean Widders; 13 Joe Westerman. Subs (all used): 15 Liam Higgins; 17 Ryan Boyle; 20 James Ford (D); 21 Sione Faumuina.
Tries: Shenton (12), Higgins (20), Dixon (23), Chase (43, 65, 67), Faumuina (46), Evans (48), Owen (57), Ford (62), Netherton (69); **Goals:** Dixon 10/11.
Rugby Leaguer & League Express Men of the Match: *Cougars:* Lee Mapals; *Tigers:* Rangi Chase.
Penalty count: 6-12; **Half-time:** 6-16;
Referee: Matthew Thomasson; **Attendance:** 3,255.

HULL FC 18 SALFORD CITY REDS 22

HULL: 24 Craig Hall; 2 Mark Calderwood; 17 Graeme Horne; 4 Kirk Yeaman; 21 Tom Briscoe; 6 Richard Horne; 7 Chris Thorman; 8 Ewan Dowes; 9 Shaun Berrigan; 10 Peter Cusack; 16 Willie Manu; 12 Danny Tickle; 11 Lee Radford (C). Subs (all used): 23 Tommy Lee; 15 Danny Washbrook; 27 Sam Moa; 19 Paul King.
Tries: Yeaman (3, 64), Briscoe (70); **Goals:** Tickle 3/3.
Sin bin: Calderwood (58) - interference.
CITY REDS: 1 Karl Fitzpatrick; 2 John Wilshere; 15 Stuart Littler; 14 Jordan Turner; 24 Dean McGilvray; 6 Jeremy Smith; 7 Richard Myler; 8 Ray Cashmere; 9 Malcolm Alker (C); 10 Craig Stapleton; 20 Luke Adamson; 12 Rob Parker; 13 Luke Swain. Subs (all used): 16 Phil Leuluai; 11 Ian Sibbit; 18 Lee Jewitt; 17 Robbie Paul.
Tries: Littler (10), Wilshere (47), Myler (77);
Goals: Wilshere 5/7.
Rugby Leaguer & League Express Men of the Match: *Hull:* Willie Manu; *City Reds:* Ray Cashmere.
Penalty count: 6-9; **Half-time:** 6-10;
Referee: Ian Smith; **Attendance:** 8,945.

LEEDS RHINOS 18 ST HELENS 22

RHINOS: 1 Brent Webb; 2 Scott Donald; 20 Ashley Gibson; 4 Keith Senior; 5 Ryan Hall; 6 Danny McGuire; 7 Rob Burrow; 8 Kylie Leuluai; 14 Matt Diskin; 10 Jamie Peacock; 11 Jamie Jones-Buchanan; 18 Carl Ablett; 13 Kevin Sinfield (C). Subs (all used): 19 Luke Burgess; 9 Danny Buderus; 12 Ali Lauitiiti; 17 Ian Kirke.
Tries: Jones-Buchanan (21), Webb (60), Senior (78);
Goals: Sinfield 3/3.
SAINTS: 1 Paul Wellens; 2 Ade Gardner; 3 Matt Gidley; 11 Lee Gilmour; 5 Francis Meli; 12 Jon Wilkin; 6 Leon Pryce; 10 James Graham; 9 Keiron Cunningham (C); 15 Bryn Hargreaves; 16 Tony Puletua; 13 Chris Flannery; 17 Paul Clough. Subs (all used): 8 Jason Cayless; 14 James Roby; 23 Maurie Fa'asavalu; 28 Matty Ashurst.
Tries: Gardner (14), Roby (27), Wellens (51), Gidley (55); **Goals:** Wellens 3/6.
Rugby Leaguer & League Express Men of the Match: *Rhinos:* Brent Webb; *Saints:* Jon Wilkin.
Penalty count: 8-9; **Half-time:** 6-10;
Referee: Phil Bentham; **Attendance:** 17,689.

ROUND 5

Saturday 9th May 2009

WAKEFIELD TRINITY WILDCATS 17 WIGAN WARRIORS 28

WILDCATS: 1 Matt Blaymire; 13 Scott Grix; 3 Tony Martin; 4 Ryan Atkins; 5 Matt Petersen; 14 Sam Obst; 7 Danny Brough; 12 Oliver Wilkes; 20 Tevita Leo-Latu; 25 Richard Moore; 11 Steve Snitch; 29 Jay Pitts; 8 Jason Demetriou (C). Subs (all used): 9 Brad Drew; 28 Kyle Bibb; 10 Danny Sculthorpe; 18 Frank Winterstein (D).
Tries: Demetriou (4), Leo-Latu (6), Martin (52);
Goals: Brough 2/3; **Field goal:** Brough (30).
WARRIORS: 21 Cameron Phelps; 2 Amos Roberts; 22 Martin Gleeson; 4 George Carmont; 5 Pat Richards; 6 Tim Smith; 7 Thomas Leuluai; 8 Stuart Fielden; 17 Michael McIlorum; 15 Andy Coley; 11 Gareth Hock; 12 Phil Bailey; 13 Sean O'Loughlin (C). Subs (all used): 10 Iafeta Palea'aesina; 14 Joel Tomkins; 19 Paul Prescott; 25 Sam Tomkins.
Tries: Carmont (18), McIlorum (25), Phelps (33), Fielden (65), S Tomkins (75); **Goals:** Richards 4/6.
Rugby Leaguer & League Express Men of the Match: *Wildcats:* Ryan Atkins; *Warriors:* Andy Coley.
Penalty count: 9-6; **Half-time:** 11-16;
Referee: Phil Bentham; **Attendance:** 4,883.

GATESHEAD THUNDER 34 OLDHAM 16

THUNDER: 5 Stewart Sanderson; 18 Robin Peers; 4 Dylan Nash; 1 Ben McAlpine; 26 Crawford Matthews; 6 Neil Thorman; 7 Luke Branighan; 17 Chris Parker; 9 Andrew Henderson; 10 Tabua Cakacaka; 32 James Cording; 12 Michael Knowles; 14 Ryan Clarke. Subs (all used): 33 Sam Crowther; 21 Ryan McBride; 15 Matt Barron; 29 Rhys Clarke.
Tries: Knowles (25), Branighan (46, 73), Barron (50), Sanderson (55), McAlpine (59); **Goals:** Knowles 5/7.
OLDHAM: 1 Paul O'Connor; 2 Andy Ballard; 3 Danny Halliwell; 24 Marcus St Hilaire; 21 Lucas Onyango; 6 James Coyle; 7 Thomas Coyle; 8 Paul Highton; 29 Steve Gibbons; 15 Jason Boults; 12 Tommy Goulden; 11 Dave Allen; 13 Rob Roberts. Subs (all used): 10 Jamie I'Anson; 14 Richard Mervill; 18 Neil Roden; 23 Chris Baines.
Tries: Goulden (13), Halliwell (62), Allen (65);
Goals: Ballard 2/3.
Rugby Leaguer & League Express Men of the Match: *Thunder:* Luke Branighan; *Oldham:* Dave Allen.
Penalty count: 10-9; **Half-time:** 4-6;
Referee: James Child;
Attendance: 929 *(at Northern Echo Arena, Darlington).*

CASTLEFORD TIGERS 35 HALIFAX 34
(after golden point extra time)

TIGERS: 23 Ryan McGoldrick (C); 2 Kirk Dixon; 3 Michael Shenton; 4 James Evans; 5 Michael Wainwright; 6 Rangi Chase; 7 Brent Sherwin; 8 Mitchell Sargent; 14 Stuart Jones; 17 Ryan Boyle; 11 Brett Ferres; 21 Sione Faumuina; 13 Joe Westerman. Subs (all used): 12 Ryan Clayton; 15 Liam Higgins; 16 Chris Feather; 20 James Ford.
Tries: McGoldrick (19, 57), Evans (26), Shenton (37), Dixon (49), Chase (53), Sherwin (77);
Goals: Dixon 2/5, Sherwin 1/2; **Field goal:** Sherwin (81).
HALIFAX: 1 Miles Greenwood; 2 Lee Patterson; 4 Shad Royston; 6 Dwayne Barker; 5 James Haley; 9 Sean Penkywicz; 7 Ben Black; 10 Dana Wilson; 14 Mark Gleeson; 16 Said Tamghart; 11 David Larder; 12 Paul Smith; 13 Bob Beswick. Subs (all used): 15 Mark Roberts; 17 Frank Watene; 21 Neil Cherryholme; 22 David Wrench.
Tries: Royston (11), Barker (42), Beswick (45, 67, 71);
Goals: Patterson 7/8.
Rugby Leaguer & League Express Men of the Match: *Tigers:* Ryan McGoldrick; *Halifax:* Miles Greenwood.
Penalty count: 7-9; **Half-time:** 16-12;
Referee: Steve Ganson; **Attendance:** 5,595.

Sunday 10th May 2009

HUDDERSFIELD GIANTS 38 ROCHDALE HORNETS 12

GIANTS: 21 Leroy Cudjoe; 19 Michael Lawrence; 11 Jamahl Lolesi; 28 Josh Griffin (D); 2 Martin Aspinwall; 26 Tom Hemingway; 7 Luke Robinson; 15 Paul Jackson (C); 24 Shaun Lunt; 17 Michael Korkidas; 14 Simon Finnigan; 30 Larne Patrick; 9 David Faiumu. Subs (all used): 8 Eorl Crabtree; 10 Darrell Griffin; 29 Keal Carlile (D); 23 Joe Walsh.
Tries: Robinson (7), Lunt (11, 44, 76), Patrick (13), Carlile (30), Lolesi (37); **Goals:** Cudjoe 5/7.
HORNETS: 1 Chris Giles; 2 John Gillam; 3 Mick Fogerty; 20 Dale Cunniffe; 19 Craig Johnson; 6 Martin Ainscough; 34 Brett Robinson; 35 David Houghton; 13 Wayne Corcoran; 12 Ian Sinfield; 25 Dayne Donoghue; 14 Adam Thomas; 33 Matthew Strong. Subs (all used): 9 Janan Billings; 17 Andrew Isherwood; 24 Chris Hough; 26 Leroy Rivett.
Tries: Fogerty (53), Ainscough (62); **Goals:** Giles 2/2.
Rugby Leaguer & League Express Men of the Match: *Giants:* Shaun Lunt; *Hornets:* Mick Fogerty.
Penalty count: 5-4; **Half-time:** 26-0;
Referee: Gareth Hewer; **Attendance:** 2,859.

FEATHERSTONE ROVERS 8 WARRINGTON WOLVES 56

ROVERS: 3 Ian Hardman; 5 Jon Steel; 4 Andy Kirk; 14 Tom Haughey; 1 Tom Saxton; 6 Iestyn Harris; 7 Andy Kain; 8 Tony Tonks; 13 Richard Blakeway; 10 Stuart Dickens; 11 Matty Dale; 18 Tim Spears; 12 Jamie Field. Subs (all used): 24 Jon Fallon; 16 Joe McLocklan; 20 Stuart Kain; 15 James Houston.
Tries: Saxton (10), Haughey (47); **Goals:** Dickens 0/2.
WOLVES: 30 Richard Mathers (D2); 23 Chris Hicks; 4 Matt King; 20 Simon Grix; 19 Chris Riley; 25 Chris Bridge; 7 Michael Monaghan (C); 16 Garreth Carvell; 9 Jon Clarke; 12 Ben Westwood; 11 Louis Anderson; 2 Paul Johnson; 24 Ben Harrison. Subs (all used): 14 Mick Higham; 18 Michael Cooper; 15 Paul Wood; 21 Matty Blythe.
Tries: Grix (22), Mathers (24, 56), Monaghan (31), Wood (39), Hicks (41, 51), Harrison (64), Riley (72), Bridge (77); **Goals:** Hicks 8/10.
Rugby Leaguer & League Express Men of the Match: *Rovers:* Tim Spears; *Wolves:* Michael Monaghan.
Penalty count: 6-6; **Half-time:** 4-20;
Referee: Ian Smith; **Attendance:** 3,127.

BATLEY BULLDOGS 4 SALFORD CITY REDS 66

BULLDOGS: 18 Jermaine McGilvary; 2 Ben Feehan; 28 Daryl Cardiss; 4 Danny Maun; 1 Ian Preece; 23 Chris Buttery; 7 Paul Mennell; 17 Craig Potter; 14 John Gallagher; 35 Jack Watson; 11 Kevin Crouthers; 8 Byron Smith; 9 Kris Lythe. Subs (all used): 13 Ashley Lindsay; 6 Mark Barlow; 20 David Tootill; 16 Jon Simpson.
Try: Maun (57); **Goals:** Barlow 0/1.
CITY REDS: 2 John Wilshere; 24 Dean McGilvray; 14 Jordan Turner; 4 Willie Talau; 3 Mark Henry; 19 Stefan Ratchford; 7 Richard Myler; 8 Ray Cashmere; 9 Malcolm Alker (C); 18 Lee Jewitt; 20 Luke Adamson; 11 Ian Sibbit; 13 Luke Swain. Subs (all used): 12 Rob Parker; 16 Phil Leuluai; 17 Robbie Paul; 15 Stuart Littler.
Tries: Wilshere (5), Myler (8), Henry (15, 36, 48, 54), Ratchford (19), McGilvray (25), Alker (28), Paul (32), Adamson (80); **Goals:** Wilshere 11/11.
Rugby Leaguer & League Express Men of the Match: *Bulldogs:* Danny Maun; *City Reds:* Richard Myler.
Penalty count: 14-7; **Half-time:** 0-48;
Referee: Jamie Leahy; **Attendance:** 1,298.

HULL KINGSTON ROVERS 34 SHEFFIELD EAGLES 24

ROVERS: 1 Shaun Briscoe (C); 2 Peter Fox; 19 Kris Welham; 4 Jake Webster; 15 Daniel Fitzhenry; 6 Paul Cooke; 7 Michael Dobson; 18 Scott Wheeldon; 9 Ben Fisher; 10 David Mills; 11 Clint Newton; 14 Stanley Gene; 21 Chaz I'Anson. Subs (all used): 12 Ben Galea; 26 Frankie Mariano (D); 22 Liam Watts; 16 Jason Netherton.
Tries: Webster (6), Gene (19), Fisher (22, 78), Newton (32), Briscoe (62); **Goals:** Dobson 5/6.
EAGLES: 1 Jonny Woodcock; 28 Damian Gibson; 3 Menzie Yere; 23 Tangi Ropati; 5 Ashley Thackeray; 6 Brendon Lindsay; 21 Aaron Groom; 8 Jack Howieson; 20 Matty Brooks; 22 Ryan Hepworth; 11 Alex Szostak; 15 Sam Barlow; 9 Grant Edwards. Subs (all used): 4 Mike

Roby; 19 Kyle Wood; 10 Mitchell Stringer; 14 Andy Boothroyd.
Tries: Yere (12), Barlow (41), Woodcock (59), Wood (70); **Goals:** Woodcock 4/4.
Rugby Leaguer & League Express Men of the Match: *Rovers:* Stanley Gene; *Eagles:* Brendon Lindsay.
Penalty count: 5-7; **Half-time:** 22-6;
Referee: Thierry Alibert; **Attendance:** 4,955.

ST HELENS 42 CATALANS DRAGONS 8

SAINTS: 1 Paul Wellens; 2 Ade Gardner; 3 Matt Gidley; 21 Gary Wheeler; 5 Francis Meli; 6 Leon Pryce; 7 Sean Long; 10 James Graham; 9 Keiron Cunningham (C); 15 Bryn Hargreaves; 11 Lee Gilmour; 13 Chris Flannery; 16 Tony Puletua. Subs (all used): 14 James Roby; 17 Paul Clough; 23 Maurie Fa'asavalu; 28 Matty Ashurst.
Tries: Meli (8, 31), Wheeler (10, 40), Wellens (49, 54), Clough (62), Pryce (69); **Goals:** Long 4/7, Wheeler 1/1.
DRAGONS: 1 Clint Greenshields; 18 Vincent Duport; 3 Steven Bell; 15 Jean-Phillipe Baile; 5 Dimitri Pelo; 4 Adam Mogg; 6 Thomas Bosc; 24 Remi Casty; 20 Kane Bentley; 10 Jerome Guisset; 16 Olivier Elima; 17 Cyrille Gossard; 13 Gregory Mounis. Subs (all used): 8 David Ferriol; 9 Casey McGuire (C); 14 Dane Carlaw; 22 Jamal Fakir.
Try: Gossard (23); **Goals:** Bosc 2/2.
Rugby Leaguer & League Express Men of the Match: *Saints:* Paul Wellens; *Dragons:* David Ferriol.
Penalty count: 10-5; **Half-time:** 18-8;
Referee: Ben Thaler; **Attendance:** 7,176.

QUARTER FINALS

Friday 29th May 2009

WIGAN WARRIORS 28 SALFORD CITY REDS 6

WARRIORS: 21 Cameron Phelps; 2 Amos Roberts; 22 Martin Gleeson; 4 George Carmont; 5 Pat Richards; 25 Sam Tomkins; 7 Thomas Leuluai; 15 Andy Coley; 9 Mark Riddell; 19 Paul Prescott; 11 Gareth Hock; 12 Phil Bailey; 13 Sean O'Loughlin (C). Subs (all used): 10 Iafeta Palea'aesina; 14 Joel Tomkins; 16 Harrison Hansen; 17 Michael McIlorum.
Tries: Hock (3, 77), Richards (26, 53, 71);
Goals: Richards 4/6.
CITY REDS: 2 John Wilshere; 15 Stuart Littler; 14 Jordan Turner; 4 Willie Talau; 3 Mark Henry; 19 Stefan Ratchford; 7 Richard Myler; 8 Ray Cashmere; 9 Malcolm Alker (C); 10 Craig Stapleton; 20 Luke Adamson; 12 Rob Parker; 13 Luke Swain. Subs (all used): 11 Ian Sibbit; 18 Lee Jewitt; 16 Phil Leuluai; 17 Robbie Paul.
Try: Adamson (12); **Goals:** Wilshere 1/1.
Rugby Leaguer & League Express Men of the Match: *Warriors:* Gareth Hock; *City Reds:* Ray Cashmere.
Penalty count: 7-10; **Half-time:** 10-6;
Referee: Thierry Alibert; **Attendance:** 9,466.

Saturday 30th May 2009

HULL KINGSTON ROVERS 24 WARRINGTON WOLVES 25

(after golden point extra time)

ROVERS: 1 Shaun Briscoe (C); 2 Peter Fox; 4 Jake Webster; 19 Kris Welham; 5 Liam Colbon; 6 Paul Cooke; 7 Michael Dobson; 8 Nick Fozzard; 9 Ben Fisher; 11 Clint Newton; 14 Stanley Gene; 12 Ben Galea; 13 Scott Murrell. Subs (all used): 17 Makali Aizue; 15 Daniel Fitzhenry; 18 Scott Wheeldon; 3 Chev Walker.
Tries: Welham (3), Newton (48), Galea (52), Webster (60); **Goals:** Dobson 4/5.
WOLVES: 30 Richard Mathers; 19 Chris Riley; 25 Chris Bridge; 20 Simon Grix; 4 Matt King; 6 Lee Briers; 7 Michael Monaghan; 8 Adrian Morley (C); 9 Jon Clarke; 16 Garreth Carvell; 11 Louis Anderson; 12 Ben Westwood; 13 Vinnie Anderson. Subs (all used): 14 Mick Higham; 15 Paul Wood; 10 Paul Rauhihi; 24 Ben Harrison.
Tries: V Anderson (17), Clarke (43), King (68), Bridge (70); **Goals:** Bridge 4/4; **Field goal:** Briers (85).
Rugby Leaguer & League Express Men of the Match: *Rovers:* Shaun Briscoe; *Wolves:* Chris Bridge.
Penalty count: 7-4; **Half-time:** 6-6;
Referee: Phil Bentham; **Attendance:** 7,671.

GATESHEAD THUNDER 6 ST HELENS 66

THUNDER: 19 Nick Youngquest; 18 Robin Peers; 1 Ben McAlpine; 25 Paul Franze; 5 Stewart Sanderson; 6 Neil Thorman; 7 Luke Branighan; 24 Kris Kahler; 14 Ryan Clarke; 33 Sam Crowther; 4 Dylan Nash; 32 James Cording; 12 Michael Knowles. Subs (all used): 17 Chris Parker; 15 Matt Barron; 21 Ryan McBride; 10 Tabua Cakacaka.
Try: McAlpine (36); **Goals:** Youngquest 1/1.
SAINTS: 1 Paul Wellens; 30 Jonny Lomax; 3 Matt Gidley; 13 Chris Flannery; 21 Gary Wheeler; 6 Leon Pryce; 7 Sean Long; 10 James Graham; 14 James Roby; 15 Bryn Hargreaves; 12 Jon Wilkin; 28 Matty Ashurst; 16 Tony Cunningham (C); 17 Paul Clough; 18 Kyle Eastmond.
Tries: Gidley (2, 57), Roby (5), Wellens (12), Flannery (26, 72), Fa'asavalu (29), Eastmond (31), Pryce (33, 64), Ashurst (51); **Goals:** Eastmond 8/8, Long 1/4.
Rugby Leaguer & League Express Men of the Match: *Thunder:* Michael Knowles; *Saints:* Maurie Fa'asavalu.
Penalty count: 3-8; **Half-time:** 6-36;
Referee: Ian Smith; **Attendance:** 4,325.

Sunday 31st May 2009

HUDDERSFIELD GIANTS 16 CASTLEFORD TIGERS 14

GIANTS: 1 Brett Hodgson (C); 2 Martin Aspinwall; 11

Huddersfield's Kevin Brown dives past St Helens' Ade Gardner

Jamahl Lolesi; 4 Paul Whatuira; 5 David Hodgson; 3 Kevin Brown; 7 Luke Robinson; 16 Keith Mason; 20 Scott Moore; 15 Paul Jackson; 18 Danny Kirmond; 13 Stephen Wild; 14 Simon Finnigan. Subs (all used): 9 David Faiumu; 8 Eorl Crabtree; 10 Darrell Griffin; 12 Andy Raleigh.
Tries: K Brown (22), Wild (70), Kirmond (76);
Goals: B Hodgson 2/3.
TIGERS: 1 Richard Owen; 5 Michael Wainwright; 3 Michael Shenton; 4 James Evans; 2 Kirk Dixon; 23 Ryan McGoldrick (C); 6 Rangi Chase; 8 Mitchell Sargent; 19 Kirk Netherton; 15 Liam Higgins; 11 Brett Ferres; 14 Stuart Jones; 13 Joe Westerman. Subs (all used): 10 Craig Huby; 12 Ryan Clayton; 16 Chris Feather; 21 Sione Faumuina.
Tries: Shenton (4), Ferres (45); **Goals:** Dixon 3/4.
Rugby Leaguer & League Express Men of the Match: *Giants:* Stephen Wild; *Tigers:* Rangi Chase.
Penalty count: 9-8; **Half-time:** 6-6;
Referee: Richard Silverwood; **Attendance:** 6,359.

SEMI-FINALS

Saturday 8th August 2009

WARRINGTON WOLVES 39 WIGAN WARRIORS 26

WOLVES: 30 Richard Mathers; 23 Chris Hicks; 25 Chris Bridge; 4 Matt King; 19 Chris Riley; 6 Lee Briers; 7 Michael Monaghan; 8 Adrian Morley (C); 9 Jon Clarke; 12 Ben Westwood. Subs (all used): 13 Vinnie Anderson; 2 Paul Johnson; 18 Michael Cooper; 10 Paul Rauhihi.
Tries: King (18, 39, 49), L Anderson (20), Briers (23), Cooper (30), Hicks (75); **Goals:** Bridge 5/7;
Field goal: Briers (71).
WARRIORS: 21 Cameron Phelps; 2 Amos Roberts; 22 Martin Gleeson; 4 George Carmont; 5 Pat Richards; 25 Sam Tomkins; 7 Thomas Leuluai; 19 Paul Prescott; 9 Mark Riddell; 15 Andy Coley; 12 Phil Bailey; 16 Harrison Hansen; 14 Sean O'Loughlin (C). Subs (all used): 8 Stuart Fielden; 10 Iafeta Palea'aesina; 14 Joel Tomkins; 26 Mark Flanagan.
Tries: Bailey (7), S Tomkins (55), Coley (60), Leuluai (68); **Goals:** Richards 5/5.
Rugby Leaguer & League Express Men of the Match: *Wolves:* Lee Briers; *Warriors:* Paul Prescott.
Penalty count: 6-6; **Half-time:** 28-8;
Referee: Steve Ganson; **Attendance:** 12,975.
(at Stobart Stadium, Widnes).

Sunday 9th August 2009

HUDDERSFIELD GIANTS 24 ST HELENS 14

GIANTS: 1 Brett Hodgson (C); 21 Leroy Cudjoe; 11 Jamahl Lolesi; 4 Paul Whatuira; 5 David Hodgson; 3 Kevin Brown; 7 Luke Robinson; 16 Keith Mason; 20 Scott Moore; 10 Darrell Griffin; 13 Stephen Wild; 6 Liam Fulton; 9 David Faiumu. Subs (all used): 24 Shaun Lunt; 8 Eorl Crabtree; 15 Paul Jackson; 18 Danny Kirmond.
Tries: B Hodgson (6), Wild (37, 75), Cudjoe (41), K Brown (51); **Goals:** B Hodgson 2/5.
SAINTS: 1 Paul Wellens; 2 Ade Gardner; 3 Matt Gidley; 19 Chris Dean; 5 Francis Meli; 6 Leon Pryce; 18 Kyle Eastmond; 10 James Graham; 9 Keiron Cunningham (C); 16 Tony Puletua; 13 Chris Flannery; 12 Jon Wilkin; 11 Lee Gilmour. Subs (all used): 17 Paul Clough; 14 James Roby; 15 Bryn Hargreaves; 24 Andrew Dixon.
Tries: Meli (13, 55, 77); **Goals:** Eastmond 1/3.
Rugby Leaguer & League Express Men of the Match: *Giants:* Brett Hodgson; *Saints:* Keiron Cunningham.
Penalty count: 11-8; **Half-time:** 10-4;
Referee: Richard Silverwood; **Attendance:** 10,638
(at Halliwell Jones Stadium, Warrington).

FINAL

Saturday 29th August 2009

HUDDERSFIELD GIANTS 16 WARRINGTON WOLVES 25

GIANTS: 1 Brett Hodgson (C); 21 Leroy Cudjoe; 11 Jamahl Lolesi; 4 Paul Whatuira; 5 David Hodgson; 3 Kevin Brown; 7 Luke Robinson; 16 Keith Mason; 24 Shaun Lunt; 10 Darrell Griffin; 6 Liam Fulton; 13 Stephen Wild; 9 David Faiumu. Subs (all used): 8 Eorl Crabtree; 15 Paul Jackson; 20 Scott Moore; 2 Martin Aspinwall.
Tries: Lunt (9), B Hodgson (37), D Hodgson (76);
Goals: B Hodgson 2/3.
WOLVES: 30 Richard Mathers; 23 Chris Hicks; 25 Chris Bridge; 4 Matt King; 19 Chris Riley; 13 Vinnie Anderson; 6 Lee Briers; 8 Adrian Morley (C); 7 Michael Monaghan; 16 Garreth Carvell; 11 Louis Anderson; 24 Ben Harrison; 12 Ben Westwood. Subs (all used): 18 Michael Cooper; 2 Paul Johnson; 14 Mick Higham; 28 Tyrone McCarthy.
Tries: Mathers (2), Monaghan (12), Hicks (14), V Anderson (61); **Goals:** Bridge 4/5;
Field goal: Briers (78).
Rugby Leaguer & League Express Men of the Match: *Giants:* Shaun Lunt; *Wolves:* Michael Monaghan.
Penalty count: 11-10; **Half-time:** 10-18;
Referee: Steve Ganson; **Attendance:** 76,560
(at Wembley Stadium).

Richard Mathers wrapped up by Martin Aspinwall and Paul Whatuira during the Challenge Cup Final

SUPER LEAGUE 2010 FIXTURES

ROUND 4
Friday 29 January
Crusaders v Leeds Rhinos 20:00
at Wrexham FC
ROUND 3
Saturday 30 January
Harlequins v Wakefield Trinity Wildcats 15:00

ROUND 1

Friday 5 February
Wigan Warriors v Crusaders 20:00
Huddersfield Giants v Bradford Bulls ......20:00 (TV)
Leeds Rhinos v Castleford Tigers 20:00
Saturday 6 February
St Helens v Hull FC................................18:00 (TV)
Sunday 7 February
Hull Kingston Rovers v Salford City Reds 15:00
Wakefield Trinity Wildcats v Catalans Dragons15:30
Warrington Wolves v Harlequins 15:00

ROUND 2

Friday 12 February
Wigan Warriors v Hull Kingston Rovers..20:00 (TV)
Hull FC v Huddersfield Giants.........................20:00
Salford City Reds v Crusaders 20:00
Saturday 13 February
Castleford Tigers v Warrington Wolves ..18:00 (TV)
Sunday 14 February
Harlequins v Catalans Dragons 14:00
Bradford Bulls v St Helens 15:00
Wakefield Trinity Wildcats v Leeds Rhinos......15:30

ROUND 3

Friday 19 February
Leeds Rhinos v Salford City Reds 20:00
Bradford Bulls v Castleford Tigers ....20:00 (TV)
Saturday 20 February
Warrington Wolves v Wigan Warriors ......18:00 (TV)
Crusaders v Hull FC ....18:00 *venue tbc*
Catalans Dragons v St Helens ....tbc
Sunday 21 February
Hull Kingston Rovers v Huddersfield Giants ..15:00

ROUND 4

Friday 26 February
Wigan Warriors v Catalans Dragons 20:00
Hull FC v Harlequins......................................20:00 (TV)
Salford City Reds v Bradford Bulls.................20:00
St Helens v Wakefield Trinity Wildcats 20:00
Saturday 27 February
Castleford Tigers v Hull Kingston Rovers18:00 (TV)
Sunday 28 February
Huddersfield Giants v Warrington Wolves 15:00

ROUND 5

Friday 5 March
Bradford Bulls v Wigan Warriors ....20:00 (TV)
Leeds Rhinos v Harlequins.............................20:00
Hull FC v Castleford Tigers.............................20:00
Salford City Reds v Catalans Dragons 20:00
Saturday 6 March
Wakefield Trinity Wildcats v Huddersfield Giants
....18:00 (TV)
Sunday 7 March
Hull Kingston Rovers v St Helens 15:00
Warrington Wolves v Crusaders.....................15:00

ROUND 6

Friday 12 March
Hull Kingston Rovers v Wakefield Trinity Wildcats
....20:00 (TV)
Wigan Warriors v Hull FC...............................20:00
St Helens v Crusaders 20:00
Saturday 13 March
Warrington Wolves v Bradford Bulls ......18:00 (TV)
Catalans Dragons v Castleford Tigers.................tbc
Sunday 14 March
Harlequins v Salford City Reds.......................14:00
Huddersfield Giants v Leeds Rhinos 15:00

ROUND 7

Friday 19 March
Crusaders v Catalans Dragons20:00 venue tbc (TV)
Leeds Rhinos v Hull Kingston Rovers 20:00
Hull FC v Bradford Bulls 20:00
St Helens v Warrington Wolves 20:00
Saturday 20 March
Harlequins v Huddersfield Giants ....18:00 (TV)
Sunday 21 March
Castleford Tigers v Wigan Warriors 15:30
Wakefield Trinity Wildcats v Salford City Reds15:30

ROUND 8

Friday 26 March
Wigan Warriors v Leeds Rhinos..............20:00 (TV)
Bradford Bulls v Harlequins 20:00
Castleford Tigers v Crusaders 20:00
Warrington Wolves v Wakefield Trinity Wildcats
....20:00
Saturday 27 March
Salford City Reds v Hull FC ....18:00 (TV)
Catalans Dragons v Hull Kingston Rovers ....tbc
Sunday 28 March
Huddersfield Giants v St Helens.....................15:00

ROUND 9

Thursday 1 April
Leeds Rhinos v Bradford Bulls ....tbc (TV)
Friday 2 April
Crusaders v Harlequins ....*venue & time tbc*
Huddersfield Giants v Catalans Dragons 19:00
Hull Kingston Rovers v Hull FC ....tbc (TV)
Wakefield Trinity Wildcats v Castleford Tigers 19:30
Warrington Wolves v Salford City Reds 15:00
St Helens v Wigan Warriors ....tbc (TV)

ROUND 10

Monday 5 April
Wigan Warriors v Wakefield Trinity Wildcats ..15:00
Harlequins v Hull Kingston Rovers.................14:00
Catalans Dragons v Leeds Rhinos ....tbc (TV)
Bradford Bulls v Crusaders 15:00
Castleford Tigers v St Helens 15:30
Hull FC v Warrington Wolves 15:15
Salford City Reds v Huddersfield Giants 15:00

ROUND 11

Friday 9 April
Huddersfield Giants v Castleford Tigers ..20:00 (TV)
Saturday 10 April
Harlequins v St Helens ....18:00 (TV)
Catalans Dragons v Bradford Bulls time tbc
Sunday 11 April
Leeds Rhinos v Hull FC 15:00
Hull Kingston Rovers v Warrington Wolves 15:00
Wakefield Trinity Wildcats v Crusaders 15:30
Salford City Reds v Wigan Warriors...............15:00

ROUND 12

Friday 23 April
Wigan Warriors v Harlequins 20:00
Hull FC v Wakefield Trinity Wildcats ......20:00 (TV)
Saturday 24 April
Crusaders v Huddersfield Giants ....18:00 *venue tbc*
St Helens v Leeds Rhinos ....18:00 (TV)
Sunday 25 April
Bradford Bulls v Hull Kingston Rovers...........15:00
Castleford Tigers v Salford City Reds..............15:30
Warrington Wolves v Catalans Dragons..........15:00

ROUND 13 - Murrayfield Magic

Weekend 1/2 May
Hull FC v Harlequins
Bradford Bulls v Crusaders
Warrington Wolves v Salford City Reds
Leeds Rhinos v Wakefield Trinity Wildcats
Wigan Warriors v Huddersfield Giants
St Helens v Hull Kingston Rovers
Castleford Tigers v Catalans Dragons
Days and times TBC

ROUND 14

Friday 14 May
Wakefield Trinity Wildcats v Bradford Bulls
....20:00 (TV)
Leeds Rhinos v Warrington Wolves 20:00
Saturday 15 May
Salford City Reds v St Helens ....18:00 (TV)
Catalans Dragons v Hull FC time tbc
Sunday 16 May
Harlequins v Castleford Tigers 14:00
Huddersfield Giants v Wigan Warriors 15:00
Hull Kingston Rovers v Crusaders 15:00

ROUND 15

Friday 21 May
St Helens v Hull Kingston Rovers 20:00
Saturday 22 May
Crusaders v Wigan Warriors ....18:00 *venue tbc*
Catalans Dragons v Salford City Reds ....tbc
Sunday 23 May
Bradford Bulls v Leeds Rhinos.......................15:00
Castleford Tigers v Hull FC.............................15:30
Wakefield Trinity Wildcats v Harlequins 15:30
Warrington Wolves v Huddersfield Giants 15:00

ROUND 16

Friday 4 June
Wigan Warriors v Castleford Tigers 20:00
Leeds Rhinos v Wakefield Trinity Wildcats......20:00
Hull FC v St Helens 20:00
Salford City Reds v Warrington Wolves 20:00
Sunday 6 June
Harlequins v Crusaders 14:00
Bradford Bulls v Huddersfield Giants 15:00
Hull Kingston Rovers v Catalans Dragons 15:00

ROUND 17

Friday 11 June
Hull FC v Salford City Reds 20:00
St Helens v Huddersfield Giants.....................20:00
Saturday 12 June
Harlequins v Leeds Rhinos............................15:00
Crusaders v Bradford Bulls ....18:00 venue tbc
Sunday 13 June
Castleford Tigers v Catalans Dragons 15:30
Wakefield Trinity Wildcats v Wigan Warriors ..15:30
Warrington Wolves v Hull Kingston Rovers 15:00

ROUND 18

Friday 18 June
Wigan Warriors v St Helens 20:00
Leeds Rhinos v Crusaders 20:00
Salford City Reds v Castleford Tigers.............20:00
Saturday 19 June
Catalans Dragons v Wakefield Trinity Wildcats....tbc
Sunday 20 June
Bradford Bulls v Warrington Wolves 15:00
Huddersfield Giants v Hull FC........................15:00
Hull Kingston Rovers v Harlequins.................15:00

ROUND 19

Friday 25 June
Hull FC v Catalans Dragons 20:00
St Helens v Salford City Reds 20:00
Saturday 26 June
Harlequins v Wigan Warriors 15:00
Crusaders v Wakefield Trinity Wildcats
....18:00 venue tbc
Sunday 27 June
Castleford Tigers v Bradford Bulls 15:30
Huddersfield Giants v Hull Kingston Rovers ..15:00
Warrington Wolves v Leeds Rhinos 15:00

ROUND 20

Friday 2 July
Leeds Rhinos v St Helens 20:00
Salford City Reds v Harlequins.......................20:00
Saturday 3 July
Crusaders v Warrington Wolves ....18:00 venue tbc
Sunday 4 July
Catalans Dragons v Wigan Warriors.....................tbc
Bradford Bulls v Hull FC 15:00
Castleford Tigers v Huddersfield Giants 15:30
Wakefield Trinity Wildcats v Hull Kingston Rovers
....15:30

ROUND 21

Friday 9 July
Wigan Warriors v Salford City Reds...............20:00
Harlequins v Bradford Bulls 20:00
St Helens v Catalans Dragons 20:00
Saturday 10 July
Huddersfield Giants v Crusaders 15:00
Hull Kingston Rovers v Leeds Rhinos 15:00
Sunday 11 July
Wakefield Trinity Wildcats v Hull FC...............15:30
Warrington Wolves v Castleford Tigers 15:00

ROUND 22

Friday 16 July
Wigan Warriors v Warrington Wolves 20:00
Leeds Rhinos v Huddersfield Giants 20:00
Hull FC v Hull Kingston Rovers 20:00
St Helens v Harlequins..................................20:00
Saturday 17 July
Catalans Dragons v Crusaders ....tbc
Sunday 18 July
Bradford Bulls v Salford City Reds..................15:00
Castleford Tigers v Wakefield Trinity Wildcats 15:30

ROUND 23

Friday 23 July
Hull FC v Wigan Warriors...............................20:00
Saturday 24 July
Crusaders v Castleford Tigers ....18:00 venue tbc
Catalans Dragons v Warrington Wolves ....tbc
Sunday 25 July
Salford City Reds v Leeds Rhinos 15:00
Huddersfield Giants v Harlequins....................15:00
Hull Kingston Rovers v Bradford Bulls............15:00
Wakefield Trinity Wildcats v St Helens 15:30

ROUND 24

Friday 30 July
Leeds Rhinos v Wigan Warriors.....................20:00
Saturday 31 July
Harlequins v Hull FC 15:00
Crusaders v Salford City Reds ....18:00 venue tbc
Sunday 1 August
Bradford Bulls v Catalans Dragons.................15:00
Huddersfield Giants v Wakefield Trinity Wildcats
....15:00
Hull Kingston Rovers v Castleford Tigers........15:00
Warrington Wolves v St Helens 15:00

ROUND 25

Friday 13 August
Wigan Warriors v Huddersfield Giants 20:00
Hull FC v Crusaders 20:00
St Helens v Bradford Bulls.............................20:00
Saturday 14 August
Catalans Dragons v Harlequins ....tbc
Sunday 15 August
Salford City Reds v Hull Kingston Rovers 15:00
Castleford Tigers v Leeds Rhinos...................15:30
Wakefield Trinity Wildcats v Warrington Wolves
....15:30

ROUND 26

Friday 20 August
Leeds Rhinos v Catalans Dragons 20:00
Saturday 21 August
Crusaders v St Helens ....18:00 venue tbc
Sunday 22 August
Bradford Bulls v Wakefield Trinity Wildcats 15:00
Castleford Tigers v Harlequins.......................15:30
Huddersfield Giants v Salford City Reds 15:00
Hull Kingston Rovers v Wigan Warriors..........15:00
Warrington Wolves v Hull FC 15:00

ROUND 27

Friday 3 September
Wigan Warriors v Bradford Bulls 20:00
Hull FC v Leeds Rhinos 20:00
St Helens v Castleford Tigers 20:00
Saturday 4 September
Harlequins v Warrington Wolves ...venue & time tbc
Crusaders v Hull Kingston Rovers ..18:00 venue tbc
Catalans Dragons v Huddersfield Giants time tbc
Sunday 5 September
Salford City Reds v Wakefield Trinity Wildcats
....15:00

PLAY-OFFS

Weekend of 10/11/12 September
Qualifying Play-offs
Elimination Play-offs

Weekend of 17/18/19 September
Preliminary Semi-finals

Weekend of 24/25/26 September
Qualifying Semi-finals

Saturday 2 October
GRAND FINAL

GRAND FINALS
1998-2008

1998

DIVISION ONE GRAND FINAL

Saturday 26th September 1998

FEATHERSTONE ROVERS 22 WAKEFIELD TRINITY 24

ROVERS: 1 Steve Collins; 2 Carl Hall; 3 Shaun Irwin; 4 Danny Baker; 5 Karl Pratt; 6 Jamie Coventry; 7 Ty Fallins; 8 Chico Jackson; 9 Richard Chapman; 10 Stuart Dickens; 11 Gary Price; 12 Neil Lowe; 13 Richard Slater. Subs: 14 Paddy Handley for Coventry (70); 15 Asa Amone for Lowe (50); 16 Micky Clarkson for Jackson (50); 17 Steve Dooler (not used). **Tries:** Baker (15), Jackson (45), Collins (49), Hall (69); **Goals:** Chapman 3.
TRINITY: 1 Martyn Holland; 2 Josh Bostock; 3 Adam Hughes; 4 Martin Law; 5 Kevin Gray; 6 Garen Casey; 7 Roger Kenworthy; 8 Francis Stephenson; 9 Roy Southernwood; 10 Gary Lord; 11 Ian Hughes; 12 Sonny Whakarau; 13 Matt Fuller. Subs: 14 Sean Richardson for I Hughes (32); 15 Andy Fisher for Lord (26); 16 David Mycoe (not used); 17 Wayne McDonald for Whakarau (70); Lord for Stephenson (40); Stephenson for Lord (70). **Tries:** Southernwood (2), Bostock (7, 25), Casey (58), Stephenson (76); **Goals:** Casey 2.
League Express Men of the Match:
Rovers: Richard Chapman; *Trinity:* Garen Casey.
Penalty count: 8-3; **Half time:** 6-12; **Referee:** Nick Oddy (Halifax); **Attendance:** 8,224 *(at McAlpine Stadium, Huddersfield).*

SUPER LEAGUE GRAND FINAL

Saturday 24th October 1998

LEEDS RHINOS 4 WIGAN WARRIORS 10

RHINOS: 1 Iestyn Harris (C); 22 Leroy Rivett; 3 Richie Blackmore; 4 Brad Godden; 5 Francis Cummins; 13 Daryl Powell; 7 Ryan Sheridan; 8 Martin Masella; 21 Terry Newton; 25 Darren Fleary; 11 Adrian Morley; 17 Anthony Farrell; 12 Marc Glanville. Subs: 20 Jamie Mathiou for Masella (25); 24 Marcus St Hilaire for Powell (40); 14 Graham Holroyd for Newton (49); 27 Andy Hay for Fleary (54); Powell for Godden (58); Masella for Mathiou (71).
Try: Blackmore (20).
WARRIORS: 1 Kris Radlinski; 2 Jason Robinson; 3 Danny Moore; 4 Gary Connolly; 5 Mark Bell; 6 Henry Paul; 7 Tony Smith; 16 Terry O'Connor; 9 Robbie McCormack; 10 Tony Mestrov; 20 Lee Gilmour; 17 Stephen Holgate; 13 Andy Farrell (C). Subs: 8 Neil Cowie for O'Connor (18BB, rev 48); 14 Mick Cassidy for McCormack (19BB, rev 27); 25 Paul Johnson for Moore (37); 12 Simon Haughton for Gilmour (27BB, rev 33); Haughton for Holgate (33); Cowie for Mestrov (54); Cassidy for Haughton (64); Holgate for Cowie (68); Haughton for Gilmour (71BB, rev 75); Mestrov for O'Connor (75BB).
Try: Robinson (37); **Goals:** Farrell 3.
League Express Men of the Match:
Rhinos: Iestyn Harris; *Warriors:* Jason Robinson.
Penalty count: 7-13; **Half-time:** 4-6; **Referee:** Russell Smith (Castleford); **Attendance:** 43,553 *(at Old Trafford, Manchester).*

1999

NORTHERN FORD PREMIERSHIP GRAND FINAL

Saturday 25th September 1999

DEWSBURY RAMS 11 HUNSLET HAWKS 12

RAMS: 1 Nathan Graham; 2 Alex Godfrey; 3 Paul Evans; 4 Brendan O'Meara; 5 Adrian Flynn; 6 Richard Agar; 7 Barry Eaton; 8 Alan Boothroyd; 9 Paul Delaney; 10 Matthew Long; 11 Andy Spink; 12 Mark Haigh; 13 Damian Ball. Subs: 14 Brendan Williams for Eaton (5BB, rev 15); 15 Sean Richardson for Haigh (50); 16 Simon Hicks for Long (25); 17 Paul Medley for Spink (50); Williams for Evans (61); Long for Boothroyd (71); Spink for Long (78). **Tries:** Flynn (27), Ball (54); **Goal:** Eaton; **Field goal:** Agar.
HAWKS: 1 Abraham Fatnowna; 2 Chris Ross; 3 Shaun Irwin; 4 Paul Cook; 5 Iain Higgins; 6 Marcus Vassilakopoulos; 7 Latham Tawhai; 8 Richard Hayes; 9 Richard Pachniuk; 10 Steve Pryce; 11 Rob Wilson; 12 Jamie Leighton; 13 Lee St Hilaire. Subs: 14 Mick Coyle for Wilson (57); 15 Phil Kennedy for Pryce (35); 16 Jamie Thackray for St Hilaire (25); 17 Richard Baker for Higgins (55); Higgins for Fatnowna (62); Pryce for Kennedy (65). **Tries:** Cook (31), Higgins (46); **Goal:** Ross; **Field goals:** Tawhai, Leighton.
League Express Men of the Match:
Rams: Barry Eaton; *Hawks:* Latham Tawhai.
Penalty count: 8-5; **Half-time:** 7-7; **Referee:** Steve Ganson (St Helens); **Attendance:** 5,783 *(at Headingley Stadium, Leeds).*

SUPER LEAGUE GRAND FINAL

Saturday 9th October 1999

BRADFORD BULLS 6 ST HELENS 8

BULLS: 28 Stuart Spruce; 2 Tevita Vaikona; 20 Scott Naylor; 5 Michael Withers; 17 Leon Pryce; 6 Henry Paul; 1 Robbie Paul (C); 10 Paul Anderson; 9 James Lowes; 29 Stuart Fielden; 15 David Boyle; 23 Bernard Dwyer; 13 Steve McNamara. Subs: 14 Paul Deacon for R Paul (53); 4 Nathan McAvoy (not used); 12 Mike Forshaw for McNamara (18); 22 Brian McDermott for Anderson (18); Anderson for Fielden (61); Fielden for Dwyer (65); R Paul for Deacon (72).
Try: H Paul (18); **Goal:** H Paul.
SAINTS: 1 Paul Atcheson; 14 Chris Smith; 3 Kevin Iro; 4 Paul Newlove; 5 Anthony Sullivan; 13 Paul Sculthorpe; 20 Tommy Martyn; 8 Apollo Perelini; 9 Keiron Cunningham; 10 Julian O'Neill; 2 Fereti Tuilagi; 21 Sonny Nickle; 11 Chris Joynt (C). Subs: 26 Paul Wellens for Martyn (52); 6 Sean Hoppe for Newlove (43); 16 Vila Matautia for O'Neill (20); 7 Sean Long for Perelini (24); Perelini for Matautia (46); O'Neill for Perelini (69). **Tries:** Iro (65); **Goals:** Long 2.
League Express Men of the Match:
Bulls: Henry Paul; *Saints:* Kevin Iro.
Penalty count: 4-7; **Half-time:** 6-2; **Referee:** Stuart Cummings (Widnes); **Attendance:** 50,717 *(at Old Trafford, Manchester).*

1998...Wakefield celebrate their win against Featherstone

1999... Chris Joynt lifts the Super League trophy

2000

NORTHERN FORD PREMIERSHIP GRAND FINAL

Saturday 29th July 2000

DEWSBURY RAMS 13 LEIGH CENTURIONS 12

RAMS: 1 Nathan Graham; 2 Richard Baker; 4 Dan Potter; 3 Brendan O'Meara; 5 Adrian Flynn; 6 Richard Agar; 7 Barry Eaton; 8 Shayne Williams; 9 David Mycoe; 10 Mark Haigh; 11 Sean Richardson; 12 Daniel Frame; 13 Damian Ball. Subs: 14 Gavin Wood (not used); 15 Paul Delaney for Mycoe (53); 16 Ryan McDonald for Haigh (30); 17 Matthew Long for Williams (23); Haigh for McDonald (64).
Tries: Eaton (2), Long (23); **Goals:** Eaton 2; **Field goal:** Agar.
Sin bin: Williams (66) - use of the elbow.
On report: Richardson (20) - high tackle on Donlan.
CENTURIONS: 1 Stuart Donlan; 5 David Ingram; 3 Paul Anderson; 4 Andy Fairclough; 2 Alan Cross; 6 Liam Bretherton; 7 Kieron Purtill; 8 Tim Street; 9 Mick Higham; 10 Andy Leatham; 11 Simon Baldwin; 12 Heath Cruckshank; 13 Adam Bristow. Subs: 14 James Arkwright for Cross (68); 15 Paul Norman for Street (36); 16 Radney Bowker (not used); 17 David Whittle for Leatham (24); Street for Norman (62).
Tries: Higham (29, 69); **Goals:** Bretherton 2.
Sin bin: Whittle (66) - retaliation.
League Express Men of the Match:
Rams: Richard Agar; *Centurions:* Mick Higham.
Penalty count: 4-4; **Half-time:** 10-6; **Referee:** Robert Connolly (Wigan); **Attendance:** 8,487 *(at Gigg Lane, Bury).*

SUPER LEAGUE GRAND FINAL

Saturday 14th October 2000

ST HELENS 29 WIGAN WARRIORS 16

SAINTS: 17 Paul Wellens; 24 Steve Hall; 3 Kevin Iro; 15 Sean Hoppe; 5 Anthony Sullivan; 20 Tommy Martyn; 7 Sean Long; 8 Apollo Perelini; 9 Keiron Cunningham; 10 Julian O'Neill; 11 Chris Joynt (C); 22 Tim Jonkers; 13 Paul Sculthorpe. Subs: 14 Fereti Tuilagi for O'Neill (20); 12 Sonny Nickle for Perelini (28); 26 John Stankevitch for Jonkers (50); 23 Scott Barrow (not used); Perelini for Nickle (52); Jonkers for Stankevitch (66); Stankevitch for Perelini (67BB); O'Neill for Hall (74).
Tries: Hoppe (7), Joynt (28, 50), Tuilagi (69), Jonkers (80);
Goals: Long 4; **Field goal:** Sculthorpe.
WARRIORS: 5 Jason Robinson; 2 Brett Dallas; 1 Kris Radlinski; 3 Steve Renouf; 26 David Hodgson; 6 Tony Smith; 7 Willie Peters; 8 Terry O'Connor; 9 Terry Newton; 10 Neil Cowie; 11 Mick Cassidy; 12 Denis Betts; 13 Andy Farrell (C). Subs: 23 Brady Malam for Cowie (30); 17 Tony Mestrov for O'Connor (43); 19 Chris Chester for Cassidy (47BB, rev 69); 14 Lee Gilmour for Betts (51); O'Connor for Mestrov (61); Cowie for Malam (67); Chester for Newton (75).
Tries: Farrell (13), Hodgson (58), Smith (61); **Goals:** Farrell 2.
League Express Men of the Match:
Saints: Chris Joynt; *Warriors:* Andy Farrell.
Penalty count: 10-6; **Half-time:** 11-4; **Referee:** Russell Smith (Castleford); **Attendance:** 58,132 *(at Old Trafford, Manchester).*

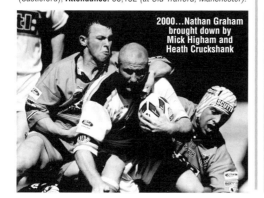

2000...Nathan Graham brought down by Mick Higham and Heath Cruckshank

2001

NORTHERN FORD PREMIERSHIP GRAND FINAL

Saturday 28th July 2001

OLDHAM 14 WIDNES VIKINGS 24

OLDHAM: 1 Mark Sibson; 2 Joey Hayes; 3 Anthony Gibbons; 4 Pat Rich; 5 Joe McNicholas; 6 David Gibbons; 7 Neil Roden; 8 Leo Casey; 9 Keith Brennan; 10 Paul Norton; 11 Phil Farrell; 12 Bryan Henare; 13 Kevin Mannion. Subs: 14 Mike Ford for Mannion (27); 15 Jason Clegg for Casey (18); 16 John Hough for Brennan (44); 17 Danny Guest for Norton (40BB, rev 54); Mannion for Henare (66); Guest for Clegg (73).
Tries: Brennan (9), Ford (74), Mannion (80); **Goal:** Rich.
VIKINGS: 1 Paul Atcheson; 2 Damian Munro; 3 Craig Weston; 4 Jason Demetriou; 5 Chris Percival; 6 Richard Agar; 7 Martin Crompton; 8 Simon Knox; 9 Phil Cantillon; 10 Stephen Holgate; 11 Steve Gee; 12 Sean Richardson; 13 Tommy Hodgkinson. Subs: 14 Andy Craig for Percival (65); 15 Chris McKinney for Gee (41); 16 Joe Faimalo for Knox (32); 17 Matthew Long for Holgate (23); Knox for Long (49BB, rev 61); Holgate for Gee (74).
Tries: Gee (17), Demetriou (38, 60), Cantillon (50), Munro (69); **Goals:** Weston 2.
League Express Men of the Match:
Oldham: Jason Clegg; *Vikings:* Phil Cantillon.
Penalty count: 8-5; **Half-time:** 4-10; **Referee:** Steve Ganson (St Helens); **Attendance:** 8,974 *(at Spotland, Rochdale).*

SUPER LEAGUE GRAND FINAL

Saturday 13th October 2001

BRADFORD BULLS 37 WIGAN WARRIORS 6

BULLS: 5 Michael Withers; 2 Tevita Vaikona; 20 Scott Naylor; 23 Graham Mackay; 3 Leon Pryce; 6 Henry Paul; 1 Robbie Paul (C); 8 Joe Vagana; 9 James Lowes; 22 Brian McDermott; 11 Daniel Gartner; 19 Jamie Peacock; 12 Mike Forshaw. Subs: 29 Stuart Fielden for McDermott (21BB, rev 65); 10 Paul Anderson for Vagana (22); 15 Shane Rigon for Pryce (40); 7 Paul Deacon for R Paul (69); Vagana for Anderson (53); Fielden for Gartner (72); Anderson for Vagana (74).
Tries: Lowes (9), Withers (11, 27, 31), Fielden (65), Mackay (72); **Goals:** H Paul 5, Mackay; **Field goal:** H Paul.
WARRIORS: 1 Kris Radlinski; 2 Brett Dallas; 4 Gary Connolly; 3 Steve Renouf; 5 Brian Carney; 6 Matthew Johns; 7 Adrian Lam; 8 Terry O'Connor; 9 Terry Newton; 20 Harvey Howard; 11 Mick Cassidy; 14 David Furner; 13 Andy Farrell (C). Subs: 15 Paul Johnson for Carney (12BB); 10 Neil Cowie for Howard (17); 12 Denis Betts for O'Connor (32); 19 Chris Chester for Farrell (59); O'Connor for Cowie (55); Howard for Newton (64); Cowie for Cassidy (72).
Try: Lam (63); **Goal:** Furner.
League Express Men of the Match:
Bulls: Michael Withers; *Warriors:* Adrian Lam.
Penalty count: 6-7; **Half-time:** 26-0; **Referee:** Stuart Cummings (Widnes); **Attendance:** 60,164 *(at Old Trafford, Manchester).*

2001...Michael Withers celebrates a try with Leon Pryce and Daniel Gartner

2002

NORTHERN FORD PREMIERSHIP GRAND FINAL

Saturday 12th October 2002

HUDDERSFIELD GIANTS 38 LEIGH CENTURIONS 16

GIANTS: 1 Ben Cooper; 2 Hefin O'Hare; 3 Eorl Crabtree; 4 Graeme Hallas; 5 Marcus St Hilaire; 6 Stanley Gene; 7 Chris Thorman; 8 Michael Slicker; 9 Paul March; 10 Jeff Wittenberg; 11 David Atkins; 12 Robert Roberts; 13 Steve McNamara. Subs: 14 Heath Cruckshank for Roberts (24BB); 15 Chris Molyneux for Slicker (53); 16 Darren Turner for March (21); 17 Andy Rice for Cruckshank (57); Roberts for Wittenberg (34); Wittenberg for Roberts (74).
Tries: O'Hare (12, 78), St Hilaire (34, 53), Thorman (46), Gene (57); **Goals:** McNamara 7.
Sin bin: Roberts (47) - fighting.
CENTURIONS: 1 Neil Turley; 2 Leon Felton; 4 Jon Roper; 3 Dale Cardoza; 5 Oliver Marns; 6 Willie Swann; 7 Bobbie Goulding; 8 Vila Matautia; 9 Paul Rowley; 10 David Bradbury; 11 Simon Baldwin; 12 Andrew Isherwood; 13 Adam Bristow. Subs: 14 Gareth Price for Bradbury (24BB, rev 35); 15 John Duffy for Swann (32); 16 John Hamilton for Bristow (46BB, rev 57); 17 David Whittle for Matautia (22); Matautia for Bradbury (53BB); Swann for Goulding (58); Hamilton for Whittle (67); Bradbury for Turley (72); Goulding for Swann (75).
Tries: Cardoza (9), Marns (18), Hamilton (70); **Goals:** Turley 2.
Sin bin: Whittle (47) - fighting; Bristow (74) - interference.
On report: Isherwood (66) - high tackle on Roberts.
Rugby Leaguer & League Express Men of the Match:
Giants: Chris Thorman; *Centurions:* Adam Bristow.
Penalty count: 11-11; **Half-time:** 14-10;
Referee: Karl Kirkpatrick (Warrington);
Attendance: 9,051 *(at Halton Stadium, Widnes).*

SUPER LEAGUE GRAND FINAL

Saturday 19th October 2002

BRADFORD BULLS 18 ST HELENS 19

BULLS: 6 Michael Withers; 2 Tevita Vaikona; 20 Scott Naylor; 15 Brandon Costin; 5 Lesley Vainikolo; 1 Robbie Paul (C); 7 Paul Deacon; 8 Joe Vagana; 9 James Lowes; 29 Stuart Fielden; 11 Daniel Gartner; 12 Jamie Peacock; 13 Mike Forshaw. Subs: 14 Lee Gilmour for Gartner (21); 10 Paul Anderson for Vagana (25); 22 Brian McDermott for Fielden (34); 3 Leon Pryce for Vainikolo (53); Fielden for Anderson (55); Vainikolo for Paul (77).
Tries: Naylor (3), Paul (44), Withers (47); **Goals:** Deacon 3.
SAINTS: 1 Paul Wellens; 5 Darren Albert; 3 Martin Gleeson; 4 Paul Newlove; 19 Anthony Stewart; 13 Paul Sculthorpe; 7 Sean Long; 8 Darren Britt; 9 Keiron Cunningham; 10 Barry Ward; 23 Mike Bennett; 15 Tim Jonkers; 11 Chris Joynt (C). Subs: 2 Sean Hoppe for Wellens (3); 12 Peter Shiels for Ward (27); 14 John Stankevitch for Britt (31BB, rev 58); 17 Mick Higham for Joynt (54); Stankevitch for Shiels (58); Joynt for Britt (75); Shiels for Jonkers (77).
Tries: Bennett (24), Long (32), Gleeson (56);
Goals: Long 3; **Field goal:** Long.
Rugby Leaguer & League Express Men of the Match:
Bulls: Paul Deacon; *Saints:* Mike Bennett.
Penalty count: 5-4; **Half-time:** 12-8; **Referee:** Russell Smith (Castleford); **Attendance:** 61,138 *(at Old Trafford, Manchester).*

2003...Alan Hunte leads the Salford celebrations

2003

NATIONAL LEAGUE TWO GRAND FINAL

Sunday 5th October 2003

KEIGHLEY COUGARS 13 SHEFFIELD EAGLES 11

COUGARS: 1 Matt Foster; 2 Max Tomlinson; 3 David Foster; 4 James Rushforth; 5 Andy Robinson; 6 Paul Ashton; 7 Matt Firth; 8 Phil Stephenson; 9 Simeon Hoyle; 10 Danny Ekis; 11 Oliver Wilkes; 12 Ian Sinfield; 13 Lee Patterson. Subs (all used): 14 Chris Wainwright; 15 Richard Mervill; 16 Mick Durham; 17 Jason Ramshaw.
Tries: M Foster (7), Robinson (74); **Goals:** Ashton 2;
Field goal: Firth.
EAGLES: 1 Andy Poynter; 2 Tony Weller; 3 Richard Goddard; 4 Tom O'Reilly; 5 Greg Hurst; 6 Gavin Brown; 7 Mark Aston; 8 Jack Howieson; 9 Gareth Stanley; 10 Dale Laughton; 11 Andy Raleigh; 12 Craig Brown; 13 Wayne Flynn. Subs (all used): 14 Peter Reilly; 15 Simon Tillyer; 16 Nick Turnbull; 17 Mitchell Stringer.
Try: O'Reilly (51); **Goals:** G Brown 3; **Field goal:** Reilly.
Rugby Leaguer & League Express Men of the Match:
Cougars: Simeon Hoyle; *Eagles:* Andy Raleigh.
Penalty count: 6-8; **Half-time:** 9-4; **Referee:** Peter Taberner (Wigan). *(At Halton Stadium, Widnes).*

NATIONAL LEAGUE ONE GRAND FINAL

Sunday 5th October 2003

LEIGH CENTURIONS 14 SALFORD CITY REDS 31

CENTURIONS: 1 Neil Turley; 2 Damian Munro; 3 Alan Hadcroft; 4 Danny Halliwell; 5 Leroy Rivett; 6 John Duffy; 7 Tommy Martyn; 8 Sonny Nickle; 9 Patrick Weisner; 10 Paul Norman; 11 Sean Richardson; 12 Willie Swann; 13 Adam Bristow. Subs (all used): 14 David Bradbury; 15 Lee Sanderson; 16 Bryan Henare; 17 Ricky Bibey.
Tries: Richardson (33), Halliwell (38), Swann (65); **Goal:** Turley.
On report: Nickle (60) - late tackle on Clinch.
CITY REDS: 1 Jason Flowers; 2 Danny Arnold; 3 Stuart Littler; 4 Alan Hunte; 5 Andy Kirk; 6 Cliff Beverley; 7 Gavin Clinch; 8 Neil Baynes; 9 Malcolm Alker; 10 Andy Coley; 11 Simon Baldwin; 12 Paul Highton; 13 Chris Charles. Subs (all used): 14 Steve Blakeley; 15 David Highton; 16 Martin Moana; 17 Gareth Haggerty.
Tries: Hunte (3, 52), Beverley (23), Littler (73);
Goals: Charles 6, Blakeley; **Field goal:** Clinch.
Rugby Leaguer & League Express Men of the Match:
Centurions: Willie Swann; *City Reds:* Gavin Clinch.
Penalty count: 10-10; **Half-time:** 10-16;
Referee: Richard Silverwood (Dewsbury);
Attendance: 9,186 *(at Halton Stadium, Widnes).*

SUPER LEAGUE GRAND FINAL

Saturday 18th October 2003

BRADFORD BULLS 25 WIGAN WARRIORS 12

BULLS: 17 Stuart Reardon; 2 Tevita Vaikona; 6 Michael Withers; 4 Shontayne Hape; 5 Lesley Vainikolo; 15 Karl Pratt; 7 Paul Deacon; 8 Joe Vagana; 9 James Lowes; 29 Stuart Fielden; 11 Daniel Gartner; 12 Jamie Peacock; 13 Mike Forshaw. Subs (all used): 10 Paul Anderson; 18 Lee Radford; 3 Leon Pryce; 1 Robbie Paul (C).
Tries: Reardon (51), Hape (59), Lowes (75);
Goals: Deacon 6/6; **Field goal:** Deacon.
WARRIORS: 1 Kris Radlinski; 5 Brian Carney; 18 Martin Aspinwall; 14 David Hodgson; 2 Brett Dallas; 15 Sean O'Loughlin; 20 Luke Robinson; 30 Quentin Pongia; 9 Terry Newton; 10 Craig Smith; 11 Mick Cassidy; 12 Danny Tickle; 13 Andy Farrell (C). Subs (all used): 4 Paul Johnson; 8 Terry O'Connor; 23 Gareth Hock; 17 Mark Smith.
Tries: Tickle (17), Radlinski (72); **Goals:** Farrell 2/3.
Rugby Leaguer & League Express Men of the Match:
Bulls: Stuart Reardon; *Warriors:* Kris Radlinski.
Penalty count: 7-6; **Half-time:** 4-6; **Referee:** Karl Kirkpatrick (Warrington); **Attendance:** 65,537 *(at Old Trafford, Manchester).*

2004

NATIONAL LEAGUE ONE GRAND FINAL

Sunday 10th October 2004

LEIGH CENTURIONS 32 WHITEHAVEN 16
(After extra time)

CENTURIONS: 1 Neil Turley; 2 Rob Smyth; 3 Danny Halliwell; 4 Ben Cooper; 5 David Alstead; 6 John Duffy; 7 Tommy Martyn; 8 Simon Knox; 9 Paul Rowley; 10 Matt Sturm; 11 David Larder; 12 Oliver Wilkes; 13 Ian Knott. Subs (all used): 14 Dave McConnell; 15 Heath Cruckshank; 16 Richard Marshall; 17 Willie Swann.
Tries: Cooper (27, 83), Martyn (61), Turley (87);
Goals: Turley 6/8; **Field goals:** Turley 2, Rowley, Martyn.
WHITEHAVEN: 1 Gary Broadbent; 2 Craig Calvert; 3 David Seeds; 4 Mick Nanyn; 5 Wesley Wilson; 6 Leroy Joe; 7 Sam Obst; 8 Marc Jackson; 9 Aaron Lester; 10 David Fatialofa; 11 Paul Davidson; 12 Howard Hill; 13 Craig Walsh. Subs (all used): 14 Spencer Miller; 15 Carl Sice; 16 Chris McKinney; 17 Ryan Tandy.
Tries: Wilson (2, 71), Calvert (45); **Goals:** Nanyn 2/6.
Rugby Leaguer & League Express Men of the Match:
Centurions: Neil Turley; *Whitehaven:* Aaron Lester.
Penalty count: 5-9; **Half-time:** 7-6;
Referee: Ronnie Laughton (Barnsley);
Attendance: 11,005 *(at Halton Stadium, Widnes).*

SUPER LEAGUE GRAND FINAL

Saturday 16th October 2004

BRADFORD BULLS 8 LEEDS RHINOS 16

BULLS: 6 Michael Withers; 17 Stuart Reardon; 16 Paul Johnson; 4 Shontayne Hape; 5 Lesley Vainikolo; 18 Iestyn Harris; 7 Paul Deacon; 8 Joe Vagana; 1 Robbie Paul (C); 29 Stuart Fielden; 12 Jamie Peacock; 13 Logan Swann; 11 Lee Radford. Subs: 10 Paul Anderson for Vagana (14); 15 Karl Pratt for Paul (23); 27 Rob Parker for Anderson (24); 19 Jamie Langley for Peacock (32); Paul for Withers (ht); Peacock for Radford (48); Radford for Swann (54); Vagana for Parker (56); Parker for Fielden (63); Fielden for Vagana (67); Swann for Langley (68).
Tries: Vainikolo (7), Hape (43); **Goals:** Deacon 0/2.
RHINOS: 21 Richard Mathers; 18 Mark Calderwood; 5 Chev Walker; 4 Keith Senior; 22 Marcus Bai; 13 Kevin Sinfield (C); 6 Danny McGuire; 19 Danny Ward; 9 Matt Diskin; 8 Ryan Bailey; 3 Chris McKenna; 29 Ali Lauitiiti; 11 David Furner. Subs: 16 Willie Poching for Furner (19); 10 Barrie McDermott for Ward (22); Ward for Bailey (29); 7 Rob Burrow for Lauitiiti (30); Bailey for McDermott (41); 20 Jamie Jones-Buchanan for McKenna (48); Lauitiiti for Ward (50); Furner for Sinfield (60); McKenna for Poching (63); Sinfield for Diskin (67); Poching for McKenna (72); Ward for Bailey (73).
Tries: Diskin (15), McGuire (75); **Goals:** Sinfield 4/4.
Rugby Leaguer & League Express Men of the Match:
Bulls: Lesley Vainikolo; *Rhinos:* Richard Mathers.
Penalty count: 5-5; **Half-time:** 4-10; **Referee:** Steve Ganson (St Helens); **Attendance:** 65,547 *(at Old Trafford, Manchester).*

2005

NATIONAL LEAGUE ONE GRAND FINAL

Sunday 9th October 2005

CASTLEFORD TIGERS 36 WHITEHAVEN 8

TIGERS: 1 Michael Platt; 2 Waine Pryce; 3 Michael Shenton; 4 Jon Hepworth; 5 Damien Blanch; 6 Brad Davis; 7 Andrew Henderson; 8 Adam Watene; 9 Aaron Smith; 10 Richard Fletcher; 11 Tom Haughey; 12 Steve Crouch; 13 Deon Bird. Subs (all used): 14 Paul Handforth; 15 Craig Huby; 16 Adrian Vowles; 17 Frank Watene.
Tries: Huby (22), Crouch (24), Blanch (26), Davis (33, 45), Haughey (52); **Goals:** Fletcher 2/3, Huby 3/4, Hepworth 1/1.
WHITEHAVEN: 1 Gary Broadbent; 2 Craig Calvert; 3 David Seeds; 4 Mick Nanyn; 5 Wesley Wilson; 6 Leroy Joe; 7 Joel Penny; 8 Ryan Tandy; 9 Carl Sice; 10 David Fatialofa; 11 Spencer Miller; 12 Howard Hill; 13 Aaron Lester. Subs (all used): 14 Carl Rudd; 15 Aaron Summers; 16 Craig Chambers; 17 Marc Jackson.
Tries: Seeds (56), Calvert (78); **Goals:** Nanyn 0/2.
Sin bin: Joe (16) - late tackle on Davis.
On report: Joe (16) - late tackle on Davis;
Sice (40) - alleged biting.
Rugby Leaguer & League Express Men of the Match:
Tigers: Brad Davis; *Whitehaven:* Wesley Wilson.
Penalty count: 4-9; **Half-time:** 26-0;
Referee: Steve Ganson (St Helens);
Attendance: 13,300 *(at Halton Stadium, Widnes).*

SUPER LEAGUE GRAND FINAL

Saturday 15th October 2005

BRADFORD BULLS 15 LEEDS RHINOS 6

BULLS: 6 Michael Withers; 3 Leon Pryce; 13 Ben Harris; 4 Shontayne Hape; 5 Lesley Vainikolo; 18 Iestyn Harris; 7 Paul Deacon; 12 Jamie Peacock (C); 9 Ian Henderson; 29 Stuart Fielden; 16 Paul Johnson; 10 Brad Meyers; 11 Lee Radford. Subs (all used): 24 Adrian Morley for Johnson (5); 19 Jamie Langley for Peacock (24); 8 Joe Vagana for Fielden (24); Johnson for Radford (24); 1 Robbie Paul for Henderson (31); Peacock for Vagana (45); Fielden for Morley (49); Henderson for Paul (54); Radford for Meyers (60); Morley for Peacock (62); Meyers for Langley (73); Peacock for Johnson (74).
Tries: L Pryce (29), Vainikolo (53); **Goals:** Deacon 3/5;
Field goal: I Harris.
RHINOS: 1 Richard Mathers; 2 Mark Calderwood; 3 Chev Walker; 12 Chris McKenna; 5 Marcus Bai; 6 Danny McGuire; 7 Rob Burrow; 8 Ryan Bailey; 14 Andrew Dunemann; 15 Danny Ward; 20 Gareth Ellis; 16 Willie Poching; 13 Kevin Sinfield (C). Subs (all used): 10 Barrie McDermott for Ward (17); 11 Ali Lauitiiti for Poching (21); 18 Jamie Jones-Buchanan for Bailey (31); Ward for McDermott (34); 9 Matt Diskin for Ellis (48); Poching for Lauitiiti (48); McDermott for Ward (54); Ellis for Poching (54); Lauitiiti for McDermott (61); Poching for Dunemann (65); Ward for Jonoc-Buchanan (68); Dunemann for Ellis (71).
Try: McGuire (22); **Goals:** Sinfield 1/2.
Rugby Leaguer & League Express Men of the Match:
Bulls: Leon Pryce; *Rhinos:* Danny McGuire.
Penalty count: 6-8; **Half-time:** 8-6; **Referee:** Ashley Klein (Keighley); **Attendance:** 65,537 *(at Old Trafford, Manchester).*

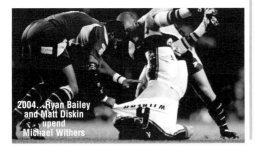

2004... Ryan Bailey and Matt Diskin upend Michael Withers

2005... Brad Davis and Adrian Vowles lift the NL1 trophy

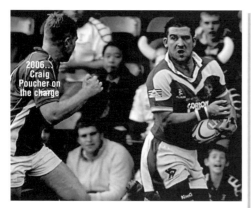

2006.. Craig Poucher on the charge

2006

NATIONAL LEAGUE TWO GRAND FINAL

Sunday 8th October 2006

SHEFFIELD EAGLES 35 SWINTON LIONS 10

EAGLES: 1 Johnny Woodcock; 5 Greg Hurst; 4 Jimmy Walker; 3 James Ford; 2 Rob Worrincy; 6 Brendon Lindsay; 7 Gavin Brown; 8 Jack Howieson; 9 Paul Pickering; 10 Mitchell Stringer; 11 Andy Hay; 12 Dale Holdstock; 13 Andy Smith. Subs (all used): 14 Craig Poucher; 15 Martin Ostler; 16 Sean Dickinson; 17 Waisale Sovatabua.
Tries: Worrincy (21, 43), Lindsay (38), Woodcock (39), Walker (51), Hay (60); **Goals:** Woodcock 5/6;
Field goal: G Brown.
LIONS: 1 Wayne English; 2 Andy Saywell; 3 Darren Woods; 4 David Alstead; 5 Marlon Billy; 6 Martin Moana; 7 Chris Hough; 8 Bruce Johnson; 9 Phil Wood; 10 Dave Newton; 11 Kris Smith; 12 Ian Sinfield; 13 Lee Marsh. Subs (all used): 14 Liam McGovern; 15 Chris Morley; 16 Danny Aboushakra; 17 Ian Parry.
Tries: Saywell (35), Alstead (74); **Goals:** McGovern 1/2.
Rugby Leaguer & League Express Men of the Match:
Eagles: Johnny Woodcock; *Lions:* Wayne English.
Penalty count: 3-4; **Half-time:** 16-4;
Referee: Peter Taberner (Wigan).
(at Halliwell Jones Stadium, Warrington).

Dewsbury Rams were National League Two Champions in 2006. This game was to determine who took the second promotion place.

NATIONAL LEAGUE ONE GRAND FINAL

Sunday 8th October 2006

HULL KINGSTON ROVERS 29 WIDNES VIKINGS 16

ROVERS: 1 Ben Cockayne; 2 Leroy Rivett; 3 Gareth Morton; 4 Jon Goddard; 5 Byron Ford; 6 Scott Murrell; 7 James Webster; 8 Makali Aizue; 9 Ben Fisher; 10 David Tangata-Toa; 11 Iain Morrison; 12 Michael Smith; 13 Tommy Gallagher. Subs (all used): 14 Pat Weisner; 15 Dwayne Barker; 16 Jason Netherton; 17 Dave Wilson.
Tries: Ford (6), Goddard (18, 36), Murrell (24), Weisner (43); **Goals:** Morton 4/6; **Field goal:** Murrell.
VIKINGS: 1 Gavin Dodd; 2 Damien Blanch; 3 Sean Gleeson; 4 Daryl Cardiss; 5 John Kirkpatrick; 6 Dennis Moran; 7 Ian Watson; 8 Terry O'Connor; 9 Mark Smith; 10 Barrie McDermott; 11 Mick Cassidy; 12 David Allen; 13 Bob Beswick. Subs (all used): 14 Aaron Summers; 15 Oliver Wilkes; 16 Jordan James; 17 Ryan Tandy.
Tries: Dodd (32), Tandy (57), Blanch (70); **Goals:** Dodd 2/3.
Rugby Leaguer & League Express Men of the Match:
Rovers: James Webster; *Vikings:* Mark Smith.
Penalty count: 8-5; **Half-time:** 22-4;
Referee: Phil Bentham (Warrington);
Attendance: 13,024 *(at Halliwell Jones Stadium, Warrington).*

SUPER LEAGUE GRAND FINAL

Saturday 14th October 2006

HULL FC 4 ST HELENS 26

HULL: 1 Shaun Briscoe; 14 Motu Tony; 4 Sid Domic; 3 Kirk Yeaman; 5 Gareth Raynor; 13 Paul Cooke; 7 Richard Horne; 8 Ewan Dowes; 9 Richard Swain (C); 10 Garreth Carvell; 11 Lee Radford; 12 Shayne McMenemy; 24 Danny Washbrook. Subs: 15 Paul King for Carvell (17); 19 Graeme Horne for Radford (23); 26 Scott Wheeldon for Dowes (27); 6 Richard Whiting for McMenemy (29); Dowes for Wheeldon (49); Carvell for King (49); Radford for G Horne (51); McMenemy for Whiting (54); King for Carvell (68); Wheeldon for Dowes (73); Whiting for Tony (76); G Horne for Radford (77).
Try: Domic (24); **Goals:** Cooke 0/1.
SAINTS: 1 Paul Wellens; 2 Ade Gardner; 3 Jamie Lyon; 4 Willie Talau; 5 Francis Meli; 6 Leon Pryce; 7 Sean Long (C); 17 Paul Anderson; 9 Keiron Cunningham; 10 Jason Cayless; 11 Lee Gilmour; 12 Jon Wilkin; 16 Jason Hooper. Subs: 23 Maurie Fa'asavalu for P Anderson (12); 19 James Graham for Cayless (25); 15 Mike Bennett for Fa'asavalu (28); 14 James Roby for Cunningham (31); P Anderson for Wilkin (33); Cunningham for Gilmour (49); Cayless for P Anderson (52); Wilkin for Hooper (56); Fa'asavalu for Cayless (58); Gilmour for Graham (66); Cayless for Fa'asavalu (72); P Anderson for Wilkin (75).
Tries: Meli (17), Pryce (29), Talau (49), Gardner (52), Cunningham (62); **Goals:** Lyon 3/5.
Rugby Leaguer & League Express Men of the Match:
Hull: Shaun Briscoe; *Saints:* Paul Wellens.
Penalty count: 4-2; **Half-time:** 4-10;
Referee: Karl Kirkpatrick (Warrington);
Attendance: 72,582 *(at Old Trafford, Manchester).*

2007

NATIONAL LEAGUE TWO GRAND FINAL

Sunday 7th October 2007

FEATHERSTONE ROVERS 24 OLDHAM 6

ROVERS: 1 Loz Wildbore; 2 Danny Kirmond; 3 Jon Whittle; 4 Wayne McHugh; 5 Ade Adebisi; 6 Andy Kain; 7 Paul Handforth; 8 Gareth Handford; 9 Joe McLocklan; 10 Stuart Dickens; 11 Jamie Field; 12 Richard Blakeway; 13 Tom Haughey. Subs (all used): 14 Jamie Benn; 15 Ian Tonks; 16 James Houston; 17 Gavin Swinson.
Tries: McHugh (39, 49), Handforth (46); **Goals:** Dickens 5/6;
Field goals: Wildbore (66, 70).
Dismissal: Blakeway (64) – head butt on Roberts.
OLDHAM: 1 Gareth Langley; 2 Byron Ford; 3 Craig Littler; 4 Adam Hughes; 5 Lucas Onyango; 6 Neil Roden; 7 James Coyle; 8 Anthony Tonks; 9 Simeon Hoyle; 10 Richard Mervill; 11 Ian Sinfield; 12 Robert Roberts; 13 Geno Costin. Subs (all used): 14 Ian Hodson; 15 Alex Wilkinson; 16 Said Tamghart; 17 Matty Brooks.
Try: Hughes (31); **Goals:** Langley 1/2.
Rugby Leaguer & League Express Men of the Match:
Rovers: Paul Handforth; *Oldham:* Robert Roberts.
Penalty count: 9-5; **Half-time:** 10-6; **Referee:** Gareth Hewer.
(at Headingley Carnegie, Leeds).

Celtic Crusaders were National League Two Champions in 2007. This game was to determine who took the second promotion place.

NATIONAL LEAGUE ONE GRAND FINAL

Sunday 7th October 2007

CASTLEFORD TIGERS 42 WIDNES VIKINGS 10

TIGERS: 1 Stuart Donlan; 2 Danny Williams; 3 Michael Shenton; 4 Ryan McGoldrick; 5 Kirk Dixon; 6 Anthony Thackeray; 7 Danny Brough; 8 Liam Higgins; 9 Andrew Henderson; 10 Awen Guttenbeil; 11 Joe Westerman; 12 Ryan Clayton; 13 Peter Lupton. Subs (all used): 14 Mark Leafa; 15 Chris Charles; 16 Michael Wainwright; 17 Ryan Boyle.
Tries: Wainwright (20), McGoldrick (29), Guttenbeil (44, 76), M Shenton (52), Westerman (62), Clayton (66).
Goals: Brough 6/9; **Field goals:** Brough (25, 55).
VIKINGS: 1 Scott Grix; 2 Damien Blanch; 3 Toa Kohe-Love; 4 Mick Nanyn; 5 Gavin Dodd; 6 Dennis Moran; 7 Joel Penny; 8 Mick Cassidy; 9 Mark Smith; 10 Oliver Wilkes; 11 Joel Tomkins; 12 Paul Noone; 13 Bob Beswick. Subs (all used): 14 Aaron Summers; 15 Jordan James; 16 Ian Webster; 17 Lee Doran.
Tries: Nanyn (35), Wilkes (69); **Goals:** Nanyn 1/2.
Rugby Leaguer & League Express Men of the Match:
Tigers: Danny Brough; *Vikings:* Scott Grix.
Penalty count: 7-2; **Half-time:** 13-4; **Referee:** Phil Bentham; **Attendance:** 20,814 *(at Headingley Carnegie, Leeds).*

SUPER LEAGUE GRAND FINAL

Saturday 13th October 2007

LEEDS RHINOS 33 ST HELENS 6

RHINOS: 1 Brent Webb; 5 Lee Smith; 3 Clinton Toopi; 4 Keith Senior; 2 Scott Donald; 6 Danny McGuire; 7 Rob Burrow; 8 Kylie Leuluai; 9 Matt Diskin; 10 Jamie Peacock; 11 Jamie Jones-Buchanan; 12 Gareth Ellis; 13 Kevin Sinfield (C). Subs (all used): 14 Ali Lauitiiti for Diskin (23); 16 Ryan Bailey for Leuluai (18); 17 Ian Kirke for Jones-Buchanan (33); 22 Carl Ablett for Kirke (57); Leuluai for Bailey (55); Jones-Buchanan for Lauitiiti (60); Diskin for Ablett (63); Kirke for Leuluai (65); Bailey for Kirke (76).
Tries: Webb (19), Lauitiiti (50), Donald (52), Smith (69), Jones-Buchanan (80); **Goals:** Sinfield 6/7;
Field goal: Burrow (55).
SAINTS: 1 Paul Wellens; 2 Ade Gardner; 3 Matt Gidley; 4 Willie Talau; 5 Francis Meli; 6 Leon Pryce; 7 Sean Long; 8 Nick Fozzard; 9 Keiron Cunningham (C); 10 Jason Cayless; 11 Lee Gilmour; 30 Chris Flannery; 12 Jon Wilkin. Subs (all used): 17 James Graham for Cayless (15); 14 James Roby for Cunningham (23); 23 Maurie Fa'asavalu for Fozzard (23); 15 Mike Bennett for Wilkin (31); Cayless for Fa'asavalu (34); Cunningham for Flannery (51); Wilkin for Bennett (55); Fa'asavalu for Cayless (55); Fozzard for Graham (57); Cayless for Fozzard (68); Graham for Fa'asavalu (68); Bennett for Gilmour (72).
Try: Roby (27); **Goals:** Long 1/2.
Rugby Leaguer & League Express Men of the Match:
Rhinos: Rob Burrow; *Saints:* Sean Long.
Penalty count: 4-5; **Half-time:** 8-6; **Referee:** Ashley Klein; **Attendance:** 71,352 *(at Old Trafford, Manchester).*

2007... Danny McGuire jumps for joy following Scott Donald's try

2008

NATIONAL LEAGUE TWO GRAND FINAL

Sunday 28th September 2008

DONCASTER 18 OLDHAM 10

DONCASTER: 1 Zebastian Luisi; 2 Dean Colton; 3 Andreas Bauer; 4 Shaun Leaf; 5 Wayne Reittie; 6 Kyle Wood; 7 Luke Gale; 8 Nathan Freer; 9 Corey Lawrie; 10 Alex Benson; 11 Peter Green; 12 Craig Lawton; 13 Josh Weeden. Subs (all used): 14 Kyle Briggs; 15 Chris Buttery; 16 Michael Haley; 17 Mark Castle.
Tries: Buttery (44), Gale (49), Briggs (73); **Goals:** Gale 3/4.
OLDHAM: 1 Paul O'Connor; 2 Gareth Langley; 3 Marcus St Hilaire; 4 Mick Nanyn; 5 Daryl Cardiss; 6 Phil Joseph; 7 James Coyle; 8 Adam Robinson; 9 Matty Brooks; 10 Richard Mervill; 11 Tommy Goulden; 12 Danny Halliwell; 13 Robert Roberts. Subs (all used): 14 Ian Hodson; 15 Luke Menzies; 16 Chris Baines; 17 Said Tamghart.
Tries: Hodson (34), Nanyn (62); **Goals:** Nanyn 1/4.
Rugby Leaguer & League Express Men of the Match:
Doncaster: Luke Gale; *Oldham:* Adam Robinson.
Penalty count: 7-8; **Half-time:** 2-6; **Referee:** Ronnie Laughton. *(at Halliwell Jones Stadium, Warrington).*

Gateshead Thunder were National League Two Champions in 2008. This game was to determine who took the second promotion place.

NATIONAL LEAGUE ONE GRAND FINAL

Sunday 28th September 2008

CELTIC CRUSADERS 18 SALFORD CITY REDS 36
(after extra-time)

CRUSADERS: 1 Tony Duggan; 2 Luke Dyer; 3 Josh Hannay; 4 Mark Dalle Cort; 5 Anthony Blackwood; 6 Damien Quinn; 7 Jace Van Dijk; 8 Jordan James; 9 Neil Budworth; 10 David Tangata-Toa; 11 Chris Beasley; 12 Darren Mapp; 13 Terry Martin. Subs (all used): 14 Aaron Summers; 15 Ian Webster; 16 Mark Lennon; 17 Neale Wyatt.
Tries: Blackwood (38), Dyer (50), J James (54), Tangata-Toa (66); **Goals:** Hannay 0/1, Lennon 1/3.
CITY REDS: 1 Karl Fitzpatrick; 2 Matt Gardner; 3 Stuart Littler; 4 John Wilshere; 5 Paul White; 6 Robbie Paul; 7 Richard Myler; 8 Paul Highton; 9 Malcolm Alker; 10 Craig Stapleton; 11 Ian Sibbit; 12 Luke Adamson; 13 Jordan Turner. Subs (all used): 14 Stefan Ratchford; 15 Steve Bannister; 16 Lee Jewitt; 17 Phil Leuluai.
Tries: White (5, 86), Gardner (26), Fitzpatrick (63), Sibbit (83), Myler (99); **Goals:** Wilshere 6/7.
Rugby Leaguer & League Express Men of the Match:
Crusaders: Tony Duggan; *City Reds:* John Wilshere.
Penalty count: 5-5; **Half-time:** 4-10; **Full-time:** 18-18; **Referee:** Ben Thaler; **Attendance:** 7,104 *(at Halliwell Jones Stadium, Warrington).*

SUPER LEAGUE GRAND FINAL

Saturday 4th October 2008

LEEDS RHINOS 24 ST HELENS 16

RHINOS: 5 Lee Smith; 22 Ryan Hall; 19 Carl Ablett; 4 Keith Senior; 2 Scott Donald; 6 Danny McGuire; 7 Rob Burrow; 8 Kylie Leuluai; 9 Matt Diskin; 10 Jamie Peacock; 11 Jamie Jones-Buchanan; 12 Gareth Ellis; 13 Kevin Sinfield (C). Subs (all used): 17 Nick Scruton; 14 Ali Lauitiiti; 18 Ian Kirke; 16 Ryan Bailey.
Tries: Smith (23), Hall (37), McGuire (49, 63);
Goals: Sinfield 4/4.
SAINTS: 1 Paul Wellens; 2 Ade Gardner; 3 Matt Gidley; 4 Willie Talau; 5 Francis Meli; 6 Leon Pryce; 7 Sean Long; 18 Bryn Hargreaves; 9 Keiron Cunningham (C); 17 James Graham; 11 Lee Gilmour; 12 Jon Wilkin; 16 Chris Flannery. Subs (all used): 8 Nick Fozzard; 21 Paul Clough; 14 James Roby; 23 Maurie Fa'asavalu.
Tries: Graham (6), Gidley (43), Gardner (59); **Goals:** Long 2/3.
Rugby Leaguer & League Express Men of the Match:
Rhinos: Jamie Peacock; *Saints:* Sean Long.
Penalty count: 6-8; **Half-time:** 12-6; **Referee:** Ashley Klein; **Attendance:** 68,810 *(at Old Trafford, Manchester).*

AMATEUR, RESERVES & ACADEMY 2009

CO-OPERATIVE RLC NATIONAL

FINAL TABLE

	P	W	D	L	F	A	D	Pts
Bramley Buffaloes	20	17	1	2	833	332	501	55
Hudds-Underbank	20	15	1	4	722	330	392	50
Featherstone Lions	20	13	2	5	795	414	381	46
Nottingham Outlaws	20	15	0	5	746	474	272	45
Hemel Stags	20	13	0	7	776	415	361	44
Warrington Wizards	20	12	0	8	714	599	115	38
L'pool Buccaneers	20	8	0	12	602	593	9	31
Dewsbury Celtic	20	5	0	15	417	774	-357	18
Carlisle Centurions	20	5	0	15	411	983	-572	16
East Lancs Lions	20	3	0	17	356	895	-539	11
Gateshead Storm	20	2	0	18	294	857	-563	8

ELIMINATION PLAY-OFFS
Saturday 12th September 2009
Featherstone Lions 40 ....Warrington Wizards 34
Nottingham Outlaws 24 ....Hemel Stags 22

ELIMINATION SEMI-FINAL
Saturday 19th September 2009
Featherstone Lions 24 ....Nottingham Outlaws 32

QUALIFYING SEMI-FINAL
Saturday 19th September 2009
Bramley Buffaloes 30 ....
Huddersfield Underbank Rangers 24

FINAL ELIMINATOR
Saturday 26th September 2009
Huddersfield Underbank Rangers 44 ....
Nottingham Outlaws 10

GRAND FINAL
Sunday 4th October 2009
Bramley Buffaloes 38 ....
Huddersfield Underbank Rangers 22
Buffaloes: T - Booth (3, 37, 54), Mulholland (19),
Nicholls (32), Flynn (43), Elliker (68); G - Drake 5/8
Rangers: T - Thorley (14, 29), Aka (65), St Hilaire (70);
G - Barrett 3/4
(at Halliwell Jones Stadium, Warrington)

NATIONAL CONFERENCE

PREMIER DIVISION

	P	W	D	L	F	A	D	Pts
Siddal	26	19	0	7	639	385	254	38
East Hull	26	17	1	8	640	466	174	35
Skirlaugh	26	17	0	9	696	436	260	34
Leigh Miners	26	16	1	9	743	548	195	33
York Acorn	26	16	0	10	697	564	133	32
Oulton Raiders	26	14	0	12	665	528	137	28
Hull Dockers	26	14	0	12	645	524	121	28
Leigh East	26	13	1	12	595	519	76	27
Wigan St Patricks	26	13	0	13	458	546	-88	26
Wigan St Judes	26	12	1	13	698	603	95	25
West Hull	26	12	0	14	654	534	120	24
Thatto Heath	26	12	0	14	638	581	57	24
Rochdale Mayfield	26	3	0	23	394	1079	-685	6
Thornhill Trojans	26	2	0	24	382	1231	-849	4

ELIMINATION PLAY-OFFS
Saturday 18th April 2009
SLeigh Miners Rangers 36 ....York Acorn 54
Skirlaugh 10 ....Oulton Raiders 42

ELIMINATION SEMI-FINAL
Saturday 25th April 2009
York Acorn 0......................................Oulton Raiders 38

QUALIFYING SEMI-FINAL
Saturday 25th April 2009
Siddal 4 ....East Hull 24

FINAL ELIMINATOR
Saturday 2nd May 2009
Siddal 22..Oulton Raiders 18

GRAND FINAL
Saturday 9th May 2009
Siddal 15 ....East Hull 8
Siddal: T - L Simeunovich (7), Hope (57); G - Attwood 3;
FG - L Gudor
East Hull: T - Brett (45), M Blanchard (65)
(at Chris Moyles Stadium, Featherstone)

DIVISION ONE

	P	W	D	L	F	A	D	Pts
Wath Brow Hornets	24	18	2	4	576	324	252	38
Ince Rose Bridge	24	17	2	5	632	406	226	36
Widnes St Maries	24	14	2	8	596	461	135	30
Saddleworth	24	13	0	11	468	377	125	26
Stanningley	24	12	1	11	510	426	84	25
Castleford Panthers	24	12	1	11	490	492	-2	25
Bradford Dudley Hill	24	11	2	11	589	498	91	24
West Bowling	24	12	0	12	534	496	38	24
Normanton Knights	24	11	2	11	516	564	-48	24
Millom	24	10	0	14	513	604	-91	20
Eastmoor Dragons	24	8	0	16	449	586	-137	16
Oldham St Annes	24	7	1	16	470	671	-201	15
Shaw Cross Sharks	24	4	1	19	294	732	-438	9

DIVISION TWO

	P	W	D	L	F	A	D	Pts
Myton Warriors	22	18	1	3	672	290	382	37
Milford Marlins	22	15	0	7	792	319	473	30
Heworth	22	14	1	7	590	457	133	29
Lock Lane	22	13	0	9	592	479	113	26
Eccles & Salford J	22	13	0	9	471	457	14	26
Ovenden	22	13	1	8	683	394	289	25
Stanley Rangers	22	11	1	10	413	534	-121	23
Crosfields	22	9	2	11	485	526	-41	20
Waterhead	22	8	1	13	453	599	-146	17
Egremont Rangers	22	8	1	13	436	705	-269	17
East Leeds	22	5	0	17	308	553	-245	10
Hull Isberg	22	1	0	21	346	880	-534	2

ACE INSURANCE NATIONAL CUP

QUARTER FINALS
Saturday 21st March 2009
West Hull 40 ....Ellenborough 10
Queens 39 ....Leigh East 20
Wigan St Cuthberts 22 ....Sharlston Rovers 16
Wednesday 25 March 2009
Saddleworth Rangers 2 ....Siddal 16

SEMI-FINALS
Saturday 11th April 2009
Wigan St Cuthberts 25 ....West Hull 24
Siddal 28 ....Queens 21

FINAL
Saturday 23rd May 2009
Siddal 38.....................................Wigan St Cuthberts 14

CO-OPERATIVE RLC PREMIER

MIDLANDS PREMIER

	P	W	D	L	F	A	D	Pts
Coventry Bears	12	8	0	4	409	278	131	16
Derby City	12	8	0	4	378	254	124	16
Bristol Sonics	12	8	0	4	346	300	46	16
Birmingham Bulldogs	12	7	0	5	316	259	57	14
Leicester Phoenix	12	7	0	5	301	249	52	14
Gloucestershire W	12	4	0	8	252	410	-158	8
Telford Raiders	12	0	0	12	118	380	-262	0

NORTH WEST PREMIER

	P	W	D	L	F	A	Diff	Pts
Lymm	12	10	0	2	325	182	143	20
Widnes Saints	12	8	0	4	376	243	133	16
New Broughton	12	7	0	5	323	252	71	14
Wigan Riversiders	12	6	0	6	434	252	182	12
Runcorn	12	6	0	6	308	330	-22	12
Blackpool Sea Eagles	12	3	0	9	210	496	-286	6
Rhyl Coasters	12	2	0	10	141	362	-221	4

YORKSHIRE PREMIER

	P	W	D	L	F	A	Diff	Pts
Kippax Knights	12	10	0	2	446	172	274	20
Moorends-Thorne M	12	9	0	3	438	267	171	18
Cottingham Phoenix	12	8	0	4	404	282	122	16
York Lokomotive	12	7	0	5	431	318	113	14
Scarborough Pirates	12	6	0	6	248	308	-60	12
Leeds Akkies	12	2	0	10	258	366	-108	4
East Riding	12	0	0	12	132	644	-512	0

SOUTHERN PREMIER

	P	W	D	L	F	A	Diff	Pts
S'th London Storm	14	14	0	0	780	234	546	28
West London	14	12	0	2	638	214	424	24
St Albans Centurions	14	11	0	3	466	305	161	22
Ipswich Rhinos	14	7	0	7	356	408	-52	14
Portsmouth NS	14	5	0	9	346	476	-130	10
Bedford Tigers	14	5	0	9	268	552	-284	10
London Skolars	14	4	0	10	319	461	-142	8
Hainault Bulldogs	14	3	0	11	248	378	-130	6
Elmbridge Eagles	14	1	0	13	226	537	-311	2

WALES

	P	W	D	L	F	A	Diff	Pts
Blackwood Bulldogs	8	8	0	0	352	104	248	16
Bridgend Blue Bulls	8	7	0	1	324	117	207	14
Valley Cougars	8	6	0	2	333	234	99	12
Cardiff Demons	8	5	0	3	220	167	53	10
Newport Titans	8	4	1	4	228	286	-58	7
NPT Steelers	8	1	2	5	146	262	-116	4
Torfaen Tigers	8	2	0	6	170	314	-144	4
Dinefwr Sharks	8	1	1	6	213	320	-107	3
W Wales Wildboars	8	1	0	7	130	312	-182	2

HARRY JEPSON TROPHY - GRAND FINAL
Sunday 13th September 2009
Coventry Bears 14 ....West London Sharks 24
(at Haslams, Derby)

CO-OPERATIVE RLC REGIONAL

NORTH EAST

	P	W	D	L	F	A	D	Pts
Jarrow Vikings	12	12	0	0	666	220	446	24
Peterlee Pumas	12	9	0	3	710	190	520	18
Newcastle Knights	12	7	1	4	476	310	166	15
Sunderland Nissan	12	7	0	5	374	438	-64	14
Northallerton Stallions	11	6	0	5	398	400	-2	12
Hartlepool	12	1	8	269	434	-165	5	
Winlaton Warriors	12	2	0	10	202	548	-346	4
Whitley Bay B	12	1	0	11	164	719	-555	2

SOUTH WEST

	P	W	D	L	F	A	Diff	Pts
East Devon Eagles	10	10	0	0	612	145	467	20
Devon Sharks	10	7	0	3	330	216	114	14
Exeter Centurions	10	6	0	4	250	286	-36	12
Somerset Vikings	10	3	0	7	244	430	-186	6
Plymouth Titans	10	2	0	8	185	312	-127	4
South Dorset Giants	10	2	0	8	162	394	-232	4

EAST

	P	W	D	L	F	A	Diff	Pts
Northampton Casuals	8	8	0	0	420	86	334	16
Bury Titans	8	5	0	3	200	264	-64	10
Norwich City	8	4	0	4	176	216	-40	8
St Ives	8	3	0	5	184	196	-12	6
Colchester	8	0	0	8	88	306	-218	0

NORTH MIDLANDS

	P	W	D	L	F	A	Diff	Pts
Parkside Hawks	10	8	1	1	362	146	216	17
Scunthorpe B	10	7	1	2	382	215	167	15
Rotherham Giants	10	6	0	4	397	190	207	12
Lincoln City Knights	10	5	0	5	267	255	12	10
Leeds Akkies A	10	1	1	8	92	384	-292	3
Nottingham	10	1	1	8	130	440	-310	3

LONDON & SOUTH

	P	W	D	L	F	A	Diff	Pts
Greenwich	8	7	0	1	332	159	173	14
Swindon	8	4	1	3	279	276	3	9
Southampton S	8	3	1	4	304	266	38	7
Guildford Giants	8	3	0	5	240	238	2	6
Oxford Cavaliers	8	2	0	6	146	362	-216	4

SCOTLAND

	P	W	D	L	F	A	Diff	Pts
Edinburgh Eagles	7	7	0	0	462	60	402	14
Carluke Tigers	7	5	0	2	310	194	116	10
Fife Lions	7	5	0	2	222	118	104	10
Moray Eels	7	5	0	2	200	260	-60	10
Hillfoots Rams	7	3	0	4	132	256	-124	6
Jordanhill Phoenix	7	2	0	5	218	238	-20	4
Easterhouse Panthers	7	1	0	6	124	288	-164	2
Victoria Knights	7	0	0	7	56	310	-254	0

REGIONAL GRAND FINAL
Saturday 13th September 2009
Jarrow Vikings 14 ....Northampton Casuals 40
(at Haslams, Derby)

RESERVE TEAM CHAMPIONSHIP

FINAL TABLE

	P	W	D	L	F	A	D	Pts
Wigan Warriors	20	19	0	1	854	298	556	38
St Helens	20	17	0	3	809	376	433	34
Huddersfield Giants	20	14	1	5	720	410	310	29
Bradford Bulls	20	12	0	8	508	526	-18	24
Warrington Wolves	20	11	0	9	555	584	-29	22
Leeds Rhinos	20	9	1	10	632	615	17	19
Hull KR	20	9	0	11	546	474	72	18
Harlequins RL	20	9	0	11	624	602	22	18
Hull FC	20	8	1	11	572	579	-7	17
Castleford Tigers	20	7	1	12	463	714	-251	15
Salford City Reds	20	5	0	15	476	691	-215	10
Wakefield Wildcats	20	5	0	15	326	812	-486	10
Celtic Crusaders	20	3	0	17	374	778	-404	6

ELIMINATION PLAY-OFFS
Saturday 5th September 2009
Huddersfield Giants 14 ....Leeds Rhinos 38
Bradford Bulls 32........................Warrington Wolves 10

QUALIFYING SEMI-FINAL
Friday 11th September 2009
Wigan Warriors 22 ....St Helens 16

ELIMINATION SEMI-FINAL
Friday 11th September 2009
Bradford Bulls 26 ....Leeds Rhinos 46

FINAL ELIMINATOR
Friday 18th September 2009
St Helens 59...Leeds Rhinos 28

GRAND FINAL
Saturday 26th September 2009
Wigan Warriors 34 ....St Helens 6
(at DW Stadium, Wigan)

RESERVE TEAM DIVISION ONE

FINAL TABLE

	P	W	D	L	F	A	D	Pts
Leigh Centurions	16	13	0	3	699	305	394	26
Featherstone Rovers	16	13	0	3	653	281	372	26
Widnes Vikings	16	11	0	5	596	350	246	22
Hunslet Hawks	16	10	0	6	586	346	240	20
Barrow Raiders	16	10	0	6	511	358	153	20
Whitehaven	16	10	0	6	401	426	-25	20
Keighley Cougars	16	8	0	8	347	568	-221	16
York City Knights	15	6	0	9	410	525	-115	12
Oldham	16	5	0	11	409	512	-103	10
Dewsbury Rams	16	5	0	11	358	524	-166	10
Sheffield Eagles	15	4	0	11	333	620	-287	8
Doncaster	16	0	0	16	176	664	-488	0

GILLETTE ACADEMY CHAMPIONSHIP

FINAL TABLE

	P	W	D	L	F	A	D	Pts
Wakefield T Wildcats	15	15	1	2	660	300	360	31
Wigan Warriors	18	14	0	4	607	340	267	28
Castleford Tigers	18	13	1	4	653	468	185	27
Warrington Wolves	18	13	0	5	615	328	287	26
Bradford Bulls	18	12	2	4	632	385	247	26
Hull KR	18	11	0	7	433	397	36	22
St Helens	18	9	0	9	636	507	129	18
Hull FC	18	7	0	11	442	500	-58	14
Widnes Vikings	18	6	0	12	422	653	-231	12
Leeds Rhinos	18	5	1	12	516	614	-98	11
Salford City Reds	18	4	1	13	404	696	-292	9
Huddersfield Giants	18	4	0	14	345	684	-339	8
Harlequins	18	1	0	17	398	891	-493	2

ELIMINATION PLAY-OFFS
Wednesday 9th September 2009
Castleford Tigers 30..Hull KR 16
Saturday 12th September 2009
Warrington Wolves 16.........................Bradford Bulls 27

QUALIFYING SEMI-FINAL
Thursday 17th September 2009
Wakefield T Wildcats 12 ....Wigan Warriors 4

ABOVE: Lee Mossop makes a break during Wigan's Reserve Team Championship Grand Final win over St Helens

BELOW: Cain Southernwood takes the ball forward for Wakefield in the Gillette Academy Championship Grand Final

ELIMINATION SEMI-FINAL
Friday 18th September 2009
Castleford Tigers 36 ....Bradford Bulls 40

FINAL ELIMINATOR
Friday 25th September 2009
Wigan Warriors 23 ....Bradford Bulls 22

GRAND FINAL
Friday 2nd October 2009
Wakefield T Wildcats 30 ....Wigan Warriors 4
(at Hearwell Stadium, Wakefield)

2009 SEASON
Stats round-up

Pat Richards

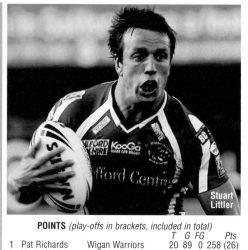

Stuart Littler

TRIES *(play-offs in brackets, included in total)*

1	Ryan Hall	Leeds Rhinos	31 (3)
2	Pat Richards	Wigan Warriors	20 (2)
3	David Hodgson	Huddersfield Giants	18 (0)
	Peter Fox	Hull Kingston Rovers	18 (1)
5	Kirk Dixon	Castleford Tigers	17 (0)
	Olivier Elima	Catalans Dragons	17 (2)
	Dimitri Pelo	Catalans Dragons	17 (3)
8	Michael Shenton	Castleford Tigers	16 (0)
	Leon Pryce	St Helens	16 (1)
	Chris Hicks	Warrington Wolves	16 (-)

GOALS *(play-offs in brackets, included in total)*

1	Kevin Sinfield	Leeds Rhinos	117 (9)
2	Michael Dobson	Hull Kingston Rovers	100 (4)
3	Pat Richards	Wigan Warriors	89 (9)
4	Brett Hodgson	Huddersfield Giants	88 (2)
5	Paul Deacon	Bradford Bulls	86 (-)
6	Thomas Bosc	Catalans Dragons	78 (8)
7	Danny Tickle	Hull FC	76 (-)
8	Danny Brough	Wakefield Trinity Wildcats	70 (0)
9	John Wilshere	Salford City Reds	59 (-)
10	Kirk Dixon	Castleford Tigers	51 (0)

GOALS PERCENTAGE *(play-offs included)*

			G	Att	%
1	Stefan Ratchford	Salford City Reds	10	10	100
2	Lee Smith	Leeds Rhinos	14	15	93.3
3	Rob Purdham	Harlequins	39	42	92.8
4	Damien Quinn	Celtic Crusaders	12	14	85.7
5	Brett Hodgson	Huddersfield Giants	88	103	85.4
6	Tony Martin	Wakefield Trinity Wildcats	28	35	80
7	Joe Westerman	Castleford Tigers	41	52	78.8
8	Danny Tickle	Hull FC	76	97	78.3
9	Paul Deacon	Bradford Bulls	86	110	78.1
10	Kevin Sinfield	Leeds Rhinos	117	150	78

(10 minimum attempts to qualify)

POINTS *(play-offs in brackets, included in total)*

			T	G	FG	Pts
1	Pat Richards	Wigan Warriors	20	89	0	258 (26)
2	Kevin Sinfield	Leeds Rhinos	4	117	3	253 (20)
3	Michael Dobson	Hull Kingston Rovers	11	100	2	246 (8)
4	Brett Hodgson	Huddersfield Giants	11	88	0	220 (4)
5	Paul Deacon	Bradford Bulls	3	86	3	187 (-)
6	Danny Brough	Wakefield Trinity Wildcats	9	70	4	180 (0)
7	Danny Tickle	Hull FC	6	76	0	176 (-)
8	Thomas Bosc	Catalans Dragons	4	78	2	174 (17)
9	Kirk Dixon	Castleford Tigers	17	51	0	170 (0)
10	Chris Hicks	Warrington Wolves	16	49	0	162 (-)

CONSECUTIVE APPEARANCES
(Super League, including play-offs, and Challenge Cup)

1	Stuart Littler	Salford City Reds	163
		(includes 2008 National League season)	
2	Malcolm Alker	Salford City Reds	57
		(includes 2008 National League season)	
3	Thomas Leuluai	Wigan Warriors	52
4	Michael Dobson	Hull Kingston Rovers	46
5	Iafeta Palea'aesina	Wigan Warriors	45
6	Paul Clough	St Helens	43
7	Neil Budworth	Celtic Crusaders	42
		(includes 2008 National League season)	
	Phil Leuluai	Salford City Reds	42
		(includes 2008 National League season)	
9	Kris Welham	Hull Kingston Rovers	41
10	Nick Scruton	Bradford Bulls/Leeds Rhinos	38

316

FINAL TABLE

	P	W	D	L	F	A	D	Pts
Leeds Rhinos	27	21	0	6	805	453	352	42
St Helens	27	19	0	8	733	466	267	38
Huddersfield Giants	27	18	0	9	690	416	274	36
Hull Kingston Rovers	27	17	1	9	650	516	134	35
Wakefield Trinity Wildcats	27	16	0	11	685	609	76	32
Wigan Warriors	27	15	0	12	659	551	108	30
Castleford Tigers	27	14	0	13	645	702	-57	28
Catalans Dragons	27	13	0	14	613	660	-47	26
Bradford Bulls	27	12	1	14	653	668	-15	25
Warrington Wolves	27	12	0	15	649	705	-56	24
Harlequins	27	11	0	16	591	691	-100	22
Hull FC	27	10	0	17	502	623	-121	20
Salford City Reds	27	7	0	20	456	754	-298	14
Celtic Crusaders	27	3	0	24	357	874	-517	6

AVERAGE ATTENDANCES

	2009 Avg	2008 Avg	Diff
Leeds Rhinos	15,312	16,756	-1,444
Wigan Warriors	13,695	13,955	-260
Hull FC	13,226	13,432	-206
St Helens	11,027	10,740	+287
Bradford Bulls	9,677	10,287	-610
Warrington Wolves	9,228	9,496	-268
Catalans Dragons	9,104	8,488	+616
Hull Kingston Rovers	8,501	8,554	-53
Huddersfield Giants	7,641	7,846	-205
Castleford Tigers	7,490	7,501	-11
Wakefield Trinity Wildcats	5,891	7,000	-1,109
Salford City Reds	4,390	3,768	+622 (NL1)
Celtic Crusaders	3,603	1,929	+1,674 (NL1)
Harlequins	3,436	3,773	-337

2009 Average	8,730
2008 Average	9,819
Difference	-1,089

BEST ATTENDANCES

		Round	Date
63,259	Leeds v St Helens	GF	10/10/09
	(at Old Trafford, Manchester)		
22,337	Hull v Hull KR	8	10/4/09
22,232	Wigan v St Helens	8	9/4/09
20,295	Wigan v Leeds	22	24/7/09
19,997	Leeds v St Helens	26	4/9/09
18,150	Catalans v Warrington	17	20/6/09
	(at Olympic Stadium, Barcelona)		
17,824	Leeds v Bradford	18	26/6/09
17,677	Leeds v Wigan	5	13/3/09
17,009	St Helens v Warrington	1	13/2/09
16,931	Leeds v Castleford	24	14/8/09

WORST ATTENDANCES

		Round	Date
1,988	Celtic Crusaders v Huddersfield	26	5/9/09
2,017	Celtic Crusaders v Castleford	11	26/4/09
2,089	Celtic Crusaders v Wakefield	6	30/5/09
2,245	Harlequins v Celtic Crusaders	15	6/6/09
2,475	Salford v Catalans	16	7/8/09
2,540	Harlequins v Catalans	8	9/4/09
2,612	Harlequins v Salford	24	15/8/09
2,927	Celtic Crusaders v Catalans	14	23/5/09
3,009	Celtic Crusaders v Harlequins	9	13/4/09
3,009	Celtic Crusaders v Salford	20	11/7/09

CHALLENGE CUP

TRIES

1	Andy Kain	Featherstone Rovers	6
	Luke Branighan	Gateshead Thunder	6
3	Lucas Onyango	Oldham	5
	Francis Meli	St Helens	5
	Paul Wellens	St Helens	5

GOALS

1	John Wilshere	Salford City Reds	17
2	Chris Hicks	Warrington Wolves	16
3	Kirk Dixon	Castleford Tigers	15
	Michael Dobson	Hull Kingston Rovers	15
5	Tim Hartley	Widnes Vikings	14
	Michael Knowles	Gateshead Thunder	14

POINTS

			T	G	FG	Pts
1	Chris Hicks	Warrington Wolves	4	16	0	48
2	John Wilshere	Salford City Reds	2	17	0	42
3	Chris Bridge	Warrington Wolves	3	13	0	38
	Kirk Dixon	Castleford Tigers	2	15	0	38
	Pat Richards	Wigan Warriors	3	13	0	38

BEST ATTENDANCES

		Round	Date
76,560	Huddersfield v Warrington	F	29/8/09
	(at Wembley Stadium)		
17,689	Leeds v St Helens	4	5/4/09
12,975	Warrington v Wigan	SF	8/8/09
	(at Stobart Stadium, Widnes)		
10,638	Huddersfield v St Helens	SF	9/8/09
	(at Halliwell Jones Stadium, Warrington)		
9,466	Wigan v Salford	QF	29/5/09

WORST ATTENDANCES

		Round	Date
221	Leeds Met Carnegie v Rochdale	3	8/3/09
	(at Headingley Carnegie, Leeds)		
251	Kells v Hunslet	3	14/3/09
	(at Recreation Ground, Whitehaven)		
314	Workington v Lezignan	3	7/3/09
320	Wath Brow v London Skolars	3	8/3/09
	(at Recreation Ground, Whitehaven)		
447	Keighley v Pia	3	7/3/09

NORTHERN RAIL CUP

TRIES

1	Shad Royston	Halifax	8
2	Jon Presley	Keighley Cougars	7
	Toa Kohe-Love	Widnes Vikings	7
4	Andy Ellis	Barrow Raiders	6
	Stewart Sanderson	Gateshead Thunder	6
	Ben Black	Halifax	6
	Paul Hughes	York City Knights	6

GOALS

1	Pat Walker	Dewsbury Rams	28
2	Andy Ballard	Oldham	24
3	Jonny Woodcock	Sheffield Eagles	18
4	Paul Noone	Barrow Raiders	17
5	Craig Hall	Widnes Vikings	16

POINTS

			T	G	FG	Pts
1	Andy Ballard	Oldham	5	24	0	68
2	Pat Walker	Dewsbury Rams	1	28	0	60
3	Jonny Woodcock	Sheffield Eagles	2	18	0	44
4	George Flanagan	Batley Bulldogs	3	13	0	38
5	Martyn Ridyard	Leigh Centurions	4	10	0	36

BEST ATTENDANCES

		Round	Date
8,720	Barrow v Widnes	F	12/7/09
	(at Bloomfield Road, Blackpool)		
3,972	Halifax v Widnes	SF	21/6/09
3,001	Widnes v Gateshead	3	21/2/09
2,783	Widnes v Oldham	2	13/2/09
2,775	Barrow v Featherstone	SF	18/6/09

WORST ATTENDANCES

		Round	Date
213	London Skolars v Doncaster	3	22/2/09
242	Swinton v Workington	1	11/3/09
314	London Skolars v Dewsbury	1	15/3/09
337	Keighley v Gateshead	1	10/2/09
371	Rochdale v Blackpool	3	22/2/09

CHAMPIONSHIP

James Nixon

TRIES *(play-offs in brackets, included in total)*

1	James Nixon	Barrow Raiders	26 (2)
2	Jermaine McGilvary	Batley Bulldogs	20 (-)
	Shad Royston	Halifax	20 (4)
4	Gregg McNally	Whitehaven	19 (0)
5	Paddy Flynn	Widnes Vikings	18 (0)
6	Ian Hardman	Featherstone Rovers	16 (1)
7	Ben McAlpine	Gateshead Thunder	15 (-)
	Nick Youngquest	Gateshead Thunder	15 (-)
	Craig Calvert	Whitehaven	15 (0)
10	Luke Branighan	Gateshead Thunder	13 (-)
	Rob Worrincy	Halifax	13 (0)

GOALS *(play-offs in brackets, included in total)*

1	Lee Patterson	Halifax	106 (9)
2	Jonny Woodcock	Sheffield Eagles	85 (2)
3	Michael Knowles	Gateshead Thunder	84 (-)
4	Nathan Wynn	Toulouse Olympique	76 (-)
5	Stuart Dickens	Featherstone Rovers	65 (1)
	Gregg McNally	Whitehaven	65 (0)
7	Ian Mort	Leigh Centurions	52 (-)
8	Paul Mennell	Batley Bulldogs	50 (-)
9	Jamie Rooney	Barrow Raiders	44 (10)
10	Tim Hartley	Widnes Vikings	42 (7)

POINTS *(play-offs in brackets, included in total)*

			T	G	FG	Pts
1	Lee Patterson	Halifax	7	106	0	240 (18)
2	Gregg McNally	Whitehaven	19	65	0	206 (0)
3	Michael Knowles	Gateshead Thunder	6	84	0	192 (-)
4	Jonny Woodcock	Sheffield Eagles	3	85	0	182 (4)
5	Nathan Wynn	Toulouse Olympique	5	76	0	172 (-)
6	Stuart Dickens	Featherstone Rovers	3	65	0	142 (2)
7	Paul Mennell	Batley Bulldogs	10	50	0	140 (-)
8	Ian Mort	Leigh Centurions	7	52	0	132 (-)
9	James Nixon	Barrow Raiders	26	0	0	104 (8)
10	Jamie Rooney	Barrow Raiders	2	44	3	99 (21)

FINAL TABLE

	P	W	D	L	BP	F	A	D	Pts
Barrow Raiders	20	13	0	7	5	632	361	271	44
Halifax	20	13	0	7	4	714	476	238	43
Sheffield Eagles	20	11	0	9	9	635	447	188	42
Widnes Vikings	20	11	0	9	6	649	438	211	39
Whitehaven	20	12	0	8	3	565	567	-2	39
Featherstone Rovers	20	12	0	8	1	619	524	95	37
Gateshead Thunder	20	9	2	9	1	610	657	-47	32
Batley Bulldogs	20	8	2	10	4	536	620	-84	32
Leigh Centurions	20	9	0	11	5	426	572	-146	32
Toulouse Olympique	20	9	0	11	3	556	582	-26	30
Doncaster *	20	1	0	19	5	257	955	-698	-1

* 9 points deducted for entering administration

** Toulouse were exempt from relegation.
Leigh were relegated as 9th placed team, but re-instated after Gateshead requested to play in Championship One in 2010.

AVERAGE ATTENDANCES

	2009 Avg	2008 Avg	Diff
Widnes Vikings	3,412	4,122	-710
Toulouse Olympique	2,372	N/A	N/A
Halifax	2,330	1,999	+331
Barrow Raiders	2,206	1,427	+779 (NL2)
Leigh Centurions	1,917	2,438	-521
Featherstone Rovers	1,754	1,338	+416
Whitehaven	1,599	1,640	-41
Sheffield Eagles	1,090	1,068	+22
Batley Bulldogs	856	970	-114
Doncaster	705	860	-155 (NL2)
Gateshead Thunder	679	490	+189 (NL2)

2009 Average	1,720	
2008 Average	2,047	
Difference	-327	

BEST ATTENDANCES

		Round	Date
11,398	Barrow v Halifax	GF	4/10/09
	(at Halliwell Jones Stadium, Warrington)		
5,236	Widnes v Gateshead	11	23/5/09
5,071	Widnes v Toulouse	1	12/3/09
4,354	Widnes v Leigh	4	10/4/09
4,039	Widnes v Halifax	18	31/7/09
3,507	Toulouse v Widnes	6	18/4/09
3,453	Widnes v Doncaster	15	4/7/09
3,296	Widnes v Featherstone	ESF	18/9/09
3,290	Widnes v Barrow	8	1/5/09
3,278	Widnes v Featherstone	13	13/6/09

WORST ATTENDANCES

		Round	Date
275	Doncaster v Sheffield	14	28/6/09
	(at Chris Moyles Stadium, Featherstone)		
337	Doncaster v Whitehaven	17	26/7/09
405	Gateshead v Doncaster	8	1/5/09
481	Doncaster v Barrow	19	9/8/09
502	Gateshead v Barrow	2	22/3/09
516	Gateshead v Toulouse	12	7/6/09
551	Doncaster v Gateshead	22	6/9/09
554	Gateshead v Batley	18	1/8/09
565	Doncaster v Batley	9	21/6/09
	(at Chris Moyles Stadium, Featherstone)		
575	Gateshead v Whitehaven	10	17/5/09

* Championship attendance figures include play-offs and Northern Rail Cup. Challenge Cup not included.

CHAMPIONSHIP ONE

TRIES *(play-offs in brackets, included in total)*

1	Andrew Bostock	Dewsbury Rams	20 (-)
2	Jon Presley	Keighley Cougars	15 (2)
3	Bryn Powell	Dewsbury Rams	14 (-)
	Thomas Coyle	Oldham	14 (2)
	Martin Ainscough	Rochdale Hornets	14 (-)
6	Kane Epati	Dewsbury Rams	13 (-)
	Liam Finn	Dewsbury Rams	13 (-)
8	Chris Baines	Oldham	12 (5)
	Danny Ratcliffe	York City Knights	12 (1)
10	Jonny Leather	Blackpool Panthers	11 (0)
	Damian Munro	Blackpool Panthers	11 (0)
	Alex Bretherton	Dewsbury Rams	11 (-)
	Chris Spurr	Dewsbury Rams	11 (-)
	Michael Brown	Hunslet Hawks	11 (2)
	Daley Williams	Keighley Cougars	11 (2)
	Lee Greenwood	Oldham	11 (0)

GOALS *(play-offs in brackets, included in total)*

1	Pat Walker	Dewsbury Rams	110 (-)
2	Danny Jones	Keighley Cougars	87 (8)
3	Carl Sneyd	Swinton Lions	73 (3)
4	Andy Ballard	Oldham	57 (-)
5	Adam Mitchell	York City Knights	50 (1)
6	Liam McGovern	Rochdale Hornets	44 (-)
7	Darren Robinson	Hunslet Hawks	43 (3)
8	Chris Baines	Oldham	33 (23)
	Jonny Leather	Blackpool Panthers	33 (0)
10	Paul Thorman	London Skolars	31 (-)

POINTS *(play-offs in brackets, included in total)*

			T	G	FG	Pts
1	Pat Walker	Dewsbury Rams	5	110	0	240 (-)
2	Danny Jones	Keighley Cougars	7	87	0	202 (28)
3	Carl Sneyd	Swinton Lions	8	73	0	178 (6)
4	Andy Ballard	Oldham	10	57	0	154 (-)
5	Chris Baines	Oldham	12	33	0	114 (66)
6	Jonny Leather	Blackpool Panthers	11	33	1	111 (0)
7	Liam McGovern	Rochdale Hornets	5	44	1	109 (-)
8	Adam Mitchell	York City Knights	2	50	0	108 (2)
9	Darren Robinson	Hunslet Hawks	4	43	1	103 (6)
10	Liam Finn	Dewsbury Rams	13	15	2	84 (-)

FINAL TABLE

	P	W	D	L	BP	F	A	D	Pts
Dewsbury Rams	18	18	0	0	0	760	223	537	54
Keighley Cougars	18	13	0	5	3	539	415	124	42
York City Knights	18	12	0	6	4	589	360	229	40
Oldham	18	10	1	7	3	618	449	169	35
Blackpool Panthers	18	9	1	8	4	532	456	76	33
Hunslet Hawks	18	10	0	8	3	472	411	61	33
Swinton Lions	18	8	0	10	3	513	516	-3	27
Rochdale Hornets *	18	6	0	12	6	500	557	-57	15
Workington Town	18	2	0	16	5	281	700	-419	11
London Skolars	18	1	0	17	2	210	927	-717	5

* 9 points deducted for entering administration

AVERAGE ATTENDANCES

	2009 Avg	*2008 Avg*	*Diff*
Dewsbury Rams	1,263	1,196	+67
			(NL1)
York City Knights	1,096	940	+156
Oldham	983	1,160	-177
Keighley Cougars	916	868	+48
Hunslet Hawks	655	558	+97
Rochdale Hornets	637	586	+51
Swinton Lions	519	537	-18
Blackpool Panthers	502	439	+63
Workington Town	474	717	-243
London Skolars	412	450	-38

2009 Average	746
2008 Average	753
Difference	-7

BEST ATTENDANCES *(figure unavailable for Grand Final)*

		Round	*Date*
3,106	York v Oldham	11	25/6/09
2,103	Dewsbury v Workington	16	16/8/09
1,726	Keighley v Dewsbury	15	30/7/09
1,705	Dewsbury v Keighley	10	11/6/09
1,501	Keighley v York	QSF	20/9/09
1,419	Oldham v London Skolars	10	6/8/09
1,413	Dewsbury v Hunslet	5	26/4/09
1,326	York v Dewsbury	9	31/5/09
1,249	Rochdale v Oldham	3	10/4/09
1,216	Dewsbury v York	1	22/3/09

WORST ATTENDANCES

		Round	*Date*
215	London Skolars v Blackpool	4	13/4/09
257	London Skolars v Oldham	6	2/5/09
257	London Skolars v Workington	15	2/8/09
265	Blackpool v Hunslet	1	22/3/09
280	Blackpool v Workington	11	28/6/09
293	London Skolars v Hunslet	9	31/5/09
319	Workington v Dewsbury	8	24/5/09
336	London Skolars v York	8	24/5/09
347	Blackpool v Rochdale	6	4/5/09
353	Workington v London Skolars	7	17/5/09

* Championship One attendance figures include play-offs and Northern Rail Cup. Challenge Cup not included.

2009 TOP SCORERS - ALL COMPETITIONS

Ryan Hall

TRIES

1	Ryan Hall	Leeds Rhinos	32
2	James Nixon	Barrow Raiders	31
3	Shad Royston	Halifax	30
4	Jon Presley	Keighley Cougars	25
	Gregg McNally	Whitehaven	25
6	Pat Richards	Wigan Warriors	23
7	Andrew Bostock	Dewsbury Rams	22
	Stewart Sanderson		
		Gateshead Thunder	22
9	Andy Ballard	Barrow Raiders	21

(includes 17 for Oldham)

	Jermaine McGilvary		
		Batley Bulldogs	21
	Luke Branighan	Gateshead Thunder	21
	David Hodgson	Huddersfield Giants	21

GOALS

1	Pat Walker	Dewsbury Rams	146
2	Lee Patterson	Halifax	126
3	Kevin Sinfield	Leeds Rhinos	122
4	Michael Dobson	Hull Kingston Rovers	115
5	Jonny Woodcock	Sheffield Eagles	112
6	Danny Jones	Keighley Cougars	106
7	Andy Ballard	Barrow Raiders	103

(includes 93 for Oldham)

8	Michael Knowles	Gateshead Thunder	102
	Pat Richards	Wigan Warriors	102
10	Brett Hodgson	Huddersfield Giants	98

POINTS

			T	G	FG	Pts
1	Pat Walker	Dewsbury Rams	6	146	0	316
2	Pat Richards	Wigan Warriors	23	102	0	296
3	Lee Patterson	Halifax	10	126	0	292
4	Andy Ballard	Barrow Raiders	21	103	0	290

(includes 254 (17t, 93g) for Oldham)

5	Michael Dobson	Hull Kingston Rovers	11	115	2	276
6	Kevin Sinfield	Leeds Rhinos	4	122	3	263
7	Jonny Woodcock	Sheffield Eagles	8	112	0	256
8	Brett Hodgson	Huddersfield Giants	14	98	0	252
9	Gregg McNally	Whitehaven	25	74	0	248
10	Danny Jones	Keighley Cougars	7	106	1	241

FIELD GOALS

1	Danny Brough	Wakefield Trinity Wildcats	5
2	Lee Briers	Warrington Wolves	4
3	Paul Deacon	Bradford Bulls	3
	Sean Long	St Helens	3
	Jamie Rooney	Barrow Raiders	3
	Brent Sherwin	Castleford Tigers	3
	Kevin Sinfield	Leeds Rhinos	3

Grassroots to World Class

Gillette proudly sponsor England Rugby League at every age level,
plus The Gillette Academy, The Gillette National Youth League
and The Gillette Regional Championship.